CLASSICAL AND MEDIEVAL LITERATURE CRITICISM

Guide to Gale Literary Criticism Series

For criticism on	Consult these Gale series
Authors now living or who died after December 31, 1999	*CONTEMPORARY LITERARY CRITICISM (CLC)*
Authors who died between 1900 and 1999	*TWENTIETH-CENTURY LITERARY CRITICISM (TCLC)*
Authors who died between 1800 and 1899	*NINETEENTH-CENTURY LITERATURE CRITICISM (NCLC)*
Authors who died between 1400 and 1799	*LITERATURE CRITICISM FROM 1400 TO 1800 (LC)* *SHAKESPEAREAN CRITICISM (SC)*
Authors who died before 1400	*CLASSICAL AND MEDIEVAL LITERATURE CRITICISM (CMLC)*
Authors of books for children and young adults	*CHILDREN'S LITERATURE REVIEW (CLR)*
Dramatists	*DRAMA CRITICISM (DC)*
Poets	*POETRY CRITICISM (PC)*
Short story writers	*SHORT STORY CRITICISM (SSC)*
Black writers of the past two hundred years	*BLACK LITERATURE CRITICISM (BLC)* *BLACK LITERATURE CRITICISM SUPPLEMENT (BLCS)*
Hispanic writers of the late nineteenth and twentieth centuries	*HISPANIC LITERATURE CRITICISM (HLC)* *HISPANIC LITERATURE CRITICISM SUPPLEMENT (HLCS)*
Native North American writers and orators of the eighteenth, nineteenth, and twentieth centuries	*NATIVE NORTH AMERICAN LITERATURE (NNAL)*
Major authors from the Renaissance to the present	*WORLD LITERATURE CRITICISM, 1500 TO THE PRESENT (WLC)* *WORLD LITERATURE CRITICISM SUPPLEMENT (WLCS)*

ISSN 0896-0011

Volume 40

CLASSICAL AND MEDIEVAL LITERATURE CRITICISM

Excerpts from Criticism of the Works of World
Authors from Classical Antiquity through the
Fourteenth Century, from the First Appraisals
to Current Evaluations

Jelena O. Krstović
Editor

Detroit
New York
San Francisco
London
Boston
Woodbridge, CT

STAFF

Janet Witalec, Lynn M. Spampinato, *Managing Editors, Literature Product*
Kathy D. Darrow, *Product Liaison*
Jelena Krstović, *Editor*
Mark W. Scott, *Publisher, Literature Product*

Elisabeth Gellert, *Associate Editor*
Patti A. Tippett, *Technical Training Specialist*
Deborah J. Morad, Kathleen Lopez Nolan, *Managing Editors, Literature Content*
Susan M. Trosky, *Director, Literature Content*

Maria L. Franklin, *Permissions Manager*
Edna Hedblad, *Permissions Specialist*
Julie Juengling, *Permissions Assistant*

Victoria B. Cariappa, *Research Manager*
Tracie A. Richardson *Project Coordinator*
Andrew Guy Malonis, Barbara McNeil, Gary J. Oudersluys, Maureen Richards, Cheryl L. Warnock, *Research Specialists*
Tamara C. Nott, *Research Associate*
Tim Lehnerer, *Research Assistant*

Dorothy Maki, *Manufacturing Manager*
Stacy L. Melson, *Buyer*

Mary Beth Trimper, *Composition and Prepress Manager*
Evi Seoud, *Assistant Production Manager*
Gary Leach, *Composition Specialist*

Randy Bassett, *Image Database Supervisor*
Robert Duncan, *Imaging Specialist*
Mike Logusz, *Graphic Artist*
Pamela A. Reed, *Imaging Coordinator*
Kelly A. Quin, *Imaging Editor*

Library of Congress Catalog Card Number 88-658021
ISBN 0-7876-4382-3
ISSN 0896-0011
Printed in the United States of America

10 9 8 7 6 5 4 3 2 1

Contents

Preface vii

Acknowledgments xi

Preface

Since its inception in 1988, *Classical and Medieval Literature Criticism* (*CMLC*) has been a valuable resource for students and librarians seeking critical commentary on the works and authors of antiquity through the fourteenth century. The great poets, prose writers, dramatists, and philosophers of this period form the basis of most humanities curricula, so that virtually every student will encounter many of these works during the course of a high school and college education. Reviewers have found *CMLC* "useful" and "extremely convenient," noting that it "adds to our understanding of the rich legacy left by the ancient period and the Middle Ages," and praising its "general excellence in the presentation of an inherently interesting subject." No other single reference source has surveyed the critical reaction to classical and medieval literature as thoroughly as *CMLC*.

Scope of the Series

CMLC provides an introduction to classical and medieval authors, works, and topics that represent a variety of genres, time periods, and nationalities. By organizing and reprinting an enormous amount of critical commentary written on authors and works of this period in world history, *CMLC* helps students develop valuable insight into literary history, promotes a better understanding of the texts, and sparks ideas for papers and assignments.

Each entry in *CMLC* presents a comprehensive survey of an author's career, an individual work of literature, or a literary topic, and provides the user with a multiplicity of interpretations and assessments. Such variety allows students to pursue their own interests; furthermore, it fosters an awareness that literature is dynamic and responsive to many different opinions. Early commentary is offered to indicate initial responses, later selections document changes in literary reputations, and retrospective analyses provide the reader with modern views. The size of each author entry is a relative reflection of the scope of the criticism available in English.

An author may appear more than once in the series if his or her writings have been the subject of a substantial amount of criticism; in these instances, specific works or groups of works by the author will be covered in separate entries. For example, Homer will be represented by three entries, one devoted to the *Iliad,* one to the *Odyssey,* and one to the Homeric Hymns.

CMLC continues the survey of criticism of world literature begun by Gale's *Contemporary Literary Criticism* (*CLC*), *Twentieth-Century Literary Criticism* (*TCLC*), *Nineteenth-Century Literature Criticism* (*NCLC*), *Literature Criticism from 1400 to 1800* (*LC*), and *Shakespearean Criticism* (*SC*).

Organization of the Book

A *CMLC* entry consists of the following elements:

- The **Author Heading** cites the name under which the author most commonly wrote, followed by birth and death dates. Also located here are any name variations under which an author wrote, including transliterated forms for authors whose native languages use nonroman alphabets. If the author wrote consistently under a pseudonym, the pseudonym will be listed in the author heading and the author's actual name given in parenthesis on the first line of the biographical and critical information. Uncertain birth or death dates are indicated by question marks. Single-work entries are preceded by a heading that consists of the most common form of the title in English translation (if applicable) and the original date of composition.

- The **Introduction** contains background information that introduces the reader to the author, work, or topic that is the subject of the entry.

- A **Portrait of the Author** is included when available.

- The list of **Principal Works** is ordered chronologically by date of first publication and lists the most important works by the author. The genre and publication date of each work is given. In the case of foreign authors whose works have been translated into English, the list will focus primarily on twentieth-century translations, selecting those works most commonly considered the best by critics. Unless otherwise indicated, dramas are dated by first performance, not first publication. Lists of **Representative Works** by different authors appear with topic entries.

- Reprinted **Criticism** is arranged chronologically in each entry to provide a useful perspective on changes in critical evaluation over time. The critic's name and the date of composition or publication of the critical work are given at the beginning of each piece of criticism. Unsigned criticism is preceded by the title of the source in which it appeared. All titles by the author featured in the text are printed in boldface type. Footnotes are reprinted at the end of each essay or excerpt. In the case of excerpted criticism, only those footnotes that pertain to the excerpted texts are included. Criticism in topic entries is arranged chronologically under a variety of subheadings to facilitate the study of different aspects of the topic.

- A complete **Bibliographical Citation** of the original essay or book precedes each piece of criticism.

- Critical essays are prefaced by brief **Annotations** explicating each piece.

- An annotated bibliography of **Further Reading** appears at the end of each entry and suggests resources for additional study. In some cases, significant essays for which the editors could not obtain reprint rights are included here. Boxed material following the further reading list provides references to other biographical and critical sources on the author in series published by Gale.

Cumulative Indexes

A **Cumulative Author Index** lists all of the authors that appear in a wide variety of reference sources published by the Gale Group, including *CMLC*. A complete list of these sources is found facing the first page of the Author Index. The index also includes birth and death dates and cross references between pseudonyms and actual names.

Beginning with the second volume, a **Cumulative Nationality Index** lists all authors featured in *CMLC* by nationality, followed by the number of the *CMLC* volume in which their entry appears.

Beginning with the tenth volume, a **Cumulative Topic Index** lists the literary themes and topics treated in the series as well as in *Nineteenth-Century Literature Criticism, Twentieth-Century Literary Criticism,* and the *Contemporary Literary Criticism* Yearbook, which was discontinued in 1998.

A **Cumulative Title Index** lists in alphabetical order all of the works discussed in the series. Each title listing includes the corresponding volume and page numbers where criticism may be located. Foreign-language titles that have been translated into English are followed by the titles of the translation—for example, *Slovo o polku Igorove (The Song of Igor's Campaign)*. Page numbers following these translated titles refer to all pages on which any form of the titles, either foreign-language or translated, appear. Titles of novels, dramas, nonfiction books, and poetry, short story, or essay collections are printed in italics, while individual poems, short stories, and essays are printed in roman type within quotation marks.

Citing *Classical and Medieval Literature Criticism*

When writing papers, students who quote directly from any volume in the Literary Criticism Series may use the following general format to footnote reprinted criticism. The first example pertains to material drawn from periodicals, the second to material reprinted from books.

T. P. Malnati, "Juvenal and Martial on Social Mobility," *The Classical Journal* 83, no. 2 (December-January 1988): 134-41; reprinted in *Classical and Medieval Literature Criticism,* vol. 35, ed. Jelena Krstovi (Farmington Hills, Mich.: The Gale Group, 2000), 366-71.

J. P. Sullivan, "Humanity and Humour; Imagery and Wit," in *Martial: An Unexpected Classic* (Cambridge University Press, 1991), 211-51; excerpted and reprinted in *Classical and Medieval Literature Criticism,* vol. 35, ed. Jelena Krstovi (Farmington Hills, Mich.: The Gale Group, 2000), 371-95.

Suggestions are Welcome

Readers who wish to suggest new features, topics, or authors to appear in future volumes, or who have other suggestions or comments are cordially invited to call, write, or fax the Managing Editor:

Managing Editor, Literary Criticism Series
The Gale Group
27500 Drake Road
Farmington Hills, MI 48331-3535
1-800-347-4253 (GALE)
Fax: 248-699-8054

Acknowledgments

The editors wish to thank the copyright holders of the excerpted criticism included in this volume and the permissions managers of many book and magazine publishing companies for assisting us in securing reproduction rights. We are also grateful to the staffs of the Detroit Public Library, the Library of Congress, the University of Detroit Mercy Library, Wayne State University Purdy/Kresge Library Complex, and the University of Michigan Libraries for making their resources available to us. Following is a list of the copyright holders who have granted us permission to reproduce material in this volume of *CMLC*. Every effort has been made to trace copyright, but if omissions have been made, please let us know.

Genesis

First book of the Bible.

INTRODUCTION

Ascribed by tradition, though not by scholars, to Moses, the book of *Genesis* chronicles the creation of the world and everything in it, as well as God's early relationship to humanity. For purposes of critical analysis, *Genesis* is often divided into the primeval history (chapters 1 through 11), which includes the stories of God's creation of the universe, as well as the Adam and Eve, Cain and Abel, and Noah stories, and the patriarchal history (chapters 12-50), which includes the narratives of Abraham, Isaac, Jacob, and Joseph. Altogether, the stories in Genesis span—according to the usual calculation—2,369 years. The sources from which *Genesis* was compiled, including Babylonian, Egyptian, and Hebrew myths and folklore, date from the tenth to fifth centuries B.C.

TEXTUAL HISTORY

Modern scholars generally agree that there are three main literary sources within *Genesis*. Among these three groups of source documents, the two oldest are designated as "Yahwist" (or "J" for the German word for Yahweh) and "Elohist" (or "E"), respectively. These terms are derived from the distinctive name by which each author referred to God, either Yahweh or Elohim. The completed texts (rather than the various source materials) for the Yahwist compositions date from circa 950 B.C., and the Elohist compositions have been dated one to two centuries later. The third, later group of source texts, referred to as "Priestly" (or "P"), is believed to have been completed circa 538 to 450 B.C. The style of the P sources is somewhat different from that of J and E, in that P is more formal and more interested in factual information, such as geneologies and precise dates. J and E sources, on the other hand, tend to be more lyrical. Many scholars believe that the chapters of *Genesis* are comprised of a number of J, E, and P source documents that were at one time combined by a redactor (sometimes referred to as "R").

PLOT AND MAJOR CHARACTERS

The principal characters of *Genesis* include God and the individuals he created. *Genesis* tells the tale of God's creation of the universe, and then traces the history of mankind from Adam and Eve, through Abraham and his descendents. *Genesis* focuses primarily upon five persons: Adam, Noah, Abraham, Isaac, and Jacob. God appears

repeatedly throughout the text, interacting with mankind largely through issuing commands and announcements, and punishing, forgiving, and testing those he created.

MAJOR THEMES

Many scholars have attempted to isolate the various themes threading their way throughout the book of *Genesis*. Some point to *Genesis*'s emphasis on power and patriarchy, with God the Creator as the initial patriarch, followed later by Abraham and his descendents. Other critics note that the theme of sin and failure is woven throughout *Genesis*, from Adam and Eve's original sin, to sins of humanity as a whole, punishable by such acts as the great flood, from which only Noah and a select few escaped. Man's alienation from God, as a result of man's failures, has also been identified as one of the primary themes in *Genesis*.

CRITICAL RECEPTION

Modern criticism of *Genesis* has centered on analysis of issues related to the composition of the text, and literary analyses focusing on such things as plot, theme, and use of literary devices. A number of critics have studied the myth sources from which, it is argued, *Genesis* was derived. Robert Graves and Raphael Patai review the deities of Hebrew myth that have found their way into the Bible, and examine the parallels between Greek and Hebrew mythology and religious attitudes, stating that one significant difference is that the Hebrew myths draw moral conclusions from the acts of their heroes. Similarly, William H. Ralston, Jr. compares the creation story in *Genesis* with other creation myths. For example, Ralston draws parallels between the story of Adam and Eve, and an older Palestinian myth; in both stories, Ralston obverses, a couple becomes alienated from one another and from God. Other commonalities have been observed as well. Peter Booth examines the relationship between the myth of Agamemnon and his sacrifice of Iphigeneia, and Abraham's near-sacrifice of his son Isaac. In addition to the study of myth as source material for *Genesis*, critics have also analyzed the method by which *Genesis*'s final form was derived. Gerhard Von Rad views *Genesis* not as an independent book but as a part of the Hexateuch (the book of *Genesis* through the book of Joshua), and examines the way the Yahwist writer developed his source material. Von Rad also outlines the widely-accepted view that the source documents comprising the books *Genesis* to Joshua were woven together by a skillful redactor. Leslie Brisman, however, challenges the traditional view that the Yahwist and Eloist strands were "reacted to" by the author of the Priestly strand; Brisman maintains that a character identified with the Yahwist strand "reacted to" a composite of the Elohist and Priestly documents.

The plot and themes in *Genesis* offer numerous avenues of critical investigation. D. J. A. Clines examines the ways in which *Genesis* provides hints about the plot and meaning of the Bible. One such way is the series of "announcements" made by God. Clines studies how these announcements are fulfilled and what they lead the reader to believe. He maintains that often the announcements made in *Genesis* are not brought to fulfillment until much later in the Bible, as late as 2 Kings 25. In conclusion, Clines states that *Genesis* foreshadows the events to come in subsequent chapters of the Bible. Thematic studies of *Genesis* are another area of scholarly analysis. Edwin M. Good examines *Genesis'* thematic irony, which Good defines as the conjunction of several episodes which all point to an ironic theme or motif. Good identifies the thematic irony in a number of stories, including the stories of creation, Cain and Abel, the flood, Abraham, Jacob, and Joseph. The ironic theme of the first eleven chapters of *Genesis*, argues Good, is the perception of the incongruity between God's purpose in creating man, and man's actual nature. Like Good, D. J. A. Clines searches for the theme of *Genesis* 1-11. Clines offers two possible versions of the theme of this portion of *Genesis*: that man destroys God's

creation, and despite God's forgiveness and/or punishment, sin continues; or: that no matter how severe man's sin, God's grace continues to save mankind from the consequences of sin. Another portion of the *Genesis* text singled out for thematic study is the story of Adam and Eve. Alan Jon Hauser contends that the theme of intimacy in *Genesis* 2 (God's creation of man and woman) is intertwined with the theme of alienation in *Genesis* 3 (man and woman's original sin against God). This dual theme, argues Hauser, integrates the narrative and is used as a literary device by the author to reveal the disruption of order that occurs in day-to-day life. While Hauser's analysis focuses on the disorder that apparently results from the sin of Adam and Eve, other critics view the end of this tale somewhat differently. Dan E. Burns studies the inconsistencies within this myth, finding that they are only problematic when viewed from a logical, rather than literary, standpoint. Burns concludes that the tale is best viewed as an awakening, rather than the fall of man. Similarly, Sam Dragga identifies several assumptions that are traditionally held about the Adam and Eve story, assumptions which yield a tragic interpretation of the myth. Dragga argues that when the connotations of these assumptions—such as the assumptions that the serpent's intentions are malicious or that God is omnipotent—are properly understood, the story may be viewed as one of man's liberation, rather than the fall of humanity.

PRINCIPAL WORKS

Principal English Translations

Authorized King James Version with Apocrypha Bible (1998)
The Holy Bible: King James Version (1999)

CRITICISM

Kenneth Burke (essay date 1958)

SOURCE: "On the First Three Chapters of *Genesis*," *Daedalus,* Vol. 87, Summer, 1958, pp. 37-64.

[*In the following essay, Burke offers an examination of the covenants depicted in* Genesis, *focusing primarily on the nature of disorder, temptation, and man's "fall."*]

INTRODUCTION: ON COVENANT AND ORDER

We want so to relate the ideas of Creation, Covenant, and Fall that they can be seen to implicate one another inextricably, along with ideas of Sacrifice and Redemption.

Creation implies authority in the sense of originator, the designer or author of the things created.

Covenant implies authority in the sense of power, sovereignty—the highest or more radical sovereignty in case the Covenant is made by God.

The possibility of a "Fall" is implied in the idea of a Covenant insofar as the idea of a Covenant implies the possibility of its being violated. One does not make a covenant with stones or trees or fire—for such things cannot break agreements or defy commands, since they cannot even understand agreements or commands.

Also, the possibility of a "Fall" is implied in the idea of the Creation, insofar as the Creation was a kind of "divisiveness," since it set up different categories of things which could be variously at odds with one another and which accordingly lack the proto-Edenic simplicity of absolute unity. Thus Coleridge observes (*Table Talk,* May 1, 1830):

> A Fall of some sort or other—the creation, as it were, of the non-absolute—is the fundamental postulate of the moral history of man. Without this hypothesis, man is unintelligible; with it, every phenomenon is explicable. The mystery itself is too profound for human insight.

Though this may be a mystery theologically, its logological analogue is not mysterious. Logologically, there is a "fall" from a prior state of unity whenever some one term is broken into two or more terms, so that we have the "divisiveness" of "classification" where we formerly had had a "vision of perfect oneness." If the title of a book could be said to sum up the nature of that book, then the breakdown of the book into parts, chapters, paragraphs, sentences, words would be technically a "fall" from the Edenic unity of the title, or epitomizing "god-term." The parts of the book reduce its "idea" to "matter." Or, as Coleridge said (*Table Talk,* October 15, 1833): "The Trinity is the Idea: the Incarnation, which implies the Fall, is the Fact: the redemption is the mesothesis of the two—that is—the Religion."

Presumably he is thinking of "religion" here in the sense of *religare* (to bind, connect, fasten)—and the logological analogue to his theory in this instance would concern our way of tying the particulars of a work together in accordance with the over-all spirit signalized by its unitary and unifying title.

Narratively, there was the Creation; then came the "Edenic" Covenant (which included the injunction against eating of the tree of the knowledge of good and evil); then the Fall; and then the "Adamic" Covenant (III, 14-19), which included punishments for Adam's first disobedience. But though this order is irreversible from the standpoint of narrative, there is a sense in which we can reverse the order. For instance, we could "begin" with the idea of a punishment; next we could note that the idea of

punishment implies the idea of some infraction which makes the punishment relevant; and such infraction implies the need for a set of conditions that make the infraction possible; and insofar as we looked for a "first" set of such conditions, the idea of them would imply the idea of the kind of Creation that allowed for disobedience.

Again, in the idea of punishment we might discern another kind of implication. Punishment being a kind of "payment" for wrong, we can see flickering about the edges of the idea of punishment the idea of redemption. To "pay" for one's wrongdoing by suffering punishment is to "redeem" oneself, to cancel one's debt, to ransom, or "buy back."

Next, since the idea of an agent is implicit in the idea of an act, we can say that in the idea of redemption there is implicit the idea of a personal redeemer. Or, if you think of redemption as a condition or situation (a "scene"), then you may extract the same implication by thinking of a redeemer as an instrument, or agency, for bringing about the condition. And this step, you will note, automatically includes the idea of a substitution: the possibility that one character may be redeemed through the act or agency of another.

The idea of such substitution, or vicarage, neatly parallels at one end of the series an idea at the other: the notion that, as one character can redeem another by suffering in his stead, so one character can impute guilt to another by sinning in his stead. This would be true of the Pauline logic whereby Adam's disobedience represents a guiltiness in Everyman with regard to Covenants ("In Adam's fall / We sinned all") and there is introduced a principle of representation whereby a "second Adam" can serve as sacrificial substitute for mankind when the categorical guiltiness is being "paid for."

More specifically, the conditions for such a doctrine of "original sin" are set up when our "first" parent who commits the crucial sin has a name at once individual and generic, a name that can be translated either as "Adam" or as "man." Thus, in his sin as "Adam," he can personate mankind in general. We shall later consider other ways in which the purely narrative style operates here, but this shift between individual and generic should be enough for the moment.

The other six great Covenants mentioned in the Bible are the Noachian, Abrahamic, Mosaic, Palestinian, Davidic, and New (as in Hebrews VIII, 8). But the two mentioned in the first three chapters (the Edenic and the Adamic) are sufficient for our purposes, except that the step from punishment to redemption is tenuous. There are the ceremony of redemption by vicarious atonement in connection with the feast of the Passover (Exodus XII) and the sacrificial slaying of the goat set apart for Azazel (Leviticus XVI). Earlier, the principle of a personal redeemer was clearly present in Abraham's offering of Isaac (*Genesis* XXII). And as early as *Genesis* VIII, 20-21 (in connection with the third Covenant), Noah makes burnt offerings "of every clean fowl" (whereat the Lord "smelled a sweet savour" and "said in his heart, I will not again curse the ground any more for man's sake").

Though the idea of a redemptive sacrifice is clear enough as regards the Biblical idea of a Covenant in general, it is but inchoately there as regards the two Covenants in the first three chapters of *Genesis*. We have tried to argue for its implicit presence by showing that the idea of redemption is a further stage in the idea of punishment, and the idea of a redeemer (hence, of vicarious atonement) is implicit in the idea of redemption. And as regards our over-all concern (with the notion that the idea of a redeemer is implicit in the idea of a Covenant in general), the later developments of the Bible itself with relation to God's "peculiar people" make this relation clear enough.

But I might add, incidentally, that one Bible I happen to be consulting, *The Scofield Reference Bible,* professes to find "the first promise of a Redeemer" in *Genesis* III, 15, where the Lord God, in cursing the serpent for having tempted Eve, decrees: "And I will put enmity between thee and the woman, and between thy seed and her seed; and it shall bruise thy head, and thou shalt bruise his heel." The editor asserts that here begins "the highway of the Seed," which he traces through Abel, Seth, Noah (*Genesis* VI, 8-10), Shem (*Genesis* IX, 26-27), Abraham (*Genesis* XII, 1-4), Isaac (*Genesis* XVII, 19-21), Jacob (*Genesis* XXVIII, 10-14), Judah (*Genesis* XLIX, 10), David (2 Samuel VII, 5-17), Immanuel-Christ (Isaiah VII, 9-14; Matthew I, 1, 20-23; 1 John III, 8; John XII, 31). Thus, however strained the point may seem, it should apply insofar as there is a continuity between the idea of temptation and the idea of a redeemer when this continuity is expressed in terms of a continuity of "the Seed," from the locus of "original sin" to the locus of its cancellation by redemptive sacrifice. Or, otherwise put: the hereditary line here listed would represent at every stage a contact with the principle of a Covenant, and the principle of a Covenant contains within itself the principles of both temptation (on the part of one who might break the Covenant) and "repayment" (or "redemption") insofar as the aggrieved party is willing to impose and accept a fine or forfeit. (The thought, incidentally, suggests how the ideas of "justice" and "mercy" will also be found implicit in the idea of a Covenant—"justice" being but the idea of a proper repayment and "mercy" the "good" word for the idea of a willingness to accept a repayment that in some notable respect is disproportionate to the gravity of the offense.)

In Rashi's *Commentary on the Pentateuch,* with regard to the opening formula ("In the beginning") another commenator is quoted to this effect: The main object of the Law (or Torah) being to teach commandments *(mitzvoth),* if this were the only consideration involved the Bible could have begun with the second verse of Exodus XII ("This month shall be unto you the beginning of months: it shall be the first month of the year to you"). Notably for our

purposes, the passage he mentions deals with the rite of the paschal lamb sacrificed at Passover, and thus contains the thought that in a notable respect this book of beginnings might have begun with the principle of sacrifice.

For our purposes, this is a most important consideration. For we are to deal above all with "firsts" (or "principles"). More specifically, we are to be concerned with the "firsts" or "principles" of Covenants. And we are to be on the lookout for the important role played by the sacrificial principle in the cycle of terms that cluster about the idea of a Covenant. So it is notable that the most famous Jewish commentary on *Genesis* begins by considering a possible alternative first, one having to do with the instituting of a sacrifice as regards the Lord's governmental contract with his chosen people.

However, we are told in the Rashi commentary that the Bible begins as it does rather than with the establishing of a paschal ceremony because the first words of *Genesis*, by showing all the world to be the property of God, make clear Israel's rights to seize the lands of the Canaanites, since God could dispose of his property as he chose, and he chose to give the lands of Canaan to the Israelites. (Incidentally, there is a sense in which the beginning of *Genesis* as we now have it would be the proper "pre-first," even for the commentator's claim: it sets up the conditions of division and dominion necessary for the idea of a Covenant by which Canaan became a promised land.)

Rashi also cites a rabbinical interpretation to the effect that God created the world for the sake of the Law (the Torah). And in connection with this position (as against the notion that the Bible is attempting to say what came first in time), he notes that there were waters before the creating of heaven and earth. (Also, the very word for "heavens" is a combination of words for "fire" and "water.")

Rashi is interested in bringing out the notion that the world was created by God not solely to the ends of justice, but first of all to the ends of mercy combined with justice. As regards our cycle of the terms implicit in the idea of a Covenant, we need but note that the ideas of both justice and mercy are present in the idea of repayment for the breaking of a contract (justice when the penalty is proportionate to the offense, mercy when the penalty is favorably disproportionate, while injustice would involve a penalty unfavorably disproportionate).

As regards Rashi's questioning of the notion that the Creation story in *Genesis* is dealing strictly with firsts in time, we should find his reservations logologically much to our purposes. Logologically, *Genesis* would be interpreted as dealing with principles (with logical "firsts," rather than sheerly temporal ones). From the very start it is dealing with the principles of governance (firsts expressed in quasi-temporal terms, since they are the kind most natural to the narrative style). That is, the account of the Creation should be interpreted as saying in effect: This is, in principle, a statement of what the natural order must be like if it is to fit perfectly the conditions of human socio-political order (conditions that come to a focus in the idea of a basic Covenant backed by a perfect authority).

To get the point, turn now to Pope's line, "Order is Heaven's first law." In Pope's formula, the idea of a "first" is ambiguous. The reader is not quite sure (nor need he be) whether it means first in time, or first in importance, or first in the sense of a logical grounding for all other laws, a kind of "causal ancestor" from which all other "laws" could be deduced or derived as lineal descendants.

Once we have brought out the strategic importance of the part played by the Biblical stress upon the idea of Covenant, there are advantages to be gained by locating our cycle of dramatistic terms about the term "Order" rather than about the term "Covenant."

The most general starting point for the dramatistic cycle of terms would be in the term "act." Under this head would belong God's creative acts in the first chapter of *Genesis,* God's enactment of the first Covenant (largely permissive, but with one crucial negative command), Adam's act of disobedience, and God's enactment of a second Covenant imposing penalties upon all mankind.

Also, of course, there would be terms for the many kinds of "rationally" purposive motion, along with their corresponding "passions," which characterize human life in all its aspects. These would be without such stress upon "sin" or "guilt" as necessarily arises when we deal with the story of a first temptation. But for this very reason, such a general approach to a dramatistic cycle of terms would not serve our present purpose. Frankly, it would not be morbid enough. We need an approach that, like the Bible itself, leads us from a first Adam, in whom all vicariously "sinned," to a "second Adam" by whom all might vicariously make atonement. For we are trying to analyze the respects in which the ideas of both guilt and redemption by vicarious sacrifice are intrinsic to the idea of a Covenant (which in turn is intrinsic to the idea of governance).

Yet the term "Covenant" is not wholly convenient for our purposes. Having no opposite in standard usage, it seems as purely "positive" as words like "stone," "tree," or "table," which are not matched by companion words like "counter-stone," "anti-tree," or "un-table" (except sometimes in the dialectic of E. E. Cummings). And perhaps the notion of "positive law" secretly contributes to one's feeling that "Covenants" can be treated as "positive," despite the all-importance of the negative in defining the conditions of Adam's fall. The term "Order," on the other hand, clearly reveals its dialectical or "polar" nature on its face. "Order" implies "disorder" and vice versa. And that is the kind of term we need.

However, when putting it in place of the word "Covenant," we should try never to forget Hobbes's emphasis upon the severities of sovereignty as integral to the kind of Order

we shall be studying. The idea of "Order" is ambiguous not only in the sense that it contains an idea of "Disorder." The term "Order" is ambiguous also because it can be applied to two quite different areas, either to such natural regularities as tides and seasons or to socio-political structures in which people can give or receive orders, in which orders can be obeyed or disobeyed, in which offices are said to pyramid in an orderly arrangement of powers and responsibilities. The double notion of God's authority (in his roles as both originator and sovereign) obviously combines both of these meanings. It joins the idea of the creative verbal fiats by which God brought the natural order into existence and the idea of a divine ruler laying down the law by words, in keeping with Hobbes's stout statement: "He only is properly said to reign, that governs his subjects by his word, and by promise of rewards to those that obey it, and by threatening them with punishment that obey it not."

Our task, then, is to examine the term "Order" by asking what cluster of ideas is "tautologically" present in the idea of Order. Such a cycle of terms follows no one sequence. That is, we may say either that the idea of Disorder is implicit in the idea of Order or that the idea of Order is implicit in the idea of Disorder. Or we might say that the idea of Order implies the ideas of Obedience and Disobedience, or that either of them implies the other, or that either or both imply the idea of an Order, and so on.

However, when such terministic interrelationships are embodied in the narrative style (involving acts, images, and personalities) an irreversibility of the sequence can become of major importance. For instance, the implications of a story that proceeds from order to disorder (or from obedience to disobedience) differ greatly from those of a story that proceeds in the other direction. We may say that "success" and "failure" imply each other, without equating the step from success to failure with the step from failure to success. There are also paradoxical complications whereby, for instance, a step from success to failure in some respects is at the same time a step from failure to success in other respects. And there is the possibility of a story so self-consistent in structure that an analyst could, ideally, begin at the end and deductively "prophesy" what earlier developments must have taken place for things to culminate as they did. But such considerations merely subtilize the narrative or temporal principle of irreversibility; they do not eliminate it.

The plan, then, is first to evolve a cluster of interrelated key terms implicit in the idea of "Order." Then we shall ask how the narrative, or "rectilinear," style of *Genesis* compares with the "cycle of terms" we have found to revolve "endlessly" about the idea of "Order." And, finally, we shall draw some conclusions from the comparison of the two styles (the "timeless" terministic cluster and the kind of "temporal" sequence embodied in the Biblical myth). The distinction is one touched upon by Coleridge ("Idea of the Prometheus of Aeschylus," in Volume IV of the Shedd edition of his *Complete Works),* where he speaks of the Biblical method as "sacred narrative" and "Hebrew archæology," in contrast with Greek "philosopheme."

TAUTOLOGICAL CYCLE OF TERMS FOR "ORDER"

First, consider the strategic ambiguity whereby the term "Order" may apply both to the realm of nature in general and to the special realm of human socio-political organizations (an ambiguity whereby, so far as sheerly empirical things are concerned, a natural order could be thought to go on existing even if all human beings, with their various socio-political orders, were obliterated). This is a kind of logical pun whereby our ideas of the natural order can become secretly infused by our ideas of the socio-political order.

One might ask: Is not the opposite possibility just as likely? Might not the terms for the socio-political order become infused by the genius of the terms for the natural order? They do, every time we metaphorically extend the literal meaning of a natural image to the realm of the socio-political. It is the point that Bentham made much of in his Theory of Fictions, his systematic procedure ("archetypation") for locating the natural images that may lurk undetected in our ideas and so may mislead us into attempting to deal too strictly in terms of the irrelevant image. For instance, if Churchillian rhetoric gets us to thinking of international relations in such terms as "iron curtains" and "power vacuums," then we must guard lest we respond to the terms too literally—otherwise we shall not conceive of the political situation accurately enough. The Arab nations are no "vacuum." Theologians have made similar observations about the use of natural images to express the idea of godhead.

But it is much more important for our present purposes to spot the movement in the other direction. We need to stress how a vision of the natural order can become infused with the genius of the verbal and socio-political orders.

Thus, from the purely logological point of view we note how, inasmuch as the account of the Creation in *Genesis* involves on each "day" a kind of enactment done through the medium of God's "Word," the sheerly "natural" order contains a verbal element or principle that from the purely empirical point of view could belong only in the socio-political order. Empirically, the natural order of astrophysical motion depends upon no verbal principle for its existence. But theologically it does depend upon a verbal principle. And even though one might say that God's creative fiats and his words to Adam and Eve are to be conceived as but analogous to ordinary human verbal communication, our point remains the same. For from the empirical point of view, there would not even be an analogy between natural origins and responses to the power of words. The world of natural, nonverbal motions must be empirically the kind of world that could continue with its motions even if it contained no species, such as man, capable of verbal action; and it must be described without any reference to a Creation by verbal fiat, whether or not there had been such.

By a dramatistic ambiguity, standard usage bridges this distinction between the realms of verbal action and nonverbal motion when it speaks of sheerly natural objects or processes as "actualities." Here even in a purely secular usage we can discern a trace of the theological view that sees nature as the sign of God's action—and thus by another route we see the theological way of merging the principle of the natural order with the principle of verbal contract or covenant intrinsic to legal enactment in the socio-political order.

But to proceed with the "tautologies":

If, by "Order," we have in mind the idea of a command, then obviously the corresponding word for the proper response would be "Obey." Or there would be the alternative, "Disobey." Thus we have the proportion: Order is to Disorder as Obedience is to Disobedience. However, there is a logological sense in which the things of nature could be called "innocent." They cannot disobey commands, since they cannot understand commands. They do not have a "sense of right and wrong" or, more generically, a "sense of yes and no." They simply do as they do—and that's that. Such would be the *non posse peccare* of natural things or even of humans insofar as their "natural" state was not bound by moralistic negatives. All was permissive in Eden but the eating of the one forbidden fruit, the single negative that set the conditions for the Fall (since, St. Paul pointed out, only the law can make sin, as Bentham was later to point out that only the law can make crime). The Biblical myth pictures natural things as coming into being through the agency of God's Word; but they can merely do as they are told, whereas with God's permission, though not without his resentment, the seed of Adam can do even what it has been explicitly told not to do. The word-using animal not only understands a thou-shalt-not; it can carry the principle of the negative a step further, and answer the thou-shalt-not with a disobedient No. Logologically, the distinction between natural innocence and fallen man hinges about this problem of language and the negative. Eliminate language from nature and there can be no moral disobedience. In this sense, moral disobedience is "doctrinal." Like faith, it is grounded in language.

Looking into the act of Disobedience, we come upon the need for some such term as "Pride" to name the corresponding attitude that precedes the act. And some such term as "Humility" names the idea of the attitude that leads into the act of Obedience.

But implicit in the distinction between Obedience and Disobedience there is the idea of some dividing line, some "watershed" that is itself midway between the two slopes. Often a word used for naming this ambiguous moment is "Will" or, more fully, "Free Will," which is thought of as a faculty that makes possible the choice between the yea-saying of Humble Obedience or the nay-saying of Prideful Disobedience (the choice between *serviam* and *non serviam*).

Ontologically, and theologically, we say that this locus of freedom makes possible the kind of personal choice we have in mind when we speak of "Action." But note that, logologically, the statement should be made the other way round. That is, whereas ontologically or theologically we say that by being endowed with free will man is able to act morally, the corresponding logological statement would be: Implicit in the idea of an act is the idea of free will. (Another version of the formula would be: Implicit in the idea of an act is the idea of freedom.)

The ontological and theological statements may or may not be true. The logological statement would be "true logologically" even if it were not true ontologically. That is, even if we hypothetically supposed, with strict behaviorists and the like, that there is no such thing as "free will," that all "action" is reducible to terms of mechanical "motion," it would still remain true that implicit in the idea of action there is the idea of freedom. If one cannot make a choice, one is not acting, one is but being moved, like a billiard ball tapped with a cue and behaving mechanically in conformity with the resistances it encounters. But even if men are doing nothing more than that, the word "act" implies that they are doing more—and we are now concerned solely with the implications of terms.

As regards the dramatistic tautology in general, an act is done by an agent in a scene. But such an act is usually preceded by a corresponding attitude, or "incipient act" (as when an act of friendliness follows a friendly attitude on the part of the agent). The scene is the motivational locus of the act insofar as the act represents a scene-act ratio (as, for instance, when an "emergency situation" is said to justify an "emergency measure"). But as the act derives from an attitude of the agent, the agent-act ratio can be narrowed to an attitude-act ratio, as when a friendly agent does a friendly act. The term "Will" is apparently designed to assign a "place" to the choice between different possibilities of attitude-act development. Here a verb is thought of as a noun; the idea of "the will" as willing is conceived after the analogy of rain raining, though we do not speak of fear as fearing. But the idea of such a locus for "the Will" brings up a further problem: What in turn influences "the Will"?

On the Disorder side, this role is assigned to the Imagination, insofar as the imagination's close connection with sensory images is thought both to make it highly responsive to the sensory appetites and to make sensory appetites more enticing. In brief, the combination of Imagination and the Senses, by affecting the Will from the side of Disorder, is said to predispose toward Temptation, except as Imagination in turn is corrected from the side of Order by the controls of Reason and Faith (which can also be thought of as having a controlling effect upon each other). Another refinement here is the notion that, once Imagination is on the side of Reason, it can contribute to Order, rather than to Disorder, by making reasonable things seem sensible and thus inducing the Wills of persons weak in Reason to none the less freely choose, as it were, reasonably and thus to act on the side of Order, eschewing Temptation.

The idea of Reason in such a system is obviously permeated with ideas of Dominion, owing to its identification with ideas of control and as indicated in the formula, "the Rule of Reason." So it brings us clearly back to the principle of sovereignty underlying the general idea of Order by Covenant. The relation between Reason and Faith becomes ambiguous because of the possible shift between the natural order and the socio-political order as grounds of Reason. For if the socio-political Order is conceived in "ultimate" terms (as it is in the idea of a Covenant derived from God), then Faith must be a kind of control higher than Reason, insofar as Reason is identified with "Natural Law" and with purely worldly rules of governance. (Incidentally, we might note the strongly verbal element in both, as indicated by the close relation between Rational and Logical and by St. Paul's statement that the doctrines of the Faith are learned "by hearing." However, there is said to be a further stage of supernatural awareness, called by St. Anselm *contemplatio* and by Spinoza *scientia intuitiva,* which would by definition transcend the verbal.)

There is also an act-agent ratio, as with the Aristotelian notion of *hexis, habitus,* the notion that a person may develop a virtuous Disposition by the practices of virtue or a vicious Disposition by repeated indulgence in vice. And this brings us to the subtlest term of all as regards the set of major dramatistic terms clustering about the idea of Order; namely, Mortification.

Of all theology-tinged terms that need logological reclamation and refurbishment, this is perhaps the most crucial. Here the motives of sacrifice and dominion come to a head in everyday living. The possibility is that most ailments now said to be of "psychogenic" origin are but secularized variants of what might be called "mortification in spite of itself." That is, if we are right in assuming that governance makes "naturally" for victimage, either of others (homicidally) or of ourselves (suicidally), then we may expect to encounter many situations in which a man, by attitudes of self-repression, often causes or aggravates his own bodily and mental ills.

The derived meaning (humiliation, vexation, chagrin) would figure here. But mainly we have in mind the Grand Meaning, "subjection of the passions and appetites, by penance, abstinence, or painful severities inflicted on the body," mortification as a kind of governance, an extreme form of "self-control," the deliberate, disciplinary "slaying" of any motive that, for "doctrinal" reasons, one thinks of as unruly. In an emphatic way, mortification is the exercising of oneself in "virtue"; it is a systematic way of saying no to Disorder, or obediently saying yes to Order. Its opposite is license, *luxuria,* "fornication," saying yes to Disorder, no to Order.

The principle of Mortification is particularly crucial to conditions of empire, which act simultaneously to awaken all sorts of odd and exacting appetites, while at the same time imposing equally odd and exacting obstacles to their fulfillment. For "mortification" does not occur when one is merely "frustrated" by some external interference. It must come from within. The mortified must, with one aspect of himself, be saying no to another aspect of himself—hence the urgent incentive to be "purified" by "projecting" his conflict upon a scapegoat, by seeking a sacrificial vessel upon which he can vent, as from without, a turmoil that is actually within. "Psychogenic illness" would occur in cases in which one was scrupulous enough to deny himself such easy outgoing relief and, instead, in all sorts of roundabout ways, scrupulously circled back upon himself, unintentionally making his own constitution the victim of his hierarchally goaded entanglements.

To complete the pattern: On the side of Order, where the natural actualities created by verbal fiat are completed in sovereignty and subjection by Covenant, with Obedience goes promise of reward (as payment for service), while on the other side goes Disobedience, with threat of punishment as enforced payment for disservice.

Then comes the Grand Rounding Out, where the principle of reward as payment (from the Order side) merges with the principle of punishment as payment (from the Disorder side), to promise of redemption by vicarious atonement. Sovereignty and subjection (the two poles of governance) are brought together in the same figure (Christ as King and Christ as Servant, respectively)—and the contradiction between these principles is logically resolved by a narrative device, the notion of two advents whereby Christ could appear once as servant and the second time as king. Here is the idea of a "perfect" victim to cancel (or "cover") what was in effect the "perfect" sin (its technical perfection residing in the fact that it was the first transgression of the first man against the first and foremost authority).

However, the symmetry of the design does not resolve the problem of the "watershed moment," the puzzle of the relation between "determinism" and "free will." The search for a cause is itself the search for a scapegoat, as Adam blames Eve, Eve blames the serpent, the serpent could have blamed Lucifer, and Lucifer could have blamed the temptations implicit in the idea of Order (the inchoate "fall" that, as we saw in the quotation from Coleridge, is intrinsic to the "creation of the non-absolute"). Adam himself has a hint of the Luciferian rejoinder when he says to the Lord God that he received the fruit from "the woman whom thou gavest to be with me." Also, from the purely imagistic point of view, there is a sense in which the Lord God has caused Adam to be tempted by an aspect of himself, in accordance with the original obstetrical paradox whereby woman was born of man.

Here would be a purely "grammatical" way of stating the case: If order, implying the possibility of disorder, implies a possible act of disobedience, then there must be an agent so endowed, or so minded, that such an act is possible to him—and the motives for such an act must eventually somehow be referred to the scene out of which he arose and which thus somehow contains the principles that in their way make a "bad" act possible.

Arrived at this point, we might shift the problem of the "watershed moment" to another plane, by recalling that the same conditions of divisiveness also make for the inchoately "holy," inasmuch as the Hebrew word for "holy," *qodesh,* means literally the "separate," the "set apart," as does the word *qudesh,* which means "Sodomite." This verbal tangle has often been commented on, and it applies also to the New Testament word *hagios,* which means both "holy" and "accursed," like its Latin counterpart, *sacer.* Here, we might say, is a purely terministic equivalent of the problem of choice, or motivational slope. The question of de-terminism narrows down to a kind of term that within itself contains two slopes (two different judgments or "crises").

As regards the matter of terms, we could move into the area of personality proper by equating human personality with the ability to use symbol-systems (centering in the feeling for the negative, since "reason," in its role as the "sense of right and wrong," is but a special case of the "sense of yes and no"). Thus, more broadly, we could say that the conception of the creative verbal fiat in *Genesis* is essentially the *personal principle.* But insofar as personal character is defined by choice (*cf.* Aristotle on *proairesis, Poetics,* VI, 24), the question becomes one of deciding how far back the grounds of choice must be traced. Since *Genesis* would depict us as arising from a scene that is the act of a super-person and redemption is thought to be got by voluntary enlistment on the side of Order, conceived sacrificially, the ultimate formula becomes that of Jeremiah XXXI, 18: "Turn thou me, and I shall be turned" (*converte me, et convertar*). Here the indeterminate watershed of "free" choice is reducible to a question of this sort: Though all men are given enough "grace" to be saved, how can anyone be saved but by being given enough grace to be sure of using it? Yet how could he have as much saving grace as that, without in effect being compelled to be saved (in which case he would not, in the last analysis, have "free will")?

Fortunately, it is not our duty, as logologers, to attempt solving this ultimate theological riddle, entangled in ideas of providence, predestination, and the possibilities of an elect, chosen from among the depraved, all of whom deserve eternal damnation, but some of whom are saved by God in his mysterious mercy and may attest to their future glory by becoming a kind of materially prosperous elite here and now.

Fortunately, as logologers, we need but consider the ways in which such ideas are interwoven with the conditions of dominion, as they prevail among human symbol-using animals. As seen in this light, the thought of all such issues leads us to revision of our initial dialectical pattern. That is, the Order-Disorder pair is not enough. And what we need now is another kind of antithesis, setting Order against Counter-Order.

Methodologically, we might say that we have now come upon the penalties resulting from our earlier decision to approach this problem in terms of "Order" rather than in terms of "Covenant." For the idea of a "Counter-Covenant" would have been somewhat different from the idea of such a mere disintegration as is usually suggested by the term "Disorder."

In sum, there is a notable qualitative difference between the idea of a mere "fall" from a position in which one still believes, but to which one is at times unequal, and the idea of a deliberate turn to an alternative allegiance. It would be a difference between being "weak in virtue" and being "strong in sin."

But perhaps we should try to sum up the line of reasoning we have been pursuing in these last paragraphs. We have been considering the problem of a possible ultimate ground for "Temptation." Logologically, "Temptation" is but a tautological aspect of the idea of "Order." It is grounded in the idea of a verbal command, which by its very nature contains possibilities of both obedience and disobedience. We do not "command" the nonverbalizing things of nature. To the best of our ability, we simply set up conditions which we think likely to bring about the kind of situation we desire. We reserve our commands (or requests!) for language-using entities that can, to varying degrees, resist. And the command is backed, explicit or implicitly, by promises or threats.

However, ontologically, or theologically, such a purely "tautological" point of view would not be enough. And we confront such problems as St. Augustine was concerned with in his battles with the Manichaeans. We may, like the Manichaeans, conceive of an ultimate Tempter, existing in his own right and with powers rivaling those of God. Or we may derive everything from a God who is by definition merciful, and good, the author of a wholly good Creation, yet who not only lets man sin but permits the existence and incessant schemings of a supernatural tempter endowed with diabolical ingenuity and persuasiveness. Hence arises the "problem of evil" (as with Augustine's urgent question, "*Unde malum?*"). We have considered in the previous talk how Augustine proposed to solve the problem theologically by his notion of evil as a "deficient cause," a kind of "eclipse."

But logologically, the question takes on a different form. Logologically, moral "evil" is a species of negative, a purely linguistic (or "rational") principle. And insofar as natural calamities are viewed in terms of moral retribution, we should say that the positive events of nature are being seen through the eyes of moral negativity (another instance of ways whereby the genius of the verbal and socio-political orders can come to permeate our ideas of the natural order). All told, "evil" is implicit in the idea of "Order" because "Order" is a polar, or dialectical term, implying an idea of "Disorder."

But there can be two kinds of "Disorder": (1) a tendency toward failure to obey completely always; (2) disobedience due to an out-and-out enrollment in the ranks of a rival force. We might call this a distinction between mere Disorder and deliberate allegiance to a Counter-Order. (There is an analogous situation in contemporary politics, since a person's disagreements with those in authority may be interpreted either as temperamental deviation from the prevailing orthodoxy or as sinister, secret adherence to an organized enemy alien power.)

Theologically, perhaps the analogous distinction would be between the kind of "Temptation" that is intrinsic to the possibility of choice and the kind that attains its ideal perfection in the notion of a Faustian pact with the Devil— the difference between ordinary "backsliding" and "heresy" or "black magic." Problems of "predestination" lie in the offing, inasmuch as different people are differently tempted or differently enlightened and such differences are not of their own choosing but arise in connection with the accidents of each man's unique, particular destiny. (In the *Confessions,* for instance, we see St. Augustine interpreting as God's will many decisions which he had made for quite different personal reasons. And no man could sell his soul to the Devil if God, who was necessarily present at the signing of the contract, but chose that moment to flood the victim's imagination with the full realization of his danger.)

At this point, we should look at Hobbes's *Leviathan,* since it illustrates so well the idea of Disorder in this more aggressive sense of a Covenant matched by a "Counter-Covenant." And in the course of doing so, it well illustrates the role of the sacrificial principle which we believe to be "logologically inseparable" from the idea of dominion.

COVENANT AND "COUNTER-COVENANT" IN
HOBBES'S LEVIATHAN

Part I of the *Leviathan* is "Of Man." But this subtitle can easily mislead us. For Part I is not just "Of Man." It is *of man in the commonwealth.* That is, the principle of Part II, which explicitly concerns commonwealth, is already implicit as a germ in Part I. Thus there is no break in continuity as we turn from Part I to Part II. The quickest way to make it obvious that the motives of commonwealth are already operating in the first section, and coloring the philosopher's view of man qua man, is to cite such chapter headings as: "Of Power, Worth, Dignity, Honour, and Worthiness" and "Of Persons, Authors, and Things Personated." Perhaps one cannot explicitly write just "of man" without implicitly writing of man in the commonwealth (or, at least, of man in the tribe), since man is, as Aristotle puts it in good Athenian fashion, a "political animal."

Similarly, in **Genesis,** though the first three Covenants have to do with man and woman, brothers, parents, and children, and though it is not until the fourth, or Abrahamic, Covenant that God deals with Israel as a nation, yet the generic and familial motives exemplified in these early Covenants are but the beginnings of such motives as come clear in terms of dominion, however theocratically conceived. This is to say that man's notion of his "pre-political" self will necessarily be seen in the light of a socio-political perspective. And all the more so because "pre-political" childhood is experienced in terms of family relationships that are themselves shaped by tribal or national conditions as a whole.

As regards Part II, "Of Commonwealth": If one reads this section along the lines of our notion that the first section is "in principle" saying the same thing, one gets the essence of Hobbes's politics. Here, near the end of Chapter XVII, occurs an almost gloriously resonant passage succinctly summing up the Hobbesian notion of a Covenant, made with a "common power" and designed to keep the covenanters "in awe and to direct their actions to the common benefit":

> The only way to erect such a common power, as may be able to defend them from the invasion of foreigners, and the injuries of one another, and thereby to secure them in such sort, as that by their own industry, and by the fruits of the earth, they may nourish themselves and live contentedly; is, to confer all their power and strength upon one man, or upon one assembly of men, that may reduce all their wills, by plurality of voices, unto one will: which is as much as to say, to appoint one man, or assembly of men, to bear their person; and every one to own, and acknowledge himself to be author of whatsoever he that so beareth their person, shall act, or cause to be acted, in those things which concern the common peace and safety; and therein to submit their wills, every one to his will, and their judgments, to his judgment. This is more than consent, or concord; it is a real unity of them all, in one and the same person, made by covenant of every man with every man, in such manner, as if every man should say to every man, *I authorize and give up my right of governing myself, to this man, or to this assembly of men, on this condition, that thou give up thy right to him, and authorize all his actions in like manner.* This done, the multitude so united in one person, is called a COMMONWEALTH, in Latin CIVITAS. This is the generation of that great LEVIATHAN, or rather, to speak more reverently, of that *mortal god,* to which we owe under the *immortal God,* our peace and defence. For by this authority, given him by every particular man in the commonwealth, he hath the use of so much power and strength conferred on him, that by terror thereof, he is enabled to form the wills of them all, to peace at home, and mutual aid against their enemies abroad. And in him consisteth the essence of the commonwealth; which, to define it, is *one person, of whose acts a great multitude, by mutual covenants one with another, have made themselves every one the author, to the end he may use the strength and means of them all, as he shall think expedient, for their peace and common defence.*

> And he that carrieth this person, is called SOVEREIGN, and said to have *sovereign power;* and every one besides, his SUBJECT.

In Part III ("Of a Christian Commonwealth") Hobbes adds a dimension, by introducing from the Bible his terms for what he calls "Christian politics." Essentially, this section involves his devices for subjecting priest-rule to the powers of secular sovereignty. That is to say: In another way, by new ingenuities, he reaffirms the principles of the commonwealth that were adumbrated in Part I and explicitly expounded in Part II. Perhaps the most quotable passage for our purposes is the last paragraph of Chapter XXVIII:

> Hitherto I have set forth the nature of man, whose pride and other passions have compelled him to submit himself to government: together with the great power of his governor, whom I compared to *Leviathan,* taking that comparison out of the two last verses of the one-and-fortieth of *Job;* where God having set forth the great power of *Leviathan,* calleth him King of the Proud. *There is nothing,* saith he, *on earth, to be compared with him. He is made so as not to be afraid. He seeth every high thing below him; and is king of all the children of pride.* But because he is mortal, and subject to decay, as all other earthly creatures are; and because there is that in heaven, though not on earth, that he should stand in fear of, and whose laws he ought to obey; I shall in the next following chapters speak of his diseases, and the causes of his mortality; and of what laws of nature he is bound to obey.

The reference to Leviathan as "King of the Proud" is perfect for our purposes. However, we have said that where Governance is, there is the goad to scapegoats.

And that brings us to Part IV ("Of the Kingdom of Darkness"). The curative victim here is not Christ, but Popery, conceived as Anti-Christ.

At this point (praise Logology!) we most decidedly need not enter the fray on Hobbesian terms. But we most decidedly should be admonished by Hobbes, in accordance with our ways of translating. And his methodologically fundamental admonition gets down to the fact that, in the light of his title for Part IV, "Of the Kingdom of Darkness," we must shift from Order-thinking back to Covenant-thinking and thereby concern ourselves with the sheerly dialectical possibilities of a Counter-Covenant, though the word itself is not in Hobbes.

Viewed here not as doctrine, but as design, Hobbes helps us realize that implicit in the idea of a Covenant is the idea not just of obedience or disobedience to that Covenant, but also of obedience or disobedience to a rival Covenant. The choice thus becomes not just a difference between seeking the light and not seeking the light, but rather the difference between eagerly seeking the light and just as eagerly seeking darkness (a "Disorder" having an "Order" all its own, however insistent the orthodoxy must be that the Satanic counter-realm can exist only by the sufferance of the One Ultimate Authority).

About the edges of all such speculations lie variants of the Manichæan "heresy," according to which Evil is a power in its own right. As we have observed before, logology must side with Augustine's attacks upon this position. For logology looks upon "evil" as a species of the negative and looks upon the negative as a linguistic invention. This would be the logological analogue of Augustine's theological doctrine that *malum* is a *causa deficiens,* a mere deficiency, like an eclipse. And from the purely dialectical point of view, we take it that all admonishment against the temptations of a Counter-Covenant are a recognition of the moral certainty that the mere stating of a position is likely to call forth some opposition. Hobbes's strongly nationalist position made it inevitable that Roman Catholicism would be his scapegoat.

But whether the scapegoat principle be conceived after the analogy of a villain, or after the analogy of arbitrarily chosen vessel that gets its function purely by appointment, or after the analogy of divine paraclete combining exhortation and guidance with victimage, the principle of Mortification is basic to the pattern of governance, as summed up in Paul's paradox (2 Corinthians, XII, 10): "Therefore I take pleasure in infirmities, in reproaches, in necessities, in persecutions, in distresses for Christ's sake: for when I am weak, then I am strong."

The idea of the Sacrificial Redeemer, in bringing together ideas of patience, repentance, and obedience to the verbalities of the faith, reproduces in the large the same principle that prevails in the minute scruples of Mortification. Here also would belong the idea of the "remnant," those especially good Jews who maintained the continuity of a blessed relation to the deity despite the backsliding of the people as a whole. And the priesthood, too, would be an extension of the principle of sacrifice, in that it involves special persons set apart for the sacrificial services. The priests extend the sacrificial principle to themselves insofar as they practice special acts of mortification deemed to fit them for their special office.

The companion principle to such an idea of graceful, voluntary subjection being, of course, sovereignty, the other side of the sovereign-subject relation is presented in terms of the ultimate rewards in store for those of good will who subject themselves to the principle of governance. That is, as with the two advents of Christ, the logical contrast between sovereignty and subjection is resolved by translation into terms of narrative sequence whereby the principle of subjection, of mortification, first prevails, but is finally followed by the sovereign principle of boundless rejoicing. And in the meantime, the notion of "grace" itself (as a way of goading the sluggish Imagination to the proper fears) is extended to include the idea that natural calamities are "acts of God," designed to warn or chasten—whereupon the principle of Mortification is introduced under another guise.

Mortification is as true of Order as mortmain is of contract.

PRINCIPLES OF GOVERNANCE, STATED NARRATIVELY

Imagine that you wanted to say, "The world can be divided into six major classifications." That is, you wanted to deal with "the principles of Order," beginning with the natural order and placing man's socio-political order with reference to it. But you wanted to treat of these matters in nar-

rative terms, which necessarily involve temporal sequence (in contrast with the cycle of terms for "Order," that merely cluster about one another, variously implying one another but in no one fixed sequence).

Stated narratively (in the style of **Genesis,** *Bereshith,* Beginning), such an idea of principles, or "firsts," would not be stated simply in terms of classification, as were we to say "The first of six primary classes would be such-and-such, the second such-and-such," and so on. Rather, a completely narrative style would properly translate the idea of six classes or categories into terms of time, as were we to assign each of the classes to a separate "day." Thus, instead of saying, "And that completes the first broad division, or classification, of our subject matter," we would say, "And the evening and the morning were the first day" (or, more accurately, the "One" Day). And so on, through the six broad classes, ending, "last but not least," on the category of man and his dominion. [The clearest evidence that this principle of "divisiveness" is itself a kind of proto-fall" is to be seen in the use made of it by the segregationists of the southern Bible belt. Members of the Ku Klux Klan refer to the classificatory system of *Genesis* as justification for their stress upon the separation of Negroes and whites. In an ironic sense, they are "right." For when nature is approached via the principle of differentiation embodied in the notion of Social Order, then "Creation" itself is found to contain implicitly the guiltiness of "discrimination." Furthermore, the Word mediates between these two realms. And the Word is social in the sense that language is a collective means of expression, while its sociality is extended to the realm of wordless nature insofar as this nonverbal kind of order is treated in terms of such verbal order as goes with the element of command intrinsic to dominion.]

Further, a completely narrative style would personalize the principle of classification. This role is performed by the references to God's creative fiat, which from the very start infuses the sheerly natural order with the verbal principle (the makings of that "reason" which we take to be so essential an aspect of human personality).

Logologically, the statement that God made man in his image would be translated as: The principle of personality implicit in the idea of the first creative fiats, whereby all things are approached in terms of the word, applies also to the feeling for symbol-systems on the part of the human animal, who would come to read nature as if it were a book. Insofar as God's words infused the natural order with their genius, and insofar as God is represented as speaking words to the first man and woman, the principle of human personality (which is at the very start identified with dominion) has its analogue in the notion of God as a super-person and of nature as the act of such a super-agent. (That is, we take symbol-using to be a distinctive ingredient of "personality.")

Though technically there is a kind of "proto-fall" implicit in the principle of divisiveness that characterizes the

Bible's view of the Creation, and though the principle of subjection is already present (in the general outlines of a government with God at its head and mankind as subject to his authority while in turn having dominion over all else in the natural realm), the Covenant (as first announced in the first chapter) is necessarily Edenic, in a state of "innocency," since no negative command has yet been pronounced. From the dialectical point of view (in line with the Order-Disorder pair) we may note that there is a possibility of "evil" implicit in the reference to all six primary classifications as "good." But in all three points (the divisiveness, the order of dominion, and the universal goodness) the explicit negative is lacking. In fact, the nearest approach to an outright negative (and that not of a moralistic, hortatory sort) is in the reference to the "void" (*bohu*) which preceded God's classificatory acts. Rashi says that the word translated as "formless" (*tohu*) "has the meaning of astonishment and amazement." Incidentally, in connection with I, 29, the *Interpreter's Bible* suggests another implicit negative, in that the explicit permitting of a vegetarian diet implies that Adam may not eat flesh.

In the first chapter of **Genesis,** the stress is upon the creative fiat as a means of classification. It says in effect, "What hath God wrought (by his Word)?" The second chapter's revised account of the Creation shifts the emphasis to matters of dominion, saying in effect, "What hath God ordained (by his words)?" The seventh "day" (or category), which is placed at the beginning of the second chapter, has a special dialectical interest in its role as a transition between the two emphases.

In one sense, the idea of the Sabbath is implicitly a negative, being conceived as antithetical to all the six foregoing categories, which are classifiable together under the single head of "work," in contrast with this seventh category, of "rest." That is, work and rest are "polar" terms, dialectical opposites. (In his *Politics,* Aristotle's terms bring out this negative relation explicitly, since his word for business activity is *ascholein,* that is, "not to be at leisure," though we should tend rather to use the negative the other way round, defining "rest" as "not to be at work.")

This seventh category (of rest after toil) obviously serves well as transition between Order (of God as principle of origination) and Order (of God as principle of sovereignty). Leisure arises as an "institution" only when conditions of dominion have regularized the patterns of work. And, fittingly, just after this transitional passage, the very name of God undergoes a change (the quality of which is well indicated in our translations by a shift from "God" to "Lord God." [Grammatically, the word for God in the first chapter, "Elohim," is a plural. Philologists may interpret this as indicating a usage that survives from an earlier polytheistic period in the development of Jewish Monotheism. Or Christian theologians can interpret it as the first emergence of a Trinitarian position, thus early in the text, with the Creator as first person of the Trinity, the Spirit that hovered over the waters as third person, and the

creative Word as second person. (Incidentally, the words translated as "Lord God" in Chapter II are *Jehovah-Elohim.* Later, in connection with the Abrahamic Covenant, the words translated as "Lord God" are *Adonai Jehovah. Adonai,* which means "master," applies to both God and man—and when applied to man it also includes the idea of husband as master.) The distinction between authority and authorship is approached from another angle in Augustine's *Confessions* I, X, where God is called the *ordinator* and *creator* of all natural things, but of sin he is said to be only the *ordinator.*] Here, whereas in Chapter I, verse 29, God tells the man and woman that the fruit of "every tree" is permitted them, the Lord God (II, 17) notably revises thus: "But of the tree of the knowledge of good and evil, thou shalt not eat of it: for in the day that thou eatest thereof thou shalt surely die." Here, with the stress upon governance, enters the negative of command.

When, later, the serpent tempts "the woman" (III, 4), saying that "Ye shall not surely die," his statement is proved partially correct, to the extent that they did not die on the day on which they ate of the forbidden fruit. In any case, III, 19 pronounces the formula that has been theologically interpreted as deriving mankind's physical death from our first parents' first disobedience: "In the sweat of thy face shalt thou eat bread, till thou return unto the ground; for out of it wast thou taken: for dust thou art, and unto dust shalt thou return."

The *Interpreter's Bible* (page 512) denies that there is any suggestion that man would have lived forever had he not eaten of the forbidden fruit. Verse III, 20 is taken to imply simply that man would have regarded death as his natural end, rather than as "the last fearful frustration." Thus, the fear of death is said to be "the consequence of the disorder in man's relationships" when they are characterized "by domination" (along with the fear that the subject will break free of their subjection). This seems to be at odds with the position taken by the *Scofield Bible,* which, in the light of Paul's statements in Romans V, 12-21 ("by one man sin entered the world, and death by sin" and "by one man's offence death reigned by one") interprets the passage as meaning that "physical death" is due to a "universal sinful state, or nature," which is "our heritage from Adam."

It is within neither our present purpose nor our competency to interpret this verse theologically. But here is how it would look logologically:

First, we would note that in referring to "disorder" and "domination," the *Interpreter's Bible* is but referring to "Order" and "Dominion" as seen from another angle. For a mode of domination is a mode of dominion, and a socio-political order is by nature a ziggurat-like structure which, as the story of the Tower makes obvious, can stand for the principle of Disorder.

If we are right in our notion that the idea of Mortification is integral to the idea of Dominion (as the scrupulous subject must seek to "slay" within himself whatever impulses run counter to the authoritative demands of sovereignty), then all about a story of the "first" dominion and the "first" disobedience there should hover the theme of the "first" mortification.

But "mortification" is a weak term as compared with "death." And thus, in the essentializing ways proper to the narrative style, this stronger, more dramatic term replaces the weaker, more "philosophic" one. "Death" would be the proper narrative-dramatic way of saying "Mortification." By this arrangement, the natural order is once again seen through the eyes of the socio-political order, as the idea of mortification in the toil and subjection of Governance is replaced by the image of death in nature.

From the standpoint sheerly of imagery (once the idea of mortification has been reduced to the idea of death, and the idea of death has been reduced to the image of a dead body rotting back into the ground), we now note a kind of "imagistic proto-fall," in the pun of II, 7, where the Lord God is shown creating man *(adham)* out of the ground *(adhamah)*. Here would be an imagistic way of saying that man in his physical nature is essentially but earth, the sort of thing a body becomes when it decays; or that man is first of all but earth as regards his place in the sheerly natural order. You would define him in narrative or temporal terms by showing what he came from. But insofar as he is what he came from, such a definition would be completed in narrative terms by the image of his return to his origins. In this sense, the account of man's forming (in II, 7) ambiguously lays the conditions for his "return" to such origins, as the Lord God makes explicit in III, 19, when again the subject is the relation between *adham* and the *adhamah:* "For dust thou art, and unto dust shalt thou return." Here would be a matter of sheer imagistic consistency, for making the stages of a narrative to be all of one piece.

But the death motif here is explicity related to another aspect of Order or Dominion: the sweat of toil. And looking back a bit further, we find that this severe second Covenant (the "Adamic") also subjected woman to the rule of the husband—another aspect of Dominion. And there is to be an eternal enmity between man and the serpent (the image, or narrative personification, of the principle of Temptation, which we have also found to be intrinsic to the motives clustering about the idea of Order).

Logologically, then, the narrative would seem to be saying something like this: Even if you begin by thinking of death as a merely natural phenomenon, once you come to approach it in terms of conscience-laden mortification you get a new slant on it. For death then becomes seen, in terms of the socio-political order, as a kind of capital punishment. But something of so eschatological a nature is essentially a "first" (since "ends," too, are principles—and here is a place at which firsts and lasts meet, so far as narrative terms for the defining of essences are concerned). Accordingly, death in the natural order becomes conceived as the fulfillment or completion of mortification in the

socio-political order, but with the difference that, as with capital punishment in the sentencing of transgressions against sovereignty, it is not in itself deemed wholly "redemptive," since it needs further modifications along the lines of placement in an undying Heavenly Kingdom after death. And this completes the pattern of Order: the symmetry of the socio-political, the natural, and the supernatural.

Edwin M. Good (essay date 1965)

SOURCE: "*Genesis:* The Irony of Israel," in *Irony in the Old Testament,* pp. 81-114, The Westminster Press, 1965.

[*In the following essay, Good maintains that "thematic irony" is developed throughout the book of* Genesis. *Good discusses* Genesis*'s use of such irony, from the creation myth through the stories of Abraham, Jacob, and Joseph.*]

An essay on irony in the book of **Genesis** should probably be of book length. Such an essay, thoroughly done, would approximate a commentary, which would necessitate attention to many subjects that must here be passed by. I cannot consider in any detail the problems of the composition of the book of **Genesis,** whether they be solved by documentary analysis, by traditio-historical criticism, by form criticism, or by any other method. I will not, therefore, weary the reader with J, E, D, and P, as the study of irony in **Genesis** does not necessitate either a positive or a negative decision regarding the documentary hypothesis. Whatever account of the composition of the book of **Genesis** is accepted, the book achieved that final form in which we now read it. This study will consider the book as it now stands. If it can be shown that failure to analyze documents has seriously distorted the perception of irony in the text, I will then be prepared to mend my ways.

EDEN TO BABEL: VARIATIONS ON AN IRONIC
THEME

Irony in narrative may take several forms. It may be a *punctual* irony, the use of words and expressions of ironic intention at particular, more or less isolated, "points." It may be *episodic* irony, the perception of an entire episode with an ironic aim or content. It may be *thematic* irony, the conjunction of a number of episodes all of which point to an ironic theme or motif. These three types of narrative irony may be interrelated. An episode may, for example, take its ironic flavor from a number of ironic expressions and words in it, and punctual irony may therefore establish episodic irony. On the other hand, the irony of a particular episode may arise from its conjunction with one or more themes of the wider context. Again, thematic irony may be recognized by a continuum of several episodes with ironic content. In the first eleven chapters of **Genesis,** we have this sort of thematic irony. The various myths of man's origins, taken separately, are filled with irony. At the same time, the common ironic theme of these episodes is set against the background of another theme that lends depth to the irony.

The ironic theme in these chapters is that of man's failure to live up to the aim of his creation.[1] Whatever the process through which the separate stories were combined into one, the passage is finally intended to have a thematic unity. The final editor (or editors) was far more than a mere compiler, but was in a true sense an "author."[2] Hence, the theory that the episode of *Gen.*, ch. 3, belongs to the J document, while the creation story of chs. 1:1 to 2:4a belongs to the P document, though perhaps true, does not prevent our recognizing a thematic effect of the latter story upon the former, which, moreover, is surely intended by the "author" who brought them together.

The creation motif, indeed, is the backdrop to all that occurs in these chapters. The drama of failure is played out against the creation of man and the earth, the motif of sin against the "very good" creation (*tôb mᵉ'ôd*, ch. 1:31). Divinely ordained as ruler of earth (ch. 1:28) and as "servant of the soil" (cf. *lᵉ'obdāh*, ch. 2:15), man misrules and denies his servitude. Disregarding his limitations (ch. 2:17), he reaches for the divine knowledge. The theme of sin and failure, therefore, is ironic in part because it is juxtaposed to the theme of the good creation.

At the same time, the myths of sin are ironic in content. The myth of the primal fall (ch. 3) betrays its irony in several ways. There is, first of all, the play on words in the primal couple's "nakedness" (*'ᵃrummîn*, ch. 2:25) and the serpent's "subtlety" (*'ārûm*, ch. 3:1), suggesting that the subtle serpent exerts an uncanny power over the naked and defenseless human beings.[3] The serpent's speech itself is an ironic overstatement: "Did God really say that you may not eat from any trees of the garden?" (v. 1). When the woman hastens to God's defense, remembering at the same time the one tree that has been forbidden, the serpent scoffs. God is "holding out" on the human beings, for that one forbidden tree is the one important source of power. "God knows that in the day that you eat of it, your eyes will be opened, and you will become like God, knowing good and evil." (V. 5.) And so she eats, and he as well. "It is not good that man should be alone." (Ch. 2:18.) With the eating of the fruit, half of the serpent's promise comes true: their eyes are opened. The other half is ironically reversed: "And they saw that they were—naked" (ch. 3:7). The fruit, touted as the source of divine power, produces not the Godlike knowledge of good and evil but only the perception of helplessness. Having grasped after the divine knowledge, man now ludicrously hides from the God he sought to displace (v. 8). With the alteration of man's relationship with God, extending even to the ironic blaming of God for the whole situation ("the woman *whom you gave to be with me*," v. 12), all of man's relationships are now changed. As soon as man's created oneness is a solidarity in sin, it splits apart. Woman is subordinated to man (v. 16),[4] and man loses the cooperation of the soil (*'ᵃdāmāh*) of whose stuff he (*'ādām*) was made (vs. 17-

18). Man's function in the creation has been fundamentally changed. He remains, as he must, "the servant of the soil" (v. 23), but the soil that has formed him represents now the frightful finis of his sojourn. "You are dust." That would have stated only fact before, but now, seen against man's pretense to divinity, it is an ironic judgment. "And to dust you shall return." If man insists on trying to achieve higher than human status, his destiny is to be less than man. Grasping for everything, Adam and Eve lose everything.

In the Cain and Abel myth, the irony is slightly different. Cain, like Adam, is the "servant of the soil" (ch. 4:2), but Yahweh's failure to accept his offering (v. 5) raises Cain's ire. Yet Yahweh disarmingly requires only "doing well," or else sin will wait in ambush.[5] But Cain's action brings out the irony in both the promise and the threat of Yahweh. He takes the course of ambush, falling upon Abel in the field. He who has been exhorted to "do well" does, on the contrary, evil. When Yahweh asks, "Where is Abel your brother?" (v. 9), Cain's famous answer carries a double irony. On the one hand, Cain does not admit that he is his "brother's keeper," and the question implies his own ironic perception of the idea. On the other hand, the obvious answer to Cain's question is affirmative, uncovering Cain's ironic failure to perceive his true relationship to his brother. There may even be a third level of irony in Cain's use of the term "keeper" (*shômēr*), perhaps alluding to Abel's vocation as shepherd, as the term is used several times of "keeping" sheep (cf. *Gen.* 30:31; I Sam. 17:20; Jer. 31:10).

With Yahweh's curse, Cain, like Adam before him, loses his vocation, and the soil, which he was to serve but which has given evidence against him (*Gen.* 4:10), now turns uncooperative (v. 12), and Cain must become a nomad. His outcry reflects his fear that the fate he meted out to Abel will now be his (*hārag*, "slay"; cf. the same verb in v. 8). Ironically, Cain is not permitted to pay off his debt so easily. On the contrary, having taken vengeance, he is now the agent by whom vengeance is to be multiplied in the world. The tragedy of vengeance comes to its savage extension with the Song of Lamech (vs. 23-24), where Lamech claims the privilege of seventy-sevenfold vengeance for very slight provocation. Here, then, is the pass brought on by one rupture of brotherly responsibility, the tragically ironic expansion of vengeance in a world where vengeance has no proper place, except as it belongs to God (v. 15). Once more man claims the divine prerogative and sounds strangely beastly as he does so.

The curious little myth in ch. 6:1-4, with its drastic perception of "total depravity" (v. 5), is very difficult to penetrate. Clearly the narrator views the marriages between the "sons of God" and the "daughters of men" as illegitimate if not incongruous, since these unions occasion the divine limitation on the length of human life. The limitation seems required because human beings continue to grasp after more than is good for them, and, if the sequence (v. 5) is the narrator's comment on the story, human aspiration to what is more than human produces nothing but evil, an ironic perception not different from that of ch. 3. Mean-while, however, we have the enigmatic reference to the Nephilim, the heroes and famous men of old (v. 4). Clearly they are connected to the illicit marriages of vs. 1 and 2. We must certainly assume that the ancient editor saw as well as we do that the name Nephilim suggests an etymology from the verb *nāphal*, "to fall."[6] The references to "heroes" and "famous men" in the context of the illicit divine-human marriages and in relationship to the name Nephilim falls, then, into line with the theme of human self-elevation noticeable throughout these chapters. Human power and fame carry an ironically illegitimate air. They are the "fallen" issue of an unnatural conjunction of powers.

Now we are confronted by the statement of utter human evil (v. 5), and the whole creation is cast in the ironic light of failure, Man has "increased" as he was told to do (cf. *rᵉbû*, ch. 1:28, and *rôb*, ch. 6:1), but what he has actually "increased" is evil (cf. *rabbāh* in ch. 6:5). The goodness of creation has gone wrong, and it is time to begin again.[7] The waters of the flood are a return to the waters of chaos, an ironic conclusion to the first act of the creation. In addition, the rain as the source of the flood in the J strand (ch. 7:4) represents an advance on man's cosmic experience, since the J creation story begins by noting that "Yahweh God had not yet made it rain on the earth" (ch. 2:5).[8] The flood is at once a retrogression, the return of the chaos from which creation came, and a progression, the introduction of a new experience, rain. In the context of the flood, however, progress is ironically undesirable.

With the conclusion of the flood, Noah attempts a return to normalcy. But the occasion of his trouble is once more the soil. Noah becomes an *'îsh hā'ᵃdāmāh*, plants a vineyard, and gets stupidly drunk on its produce (ch. 9:20-21). Now, the son may—and does—sarcastically lord it over the father, and the curse is again present in the earth (vs. 22-27).[9] The irony is twofold. On the one hand, the sphere of the fertility cults with their looking upon nakedness[10] and their drunkenness is the condition into which Noah, the righteous and perfect man (cf. ch. 6:9), falls. On the other hand, Noah curses Canaan, who bespeaks precisely that fertility realm, forbidden to the Israelite, into which he himself has fallen.

Noah's sons now proceed to populate the earth, thus leading to the dangerous unity of the tower-building (ch. 11:1-9). The tower, indeed, is built at Shinar in the territory of Nimrod, Ham's grandson (ch. 10:10), suggesting again that Ham is the source of trouble. But the irony of the story of the Tower of Babel lies principally in its completing and rounding out the theme of man's exclusion from Eden. Here men attempt an anti-Eden, a humanly constructed paradise from which God is to be excluded.[11] The tower (*migdāl*) is defensive security against God, that man may be free to pursue his technologically assured salvation. But man's unity is ruptured by the humorously economical means of the confusion of language. We might expect Yahweh to fling people and bricks about the

landscape with a mighty arm. The narrators give us a more subtle and, I believe, ironic perception of the Deity's workings. The breaking of man's linguistic unity produces precisely what the entire project was designed to prevent, the scattering of man over the earth (ch. 11:8). The narrator has capped the irony by identifying the tower with Babylon, the location of Judah's exile (v. 9), and by sardonically connecting the name Babel with the verb *bālal*, "to confuse." This type of ironic humor is to be found in every underground movement, and perhaps it implies a sixth-century B.C. "demythologization" of the story.

The ironic theme in these chapters is the perception of incongruity between the purpose of man's creation and how he actually acts, between the "is" and the "ought." It is expressed through the piling up of ironic episodes in which man, reaching beyond the Creator's limitations, is hurled down below his proper place, in which he causes his own downfall by attempting his own elevation. Another thread of an ironic theme running through these chapters is the juncture of *'ādām* and *'ᵃdāmāh*, man's relationship to the soil. Somehow, whenever man acts in his appointed role as "servant of the soil," trouble ensues, for Adam, for Cain, for Noah. The irony of this theme may imply the danger of man's dependence on the soil for his life, because of the powerful impetus to fertility-centered worship. Or it might simply convey the fact that man, even engaged in his appointed pursuits, finds a way to try to lift himself toward divinity. Whatever the precise meaning of the theme, a careful look both at the details of the section and at their effect emphasizes a fundamentally ironic portrayal of man.

ABRAHAM: THE IRONIES OF PROMISE

The thematic unity of the Abraham story is woven about the thread of promise. The continued narrowing of the genealogical tables in chs. 10 and 11, until finally, at ch. 11:26-32, we have settled down with Abraham, suggests that Abraham represents the solution to the ironic theme of man as sinner set in chs. 1 to 11. But with Abraham the solution remains provisional, not yet achieved but a promise for the future.

The promise has two interconnected aspects, both implied in Abraham's vocation (ch. 12:1-2): "Go out from your land, from your relatives, and from your family, to the land I will show you. And I will make of you a great nation, and I will bless you and will give you a great name." The two themes are the promise of the land, which becomes a definite promise of possession only in v. 7, and the assurance that Abraham's descendants will be a great nation. With the former, we have in prospect the solution to man's homelessness, vividly related in the expulsion from Eden (ch. 3:23-24), the curse on Cain (ch. 4:16), the dispersion of Noah's sons (ch. 10), and the scattering of men from the Tower of Babel (ch. 11:8). With the promise of descendants, the centrifugal movement of man is to be arrested, for around the Abrahamic nation will gather the blessedness of mankind ("all the clans of the soil" [ᵃdāmāh]). Hence, Abraham's "great name" sets the legitimate counterpoise to the illegitimate "name" sought by the tower builders (ch. 11:4), for this power and identity are not grasped by man for himself with the object of excluding God but are presented to man by God.

But here is promise, not actuality. The land will be given to Abraham's descendants (ch. 12:7), not to Abraham, who journeys through and within it. Yet Abraham's greatness of name begins to pay off even in Egypt (vs. 10-20), where, for all his timidity, Pharaoh treats him with respect both before and after the near-disaster over Sarah's temporary sojourn as his wife.¹² As he finds himself once again in Canaanite territory, his wealth might make us think the promise has already come. His possessions and Lot's are so vast that "the land could not support them both together" (ch. 13:6). In their times of trouble, the hearers of that remark ironically compared their own tenuous hold of the land with Abraham's power, as Ezekiel tells us from the Babylonian exile: "Son of man, the dwellers in these wastes on Israel's soil are saying, 'Abraham was but one man, and he possessed the land, whereas we are many. We should be given possession of the land'" (Ezek. 33:24).

Yet the very prosperity of Abraham and Lot causes them to separate, Abraham to the barren hills, Lot to the fertile Jordan valley. But Lot's country retains the problems that plagued man in the beginning. "The people of Sodom were very wicked and sinful against Yahweh." (**Gen.** 13:13.) In the interest of his comfort, Lot has regressed, passing his life among those who represent mankind before Abraham. Abraham, however, receives the reiteration of the double promise, that the land will be given to his descendants and of these there will be many (vs. 15-17). Yet the blessing remains Yahweh's; the earth's families have not yet bestowed it.

In the next episode, a glimmering of the universal blessing appears (ch. 14). Some of earth's families are bent on displacing the heir to the land, though they come only as far as poor, hapless Lot. But from Salem comes the blessing of Melchizedek (vs. 19-20). The story has given exegetes a great deal of difficulty. Not only does it not fit into any of the Pentateuchal strata; it is also enigmatic in language and background. In the context, the story reflects the ambiguity of Lot's decision in ch. 13, which will come to its climax in ch. 19, and it also reflects the beginnings of the actualization of the promise to Abraham. From Salem the blessing comes, and hearers of the story would have made the same connection between Salem and Jerusalem that we make. They knew perfectly well that Jerusalem became an Israelite city only with David (II Sam. 5:6-10). The blessing comes also from Melchizedek, a name that we may suppose they would understand to mean "My king is righteous." The episode conveys, then, both the eschatological universality of blessing on Abraham from the earth's families and the certainty of Israel's establishment in the land, where Jerusalem will be the seat of the righteous kingship. The promise begins to have its fulfillment, then, even with Abraham himself.

But the promise remains unfulfilled, for Abraham cannot possess the land without decendants. It is all very well for Yahweh to promise Abraham that his "reward is great indeed" (ch. 15:1). Abraham protests with more than a hint of irony: "O Lord Yahweh, what are you going to give me? I am still childless" (v. 2).¹³ The promise is repeated, the number of Abraham's descendants being compared to the stars (v. 5)—previously they were compared to the grains of dust (ch. 13:16). The covenant ceremony seals the promise (ch. 15:7-21).

We must continue to await its fulfillment, however. The birth of Ishmael (ch. 16:1-16) and the vexation he causes Sarah (ch. 21:9-21) provide an ironic suspense to the promise of descendants. The fact that the custom of giving a maid to a man to provide heirs is attested elsewhere in the Old Testament (cf. its practice in ch. 30:3-13) and in the ancient Near East does not efface the fact that Ishmael is clearly not the promised heir, any more than the children of Bilhah and Zilpah in ch. 30 are on an equality with the children of Leah and, finally, Rachel. The struggle between Hagar and Sarah underscores the relative—though not absolute—illegitimacy of Ishmael. Hagar's arrogance too lends irony to Ishmael's position, for however sympathetic we are intended to be to Hagar in her two excursions into the desert (chs. 16:7-14; 21:14-21), the narrator intends us to remain convinced that Ishmael's birth is an interlude between promise and fulfillment. There is in addition a certain etiological irony, similar to that on Moab and Ammon (ch. 19:30-38), that Ishmael, while blessed as the son of Abraham and circumcised covenantally with him, passes to his Ishmaelite descendants the relative illegitimacy that he received through his mother.

But the fulfillment of the promise still awaits its actuality. The heir will not be born until ch. 21, and we have barely reached ch. 17. The continued promise in the priestly circumcision-covenant narrative retains its irony in the explanation of Abraham's new name, "father of a multitude" (v. 5), since Abraham is not as yet father of anyone. The promise of a son moves Abraham at last to laughter: "Shall a son be born to a centenarian? And can Sarah—can a ninety-year-old woman—give birth?" (v. 17). The idea, of course, is ridiculous. But God will have the last laugh. "You shall call him Isaac" (*yitschāq,* "he laughs"). (V. 19.) One wonders how anyone could say, as Alfred North Whitehead commented, that there is no humor in the Old Testament.¹⁴ The laughter rings out again in ch. 18 when Sarah, eavesdropping on the conversation between Yahweh and Abraham, laughs to herself (v. 12): "After I am decrepit, do I get some pleasure? And with an elderly husband?" Not often in the Old Testament do human beings laugh at Yahweh, and Sarah hastily denies having laughed (v. 15). Certainly, however, the rhetorical questions expressing the incongruity of old folks' bearing babies are ironic.¹⁵

But when, having been told Yahweh's intention to wipe out Sodom and Gomorrah, Abraham begins to argue, the irony is far different. Clearly he intends an escape clause for Lot, as he bargains Yahweh down from fifty to ten righteous people as sufficient to avert the catastrophe. The ground of the argument, however, is a moral one: "Are you really going to destroy the righteous along with the wicked? . . . Far be it from you to do such a thing, to kill the righteous along with the wicked, the same thing happening to both. Far be it from you! Should not the whole world's judge do justice?" (vs. 23, 25). The final question contains an ironic wordplay: "Should not the *shôphēt* of the whole world do *mishpāt?*" Yahweh's function as "judge" implies his pursuit of "justice." Abraham pleads not for the evil cities or even primarily for his nephew but for the divine consistency. The proposal to wipe out the righteous with the wicked seems to him an incongruity, and he is prepared even to tackle Yahweh with its irony.[16]

With the imminent destruction of Sodom and Gomorrah, Lot's ludicrous delay is comically ironic (ch. 19:16-22). Lot does not want to leave Sodom. He "dawdles" (*yithmah^emāh*, v. 16) and must be coerced out of the city. Told to flee to the hills, he protests that he is as much afraid of the hills as of the city (v. 19). Here we are, waiting for the fire and brimstone to strike the city to ashes, and Lot stands around arguing about the escape route! "That city over there is nearer to flee to." (V. 20.) Lot even wants as easy a journey as possible, not considering that proximity to Sodom is, to say the least, unhealthy. Furthermore, that city over there is "a little one," presumably beneath the notice of fire and brimstone. It must nevertheless be specifically exempted by the angel from the destruction, and we receive the impression that the exemption is granted in irritated desperation and haste (vs. 21-22).

Before Abraham's promised child comes, another episode builds up the suspense when, for the second time, Abraham almost gives away Sarah on whom the promise of the heir depends (ch. 20:1-18).[17] Abimelech is completely taken in, believing everything he is told in utter innocence (vs. 4-5). Confronted with his perfidy, Abraham has his own rationalization. He feared the pagans (v. 11), and anyway, there is a sense—a very tenuous sense, to be sure—in which Sarah is his sister, since she is the daughter of his father though not of his mother (v. 12).[18] There is no other reference to this fact, and it seems quite possible that the writer intends it as pure fabrication on Abraham's part. Nor can we miss the irony in Abraham's remark that he asked Sarah to report him as her brother out of "loyalty" (*chesed*, v. 13). That is the "loyalty" of wife for husband! In this version of the story, Abimelech adds his own subtle touch of irony. He gives Abraham the rights of the countryside. "And to Sarah he said, 'See, I have given a thousand pieces of silver to your—brother.'" (V. 16.)

The laughter to which we have alluded before now comes to its fruition, with the birth of the child who will be a living and walking laugh. Yet no sooner has the promised child been born than the trail of threats to the actualization of the promise comes to its climax. "Take your son, your only son, whom you love, Isaac, and go to the land of

Moriah, and offer him there as a burnt offering on one of the mountains which I will designate." (Ch. 22:2.) The command piles up the terms of endearment in a concentrated tragic irony, capped by the mention of the boy's name, with its echo of the laughter that greeted the promise and the actuality of his birth. When they reach the mountain, Abraham's response to Isaac's question about the offering is profoundly ironic: "God will see to the offering, my son" (v. 8). The answer satisfies the boy, intensifying the irony of its double meaning. We may also note the possible connection of the name Moriah with the verb that Abraham uses here (*yir'eh*) and the name that is finally given the mountain in v. 14: *Yahweh yir'eh*, "Yahweh will see." This is even clearer in the reading of the Samaritan Pentateuch, *môrā'āh* for *môriyyāh* in v. 2, reflected in the LXX reading (*optasias*) and the Vulgate (*visionis*). Vision, the seeing that produces understanding, is a central theme in the story, but, in the shadow of the all but unbearable beginning, Abraham is blind to it until the surprising end.

At the same time, we must connect the passage to the larger theme of the Abraham story, the provision of an heir to the covenantal promise. Lot, the first potential candidate, separated himself from Abraham and fell from consideration. Abraham apparently considered adopting Eliezer the slave. The birth of Ishmael was only an apparent solution to the problem of Sarah's sterility, for with Isaac's birth, Ishmael and his mother had been cast out. Everything then rests on Isaac's shoulders. Immediately comes the command to sacrifice the child of the promise, whose coming has seemed so dubious for so long. In the structure of the Abraham story, this episode is the culmination of the continual frustration of Yahweh's plans for Abraham, up to the point (v. 11) where the angel of Yahweh calls him.[19] The suspense, creating almost unbearable tension, could have approached the character of *The Perils of Pauline*, save for the sober restraint of the narrator. And the episode's irony finds its depth from the context, which at the same time gives the passage its meaning.

The problem of descendants solved, half of Yahweh's promise to Abraham (ch. 12:1-2) bears the likelihood of actualization. But the other half of the theme, the promise of possession of the land, which has been subordinated for several chapters, casts an ironic reflection on an otherwise rather isolated episode, the purchase of the cave of Machpelah (ch. 23:1-20). At first glance, the purchase of land for a tomb is not promising material for irony. Yet the story possesses not only irony but also humor, in what may be taken as a mild satire on commercial bargaining customs (vs. 3-16).[20] Who would haggle over a price at a time like this? Abraham would (by implication, perhaps, his descendants as well), and so would the Hittites. And the studied casualness with which Ephron, having urged Abraham to take the land for nothing and knowing that he would not, mentions the value of the plot (v. 15) is certainly humorous. The irony of the episode arises out of the theme of God's promise of the land to Abraham. The first time Abraham arrives in Canaan, the promise is given (ch. 12:7), and it is reiterated when he and Lot separate (ch. 13:14-17), in the covenant ceremony (ch. 15:7, 16, 18-21), and in the promise related to the circumcision (ch. 17:8). The land is Abraham's by promise. Yet he must bargain with a Hittite over the purchase of a piece of it for a burial ground.[21] "I am an alien and a sojourner among you." (Ch. 23:4). It is the irony inherent in the promise that remains only promise. And when the servant must be sent off to Abraham's relatives in Mesopotamia to find a wife for Isaac (ch. 24), the irony is deepened. For all the promise, Abraham remains an alien in the land that is his.

The Abraham story is a tightly structured whole, carrying its double theme of the promised heir and the promised land by the constant contrast of promise and ironic actuality. Indeed, that irony is finally intrinsic to the theme of promise in the Abraham tradition. Wherever the promise is not and cannot be actualized, those who await its fulfillment are inevitably entangled in the ironic incongruity between what is and what will be.

JACOB: THE IRONY OF BROTHERHOOD

It is surprising that God appears so rarely in the Jacob story, as compared to his almost constant confrontation of Abraham. To be sure, the points of the divine interjection are crucial: the oracle to Rebekah about her sons (ch. 25:23); the vision at Bethel (ch. 28:11-17); the intervention on behalf of Leah (chs. 29:31 to 30:24); the meeting and wrestling with Jacob at the Jabbok (ch. 32:1-2, 22-32); Jacob's movement from Shechem to Bethel (ch. 35:1-15). It has been argued that the second and fourth of these episodes afford the theological grounds for the understanding of the entire Jacob story.[22] In the one (ch. 28:11-17) he receives the covenantal promise of the land; in the other (ch. 32:22-32), the covenantal name, Israel. We should not miss the irony of the fact that in the former episode, Jacob receives the promise of the land at just the moment that he is hotfooting it away from the land. Nor should we overlook the irony that the name Israel, whose meaning is disputed but which perhaps signifies something like "he strives with God," is given at just the moment that Jacob, in abject terror, is about to meet his estranged brother Esau.

It is equally noticeable, however, that those two episodes stand structurally between the two major groups of stories in which Jacob is central. Chapter 28:11-17 is the episode of transition between the first set of Jacob-Esau stories and the Jacob-Laban cycle; ch. 32:22-32 is the transition from the Jacob-Laban cycle to the second part of the Jacob-Esau cycle. We have, therefore, to do with Jacob's actions with Esau on the one hand and with Laban on the other. In these contexts the Jacob tradition must be understood. And the narrator, by judicious placement of the revelations to Jacob, has set the human interactions in the context of the divine action.

The Jacob-Esau conflict begins before the twins' birth. The oracle to Rebekah expresses an ironic reversal of normal inheritance pattern; the younger will dominate the older (ch. 25:23).[23] That theme brings the relation between Jacob and Esau to its focus. The conflict of the brothers is foreshadowed in the comment, rich in ironic potential, of ch. 25:28: "And Isaac loved Esau because of the meat in his [Isaac's] mouth; but Rebekah loved Jacob." We have already seen the reason for Rebekah's preference for Jacob: he is destined for primacy. Rebekah looks to the future; Isaac thinks only of his stomach.

Esau too thinks only of his stomach. The caustic gibe cast at the Edomites by referring to their descendance from Esau (v. 30) in the context of his stupid abandonment of his inheritance for a bowl of lentil soup perhaps reflects the late exilic or early post-exilic enmity between Israel and Edom. Jacob's mulcting Esau of his birthright (vs. 29-34) shows how easy is the supplanting, adumbrated in the oracle to Rebekah and in the birth narrative (v. 26). Esau has only to be momentarily hungry to "despise" his inheritance rights.

From the private transaction, we move to the more nearly public one (ch. 27). Isaac is prepared to pass the blessing to Esau, the rightful heir. We know, from the previous episode, that Esau has forfeited his right to the blessing. Yet ironically, Jacob must resort to deception to gain the blessing. Rebekah presumably knows nothing of the bartered birthright. She knows only the oracle given her, and she now takes into her own hands the assurance of its fulfillment. She has everything well in hand, including Jacob's fearful anxieties that the scheme may not succeed (ch. 27:5-17).

The dialogue between Jacob and Isaac (vs. 18-29) is filled with dramatic ironies. Isaac is very suspicious. "Who are you, my son?" (V. 18.) "How is this? You have been so quick to find [game], my son." (V. 20.) "Come here and let me feel you, my son. Are you really he, my son Esau, or not?" (V. 21.) "The voice is Jacob's, but the hands are Esau's." (V. 22.) Finally, almost the last gasp of suspicion: "Are you really he, my son Esau?" (v. 24).[24] Isaac seems satisfied, and yet, after the meal, he must check once again. "Come here and kiss me, my son." (V. 26.) Isaac wants to smell his son, and that leads into the opening metaphor of the blessing. The poem, conveying the irretrievable blessing and inheritance, is thoroughly ironic, intended as it is to apply to Esau and metaphorically inapplicable to Jacob:

> See, my son's smell
> Is like the field's smell,
> Which Yahweh has blessed.
> May God give you the heaven's dew
> And the ground's fat things,
> Much of grain and of wine.
> Peoples shall serve you,
> Nations bow to you.
> Be master over your brothers,[25]
> And may your mother's sons bow to you.
> Cursed be those who curse you,
> But blessed those who bless you.

(Vs. 27-29.)

Dramatic irony is enhanced by the timing of the ensuing action: "As Isaac had finished blessing Jacob, and just as Jacob had gone out from Isaac his father, Esau his brother came in with his game" (v. 30). Isaac's bad news arouses Esau's bitterly ironic criticism of Jacob. "Is his name not properly Jacob [supplanter]? He has supplanted me twice: he took my inheritance right, and now he has taken my blessing." (V. 36.) The bitter play on the name, *ya'ᵃqōb*, with the verbal form, *wayya'qᵉbēnî*, takes us back to the boys' birth and to the oracle to Rebekah (ch. 25:23). All Isaac has left for Esau is the curse, the very reverse of what he has given Jacob (ch. 27:39-40).

The parental preference, then, has deepened the ironies of the brothers' relationships. Isaac's preference for Esau has perhaps made both of them careless. Rebekah's fondness for Jacob leads to her underhanded machinations on his behalf, which are not yet complete. She manages to get Isaac not only to approve but to suggest Jacob's disappearance before Esau can kill him (chs. 27:46 to 28:2).

The sojourn in Padan-aram, which occupies the next chapters, sets out the conflict between Jacob and Laban. Here is presented, with an almost Aristophanic gusto, the comic confrontation of *eirōn* with *alazōn* (cf. Chapter I), of the ironical man with the impostor. The stories are told from the Israelite bias, of course, and Jacob therefore finally triumphs over his sometimes dense but occasionally too shrewd kinsman.

The first episode, at least, is Laban's triumph (ch. 29:15-30). Jacob, desiring to marry Rachel, contracts to do so, but Laban slips Leah into the tent in the dark. Jacob is furious, Laban bland. "It simply is not done around here, to marry off the younger daughter before the elder." (V. 26.) Undoubtedly Laban sees Leah's chances of a good match to be inferior to Rachel's, since Leah has poor eyesight (v. 17). But Jacob must swallow defeat and work seven years more for nothing. The *alazōn* has won the first round, and Jacob has learned the hard lesson: *caveat emptor.* In the second, Yahweh enters the action. "Now Yahweh saw that Leah was hated, and he opened up her womb; but Rachel was barren." (V. 31.) The trick is hard on Rachel, but, we sense, hardly easier for Leah. Her pathetic explanations of the naming of each child underline her awareness that she is not loved (cf. chs. 29:32-35; 30:11, 13, 18, 20). At the last, Rachel finally is able to bear a son, which caps the perception of Yahweh's ironic preference for the underdog.

Jacob now wants to leave for home (ch. 30:26), and he asks for severance pay. Laban is ostensibly generous but has some trickery up his own sleeve. When Jacob offers to take only the speckled and spotted sheep and goats and the black lambs, Laban's agreement is accompanied by the removal of all those animals from Jacob's ken (vs. 32-36). But the *eirōn* has profited from his experience, and pulls the breeding trick that enriches him and impoverishes Laban (vs. 37-43). Any animal husbandman will testify that the trick is impossible, though it reflects old wives' tales

that are still abroad. Yet the very comic improbability of the action provides the irony. Laban seems to have won again, certainly thinks he has won, but Jacob outsmarts him. The narrator's comment (ch. 31:2) is a masterpiece of ironic understatement: "And Jacob perceived in Laban's face the fact that he was not, as before, on his side."[26] A convenient order from Yahweh (v. 3) is an excuse to get under way, but Jacob wins his wives to his side with a rather demagogic speech, designed to set them against their father (vs. 5-13). The response is as indignant as he had hoped: "Have we still any portion or inheritance in our father's family? Does he not consider us foreigners? For he sold us, and now he is using up our money. All the wealth that God has taken from our father is ours and our children's. So now, do whatever God has told you" (vs. 14-16). They are thoroughly in Jacob's camp, and Rachel even spirits away Laban's *terāphîm*, which will anger him more than anything else.

The chase is on, and when Laban overtakes them and launches his furious accusation, Jacob replies—for him—quite calmly: he knows nothing about Laban's *terāphîm*, and encourages Laban to look for them. Rachel having hidden them under the camel saddle pleads that she cannot get up "for the way of women is upon me" (v. 35). Laban, rummaging through the tent—we have the unforgettable picture of the old man flinging goods and chattels in all directions—fails, ironically, to find them. It is another feather in the cap of *eirōneia*. Now Jacob in his turn lambastes Laban with real indignation (vs. 36-42). But we must sense the narrator's irony: Jacob has not been so single-mindedly occupied with Laban's welfare; rather, his own as he avers. The ensuing covenant is at best a truculent one. The famous Mizpah benediction (vs. 49-50) is an ironic warning, in which Laban's concern for his daughter's welfare is very different from the attitude they had perceived (vs. 14-16).

We now move back to the Jacob-Esau cycle (chs. 32-33). As Jacob left Canaan in fear of Esau, he returns in fear. This is clear from his reaction to the news that Esau is coming to meet him and his careful refusal to go anywhere with his brother. Why, then, does he send messengers to Esau (ch. 32:3)? I think we must find the meaning in the connection between the otherwise strange naming of Mahanaim in vs. 1-2 and the sending of the messengers in vs. 3-5. At first blush, vs. 1-2 looks like a simple etiology. However, those who meet Jacob are "God's messengers, angels" (*mal'ᵃkē 'ᵉlôhîm*), and Jacob exclaims, on seeing them, "This is God's army" (*machᵃneh*). In v. 3, Jacob sends his own "messengers" (*mal'ākîm*) to Esau. He is certainly not requesting a reunion. The message says only that Jacob has amassed considerable wealth and power, and he tells this to Esau in order "to find favor" in his sight. Jacob is bluffing. His wealth and the presence of "God's army" give him a sense of security, and he sends his *mal'ākîm* to Esau as God sent *mal'ākîm* to him. The otherwise odd passage, vs. 1-2, provides a partial motivation for Jacob's bluff.

Ironically, as soon as the bluff is called, or Jacob thinks it is called, his security leaves him. The reply brought by the messengers is artfully casual: "We came to your brother Esau, and he too is coming to meet you—and four hundred men with him" (v. 6). Jacob is now really frightened, and divides his forces into two "companies" (*mach*[a]*nôth*, recalling the *mach*[a]*neh* of v. 2). This, however, is for purely defensive reasons. The rather pitiful prayer (vs. 9-12) must strike us as "foxhole piety." In the following verses (vs. 13-23)[27] the very confusing account of the movements of companies, flocks, herds, persons, and Jacob himself is perhaps deliberately intended to convey Jacob's terrified fluttering over this unexpected catastrophe.

Clearly, Jacob expected to move unhindered into Canaan, the Land of Promise, as his message to Esau would suggest. When he misunderstands Esau's response—as we see from ch. 33:4—the realization of the promise seems hopeless. He even goes so far as to arrange things so that his vaunted wealth may conceivably fall into Esau's hand in the interest of his own survival (cf. ch. 32:8, 11, 20). But before he can meet Esau, he must face an even greater challenge, the night-long battle on the bank of the Jabbok (vs. 22-32). The passage is crucial to the structure of the entire Jacob tradition, and it has received a great deal of attention in terms of questions with which we cannot here be concerned. Has it an ironic effect or content? I think it does. On the one hand, Jacob, in mortal dread of confronting Esau, finds himself instead wrestling with God.[28] The fulfillment of the promise to Jacob rests finally not with his success over against Esau and Laban but with his success with God. "You have battled with God and with men, and you have overcome." (V. 28.) On the other hand, however, Jacob does not emerge unscathed; he limps (v. 31).

But when, barely surviving the crucial fight with God, he now has immediately to face Esau, his fright has not abated, though his nerve has abated no less. The brothers weep on meeting (ch. 33:4), and the suggestion that, where Esau's weeping is that of joy, Jacob's is the weeping of sheer relief, has much to commend it.[29] Jacob, making a vastly obsequious and overstated speech (vs. 10-11), practically forces Esau to take the gift he has given. When Esau offers to journey on to Edom with him (vs. 12-14), Jacob protests his necessary and inconvenient slowness. Jacob wants no part of Edom! Finally, he refuses Esau's offer of a bodyguard (v. 15). Once more, the *eirōn* is at work, pretending to Esau that he is coming south with him, letting Esau's assumption to that effect go unchallenged. Note also the ironic word that describes Jacob's arrival at Shechem, back in Canaan: "And Jacob arrived healthy (*shālēm*) at the city of Shechem" (v. 18). At last, like Abraham, the father of promise, Jacob must purchase a plot of land in the country promised him on which to pitch his tent (v. 19; cf. ch. 23).

Having withstood forces against him outside the land, Jacob must now withstand the foolishness of his sons. The episode at Shechem (ch. 34:1-31) has at least that thematic

irony to it. It has, further, two bits of punctual irony. The men of Shechem are to be circumcised so that Dinah, Jacob's daughter, will be free to marry young Shechem. But where that reason will satisfy Hamor and his son Shechem, it will by no means satisfy the populace. Another reason must be given: "Their flocks, their goods, their cattle— will they not be ours?" (v. 23). Appeal to economic gain is more persuasive to the men of the city than the desires of a love-struck young prince. But the irony of the question rests both on its incompatibility with the intentions of the brothers (v. 13) and on the ensuing slaughter, which takes place when all the men are still in pain from being circumcised and hence are unable to fight (v. 25). Jacob has at least the grace to castigate Simeon and Levi for this indiscretion, and it provides some motivation for the move from Shechem to Bethel.

The irony in the Jacob story, as we have seen it, is for the most part a comic irony, involving the triumph of Jacob over his adversaries. Where Jacob regards Esau as having the upper hand and works to wrest it from him, he regards Laban with a certain amount of contempt. The story is, of course, related to the nationalistic pleasure of Israel at the discomfiture of its foes, Aram and Edom, and it is by no means unlikely that the national enmity with those nations has helped to shape the story. At the same time, Laban and Esau are not the only objects of irony. Jacob too—and with him, Israel—receives the ironic treatment at several places in the story, in relation both to Esau and to Laban. Insofar as the Jacob story contains the reflections of the national mind upon itself vis-à-vis its inimical neighbors, we must recognize Israel's capacity to laugh at its own pretensions.

JOSEPH: THE IRONY OF PROVIDENCE

In the complexes of tradition about Abraham and Jacob the irony was primarily perceptible within the episodes themselves, and secondarily in the relation of episodes to themes. In the Joseph story we have to do with an overarching ironic theme which is reflected to a lesser degree in the individual episodes. That is not to say that we have neither punctual nor episodic irony in the Joseph story. We do have both. But the lesser ironies do not really add up to the greater. We need, nevertheless, to consider these instances of irony, postponing the thematic irony for the present.

The reaction of the brothers and Jacob to Joseph's recounting of his magniloquent dreams is at least ironic and probably sarcastic, greeting Joseph's prophecy of his dominion with what comes to "Oh, is that so!" (ch. 37:8, 10). The same sarcasm occurs later in the chapter, when Joseph comes with his father's message to Dothan: "Look, here comes that master dreamer [*ba'al hach*[a]*lômôth*]" (v. 19). They propose to kill him then and there, "so we can see what comes of his dreams" (v. 20). But when, having paused to eat before disposing of Joseph, and seeing the Ishmaelite caravan coming along, the brothers decide instead to sell the boy into slavery, it appears that the

Midianites beat them to it (vs. 25-28).[30] The brothers, then, receive no profit at all from their underhanded plot, unless their satisfaction at having the troublesome and arrogant youth disposed of is sufficient. Jacob's complete acceptance of the trumped-up story bears the dramatic irony of the difference between what Jacob is told and what the brothers know, as well as between what Jacob knows and what we know.

The ironic episode of Judah and Tamar is probably not integral to the Joseph legend.[31] It provides a sort of "meanwhile, back at the ranch" interlude while Joseph gets to Egypt, when the story line can be picked up once more. The incident revolves around the custom of levirate marriage, legislated in Deut. 25:5-6. When Tamar's first two husbands, Judah's elder sons, have died, Judah is reluctant to give her his youngest son, Shelah, perhaps feeling that Tamar is bad medicine. He promises Shelah to Tamar when he comes of age, and Tamar goes home to her father. The position of the young, childless window in the ancient world was a precarious one, and it is important for Tamar that the promised marriage be carried through. When she finds that Shelah has come of age, but Judah has not suggested the promised marriage (*Gen.* 38:14), she takes the matter into her own hands. That Tamar perpetrates virtual blackmail on Judah is certainly condoned by narrator and hearers alike, for Judah has treated her badly. His readiness to go to a roadside prostitute increases the comic irony, as does her insistence on a pledge of payment, which prepares us for the conclusion. We must also perceive the irony of the fact that two words for "prostitute" are used in the story: *zônāh,* the ordinary type, and *q*ᵉ*dēshāh,* a cultic prostitute. Along the road (v. 15), the narrator uses *zônāh,* and when, in v. 24, Judah is told of Tamar's indiscretion, we have the verb *zānāh,* "to engage in prostitution," and the noun *z*ᵉ*nûnîm,* "acts of prostitution." When, however, Judah sends his friend the Adullamite to Enaim to make his payment, he asks after a *q*ᵉ*dēshāh* (v. 20). Certainly the alternation of terms is not accidental. Judah is not about to inform strangers that he runs around after ordinary prostitutes, while anyone would assume perfect respectability in the search for a cultic prostitute. Ironically, had Judah's friend inquired for a *zônāh,* the men of Enaim might have recalled Tamar. When Tamar turns out to be pregnant, Judah is furiously indignant: "Bring her out and have her burned" (v. 24). Tamar is far ahead of him, however, producing with devastating irony Judah's property. Judah must accept the humiliation he was so eager to avoid. "She is righteous rather than I, since I did not give her to my son Shelah." (V. 26.)

As we pick up the Joseph story again, we must perceive a certain irony in the incident with Potiphar's wife (ch. 39:6b-23), where the innocent and guileless lad is thrown into prison on the word of a perjuring nymphomaniac. An ironic, if macabre, wordplay occurs in Joseph's interpretations of his fellow prisoners' dreams. To the butler, he says, "Within three days, Pharaoh will lift up your head" (*nāsā' rôsh,* "will take you back," ch. 40:13). To the baker, he says, "Within three days, Pharaoh will lift your head

too—from your shoulders" (v. 19). We may even perceive a tiny piece of irony, perhaps unintended, in the list of presents that Jacob has the brothers take to the great man in Egypt (ch. 43:11), which includes some of the same materials that were being carried by the Ishmaelite caravan with whom Joseph went to Egypt in slavery (ch. 37:25). There is a hint of the ironic in Joseph's careful advice to his kinsmen not to tell Pharaoh that they are shepherds, since shepherds are disliked by Egyptians (ch. 46:33-34).[32] But when the family chooses the course of honesty with Pharaoh (ch. 47:3), the explosion Joseph apparently expected does not come.

We have, finally, some irony, both obvious and subtle, in the "Blessing of Jacob," ch. 49:2-27. The passage is difficult, full as it is of metaphors and allusions whose precise connotations escape us. Some of the blessings on the individual tribes probably refer to specific historical incidents which we no longer know; this would seem to be the case in the blessings on Gad (v. 19), Asher (v. 20), Naphtali (v. 21), and Benjamin (v. 27). Though the blessing on Issachar (vs. 14-15) may also allude to some now unknown incident, we can recognize some irony in it. We were told earlier that Issachar's name has to do with *śākār,* wages (ch. 30:18). For the sake of comfort, however, Issachar turns his "hired labor" into abject slavery. In addition, the poet describes Issachar with the image of the "castrated ass," the fruitless beast of burden.[33] With the blessing on Gad (v. 19), we have, as with several of the other blessings, a virtuoso play on the sound of the name: *gād g*ᵉ*dûd y*ᵉ*gûdennû, w*ᵉ*hû' yāgûd 'āqēb.* In the oracle on Dan (vs. 16-18)[34] is also a wordplay on the name in "Dan shall judge" (*dān yādîn*), but the sudden shift to an animal metaphor, of which this set of blessings has several (cf. vs. 9, 14, 21, 27), that of the snake, seems to suggest an ironic reversal of Dan's judicial function.[35] Certainly the implication of the snake's ambush on the horse is a shift in tone from the previously implied, straightforward confrontation in the courts. If the two images are not simply to be regarded as clumsily juxtaposed materials from diverse sources, their coherence would appear to lie in irony.

Finally, the first three blessings, those on Reuben, on Simeon and Levi, and on Judah, reflect an ironic perception of incidents involving those persons. The blessing on Reuben (vs. 3-4) plays on double meanings and refers as well to an earlier incident. Reuben is the "eldest," and therefore he has a certain "primacy" (*yether,* v. 3), which is not, however, constant (v. 4a: *'al tôthār*). *Yether* can also carry the connotation of "excess," and v. 3c could be translated: "excessive of pride, excessive of might." The first-born, of course, participates in a special way in the virile power of the father; hence Reuben can be called "my strength and the beginning of my power" (v. 3b: *kôchî w*ᵉ*rēshîth 'ônî*). Yet *'ôn,* "power," can also have another meaning: "sorrow" (cf. *ben-'ônî,* "son of my sorrow," ch. 35:18). And that very portion in the father's virile power is the source of Reuben's downfall: "You went up to your father's bed; then you defiled it—going up to my couch" (v. 4b-c). The reference is to the barely mentioned incident in ch. 35:22, where Reuben had slept with Bilhah, Jacob's concubine.

The blessing on Simeon and Levi (ch. 49:5-7) is actually a curse, denouncing their action at Shechem (ch. 34). In that it implies a virtual disinheritance of these two tribes (and in the later settlement neither tribe possessed independent territory), we might perceive a kind of thematic irony in the passage that is not made explicit in ironic language. With the blessing on Judah, however (ch. 49:8-12), we have a devastating irony by means of very subtle allusions and metaphors.[36] Wordplay appears again in Judah (*y*ᵉ*hûdāh*) and "praise" (*yôdû*), with an additional sound-play in "your hand" (*yād*ᵉ*kā*). The metaphor of the lion suggests the part Judah played in the deception of Jacob over Joseph's departure for Egypt in ch. 37:31 f. This is also the source of the allusion to dipping the garment in wine (note "blood of grapes," ch. 49:11). But vs. 10-11b and 12 make sense only when read as ironically symbolic allusions to the incident with Tamar (ch. 38). The scepter and judges' rod suggest the staff that Judah gave the "harlot" as collateral, the expression "between his feet" is certainly a euphemism for the sexual organs, reflecting the intercourse between them, and the enigmatic *shîlôh* of MT v. 10c is best read *shēlāh,* the name of the boy promised to Tamar as husband. We note further the connection of the term *śôrēqāh* "choice vine" (v. 11a) with the Valley of Soreq, near Timnah, the place to which Judah was going to shear his sheep on that occasion. And the foolishness of tying an ass to a vine, particularly to a fine vine like a *śôrēqāh,* reflects the irony of Judah's act with Tamar. Finally, the reference in v. 12 to the redness (?) of his "eyes" (*'ēnaim*) recalls the name of the town where the encounter between Judah and Tamar took place: Enaim. Viewed as a group of very subtle allusions to two earlier misdeeds of Judah, one with Joseph and the other with Tamar, the entire oracle masks a biting irony behind what looks like strong praise and high expectation.

The thematic irony of the Joseph legend does not depend on the punctual or episodic irony within it, nor does it emerge as the sum of the lesser ironies. We must now turn to the overarching irony of providence that provides the theme of the entire story. Modern psychologists did not invent "sibling rivalry." Jacob loves Joseph too well, a theme that we saw also behind the irony of his own career. But the father's too evident preference for the young boy quite naturally causes the other sons to hate him. All of this is succinctly put in ch. 37:3-4. And on this ironic incongruity—that love should produce hate—the entire story depends.

For the desire of the brothers to rid themselves of the young pest comes both out of their own hatred for him and out of their assumption that to get rid of him will reinstate them in Jacob's affections. Their spontaneous scheme is successful—though it would appear that someone else collects the cash (v. 28). But Joseph seems able to turn all he touches to gold. His expert interpretation of dreams in prison (ch. 40) makes possible his interpretation of the Pharaoh's dream (ch. 41:1-36), and the rags-to-riches theme of his success comes to its astounding climax (vs. 37-45). That much in itself would

have been enough to establish the ironic theme of the Joseph story. When, however, the storyteller weaves the family back into the story in conjunction with the famine (ch. 42:1-5), the irony deepens still further. The boy, disposed of into slavery, now can dispose of his brother's destinies. Where his own dreams brought him to grief with his brothers before, now his interpretation of others' dreams have brought him to Pharaoh's favor and therefore to his position over the brothers. Their ignorance of his identity adds to the irony hanging over their abject request to buy food (ch. 42:6-38). We have, therefore, the dramatic irony of the difference between the character's perception of his situation—that he is dealing with an evil and tight-fisted Egyptian—and the reality of the situation—that he is dealing with his little brother. But this is simply the underlying irony of the whole, which is finally explicated in two different but related ways:

> But now, do not be dismayed or displeased with yourselves, having sold me here. To maintain life, God sent me on before you. For these two years, famine has been in the land, and for five years more there will be neither plowing nor harvesting. But God sent me before you to make you a remnant in the land, and to maintain your life for great survival. So now, it was not you who sent me here but God, and he has made me like a father to Pharaoh and a lord to his whole household and a ruler in all the land of Egypt. (Ch. 45:5-8.)

After Jacob's death, attempting to forestall any grudge Joseph might have borne them, the brothers concoct a message from Jacob requiring Joseph to forgive them for their previous misdeed. Joseph's reply is the epitome of magnanimity, and it also expresses the fundamental irony of the entire story:

> Do not be afraid. For am I in God's place? You planned evil for me; God planned it for good, in order to make sure the survival of a numerous people as on this day. (Ch. 50:19-20.)

The ascription of ultimate causality to God caps the ironic theme of the story. To that point, we note some curiously twisted circumstances. When the divine intention is made explicit, however, the circumstances become something far more profound. Human beings do not finally override the divine purpose. "Surely the wrath of men shall praise thee." (Ps. 76:10.) Man's evil intentions may produce good; conversely, man's good intentions may produce evil. We have both in the Joseph story. Jacob's intentions of love give him only grief over Joseph. The brothers' intentions of hatred produce their survival in the famine. The providence of God rules and overrules the plans of men. Even the Pharaoh of Egypt cooperates with the God of Israel, more urbanely in this story than a subsequent Pharaoh does in the later events of the exodus. That Pharaoh, to be sure, "did not know Joseph" (Ex. 1:8).[37]

The book of *Genesis* might stand as an exhibit of the different kinds and uses of irony in narrative. We have seen small points of irony, unrelated to larger context; we have seen ironic episodes, humorous or critical; we have seen

the large canvases of ironic themes. We might be surprised at the amount of irony here, since the book of *Genesis* is occupied with the great themes of Israel's creation and election, with the covenant faith and the providential activity of God. Yet Israel's ironic vision comes to the fore precisely in conjunction with those august and solemn themes. In the final analysis the book is perhaps not ironic about God, though it proposes more than once that God is ironic about Israel. Equally, Israel is ironic about itself. Something about Israel's faith opens out to the free play of irony.

Notes

1. I would refer the reader also to my discussion of these passages in *You Shall Be My People: The Books of Covenant and Law* (The Westminster Press, 1959), pp. 78-84.

2. Cf. the perspicacious remark of F. van Trigt, made in another connection, in "La significance de la lutte de Jacob près du Yabboq, *Gen.* xxxii 23-33," in *Oudtestamentische Studiën,* deel XII, "Studies on the Book of *Genesis*" (E. J. Brill, Leiden, 1958), p. 302: *"En effet, à moins de fermer entièrement les yeux sur la composition exceptionelle de l'ensemble des récits, nous y découvrons des 'auteurs' qui sont bien plus que des compilateurs des données d'une vieille tradition."*

3. I suggested, without documentation, in *You Shall Be My People,* p. 79, that nakedness (*'ērôm*) connotes helplessness. Cf. the uses of *'ērôm* in Ezek. 18:7, 16, in parallel with "hungry"; in ch. 16:7, 22, 39, of the personified young Jerusalem in her helplessness without God; in ch. 23:29 of Oholibah in her deliverance to those whom she hates; in Deut. 28:48, where nakedness, hunger, thirst, and want are the conditions under which Israel will serve her enemies, i.e., that nothing is of any help against those conditions. The cognate *'ārôm,* used in *Gen.* 2:25, is found in Hos. 2:5 in a context very much like that of Ezek., ch. 16; in Micah 1:8, perhaps of a symbolic act of the prophet somewhat like that of Isa., ch. 20, which also uses the word; in Amos 2:16 of the flight of ignominiously defeated warriors; in Isa. 58:7 in the same sense as in Ezek. 18:7, 16; in Job 22:6 of the weakness of the poor before the mighty; in Job 24:7, 10 of the sad state of men whom God ignores; in Job 26:6 of the openness of Sheol before God; and in Job 1:21 of man's condition before God at birth and death alike. Taken together, these passages suggest to me that the connotation of *'ērôm* and *'ārôm* is not sexual but situational, nakedness as the absence of defense against threatening powers. For other opinions of the symbolic connotations of nakedness in *Gen.,* ch. 3, see Robert Gordis, "The Knowledge of Good and Evil in the Old Testament and the Qumran Scrolls," *JBL,* Vol. 76 (1957), pp. 123-138, and literature cited there; Walter Zimmerli, *1. Mose 1-11: Die Urgeschichte,* 2te Auflage (Prophezei, Zwingli Verlag, Zürich, 1957), p. 147.

4. Is it not surprising that, in a culture where the subordation of woman to man was a virtually unquestioned social principle, the etiology of the subordination should be in the context of man's primal sin? Perhaps woman's subordination was not unquestioned in Israel.

5. This remark is closely related to the curse on the woman in ch. 3:16. Here, "its [sin's] desire [*t^eshûqāh*] is centered on you, but you must master [*māshal*] it"; there, "your desire [*t^eshûqāh*] is centered on your husband, but he must master [*māshal*] you." Cain's relationship to sin ought to be like man's relationship to woman. The statement rings loud with irony, in both itself and the context of the Eden myth. Cf. Zimmerli, *op. cit.,* p. 212.

6. Not until the Ethiopic Enoch in the second century B.C. is this myth, rather than that of Adam and Eve, used as the primal myth of the Fall. Cf. I Enoch, chs. 6 to 8.

7. To be sure, the "goodness" of creation is a theme of the P creation story, and ch. 6:5-8 is normally analyzed as J. Nonetheless, we cannot ignore the fact that the "sources" have been combined into a unity, and it is illegitimate to avoid the conjunctions of images and themes in what is now a single story.

8. Cf. U. Cassuto's reading of ch. 2:5 in *A Commentary on the Book of Genesis, Part One: From Adam to Noah* (Magnes Press, Jerusalem, 1961), pp. 102-104.

9. The curse was certainly originally on Ham, but was transferred to Canaan because Canaan was Israel's immediate religious problem. Von Rad, *Genesis,* tr. by John H. Marks (The Westminster Press, 1961), pp. 131-132, argues, however, that "Ham the father of" in vs. 18 and 22 is a harmonizing gloss.

10. Also a mark of the fertility cult. Cf., e.g., Ex. 20:26. See also the remarks above, note 3, on the nakedness motif in *Gen.,* ch. 3.

11. I owe this interpretation to remarks in a lecture by Prof. A. J. Heschel at Stanford in May, 1963. A rather similar interpretation is proposed by Walter Zimmerli, *op. cit.,* pp. 399-404, but on pp. 405-407 Zimmerli seems to me to confuse the point by referring to the Tower of Babel as the Marduk temple in Babylon. The point of the tower is that it is a defense tower, not that it is a pagan temple.

12. The story has its ironic potential, best realized in the second version, ch. 20:1-18. Discussion will be postponed for that version. The same story, of course, is told of Isaac in ch. 26:6-11.

13. V. 2b is in a hopeless textual state. It appears to say that Abraham will be forced to adopt a slave in order to have an heir. V. 3 is not very much help. RSV has interpolated "slave," which may be the sense of it, though the expression *ben bēthî,* "son of my house," is not clear. L. A. Snijders, "*Genesis* XV. The Covenant with Abraham," in

Oudtestamentische Studiën, deel XII, pp. 269-270, has suggested the reading *ben mashshāq* for *ben mesheq* in v. 2a, meaning "the attacker, he who forces himself on one" (cf. Isa. 33:4). The gloss, "that is, Damascus" (*dammesheq*), is a deliberate pun, according to Snijders. The idea is by no means impossible, but the syntax remains obscure, and I am not convinced.

14. *Dialogues of Alfred North Whitehead,* edited by Lucien Price (The New American Library of World Literature, Inc., 1956 [originally published by Little, Brown and Company, 1954]), p. 163.

15. In the Canaanite story of Aqhat, Dan'el, the prospective father, also laughs at the news, but his laughter is that of sheer pleasure: "He parted his jaws and laughed" (AQHT A.ii.10; cf. *ANET,* p. 150). In a brief note, "Abraham and the Aqhat Legend," *JBL,* Vol. 77 (1958), pp. 72-73, I argued for a connection in tradition between the Aqhat story and the continuum of episodes leading up to the birth of Isaac.

16. Cf. von Rad, *Genesis,* pp. 206-210, who fails to mark the irony of the question. I have often wondered whether the narrator intended a certain irony in the fact that Abraham ceases his bargaining with ten. As it turns out, there are only four righteous in Sodom (ch. 19:15). Is the narrator saying, with extreme subtlety, that if Abraham had carried his boldness far enough—say, to four—Sodom might have been spared? Perhaps the point rests on silence, which cannot establish it.

17. The story is told again of Isaac (ch. 26:6-11), and the contention of Noth, *Überlieferungsgeschichte des Pentateuch* (W. Kohlhammer Verlag, Stuttgart, 1948), pp. 115-116, that the tale originated with Isaac, is probably correct.

18. It has often been noted that the remark presupposes a matriarchal system, for a man marrying the daughter of his father would avoid incest only on the assumption that the blood-line passes through the mother.

19. Note the expression *mal'ak yhwh* in an allegedly E passage.

20. So also von Rad, *Genesis,* p. 242. The humor is in a passage universally analyzed as P. The Priestly writers are not ordinarily singled out as purveyors of the comic.

21. R. de Vaux, O.P., *La Genèse* (BJ, Les Éditions du Cerf, Paris, 1962), p. 109, makes the connection of this story with the theme of promise but fails to mark its irony.

22. Cf. Napier, *From Faith to Faith,* pp. 85-87.

23. The pattern occurs so often that perhaps it is virtually normal. Note the younger sons in the Old Testament who attain preeminence: Isaac, Jacob, Joseph, Ephraim (*Gen.* 48:14), Othniel (Judg. 3:9), David, Solomon.

24. Reading, with Samaritan Pentateuch, *ha' attāh.* Only with the interrogative prefix would we expect Jacob to answer as he does, "I am."

25. LXX and Targum Onkelos read the singular, "your brother," an ironic reference to Jacob. The counterpart, spoken to Esau in v. 37, is in the singular, suggesting the propriety of the singular here. It requires only repointing from *'achekā* to *'achîkā.*

26. That is a paraphrase. The sentence reads literally: "And Jacob saw the face of Laban, and behold, he was not with him as previously."

27. Cf. John L. McKenzie, S.J., "Jacob at Peniel: Gn 32, 24-32," *CBQ,* Vol. 25 (1963), pp. 71-76, for an account of efforts to sort out the confusion by source analysis.

28. I speak of the story in its present form. Its origins and developments do not concern me here. For a thorough and penetrating consideration of the entire passage, cf. F. van Trigt, *loc. cit.,* pp. 280-309.

29. Napier, *From Faith to Faith,* p. 90.

30. The confusion between v. 27, which seems to mean that the brothers actually sold Joseph to the Ishmaelites, and v. 28, where passing Midianites do the job, has often been used to distinguish sources. I do not see the necessity of that conclusion.

31. Cf. von Rad, *Genesis,* p. 351.

32. In view of v. 34, the phrase "the men are shepherds" (v. 32) is probably to be excised as a gloss from some uncomprehending reader.

33. For this interpretation of a difficult text, cf. Samuel I. Feigen, "*Hamôr Gārîm,* 'Castrated Ass,'" *JNES,* Vol. 5 (1946), pp. 230-233.

34. V. 18 is probably a gloss.

35. The connection between vs. 16 and 17 is otherwise extremely tenuous. Cf. von Rad, *Genesis,* p. 422, who dismisses v. 17 as a later gloss.

36. I have argued the case at greater length in "The 'Blessing' on Judah, *Gen.* 49:8-12," *JBL,* Vol. 82 (1963), pp. 427-432.

37. In *You Shall Be My People,* pp. 69-70, I used this notice, together with Joseph's marriage to a daughter of the priest of On (*Gen.* 41:45), to date the descent of the Joseph tribes into Egypt in the Amarna period. I am now very dubious about using this material for that purpose, since I would see the Joseph story as fiction, written much too late to reflect accurate memory of Egyptian events and politics in pre-Mosaic times. As Noth points out (*Überlieferungsgeschichte des Pentateuch,* p. 226), the literary function of the Joseph story is to make the transition from the patriarchs of the promise to the exodus, to get Jacob and his family into Egypt in order that Yahweh may then get them out again. I do not therefore believe that the Joseph story has

any historical basis. The notice of Ex. 1:8 serves the purpose of motivating the Egyptian persecution of the Israelites.

Abbreviations

ANET: *Ancient Near Eastern Texts Relating to the Old Testament,* ed. by James B. Pritchard (2d ed., Princeton University Press, 1955)

AQHT: "The Tale of Aqhat," a Ugaritic legend

ATD: Das Alte Testament Deutsch

BJ: La Sainte Bible (Bible de Jérusalem)

CB: The Cambridge Bible

CBQ: *Catholic Biblical Quarterly*

HAT: *Handbuch zum Alten Testament*

HKAT: *Handkommentar zum Alten Testament*

IB: *The Interpreter's Bible*

ICC: The International Critical Commentary

IDB: *The Interpreter's Dictionary of the Bible*

JBL: *Journal of Biblical Literature*

JNES: *Journal of Near Eastern Studies*

K-B: Ludwig Koehler and Walter Baumgartner, *Lexicon in Veteris Testamenti Libros* (2d ed., E. J. Brill, Leiden, 1958)

LD: Lectio Divina

LXX: The Septuagint

MT: Masoretic Text

RPh: *Revue Philosophique*

RSV: Revised Standard Version of the Holy Bible

TR: *Theologische Rundschau*

VT: *Vetus Testamentum*

ZAW: *Zeitschrift für die alttestamentliche Wissenschaft*

Jay Y. Gonen (essay date 1971)

SOURCE: "Then Men Said, 'Let Us Make God in Our Image, After Our Likeness'," *Literature and Psychology,* Vol. XXI, No. 2, 1971, pp. 69-79.

[In the following essay, Gonen analyzes the analogous relationship between Genesis*'s account of man's nature, and psychoanalytic ideas regarding man's nature. Gonen concludes that the description of God in* Genesis *reflects man's own image of what he is and what he would like to be.]*

The story of man's banishment from the Garden of Eden has fascinated many thinkers who discovered a variety of meanings in the story. For example, Erikson (1950) sees this banishment as symbolizing the first ontogenetic catastrophe which occurs with teething. He asserts that at this particular point of time, the mother figure—the blissful and nourishing maternal environment which was always with the infant and which he trusted up to that time—begins to separate from him in response to his bites.

This evokes what is to become a life long conflict between a basic sense of "trust" and a basic sense of "evil". In another example, May (1967) sees in this story an Hegelian "fall upward" of man. After existing in a state of naive and pre-human happiness without anxiety and conflicts, Adam and Eve revolt against the benevolent dictatorship of God, develop human and moral consciousness, and differentiate themselves as persons. In doing this, however, they pay the inevitable prices of the human condition—conflict, shame, and anxiety. Thus, Erikson regards this first revolt of man against God as an expression of the inevitable anger and basic sense of evil which the teething infant feels toward the mother who tears him away from the nipple, while May sees in this revolt man's age-old existential struggle to realize his human condition. Obviously myths such as these can have many meanings.

The multiple meanings of myths frequently stem from an extensive use of symbols rather than use of more narrowly defined terms. The wealth of connotative meanings of symbols provides man with an opportunity to become aware of his many potentialities. This point has been emphasized by May (1960) who regards the creation of myths as part of man's constant struggle to understand himself, and to structure for himself a role in his universe. In this process of forming his own image through myths, man crystallizes numerous themes which are central to the human condition and which are as old as man. Not the least among them is the creation of a God who sets the rules for man and his world. From a psychological viewpoint, this creation is a projection of man's image of himself not only as he is, but as he would like to be. The successes and failures of such a God are the successes and failures of man himself. From this viewpoint, the early myths of creation and man's banishment from Eden constitute a monumental effort to understand man and his universe. As such they reveal a complex image of man and include themes which have preoccupied humanity throughout the ages. It is therefore not surprising to discover that some of these themes are also the subject of modern day psychoanalytic inquiry and that some analogies exist between Biblical and psychoanalytic notions concerning man's nature. An inquiry into these themes must necessarily begin with the particular sequence of events in the Biblical text.

The Sequence of the Early Tales

It is not possible to determine the original order of the various fragments which comprise the first three chapters of *Genesis.* These fragments may not have even belonged together at first.[1] However, the final sequence of events which has been established in *Genesis* and preserved for posterity does not seem coincidental and alludes to some important ideas. This interesting sequence can be summed up as follows:

(1) God created the world including life in it.

(2) God or possibly Gods (*Elohim*) created man, male and female, in his or their own image.

(3) Adam was created first, placed in Eden, and forbidden under the threat of death to eat from the tree of knowledge of good and evil.

(4) Adam was not satisfied living alone and God recognized this fact.

(5) Eve was created from Adam's rib and, under the influence of the serpent, led Adam to transgress God's command, and, thus, learn the meaning of nakedness and good and evil.

(6) This act of learning was punished by God with banishment from the blissful environment of Eden, thus insuring that man would (a) have to work to survive and (b) not eat from the tree of life and become immortal.

From a psychological viewpoint, which assumes that stories about the deity represent deep-rooted projections concerning the nature of man, this sequence is very revealing. Some of its most striking features are as follows:

(1) There is a switch from a singular to a plural form of describing God's deeds when it comes to the creation of man, male and female, in the image of God.

(2) God's attempt first to keep Adam alone and sexually naive or repressed, and later on to suppress and prohibit his sexual curiosity, resulted in failure.

(3) The transgression which followed the prohibition casts man in the role of an original sinner.

(4) The punishment for original sin is banishment and death. Each of these themes will now be discussed in turn.

THE DUALITY IN THE DEITY

In order to explore the first theme we need to investigate the specific use of language in the original Hebrew text. The story begins (*Genesis* I) with God creating the universe. God (*Elohim*) is repeatedly referred to in the third person pronoun until the first deviation from this mode which occurs in verses 26 and 27: "Then God said, 'Let us make man in our image, after our likeness; and let them have dominion over the fish of the sea. . . .' So God created man in his own image, in the image of God he created him; male and female he created them". It is interesting to note that *Elohim* in a literal translation means Gods and is the plural form of *Eloha*. This plural form usually serves merely as a form of reverence without implying a plurality in the deity. However, while it is a common practice in the Old Testament to refer to God's name in the plural form, it is unusual to do this with his speech and actions as is the case above. It is also important to note that the use of God's speech in the plural form appears for the first time in the description of the creation of man, male and female, in the image of God. All three themes—plurality in God's speech, differentiation of gender, and creation of man in the image of God—appear for the first time and together in these two verses. This

juxtaposition suggests that in the beginning "Gods" (literally *Elohim*) created Adam after their own image and later on created Eve out of Adam. Originally, therefore, there is a masculine-feminine duality in God and man, with the feminine component being censored (Adam was first created alone) perhaps because of its potential for sin. This potential was subsequently realized with Eve and the serpent playing important instrumental roles.

Interestingly enough, the idea that God has a potential for sin and needs to struggle and purge himself from an evil element within him was emphasized later on in various Jewish mystical traditions such as the Kabbalistic school of Isaac Luria (Sholem, 1954). In these traditions a similar emphasis was put on a masculine-feminine duality within the deity. Indeed it is very likely that the original mythical material on which the Biblical text is based included more than one God. This is the opinion of Gunkel (1964) who has suggested that the early pre-Biblical accounts of these tales were probably in poetic form rather than in prose, were action rather than speech oriented, included more personages who were involved in a conflict between God and Chaos, and consisted of dialogues rather than monologues by God alone. Be that as it may, it is important to reflect upon the fact that, from the start, the images of God—Adam and Eve—display a differential predisposition toward sin. Eve the female rather than Adam the male is cast in the role of the main culprit. Therefore, at least on a manifest level, sin and evil are mostly attributed to Eve and the serpent rather than to Adam and God. On this manifest level, which disregards the symbolic meaning of the serpent, the masculine component is nobler and does not originate evil as much as does the feminine component. Not only is the masculine element nobler but it is also the original one from which femininity was carved out later on. From this, one may conclude that Eve, or women in general, are of an inferior quality as compared to men and the root of all trouble. This is a popular notion which found frequent expression in world literature and which represents an old masculine bias. The Biblical text definitely suggests that before there was a woman there was only a potential for sin and that actual knowledge of good and evil, i.e., sexuality, comes about only through the "knowledge" of a woman. This equation of "knowledge" with sexual activity accounts for the frequent Biblical term which appears for the first time in *Genesis* IV, 1: "Now Adam knew Eve his wife, and she conceived and bore Cain . . .". Thus, the forbidden knowledge of good and evil is also knowledge of women and can come about only through companionship with women.

The belief that women are evil or inferior is of course a masculine bias. This is both an old and new bias as indicated in Biblical and psychoanalytic thinking with some amazing analogies between the two. In this connection, one may recall Karen Horney's (1939) bitter controversy with Freud over such issues as whether originally both boys and girls know only one sex, the masculine; whether libido, the Freudian theoretical construct of psychic energy, is primarily masculine and active in nature; and whether women are essentially masochistic, a trait which is at least inferior if not evil. Freud had his strong biases which persisted through time in spite of the Biblical idea that all human beings are equal before God and the psychoanalytic idea that the egos of both sexes develop out of a similar and undifferentiated instinctual substrate. The bias survived and for generations Jewish men were saying a prayer blessing the Lord for not making them women. In a similar fashion, Freud may have blessed his biological luck for being a man so as to be spared the specific feminine agonies of penis envy and a masochistic fate.

All in all, this sequence of events presented above suggests that man was created male and female after the image of Gods and that, therefore, Gods, like men, experience a bisexual polarity. This polarity contains an original and "good" masculine component which is relatively unsuccessful in resisting the temptations of the opposite feminine component which shares in evil and produces sin. Watts (1969) who also thinks that "Man makes God in his own image" underscores the fact that in western cultures the underlying unity of light and dark or good and evil forces is denied and a perpetual conflict is assumed to exist between the two. This image of internal conflict is not new when applied to man but is considered revolutionary when applied to God. At this point it is important to note that this attribution of internal conflict to God was later on underscored in the Kabbalistic and several other Jewish mystical traditions as indicated by Sholem (1954). This idea has been regarded as a revolutionary development in Judaism. It all may sound less revolutionary, however, when one adopts the point of view that God was created in the image of man. In this latter case, attributing shortcomings and internal conflicts to the deity amounts to no more than delineating the imperfect human condition as a given fact of life. It is sort of an ancient mode of "telling it like it is." It follows from this view that God, like man his creator, is imperfect, conflicted, and bound to fail occasionally in what he sets out to accomplish. One such example is his failure in the role of a censor. This will be the subject of our next discussion.

The Failure of the Censor

The text indicates that even before Eve was created Adam was already forbidden to eat the fruit of the tree of knowledge of good and evil, a knowledge which includes the understanding of the meaning of nakedness and presumably sexuality. The state of man's being alone symbolizes a state of naiveté or lack or sexual awareness, a state imposed by God as a preventive measure against sexuality. However, there is something peculiar about God's behavior toward the lone Adam. It is as if God had imposed a state of sexual ignorance on man, but in a most clumsy fashion. Although at first he created Adam alone so as to keep him sexually naive, he later on showed him the forbidden fruit and warned him against tasting it, thus defeating his own purpose. Instead of placing man in a true state of unawareness, thus precluding temptation, God

made him keenly aware of the forbidden. This psychological state inevitably led to the transgression of God's command and simply does not qualify as a true state of naiveté. To top it all, God himself became dissatisfied with Adam being alone and created Eve out of him. Thus, God in the role of a repressor or censor falls short of his ultimate goals. What is more, too much success in his work of repressing instinctual forces in man may leave God dissatisfied and he will then help man in seeking objects of gratification and, if need be, will even produce them for him. Thus, God created Eve who was subsequently instrumental in tempting Adam.

It should be borne in mind, however, that an important part was also played by the "subtle" serpent. The term "subtle", by the way, is the English translation of the Hebrew word "Arum" which has two meanings. One meaning is "sly" or "clever" and the other is "naked". This double meaning alludes to the above-mentioned connection between sexuality and knowledge. If the serpent or snake is taken to be a phallic symbol, then the role played by the male Adam in tempting the female Eve is being externalized. This again indicates a bias in the Biblical text in favor of masculinity. It also suggests a conceptualization of the working of instincts as largely independent of intellectual control. Supposedly Adam's head did not know what his "snake" was doing or at least could not control it. The outcome of the Biblical story therefore points toward the concept of the limited capability of repressive forces whether of God or Adam.

In summary, the sequence of events mentioned above suggests that God did not really believe in the idea of a naive and sexless man and therefore created all the conditions which make subsequent transgression of his own commands virtually inevitable. First, the repression of sexuality failed when God presented the lone Adam with Eve, and later the suppression of sexuality failed when God tempted Adam and Eve with a snake and forbidden fruits. This peculiar behavior can be understood as the works of a malicious God who springs a trap for man and insures that man will both sin and be punished. However, it can be better understood in terms of a censor who tries to do a job but fails. In this latter case, God who was created in the image of man is doomed to fail since he can no more stamp sexuality out of his nature than can his creator. Why he tried in the first place or why sexuality is viewed as evil in the first place is a question whose answer requires a discussion of the concept of original sin.

Original Sin

The failure of censorship and the inevitable manifestation of sexuality despite divine prohibitions cast man in the role of an original sinner. It is interesting to note how deeply the idea of original sin, which later on was emphasized so much in Catholicism, is already embedded in the Old Testament and finds subtle expression in the early tales of God and man. The root of the problem is that God creates man as a sexual being but prohibits sexual awareness. This paradoxical behavior casts God in a role similar to that of a Haleyan therapist (Haley, 1963) who constantly gives his patients conflicting messages. The conflicting message in this case is "I do not want you to display sexuality but of course I expect you to." This kind of message can occasionally anger patients and result in vituperative reactions. Indeed, Ayn Rand (1959) had such a reaction to God's message in *Atlas Shrugged:* ". . . the good is that which is non-man. The name of this monstrous absurdity is Original Sin. . . . To hold man's nature as his sin is a mockery of nature. To punish him for a crime he committed before he was born is a mockery of justice . . . it is not his errors that they hold as his guilt, but the essence of his nature as man. Whatever he was—that robot in the Garden of Eden, who existed without mind, without values, without labor, without love—he was not man".

This reaction misses a point or two. For one thing, this kind of double message is used in therapy as a part of the struggle for control of the relationship between therapist, and patient, and it has healthy growth-inducing aspects. Its purpose is to help patients assume control and responsibility for their own behavior. In a similar fashion, this paradoxical message by God to Adam and Eve leads to a struggle over the control of the relationship and results in man's rebellion and his "fall upward" as mentioned above. Thus, God, who at the very same time demands obedience and encourages rebellion, can be perceived not as a mean and arbitrary dictator but as a challenging therapist. In similar fashion, man's original sin may be perceived not as a sin but as a state of mind of uncertainty and fallibility which is a definer of the human condition and which accompanies all growth and acquisition of autonomy. Therefore, man's being held guilty by an arbitrary definition, which is probably what maddened Ayn Rand so much, involves a conception of man's nature which is far from arbitrary and which is rather multiply determined. We shall now explore some of the meanings of this guilt.

Why sexuality, i.e., original sin, is regarded as evil has already been suggested by Freud in *Totem and Taboo.* The various prohibitions of sexuality are invoked as regulatory mechanisms of the small social unit to prevent fraternal and paternal killings among the male members. Allowing the sexual rivalry to go on unchecked could result in disruptions which would threaten the survival chances of the small familial or tribal unit. Usually Oedipal-like and sibling rivalry-type dynamics are involved in the discharge of uncontrolled aggression. Uncontrolled sexuality involving such dynamics is therefore "evil," in a sense, and survival dictates certain prohibitions. The Biblical point of view may therefore be similar to that of later-day psychoanalysis as well as ethology in assuming that some kind of regulation of the aggression which accompanies sexual drives is a cornerstone for the survival and development of civilization. Thus original sin and guilt create the necessary motivation for checking aggressive and sexual behavior so as to make it serve survival rather than militate against it. There are additional meanings to original sin and guilt which involve the concept of punishment and which will be discussed next.

DEATH AS A PUNISHMENT

There are some aspects to original sin and guilt which involve the resulting punishment of banishment and death. This punishment is the fourth major theme suggested by the particular sequence of events as told in the Biblical text. Usually it is guilt which calls for punishment but in a sense it can also be vice versa. If punishment is a given, by definition, as death is sometimes perceived to be, then sin and guilt are needed to retroactively make sense out of this punishment. Otherwise, man may perceive himself as a meaningless and helpless creature at the hand of an arbitrary and cruel fate. Such a philosophy is very hard to live by and the Old Testament tells us that even the strong-willed Job could not abide by it for very long. However, since death as punishment is a primitive and easy-to-arrive-at concept, man has to grope with it frequently and he has to find his way out of a gloomy philosophy of arbitrariness. The Biblical text suggests a way out of this predicament.

Adam was threatened with death were he to eat from the tree of knowledge of good and evil. This conception of sexuality as an original sin and an inescapable guilt is perhaps a desperate attempt on the part of men to make some sense out of death by providing a crime which fits the given punishment. The tying together of sex and death, Eros and Thanatos if one prefers Freudian terms, as crime and punishment, is another theme which is perhaps as old as man. The way a specific connection between the two is established in the Biblical text will now be described. In developing sexual awareness Adam and Eve became more similar to the deity. This is indicated in *Genesis* III, 22-23: "Then the Lord God said, 'Behold, the man has become like one of us, knowing good and evil; and now, lest he put forth his hand and take also the tree of life, and eat, and live for ever'—therefore the Lord God sent him forth from the Garden of Eden, to till the ground from which he was taken." It is as if by yielding to sexual temptation man learns to distinguish between good and evil, like God. Original sin, therefore, is the sin of man's so resembling God to the point where the only remaining difference between him and God is immortality.

As man comes to resemble God, he experiences the same duality which is already inherent in the deity—a bipolarity of masculinity-femininity which may overlap to some extent the bipolarity of good-evil. God may have tried to save man from the agony and conflict of being caught between these polarities, but to no avail. There is a rupture in the deity itself which, from a psychological standpoint, is the mirror image of this rupture in man. There is a schism in man between dualistic tendencies which cannot be reconciled very well. Perhaps the best modern expression of this age-old bipolarity appears in *Narcissus and Goldmund* by Herman Hesse (1968). In this novel, an unbridgeable gap between and within men is developed between two sets of related ideas and images. One set of connected ideas includes Narcissus, father, mind, good and masculine and the other set of related images includes

Goldmund, mother, senses, sinful and feminine. In the book of *Genesis* this old theme of a bipolar tension between masculine as good and disciplined and between feminine as sinful and uncontrolled is a given, i.e., it is the inevitable lot of man. Thus, the text clearly indicates that man is born to experience sexuality or knowledge of good and evil, i.e., man is born to sin and is doomed to yield to evil through the knowledge of the pleasures of the flesh. One may speculate that God himself is similarly doomed and that this is why his clumsy attempts to mold man differently have never had a fighting chance. All that God can do in order to put a stop to man's activities is put a time limit on man in the form of death. Man's progressive resemblance to God through the development of knowledge, moral sense and autonomous will is thus limited by an upper ceiling. Only God can be not only what man is, but also what he wishes to become.

In spite of the threat of death Adam and Eve were not actually killed following their sin. They were only banished and sentenced to hard labor. God made sure, however, to deny them the tree of life, thus protecting an important difference between himself and man. While God is an immortal sexual being, at least conceptually by virtue of possessing "knowledge" of nakedness and good and evil, man is a mortal sexual being. Adam is what man actually is while God is what man occasionally wishes to become. Immortal God is therefore a projection of man who wishes to escape his lot. However, the banishment of man from Eden suggests that God's punishment, i.e., man's inescapable fate, while not necessarily for him to be killed, is that he eventually and inevitably die. His days are numbered. While he is alive he is forced to *work* for a living as sentenced by God and chooses to *love* for joy as he has already chosen prior to his banishment. Thus, until man's days on this earth are over, he can *work* and *love* or *arbeit und lieben* as recommended much later by Freud.

It is not surprising that under this set of rules as set forth by God man occasionally wishes to escape the human condition and become immortal. This is an intriguing psychological issue and appears in many cultures. The old Mesopotamian saga, *The Epic of Gilgamesh* (Sandars, 1964), tells of the renowned hero Gilgamesh who, after accomplishing nearly every feat which human beings could possibly accomplish, finally sets on a journey in search of immorality. He was doomed to learn in a hard, bitter way that man cannot abide with the Gods and live forever.[2] On the other hand, Homer's *The Odyssey* tells us of a hero who did not have to learn this particular lesson the hard way. Ulysses was abiding with Circe and enjoying what might have become eternal sexual life. For a brief period of time he left Circe and descended to the land of the dead where he listened to the plight of former kings and heroes of the Trojan war who urged him to escape the miserable fate of mortals. Nevertheless, he adamantly refused to abandon the unique agonies and joys which are rooted in the human condition and perspective of mortality. Somehow, eternal sexual pleasures with the enchanting Circe did not make adequate sense and lacked meaning so

that he decided to cast his lot with mortal humans rather than with the immortal gods. Ulysses of course was wiser than Gilgamesh in accepting and loving the human condition rather than looking for hopeless escapes.

Similar ideas are also embedded in the Old Testament. *Genesis* VI, 2, tells us of the sons of God who married daughters of men. These sons of God may have traded their own or their descendents' immortality for the joys of the flesh. That this indeed has been the price, we learn from God's subsequent decision (*Genesis* VI, 3): "Then the Lord said, 'My spirit shall not abide in man for ever, for he is flesh, but his days shall be a hundred and twenty years." This is a reiteration of the earlier and similar verdict which God passed in Eden numbering the days of man after Adam and Eve sinned. It is important to note that, unlike sexuality which was offered by God to man, even though as a forbidden sin, immortality was denied him. Immortality can remain man's dream never to be fulfilled, and man is doomed to retain the human condition and perspective. In this connection one is reminded of the existential notion that a very important part of being human is to encounter the idea of death. The idea of death, though, relates by definition to the idea of life, including perpetuation of life, i.e., sexuality. Death therefore becomes intertwined with Eros not merely as a punishment for the latter but also as a definition of the human condition which necessarily relates to the other definitions. Thus, it is as if God the definer of the human condition rather than God the punisher has said to Adam that he who choses sexual propagation should die. Otherwise, his choice is rendered meaningless. It is as if man, by choosing sexuality, has also chosen death, even if in fantasy he wishes to choose the former without the latter.[3] That the Biblical text is preoccupied with this theme both in man and sons of God, is an indication that the intricate relationship between life- and death-wishes which has preoccupied Freud's thinking so much is one other theme which is as old as man.

In summary, the whole concept of original sin or of guilt by definition is explicable in terms of coping with the idea of death. If death is perceived as an inevitable punishment, the notion of original sin is needed to make sense out of it by providing the missing crime. If death is perceived in a more sophisticated fashion as one of the conditions which define the fallibility, brevity, and sensuality of human life, then original sin also becomes a definer of the human condition and alludes to the unpredictability and uncontrollability of human action as well as to the terrible self-doubts which inevitably accompany men who chart autonomous courses for themselves. In this latter sense original sin implies existential doubts rather than inevitable masochistic guilt as a form of primitive punishment. The mythical stories lend themselves to both interpretations and perhaps some others as well. However, the whole notion of original sin seems less abhorrent when understood as part of an existential struggle with the meanings of life and death and does not call for the kind of vehement reaction evidenced by Rand (1959).

CONCLUDING REMARKS

The main contention of the present article is not new. The Greek philosopher Xenophanes of Kolophon has already expressed it as follows: "Yes, and if oxen and horses or lions had hands, and could paint with their hands, and produce works of art as men do, horses would paint the forms of gods like horses, and oxen like oxen, and make their bodies in the image of their several kinds" (Burnet, 1957). In a similar fashion, in the story of creation God was created in the image of man both as man is and as he would like to be. It is therefore not surprising that the emerging picture of God is *not* always that of an omnipotent being. After all, the image of man includes internal rifts and incomplete mastery over his own actions. Thus, the projected image of God is that of an immortal, but by no means omnipotent, being. He suffers from a schism between masculine and feminine components which, to a certain degree, stands for good and evil. Because of the internal rift within himself he fails in his role as a censor of sexual awareness. This failure is not only inevitable but may even constitute a part of God's deliberate plan to goad man to gain knowledge and realize his human condition.

The official Biblical point of view is of course that man was created in the image of God and not vice versa. Our point of view, however, is that God's and man's images reflect each other. Thus, both man and God experience sexual and moral conflicts but God, who has access to the Garden of Eden and the tree of life, is the only being who "knows" and is immortal. As such, he is a projection of man's wishes to escape his human condition and his mortal fate. The story, however, clearly indicates that this wishful escape is impossible. Sexuality and procreation do not go together with immortality, and man either makes his choice as Ulysses did, or is simply fated to have the one but not the other as both the Biblical text and the Gilgamesh saga imply. On the whole, these early myths constitute a marvelous success in man's attempt to deineate an image of himself. Nowhere is this better illustrated than by the two simple facts that on the one hand God could not succeed in stamping out man's sexual awareness and on the other hand man could not achieve immortality. God could no more deny man the tree of knowledge than man could reach the tree of life. This is a beautiful, simple, but forceful symbol, which illustrates how both God and man are bound by inviolable laws of human nature which the early Biblical myths tap so ingeniously.

It is interesting to note that in many phases of its history, especially during periods of resurgent mystical traditions, Judaism included beliefs in a dualistic deity, be it separate good and evil deities or a single deity undergoing a breach between inherent good and evil components and occasionally between masculine and feminine components. This is true of other religious traditions such as the Persian and the Gnostic. The text of *Genesis,* however, is among the oldest religious texts and precedes these latter developments. It consists of very old mythological writings which contain the first comprehensive monotheistic credo in the history of ideas as well as some polytheistic remnants, such as the sons of God mentioned above, which were not fully suppressed. In view of the antiquity of the book of *Genesis* it is doubly fascinating that this text alludes to certain psychological insights which bear a remarkable resemblance to the ideas advocated by Freud. However, fascinating as this parallel is, it should not come as a surprise. This parallel between insights derived from clinical observations of patients and the intuitive insights which are embedded in myths results from attempts to cope with similar problems. Throughout the ages, man has tried to deal with the anxieties generated by regularly recurring but to a large degree inexplicable life events. These events relate to the inevitable life cycle of birth, growth, decline, and death, and to basic personal and social issues such as authority, rebellion, and autonomy. In his efforts to cope with these events, man created God after his own image and crystallized his notion of humanity.

Notes

1. For a discussion of the various fragments, including non-Hebrew sources, from which the present Biblical text was constructed, see the discussion on Hebrew mythology in Hooke's (1963) book.

2. The story of Gigamesh, whom Sandars characterizes as the first tragic hero of whom anything is known, bears great resemblance not only to the early Biblical tales with which it shares some common origins, but also to the *Odyssey.* Sanders regards it as an historical possibility that the poet of The *Odyssey* was familiar with this epic. Of the many similarities between the Gilgamesh saga and the early Biblical tales perhaps the most striking relates to Enkidu, the closest friend of Gilgamesh. Enkidu was expelled from animal society and forced to abide with humans after succumbing to the temptations of a harlot. After making love to her "Enkidu was grown weak, for wisdom was in him, and the thoughts of a man were in his heart. So he returned and sat down at the woman's feet, and listened intently to what she said. 'You are wise, Enkidu, and now you have become like a God' (Sandars, 1964, p. 63)." In this saga, as in *Genesis,* becoming more human involves sexual activity which brings knowledge and makes men resemble God.

3. A brilliant discussion of an exactly opposite theme, that she who chooses death chooses sexuality as well, appears in David McClelland's (1963) article, *The Harlequin Complex.* In the article the author traces the appearance in literature of the theme of death who comes as a lover to take the woman away.

References

Burnet, J. *Early Greek Philosophy.* New York: Meridian, 1957, p. 119.

Erikson, E. *Childhood and Society.* New York: Norton, 1950.

Gunkel, H. *The Legends of Genesis.* New York: Schocken, 1964.

Haley, J. *Strategies of Psychotherapy.* New York: Grune & Stratton, 1963.

Hesse, H. *Narcissus and Goldmund.* New York: Farrar, Straus & Giroux, 1968.

Hooke, S. H. *Middle Eastern Mythology.* Baltimore, Maryland: Penguin, 1963.

Horney, K. *New Ways in Psychoanalysis.* New York: Norton, 1939.

McClelland, D. "The Harlequin Complex." In R. W. White (Ed.), *The Study of Lives.* New York: Prentice-Hall, 1963, Pp. 94-119.

May R. *Psychology and the Human Dilemma.* Princeton, New Jersey: Van Nostrand, 1967.

May, R. "The Significance of Symbols." In R. May (Ed.), *Symbolism in Religion and Literature.* New York: George Braziller, 1960, Pp. 11-49.

Rand, A. *Atlas Shrugged.* New York: Signet Books, 1959, Pp. 951-952.

Sandars, N. K. *The Epic of Gilgamesh.* Baltimore, Maryland: Penguin Books, 1964, p. 63.

Sholem, G. G. *Major Trends in Jewish Mysticism.* New York: Schocken, 1954.

Watts, A. W. *The Two Hands of God; The Myths of Polarity.* New York: Collier, 1969, p. 31.

Gerhard Von Rad (essay date 1972)

SOURCE: Introduction to *Genesis: A Commentary,* revised edition, pp. 13-43, The Westminster Press, 1972.

[*In the following essay, Von Rad asserts that the book of* Genesis *should not be viewed as an independent work; rather, it is "significantly related" to the five Biblical books that follow it. Together, these six books—Genesis, Exodus, Leviticus, Numbers, and Deuteronomy—are commonly designated as the Hexateuch. Von Rad goes on to discuss the theme of the Hexateuch, and the development of the source materials into their current Biblical form.*]

1. GENESIS AS PART OF THE HEXATEUCH

Genesis is not an independent book that can be interpreted by itself. On the contrary, the books *Genesis* to Joshua (Hexateuch) in their present form constitute an immense connected narrative. It matters little whether one is more interested in the great individual narrative sources that make up the book or in the composition as a whole which arose when a final redactor skillfully combined these individual sources. In either case, whereever he begins, the reader must keep in mind the narrative as a whole and the contexts into which all the individual parts fit and from which they are to be understood. The present, pronounced division of this originally unified material into the books of *Genesis,* Exodus, Leviticus, etc., is merely a subsequent partition of the massive material into single intelligible sections; one must not lose sight of the great unit of which these are only parts.

A work of such dimension and with such remarkable content—it takes us from Creation to the entrance of the tribes into Canaan—must be investigated carefully with regard to its purpose and theological character. Much has already been done with respect to its literary characteristics, and today we understand tolerably the nature and origin of many individual bits of material. But there has been much too little inquiry into what the Hexateuch is as a whole, what its basic theme really is, and therefore the exposition of *Genesis* has often been somewhat atomistic. Little, if any, attention has been paid to the fact that this book is significantly related to those events reported in the later books of the Hexateuch.

The basic theme of the Hexateuch may be stated as follows: God, the Creator of the world, called the patriarchs and promised them the Land of Canaan. When Israel became numerous in Egypt, God led the people through the wilderness with wonderful demonstrations of grace; then after their lengthy wandering he gave them under Joshua the Promised Land. If we compare this table of contents with the Hexateuch itself, we are struck with the incongruity between the theme and its actual development, with this colossal massing and arranging of the most varied kinds of material around so simple a basic design. From this observation we draw an immediately illuminating conclusion: this way of structuring the material for so simple a theme must represent a final conception, the last and last possible. This baroque fashioning of the basic theme into such gigantic proportions, when considered from the viewpoint of the history of literature, cannot have been a first conception, not even one that blossomed into classic maturity and balance. Rather, it is a final conception that has burgeoned from earlier stages to the limits of the possible and readable.

If we examine the Old Testament with the question of the theme of the Hexateuch in mind, our attention is drawn to a whole series of shorter or longer texts. For example, the prayer to be spoken when the first fruits were delivered to the sanctuary is especially ancient:

> A wandering Aramean was my father; and he went down into Egypt and sojourned there, few in number; and there he became a nation, great, mighty, and populous. And the Egyptians treated us harshly, and afflicted us, and laid upon us hard bondage. Then we cried to the Lord the God of our fathers, and the Lord heard our voice, and saw our affliction, our toil, and our oppression; and the Lord brought us out of Egypt with a mighty hand and an outstretched arm, with great

terror, with signs and wonders; and he brought us into this place and gave us this land, a land flowing with milk and honey.—Deut. 26.5-9.

There can be no doubt that this is how men really spoke in ancient times, and we see that within the cultic framework it was customary, among other things, to recite a short form of the sacred history as a confession. For what we find here is a kind of credo, not a personal prayer of thanksgiving. There is no divinely addressed Thou. Rather, the speaker recapitulates the great, sacred facts that constitute the community. He abstains from all individual concerns and in this moment identifies himself completely with the community; that is, he makes a confession of faith.

A similar summary of the sacred history in a creed occurs in Deut. 6.20-24. The text, which is now completely imbedded in the great paraenetic context, is easily recognizable as having been originally independent, with regard both to form and to content.

> When your son asks you in time to come, "What is the meaning of the testimonies and the statutes and the ordinances which the Lord our God has commanded you?", then you shall say to your son, "We were Pharaoh's slaves in Egypt; and the Lord brought us out of Egypt with a mighty hand; and the Lord showed signs and wonders, great and grievous, against Egypt and against Pharaoh and all his household, before our eyes; and he brought us out from there, that he might bring us in and give us the land which he swore to give to our fathers. And the Lord commanded us to do all these statutes, to fear the Lord our God, for our good always, that he might preserve us alive, as at this day."

We may add still a third example, the speech of Joshua before the assembly at Shechem. It is somewhat more extensive because of a few embellishments, but there can be no doubt that basically this historical review is not a distinct literary creation. Here too, apparently, an essentially fixed form is used, a form with which one can take only minor liberties.

> Thus says the Lord, the God of Israel, "Your fathers lived of old beyond the Euphrates, Terah, the father of Abraham and of Nahor; and they served other gods. Then I took your father Abraham from beyond the River and led him through all the land of Canaan, and made his offspring many. I gave him Isaac; and to Isaac I gave Jacob and Esau. And I gave Esau the hill country of Seir to possess, but Jacob and his children went down to Egypt. And I sent Moses and Aaron, and I plagued Egypt with what I did in the midst of it; and afterwards I brought you out. Then I brought your fathers out of Egypt, and you came to the sea; and the Egyptians pursued your fathers with chariots and horsemen to the Red Sea. And when they cried to the Lord, he put darkness between you and the Egyptians, and made the sea come upon them and cover them; and your eyes saw what I did to Egypt; and you lived in the wilderness a long time. Then I brought you to the land of the Amorites, who lived on the other side of the Jordan; they fought with you, and I gave them into your hand, and you took possession of their land, and I destroyed them before you. Then Balak the son of Zippor, king of Moab, arose and fought against Israel; and he sent and invited Balaam the son of Beor to curse you, but I would not listen to Balaam; therefore he blessed you; so I delivered you out of his hand. And you went over the Jordan and came to Jericho, and the men of Jericho fought against you, and also the Amorites, the Perizzites, the Canaanites, the Hittites, the Girgashites, the Hivites, and the Jebusites; and I gave them into your hand. And I sent the hornet before you, which drove them out before you, the two kings of the Amorites; it was not by your sword or by your bow. I gave you a land on which you had not labored, and cities which you had not built, and you dwell therein; you eat the fruit of vineyards and oliveyards which you did not plant."—Josh. 24.2-13.

None of the three passages mentioned above contains even a parenthetical recollection of anything historical; rather, each one is considered a recitation, elevated in form and in direct discourse. Obviously they are constructed according to a scheme, i.e., they follow a canonical pattern of the sacred history, long established in all its essentials. Though this virtually creed-like recitation of the sacred facts may appear far removed from our Hexateuch in its final form, still the uniformity here and there in thought and theme is often surprising. At bottom there is one and the same extremely simple train of thought, and Josh. 24.2-13 can be characterized as a "Hexateuch" *in nuce*. If one now surveys the beginning and end of the process, one gains some notion of the persevering power of the essential content of Old Testament faith. For no matter how numerous the additions to it are or how intensive its revision is, still there is always a fixed datum, a basic apprehension of faith, beyond which the Hexateuch in its final form did not and would not go.

The text Deut., ch. 26, bears clear signs of a later revision. So it is hard to say when such historical summaries arose and came into use. In our view there is no difficulty in supposing that they existed as early as the time of the Judges. At the other extreme it would be impossible to take these historical summaries to be later résumés of the great historical outlines of the Hexateuch. Were that the case they would inevitably have a different appearance. This applies above all to the absence of the Sinai event, which must be discussed immediately.

The Yahwist, however, wrote in a period quite different from that of the Deuteronomist. No very great span of years lay between him and the time of the old Israelite amphictyony (we have reason to assume that he wrote at the time of Solomon or a little later), but even so, much had changed culturally and cultically between the time of the amphictyony and his own day.

For a thorough understanding of the first books of the Bible it is crucial that this notation "J" lose its schematic character and that we come to a realistic view about the formation of the literary tradition. For it was the Yahwist who, so far as we can see, gave to the entire Hexateuch its form and compass. The Yahwist marks that decisive line of demarcation in the history of culture which we can observe for so many peoples: he was the collector of the countless old traditions which until then had circulated freely among the people. With him began the writing down of those poetic or cultic narratives which previously had circulated orally and without context among the people. It seems probable that this process was not one in which a great literary work issued at a stroke. Perhaps the Yahwist followed earlier works about which, of course, we know nothing. Such a collecting and refashioning of old material cannot, of course, be ascribed to the initiative of the Yahwist alone; the time must have been ripe for it. Indeed, what is most important is that the presuppositions for this collecting and refashioning must have been present in the ancient material itself. The majority of these old narratives were aetiologies, i.e., their purpose was to explain some facts in tribal history, about a place, or in the cult. Previously the validity of these traditions and the interest in them had been regionally limited to that area in which the question was alive and to which the existing aetiological narrative would give the answer. This is especially easy to comprehend in the case of cult legends.

The old cultic traditions in particular were previously unthinkable outside the sacred framework. Only in the course of the cultic act could one meet and experience them. These sacred traditions were not some kind of ornamental addition to the cult; rather, they were its inmost nerve, by which it lived and from which proceeded the content and form of the festivals.[1] What a profound change occurred when materials from the most dissimilar cult centers became unified and even substantially altered by a superimposed plan, when, in a word, they became available as literature! For that to happen it was necessary, as we have said, for the presuppositions to be present in the material itself. A slackening (harmful to the cult!) must already have occurred in the connection between the materials and their hereditary cultic points of reference. At the time of the first kings a crisis seems to have occurred in the genuine, naïve, ancient cult; its spiritual fundamentals began to change, and in this process those traditions were gradually liberated from their imprisonment in the hereditary sphere of the sacred cult.

This was the great crisis that went hand in hand with the formation of the Israelite state. Connected with the crisis was the decline of the ancient Israelite tribal unity, which took place toward the end of the period of the Judges, and the crisis reached its first high point in the enlightenment of the Solomonic era. No matter where one dates the Yahwist, when he is judged by the age of the traditions on which he worked he signifies a *late* phase. One must realize, therefore, that becoming literature meant in a sense an end for this material, which until then had already had a varied history behind it.[2]

But at the same time it meant the beginning of a much longer history! Above all, there occurs at this stage a profound inner shift in the meaning of those narratives.

One need only ask how much of the old meaning is still left when a cult legend is deprived of its cultic aetiological point! The same can be said of the old ethnological tribal sagas, which at that time were also bound to a limited area. When they were uprooted they were open to every kind of spiritualized literary application. For what is the content of *Gen.*, ch. 18, if the narrative no longer serves to legitimize the cultic center of Mamre? What is the content of ch. 22 if the narrative no longer legitimizes the abolition of child sacrifice? What is the meaning of ch. 28 if the narrative no longer legitimizes the sacredness of Bethel and its customs? What is the meaning of ch. 16—to take an ethnological saga—if the narrative no longer answers the question of the origin and way of life of the Ishmaelites? (The Yahwist himself probably no longer had any interest in the aetiological question because the Ishmaelites at his time no longer existed as a tribe.) These questions indicate one of the most important tasks that face anyone who interprets the stories in *Genesis* today. In many narratives he can ascertain with a probability verging on certainty the meaning and purpose which the material once had in an earlier, pre-literary phase. But he must not forget that the narrative has changed by virtue of the context in which the Yahwist has put it. Sometimes he must reckon with profound changes, since when the old aetiological focus of a story is diffused, its whole structure can collapse. Thus once again we face the question of the meaning of the whole of the Yahwist's work.

Suppose we visualize the matter roughly. On the one hand he had one of those summaries of salvation history (from the patriarchs to the conquest). On the other hand he had a very great number of loose compositions, of which a few perhaps had already coalesced into smaller compositions. Most of them, however, were certainly short and without context. The astonishing creative accomplishment was that by means of the simple plan of that credo of sacred history he was successful in forging the immense mass of narrative detail into a supporting and unifying basic tradition, and indeed in such a way that the simple and manifest thought of that credo remained dominant and almost unchanged in its theological outline. It is scarcely possible to determine all the single traditions which the Yahwist incorporated into his work. Perhaps he had earlier models to follow. However, his inclusion of traditions that could not immediately be incorporated into the old pattern is of theological interest. The result of such inclusions and additions was naturally an over-extension of the old plan and a theological diffusion of its original basis. This is particularly striking at three main points: (*a*) the incorporation of the Sinai tradition, (*b*) the extension of the patriarchal tradition, and (*c*) the inclusion of the primeval history.

A. The Incorporation of the Sinai Tradition

If one looks over the data of the sacred history in the short compositions introduced above, one is struck by the complete absence of any mention of the Sinai episode. In Josh., ch. 24 especially, it seems that the greatest event of the desert wandering could well have been mentioned alongside many less important recollections, if its mention were at all demanded by the canonical tradition. The conjecture that this plan of the old tradition about the conquest did not originally contain the Sinai event first becomes a certainty when we examine the free modifications of the credo in poetry (Ps. 78; 105; 135; 136; Ex., ch. 15), and secondly when we notice the remarkable position of the Sinai pericope in its present context. The Sinai tradition, too, probably owes its form (as the exposition of Exodus will show) to a cult festival, but in the history of the cult as in the history of the tradition it must be separated from our conquest tradition. Remarkably, this material, which is without doubt particularly old, had its own history.³ The Yahwist (and perhaps even his predecessor) was the first to unite these widely separated traditions and to incorporate the Sinai tradition into the conquest tradition. Most important, however, is the great theological enlargement that was accomplished by the union of both traditions. The conquest tradition in our credo is a witness to God's gracious leading; it is sacred history. The Sinai tradition celebrates God's coming to his people, and at its center is the demand of Yahweh's lawful will, the revelation of the great sovereign right of God over Israel. Without question the simple, soteriological motif of the credo receives powerful support from the Sinai tradition. In the union of these traditions the two basic elements of all biblical proclamation are outlined: law and gospel.

B. The Extension of the Patriarchal Tradition

The summaries made only brief mention of the patriarchal period (Deut. 26.5; Josh. 24.2; I Sam. 12.8). In our *Genesis* the narrative material extends over thirty-eight chapters. How can we analyse such extremely complex material? There is now no fundamental dispute that it is to be assigned to the three source documents J, E, and P, and there is even agreement over detail. But it is equally certain that the narratives incorporated into the source documents already have a long history behind them. So where do they come from, and what is the nature of the information that they give about Abraham, Isaac, and Jacob? If we examine the geographical area within which they move, the "local points of reference" of the narrative material, we find that they are spread over Palestine in a remarkable way. With their connections with Shechem (*Gen.* 33.18f.), Bethel (*Gen.* 28.11 ff.; 35.3 ff.) and Penuel (*Gen.* 32.22 ff.), the Jacob stories are clearly rooted in central Palestine, whereas the Isaac stories never leave the area of Beersheba in the extreme south (*Gen.* 26). The Abraham stories cannot all be located so clearly, but they too surely belong in the south (Mamre, *Gen.* 18). The only explanation of this remarkable position is that as the semi-nomadic ancestors of what later became Israel gradually settled in Palestine, they transferred the traditions which they had brought with them to the sanctuaries there. This transplantation of their traditions to ancient Palestinian sanctuaries meant that their religion, which was probably a cult of an ancestral God,⁴ was mixed with ancient Canaanite tradi-

tions. So while we may not doubt that as "recipients of revelation" and "founders of cults" (A. Alt), Abraham, Isaac, and Jacob were historical personalities, it is no longer possible to use the narrative material for biographical accounts. It has passed through too many hands. The narratives offer little more than a few indications of the characteristic cultural situation that governed the living conditions of these clans. Nor do they offer any point of reference for even an approximate dating of the patriarchs. The living conditions of these semi-nomadic groups remained the same for hundreds of years, and they never made history. If one assumes (with J. Bright) that they lived early in the second millennium, then something like nine hundred years lay between them and the narratives of the Yahwist!

So it is the Yahwist who tells us of the experiences of the ancestors of Israel. But he does not think in terms of interpreting the old traditions (as a modern historian would do) completely from the conceptions of the "religion of the fathers" held at that early period. Rather, quite "anachronistically," he incorporated them into the view which he and his time had of the action of Yahweh toward men, and thus almost made them his contemporaries.

To weld the very varied and often unwieldy material of the patriarchal narratives into a great narrative complex required a thoroughgoing redactional technique. These many individual narratives, together with the larger units that had already been formed, the so-called "saga clusters" (e.g. the Lot-Sodom and the Jacob-Laban complexes), did not come together of their own accord to form a continuous narrative that was also governed by a particular theological theme. The internal connection between individual narratives can be seen above all in the way in which they are now all subordinated to the theme of the "promise to the patriarchs": especially the promise of land, but also the promise of descendants. In some cases this promise was already rooted in the narrative material before it was taken over (*Gen.* 15.18; 26.4, 24), but elsewhere we can see that it was only woven into the narrative later, by the Yahwist (e.g., *Gen.* 18.13; 22.17; 50.24). At least the promise of land is an element which goes back to the time of the "religion of the fathers". This earliest promise in the patriarchal sagas was, of course, at that time an immediate one. It promised possession of cultivated land to those semi-nomadic "patriarchs" who were then living. Thus originally it did not reckon at all with an imminent abandonment of the land and a second conquest (under Joshua). But because of the inclusion of this patriarchal tradition in the great salvation-historical scheme of historical summaries, that first ancient promise appears strangely broken. Now the reader must understand the promise mediately, because it now refers to the conquest under Joshua. Thus the relation of the patriarchs to the land in which they live appears as something temporary; indeed, the entire patriarchal period thus becomes theologically a peculiar intermediate state, a wandering from promise to fulfillment which gives to all events the character of temporariness and at the same time mysterious portent.

The Hexateuch was already laid out by the Yahwist around the great theological pragmatic plan: patriarchal period and promise, conquest and fulfillment. Even the covenant with Abraham, as an element of tradition, probably belongs to that ancient religion of the fathers (cf. below on *Gen.* 15.17 ff.). Now, however, it is obviously related to the covenant at Sinai. The relation of the patriarchs not only to the land, but especially to God, is temporary; it finds its fulfillment in God's revelation at Sinai and in the sequestering of the people who had descended by God's will from the patriarchs.

Finally, the content of the patriarchal narratives was broadened because all events of the patriarchal period were connected with *all* Israel by being oriented toward the conquest under Joshua. If one remembers that the old cultic traditions of the pre-Mosaic period always belonged only to a very small cultic community and that formerly the numerous aetiological narratives likewise had only a limited regional validity, then one will comprehend the full importance of that broadening and orientation toward the Israel of the twelve tribes.

The Yahwist worked to join the traditional material together in yet another way, by the occasional insertion of "interludes". These are sections which, as can be seen relatively easily, do not go back to ancient tradition but represent short bridges between early narrative material (thus e.g., *Gen.* 6.5-8; 12.1-9; 18.17-33). These "interludes" are characterized by a higher degree of theological reflection, and for that very reason they are particularly important to us for determining the religious ideas of the Yahwist himself, which otherwise we can discover only in an indirect way.

C. The Inclusion of Primeval History

By including a primeval history (chs. 2.4b to 12.3) the Yahwist shows the greatest independence of that sacred tradition which otherwise supports him. The tradition of the conquest began with the patriarchal stories, and never did it contain anything of the primeval history, creation, etc. But where it left the Yahwist in the lurch he was quite self-reliant and free to unfold his own conceptions. Strict proof that the Yahwist had no precursor in that theological union of primeval history and sacred history is, of course, not available. On the other hand, there are no indications that the Yahwist was here following a received tradition. This view is thus unique, and one may still be able to sense the boldness of the first draft in this loosest part of the whole composition.

The primeval history, which the Yahwist constructed from elements of very different kinds, proclaims first of all with impressive one-sidedness that all corruption, all confusion in the world, comes from sin; but it also testifies that the continually widening cleft between God and man is matched by a secret increasing power of grace. The stories of the Fall, of Cain, and of Noah show God's forgiving and supporting act of salvation. Only in the story of the

Tower of Babel, when the nations are scattered and the unity of mankind is lost, does the judgment of God seem to be the last word. But here primeval history dovetails with sacred history: Abraham is called from the multitude of nations, "that in him all generations of the earth should be blessed." Thus the insertion of sacred history gives the answer to the unsolved question of primeval history, the question about the relation of God to all peoples. This entry of sacred history in ch. 12.1-3 is thus not only the conclusion to primeval history but the actual key to it. In this close union of primeval history and sacred history the Yahwist does justice to the meaning and purpose of the conditions of salvation which Yahweh has granted to Israel. He gives the aetiology of all aetiologies in the Old Testament and becomes at this point a true prohet, for the proclaims the distant goal of the sacred history effected by God in Israel to be the bridging of the cleft between God and all mankind; and he announces it neither as being rationally grounded nor as being already comprehensible in its details. The promise in *Gen.* 12.1 ff. contains three promises of blessing: (1) Abraham will be blessed and become a great nation, (2) Yahweh will give the land to Abraham's seed (v. 7), (3) in Abraham all nations of the earth will be blessed (v. 3). The first two promises were already known to the Yahwist from the tradition of the patriarchal sagas, the third, however, obviously arose from none of the older traditions but directly from the authority of his prophetic inspiration (commentary on chs. 11.28-30; 12.1-3).

2. The Three Narrative Sources

The preceding discussion presupposes the recognition of a fact that has become accepted in contemporary Old Testament science after almost 200 years of research: The books *Genesis* to Joshua consist of several continuous source documents that were woven together more or less skillfully by a redactor. The oldest source documents are known as "Yahwist" (J) and "Elohist" (E) because of their distinctive use of the name for God. The Yahwist may be dated ca. 950, the Elohist perhaps one or two centuries later. Deuteronomy (D) is literarily distinct; we have it in the book of Deuteronomy, but Deuteronomistic additions and revisions occur also in the Book of Joshua. The latest source is the Priestly document (P); its actual composition (without the later additions, of course) falls in the postexilic period, ca. 538-450.

The importance of these dates must not be overestimated, both because they are in every instance only guesses and, above all, because they refer only to the completed literary composition. The question of the age of a single tradition within any one of the source documents is an entirely different matter. The youngest document (P), for example, contains an abundance of ancient and very ancient material.

This is not the place for even a partially exhaustive characterization of the descriptive method of the sources. We shall be content with a few indications. As regards the creative genius of the *Yahwist's narrative* there is only admiration. Someone has justly called the artistic mastery in this narrative one of the greatest accomplishments of all times in the history of thought. Wonderful clarity and utter simplicity characterize the representation of the individual scenes. The meagerness of his resources is truly amazing, and yet this narrator's view encompasses the whole of human life with all its heights and depths. With unrivalled objectivity he has made man the subject of his presentation—both the riddles and conflicts of his visible acts and ways of behaving as well as the mistakes and muddles in the secret of his heart. He among the biblical writers is the great psychologist. However, he is concerned, not with man who with his desires and despair believes himself to be alone in the world, but rather with man to whom the living God has been revealed and who therefore has become the object of divine address, a divine act, and therefore a divine judgment and divine salvation. Thus in the primeval history he subjects the great problems of humanity to the light of revelation: creation and nature, sin and suffering, man and wife, fraternal quarrels, international confusion, etc. But above all, he investigates God's activities in the beginnings of Israel, both their visible wonders and their hidden mysteries. He sees the complete mystery of the election of the Old Testament community, and in *Gen.* 12.3 he answers the riddle of this divine act with prophetic authority. "Yahweh is the God of the world, his presence is felt everywhere with profound reverence." (Pr.) Yet precisely the Yahwistic narrative is full of the boldest anthropomorphisms. Yahweh walks in the garden in the cool of the evening; he himself closes the ark; he descends to inspect the Tower of Babel, etc. This is anything but the bluntness and naïveté of an archaic narrator. It is, rather, the candor and lack of hesitation which is only the mark of a lofty and mature way of thinking. This glasslike, transparent, and fragile way of thinking in the Yahwistic narratives makes of every exposition, which inevitably coarsens the original text, a difficult and almost insoluble task.

The work of the *Elohist* probably arose one or two centuries later. Soon, it was closely intertwined with the work of the Yahwist by a redactor. Even so, it differs rather distinctly from the work of the Yahwist. As a whole, it does not attain the splendor and brilliant perfection of the Yahwistic account. The fabric is much less finely woven. Thus, for example, the spectacular aspect of the miracles is much more strongly emphasized. The work does not require the same degree of reflection from its readers and expositors; it is more "popular", i.e., it has taken over the old sacred folk tradition with less modification and spiritualization. This accounts for the fact that the Elohist cannot create so many great, overlapping contextual units. (Compare the singleness of purpose in the Yahwistic stories of Abraham or Jacob!) His dependence on popular tradition is especially recognizable in the total plan. The Elohist begins with Abraham and therefore does not have a primeval history. Thus he stands closer than the Yahwist to the old canonical form of the sacred history. The Yahwist, by including the primeval history, deviated from the old

tradition more than the Elohist, who felt more bound to the old form of the credo, which had been hammered into the religious consciousness of the people by the tradition of centuries.

This description would be false, however, if the fact were not mentioned at once that the Elohist has clear statements of theological reflection which go beyond what is simply popular. In many places one can recognize almost a systematic theological revision of the old traditions. We will mention only two peculiarities of the Elohist: (1) The immediacy of God with man, his appearances, his movement on earth is severely limited. The angel of Yahweh calls down from heaven, and is therefore no longer thought of as walking on earth (*Gen.* 21.17; 22.11, 15). Related to this removal of God from men and from anything earthly is the great significance given to dreams. They are now the spiritual plane on which God's revelation meets men. The more neutral sphere of the dream is to some extent the third place where God meets man. But even here man is given no direct access to God's revelation, for man cannot simply interpret the dream except through the power of special inspiration which comes from God (*Gen.* 40.8; 41.15 f.).

(2) This loss of immediacy with God and his revealed word in the Elohistic work is matched by the great significance that is given to the prophet and his office. The prophet is the properly qualified mediator between God and men; he is the one who receives God's revelation, and he is the one who brings the concerns of men in supplication before God (*Gen.* 20.7, 17; Ex. 15.20; 20.19; Num., ch. 11; 12.6 ff.; 21.7). The Elohist's concern for the prophet and his tasks is so strong that much can be said for the conjecture that the entire work arose in old prophetic circles. Our exposition, however, does not conceive as its task a thorough elaboration of this narrative in its original form. The interweaving with the Yahwistic narrative is so thorough that any separation can be made only with great damage to the text. Attention will be given in every instance to the theological distinctiveness of the Elohistic tradition.[5]

The *Priestly narrative* is quite different from the sources characterized above. Its text can be recognized even by laymen because of its striking peculiarities with regard to form and content. One may not consider this document a narrative at all. It is really a Priestly document, i.e., it contains *doctrine* throughout. It is the result of intensive, theologically ordering thought. Consequently the manner of presentation is quite different. The language is succinct and ponderous, pedantic and lacking artistry. Only at the points of primary interest does the usual, excessively terse diction become relaxed and more detailed in an effort to paraphrase the matter conceptually (e.g., *Gen.*, chs. 1; 9; 17). If in the Yahwist we found a narration of overpowering simplicity without anything doctrinal (in the narrower sense of the word), in the Priestly document we find a minimum of vivid narration and artistic movement. In this respect the writing is divested of every impressive ornament. To be sure, the greatness of the work lies precisely in that renunciation, for this sober objectivity is in reality the deepest concern, the most intense concentration on what is revealed by God. Here everything is written after reflection; nothing is without theological relevance, for in this work we have the essence of the theological labor of many generations of priests. No effort is given to depicting man as the recipient of revelation or to the circumstances, the conflicts, the spiritual or social uncertainties attending that experience. The figures of the Priestly account are in this respect completely colorless and shadowy. The whole interest is focused exclusively on what comes from God, his words, judgments, commands, and regulations. Thus it describes a course of history only with respect to God's revealed judgments and regulations, with respect to divine regulations which with increasing number establish and assure the salvation of God's people. It presents history, not of men, but of divine regulations on earth, in so far as one can speak of history in this way. The "composition" of such a work with its infinitely slow growth of such sacred traditions cannot be determined in terms of a year or a century. Even though it may really have received its final form only in the postexilic period, still, along with later material and material that has been considerably revised theologically, it also preserves very ancient matter in almost unchanged archaic garb.

The interweaving by the redactor of this document with the previously united Yahwist and Elohist documents ("the Jehovist") could not, of course, be done organically. The Priestly texts are as a rule simply recorded, each in its place, in the composition of the Hexateuch. In *Genesis,* apart from minor insertions from the Priestly document, the redactor found himself forced to unite the tradition of P and J to *one* text only in the story of the Flood.

The Hexateuch in its present form arose by means of redactors who heard the peculiar testimony of faith of each document and considered it binding. There is no doubt that the present Hexateuch in its final form makes great demands on the understanding of every reader. Many ages, many men, many traditions and theologies, have constructed this massive work. Only the one who does not look super-ficially at the Hexateuch but reads it with a knowledge of its deep dimension will arrive at true understanding. Such a one will know that revelations and religious experiences of many ages are speaking from it. *For no stage in this work's long period of growth is really obsolete; something of each phase has been conserved and passed on as enduring until the Hexateuch attained its final form.*

3. The Theological Problem of the Yahwist

One further question most be answered if one is to understand the Yahwistic (and also Elohistic) work. A great number of old cultic traditions are included in the Yahwist's work, materials that were created, formed, and preserved by the cult through long periods of time. But now this cultic attachment and orientation, without which

these materials were at one time unthinkable, has been absolutely stripped away, as we saw; it is as though they had changed into a chrysalis and now emerged in new, free form. They all have risen high above their sacred, native soil, and now, having grown independent, they move in a partially or even completely "cult-less" atmosphere. The Yahwist's distinctively spiritual method, which, by the way, is almost without parallel in Old Testament religious history, seems to us like a cool breath from the freethinking era of Solomon. The question now is whether this process by which the traditions outgrew their origins was a necessary secularization, or whether the loss that these traditions suffered by being separated from the cult was compensated for by a new but different kind of theological attachment. A witness in the theological sense of the word arises only in relation to a preceding divine act of revelation; and it is really quite unthinkable that the Yahwist spoke to his people without such a backing for his words.

It is surely not unprofitable to inquire after the divine fact which formed the background against which the Yahwist plotted his entire work. *Ancient* Israel considered God's speaking and acting for man's salvation as confined to the sacred institutions, particularly to the narrower cultic sphere of sacrifice and divine decision mediated by the priest. But men also experienced God's gracious, saving act in the wider cultic sphere, in the holy war, the *charisma* of a qualified leader, the "terror of God" which fell upon the enemy without human agency, or in other miracles that occurred because of the presence of the sacred Ark. The Yahwist, however, considers God's activity in a fundamentally different way. He does not challenge the possibilities with which his forebears reckoned, but he goes far beyond these notions of faith. He sees God's leading in the facts of history as well as in the quiet course of a human life, in the sacred things, but not less in the profane, in great miracles as well as in the innermost secrets of the human heart. (In the story of Jacob and Joseph we are brought close to the thought that God works even in and through man's sin!) In a word, the chief importance of God's activity suddenly lies outside the sacred institutions. It is thereby perhaps more concealed from the natural eye because the entire profane sphere is also the domain of God's activity; but it is nevertheless looked at more inclusively, not intermittently, but much more continually. The Yahwist presents one story of divine guidance and disposition; God's providence is revealed in all areas of life, the public as well as the private.

This view, which did not consider God's activity as confined to the old sanctified sacred institutions but which ventured to discover it retrospectively in the tortured paths of political as well as personal fortune, was something new when compared to the old conception of the patriarchal cult. But it is in fact connected very closely with the great historical events of the Davidic period especially. The ancient sacred union of tribes (in the period of the Judges) had dissolved, and national life had begun to shed its old forms and to become profane. By the time of Saul the national mind had already become emancipated from the old cultic regulations, and this process certainly made further progress under the much more systematically constructed state apparatus of David, with its newly organized court and military life. Ordinary life in its details became more autonomous and demanding. At all events, the period had ended when sacred regulations on principle took precedence over all other legitimacies of life. Had Israel thus slipped from the hand of its ancient God, the God of the patriarchs and of Moses? Had she thus departed from the domain of his salvation and his leading? That was the great question.

The reader will not find it hard to read the answer from the Yahwist's work. This narrative displays boundless confidence in the nearness of Yahweh, in the immediacy of his rule and in the possibility of speaking of all this, in the simplest possible terms, in the new religious language. Of course, to discover the whole range of the Yahwist's thought it is necessary to add to his stories of the patriarchs the narratives about Moses, the event on Sinai and the wandering in the wilderness, as they are contained in Exodus and Numbers. It then becomes quite clear that the old times, including the period of the Judges, lie far behind him. It can, however, be ascertained that the historical situation presupposed by the Yahwist's work must have arisen in the period immediately following the formation of the state. It is striking that the tribes have given up their political independence, but that we can discover no reference to the deep division of Israel into two kingdoms.[6]

More important than the political changes that can be inferred is, however, the change in religious conceptions which have become more "modern" than those of the archaic period of the Judges. Behind the work of the Yahwist stands a new experience of God. Throughout this work, which is still a unique history of miraculous and hidden guidance and divine providence, one feels able to trace the freshness of the joy of a new discovery. These remarks have to be made to warn the reader of these stories against deceiving himself by his familiarity with them, and to urge him to understand their revolutionary contemporary character against their special background.

4. HERMENEUTICAL PROBLEMS OF THE GENESIS NARRATIVES

At first, knowledge of the long process to which individual traditions were subjected before they received their final and present form in our book of *Genesis* makes the work of the exegete difficult. Above all, there are two groups of hermeneutic questions that we must wrestle to answer. For a long time Old Testament science has called these traditions "sagas." Thus one of the first tasks of the exegete is to give an exact account of this term, the possibility and the limits of its use. A second task arises from the fact that the narratives, which formerly began in isolation, are now related to a large overarching context and obviously must be interpreted within this context, from the particular spot that has been assigned to them within the whole. Finally, as a result of putting together the source documents, there

have arisen relationships and theological interplay between the individual texts which demand discussion. In connection with this last problem the question about the historicity (*Geschichtlichkeit*) of these narratives (in their present form) must be raised anew and answered.

It is to the undying credit of H. Gunkel that in his great commentary on *Genesis* he separated the original narrative units from the larger whole and analyzed them with a distinctive aesthetic *charisma*. These individual traditions were of very different kinds. As we have seen, a number of them were cultic aetiological narratives. Others arose from the need to explain the origin of certain curiosities in the relationship of the tribes and the nations to one another; these are traditions with an ethnological aetiology. Some narratives are like rather short novellistic poems. Indeed, one may not refuse on principle to accept an originally vacillating character of one or another narrative in its oldest form—we are speaking now of the oldest *pre*literary form of these single traditions! But that these very old traditions are for the most part *sagas* is a fact, the background of which we can investigate no further. What does this fact, which today is neither new nor scientifically disputed, and yet concerning which so much lack of clarity still prevails, mean for the exegete?

Suspicion of saga begins as a rule with doubt concerning its "historical" content. It is considered a product of poetic fantasy, and as such it has at best a broken relation to historical reality, or none at all. Consciously or unconsciously this depreciation proceeds from a one-sided overestimation of historical writing, which records exactly and trustworthily everything the saga mentions unclearly and often with distortion.[7] This way of judging—one could call it historical materialism—contains an extremely crass misunderstanding of the essence of saga; it was, however, by and large a characteristic of the nineteenth century, which was otherwise so well schooled in historical perception.[8]

No, the saga is the result of a kind of intellectual activity quite different from that of history (*Historie*), and it is advisable to compare history (*Historie*) with sagas as little as possible. To be sure, there exists one point in common—and it was the cause of all fatal comparisons: both are concerned with history (*Geschichte*). That is true of the biblical saga even when it is concerned with apparently unhistorical material. Whatever saga we examine, we find with respect to its simplest and most original purpose that it narrates an actual event that occurred once for all in the realm of history. It is therefore to be taken quite seriously (as distinct, for example, from fairy tales, which serve primarily to entertain)—it is to be "believed."[9] In all that follows, therefore, let us hold fast to this: by no means is saga merely the product of free-ranging fantasy; it, too, conjures up history. It is the form favoured by a people for depicting its early history. Of course it does not feel bound by the modern demand for exactness. The saga[10] comes from a quite different period of the people. Its roots are in a form of society preceding that of the state, which means that it lives and grows at a time when the power of rational and logical, historical perception is not yet fully liberated, at a time, however, when the powers of instinctive, intuitively interpretative, one could almost say mantic, understanding dominate all the more freely. In its sagas a people is concerned with itself and the realities in which it finds itself. It is, however, a view and interpretation not only of that which once was but of a past event that is secretly present and decisive for the present. Thus, just as for an individual certain events or decisions of the past determine his whole life, so in the life of tribes and peoples past events have a direct influence on the present and mold it. It is the saga, much more than historical writing, that knows this secret contemporary character of apparently past events; it can let things become contemporary in such a way that everyone detects their importance, while the same events would probably have been overlooked by historical writing (if it can be thought to have existed at the time). For there is another history that a people makes besides the externals of wars, victories, migrations, and political catastrophes. It is an inner history, one that takes place on a different level, a story of inner events, experiences, and singular guidance, of working and becoming mature in life's mysteries; and for Israel that meant a history with God. One can see that the subject-matter of saga is quite special; above all, the way in which it describes and re-presents the past has unmistakable characteristics. For example, it is simply a fact—to begin with something general—that the sagas about the patriarchs, in spite of their complexity, preserve a mood, a spiritually religious atmosphere, if one may put it this way, that was obviously a characteristic of the pre-Mosaic period. And one can say that the prerogative of the saga over all "more exact" traditions is just to preserve these imponderable, intimate experiences from a people's youth. Thus occasionally the things of which the saga takes possession are trifling. And yet, even then it is often concerned with facts and events of much greater inner significance than many things that history (*Historie*) puts down, because they have a longer aftereffect and therefore remain decisive for the existence of posterity. There is often an entire world of events— actual, experienced events!—enclosed in a single saga. The saga, therefore, has a much higher degree of density than has history (*Historie*).

This is also expressed in the style. Through centuries of being told and heard, that primitive art, which can speak simply of small as well as quite important things without diminishing their substance, grew equal to the task of describing all human experience. Indeed, this art was the first to appear as the only monumental form appropriate for such content. The biblical traditions are characterized by a thorough-going economy of expression on the emotional side. What men thought or felt, what moved them, is subordinate to the objective events. When the narrator does say something about the fright or anxiety that took hold of a man (*Gen.* 15.12; 32.7), his remark seems all the more primitive precisely because of its rareness.

Anyone who wants to understand such sagas correctly must acquire a broader and more profound conception of "history" (*Geschichte*) than what is often accepted today. At the beginning, the saga in most cases certainly contained a "historical" fact as its actual crystallizing point. But in addition it reflects a historical experience on the relevant community which extends into the present time of the narrator. This second constructional element is, as a rule, the stronger, often dominating to such an extent that it can expand and elevate the material to a historical type behind which the original historical fact more and more disappears. In other cases the degree of inner revision and fashioning of the material by those who came later is much smaller, as for example in the tradition of God's covenant with Abraham (*Gen.* 15.7 ff.), a cult saga that in all essential points was obviously left in its archaic form.

Despite the great differences in style and theme which distinguish the individual stories of Abraham, Isaac, and Jacob from each other, they have one common factor: with the exception of *Gen.* 14 they all move in the same social and political sphere, that of the independent family.[11] The family in which so many astounding things happen, the family which has to sustain such severe tensions, is not one partial sphere of communal human life here, set over against other forms. Rather, it is the total sphere of all human communal life; it is the framework of all human activity, politics and economics as well as religion. In this sphere, events like the birth of a child or a quarrel have a special importance which is only attached to them here. The way in which the narrative material is thus rooted in the family or the clan is a sign of its antiquity. Of course, both its form and its content changed a great deal as it was handed down. Thus one may reckon correctly with subsequent expansion of old traditions by means of material, even by means of fairy-tale motifs.[12] This does not endanger the "historicity" of the saga in any way, in so far as with the help of such means it elucidates real events and experiences; for the saga cannot report in abstract formulas, but its manner of communicating is highly figurative. History has therefore not directly merged with saga, so to speak, but rather its form has been changed by long thought and is reflected somewhat brokenly in single images. This peculiar process of symbolization attempts primarily to demonstrate, through the experiences of a single individual, historical facts that originally belonged completely to the group. In Abraham and Jacob, Israel saw, increasingly, simply the need and the promise of its own existence before God. That does not mean, of course, that these figures and the traditions about them are nothing more than subsequent projections of popular faith back into the primeval period. It means, rather, that this material did not lie in the archives untouched but was molded and substantially enlarged by being handed down for centuries. Certainly one would understand the saga of Jacob's nocturnal struggle at the Jabbok, for example, only superficially, and would miss its primary meaning, if one were to suppose that its concern were exhausted in describing the details of an event of the distant past as objectively as possible. No! The saga *Gen.* 32.22 ff. in its present form, in the garb and style of a narrative of bygone events, tells of things that at the same time are thoroughly present. Israel recognized something of her own relation to God in what Jacob experienced at that time. Thus the saga has a wonderful transparence of its own, and only in this character has it become the witness of a past, and at the same time completely contemporary, act of God.

In ancient Israel the principal power in the forming of saga was faith. In any case, we do not have a single saga that has not received from faith its decisive stamp and orientation. In every instance the degree of this revision, stamp, and orientation is completely different. There are sagas—especially those which formerly were cult sagas—which through many generations, from their beginning until their mature final form, were under the formative influence of faith. Other material existed popularly for a long time in more worldly narratives (perhaps even of doubtful value!) before it was incorporated into the religious realm. One must not think, however, that this religious requisition, even if it changed the content of the saga only at a relatively late period, was therefore only superficial and did not touch its essential content. The opposite is true. The later the version of a saga, the more theologically reflective and less naïve it is. Even if this transformation altered the external form of the text only slightly, even if it is true that on occasion only the name of Yahweh was subsequently added, that change is nevertheless radical, for this inserted name, Yahweh, is something very presumptuous.[13] When this ancient material was related to Yahweh, when Yahweh loomed above the previous substance of the saga, which was perhaps profane, this meant a complete abrogation of its ancient immanental meaning and a new illumination of all parts of the narrated material. Thus we must reckon with the fact that certain individual characteristics, formerly belonging to the insignificant accessories, have now become extremely significant. This requisition of ancient saga by theological reflection mirrors nothing other than what all Israel experienced by the revelation of Yahweh: the requisition of all areas of life, of all profane spheres, by God's exacting and promising will.

To bring out the point, one might even say that the patriarchal narratives deal more with God than with men. Men are not important in themselves, but only as the objects of divine planning and action. Above all, one must ask where and in what sense Abraham, Jacob, or Joseph are meant by the narrator to be understood as models, by virtue of their own actions or of divine providence. In some cases—e.g., *Gen.* 13; 15.6; 22.1 ff.—that is probably indeed the case. Such narratives are meant to encourage imitation, "discipleship." But they are in the minority. The figures of the patriarchs are presented with a matter-of-fact realism which by no means suppresses those things that move and concern mankind, and on some occasions weakness and failure are brought out with unrelieved harshness. One need only think of the three variations on the narrative of the "endangering of the ancestress" (*Gen.* 12.10 ff.; 20.1 ff.; 26.7 ff.).[14] The patriarchal narratives are remarkably free of that urge to transfigure and idealize the figures

of earlier times, which plays such a great role in popular literature. The patriarchal narratives do not fall short of the rest of the Old Testament in drawing a picture of man which Israel only found through a long conversation with Yahweh. It is the picture of a man who is directed to hear the divine address and who is sheltered by the guidance of this God.

Of course, one can now ask whether the designation "saga" is still appropriate for this material which is so permeated through and through by faith. It is certainly misleading if we apply it to the present forms of the Old Testament traditions, for from a literary point of view we have here narratives which have reached a high degree of artistry and which venture to depict God's ways in sacred history by means of constantly new pictures.

The measure of freedom that J, E, or P could exercise in their literary modification of the available material was scarcely great. In any case this freedom was much more limited than any modern Western author would be permitted to claim for himself. The Yahwist, in shaping the individual narrative, probably did not go beyond some trimming of the archaic profiles and making definite fine accents. He could naturally act much more freely when joining originally independent narratives. And even if some attempts at uniting various traditions into a small unit in a few cases have been made, nevertheless the actual composition of the narratives in *Genesis* is without question his work. And the important thing is this: the individuality of the Yahwist, his basic theological conceptions, are much less apparent within the individual narratives than in the character of the composition as a whole. The Yahwist's theology of history is essentially expressed in the way he has linked together the materials, connected and harmonized them with one another. This theological conception of the Yahwist is important for the exegete because it became the canon to a certain extent for the interpretation of the other source narratives and thereby also became definitive for the final form of *Genesis.*

The way the Yahwist, from the most varied kinds of building material, formed in the primeval history (chs. 2 to 11) a story of mankind's increasing alienation from God has already been indicated (in the section "The Inclusion of the Primeval History"). He obviously set as the theme of the Abraham narratives the postponement of the promise. The outstanding characteristic of the Yahwistic (also of the Elohistic) narratives in contrast to the Priestly document is that they summarize with particular minuteness of detail the subjective situation of the one who receives the promise. They note the characteristic conflicts, temptations, and errors into which the patriarchs fell precisely in receiving the promise, both because of its increasing expression and because of its delay.

Compare the narratives of ch. 12.10 ff. (Sarah in Egypt) and ch. 16 (Hagar)! In ch. 12.10 ff. immediately after receiving the great, divine promise—enhanced meanwhile by the promise of land in v. 7—Abraham is beset with great difficulties (famine in the Promised Land!). He acts as though God's promise could not be relied upon at all, that is, in complete unbelief. God saves her who is to be the mother of Israel and carries forward his promise over all the chasms of despair regarding the heir of promise. This narrative, which recurs in three forms in *Genesis* (chs. 20; 26), obviously was especially important to the ancients. It shows something of the confusion and perplexity that the divine promise evoked in men, but more than that, it shows the faithfulness of Yahweh, who stands by his plan of salvation which is often betrayed by men. In ch. 16, judging by human standards, the possibility of receiving the heir of promise from Sarah is past. This dilemma causes those concerned to take matters into their own hands, and men try to force the fulfillment of the promise because they do not trust God for it. But this Ishmael, begotten in defiance and lack of faith, cannot be the child of promise. God will be with him indeed, but he will be a brute (!) fighting against everyone and everyone against him. With respect to the psychology of faith, both narratives illustrate Abraham's extremely different reactions to the promise. Two basic attitudes appear as almost typical: (1) disregard for, and (2) arbitrary wresting of, the divine offer. In both cases a difficulty that has emerged over the bearer of the promise gives rise to an action which works against Yahweh's plan. This conviction of a historical plan conceived by Yahweh and the assurance with which this plan is contrasted with human action is very reminiscent of the authority of the prophets, who in other circumstances claimed to know the long-term divine plan for history. The necessity for psychological uniformity in the human portrait that was being sketched was foreign to these narrators.

Naturally one cannot expect complete thematic consistency in a composition that joins together the most varied preformed materials. Occasionally the narratives are even unyielding toward one another. In the stories of Laban, for instance, one cannot help feeling that the individual traditions to which the Yahwist was bound by the history of tradition had resisted thematic permeation more than others because of their specific weight and particular character. And yet the plan for a thematic synopsis of the whole cannot be misunderstood. The Jacob story in its "Jehovistic" form is like a bridge supported from within by two pillars: by the Bethel story (ch. 28) on the one hand and the Peniel story (ch. 32.22 ff.) on the other. And, what is more, the paradox of the divine act in each of the two incidents is extremely harsh. Where Jacob has experienced bankruptcy, where everything seems done for, blessing turned to curse, there God gives him the promise. And where the narrative shows him prosperous, where he thinks he has only to survive a quarrel with Esau, there God falls on him like a nocturnal ghost. And here again the point is the blessing! (v. 26.) Obviously these striking narrative sections are meant to indicate the leading theological ideas and cause the reader to read the entire story of Jacob with respect to the inscrutability and freedom of God's ways.

Any scholarly commentary must attempt to understand the narrative material of *Genesis* primarily in the way in which it was understood in the context of the great narrative works J, E, and P, that is, as it was understood in Israel between the ninth and the fifth centuries B.C. This is difficult, because the narrators do not interpret the events directly, but are quite restrained in their judgments. They do not hand over an explanation to the reader, but take him through the events without assessing men's actions and experiences, evidently on the presupposition that these events are able to speak for themselves to the reader or hearer. For this reason, the interpreter has to give up from the start any search for one meaning which is the only meaning that the narrator can have intended. He will have to concede that it could have prompted the reflections of the reader in more than one direction. Equally, however, the exegete must reserve for himself the right to reject interpretations which are inappropriate to the narrative or to the understanding of the reader. If he is to keep on the right lines, he needs to read the material very carefully. The interpreter will find great help in the leading ideas which permeate the narratives, for example the theme of promise, which was discussed above (pp. 22f.). Whatever happened to the patriarchs was part of the divine plan for history, which was directed beyond the life of these men toward a still distant goal.

If the reader of today raises the question of the "historicity" of the events, he must first realize that the ancient narrators were simply not aware of this question that so often troubles modern man. Still less did they see an "either-or" here. So we must attempt to answer the question in an indirect way, i.e., in terms of the very nature of these stories. What we have said so far has already suggested one thing: the old, naïve idea of the historicity of these narratives as being biographically reliable stories from the life of the patriarchs must be abandoned. If the narratives of *Gen.*, chs. 18; 22; 28; 32 were once very early Palestinian cult legends (and therefore pre-Israelite and pre-Canaanite), and if the tradition of the patriarchs was only interwoven with these narratives after the Israelite incursion, we can no longer accept them as documents from the life of the patriarchs. The same is true of most of the patriarchal narratives. (This is not to deny that individual elements—now bound up with these narratives—in fact go back to the "patriarchal period"; but that does not alter the general picture.) The stories are about the past, indeed the distant past, but the God who directs events and speaks to the patriarchs is Yahweh, who was as yet unknown to the pre-Mosaic ancestors of Israel (Exod., 3.13 ff.; 6.6). Similarly, the religious field of tension in which the faith of an Abraham had to make its choice between temptation and faith, is much less that of the ancestors of Israel than that of the narrators and their time. They were not concerned to revive a long past religious situation. On the contrary, these narratives express everything that Israel had learnt from her association with Yahweh right down to the narrator's own time. By the medium of these sagas, the narrators express many of the essentials of what Israel had learnt in her history with Yahweh. In this sense the narratives are deeply rooted in history. So it is no longer possible to discover what historical event lies behind the narrative of the jeopardizing of Sarah; we must, in fact, assume that the transfer of the material to Abraham and Sarah was only made subsequently (see the expositions on chs. 12; 20; 26). Therefore one could say pointedly that this narrative is not "historical"; but the experience that God miraculously preserves the promise beyond human failure was eminently historical (*geschichtlich*) for the community. These narratives have a very high degree of compactness because they compress experiences that faith brought to the community slowly, perhaps over centuries. And this is primarily what gives the narratives their proper characteristic witness. So much is clear: if the historicity of the patriarchal narratives now rests essentially upon the community's experiences of faith, then that fact has far-reaching consequences for exegesis. No one will deny that dangers threaten this kind of exegesis. Even though we stand for a high degree of spiritualizing—in our opinion the subtle spirituality of these narratives has been greatly underestimated even in their first literary version— nevertheless, this way of exegesis threatens to evaporate into purely allegorical interpretation, a tendency that must nevertheless be resisted. One needs to understand that the communal theological element of which we are speaking may never be declared the sole content of the narrative. It is indeed an important component that again and again must be freshly considered; but with it in individual tradi-tions there have been preserved characteristics of a more ancient, indeed, most ancient, meaning, which the exegete may not overlook. Therefore, it is impossible even for the most carefully thought out hermeneutical rule to mark the middle course which will preserve in these narratives their characteristic uniqueness for sacred history. Under no circumstances may the narratives be deprived of this imponderable element of historical moment.

The long process of tradition which many narratives have undergone has left a number of traces behind in them. Usually it is a matter of some inner unevennesses or dislocations in the structure of a particular narrative. These are nowhere so obvious as in the narrative of Jacob's struggle in *Gen.* 32.10 ff., where in one and the same story quite different conceptions of the event have been preserved side by side (see the commentary). The question of the nature of the narrative material at a pre-literary stage has been discussed most perceptively by H. Gunkel in his great commentary. It is still largely open, even today, as in the meantime the way of posing the problems it raises has shifted, and Gunkel's explanations are no longer always adequate. Occasionally the question must be posed in an entirely new way. However, one should not investi-gate the earlier history of the material with the expectation of finding what is really "authentic" at the lowest level at-tainable, of coming upon the historical tracks of the patriarchs themselves. Quite apart from the fact that this will very rarely be the case, the narrative never for a mo-ment leaves us in doubt that it does not share this interest in its earliest level. Consequently, I feel that it is particularly important today that we should turn once again to exegesis of the texts in their present form, that is, that we should take up the question of the meaning that was gradually attached to them, not least through their incorporation into a great narrative complex with its specific themes.[15] Is there unanimity among exegetes about the meaning of the narrative of the "sacrifice of Isaac" in its present literary (*not* its preliterary) form? Furthermore, the exegete must take into account the fact that the sources are no longer separate from each other, but have been combined together. Must one not say that the two creation stories are in many respects open to each other? In the exposition it will be pointed out that the Yahwist has an intimate world constructed around man (the garden, the trees, the animals, the wife), while P paces the great cosmos in all dimensions before he treats the creation of man. *Genesis,* ch. 2, complements ch. 1 by its witness to God's providential, almost fatherly, act toward man, etc. Futhermore, the story of the Fall can no longer be expounded without reference to the "very good" in ch. 1.31. And for the patriarchal stories it must at least be kept in mind that the God of Abraham, Isaac, and Jacob is also the Yahweh who grants forgiveness in the cultic sacrifice in the Taber-nacle. True, in *Genesis,* the redactor has in many instances given precedence to the Yahwistic-Elohistic tradition over the Priestly document. But in the book of Exodus the situation is reversed, and since *Genesis* and Exodus are not two separate "books," that must be considered in the exegesis.

Franz Rosenzweig once remarked wittily that the sign "R" (for the redactor of the Hexateuch documents, so lowly esteemed in Protestant research) should be interpreted as Rabbenu, "our master," because basically we are dependent only on him, on his great work of compilation and his theology, and we receive the Hexateuch at all only from his hands.[16] From the standpoint of Judaism, that is consistent. But for us, in respect to hermeneutics, even the redactor is not "our master." We receive the Old Testament from the hands of Jesus Christ, and therefore all exegesis of the Old Testament depends on whom one thinks Jesus Christ to be. If one sees in him the bringer of a new religion, then one will consistently examine the chief figures of the patriarchal narratives for their inward religious disposition and by, say, drawing religious "pictures from life" will bring into the foreground what comes close to Christianity or even corresponds with it. But this "pious" view is unsatisfactory because the principal subject of the account in the *Genesis* stories is not the religious characteristics of the patriarchs at all. Any mention of them is almost an aside. Often the details have to be drawn from the reader's imagination. The real subject of the account is everywhere a quite definite act of Yahweh, into which the patriarchs are drawn, often with quite perplexing results. So the first interest of the reader must be in what circumstances and in what way Yahweh's guidance is given, and what consequences result from it. In all the variety of the story, can we perhaps recognize some things that are typical of the action of God towards men? Then we must go on to raise the chief question: can we not recognize a common link even between the revelation of God in the old covenant and that in the new, a "type"? The patriarchal narratives include experiences which Israel had of a God who revealed himself and at the same time on occasions hid himself more deeply. In this very respect we can see a continuity between the Old Testament and the New. In the patriarchal narratives, which know so well how God can conceal himself, we see a revelation of God which precedes his manifestation in Jesus Christ. What we are told here of the trials of a God who hides himself and whose promise is delayed, and yet of his comfort and support, can readily be read into God's revelation of himself in Jesus Christ.

Notes

1. By cult legend or *hieros logos* we mean a sacred story that tells of a god's appearance and revelation at a place which for that reason became a cultic center. Such traditions were, of course, carefully cultivated at the shrines and passed on, for from them alone derived the legitimacy of a cult center. Everything depended upon this legitimacy. Men did not believe it necessary to pray and offer sacrifice everywhere, of course, but only where God had already revealed himself and where he had prescribed the manner for prayer. (The narrative in *Gen.*, ch. 18, was once the cult legend of Mamre, that in ch. 28, the cult legend of Bethel. See further Judg. 6; 13; II Sam., ch. 24; etc.) The great festivals too were based on a sacred story; by it they were justified and shaped, often to the extent of becoming part of the cult drama

2. It is well to consider what in all probability would have happened to these traditions if they had not been united in a fixed literary form. Without doubt the fact that some traditions were detached from the cultic sphere meant that their content was heavily spiritualized. Nor will it be denied that this liberation from a musty and materialistic cult was a fortunate occurrence, which opened up the possibility of unsuspected development of the subject of this material. But by the same token, the traditions would be more and more subject to inner dissipation. Every such spiritualization is at the same time a dangerous process of dissolution working at the marrow of the material, for every spiritualization is also a rationalization. One no longer finds oneself before the material in the naïve attitude of reverential acceptance, but rather, one begins to stand over it and to interpret and reform it according to one's own reason. Take an example in which this process can be well observed, the Manna story (Ex., ch. 16). The older Manna story (especially vs. 4-5, 13b-15, 27-30) is meant to be understood quite objectively and is full of historical difficulties. The version of the Priestly document is quite different (vs. 2-3, 6-13a, 16-26). The event is apparently described concretely, yet in such a way that no reader is detained by the external details, but rather its secret spiritual meaning becomes clear as day. A miracle, limited in space and time, becomes

something universal, almost timelessly valid. Here no storyteller is speaking, but rather a man who is theologian through and through, who has clothed his reflections in the very transparent garb of a historical narrative. But the Deuteronomist has taken a great step even beyond this position.

"And he humbled you and let you hunger and fed you with manna, which you did not know, nor did your fathers know; that he might make you know that man does not live by bread alone, but that man lives by everything that proceeds out of the mouth of the Lord."—Deut. 8.3.

Where the Priestly document externally preserved the old form of the report throughout—the spiritualization existed only in a certain transparency of the narrative—the Deuteronomist gave up the old meaning altogether. He speaks only indirectly of actual eating to still hunger and substitutes for it feeding on God's word. Bluntly he tells what spiritual meaning actually lay behind the material event at that time. Here too it must be said that the old, simple story has been beautifully and significantly enlarged by that spiritualization; but one cannot deny it was providential that free reign for such progressive spiritualization and religious transformation was not given to all traditions of the Hexateuch. One can only surmise that process of dissolution which was arrested when the traditions were written down. This much in any case can be observed: when the material was written down, it became fixed at a phase of its development in which a certain religious transformation had already occurred, but when, notwithstanding, the historical element was preserved undissipated and with the full import of uniqueness.

3. M. Noth, *Überlieferungsgeschichte des Pentateuch,* ³1963, pp. 63 ff.

4. A. Alt, "The God of the Fathers" (1929), in: *Essays on Old Testament History and Religion,* 1966.

5. On the Elohist, see H.-W. Wolff, "Zur Thematik der elohistischen Fragmente im Pentateuch," *Evangelische Theologie* 1969, 59 ff.

6. More details in H. W. Wolff, "Das Kerygma des Jahwisten," *Gesammelte Studien zum AT,* 1964, 345 ff.

7. "The form which we have provisionally called history (*Historie*) acts as an enemy of the saga; it threatens it, it waylays it, it slanders it and perverts the words in its mouth. That which was positive in the saga becomes negative in history. That which was truth becomes falsehood. The tyranny of history is in fact able to assert of the saga that it simply does not exist but is only a kind of timid preparation for history itself." (A. Jolles, *Einfache Formen*², 1956, 64.)

8. Thus even in Grimm's dictionary this term "saga" is defined as information about events in the past which lack historical verification.

9. A. W. Schlegel, *Sämtliche Werke* XII, 1847, 387; K. Wehrhan, *Sachwörterbuch der Deutschkunde,* 2, 1930, s.v. "Sage."

10. For the saga in ancient Israel, now see K. Koch, *The Growth of the Biblical Tradition,* 1969, §12.

11. C. Westermann, "Arten der Erzählung in der *Genesis*", *Forschung am Alten Testament,* 1964, 35-39.

12. O. Eissfeldt, "Stammessage und Novelle in den Geschichten von Jakob und seinen Söhnen," in: *Eucharisterion für H. Gunkel,* I, 1923, 56 ff.

13. "One need delete only the name of Yahweh to remove almost all the varnish with which Israel covered the strange pictures." H. Gressmann, ZAW, 1910, 24 f.

14. Delitzsch says of the Tamar story (*Gen.,* ch. 38): "Thus . . . the beginnings of the tribe of Judah were shaped by the remarkable interaction of human sin and divine guidance. . . . How simple are the images of Israel's ancestors! They have almost more shadow than light. National ambition did not add to them or change them. No trace of an idealizing myth is noticeable. The nobleness of these figures consists in the fact that they conquer in the strength of the grace granted to them, and when defeated, they arise again and again. Their mistakes are the foils of their greatness for sacred history. By the yardstick of the Old Testament even Tamar, with all her going astray, is a saint because of her wisdom, her tenderness, her nobility." (451 f.)

15. See now H. W. Wolff, "Kerygma", cited p. 31 above.

16. M. Buber and Franz Rosenzweig, *Die Schrift und ihre Verdeutschung,* 1936, 322.

William H. Ralston, Jr. (essay date 1973)

SOURCE: "That Old Serpent," *The Sewanee Review,* Vol. LXXXI, No. 3, July-September, 1973, pp. 389-428.

[*In the following essay, Ralston examines the composition and themes of* Genesis, *maintaining that the book emphasizes man's separation from God.*]

I.

The anonymous author of the primary literary document of the Old Testament, whose imagination has been determinative for the rest of Biblical literature, begins the story of his people, a narrative he was impelled to write by his experience of the person and the kingdom of David, with an account of creation. For this writer, the form of history, without which the events and circumstances of human life would hold no meaning, was Jahveh (a particular tribal name for the God whose own name was unknown, and who therefore remained beyond definition), whose power had created the physical world, and placed man within it. His nature was the ultimate origin, as his power was the final determinant, of "the way things are".

The book of *Genesis* was revised again and again by the later Hebrew writers, but the basis of it has remained the mind of its primary anonymous author. In particular it is the third chapter of *Genesis,* the story of "man's first disobedience and the fruit of that forbidden tree", which comes to us virtually unaltered from his hand, that is the key to his imagination and that continued to be the fundamental source for the Biblical understanding of two things: the nature of man's separation from God; and the tragic consequences of that separation in the disordering of all man's knowledge of himself and others. The writers of the Gospels, in presenting the death of Christ as the sufficient and necessary act of restoration and remedy, assume as truth the description set forth by the original writer in *Genesis.*

This writer began, however, with a creation-story. In the form in which we now have it the opening of *Genesis* is completely overwhelming:

> In the beginning God created the heaven and the earth.
>   (v. 1)
> And the earth was without form, and void; and
>   darkness was upon the face of the deep. And the
>   Spirit of God moved upon the face of the waters.
> (v. 2)
> And God said, Let there be light: and there was light.
> (v. 3)

It is no wonder that Longinus cited as "sublime" this vision of the universe as the effortless expression of a God whose Word can empower things that are not to become what they are. If one accepts a Rabbinic tradition of pointing the text, the first verse would read, "In the beginning of God's creating . . . ," which makes his act yet more absolute and unconditional. These verses in their present form represent a literary history of enormous complexity. It is the second verse which remains to us from the original version, and it is this verse which suggests the mystery which the original writer was trying to convey, and which the more orthodox later revisions of the priestly editor did not remove.

The account as we have it goes on to say that Jahveh made man "in his own image" ("after our likeness"), and it is here that the central mystery of what it means to *be made,* to be a *creature,* begins to be seen. Allusively, in terms of the myth, we learn that Jahveh, by creating man from the dust of the ground in his own image, has given his creature a share of that quality which is Jahveh's supreme attribute—to wit, his power to be always himself. This power is the source of God's freedom, and to be the creature of such a God places man in terrible danger.

For if God is free in every way to be always himself, something of this freedom must be given to the creature made after his likeness. The very name itself of God specified this power, which is not only the supreme power, but, more simply, all the power there is: "I am what I am" or "I will be what I will be." For this writer God was not the other end of a personal relationship, and certainly not an "object" of faith. He was Jahveh, the great God of the desert storm and volcano, who simply and completely and everywhere is what he is.

> He bowed the heavens also and came down, and it was dark under his feet.
> He rode upon the cherubim, and did fly; he came flying upon the wings of the wind.
> He made darkness his secret place, his pavilion round about him with dark water, and thick clouds to cover him.

The peril of being created in the image of such a God is felt at every level throughout the Bible. David is terrified at the destruction of Uzzah; the Wisdom writers know that the beginning is fear; it would be better for Judas never to have been born; and the terror of falling into the hands of the living God remains a fact for a Christian of the New Testament.

The profound mystery of being created and of what it means to be a creature—in a later idiom, of what it means to be "here"—is the subject of all creation myths. One of these stories, found in a variety of forms all over the ancient Near East, had been current in Palestine for centuries before the writer in *Genesis* reshaped it to his own understanding. This story, probably Babylonian in origin, had at its center the familiar element of conflict between the creator-god, whatever his name, and the material out of which he made the world. The primary physical stuff of the creation was, in every instance of these stories, invariably chaotic. The abyss of chaos, of sheer meaninglessness, stands—perhaps destructively, but always threateningly—over against the creator-god. The world is made when this god either subdues or conquers chaos, most often by killing a monster who is the dramatic embodiment of chaos. Creation is the imposition of order upon disorder. The second verse of *Genesis* is an unmistakable echo of such a story:

> . . . the earth was without form, and void; and darkness was upon the face of the deep.

Bound up in this is the basic meaning of language. The primary function of a word, whether the Word of God or any other word, is its power to give sense to what otherwise makes no sense, to provide meaning for what otherwise is meaningless, to bring light to what otherwise is darkness. It is, in short, the power to "name" things, and the writer of the primary account of creation in *Genesis* makes absolutely concrete his statement that man is made after God's likeness when Jahveh brings to Adam all living creatures to receive their names. Language, in this writer's understanding, is statement—an activity proper to the creature man in direct imitation of Jahveh who created him. Thus words are meant for the articulation of truth. They are means of discrimination between the things that are and that are not.

In the mind of the Biblical writer the chaos which Jahveh subdued was not destroyed. It was ordered, but it remained potentially chaotic, and in some way a threat. In the story as he found it there was no certainty that chaos might not reassert itself, reducing creation again to darkness and the abyss. In his own history the story of the flood, following almost at once the story of the garden, was an account of just such an occurrence. There is no doubt that these stories, firmly embedded in the much-edited version of *Genesis* we now possess, reflect with uncanny precision the experience of ancient man of his world—a world mysterious, inexplicable, and not dependably interested in man or his fate, but upon which all human life nonetheless depended absolutely. It is a sense of things awesomely present again in every representative form in the imagination of the twentieth century.

> Doom is dark and deeper than any sea-dingle.
> Upon what man it fall
> In spring, day-wishing flowers appearing,
> Avalanche sliding, white snow from rock-face,
> That he should leave his house,
> No cloud-soft hands can hold him, restraint by women,
> But ever that man goes
> Through place keepers, through forest trees,
> A stranger to strangers over undried sea,
> Houses for fishes, suffocating water. . . .

It is important that this insecurity—the sense of being a stranger in the creation; the sense of our fragile hold upon life—not be interpreted as a consequence of sin. A usual metaphor for it was "the hostility of the gods", and one catches this note throughout Greek literature. The jealousy of the gods, with whom man may be in conflict, and at whose mercy he certainly is at every moment, is not due to human sin. It is simply there, something given. If the meaning of life is to be understood this fact has to be accepted as a prior condition. There was undoubtedly an intuitive awareness that this uneasy insecurity in the world—man's sense of conflict with Nature and with his own nature—had been aggravated by sin; but it was not caused by sin, and did not originate in man's experience of sin.

When the old story was taken over by the Biblical writer he did not exclude from it this essential note of insecurity and incipient disorder. He removed from it any traces of polytheism, and what would seem to him the unimaginable crudity of representing Jahveh as envious of man or hostile to what he had made in his own image. The conflict was inherent in creation, between Jahveh and the chaos he had conquered. This primary account has been modified by the later editors of the Old Testament, but it remains apparent beneath the theological cover they supply. It retained its hold upon the imagination of subsequent Biblical writers, and it remained a profound part of the traditional popular religion. Allusions to it and traces of it are everywhere in the Bible, where it is spoken of primarily in terms of the sea. The sea is primaeval chaos, the waters of disorder and darkness, the home of the chaos monster. We have our own metaphors for this absence of form—the absurd, the unknown, the unconscious—and our own emotional terms for the insecurity we experience as a consequence of it. The Biblical writers remember that the monster was a great dragon, a serpent one of whose familiar names was Rahab. Deutero-Isaiah recalls it four hundred years later:

> Awake, awake, put on strength, O arm of the Lord;
> awake, as in the ancient days, in the generations of old.
> Art thou not it that hath cut Rahab, and wounded the dragon?
> Art thou not it which hath dried up the sea, the waters of the great deep; that hath made the depths of the sea a way for the ransomed to pass over?

The literary allusion is extremely complex. One is taken back in imagination not only to the primary act of Jahveh in creation, but also to the storm of waters and the drying up of the sea at the time of the Exodus. The poet sees in the triumphant victory over Babylon and the return of his people from exile another unmistakable sign of Jahveh's power to make energies inherently chaotic work to his purposes. The Psalter is laced with such references and allusions, some of them humorous:

> The floods are risen, O Lord, the floods lift up their voice. . . .
> The waves of the sea are mighty, and rage horribly, but yet the Lord which dwelleth on high is mightier.
> There go the ships, and there is that Leviathan, whom Thou hast made to take his pastime therein [or, more literally: "that Thou might play with him"].

These reminiscences and allusions, omnipresent in the Bible, are one of the most moving and disturbing parts of this literature.

The story in *Genesis* of the flood is the one most readily familiar. Jahveh allows the waters of chaos almost to destroy the earth, not so much as a punishment for human wickedness, but as a sign that the wickedness of man has released chaos into the world again. One must beware constantly in the Old Testament of the schematic moral theology of rewards and punishments which the later Deuteronomist editors have brought to bear upon this literature at nearly every point. They are serious men, and they have their value; but their hand is heavy, and the total effect of their redactions mechanical and boring. In the mind of its original author the flood is a dramatic representation of a tremendous experience of actual chaos, moral and physical, individual and political.

He has precisely defined his understanding of this experience in the comment he makes on the horrendous stories of the collapse of religious, personal, and social life at the end of the time of the Judges:

> In those days there was no King in Israel.
> Every man did that which was right in the sight of his own eyes.

There is no question that either he, or a writer close to him and identical in outlook, represents the increasing disorder in David's kingdom toward the end of his reign, a disorder which culminates in the blood-bath and horror of Solomon's seizure of the throne and his subsequent tyranny, as yet another manifestation of our fearful freedom to release the flood of chaos into our world. Over the waters of the great flood the rainbow finally arches, the sign of Jahveh's power as creator and of his faithfulness to his creation. He will not "let it go". Hopkins has caught this magnificently:

> I admire thee, master of the tides
> Of the Yore-flood, of the year's fall;
> The recurb and the recovery of the gulf's sides,
> The girth of it and wharf of it and the wall;
> Stanching, quenching ocean of a motionable mind;
> Ground of being, and granite of it: past all
> Grasp God, throned behind
> Death with a sovereignty that heeds but hides, bodes
> but abides;
>
> With a mercy that outrides
> The all of water, an ark
> For the listener. . . .

In the New Testament the sea is still the symbol of chaos. When Jesus stills the storm there is no question what this means to the disciples, with their long racial memory of the waters of chaos and God's supremacy over them. Or, even more, when Jesus appears walking on the water, there could be no sign more mysterious and compelling to these men that the power in him is derived from the basic power in the universe, the power which is God's alone. Perhaps the most moving of all these echoes is in the Apocalypse:

> And there shall be no more sea.

At the very end chaos will disappear forever in the final triumph and perfection of God's Kingdom. The idea persists at the fundamental level in the dramatic exorcism of the water at Baptism. The invocation of the Holy Spirit to come into the baptismal water is a literal recapitulation of its archetype:

> And the Spirit of God moved upon the face of the waters.

(In the original story the reference was doubtless to Jahveh alone, since there was no thought of his "Spirit" in this metaphysical sense in the middle of the tenth century B. C.) It is wonderful that Milton, in so many ways straitened by his theology, should at this point respond as poet rather than as Calvinist:

> Thou from the first
> Wast present, and with mighty wings outspread
> Dove-like sat'st brooding on the vast Abyss
> And mad'st it pregnant.

Underneath the sublime representation in *Genesis* of a creation by God *ex nihilo* is this more primitive story of Jahveh's contention with chaos, when the earth was without form, and void, and darkness was upon the face of the deep. One of the constantly recurring miracles of the literature of the Bible is the capacity of these writers to assimilate all the materials accessible to them, transforming them and weaving them into their own design. This power to transform by incorporation materials of the most ordinary, or even dreadful, types is a literary analogue to a claim even more momentous in the New Testament—that Jesus is the "redeemer" of all mankind. Such a claim is not an aberration from the Old Testament. It is consonant with the kind of enabling power God is everywhere shown to possess.

Even when the Old Testament writers were led to the explicit affirmation that there was one God, and one only, and that his power therefore is the only power and the source of all power whatsoever in his creation—even then, these same writers could not forget, and therefore did not negate the original fact of experience given concretely by the primary writer, the fact that creation somehow stands over against the creator, in partial separation from him, and in potential if not actual conflict with him. This is a direct consequence of its being "made". Whatever share it may have in its own further making is entirely after that fact.

Even more, since man not only is part of creation, a "made thing" like everything else, but also is in some more mysterious way made "in God's image", the mystery of being a creature shows itself in him more dramatically and more poignantly in terms of his conflicts with himself as well as with his world. The assertion that chaos is not "with God" from the beginning, but actually comes from God's own hand, is part of the philosophical theology of Deutero-Isaiah, and itself a profound and necessary transformation of the idea of the earlier writer:

> I form the light, and create darkness; I make good,
> and create evil;
> I, God, do all these things.

The idea that in being created we are separate, made "apart", the early writer states in terms of his primary creation myth: we are creatures sprung from the dust, a chaos which exists under God's hand, but a primary condition of his activity as Creator and of our lives as creatures. This insecurity of being is simply there; it is given. In psychological terms it is our sense of being "alone"; in philosophical terms it is our sense of being "out here" or "out there"; in religious terms it is our sense of being "away".

> Here is non home, here nis but wyldernesse . . .

In whatever mode of apprehension, it is a sense of separation from God, of existing somehow independent of the very Being on whom we are at the same time utterly dependent. Plato has his own version of it. We occupy the realm of becoming and opinion, a place between being and non-being, between knowledge and ignorance.

This strange sense we have of our existence is not a sense of alienation. Alienation is the result of sin. Behind alienation is separation—the sense of standing apart; of existing alone; of the insecurity of being a creature. The Bible everywhere insists that this sense of separation, with its implied possibility of isolation and annihilation, is no morbid figment of our imaginations. Nor is it a neurotic preoccupation with our own security which has no foundation in fact. It is part of what it means to be human, and is the embodied actuality of our status as creatures. In the mind of the Biblical writer it is simply "the way things are", and therefore, however terrifying it may have become to us, it must be accepted. It is through refusal to accept this fact and from rebellion against it that sin enters, and our alienation begins. The fact itself, and its effect upon us, is not evil, and not a necessary occasion for sin. There is no sin in being a creature. To live as a made thing is not to exist in an evil plight. To be a creature asks of us not repentance, but acceptance. It is a matter of knowledge.

The Biblical writer explains that man was formed out of the dust and woman formed from a rib of his side "because it was not good that the man should be alone"—that is, the only one of his kind. Yet in making a creature to share creation with man God must separate that creature from him. Therefore the mystery of creatureliness is true not only for us, but of us and between us as well. If the Biblical writer had failed to do justice to our sense of a lost wholeness in the human nature common to us all, he would scarcely deserve consideration. All the speeches in Plato's *Symposium* turn on this. They lead initially to Aristophanes' tragi-comedy of our split natures, and finally to Socrates' sublime eros of our recovered wholeness. The Biblical writer is no less certain in his formulation of the mystery. There is no way for us to know ourselves, to find out "who" we are, until we know what kind of thing we are, what our nature is. The question is put categorically in the Psalter: "*What* is man . . . ?" The great story in the third chapter of *Genesis* is the writer's account of how the refusal to accept the fact of his creatureliness—that is, to know what he is—led man to assert his own power, and how this assertion of himself drove him into alienation from his fellow-creature, from himself, from God, and from the rest of creation.

> And he looked for judgment, but behold oppression;
> For righteousness, but behold a cry.

In the opinion of the New Testament writers the resolution of this failure and the reconciliation of the creature responsible for it come only on Good Friday, at its deepest moment, which the Church has always recognized as the darkest of dark nights of the soul. It is the primaeval darkness of chaos come again:

> There was darkness over all the land from the sixth
> until the ninth hour. And about the ninth hour Jesus
> cried with a loud voice, 'Eli, Eli, lama sabachthani.'

As we look at this in the whole pattern of Biblical literature, it is not a cry of human pain. Nor is it a cry of agony for sin. It is the pit of loneliness, the acceptance by Jesus of the full weight of what it means to be a creature of God in the world God has made. He received this mystery into his own life at the moment of his death. In the mind of the New Testament writers, since Jesus was what he was, he also took the full weight of it into the life of the Creator-God himself, to whom therefore even this creatureliness is not any longer foreign. If it is true in the theology of Deutero-Isaiah that chaos comes from God, the circle is completed in the life of Jesus, God's son, in his returning with it to his Father. This moment in Jesus' life recalls us to that chaos stated by the original Biblical writer as a first condition of creation by God—to that time when the earth was without form, and void, and darkness was upon the face of the deep. The cry of the Incarnate Word of God on the cross is the response of the creation to that Word which God spoke to the dark, primordial waters "in the beginning".

II.

Not the way of acceptance, however, but the other way of assertion of ourselves against chaos, against the very condition of our lives as creatures, is what we have tried, and this has resulted in an alienation from God which is desperately unnatural to us. From this alienation have come a fear, an impotence, and a confusion from which, by our own efforts, we cannot extricate ourselves. This mode of our self-assertion—which is not disobedience, but rebellion—is made actual at the foot of that tree from which the old serpent first spoke to us.

As we read it now, the story is from the tenth century before Christ. Underlying it, as with the author's story of creation, is an older myth, the origins of which are lost to us, but which must have been current in Palestine when the Hebrew tribes were entering the country three centuries earlier. It is important to note what the Biblical writer has done with it.

The Palestinian story was a variation of the chaos myth. It was an attempt to account for man's tragic plight, but in this story man was the innocent victim of the jealousies and rivalries of the gods. His sense of loneliness and deprivation is not attributed to the fact of his being a creature. Rather, it is due to his being trapped by the powers that govern his existence. It is no longer an internal constituent of his nature, but a set of circumstances external to him, in which he is imprisoned. Almost any of Hardy's best poems give this sense of a captured creature at the mercy of imbecilic, indifferent, or inimical powers. The feeling of being trapped is once again a part of contemporary sensibility. Hardy extends the sense to cover the whole range of physical objects:

> We wonder, ever wonder, why we find us here!
>
> 'Has some Vast Imbecility,
>   Mighty to build and blend,
>   But impotent to tend,
> Framed us in jest, and left us now to hazardry?

> 'Or come we of an Automaton
>   Unconscious of our pains? . . .
>   Or are we live remains
> Of Godhead dying downwards, brain and eye now gone? . . .'

The old Palestinian story was apparently well-known, and highly popular. The Biblical writer thought it was also highly dangerous, and subversive of the fundamental understanding of God which his people had brought with them from the desert. He had behind him the knowledge of the independent, uncontrollable power of the God of storm and volcano, a knowledge vastly enriched by the Mosaic interpretation of the operations of that power beside the Red Sea. Matthew Arnold's formulation of this Mosaic interpretation remains classic: "a power that makes for righteousness". The final expression of this truth in the Old Testament comes, again, from Deutero-Isaiah:

> I am the Lord, and there is no god beside me; a just God and a Saviour.
> I am God, and there is none else.

In however inarticulate and unphilosophical a way, the early Biblical writer shared this faith. There is no question that for him Jahveh was the only god of any importance, since he was the only god of any real power. The crude polytheism of the Palestinian story concerned him in two ways. Because it was ignorant of Jahveh and the nature of his power, its effect would be disastrous, first for the minds of his people, and hence for their religion. At every point in Biblical literature the failure to "know" God invites immediate destruction of oneself, and of one's society.

The old story was not entirely untrue. It held a convincing account of our experience of frustration, and of our sense of standing over against the gods (the "powers of being"), with whom we are at least potentially in conflict, and who, in any actual encounter, can destroy us. The story preserved the whole negative side of human existence as we experience it, in all its incomprehensible confusion of meanings, and its equally riddling and continuous threats of annihilation. All these were facts to be accepted. They indicated an aspect of reality which man would act as a fool to ignore. The danger was the way the old story accounted for this. The writer of **Genesis** has accepted all the features of the old story which gave it the partial truth it had, but has given them an entirely new meaning.

He says that when God made man out of the dust he put him into a garden to live. To man was given the power to name the other creatures. It is this power which is the evidence in him of the divine power in whose image he is made. To name a thing is to bring upon it the power of the word. It is to act in imitation of the God whose Word informs the whole of Nature, including man. When Coleridge did his mischief in setting up the artist as "creator", he remembered his theology well enough to qualify the sense in which he meant creator. Later enthusiasts for man as artist have ignored it to their peril. In any case, it is the classical theory of art as imitation which is consonant with the kind of imaginative authority God gave Adam in the garden.

God then provided the man with a wife. The two lived together—in innocence and happiness, and in accord with their own nature as creatures. The most comprehensive and, indeed, perfect metaphor for this was found by the writer:

> They were naked, the man and his wife, and they were not ashamed.

The serpent, who now speaks to the woman, had been in the original form of the story a god, a god who was at enmity with the god of the garden, jealous both of his ownership of it and of the man and woman who lived in it. In this older story enmity, jealousy, and deceit are of the very fabric of things. They exist among the gods. Thus the frustrations of men are nothing more than a reflection of the frustrations of the gods. One side of Homer's theology reflects this, and Wagner's *Der Ring des Nibelungen* is wholly based upon it. No wonder Brünnhilde, wish-maiden to Wotan, semi-divine, and finally mortal woman, burns the whole thing up. For if this deceit is inherent in the gods, then the pain is irremediable and unreconcilable.

> As flies to wanton boys, are we to the gods.
> They kill us for their sport.

The universe is a vast trap of lies from which there can be no release short of destroying it.

In the Biblical version of the story the serpent is not a god. He is a creature of God, Jahveh of the desert and the Red Sea. Even as in the creation-story chaos is brought within the range of God's power, so too is the serpent in the garden—the serpent who is, to be sure, the chaos monster in another form. If, in this story, chaos is itself embodied in a creature of God, we are imaginatively on the way to the Isaianic transformation of the whole theology of creation, in which chaos originates from God. In this case, as with all the greatest imaginative writers, the author of *Genesis* has surpassed what he thought he knew.

The serpent is a creature, and he is also a liar. This is one of the master-strokes of the writer. For what is it to lie? It is to say the thing that is not, to give it a ghostly substance, a semblance of truth, just as the old Palestinian story had such a semblance, and derived its power from it. The lying, hissing serpent is precisely the threat of chaos to truth. The nature of his lie makes his identification with chaos very clear.

There was a tree in the midst of the garden, forbidden to the man and the woman even to touch, on pain of death. It is at this point that the *Genesis* story has been misread, even by the Deuteronomist editors, let alone Calvin and Milton, and one must be careful. In the old version of the story the command was in fact arbitrary, an attempt by the god of the garden to keep man in his place by preventing him from acquiring the power which would enable him to challenge the superior power of the gods. In the story we have in *Genesis* the command is entirely different. There is no suggestion that the tree is forbidden because God is afraid of man, or jealous of his own divine prerogatives. Such an idea would have been fantastic to the Biblical writer, with his knowledge of the mighty, austere, and just God of the desert and the Red Sea and the kingdom of David. If it is true that man must be kept in his place, the reason for it is that man may thereby be himself, may continue to be the creature he is, may continue in accord with his own nature. The command becomes in the hands of the Biblical writer a concrete embodiment of the limits of man as creature, of that fact about himself which he must accept if he is to be himself. It is therefore not a command in any prescriptive sense. It is a statement of a condition *sine qua non*. The mood is not imperative; it is indicative. The essence of Biblical morality is always this. Its basic mode is: Be good, because I am God, and you are made in my image. Evil, in whatever form, is the invitation of chaos.

The serpent becomes then the concrete symbol of the temptation men are under to escape from the apparent insecurity of being a creature into a state of self-sufficiency. It is the temptation of the chaos out of which we were made to return to chaos. In the story the serpent is not evil; he is the tempter. At first he speaks; he learns later to hiss. In our own experience, it is not our temptations which are evil. They become evil as we act upon them, whether by harboring them in our minds, feeding them with our hearts' blood, or implementing them by our wills. Chaos is not evil except as we live by it and act upon it. There is nothing wrong with being a creature. The serpent *becomes* the devil as we act on his temptation of us. He has no substance until we give it to him by such acting. "Evil casts no shadow."

The lie is in the soul, where it has always been. The serpent tells the woman that if she and her husband will eat of the forbidden tree they will become "as gods, knowing good and evil". The desire to be like God is reasonable, because natural to us. We are possessed of this possibility by being made in God's image. There is no morality in Biblical literature apart fom this fundamental religious apprehension. It is categorical in Jesus:

> Be ye perfect, as your Father in heaven is perfect.

The later New Testament writers are equally clear about it:

> He hath made us to be partakers of the divine nature
> . . .

This potentiality can be fulfilled for man only as man lives in imitation of God, and this means that he can come to himself as man only as he lives in accord with the character of the divine nature whose likeness he bears. No type of assertion of himself against the God who made him can issue in less than his ruin.

The serpent tells the woman that by eating of the forbidden fruit she and her husband would at once become as gods. They would achieve likeness to God not through increasing knowledge of God, which comes through accepting the fact of their creatureliness—a fact concretely embedded in the commandment about the tree—but by means of a knowledge of good and evil which was to be acquired by an act of defiance, of self-assertion. Such knowledge is not true knowledge. It is magic, a thing by which control is exercised over the powers of existence. If superstition is the ancestor of religion, and is bad religion; then magic is the ancestor of science, and is false knowledge. We fell in the garden into both perils.

Nothing is said by the serpent about the "power to choose the good and refuse the evil", which is the true power of freedom, and the true likeness we can have to the freedom of God. This likeness comes only through increasing knowledge of him, and produces in us likeness to him in character, which is the only likeness to him we can have. It is not within our grasp as creatures to become like the Creator as he is in himself. In the temptation good and evil have nothing to do with character. They have been made objects external to the mind. The sophists of Plato's day had done this with "virtue", as did Protagoras; and with "rhetoric", as did Gorgias. Plato knew as certainly as did the writer in *Genesis* that to make language and knowledge external to the mind which uses and holds them is immediately to invite degeneracy, both of individual and society. When knowledge is considered as a thing to be valued for its own sake, a thing objective to the person whose knowledge it is, then the temptation to acquire knowledge, even the knowledge of good and evil, is not a temptation to knowledge. It is a most subtle temptation to power. The writer in *Genesis* interprets it as power to escape from the bond of our creatureliness, to become independent of any external condition of our existence, to be in control of our own destinies.

In the mind of the writer, however, it is only as creatures, and in the knowledge of our limitations as creatures, that we can ever come to fullness of being, to a fulfillment of our likeness to the divine nature. The insecurity rooted in our creatureliness is necessary to the emergence of the person because it is an essential part of what we are. Time after time this writer makes his point. The insecurity of Jephthah's birth from a harlot and his lack of any social standing within his tribe lead him to bargain with God for success in battle. The cost of such an attempt to insure himself against this insecurity is his child's life; but the temptation was very great, as it always is. From a man impelled by ecstasy to save his neighbors at Jabesh-Gilead Saul declines into a superstition mean enough to prompt him to sacrifice his son for tasting honey. David is warned by the death of Uzzah, who had put out his hand to secure Jahveh's ark, not to try to lay hold of divine power as a guarantee for his throne, and he understands. When he finally brings the ark into Jerusalem he strips himself to sing and dance before it. And it is Michal, with all the bitterness of the past, who interprets the nakedness of the

creature as the vileness of the King. At the climactic moment of his reign, leaving Jerusalem, which he loves too much to subject to siege, fleeing from the treachery of a son he adored into a wilderness of uncertainty and insecurity, David sends the ark back:

> Carry back the ark of God into the city: if I shall find favor in the eyes of the Lord, he will bring me again, and show me both it, and his habitation;
> But if he thus say, I have no delight in thee; behold, here am I, let him do to me as seemeth good unto him.

It is more because of such understanding than for the glory of his reign that David's house and lineage are held to be that from which Messiah will come.

When man refuses to accept the conditions of his own humanity, symbolized in the prohibition of the fruit of the one tree, the desire to be like God, a desire natural to us and divinely planted within us, becomes first the desire to be *as* God, and then the conviction—growing insensibly and unconsciously, and never spoken, even to oneself—that we *are* God. This is what sin is, and it enters the human heart and infects the world through envy—envy of the God whose creatures we are and whose power as Creator we are determined to share, not as his gift to our nature, but by our own right. This is the root sin ("original sin"); and, because of this, sin is our deadly enemy, for it is destructive of the very first condition of our life as creatures made in the image of God. It is for this reason that Jesus so often resorts to hyperbole and paradox:

> He who would save his life shall lose it;
> And he who would lose his life . . . shall save it.
> . . .

He knows how desperate the peril is. When that same old serpent had hissed in his ears before his own ministry, a devil now long experienced in evil and even more subtle than before, the first approach was in terms of creaturely limitation—the temptation to make bread of stones, or prove oneself superior to the natural law. When he has been twice rebuffed, it becomes very plain:

> Again the devil taketh him up into an exceeding high mountain, and sheweth him all the kingdoms of the world, and the glory of them; and saith unto him, All these things will I give thee, if thou wilt fall down and worship me.
> Then saith Jesus unto him, Get thee hence, Satan: for it is written, Thou shalt worship the Lord thy God, and him only shalt thou serve.

It is this refusal to have all the world can give on the only terms on which the world will provide it that gives the devil occasion to take his leave. Fixed to another tree, and in the grip of death, Jesus will hear the old voice for the last time:

> He saved others; himself he cannot save. Let Christ, the Son of God, come down from the cross.
> We will see and believe.

It is again the aboriginal temptation to grasp equality with God, to assert the power one has in oneself. Jesus' refusal rests upon the "first and great commandment", and is the religious reason why the Creed begins with the statement:

> I believe in God the Father Almighty, Maker of heaven
> and earth, and of all things, visible and invisible. . . .

The story proceeds as the woman, looking at the tree, finds that it is "good for food", a "delight to the eyes", and "to be desired to make one wise". The insinuation, enormously subtle, is that God would hardly have been so unreasonable as to forbid such obviously good things, and therefore there can be no harm in the satisfaction of such normal desires. We need food; beauty is to be appreciated; and the desire for wisdom is the pull of the divine mind upon us. By any sensible argument, how is it plausible that God should forbid the satisfaction of such desires by forbidding the fruit of the tree?

It has already been made plain by the writer that none of these desires had been either forbidden or left without means of satisfaction. God had provided abundantly for them in the garden which the man and woman inhabited. What God had done was warn the man and woman that satisfaction of these desires, wholly natural to us in themselves, could never come through eating the forbidden fruit. He had warned that if the man and his wife did not accept the fact that they were men, and not God, the penalty would be death. The fatal irony in the temptation is that the commandment and its mysterious prohibition had already furnished the man and the woman the only "knowledge of good and evil" which would be of any value to them in living as themselves. The desires of which the satisfaction is promised in the tree are expressive of the deepest needs of human nature. The attempt to satisfy them in a way other than that which God had provided was to attack this nature at its center.

The attack begins on the woman—that is, ostensibly, on our creaturely separateness from each other; but in reality it is an attack on our creatureliness before God. The woman, deceived by the serpent, deceives herself. It is not food, nor beauty, nor wisdom she desires. It is the power to satisfy these needs for herself. It is not even the power to be "as gods". It is the power to *be* God, to take his place for oneself. Neither she nor any of us might admit this, nor need we be aware of it in a self-conscious way, but this is what the writer in *Genesis* has found beneath all our rationalizations.

He goes on to tell us what happened when the self-deception was complete:

> . . . She took of the fruit . . . and did eat, and gave
> also unto her husband, with her; and he did eat.
> And the eyes of them both were opened, and they
> knew that they were naked; and they sewed fig leaves
> together, and made themselves aprons.

From rebellion—pride released through envy—comes neither power nor equality with God, but an ashamed awareness of their own nakedness, of a creatureliness for which they are now guilty and embarrassed. The writer has unerringly chosen the overwhelming symbolic form of "nakedness", a helplessness and innocence natural to us as creatures, and in itself without fear or shame. The unique pathos of the story arises directly from this form of statement, with its powerful erotic and metaphysical suggestions. Among other things, it allows this writer to show that the knowledge which had bound the man and the woman together as man and wife—a knowledge that both were creatures, whose bond of being derived from their common dependence on God as their form of life—was now entangled in confusion, apprehension, shame, and fear. The alienation from each other, of which they are both immediately aware, is in fact only the surface of the real alienation from their very "ground of being". Psychological awareness comes first in the order of perception; but it is secondary in the order of being and knowing. The next part of the story begins the process of recollection which, since the fall, has defined our means of acquiring knowledge.

In the original version of the myth we may suppose that the man and the woman obtained the power they desired. The story would then become an analogue to the Prometheus myth. The gods of the garden could not tolerate such a threat to their supremacy, and drove the man and his wife immediately away, before they could eat of the other magic tree growing there, the tree of life, thus making themselves immortal and equal to the gods. Whatever insight there is in this kind of story, it is a long way from the mind of the author in *Genesis.* The differences in his version of the story are precise reflections of the differences in the nature of the God whom he knew, the immense God of power and righteousness whom his people had known for centuries in the desert, before they ever came into Palestine. That this God should in any way be afraid of man was impossible. That he should in any way be motivated by a concern for his own supremacy was equally impossible. Neither idea was consonant with what this man knew of God's nature. If it is unthinkable that man's rebellion against God can harm God, then the only harm it can do is to man. The harm it did reaches to the very roots of our being.

III.

The metaphor adopted by the writer to state this fact is dependent on our experience of ourselves as sexual beings. His use of it indicates a careful analysis of the popular religion of Palestine in his time. This religion was a fertility cult, tied, as these cults normally are, to the fecundity of the soil and the rotation of the seasons. To desert people such an experience was strange, but it could scarcely have failed to fascinate them when they encountered it in the country in which they were settling. The purpose of the religion and its cult practices was to insure that the gods would maintain their benign and fructifying interest in the land. Such a concern is completely natural and comprehensible. It led, as it almost always leads, to a preoccupation with the reproductive energies of nature as such, and thus to a fascination with sexuality that had become the dominant element in the cult. In the interest of propitiating the deities of the earth, the "dark powers" who demand and come to control even the "father" gods of the air and water, all restraints are discarded. The sexual experience takes on a secretive and morbid fascination, the more frustrated in direct proportion to the orgiastic licence encouraged by the cult. It is another form of chaos, the worship of the womb, of the waters of undifferentiated fecundity.

> Down the mountain walls
> From where Pan's cavern is
> Intolerable music falls.
> Foul goat-head, brutal arm appear,
> Belly, shoulder, bum,
> Flash fishlike; nymphs and satyrs
> Copulate in the foam.

The preoccupation with the powers of reproduction in themselves is exactly parallel to the making external of the knowledge of good and evil by the serpent in the tree. Traces of this morbid fertility religion are everywhere in *Genesis,* most notoriously in the story of Sodom and Gomorrah, which became a byword in Biblical literature for the thing. There is, for another example, more than a suggestion that underlying the enormously popular cycle of legends about Samson is a myth of the earth-mother overcoming the sun.

It is obvious to the writer in *Genesis* that neither the "baals" nor the dark powers of the earth were Jahveh. It was equally obvious to him that in this sex-ridden religion of the land were embodied truths very powerful, in their intimacy and emotional significance, which had to be brought within the range of an experience of God hitherto exclusive of them. Life in a settled country, defined by fields rather than oases, was something more than moments of ecstatic surrender to the great God of storm and volcano. If there was no way that the baals could be Jahveh, then it had to be shown that in some way Jahveh could do what the baals do, that their power in fact was his power. When the power was recognized as Jahveh's, this writer was convinced that the whole experience of the religion of the land could be recovered from the chaos of mechanical sexuality to some kind of ethical order. If we think of baalism as the "secular gospel" of his time, it is apparent that this writer was certain there could be no question of adjusting God to baalism. The only possible thing was to see how God's power could and did encompass the baals. When, more than a millennium later, St. Athanasius was led to say something about the mode of the Incarnation, he was very clear that it was *not* by the conversion of Godhead into manhood, but by the taking of manhood into Godhead, that the miracle occurred. It is this kind of miracle which the writer in *Genesis* was empowered to perform in his story.

The essence of the question is the nature of power. It is because the Biblical writer grasped this question from the very first that the Bible is unique in its idea of God. The essential experience of Old Testament religion is of surrender to the fundamental conditions of power, manifested initially in the power of the storm. The energies of the deities of the earth were a fact. In the mind of the Biblical writer surrender to them had become an insidious way to manipulate them to man's own purpose, and, because this was finally impossible, they worked to destroy the integrity of human life at its emotional center. In his mind it was yet another manifestation of the way in which we have turned against ourselves the very conditions of our life as creatures. He saw that this failure of knowledge—the word in Hebrew as in Greek connotes participation and erotic union—had rotted the whole civilization of the country into which his people had entered. No more horrible metaphor of destruction exists in the Bible than Hosea's:

> Therefore will I be unto Ephraim as a moth, and to the house of Israel as rottenness.

The continuity of tradition is precise, but most terrible in the poet's vision of a perverse knowledge of God turning God into the destroyer.

This element of surrender is present in true science as in true religion. It is neither magic nor superstition, both of which worship the power with a view to bringing it under control. The genuine discipline of science and religion to the basic facts and energies of the experienced world is a discipline of understanding. In religion it is also a discipline toward the further knowledge which is participation. In both science and religion there is the recognition of the absolute priority of the "given", of the "not-myself". For both, reality does not start with myself and my modes of apprehension. Whatever these modes may be, there is something to be apprehended, and if I gain real knowledge of it, such knowledge is not an object, giving me power over the thing known. Knowledge comes as the consequence of reverent exploration, as in science; or of adoration, as in religion. Both are modes of communion with the power.

The fundamental energies of life celebrated in the popular religion of Palestine in his day were thought by this writer to be benign. He saw very clearly that the generosity of the earth, and the immediate affairs of family life and society, must reflect divine sanction and protection. The first insight was a direct consequence of his story of creation. I do not think there can be much question that the other came through his reflection upon the momentous implications of the family histories of Saul and David. If the whole thing had gone wrong, the clue to it was in the sexual experience and its abuse. This man knew that David had seen an exceedingly lovely woman bathing on her roof in the cool of the day, and from his lust had come lying, treachery, murder, rebellion, and, finally, the tyrant Solomon, his child of her. If the sexual experience was of such power that it could thus affect all of life, then in some way it is an experience basic to all others, and also, in some way, determinative of them. If it was wrong, all else might be wrong with it. The drunkenness of Noah and his curse upon Ham (Canaan) is part of the ambience of this thinking.

Even more, however, this writer says that if the God who had created the world and placed man and woman in it was righteous, then the horror and destructiveness into which knowledge between man and woman had fallen reflected and was tied intimately into a yet more fundamental and destructive alienation from God himself. This alienation was the direct consequence of man's refusal to accept what he is—a creature of God. His picture of life prior to this refusal is based on a truth acutely perceived: that communion is basic to us as creatures, and integral to our being persons. He has put this very simply and concretely:

> And the Lord God said: It is not good that the man should be alone.

In the purpose of God, sexual knowledge, and knowledge of every kind whatsoever, is not a matter of control, domination, and subjection, but of deep mutuality, surrender, and delight.

The writer tells us that sin has destroyed this. To the man, hiding in the confusion and shame of his creatureliness among the trees of the garden, in his pitiful, self-made clothing, comes the voice of the Lord God:

> Adam, . . . where art thou?
> And he said, I heard thy voice in the garden, and I was afraid because I was naked; and I hid myself.
> And he said, Who told thee that thou wast naked? Hast thou eaten of the tree, whereof I commanded thee that thou shouldest not eat?
> And the man said, The woman whom thou gavest to be with me, she gave me of the tree, and I did eat.
> And the Lord God said unto the woman, What is this that thou hast done?
> And the woman said, The serpent beguiled me, and I did eat.

The narrative proceeds at once to state the inevitable effect of this rebellion and self-deception upon the human soul. The curses only make explicit what is already evident in his narrative. These sentences—passed upon the serpent, the woman, and the man—are not the arbitrary judgments of a vindictive God, any more than the original prohibition was a mere command to be obeyed simply because it was commanded. It would have been as impossible for this writer to think of God as vindictive as it would to think of him as fearful of man. Jahveh is neither arbitrary nor vindictive. On the contrary, he is always and everywhere himself. That is what the "power" of God means. If, in addition, the character of that power is everywhere and always "to be righteous", then this is the way God's power works to make and to keep him free. The primal conditions of life as a creature are determined by this "holiness" of God, whose power is the inescapable energy constantly informing the whole creation. There is no power by which God can be other than God. The disorder into which hu-

man life is thrown by our refusal to live as creatures was inevitable, but the inevitability is rooted in the righteous power of God. We are at the beginning of an understanding which will not be complete until John hymns the Word made flesh. The mid-point, as before, is Deutero-Isaiah:

> My Word which I utter shall not fail of the purpose for which I sent it.
> It shall not return unto me void, but it shall accomplish the thing for which I sent it.

The writer in *Genesis* employs the narrative form of a curse to state all this. The references to the physical characteristics of the serpent are relics of the primitive story, without particular significance, except for the emphasis on the association with chaos by placing the serpent in the dust. The important thing is the next:

> . . . I will put enmity between thee and the woman, and between thy seed and her seed; it shall bruise thy head, and thou shalt bruise his heel.

Throughout the story there has been an implied identification of the serpent with the monster who is the narrative symbol for the waters of chaos—with its absence of form, its darkness and depths. Yet it is only in terms of this chaos—not evil in itself—that human life can come to fullness of being, through the exercise of creaturely freedom in imitation of God. Only by taking the risk of chaos can God make a creature "in his likeness". The consequence of our refusal to imitate him by bringing order to the chaos essential to our own being as men is the curse. The enmity between us and the serpent is the schism in our own nature, the conflict with the primary condition of our life as creatures. We have refused the necessities of our own humanity, and are alienated from ourselves. The obscurity of the reference to bruising the serpent's head nonetheless carries with it the one element of hope in the whole tale. If Jahveh's righteous power is that in which the inevitability of our tragedy is rooted, it is also the security of a further inevitability—another victory of God over chaos, a chaos now made inimical to our well-being as creatures, and therefore demanding redemption and reconciliation. How this would come, the author could not know, but he saw in the emergence of the monarchy of David an unmistakable sign of it:

> And David perceived that the Lord had established him King over Israel, and that he had exalted his kingdom for his people Israel's sake.

He saw in the way the monarchy collapsed and failed an equally unmistakable confirmation of the truth of our fall in the garden. The story of the flood completes his introductory triptych of myths, which he placed as a preface to his history, and its implications are consistent with this hopeful expectation of a future victory of Jahveh in time.

Now God speaks to the woman. The curse begins with a reference to the pain of childbirth, the peril of bringing another creature to light from the darkness which chaos has again in large part become. Seven centuries later Job will cry out:

> Let the day perish wherein I was born, and the night in which it was said, There is a man child conceived. Let that day be darkness; let not God regard it from above, neither let the light shine upon it. . . .
>
> As for that night, let darkness seize upon it, . . . Because it shut not up the doors of my mother's womb. . . . Why died I not from the womb? why did I not give up the ghost when I came out of the belly?

"We came crying hither; / Thou know'st, the first time that we smell the air / we wawl and cry." A contemporary poet understands this:

> What youthful mother, a shape upon her lap Honey of generation had betrayed, And that must sleep, shriek, struggle to escape As recollection or the drug decide, Would think her son, did she but see that shape With sixty or more winters on its head, A compensation for the pang of his birth, Or the uncertainty of his setting forth?

The curse proceeds:

> Thy desire shall be to thy husband and he shall rule over thee.

This describes accurately the position of woman in the society in which this author lived. She was man's chattel, subject to his desire and his wishes, however irresponsible and cruel. She was possessed as a property, with no inherent rights as a person. This is represented by the author as categorically and unequivocally unnatural, here a thousand years before Christ. It is the result of sin, of the schism in the human soul that has come from alienation from God. The brutal story of the rape and murder and dissection of the Levite's concubine at Gibeah, which includes not only the utter barbaric callousness of the priest but also the willingness of the old man who is host to throw his daughter to the human wolves outside his door, brings from this author one of his few personal intrusions into his narrative:

> And it was so, that all who saw it said, There was no such deed done nor seen from the day that the children of Israel came up out of the land of Egypt unto this day:
> Consider of it, take advice, and speak your minds.

He has certainly spoken his. It is astonishing that his story of the garden could have been used to support the exact opposite of what it says. Milton's confidence that God's universal law sustained his subjugation of his wife and daughters only proves the continuous darkness of mind that chaos has become for us.

It is not domination and subjection, but mutuality and communion, which must characterize this most basic form of human knowledge of each other. Othello recognizes this communion as the absolute condition of his life:

> Perdition catch my soul
> But I do love thee: and when I love thee not,
> Chaos is come again.

When this love is cankered by Iago's monstrous insinuations, perdition does catch his soul and the threat is made actual:

> O blood, blood, blood! . . .
> Like to the Pontic sea,
> Whose icy current and compulsive course
> Ne'er feels retiring ebb, but keeps due on
> To the Propontic and the Hellespont,
> Even so my bloody thoughts, with violent pace,
> Shall ne'er look back, ne'er ebb to humble love,
> Till that a capable and wide revenge
> Swallow them up. . . .

The kind of meaning the **Genesis** story gives human sexuality is of the highest significance. If disorder has attacked us here it will infect all other modes of knowledge and communion—between groups, classes, and nations. The natural desire we have to share our life with others in mutuality and trust and joy, a desire inherent in us, has been twisted and deranged. Defiance of God has bred in us an insidious, daemonic ruthlessness in our dealings with other people, for we must force them to meet our desire in order to quiet the fear for our own security now unleashed in our hearts. We must convince ourselves that we are "all right". In some subconscious way we must, I suppose, assure ourselves that our claim to be God is a valid claim, and that reality begins and ends with our sense of it. Thus we must try to subdue to our need those others whom we know we need, and, if we are successful, a momentary satisfaction is the result. Our eventual defeat is certain, for such knowledge of another, devoid of communion, is no knowledge. It remains external to us, a possession which fails of union. Without participation the need of the soul remains unsatisfied. The false security of having subdued to our will everything and everyone whom we think we need, leaving ourselves the only one, is a state of tyranny, and, as Plato knew, the tyrant is the loneliest man in the world.

We have fallen from the essentially good and benign aloneness of being a creature, with all its wonderful and creative possibilities of knowledge of God and communion with the whole range of our fellow-creatures, into the tyrannical loneliness of alienation and of ruthless self-assertion. Having entered on the path of domination as a way of escape from this self-imposed alienation, we do not know how to turn back, and therefore we go on, with ever-increasing appetite, and a fear insatiable because incapable of satisfaction, sinking deeper and deeper into frustration and ceasing moment by moment to be human. Through envy sin entered the world, and through envy sin is perpetuated. It is Dante's she-wolf, hungry after being fed.

IV.

All of this is brought together in the curse pronounced on the man:

> Cursed is the ground for thy sake; in sorrow shalt
> thou eat of it all the days of thy life. . . .
> In the sweat of thy face shalt thou eat bread, till thou
> return unto the ground, for out of it wast thou taken:
> For dust thou art, and unto dust shalt thou return.

The most powerful note in this curse is that of frustration, the frustration of drudgery and defeat, a ceaseless going-round, and in the end the fact of death, which is inescapable. It is an existence of horror, an accurate description of what things have become:

> Vanity of vanities, . . . all is vanity . . . there is no
> new thing under the sun.
> Is there any thing whereof it may be said, See, this is
> new? It hath been already of old time, which was
> before us . . .
> Therefore I hated life; because the work that is
> wrought under the sun is grievous unto me:
> For all is vanity, and vexation of spirit.

It is a world of hollow men, whether quietly desperate and cold, or savagely aggressive and violent. It is a world in which the very righteousness of God has become a law of death for men who have refused to live by it. Dante sees such a law written on Hell's gate:

> Divine power made me, and supreme wisdom, and
> eternal love.
> Before me nothing was created but eternal things, And
> I endure eternally. . . .
> Abandon every hope, ye who enter here.

The most tragic of Shakespeare's tragedies takes up these same themes of acceptance and alienation. Cordelia cannot play the game of compliments with her sisters, whose rhetoric of love is the mask for their desire of power. The game is not true, and therefore for Cordelia there can be no charity in it. Even if she could "heave her heart into her mouth" and say what King Lear wants to hear, no reconciliation is possible at this point, for her father also wants power and is playing with it. So what can poor Cordelia speak?—"Love, and be silent." Such silence is the equivalent of Isaiah's "their wisdom is to sit still." It is the silence Jesus knew how to maintain, when no word of his would avail anything. If *King Lear* is the most tragic, it is also the most redemptive and reconciling of Shakespeare's tragedies. At the end of the play everyone and everything that can be redeemed is redeemed. Shakespeare does not deny the evil that comes from love's violation one whit of its effect. King Lear, against every caution, has himself unleashed the storm of chaos which overwhelms his mind and body:

> Come not between the dragon and his wrath.

Shakespeare knows that such ignorance of the form of love must work itself out in full measure to its final consequence. Yet love is not destroyed. King Lear dies, stretched out on the rack of this tough world, but he dies reconciled with Cordelia—with love itself, in her person:

> Come, let's away to prison.
> We two alone will sing like birds i' th' cage.
> When thou dost ask me blessing, I'll kneel down,
> And ask of thee forgiveness. So we'll live,
> And pray, and sing, and tell old tales, and laugh
> At gilded butterflies. . . .

No poet has seen the horror and vanity of our plight more clearly than Eliot:

> Our dried voices, when
> We whisper together
> Are quiet and meaningless
> As wind in dry grass
> Or rats' feet over broken glass
> In our dry cellar . . .
> Is it like this
> In death's other kingdom
> Waking alone
> At the hour when we are
> Trembling with tenderness
> Lips that would kiss
> Form prayers to broken stone.

In relation to the Biblical story it is sometimes held that if man had not sinned he would not have to die. If the author of *Genesis* had been this naive he would hardly have been capable of the profound understanding of man's predicament which he has shown. He is not thinking of death as the physical fact of dying. He is thinking of death as we "feel" it and "experience" it—as the final frustration, as the inescapable seal of separation, as the dreaded and fearful King of terrors. He is thinking of death as exhaustion, the final negation of meaning and communion. He would know what Macbeth means:

> It is a tale told by an idiot, full of sound and fury,
> signifying nothing.

It is more than what Hamlet says he fears:

> Who would fardels bear
> To grunt and sweat under a weary life,
> But that the dread of something after death,
> The undiscover'd country from whose bourn
> No traveller returns, puzzles the will,
> And makes us rather bear those ills we have
> Than fly to others that we know not of?

In the *Genesis* story it is the fear itself of death, not fear of the consequences that follow death, which is the result of the sin in the garden. If in this fear all other fears are bound up, it is because one dies in sin; it is not the ceasing to be physically, but the dying evilly. St. Paul sees it: the *sting* of death is sin. This disorder has distorted our souls, so that physical death has become for us the terror and the fascination of sheer annihilation or oblivion. To secure ourselves from death we have become predators of each other, preying upon ourselves "like monsters of the deep"—and the life of man, "solitary, poor, mean, nasty, brutish, and short". Nor is there any escape through drawing ever more tightly about oneself a cloak of insensibility to the rest of the creation. At the end we will have to stand forth naked, with every self-made covering stripped away, and God will call to us, and we will again be dust.

The writer of this story, as we have said, saw in the reign of David what he took to be the beginnings of God's victory over this chaos in the life of man, a life now become terrible and monstrous: "every man did that which was right in the sight of his own eyes." He is very clear that such a victory is wholly dependent upon the God who in the very beginning gave his Word to the primal chaos. He is equally clear that the lust for Bathsheba is the act in which the whole defect of David's kingdom is embodied—an act which leads implacably toward its tragic end, the blood-bath of Solomon's accession in which the very chaos the monarchy was inaugurated to heal re-emerges in all its fury. The end of his history is inconclusive and questioning, but there is no question about the source of whatever victory may come, nor any doubt of the power Jahveh has to accomplish a reconciliation "in the fulness of time".

> Be adored among men,
> God, three-numbered form;
> Wring thy rebel, dogged in den,
> Men's malice, with wrecking and storm . . .
> Make mercy in all of us, out of us all
> Mastery, but be adored, but be adored King.

The narrative chronicle of David's court is an historical analogue of the myth of the garden in *Genesis.* It is a concrete parable of the fall of man in history, of the resurgence of chaos, and of the kinds of thing that release it.

The story ends:

> Behold, the man is become as one of us, to know good and evil: and now, lest he put forth his hand, and take also of the tree of life, and eat, and live forever: Therefore the Lord God sent him forth from the garden of Eden, to till the ground from whence he was taken. So he drove out the man; and he placed at the east of the garden of Eden cherubims, and a flaming sword which turned every way, to keep the way of the tree of life.

The knowledge of good and evil—our self-awareness of our creatureliness—since it was corrupted by the heart which had received it, had not brought with it likeness to God, but alienation. In the older version of the story the other tree growing in the garden, the tree of life, was also a magic tree, with the power to confer eternal life. For the Biblical writer there is no magic by which "good and evil" or "life" can be brought within our power. Both of these are gifts and are realized in us as we live in imitation of the freedom of Jahveh, in whose image we were made.

The real tragedy of the *Genesis* story here becomes apparent. The knowledge which the lie of the serpent suggested would give the man the power to become as a god has brought no power. It has brought instead the frustration of knowing a good unattainable and inaccessible, to have which we are completely impotent, and the stark terror of a knowledge of death which, however we may struggle, remains inescapable.

If rebellion has stripped us of the power to become like God, a power divinely implanted in us and proper to us, and if every moment of our lives recalls to us the knowledge of what we have lost and still desire, such a state cannot be allowed to be perpetual. To bar the way to the tree of life is a supreme mercy. It leaves the fear of death as inescapable evidence, however twisted and distorted, of our creatureliness. Should we lose this awareness our salvation would be impossible, and we would condemn ourselves eternally to the misery of our condition. Dante has read the Bible accurately when he calls that state "hell". The necessity of dying has become for us in our state of alienation our only hope for restoration of life. The threat of a relapse into chaos, now become a certainty, is at least a finite threat, and death's inescapable presence a primary means of restoring to us the knowledge of what we are.

> No, no, no life?
> Why should a dog, a horse, a rat, have life,
> And thou no breath at all? Thou'lt come no more,
> Never, never, never, never, never.
> Pray you undo this button. Thank you, sir.
> Do you see this? Look on her! Look her lips,
> Look there, look there.

And so the New Testament sees that it is only "by means of death"—not our own, but another's—that the curse of Eden can be reversed. The Church sings of this at Easter: "who by his death hath destroyed death". It is not physical dying which is meant, or has ever been meant; rather, the fear of death:

> O death, where is thy sting?
> O grave, where is thy victory?

Only when the fear of death is done away can we pass the cherubim and the flaming sword, to approach the tree of life.

> . . . the end of all our exploring
> Will be to arrive where we started
> And know the place for the first time.
> Through the unknown, remembered gate
> When the last of earth left to discover
> Is that which was the beginning . . .

In the meantime, and apart from this triumph,

> What shall we say who have knowledge
> Carried to the heart? Shall we take the act
> To the grave? Shall we, more hopeful, set up the grave
> In the house? The ravenous grave?
>   Leave now
> The shut gate and the decomposing wall:

The gentle serpent, green in the mulberry bush
Riots with his tongue through the hush—
Sentinel of the grave who counts us all.

Peter Booth (essay date 1974)

SOURCE: "Abraham and Agamemnon: A Comparative Study of Myth," *The Humanities Association Review,* Vol. 25, No. 4, Fall, 1974, pp. 290-97.

[*In the following essay, Booth analyzes the commonalities between the Greek myth of Agamemnon's sacrifice of Iphigeneia, and Abraham's near-sacrifice of Isaac in the book of* Genesis. *In particular, Booth studies the similarities in story patterns and aetiological features.*]

The myths of Agamemnon's sacrifice of Iphigeneia and Abraham's near-sacrifice of Isaac have much in common. Out of similarities in story patterns emerge narrative unities of comparable primary characteristics suggesting variations on a single theme, a common matrix, and a spiritual dimension not characteristic of particular and independent legends.

Myth may be defined as traditional oral narrative transmitted from generation to generation by a pre-literate society or an illiterate segment of a society. Myth is a social not an individual phenomenon arising from group experience and reflecting, recollecting or expressing that experience in narrative form. Myths are usually classified according to the nature (as best it can be ascertained) of the original stimulus, as aetiological, liturgical, historical and what I shall call psyche myths. Myths of the historical type, usually called legends or sagas, may be either directly reminiscent of actual events in history or indirectly reflective; myths of this latter type either reflect customs and change indirectly by changes within the narrative itself or by disguising the doings of men as the doings of gods. Myths of the psyche type are usually called either Märchen or folktales and not taken seriously enough or taken too seriously, too clinically that is, as Jungian archetypes. Unlike myths of the first three categories they are stimulated by an inner impulse and express mental perceptions concerning life and death and social intercourse, and man's relation to the powers that be. Myths of this kind convey conceptual frameworks within which myths of the other three categories may be interpreted. The mythologizing of pre-literate societies is a rationally respectable process. A culture may give birth to or adopt perceptions manifesting validity in the light of its own experience, and retain and transmit the myth-expressions of these perceptions, and use them interpretatively to understand its own unfolding history. The ancient Greeks like the ancient Israelites entered and occupied territory inhabited by foreign and more highly evolved civilizations and over a long period of time acquired with that land many new ways of living and many new ways of thinking. They did not come into contact with the same peoples but with peoples among whom many practices and conceptions had been enabled by generations of relative peace and commercial intercourse to develop commonly.

Myth ceases to be myth when the free-floating oral tradition is caught, crystallized, first as oral poetry with its formulaic rigidity and then as written literature. We have no immediate knowledge of either of the myths of Abraham and Agamemnon; we are acquainted with them by the mediacy of crystallizations like those of Aeschylus and Euripides and the work of one of two authors compiling Pentateuchal traditions possibly during the early days of the Israelite monarchy. These two authors, the Yahwist and Elohist, distinguished by their respective names for God (Yahweh and Elohim), appear to have used a common source and added, each one, special material of his own.[1] The Abraham myth with which we are concerned, like the preceding account of Abraham's dealings with Abimelech at Beer-sheba, is part of the Elohist's special contribution. He crystallized an oral tradition, or made use of an already crystallized version, either unknown to or simply unused by either the Yahwist or their precursor, just as Aeschylus and Euripides used varying versions of the Agamemnon tradition either unknown to or simply unused by Homer. In order to catch a glimpse of the myths thus crystallized it is necessary to take into account what is known both of the way myth passes from generation to generation and of the motives of each author who selects from the versions one that suits his own ends. This inquiry constitutes the first step in a two-step retrospective process, decrystallization of extant literary expression using all available methods of textual and form criticism in order to hypothesize the narrative as it must have existed during not less than fifteen generations of oral transmission as myth.

The second step is that of de-mythologizing—going behind the narrative itself to glimpse the kind of stimulus that gave rise to it. Are these myths basically aetiologies? Are they liturgical, accompanying a particular act of worship? Do they owe their origin as legends to actual events in history? Or do they fall rather, as psyche myths, into that fourth category whose impetus is from within the mind?

Considering first the Agamemnon tradition we are struck at once by the co-existence of sacrifice and substitution versions. We assume the priority of the former. Farnell notes that this is a strong tradition but records doubt concerning the identity of Iphigeneia—the name is a title and could serve either mortal or immortal (it does appear as cult title of Artemis).[2] The tradition has no necessary connection either with the house of Atreus or with the war to which it now appears preliminary. De-crystallization notes primary and secondary features: among the latter the particular motivation for the act, and the particular identities of participants; among the former: a national crisis, the father's rank, the father-first-born relationship, a local association, the goddess Artemis. No one of these primary features is altered by the suggestion that the myth was originally told in a non-Greek (specifically pre-Greek Mediterranean) context of non-Greek participants and that the myth was assimilated along with the Artemis cult at one of the cult centres into the main body of Mycenaean and subsequent Greek mythology around the figure of Agamemnon, a figure corresponding in position and prominence to that about whom the myth had originally been told.

Turning to the Abraham tradition we are struck not by the coexistence of versions but by an awkwardness of context that begs explanation. Abraham is commanded to sacrifice his only son Isaac, the son for whom he had waited years past human hoping, and the means through whom God's earlier promise of land and the posterity to inherit it would finally have been possible. The explanation provided by the text, that this is a test of faith, frightens rather than satisfies.[3] And if, for the same reasons that led us to assign priority to the sacrifice over the substitution version of the Agamemnon myth, we hypothesize an earlier telling in which the sacrifice was completed, then the reason here given becomes a question clearly of context. Doubt expressed concerning the identity of Iphigeneia is mirrored by the question concerning the name of Abraham's first-born. Originally Abraham and Isaac seem to have been patriarchal figures for related but distinct tribal groups. Having in common the promise of land and descendants to prosper in it they merged, as did their tribes, into a father-son relationship reflecting the ascendency of the Abraham group. Had the myth of Abraham's sacrifice of his first-born been modified by the time of the merging into a substitution account comparable to that of Iphigeneia, the identification of that son with Isaac would have been readily facilitated. The tradition of Isaac's near-sacrifice has not only no necessary connection either with the identity of the participants or with the promise of land and posterity but even counters this latter in a most awkward manner. De-crystallization once again notes primary and secondary features: and again among the latter the particular motivation for the act, and the particular identities of participants; and among primary features a crisis situation (mirrored in the father's suffering), the father's rank, the father-first-born relationship, a local association, the god who is identified as El. And once again no one of these primary features is altered by the suggestion that this myth also was originally told in other than its present context and of other participants (specifically pre-Israelite Mediterranean) and that the myth was assimilated along with the cultic worship of El at Beer-sheba into the mainstream of Israelite mythology around the figure of Abraham, a figure corresponding in position and prominence to that about whom the myth had originally been told.

To demythologize is to cast about for the kind of stimulus which gave rise to a myth or to consider the manner of a myth's inception, and to arrive at some understanding thereby of the kind of myth concerned and the essence reflected, recollected or expressed by its narrative unity.[4] That that essence is conveyed by the narrative unity is an important tenet inasmuch as during a long and multicultural evolution such as that exhibited by the type of myth with which we are dealing the marks of stimuli other than the essential one may well appear but always in a secondary manner. This fact becomes clear when each potentially essential stimulus is viewed in the light of the narrative unity.

Both myths exhibit aetiological features but of a secondary nature. The Abraham myth concludes with an explanation of the name of the mountain on which God provided a substitute for Isaac, but this is an incidental aetiology comparable to that which explains Corinthian initiation rites at the temple of Hera Akraia in terms of the slaughter of Medea's children.[5] Both myths have on occasion been explained as aetiologies of particular sacrificial practice: the sacrifice of a she-bear dressed in clothing to the she-bear goddess Artemis at Brauron (Farnell, p. 57) and the substitution of a ram for a child symbolically bound and placed on the altar at Beer-sheba (Noth, pp. 114f.). The likelihood is greater that the substitution versions of the myths were adduced, like the story of Zeus' and Hera's falling out and the Plataean Daedala (Kirk, p. 17), to explain an independent practice the meaning of which had long since disappeared. The secondary nature of the aetiological factor, however, is most clearly seen in the fact that it doesn't really affect the primary features of the myth itself whether the sacrifice or the substitution version is accepted. Tradition left Iphigeneia free to come or go (to the land of the Taurians) as she pleased; Isaac had no choice but to be spared.

Although both myths have profound theological implications and appear to have been perpetuated at particular cult centres because of the nature of the rite and the person of the deity concerned, they seem not to be essentially liturgical expressions; unlike the myth of Hyacinthus' annual death or the passover tradition shared by each and every household they are concerned with a once-and-for-all emergency measure effected by the king or tribal leader on the people's behalf. Both the status of the father and the efficacy of the sacrifice of the only-begotten or first-born indicate the secondary nature of the liturgical association. Better comparison would be with the emergency ritual prescription of the Roman *devotio*, both in the rank of the agent and the singleness of the act.

Even actual historical occurrence as stimulus giving rise to legend, on the face of it the most obvious (and certainly the guise under which the ancients themselves transmitted the myths), is seen on examination once again in the light of the narrative unity and those features revealed as primary to be less significant than one might assume. As stated earlier myth of this type may reflect indirectly. The substitution accounts may well reflect either a modification in popular practice over a long period of time and a corresponding and spontaneous updating of the myths or, as seems quite likely in this case, the assimilation from a culture accepting the practice of human sacrifice to cultures rejecting it outright or never fully accepting it. Human sacrifice seems not to have been an Israelite custom even in the earliest stages of which traces can be found; among the Greeks as well, although the point is debatable, it seems not to have been a native custom. (It is worth nothing, for example, that the comparable reference to the sacrificing in a war with the Eleusinian Eumolpus is to the daughter of the autochthonous king Erechtheus.[6]) As for direct recollection, as opposed to indirect reflection, the possibility cannot, of course, be ruled out that either Agamemnon or Abraham or both did indeed do what the myths recount and that the myths in question are essentially historical. Nevertheless, there are problems, as we have seen. But even if the myths do ascend through greater antiquity to more ancient, foreign figures of comparable status and the myths for that reason be considered essentially historical, once again, viewed in the light of the narrative unity the historical feature loses its primacy. If and when and whoever actually effected such rites, the practice was done in accord with the kind of emergency ritual prescription to which we earlier referred.

To suggest that we are dealing with a ritually prescribed procedure not native to either Greeks or Israelites but assimilated by them independently from a common source in a civilization or complex of civilizations preceding both along the shores of the Eastern Mediterranean would not be to lack parallel elsewhere. Roland de Vaux suggests that the ritual burning of part or all of the sacrifice, like the mounds or knolls (Hebrew *bamôth*, Greek *bōmoi*) raised for the purposes of cultic worship, were neither Israelite nor Greek in origin.[7] Glotz lists *bōmos* among Greek words of identifiably Cretan origin and makes reference in the same context to *Britomartis* "the sweet maiden" or "the good maiden" whom the Greeks revered as Artemis wherever the Minoans had settled.[8] The god El of the Abraham myth was in all probability the local manifestation at Beer-sheba of the Canaanite-Phoenician deity El, addressed in the preceding segment of the Elohist's special material as El-Olam, El of Eternity (de Vaux, p. 293). Abimelech the king mentioned in that same passage bears a typically Canaanite dynastic name and calls to mind the Tyrian Abi-milki of the Amarna tablets (Noth, p. 155).

Nor is evidence for the specific pattern which seems to emerge out of similarities between the Abraham and Agamemnon myths lacking for either the Phoenicians or Canaanites. Eusebius in his *Praeparatio Evangelica* (I, 10), citing a Phoenician myth, attributes to Kronos, king of Phoenicia, the sacrifice in time of war of his only begotten son. The second book of Kings (3: 26-27) records the sacrifice by Mesha of Moab, beset by the combined armies of Israel and Judah and beseiged within his last stronghold, of his eldest son who was to reign in his stead, as burnt offering upon the city wall in full view of the beseiging armies. Their immediate panic and withdrawal gives clear indication, even in the understandably slight Old Testament reference, of the comprehension of an act bound by its gravity to bring down upon them the terrible anger of Chemosh, god of Moab, an anger thus effectively transferred from Moab herself to her enemies outside the walls.[9]

Now inasmuch as we are speaking of a prescribed procedure, a once-and-for-all stratagem to be employed in time of dire national calamity, it is not legend with which we are concerned, even though particular legends may well have arisen out of particular applications. We are concerned rather with a perception of reality, a feeling that the greatest common peril can only be overcome by the greatest common sacrifice. The perception is not individual but tribal or national; it arose out of the experience of the mind and in this sense is embodied in psyche myth. Only the psyche myth category fulfills all the primary features of the narrative unity: the formula is applied in time of dire national crisis; the king as father and representative of his people performs the sacrifice; he sacrifices the most valuable thing, the first-fruit of his own loins, his only begotten; he does this at the cult place of the deity as an act of propitiation to appease the anger of the deity and to save his people from the wrath of God.

The civilization among which this perception came into being perpetuated it as a prescription of life-and-death gravity and applied it as required. The Greek and Israelite nations who assimilated it through legends of particular application did so because they intuitively recognized in it chords resonant with their own experience. Historical myth, springing from historical actuality, lacks the conceptual or spiritual dimension of the psyche myth; history is subject to interpretation—and theological interpretation of the most profound sort—especially in the tradition of Israel, but only when the psyche framework already exists within which to read the times.

Theologically embedded in their respective literatures, the Greek myth by Aeschylus, the Israelite by the Elohist, these variants on a single theme continued to evoke the response prompted by their psyche dimension, continued, that is, to provide the conceptual framework within which national experience could be interpreted. Significantly that response was triggered on both sides by the experience, on a collective or national scale, of suffering. For the Greeks, Dionysiac tragedy, a dramatic expression of the inevitability of suffering, would become the vehicle par excellence of this perception. Agamemnon's dilemma is that of a suffering king and suffering father, and he becomes a type of the tragic hero, obeying divine injunction to break divine law. His agony and Abraham's are identical, and Aeschylus' words could well be put on the lips of the Israelite:

> A heavy doom indeed is disobedience,
> but heavy, too,
> if I rend my child

> which of these courses is without evil?

For the Israelites, repeated political disaster would express itself in the figure of the Suffering Servant and, in the new Israel, of the beloved son suffering the ultimate at the Father's will on the nation's behalf. The extent to which this perception, in origin foreign to both Israel and Greece, was to become vehicle for the most profound theological speculations, speculations so widely differing as Greek tragedy and Christian kerygma, is shown by the use to which it was put by the authors of the *De Rerum Natura* and the fourth gospel. It has been pointed out that Lucretius could have illustrated his point with an example drawn from recent Roman history;[10] he chose the sacrifice of Iphigeneia, however, not only because of its familiarity and dramatic potential, but above all because of the position it had come to occupy in Greek theology. He uses the story, moreover, with a view to overturning that entire theology by utterly invalidating the basic premiss of that narrative unity:

> tantum religio potuit suadere malorum

It is a radically distorted perspective that sees man in any sense inculpated by divine discord. John, on the other hand, tacitly confirms the validity of the ancient perception. It is in the interpretative fourth gospel that the Lamb of God, publicly attired and most emphatically proclaimed King of the Jews, goes to his death at the time when the Paschal lamb is being slain in the temple.

> For God so loved the world, that he gave his only begotten Son.

Notes

1. Martin Noth, *A History of Pentateuchal Traditions,* trans. Bernhard W. Anderson (Englewood Cliffs, N.J.: Prentice-Hall, 1972; Stuttgart: W. Kohlhammer Verlag, 1948), pp. 38 ff.

2. *Greek Hero Cults and Ideas of Immortality* (Oxford: The Clarendon Press, 1921), pp. 55 ff.

3. Compare, for example, Kierkegaard's treatment in *Fear and Trembling.*

4. One must bear in mind the importance of the narrative or plot element of a myth, providing as it does the only rigidity of form (as distinct from the rigidity of expression characteristic of oral poetry and the conservatism of the written word), and thus insuring the myth's perpetuation through generations of oral transmission.

5. G.S. Kirk, *Myth: its Meaning and Functions in Ancient and Other Cultures* (Cambridge: The University Press, 1971), p. 18.

6. H.J. Rose, *A Handbook of Greek Mythology* (London: Methuen and Co. Ltd., 1928, 6th edition, 1958), p. 262.

7. Roland de Vaux, *Ancient Israel: its life and institutions* (New York: McGraw-Hill, 1961), pp. 440-441.

8. Gustave Glotz, *The Aegean Civilization* (New York: Barnes and Noble, 1968; London: Kegan Paul, Trench, Trubner and Co., Ltd., 1925), p. 387.

9. John Gray, *I and II Kings: a commentary* (Philadelphia: The Westminster Press, 1963), p. 439.

10. John Masson, *Lucretius, Epicurean and Poet* (London: John Murray, 1907), p. 434, n. 2.

D. J. A. Clines (essay date 1976)

SOURCE: "Theme in *Genesis* 1-11," *The Catholic Bible Quarterly,* Vol. XXXVIII, No. 4, October, 1976, pp. 483-507.

[*In the following essay, Clines studies the theme of the first eleven chapters of* Genesis, *emphasizing that this thematic investigation focuses on these chapters as a portion of Penteteuchal text, rather than on the individual sources from which* Genesis *was created. Clines goes on to survey the historical setting and literary pre-history of* Genesis.]

I. The Nature of "Theme"

Most recent studies of theme in the Pentateuch turn out to be investigations of the theme of the individual sources of the Pentateuch. Even though the chorus of dissent from the classic four-source analysis is swelling,[1] most scholars still believe that the Graf-Wellhausen theory is the best we have,[2] and articles and books are being written on "The Kerygma of the Yahwist,"[3] *The Yahwist. The Bible's First Theologian,*[4] "The Elohistic Fragments in the Pentateuch,"[5] "The Kerygma of the Priestly Writers,"[6] and so on.

The aim however of this article is to enquire about the theme of a unit of Pentateuchal text, *Gen* 1-11, considered in and by itself. Almost everyone acknowledges that disparate materials went into the fashioning of *Gen* 1-11, and most believe they can distinguish at least the major blocks of those materials. But my primary concern here is with the text in its final form,[7] asking, "What is the theme of *Gen* 1-11 as it stands?" G. von Rad has already pointed us in the direction of such a concern in some comments he made on *Gen* 2-3:

> Reconstruction of the original texts . . . is not the primary task of exegesis. . . . No matter how much a knowledge of the previous stages of the present text can preserve us from false exposition, still there is no question that the narrative of chs. 2f., in spite of certain tensions and irregularities, is not a rubble heap of individual recensions, but is to be understood as a whole with a consistent train of thought. Above all else, the exegete must come to terms with this existing complex unity.[8]

I should like to apply that approach to *Gen* 1-11 as a whole.

Since my subject is the *theme* of *Gen* 1-11, a few remarks about what I mean by "theme" are in order. My understanding of "theme" can best be presented by distinguishing "theme" from similar terms: "intention," "motif," "plot," and "subject."

"Theme" is both *narrower and broader* than "the intention of the author." It is narrower in that it may express only one aspect of an author's intention. That intention may be, variously, to influence a particular historical situation (e.g., of controversy), or to meet a psychological need on the author's part, or even to make money or gain prestige. "Theme" could only refer to that aspect of the author's intention that is expressed in the shape and development of the literary work. But "theme" is broader than "author's intention" in that it cannot always be stated adequately in terms of what the author had consciously in mind: on the one side, authors do not necessarily formulate the theme of their work even to themselves (see further the last paragraph of this section I), and on the other, the reader is under no constraint to make his statement of theme in terms of the author's intention (rather than in terms of the work) when he has no access to that intention apart from the work itself.

"Theme" is *broader* than "motif" or "topos"[9] or "typical scene"[10] or "narrative pattern"[11] or "theme" in the sense used by Parry and Lord in their studies of South Slavic epic[12] and adopted by other students of techniques of oral composition. It relates to larger units than do these other terms. I am concerned with theme in the sense of the theme of the whole work; one could not speak of the motif or typical scene of a work. Even a recurrent motif[13] does not necessarily constitute a theme. Theme and motif are of the same substance, however, for the theme of a pericope may become a motif of a larger work into which the pericope is incorporated.

"Theme" is *deeper* than "plot." "Plot" may be defined as a kind of story, namely, a story with the emphasis on causality;[14] "theme" tends to conceptualize plot, to focus its significance, and state its implication; it may be said (in a narrative work) to be "plot with the emphasis on meaning."

To discern the "theme" of a work is a *more perceptive* undertaking than to discover its "subject." Both theme and subject may be answers to the question, "What is the work *about*?" But to identify its subject is merely to classify, while to discover its theme is to see "the attitude, the opinion, the insight *about* the subject that is revealed through a particular handling of it,"[15] that is, to *understand* the work more deeply than knowing its "subject." Theme of course arises out of the subject, but because it is a matter for deeper perception its identification is more complex and involves more subjective considerations than does an enquiry about the "subject." In a literary work, unlike a scientific or technical work, theme is not usually explicit.

Four further questions about theme are relevant to the present study:

(i) Can there be more than one theme in a literary work? I think not. When different, divergent, or contradictory themes emerge other than the theme the critic has first identified, he has to adapt his statement of the theme to take account of them. There may indeed be different *levels* on which theme is sought, identified, and articulated. Thus a novel whose theme is the declining fortunes of a family may also be seen as developing the theme of the decay of a society or an empire. If both themes can be shown to

belong to the intention of the writer, a statement of the novel's theme would have to express the author's sense of the relationships between the family and the society. But if the latter theme was not consciously part of the author's intention and identified only as the "deep structure" of the plot, we are dealing with theme on quite another *level*, on which to speak also of the author's theme would be out of place. Unity of theme is a function of the unity of the literary work.[16] Of course, in the case of a work like *Gen* 1-11, which is self-evidently a composition from other works, the possibility exists that it has no unity and no unified theme. So a second question arises:

(ii) How can the existence of a given theme in a literary work be demonstrated? There is no way of *demonstrating* a theme to everyone's satisfaction. The only formal criterion for establishing a theme is: the best statement of the theme of a work is the statement that most adequately accounts for the content, structure and development of the work. To state the theme of a work is to say what it means that the work is as it is.

(iii) How can theme be discovered? I know of no technique for exposing an implicit theme apart from: trial and error. Since theme arises from subject, is a conceptualization of plot, and is of the same substance as motif, the critic has already defined for him an area within which to move. All he can do then is to examine likely candidates. That is the method I propose following in this study of theme in *Gen* 1-11.

(iv) One more preliminary question raises itself: Does our theme need to have been in the mind of the author? Not necessarily. "Theme" is an item from the conceptual equipment of the literary critic, and not necessarily of the creative artist. The function of enquiry about theme is orientation to the work. The author needs no orientation to his own work, and he may not conceptualize its theme. If theme encapsulates the meaning of the work, the theme and the work are created together in the author's mind. It is the critic or reader, looking for a way into the work, for what makes this work the work it is and not another, and for what makes it hang together, who needs to think about theme. None of this is to say that an author cannot or does not perceive the theme of his work or that he is not in many cases far better able to state the theme of his work than any of his readers or critics. All I am asserting is that we do not need to assure ourselves that such and such a theme could have been present in the mind of the author or conceptualized by him before we allow the possibility that such and such is the theme of the work.

II. SUGGESTED THEMES

1. A SIN—SPEECH—MITIGATION—PUNISHMENT THEME

The first theme to be considered is realized in the plot or story pattern of the major narratives of *Gen* 1-11. G. von Rad has pointed out how the narratives of the fall, Cain and Abel, the "sons of God," the flood and Babel each exhibit a movement from (a) human sin to (b) divine punishment to (c) divine forgiveness or mitigation:

> God reacts to these outbreaks of human sin with severe judgments . . . [Yet] the Yahwistic narrator shows something else along with the consequences of divine judgment. . . . Each time, in and after the judgment, God's preserving, forgiving will to save is revealed.[17]

Although von Rad does not state the theme in quite this fashion, he obviously understands the theme of these narratives to be: whenever man sins, God's response is just, yet gracious; he punishes, yet he forgives. Since these are narratives about the human condition, and not about historical actuality, the theme is an affirmation about the character of God's relationship with mankind.

At this point two questions arise: (i) Can the narrative pattern exemplified in these narratives be differently, or better, analyzed? and (ii) Are the *narratives* of *Gen* 1-11 an adequate basis for establishing the theme of **Gen** 1-11 as a whole?

To (i) we can reply, first, that Claus Westermann's analysis of the narrative pattern[18] brings to light another significant element. He observes that there always intervenes between the act of sin and the act of punishment a divine *speech* announcing or deciding the penalty. Accordingly he draws up the following table:

	I.	II.	III.
	Sin	*Speech*	*Punishment*
1. Fall	3:6	3:14-19	3:22-24
2. Cain	4:8b	4:11-12	4:16b
3. Sons of God	6:1-2	6:3	—
4. Flood	6:5-7	6:5-7	7:6-24
5. Babel	11:4	11:6-7	11:8-9
6. (Canaan)	9:22	9:24-25	—

Westermann very properly sees a theological significance in this recurrent element of the divine speech. It means, he says, first that God's acts of judgment are always related to a particular sin and so are the very opposite of arbitrary; secondly that there is but one God, who is responsible for woe and weal alike; and thirdly that it is the character of that God to be a judge and to hold himself responsible for detecting and punishing human sin.

But, secondly, we observe that Westermann does not include within his analysis the important element of mitigation, to which von Rad has drawn attention. And neither Westermann nor von Rad has noted that this element of mitigation or grace occupies a significant place in the pattern of these narratives: it is always to be found after the speech of punishment and before the act of punishment. That is to say, God's grace or "forgiving will to save" is not only revealed "in and after the judgment," as von Rad says,[19] but even *before* the execution of judgment. The structure of the narratives may then be exposed thus:

	I.	II.	III.	IV.
	Sin	*Speech*	*Mitigation*	*Punishment*
1. Fall	3:6	3:14-19	3:21	3:22-24
2. Cain	4:8	4:11-12	4:15	4:16
3. Sons of God	6:2	6:3	?6:8, 18ff.	?7:6-24
4. Flood	6:5,11f.	6:7,13-21	6:8,18ff.	7:6-24
5. Babel	11:4	11:6f.	?10:1-32	11:8

To observe that all the narratives of the primeval history conform to a pattern does not destroy the individuality of the narratives, but rather highlights it. Some significant differences exist among the various exemplifications of the overall pattern. In nos. 1 and 2 it is individuals who sin and are punished, in 3-5 it is communities. 1 and 2 contain the element of God's investigation of the crime, while in 3-5 the sins are public and in 3 and 5 God only needs to "see" the crime (6:5, 12; 11:5). In 1 and 2 the same persons sin, are punished, and are partly relieved of the severity of their punishment. In 3 more than those who have sinned are punished, and it is uncertain whether there is any mitigation.[20] In 4 the vast majority of those who have sinned are punished and the mitigation operates only for one man and his family;[21] in 5 all those who have sinned are punished, and there is no direct mitigation. These variations are not insignificant. Where God's relationship with individuals is concerned, his dealing can be highly personalized (note especially the differing punishments for the three protagonists of the fall story). But where a whole community's relationship with God is involved, the operation of justice in punishment can sometimes be undifferentiated, as in the sons of God episode, where all mankind's lifespan (or, the period before the flood) is shortened because of the sins of the sons of God and the daughters of men, but sometimes differentiated, as in the flood story, where Noah escapes. In each case, however, except perhaps for the last, there is an outworking of the basic pattern of sin—speech—mitigation—punishment. Can this pattern, then, form the basis for a statement of the theme of **Gen** 1-11?

That brings us to our question (ii): can the narratives alone form an adequate basis for establishing the theme of **Gen** 1-11 as a whole? It is indeed correct that the theme of a narrative work often emerges from a consideration of its plot or narrative pattern, or, as could in principle be the case here, from a narrative pattern repeated in every episode of the narrative. But can the plot of the narratives of **Gen** 1-11 account for the presence of the creation account (**Gen** 1), the genealogies (4:17-26; 5; 11:10-26), and the table of nations (10)? I think not. If "theme" is a statement of the content, structure and development of a work, as I have suggested above, the "sin—speech—mitigation—punishment" pattern, significant though it is, can only be called a recurrent motif in the primeval history, and not the unifying theme of **Gen** 1-11 as a whole. G. von Rad himself, we should note, spoke only of the "*Yahwistic* Primeval History" when developing his "sin—punishment—mitigation" schema. Although he regarded the Yahwistic scheme as the foundation of the final canonical shape of *Gen* 1-11, he did not directly express his understanding of the significance of *Gen* 1-11 in its final form, and so falls short of his own excellent goal of understanding the work "as a whole with a consistent train of thought."[22]

2. A SPREAD-OF-SIN, SPREAD-OF-GRACE THEME

a. *Statement.* Another element in G. von Rad's understanding of the theme of *Gen* 1-11, which I have left aside hitherto for the sake of our analysis of themes, is the theme of the "spread of sin," to which corresponds increasingly severe punishment, and a spread of "grace" on God's part.[23] That is: (i) From Eden to Babel by way of the sins of Cain, Lamech, the "sons of God," and the generation of the flood, there is an evergrowing "avalanche" of sin, a "continually widening chasm between man and God." There is a movement from disobedience to murder, to reckless killing, to titanic lust, to total corruption and violence, to the full disruption of humanity. (ii) God responds to the extension of human sin with increasingly severe punishment; from expulsion from the garden to expulsion from the tillable earth, to the limitation of human life, to the near annihilation of mankind, to the "dissolution of mankind's unity." (iii) Nevertheless, these are also stories of divine grace: God not only punishes Adam and Eve, but also withholds the threatened penalty of death; he not only drives out Cain, but also puts his mark of protection upon him; not only sends the flood, but saves the human race alive in preserving Noah and his family. Only in the case of the Babel narrative does it appear that the element of "grace" is lacking—a subject to which we shall return in section III below.

b. *Development.* Such a statement of the theme of *Gen* 1-11 is initially open to the same objection as was raised above: it speaks only to the *narratives* of these chapters. However in the case of this theme there is the possibility that it can be extended to parts of *Gen* 1-11 outside the main narratives, i.e., that it can account for the content, development and shape of the material as a whole.

(i) *The creation account* (*Gen* 1). The connection of this chapter with the spread of sin theme becomes clear if we accept the perspective of D. Kidner: he sees *Gen* 1-11 as describing "two opposite progressions: first, God's orderly creation, to its climax in man as a responsible and blessed being, and then the disintegrating work of sin, to its first great anticlimax in the corrupt world of the Flood, and its second in the folly of Babel."[24] That is, the theme of the spread of sin is only the negative aspect of the overall theme—which remains yet to be defined. We may take this insight further and observe that the pattern according to which creation proceeds in chap. 1 is in fact the positive aspect of the sin-judgment motif: here it is a matter of obedience followed by blessing, not sin followed by curse. So, for example, light comes into being in prompt obedience to the word of God (1:3), whereupon the divine judgment is pronounced: God saw that it was good. The chapter as a whole moves towards "blessing," first upon the living

creatures (1:22), then upon man (1:28), and finally upon the seventh day (2:3). *Gen* 1 is thus the positive counterpart to the remainder of the primeval history (though the remainder is not unrelieved gloom).

(ii) *The genealogies* (*Gen* 4:17-26;5; 11:10-26). Since the kind of theme appropriate to *Gen* 1-11 is obviously theological, we may wonder whether the genealogies can in any way be integrated with the overall theme of these chapters. The genealogies have indeed not usually been thought to serve some theological function, but have often been regarded simply as ancient material reproduced here only because of the chronological relationship of their contents to the narratives of *Gen* 1-11.[25] Yet there are some clues in the narrative sections of *Gen* 1-11 which point to the validity of a theological interpretation of the genealogies; that is, to the likelihood that the final author of the primeval history intended them to express some theological purpose.

The first clue lies in some statements about the multiplication of the race. In 1:28 the procreation of the human race stands under divine command and blessing: "And God blessed them, and God said unto them, Be fruitful and multiply, and fill the earth." To the same effect are the statements by Eve at the birth of Cain and Seth: "I have gained (or, created) a man with the help of Yahweh" (4:1),[26] and "God has appointed for me another child" (4:25). Just as the birth of Eve's children is a token of the divine aid, so the whole growth of the human family witnessed by these genealogies is to be viewed under the sign of the divine blessing.[27]

The second clue to the theological significance of the genealogies is provided by their form. No reader of *Gen* 5, to take one example, fails to be impressed by the recurrent phrase "And he died," which baldly and emphatically concludes the entry for each of these antediluvians. The whole movement of the regular form of these notices is toward death. The form is:

1. When A lived x years, he begat B.
2. A lived after the birth of B y years, and had other sons and daughters.
3. All the days of A were z $(x + y)$ years.
4. And he died.

Items 3 and 4 are logically unnecessary. They add nothing to the information given in items 1 and 2. Their function is to emphasize a finality about each of these lives; though possessed of an excess of vitality by ordinary human standards,[28] these men also die. The thrust of the *Gen* 5 genealogy is toward death, even though human life continues.

A further hint of progression toward death may be given by the diminishing life-spans attributed to the personages of the primeval history. While the antediluvians usually live 800 or 900 years,[29] the generations after the flood live ever shorter lives, from 600 years for Shem (11:10) to 205 for Terah (11:32).[30] This decline may perhaps be seen as a deterioration of man's "original wonderful vitality, a deterioration corresponding to his increasing distance from his starting point at creation . . . thus *Gen* 5 describes something like a 'transitional period, during which death caused by sin broke the powerful resistance of primitive human nature.'"[31]

As for the genealogical material of chap. 4, its function within the primeval history becomes clearly visible when it is viewed from the perspective of the spread of sin theme. The Cainite genealogy of 4:17-24 has the same dialectic significance as the Sethite genealogy of chap. 5.[32] In chap. 4, while the genealogy appears on the surface to be a list of the founders of the arts of civilization (the city, cattle-breeding, music, metal-working),[33] and was perhaps originally transmitted as such, it is made clear by the point to which the progress of civilization reaches, namely Lamech's tyrannous boast (4:23f.), that this has been a progress in sin as much as in civilization.[34] In the seven generations of the line of Cain history has seen a "progress" from an impulsive act of murder to a deliberate reign of terror. But, by affixing the beginning of a Sethite genealogy (4:25f.) to the cainite list, the author of *Gen* 4 has affirmed that the world of men is not totally given over to the cainite life-style. Even while the race of Cain is increasing in congenital violence, he means to say, elsewhere there is a line of men who have begun to "call on the name of Yahweh" (4:26).

Thus, whatever may have been the origin of the genealogies or their original function, the present form of *Gen* 1-11 permits us to interpret them as displaying a theological purpose analogous to that outlined by von Rad for the narratives. Here also in the genealogies there is in the monotonous reiteration of the fact of death, which increasingly encroaches upon life, a pessimistic note which corresponds to the narrative theme of the continuing spread of sin. But as in the narratives, history is not simply a matter of sin and punishment; where sin abounds, grace much more abounds. Even though the divine grace is experienced not in dramatic acts of deliverance, as it is in the narratives, but in the steady silent expansion of human life, it is the divine grace all the same. To the grace that appoints for Eve another child to take the place of the dead Abel is owed also the furtherance of mankind's growth throughout the genealogy of *Gen* 5; and to the grace that preserves the human race through the dramatic rescue of Noah and his family from the flood is due also the repeopling of the earth after the flood (*Gen* 10).

(iii) *The Table of Nations* (*Gen* 10). It is a remarkable feature of the structure of the primeval history that the Table of Nations (chap. 10) is located not after the story of the tower of Babel (11:1-9) but before it. Since chap. 10 recounts the "spreading" (*pārad*, vv 5,32) or "scattering" (*pûs*, v 18) of men, "each with his own language" (v 5, cf. vv 20,31), it would seem more logically placed after 11:1-9 where the "scattering" (*pûs*) of men "over the face of all the earth" and the division of languages is narrated.

A thematic explanation for this dischronologization is ready to hand in the "spread of sin, spread of grace" theme

as we have been developing it. If the material of chap. 10 had followed the Babel story, the whole Table of Nations would have to be read under the sign of judgment; where it stands it fancations as the fulfillment of the divine command of 9:1 "Be fruitful and multiply, and fill the earth," which looks back in its turn to 1:28. All this means that the final author of the primeval history understands that the dispersal of the nations may be evaluated both positively (as in chap. 10) and negatively (as in chap. 11). Since Babel, mankind stands under both the blessing and the curse of God; the division of the peoples and their languages is both a token of the divine judgment and a natural concomitant of man's fulfillment of the divine command and so part of the divine "blessing" (9:1). With this ambivalence in the relationship of God with man the primeval history comes to a conclusion. The final author or redactor of the primeval history has, by the sequence in which he has arranged his materials on the dispersal of mankind, made the same theological point as have the narratives and genealogies in the preceding chapters: that though the judgment of God rests upon men as sinful, they experience not only his judgment but also his grace.

c. *Criticism.* So far the statement of the "spread of sin" theme with which this section began has proved productive of insight into material which von Rad did not himself connect with the theme. But next we should consider whether there are any difficulties in regarding the "spread of sin" as the unifying theme of these chapters.[35]

(i) While it is readily granted that a "spread" of sin and an intensification of punishment from Adam to Cain and from Cain to the generation of the flood is clear, it may well be asked whether any such extension or intensification can be discerned when the flood and the Babel narratives are compared. Can the theme of *Gen* 1-11 properly be said to be the increasing spread of sin when the last exemplification of the theme, the Babel story, depicts neither a sin so drastic as that which brings on the flood nor a punishment so severe and universal as the flood?[36]

This issue will depend to some extent on how precisely the sins of *Gen* 6:1-4 and 11:1-9 are understood. It is possible, for example, to interpret the sin of the "sons of God" in 6:1-4 not, as is commonly thought, as the unnatural mixing of the divine and the human, but as a sin of violence on the purely human plane.[37] Then, if the sin of the "sons of God," which is partly if not wholly the cause for the flood, is perhaps not so fundamental as some interpreters have claimed, the sin of the tower builders may not be so trivial as at first sight appears. Their sin may be seen not as a mere expression of human self-importance and self-reliance, but as an act of *hybris,* matched in its defiance of God only by the first sin in the garden; like the eating of the forbidden fruit the tower-building may be an assault on heaven, an attempt at self-divinization.[38] Such an interpretation is confirmed by the fact that, so understood, the primeval history would exhibit the common literary technique of *inclusio,* with the final episode in the story of human sin repeating and balancing the first.

But if the sin of the generation of the flood is not necessarily more heinous than that of the tower-builders, is the scattering of mankind a more severe punishment than the flood? It may be replied that in two ways at least the scattering is more drastic than the flood. First, the flood left no permanent mark on humanity; though the generation of the flood was destroyed, mankind was preserved, and continued to grow. The scattering of mankind is, however, of lasting effect. There are no survivors of Babel. Secondly, what is destroyed at Babel is the community of mankind as a family; hitherto, as the genealogies have witnessed, mankind is one family, and the flood has only accentuated that fact by making one family in the narrowest sense of the word co-terminous with humanity. But the punishment of Babel divides men irrevocably from one another (as did also the first sin in its own way); now mankind is no longer one "people" or "kin-group" (*'am,* 11:6), but "nations" (10:32).

In sum, this criticism of a theme of spread of sin from the fall to Babel can be met by a more exact interpretation of the significance of the flood and Babel narratives.

(ii) Another criticism of the spread of sin theme from Eden to Babel arises from the opinion that it is *Gen* 8:21 (at the close of the Yahwistic flood narrative) and not the Babel story that brings the primeval history to a close. In his influential study,[39] Rolf Rendtorff claims that this verse should be translated: "I will no longer curse the earth," or "I will no longer regard the earth as cursed, and treat it as such." It is not that God will not *again* curse the earth, but that at 8:21 the period of the curse uttered by God in 3:17, "Cursed is the ground because of you," is concluded. "From now on it is no longer curse that rules the world, but blessing. The time of the curse is at an end, the time of blessing has arrived."[40] Some who have followed Rendtorff's view have expressed the contrast rather less starkly. Thus W. M. Clark says, "The power of that initial curse to work disruption is limited,"[41] and T. E. Fretheim writes: "The idea of blessing . . . is here introduced for the first time (v.22). Since the beginning of man's sin the curse has been predominant in the created order of things, leading to the catastrophe of the Flood. This will not continue to be the case. Now blessing stands alongside of the curse and begins to have its beneficial effects on the earth, breaking down the effects of the curse (3:17). This is made concretely evident for the first time in the following story (in J) of Noah and his vineyard."[42] If this view is correct, there is of course no point in seeking for a theme of *Gen* 1-11, since those chapters do not form a literary unit.

The view of Rendtorff and his followers, however, does not appear to me to be well-founded in its central contention.[43] The curse that will not again come upon the ground (8:21) is not the curse of 3:17. There the curse upon the ground is that it will bring forth thorns and thistles; and that curse is not said in 8:21 to be lifted, nor is it easy to see how the Yahwist, or any author, could have claimed from his own experience that it had been lifted. In 8:21

the curse has been the smiting of the earth with a flood. It is true, as Rendtorff points out,[44] that the introduction to the flood story does not specifically view the flood as a "curse," but that is not a very strong counter-argument to the plain structure of 8:21. Here the clause "I will not again curse the earth" seems clearly parallel to "I will not again smite all living beings,"[45] as God has done by means of the flood. There is indeed a verbal connection between 3:17 and 8:21 ("Cursed is the ground because of *[ba'ǎbûr]* thee" and "I will not curse the ground because of *[ba'ǎbûr]* man"), but the content of the two passages is different, and we are dealing simply with the repetition of a verbal motif which takes on new light in different settings.[46]

A further weakness in the view that 8:21 ends the period of the curse lies in its interpretation of the narrative of Noah's vineyard (9:20-27). According to W. M. Clark, that narrative "does not convey the idea that wine relieves the toil of mankind, but rather is a verification that the curse has been lifted off the ground which can henceforth produce vineyards, a symbol of fertility."[47] But this is to misunderstand the clear connection between the vineyard story and the birth-oracle of Noah in 5:29: "Out of the ground which Yahweh has cursed this one [Noah] shall bring us relief from our work and from the toil of our hands"; that is, the "relief out of the ground" is the discovery of the cultivation of the vine and the making of wine.[48] The curse is not lifted from the ground, but even the cursed ground can produce some comfort and enjoyment for man. The pattern of punishment relieved by divine grace is visible here too, though it is not as explicitly spelled out as it is in some of the longer narratives.

It may finally be objected to the view of Rendtorff, especially as developed by Clark, that the remainder of J's post-flood primeval history cannot be satisfactorily interpreted as belonging to an age of blessing rather than of curse. What immediately follows the story of Noah's drunkenness is not blessing but curse—the curse of Canaan (9:25ff.). And even though there is contained in this curse a blessing on Shem and Japheth, the first explicit blessing in J, as Clark says (though not the first in the primeval history as it now stands; cf. 1:22, 28; 2:3; 5:2; 9:1), the structure of vv 25ff., which begin with "Cursed be Canaan," and in which each blessing is followed with "And let Canaan be his slave," shows that attention is focused on Canaan and the curse rather than the blessing. Furthermore, it is difficult to see how Clark can interpret the vineyard and Babel narratives as a "recapitulation of the events prior to the flood . . . a story of sin on the individual level followed by a story in which sin threatens to reach cosmic dimensions again" without understanding them as developing a "spread of sin" theme, which is hardly appropriate for the age of blessing.[49]

It seems incorrect, therefore, to regard *Gen* 8:22 as marking the major turning-point in the Yahwist's primeval history; the "spread of sin" both includes the flood and extends beyond it.

(iii) A quite different suggestion which would cast doubt on the "spread of sin" as the unifying theme of *Gen* 1-11 is that of W. Brueggemann in his study, "David and His Theologian."[50] He argues that the sequence of episodes in the J material of *Gen* 1-11 is "dependent upon the career of the sons of David in the quest for the throne."[51] The four stories of sin in *Gen* 3-11 (Adam and Eve; Cain and Abel; Noah and the Flood; the Tower of Babel) correspond to the four major episodes of the Succession Narrative (David and Bathsheba; Amnon and Absalom; Absalom and David; Solomon and David). *Prima facie*, if this is so, the structure of *Gen* 1-11 is essentially (at least as far as the J material is concerned) shaped by the course of history and not by a conceptual theme such as "the spread of sin."

Brueggemann is indeed able to point to many striking correspondences of language and motif between the primeval history and the Succession Narrative. But two considerations make his view rather unlikely, in my judgment:[52] (i) The correspondence between Absalom's rebellion and the flood story is not very strong,[53] as Brueggemann himself candidly acknowledges;[54] and one major disruption of the pattern spoils the argument about sequence, which is crucial to the present discussion. Even if some narratives in *Gen* 1-11 are reflections of the Davidic history, the sequence of those narratives is not clearly dependent upon it. (ii) Striking parallels of motif and language can also be traced between the Succession Narrative and other sections of J,[55] and a special relationship with *Gen* 1-11 cannot be claimed.[56]

Furthermore, even if there is a sequential correspondence between the two works, there is no clear evidence that the Davidic narrative is prior to the primeval history, nor that the telling of the David story has not been influenced—in its selection of episodes and in its language—by the primeval history.[57] It is unnecessary, therefore, to regard Brueggemann's view, stimulating though it is, as an obstacle to uncovering a conceptual link between the narratives of *Gen* 1-11, namely the "spread of sin" theme.

To summarize to this point: The theme of the spread of sin accounts for the vast majority of the content of *Gen* 1-11. It is visible, not just in the narratives, but also in other literary types in these chapters. It is more than probable that, even if this suggested theme alone does not adequately express the thrust of *Gen* 1-11, its pervasiveness ensures that it will have to be taken into account in any statement of theme in the primeval history.

3. A CREATION—UNCREATION—RE-CREATION THEME

We have already noted that the flood episode has given rise to some criticisms of the "spread of sin" theme. While those criticisms can be met, the fact remains that the flood narrative does not function simply as yet a further stage in the development of human sin, but imports concepts of "end" and "re-creation" into the primeval history.[58] When chap. 1 is also taken into consideration, some case can be made out for suggesting that the theme of the primeval history is "creation—uncreation—re-creation."

It is very plain that the flood is represented not just as a punishment for the sin of the generation of the flood, but as a reversal of creation—"uncreation," as Joseph Blenkinsopp has put it: "The world in which order first arose out of a primeval watery chaos is now reduced to the watery chaos out of which it arose—chaos-come-again."[59] While *Gen* 1 depicts creation as largely a matter of separation and distinction, *Gen* 6f. portrays the annihilation of distinctions. If in *Gen* 1:6ff. a firmament is established to keep the heavenly waters from falling upon the earth except in properly regulated measure, 7:11 has the "windows of heaven" opening to obliterate this primal distinction. Similarly, the distinction between the lower waters and the earth in 1:9 is done away with by the breaking forth through the earth of the "fountains of the great deep" (7:11). The binary nature of created existence gives way to the formlessness of the *tōhû wābōhû* before creation. And significantly, the destruction follows much the same sequence as the creation: earth, birds, cattle, wild animals, swarming creatures, man (7:21).

Re-creation occurs, in the first place, by the renewed separation of sea and land: the waters recede from and dry up from the earth (8:3, 7, 13). Then comes the renewal of the divine order to living beings to "breed, be fruitful, and multiply" (8:17). There follows God's guarantee of the binary structure of existence: seedtime and harvest, cold and heat, summer and winter, day and night are re-established (8:22). Finally, the creation ordinances are re-announced, albeit in somewhat altered form (9:1-7),[60] the separation of sea and land—a fundamental element in the creative process (1:9ff.)—is assured (9:8-17), and mankind begins to be re-created (by procreation, chap. 10), and to fill the earth at God's command (10:32).[61]

As for the intervening material of *Gen* 1-11 between creation and flood, when it is viewed from the perspective of the theme "creation—uncreation—re-creation" new understandings emerge. Chief among them is the recognition that chaps. 3-6 are not simply the story of human sin matched by divine grace, but the story of the undoing of creation. The flood is only the final stage in a process of cosmic disintegration which began in Eden. While chap. 1 views reality as an ordered pattern which is confused by the flood, chaps. 2-3 sees reality as a network of elemental unions which become disintegrated throughout the course of the narrative from Eden to the flood.

Thus, in *Gen* 2, as in *Gen* 1, reality has a binary structure; but here creation has not proceeded by distinction and separation, but by the forging of bonds: between man and soil, man and the animals, man and woman, man and God. In ch. 3 the relationship of harmony between each of these parts is disrupted. The communion between God and the man who breathes God's breath (2:7) has become the legal relationship of accuser and defendant (3:9ff.); the relationship of man and woman as "one flesh" (2:24) has soured into mutual recrimination (3:12); and the bond of man *ădām*) with the soil (*'ădāmâ*) from which he was built has been supplanted by "an alienation that expresses itself in a silent, dogged struggle between man and soil"[62] (3:17ff.); the harmonious relationship of man with beast in which man is the acknowledged master (2:19ff.) has become a perpetual struggle of intransigent foes (3:15). In *Gen* 4 another union, of twin (?)[63] brothers, which might have been expected to be paradigmatic of human friendship,[64] is broken by the ultimate act of enmity, murder. Cain is further alienated from the soil, by being driven out from the tillable earth (4:11), and the bond between man and the soil is further loosened. The disintegration of the most intimate bond of all—of man with the divine breath (2:7)—first sets in with the murders by Cain and Lamech (4:8, 23), broadens its scope with the successive deaths of each descendant of Adam in the genealogy of chap. 5, and reaches its climax with the simultaneous death of all mankind in chap. 7, The destruction of mankind is significantly expressed in language reminiscent of creation: Yahweh determines that he will "blot out man whom I have created" (6:7), whereupon "all in whose nostrils was the breath of the spirit of life" *(nišmat - rûah hayyîm)*" died (7:22), an echo of Yahweh Elohim's breathing into man's nostrils the "breath of life *(nišmat hayyîm)*" (2:7). With this, the creation of man is undone.

The movement towards uncreation viewed as the dissolution of unities begins again directly after the flood. Ham's incest with his mother—if that is the significance of 9:20-27[65]—strikes at the bond between man and wife (2:23f.), and the scattering of mankind after the building of Babel (11:9) is a potent symbol of the disintegration of mankind's unity. Man's tendency has not been changed by the flood: the "imagination of man's heart is evil from his youth" (8:21) as much after the flood as before it.

There can be little doubt that the theme "creation—uncreation—re-creation" is firmly fixed in *Gen* 1-11, and needs to be taken into account in our general statement of the theme of the work.

III. A Statement of Theme

There seem to be two ways in which the insights about theme gained from considering the foregoing suggestions can be incorporated into a general statement of the theme of *Gen* 1-11. The theme of these chapters may be said to be, either:

(a) Mankind tends to destroy what God has made good. Even when God forgives human sin and mitigates the punishment sin continues to spread, to the point where the world suffers uncreation. And even when God makes a fresh start, turning his back on uncreation forever, man's tendency to sin immediately becomes manifest. Or:

(b) No matter how drastic man's sin becomes, destroying what God has made good and bringing the world to the brink of uncreation, God's grace never fails to deliver man from the consequences of his sin. Even when man responds to a fresh start with the old pattern of sin, God's commitment to his world stands firm, and sinful man experiences the favor of God as well as his righteous judgment.[66]

Each of these readings does justice, I hope, to the perspectives of our foregoing discussion. But their thrust is in quite opposite directions. How can we decide between these statements?

At this point two issues that have been ignored up to this point have to be brought into the discussion: (i) What is the precise terminus of the primeval history? and (ii) What is the relationship of the theme of *Gen* 1-11 to the theme of the Pentateuch?

(i) Although we have been able to speak previously rather loosely of "*Gen* 1-11," here the exact terminus of this literary unit becomes critical. If it concludes with the last narrative of these chapters (11:1-9), some color is lent to von Rad's claim (rather strongly expressed) that the absence of the mitigation element in the Babel story means that "the whole primeval history . . . seems to break off in strict dissonance" and that the question arises: "Is God's gracious forebearance now exhausted; has God rejected the nations in wrath forever?"[67] A sharp disjunction can then be made between universal history (*Gen* 1-11) and "salvation history" (*Gen* 12 onward), with the themes of the two units being set in contrast: universal history leads only to judgment, whereas the narrowing of vision to Abraham opens the way for an era of blessing, that is, for salvation history. Our statement (a) of the theme of the primeval history would thus appear to be appropriate.

However, it is most significant that there is no clear-cut break at the end of the Babel story. Clearly the Abraham material begins a new section of the Pentateuch, but the precise beginning of the Abraham material—and therewith the conclusion of the pre-Abrahamic material—cannot be determined.[68] In the final form of *Genesis* there is at no point a break between primeval and patriarchal history—11:10 (descendants of Shem) resumes from 10:21-31 (family of Shem) and is directed toward 11:27-30 (Abram and Sarai). Where there is a developed transitional passage from the one unit to the other, the probability of their being set in opposition thematically is minimized. If the patriarchal history unfolds the fulfillment of the blessing promise (12:2f.), the more positive reading of the theme of the primeval history [statement (b) above], with which it is integrated, is to be preferred. The patriarchal narratives then function as the "mitigation" element for the story of mankind's dissolution at Babel.[69]

(ii) If we broaden our focus beyond *Genesis,* and consider the function of the primeval history within the Pentateuch as a whole, again I would suggest that the theme of *Gen* 1-11, as expressed in statement (b) above, is closely parallel to the theme of the Pentateuch. Broadly speaking, the theme of the Pentateuch may be said to be: in spite of Israel's propensity to sinfulness, it experiences not only God's judgment but also his determination to save. Thus despite the patriarchs' deceitfulness and faithlessness, for which they suffer danger and exile, the promise of progeny is fulfilled, and despite Israel's rebellions, for which they suffer a generation's delay in entering the land and the

Engraving depicting Cain fleeing from an angry God who has witnessed the murder of Abel (Genesis IV: verse 10).

death of their leader, they stand, at the end of the Pentateuch, on the brink of the fulfillment of the promise. That can only be a provisional, and doubtless over-ambitious, attempt to formulate the theme of this vast work, but in so far as it is an appropriate formulation it corresponds well to our reading of the theme of its initial eleven chapters. *Gen* 1-11, therefore, works out on the plane of universal history the same theme that is developed in the Pentateuch as a whole.

It may finally be as well to make some remarks about what has and what has not been achieved by attempting to state the theme of *Gen* 1-11. The reader may well wonder whether the seemingly banal, or at least rather unexciting, conclusion to which our quest for theme has led us has been worth the journey. Yet the very banality of statements of "themes," of whatever literary work, is evident proof of what they are not: they are not themselves literature, and they are not in any sense substitutes for the work itself. While they may point to the essential message of the work, they do not make the work a disposable packaging to be thrown away once the theme or the point has been extracted. At best their function is to orient the reader to

the work, or at least to one critic's reading of the work; at most they serve to guide the reader away from possible misconceptions about the work; and one of their greatest values is when they convince the reader—as hopefully may happen in the present case—that the work *is* a literary work, and not a rag-bag or a scissors-and-paste job. In the end the quest for theme is only really successful if it returns the reader to the text.

IV. HISTORICAL SETTING AND LITERARY HISTORY

Up to this point our quest for theme in *Gen* 1-11 has been pursued entirely within the boundaries of the text itself in its final form. No consideration has been given to the historical setting of the work or to its literary pre-history. This procedure does not imply any objection in principle to the relevance of such considerations, even although there are some literary critics who assert that a literary work is autonomous and must be understood independently of the circumstances of its origin.[70] Rather, since in the case of the Pentateuch we have little hard evidence concerning its historical and literary origins, we do better, I think, to rest the weight of our study largely upon what we do have—the work itself—however subjective our understanding of it has to be, than upon hypotheses, however much they deal with "objective" data like dates and sources.

Nevertheless, if our reasoned intuitions about the theme of the work fit with current hypotheses about Pentateuchal origins, well and good; that may provide some confirmation of our proposal about theme. Ultimately, of course, our proposal about theme stands or falls with its applicability to the work itself.

I assume, following K. Elliger,[71] W. Brueggemann,[72] and others,[73] that the Priestly work belongs to the period of the exile as a message to the exiled, and I would argue further, that the Pentateuch as a whole relates to the same situation. It would not, however, affect the argument significantly if the more common date for the Pentateuch—the fifth century—were adopted, and the work were interpreted as addressed to diaspora Jewry before the time of Ezra.

Most significantly, the Pentateuch concludes with Israel outside the promised land, but on the brink of entry under a new leader. This is exilic Israel's situation before the return. *Genesis* through Numbers incorporates Israel's canonical traditions of God's relationship with Israel, while Deuteronomy, a farewell discourse in the mouth of Moses, relates those traditions to Israel's present existence by declaring Israel, even on the eve of fulfillment, to be still open to the possibility of curse as well as of blessing.

Read from this point of view, *Gen* 1-11 also takes on new light. The primeval history is not just about the nations, nor about God and man, but is heard in exile as a story of God and Israel. The dispersion of the nations (chap. 11) is Israel's own diaspora, the flood is the uncreation of Israel's life at the destruction of Jerusalem, the judgments of God upon primal sin are his righteous judgments upon sinful Israel. But the movement towards life and salvation which the primeval history evidences is a word of hope to the exiles, a remnant is saved alive through the disaster of uncreation, a divine promise guarantees that such disaster will not recur, and an unbroken line stretches from the moment of dispersion to the summons "Go forth . . . to the land . . . ; I will make of you a great nation" (12:1f.). Although sin is congenital even in a re-created Israel, God's commitment to Israel stands as firm as the promise to Noah (so also Isa 54:9f.). Thus the traditional material of *Gen* 1-11 not only is bound together by a unifying theme, and not only realizes *in parvo* the theme of the Pentateuch, but also speaks to a historical situation.

Our historical-critical inclinations compel us to ask one more question: *Whose* is the theme of *Gen* 1-11? Clearly it is the final redactor who has worked out the theme we have attempted to discern, but he has been using traditional materials. Assuming the essential correctness of the usual analysis of J and P in *Gen* 1-11, the theme-element "Creation—uncreation—re-creation" comes from the P source (*Gen* 1;6-8 [*partim*]; 9), though the sequence

creation—flood—re-creation is as old at least as the Atrahasis epic.[74] P does not depict in narrative episodes the human movement towards uncreation; for him it suffices to observe: "The earth was corrupt in God's sight . . . and God saw the earth, and behold it was corrupt, for all flesh had corrupted their way upon the earth" (6:11f.). For P, of course, the genealogy of chap. 5 does not signify the encroachment of death upon life; to him death is a natural part of life, not the result of sin. Only when his genealogy follows the Yahwist's account of the origin of death (2:17; 3:19) does it take on that significance. From the Yahwist, we may be sure, comes the theme-element of the "spread of sin." The narratives of the primeval history are his,[75] and so especially is their sequence. Particularly if both *Gen* 3 and the Cain and Abel story were previously told as tales of the *first* sin, and were first linked by him, his ordering of the narratives will have been in conformity with the theme of his work: the spread of sin cannot defeat, or, has not defeated, the purposes and blessing of God.[76] I take it that the narratives of the Yahwist's primeval history are older than his work. The fact that they have in common a narrative pattern, the "sin—speech—mitigation—punishment" pattern discussed earlier, is not surprising; this may well be a narrative patterning from oral tradition.

The theme of *Gen* 1-11, then, from the point of view of the history of tradition, is an amalgam of which the main elements correspond to the layers of the tradition. The amalgam, however, is a new unity, which makes sense and has a meaning independent of the meanings of its sources as they may be uncovered by literary archeology.

Notes

1. So, e.g., D. B. Redford, *A Study of the Biblical Story of Joseph (Genesis 37-50)* (VTSup 20; Leiden: Brill, 1970); R. N. Whybray, "The Joseph Story and Pentateuchal Criticism," *VT* 18 (1968) 521-8; S. Sandmel, "The Haggada within Scripture" *JBL* 80 (1961) 105-22; M. Kessler, "Rhetorical Criticism of *Genesis* 7," in *Rhetorical Criticism. Essays in Honor of James Muilenburg* (ed. J. J. Jackson and M. Kessler; Pittsburgh: Pickwick, 1974) 1-17 (16f.).

2. So some time ago H. H. Rowley, *The Changing Pattern of Old Testament Studies* (London: Epworth, 1959) 12: "If a more satisfactory view can be found, I will eagerly accept it"; similarly more recently W. Richter, "Urgeschichte und Hoftheologie," *BZ* 10 (1966) 96-105 (96).

3. H. W. Wolff, *Int* 20 (1966) 131-158, originally published in *EvT* 24 (1964) 73-97.

4. P. F. Ellis, *The Yahwist. The Bible's First Theologian* (London: Chapman, 1969).

5. H. W. Wolff, *Int* 26 (1972) 158-173, originally published in *EvT* 27 (1969) 59-72.

6. W. Brueggemann, *ZAW* 84 (1972) 397-414.

7. On such terms of reference, see J. F. A. Sawyer, "The Meaning of . . . ('In the Image of God') in *Genesis* I-XI," *JTS* 25 (1974) 418-26 (418f.), and

for a similar undertaking see M. Fishbane, "Composition and Structure in the Jacob Cycle (*Gen* 25:19-35: 22)," *JJS* 26 (1975) 15-38.

8. G. von Rad, *Genesis* (rev.ed.; Philadelphia: Westminster, 1972) 75. Von Rad, however, did not follow his own principle when he came to expound *Gen* 6-9, where he dealt with the J and P material separately.

9. R. Scholes and R. Kellogg, *The Nature of Narrative* (New York: Oxford University, 1966) 27, define a *topos* as consisting of a narrative and a conceptual element; e.g., a combination of (narrative) motif of a hero's descent to the netherworld and a (conceptual) "theme" of the search for wisdom.

10. As in W. Arend, *Die typischen Scenen bei Homer* (Berlin Weidmann, 1933); B. Fenik, *Typical Battle Scenes in the Iliad: Studies in the Narrative Techniques of Homeric Battle Description* (Wiesbaden: Steiner, 1968).

11. As the term has been used by my colleague D. M. Gunn, "Narrative Patterns and Oral Tradition in Judges and Samuel," *VT* 24 (1974) 286-317 (see especially 314 n.2).

12. A. B. Lord defined theme as "a recurrent element of narration or description in traditional oral poetry" ("Composition by Theme in Homer and Southslavic Epos," *TAPA* 82 [1951] 71-80 [73]). and elsewhere as "groups of ideas regularly used in telling a tale in the formulaic style of traditional song" (cited from Scholes and Kellogg, *Nature of Narrative* 26).

13. E.g., the theme of expulsion in *Gen* 1-11 (Adam, Cain, the tower-builders).

14. "A plot is . . . a narrative of events, the emphasis falling on causality. 'The king died and then the queen died' is a story. 'The king died, and then the queen died of grief' is a plot. The time sequence [sc. of the story] is preserved, but the sense of causality overshadows it" (E. M. Forster, *Aspects of the Novel* [Harmondsworth: Penguin 1962; originally published, 1927] 93f.).

15. R. and M. Thompson, *Critical Reading and Writing* (New York: Random House, 1969) 15.

16. Cf. the definition of "theme" offered by W. F. Thrall and A. Hibberd, *A Handbook to Literature* (New York: Odyssey, 1960) 486, as "the central or dominating idea in a literary work . . . the abstract concept which is made concrete through its representation in person, action, and image in the work" (cited from D. L. Petersen, "A Thrice-Told Tale: Genre, Theme and Motif," *BR* 18 [1973] 30-43 [36]).

17. Von Rad, *Genesis* (rev. ed.) 152f.

18. C. Westermann, "Arten der Erzählung in der *Genesis*," in *Forschung am Alten Testament* (Munich: Kaiser, 1964) 9-91 (47).

19. Von Rad, *Genesis* (rev.ed.) 153.

20. Westermann, *Forschung* 56, sees a mitigation in the fact that the punishment is *only* a shortening of life; but this view is unlikely since no hint is given in the narrative that the punishment could have been more severe. If the sons of God episode is closely connected with the Flood narrative, the element of mitigation can be seen in the deliverance of Noah.

21. On the question whether Noah is regarded as typical of his generation or as "righteous" only in view of God's deliverance of him, see W. M. Clark, "The Righteousness of Noah," *VT* 21 (1971) 261-80; A. N. Barnard, "Was Noah a Righteous Man?" *Theology* 84 (1971) 311-14.

22. *Genesis* (rev.ed.) 75.

23. *Genesis* (rev.ed.) 152f.; cf. also his *Theology of the Old Testament* (tr. D. M. G. Stalker; Edinburgh: Oliver and Boyd, 1962) I, 154ff. Similarly already H. Gunkel, *Genesis* (6th ed.; Göttingen: Vandenhoeck und Ruprecht, 1964) 1, noting themes of human sin, God's wrath, God's grace; and J. Skinner, *A Critical and Exegetical Commentary on Genesis* (*ICC;* 2d ed.; Edinburgh: T. and T. Clark, 1930) 2, who thought that the units of the primeval history were arranged "with perhaps a certain unity of conception, in so far as they illustrate the increasing wickedness that accompanied the progress of mankind in civilisation."

24. *Genesis* (*Tyndale Old Testament Commentaries;* London: Tyndale Press, 1967) 13.

25. Cf., e.g., M.D. Johnson, *The Purpose of the Biblical Genealogies with special reference to the setting of the genealogies of Jesus* (SNTSMS 8; Cambridge: University Press, 1969) 14, 26ff., who distinguishes between the genealogies of J and P, finding in the genealogies of J no particular purpose beyond showing the "interrelation of a certain number of tribes," but in P certain theological purposes, notably to set the stage for the emergence of the chosen people and to trace the narrowing of the line down to Aaron.

26. On the precise significance of the phrase, see most recently I. M. Kikawada, "Two Notes on Eve," *JBL* 91 (1972) 33-37.

27. So C. Westermann, *Genesis* (BKAT I/1; Neukirchen: Neukirchener Verlag des Erziehungsvereins, 1966) 24.

28. Even in the eschatological age pictured in Isa 65:20, 100 years is the normal span of life.

29. The two exceptions are Enoch (365 years) and Lamech (777 years). It seems undeniable that both these figures have a symbolic significance: the 365 years of Enoch correspond to the number of days of the solar year, Enoch's counterpart (the seventh) in the Sumerian King List being Enmeduranki, king of Sippar, the centre of sun-worship (cf.e.g. E.A. Speiser, *Genesis* [AB; New York: Doubleday, 1964] 43). Lamech's 777 years are presumably to be

related to the "sword-song" of the Lamech of 4:24: "If Cain is avenged sevenfold, truly Lamech seventy-sevenfold."

30. The progressive decline, both for antediluvians and postdiluvians, is most consistent in the Samaritan version, but the text-critical value of this version at this point is dubious. A similar progressive decline is apparently exhibited in a portion of the Sumerian King List relating to the first six kings of Kish (they reign 1200, 900 [variant 960], 670, 420, 300, 240 years, though the parallel with *Genesis* 5 has recently been held to be merely fortuitous (T. C. Hartman, "Some Thoughts on the Sumerian King List and *Genesis* 5 and 11B," *JBL* 91 [1972] 25-32 [30 n. 19]). We might compare also Hesiod's picture of history as a declining succession of metals (*Works and Days* 1.148) as further evidence of an ancient conception of history as a decline.

31. Von Rad, *Genesis* 69f., quoting F. Delitzsch. A Connection with the "tree of life." of chap. 3 as the explanation of the longevity of the patriarchs is however too fanciful.

32. The fact that the two genealogies derive from different sources, according to the usual analysis, is not relevant to our present concern with the final form of the text.

33. We may perhaps compare with the Cainite genealogy the list of the Seven Sages of antediluvian times who appear in Mesopotamian texts to be the founders of the arts of civilization; cf. J. J. Finkelstein, *JCS* 17 (1963) 50 n.41; and E. Reiner, "The Etiological Myth of the Seven Sages," *Or* 30 (1961) 1-11.

34. Cf. T. E. Fretheim, *Creation, Fall and Flood. Studies in Genesis 1-11* (Minneapolis: Augsburg, 1969) 101; and J. L. McKenzie, "Reflections on Wisdom," *JBL* 86 (1967) 1-9 (6): "The culture myths have been woven into a sequence of events in which the progress of culture marches with the growth of human pride and wickedness."

35. I leave aside the criticism of I. Soisalon-Soininen ("Die Urgeschichte im Geschichtswerk des Jahwisten," *Temenos* 6 [1970] 130-41) that there is no need to attribute any theological plan to the Yahwistic primeval history and that his traditional material effectively determined its own position in his narrative (brother-murder must follow creation of primeval pair; flood that almost annihilates mankind must follow genealogy of mankind's multiplication and story of its motivation, the angel-marriages and so on). On one level that may be so; but we are here considering whether the work (of Yahwist or final redactor) has any conceptual theme beyond a merely "logical" development.

36. So R. Rendtorff, "*Genesis* 8:21 und die Urgeschichte des Yahwisten," *KD* 7 (1961) 69-78 (75); W. M. Clark, "The Flood and the Structure of the Pre-Patriarchal History," *ZAW* 83 (1971) 184-211 (206); Fretheim, *Creation, Fall and Flood* 20.

37. That is, that the "sons of God" are dynastic rulers; cf. M. G. Kline, "Divine Kingship and *Genesis* 6:1-4," *Westminster Theological Journal* 24 (1962) 187-204; F. Dexinger, *Sturz der Göttersöhne oder Engel vor der Sintflut?* (Vienna: Herder, 1966). I would want to add that they are *also* (semi-) divine beings, like Gilgamesh, two-thirds god and one-third human (Gilgamesh I ii 1; *ANET* 73 b).

38. "Man's attempt to overstep the bounds of creatureliness" (Fretheim, *Creation, Fall and Flood* 123). On the theme of *hybris,* see P. Humbert, "Démesure et chute dans l'A.T.,"-*maqqél shâqédh. La Branche d'Amandier. Hommage à Wilhelm Vischer* (Montpellier: Graille, Castelnau, 1960) 63-82.

39. See note 36 above.

40. Rendtorff, *KD* 7 (1961) 74.

41. Clark, *ZAW* 83 (1971) 207.

42. Fretheim, *Creation, Fall and Flood* 113.

43. For an independent examination of Rendtorff's view, reaching similar conclusions, see O. H. Steck, "*Genesis* 12:1-3 und die Urgeschichte des Jahwisten," in *Probleme biblischer Theologie Gerhard von Rad zum 70. Geburtstag* (Ed. H. W. Wolff; Munich: Kaiser, 1971) 525-554 (527-542).

44. *KD* 7 (1961) 70.

45. *lo'-'ōsip l^{e}qallēl 'ôd 'et-ha'ādāmâ* parallel to *lo'-'osip 'ôd l^{e}hakkôt 'et-kol-hay.*

46. For a parallel, cf. 3:16 "your desire [the rare word *tušûqâ*] shall be toward your husband, but he will rule *(māšal)* over you," with 4:7 "[sin's] desire *(tešûqâ)* is toward you, but you will rule *(māšal)* over it." There is no connection of substance between the content of these passages. For another parallel, see n. 48 below.

47. Clark, *ZAW* 83 (1971) 208; cf. Rendtorff, *KD* 7 (1961) 74.

48. H. Holzinger, *Genesis (Kurzer Hand-Commentar zum Alten Testament;* Freiburg: J. C. B. Mohr, 1898) 60f.; Gunkel, *Genesis* 55; Skinner, *Genesis* 133f. The observation made by U. Cassuto, *Commentary on Genesis*(Jerusalem: Magnes Press, 1961) I, 303, that the roots of "relief," "work," and "toil" (*nhm, 'śh, 'sb*) in 5:29 occur in the same sequence in 6:6, does not destroy the connection of substance between 5:29 and 9:20. 6:6 provides another example of verbal mimicry to add to those mentioned above (n.46).

49. It may also be objected that the strongly marked element of mitigation in *Gen* 3-8 makes it inappropriate to label this an age of the curse.

50. *CBQ* 30 (1968) 156-81.

51. Ibid., 158.

52. For another critique, see Clark, *ZAW* 83 (1971) 201f.

53. Being confined to motifs of wickedness which is punished, but from which Yahweh delivers Noah/David and makes a new beginning.

54. Ibid., 167 and n.45.

55. T. Klaehn, *Die sprachliche Verwandschaft der Quelle K (2 Sam.9ff) der Samuelisbücher mit J des Heptateuchs* (Borna-Leipzig: Noske, 1914); J. Blenkinsopp, "Theme and Motif in the Succession History (2 Sam XI 2ff.) and the Yahwist Corpus," VTSup 15 (1966) 44-51.

56. From another point of view, a relationship between the primeval history and Jerusalem court traditions in general—not specifically David material—has been claimed by W. Richter, "Urgeschichte und Hoftheologie," *BZ* 10 (1966) 96-105.

57. Even if the Davidic narrative is historically reliable—a view that seems much less certain now than in 1968 when Brueggemann's article was published—(cf., e.g., the role of traditional story-telling elements within it; see D. M. Gunn, "Traditional Composition in the 'Succession Narrative,'" *VT* 26/2 [1976])—the conception of the work and the choice of material from the doubtless greater bulk of Davidic material available could well follow a traditional or developmental sequence such as is displayed in the primeval history. Brueggemann's case depends on the assumptions that the David story is "(a) historically reliable, and (b) chronologically prior to the other piece" (*CBQ* 30 [1968] 158 n. 17).

58. See also D. J. A. Clines, "The Theology of the Flood Narrative," *Faith and Thought* 100 (1972-73) 128-42.

59. Blenkinsopp, in J. Blenkinsopp *et al., The Pentateuch* (Chicago; ACTA, 1971) 46f.

60. See Clines, *Faith and Thought* 100 (1972-73) 138f.

61. Traditional source analysis, assigning 8:3, 7,13a,22 and parts of chap. 10 to J and 8:13b,17; 9:1-17 and parts of chap. 10 to P, fails to observe how deeply imprinted this element is upon the whole text in its final form.

62. G. von Rad, *Genesis* (rev.ed.) 94.

63. Does not our text of *Gen* 4:1f., in which one conception but two births are spoken of, already imply this interpretation, common in rabbinic exegesis? Cf. Ps.-Jonathan *in loc.;* Ber.R. xxii.2; TB San. 38b. Even Skinner, *Genesis* 103, acknowledges that this "may very well be the meaning."

64. It is no disproof of this belief that the Cain and Abel story belongs to the well-known folktale type of "the hostile brothers" (cf. Westermann, *Genesis* 428 ff.). Such stories are popular just because they are contrary to expectation, like tales of "the unlikely hero."

65. So F. W. Bassett, "Noah's nakedness and the curse of Canaan," *VT* 21 (1971) 232-7; though cf. also G. Rice, "The Curse that Never Was," *JRT* 29 (1972) 5-27 (11ff.) for criticism of this view.

66. Cf. similarly Brueggemann, *CBQ* 30 (1968) 175f.

67. Von Rad, *Genesis* (rev.ed.) 153.

68. Hence, I suppose, von Rad's indecisiveness on this question. On p. 152 of his *Genesis* (rev.ed.) we find the Babel story is the end of the primeval history, on p.154 the "real conclusion" is 12:1-3, and on pp. 161ff. 12:4-9 is included in the primeval history.

69. Von Rad's view of the relation of the primeval and patriarchal histories is essentially similar (*Genesis* 154); my criticism of his exposition is principally that he over-dramatizes the significance of the Babel story, finding tension where none exists.

70. So E. Staiger, *Die Kunst der Interpretation* (4th ed.; Zürich: Atlantis, 1963); cf. M. Kessler, "Narrative Technique in 1 Sm 16, 1-13," *CBQ* 32 (1970) 543-54 (544); J. Blenkinsopp, "Stylistics of Old Testament Poetry," *Bib* 44 (1963) 352-8 (353); and for an extreme expression of this point of view, M. Weiss, "Wege der neuen Dichtungswissenschaft in ihrer Auswendung auf die Psalmenforschung," *Bib* 42 (1961) 255-302 (259). Cf. also R. E. Palmer, *Hermeneutics. Interpretation Theory in Schleiermacher, Dilthey, Heidegger, and Gadamer* (Evanston; Northwestern University Press, 1969) 246f.: "One's interest is in 'the thing said' itself, not in [the author's] intentions or personality. In the text a 'reality' is brought to stand. In the Garden of Eden scenes in *Paradise Lost,* a reality is brought to stand; one is not deeply interested in whether Milton actually had these feelings, nor does one really care whether Adam and Eve 'actually' had them, for in them something deeper and more universal is coming to expression: the possibilities resident in being, lighted up now for a moment in their truth."

71. Sinn und Ursprung der priesterschriftlichen Geschichtserzählung," *ZTK* 49 (1952) 121-43.

72. "The Kerygma of the Priestly Writers," *ZAW* 84 (1972) 397-414 (398,409 n.38).

73. E.g., A Eitz, *Studien zum Verhältnis von Priesterschrift und Deuterojesaja* (Heidelberg Diss., 1970) (cf. *ZAW* 82 [1970] 482). The recent study of A. Hurvitz, "The Evidence of Language in Dating the Priestly Code," *RB* 81 (1974) 24-56, arguing for a pre-exilic date for P, seems to rest on too narrow a base.

74. See A. R. Millard, "A New Babylonian 'Genesis' Story," *Tyndale Bulletin* 18 (1967) 3-18; Clark, *ZAW* 83 (1971) 184-88.

75. Cf. M. Noth, *A History of Pentateuchal Traditions* (Englewood Cliffs, N.J.: Prentice-Hall, 1972) 237f.

76. While Wolff, *Int* 20 (1966) 131-58, may well be correct in reading the Yahwist's work as addressed to the Israel of David and Solomon, and in focusing on the theme of blessing, I am not convinced that the Yahwist is proclaiming a message about Israel's responsibility to be a channel of blessing for the nations (e.g., p. 155), since the alternative interpretation of *Gen* 12:3 seems far preferable; see B. Albrektson, *History and the Gods. An Essay on the Idea of Historical Events as Divine Manifestations in the Ancient Near East and in Israel* (Lund: Gleerup, 1967) 78-81.

Bernhard W. Anderson (essay date 1978)

SOURCE: "From Analysis to Synthesis: The Interpretation of *Genesis* 1-11," *Journal of Biblical Literature,* Vol. 97, No. 1, March, 1978, pp. 23-39.

[*In the following essay, Anderson argues that while scholars have often examined the source materials of* Genesis, *and how these materials were formulated into the final version of* Genesis, *a new critical approach examines* Genesis *as a synthesized whole. Anderson follows this approach in examining the flood story in* Genesis.]

The vitality of biblical scholarship is shown by a disposition to test and challenge working hypotheses, even those that are supported by a broad consensus. Today there are new signals that call for advance, like the rustling of leaves in the tops of the balsam trees, to cite a biblical figure of speech (2 Sam 5:24).[1] The purpose of this essay is to reexamine some old-fashioned views that have constituted the critical orthodoxy of the twentieth century and to look toward the new era of biblical study that is dawning. Attention will focus on the book of *Genesis* which has been a storm-center of biblical criticism in the modern period. In order to make the task somewhat manageable, however, I shall bracket out the patriarchal history and consider only the primeval history (*Gen* 1:1-11:26). But even this is too much to deal with; so, within the primeval history, I shall concentrate on the flood story. Everyone will admit that we have more than enough problems to handle within this pericope!

I. THE GENESIS OF *GENESIS*

Before coming to the flood story, let us consider briefly the methodological crisis in which we find ourselves. As we look back over the history of pentateuchal criticism in the twentieth century, it is clear that the mainstream of biblical scholarship, as represented by the Society of Biblical Literature, has been concerned with the genetic development of the biblical materials. Otto Eissfeldt's little book, *Die Genesis der Genesis* (1958), the German version of his article on "*Genesis*" in *IDB,* is symptomatic of the major interest of past generations. In this period the interpretive task has been both analytic and diachronic: analytic in the sense that one dissects the received text

into its component parts, and diachronic in the sense that one seeks to understand the genesis of the text from its earliest origin to its final formulation. Thus the source critic begins by analyzing the text into its component "documents" on the basis of criteria applicable to literary texts. As Eissfeldt points out, however, these "narrative threads" have had a prehistory. Accordingly, it is the task of the form critic, following the lead of Gunkel, to venture behind the literary sources into the previous period of oral tradition and to recover the *Urform* of a particular text and its setting in life. Finally, the task of the historian of traditions is to realize Gunkel's goal of presenting a *Literaturgeschichte,* that is, a reconstruction of the whole genetic development from the early phase of oral tradition through the stages of various literary formulations to the end-result of the pentateuch which we have received.

It is not my intention to denigrate this period of scholarship, for it has contributed to our understanding of the depth-dimension of the texts. To borrow a figure of speech used by Gerhard von Rad in his **Genesis** commentary and employed effectively by Brevard Childs in his commentary on Exodus, the final text must not be read on a flat surface, "superficially," but in a dimension of depth,[2] that is, with sensitivity to the voices of the past—the whole history of traditions—that resound in the final polyphonic presentation. Nevertheless, we ought to be aware of the assumptions that have governed this genetic interpretation. Let me list three of them. First, the early period of tradition, which we seek to recover, is the creative stage of tradition. This was clearly Gunkel's conviction, apparently influenced by romanticism;[3] and it survives in a modified form in von Rad's emphasis on the primacy of the Yahwist's epic which, being based on early creedal formulations, provided the determinative ("canonical") tradition that was accepted basically in the final priestly formulation of the traditions. Secondly, the earliest stages of the transmission of traditions are reconstructed with help from the literary models employed in source or documentary criticism. Tensions in the text, as evidenced by literary style, vocabulary, inconsistencies, and duplications, are transferred from the literary stage to an earlier, preliterary stage. Using these accepted literary criteria, one attempts to reconstruct the prehistory of the written text, that is, "scripture." And thirdly, it has been assumed that the way to understand the combination of strata in the final text is to explore their origin and development. As Eissfeldt's essay on "the genesis of *Genesis*" indicates, excursions into the prehistory of the text are motivated by a concern for historicity, that is, criticism enables us to make judgments about the historical value of narratives for the time about which they claim to speak or about their place in religious history.[4] This seems to imply that the scriptural text points to a meaning that lies, to some degree, outside of the text: in the history of the ancient world or in the ideas or customs reflected in various circles during the history of traditions.

If I am not mistaken, a new generation of biblical scholars has arisen that wants to move beyond this kind of analysis to some sort of synthesis, beyond a method that is rigidly diachronic to one that gives appropriate weight to the synchronic dimension of the text. Without attempting to survey the whole scholarly scene, let me mention several scholarly impulses that are potentially significant for the study of *Genesis.*

First of all, let me call attention to the stylistic or rhetorical criticism that was given new impetus by James Muilenburg's presidential address to this society a few years ago on "Form Criticism and Beyond."[5] My esteemed teacher certainly did not intend to throw overboard the substantial contributions of past scholarship, including Wellhausen, in spite of increasing reservations about his kind of historical criticism and Gunkel from whom he learned most. An essay that summarizes his career concludes: "'We affirm the necessity of form criticism,'—and that demands appropriate exploration of the prehistory of the text; 'but we also lay claim to the legitimacy of what we have called rhetorical criticism'—and that requires attention to the text itself: its own integrity, its dramatic structure, and its stylistic features."[6]

This type of study is evidenced in a recent book by J. P. Fokkelman, dealing with various specimens of narrative art in *Genesis;*[7] and his study, in turn, is influenced by the so-called new literary criticism advocated, for instance, by René Wellek and Austin Warren who call into question scholarly preoccupation with questions of authorship, social context, and prehistory of the text and insist that the proper task of the literary critic is the study of the work itself.[8] Using a vivid figure of speech, Fokkelman writes:

> The birth of a text resembles that of man: the umbilical cord which connected the text with its time and the man or men who produced it, is severed once its existence has become a fact; the text is going to lead a life of its own, for whenever a reader grants it an adequate reading it will come alive and become operative and it usually survives its maker. Whereas the creation of a text is finite, finished after hours, years or centuries, its re-creation is infinite. It is a task for each new age, each new generation, each new reader, never to be considered complete.[9]

Frankly, I must admit to misgivings about some exercises in rhetorical criticism which seem to be purely formal, almost mathematical, and lack a dimension of depth that adds richness to the text. Moreover, some biblical theologians wonder whether this new form of literalism, which disavows interest in historical questions, leads us to a docetic view of revelation, if indeed revelation is considered a meaningful term at all. Despite these reservations, one is compelled to agree that the proper starting-point methodologically is with the text as given, not with the reconstruction of the prehistory of the text which, as Fokkelman observes, is usually "an unattainable ideal." Something more is involved, however, than the epistemological problem that the prehistory of the texts is unknowable in any certain sense. What is at stake is the question, to which Hans Frei has directed our attention, as to whether the narrative can be split apart from its meaning (a hermeneutical presupposition inherited from the 18th century) or whether, alternatively, "the story is the meaning," as he puts it.[10] The beginning and end of exegesis is the text itself—not something beyond it. Given this textual basis, excursions behind the text are appropriate and often illuminating; but, as Amos Wilder has reminded us, we should be on guard against "the historicist habit of mind" that "may operate unconsciously to handicap a free encounter with a writing in its final form."[11]

Secondly, recent studies in oral tradition should make us more cautious about basing our study of the depth-dimension of the text on the literary presuppositions which, in the past, have been applied by both source criticism and form criticism (i.e. differences in style and vocabulary, seams and inconsistencies, duplications and repetitions). Field studies in oral tradition, to which scholars like R. C. Culley and recently Burke Long have drawn our attention,[12] challenge the view, near and dear to source and form critics, that it is possible to recover an *Urtradition* and even an *Urtext* behind the final, written formulation of the pentateuch as we have received it.

This problem struck me as I was reviewing the work of Martin Noth and Claus Westermann. Careful rereading of Noth's study of pentateuchal traditions[13] will disclose that, although he was in bondage to the literary model of source criticism and could even "out-Wellhausen" Wellhausen in refined source analysis, he was somewhat sensitive to the fluid, dynamic character of the transmission of the traditions, based on major themes and their elaboration. This central thrust of Noth's work has not escaped the attention of Westermann, a consistent form-critic who has carried Gunkel's work to a logical and brilliant conclusion. "Gunkel's new impulse," Westermann observes, "was that he elevated the significance of the preliterary history of the individual narrative"—a narrative that had its own life (*Eigenleben*) and that was governed by "laws other than that of a written text;" but, Westermann insists, Noth fails to stress "the smallest literary units" and their respective forms, and, instead, he concentrates on the major themes of the Israelite tradition that were elaborated and filled out in the course of their transmission.[14]

Almost everyone will admit—even conservative scholars like Umberto Cassuto and Benno Jacob—that ancient traditions have been utilized in the final formulation of the pentateuch. The debatable question is twofold: (a) whether these traditions were cast into a *fixed* form, and (b) whether we are in a position to recover the *Urform* or *Vorlage*. In the past, scholars have proceeded on the assumption that, as Albert Lord puts it in the context of a study of Homeric texts, poets "*did* something to a fixed text or a fixed group of texts," as though they composed "with pen in hand."[15] This *scribal* view of composition does not do justice to the dynamic of oral performance which involves the role of the narrator, the response of a live audience, and improvisation on traditional materials in various and changing settings. Some of the phenomena which in the past have prompted source or form critical analysis, such as repetitions or inconsistencies, may well be the *stigmata* of oral transmission. Burke Long wisely reminds us that, in view of our limited knowledge of the sociology of ancient Israel and the nature of oral composition, we should be cautious about attempting to reconstruct the original wording or *Vorlage* of a text that comes to us only in its final, written form.[16] I would add a further caveat: since efforts to recover preliterary stages lead us away from the givenness of the text itself into the realm of hypothesis, it is not valid to regard the reconstructed *Urform* as normative for interpretation or as having some superiority to scripture itself. Whatever excursions into the prehistory of the text are possible or necessary, the beginning and end of interpretation is "a free encounter with a writing in its final form" (Wilder).

There is a third scholarly movement which I mention with some hesitance, for I do not claim to understand it fully or sympathetically, and therefore I shall treat it with an undeserved brevity. Structuralism is an invitation to explore the "depth dimension" of biblical texts in a new way: not by analytically juxtaposing various levels of tradition and tracing a genetic development to the final composition, but by exploring the sub-surface unity, coherence, and even dramatic structure at "deep levels" of language that generate the text as it is heard or read. In the view of one of the advocates of this method, Hugh White, it is structural exegesis that lies beyond form criticism and beyond redaction criticism; for the "artistic power" of the narrative art that we have received cannot be accounted for adequately by understanding the text as a function of an ancient *Sitz im Leben,* whether social or cultic, nor can "the large contours of the narrative" be simply the product of "a more or less insensitive redactor of relatively fixed traditional materials." In his judgment, "the enormous role played by the narrator of ancient tales in the formation of the structure and texture of the form of literature" (as emphasized by Lord, Culley, Long, *et al.*) calls for a method that enables us to penetrate and articulate the deep linguistic and dramatic structure that is implicit in the narrative.[17] Whatever more should be said about structuralism, at least this deserves attention: in contrast to analytic methods of the past, this method attempts to grasp wholes or totalities (*l'attitude totalisante*).

II. PAST ANALYSIS OF THE FLOOD STORY

Thus various scholarly impulses have moved us away from an excessive preoccupation with the genetic development of the text to exegesis that takes with greater seriousness the style and structure of the received texts and that considers how these texts function in their narrative contexts. In a previous essay,[18] I tried to show that form and content are so inseparably related that attempts to separate out traditions (*Tatbericht and Wortbericht*) are not successful. That endeavor was facilitated by the general recognition that the present creation story is homogeneous (P). Now, however, I turn to a pericope, the flood story, about which there is just as great scholarly agreement, only in this case it is agreed that the text is composite (a combination of J and P).

Evidences for the disunity of the story in its present form can be recited easily. (1) Some passages prefer the divine name Yahweh, others Elohim (e.g., 6:13 and 7:1). (2) There are irregularities and inconsistencies: (a) some passages speak about a downpour (*gešem*) lasting forty days and forty nights (7:4, 12, 17a), others of a cosmic deluge (*mabbûl*) whose waters maintained their crest for 150 days (7:11, 24); (b) some passages make a distinction between clean and unclean animals—seven pairs of the former and a pair of the latter (7:2-3), while others speak only of the pairing of every kind of animal (6:19-20). (3) There are instances of parallel or duplicate passages; for instance, the command to enter the ark (6:18b-20) seems to be paralleled in 7:1-3, and the execution of the command (7:5, 7-9), is paralleled in 7:13-16a. (4) Peculiarities of style and vocabulary suggest that the story is not of one piece (see the standard commentaries). In his monumental commentary on *Genesis,* Hermann Gunkel declared that the analysis of the story into separate sources, J and P, is "ein Meisterstück der modernen Kritik." According to him, the redactor had at hand two full and distinct versions of the flood story, quite similar in structure and sequence. "The Redactor," he averred, "attempted to preserve both accounts as much as possible" and allowed no *Körnlein* to be lost, especially from the priestly version that he highly esteemed.[19]

Since Gunkel's time, there has been a broad consensus regarding this scribal view of the composition of the flood story. Commentators have agreed that the *first step* is to separate analytically the two component parts and to comment on each independently, although—like Gunkel— giving only short shrift to the artistic work presented in the whole, that is, the accomplishment of the "redactor." Take as an example the excellent commentary by the late Gerhard von Rad. In his introduction, von Rad draws attention to Franz Rosenzweig's observation that the underrated siglum "R" (redactor) should be understood to mean *Rabbenu,* "our master," because it is from his hands that we have received the scriptural tradition as a finished product. In this context, however, von Rad jumps immediately to the question of what it means in the Christian community to receive the OT "from the hands of Jesus Christ," *Rabbenu.*[20] True, von Rad stresses the overall thematic unity of the hexateuch in which the themes of the early Israelite credo are elaborated; but in exegetical practice he does not reflect on the final shape of the pentateuchal (hexateuchal) tradition. Hence, in his exegesis of the flood story he comments separately on the isolated J and P versions and even resorts to textual rearrangement to restore the putative original texts.

It is noteworthy that the Jewish scholar, E. A. Speiser, who accepts the view that "the received biblical account of the Flood is beyond reasonable doubt a composite narrative, reflecting more than one separate source," admits to misgivings about "reshuffling the text" in violation of "a tradition that antedates the Septuagint of twenty-two centuries ago."[21] He does not follow up on the possible implications of his caveat, however, but settles for translating the received text with slash marks to indicate J and P sources. It is a fact, of course, that at least since the time of the LXX translation the flood story has functioned in its final form in Judaism and Christianity, rather than in separable traditions lying behind the text; and it is in this form that the story continues to make its impact upon the reader today.

These scholars, though operating within the scholarly consensus of the twentieth century, seem to raise questions about the relative priority of a genetic vs. a synthetic, a diachronic vs. a synchronic approach to the task of exegesis. Claus Westermann, in his massive and impressive commentary on the *Urgeschichte,* also addresses himself to this issue. At one point he observes:

> To interpret the flood story of J and P separately, as in most commentaries, threatens a neglect of the peculiarity of the narrative form as it has been transmitted to us. It cannot be denied that the formulation of the combined narrative by R represents an important voice of its own, and that the subsequent impact [*Wirkungsgeschichte*] of the flood story is neither that of J nor of P, but that of R.[22]

In exegetical practice, however, Westermann juxtaposes J and P and at times relocates verses for the sake of emphasizing the separate identity of the two sources. In his view, the unity of the flood story lies primarily in a prehistory of tradition that is refracted separately in the two sources. At the conclusion of his commentary, however, he devotes a couple of paragraphs to the work of the redactor whose intention, he maintains, was to preserve the *Mehrstimmigkeit* of the tradition—a musical figure suggesting a polyphonic performance in which each voice sings its own part according to fixed texts. He writes: "R created out of both [i.e., J and P] a new, flowing, self-contained narrative composition" in which the separate voices of J, P, and R are heard; and this was possible because all three shared the same "basic view of the primeval event and of reality."[23]

Westermann's commentary is a laudable witness to the need to go beyond analysis of separate sources to interpretive synthesis, to grasping the text as a whole. Even in this endeavor, however, he falls into the genetic fallacy of the past in that he posits a unity outside of and before the text which, he maintains, may be recovered by a phenomenological exposition of the religious consciousness expressed in ancient myths. The creativity of R(edactor) is evidenced in his ability to combine texts, each of which gives its own variation on the basic mythical datum. The question is whether this view is adequate to account for the final narrative which, to use Westermann's adjectives, is "new," "flowing," and "self-contained." Similar claims for the final composition have been made by others, for instance by Eduard Nielsen, a representative of the Scandinavian circle. "Our present text," Nielsen observes (speaking of the flood story), "is a work of art, composed of different traditions, it is true, but in such a way that a unified work has been the result."[24] If we are dealing with "a work of art," however, is not the final whole greater—or at least, different—than the sum of its parts? This, it seems to me, is the basic issue. Without denying the legitimacy of excursions into the prehistory of the text in their proper place, the question is whether the present narrative art can be understood and appreciated by a genetic study of its origin and development.

Finally, the symbol R constitutes a special problem.[25] R(edactor) is a shadowy figure, to whom virtually nothing is attributed except the synthesis of discrete traditions, J and P. Gunkel said precious little about this mystery man in his commentary and, as indicated above, Westermann devotes very brief space to him in the lengthy conclusion to his commentary on the *Urgeschichte.* R is merely a synthetic agent; and statements about him are inferences from the fact that traditions have been reworked or reshaped so as to produce a new totality. My own study of the primeval history has corroborated the judicious proposal of Frank Cross that P and R should be merged into one. While accepting the broad results of source criticism, Cross observes that "the Flood story has been completely rewritten by P." "The interweaving of the sources," he writes, "is not the work of a redactor juxtaposing blocks of materials, but that of a tradent reworking and supplementing a traditional story."[26]

This tantalyzingly brief reference to the flood story contains implications that may lead us beyond the rather artificial source analysis of the past. This story is not a mere combination of discrete texts (J juxtaposed to P and conflated by R), according to the usual understanding; rather, we have a story from the priestly circle or "tradent" into which traditional epic material has been incorporated. The priestly version is a reworking and recasting of the story, not just a preservation of past traditions in their *Mehrstimmigkeit.* The re-presentation of the flood story in this elaborated and expanded form is a work of art in its own right, and deserves to be considered in the form in which it is given. We must admit our ignorance about the circumstances of the composition. Was the story the scribal result of retelling in situations of performance? Was it the result of purely literary activity in the time of the exile? There is much that we do not know. However, the important point is that, whatever the history of transmission or whatever the immediate occasion of final composition, the priestly "tradent" shaped the story to produce a dramatic effect as a totality.

III. THE DRAMATIC MOVEMENT OF THE STORY

Let us turn, then, to the flood story itself and consider some of the structural and stylistic features that make it a dramatic unity in its present form.

In an important monograph on the priestly work, Sean McEvenue shows that priestly narrative style, far from being pedantic and unartistic, displays rhetorical and structural features that are characteristic of narrative art generally, such as a sequence of panels in which formulaic patterns are repeated. (He uses the homely example of the story of "The Little Red Hen.")[27] With specific regard to the flood story, he maintains that in the P version the narrative builds up dramatically to the turning point reached in 8:1a: "However, God remembered Noah and all the wild and tame animals that were with him in the ark." The narrative, as he puts it, "swells toward the climax" and, after the turning point is reached, moves "toward repose."[28] His stylistic study, it should be noted, is based exclusively on the juxtaposition of J and P components of the story. He maintains that P was "writing from a Yahwist narrative, which he either knew by heart or had in front of him;" and he aims to understand the divergences of P from J—divergences that are all the more striking since "P has stuck so closely to his source."[29] McEvenue, however, does not take the step that we are advocating and that is implicit in his own view that P reworked J tradition, namely, to consider the narrative as a totality in which the priestly tradent has absorbed into his composition elements of old epic tradition.

Since the story in its final form has been shaped by the priestly tradent, McEvenue's observation about the dramatic movement of the P narrative applies also to the story as a whole—as people read it today. Indeed, it is not surprising that the Jewish scholar, Umberto Cassuto, who rejects source analysis,[30] makes a similar observation. According to Cassuto, the story is organized into a series of "paragraphs" that move in crescendo toward a climax as the rising waters of chaos lift up the ark on their crest and then, after the turning point in 8:1 ("God remembered Noah"), falls away in decrescendo as the waters of chaos ebb and there is the beginning of a new creation. Of the twelve paragraphs that comprise the story, according to his division, he writes:

> The first group depicts for us, step by step, the acts of Divine justice that bring destruction upon the earth, which had become filled with violence; and the scenes that pass before us grow increasingly gloomier until in the darkness of death portrayed in the sixth paragraph there remains only one tiny, faint point of light, to wit, the ark, which floats on the fearful waters that have covered everything, and which guards between its walls the hope of future life. The second group shows us consecutively the various stages of the Divine compassion that renews life upon earth. The light that waned until it became a minute point in the midst of the dark world, begins to grow bigger and brighter till it illumines again the entire scene before us, and shows us a calm and peaceful world, crowned with the rainbow that irradiates the cloud with its colours—a sign and pledge of life and peace for the coming generations.[31]

Readers who submit to the text of the story in its present form find themselves caught up in this rising and falling movement, corresponding to the tide and ebb of the waters of chaos. At the climax, God's remembrance of Noah and the remnant anticipates the conclusion, where God promises to remember the "everlasting covenant" that signals the beginning of a new humanity and, indeed, a new creation, paralleling the original creation portrayed in

Genesis 1. In short, the flood narrative in its present form is composed of a sequence of episodic units, each of which has an essential *function* in the dramatic movement of the whole. The story as a totality deserves attention.

To begin with, notice the immediate context in which the story is placed, namely, the genealogical outline followed by the priestly tradent. Between 6:1 and 9:27 we find a long block of narrative material dealing with Noah's lifetime which has been inserted into the heart of Noah's genealogy as presented in the toledoth document (5:1). In this document the genealogies follow a fixed lineal, rather than ramified, pattern: (a) N lived x years, (b) and he fathered S; (c) after the birth of S, N lived y years; (d) he fathered sons and daughters; (e) the lifetime of N was z years; and (f) then he died. Now, the first two elements of Noah's genealogy (a and b) are found in 5:32, right at the end of a series of excerpts from the toledoth document, namely, (a) Noah lived 500 years, and (b) he fathered Shem, Ham, and Japheth. The conclusion of the genealogy is found in 9:28-29, although the pattern is modified to refer to the flood, the principal event in Noah's lifetime: (c) After the flood Noah lived 350 years; (d) . . . ; (e) the lifetime of Noah was 950 years; and (f) then he died. Whether the Noachic entry in the toledoth document once contained a brief reference to the flood, on the analogy of some editions of the Sumerian King List,[32] cannot be said with confidence. In any case, the narrative material extending from the episodes that deal with the promiscuity of the celestial beings (6:1-4) and the "Sorrow of Yahweh" (6:5-8) to the post-diluvian story of Noah's intoxication and the condemnation of Canaan (9:20-27), is encased within the genealogical frame. According to this sequence, the initial epic material constitutes the prologue to the flood, or as Speiser phrases it, "Prelude to Disaster," and the subsequent material, dealing with Noah's post-diluvian situation, is an epilogue.

The priestly drama proper begins with the transitional passage concerning the *saddîq,* Noah and his three sons, which is formulated in the style of the toledoth document (6:9-10); and at the end of the priestly story we find another transitional passage (9:18-19) which both recapitulates previous elements and prepares for the sequel by saying that the sons of Noah who went forth from the ark were Shem, Ham, and Japheth, and that from them the whole earth was repopulated.[33] In between these boundaries the drama of the flood unfolds in a succession of episodic units, each of which has a definite function in relation to the whole. Let us follow the sequence as it is given to us, at the expense of paying closer attention to details.

(1) The keynote is struck in 6:11-12: violence and corruption in the earth—first announced as an objective fact (v. 11) and then reiterated in terms of God's perception (v. 12). These verses display noteworthy stylistic features, such as the emphasis achieved through repetition, the play upon the verbal root *šāhat* in three variations ("become corrupt," "spoil," "ruin"), and the climactic use of the particle *kî* ("for") to provide explanation (v. 12b). The

discordant note struck at the beginning is resolved at the end with the restoration of harmony and peace in God's creation (9:1-17).

(2) The main action of the drama begins in 6:13-22, introduced by the declarative formula, "Then God said." God's first address, in good priestly narrative style, is structured according to a twofold announcement-command sequence: announcement of God's resolution to destroy (6:13) followed by the command to build the ark (vv. 14-16); repeated announcement of the imminence of the *mabbûl* waters (vv. 17-18), followed by a command that deals mainly with laying away supplies of food for those to be saved (vv. 19-21). This passage concludes with the execution formula: "Noah did this. Just as Elohim commanded him, so he acted" (6:22).

(3) The divine command to load the ark with its passengers is the subject of the next unit in 7:1-10, usually ascribed to J (except for the chronological notation in v. 6). Strikingly, the second divine address is introduced by the declarative formula, "Then *Yahweh* said." Also, the execution of the command is indicated in the formula, "Noah did just as Yahweh commanded him" (7:5), though at the conclusion of the unit (7:9) we find "just as Elohim commanded him." It is incontrovertible, in my judgment, that in this passage the priestly tradent has drawn upon and reworked old epic tradition whose pecularities are evident in various matters of content (for instance, seven pairs of clean animals and a pair that are not clean, 7:2-3; but cf. 7:8-9), and in turns of speech (e.g., "a male and his mate" rather than "male and female," 7:2; but cf. 7:9).[34] However, the question is whether these phenomena, which we perceive as inconsistencies, actually disturb the structure and movement of the narrative in its final form.[35] I do not see that this is the case. On the contrary, this unit, which is also formulated in a command-execution sequence, advances the motion of the previous unit by showing that the disaster is at hand, only seven days away, and therefore it is time to get on board the ark! In spite of modern views based on alternation in the usage of divine names in the book of *Genesis,* the priestly tradent seems to have had no compunction about using both names, Yahweh and Elohim, in his reworking of the pre-Mosaic traditions.[36]

(4) The two divine addresses are followed by a unit found in 7:11-16 which source critics have credited to priestly tradition, except for the statement about the forty-day downpour (*gešem*) in 7:12 and the brief anthropomorphic touch in 7:16b, "Yahweh closed him inside." This unit clearly involves repetition, for it resumes and summarizes the earlier narrative, beginning with the point reached in 7:10 of the previous episode ("At the end of seven days the waters of the Flood were upon the earth") and harking back to the command regarding the saving of animals and humans, anticipated in 6:18b-21 and definitely mandated and executed in 7:1-10. The new element in the dramatic movement of the story is the announcement of the manner in which "the waters of the flood" came upon the earth (vv. 11-12). Clearly the priestly tradent sought to rework

the received tradition of a violent forty-day rainstorm into his own conception of the *mabbûl* as a cosmic catastrophe which threatened the earth with a return to primeval chaos. The chief function of this unit, however, is to indicate the inception of the disaster, and this provides the opportunity to rehearse once again the number of those whom God commanded to be saved in 7:13-16a, a passage that harks back to the priestly command passage in 6:18b-21 by way of resumption and inclusion. Notice that the recapitulation of the divine command is indicated once again by the obedience formula: "just as Elohim had commanded him" (7:16a). This is followed by the celebrated sentence, "Then Yahweh closed him inside." Usually this is regarded as a fragment of the J epic because of the usage of the name Yahweh and the anthropomorphism which allegedly is out of keeping with priestly tradition. However, this brief sentence—a snippet of only three Hebrew words (*wayyisgōr YHWH bă 'adô*) in a predominantly P context, calls into question the analytical procedure of the past. How does this notice *function* in the received text? Coming after the summarizing recapitulation of the divine command to enter the ark and its execution, these words serve as a final punctuation of the unit and at the same time they anticipate what follows, God's "remembrance" of those who were sealed in the ark—the anthropomorphism stressed in the priestly recension (cf. Exod 2:24-25).

(5) The storm is now raging, as indicated in the next unit, 7:17-24. This unit is framed within two chronological statements, the first (7:17) stating that the *mabbûl* innundated the earth for forty days (apparently the priestly tradent's reinterpretation of the epic tradition [7:4] to mean the time required for the ark to be buoyed on the waters), and the last (7:24) giving the total duration of the cresting waters, that is, 40 + 110 + 150 days. The swelling of the waters is vividly portrayed by the repeated use of the key words "the waters prevailed" to create an ascending effect.

wayyigbĕrû hammāyim

(v. 18)

wĕhammāyim gābĕrû

(v. 19)

gābĕrû hammāyim

(v. 20)

Source critics find traces of old epic tradition (J) in vv. 22-23, largely because these verses seem to repeat the content of vs. 21, "All flesh died that moved upon the earth. . . ." But in the reworking of the tradition, the repetition serves to heighten the dramatic contrast between the perishing of "every human" (v. 21) and the climactic statement, "Only Noah was left [the verb suggests the "remnant"], and those that were with him in the ark" (7:23b).[37] Thus the narrative swells to a climax, with the ark and its precious remnant tossed on the waters of chaos. "We see water everywhere," Cassuto comments, "as though the world had reverted to its primeval state at the dawn of Creation, when the waters of the deep submerged everything."[38]

(6) The next unit, 8:1-5, brings us to the turning point of the story with the dramatic announcement of God's remembrance of Noah and the remnant with him in the ark. The statement, "God caused a wind to blow over the earth," which recalls the "wind from God" (*rûah 'Elōhîm*) of *Gen* 1:2, introduces by way of contrast the theme of the new creation which becomes explicit in 9:1-17 where the *imago Dei* reappears. Source critics attribute this passage to P, with the exception of the notice about the restraining of the downpour (*gešem*) from the sky (8:2b). This traditional element, however, should not be separated out, for the priestly tradent, as we have already noticed, has absorbed the forty-day rainstorm into his view of a cosmic deluge and into his chronology. The effect of the text at this point is to show dramatically that when all seems to be lost, from a human point of view, God's faithfulness makes possible a new beginning.

(7) The decrescendo from the climax is effectively carried out in the next unit, 8:6-14. The first part, the vignette about the release of the birds (8:6-12), is derived from old epic tradition (J). This material, however, should not be detached from its present context, for it now has a definite narrative function, namely, to portray the gradual ebbing of the waters from their crest and the emergence of the dry land, as at the time of creation (cf. 1:9-12). The dramatic action is retarded and extended over a span of time so that the hearer or reader may sense in Noah's experiment with the birds (including his tender treatment of the dove, vv. 8-9!) the wonder of what was taking place. The unit concludes by dating the emergence of the dry land, and therefore the possibility of the earth's renewed fertility, in relation to the New Year, which was also the 601st anniversary of Noah's birth. This wonderful event is indicated in two ways (as in 6:11-12): one in terms of Noah's perception (8:13b) and the other as an objective fact (8:14)—sentences that source critics attribute to J and P respectively.

(8) After the drama of the rising and the falling of the waters, the story returns to a scheme of divine addresses, as at the beginning. Notice that the address in 8:15-19, which is attributed to priestly tradition, is also structured in a command-execution sequence. In this case, the theme is God's command to leave the ark (vv. 16-17), accompanied by a special word that the animals should swarm, be fertile, and increase on the earth, and the fulfillment of that command (vv. 18-19).

(9) Next comes a unit, 8:20-22, dealing with Noah's sacrifice and Yahweh's resolution never again to engage in wholesale destruction but, rather, to maintain the regularities and rhythms on which earthly existence is dependent. It is true that this episodic unit, derived from old epic tradition, harks back to the passage about "The Sorrow of Yahweh" (6:5-8) and forms an inclusion with it.[39] The episode, however, has an important function in its present narrative context. On the one hand, it provides the appropriate sequel to disembarking from the ark, namely, a human act of praise; and, on the other, the divine response

to the sacrifice (i.e., Yahweh's resolution) serves as a transition to the final priestly discourse which elaborates God's pledge in the theological perspective intended to govern the whole story.

(10) The final unit, 9:1-17, is also cast in the form of a divine address, though this one is articulated in three parts, each marked by the declarative formula, "Then God said" or variations of it (9:1, 8, 12). In the fourth address the narrator rounds off the story by re-sounding tones that were heard earlier. God's promise to establish his covenant with Noah (6:18a) is fulfilled in the "everlasting covenant" (*běrît 'ôlām*)—a covenant that is made, however, not just with Noah but with "every living creature of all flesh that is upon the earth" (9:8-11). God's remembrance of Noah and the remnant in the ark (8:1a) is consummated in his pledge to "remember" his covenant, whose visible sign is the rainbow (9:12-17). And above all, the initial discordant note—violence in God's creation (6:11-12)—is resolved into the harmony of a new creation, as shown by the renewal of the blessing given at the original creation (9:1: "Be fertile, multiply, and fill the earth"), by a restatement of the role of man who is made in the image of God (9:6), and by the creator's pledge, based unconditionally on his faithfulness, that the earth would not be threatened by a return to pre-creation chaos.

IV. THE OVERALL DESIGN

Thus the present flood story, in which the priestly tradent has incorporated old epic tradition into his narrative, discloses an overall design, a dramatic movement in which each episodic unit has an essential function. McEvenue attempted to demonstrate that the story displays a chiastic structure—or, as he prefers to put it, "a rough palistrophe."[40] He would have had more success in tracing a symmetrical design had he not restricted his attention to the analysis of P, regarded as a discrete document, and had he concentrated, instead, on the total priestly revision of the tradition. It is indeed striking that the story in its final form flows in a sequence of units toward a turning-point and then follows the same sequence in reverse, as the following outline indicates:

> Transitional introduction (6:9-10)
> . 1. Violence in God's creation (6:11-12)
> . . 2. First divine address: resolution to destroy (6:13-22)
> . . . 3. Second divine address: command to enter the ark (7:1-10)
> . . . . 4. Beginning of the flood (7:11-16)
> . . . . . 5. The rising flood waters (7:17-24)
> . . . . . . GOD's REMEMBRANCE OF NOAH
> . . . . . 6. The receding flood waters (8:1-5)
> . . . . 7. The drying of the earth (8:6-14)
> . . . 8. Third divine address: command to leave the ark (8:15-19)
> . . 9. God's resolution to preserve order (8:20-22)
> . 10. Fourth divine address: covenant blessing and peace (9:1-17)
> Transitional conclusion (9:18-19)

The first part of the story represents a movement toward chaos, with the hero Noah and the remnant with him as survivors of the catastrophe. The second part represents a movement toward the new creation, with Noah and his sons as the representatives of the new humankind who were to inherit the earth.

As I see it, there is no need to try to harmonize the flood story by denying the irregularities and inconsistencies which source analysis has sought to understand in its own way and according to its presuppositions. The question is whether we are to be bound exclusively or even primarily by this analytical method. This method demands that we *begin* by analyzing and juxtaposing "sources" or "levels of tradition" under the assumption that by charting the genesis of the text we can best understand the text itself, which is regarded as a conflation of discrete, identifiable traditions, loosely joined together by a redactor. There is an alternative to this analytical method which, I believe, is overdue, namely, to begin by examining the structural unity of the story that we have received from the priestly tradent who is actually *Rabbenu,* to recall once again the remark of Rosenzweig. In this case, our first priority would be to understand the text in its received form and to consider what George Coats has termed its "functional unity;"[41] and after that we would turn—as our second priority—to an investigation of the prehistory of the text, hoping to find further light on the richness and dynamic of the text that we have received. In regard to the flood story, this set of priorities is dictated by at least two considerations. First, the priestly tradent has absorbed the old epic tradition into his presentation, though under circumstances that are not as yet clear to us; and second, the result of this reinterpretation of the tradition is not a literary patchwork but a story whose overall design and dramatic movement make it a work of art, one that even yet stirs and involves the hearer or reader.

It is not enough, however, to consider the dramatic unity of the story by itself, in isolation. If we are to understand the story theologically, it is equally important to consider how this story functions in its present context in the book of *Genesis* and specifically within the toledoth scheme used by the priestly tradent to organize the primeval history. When the priestly revision of the story is regarded as a separate pericope, the *hāmās* ("violence," "lawlessness") that prompted God's resolve to bring the flood hangs in the air (6:11, 13), and the prohibition against murder in 9:6 is unmotivated. "P's summary statement referring to violence and corruption," Frank Cross observes, "must presume a knowledge of concrete and colorful narratives of the corruption of the creation. Otherwise, it has neither literary nor theological force."[42] By appropriating the old epic tradition, the priestly tradent has provided a vivid portrayal of the disorder rooted primarily in creaturely freedom, as illustrated in the stories of primeval rebellion in the garden, fratricide in the first family, Lamech's measureless revenge, and the marriage of celestial beings with human daughters.[43] Thus the *Urgeschichte* in its final form displays an overall design: a dramatic movement from the original harmony of creation, through the violent disruption of that order and the near return to chaos, and finally to a new creation under the rainbow sign of the everlasting covenant.

Notes

1. Recent examples, *inter alia,* of the new ferment are Hans Heinrich Schmid, *Der sogenannte Jahwist: Beobachtungen und Fragen zur Pentateuchforschung* (Zurich: Theologischer Verlag, 1976) and Rolf Rendtorff, *Das überlieferungsgeschichtliche Problem des Pentateuch* (BZAW 147; Berlin/New York: de Gruyter, 1977).

2. Gerhard von Rad, *Genesis* (2d ed.; Philadelphia: Westminster, 1972) 28.

3. See my introductory essay, Martin Noth, *A History of Pentateuchal Traditions* (Englewood Cliffs: Prentice-Hall, 1972) xviii-xx.

4. *IDB,* 2. 378-80.

5. *JBL* 88 (1969) 1-18. See further my essay, "The New Frontier of Rhetorical Criticism," in Jared J. Jackson and Martin Kessler, eds., *Rhetorical Criticism* (Pittsburgh: Pickwick, 1974) ix-xviii.

6. "The New Frontier of Rhetorical Criticism," xviii.

7. J. P. Fokkelman, *Narrative Art in* Genesis: *Specimens of Stylistic and Structural Analysis* (Amsterdam: Van Gorcum, 1975).

8. R. Wellek and A. Warren, *Theory of Literature* (3rd ed.; London: Harcourt, Brace & World, 1963).

9. *Narrative Art,* 3-4.

10. Hans Frei, *The Eclipse of Biblical Narrative: A Study in Eighteenth and Nineteenth Century Hermeneutics* (New Haven/London: Yale University, 1974).

11. Amos N. Wilder, "Norman Perrin, What is Redaction Criticism?" in *Christology,* Norman Perrin Festschrift (Claremont, CA: The New Testament Colloquium, 1971) 153.

12. Burke O. Long, "Recent Field Studies in Oral Literature and their Bearing on Old Testament Criticism," *VT* 26 (1976) 187-98, who carries forward the discussion of R. C. Culley, "An Approach to the Problem of Oral Tradition," *VT* 13 (1963) 113-25.

13. *A History of Pentateuchal Traditions,* my translation of a basic study first published in German in 1948.

14. Claus Westermann, *Genesis* (BK 1; Neukirchen-Vluyn: Neukirchener Verlag, 1976) 765. See further my reviews of this work; *JBL* 91 (1972) 243-45 and 96 (1976) 291-94.

15. Albert B. Lord, *The Singer of Tales* (Cambridge: Harvard University, 1960) 11; cf. 57.

16. "Recent Field Studies," 194-98.

17. Hugh C. White, "Structural Analysis of Old Testament Narrative," unpublished manuscript (Sept. 1975) 5.

18. "A Stylistic Study of the Priestly Creation Story," in *Canon and Authority: Essays in Old Testament Religion and Theology,* ed. G. W. Coats and B. O. Long (Philadelphia: Fortress, 1977) 148-62.

19. Herman Gunkel, *Genesis* (HKAT; Göttingen: Vandenhoeck & Ruprecht, 1910) 137. See his brief treatment of the redactor, 139-40.

20. *Genesis,* 41.

21. E. A. Speiser, *Genesis* (AB; Garden City: Doubleday, 1964) 54.

22. *Genesis,* 580.

23. Ibid., 797-98.

24. Eduard Nielsen, *Oral Tradition* (London: SCM, 1954) 102. For his criticism of source analysis of the flood story, see pp. 93-103.

25. This has already been observed by Samuel Sandmel in "The Haggada within Scripture," in Sandmel, ed., *Old Testament Issues* (New York: Harper & Row, 1968), esp. 97-98; reprinted from *JBL* 80 (1961) 105-22.

26. Frank M. Cross, "The Priestly Work," *Canaanite Myth and Hebrew Epic* (Cambridge: Harvard University, 1973) 305. See also Samuel Sandmel, "The Haggada within Scripture," 106.

27. Sean E. McEvenue, *The Narrative Style of the Priestly Writer* (AnBib 50; Rome: Biblical Institute, 1971) chap. 1. See further Joseph Blenkinsopp. "The Structure of P," *CBQ* 38 (1976) 275-92.

28. Ibid., 36.

29. Ibid., 27. McEvenue adopts as a working basis K. Elliger's delimitation of P set forth in Elliger's "Sinn und Ursprung der priesterlichen Geschichtserzählung," *ZTK* 49 (1952) 121-42, esp. 121-22.

30. See U. Cassuto, *The Documentary Hypothesis* (Jerusalem: Magnes, 1961).

31. Cassuto, *Commentary on Genesis*(Jerusalem: Magnes, 1964) 2. 30-31.

32. *ANET,* 265-66.

33. Usually these verses are assigned to J, mainly because P has already mentioned Noah's sons by name (6:10; 7:13) and a third mention seems too repetitious, and because the scattering-verb (*nāpĕsâ*) is found in other passages that must be assigned to J. Westermann (*Genesis,* 650) quotes with approval Gunkel's dictum: "The expression has its *Sitz* in the Babel story." But these arguments are questionable. The argument based on repetition is not strong when dealing with priestly material; and there is no reason why the priestly tradent could not have used the scattering-verb, one that is prominent in his approximate contemporary, Ezekiel. Furthermore, the participial expression "those who went forth [*hayyôsĕ'îm*] from the ark (9:18) corresponds to the same formulation in the preceding priestly material (9:10: *yôsĕ'ê hattēbâ*). In any case, the passage now has a transitional function in the overall narrative.

34. See the commentaries for a treatment of words and phrases characteristic of J and P. It is noteworthy that in the execution passage (7:7-9) it is stated that the animals, clean and unclean, went into the ark by pairs, "two and two." The priestly tradent, who reworked the epic tradition, may have been concerned at this point with the sexual pairing of the animals, not the total number of clean and unclean.

35. The same question is asked by George Coats in his study of the Joseph Story, *From Canaan to Egypt: Structural and Theological Context for the Joseph Story* (CBQM S4; Washington: Catholic Biblical Association, 1976) 57.

36. Arguments based on the alternation of divine names in *Genesis,* which appeal to Exod 6:2-3 for support, perhaps need to be reexamined. It is noteworthy that the priestly tradent clearly uses the divine name Yahweh in *Gen* 17:1 ("Yahweh appeared to Abram, and said to him, 'I am El Shaddai."); and he has even hyphenated Yahweh and Elohim in the paradise story.

37. See Martin Kessler, "Rhetorical Criticism of *Genesis* 7," in *Rhetorical Criticism* (see note 5) 1-17.

38. *Genesis,* 2. 97.

39. See McEvenue, *Narrative Style,* 28.

40. Ibid., 31.

41. *From Canaan to Egypt,* 7-8.

42. "The Priestly Work," 306.

43. See Paul D. Hanson, "Rebellion in Heaven, Azazel, and Euhemeristic Heroes in I Enoch 6-11," *JBL* 96 (1977) 195-233, who points out that in old epic tradition (J) the mythic fragment in 6:1-4 serves to illustrate the degeneration of humankind and specifically to highlight two related themes: "the divinely ordained separation of heaven and earth as two distinct realms, and the enforcement of distinct limits upon the human race" (p. 214). Clearly the priestly tradent saw in this enigmatic episode the final evidence of "violence" and "corruption" in God's creation.

Alan Jon Hauser (essay date 1982)

SOURCE: *"Genesis* 2-3: The Theme of Intimacy and Alienation," *Art and Meaning in Biblical Literature, Journal for the Study of the Old Testament,* Supplement Series, 19, 1982, pp. 20-36.

[In the following essay, Hauser examines the literary devices and techniques by which the author of Genesis *develops the theme of intimacy in chapter two of* Genesis,*

and alienation in chapter three. Hauser maintains that the author uses this intimacy/alienation theme as a motif to both focus and integrate the narrative, and to emphasize the disorder and divisiveness of human life.]

The narrative in **Genesis** 2-3 is one of the better-known pieces of Western literature, largely because it has the ability to focus the reader's attention on key issues relating to man's existence. The writer has artfully woven his story, using a limited number of characters and objects to present in brief but moving form the story of man's fall. Any attempt to make a complete analysis of this writer's work would be a major undertaking, especially when one considers the complexity of issues such as the role and identity of the serpent, or the form and function of the knowledge that woman so strongly desires. In this study I have a fairly limited goal: to analyze the writer's development of the two-dimensional theme of intimacy and alienation. These are my words, not his, but it is my conviction that they clearly express a major motif the writer has used to focus and integrate his narrative. As I analyze this motif, I will pay special attention to the ways in which the writer leads his audience, by means of numerous literary devices, to experience the shattering of the closely-knit created order and the onslaught of that divisiveness which both writer and reader know to be a part of their everyday life.

Of necessity, this study will fall into two parts. The first will treat the development of the theme of intimacy in **Genesis** 2. The second will analyze the theme of alienation as it unfolds in **Genesis** 3.

I

In ch.2 the writer weaves several components into an intimate picture of harmony, with all revolving around man, the first and central element in the created order. These components are: the ground (*h'dmh*); the Lord God (*yhwh 'lhym*); the garden (*hgn*) and its trees (*kl 'ts*); the animals; and woman (*'shh*). A study of select verses from this chapter will show in detail how the writer has used various stylistic devices to convey the theme of intimacy.

Verse 7. *wyytsr yhwh 'lhym 't h'dm* (then the Lord God molded man). The verb *ytsr* (to form, mold) underlines the intimacy between God and man. God does not simply create man or bring him into being: he takes pains with him, just as a potter would in forming a fine vessel. Man is therefore most special.

'pr mn h'dmh (dust from the ground). This phrase points to man's close association with the ground: *'dm* is taken from *'dmh*. The Hebrew mind viewed the similarity of sounds, as here with the words *'dm* and *'dmh,* as a key to the interrelatedness of the persons, objects, or concepts embodied in the words. In subsequent verses the writer will develop this association of man with the ground, as when God causes trees to grow out of the ground to provide food for man (2:9,16), or when God forms animals out of the ground as companions for man (2:19). Further-

more, the phrase *'pr mn h'dmh* forms an *inclusio* with 3:19. Man is formed by God from the dust of the ground (2:7): after man has disrupted creation he must return to the ground as dust (3:19). Significantly, even though *'dmh* is used repeatedly in chs. 2 and 3, 2:7 and 3:19 are the only two points where *'dmh* and *'pr* are directly associated with one another. As a result, the statement of consequences in 3:19 harks back directly to the time of beginning, making more poignant man's fall.

wypch b'pyw nshmt chyym wyhy h'dm lnpsh chyh (and he breathed into his nostrils the breath of life, and man became a living creature). In addition to further developing God's closeness to man during the act of creation, these words stress through repetition the gift of life that man has received. In a fashion reminiscent of Hebrew poetry, the writer parallels *nshmt chyym* (breath of life) with *lnpsh chyh* (living creature). The rest of ch.2 continues to stress the gift of life, life which is created for the benefit of man and in order to provide him with companionship. It is in 3:19 that the gift of life is withdrawn; thus, the life-death sequence forms a further link between 2:7 and 3:19.

Verse 8. The garden is created for man. The writer emphasizes this fact by having God plant it immediately after man receives life, and by having God set the man in the garden immediately after it is planted.[1] *wysm shm 't h'dm 'shr ytsr* (and there he set the man whom he had formed). It would have been adequate for the writer to say, "And there he set the man." He chooses, however, to add the last two words, using the identical verb (*ytsr*) from v.7, so that he may again stress the close association between man and God.

Verse 9. God causes the trees to grow *mn h'dmh* (from the ground). Man, who himself was taken from the ground, is able to enjoy through sight and taste the produce God has brought forth for him from the ground. Here man's enjoyment of the trees through sight and taste is part of God's plan. This sets the stage for 3:6, where enjoying the tree in the midst of the garden belongs to the sequence of disruption.

Verse 15. Man's closeness to the garden is again stressed. He lives in harmony with it, having the responsibility of caring for it, even while he enjoys its fruit (v.16). The verb *'bd* (to till, care for) points back to v.5, where there were as yet no plants, because there was no man to till (*'bd*) the ground. Now, however, it is appropriate that God has planted trees in the garden: there is a man to care for them.

Verse 18. The writer now turns to the element of creation closest to man. He tells us this not only by using the programmatic clause, "It is not good that man should be alone," but also by means of the phrase *'zr kngdw* (a companion corresponding to him, a helper like him). The writer also makes his point by means of a word play: although man is part of the created order, in close harmony with God and the garden, for which he cares (*ᶜbd:* v.15), he is alone (*lbd*), lacking a close companion, someone to care for him. The fact that a suitable companion is not found immediately, but only after prolonged effort by God, helps to emphasize the closeness to man of the ultimate companion, woman.

Verse 19. Like man, the animals are formed (*ytsr*) from the ground (*'dmh*). The writer thus represents God as attempting to create a companion for man who is as much like him as possible, being formed in the same way and being taken from the same source. This sets up the failure at the end of v.20, where none of the animals proves acceptable as man's companion. In light of this failure, woman, who is the appropriate companion, must be seen to be *very* close to man.

Verses 19-20. The writer places great stress on the naming of the animals by man. Three times the verb *qr'* (to name) is used, and the noun *shm* (name) is used twice. The writer does not have God name the animals, because the man must examine each thoroughly and discern for himself a companion. This is stressed by the clause *wyb' 'l h'dm lr'wt mh yqr' lw* (and he brought them unto the man, to see what he would name them). This clause, the two lists naming categories of animals God has created (vv.19 and 20), and the clause *wkl 'shr yqr' lw h'dm npsh chyh hw' shmw* (and whatever the man named each living creature, that was its name), all serve to elongate the process of man's careful scrutinizing of the animals. The writer has chosen to employ this repetition so that the last phrase in v.20 will be even more emphatic: *wl'dm l' mts' 'zr kngdw* (but there was not found for man a companion like him). Despite God's efforts to make the animals as much like man as possible, the long search is fruitless, and man is still alone. Man's being alone is especially stressed by the repetition of the phrase *'zr kngdw* (a companion like him) from v.18, which described the beginning of the search.

Verse 21. God now causes a deep sleep to fall upon man, because the creation of a companion for man literally requires that God take a part of man himself: *wyqch 'cht mtsl'tyw* (and he took one of his ribs). The animals, like man, were taken from the ground, but this does not give them the closeness to man which woman will possess. The closing up of the wound with flesh (*bsr*) enables the writer to anticipate the end of the scene in v.24 where man and woman are described as one flesh.

Verse 22. The writer repeats the phrase "the rib which he had taken from man" in order to stress again the intimate connection between man and woman. *wybn* (and he built): the writer uses the verb *bnh* in order to stress the uniqueness of woman's creation; for whereas God formed (*ytsr*) man and the animals from the ground, he builds up woman from man's rib. While *bnh* normally means "to build," in this context it carries the connotation of "building up," since from a small part of man God fashions a companion for him.

wyb'h 'l h'dm (and he brought her to the man). These words echo God's bringing the animals to man in v.19.

The writer deliberately parallels the wording in the two scenes so that the reader will keep the former scene in mind, and thereby focus on the contrast between woman, who indeed is man's *ᶜzr kngdw* (companion like him), and the animals, which are not. This phrase also suggests the way in which a father brings to a man his bride (cf. ***Gen.*** 29:23), thereby preparing the reader for v.24.

Verse 23. The writer uses this short piece of poetry to bring to a climax the search for man's *'zr* (helper). The demonstrative pronoun *z't* (this)[2] is used three times in order to single out woman emphatically as *the* one who is suited to be man's companion. The poetry begins with man exclaiming *z't,* as if he has been watching a long parade of nominees and now suddenly sees the right one. The next word, *hp'm* (at last, finally), strengthens the image, declaring man's exasperation over the long wait. The second use of *z't,* at the beginning of line two, again accentuates woman as she receives a name indicating her closeness to man. The final *z't,* at the end of the short poem, forms a neat *inclusio* with the opening word, recalling man's earlier word of joy upon having at last found his companion. It also serves to emphasize for a third time woman's suitability as the writer repeats, in language closely parallel to v.22, the fact that woman is taken from man (*m'ysh lqchh z't*).[3]

'tsm mᶜtsmy wbsr mbsry (bone of my bone and flesh of my flesh). This phrase is often used in the OT to express intimate family ties, as in ***Gen.*** 29:14; Judg. 9:2; 2 Sam. 5:1, 19:12-13. In such cases, a common ancestry is assumed. Here, however, woman is literally man's bone and flesh (see the writer's earlier setting of the stage in v.21). The writer knew that the special twist he was putting on the common phrase would seize the attention of his reader and therefore stress even more the intimacy of man and woman.[4] Furthermore, *ᶜtsm* (bone), because of its vocal similarity to *'zr* (companion), calls to the reader's attention the fact that woman, who is *ᶜtsm* of man's *ᶜtsm,* is also man's *ᶜzr.*

lz't yqr' 'shh (for this will be called "woman"). As with the animals, man names the woman, except that in this case he clearly perceives the *woman* to be his *'zr kngdw* (companion like him). The writer does not specifically use that phrase here. Rather, he employs a word play between *'shh* (woman) and *'ysh* (man) to make his point. While there is no etymological relationship between the two words[5], the phonetic similarity makes a "common sense" case for the closeness between man and woman. Thus, while man's observation of each animal led him to give each a name, so his perception of woman causes him to give her a name closely akin to his.

Verse 24. Again the writer makes his point about woman being one flesh with man. As close as man is to his parents, who have given him life, he will be even closer to his wife, to whom he will cleave (*dbq*), and with whom he will become one flesh. But in this first instance the relationship is even closer, since the writer is clearly alluding to v.21, where the first woman is taken directly from man.[6] Thus, the theme of alienation in ch.3 becomes even more tragic in light of this special oneness of the first man and woman.

Beginning with v.24, the word is not simply "woman," but rather "his woman." While the root word in Hebrew, *'shh*, is the same as that used in vv.22-23, the sense of the passage makes "his wife" a better translation.

Verse 25. The reference in v.24 to being one flesh does not refer only to sexual relations (nor does it exclude them). In v.25 the sexual overtones are more pronounced. Throughout the OT there is basically a reserved attitude towards nakedness, with it being presumed that one's nakedness is, with only rare exception, to be shielded from the eyes of others. To expose someone's nakedness was to lay them bare before the world, to make them open and vulnerable, in a most thoroughgoing sense (**Gen.** 42:9,12; Isa. 20; Ezek. 16:22,39; 23:22-35; Hos. 2). It often means to expose one to shame (1 Sam. 20:30; 2 Sam. 10:4-5; Isa. 47:3; Nah. 3:5). Clearly, one's nakedness was seen as a very personal thing, a key to one's innermost self. It is for this reason that the phrase "to expose the nakedness of . . ." is often used to refer to sexual intercourse (Lev. 18; 20), wherein two people open themselves to one another in the most complete way possible. Thus, in v.25 man and his wife stand naked before one another, expose themselves completely to one another, and are not ashamed.[7] Their vulnerability causes no anxiety, and their intimacy is complete. This sets the stage for ch.3, where the intimacy is disrupted, as expressed in part through the urgent need of man and woman to cover up their nakedness.

II

As we move into ch.3, the writer dramatically shifts the course of his narrative. The world of harmony and intimacy becomes a world of disruption and alienation. The sudden introduction of the serpent[8] alerts the reader that he is entering a new stage of the narrative, as does also the format of the opening words, which may be translated "Now the serpent was . . ." The word *'rwm* (cunning) also presents a new element, one which is accentuated by the writer's word play between it and the similar—sounding *'rwmym* (naked) from the previous verse. The nakedness of man and woman had given expression to their intimacy. Now, however, the cunning of the serpent injects into the created order a disruptive feature which grows until it reaches a climax in vv.12-13. The intimacy of ch.2 dissolves in a rapid sequence of events.

Verses 1-6. In the encounter between woman and the serpent, the writer subtly but firmly continues to stress the intimacy between man and woman. Throughout vv.1-6, plural verbs are used when the serpent addresses woman, as though man were also being addressed (e.g., v.5 *whyytm k'lhym,* and you will be like God), plural verbs are used to summarize God's command concerning the fruit of the trees (e.g., v.3 *l' t'klw,* you shall not eat)[9], and woman in

speaking of herself and man uses a plural verb (v.2 *n'kl,* we may eat). The writer's use of these plural verbs[10] implies that man and woman are one, that they cannot be dealt with or addressed apart from one another. When woman eats the fruit of the forbidden tree, her first act thereafter is to give some to man, and the writer further stresses the intimacy by using the phrase *l'yshh 'mh* (to her husband with her). While the intimacy between man and woman continues to be stressed in the opening verses of ch.3, it will soon dissolve into open animosity between the two (especially in vv.12-13).

But if the intimacy between man and woman continues in vv.1-6, other elements of the intimate world described in ch.2 are already being torn apart. In a series of steps, the serpent moves woman from correcting the serpent's false statement about God's command, to doubting God's truthfulness, craving the forbidden fruit, and desiring to be wise like God. The intimacy with God is being destroyed by the serpent's cunning even before woman eats of the fruit.

Thus, in vv.1-6 the writer has artfully woven together his themes of intimacy and alienation. The intimacy of man and woman, the most complete form of intimacy described in ch.2, temporarily continues as a remnant of the harmonious world of ch.2, even while the disruption between God and his creatures grows at a rapid pace.

The writer has used the verb *yd'* (to know) to strengthen the image of alienation. It is first used at the beginning of v.5, where the woman is told, "God knows that when you eat of it, your eyes will be opened." The tone of this statement is that God is deliberately withholding information, desiring to keep his creatures in their place. Thus, woman is led to doubt God. Furthermore, the writer is using a word play, for at the end of v.5 there is the phrase "knowing good and evil." Both forms of *yd'* are participles. One might loosely paraphrase the sense of this word play as follows: God knows that . . . you will know good and evil (and he doesn't want you to know!). This use of *yd'* in v.5 sets the stage for the knowledge that is actually received in v.7.

The writer also stresses the divine-human alienation by means of the clause *whyytm k'lhym* (and you will be like God) in v.5. It is noteworthy that, unlike **Genesis** 1, which stresses the intimacy between God and man by man's being made in the image and likeness of God, **Genesis** 2-3 stresses this intimacy by means of God's great care in the creation of man and man's companion. Although God forms man and breathes into him the breath of life, man is different from God, and has a clearly-defined place as God's creature (as in 2:16-17,18,21-22). Thus, any human desire to be like God places the creature in rebellion against his creator. He becomes estranged from God.

Beginning in v.5, the writer places great stress on the motif of seeing. Woman is told that their eyes (*'ynykm*) will be opened if they eat the fruit of the tree (v.5). She saw (*wtr'*) that the tree was good for food (v.6), and that it was a delight to the eyes.[11] It is therefore ironical that after the fruit has been eaten (v.6), man and woman desire that *they* not be seen. Although the tree was a delight (*t'wh*) to the eyes (v.6), the "eye opening" experience they have after eating the fruit is anything but delightful, and there now is an attempt to cover up (vv.7-11). The writer uses this fear of being seen as a key means to express the alienation that destroys the harmony of ch.2.

The writer has devoted only a bare minimum of words to the act of eating, and even a majority of these words are used to indicate that man and woman take part in the act together.

Verse 7. Here the writer's interweaving of the themes of intimacy and alienation continues. As a result of their eating, both man and woman have their eyes opened. While they experience this together[12], the knowledge they have gained separates them. They can no longer tolerate being naked in one another's presence. Since, as noted earlier, one's nakedness is a key to one's innermost self, man and woman are pulling apart from one another: their intimacy is no longer complete.

The clause, "Then the eyes of the two of them were opened," is rather surprising, given all the seeing that has taken place in the previous verses. The writer is using this clause to express the dramatic change that has come about as a result of the forbidden act. As a consequence of their rebellion against God, the man and woman see things very differently. The writer has also stressed this change by means of the word play on *yd'* (to know). While knowing had appeared very attractive in v.5, now man and woman know that they are alienated from one another, and they make clothes.

The influence of alienation is not yet complete. There is a remnant of togetherness, as indicated by the plural verbs describing the making of clothes, and by the plural *lhm* (for themselves).

Verses 8-10. God has been absent since 2:22, his absence being part of a deliberate pattern by the writer. In ch.2 God and man had been quite intimate, but the chapter closes by stressing the complete intimacy of man and woman (vv.23-25), and God recedes into the background. In ch.3 God continues to be absent as the forces of disruption are turned loose. His reappearance in v.8, however, brings the theme of alienation to its climax. Thus, not only does God create the most complete form of intimacy (2:22); he also brings out into the open all the divisive consequences of man's rebellion (3:9-13).

Upon hearing God, man and his wife hide themselves (*wytchb'*) in the midst of the trees of the garden. This act, their mutual hiding from God, is the last remnant of the "togetherness" of man and woman. Hereafter they act as individuals, and the plural verbs of vv.1-8 are absent. Similarly, the phrase "the man and his wife" (*h'dm w'shtw*)

is the last time the two words are used in relation to one another to express intimacy. The complete phrase appears earlier in 2:25, and singly the words "his wife" (*'shtw*) and "her husband" (*'yshh*) appear in 2:24 and 3:6, respectively. This usage, along with the stress in 2:23-24 on man and woman being one flesh, is in stark contrast to the way man refers to woman in 3:12.

The phrase *btwk 'ts hgn* (in the midst of the trees of the garden) points back to v.3. Woman had told the serpent that they were forbidden to eat the fruit of the tree in the midst of the garden (*h'ts 'shr btwk hgn*). But she and her husband did eat of it. Thus, by using the same words (slightly rearranged) in v.8 the writer again brings to the reader's attention the offense that unleashed the forces of disruption and alienation, and now causes man and woman to hide from the presence of God (*mpny yhwh 'lhym*), with whom they formerly had been intimate. The writer is also being ironical: man and woman eat of the fruit of the tree in the midst of the garden in order to be like God (v.5); now, as a consequence of their eating, they hide from God in the midst of the trees of the garden.[13] They sin by means of a tree; yet, they must hide among the trees. Thus, they cannot escape what they have done. Indeed, from this point on, everywhere man and woman turn they encounter as symbols of alienation what had formerly been elements of the created world of harmony.

Significantly, in v.9 God does not address man and woman together, but rather calls to man (*wyqr' yhwh 'lhym 'l h'dm*). To stress further that God is speaking to man alone, the writer adds *wy'mr lw* (and he said to him), and *'ykh* (where are you?), the latter having a second person masculine singular ending.[14] The writer is thus suggesting, as he soon will stress more bluntly (v.12), that man and woman no longer are one.

Man's response (v.10) to God's question emphatically stresses man's aloneness. Verse 8 had begun by stating, "and they heard (*wyshm'w*) the sound (*qwl*) of the Lord God walking in the garden (*bgn*)." In v.10 the words *qwl, gn,* and the root *shm^c* are repeated, so as to underline the parallelism between vv.8 and 10. This makes the singular form of *shm'ty* (I heard) in v.10 stand out all the more in contrast to the plural form of v.8. Thus, in v.8 man and woman hear together; in v.10 man has become alienated to the point that he now perceives himself to have heard alone. Man's alienation is further underlined by the final verb *w'chb'* (and I hid myself), which contrasts with the plural *wytchb'* of v.8. The writer also stresses man's aloneness through the singular verb *w'yr'* (and I was afraid) and through the phrase *ky ^cyrm 'nky* (because I was naked).

While the contrast between the plural forms of v.8 and the singular forms of v.10 stresses the alienation of man from woman, the writer also emphasizes man's alienation from God. Man hears God's voice in the garden, and is afraid. God heretofore has been very intimate with man, forming him from the dust of the ground, planting the garden for him, forming animals for him from the ground, and building up woman from the rib taken from man's side. All this, however, is now gone, as man fears the very one who has given him life and his world. Man is afraid, "Because I am naked," and he hides himself. As noted earlier, one's nakedness was seen as a key to one's innermost self; as a consequence, being comfortably naked in another's presence was a sign of real intimacy. But now man must cover up, since he fears having God see him as he is.

Verse 11 stresses man's act of rebellion against God, which more than anything else is what he wishes to hide. It was after his eating that man became conscious of his nakedness, of his alienation. The writer uses God's questions to recall that for the reader: "Who told you that you were naked? Have you eaten of the tree of which I commanded you not to eat?" The double use of the verb *'kl* (to eat) focuses the reader's attention even more sharply on the act, since this is the same verb used three times in v.6 to describe the act.[15] Furthermore, the writer's emphasis on the fact that *God* commanded man not to eat of the tree helps stress even more man's alienation from God. The writer also continues to underline man's alienation from woman by having God address man with singular verbs and pronouns. Thus, man stands before God completely alone.

Verse 12. The motif of man's alienation from God and from woman reaches its climax in v.12. In previous scenes the intimacy between man and woman has been thoroughly developed, especially through the idea that man and woman are one flesh (2:23-25). Furthermore, when woman's relationship to man has been described, she has consistently been referred to as *'shtw* (his wife; 2:24,25; 3:8). Now, however, man coldly passes the blame for his deed to "*the* woman" (*h'shh*):[16] "*she* gave to me" (*hw' ntnh ly*).[17] To man she has become an object, not a companion, and the clause *'shr ntth 'mdy* (whom you gave to be with me) points the reader back to an earlier situation of intimacy which no longer exists. The alienation of man from woman is complete.

While God's question in v.11 called for a simple yes or no answer, man refuses to accept responsibility for what he has done. It is not only woman who is blamed, however, as indicated by the words *'shr ntth 'mdy* (whom you gave to be with me)[18], which closely parallel the immediately following words *hw' ntnh ly* (she gave me). Man is clearly saying that God is to blame, since God gave to man the woman who led him astray. Thus, not only has man ceased to see woman as a companion: he also has ceased to see God as a well-intentioned creator who provides man with all good things. The alienation of man from God is also complete.

As previously noted, *'kl* (to eat) is used to point to the act of rebellion, most importantly in the twofold usage in v.11 and in the threefold usage in v.6. In v.12 it again serves this function in the clause *hw' ntnh ly mn h'ts w'kl* (she gave to me from the tree, and I ate), which closely parallels the wording in v.6, *wttn gm l'yshh 'mh wy'kl* (and she

gave also to her husband with her, and he ate). Furthermore, the double use of *ntn* in v.12 helps recall woman's giving of the fruit to man in v.6, and the use of *'mdy* (with me) in v.12 points back to *'mh* (with her) in v.6. Thus, in v.12 the writer has carefully constructed a number of links with the description of the act of rebellion in v.6. This is most appropriate, since it is in v.12 that the consequences of the act are most sharply focused.

Finally, man's concluding word, *w'kl* (and I ate) points once again to man's aloneness, since the verb is in the singular. This directly parallels the aloneness of woman in v.13, where her concluding word is exactly the same.

Verse 13. As was the case with man (v.12), woman refuses to shoulder any blame. She ignores man's claim that she had led him to sin, and instead passes to the serpent the blame for her own deed. Nevertheless, God's question to woman, "What is this that you have done?," underlines the devastating nature of woman's deed. The tone of God's question is, "How could you do such a horrible thing?"[19] The final word *w'kl* (and I ate), being in the singular, further stresses woman's aloneness and alienation from man.

Verses 14-19. There are a number of ways in which the writer expresses his motif of alienation in the poetry of these verses:

1. As in the previous section (3:9-13), the principal figures are each addressed separately by God. Their relationship to one another is consistently depicted as one of animosity and separation. There will be enmity and strife between the serpent and woman, and between the serpent's seed and woman's seed (3:15), which means all mankind (cf. 3:20). While man and woman remain together, they no longer are intimate in the way they were previously, since man will rule over his wife (3:16), and the woman will desire her husband (cf. 2:24-25).

2. The serpent is singled out from the cattle and the creatures of the field and cursed (3:14), because of what he has done.[20] The writer has stressed the serpent's role in causing alienation by paralleling *'rwr 'th mkl hbhmh wmkl chyt hsdh* (cursed are you more than all the cattle and all the creatures of the field) with *'rwm mkl chyt hsdh* (more cunning than all the creatures of the field) from 3:1. Because the serpent was cunning (*'rwm*), leading woman to eat of the fruit of the tree, he is now cursed (*'rwr*).

3. Man has become alienated from the ground. Although God formed man from the dust of the ground (*h'dmh;* 2:7), and from the ground created for man the trees of the garden (2:9) and the animals (2:19), man must now cope with a ground that is cursed, that has become his enemy (3:17-19). He must constantly wrestle with it to sustain his life, yet in the end his life must be surrendered to the ground. Thus, although he is one with it in his creation and in his death, he will throughout his life be alienated from his source. As noted previously (see my comments

on 2:7), the writer uses *'pr* (dust) in conjunction with *'dmh* in only two places: 2:7, where God forms man from the dust of the ground and in 3:19, where man's death is described. The writer thus gives the reader a subtle reminder of what could have been, man's ongoing, intimate relationship with God and the ground, even while the writer stresses the devastating consequences of man's rebellion against God.

4.The main verb used to describe man's rebellion against God was *'kl* (to eat: cf. 3:1,2,3,5,6,11,12,13). The writer continues to use this verb in 3:17-19 in order to link the fact of man's rebellion with the consequences that follow. This is most clearly focused in v.17: because man ate of the tree from which God had forbidden him to eat, the ground will henceforth be cursed, causing man to eat in toil all his days (cf. also v.19). He will struggle with it, but it will bring forth thorns and thistles (v.18). Significantly, man will eat *ᶜsb hsdh* (the plants of the field): now that he has eaten of the tree in the midst of the garden, all the trees of the garden become unavailable to him.

5.The writer employs a word play between *ᶜts* (tree) and *ᶜtsb* (pain). *ᶜts* has consistently been used to develop the theme of man's rebellion (3:1,2,3,6,8,11,12). Consequently, *ᶜtsb,* with its similar sound, reminds the reader of the human rebellion even while describing woman's pain in childbearing (v.16) and man's toil in raising food (v.17). The offense of man and woman concerning the *'ts* results in their *'tsb.*

Verse 21. The act of "covering up" had earlier symbolized the first awareness of man and woman that they were alienated from God and from one another (vv.8-11). Now, the permanence of that alienation is stressed. The creator, who had made man and woman naked, in the most perfect form of intimacy, covers their nakedness, thereby acknowledging the ongoing nature of the divisiveness which man and woman have brought upon themselves. The fact that he makes for them garments of skins, as compared to the hastily-sewn aprons of fig leaves they had made for themselves, helps to emphasize the permanence of their need to cover up.

The words *l'dm wl'shtw* (for man and for his wife) hark back to the earlier intimacy described in 2:21-25, but they do so in a melancholy manner. As man and woman's clothing indicates, their relationship to one another will henceforth be quite different from what it was before the fall. The writer emphasizes this by repeating *wylbshm* (and he clothed them) after *wyᶜs . . . ktnwt ᶜwr* (and he made . . . garments of skins).

Verse 22. Chapter 2 shows man being given specific roles and functions within the created order, with definite bounds being set for man (e.g., 2:16-17). Most notably, although man is intimate with God, he is clearly subordinate to him (as in 2:18,21). In 3:22, however, emphasis is placed on man's attempts to be like God. Thus, man has stepped beyond the bounds set for him as creature, desiring instead to make himself creator.

hn h'dm hyh k'chd mmnw ldᶜt twb wrᶜ (Behold, the man has become like one of us, knowing good and evil). These words echo the serpent's statement to the woman in 3:5, thereby reminding the reader at the close of the account of man's rebellion against his creator. It is not just that man has transgressed the bounds set for him: he threatens the creator's supremacy as creator.

This is especially brought out by the second half of v.22. Traditionally in the ancient Near East, one of the key boundaries between man and the gods is the fact that man is mortal whereas the gods are eternal (as, for example, in the Gilgamesh epic). In 3:22 God fears that man will attempt to transgress this boundary also (*gm*), since he has already acquired the knowledge of good and evil. Thus, man could attempt to be even more like God (3:5). The writer uses the idea of eating (*'kl*) from the tree (*ᶜts*) of life to parallel man's potential deed with his earlier act (3:1-6,11-13,17). God's status as creator is sorely threatened by man, and God takes stringent measures (vv.23-24) to guard this last divine possession from man.

Verse 23. Man was originally formed from the dust of the ground, and the writer throughout ch.2 (vv.7,9,19) notes the importance of the ground in the creation of man's world. As noted above, in 3:17-19 the writer stresses man's alienation by emphasizing the antagonism between man and the ground which has been brought about by man's act of rebellion. Verse 23 re-emphasizes that point through the words *lᶜbd 't h'dmh 'shr lqch mshm* (to till the ground from which he was taken). Thus, the result of man's alienation from God (v.22) is man's alienation from the very ground from which God had formed him.

Verse 24. In v.23 God had sent (*shlch*) man forth from the garden. Verse 24 repeats this for emphasis, only in stronger terms: *wygrsh 't h'dm* (and he drove out the man). Man must not have access to the tree of life![21] This leads well into the final image of these two chapters. God places the cherubim and a flaming sword to guard the way to the tree of life. There is now no turning back. Man has striven to be like God, and will always do so. God must take strong measures to see that man is kept in his place. The fact that God must act so decisively to keep his creatures in line re-emphasizes the radical victory of alienation.

SUMMARY

One of the main themes the writer of *Genesis* 2-3 has used to tie his story together is the motif of intimacy and alienation. This motif is developed in ch.2 by: the writer's depiction of God's care in forming man from the dust of the ground; God's creation of the garden for man, with its trees growing from the ground and providing man with food; God's forming the animals from the ground in an attempt to create a companion for man; God's creation of a companion for man who is literally a part of man; and the picture of man and woman being one, naked but yet completely at ease in one another's presence. This intimate world of harmony developed in ch.2 is shattered in ch.3.

Although man and woman have a set place in the created order, the writer pictures woman striving, at the serpent's urging, to become like God, knowing good and evil. Man and woman act together in eating the fruit of the tree, but their intimacy is beginning to be shattered as the writer portrays them making clothes to cover themselves. Furthermore, their striving to be like God in fact results in their being alienated from him: they hide from him. But this is their last act together. God's probing questions expose the alienation of man and woman not only from God, but also from one another. The use of singular nouns and verbs, along with the tendency of man (and subsequently of woman) to blame everyone but himself, shows that the alienation of the various elements of the created order from one another and from God is complete. The poetry of 3:14-19 gives clear expression to this state of alienation, and appropriately presents the picture of man returning to the ground, from which he was taken at the beginning of the narrative. Finally, the permanence of alienation is stressed both by the clothing God makes to cover man and woman's nakedness and by God's decisive measures to keep man out of the garden and away from the tree of life.

Notes

1. The creation of the garden for man is further stressed by the repetition in v.15 of the idea that God placed man in the garden, specifically using the verb *nwch* (to place, to cause to settle).

2. The writer could have used *hw'* (she) in some or all of the instances where *z't* is used, but that would have reduced the emphasis on woman provided by the demonstrative pronoun. On the use of *z't* for emphasis, see Ludwig Koehler and Walter Baumgartner, *Lexicon in Veteris Testamenti Libros* (Leiden: Brill, 1958) 250.

3. See also the use of the verb *lqch* in v.21.

4. See the discussion of Umberto Cassuto, *A Commentary on the Book of Genesis: Part I* (Jerusalem: Magnes Press, 1961) 135-36.

5. E.A. Speiser, *Genesis: Introduction, Translation, and Notes* (AB; Garden City, N.Y.: Doubleday, 1964) 18.

6. It is precisely this point which allows the writer to stress in v.24 the fact that man and woman become one flesh.

7. The writer stresses their standing in each other's presence both by using *shnyhm* (the two of them) and by specifically mentioning each, *h'dm w'shtw* (the man and his wife).

8. The inverted word order, with the noun *hnchsh* (the serpent) coming first, places even greater emphasis on the serpent.

9. This despite the fact that woman has not yet been created when man alone receives the command from God in 2:16-17.

10. Interestingly, almost all these plural verbs are second person masculine, even when woman alone

is addressed (vv.4-5). The writer thus makes it impossible for the reader to think of woman apart from man in vv.1-6.

11. This wording parallels 2:9, except that in 3:6 there is the additional clause, "and that the tree was to be desired to make one wise." The addition of this clause in 3:6 helps contrast the situation there, where disruption is breaking into the created order, with earlier conditions where the created world was in harmony.

12. As indicated by the phrase *'yny shnyhm* (the eyes of the two of them). It should further be noted that the verbs throughout v.7 are plural, continuing the pattern of vv.1-6, where the plural verbs indicate the oneness of man and woman.

13. As noted above, there was great stress on the delight of seeing in vv.5-6, whereas in vv.7-11 man and woman cannot bear to be seen, either by God, or by one another.

14. See A.E. Cowley (ed.), *Gesenius' Hebrew Grammar as Edited and Enlarged by the Late E. Kautzsch* (Oxford: The Clarendon Press, 1910) 256.

15. Note also the usage in vv.1,2,3, and 5.

16. Prior to 3:12, the writer has used *h'shh* only in 3:1-6, where he describes the serpent's tempting of the woman.

17. Note the stress that is placed on *hw'* (she), both by the fact that it is an added element, not really required in its clause, and by its position at the beginning of the clause, which is opposite to the normal verb-subject word order in Hebrew.

18. The writer has used the longer spelling, *ntth*, as opposed to the shorter *ntt* (see Gesenius, 121, 175), so as to make a more perfect parallel to the subsequent *ntnh*.

19. See Cassuto, 158.

20. Note the parallelism of *ky 'syt z't* (because you have done this) to *mh z't 'syt* (What is this that you have done?) in v.13.

21. The word play on *shlch* in vv.22 and 23 helps strengthen this point. God sent man forth (*wyshlchhw*) from the garden (v.23) so that he would not stretch out (*yshlch*) his hand to take and eat from the tree of life.

James S. Ackerman (essay date 1982)

SOURCE: "Joseph, Judah, and Jacob," in *Literary Interpretations of Biblical Narratives,* Vol. II, edited by Kenneth R. R. Gros Louis with James S. Ackerman, pp. 85-113. Abington, 1982.

[*In the following essay, Ackerman explores the use of doubling in the Joseph narrative, noting that the author employs an "unusual" amount of doubling of speech and actions. Ackerman argues that this doubling is intentional and used for emphasis.*]

Scholars have long noted the unusual amount of doubling in the Joseph story: three sets of dreams occur in pairs—by Joseph, by his fellow prisoners, and by Pharaoh.[1] Joseph is twice confined—in the pit and in prison. The brothers make two trips to Egypt for grain, have two audiences with Joseph on each occasion, twice find money in their grain bags, make two attempts to gain Jacob's permission to send Benjamin to Egypt, and finally receive two invitations to settle in Egypt. Both Potiphar and the prison keeper leave everything in Joseph's hands. Potiphar's wife makes two attempts to seduce Joseph and then accuses him twice. Joseph serves two prominent prisoners (and two years elapse between their dreams and those of Pharaoh). Joseph twice accuses his brothers of spying, devises two plans to force the brothers to bring Benjamin to Egypt, and on two occasions places money in their sacks. Finally, the same goods (gum, balm, and myrrh) are twice brought from Canaan to Egypt—first with Joseph and later with Benjamin.[2]

Doubling appears in speeches as well as actions. In some instances characters repeat a phrase in one episode (eg., 41:25/28; 42:15/16; 43:3/5). Elsewhere, speeches recapitulate and supplement events reported earlier in the story (e.g., 40:15; 42:21-22; 42:31-34; 43:7; 43:20-23; 44:3-7; 44:18-34; 50:17).

The common assumption has been that much of the doubling is a result of the conflation of sources—an assumption I shall not question here. My concern is to point out the effect that doubling has as a literary device in the story. D. B. Redford, for example, has noted that doubling can often be used for emphasis: "The certainty of the dreams' fulfillment is thus stressed, as well as the stubbornness of Jacob, Joseph's determination to treat his brothers as spies, Egyptian initiative in making possible Israel's settlement in Egypt, and so on."[3] A second effect of doubling, Redford believes, is plot retardation in some crucial instances. For example, while the doublets are emphasizing Jacob's stubbornness and Joseph's determination, they are also delaying the recognition scene in which the brothers will discover the identity of the Egyptian lord.[4]

Acknowledging the many instances of these kinds of doubling, I would argue that there is a deeper, structural doubling in the Joseph story—occasioned by the unexpected turn of events in chapter 42 when the brothers first come to Egypt to bring grain. "And Joseph's brothers came, and they did obeisance to him—nostrils to the ground. . . ."[*] (All asterisked biblical quotations have been made directly from the Hebrew text.) This is the outcome envisioned in Joseph's first dream of ascendancy over the rest of his family (37:5-7). We hadn't known what to make of those dreams: had special favor been thrust on the youth, or did he grasp after it by tattling on his brothers? Did the dreams indicate divine choice, or were they the ambitious imaginings of a lad who would play the role of deity? Like Day Star, who had tried to replace the deity, Joseph is cast into the pit (Isa. 14:12ff); and then he is taken down into Egypt. But a recurring motif is God's presence with Joseph in Egypt, whether he is in Potiphar's house or in Pharaoh's prison. The reader notes with satisfaction that Joseph's rise to power in Egypt results from a combination of pious behavior, divine help, and his wise advice at court.

When the brothers come to Egypt for grain, the reader is prepared for the denouement. When they do obeisance before Joseph, we remember the dreams before he does. We assume that the story will soon end, showing how human beings cannot thwart the divine purpose. We have been prepared for this conclusion by chapter 41: after hearing and interpreting Pharaoh's dreams, Joseph tells him that the matter is fixed by God when a second dream repeats the first (41:32). Then, as Joseph predicted, the seven-year cycles of plenty and drought take place. Thus as the brothers fulfill Joseph's dreams by bowing down before him, the lesson of God's control of history is played out again, and the reader may consider the main story at an end.

The denouement does not fulfill our expectations, however, as Joseph turns with apparent vengeance on his brothers. Scholars who question Joseph's morality or who see him reverting to his earlier adolescent behavior are overlooking a literary device used by the storyteller: "And Joseph recognized his brothers; but as for them, they did not recognize him. And Joseph *remembered the dreams* that he had dreamed about them. And he said to them, 'Spies you are—to see the nakedness of the land'"[*] (42:8-9a).

At this crucial moment of confrontation, the prostrated brothers bring to his mind an image from the past. Like the reader, Joseph remembers not the betrayal or suffering wrought by his brothers, but his dreams.[5] We have been seduced by the baker-butler and the Pharaoh dream sequences into assuming that dreams indicate that what has been fixed by God will inevitably come to pass. Here is the climactic instance: Joseph's brothers are bowing down before him. We are not prepared for further plot complications.

In the unusual description of Joseph's thoughts in 42:9, the syntax connects his remembering the dreams with his accusing his brothers, launching a new series of events. That syntactical connection suggests that everything that follows is related to his dreams. We have just been told how Joseph, in naming his Egyptian-born sons, had put the past behind him: "God has made me forget all my hardship and all my father's house (and) made me fruitful in the land of my affliction" (41:51, 52). Now events remind him of his dreams. And somehow, from Joseph's point of view, the dreams have not yet been *completely* fulfilled.

As we read further it quickly becomes clear that Joseph's immediate purpose is to have the brothers bring Benjamin to Egypt. Then we recall: *all* the brothers' sheaves had bowed to Joseph's sheaf, and Benjamin is still in Canaan. The lad must join the brothers in Joseph's presence. And Joseph must continue to dissemble, since the first dream depicts his being treated as lord rather than brother.

We might wonder why Joseph focuses on bringing only Benjamin to Egypt. He does ask after Jacob's welfare, but makes no effort to include the patriarch in his machinations with his brothers. When we look more closely at Joseph's dreams, however, we see that they were not so closely doubled as were Pharaoh's. The motif of obeisance appears in both dreams; but the first points only to the brothers, while the second includes the whole family. Thus Joseph's dream sequence establishes the pattern for his course of action after his brothers come to Egypt: obeisance of all the brothers is of first importance.

Joseph may not yet be conscious of the full meaning of his dreams. With the dreams of the butler-baker and Pharaoh, the pattern had been dream-interpretation-fulfillment. In Joseph's own case, however, the interpretation will not be clear to him until after the dreams have been fulfilled—possibly because he himself must play a role in bringing the dreams to fulfillment.

Both the recognition of the brothers and the recollection of the dreams are one-sided. As a plot device, they force the reader to see what follows in the light of what has preceded. But what of the actors in this drama? Will Joseph come to understand the connection between his dreams and the new sequence of events? Will the brothers come to the same understanding? Will they not have to relive Joseph's suffering so they can fully realize what they did to him?

The brothers soon recall their past crime and interpret their present misfortunes as a long-delayed retribution, but there is room for further growth. Joseph recalls his dreams, but is not yet able to interpret their meaning. Thus after the climactic meeting the story is so arranged that Joseph, in acting out his dreams, will embark on a twice-told tale through which he will both fulfill and learn the divine purpose for his life.

One result of this plot device is a series of dramatic ironies, some apparent to Joseph, some appreciated only by the reader:

(a) "We are all sons of one man," say the brothers in 42:11, not realizing that their statement includes the strange lord standing before them.

(b) "You will be tested . . . Send one of you and let him bring your brother . . . so that your words may be tested, whether '*emet* [a word that means both *truth* and *faithfulness*] is with you,"* says Joseph in 42:15-16. The brothers pass half of the test in chapter 43. There was '*emet/truth* with them: they have proved they were the family unit they had claimed to be, rather than a group of spies, by

producing the youngest son. But they will soon discover that the test has not ended. It is yet to be determined whether or not '*emet/faithfulness* was with them.

(c) When Jacob finally relents and agrees to send Benjamin, he prays in 43:14 that God will prosper the journey "so that he will send to you your brother, another, and Benjamin."* The father may be referring to Simeon, the brother kept hostage in Egypt. But Jacob did not say "your other brother." The syntax leaves the meaning just ambiguous enough for the reader to know that it can also refer to Joseph.[6]

(d) In 42:21 we are told that Joseph had earlier pleaded for "favor" (*hnn*) for himself, but his brothers would not listen. When Joseph first meets Benjamin, he gives the pious, traditional greeting "May God grant you faovr [*hnn*], my son"* (43:29). Those words will have a deeper significance as the plot develops. Will the other son of Rachel find "favor" from the brothers when they are asked to leave him enslaved in Egypt and return to their father?

(e) When the brothers return to the Egyptian lord after the divining cup has been discovered in Benjamin's sack, Judah's defense should be *nolo contendere:* they cannot defend themselves against the charge, even though they consider themselves not guilty. Instead, however, Judah exclaims, "God has found out the guilt of your servants" (44:16). Does he mean that the Egyptian should accept the statement as an admission of guilt regarding a deliberate theft, or something else? The guilt that Judah acknowledges God has "found out"—we and his brothers know—is for an incident that took place long ago.

A second result of the narrative device of delayed fulfillment is the doubled plot. Readers can see the brothers suffering, in part at least, measure for measure for what they did in the past:

(a) In *Genesis* 37, as Joseph approached his brothers in Dothan, "they *saw* him . . . and they conspired [*vayyit-nakkᵉlû*] against him." Finally they returned with the bloody garment to their father, saying "This we have found; *recognize* now—cloak of your son—is it or not?"*[7] Twenty years later, when the brothers first appear before Joseph, "he *saw* his brothers, and he *recognized* them; but he acted unrecognizably [*vayyitnakkēr*] unto them"*—the significant pun, in a technique characteristic of the whole story, reinforcing the moral pattern of measure for measure. Joseph's dissembling echoes the brothers' conspiring. In 37:4 "they were not able to speak peaceably to him."* Now Joseph "speaks harshly to them"* (42:7). Those who had duped their father into "recognition" are now recognized. The deceivers are deceived. The ones who had seen Joseph and conspired against him are now on the receiving end, and the key to the deception is Joseph "acting unrecognizably."

(b) Joseph then falsely accuses the brothers of coming "to see the nakedness of the land"* (42:9). In the biblical tradition "nakedness" consistently occurs in texts referring to sexual misconduct.[8] Are we not being asked to recall Joseph's plight in **Genesis** 39, when Potiphar's wife falsely accused him of sexual misconduct, causing his angry master to throw him in prison? Now Joseph falsely accuses his brothers and has them bound over into prison for a period of three days.

(c) In 40:15 Joseph, interpreting the butler's dream, uses language that equates his Egyptian imprisonment with an earlier event in his life: "For I was indeed stolen from the land of the Hebrews, and also here I have not done anything that they should place me *in the pit.*"* Joseph is linking his brothers' betrayal with his imprisonment, so that the memory of his suffering is doubly tied to the pit. Thus when he imprisons his brothers, he is forcing them to relive two separate experiences from the past: his imprisonment by Potiphar, and his being cast into the pit by his brothers.

(d) While in prison, the brothers must decide which one will return to tell Jacob that nine more of his sons have been taken and that Benjamin must also come down to Egypt; they realize that Jacob will hold back. Desolately, the brothers in the prison/pit contemplate the prospect of death or slavery—just as Joseph had earlier sat in their pit awaiting death. He is meting out, measure for measure, what he had suffered in the past.

The outburst of "measure for measure" activity soon ends. After three days Joseph changes his mind and allows the brothers to return to Canaan, keeping only Simeon as a hostage. Why do we find the seemingly unnecessary change of plan after this short interval? Joseph's first response to his brothers had been punitive. He had wanted his brothers to relive in part the hardships that he had experienced. But his major purpose is to bring his dreams to fulfillment, and this necessitates a change in strategy. He also must realize that sending only one brother back home would be a certain overkill that would cause Jacob to dig in his heels, frustrating his intention. Thus he carefully modifies his course of action.

This change initiates a chain of events that will be part of a third plot doubling. The result of Joseph's changed course of action is to bring the brothers' long-repressed guilt to the surface. Only now will there be discussion and recriminations among them concerning what had happened twenty years before. Why does this happen? It is unclear whether Joseph intends it or not, but the changed course of action—ostensibly aimed at fulfilling the dreams—is subtly forcing the brothers to relive their earlier crime.[9] Thus with 42:18ff we move from a "measure for measure" punitive reaction to a more subtle "play within a play" in which, like Hamlet's uncle, the brothers will be forced to relive the past and face its horror.

The first expression of guilt comes as soon as they learn that they must return to their father to fetch Benjamin (42:21-22). Why is this? Surely part of the reason is a growing sense of *déjà vu* among the brothers. They must return to their father with the dreadful news of a second lost brother—this time, Simeon; and at the same time they must demand that Jacob surrender the other son of Rachel. Their imprisonment had forced them to relive Joseph's pit/imprisonment experiences. Now they must reenact their earlier crime.

On the homeward journey one of the brothers discovers silver in his sack. "What is this that God had done to us?" they exclaim. They are horrified by the discovery of what, in other circumstances, could have been construed as an act of kindness. Surely, their reaction is to some extent caused by fear that the money is part of a setup: it will be used as an occasion for a second false accusation that will result in imprisonment, slavery, or death when they return to Egypt. But the silver gained in the context of losing another brother also echoes their grim plan to sell Joseph into slavery for silver. That time, the Midianites had foiled their plan and received the silver instead. Now as the brothers return to their father minus another brother and with silver in their sacks, we (and possibly also the brothers) may well feel that the payoff for their earlier crime was twenty years delayed in coming.

The brothers have changed. As the story repeats itself, we must notice the great difference between their attitude toward Jacob's suffering over the report of Joseph's loss with the bloody garment and their description of why Simeon was taken and what they must do with Benjamin. They are now sincere, compassionate for their mourning father, desperate to set things straight. Reuben offers the lives of his two sons if Benjamin does not return. But Jacob pitifully turns them away. If Benjamin is lost, "you would bring my gray hairs in sorrow to Sheol."* This echoes Jacob's response to the loss of Joseph: "I will go down to my son mourning—to Sheol"* (37:35).

The parallels continue, as the reader picks up an irony that must elude the brothers. Jacob, after a long struggle, has finally been convinced that the family will not survive if Benjamin is not sent to Egypt. The wily father hopes for the best and does what he can by sending gifts to the Egyptian lord (43:11). Thus Benjamin departs for Egypt; and with him go balm, honey, gum, myrrh, pistachio nuts, and almonds—the very goods that accompanied Joseph twenty years before (37:25). The brothers had been indirectly responsible for Joseph's earlier descent into Egypt. This time they must take Benjamin in their own caravan. The allusion to the items of transport suggests that this time the brothers are reenacting the role of the Ishmaelite traders, bringing the other son of Rachel to an uncertain fate.[10]

When the brothers arrived in Egypt with Benjamin, "they did obeisance before him to the ground"* (43:26). With this statement, the narrator stresses that the first dream has been completely fulfilled. We can assume the same of the divine purpose contained in the dream. As for Joseph's own reported purpose, the brothers have demonstrated that '*emet* is with them by producing Benjamin; they have told the truth. Joseph generously provides a banquet for his brothers; and they all feast, drink, even become drunk together. As chapter 43 draws to a close, the writer would have a perfect opportunity to describe Joseph's revelation of his true identity; but Joseph bypasses it.

Why not tell all right now? Joseph proceeds on a course of action that is puzzling (why pick on Benjamin, the one innocent brother?) and that goes beyond the dreams. We should remember, however, that Pharaoh's dreams told only what was fixed by God: seven years of plenty, followed by seven years of famine. They did not hint at the appropriate mode of human response to the fixed divine action, so that the human community would gain the maximum benefit. The appropriate response required a discreet and wise person in whom was the spirit of God. Similarly, Joseph's dreams had disclosed only the course of events that God would ultimately bring about within the family of Jacob: the young Joseph would rise to ascendancy over his brothers and parents. His dreams did not disclose the appropriate response to what they foretold. May we not assume that, as Joseph's response to Pharaoh's dreams had benefited all of Egypt in chapter 41, his mysterious course of action with the divining cup in chapter 44 will somehow benefit the family of Israel?

The first allusion to Joseph's dreams in 42:8-9 begins a plot doubling in which the brothers go through two distinct stages:

A. Measure for measure. First they suffer fit retribution for their crime against Joseph and for his tribulations in the land of Egypt—false accusation and imprisonment, with the fear of death or slavery.

B. Reenactment of the crime. As they return to their father minus a brother and with silver in their sack, hear their father's renewed anguish, and bring the second son of Rachel into Egypt, they are forced to relive painful scenes from the past that bring their guilt to the surface.

Both stages take place as part of Joseph's need to bring his dream to fulfillment. Note also that the brothers' experience is the chronological reverse of the earlier plot: first they suffer what had happened to Joseph during and after the crime; then they relive the crime. Chapter 43, verse 26 describes the literal fulfilling of Joseph's dream and initiates the final doubling that must precede the great climax and denouement of the story. In Aristotle's terms, we have had the major reversal and a one-sided recognition scene. Yet to come are the full recognition scene ("I am Joseph") and the final working out of the plot.

The third stage of the doubling is carefully planned to push events back to the point before the crime took place. When the brothers return to the Egyptian lord after the divining cup has been discovered in Benjamin's sack, the chronology has suddenly shifted. They are no longer acting out an earlier crime. Instead, they are given a chance

to commit a new one. The plot doubling has structured events so that history can repeat itself and they can again be rid of the favored son.[11] This time, however, they will be guiltless. All they have to do is go home and tell their father exactly what happened. Despite Judah's offer that all the brothers remain enslaved, Joseph tells them to return to their father "in peace." They surely recall Jacob's reaction to the loss of Joseph and their fruitless efforts to console him; the loss of the only other son of Rachel would destroy their father. Realization of this leads to Judah's moving speech in which he offers himself as a slave in Benjamin's stead so that the younger brother can return to his father.

When Joseph saw his eleven brothers bowed before him in 43:26, he knew that the divine plan foreshadowed in his first dream had been fulfilled. As a youth he could not have known why his ascendancy to power would be an important part of the divine plan to keep alive the family of Israel. As Joseph proceeds with the divining cup ruse, the narrative gives no indication that he has plumbed the relationship between his past suffering and his present power. Joseph's ploy with the divining cup is in no way related to the explanation he finally expresses to his brothers in 45:5-7. In chapter 44 Joseph's motivation is to test his brothers. They have proved their '*emet*/truthfulness by producing Benjamin. Now he wants to learn whether they have grown and changed—whether there is the possibility of reestablishing brotherhood with them. (Paradoxically, as the brothers pass the test, Joseph will learn more than he had expected. Judah's speech will give him the key for interpreting the mystery of his *own* life. We will return to this later.)

The first dream has been fulfilled in 43:26, but the blessing of reconciliation among the brothers has not been realized. In this story a wise, human response is required to complement and complete the divine activity. Thus, structurally, the divining cup incident is to the fulfillment of Joseph's first dream what the construction of store-cities was to Pharaoh's dreams. The store-cities will contain the blessing of the harvest; the divining cup is the final test of '*emet*/faithfulness that, if passed, may bring the blessing of reconciliation among brothers.

Although the dominant theme of this story may be the providential care of the family of Israel through Joseph's career, reconciliation among brothers is a strong and closely related sub-theme: family survival involves both escape from famine and reconciliation among brothers. In chapter 37 the brothers were angry at Joseph when he tattled and jealous when he received the special garment—"they hated him, and could not *speak peaceably* to him" (37:4). These feelings were intensified by Joseph's dreams (37:5, 8, 11). The narrator reports no word spoken to Joseph as they cast him into the pit. In fact, when the brothers recall that incident in 42:21-22, they describe it as not listening to his entreaties.

The alienation theme is continued on Joseph's part as he "*speaks harshly*"* to his brothers when they first come down to Egypt (42:7); and in their first four encounters they are separated by an interpreter. The descriptions of Joseph's weeping indicate a gradual change in his attitude toward his brothers as he perceives that they have changed. But even in the banquet scene, which might have made a fitting climax, the narrator stresses the physical separation of Joseph from his brothers (43:32). They sat "before him." The language suggests a royal court in which the brothers are placed in subservient positions to the ruler. Even the phrase "They drank and became drunken with him *['immô]*"* suggests the same court background.[12] The brothers are together, but they are not a family. Only after they have passed the test in chapter 44 does reconciliation begin: "And he kissed all his brothers, and he wept upon them. And after that his brothers *spoke with* him" (45:15).[13]

It had been Joseph's reports of his dreams that exacerbated the brothers' ill will toward the youth. They had interpreted the dreams as both a claim to divine favor and a sign of an overweening pride that was nurtured by Jacob's special love for Joseph. They naturally refused to see anything providential in a plan that would cast them down before any brother. There was a strong antimonarchical strand in early Israelite history, shaped by centuries of oppression at the hands of rulers who claimed to be benevolent shepherds of their people.[14] The last thing that Joseph can do, if he wants to reestablish his place as brother in the family, is to overwhelm his brothers with his power. Conversely, the brothers must pass the divining-cup test so that Joseph can again become a brother and part of the family.

The theme of favoritism producing conflict runs throughout the book of *Genesis.* At the human level it begins in the rivalry between Sarah and Hagar, forcing Abraham to favor Isaac and drive out Ishmael. It continues in the rivalry between Isaac's sons, Jacob and Esau—each favored by one parent. The struggle between brothers continues in the next generation, caused in large part by Jacob's special love for Rachel and her offspring over Leah and hers. In all these stories the younger son wins out over the older, and geographical separation helps resolve the conflict. Ishmael becomes a wilderness dweller as he and Hagar disappear from the story. Jacob flees to Haran, at Rebekah's behest, so that Esau will have time to forget what was done to him. When the brothers again meet twenty years later, Esau has indeed forgotten. He falls upon Jacob's neck and kisses him. Then each brother departs to his own special country.

The Joseph story continues these themes and brings them to a new resolution. Favoritism and deception play crucial roles in chapter 37. Like Sarah and Isaac, Rachel and her sons are the husband/father's favorites. As with the three earlier sets of brothers, parental favoritism sets up serious sibling rivalries. As with favoritism, so with deception. Just as Isaac had been unable to recognize *(nkr)* the disguised son he was blessing, Jacob, who had deceived his father and won that blessing, was himself deceived by his sons when he recognized *(nkr)* Joseph's bloodied gar-

ment and drew the wrong conclusions. Joseph also lived separated from his brothers for twenty years and finally had forgotten all his hardship and all his father's house (41:51). But at the crucial time of confrontation Joseph remembers his dreams and undertakes a series of actions that eventually results in reconciliation among the brothers. This reconciliation, however, will not be an uneasy peace best preserved by geographical separation. It is a reconciliation that results in the geographical reunification of the family of Israel.

It is a commonplace that *Genesis* 1-11 provides the prologue to inintroducedthe story of Israel by depicting the ever-increasing alienation within the human community. Humankind had been created to live in Eden, in close proximity to God. *Genesis* 11 ends with a fragmented humanity—scattered and no longer able to understand one another's tongue.

One might assume that when Abraham is introduced, the story will describe how God begins to overcome the alienation among humans through the covenant community of Israel. But strangely the rivalry and hatred among brothers that had begun with Cain and Abel are continued within the family of Abraham. In fact, these themes that were present but muted in the generation of Isaac and Ishmael become increasingly intensified, culminating when the sons of Jacob behold the approaching "master dreamer" and determine that he shall die.

Paradoxically, divine favor has played a crucial role from the beginning in catalyzing the conflict among the brothers. We first note its appearance as God prefers Abel's sacrifice to Cain's. In the story of Israel divine favor is carried out through a parent. Abraham is driven to heed Sarah's words and turn against Ishmael when he learns that Isaac will be the child of promise. Rebekah's special love for Jacob may be traced directly to God's decree, given to her alone, that the second-born will ultimately prevail over the first-born. Divinely inspired dreams, given to a younger son who wears a special garment, continue and intensify the theme of divine and parental favoritism that produces conflict.

In *Genesis* 45 the conflict of brothers begins to be resolved. The brothers, through Judah's bold action in *Genesis* 44, have passed the crucial test. When they discover Joseph's true identity, he is no longer a vengeful sovereign for them but a brother; more important, he is not a vengeful brother but a forgiving brother. They have earned forgiveness for their crime against their brother.

Full reconciliation, however, cannot take place until they can resolve the issue that had partially instigated that crime: divine favoritism. Only when Joseph explains that the dreams indicated a specially ordained family role rather than a personally privileged divine love are the brothers able to approach him. Only when they perceive that Joseph's suffering and survival had played a key role in continued life for the family of Jacob-Israel are they able to "speak with him." The survival of the family had been the key issue in Judah's entreaty to Jacob to send Benjamin with them to Egypt. And the survival of Jacob-Israel had been the key theme in Judah's desperate plea before the Egyptian lord. The brothers have come in the course of the story to choose unity over separation, even if it means a shared slavery that could easily be avoided. They have also changed from a hatred that wills death for a favored one to an urgent concern for the life of the entire family. In fact, it is Judah's stress on the survival of "the little ones"—the next generation—that finally moves Jacob to risk the death of his last beloved son, Benjamin.

I have tried to show how the divining-cup incident in *Genesis* 44 is the culmination of the plot-doubling device begun in chapter 42. It places the brothers in a position of having to choose whether or not to repeat their crime of *Genesis* 37. Will yet another favored brother be sacrificed, escalating the danger to the life of Jacob-Israel—both as father and as symbol of family cohesion? Their action indicates that they now prefer the life and survival of all over the death/cutting off of any. The long history of the sibling rivalry motif that began with Cain and Abel was introduced into the Joseph story by 37:4 ("but when his brothers saw that their father loved him more than all his brothers, they hated him . . ."). It now moves toward resolution as they fall on one anothers' necks and kiss one another. The Babel motif of alienation resulting in a breakdown of communication, also introduced into the Joseph story in 37:4 ("and [they] could not speak peaceably to him"*) and intensified by the role of the court interpreter, moves toward resolution as "after this his brothers spoke with him"* (45:15).

The remainder of this paper will discuss another key doubling in the Joseph story: Reuben/Judah. Many scholars see both playing the "good brother" role in *Genesis* 37. In the original version there was one good brother, they claim, and the present confusion in the text results from a conflation of sources.[15] Redford goes on to say, in fact, that Judah's role is not only a secondary intrusion into the narrative, but it also represents a diminution of the story's overall literary artistry.[16] There may indeed be a conflation of sources, but I will argue that the redactor displays great artistry. In the final redaction Reuben and Judah play contrasting roles. Whereas Reuben will gradually weaken and disappear as the story unfolds, Judah will undergo the most important change of any of the characters so that he will play *the* key role in catalyzing the reconciliation. To what extent has the narrative prepared us for Judah's dramatic rise in *Genesis* 43-44?

Reuben, the firstborn, is described as the good son in chapter 37. When the brothers see Joseph coming in the distance and plan to kill him, it is Reuben who seeks to foil the plan. Whereas the brothers plot a violent death for Joseph, Reuben sets limits: "let us not smite a life."* Acceding to part of the brothers' plan, he suggests that Joseph be thrown into a nearby pit alive rather than dead. The basis for his request is the prohibition against shedding

blood. But the text makes clear that Reuben's interest is to rescue Joseph and restore him to his father. When the unexpected intervention of Midianites foils Reuben's plan, he bursts out in lamentation for himself: "and I, where shall I go?" (37:30). This may mean merely, "How can I face my father?" But might he see himself as banned fugitive, unable to return to his father because he has not lived up to the responsibility of firstborn in protecting his brother?

Judah, the fourth-born of Leah, plays a role that sets him in contrast with Reuben. The text makes no mention that Judah's interest is to rescue Joseph. Instead Judah piously speaks of not laying a hand on a brother; but the effect of his suggestion is not so different from murder: Joseph will be removed from their midst and reduced to slavery. In many ways biblical law equates selling a person into slavery with murder.[17] Judah wants the same results as his other brothers, but he seeks profit from the deed (37:26-27).

Both plans—Reuben's to save and Judah's to profit—are foiled. Out of nowhere come the Midianites, and in a half verse they carry out the action contemplated by the brothers. Like the nameless stranger who met Joseph at Shechem and told him his brothers had moved on to Dothan, the Midianites are mere agents of the plot. They appear suddenly in the story to foil the opposing machinations of Reuben and Judah and disappear after they have served their function.

N. Leibowitz, backed by midrashic interpretation, sees Joseph's nameless stranger as a divine emissary.[18] Given the normal economy in biblical narrative style, there seems to be no need to tell us that Joseph was sent first to Shechem but then redirected to Dothan. Like the Midianites, the stranger appears from nowhere. He engages Joseph in a conversation that could easily have been omitted, and then he disappears from the story. Leibowitz infers that the narrator is going out of his way to emphasize the divine intent behind Joseph's fateful encounter with his brothers. I would argue the same thing for the role of the Midianites. They frustrate the plans of Reuben and Judah, but their sudden intervention into and disappearance from the story may cause us to anticipate that a larger plan, not yet revealed to characters or reader, is being carried out.

One must examine the larger context of the Joseph story to determine why Reuben and Judah play these opposing roles. Deriving his line of argument from midrashic interpretation, J. Goldin points us in a fruitful direction by referring to *Genesis* 34-35.[19] In 35:22 we learn that Reuben had sexual relations with his father's concubine, Bilhah. He may have been attempting to assert the rights of primogeniture and assume the role of the father,[20] but we learn from *Genesis* 49:3-4 that in fact his premature action had caused him to lose this status in his father's eyes. Goldin suggests that, besides fulfilling his special responsibility as firstborn, Reuben may have been desperately attempting to regain his lost/threatened status by saving

Joseph's life.[21] When Reuben finds the pit empty, his response, as translated by Goldin, is "what now is left me" (37:30*b*).[22] This alternate translation, like the conventional translation used above, leaves Reuben bemoaning his own fate as a response to Joseph's tragedy.

What about Judah, the fourth-born? His star may be on the rise. Levi and Simeon, the second- and third-born sons, had fallen from favor through their deceitful destruction of the city of Shechem (*Genesis* 34). Jacob rebukes them for their recklessness (34:30) and refers to it again in *Genesis* 49:5-7 in declaring their reduced status. Judah is next in line. If he stays out of trouble, and if Reuben does not regain favor, the special status of family leadership may fall to him. The only remaining rival is Joseph, the son favored by his father. Thus not only does the larger context of *Genesis* 37 show us how important it is for Reuben to save Joseph and return him to his father; it also reveals how much Judah stands to gain by being rid of the only other rival for special status among his brothers.[23]

When the harsh-speaking Egyptian lord begins to test the brothers in chapter 42, Reuben still appears to be the "good brother." But there are now further ambiguities: his goodness has even more self-centeredness than before. The brothers speak with one accord in remembering and repenting their guilt; they admit that they did not heed Joseph's appeals for mercy. Only Reuben breaks the brothers' eloquent solidarity. Shrilly he turns on them with an "I told you so," refusing to accept the guilt while recognizing that he must share the judgment. The brothers remember not heeding Joseph. Reuben attempts to identify himself with the innocent, wronged younger brother—reminding them that they also did not heed him earlier. But they had indeed followed his lead in chapter 37. It was Reuben's advice to throw Joseph into the pit, as part of his plan to save the lad and return him to his father. Reuben's goodness was ineffective. His plan did not work, and we learn later that if it had worked, Jacob's family would not have survived the famine. As chapter 37 concluded, we found Reuben proclaiming his tragic isolation. The brothers did not heed his words, probably because of their irrelevance to the problem of explaining Joseph's disappearance to their father.

Reuben's goodness is similarly ineffective in chapter 42. The threatening situation before the Egyptian lord did not require a querulous expression of innocence that resulted in division and recrimination. The true firstborn should provide leadership that assumed at least a shared responsibility for the situation. He should be the spokesman, coming up with an imaginative response to the Egyptian lord's accusation that would enhance the unity of the family and deliver the brothers from their peril. His lack of leadership here is a foil for the later doubling situation. Chapter 44 will portray another brother taking action before the Egyptian lord in even more threatening circumstances with vastly different results; and the reader is forced to compare the two spokesmen in these analogous situations.

When the brothers return to Jacob and describe their Egyptian adventures, they try to soften the severity of their position. Simeon is not a hostage bound over into prison, but simply a brother left to stay with the Egyptian. There was no threat of death to Simeon for failure to bring Benjamin to Egypt—only the promise to hand over Simeon and to allow the brothers to purchase grain in Egypt. The aged Jacob's response to this news is full of self-pitying, ineffective recrimination. After twenty years he still grieves for Joseph. Because he fears for Benjamin's life, he is incapable of an imaginative response. Here Reuben steps forward, making a statement more reckless than Jephthah's, offering the life of two sons as pledge for Benjamin's.

Reuben's language reminds readers of his earlier intent "to *bring him* [Joseph] *unto* his father"* (37:22). In chapter 42 the same words are used to express Reuben's promise regarding Benjamin: "two of my sons you may kill if I do not *bring him unto* you"* (42:37). We know that Reuben tried and failed before. If Reuben fails again, his suggested resolution will wreak further death in Jacob's family. Many years ago Jacob had jumped to secure the birthright of Esau—the foolish, impulsive firstborn. Now as a father he must be haunted to see Esau's traits reappear in his firstborn, Reuben—so desperate to win favor that he will risk cutting off his own descendants. Jacob's impulse is to refuse, to cut his losses and take no further risk of lives in the family. Simeon's fate remains in abeyance until the grain sacks are emptied as the famine continues.

When the famine had first hit, Jacob had been quick to seize the initiative in preserving life among the family (42:1-2). The key words here are "so that we might live and not die."* The brothers, on the other hand, are depicted as "staring at each other," helpless and paralyzed, incapable of taking productive measures. Now in chapter 43 we see a feeble, pitiful old man, unwilling to risk Benjamin's life, begging his sons to "return, bring for us a little food."* With the wisdom of the senile, he does not mention Benjamin, hoping that his sons have forgotten the awful terms. Perhaps they can secure a few scraps without risking Benjamin's life. At this point Judah intervenes to make things clear to his father. Joseph had told the brothers that if they did not bring Benjamin with them they would die (42:20). He knew that the famine would continue and that the brothers would be forced to return to Egypt to survive. Judah had understood Joseph's meaning precisely, and he twice repeats that if they do not bring Benjamin they will not have access to the Egyptian who is the sole dispenser of the grain.

Judah has become the spokesman and leader. The main turning point is reached, however, when Judah offers to assume personal responsibility for Benjamin's life in verses 8-10. Just as chapter 37 forced us to contrast the two brothers' attempts to deliver Joseph from death, the analogy between the offers of Reuben and Judah to be responsible for Benjamin forces us to contrast their words in order to see why Reuben's offer hardened Jacob's resolve not to send Benjamin, whereas Judah's words won

him over. Unlike Reuben, Judah is successful because he
sets Jacob's decision in a larger context. He sees clearly
that the continuation of the whole family is at stake, and
he is able to get this insight through to his father by pick-
ing up and building on the same phrase Jacob had used in
42:2 to respond to the famine: "*so that we might live and
not die*—also we, also you, also our offspring."* Whereas
Reuben offered to destroy part of the next generation if he
could not return Benjamin to his father, Judah emphasizes
the necessity that the next generation must continue. He
shows Jacob that Jacob's efforts to save the life of the
younger, favored son are threatening the continuation of
the entire line. How was Judah led to that conclusion?

Although the midrashic tradition was aware of many of
the parallels between *Genesis* 37 and 38, Robert Alter has
demonstrated how these parallels create a new literary
unity, integrating the themes of the Judah-Tamar story into
the Joseph narrative.[24] Alter concentrates primarily on the
integration between chapter 38 and chapters 37-39 of *Leitwörter*, images, and themes: Judah goes down from his
brothers and Joseph is brought down to Egypt; Jacob
mourns for "dead" Joseph, and Judah mourns for his dead
sons; the brothers send the bloodied garment—"Please
recognize . . ."*—to unmask deception; a garment is
dipped in kid's blood, and a pledge is taken by Tamar for
a kid; Tamar's successful seduction is deemed righteous,
but Potiphar's wife's attempted seduction is a sin against
God.

Earlier I tried to show how many of these themes,
especially deception and recognition, go back to Jacob's
early struggle with Esau for the blessing and at the same
time look forward to Joseph's recognizing his brothers
while they were unable to recognize him. Just as Jacob
had put kidskins on his arms and neck to deceive Isaac
and as Tamar had changed her garb from widow to harlot
to deceive Judah, so Joseph's royal garb, given much attention in the narrative, effectively prevents the brothers
from recognizing him.

Another key thematic relationship between *Genesis* 38 and
the Joseph narrative has not been pointed out by other
scholars. It is introduced in Judah's interior speech in
38:11. After losing Er and Onan, Judah sends Tamar back
to her father's house until his younger son shall grow up.
Readers learn instantly what only gradually becomes apparent to Tamar: Judah's action is a ruse to protect the life
of his youngest son, "for he thought 'lest he die also like
his brothers.'"* Marriage to Tamar seemed to invite death.
Chapter 38 proceeds to describe the desperate risk that
Tamar takes so that she may bear a child—and the family
of Judah will continue. She deceives the deceiver. Tamar
becomes pregnant by Judah; and when the patriarch
recognizes the pledge tokens and realizes the meaning of
her action, he says, "She is more righteous than I, because
I did not give her to Shelah, my son."* Thus we see
Judah's growth in *Genesis* 38 as he moves from an
understandable desire to protect his youngest son, given in
interior speech, to a public proclamation of his wrong. The

episode ends with a description of Judah's line continuing—not through Shelah, who remains outside this story—
but through the twin offspring of Tamar.

As Seybold has pointed out, Onan's selfish refusal to
continue the family of his dead brother through Tamar
establishes a thematic parallel with the action of the brothers in *Genesis* 37, who become callous wasters of life
through their hatred of Joseph.[25] The real point of *Genesis*
38, however, is that Judah is at first also a waster. Ironically he becomes a waster by trying to safeguard the life
of Shelah, his youngest son.

By now it should be clear why it is Judah who can step
forward to convince Jacob to send Benjamin. We have
noted that Jacob has changed from the bold initiator of
chapter 42 who saves his family from famine to the
pathetic pleader in chapter 43, shriveled into paralysis
because he has put Benjamin's safety above all other
considerations. In chapter 38 Judah learned the crucial
importance of the continuation of the family. He is able to
bring Jacob back to his senses by demonstrating that his
protective favoritism for Benjamin will destroy the future
generation of the family of Israel. Judah demonstates to
Jacob that Israel must live into the future. Whereas he left
personal items in pledge (*'rbn*) to Tamar until the kid be
brought, he now pledges himself (*''rbn*) to Jacob until
Benjamin be returned home safely. If not, says Judah, he
(not his sons, the next generation) will bear the guilt all
his days. That is, Judah is now willing to risk giving up
the firstborn/favored status he's schemed to win in chapter
37.

After the divining-cup incident Judah again emerges as the
brothers' spokesman before the Egyptian lord. Whereas
Reuben turned against his brothers and proclaimed his innocence in a similar setting (42:22), Judah admits to
Joseph that God has "found out the guilt of your servants"
just as surely as the cup had been "found" in Benjamin's
sack.

Judah's speech before the Egyptian lord also takes a different direction from his speech to Jacob. Whereas he
stressed the preservation and continuation of the family in
confronting his father, Judah now focuses on the preservation of the father in addressing the Egyptian lord. As he
summarizes the past (once more tying past crime to present
predicament), Judah highlights the old man's fragility, his
total attachment to the one remaining son of Rachel, and
the threat that if harm befall Benjamin the brothers will
"bring down . . . my father, mourning, to Sheol."*
Whereas he had told Jacob that not risking the life of the
son will be the death of Israel as a continuing family,
Judah now tells the supposed Egyptian that the life of the
father is bound to the life of the youngest son, and that the
loss of Benjamin will be the death of Israel, the family's
progenitor. True, Judah is himself the pledge for Benjamin's safety, but his speech shows that his father's life is
more important to him. Thus he offers to remain in Egypt
as slave so that Benjamin may go up with his brothers and
so that Israel may live.

Joseph's dreams were partially interpreted by his brothers and father in chapter 37, but not until Judah's speech are we (and Joseph) given sufficient narrative perspective to reach a more complete interpretation. Judah's speech shows what the brothers have learned—that the loss of a brother would be the death of Jacob-Israel. Perhaps Joseph did not realize what additional grief to his father his test of the brothers would cause. Paradoxically, there is something more important that *Joseph* must learn from *Judah:* the risking / offering up / suffering / descent of a brother can mean life for the family of Israel.

Judah twice alludes to the Sheol descent motif in his speech before Joseph. As Seybold and others have pointed out, the pattern of the opening chapters of the Joseph story is a threefold descent: into the pit, into Egypt, and into prison.[26] Both in the narrative structure and in the mind of Joseph, the hero who had dreamed of dominion was descending. The brothers see Joseph coming and ambiguously refer to him as "ba'al of the dreams." This means something like "hot shot dreamer"; but the allusion to Baal—the Canaanite vegetation god who annually descends into the pit and then arises—underscores the mythic descent pattern of the hero. This pattern is further underlined by Jacob's outburst upon learning of Joseph's death: "I will go down *[yrd]* unto my son, mourning, to Sheol"[*] (37:35). Meanwhile, we learn, Joseph was "brought down" *(yrd)* to Egypt (39:1). In 40:15 Joseph comments to the butler and banker on his innocent suffering, designating the prison in which he remains as "the pit"—a term synonymous with Sheol in biblical tradition and used only one other time in the Hebrew Bible for a prison.[27]

When Judah offers to remain enslaved in Egypt so that Israel will not enter Sheol and "the lad might go up with his brothers," Joseph is finally able to perceive the full meaning of his life. In chapter 45 he correlates his dreams of ascendancy with his past suffering: "You sold me here [descent] . . . but God . . . has made me a father to Pharaoh [ascendancy]" (45:5, 8). And the purpose of it all, Joseph now sees, is "God *sent* me before you to *preserve life* . . . to *keep alive* for you numerous survivors"[*] (45:5, 7).

Judah did not realize that, in offering to remain enslaved so that Benjamin could return, he was helping this strange Egyptian understand the meaning of his own life. In fact, however, Joseph was learning the same lesson that Judah had taught Jacob. The narrator underscores this by developing the symmetry between what Joseph claims that God has done with him and what Judah had earlier insisted that Jacob must do with Benjamin: "*Send* the lad with me . . . that we may *live* and not die . . . also our offspring."[*] That is, the favored one must descend/be offered up/be risked so that "Israel" (referring both to the father and to the clan) might not perish.

Joseph's speech before his brothers in chapter 45 suggests analogies with Abraham, Judah, Jacob, and God in the *Genesis* story: what Abraham had done willingly with Isaac, what Judah could not do with Shelah, and what Jacob had done grudgingly with Benjamin, God did with Joseph. As the brothers learn that the divine favoritism they had once hated involved the risking/descent of the chosen one so that Israel might live, they can now perceive Joseph's dreams of ascendancy in a new light. But reconciliation among the brothers—a major theme in the *Genesis* tradition—can begin only as the brothers realize that they have passed the test. They have affirmed their solidarity with Benjamin by returning with him to Joseph's city. And one of their number has gone even further, offering up not his son but himself so that Israel would not enter Sheol and "the lad might go up with his brothers."

Joseph's self-revelation to his brothers in chapter 45 prepares for the larger family reunion involving Jacob that will fulfill Joseph's second dream. The Joseph story has reached its climax and is winding down, but we should remember that it is an episode within the larger story of Jacob. As the second dream unfolds toward its unusual fulfillment, the ancient patriarch again assumes center stage, and the brothers move off to the wings. In the preceding chapters Jacob the heel-grabber had become Jacob the son-grabber—unwilling to risk Benjamin's descent so that the family might live on. When he hears that Joseph is alive, Jacob impulsively determines to go down to see him before dying. The father who once moaned that he would go down, mourning, to Sheol to seek out his dead son Joseph now prepares to go down to Egypt to meet a living ruler. But as he reaches the border, he hesitates, offering "sacrifices to the God of his father Isaac" (46:1). Sheol and Egypt have become analogous in the story. Jacob is about to leave the land of promise, about to enter Egypt. Jacob and the reader must recall earlier episodes involving the ancestors and Egypt in the context of famine: Sarai and Abram go down in 12:10-20 with ambiguous results: was it an act of foolishness or faith? More recently, Isaac was commanded by God not to go down to Egypt when famine again struck the land (26:2ff). Small wonder that Jacob holds back. Is he risking the promise through this descent into Egypt? Will "the God of his father Isaac" sanction this going down?

The descent-ascent motif continues as God addresses Jacob in a night vision. Here the patriarch must appreciate the lesson his sons have learned—he should not fear descent, for "I will go down with you" (46:4). As God's presence prospered Joseph in Potiphar's household and in prison (39:3-5, 21-23), so God's presence will prosper Jacob in his descent, making Israel a thriving nation down in Egypt. "And I will also bring you up again." As God caused Joseph's ascendancy in Egypt, delivering the family and land from famine, so Jacob will be brought up again to Canaan—his body returned amidst the pomp and circumstance of an Egyptian ceremony.

Any reader should now know that the experience of father and son will continue in the descendants: Israel will "go down" as she enters bondage in Egypt. But she also will prosper in her bondage (Exod. 1:5), and finally God will say to Moses: "I have *come down* to deliver [Israel] . . . and to *bring them up* . . . [to] a land flowing with milk and honey" (Exod. 3:8). The belly of Sheol is transformed into a nurturing womb. Although evil was feared or intended at every stage, God has intended it for good (cf. 50:20).

The second dream is nearing fulfillment. In 46:29, as father and lost son finally meet, the text says "and he [Joseph] *appeared* unto him (Jacob)"*—using a Hebrew word that consistently describes a theophany in the Bible. The narrator metaphorically suggests Joseph's royal splendor, but the reader is also asked to remember the cosmic dreams of the sun, moon, and stars. After Joseph has settled the family in Goshen, Jacob prepares for death. His primary concern is that he be buried in Canaan. When Joseph vows that he will carry out the proper burial, Jacob "bowed down *[vayyištahû]* on the head of the bed"* (47:31). The dream has been fulfilled in its own way, with the object of the verb left ambiguously unstated. When Joseph agrees to be the agent through whom the divine promises made to Jacob in 46:4 are to be carried out, the patriarch "bows down"—in gratitude to the son, but, more important, acknowledging and accepting the mysterious arrangements of providence.

In the following episode, with Jacob hovering near death, Joseph brings his Egyptian-born sons for a blessing and possibly for adoption. Surprisingly, Jacob states that Ephraim and Manasseh are "as Reuben and Simeon." That is, Joseph's offspring are to assume the role of firstborn in Israel. Paternal choice and special roles continue. The narrator stresses Jacob-Israel's dim vision "so that he could not see" (48:10). But, says the patriarch, "God has caused me to see your seed"* (48:11). Jacob-Israel will see not as man sees, but as God causes to see.

Jacob continues the motif of divine favoritism—of Ephraim, the younger, over Manasseh. Joseph protests, but Jacob answers "I know, my son, I know" (48:19). We remember the blind Isaac, who gave the blessing to the right son, though unwittingly. Unlike his father, Jacob sees truly. God has shown him through his experience that although brothers may be reconciled, divine favoritism remains. The offspring of Joseph will play out that drama in Israel's future. Through his ordeal with Joseph and Benjamin, and through his final vision of the deity upon leaving Canaan, Jacob has acquired a new perspective. He is now content to accept a mysterious providence that has brought and will continue to bring blessing and tempered reconciliation out of favoritism and conflict. Jacob sees—that his god has firm and knowable purposes that are nevertheless brought to fruition in paradoxical and surprising ways.

Scholars have generally regarded *Genesis* 49, in which Jacob gives final blessings to his sons, as an example of early Israelite poetry that reflects the political prominence of the tribes of Joseph and Judah in the early monarchical period. Others see the blessing of Judah as eschatological-messianic, pointing to a distant age beyond the time of the writer. It has rarely been noted how well the song dovetails into the larger story of Jacob, with *Leitwörter* and motifs that link the song to earlier episodes in his life. Now at the point of death, Jacob assumes an almost omniscient point of view, as he sees the future emerging from the past. At no point is the playful wonder of his retrospective vision into the future more evident than here: "it started out or looked like X, but lo, it became Y" is a recurring motif. Reuben—the first of Jacob's procreative strength—is no longer first because he "went up" to his father's bed in a premature attempt to assume the rights of primogeniture and the role of the father (cf. 35:22). Simeon and Levi are strong in anger, with implements of violence (their "cutters/cutting" perhaps punning on the cutting of covenant by cutting of foreskins in 34:13-31) that resulted in the slaying of Shechem and Hamor (the man and the ox of 49:6?) with the "edge of the sword." Like the people of Babel who were scattered (*pûs*) for building a city, Simeon and Levi will be scattered (*pûs*) for conquering Shechem.

We have seen that Judah is a main character in the Joseph story, and that he and Joseph are the two people whose development is most clearly documented. Judah played a leading role in selling his brother into bondage; yet he becomes the key to a positive resolution of the plot. He convinces Jacob to send Benjamin to Egypt and then helps Joseph understand the meaning of his dreams when he describes Jacob's distress and offers to remain in Egypt in Benjamin's stead. I have tried to argue that the incident that changed Judah's perspective was his encounter with Tamar in chapter 38. Is it possible that, in his last words on Judah, Jacob is playfully pondering a son's foibles that led to blessing?[28]

Many of Jacob's final blessings in chapter 49 contain words that play on the names of the sons. In the case of his fourth-born, "Judah" (*yᵉhûdâ*) is closely followed by "praise you" (*yôdûkā*) and "your hand" (*yādᵉkā*). The end result, for Judah, will be domination over his enemies, with his brothers *bowing down* before him—precisely the role he may have been aiming at by getting rid of Joseph.

"From the prey *[teref]*, my son, you have gone up." Are we being invited to compare and contrast Reuben's "going up" to his father's couch with Judah's "going up" from "the prey"? In 37:33 Jacob had exclaimed, upon seeing Joseph's bloody garment: *[tārôf tōraf yôsēf* ("Joseph has surely become a prey"*). Jacob had assumed it was a wild beast that had killed his son, and in *Genesis* 49 he refers to Judah as a lion's whelp that had gone up from the prey. Is the father identifying the guilty son? A further ambiguity appears when Jacob says, "From the prey, *my son,* you have gone up." Is he referring to Joseph or to Judah when he says "my son"?

Jacob shifts from the image of the brothers bowing before Judah to Judah as a bowing/couching, stretched-out lion. The first term can have a sexual connotation,[29] especially when reinforced in the first half of verse 10 by the reference to the ruler's staff "between his feet" (a sexual euphemism). In this sexual context when Jacob speaks of the "staff not departing from Judah," we are reminded of Judah's sexual encounter with Tamar in which he left his staff with the woman in pledge of payment.[30]

Judah had met Tamar on the road to Timnah, which is located in the valley of Sorek ("vineyard"). This may be the reason that the poet shifts to vineyard imagery *(gefen / śōrēkâ)*. Judah had tarried, binding his ass to the vine (49:11). The two words for "ass" *('îr / 'ᵃtōn)* may recall the names of Judah's oldest sons *'er* and *'ônān*.[31] Vines will break; they are not strong enough to hold a tethered ass. The actions and fate of Judah, Er, and Onan threatened the life of the family vine. Whereas Judah earlier participated in the deception of his father by dipping Joseph's cloak in kid's blood, he must now wash his own garments in the blood of the grape flowing from the broken stock, as he experiences the death of Er and Onan.[32]

While smiling grimly over his son's shady past, perhaps seeing analogies to his own youthful days. Jacob ponders its relationship to Judah's blessed future. The son who had schemed mightily to assume the role of the firstborn and had then been willing to give it all up in Egypt will indeed have his brothers bow down before him in days to come. The son who had let his staff depart from him—given to Tamar because he had been unwilling to send Sheleh to her—will indeed not lose his staff/scepter of rule again "until Shiloh [Shelah?] comes."[*33] Judah's folly had resulted in the near breaking of the family vine, as Joseph was sold into Egypt, as Er and Onan both perished. Tamar turned the tables, however; and the end result of the rule of Judah's line will be a paradisiacal abundance with grapes and milk in such great supply that clothes can be washed, wine can be drunk, and asses can be tethered without concern for the waste of broken vines.

In most cultures of the ancient Near East, cosmic unity and stability could not be assumed. The world order reflected an ongoing conflict between deities whose power and mood were in constant flux. There was an ever-present threat that the precarious order of creation could slip back into the chaos whence it had come. The primary goal of each culture's myth and ritual was to reestablish and preserve the cosmic order. In later times the pre-Socratics, while scorning mythology, would attempt to reach the same goal through philosophical constructs. Although Israel had her origins among the peoples of the ancient Near East, she reached a different world view at a relatively early stage of her history. The deity who spoke to Moses and the patriarchs could not be fully fathomed, but a unified, stable order underlying the cosmos could be assumed. Israel's covenant ritual affirmed and celebrated the new order that had been manifested in her early history.

Writing of the "revolution of consciousness" sparked by monotheism, R. Alter describes the effect that the Israelite world view had on biblical narrative.[34] He aptly suggests "prose fiction" as the most appropriate category for understanding biblical narrative, calling it a "mode of knowledge" and "form of play" that gives the writer freedom to explore, shape, and order the close-up nuances and panoramic vistas of human experience.[35] A unified cosmos is presupposed, liberating the writer to focus on the foibles and often mundane quality of human activity. The narrator assumes an omniscient voice, but the reader receives only fleeting glimpses of perfect knowledge.[36]

In concurring with Alter, I am not denying the presence of tribal etiologies, Egyptian background, or conflated sources in the Joseph story. I am maintaining, however, that all these elements have been subsumed in a powerful work of imagination that depicts human beings deciding and acting, both foolishly and wisely, in a world where mortals shape their destiny within a divine plan. The story's conclusion was not predetermined. Dreams may envision what is divinely determined, but they do not delineate the appropriate human response. Joseph could have rejected his brothers when he first saw them in Egypt; Jacob could have refused to send Benjamin; Judah could have allowed Benjamin to remain enslaved in Egypt. The characters brought the story to its fitting conclusion. But the narrator makes it clear that the characters were able to learn and grow only because they were placed in a cosmos that, given proper cooperation from its supporting cast, brings life out of death and transforms evil into good.

Notes

1. I wish to acknowledge my indebtedness and express my gratitude to Robert Alter, Thayer Warshaw, and George Savran for their many helpful suggestions.

2. For a convenient listing and brief discussion of the doubled elements, see H. Donner, *Die literarische Gestalt der alttestamentlichen Josephsgeschichte* (Heidelberg: Carl Winter, 1976), pp. 36-43.

3. D. B. Redford, *A Study of the Biblical Story of Joseph (Genesis 37-50),* vol. 20 of *Supplements to Vetus Testamentum* (Leiden: E. J. Brill), p. 75.

4. Ibid., pp. 75-76.

5. N. Leibowitz, *Studies in the Book of* Genesis (Jerusalem: World Zionist Organization Department for Torah Education and Culture, 1972), pp. 458-59.

6. Leibowitz, pp. 480-81. Both the Septuagint and the Samaritan Pentateuch read "your one *[hā 'ehad]* brother" rather than "your brother-another *['ahēr]*." While it must be admitted that the Hebrew syntactical construction is unusual, the Septuagint and Samaritan Pentateuch renderings seem to be emendations based on *Gen.* 42:19. The two contexts require different meanings.

7. It is interesting to note that Deut. 21:15-17, in discussing the duty of a man having two wives toward the firstborn when he is the son of the hated wife, states that he must "recognize" him as the firstborn. Are the brothers ironically alluding to this

legal custom in asking Jacob to "recognize" the garment of his favored son?

8. E.g., *Gen.* 9:22-23; Exod. 20:26; Lev. 18:6-18; 20:11-21.

9. See Leibowitz, pp. 464-67.

10. L. Ruppert, *Die Josephserzählung der* Genesis (Munich: Kösel, 1965), p. 102.

11. G. von Rad, *Genesis* (Philadelphia: Westminster Press, 1966), p. 388.

12. Exod. 8:8, 26; 9:33; 10:6, 18; 11:8; I Sam. 20:5; cf. 9:19.

13. See F. Brown, S. R. Driver, and C. A. Briggs, *A Hebrew and English Lexicon of the Old Testament* (Oxford: Clarendon, 1955), p. 87: "'*ēt* expresses closer association than '*im*'—comparing I Sam. 14:17—Saul's "Who has gone from those about us [*mē 'immānû*]"—with *Gen.* 44:28—Jacob's "and the one has gone from with me [*mē 'ittî*].

14. Cf. Exod. 2:14; Judg. 9:7-15; I Sam. 8, etc.

15. H. Gunkel, *Genesis* (Göttingen: Vandenhoeck & Ruprecht, 1917), p. 401; G. Von Rad, *Genesis,* pp. 348-49; E. A. Speiser, *Genesis* (Garden City, N.Y.: Doubleday, 1964), pp. 293-94; B. Vawter, *On Genesis: A New Reading* (Doubleday, 1977), pp. 386-87.

16. Redford, pp. 132-35.

17. Cf. Exod. 21:16; Deut. 24:7. M. Greenberg, "Some Postulates of Biblical Criminal Law," in J. Goldin, ed., *The Jewish Expression* (New Haven: Yale University Press, 1976), pp. 24-29, demonstrates that biblical law, in distinction from Babylonian or Hittite, prescribes the death penalty for murder and prohibits the death penalty for theft. Since kidnapping involved selling a person into slavery, Israelite law treated it as a form of murder.

18. Leibowitz, pp. 396-97.

19. "The Youngest Son or Where Does *Genesis* 38 Belong?" *Journal of Biblical Literature* 96 (1977): 27-44.

20. Cf. II Sam. 3:7-11; 16:20-23; I Kings 2:22.

21. "The Youngest Son," pp. 38-40.

22. Ibid., p. 40.

23. Ibid., esp. pp. 38-42.

24. "A Literary Approach to the Bible," *Commentary* 60 (1975): 70-77.

25. "Paradox and Symmetry in the Joseph Narrative," in *Literary Interpretations of Biblical Narratives,* ed. K. R. R. Gros Louis, with J. S. Ackerman and T. S. Warshaw (Nashville: Abingdon, 1974), pp. 67-69.

26. Ibid., 62-64.

27. Jer. 37:16.

28. My interpretation of *Gen.* 49:8-12 is following the general lines of E. M. Good, "The 'Blessing' on Judah, *Gen.* 49:8-12," *Journal of Biblical Literature* 82 (1963): 427-32, although I do not agree with Good's conclusion that the poem in its present setting is a polemic against Judah. Cf. also C. Carmichael, "Some Sayings in *Gen.* 49," *Journal of Biblical Literature* 88 (1969): 435-44.

29. Job 31:10; perhaps Judg. 5:27 is playing on this connotation in describing Sisera's encounter with Jael.

30. The Hebrew term for "staff" in *Gen.* 49:10 is not the same as in *Gen.* 38:18, 25; but both terms occur in poetic parallelism in Isa. 14:5 and Ezek. 19:11, 14.

31. Carmichael, "Some Sayings in *Gen.* 49," 441-42.

32. Ibid.

33. The Hebrew text (*'ad kî yābō' šîlô*) is very problematic.

34. "Joseph and His Brothers," *Commentary* 65 (1980): 59-69.

35. Ibid., esp. pp. 59-61, 69.

36. Ibid., p. 60.

Allen Scult, Michael Calvin McGee, and J. Kenneth Kuntz (essay date 1986)

SOURCE: "*Genesis* and Power: An Analysis of the Biblical Story of Creation," *The Quarterly Journal of Speech,* Vol. 72, No. 2, May, 1986, pp. 113-31.

[*In the following essay, the critics use two sections of* Genesis, *believed by many scholars to have been written by different authors, in order to examine the relationship between discourse and power. The critics maintain that the two texts complement one another and present a complete, balanced, persuasive vision of God's power.*]

The relationship between truth and power has fascinated philosophers and rhetoricians for centuries. The basic problematic of the relationship may be traced to the truism that truth claims are made through discourse, and, as such, must be made persuasively. Therefore, the will to truth would seem to be subsumed by the will to power. On the other hand, in those areas that matter to us and in which we consider ourselves to be expert, we assume we can somehow break out of whatever persuasive power the discourse holds over us, compare it with something else, and thus assess its truth or falsity. Such has been the starting point of academic positivism in all its manifold forms, claiming to produce "truths," and thus suggesting that the will to power can be subsumed by the will to truth, if the will to truth is properly enacted.

It is perhaps a desire to undermine the claims of positivism that has led thinkers in the Twentieth Century to want to develop a discourse-centered theory of power—to discover that quality of discourse which gives the discourse sufficient power to determine what people will take to be truth.[1] We are in sympathy with this theoretical direction, but believe it may be easier to clarify the relationship between discourse and power by analyzing a clear example of discourse that has had and continues to have a presumption not just that it represents truth, but that it *is* truth. In history, such presumptions are associated with sacred literature, writing that purports to be divinely authorized by a god or gods. In Judeo-Christian cultures the most commonly recognized sacred text is the Hebrew Bible, what Christians call the Old Testament. We believe that an analysis of this text will reveal the peculiar quality of discourse that makes it seem powerful enough to establish the conditions of knowledge.

There are, of course, many types of discourse within the biblical corpus: narratives, legal codes, prophetic speeches, psalms, and wisdom, to name the most salient. We choose to concentrate on narrative, for narrative seems to embody that "form of life" in which people are most likely to find truth. As Alasdair MacIntyre has observed, "He [man] is not essentially, but becomes through his history, a teller of stories that aspire to truth. I can only answer the question what am I to do if I can answer the prior question, of what story do I find myself a part."[2] What we take for truth and what we respond to as powerful appears to be a feature of narrative structure.[3]

With few exceptions to date, those who have attempted a discourse-centered theory of power have approached discourse from an aesthetic perspective.[4] Those investigating narrative in contemporary biblical studies have likewise approached narrative primarily against the background of literature and poetics.[5] Such terms as "art," "beauty," and "timeless truths" come to mind as associated with this enterprise. Literary or poetic concerns, in other words, incline us to see narrative structures as if they were involved primarily with the will to truth rather than the will to power, as competitors with positivism seeking after the same goal, different only by measure of method and attitude. Thus biblical critics have sought to understand the power of the text by establishing its aesthetic truth, its historical truth, or in extreme cases, its status as ultimate religious truth. While different aspects of the text's character have been illuminated by these approaches, its power has remained beyond their grasp.

But there is another route to follow, the route of Isocrates and Cicero, where the focus is still on narrative, but narrative considered primarily as rhetoric rather than as poetry. The words of the Bible mean to persuade its audience to right action, or what the Bible considers to be right action, and the success of the text as persuasive discourse would seem best to account for the power of these words to endure through time.[6] There were many good stories, detailed histories, and forceful testimonies that did not survive. The Bible assumes the narrative shape that it does, not because it is most beautiful or most truthful, but rather because this is the form that is most persuasive. The whole tone of the Bible is what Northrop Frye calls "concerned address."[7] Such discourse finds its end not in what its words are, but in what they do to and for an audience. If our object is a theory of power, it would seem better to think of the narratives which contain it as rhetoric, intimately and primarily concerned with the will to power.

The will to power is perhaps most evident in *Genesis* 1-3. These first three chapters were part of the primeval history that was later added to the already existing sacred history which begins with the patriarchal narratives in *Genesis* 12. Commentators have perennially asked why the Bible does not simply begin with these received sacred traditions which recount Yahweh's choosing of Israel as his people and the making of the covenant which promises Israel a land if she will obey Yahweh's law.[8] This sacred history presumes Yahweh's power in the world, but does not account for it. *Genesis* 1-3 prefaces this history with an account of his power that is forceful enough to sustain the story of Yahweh's miraculous interventions which follow. The power of *Genesis* 1-3 is great enough to have enabled the story of creation it contains to endure to this day even after the onslaught of scientific evidence which contradicts its details. *Genesis* 1-3 is also powerful enough to have established the sacredness of the discourse it introduces. Thus, we have chosen *Genesis* 1-3 as the textual focus of our study not only because it is about power, but also because the discourse itself *is* powerful enough to establish the conditions of sacred knowledge.

THE TEXT

Analysis of *Genesis* 1-3 is complicated by the fact that it is not one text but two. The formalistic text of *Genesis* 1:1-2:4a, with its precisely measured disclosure of God's creative work and its use of the formal generic term, *Elohim,* for God, is attributed by biblical scholars to the Priestly school, or "P."[9] The manifestly engaging text of *Genesis* 2:4b-3:24, with its less formal, more story-like reporting of God's creation and the Man and Woman's adventure in Paradise, is attributed to the Yahwist or "J," after the German spelling of the Divine name *Yahweh,* which the author uses instead of *Elohim.* It has become rather common practice to date the "J" and "P" strata in the Tenth and Sixth Centuries, BC, respectively.[10]

The division of the biblical text into its original separate documents has presented biblical scholars with a dilemma. Even though the text might have been originally composed as separate accounts of creation, it has been read by both the traditional Jewish and Christian communities as an integrated whole. How, then, can one be faithful to both the integrity of the separate documents discovered by biblical scholarship and the integrity of the whole as intended by the final redactor and as read by the intended audiences?

We decided to deal with this dilemma by a "best-of-both-worlds" reading, one that first examines J and P as each reads independently of the other, and then, based on the meanings obtained from each individually, reads them together as a single narrative. Our examination of P and J together also takes account of the fact that P was composed later, but then placed before J in the text. This would seem to indicate that P is meant to comment upon or interpret J in some superordinate way to subsequent readers.

The differences between P and J in both form and content are covered well by biblical scholars.[11] Our approach to reading the two texts both separately and as one, however, yielded a distinctive view of the relationship between P and J, especially against the background of a search for a discourse-centered theory of power. We shall argue that each text contains both a different view of God's power in the world and a distinctive way of representing that power to a human audience as "truth." When read separately, each text, as an account of the power of God and an example of the power of discourse, is incomplete. But each is permitted to realize fully the part of the picture it represents because each is complemented by the other. We will show that together the texts of *Genesis* 1-3 contain a full-bodied, balanced, and persuasive expression of a complete vision of power. We now proceed to our examination of each text separately in the chronological order of their composition, beginning with J, or the Yahwist.

"J"

The primary interest of the Yahwist account is not really in the origins of the universe or even in human origins *per se,* but rather in the origins of the human condition: How did human beings come to their present predicament in relationship to God? Thus, unlike his colleague in Chapter 1, J dispenses with the details of creation rather perfunctorily (2:4b-7). He expends little effort in establishing the precise sequence of creation and is unconcerned about the amount of time involved. For J, God's power is best understood not by standing in awe before the "facts" of creation, but by a sensitive narrative comprehension of how his relationship to humankind is constructed. Consequently, rather than dwelling on the details of how the world was created, his story of "creation" emphasizes the important elements which set the scene for the crucial conflict in the Garden which follows. These elements are the creation of man and woman, the simple joys of life in the Garden before the eating of the fruit, and, of course, the prohibition against eating of the "Tree of Knowledge." Each of these elements is narrated in a way which heightens the dramatic intensity and gives us insight into the relationships among the characters. The burden of J's account of creation, which takes up the rest of Chapter 2 and all of Chapter 3, builds upon these dramatic elements to tell the story of Eve's temptation by the serpent, her enticing Adam to share the forbidden fruit, God's confronting Adam and Eve with their mistake, and finally their expulsion from the Garden.

To appreciate fully the rhetorical choices made by J to lend power to his account, let us first examine the pos-

sibilities he rejected. His account clearly is not an encomium to the glory of divine creation. Unlike P, J does not bring power to his story by means of an awe-inspiring description of how order was created out of chaos. He also does not make any substantial use of the ancient mythic formulas from other traditions which would have resonated authoritatively for his Mesopotamian-bred audience.[12] He chooses to begin his story outside the bounds of the ancient core of sacred history that we find repeated in numerous places throughout the Pentateuch.[13] In short, J's story seems conceived rhetorically to deliberately avoid drawing power from sources outside itself.

Instead, J chooses to compose, almost *de nova,* a very human "pastoral." Rather than a divine presence controlling the forces of creation from above, God enters the scene as a very human character. The story itself unfolds not as a pure expression of divine will ("Let there be light . . . and it was so" [*Gen.* 1:3]), but as a description of the actions and interactions of the characters in the story. J, as narrator, appears to bargain in good faith with his characters, letting them dictate the flow of the story, rather than declaring his message through a series of pronouncements about God. It seems that J chooses to depend entirely on the story he has to tell to give his message whatever power it will have. Thus J's text provides us with an extraordinary experiment in the use of the narrative form to lend power to sacred knowledge.

The power of a sacred text may be seen as enabling it to reach beyond the temporal limitations of the author—to communicate its truths to audiences far removed from the author in time and space.[14] While the original author may lay claim, implicitly or explicitly, to divine revelation as the source of his authority, once written down, the knowledge contained in a sacred text can no longer be revealed oracularly to succeeding generations. Cast into a narrative form like J's, a sacred text depends primarily on the universal appeal of its characters: Adam must indeed be "everyman" and Yahweh everyman's God. J's appropriation of the narrative form also requires that his ideas about human beings and God be conveyed through the deeds and experiences of his characters, rather than simply pronounced "*ex cathedra.*"

Adam's creation from an amalgam of divine breath and earthly matter is a narrative reflection of the ambiguities of human nature. The earthly matter represents the limits of our bodies, and the divine breath, the seemingly infinite possibilities of our minds and its fantasies of what could be. The Tree of Knowledge of Good and Evil and the prohibition against eating its fruit express the implications of this ambiguity. The world contains what appear to be the material agents, that, if used effectively, would enable us to realize our grandiose fantasies of being like gods, but, at the same time, to contain the seeds of our inevitable destruction.

The god of the story is highly anthropomorphized. From the very start, he is more of this world than a higher one.

The verbs used to describe his creative work are descriptive of an earthly craftsman: God "forms," "fashions," and "plants," and the material he works with is all of this earth. Most of his action is in fact *re*action to what the man and woman do. He does not so much create a world and determine its course as he sets a scene and responds to the other actors within the bounds of that scene. He is, like J, a narrator, waiting to see what his characters will do to see how the story will turn out. The "sources of action" in the story are as many as the characters present in the scene, and the course of the story hinges upon the exercise of free will within the limits and possibilities of each character's nature.

J's representation of God's power is not an abstract presentation of propositions that would depend on the particular biases of a cultural situation for their authority, but rather is expressed through the universally appealing concreteness of an archetypal confrontation between humans and God. The scene in the Garden between God and human beings after the eating of the fruit epitomizes this communication of theology through the dynamics of the narrative form. The scene is a pastoral evocation of a father discovering his child with his hands in the proverbial cookie jar. God's calling to Adam, "Where are you?" (3:9) might be more accurately rendered in this context as "And what have you been up to just now?"[15] As the archetypal child, Adam, of course, first tries to shift the blame. God's response is sure and swift punishment, but with a father's solicitude for his children's physical and psychic well-being (3:21).

This is not the awesome God, creator of heaven and earth, but God as stern but loving father to the man-child Adam and by narrative implication to the audience as well. As the narrative progressively reveals the father-child relationship, the audience is invited to experience itself in the same relationship to God through identification with the very real and universal characters. As the story takes Adam and Eve from the innocence of childhood to the hard realities of adulthood, the audience is led from its reminiscence of a childlike relationship to God as father to a new understanding of its separation from God and its urge to return. The story speaks not of God as an independent divine entity, but God as the audience might experience him in the story of its own life. God's power has no existence outside of his interaction with the human beings in the story. His power is disclosed to the audience through the audience's own identification with the human characters and the appeal of God's character in the story as father.

The narrative is thus not an argumentative imposition upon the audience's thinking, but a transaction with its experience. Its "truth" depends on its capacity to evoke the isomorphic meanings in human experience as lived by the characters in the story and as lived by the audience. Its attempt at this evocative truth is transparent. The narrator has nothing to hide behind. If this is not the way life is, that fact will be readily apparent to the audience. J tells us not only that he sees man's relationship to God as a father-child relationship, but he also shows us how he came to conceive of the relationship in this way and how he would have us conceive of it. The narrator tries to tell the story as truly as he can, but the process of his trying is there for the audience to see and assess. The audience might say the telling does not ring true, and the narrator must accept that judgment, for all his claims to authority are there in the telling. He holds nothing over his audience save the power that the story might have over both of them; thus J permits his authority to remain potential, to wait upon his audience's response to the unfolding of the characters and the events of his story.

J's narrative contract with the audience also involves telling only about that which both the author and the audience might know. He does not move beyond the transaction and elevate himself above his audience by dwelling on his personal knowledge of the deity and the deeds of the deity that lie beyond the audience's understanding. Nothing of what God does in the story subsequent to the actual creation is peculiarly divine. They are the actions of any parent in a similar situation, though the range of God's "parenting" permits his judgments to take place on a much wider scale.

Thus J's narratological inquiry into the relationship between human beings and God is conducted through a story that is firmly grounded in the material world in which the author and audience both live. He brings his thoughts about God down to a level where they can be subjected to the judgment of his audience. His anthropomorphisms make God accessible to human knowing. God's relationship to human beings unfolds in a story which can be about every person who reads it, and every person who reads it can judge for himself the truth of the telling and the truth of the actions being told. J therefore solves the problem of making his text powerful by his skillful appropriation of the narrative form.

J's use of the narrative form to give his discourse power is intimately bound up with his vision of Yahweh's power. As the power of the text is a function of the transaction between the experience of the characters in the story and the experience of the audience, so the power of Yahweh grows out of a transaction of wills in conflict with one another. God does not impose his power on his human creations, but rather lets it emerge out of the conflict between his character and the aspirations and limitations of human nature.

God creates Adam, but part of the creation is the very intimate sharing of breath with him. God then invites Adam to participate in the completion of creation as a kind of partner by naming the animals which God makes, tilling the Garden which God plants, and even having woman built with a part of himself, as God gave a part of himself to the creation of man. The seeming invitation to partnership in creation suggests an ambiguity in God's power. The ambiguity continues to manifest itself as God completely leaves the stage, and Man and Woman are left to act on their own. Without God's continued presence, the limits he sets seem surmountable. It appears to be very much the human's Garden and the possibilities without limit.

The relationship between God and human beings as we know it is an outgrowth of a transaction—a transaction that follows in elegant narrative logic from the ambiguities in God's power and the response of human nature to those ambiguities. Human beings want the power of the god-head: to know good and evil and to be full partners in the creation of the world. But their knowledge is not to be as powerful as God's. God punishes them by "uncreating," by diminishing the partnership as originally conceived and by distancing humans from himself and the creative process. Human beings will have to work and bear great pain to keep themselves alive and to procreate. Outside the garden, they will also have to decide continually between good and evil. Before eating of the forbidden fruit, their intimate partnership with God made those decisions unnecessary. Once they tried to become more like God through gaining knowledge of good and evil, they were burdened with the indeterminate moral quality of their action. They would never know for sure if their actions were good or evil in God's eyes. They would need God's law to guide their actions, but they could never be certain of how God might judge those actions.

The only certainty J expresses about God's power is that it follows the logic of a story that rings true. But this certainty is crucial given the insecurity engendered by God's seemingly arbitrary choice of Israel described later in the sacred history and the implicit possibility of an equally arbitrary rejection. J's preface asserts that this awesome power to choose and reject follows a story line that carries with it a predictable course. God's expulsion of Adam and Eve from the Garden was not a premeditated act, but a response to Adam and Eve's disobedience of God's cardinal rule. God participated in the story that Man and Woman helped create by their own actions. The prophets would later pick up this theme and apply the same narrative logic both to explain what happened to Israel and to predict what would happen. Man and Woman were thus co-creators of their own destiny. We call this vision of power "authority."[16] It arises out of the give and take of divine and human action, each conceived as having more or less equal force. It results from the conflict and negotiation of wills rather than being imposed unilaterally from above.

J asserts, contrary to the Hebrew prophets, that God's ways are in fact our ways.[17] His power is not inexplicable willfulness, but a transaction framed by narrative logic. The outrageous forces loose in the universe funnel down to us in an ordered form through the narrative contract between God and human beings. J's story is a persuasive rendition of how that contract is realized in our world.

"P"

Genesis 1:1-2:4a is a dignified liturgy which depicts the seven days of creation in a manner that seems deliberately measured and balanced. Each day is filled with a discrete and unique activity, contributing to the fullness of creation. Each of these acts is introduced and concluded in a starkly styled phrase which, through repetition, becomes a motif: "And God said, 'Let there be'," "and it was so," "and God saw that it was good," "and there was evening and there was morning, a . . . day." In its worst light, P's phrasing could be thought impersonal and ingenuously studied; but in its best light, such language can be perceived as a stately, grand, decorously underplayed portrayal of an almost unimaginable act of will, the act of creating a universe.

Stylistically, P confines himself to a series of claims about God's activity in the world. The argumentative space around the claims is not filled in with the accouterments of the narrative form. The claims simply stand, without the support of surrounding story. By confining himself to claims about divine activity with which the audience has no experience, the author essentially demands assent from the audience rather than appealing to its experience for corroboration as does J. The audience's participation in this form of sacred discourse is minimal. The audience either accepts the claims made by the author or rejects them at its peril.

Where J achieved the power of sacredness by creating intimacy with the audience through the universal appeal of his characters, P imbues his text with power by creating distance from the audience. He speaks to his auditors from on high, overpowering them with his knowledge of the mysteries of divine creation—knowledge which to them is unfathomable. His vision of God's power predisposes him to eschew the intimacy and parity with the audience of literary narrative.

There are at least four important impressions attendant upon the content of P's account: (1) First, it is crucial that God speaks directly. God always appears as the subject of P's sentences, a cosmic organizer who in his speaking exercises full control over primordial chaos. He creates through the active power of his word, determining in the speech act itself that the word spoken will become the word fulfilled. (2) Further, unlike more primitive creation myths in Mesopotamia, P presents creation as the work of one deity who has no female consort and needs not battle other divine wills.[18] Sun, moon, and stars were independent deities in Babylonian tradition, but in *Genesis* 1:16-18 they are divested of divinity and made vassals responsible to one sovereign deity. (3) Additionally, P recognizes the innate excellence of creation and celebrates it in the frequent formal refrain, "And God saw that it was good," and in the climax reached in v. 31, "And behold, it was very good." No asceticism is fostered here. Rather, P proposes that before human beings praised Elohim for the wondrous work of creation, the deity contemplated his own creative work and delighted in its integrity and inherent beauty. (4) Moreover, P seems to build an irony into his description of the relationship between God and human beings. At first, one is impressed with the dignity and power of humanity's place in God's creation: Made in the divine image, human beings are God's representatives on earth who will govern the plant and animal environment. Yet, on closer study, one notes that human beings are never the subject of a P sentence; they are confined always to grammatical objectivity. So there is the distance between God and humanity that exists between active subject and passive object: Human existence and sovereignty derive solely from Elohim.

From a purely literary or dramatistic perspective, it seems difficult to think of P's account of creation as a narrative. There is but one character who acts without reason, passion, or purpose in a scene specifically described as a void and formless waste of water and darkness. The created world is a scene, but for human and not divine action— God superintends but does not participate or "live in" his own creation. He is of the Heavens and not of this world, so we know only what he does, never what he is, or what motivates him. There is no conflict in creation and no mystery regarding the capacity of God to create something from nothing. The only mark of literary or dramatistic narrative is the structure of P's account: Action is divided into seven parts, and each of the parts is related in such a way as to mark the passage of time, suggesting that creation was a staged or planned process.

From a rhetorical perspective, however, P's account is a narrative by measure of its *function*. In rhetoric, *narratio* is not a *form* of discourse, but a *feature* of discourse—that part of the written or spoken oration which describes and limits the reader's or audience member's field of action.[19] In courts of law, for example, a juror must hear the defendant's "story" as told by defense counsel and by the prosecutor before judgment as to innocence or guilt is possible: That which the contending parties will argue about is established early on as the "story of the crime." It is, from this perspective, impossible for a "narrative" to "stand alone" as it may in literature or drama. All rhetorical narratives necessarily require interpretation and are incomplete until arguments and proofs are marshalled to advise readers and audience members what it is they must do or believe as a result of the story they have heard. If there appears to be a naked narrative, we should understand that arguments, proofs, and actions are implicit, for narratives either recommend and promote or condemn and repress the action they portray.

If biblical scholars are correct in their inference that P's *narratio* was attached as a prologue to the older J account, it is important to realize that P stood in relationship to an inherited text as critic and interpreter, in precisely the same relationship we now stand. J was a part of P's world, something to contemplate, a story with a moral to discover and appreciate. P, however, did not merely criticize as a result of his contemplation of J. Rather, he tampered with a sacred text. Now he did not, so far as we know, take his blue pencil to J, changing this word and that phrase to suit his felt need; but he did *add to* J, attaching *narratio* to narrative as one would add an adjective to a noun. Why?

Among those who see differences in the *Genesis* account of creation, there has never been a doubt that, at least in comparison with J, P's contribution to the Torah is rhetorical; indeed, the very designation "Priestly account" is, as we have already remarked, an indication that P's writing seems to communicate the attitudes of a theocracy. Simply conceiving that P writes from the viewpoint and to the advantage of a priestly class establishes that the account is rhetorical. But there seems more to learn from understanding that P's operations are the same as an advocate's: What impression of J did P want us to develop? Why would P want to alter our perception of the tradition itself rather than simply criticize or comment upon an unchanging, immutable text?

If P's account is rhetorically a *narratio*, its adjectival appendage to J seems to recommend that we read J as an argument and an interpretation, a series of proofs which illuminate or amplify P's stating of the case—P's story, not of a crime, but of the act of creation. P evidently conceived that there was a lack in J of a frame of reference, and that feeling was so strong that it justified tampering with the sacred. Now we have already tried a preliminary interpretation of J, and we will in the next section interpret P and J together, but it seems useful here to read P alone, seeing J, anticipating J, through the terms and resources of P's rhetoric. If we had not read J and knew only that P was establishing a frame of reference for J, what can we learn about what P thought lacking in J? Reviewing our preliminary impressions of P's *narratio* should provide some answers:

1. God speaks directly, is always the subject of P's sentences, and creates through the active power of his word. The power portrayed seems quite literally authorial, the same power over all of life that writers enjoy over their sentences. As we may choose one word and not another, rub one out, or rip up the sheet on which we write, so God simply chooses things, rubs them out, rips them up, and so has an absolute power. J, in other words, must in P's mind be read in the frame of realizing that God is the author of the universe and is thus not only *above* all other powers, but *prior to* them: P tried mightily to communicate the idea of *nothing*, and from nothing *something*, portraying the awesome intervening force that made the difference. P's *narratio* leaves J enough argumentative or interpretive space to be read equivocally, now *presuming* God's authorial power, now *proving* such power, now exploring the consequences of such power in interaction with human will.

2. Unlike other deities in other religious systems, God is *alone* in the scene of creation. This portrayal qualifies authorial power in an important way: This essay, for example, is a collaboration, written by three authors. As these words were written, one of us had an apparent authorial power to choose this or that word and to rub out what seemed wrong or inappropriate. When the three of us came together, however, each of us had to negotiate to keep a pet sentence or to strike another's phrase that grated on

the ear. God did not have to negotiate in the act of creation, according to P; he worked alone, with no other creature or force to say him nay. So whatever J says must be read in the frame of realizing that there is no appeal from authorial power save to the author himself—God, and only God, can alter the words that have been written.

3. What God created is *intrinsically* good: In P's account, God does not *infer* that his creation is good, nor does he search for confirmation of the quality of his creation; rather, God *sees* that it is good, *says* that it is good, and that settles it. What can be seen and proclaimed must be self-evident. Now goodness is a quality, not an object—none of us has ever seen a "good" walking down the street. But God *sees* goodness; even as a quality it is self-evident in his eyes. Whatever J says, in other words, should be read in the context of knowing that authorial power like God's extends even to evaluations of creation. Unlike writers or actors, God needs no favorable review or applause, for his art is so perfect that it contains its own self-evident goodness.

4. God exalts human beings in P's frame, but he keeps them always in the objective case. Humans matter, but not because they are individual subjects, capable of being actors on the stage God occupies. Like actors performing the script of a playwright, men and women can only act out what has been written, "strutting and fretting their brief hour upon the stage." If there is villainy or heroism, accomplishment or failure, P wants it understood that the author is ultimately responsible, not the actors; humanity is as significant as a playing piece at chess. In P's mind, whatever J says should be read in the frame of realizing that freedom of will in human beings exists only as the actor's craft in relation to an author's script. Human will, in other words, is a matter of style, nuance, balance, and emphasis, not a matter of creativity or authorship.

In sum, P seems to have decided that the lack in J was an understanding of the nature of divine power, specifically the power of authorship. Each important feature of P's narrative describes or qualifies the kind of power writers and speakers have over choice of word, phrase, content, and outcome of what is written or spoken. With regard to the nature of authorial power, P asserts that God-as-author possessed an absolutely unqualified capacity to create, constrained neither by the task of creation nor by need to take other similar powers into account. With regard to the consequences of authorial power, P wants it understood that products of creation are intrinsically good no matter what opinion an audience or critic might have. Further, he wants it understood that authorial power extends even into the arena of human will, restricting a most favored creation to the status of objects able to initiate action only as nuance or emphasis. If P's *narratio* is an adjectival appendage to J's narration, we may infer that the concept of divine power J presupposes is incomplete, or easily misunderstood, without a frame of reference to establish what the power of authorship consists of. It remains for us to describe P and J together, as a whole, to see what *power*

of a piece may be, what adjective and noun mean as a unity of expression.

"P—J"

The human need that correlates with the authorial dimension of power would seem to be the need for certainty: to know what is right and to do what is right. P responds to this need with the directness it requires in its most passionate moments. But there are also moments of doubt and even of arrogance. At times we question with the same passion that moves us at other times to believe. We feel our power to be equal to that of anyone who might make claims on us through actions or words. We deserve to be reckoned with. Enter J.

As suggested earlier, J is not really a creation story at all. Whatever is "created" in J has the quality of a set or a scene being built in which the real action will take place. God's creation waits upon what humans will do for it to become whatever it will be. God's power in this scene is potential. J then tells the story of the conflict between God's authority (potential power) and human free will. As the story ends, we have more of a clarification than a resolution. We understand the conflict better as it emerges from the primeval haze, but the story of the conflict continues. The action of the human characters and God's response has effectively moved the scene from paradise to the world of the audience. The primeval story becomes their story. God's authority as a transaction with human beings began in Paradise and continues in our world. J's narrative of God's power is necessarily incomplete.

We indicated earlier that P stands as an adjectival appendage to J. We can now see that adjectival relationship as embodying P's version of the interplay between the two dimensions of power. Without authorship, authority remains embroiled in the indeterminacy of conflict. There is no circumscribing force that can determine the outcome. Because human beings are not part of a completed vision of perfection, their action emanates from their own ambiguous nature and is not drawn towards a definite end. It unfolds in endless story. P adjectivizes J by elaborating a claim that the universe is a perfectly ordered hierarchy with God ruling over all as the only significant actor. He brings his account to a close with a statement which suggests that both the creation and the story have been completed perfectly: "Such is the story of heaven and earth as they were created" (2:4a). This liturgical gloss has the ring of a claim. God created perfectly and the story of that creation has been perfectly told.

But P's account leaves God as author with nothing to do but "uncreate" if his vision is significantly violated. This is, of course, precisely what happens in the flood story (*Gen.* 6-9). Humans have no creative potential of their own to serve as the basis for more story (other than the story of uncreation). P's vision of God's authorship thus forecloses any significant story that might follow. There is nothing more of interest that might happen. Perfection has realized itself.

By joining his account to J's, P not only adds the circumscribing claim of authorship to J's story of God's authority, but he also permits himself to make that claim in the perfect rhetoric that befits it. By introducing conflict rather than authorial creation as his primary motif, J provides that dimension of God's power which invites more story. J's account ends not with a claim of closure but with the scene set for the story of man in his "fallen state."

His subject, God's authority, leads J to compose an "imperfect rhetoric" that opens itself up to the future, just as P closes his account in the perfect past. Human actors and audiences can continue the story that God and J begin. God's authorship in P necessarily lacked the appeal to the questioning, active side of human beings. P leaves nothing for people as actors or audiences to do. J's narrative in *Genesis* has been recognized by critics as possessing a universal appeal, a claim not made about P.[20] It is perhaps more accurate to say that J appeals to audiences in a wider range of mood than does P. P can offer only a vision of the perfect grandeur of God's created world to people who are in a mood receptive to such a vision. J leads his audience indirectly through a wide assortment of interpretive possibilities that can extend God's power to a more universal range of human experience.

So J apparently complements P's vision of power, just as P complements J's. But the complementarity of the two texts does not leave authorship and authority as equal partners with one another. As human beings live through the story of their relationship with God, their participation in creation is circumscribed by God's authorship. In the P-J text, authority is dialectically circumscribed by authorship. We call the circumscription dialectical because it arises out of the complementary interplay between authorship and authority in the two accounts.

One pole of the dialectic is represented in P by God's pronouncement that his creation is "good." God's authorship permits him to enact what he knows to be good and to judge it so. The other dialectical pole is acted out by Adam and Eve, according to their nature. They must try to realize the possibility of authorship, of becoming like God. Their achievement is realistically ambiguous. They know more than they did before, but they are at a loss about how to act on their knowledge. They know good and evil, but cannot be certain about the difference. They do not have the power of authorship wherein knowledge, act, and judgment are one. God's power as author circumscribes the power of human beings to transact with him as authority.

In J's story of God's authority, the human capacity to construct history through their own choices and actions is recognized. In P-J, the human construction of history (J's developing story) meets dialectically with God's perfectly created world (P's completed story). God's vision of perfection arises as the dominant force out of the P-J narrative. Human beings cannot engage the world presented

to them as co-creators. God's authorship provides the "true" construction of reality which must be sought as the final arbiter of human action. God's original creation must eventually circumscribe human action. The dialectical circumscription of authority by authorship can thus be seen as the progenitor of eschatology. "In the end it will be as it was in the beginning."

POWER AND RHETORIC

We conclude that *Genesis* 1-3, P's *narratio* read as adjectivally appended to J's narration, is less about creation as such than about the dimensions of power. Our reading of the text strongly indicates that P's adjective of authorship dialectically circumscribes J's vision of God's power as authority. There are, of course, other possible readings. But we contend that they too would have to grow out of the dialectical relationship between the P and J accounts of power that is there in the text. This relationship is dialectical in an Hegelian sense, as unity in opposition, a "natural harmony" of opposites such that one cannot exist without the other: P's "authorship" is the capacity to make and unmake. It is absolute, the kind of power that does not recognize human choice and does not brook, or even tolerate, the possibility of resistance, dissent, or conflict. It is self-willful, existing without equal or opposite will and with no notion even of the desirability of negotiation. It is perfect and permanent. J's "authority" is the capacity to lead, advise, and inspire. It is relative to the choice of human beings to recognize it, and it unfolds across time in interaction or negotiation with others. The need to recognize others as agents capable of will themselves makes J's power more comfortable to bear and easier to exercise among those who respond favorably to leaders (and gods) who care. As a circular continuum, authorship-to-authority and back again, P's *narratio* and J's narration account for every possible form and function of divine power. God's place in human affairs will be determined by how people, as individuals or in groups, settle upon a particular, formal conception of the relationship between authorship and authority, a point on the continuum. But whatever point is chosen, however one constructs the "ideal" relationship between authorship and authority, an ambiguity and a tension remain in the settlement. From one direction, human will pulls against acknowledgement that a God has authored us; and from the other direction, knowledge that *genesis* is a biological fact (if it is nothing more) pulls against an always-unsure-of-itself human will. To escape the uncomfortable consequences of the human condition, we would like to be free and to be determined both at the same time, and we are necessarily unsure of how to manage that.

Now it is important that *genesis* is not just an interesting literary allusion to other Mesopotamian creation myths which also began, "In the beginning." In a sense, each human life is a reenactment of beginnings. Each child experiences the presence of giant parents who formulate mysterious rules, praise and punish, and who exist in relation to him/her literally as biological authors of existence. The feeling that *Genesis* 1-3 circumscribes a kind of truth seems to be a product of comparing the P and J narratives against our own primitive experiences in what Walter Benjamin describes as a "dialectical engagement":

> To articulate the past historically does not mean to recognize it "the way it really was" (Ranke). It means to seize hold of a memory as it flashes up at a moment of danger. Historical materialism wishes to retain that image of the past which unexpectedly appears to a man singled out by history at a moment of danger. The danger affects both the content of the tradition and its receivers. The same threat hangs over both.[21]

Genesis 1-3 purports to be more than sacred speculation about how God set the world in motion; it is *history,* an account of what happened in sacred time. It is to be taken as fact, established by the text in itself, not by documentary evidence, anthropological artifacts, or close textual comparisons with *Enuma elish,* the ancient Babylonian myth of origins. It captures an *image* of the way it was, and, like any figure, the image is recognized as accurate only as it touches the radical experience of those who hear it. Biological *genesis* experienced by each individual stands as a ready touchstone to establish the propriety of any image of human origins generally. Thus there is a "ring of truth" in *Genesis* 1-3 independent of its status as a sacred document or its context. The text, however, is clearly not a science fiction account similar to stories of rapacious aliens somehow attracted sexually to naked, ugly ground apes. It is sacred, claiming to transcend all human motives. And it is *historically material;* that is, it has been taken for centuries as a figurative paradigm of social and political power. Absolute monarchs such as James I of England, for example, described and justified their power as authorial, *like* God's:

> If you will consider the Attributes to God, you shall see how they agree in the person of a King. God hath power to create or destroy, make or unmake at his pleasure, to give life or send death, to judge all, and to be judged nor accountable to none. . . . And the like power have Kings: they make and unmake their subjects; they have power of raising, and casting down; of life and of death; judges over all of their subjects, and in all causes, and yet accountable to none but God only. They have power to exalt low things, and abase high things, and make of their subjects like men at the Chess. A pawn to take a Bishop or a Knight, and to cry up or down any of their subjects as they do their money.[22]

The P-J narrative establishes a structure which could be used, and was used, to organize the facts of social existence in such a way as to justify the existence of human authors, Kings with the absolute power of a creator. The argument is a fascinating and intricate tautology: Scripture is holy by decree, God's own word, and that decree is recognizably genuine because it "rings true" against the shadowy memory of one's own biological *genesis.* The story is retold with Kings in place of God and subjects in place of Adam and Eve. This second account is recogniz-

ably genuine because it "rings true" against the textualized memory of human origins recorded in *Genesis* 1-3. Consequent acceptance of hierarchical social-political order makes *Genesis* 1-3 seem even more "authentic" and the materially-reinforced sacred text makes monarchy seem more "natural."

All contemporary governments derive in one way or another from an absolute monarchy justified in its power claims by appeal to the sacred. A god or gods were said to "authorize" the practice of treating a human agent as if she/he were the "author" of his/her community. Since most modern governments have reformed that conception by diffusing power, it is common to think of power as beginning with authorship and gradually (or explosively) changing *in form* to authority. So it has been common to classify "forms" of government on the basis of determining how much authorship remains, who the authors are, and describing the rhetorical gymnastics authors must practice to seduce the polity into attributing authority to the governmental system. Power thus becomes something one *has* in some proportion or another in relation to other members of one's society. And the reification is complete in that theorists rarely discuss the power of Kings any more, but instead suggest that *all* members of the polity *have* "autonomy" in some degree and are simultaneously in some degree "dependent."

> All power relations, or relations of autonomy and dependence, are reciprocal: however wide the asymmetrical distribution of resources involved, all power relations manifest autonomy and dependence "in both directions." A person kept thoroughly confined and supervised, as an individual in a strait-jacket, perhaps has lost all capability of action, and is not a participant in reciprocal power-relation. But in all other cases . . . power relations are two-way. This accounts for the intimate tie between agency and suicide. Self-destruction is a (virtually) always-open option, the ultimate refusal that finally and absolutely cancels the oppressive power of others.[23]

This "dialectic of control" is anchored in a fixed and incomplete idea of power, for it thinks of power only as negated, in regard to a motive to resist—power is that claim on behavior and belief that we would like to be able to negate. This notion is fixed on the history of the western resistance to claims of absolute monarchs and on the view that an inherently more "legitimate" kind of power developed in consequence of altering the form of government. Such an idea is incomplete because it wrongly supposes that power is fixed in a structure, that, for example, the power of Kings was in reality as authorial as their rhetoric would have indicated.

Power in fact is pure function—it is, in the Weber/Parsons/Luhmann vocabulary, a generalized medium of communication.[24] A monarch's claim to "absolute" power was "rhetorical" in both senses of that word: It was figurative in the metaphor James I developed in arguing that temporal power is the mirror-image of God's power over all of creation. It was also persuasive, in the attempt to *seduce* a polity into granting authority and suppressing awareness that even the power of God is ultimately dependent upon acknowledgement of him by this or that Adam and Eve bound in the time and space of one or another garden. Those who opposed such claims as that of James I were neither power-hungry, impious, nor opposed to power; rather, they wanted, and eventually insisted upon, power conceived and justified as authority. There was not so much a desire to re-*form* government as to re-*gain* the "love and care" of another "absolute" monarch, Elizabeth I:

> I do assure you that there is no prince that loveth his subjects better, or whose love can countervail our love. . . . There will never queen sit in my seat with more zeal to my country, care to my subjects, and that will sooner with willingness yield and venture her life for your good and safety than myself. And though you have had and may have many princes more mighty and wise sitting in this seat, yet you never had or shall have any that will be more careful and loving. . . . I know the title of a king is a glorious title; but assure yourself that the shining glory of princely authority hath not so dazzled the eyes of our understanding but that we will know and remember that we also are to yield an account of our actions before the Great Judge. . . . For myself, I was never so much enticed with the glorious name of a king, or royal authority of a queen, as delighted that God hath made me His instrument to maintain His truth and glory, and to defend this kingdom, as I said, from peril, dishonour, tyranny, and oppression.[25]

Elizabeth claimed to be an authority exercising the remanded power of God; James claimed to be an author exercising his own god-like, autonomous power. The claims were made eight years apart and in the context of very nearly the same interpenetrating religious/political/economic/social structure. In Michel Foucault's terms, it is significant that the two monarchs presented different "bodies" to the polity, one exuding "maleness" and the other undeniably "feminine."[26] But the difference is not merely between matriarchy and patriarchy, for these are but flip sides of the same coin, the idea of parentage and the power of *genesis*. The significant difference is a matter of *rhetorical style:* One cannot in fact *have* power; rather, even Kings *do* power by creating discourse that manages the contradiction between authorship and authority. No matter what form society assumes, power relations within it are determined by the need to cooperate, not the need to resist. That is, a polity must be persuaded not to resist, and such persuasion proceeds from some combination of appeals to *genesis* and simultaneous acknowledgement of the human will as it exists independent of its origins or parentage.

The problem with a reified idea of allegedly "pure" power is its lack of *authenticity* or "genuineness." Each of us has internalized an idea of parentage and recognizes a "right" deriving from it—a right to obedience at one stage of life, honor and respect at another. This right is "authentic" when claimed by real parents who behave as we are taught

to think parents should behave. The fact of parentage (authorship) is consonant with perceptions of parentage (authority), and we are bound in the power of *genesis*. When those who are not parents try to treat us *like* "sons/daughters," the claim to authorship is inauthentic on its face, and power is wholly dependent on authority. And when those who are parents do not act the part, the claim to authority is on its face inauthentic, and power is wholly dependent on authorship. It is never in the interest of power users to characterize their power as wholly authorial because the claim of a King to be "father to his people," or of a Henry Ford to be "head of the family," or of the Presidium "to speak for" the people of the Soviet Union is always literally false, a metaphor always subject to unmasking *as* a metaphor. So James I felt the bitterness of metaphorical "sons and daughters" who saw nothing at all father-like or god-like in his behavior. Similarly, it is never in the interest of power users to characterize their power as entirely authoritative, for it is the radical perception of *parentage* that makes a claim to "know better what is good for you" credible. The claim to love and care is easy to make, even by gigolos and harlots, but it is believable only from the mouth of one who is perceived as father/mother/"god." So Elizabeth I was devilled by the charge that she was a "bastard" and had no "legitimate" claim to the throne—and, in light of her rhetorical style, no "legitimate" claim to the rights of parentage. Authentic power, exercised in or on any social-political structure, emphasizes the fact of parentage when authorship may be doubted and parental behavior when authority may be doubted—and in either case, the goal of the rhetoric is to create a unity of power such that no metaphorical "son" or "daughter" would think to resist any more than real daughters and sons would think to strike an aged and loving parent.

The true "dialectic of control," we conclude, is the same as that circumscribed in the P and J narratives of human origins. "Authorship" and "authority" have meaning only in relationship to one another and in the context of the omnipresent problem of *genesis,* a problem reproduced biologically as each generation grows from the awe-ful dependence of a child to the relatively will-ful "autonomy" of an adult, from the innocence of Adam and Eve to the knowledge-ability of Cain and Abel.

There are two perspectives from which to consider this dialectic: One could believe that J, and particularly P, were extraordinarily insightful or divinely inspired in constructing a sacred narrative that successfully circumscribed all possibilities of power, divine and profane. Such an interpretation would emphasize the structural repetition of the P/J dialectic in all times and situations where power exists—power would be functional, tied to discourse, in that it derives from the bio-logic of the human condition *per se,* not from the form and structure of institutions. One could also believe that *Genesis* 1-3 is historically material, the point of embarkation for all western governments and, in consequence, for all western theories of power. Such an interpretation would emphasize the largely forgotten role of Judeo-Christian religion in establishing the practices of power about which we theorize—power in this view would be functional, tied to discourse, in that it originates in much quoted and oft-reproduced sacred narratives, not in the present shape and structure of society.

For our present purposes, the result is the same: Whether *Genesis* 1-3 is "sacred" because it captures the logic of a human condition or materially determinant because it has been taken as "sacred," it is nonetheless an accurate, "authentic" account of power as it now exists and as it has existed in western cultures. Power *does* rather than *is*. One does not have it by virtue of a "place" within the social-political structure so much as one creates it as a rhetoric that must be performed within the possibilities of the authorship/authority dialectic.

Notes

1. See H. Goldhammer and Edward A. Shils, "Types of Power and Status," *American Journal of Sociology*, 45 (1939), 171-82; Gustav Ichheiser, *Appearances and Realities* (San Francisco: Jossey-Bass, 1970); Alvin W. Gouldner, *The Future of Intellectuals and the Rise of the New Class* (New York: Seabury Press, 1979), pp. 28-47; Renate Mayntz, ed., *Theodor Geiger on Social Order and Mass Society*, trans. Robert E. Peck (Chicago: University of Chicago Press, 1969), pp. 132-65; Louis Althusser, *Lenin and Philosophy and Other Essays*, trans. Ben Brewster (1966-70; Eng. trans. New York: Monthly Review Press, 1971), pp. 127-86; Karl Mannheim, *Essays on Sociology and Social Psychology* (London: Routledge and Kegan Paul, 1953), pp. 74-153; Helmut Dubiel, *Theory and Politics,* trans. Benjamin Gregg, (1978: Eng. trans. Cambridge, MA: The MIT Press, 1985); Anthony Giddens, *Central Problems in Social Theory* (Berkeley: University of California Press, 1979), esp. pp. 9-48, 145-50; Paul Ricoeur, *History and Truth*, trans. Charles A. Kelbley (1955; Eng. trans. Evanston, IL: Northwestern University Press, 1965); Paul Ricoeur, *Time and Narrative* (1983; Eng. trans. Chicago: Univ. of Chicago Press, 1984); and Jürgen Habermas, *Theorie des kommunikativen Handelns,* 2 vols. (Frankfurt am Main: Suhrkamp Verlag, 1981).

The line of thinking that results in a discourse-centered conception of power begins in defining power as complex sociopsychological inducements to action or inaction (e.g., see Goldhammer and Shils). In Ichheiser's tale, power was originally the "biopsychological superiority of the individual." As societies grew larger and more complex, there was a double shift in the bases of power: (1) The individual's physical strength came to be less significant than his or her mental cleverness, and, at the same time (2) the personal power of individuals became less significant than "socially acquired and transmitted indirect means of power." Concomitantly, there was a shift in moral standards applicable to power: Overt physical types

of coercion were stigmatized, while society increasingly pretended that "psychological and indirect" power did not exist or was in some way "legitimate" (pp. 136-38). Effective power was thus increasingly invisible.

The social theorist, being an active promoter of what Alvin Gouldner called "the culture of critical discourse," made a professional obligation out of "telling the truth" about power. In the past, sociologists have favored a *situation-centered* account of the relationship between truth and power. "Telling the truth" about power consisted of demonstrating that the truth-claim of an "ideological" proposition is actually a power-claim that functions to obscure perceptions of "objective reality" (Geiger, pp. 132-65). Discourse was portrayed either as "scientific" (hence "truthful") or as a determined product of the political economy (of Althusser's "ideological state apparatus," for example).

Another alternative, now more fashionable, is *discourse-centered:* Anti-positivists (e.g., Mannheim) claimed that even scientific theories (the "truths" that social theorists tell about power) are power-claims that function to alter or reproduce the conditions of a "social reality." "Telling the truth" about power thus requires an accounting of the social integration of "truth" and "power." As Giddens argues, this entails a more sophisticated understanding of the relationship between discourse and reality. Whether conceived as "objective" or as "social," reality is itself a cultural product, perhaps a "text" (Ricoeur), maybe an elaborate "speech-act" (Habermas), most certainly a discursively-constituted phenomenon obedient to the principles of text-construction. Both truth and power (as well as their opposites) are thus *features of discourse,* objective or material only if discourse is conceived as (semiotically) objective or (historically) material. To theorize power, we must show how discourse *consists of* an integrated power/truth.

2. Alasdair MacIntyre, *After Virtue* (Notre Dame: Univ. of Notre Dame Press, 1981), p. 201.

3. Walter R. Fisher develops this idea quite fully in his landmark essay, "Narration as a Human Communication Paradigm: The Case of Public Moral Argument," *Communication Monographs,* 51 (1984), 1-22. See also Walter R. Fisher, "The Narrative Paradigm: An Elaboration," *Communication Monographs,* 52 (1985), 347-67.

4. See Allan Megill, *Prophets of Extremity: Nietzsche, Heidegger, Foucault, Derrida* (Berkeley: University of California Press, 1985); Clifford Geertz, "Ideology as a Cultural System," in David Apter, ed., *Ideology and Discontent* (New York: Free Press, 1964); Roland Barthes, *S/Z,* trans. Richard Miller (1970; Eng. trans. New York: Hill and Wang, 1974).

In traditional usages, as Megill notes (p. 2), the "aesthetic perspective" would emphasize the priority of "a self-contained realm of aesthetic objects and sensations" over a "'real world' of nonaesthetic objects." One major theme of post-modernism, however, is an "attempt to expand the aesthetic to embrace the whole of reality." As evinced in the work of such seminal thinkers as Michel Foucault and Jacques Derrida, "aestheticism" is "a tendency to see 'art' or 'language' or 'discourse' or 'text' as constituting the primary realm of human experience." Social scientists who turn to discourse analysis (e.g. Greetz) treat "the real world" as if it were a text in need of aesthetic critique, and literary critics who turn to "the real world" (e.g. Barthes) treat literary texts as if aesthetic representations capture all significant realities. Megill sees a changing of "ironies": "The irony that pervaded modernism tried to uncover a Man or Culture or Nature or History underlying the flux of surface experience. In post-modernism, this has given way to a new irony, one that holds these erstwhile realities to be textual fictions. We are seen as cut off from 'things' and confined to a confrontation with 'words' alone." (p. 2).

5. Perhaps the most influential contemporary work on the Bible as narrative art is Robert Alter, *The Art of Biblical Narrative* (New York: Basic Books, 1981).

6. Kenneth Burke begins his "logological" study of religious discourse with a similar observation regarding the relationship between religious scriptures and persuasion: "Religious cosmogonies are designed, in the last analysis, as exceptionally thoroughgoing modes of persuasion," *The Rhetoric of Religion: Studies in Logology* (Berkeley: University of California Press, 1961), p.v. See also Allen Scult, "The Rhetoric of the Pentateuch: An Analysis of the Argument for the Hebrew Concept of God," Diss. University of Wisconsin-Madison, 1975, for an analysis of the Pentateuch considered as persuasive discourse.

Two other points of convergence between Burke's study and our own bear mentioning. He also chooses *Genesis* 1-3 for his "text," because it so nicely embodies the basic principles of motivation he is discussing. We read the text very differently and, not incidently, our method of exegesis differs markedly from Burke's. The other point of convergence is mere coincidence. Later in our study, we use the terms authorship and authority to describe the two dimensions of power we find represented in the *Genesis* text. Burke uses these same terms with very different connotations to make a minor point in his "map" of the "Cycle of terms Implicit in the Idea of Order" (p. 9).

7. Northrop Frye, *The Great Code: The Bible and Literature* (New York: Harcourt, Brace, Jovanovich, 1982), p. 29.

8. The influential Medieval commentator Rashi begins his commentary on *Genesis* by asking this very question. See *The Pentateuch with Rashi's Commentary* (London: Shapiro, Vallentine, 1946), p. 2.

9. For an analysis of the several narrative sources in the book of *Genesis,* along with helpful characterization of their essential features, see Gerhard von Rad, *Genesis,* trans. John H. Marks (Philadelphia: Westminster Press, The Old Testament Library, rev. ed., 1972), pp. 24-28; and E. A. Speiser, *Genesis* (Garden City, NY: Doubleday, The Anchor Bible, 1964), pp. xxii-xxxvii.

10. The following considerations speak for a Tenth Century B.C. date for J and even for dating his epic in the reign of Solomon (961-922): (1) The Davidic history recorded in 1 Samuel 16-31 and the history of the throne succession contained in 2 Samuel 9-20; 1 Kings 1-2, both thought to date in the era of David-Solomon, match the Yahwist's work in terms of mentality and psychological approach. (2) The peace and prosperity of Solomon's rule along with the leisure that fosters intellectual inquiry would easily have encouraged the writing of such a theologically-oriented saga as that of J. (3) Nowhere in the Yahwist's saga is there any hint of the devastating rupture which the United Monarchy experienced immediately following Solomon's death in 922. When it comes to the dating of P, the link between P and the theological perspective of two exilic prophets, Ezekiel and Second Isaiah, is impressive. The judgment of R. E. Clements makes good sense: "there is much to favour a date in the last quarter of the sixth century B.C." See his "Pentateuchal Problems," in G. W. Anderson, ed., *Tradition and Interpretation* (Oxford: Clarendon Press, 1979), p. 106.

11. In addition to the *Genesis* commentaries of von Rad and Speiser already cited, see Bruce Vawter, *On Genesis: A New Reading* (Garden City, NY: Doubleday, 1977), pp. 15-24, and especially, Claus Westermann, *Genesis 1-11,* trans. John J. Scullion (Minneapolis: Augsburg Publishing House, 1984), pp. 569-600.

12. While one finds occasional evocations of such formulas, they appear to be merely vestigial conventions of language shorn of any mythical context that would give them power in and of themselves. For an examination of the use of such mythical language in the Bible, see Yehezkel Kaufmann, *The Religion of Israel, From Its Beginnings to the Babylonian Exile,* trans. Moshe Greenberg (Chicago: Univ. of Chicago Press, 1960), pp. 60-121.

13. Gerhard von Rad identifies the two most influential "core histories" in Deuteronomy 6:20-24 and 26:5b-9 as "historical creeds." Gerhard von Rad, "The Problem of the Hexateuch," in *The Problem of the Hexateuch and Other Essays,* trans. E. W. Trueman Dicken (New York: McGraw Hill, 1966), pp. 1-78.

14. While one might assume that this power is granted to the text by the "believer," it might be more accurate to identify the power of sacredness as a rhetorical function of a particular relationship between text and auditor. See Allen Scult, "The Relationship Between Rhetoric and Hermeneutics Reconsidered," *Central States Speech Journal,* 34 (1983), 221-28. Michael McGee has another view. He conceives of sacred power as growing out of a perception of structural isomorphism between a sacred narrative and the story that might be told about present life circumstances. See his analysis of Judges 19-21 in "Secular Humanism: A Radical Reading of 'Culture Industry' Productions," *Critical Studies in Mass Communication,* 1 (1984), 1-33.

15. This translation is suggested by E. A. Speiser's characterization of J's image of the relationship between God and Adam at this point as father to small child. See Speiser, p. xxvii. The actual translation does not appear in the book, but was offered by Speiser in a graduate seminar on *Genesis,* University of Pennsylvania, Fall, 1964.

16. Cf. Hannah Arendt, *On Revolution* (1963; emended, New York: Penguin Books, 1977), pp. 155-60, 178-202; Carl J. Friedrich, *Tradition and Authority* (London: Pall Mall, 1972), esp. p. 48; and Jürgen Habermas, "Hannah Arendt's Communications Concept of Power," *Social Research,* 44 (1977), 3-24.

17. See Isaiah 55:8 where the deity is portrayed as saying, "For my thoughts are not your thoughts, neither are your ways my ways"; similarly, Hosea 11:9, "I am God and not man, the Holy One in your midst."

18. The contrast may be seen in the Babylonian account of creation, *Enuma elish,* available, for example, in James B. Pritchard, ed., *Ancient Near Eastern Texts Relating to the Old Testament,* 3rd ed. (Princeton: Princeton Univ. Press, 1969), pp. 60-72.

19. Since Fisher's synthesis of social-theoretical work on narrative (Fisher, 1984, 1985), a number of rhetoricians have attempted to accommodate the essentially aesthetic concept "narrative" with the more pragmatic rhetorical concept "argument." McGee has argued for the "re-creation" of argumentation as "the art of moral reasoning," featuring narrative as a logical operation: "Particular cases that require moral judgment must be 'translated' into the cultural patterns of those charged to judge. The vehicle of translation is *narratio,* a story that structures facts according to the expectations of 'native speakers' of a particular culture. . . . *Narratio* is to moral reason what the equation is to mathematics, the syllogism to dialectic, and the enthymeme to Aristotelian rhetoric—it is the discourse structure that is uniquely capable of signifying [human conduct]," (pp. 51, 53). Michael Calvin McGee, "The Moral

Problem of *Argumentum per Argumentum*" and "Recreating a Rhetorical View of Narrative: Adam Smith in Conversation with Quintilian," in J. Robert Cox, Malcolm O. Sillars, and Gregg B. Walker, eds., *Argument and Social Practice: Proceedings of the Fourth SCA/AFA Conference on Argumentation* (Annandale, VA: Speech Communication Association, 1985), pp. 1-15, 45-56.

20. See J. Kenneth Kuntz, *The People of Ancient Israel: An Introduction to Old Testament Literature, History and Thought* (New York: Harper and Row, 1974), pp. 213-15.

21. Walter Benjamin, *Illuminations,* ed. Hannah Arendt, trans. Harry Zohn (New York: Schocken Books, 1969), p. 255.

22. James Stuart (King James VI of Scotland, James I of England), "The State of the Monarchy and the Divine Right of Kings," speech at Whitehall, 21 March 1609, in *British Orations from Ethelbert to Churchill* (London: J. M. Dent, 1960), p. 18.

23. Giddens, *Central Problems,* p. 149.

24. See Niklas Luhmann, "Generalized Media and the Problem of Contingency," in J. Loubser, R. Baum, A. Effrat, and V. Lidz, eds., *Explorations in Theory in Social Science: Essays in Honor of Talcott Parsons* (New York: Free Press, 1976), pp. 507-32; and Niklas Luhmann, *Trust and Power,* trans. Gianfranco Poggi (New York: John Wiley, 1979).

25. Elizabeth Tudor (Queen Elizabeth I of England), "Speech of the Queen," 30 November 1601; in Carl Stephenson and Frederick George Marcham, trans. and eds., *Sources of English Constitutional History* (New York: Harper and Row, 1937), p. 376.

26. Michel Foucault, *The History of Sexuality: An Introduction,* trans. Robert Hurley (1976; Eng. trans. New York: Random House, 1978). See also Jacques Lacan, *Feminine Sexuality,* ed. Juliet Mitchell and Jacqueline Rose, trans. Jacqueline Rose (1966-75; Eng. trans. New York: W. W. Norton, 1982), pp. 137-48; Michael Calvin McGee, "The Origins of 'Liberty': A Feminization of Power," *Communication Monographs,* 47 (1980), 23-45; and Michael Calvin McGee, *On Feminized Power,* The Van Zelst Lecture in Communication (Evanston, IL: Northwestern Univ. School of Speech, 1986).

Dan E. Burns (essay date 1987)

SOURCE: "Dream Form in *Genesis* 2.4b-3.24: Asleep in the Garden," *Journal for the Study of the Old Testament,* No. 37, February, 1987, pp. 3-14.

[*In the following essay, Burns analyzes the apparent inconsistencies in the Adam and Eve story, maintaining that such inconsistencies are only problematic when viewed from a logical, rather than literary, standpoint.*]

The story of Adam and Eve as told in **Gen.** 2.4b-3.24 contains a number of apparent inconsistencies that challenge interpreters, and that draw the careful reader in for a closer look. The garden in Eden contains not one but two talismanic trees, the tree of knowledge and the tree of life, yet the central part of the narrative knows nothing of the tree of life. Additionally, God warned Adam not to eat from the tree of knowledge, 'for in the day that you eat of it, you will surely die'; nevertheless, Adam goes on to live nearly a thousand years. Gerhard von Rad, Jerome Walsh, John McKenzie, and more recently Crossan, Jobling, and Boomershine have attempted to resolve the apparent inconsistencies with varying degrees of success. There are, as Robert Alter has observed, 'aspects of the composite nature of biblical narrative texts that we cannot confidently encompass in our own explanatory system', a fact which leads to the nagging suspicion that 'the Hebrew writer may have known what he was doing but we do not' (p. 136).

Yet previous criticism points the way. Erich Auerbach's *Mimesis* contrasts two styles of narrative: the Homeric and the biblical. The Homeric style, says Auerbach, 'leaves nothing it mentions in half darkness and unexternalized'; the biblical technique, on the other hand, with its much sparser narration, creates both a foreground and a background, 'resulting in the present lying open to the depths of the past' (p. 7). The result, as in Hawthorne, is that the narrative is multilayered: the biblical authors 'are able to express the simultaneous existence of various layers of consciousness and the conflict between them' (p. 13).

It seems to me that what Auerbach calls the hallmarks of the biblical tale—recurrence, parallels, analogy, and 'backgrounding'—are similar to narrative devices characteristic of romance as well as modern fiction, particularly the modern short story: recursion, multivalence, nesting, isomorphism, self-reference, mirroring, and use of intrareferential motifs characteristic of Gogol Chekhov, Joyce, Hawthorne, Barth, Barthelme, Borges, Kafka, Nabokov. These techniques result in formal structures capable of symbolizing multiple and even contradictory levels of meaning. Whatever else it may be, **Gen.** 2.4b-3.24 is clearly a literary construct; its inconsistencies are problematic only if we expect the narrative to conform to logical standards, rather than literary ones. My approach is to use the tools, techniques, and critical vocabulary that have evolved to deal with fiction, especially modern and contemporary literature, applying those tools to an analysis and interpretation of **Gen.** 2.4b-3.24. I compare the story with later fictions that resemble it in structure, asking what **Gen.** 2.4b-3.24 might be saying when read through the conventions associated with what I have come to think of as dream form.

Gen. 2.4b-3.24 is similar to an ancient prototype of literature whose structure is invested in the fairy tale. The fairy tale, which has its roots in the Breton lay and in Germanic folklore, is triptych in form, consisting of panels

that correspond to 'before', 'during', and 'after'. Typically, the central part of the narrative—the central panel of the triptych, if you will—is numinous, and has the characteristics of dream, including transformation, sudden juxtaposition, paradox, riddle, and masking.[1] Motifs from the framing sections appear in the dream section transformed or disguised, just as, in 'The Wizard of Oz', the farm hands from the opening section appear to Dorothy in her dream as the tin woodsman, the straw man, and the lion (Cinderella, Jack and the Beanstalk, and Little Red Ridinghood fit this pattern). We see a similar structure in James Joyce's short story 'An Encounter': motifs from the mundane setting of the school and neighborhood—the green eyes, the whipping, the Priest, the chase—reappear, transformed, in the marvelous dream-like section at the center.

Gen. 2.4b-3.24 partakes of this numinous structure. The text locates Eden at the hub of four rivers. Together, they encompass the Indo-European civilizations of the ancient world. Two of them, the Tigris and Euphrates, are identified with the rivers we know by those names, and commentators have linked the remaining two rivers with the Nile and the Indus, which in reality are nowhere closer than thousands of miles apart. Geographically speaking, then, as McKenzie has pointed out, Eden is nowhere. Rather, it is a never-never land located in a mythological landscape which, like the imaginary continents protrayed on an ancient cartographer's map, begins where the known world leaves off. Textual evidence suggests, furthermore, that Eden is located at the very center of that mythological world: the description of the garden as guarded by a cherub with sword 'pointing in every direction' implies that the angel is standing at the earth's pole.

Furthermore, the paradise story is triptych in form. The opening panel (2.4b-20) sets the stage. Then Adam is put to sleep (2.21). Events in the center of the narrative (2.22-3.6), which may be read as if it were Adam's dream, are characterized by numinous qualities, including transformation, juxtaposition, paradox, and disguise. Finally, after Adam and Eve eat from the forbidden tree, their eyes are opened (3.7), and the narrative concludes with an emergence of motifs from the opening section. Four of the major motifs in the story—Eve, the tree, and the serpent—may be traced throughout the triptych, where they evolve through the dream form. Reading **Gen.** 2.4b-3.24 in terms of its dream structure resolves the inconsistencies in the text, and leads to a new and revealing interpretation of this marvelous story—an interpretation that broadens and deepens the tradition and has important implications for us in the nuclear age, with our recently heightened awareness of good and evil.

EVE

Phyllis Trible has pointed out that grammatical gender ('*ādām* is a masculine word) is not sexual identification, and has argued that 'the earth creature', as she calls Adam, is in the opening section of the text sexually undifferentiated (p. 80). Though Trible's efforts to dispel notions of sex roles based on the myth seem to me to raise even more formidable questions, her close and skillful analysis of the text reveals some interesting patterns. She notes, for example, that the unit *'îš* and *'iššâ* (man and woman) functionally parallels *hā-'ādām* and *hā'ªdāmâ*, highlighting the fact that dream woman is formed from Adam just as Adam was formed from earth.[2] Trible's analysis provides evidence which suggests that Eve appears in Adam's dream as a projection of his unconscious, that she acts out his prohibitions, and that she is externalized when his eyes are opened, at which point procreation can begin.

Analytical psychologists will recognize the process described here as a crucial step in what Jung called individuation: a transformation in which the center of the personality shifts from the conscious ego to a balancing point between the ego and a subconscious 'shadow', releasing, in the process, an inner figure. Individuation occurs in stages marked by dreams. If the dreamer is a man he will project the inner figure as a female personification of his unconscious (if the dreamer is a woman, the sex roles are reversed). The Jungian term for this dream woman is the *anima*—the woman within.

The dream figure and the dreamer, who are 'bone of bone and flesh of flesh', function here as if they were in fact united in one person: the serpent addresses the woman in plural verb forms (3.4); the woman knows the prohibition, though in the story no one tells her (3.3); Adam is silent and invisible during the dream section, yet we are told in 3.6 that he is *'immāh,* 'with her' (Trible, p. 113). All in all, the textual evidence is consistent with the view that the woman is, in Jungian terms, a projection of Adam's inner self.

At the climax, however, the dream and the dreamer are both externalized. At that point, which corresponds to the birth of self-consciousness, individuation occurs. As evidence of the change, God addresses the man and the woman as separate persons, using singular verb forms. For the first time, the man and the woman use the pronoun 'I': four times, Adam speaks of himself: 'I heard'; 'I was afraid'; 'I was naked'; 'I hid' (*'iššâ*'s response parallels Adam's; self-centeredness prevails). As further evidence of the change, Adam renames the woman, using a verbal formula which, as Trible observes, 'chillingly echoes the vocabulary of dominion of the animals'. He calls her name Eve, a Hebrew word which resembles in sound the word *life,* 'because she was the mother of all living' (3.20). Eve reflects the womb-like fertility of Eden itself, which in a sense gives birth to everything else. Thus we have a series of analogous plot segments whose ends touch, forming a circle: the earth, inspired by God, gives birth to Adam, who through his dream gives birth to Eve, who then as a result of verbal intercourse with the serpent becomes the mother of all living, while Adam goes forth to till (or bring fertility to) the barren earth.

The encompassing theme of the narrative, as von Rad has pointed out, is *'ādām/'ªdāmâ:* man/earth. It is a theme which begins and ends the narrative: first in the creation of man (from the earth), then in his return to it (dust to dust). Additionally, the narrative is circular in form. Man was formed of the ground outside the garden, was placed in the garden, and ended his life outside of it. The circular form raises the expectation of a return. Jobling has suggested that the program of the story, in structuralist terms, is to establish a race of human beings to till the soil, which at the beginning of the narrative is barren: 'no bush of the field was yet on earth, no plant of the field had yet sprung up . . .' (2.5). '"Inside"', says Jobling, 'there was one male, born autochthonously. "Outside", there is a multiplicity of people, born sexually. The creation of the woman is both the cause of the transition and the ground of its possibility' (p. 45). What Jobling is suggesting, it seems to me, is that Eve is a personification of the archetypal earth mother. Eliade has noted that the ancient Greeks and the Romans associated tilling the soil with the act of generation, and that, throughout Mediterranean folklore, the soil is identified with the uterus: 'the earth produces living forms; it is a womb which never wearies of procreating' (p. 261). Pushed far enough, the image of Eve as 'mother earth' gives us a picture of a cosmic marriage between God the Sky Father and Eve the earth mother, with Adam both as surrogate father and as son—a relationship which adumbrates the image of God the Father; the Virgin Mary, mother of God; and Christ, the divine son. (Jung's analytical psychology suggests that the Trinity—Father, Son, and Holy Spirit—implies a fourth figure, projected as Mary, who in some medieval representations contains all three.) Pushed even further, perhaps too far for orthodox Christianity, the image would yield a vision of the Godhead endlessly giving birth to itself through sexual reproduction, with the sexes containing each other.

TREES

In the opening section of the triptych, there are apparently two trees, for we are told that God caused to grow 'the tree of life in the midst of the garden, and the tree of the knowledge of good and evil' (2.9). The numinous section, however, says nothing of the tree of life, speaking only of the tree of knowledge. In the final framing section, the missing tree reappears: God fears that Adam will 'take also from the tree of life and eat, and live forever' (3.22).

The discrepancy is one of the 'seams' that trouble critics; it is evidence, some conclude, that the narrative is crafted imperfectly. Von Rad confesses that he can scarcely suppress the suspicion that the duality of trees is 'the result of a subsequent combination of two traditions' (p. 78). The dream form, I think, explains the discrepancy: the two trees simply fuse in the numimous section to create what Clark has called 'the tree of command'. The underlying question posed by the text, then, is not how many magic trees grow in Eden; it is, rather, how knowledge and immortality are related. 'Is there an organic and necessary rapport between the theme of knowledge and that of immortality?' asks Humbert. 'The entire meaning of the myth hangs on that question' (p. 21).

Serpent

One detects in the pious criticism of *Gen.* 2.4b-3.24 a barely concealed nervousness about the role of the serpent. Brueggemann, for example, protests that the serpent has been excessively interpreted. 'Whatever the serpent may have meant in earlier versions of the story', he instructs us, 'in the present narrative it has no independent significance. It is a technique to move the plot along' (p. 47). But Brueggemann protests too much. The serpent is more than mere stage machinery; it is an indispensable member of the cast. Its job is to urge the woman to opt for knowledge (and implicitly for immortality), and to prophesy the result.

The serpent is admirably suited to its role. In folklore, as Gaster notes, the serpent is associated with wisdom: since it creeps into the earth and frequents tombstones, it is believed to embody the sapient dead. Moreover, because it sloughs its skin, the serpent is continually rejuvenated and therefore, like the gods, believed to be immortal. According to the beliefs of ancient Greeks and other Mediterranean people, the serpent is mantic. 'Serpents were kept in Greek temples', reports Gaster, 'so that oracles might be sought from them' (p. 36). Finally, if there are any doubts about the suitability of the serpent for its role as delator, Eliade's exhaustive study of Mesopotamian iconography and folklore should lay those doubts to rest. Eliade identifies the underlying archetype: the serpent, throughout the Near East, is frequently imaged as guardian of the sacred trees of spring, and is supposed to bestow fecundity, knowledge, and immortality (p. 164).

With these supernatural qualities in mind, it is interesting to note that the Hebrew word that names the serpent, *nāhāš*, is presumably related to the word meaning bewitchment or magic curse (Holladay, p. 235). The root affinity between the words is evidently the source of the nervousness displayed by such critics as Brueggemann. It has, as von Rad notes, 'led to the supposition that at the basis of the narrative there is a very different older form, in which only two acting partners appear: a man and a serpent-deity'. ('Nothing of the kind', he hastens to add, 'is evident now'.) What is evident now, I think, is much more interesting. In the numinous section of the narrative, *Yahweh-Elohim* does not appear; in his place, we have the *nāhāš*. The conventions of the dream genre, in which motifs from the waking section appear transformed in the numinous section, suggest that the serpent 'is' God, 'in disguise'. John Crossan approaches a similar conclusion by very different means. Noting that the serpent does not speak to God, he reasons as follows: 'When I speak within my own consciousness I can say to myself: "*I* think that *You* are wrong". But if I wish to answer back and contradict myself, I can only do so by saying "*I* think that *You* are not wrong". That is: there can be no mutual and reciprocal *I-You* spoken within the same consciousness'. Thus, when we consider the narrative as a whole, 'The omnipresence of the Divine *I* and the complete absence of the Serpent *I* bespeak a common consciousness' (pp. 108-109).

The central panel of the triptych has as its focus the temptation scene, and in the middle of that scene the serpent makes a statement that is central thematically as well. 'Die, you will not die!', it says, speaking of the consequences of eating from the forbidden tree. 'Rather, God knows that on the day that you eat from it, your eyes will be opened, and you will become like gods, knowing good and evil' (3.4-5).

The structural outlines of the plot are thrown into relief when we recognize that the serpent's statement is an oracle—appropriately couched, as Walsh observes, in Delphic ambiguity. Eating from the tree is declared to be a capital offense, and the consequences are clear and immediate: 'For on the day that you eat from it, you must die, yes, die'. But it is worth remembering, as nearly everyone notes, that no one dies in this text. From one point of view, then, the serpent is telling the truth: Adam and Eve do not die, their eyes are indeed opened (3.7) and they do become like gods, knowing good and evil (3.22). The apparent contradiction is resolved when we recognize that *Gen.* 2.4b-3.24 is the type of tale informed by an oracular pronouncement that is in fact an encryption of the plot (examples of this kind of narrative include *Oedipus Rex, Tristan and Iseult,* Chaucer's 'Pardoner's Tale', and *Macbeth*). In stories that share the dream form structure, the true and usually sinister meaning of the oracle, which typically takes the form of a riddle or enigmatic divination concerning the fate of the protagonist, is hidden during the exposition and development, to be revealed in an ironic epiphany at the climax.

The serpent's oracle, in its ambiguity, appears in various permutations in all three panels of the triptych: as prohibition ('on the day that you eat of it, you will die'), divination ('Die, you will not die!'), and curse ('dust thou art, and to dust thou shalt return'). More important, it implies the key questions that echo beyond the narrative: what does it mean to have one's eyes opened? to 'know good and evil'? to be 'like God'?

To answer these questions, we must assume that the story is both paradoxical and multivalent, saying apparently contradictory things at different levels.[3] Yet if we attempt to disengage the elements which may originally have been independent, the narrative falls apart. Perhaps the paradoxical nature of the story is a function of its duality: the fact that it is a potentially explosive package of myths wrapped together in the awesome and terrible cloak of God. If so, a new reading of the narrative based on an understanding of its structural principles could well transform our understanding of the story.

Consider the matter of being 'like *Elohim*'. What is God like? His chief attribute, as revealed by example in the first two chapters of *Genesis,* is neither immortality nor omniscience, but *creativity*. In the text he plants a garden, causes trees to produce fruit, and brings forth living creatures. Similarly, after eating from the forbidden tree, Adam and Eve take up horticulture and childbearing

(God's commandment to 'be fruitful and multiply' is expressed negatively in *Gen.* 3.16 as a curse). They are not as good at creation as God is—they are not quite like God—but that was not predicted in the oracle.

Consider also the question of knowing good and evil. The meaning of the phrase 'good and evil' is the subject of a vast literature, which has failed to lay the question to rest. Bonhoeffer, however, strikes out in the right direction. He suggests that '*tob* and *ra* have a much wider meaning than "good and evil" in our terminology. . . . The essential thing about them is that they belong inseparably together' (p. 53). It is possible, then, to read the words 'good and evil' as a pair meaning, in essence, 'everything'. However, to focus attention exclusively on the meaning of 'good and evil' is to miss the mark. It is also important to consider the word 'know'. The Hebrew verb *yd'*, von Rad points out, never signifies purely intellectual knowing, but carries the much broader meaning of 'to become acquainted with' or 'to experience' (p. 81). To know good and evil, then, does not imply a new moral capacity but a new program for life. Freedom, like power, is something that cannot be given; it can only be taken. What Adam and Eve took was the one thing God could not build into his creatures: control, however imperfect, of their destinies. It seems at least arguable that Adam and Eve did not fail the tree test, but passed it—a possibility which suggests, to borrow the words of John Crossan, that *Gen.* 2.4b-3.24 'is in both senses of the word the first plot'.

Is there, then, in Humbert's terms, an organic rapport between the tree of knowledge and the tree of life? I believe so. Mythologically speaking, if Eden is at the center of the world, and the forbidden tree is at the center of Eden, it becomes, as Northrop Frye has suggested, an *axis mundi,* 'the vertical perspective of the mythological universe' (p. 149). The tree of knowledge in *Gen.* 2.4b-3.24 is, then, a manifestation of the tree in the German medieval conundrum which speaks of a tree whose roots are in hell, and whose summit is at the throne of God, and whose branches contain the whole world (Eliade, p. 294). Its function in the present context becomes clear when one considers the iconography of the tree in western culture: the cross, the Christmas tree, the burning bush. Christianity, the Son of God dying on the tree of life certainly one of its central images, could be categorized as a tree cult by a being innocent of our culture. Like the oracle, the tree has a double meaning: through the crucifixion Christ (the new Adam), the tree of life and the tree of death merge in the cross. Thus, the link between the tree of knowledge and the tree of life becomes explicit when we recognize that the Eden story is the germinal episode in an encyclopedic narrative that begins in *Genesis* and ends in Revelation. For the Eden story seems to be saying that man must have knowledge, with its attendant conditions sorrow and death, before he can achieve immortality: that man must die to be like God. Thus, *Gen.* 2.4b-3.24 tells the story of a liberating event in the guise of a restrictive or imprisoning one. It is as if, in Adam's fall (if that term is indeed appropriate) we fell not just into the world of imprison-

ment, but *through* it to a new dimension of freedom, like Virgil passing through Dante's hell to the world of grace beyond.

Schneidau notes that 'When Shakespeare promises us that the "Great Globe itself", the theater, the audience, and the world, will fade away and leave not a rack behind, he voices the fundamental Yahwist insight into the constructedness of created things. Not only the fictions but we ourselves are made, and something made is not real in its own right, but that of its maker; so that the easy distinction between real and fictional breaks down' (p. 277). *Gen.* 2.4b-3.24 seems to be heading toward some such revelation. Form, content, and meaning are related in the sense that the dreamer is contained in his own dream. Furthermore the dream is nested inside a frame—the triptych—which expands when Adam and Eve's eyes open, and the dreamers awaken. God creates the earth; the earth gives birth to Adam; Adam gives birth to Eve who, breaking out of his dream, becomes the mother of all living. Each possibility is nested within the previous level of creation; each level is isomorphic to the next. But where does the process end?

As it stands, the Eden story is a systematic reversal of Eliade's 'quest for the center'. Rather than winding inward toward a never-never land, man winds outward toward a broader world. We have, at the end, an image which suggests that Adam and Eve, literally disenchanted, leave the garden and go forth to experience the worst that life has to offer, and the best. The image suggests among other things, that interpreters have got their directions reversed. One 'falls' asleep, but one wakes 'up', and *Gen.* 2.4b-3.24 appears to be better understood not as a fall, but as an awakening. The future, and the imaginative experience of life which we call literature, lie before them.

Notes

1. 'Images from the phenomenal world', as Burns and Rohrberger have suggested, 'are transposed to the numinous realm, where they are free to operate in the reader's mind metaphorically, as in dream' (p. 6). See Dan Burns and Mary Rohrberger, 'Short Fiction and the Numinous Realm', *Modern Fiction Studies* 28 (1982), pp. 5-12.

2. The word for Adam's 'rib' may be accurately translated as 'side', suggesting that the creation of *'iššâ* occurs as the result of a process closer to meiosis or cell fission than to plastic surgery.

3. One way to look at the story is as a fusion of sources, with a Sumerian paradise story tucked into the central or numinous section. Thomas Boomershire has observed that 'the underlying semantic code has been definitively shaped by the antinomies between Yahwism and the Canaanite fertility cult' (p. 127). As McKenzie has pointed out, speaking of cultic practices which may have generated the central part of this tale, 'The fertility rite was a mystic communion of the worshiper with

his gods; by intercourse under the auspices of the rites he shared the divine prerogative of procreation; he became, in a sense, the master of the force of life' (pp. 570-71). McKenzie goes on to say that 'This mastery, this communion with *Elohim,* is what the serpent promises'.

Select Bibliography

Alter, Robert, *The Art of Biblical Narrative,* New York: Basic Books, 1981.

Auerbach, Erich *Mimesis: The Representation of Reality in Western Literature,* trans. Willard R. Trask; Princeton: Princeton University Press, 1953.

Bonhoeffer, Dietrich, *Creation and Fall: A Theological Interpretation of Genesis 1-3,* trans. John C. Fletcher; London: SCM Press, 1962.

Boomershine, Thomas E., 'The Structure of Narrative Rhetoric in *Genesis 2-3*', *Semeia* 18 (1980), pp. 113-31.

Boscawen, W. St. Chad, *The Bible and the Monuments: The Primitive Hebrew Records in the Light of Modern Research,* London: Eyre and Spottiswoode, 1896.

Burns, Dan, and Mary Rohrberger, 'Short Fiction and the Numinous Realm', *Modern Fiction Studies* 28 (1982), pp. 5-12.

Brueggemann, Walter, *Genesis: A Bible Commentary for Teaching and Preaching,* Atlanta: John Knox Press, 1982.

Cassuto, Umberto, *A Commentary on the Book of Genesis,* 2 vols., trans. Israel Abrahams; Jerusalem: Magnes Press, 1961-1964.

Clark, Malcolm W., 'A Legal Background to the Yahwist's Use of "Good and Evil" in *Genesis 2-3*', *JBL* 88 (1969), pp. 266-78.

Crossan, John Dominic, 'Response to White: Felix Culpa and Foenix Culprit', *Semeia* 18 (1980), pp. 107-13.

Culley, Robert C., 'Action Sequences in *Genesis 2-3*', *Semeia* 18 (1980), pp. 25-35.

Dillman, August, *Genesis, Critically and Exegetically Expounded,* Vol. I, trans. Wm. B. Stevenson; Edinburgh: T. & T. Clark, 1897.

Eliade, Mircea, *Patterns in Comparative Religion,* trans. Rosemary Sheed; New York: Sheed & Ward, 1958.

Fokkelman, J.P. *Narrative Art in* Genesis: *Specimens of Stylistic and Structural Analysis,* Amsterdam: Van Gorcum, 1975.

Fox, Everett, *In the Beginning: A New English Rendition of the Book of Genesis,* New York: Schocken Books, 1983.

Frye, Northrop, *The Great Code: The Bible and Literature,* New York: Harcourt Brace Jovanovich, first Harvest/HBJ edn, 1983.

Gaster, Theodor H., *Myth, Legend, and Custom in the Old Testament: A Comparative Study with Chapters from Sir James G. Frazer's Folklore in the Old Testament,* New York: Harper & Row, 1969.

Holladay, William L. (ed.), *A Concise Hebrew and Aramaic Lexicon of the Old Testament,* Grand Rapids: Eerdmans, 1971.

Humbert, Paul, *Etudes sur le récit du paradis et de la chute dans la Genèse,* Mémoires de l'Université de Neuchâtel, 14 (1940), pp. 1-193.

Jacob, Benno, *The First Book of the Bible,* Genesis, *Interpreted by B. Jacob,* ed. and trans. Ernest I. and Walter Jacob; New York: KTAV, 1974.

Jobling, David, 'The Myth Semantics of *Genesis* 2.4b-3.24', *Semeia* 18 (1980), pp. 31-51.

Jung, Carl G., M.-L. von Franz, *et al., Man and His Symbols,* ed. Carl G. Jung and M.-L. von Franz; New York: Dell, 1968.

McKenzie, John L., 'The Literary Characteristics of *Genesis 2-3*', *Theological Studies* 15 (1954), pp. 541-72.

Patte, Daniel and Judson F. Parker, 'A Structural Exegesis of *Genesis 2-3*', *Semeia* 18 (1980), pp. 55-77.

Rad, Gerhard von, *Genesis: A Commentary,* trans. John H. Marks; Philadelphia: Westminster, 1972.

Ryle, Herbert, *The Early Narratives of* Genesis: *A Brief Introduction to the Study of* Genesis *I-XI,* New York: Macmillan, 1904.

Schneidau, Herbert N. *Sacred Discontent: The Bible and Western Tradition,* Berkeley: University of California Press, 1977.

Simpson, Cuthbert and Walter Bowie, 'The Book of *Genesis*', in *The Interpreter's Bible,* ed. Nolan B. Harmon, *et al.;* Vol. I; New York: Abingdon, 1952.

Smith, George, *The Chaldean Account of* Genesis, New York: Scribner, Armstrong, 1876.

Trible, Phyllis, 'A Love Story Gone Awry', in her *God and the Rhetoric of Sexuality,* Philadelphia: Fortress Press, 1978, pp. 72-142.

Vawter, Bruce, *On Genesis: A New Reading,* Garden City, N.Y.: Doubleday, 1977.

Walsh, Jerome T., '*Genesis* 2.4b-3.24: A Synchronic Approach', *JBL* 96 (1977), pp. 161-77.

Westermann, Claus, *Genesis 1-11: A Commentary,* trans. John J. Scullion; Minneapolis: Augsburg, 1984.

White, Hugh C., 'Direct and Third Person Discourse in the Narrative of The "Fall"', *Semeia* 18 (1980), pp. 91-107.

David J. A. Clines (essay date 1990)

SOURCE: "What Happens in *Genesis*?" in *What Does Eve Do to Help? and Other Readerly Questions to the Old*

Testament, Journal for the Study of the Old Testament, Supplement Series, 94, 1990, pp. 49-66.

[*In the following essay, Clines examines the plot of* Genesis, *and argues that the book, by way of the announcements made by God in it, foretells the direction in which the narrative of later books of the Bible, extending through 2 Kings 25, will follow.*]

What happens in *Genesis*? *Genesis* looks like a narrative book, with events being told in roughly chronological order and characters remaining reasonably recognizable throughout their appearances. So it is a proper question, when opening the book, to ask, What happens in this narrative? That is to say, plot is the subject of this enquiry. Of the author or sources of *Genesis* I confess (or allege, it is the same thing) that I know nothing, and so I assume nothing. But, like most readers everywhere, I expect narratives to have plots. Only after I have tried hard to discern a plot, and failed, will I decide that this book as a whole is no plotted story, but merely a chronicle or merely some incoherent collection of episodes.

But if I go looking for plot in *Genesis,* is there not perhaps a danger of inventing a plot where none exists? A possibility, perhaps, but not a danger. I have decided not to wince at the possibility of being caught out in the act of thinking something about a work that its author never thought. If such boldness may be forgiven, I would even ask, What could be a more appreciative reading of a text than to find a coherence never before discerned, not even by its original author? It is being seen these days more clearly than ever before that we readers always have a goodly share in creating meaning out of texts—though not, if we are wise, arbitrarily or individualistically or completely subjectively. The words on the page are an objective reality that we must always measure up to, take account of, fall in with. But they do not wear their meanings or the way they hang together—their coherence—on their face or on their sleeve. Making meaning, making sense, making coherence, is our task, not theirs.

Texts of course do not always leave everything up to the reader; they have ways of dropping clues about plot or meaning. This text of *Genesis* uses three such ways at least. One is the Headline. 'After these things God tested Abraham' (22.1) signals how we are to read the story of the near-sacrifice of Isaac, not as a Hitchcockian suspense thriller, nor as one of Phyllis Trible's texts of terror, nor as an aetiological legend, but as a test of Abraham's reflexes—not just whether he will obey the insane command to slaughter the promised son, but also whether he will be ready to stay his hand when a voice from the sky announces that the previous command is now inoperative.

Second is the Punchline, as when Joseph tells his brothers in 45.8 that it was not they but God who sent him into Egypt, or in 50.20 that while they were devising an evil plot against him, God was devising a plot of blessing for the ancestral family and many others. Another punchline

was 3.24 where we learned only in the very last phrase of the Eden story what the purpose of the expulsion was: to guard the way to the tree of life.

Third among the text's clues to plot is the Announcement of how the story may be expected to develop. The Announcements may in principle be made by the narrator or by the characters, but in *Genesis* they are all put in the mouths of characters in the narrative. They take the form of a divine command or prediction, a father's birth oracle, and a boyhood dream. They contain either a reversal of the prevailing situation or an inversion of what might reasonably be expected. So in ch. 1 the Announcement is that the human species are to be fruitful and multiply and also to 'subdue' the earth and take the mastery over the animals. In ch. 12 it is that a childless octogenarian will become the father of many descendants. In ch. 25 it is that the elder son will be servant to the younger. In ch. 37 it is that the second-youngest son is to be lord over his eleven brothers and his parents.

I shall be concentrating on these four Announcements in this quest for plot, asking, Do things turn out as the Announcement leads us to believe? And if not, In what way not? These are indeed not entirely novel questions to ask, but no one seems previously to have identified these Announcements as markers against which the development of the plot of *Genesis* is to be measured.[1]

1. THE FIRST ANNOUNCEMENT (1.26-28)

Then God said:
Let us make humankind in our image, after our likeness;
    and let them have dominion over the fish of the sea,
        and over the birds of the air,
        and over the cattle,
        and over all the earth,
        and over every creeping thing that creeps upon the earth . . .

And God blessed them, and God said to them:
Be fruitful and multiply,
    and fill the earth and subdue it;
    and have dominion over the fish of the sea,
        and over the birds of the air,
        and over every living thing that moves upon the earth.

In this first Announcement of how the plot of *Genesis* may be expected to develop, three elements come to the fore:

1. Be fruitful
2. Subdue the earth
3. Have dominion over the animals.

Reader-responsively, that is, reading as if for the first time, we are bound to ask, So, do these divine injunctions get fulfilled? Do they form the framework for the plot of *Genesis*? For—must we not suppose?—if those are the three things that God tells humans to do on the first page of *Genesis,* the rest of the pages ought to be telling us how the humans carried out the commands, or—at the very least—how they failed to carry out the commands.

Now the one thing that the humans of the early chapters of *Genesis* seem to be quite successful at is multiplying. By ch. 6 they have begun to multiply on the earth (6.1), and the genealogies of chs. 4, 5, 10, and 11 testify to the quantify of begetting that has been going on. In fact, the only obstacles in the path of the fulfilling of this command are those put there by God himself. For, first, he makes childbearing painful (3.16), then he determines to 'blot out' the whole of the human race with a flood (6.7), and then in ch. 12 he more or less turns a blind eye to the majority of the human race who since the flood have been doing their utmost all over again to be fruitful and multiply (ch. 10), and focuses an almost exclusive attention on one man, as if the whole process has to start afresh from the very beginning.

What this goes to show for the plot of *Genesis* is that God's commands, even when accompanied by a blessing, do not easily shape themselves into reality, especially because one can never be sure that God himself is not going to sabotage them. The reader can hardly be expected to blame the human race or the patriarchal family for the fact that *Genesis* ends up with no more than 70 humans who really count for the narrative (46.27), a birthrate of less than one and a half per chapter. It does seem somewhat thoughtless, not to say perverse, to insist on the command to fruitfulness being executed by a family with so many old men and barren women in it.

How does the expectation of subduing the earth fare, then? Adam in Eden no doubt thinks himself master of all he surveys, but the readers know, even if Adam has not yet realized it, that he is to be the 'servant' of the soil, that he has been put in the garden to . . . ('till', 'serve', 'work') it and . . . ('keep') it.[2] So that we wonder who exactly is the master, the poor lonely naked ape himself, or the tropical garden that threatens to run rank if the earth-creature does not solicitously tend it with whatever energy he can muster on his rigorous fruitarian diet. Nothing very masterful happens thereafter, either. East of Eden the earth will yield its produce to hungry humans only if the said humans have sweated over eradicating thorns and thistles from it. And when it comes to the flood story, who is the master then? The humans or the earth they have been supposed to be subduing but which now floods the breath of life from them (6.17)? No doubt the humans bear a fair share of responsibility for what happens to them; but it is hard to deny that the primary reason why the humans do not manage to subdue the earth is because God is constantly making the earth more ferocious and less tameable.

Reading on, then, through the ancestral narratives, we fail to find very much about the humans subduing the earth. They seem to live a fairly precarious and marginal existence, what with famines and the problem of finding water and the perpetual movement in search of more hospitable environments. The only time nature comes near to being tamed is when Joseph forestalls the effect of the famine in Egypt by ware-housing grain for seven years. Was this 'subduing of the earth' the kind of thing God had in mind in ch. 1, or did he not foresee the social or economic or ecological consequences of Joseph's control of the environment? What is to happen, for example, in the next famine, when the peasants of Egypt have no more land to sell to the pharaoh (47.19)?

Having dominion over the animals, the third element in the primal agenda, also proves to have some nasty surprises in store. Who would have thought, innocently reading *Genesis* 1, that on the next page, after its undoubtedly impressive demonstration of linguistic skills (2.19), the very first animal in the Bible who does anything very decisively has dominion over the humans. This does not seem to be what was intended.

In this case, though, God himself is not too happy about the way the agenda is developing. So first he makes the snake slide on the ground so that the dust will get into its mouth every time it tries to start another theological conversation (3.14). Then, a little later, he decrees that the form the human dominion over animals will take is that humans will cut animals up into little bits and proceed to masticate them (9.3). This surprising turn of events is almost as bad for the humans as it is for the animals, who having only recently been saved from a watery doom by Noah have reason to think affectionately of the humans. From the humans' point of view as well, this provision of protein has its drawback: for who wants to walk through the world with every living thing being 'in fear and dread of you', quite apart from the nausea that comes of knowing that 'every moving thing will be food for you' (9.3). Slugs?

Thereafter dominion over the animals does not figure very prominently in *Genesis,* aside from occasional sacrifices or feasts. The form it generally takes in the tales about the Hebrew ancestors is the ownership of a very few species of animals by the protagonists: mainly sheep, oxen, asses and camels (e.g. 12.16). And the execution of this element of the first Announcement is not entirely straightforward. For in fact having dominion over animals can be something of a liability when famines hit the land of Canaan and the ancestors have more than their family's empty stomachs to worry about. And by the end of *Genesis,* being encumbered with flocks of sheep proves to be even worse than a constant source of anxiety; for on arrival in Egypt the sheep-herding patriarch Jacob suddenly discovers that 'every shepherd is an abomination to the Egyptians' (46.34) and finds himself installed in lonely apartheid in Goshen some way from his favourite son.

What all this means to say is that the initial programme of *Genesis* is very inefficiently executed. And it is not all the fault of the humans, either.

2. THE SECOND ANNOUNCEMENT (12.1-2)

Go from your country and your kindred and your father's house

> to the land that I will show you.
> And I will make of you a great nation,
>   and I will bless you, and make your name great.
> And be a blessing!

With this second Announcement of how the plot of *Genesis* may be expected to develop the first Announcement is not set on one side but, apparently, added to. The reproduction element is turned from a command (1.28) into a prediction (12.2) and two further expectations are introduced.

The three elements of this Announcement take three different forms. There is the prediction ('I will make of you a great nation'), the command ('Be a blessing') and a combination of command and prediction ('Go to the land I will show you'). I will discuss them in this order:

1. Go to the land I will show you
2. Be a blessing
3. I will make of you a great nation.

The first item on this agenda gets off to a shaky start, but before long seems to be realized firmly enough. The cryptic command, 'Go to the land I will show you', obviously takes some decipherment on Abram's part. For though everyone knows the way to the land of Canaan, what is the way to the land the Lord will show you? Abram will only know which is the land when he gets there and the Lord 'shows' him that it *is* the land. In fact, the first time Abram arrives in the land of Canaan he walks right through it and out the other side (12.5, 9, 10), presumably because God has not yet said, 'This is the land!' What God does say when Abram reaches Canaan is, actually, 'This is the land I am going to give to your descendants' (12.7)—which Abram can only take to mean, 'But not to you'. Not until the end of ch. 13, after Abram has been deported from Egypt, and is back at Bethel, does God actually 'show' him the land. This time God actually does say, 'to you' as well as 'to your descendants' (13.15), so Abram at last knows he has arrived.

The second agendum is, Be a blessing (we note the imperative in 12.2).[3] This blessing that Abram and his descendants are to spread around is obviously destined for 'all the families of the earth' (12.3); whether they are to find blessing streaming to them through the Abrahamic family (as the niphal would suggest in 12.3; 18.18; 28.14) or count themselves fortunate in being associated with the family (as the hithpael would suggest in 22.18; 26.4) is not perhaps very important to settle; either way it amounts to much the same thing.

Given this agendum, we are bound to ask, So do the families of the earth in fact find the Abrahamic family a blessing? We observe that the first foreigners to be met with in the narrative are the Canaanites. In two successive sentences we read: 'At that time the Canaanites were in the land. Then the Lord . . . said to Abram, To your descendants I will give this land' (12.7-8). This promise can only be described as good news for Hebrews but bad news for Canaanites. With blessings like this, who needs curses? Things do not improve a great deal when Abram and Sarai reach Egypt, and encounter their next set of blessable foreigners. The blessing the Egyptians get through the ancestral family are 'great plagues' from the Lord on the Pharaoh and his household. In a cordial exchange of blessings Abram for his part gets, not plagues, but sheep, oxen, he-asses, men-servants, maid-servants, she-asses and camels (12.16), the Egyptian men-servants and maid-servants no doubt reckoning themselves to be greatly blessed being chattels of Abram even though ranking somewhere between he-asses and she-asses.

In the next chapter we find Abram extending his blessing to the four kings who have been reckless enough to include Lot in their booty from Sodom. As if to spread the blessing as widely as possible, Abram pursues the kings as far north as Hobah, beyond Damascus (14.15), routing among others 'Tidal, king of nations' (. . . 14.9), a neat symbolic gesture of the ancestral family's relation to the wider world. One does not need to be a particularly jaundiced reader of *Genesis* to observe that the best way to receive this famous Abrahamic blessing is to keep out of the way of the Abrahamic family as far as possible. We have only to think of the fate of the Egyptian Hagar, or of the divine pronouncement to Abimelech king of Gerar, 'You are a dead man because of the woman . . . she is a man's wife' (20.3), to be reminded of the effect upon foreigners of the family of Abram and Sarai.

From this perspective the story of Isaac in Gerar takes on fresh meaning. Nothing so drastic happens as when his father had attempted to pass off his wife as his sister, though Isaac has indeed exposed the whole town to the risk of sleeping with Rebekah. 'One of the people might easily have lain with your wife', Abimelech says, none too gallantly, but with understandable trepidation. The worst effect of Isaac's presence in the town is that the perfectly innocuous Philistines have to witness Isaac 'sowing in that land', their land, and 'reaping in the same year a hundredfold' (26.12)—which makes the Philistines realize how fortunate they are to be host to a man so singularly 'blessed of the Lord' (26.12, 29) even though they are not personally having any of the action and the bottom has fallen out of the wheat market. We are saddened to read that they 'became envious' (26.14).

The only item on the other pan of the scale is the undoubted benefit the opportunistic Joseph does to the Egyptians and, for that matter, to 'all the earth' (41.57) by averting the worst effects of the famine. Joseph's plan is of course a blessing only if one would rather be a live slave than a dead peasant. The narrative makes no bones about it, though the Masoretic text is understandably squeamish: the narrative is no doubt meant to say that Joseph 'made slaves of them from one end of Egypt to the other' (47.21). . . . It is the Samaritan text that preserves the unpleasant truth which the Masoretes could only attempt to palliate when they chose as their text . . . , 'removed them to the cities'—itself a less than brilliant solution to the problems of a food shortage.

The third element of the Announcement, 'I will make of you a great nation', does not lead to total disappointment, but neither can there be said to be a truly adequate success in fulfilling it. There should be, since the execution of this element, is very largely if not entirely up to God. There would no doubt be rather more success if the Lord did not persist in making things so difficult for himself, engineering matriarchal barrennesses, famines, and murderous feuds between brothers.

The only progress that has been made by the end of *Genesis* towards establishing a great nation is that there are seventy persons of the house of Jacob in 46.26, admittedly not including Jacob's sons' wives, or, presumably, Jacob's sons' wives' maid-servants. Considering the difficulties, we could perhaps allow that a promising start has been made. The fact that they are now all in the wrong country hardly seems to matter.

What then can we say happens to the Abrahamic Announcement of ch. 12 by the end of *Genesis*? The first element ('Go to the land I will show you') has, near enough, been fulfilled, both the going and the showing. The fact that the ancestral family ends up out of the land is not an insurmountable problem, because they are very conscious that they are headed back toward the land in the near future, Joseph solemnly promising his older brothers as he dies at the advanced age of 110 that they will return to Canaan, carrying Joseph's bones (50.25). No record is given of how his centenarian brothers responded to this parting shot by Joseph who is evidently still intent on wreaking his revenge on them for getting him to Egypt in the first place. Fortunately, from their point of view, Joseph was wrong by a factor of 430 years, according to Exod. 12.40, and this little announcement of the future on Joseph's part is not translated into reality in just the way it might have been expected to be.

The second element, 'Be a blessing', is an almost complete disaster, the one foreigner to benefit unambiguously from the patriarchal family's existence being the pharaoh who now rules a nation of slaves. It comes as a disappointment to readers anxious for the fulfilment of the announcements of plot to learn, when they get into Exodus 1, that there has arisen a pharaoh who does not know Joseph. For this implies that the one blessing the Hebrew ancestors ever did for any of the 'families of the earth' is now completely forgotten.

The third element, 'I will make of you a great nation', is at least on the road to execution by the time *Genesis* ends. It is a little disconcerting, all the same, to find, when the family does re-appear in Canaan in ch. 50 for the burial of Jacob in a proleptic mini-exodus, that 'all the servants of Pharaoh . . . and all the elders of the land of Egypt' accompany them (50.7), and the gawping Canaanites remark on what an impression these 'Egyptians' are making (50.11). This cannot be an entirely satisfactory episode for a family expecting to become a 'great nation' in its own right.

3. THE THIRD ANNOUNCEMENT (25.23; 27.27-29, 39-40)

Two peoples, born of you, shall be divided;
   the one shall be stronger than the other,
   the elder shall serve the younger.

(25.23)

May God give you [Jacob] of the dew of heaven,
   and of the fatness of the earth
   and plenty of grain and wine.
Let peoples serve you,
   and nations bow down to you.
Be lord over your brothers,
   and may your mother's sons bow down to you.

(27.28-29)

Behold, away from the fatness of the earth shall your
   dwelling be [Esau]
   and away from the dew of heaven on high.
By your sword you shall live,
   and you shall serve your brother.

(27.39-40)

The Announcement relating to Jacob and Esau is contained in three passages. The first is the birth oracle (25.23) which predicts that the two twins will be divided from one another and the elder son will serve the younger. The second and third are Isaac's blessings on the two sons. A large number of motifs are deployed in these blessings; for convenience' sake we may group the principal motifs under three headings:

1. service
2. fertility
3. division.

The first element, service, is the idea that Esau should serve Jacob. . . . We are therefore expecting the narrative to tell us of this serving. The fact is, however, that apart from passages that promise or desire that Esau should serve Jacob, all the 'serving' that gets done in the Jacob story is by Jacob. . . . Jacob serves his uncle Laban (29.15), not only for money but even for his wives, even though they are of the same family (29.20, 30). He even gets himself 'hired out' as a serving man to satisfy Leah's sexual appetites (30.16). Much more significant, though, is the way he projects himself, in his meeting with Esau. 'When my brother Esau meets you', he says to his retainers, 'you shall say, These belong to your servant Jacob' (32.17, 18). No matter that this is Jacob at his most obsequious; his words in fact amount to an inversion of the blessing he had earlier risked so much to gain. And whereas in 27.29 Isaac had hoped that nations would bow down . . . to Jacob, the only bowing down in the whole Jacob cycle is done by Jacob and his family, in a comic surfeit of prostration, himself seven times, then the secondary wives and their children, then Leah and her children, then Joseph and Rachel (33.3, 6-7). Jacob serves everyone; no one serves Jacob. So much for the blessing.

The second element in what is wished for Jacob is fertility—with corresponding infertility for Esau (27.28, 39).

Now it is true that this is realized for him: he becomes 'exceedingly rich, with large flocks, maidservants and manservants, and camels and asses' (30.43, the servants ranking this time after the flocks and before the camels). There is the slight difficulty that his favourite wife is barren, but otherwise fertility is the rule of the house. What is surprising about the outworking of the fertility wishes is that Esau, who by all expectation ought to be getting a negative blessing, is also prospering quite satisfactorily. Being without the birthright and the first son's blessing has not obviously done him much harm, not if he can bring to the meeting with Jacob a band of 400 men (32.6; 33.1) which are obviously so many more than Jacob's company that Jacob is frightened out of his wits (32.7). And when Jacob gingerly invites Esau to accept his 'present', calling it with unimaginable insensitivity his 'blessing' . . . , Esau can say with equal truth and equanimity, 'I have enough, my brother; keep what you have for yourself' (33.9). The brother with the blessing is more needy than the one without.

The third element is division, the implication of the birth oracle being that the division between the brothers will signify hostility and dissension. This is indeed what happens throughout the greater part of the narrative. But the surprise the story has in store for us is that after what seems like a lifetime of division, including murderous plans by Esau (27.41) and physical separation, the narrative moves towards an effectual reconciliation. Esau holds nothing against Jacob any longer, but runs to meet him, falls on his neck and kisses him, and they both weep (33.4). They separate physically again but not emotionally. The official explanation given by the narrator in 36.6-8 for why the brothers do not live together is that they simply do not have enough room for their cattle, Esau no less wealthy than Jacob. The scene reminds us of the separation of Abram and Lot, a separation that was equally amicable and equally constructive for the growth of the ancestral family. The primal birth oracle is not exactly overturned, because it was somewhat Delphic in its wording anyway. But, following on the uterine conflict of the twins, it led us to imagine the worst for the relationship of the brothers. In that respect we were not deceived—not, that is, till the close of the story where a quite different nuance was laid upon the term 'divide', and we discovered that it meant mere physical separation without any emotional dissension.

In sum, the Announcements that preface the Jacob story are on the whole misleading about the course that the action of the narrative will take.[4]

4. THE FOURTH ANNOUNCEMENT (37.5-10)

> Now Joseph had a dream . . .
> Hear this dream, which I have dreamed:
> behold, we were binding sheaves in the field,
> and lo, my sheaf arose and stood upright;
> and behold your sheaves gathered around it,
> and bowed down to my sheaf . . .
>
> (37.5-7)

> Then he dreamed another dream . . .
> Behold, I have dreamed another dream;
> and behold, the sun, the moon, and the eleven stars
> were bowing down to me.
>
> (37.9)

The fourth Announcement of *Genesis* takes the form of two dreams of Joseph purporting to foretell the future. They predict, according to the interpretations of them proffered in vv. 8 and 10, that:

> 1. Joseph's brothers will bow down to him
> 2. The brothers, and the father and mother, will bow down to him.

What happens to this Announcement, in brief, is that the first element comes true, and the second does not. The brothers bow down before him four times in Egypt (42.6; 43.26, 28; 44.14). But his father never does. In fact it is Joseph who bows before Jacob (48.12).[5] And his mother of course cannot. For Rachel has already died in 35.16-19 in childbirth with Benjamin, as Jacob will remind us in 48.7. Benjamin is certainly alive in ch. 37 because there are eleven stars bowing down to him. But his mother is dead. So Jacob knows that Joseph's dream cannot be fulfilled. Well, not exactly. But he is pious, or superstitious, enough to wonder whether there may not be some truth in it even so. So he keeps his options open, or as the Hebrew has it, 'kept the matter'. . . . But he makes not the slightest effort to fulfil his part in bringing it to pass.

CONCLUSION

Joseph's dreams may be taken as a paradigm for how Announcements function in *Genesis*. Because they have been spoken by someone with authority, like God or a patriarch or a dreamer, the reader must reckon with the possibility that they may be executed. But only the possibility. Reality as it develops in *Genesis* has a rather unpredictable connection with the Announcements disclosing how it is supposed to develop.

If we are trying to guess the likelihood of an announcement becoming reality, we cannot proceed by distinguishing between what God says and what humans say, as though divine words were bound to be more reliable predictors of coming events.[6] Nor do we have any more success if we discriminate between what is commanded, what is promised, and what is wished for. Nor is it always very clear whether a particular thing announced has actually come about or not.

Perhaps there is a basic flaw in the approach I have adopted. Was I right in supposing that what is announced in *Genesis* should be expected to be fulfilled in *Genesis*? It seemed to be a reasonable assumption, but let us allow that it might be more apt to regard *Genesis* as simply the first volume in a larger sequence of narrative works *à la recherche du temps perdu*, *Genesis*-2 Kings. It is indeed incontrovertible that the narrative begun by *Genesis* does not really come to a pause—as a narrative—until the end of 2 Kings; but there it does come to a full stop, and any extension of the narrative can only be possible by telling the story all over again from the beginning, starting again with Adam, Seth, Enosh (1 Chr. 1.1).

Genesis, that is to say, starts a narrative chain that concludes with 2 Kings 25. So, in order to answer our initial question more comprehensively, perhaps we need to ask, What happens to the Announcements by the point the narrative has reached at the end of 2 Kings? Perhaps 'what happens in *Genesis'* can only be stated once we have read to the end of the story as a totality. So, what *has* happened?

The first set of announcements, in *Genesis* 1, presents an agenda that is not explicitly said to have been carried out, but neither has it failed. Even though by the end of 2 Kings the Jewish people is decimated, the human race at large has been adequately prolific and there is at least no shortage of Chaldaeans and Egyptians. The earth has been filled and subdued: there are no more famines, in the land or out of it, that may be laid to the account of the earth; only humans create starvation (2 Kgs 25.2-3). Wild animals are no threat to the stability of states, and human dominion over animals as beasts of burden and as food is too much taken for granted to be remarked upon. The animal kingdom has indeed experienced a major reprieve through the destruction of the Jerusalem temple, but no one represents that as any derogation of human power over the animals.

But with the second set of Announcements things are quite different. If *Genesis* 12 announces that the Abrahamic family is to become a great nation, 2 Kings tells us that in the end this did not happen. The 10,000 significant members of the nation still surviving at the end of the narrative sequence (2 Kgs 24.14) are carried into Babylon, where they may be presumed to lose the status of a nation. And the insignificant members go, 'all' of them (25.26), to Egypt, and equally to oblivion. Whatever happened to the promise between *Genesis* and 2 Kings, and whatever nationhood the Abrahamic family acquired in the bygoing, has been undermined by the end of 2 Kings.

And if *Genesis* announces that Abraham and his descendants will be given a land, 2 Kings reports that in the end the family of Abraham ended up precisely in Babylonia and Egypt, for all the world as if they had never left Ur or as if Abram, Sarai and Lot had never escaped from *Genesis* 12. In case we needed the point spelled out, 2 Kgs 25.21 observes, amazingly laconically: 'So Judah was taken into exile out of its land'. It does not need to say, The land promised by Yahweh. We know that.

And then if *Genesis* announces divine blessing for the Abrahamic family, and a covenanted divine-human relationship, 2 Kings reports: 'It came to the point in Jerusalem and Judah that he cast them out of his presence'. And as for the intended blessing to the nations, we wonder whether the arrival of 7000 mercenaries and 1000 carpenters and smiths in Babylon, along with their numerous dependants and various nonentities (2 Kgs 24.16; 25.11) constitutes a blessing commensurate with the effort expended in getting all the way from *Genesis* to 2 Kings.

In short, Israel's Primary History, the narrative sequence of *Genesis*-2 Kings, is a narrative of (in the end) unmitigated disaster, and *Genesis'* story of the failure to meet the programme set forth by its Announcements is no contrast to the Primary History as a whole, but rather presages the direction in which the larger story is headed. In fact, *Genesis* distracts us, to a certain extent, from recognizing what the future course of events in the Primary History will inevitably be by suggesting that to some degree the Announcements are coming true. For, according to the narrative of *Genesis* to 2 Kings, despite appearances, they do not.[7]

Notes

1. Others have indeed noted from time to time the programmatic nature of the texts we have identified as 'Announcements'. On 1.28 Walter Brueggemann, 'The Kerygma of the Priestly Writers', *ZAW* 84 (1972), pp. 397-414 (400), suggests that 'the formidable blessing declaration of *Gen* 12.8 provides a focus for understanding the kerygma of the entire tradition'. However, Brueggemann limits his discussion to the so-called P tradition. On 12.1-3, John C.L. Gibson, *Genesis* (DSB; Edinburgh: Saint Andrew Press, 1982), vol. 2, p. 12, comments: 'Everything he does following his call and everything that happens to him are either directly related to them [i.e. the promises of 12.1-3] in the narratives or may be brought into connection with them by the exercise of a little imagination . . . the working out of the promises supplies both the main element of tension in the plot of the stories and the primary key to their interpretation.' On 25.21-28, Gerhard von Rad, *Genesis: A Commentary* (OTL; tr. John H. Marks; Philadelphia: Westminster Press, revised edition, 1972), p. 265, sees these verses as 'form[ing] an expository preface to the whole [Jacob story]' and 'acquaint[ing] the reader with those facts which are important for understanding the following stories'. On the Joseph story, Walter Brueggemann writes: 'The power and validity of the dream in 37.5-9 emerge as a main issue. The dream functions in the Joseph narrative as the oracle does for the Jacob materials'; '. . . the dream of chapter 37 governs all that follows' (Genesis: *A Bible Commentary for Teaching and Preaching* [Atlanta: John Knox Press, 1982], pp. 290, 296).

2. What danger will it run if it is not 'kept'?, we wonder.

3. Most scholars evade the force of the imperative with proposals which usually necessitate revocalization. Cf. various proposals by: John Skinner, *A Critical*

and Exegetical Commentary on Genesis (ICC; Edinburg: T. and T. Clark, 2nd edn, 1930), p. 244; E.A. Speiser, *Genesis* (AB, 1; Garden City, NY: Doubleday, 1983), pp. 85, 86; George W. Coats, *Genesis: With an Introduction to Narrative Literature* (FOTL, 1; Grand Rapids: Eerdmans, 1983), pp. 107-108; Theodorus C. Vriezen, 'Bemerkungen zu *Genesis* 12.1-7', in M.A. Beek *et al.* (eds.), *Symbolae biblicae et Mesopotamiae F.M.T. de Liagre Böhl dedicate* (Leiden: E.J. Brill, 1973), p. 387; Claus Westermann, *Genesis 12-36: A Commentary* (tr. John J. Scullion; Minneapolis: Augsburg, 1985), p. 144.

4. This view differs from that of most commentators; e.g. Brueggemann, *Genesis,* p. 208: 'Without a very explicit statement, the narrative [33.1-17] affirms that the initial oracle of 25.23 has come to fruition'.

5. Commentators regularly fail to see this point; cf., for example, von Rad, *Genesis,* pp. 352, 383. Robert Alter, commenting on 42.6 in 'Joseph and His Brothers', *Commentary* (November, 1980), pp. 59-69 (62) (= *The Art of Biblical Narrative* [London: George Allen and Unwin, 1981], p. 163), states, 'Joseph's two dreams are here literally fulfilled'. Yet, to reach this conclusion he is compelled to interpret the imagery of the sun, moon and stars as foreshadowing Joseph's role as Egyptian vizier—which is certainly not how Jacob understands the dream! (cf. further Alter, *The Art of Biblical Narrative,* p. 169). Eric I. Lowenthal, in *Commentary* (February, 1981), pp. 17-18 (18), responding to Alter, rightly takes him to task by pointing out that, whereas the dream spoke of eleven stars, only ten brothers bow down in 42.6. Unfortunately, he does not develop this insight. Gibson, *Genesis,* vol. 2, p. 273, writes: 'We are left in no doubt that this was a fulfilment, partial maybe but real, of the dreams in chapter 37'. It would be closer to the truth to say that the first dream is eventually fulfilled (with Benjamin's bowing down in 43.26), but that only one of the three elements of the second dream (obeisance of the eleven brothers) has been fulfilled. Donald A. Seybold, 'Paradox and Symmetry in the Joseph Narrative', in Kenneth R.R. Gros Louis, with James S. Ackerman and Thayer S. Warshaw (eds.), *Literary Interpretations of Biblical Narratives* (Nashville: Abingdon Press, 1974), p. 69, points out that in 42.6 'the second dream remains unfulfilled,' but he is very vague on any actual fulfilment of it (cf. p. 72). Wolfgang Richter, 'Traum und Traumdeutung im AT: Ihre Form und Verwendung', *Biblische Zeitschrift* 7 (1963), pp. 202-20 (208), believes that the fulfilment of the first dream (42.6ff.) prepares the way for the fulfilment of the second, which is achieved, though not literally (*wörtlich*), in ch. 47. He too remains vague on how the second dream works out. We may ask, If it is not fulfilled literally, how can it be said to have been fulfilled at all, when all other dreams in the Joseph story are fulfilled literally? Apparently the only scholar to read 48.12 in the light of 37.5-11 is Gibson, *Genesis,* vol. 2, pp. 230-31, who comments on Joseph's prostration before Jacob: 'It is not so commonly pointed out however, that the second dream is not fulfilled in the epic . . . Joseph's dream of the sun and moon and stars must have been a false one, suggested by his own arrogance and ambition, and not at all by God's prompting.'

6. This is in opposition to the view of Peter D. Miscall, 'The Jacob and Joseph Stories as Analogies', *JSOT* 6 (1978), pp. 28-40 (32), who believes that one must distinguish in biblical narrative between divine and human words in the following way: with divine words (e.g. prophecy, oracle), 'it is a question not of whether it will be fulfilled but of how it will be fulfilled', whereas with human words (e.g. blessing, prediction), 'it is a matter of whether it will be fulfilled, and not just of how'.

7. For further elaboration of this reading of the Primary History, see Chapter 4 below.

Leslie Brisman (essay date 1990)

SOURCE: "Introduction: The Documentary Hypothesis and Family Romance," in *The Voice of Jacob: On the Composition of Genesis,* pp. ix-xviii, Indiana University Press, 1990.

[*In the following essay, Brisman highlights the method by which Biblical scholars study the composition of* Genesis, *and suggests that literary motivations, rather than sociological ones, guided the development of the source material of* Genesis *into its final form.*]

In the King James translation, the Decalogue begins (or almost begins) with the injunction "Thou shalt have no other gods before Me." Although the Hebrew *'al pānaî* (as opposed to *lĕpānaî*) clearly means "to my face" rather than "before my time," there is a familiar truth represented in the English "before Me": God's insistence on unrivaled priority of importance seems to require also a denial of antecedents. Christians and Jews may differ about whether the command is the first or the second in the Decalogue, but it is not hard to agree that the added ambiguity of the English accords with a theological absolute: This god tolerates no rivals, mediators, or predecessors. He is *the* original.

Human originality is a more problematic thing. Did any biblical writer "begin at the beginning," or were all forever collecting, revising, transmuting material in more or less complicated relationship to the past? Today we are fascinated by Babylonian and Canaanite analogues or sources for Elohim and Yahweh stories, and modern scholarship routinely questions whether there was an original unity between the Elohim who is to have no others before him and the Yahweh (right before him—in the preceding verse) who spearheads the Exodus. We have come to regard the active worker who forms Adam from the earth in *Genesis* 2 as a very differently conceived character from the sublimely white-collar deity of chapter 1. The question "Which version of the creation of man is the more original?" may be in part a question about the relative antiquity of the various strands of Pentateuchal narrative, but it mingles easily with the literary question about which seems the more "original" in the sense of the stronger, more imaginative achievement.

From the literary study of the Pentateuch, there has emerged a general consensus about the "originality" of the J author in both the temporal and evaluative senses—at least when a major J author-compiler is distinguished from source-fragments, redactions, or additions "in the school of J." For most readers who regard J as *an author,* he is the Pentateuchal author most gifted in producing the uncanny, most oblivious of the moral sensibilities and institutional needs that have been thought to mark other Pentateuchal sources. From the classical documentary study of the Pentateuch—i.e., the work of Graf, Wellhausen, and their followers—there emerged a consensus about the antiquity of J in relation to the other sources, a consensus regarded, for a hundred years, as close to fact as the Darwinian hypothesis of natural selection. Even in the flurry of recent challenges to the neatness of the documentary hypothesis, there have hardly been any adherents of the old notion of Hermann Hupfelt that (what we now call) P is the precursor text and groundwork for redactional additions.

Although there was some philological evidence for the relative earliness of J, the Wellhausen hypothesis was advanced less by the rigors of a scientific discipline than by the lure of a single, sweeping idea about the development of the text. Despite subsequent refinements in the history of religion and appreciation of narrative differences, the consensus about the earliness of J remains buttressed by the overwhelming simplicity of the idea of a melancholy progress from the amoral to the moral, from the lawless to the regulated, from the naïve to the partisan, from the unexpurgated to the decorous. In this assumption, the orthodox and the irreverent have stood united: Cynics—with Wellhausen at their lead—pointed to the pristine qualities of J and the loss as we give up his "many-colored robe of fancy" for the somber dress of scribe and priest; looking at the same facts but reading black where others saw white, some pious critics who took over the study of higher criticism pointed to the grand scheme of revelation, the unfolding in time of greater and greater understandings of religious truth.

Let us consider a well-known example of Wellhausen arguing for the priority of J. One of the most shocking and indisputably J verses of the Pentateuch is Exodus 4:24: "On the way, at a rest spot, Yahweh met [Moses] and sought to kill him." Wellhausen assumes that Moses at this point in the narrative is uncircumcised, that he ought to have been, and that Yahweh is more disturbed by this omission than he was by Moses' uncircumcision of the lips. Here is the leader of the people about to take office, and the congregational subcommittee of One uncovers a troublesome flaw that can kill the nomination—strikingly troped as killing the nominee. But just what expectation of circumcision was there? Wellhausen argues that there must have been a tradition of circumcision before marriage, and that J recognized such a practice here as in *Genesis* 34, the story of Shechem. When Zipporah circumcises her son instead of her husband, throwing the son's foreskin at Moses' genitals and thus symbolically making him a *hᵃtan dāmîm* (bridegroom of blood), she delivers her husband from the wrath of Yahweh—and inaugurates the concept of infant circumcision as a milder substitute for the nasty adult practice.

This much is undoubtedly an impressive interpretation in its own right, and perhaps it gains further weight if we see Wellhausen's reading of the Zipporah story as an etiology of circumcision in line with his reading of the Adam and Eve story as an etiology of human misery. Both J texts get rewritten, in the Priestly accounts of circumcision and creation respectively, as part of "the convulsive efforts of later Judaism to deny that most firmly established of all the lessons of history, that the sons suffer for the sins of the fathers" (*Prolegomena,* II.viii.I.i). Both the narrative act of rereading an obligation and the representation of a central Hebrew ritual as being *about* revision (substituting a milder for a harsher cult practice) make the Exodus 4 passage too sophisticated for Wellhausen to claim that he spots the amoral, folkloric element in unadulterated form. But he holds on to the judgment that we have here a great piece of J narrative, in distinction from the circumcision story of *Genesis* 17, where the institution of the ritual "throws into the shade and spoils the story out of which it arose" (*Prolegomena,* II.viii.II.3). Wellhausen hails the imaginative triumph of the J story by reading it as revisionary in relationship to a ritual practice, though "original" in relationship to the belated *Genesis* 17 story.

The most surprising element of Wellhausen's interpretation remains his assumption of a sin of omission on Moses' part: Wellhausen so readily normalizes the sudden declaration of Yahweh's uncanny hostility! Usually such normalization is attributed to a belated, priestly writer or the redactor of the text. Suppose, however, that the J writer gains his power by *unwriting* a more normative account of the circumcision of the son. Suppose, that is, that behind the eerie encounter as we have it lay not the historicity of adult circumcision in Israel but a milder story of the institution of child circumcision at the time of Moses, or even a story like the Binding of Isaac, where God's apparent bloodthirsty will is a fictional "given," necessary for the story's subsequent representation of a truer, kindlier divine nature. We can believe that Wellhausen's supposition about the uncircumcised Moses is more J than the normative, rabbinic readings that Moses failed only in regard to the circumcision (or the hour of circumcision) of his son—but we can do so without accepting the assumption that the story was invented to change, or to reflect a real change, in the practice of circumcision. If Zipporah calls upon Yahweh to "read" the circumcision of her son as the circumcision of Moses, J can call upon us to read the whole episode as a strong quarrel of man (woman) with god—or poet with precursor. The suddenness of Yahweh's attack on Moses would then be not a sign of a story that has been wrested from its introduction, but the story's own best wrestling move against the god of Stories Old. It would be in line with the argument developed in this book that if we suppose the Priestly account of circumcision in *Genesis* 17 to be a prevenient text, or if we let it represent the *sort* of text in the context of Mosaic materials that J encountered, then we can better appreciate the uncanny Exodus legend. Zipporah's moral initiative remains as surprising as Abraham's passive obedience to a no less terrible command, but we need no more suppose a history of adult circumcision than a history of child sacrifice in Israel. Zipporah's response—and the fact that only her voice endorses her response—accords with the dramatic attack of Yahweh in the same way that Abraham's silent response suits the Elohist's story of a god who does not take argument for piety. The originality of each author may be both a product of the writer's reworking of a more pallid precursor text and a theme exhibited in the characters and action of the text itself.

If it is incorrect to turn the tables on Wellhausen and to suppose the priority of *Genesis* 17, or even the priority of a Mosaic legend instituting circumcision in the way that *Genesis* 17 does, one might in any case suppose the priority of the expression $h^a tan\ d\bar{a}m\hat{\imath}m$, a minimal text, perhaps, but a text all the same and not simply a sociological fact. The general point is that the originality of J does not depend on the absence of prevenient Elohistic or Priestly stories and laws, and that creative reworking of a legend and brilliant redactional tinkering may be activities of the same sort of mind—or the very same hand. If I close my books of Higher Criticism and read the Pentateuch itself, the originality of J often seems to me equally or better explained as involved in a swerve from a text like that which we also find preserved in scripture as we have it. For certain stories, therefore, the non-J material might best be appreciated as though it were in fact the scripture as J read it. On the other hand, it is not clear to me that in the evaluative sense of "original" J has a total monopoly on the quality. Some of the passages attributed to E in classical source-criticism are strikingly original, and there are a few P texts that on the basis of literary merit could hardly be passed off as belated, partisan, hack writing. To read the Pentateuch with a sense of its composite structure but without a predisposition toward the particulars of the attributions and datings of the Higher Critics is to confront a complex agon of voices that compete for authority, originality, or what is sometimes represented as "blessing." We may feel that we know the tension to be fictitious since a redactor has assembled pieces of text from strands that do not have single authors or from strands whose authors were not conscious of one another. But actually

we know no such thing, at least not while we are engaged in the actual reading of the text, however composite. We may have been repeatedly told such things, but the experience of reading the Pentateuch, and *Genesis* in particular, is an experience of confronting the copresence of voices that someone has assembled into some sort of uneasy harmony with one another. As soon as we add to the idea of tension the dimension of time—whether we regard sequentiality as relevant to the narrative strands themselves or only to the relation between the strands and a redactor—we introduce the analogies, and perhaps the models, of writer and precursor, man and God. Like Jacob wrestling with the angel, the writers of the various documentary strands make of their strife the quintessentially Israelite experience, where that adjective ambiguously denominates "mastery of" or (to borrow William Blake's term) "incorporeal war with" the God who has none other before him.

If most scholars of biblical studies dismiss the thought of influence or tension between the strands, strands representing single individuals at least one of whom was aware of others, purists of literary analysis scorn the personification of literary strands as themselves authors, persons with anxieties, debts, and wills to power. Yet if we are to pursue the literary study of scripture as anything other than the technical study of the redaction of the text, we do need to hypothesize authorial voices, with personality and intention. Or at least *I* need to do so, for my purpose in this book is to experiment with the thought of a truly literate and literary composition of *Genesis.* By *literate* I mean to suggest the possibility of one author actually able to read a text of another author, just as the author of Matthew could read the Gospel of Mark (most scholars believe) or the talmudic midrashist could read the text of the Pentateuch. By *literary* I wish to suggest the primacy of intertextual, as opposed to sociological or political, motives for invention. I cannot really hope to restore the dating of the documents as understood by Hupfeld; but I can hope to tilt the course of the literary study of the Bible, however slightly, from form criticism to literary criticism, from typological to agonistic models, from what Northrop Frye has popularized as *the* great code to what I would regard rather as the great competition, or the great competing *codes* of scripture. My immediate desire is to experiment, for once, with the thought of "originals" or originators of *Genesis* in inspired competition for divine benediction—or readers' allegiance.

In a startling parody of such a competition, Henrik Ibsen offers us, in *Hedda Gabler,* a helpful word of caution. The dreaded competition in the play concerns a professorship in history, valued as a stable source of income; Ibsen does not allow us to romanticize the competition into so noble a thing as a rivalry for a lady's affections or a mutually inspiring effort at great writing. Both Eilert Løvborg, the unconventional, J-like writer, and George Tesman, the priestlike groveler "best at putting other people's papers in order," show themselves to be insufferable egoists who botch both life and work, and we can hardly consider it the moral reformation or spiritual self-transcendence of Tesman when (whether out of guilt or pure addiction to old scraps) he undertakes to piece together and preserve something of the dead Løvborg's work. When he first hears that Løvborg has published a new book, his immediate reaction is, "It must be something he has had lying around from his better days." This careless, dismissive remark has haunted me for years as a representation of what we too often assume in supposing a Pentateuch that has been compiled by George Tesman. Løvborg's published book is new work, not something that has been lying around, and his really great book is very new work, still in manuscript. I cannot deny the basic truth of the Graf-Wellhausen hypothesis that the biblical equivalent of Løvborg's work falls, at some point, into Tesman-like hands. But scholars of the documentary hypothesis have tended to assume that the J stories must be relics of former days, and that the sorters and redactors have sometimes devotedly preserved, sometimes piously rewritten, the old J fragments, never matching their pure inspiration. Even Van Seters, perhaps our most creative proponent of a late J strand, does not return us to an aboriginal P source. He assumes that a more refined J version is a later version, but he still imagines a Tesman rewriting a Løvborg, not a young Løvborg making inspired use of the scraps left by a Tesman.

Although my aim is exegesis, not dramatic fiction, I need, like Ibsen, to flesh out the portraits of two characters—for whom I want names rather than just capital letters so as to keep in mind the idea of individuals rather than anonymous collections of materials from better days. When I started this experiment, I began with four names for four characters whom I expected to identify, more or less, with the traditional J, E, P, and R (redactor). Yet it soon became clear that my business in pursuing the thought of literary composition was to challenge the distinction between *strand* (ancient source) and *redaction* (the actual composition of the text as we know it). I wished to consider the possibility that literary motives, rather than sociological ones, were responsible for the differences between the strands, strands that emerged not as separate records of oral traditions but as text and ur-text, with an inspired author reading, modifying, recasting, or undoing his sources. In short, I wished to consider that *Genesis* had been composed in something of the way that the history plays of Shakespeare were composed—by one author of distinct personality quoting or revising freely the work of his sometimes noble, sometimes pedestrian predecessors. The analogy may seem particularly frail if we conceive of the strong revisionist in *Genesis* having the added obligation of being, unlike Shakespeare, the preserver of the very precursor text he is modifying and reshaping, but the analogy may be useful for reminding us of a distinction between what was history (at least familiar, authoritative text) and what is being introduced or rewritten for literary reasons.

My approach led me further into speculation about the literary methods and the psychology of the later author but

revealed little about the separate identities or strands that made up the "precursor" text. Indeed, it seemed to me more and more to be the case that however composite in origin, the precursor held—for the revisionist—the status of *a* sacred text and is therefore best thought of as *an* ancestor rather than several. Granted the possibility of such intertextuality, one still must choose between two broad outlines of the history: In one, a character more or less to be identified with the author of the P strand reacted to a composite of the J and E texts; in another, a character more or less to be identified with the author of the J strand reacted to a composite of the E and P texts. The present book is the result of my gradual conviction that, despite more than a century of scholarly work affirming the historicity of the former of these hypotheses, the second has much more to commend it for the understanding of the Bible *as literature*. This book makes no claim to refute, on scholarly grounds, the documentary history as it has come to be generally accepted; my subject is speculation on a possible history of the literary imagination in *Genesis*—a subject necessarily more involved with fancy than with demonstrable facts, however hard one tries not to betray the philological facts. I realize that I may be naïve in trying to understand how the same person could introduce some of the most bizarre tales and some of the most normative, nationalistic formulas. I realize that I may be wrong in working with some of the documentary strands as though they actually constituted a precursor text, *the* precursor text, available *as text* to a midrashically imaginative revisionist. And I realize how much I endanger the credibility of a few "strong misreadings" by working through the same hypothesis for a multitude of what may be weak, redactional tinkerings. Yet even if these shadows of doubt were to grow into "presences that are not to be put by," I would hold that a student of *Genesis* might come to a better understanding of the competition of theologies, the agon of literary voices, by supposing—at least for the "interposed ease" of this study's "false surmise"—that a belated author had before him an ur-text corresponding to the work actually preserved in certain fragments of our present text.

I shall call the belated author *Jacob,* after the character in *Genesis* who is his special hero and representative. To keep in mind the prevenience of the non-Jacobic material, I would like to call its author *Isaac.* But to suggest the association of this precursor with the (currently unpopular) idea of an Elohist, I shall indulge in the solecism of *Eisaac* when I mean the author rather than the character. My Jacob and Eisaac are not exactly J and E, for I am aware of the fiction by which I am substituting E and P texts for a hypothetical ur-text available to J. I will also be attributing more Priestly text to Eisaac than any scholar since Hupfeld has assigned to E, and I will be attributing additional passages and some "redactional misprisions" to Jacob. But concomitant with the reattributions, a certain consistency in what Wallace Stevens calls the "motive for metaphor" will typify these authorial characters.

In borrowing biblical names for our authors, I would like to borrow also something of the histories of the eponymous heroes, and we might begin with what could be called their birth trauma. Isaac is born of Sarah's desiccated loins and is named (at least as interpreted by Sarah) to suggest not joy or laughter but embarrassment: "God made a joke of me; everyone who hears will laugh at me" (*Gen.* 21:6). The traumatic event that Eisaac is destined to repeat and represent is the conflation of the sublime and the risible. Isaac is the most sage and serious of the patriarchs and would like to be regarded as "child of the Promise," but his name invariably suggests "playing around," sometimes specifically sexual playing, and is thus a reminder that children are engendered in the loins, not in the mental "conception" or wishful thought of their parents. As a scriptural voice, Eisaac represents the aspiration for dignity and the suppression of the risible, of the all-too-human. From the perspective of the dreaded Jacobic irony, Isaac is an "accident," a quirk of late menopause. But from an Eisaacic context, Isaac's birth is an emblem of timely deliverance from childlessness and therefore from death. Insofar as he is born to Sarah he is a welcome embarrassment, a natural joy, but insofar as he is born to Abraham he is an object of sacerdotal care, and the very sentence announcing his birth proclaims the moment to be a religious occasion: "Sarah bore, to Abraham, a child against his old age [a defense "against" old age or death], on the timely occasion of which God spoke" (21:2). The word I have translated as "timely occasion," rendered in the King James as "set time," is also the Hebrew word for religious holiday. And so it has justly become in Jewish history: The birth of Isaac is the scriptural reading for the first day of the Jewish New Year's holiday, symbolizing the opportunity for rejuvenation that distinguishes this new year from the seasonal one. Isaac's birth trauma, then, is the jolt that turns naturalistic fact into religious occasion. Not himself a priest, he becomes the very essence and emblem of priestly activity, the child bound to or on the altar. Though the episode we call "the binding of Isaac" is of course about the eventual release of Isaac, it is the binding that constitutes Eisaac's human bondage to a religious institution's representation of substitution or the deferment of death. Isaac will go free, but he will go forth ever fixated on the hill of Moriah, ever fixed in our consciousnesses as the emblem of the sacerdotal. It is small wonder that the text represents Sarah as dying immediately after; the natural child dies in Isaac as though it had gone up in smoke, and the loss of the natural child is all that his mother can bear. Henceforth no youthful Form of Love, Isaac will be married off when the servant who is his alter ego substitutes filial piety for sexual desire.

One of the indications of the enormous pathos surrounding the sacrifice of the natural man to the "Eisaac" idea is that, from Isaac's birth to his parents until the death of his father, Isaac speaks but one line: "Here is the fire and the wood, but where is the lamb for sacrifice?" This is a deeply moving moment, regardless of whether it is part of an Eisaacic narrative or a Jacobic interpolation. What must strike us, at the start of a quest for the Eisaacic line in *Genesis,* is the irony implicit in the idea of "Isaac's lines" (what he says in the Eisaacic script): to Isaac the character

belong the most awesome silences, for his destiny has been written before his birth. To Eisaac the writer likewise belong the most awesome silences, for his piety translates composition into transmission, telling into retelling. What he "made up" he made in the image of what he received, always effacing selfhood. Himself "already written," as it were, Eisaac becomes the symbol of the preservative character of religious tradition. The tradition may help preserve us from the terrors of facing ourselves as isolate, cut off before and aft, but in preserving our sense of continuity with generations past and to come, it preserves also itself. The Eisaacic text is carved in the altar stones, always already inscribed.

Jacob's birth is attended by a trauma of a different order. Born to succeed—at least in the sense of being second in the patriarchal roster—Eisaac's characteristic anxiety is that he might trespass beyond the limits of prescribed secondariness. But Jacob's birth is attended by no annunciation of comparable status, and Jacob's characteristic anxiety is that a less desirable secondariness might prove his lot in life. Where Isaac's birth is announced by an angel, Jacob's has to be specially entreatied of a God who may have slumbered. Where Isaac is born sole child of his mother, and is specially welcomed into the faith with the first party in scripture, Jacob has to share his birth with his brother, and his childhood is completely elided from the biblical account. We can fill in the childhood traumas, however, by voicing for the child a midwife's observation raised beyond natural taunt to nightmarishly internal threat: "Jacob, you are a heel, a hanger-on, an afterbirth or afterword, a secondary talent and no original!" It is against this that Jacob asserts himself as *the original,* patron of writers who achieve that mastery we call having one's own voice. Crucial to this idea of Jacob is the distinction between the prophecy about Isaac, made to Abraham, and the prophecy about Jacob, made to Rebecca alone. She has to solicit God for some word of comfort concerning the painful struggle in her womb, and God responds, as I understand it, to Rebecca—not to Rebecca and Isaac. What is known to her alone, and absorbed in the very marrow of Jacob's bones, is not only the final outcome but the ferocity of the struggle for priority in matters that count. We can hear, in that prophecy of the two brothers struggling for preeminence, some of the fierce nationalism that so distinguishes the agonistic God of Jacob from the more dignified and distant universal ruler his father worshiped.

It is convenient to represent the theological differences between Eisaac and Jacob by giving the god each worships a separate name. We can call Eisaac's god *Elohim,* thus transliterating the general name by which he is called. More often we can just say "God." But Jacob's god has a proper name as well as some other, more human attributes or appearances. This is not a scholarly book, in step with Anglo-American successors to the justly revered Germanic tradition, and so to avoid the scholarly "Yahweh," and to suggest something of the familiarity bordering on sacrilege that is associated with the appearance and naming of the deity in Jacobic narratives, I shall coin the transliteration

Yava. If the coinage in Hebrew really belongs to Jacob, a Jacob who can read and react to Eisaac's text and Eisaac's god, we will not be surprised to find Jacob occasionally referring to Elohim; Jacob can talk about and name the Eisaacic god. The name *Yava,* on the other hand, is totally absent from the Eisaacic text. Perhaps we can say that the development of the concept of Yava from its Eisaacic predecessor represents, in brief, the development of the voice of Jacob.

Sam Dragga (essay date 1992)

SOURCE: "*Genesis* 2-3: A Story of Liberation," *Journal for the Study of the Old Testament,* No. 55, September, 1992, pp. 3-13.

[*In the following essay, Dragga surveys the assumptions that typically color one's understanding of the Adam and Eve story. Dragga argues that when these assumptions and their connotations are revealed and understood, the story may be viewed as one of the liberation of humans, rather than one of their fall.*]

Genesis 2-3 is typically characterized as a tragic narrative of human failure and disgrace. This perspective, however, assumes that the human couple of the narrative is procreative prior to their act of disobedience, that the serpent who elicits their disobedience has malicious motivations, that the disobedience of the man and woman is disastrous, that the creator of the human couple is omnipotent, and that the removal of the man and woman from the garden of their creator constitutes a loss of paradise. Without the coloring of this series of assumptions, *Genesis* 2-3 might be interpreted as a story of liberation, a vivid and inspiring portrait of the origins of the human family.

THE PROCREATIVE COUPLE

In *Genesis* 2-3, the original human being is androgynous—*hā'ādām.*[1] It is the androgynous human being who receives Yahweh's command: 'You may freely eat of every tree of the garden; but of the tree of the knowledge of good and evil you shall not eat, for in the day that you eat of it you shall die' (*Gen.* 2.16-17).[2] Though the tree of knowledge is thus proscribed, eating of the tree of life 'also in the midst of the garden' (*Gen.* 2.9) is obviously permitted, indicating Yahweh's intention that this individual achieve immortality. *Gen.* 3.22-24 reinforces this reading: following the human disobedience, the absence of a prohibition regarding the tree of life leaves Yahweh apprehensive.

The significance of the tree of knowledge of good and evil, and specifically its association with sexual knowledge,[3] is obvious only following the human couple's eating of the fruit and their immediate and single discovery of their nakedness, their sexual differences (*Gen.* 3.6-7). The divine command to abstain from the fruit of the tree of knowledge of good and evil is thus designed to preclude

the human discovery of procreativity. Obviously this prohibition has little relevance to the isolated and androgynous human being; once the differentiation of the sexes occurs in *Gen.* 2.21-25, however, procreativity is a genuine option, and the prohibition is crucial to Yahweh's dominance of creation. Yahweh desires the human beings to abide as two naïve children without sexual knowledge. Yahweh intends to create only two human beings, two children eternally worshipful of their creator. Once the two have disobeyed, however, and have knowledge of procreativity, there is nothing to stop them from multiplying, from being creators themselves.

Possibly the unjustified assumption regarding the procreativity of the human couple is a consequence of the editorial juxtaposition of the Priestly creation narrative (*Gen.* 1) and the earlier Yahwist version (*Gen.* 2-3). Specifically, *Gen.* 1.22 ('And God blessed them, saying, "Be fruitful and multiply and fill the waters in the seas, and let birds multiply"') colors the reader's perception of *Genesis* 2-3, leading to the assumption that this blessing is also given to the man and the woman of the Yahwist's narrative. This assumption clouds the association of the tree of knowledge of good and evil with sexual knowledge and obscures the import of Yahweh's command regarding the eating of its fruit. This assumption thus also distorts Yahweh's motivation in creating the human beings and the serpent's motivation in directing the woman to eat the prohibited fruit.

THE WICKED SERPENT

In *Gen.* 3.1, the serpent is introduced and immediately associated with fertility through its identification as 'more *'ārûm* (wise or prudent) than any other wild creature', versus the immediately preceding description (*Gen.* 2.25) of the man and woman as *"rûmmîm* (naked),[4] again establishing a clear association between knowledge and sexuality. The serpent is also a traditional symbol of immortality; thus, though its location is never specified, it is only appropriate if the serpent is stationed at the tree of life 'in the midst of the garden' (*Gen.* 2.9), dutifully protecting the fruit of the tree from being eaten. Such a guardian of immortality is a figure common to the literature of the ancient world (e.g. the *Epic of Gilgamesh*).[5]

Traditional readings of *Genesis* 2-3, however, characterize the serpent as a deceiver. Thus, though the descriptive word *'ārûm* has the meaning 'prudent' (e.g. Prov. 14.8) as well as 'cunning' (e.g. Job 5.12),[6] translations and interpretations of *Gen.* 3.1 emphasize the pejorative meaning, thereby immediately impugning the serpent's motivation and biasing the reader's perception of its characterization. For example, RSV gives 'more subtle', NAB has 'most cunning', NEB has 'more crafty', and the AB gives 'sliest' as its translation. This assumption also yields subsequent interpretations and elaborations that identify the serpent as a demon who tempts the woman and the man to commit the capital crime of disobedience.[7]

Though the serpent's characterization as a demon has been widely rejected as anachronistic, the association of the serpent with specified or unspecified evil is tenacious, especially because the rejection of this association essentially eradicates the serpent's motivation.[8] The alternative characterization of the serpent as representative of a rival deity, and specifically a fertility deity,[9] though genuinely attractive because it allows a legitimate motivation and reinforces appropriate associations of the serpent with sexuality, is ultimately unsatisfactory. *Gen.* 3.1 itself identifies the serpent as a 'wild creature that the Lord God had made'.

The perception of the serpent as the guardian of the tree of life is thus a superior alternative, offering a cohesive characterization and a compelling motivation—exploiting the serpent's associations with fertility as well as immortality, the Yahwist has the guardian of the tree of life direct the man and woman to the tree of knowledge to discover human sexuality. In addition, because the serpent is 'more subtle than any other wild creature' (*Gen.* 3.1), its protection of the tree of life through physical violence is unnecessary, since it has the capacity verbally to dissuade all who come to eat of the precious fruit. That is, as the woman reaches to pick the fruit of the tree of life, the serpent asks, 'Has God forbidden you to eat from the trees in the garden?' The woman is stopped, and she answers by identifying the forbidden tree. The conversation is shifted to the tree of knowledge and the serpent's defensive distraction is a success.

In addition, the serpent's assertion regarding the tree of knowledge, 'You will not die. For God knows that when you eat of it your eyes will be opened, and you will be like God, knowing good and evil' (*Gen.* 3.4-5), is in direct opposition to Yahweh's earlier declaration: 'in the day that you eat of it you shall die' (*Gen.* 2.17). And though neither the serpent nor Yahweh reveals the entire significance of the tree of knowledge (i.e. the association with sexual knowledge), neither is deceptive.[10] Indeed, the Yahwist seems to emphasize the truth of the serpent's assertion through the narrator's immediate echo of the serpent's words to describe the effects of eating the fruit of the tree of knowledge: 'Then the eyes of both were opened' (*Gen.* 3.7). The serpent's accuracy is again reinforced with Yahweh's echo of its words: 'The human being (*hā'ādām*) has become like one of us, knowing good and evil' (*Gen.* 3.22). No similar repetition of Yahweh's words occurs.

The truth of their opposing promises, however, hinges of the meaning of mortality-immortality. To Yahweh, it seems that the individual dies unless he or she chooses the personal immortality that the tree of life offers. To the serpent, a different immortality is possible. This immortality is linked to the discovery of fertility: 'and they knew that they were naked' (*Gen.* 3.7). This immortality is achieved through the procreativity that the tree of knowledge allows, with the individual living on through his or her children.[11]

THE TRAGIC DISOBEDIENCE

In *Gen.* 3.6, the woman consciously chooses: she sees, assesses, judges and acts, without a single thought to the

prohibiting divine words. It is important to note here that the woman's role is active and the man's essentially passive acquiescence. It is she who observes the merits of the fruit of the tree, who perceives it as desirable, who picks the fruit, eats it, and gives it to the man. This series of active verbs in describing the woman's role is followed by the single verb regarding the man's role: he ate.[12] The man's role is thus minimized—he neither sees nor takes nor thinks; he just eats. He eats because she has eaten, siding with the woman in disobedience of Yahweh. This accords with the earlier and prophetic description of the relationship between husband and wife: 'Therefore a man leaves his father and mother and cleaves to his wife and they become one flesh' (*Gen.* 2.24). This description is especially emphatic because it is the opposite of Jewish tradition, which has the woman leave her family to be united to the man.[13]

Because the responsibility of the conscious choice is thus given to the woman, the significance of the choice is critical to a genuine appreciation and evaluation of the woman's characterization. If it is the guardian of the tree of life guiding the woman to human sexuality, the woman deserves praise: she gives human beings the opportunity of life, sacrificing personal immortality to acquire fertility. If, however, it is the spirit of evil tempting the woman to commit evil, the woman merits condemnation because she yields to the temptation and causes the man to yield also. In doing so, she deprives human beings of the opportunity to achieve immortality. Various elaborations and interpretations of *Genesis* 3 echo the misogynous interpretation of the woman's choice.[14]

The comic episode (*Gen.* 3.8-13) following the eating of the fruit, however, solicits a positive perception of the woman's choice. If the disobedience were genuinely tragic, it is unlikely that the Yahwist would minimize this ethical failure with the humorous detailing of the couple's naïve behavior. First, they foolishly hide among the trees upon hearing the approach of their creator. Secondly, they inadvertently reveal their guilt ('And he said, "I heard the sound of thee in the garden, and I was afraid, because I was naked; and I hid myself". He said, "Who told you that you were naked? Have you eaten of the tree which I commanded you not to eat?"'). Thirdly, they ineptly pass the buck ('The man said, "The woman whom thou gavest to be with me, she gave me fruit of the tree, and I ate". . . . The woman said, "The serpent beguiled me, and I ate"'). This episode thus serves to diminish the reader's perception of the gravity of the human disobedience and the reader's expectation of the severity of the divine discipline likely to occur.

THE OMNIPOTENT GOD

Gen. 3.14-19 is typically perceived as appropriately punitive of the cosmic evil that the human couple has committed. And various elaborations of the *Genesis* 3 passage emphasize this perception.[15] Possibly it is the juxtaposition of the Priestly creation narrative, with its repetition of

'God said' (**Gen.** 1.3, 6, 9, 11, 14, 20, 24, 26, 28, 29), and thus with its emphasis on the power of the divine word, that yields traditional readings of **Gen.** 3.14-19 as the righteous conviction and bitter condemnation of the guilty. In **Genesis** 1, the creator speaks and thereby brings to being—the creator's word has power. In **Genesis** 2, however, Yahweh chiefly acts: forming, breathing, planting, taking, putting, and so on. Yahweh avoids words, giving to the human being the responsibility of naming 'every living creature' (**Gen.** 2.19). And whereas the serpent's words prove sufficient to protect the tree of life, Yahweh's words fail to guard the tree of knowledge. This exhibition of Yahweh's verbal impotence obviously diminishes the punitive power of the **Gen.** 3.14-19 monologue. A superior interpretation, consistent with the import of the earlier comic episode, therefore, is that **Gen.** 3.14-19 is a judicious explanation of the consequences of a disappointing disobedience.

In this monologue, it is critical that Yahweh initially silence the serpent, giving it no opportunity to speak because its verbal powers have earlier proved superior to Yahweh's. Conversation between the serpent and humanity is henceforth impossible. In its ability to molt, however, the serpent communicates the missed immortality of the man and woman, the personal immortality that this woman and man forfeited in order to establish a human family. Simultaneously, each child of the man and woman serves as a reminder to the serpent of the cause of its lowly and despised condition: by guiding the man and woman to fertility, the serpent has forfeited its privileged position as guardian of immortality.

The woman also experiences consequences. The creation of life is agonizing, bringing with it important responsibilities (as Yahweh has discovered), and it is the woman who especially is to experience this anguish. **Gen.** 3.16 describes the dominance of the man over the woman on issues pertinent to childbearing; because it is the woman who actively sacrifices immortality to possess fertility, it is the woman who carries the child, who is physically and emotionally drained during pregnancy, who has the pains of labor and birth, whereas the man is never thus oppressed.[16] The man is assigned the similarly creative toil of cultivating crops to nourish the human family, thus tilling *hā'ᵃdāmâ* to raise *hā'ādām*.

It is important, however, that only verses 3.14 ('cursed are you above all cattle, and above all wild animals') and 3.17 ('cursed is the ground because of you') are performatives (i.e. '*rr*), causing by verbalizing; that is, the serpent is accursed by virtue of Yahweh's cursing of it. The remainder of the monologue is all promises: 'I will put enmity between you and the woman', 'I will greatly multiply your pain in childbearing', and so forth. The only promise that Yahweh reinforces by subsequent action is the promise regarding human mortality: 'you are dust, and to dust you shall return' (**Gen.** 3.19). And the promise to the woman of anguish during childbearing is itself minimized with

Eve's exclamation after the initial birth experience: 'I have gotten a man *with the help of* Yahweh' (**Gen.** 4.1, emphasis added).

The frailty of Yahweh's words is also evident in the reaction of the man to this divine monologue. In his earlier behavior (**Gen.** 3.6 and 12), the man has displayed little courage or initiative. Immediately following Yahweh's explanation that human mortality is the consequence of their disobedience, however, the man reveals neither remorse nor regret. Instead, in spite of Yahweh's words, the man seizes the earlier awarded responsibility of naming 'every living creature' and praises the choice of human fertility by giving to the woman the honorific title of Eve, mother of all living.[17] Without the woman's choice of fertility, he declares, the human family would have been impossible—a single man and a single woman would have composed humanity. Again the man sides with the woman.

Yahweh's only answer to the man's assertive words is again to act, giving the man and woman clothing, conferring on the human couple the symbols of civilization, the symbols of their sexual, social and psychological maturation. The naïve children have passed through rebellious adolescence, emerging as responsible adults.

THE LOSS OF PARADISE

Because two human beings who possess fertility and immortality constitute a god, with the capacity of giving birth to additional gods, Yahweh also acts on the earlier promise of mortality. The human couple is henceforth physically prohibited from eating the fruit of the tree of life. The previous guardian of the tree—the serpent—shielded the fruit of immortality with words, sacrificing the fruit of the tree of knowledge. Yahweh therefore silenced and banned the serpent. The newly appointed guardians are cherubim, figures with similar mythological associations.[18] They wield swords of fire and, equally important, speak no words.

Traditional interpretations of **Genesis** 3, however, characterize this episode as the violent expulsion of a grieving human couple, and elaborations of **Genesis** 3 echo this reading.[19] The assumption here is that a life of luxurious dependence inside the garden is superior to a life of rigorous self-sufficiency outside the garden. The world *šlḥ* (3.23) is therefore given the reinforcing translation 'drove out' (NEB) or 'banished' (NAB and AB), as opposed to the milder and morphologically appropriate 'sent forth' (RSV), which clarifies the relationship with 'put forth' of 3.22 ('lest he put forth his hand and take also of the tree of life'). Also possible, however, is a translation of 'set free' or 'let loose', emphasizing the liberation of the human beings from the cage of their creator. Similarly, the word *grš* (3.24) is given the ferocity of 'drove out' (RSV), 'cast out' (NEB), or 'expelled' (NAB and AB), as opposed to the civility of 'put out' or 'took out'.[20]

Without the assumptions regarding the procreative couple, the wicked serpent, the tragic disobedience, the omnipotent god and the loss of paradise, **Genesis** 2-3 is a radically different narrative, with different characterizations, motivations and meaning. It describes the origins of the human family as comic and heroic. It pictures the man and the woman developing as human beings, from timid dependence to aggressive irresponsibility to courageous maturity. It displays the woman choosing fertility and the man joining the woman, together forfeiting personal immortality, blessed and cursed with the ability of creativity, proud of their choice, and given their liberty by a sympathetic creator.

Notes

1. M. Bal, *Lethal Love: Feminist Literary Readings of Biblical Love Stories* (Bloomington: Indiana University Press, 1987), pp. 112-14; L. Swidler, *Biblical Affirmations of Woman* (Philadelphia: Westminster Press, 1979), pp. 76-81; P. Trible, *God and the Rhetoric of Sexuality* (Philadelphia: Fortress Press, 1978), pp. 94-99; all identify the original human being as sexually undifferentiated. In the creation of the companion and the differentiation of sexes, the man is identified as 'îš and the woman as 'iššâ (*Gen.* 2.22-24). Thereafter, the world hā'ādām indicates the man if it is paired with 'iššâ (*Gen.* 2.25; 3.6, 8, 12, 17, 20, 21), and it identifies collective humanity without this pairing (*Gen.* 3.9, 22-24). If there is no pairing with 'iššâ, the man is referred to as 'îš (*Gen.* 3.16).

2. Translation is RSV unless otherwise indicated. Citation of the *Book of Jubilees*, the *Apocalypse of Moses* and the *Life of Adam and Eve* is according to the translations in J.H. Charlesworth (ed.), *The Old Testament Pseudepigrapha*, II (Garden City, NY: Doubleday, 1985).

3. See, for example, Bal, 'Lethal Love', pp. 121-22; T.E. Boomershine, 'The Structure of Narrative Rhetoric in *Genesis* 2-3', in D. Patte (ed.), *Genesis 2 and 3: Kaleidoscopic Structural Readings* (Chico, CA: Scholars Press, 1980), pp. 123-24; E. Leach, *Genesis as Myth and Other Essays* (London: Jonathan Cape, 1969), pp. 14-15; S. Niditch, *Chaos to Cosmos* (Chico, CA: Scholars Press, 1985), p. 30; J.W. Rosenberg, 'The Garden Story Forward and Backward', *Prooftexts* 1 (1981), p. 17. In *Genesis 1-11* (Cambridge: Cambridge University Press, 1973), R. Davidson acknowledges the attractiveness of this interpretation; he points to the recognition by the man and woman of their nakedness after eating the fruit, and to the consequences to the woman of intensified pain in childbirth. He also sees associations with the *Epic of Gilgamesh* episode that has a prostitute seduce the naïve Enkidu, who thus acquires wisdom. But, having admitted all this, Davidson proceeds to reject this interpretation as unnecessarily limiting, preferring to perceive knowledge of good and evil as knowledge of everything, 'the totality of knowledge' (pp. 34-35). J. Bailey ('Imitation and the Primal Woman in

Gilgamesh and *Genesis* 2-3', *JBL* 89 [1970], pp. 144-47) reviews the critical literature on this issue and, curiously, sides with the 'totality of knowledge' interpretation, proposing that this passage minimizes the sexual associations of its mythological sources. There is, however, no evidence that after eating the fruit the man and woman have acquired knowledge in addition to that which is associated with sex. The passage itself identifies a single change in their consciousness: recognition of their nakedness. In *The Sons of the Gods and the Daughters of Men: An Afro-Asiatic Interpretation of Genesis 1-11* (Maryknoll, NY: Orbis Books, 1984), M. Oduyoye describes the covering of nakedness as a consequence of civilization as opposed to sexual knowledge (pp. 46-47). He also declares, however, that, among primitive peoples, 'Children were expected to go naked—and you were a child until puberty rites for girls and circumcision at initiation for boys' (p. 46). This indicates that nakedness accompanies childhood, which stops at adolescence and is itself inextricably linked to sexual maturation.

4. G.W. Coats, *Genesis: With an Introduction to Narrative Literature* (Grand Rapids: Eerdmans, 1983), p. 54. See also J. Campbell, *The Masks of God: Occidental Mythology* (New York: Viking Press, 1964), for a pertinent analysis of serpent symbolism: 'The phallic suggestion is immediate, and, as swallower, the female organ also is suggested; so that a dual image is rendered, which works implicitly on the sentiments' (p. 10). See also K.R. Joines, *Serpent Symbolism in the Old Testament* (Haddonfield, NJ: Haddonfield House, 1974), pp. 64-67.

5. M. Eliade, *Patterns in Comparative Religion* (trans. R. Sheed; Cleveland, OH: World Publishing, 1963), pp. 288-91. See also Joines, *Serpent Symbolism*, pp. 17-21.

6. H.C. White, 'Direct and Third Person Discourse in the Narrative of the Fall', in Patte (ed.), *Genesis 2 and 3*, p. 97.

7. See, e.g., *Apoc. Mos.* 16.5; *LAE* 33.3; Rev. 12.9; Wis. 2.24.

8. See, e.g., B. Vawter, *On Genesis: A New Reading* (New York: Doubleday, 1977), p. 81: 'No explanation is given why the serpent chose to interfere in the affairs of men or to assist in the disruption of good relations between God and man. . . . The serpent remains as a consequence the symbol of an unexplained source of mischief and wrong for which no accounting is given.' See also Trible, *Rhetoric of Sexuality*, p. 113: 'The motives of this animal are obscure. . . . A villain in portrayal, he is a device in plot. The ambiguity of his depiction highlights the complicated dimensions of his nature without explaining or resolving them.'

9. M. Stone, *When God was a Woman* (New York: Harcourt Brace Jovanovich, 1976), pp. 198-223.

10. Bal, *Lethal Love,* p. 124.

11. Bal, *Lethal Love,* p. 122.

12. Trible, *Rhetoric of Sexuality,* p. 113.

13. Davidson, *Genesis 1-11,* p. 38.

14. See, e.g., *Apoc. Mos.* 20.1-21.6; *Jub.* 3.20-21; *LAE* 35.1-2; 1 Tim. 2.14.

15. See, e.g., *Apoc. Mos.* 24.2-4 and *LAE* 34.1-2.

16. This passage is widely interpreted as circumscribing the relationship of men and women; see, e.g., Davidson, *Genesis 1-11,* pp. 43-45. However, because the subject of this passage is only the woman's experience during pregnancy and giving birth, it is wiser to consider the dominance of the man as limited also to this single experience. See also Bal, *Lethal Love,* pp. 126-28.

17. See J. Bailey, 'Imitation and the Primal Woman', p. 150; I. Kikawada, 'Two Notes on Eve', *JBL* 91 (1972), p. 34. According to Bal, this is a 'dubious title of honor' that leaves the woman 'imprisoned in motherhood' (*Lethal Love,* p. 128), identified by sexual function only. It is, however, through the woman's eating of the fruit that human sexuality is discovered and the human family is established; it is, therefore, the only appropriate title that the man might give. The man's naming of the woman is also traditionally perceived as indicative of his superiority: see, e.g., Davidson, *Genesis 1-11,* p. 47. This interpretation, however, assumes the wider meaning of *Gen.* 3.16 regarding the man's dominance of the woman. It also ignores a critical point: if Yahweh names the woman, this emphasizes a childish dependence on the divine, contradicting the narrative's focus at this point on the liberation of the human couple. And it is inappropriate for the woman to name herself; in the writings of the Yahwist, the only self-appointed name is *Yahweh.*

18. Campbell, *Masks of God,* pp. 9-16.

19. See, e.g., *Apoc. Mos.* 27.2 and *LAE* 1.1.

20. Obviously *grš* has a range of meanings. In *Gen.* 4.14, for example, the Yahwist has Cain describe his exile using this word: 'thou hast driven me this day away from the ground'. According to *Theological Wordbook of the Old Testament* (ed. R.L. Harris, G.L. Archer, Jr and B.K. Waltke; Chicago: Moody Press, 1980), I, pp. 173-74, however, this word always emphasizes a physical (as opposed to verbal) dismissing or discharging of individuals; it is thus especially appropriate to this passage, given the Yahwist's focus on the ineffectiveness of the divine word.

FURTHER READING

Bibliography

Watson, Duane F. and Alan J. Hauser. *Rhetorical Criticism of the Bible: A Comprehensive Bibliography with Notes on History and Method.* Leiden: E. J. Brill, 1994, 206 p.

> Discussion of two types of rhetorical criticism of the Bible—source and form criticism—followed by a bibliography that includes *Genesis* studies.

Criticism

Cassuto, U. *Commentary on the Book of Genesis. Part I: From Adam to Noah. Genesis I-VI 8.* Jerusalem: The Magnes Press, Hebrew University, translated from the Hebrew by Israel Abrahams, 1944, 323 p.

> Critical analyses of the creation story, the story of the Garden of Eden, the story of Cain and Abel, and the Book of the History of Adam.

Coats, George W. *Genesis, with an Introduction to Narrative Literature.* Grand Rapids, Mich.: William B. Eerdmans Publishing Co., 1983, 322 p.

> Critical commentary on each of the following: the structure of the Pentateuch/Hexateuch, the theme of patriarchy in *Genesis,* the primeval history, and the stories of Abraham, Isaac, and Jacob.

Crenshaw, James. "Journey Into Oblivion: A Structural Analysis of *Gen.* 22:1-19. *Soundings* LVIII, No. 2 (Summer 1975): 243-56.

> Examination of the literary structure of the story of Abraham's near-sacrifice of his son Isaac.

Curtis, Edward M. "Structure, Style and Content as a Key to Interpreting Jacob's Encounter at Peniel." *Journal of the Evangelical Theological Society* 30, No. 2 (June 1987): 129-37.

> Maintains that the literary structure and style of the Jacob narrative offer subtle but accurate guidance toward interpreting the events portrayed in the text.

Graves, Robert. "The Argument." *Adam's Rib and Other Anomalous Elements in the Hebrew Creation Myth,* pp. 1-19. Boissia, Clairvaux, Jura, France: Trianon Press, 1955.

> Argues that the composition of *Genesis* can be properly understood when based on the assumption that the book's author used the process of "iconotropy," that is, misinterpreting ancient icons and holy emblems in the service of a new religious motivation.

Hauser, Alan J. "Linguistic and Thematic Links Between *Genesis* 4:1-16 and *Genesis* 2-3." *Journal of the Evangelical Theological Society* 23, No. 4 (December 1980): 297-305.

> Challenges the notion that the Cain and Abel story was originally independent of the Adam and Eve story, and analyzes the structural, linguistic, and thematic interrelatedness of the two stories.

Kierkegaard, Soren. *Fear and Trembling. Fear and Trembling* and *the Sickness Unto Death,* translated by Walter Lowrie, pp. 21-132. Princeton: Princeton University Press, 1941.

Originally published in 1843, Kierkegaard presents a philosophical "dialectical lyric" on the Abraham / Isaac story. The translator cites Kierkegaard's notes for the project, in which the philosopher states that "Abraham's conduct was genuinely poetic, magnanimous, more magnanimous than anything I have read of in tragedies."

Kikawada, Isaac M. "A Quantitative Analysis of the 'Adam and Eve,' 'Cain and Abel,' and 'Noah' Stories." *Perspectives on Language and Text,* edited by Edgar W. Conrad and Edward G. Newing, pp. 195-203. Winona Lake, Ind.: Eisenbrauns, 1987.

    Contends that the themes and motifs of these three stories are repeated in each story, in the same sequence. Each story, states Kikawada, recounts a threat of death to mankind, followed by salvation from death and extermination.

Redford, Donald B. *A Study of the Biblical Story of Joseph (Genesis 37-50).* Leiden: E. J. Brill, 1970, 290 p.

    Booklength analysis of the Joseph story, discussing the following: the present context of the story, its syntax, the narrative as literature, the source and its plot and style, the Egyptian background of the story, and the date of its composition.

Sharpless, F. Parvin. Introduction to *The Myth of the Fall: Literature of Innocence and Experience,* pp. 1-17. Rochelle Park, NJ: Hayden Book Company, Inc., 1974.

    Discusses the original fall of Adam and Eve as depicted in *Genesis,* and highlights pertinent themes that may be sought in the other works of literature, inspired by the *Genesis* story, contained in the volume.

Vawter, Bruce. *On* Genesis: *A New Reading.* Garden City, NY: Doubleday and Company, Inc., 1977, 501 p.

    The introduction to this volume studies the sources, materials, and various interpretations of *Genesis,* and is followed by commentary on the primeval and patriarchal histories.

van Wolde, Ellen. "The Story of Cain and Abel: A Narrative Study." *Journal for the Study of the Old Testament* 52 (1991): 25-41.

    Offers a narrative approach to the Cain and Abel story, examining the actions of the protagonists (God, Cain, and Abel), in an attempt to clarify a story often held to be incoherent and ambiguous. Also maintains that the story is closely related to *Genesis* 2-3 (the Adam and Eve story).

Eclogues
Vergil

The following entry contains criticism on Vergil's *Eclogues*. For additional information on Vergil's life and works, see *CMLC*, Vol. 4.

INTRODUCTION

Vergil's *Eclogues* is a collection of ten pastoral poems inspired in part by Theocritus's *Idylls*. While the order of composition of the poems is sometimes the subject of critical debate, the collection has been dated to the 30s and 40s B.C.; the poems thus represent Vergil's earliest works. The relation between Vergil's poems and their earlier Greek counterparts, the *Idylls,* is of major interest to critics, as is the Arcadian setting of the *Eclogues.* Other scholars are more interested in the individual poems, or in the relation of individual poems to the collection as a whole.

TEXTUAL HISTORY

The *Eclogues* constitute the first extant collection of such poetry. Early readers, including Ovid and Probus, indicate that Vergil selected the poems for the book of *Eclogues* himself. Textual references also show that the *Eclogues* were published by Vergil in the order in which they appear in modern editions.

PLOT AND MAJOR CHARACTERS

In general, the heroes of the *Eclogues* are shepherds who live in the land of Arcadia and sing of their loves, their flocks, and the beauty of the countryside. Many of the *Eclogues* reproduce such features of the *Idylls* of Theocritus as the banter between shepherds and the contests between shepherds in the form of song. Such songs, incorporated within the *Eclogues,* often play a large role in the collection. In many of the poems, the plot focuses on competition between shepherds, or on love and loss experienced by a particular shepherd. The plots and characters of *Eclogues* One and Nine are of special interest to many students and critics of Vergil because biographers have drawn parallels between these poems and Vergil's own life—especially the threat of eviction from the family farm that Vergil and his family faced. In both *Eclogues* One and Nine, one shepherd faces exile, while another remains in the pastoral world. In *Eclogue* One, Meliboeus's exile is contrasted with the pastoral bliss enjoyed by Tityrus, and the two shepherds engage in a dialogue which highlights this tension. Most critics agree,

however, that the biographical parallels within these poems should not be viewed as straight allegory.

MAJOR THEMES

Critics have identified surprisingly complicated themes within the simple pastoral setting of the *Eclogues*. Vergil uses the pastoral as representative of the life of imagination and of the individual's struggle to identify his or her place within society and nature. Similar themes are expanded upon in Vergil's later works, such as the *Aeneid*. Love is also a central theme in many of the *Eclogues*, especially *Eclogues* Two, Eight, and Ten, and is often discussed in terms of lamentation and wooing, although Vergil also incorporated some humor into these often somber poems. Other themes explored by the *Eclogues* include piety and the pleasures of the countryside, and, especially in *Eclogue* Six, passion and violence.

CRITICAL RECEPTION

Many critics have studied the way in which Vergil adapts his source material, the *Idylls* of Theocritus. W. Y. Sellar, for instance, observes that in both form and content, many of the *Eclogues* imitate the work of Theocritus in that they make use of dialogue to reproduce the banter of shepherds and their singing contests. Sellar maintains that although the earlier *Eclogues* are highly imitative, the later *Eclogues* demonstrate Vergil's command over the form, as well as of the rhythm and diction, of pastoral. Furthermore, Sellar notes that while Vergil's work is inferior to the Greek *Idylls* in terms of dramatic power, the strength of Vergil's poems lies in their "truth of feeling" and in Vergil's mastery over the pastoral form. Like Sellar, Robert Coleman notes both the conventional and the praiseworthy in Vergil's poems. Coleman states that while Vergil's range of themes is not unique, his details are original and his technique is more mature than that of Theocritus. Vergil's use of quatrains over couplets, Coleman asserts, allows his themes to be more fully explored. R. W. Garson maintains that many analyses of Vergil's poetry in which the *Eclogues* are compared with Theocritus's *Idylls* are flawed in that such studies only list parallel passages, and often label the *Eclogues* "pastiche." Taking a different approach, Garson reviews the mechanics of Vergil's composition, particularly in *Eclogues* Two, Three, Five, Seven, and Eight, in which the Theocritean elements are of primary importance.

While Theocritus used the same Arcadian setting for his poems, Vergil's depiction of it is less realistic and more fantastic than Theocritus's treatment. The role of Arcadia in Vergil's poems is a major focus of modern criticism. Bruno Snell argues that the "air of unreality" captured in Vergil's poems can be explained by the fact that Vergil attempts to approximate Theocritus's Arcadia and the world of myth. In doing so, Snell explains, Vergil manipulates the mythology surrounding Arcadia to a greater degree than a Greek poet would have been able to do. Like Snell, John B. Van Sickle highlights the importance of the Arcadian setting to Vergil's poems. Van Sickle describes Vergil's Arcadia as the key to understanding the unity of the *Eclogues* in that it operates as a poetic symbol of both hope and remembrance, and at the same time establishes a framework for the *Eclogues* as a whole.

PRINCIPAL WORKS

Principal English Translations

The Bucolics and Georgics of Vergil Rendered in English Hexameters (edited by A. F. Murison) 1932

The Eclogues of Vergil (edited by A. S. Way) 1933
The Pastoral Poems (edited by E. V. Rieu) 1949
The Eclogues of Virgil (edited by A. J. Boyle) 1976

CRITICISM

W. Y. Sellar (essay date 1908)

SOURCE: *"The Eclogues"* in *The Roman Poets of the Augustan Age: Virgil*, Clarendon Press, 1908, pp. 130-73.

[*In the essay below, Sellar discusses the order of composition of Vergil's* Eclogues *and maintains that Vergil's earlier poems are imitative of Theocritian poetry. After Vergil mastered the form, rhythm, and diction of the pastoral, Sellar notes, he increasingly demonstrated originality in his choice of subject and in the truthful manner in which he treated his subject.*]

I.

The name by which the earliest of Virgil's recognised works is known tells us nothing of the subject of which it treats. The word 'Eclogae' simply means selections. As applied to the poems of Virgil, it designates a collection of short unconnected poems. The other name by which these poems were known in antiquity, 'bucolica,' indicates the form of Greek art in which they were cast and the pastoral nature of their subjects. Neither word is used by Virgil himself; but the expressions by which he characterises his art, such as 'Sicelides Musae,' 'versus Syracosius,' 'Musa agrestis' and 'silvestris,' show that he writes in a pastoral strain, and that he considered the pastoral poetry of Greece as his model. He invokes not only the 'Sicilian Muses,' but the 'fountain of Arethusa.' He speaks too of Pan, and Arcadia, and the 'Song of Maenalus.' His shepherd-poets are described as 'Arcadians.' The poets whom he introduces as his prototypes are the 'sage of Ascra,' and the mythical Linus, Orpheus, and Amphion. He alludes also to Theocritus under the name of the 'Syracusan shepherd.' The names of the shepherds who are introduced as contending in song or uttering their feelings in monologue—Corydon, Thyrsis, Menalcas, Meliboeus, Tityrus, etc.—are Greek, and for the most part taken from the pastoral idyls of Theocritus. There is also frequent mention of the shepherd's pipe, and of the musical accompaniment to which some of the songs chanted by the shepherds are set.

The general character of the poems is further indicated by the frequent use of the word 'ludere,' a word applied by Catullus, Horace, Propertius, Ovid, and others to the poems of youth, of a light and playful character, and, for the most part, expressive of various moods of the passion of love. Thus at the end of the *Georgics* Virgil speaks of himself thus:—

Carmina qui lusi pastorum, audaxque iuventa,
Tityre, te patulae cecini sub tegmine fagi.[1]

This reference shows further that the poem which stands first in order was placed there when the edition of the Eclogues was given to the world. But other references (at v. 86-87 and vi. 12) seem to imply that the separate poems were known either by distinct titles, such as Varus, the title of the sixth, or from their opening lines, as the 'Formosum Corydon ardebat Alexim,' and the 'Cuium pecus? an Meliboei?' It has been also suggested, from lines quoted in the ninth, which profess to be the opening lines of other pastoral poems, that the ten finally collected together were actual 'selections' from a larger number, commenced if not completed ('necdum perfecta canebat') by Virgil. But these passages seem more like the lines attributed to the contending poets in the third and seventh *Eclogues,* i.e. short unconnected specimens of pastoral song.

Nearly all the poems afford indications of the time of their composition and of the order in which they followed one another; and that order is different from the order in which they now appear. It is said, on the authority of Asconius, that three years, from 42 B.C. to 39 B.C., were given to the composition of the *Eclogues.* But an allusion in the tenth (line 47) to the expedition of Agrippa across the Alps in the early part of 37 B.C. proves that a later date must be assigned to that poem. The probable explanation is that Virgil had intended to end the series with the eighth, which celebrated the triumph of Pollio over the Parthini in 39 B.C.,—

A te principium, tibi desinet,—

But that his friendship for Gallus induced him to add the tenth, two years later, either before the poems were finally collected for publication, or in preparing a new edition of them. They were written at various places and at various stages of the poet's fortunes. They appear to have obtained great success when first published, and some of them were recited with applause upon the stage. The earliest in point of time were the second and third, and these, along with the fifth, may be ascribed to the year 42 B.C. The seventh, which has no allusion to contemporary events and is a mere imitative reproduction of the Greek idyl, may also belong to this earlier period, although some editors rank it as one of the latest. The first, which is founded on the loss of the poet's farm, belongs to the next year, and the ninth and sixth probably may be assigned to the same year, or to the early part of the following year. The date of the fourth is fixed by the Consulship of Pollio to the year 40 B.C.; that of the eighth to the year 39 B.C. by the triumph of Pollio over the Parthini. The opening words of the tenth show that it was the last of the series; and the reference to the expedition of Agrippa implies that it could not have been written earlier than the end of 38 B.C. or the beginning of 37 B.C. The first, second, third, and fifth, were in all probability written by the poet in his native district, the sixth, ninth, and perhaps the seventh, at the villa which had formerly belonged to Siron ('villula quae Sironis *eras*'),

the rest at Rome. The principle on which the poems are arranged seems to be that of alternating dialogue with monologue. The eighth, though not in dialogue, yet resembles the latter part of the fifth, in presenting two continuous songs, chanted by different shepherds. The poem first in order may have occupied its place from its greater interest in connexion with the poet's fortunes, or from the honour which it assigns to Octavianus, whose preeminence over the other competitors for supreme power had sufficiently declared itself before the first collected edition of the poems was published.

In the earliest poems of the series the art of Virgil, like the lyrical art of Horace in his earlier Odes, is more imitative and conventional than in those written later. He seems satisfied with reproducing the form, rhythm, and diction of Theocritus, and mingling some vague expression of personal or national feeling with the sentiment of the Greek idyl. That the fifth was written after the second and third appears from the lines v. 86-87, in which Menalcas, under which name Virgil introduces himself in the *Eclogues,* presents his pipe to Mopsus:—

Haec nos 'Formosum Corydon ardebat Alexin,'
Haec eadem docuit 'Cuium pecus? an Meliboei[2]?'

From these lines also it may be inferred as probable that the second poem, 'Formosum pastor Corydon,' was written before the third, 'Dic mihi, Damoeta, cuium pecus? an Meliboei?'

A tradition, quoted by Servius and referred to (though inaccurately) by Martial[3], attributes the composition of the second *Eclogue* to the admiration excited in Virgil by the beauty of a young slave, Alexander, who was presented to him by Pollio and carefully educated by him. A similar story is told of his having received from Maecenas another slave, named Cebes, who also obtained from him a liberal education and acquired some distinction as a poet. It is not improbable that Virgil may have been warmly attached to these youths, and that there was nothing blameable in his attachment. Even Cicero, a man as far removed as possible from any sentimental weakness, writes to Atticus of the death of a favourite slave, a young Greek, and evidently, from the position he filled in Cicero's household, a boy of liberal accomplishments, in these words: 'And, I assure you, I am a good deal distressed. For my reader, Sositheus, a charming boy, is just dead; and it has affected me more than I should have thought the death of a slave ought to affect one[4].' It remains true however that in one or two of those *Eclogues* in which he most closely imitates Theocritus, Virgil uses the language of serious sentiment, and once of bantering raillery, in a way which justly offends modern feeling. And this is all that can be said against him.

There are more imitations of the Greek in this and in the next poem than in any of the other *Eclogues*[5]. The scenery of the piece, in so far as it is at all definite, combines the mountains and the sea-landscape of Sicily with Italian woods and vineyards. Corydon seems to combine the features of an Italian vinedresser with the conventional character of a Sicilian shepherd. The line

> Aspice aratra iugo referunt suspensa iuvenci[6]

applies rather to an Italian scene than to the pastoral district of Sicily; and this reference to ploughing seems inconsistent with the description of the fierce midsummer heat, and with the introduction of the 'fessi messores' in the opening lines of the poem. These inconsistencies show how little thought Virgil had for the objective consistency of his representation. The poem however, in many places, gives powerful expression to the feelings of a despairing lover. There are here, as in the Gallus, besides that vein of feeling which the Latin poet shares with Theocritus, some traces of that 'wayward modern mood' of longing to escape from the world and to return to some vague ideal of Nature, and to sacrifice all the gains of civilisation in exchange for the homeliest dwelling shared with the object of affection:—

> O tantum libeat mecum tibi sordida rura
> Atque humiles habitare casas, et figere cervos[7];

and again,

> Habitarunt di quoque silvas
> Dardaniusque Paris. Pallas quas condidit arces
> Ipsa colat, nobis placeant ante omnia silvae[8].

The third *Eclogue,* which is in dialogue, and reproduces two features of the Greek idyl, the natural banter of the shepherds and the more artificial contest in song, is still more imitative and composite in character. It shows several close imitations, especially of the fourth, fifth, and eighth Idyls of Theocritus[9]. In this poem only Virgil, whose muse even in the *Eclogues* is almost always serious or plaintive, endeavours to reproduce the playfulness and vivacity of his original. Both in the bantering dialogue and in the more formal contest of the shepherds, the subjects introduced are for the most part of a conventional pastoral character, but with these topics are combined occasional references to the tastes and circumstances of the poet himself. Thus in lines 40-42,

> In medio duo signa . . . curvus arator haberet,

allusion is made to the astronomical studies of which Virgil made fuller use in the *Georgics.* In the line

> Pollio amat nostram quamvis est rustica Musam,

and again,

> Pollio et ipse facit nova carmina[10],

he makes acknowledgment of the favour and pays honour to the poetical tastes of his earliest patron, whom he celebrates also in the fourth and eighth *Eclogues.* The line

> Qui Bavium non odit amet tua carmina, Maevi[11]

has condemned to everlasting notoriety the unfortunate pair, who have served modern satirists as types of spiteful critics and ineffectual authors. At lines 10-11 there is, as in *Eclogue* ii., an apparent blending of the occupations of the Italian vinedresser with those of the Sicilian shepherd. In the contest of song there is no sustained connexion of thought, as indeed there is not in similar contests in Theocritus. These contests are supposed to reproduce the utterances of improvisatori, of whom the second speaker is called to say something, either in continuation of or in contrast to the thought of the first. The shepherds in these strains seek to glorify their own prowess, boast of their successes in love, or call attention to some picturesque aspect of their rustic life.

The fifth *Eclogue* is also in dialogue. It brings before us a friendly interchange of song between two pastoral poets, Mopsus and Menalcas. Servius mentions that Menalcas (here, as in the ninth *Eclogue*) stands for Virgil himself, while Mopsus stands for his friend Aemilius Macer of Verona. Mopsus laments the cruel death of Daphnis, the legendary shepherd of Sicilian song, and Menalcas celebrates his apotheosis. Various accounts were given in antiquity of the meaning which was to be attached to this poem. One account was that Virgil here expressed his sorrow for the death of his brother Flaccus[12]. Though the time of his death may have coincided with that of the composition of this poem, the language of the lament and of the song celebrating the ascent of Daphnis to heaven is quite unlike the expression of a private or personal sorrow. There seems no reason to doubt another explanation which has come down from ancient times, that under this pastoral allegory Virgil laments the death and proclaims the apotheosis of Julius Caesar. It is probable[13] that the poem was composed for his birthday, the 4th of July, which for the first time was celebrated with religious rites in the year 42 B.C., when the name of the month Quintilis was changed into that which it has retained ever since. The lines 25-26,

> Nulla neque amnem
> Libavit quadrupes nec graminis attigit herbam,[14]

are supposed[15] to refer to a belief which had become traditional in the time of Suetonius, that the horses which had been consecrated after crossing the Rubicon had refused to feed immediately before the death of their master[16]. In the lines expressing the sorrow for his loss, and in those which mark out the divine office which he was destined to fulfil after death,—

> Ut Baccho Cererique, tibi sic vota quotannis
> Agricolae facient, damnabis tu quoque votis[17],—

as in the lines of the ninth, referring to the Julium Sidus,—

> Astrum quo segetes gauderent frugibus, et quo
> Duceret apricis in collibus uva colorem[18],—

allusion is made to the encouragement Caesar gave to the husbandman and vine-planter in his lifetime, and to the honour due to him as their tutelary god in heaven. And these allusions help us to understand the 'votis iam nunc adsuesce vocari' of the invocation in the first *Georgic.*

Nothing illustrates more clearly the unreal conceptions of the pastoral allegory than a comparison of the language in the 'Lament for Daphnis,' with the strong Roman realism of the lines at the end of the first *Georgic,* in which the omens portending the death of Caesar are described. Nor can anything show more clearly the want of individuality with which Virgil uses the names of the Theocritean shepherds than the fact that while the Daphnis of the fifth *Eclogue* represents the departed and deified soldier and statesman, the Daphnis of the ninth is a living husband-man whose fortunes were secured by the protecting star of Caesar,—

Insere, Daphni, piros, carpent tua poma nepotes[19].

The peace and tranquillity restored to the land under this protecting influence are foreshadowed in the lines 58-61—

Ergo alacris . . . amat bonus otia Daphnis;

and the earliest reference to the divine honours assigned in life and death to the later representatives of the name of Caesar, is heard in the jubilant shout of wild mountains, rocks, and groves to the poet—

Deus, deus ille, Menalca.

Although the treatment of the subject may be vague and conventional, yet this poem possesses the interest of being Virgil's earliest effort, directed to a subject of living and national interest; and many of the lines in the poem are unsurpassed for grace and sweetness of musical cadence by anything in Latin poetry.

There is no allusion to contemporary events by which the date of the seventh can be determined; but the absence of such allusion and the 'purely Theocritean[20]' character of the poem suggest the inference that it is a specimen of Virgil's earlier manner. Two shepherds, Corydon and Thyrsis, are introduced as joining Daphnis, who is seated under a whispering ilex; they engage in a friendly contest of song, which is listened to also by the poet himself, who here calls himself Meliboeus. They assert in alternate strains their claims to poetic honours, offer prayers and vows to Diana as the goddess of the chase and to Priapus as the god of gardens, draw rival pictures of cool retreat from the heat of summer and of cheerfulness by the winter fire, and connect the story of their loves with the varying aspect of the seasons, and with the beauty of trees sacred to different deities or native to different localities. Though the shepherds are Arcadian, the scenery is Mantuan:—

Hic viridis tenera praetexit harundine ripam
Mincius, eque sacra resonant examina quercu[21].

Meliboeus decides the contest in favour of Corydon:—

Haec memini, et victum frustra contendere Thyrsin.
Ex illo Corydon Corydon est tempore nobis[22].

These poems, in which the conventional shepherds of pastoral poetry sing of their loves, their flocks and herds, of the beauty of the seasons and of outward nature, in tones caught from Theocritus, or revive and give a new meaning to the old Sicilian dirge over 'the woes of Daphnis,' may be assigned to the eventful year in which the forces of the Republic finally shattered themselves against the forces of the new Empire. There is a strange contrast between these peaceful and somewhat unreal strains of Virgil and the drama which was at the same time enacted on the real stage of human affairs. No sound of the 'storms that raged outside his happy ground' disturbs the security with which Virgil cultivates his art. But the following year brought the trouble and unhappiness of the times home to the peaceful dwellers around Mantua, and to Virgil among the rest. Of the misery caused by the confiscations and allotments of land to the soldiers of Octavianus, the first *Eclogue* is a lasting record. Yet even in this poem, based as it is on genuine feeling and a real experience, Virgil seems to care only for the truth of feeling with which Tityrus and Meliboeus express themselves, without regard for consistency in the conception of the situation, the scenery, or the personages of the poem. Tityrus is at once the slave who goes to Rome to purchase his freedom, and the owner of the land and of the flocks and herds belonging to it[23]. He is advanced in years[24], and at the same time a poet lying indolently in the shade, and making the woods ring with the sounds of 'beautiful Amaryllis[25],' like the young shepherds in Theocritus. The scenery apparently combines some actual features of the farm in the Mantuan district—

Quamvis lapis omnia nudus
Limosoque palus obducat pascua iunco[26],

with the ideal mountain-land of pastoral song—

Maioresque cadunt altis de montibus umbrae[27].

A further inconsistency has been suggested between the time of year indicated by the 'shade of the spreading beech' in the first line, and that indicated by the ripe chestnuts at line 81[28]. The truth of the poem consists in the expression of the feelings of love which the old possessors entertained for their homes, and the sense of dismay caused by this barbarous irruption on their ancient domains:—

Impius haec tam culta novalia miles habebit?
Barbarus has segetes? En quo discordia civis
Produxit miseros[29]!

Virgil's feeling for the movement of his age, which henceforth becomes one of the main sources of his inspiration, has its origin in the effect which these events had on his personal fortunes, and in the sympathy awakened within him by the sorrows of his native district.

The ninth *Eclogue,* written most probably in the same year, and in form imitated from the seventh Idyl—the famous Thalysia—of Theocritus, repeats the tale of dejection and alarm among the old inhabitants of the Mantuan district,—

> Nunc victi, tristes, quoniam fors omnia versat[30],—

and touches allusively on the story of the personal danger which Virgil encountered from the violence of the centurion who claimed possession of his land. The speakers in the dialogue are Moeris, a shepherd of Menalcas,—the pastoral poet, who sings of the nymphs, of the wild flowers spread over the ground, and of the brooks shaded with trees,—and Lycidas, who, like the Lycidas of the Thalysia, is also a poet:—

> Me quoque dicunt
> Vatem pastores, sed non ego credulus illis.
> Nam neque adhuc Vario videor nec dicere Cinna
> Digna, sed argutos inter strepere anser olores[31].

After the account of the fray, given by Moeris, and the comments of Lycidas, in which he introduces the lines referred to in the previous chapter, as having all the signs of being a real description of the situation of Virgil's farms—

> qua se subducere colles incipiunt—

Moeris sings the opening lines of certain other pastoral poems, some his own, some the songs of Menalcas. Two of these—'Tityre dum redeo' and 'Huc ades O Galatea'—are purely Theocritean. Two others—

> Vare tuum nomen, superet modo Mantua nobis,

and

> Daphni quid antiquos signorum suspicis ortus[32]—

indicate the new path which Virgil's art was striking out for itself. There is certainly more real substance in this poem than in most of the earlier *Eclogues.* Lycidas and Moeris speak about what interests them personally. The scene of the poem is apparently the road between Virgil's farm and Mantua. There seem to be no conventional and inconsistent features introduced from the scenery of Sicily or Arcadia, unless it be the 'aequor' of line 57—

> Et nunc omne tibi stratum silet aequor[33].

But may not that be either the lake, formed by the overflow of the river, some distance above Mantua, or even the great level plain, with its long grass and corn-fields and trees, hushed in the stillness of the late afternoon?

The sixth *Eclogue* was written probably about the same time and at the same place, the villa of Siron, in which Virgil had taken refuge with his family. It is inscribed with the name of Varus, who is said to have been a fellow-student of Virgil under the tuition of Siron. But, with the exception of the dedicatory lines, there is no reference to the circumstances of the time. Though abounding with

rich pastoral illustrations, the poem is rather a mythological and semi-philosophical idyl than a pure pastoral poem. It consists mainly of a song of Silenus, in which an account is given of the creation of the world in accordance with the Lucretian philosophy; and, in connexion with this theme (as is done also by Ovid in his Metamorphoses), some of the oldest mythological traditions, such as the tale of Pyrrha and Deucalion, the reign of Saturn on earth, the theft and punishment of Prometheus, etc., are introduced. The opening lines—Namque canebat uti—are imitated from the song of Orpheus in the first book of the Argonautics[34], but they bear unmistakable traces also of the study of Lucretius. There seems no trace of the language of Theocritus in the poem.

Three points of interest may be noted in this song: (1) Virgil here, as in *Georgic* ii. 475, etc., regards the revelation of physical knowledge as a fitting theme for poetic treatment. So in the first *Aeneid,* the 'Song of Iopas' is said to be about 'the wandering moon and the toils of the sun; the origin of man and beast, water and fire,' etc. The revelation of the secrets of Nature seems to float before the imagination of Virgil as the highest consummation of his poetic faculty. (2) We note here how, as afterwards in the *Georgics,* he accepts the philosophical ideas of creation, side by side with the supernatural tales of mythology. He seems to regard such tales as those here introduced as part of the religious traditions of the human race, and as a link which connects man with the gods. In the *Georgics* we find also the same effort to reconcile, or at least to combine, the conceptions of science with mythological fancies. In this effort we recognise the influence of other Alexandrine poets rather than of Theocritus. (3) The introduction of Gallus in the midst of the mythological figures of the poem, and the account of the honour paid to him by the Muses and of the office assigned to him by Linus, are characteristic of the art of the *Eclogues,* which is not so much allegorical as composite. It brings together in the same representation facts, personages, and places from actual life and the figures and scenes of a kind of fairy-land. In the tenth Eclogue Gallus is thus identified with the Daphnis of Sicilian song, and is represented as the object of care to the Naiads and Pan and Apollo. While Pollio is the patron whose protection and encouragement Virgil most cordially acknowledges in his earlier poems, Gallus is the man among his contemporaries who has most powerfully touched his imagination and gained his affections.

The *Eclogue* composed next in order of time is the 'Pollio.' It was written in the consulship of Pollio, B.C. 40, immediately after the reconciliation between Antony and Octavianus effected by the treaty of Brundisium, and gives expression to that vague hope of a new era of peace and prosperity which recurs so often in the poetry of this age. In consequence of the interpretation given to it in a later age, this poem has acquired an importance connected with Virgil's religious belief second only to the importance of the sixth *Aeneid.* Early Christian writers, perceiving a parallel between expressions and ideas in this poem and those in the Messianic prophecies, believed that Virgil was here the unconscious vehicle of Divine inspiration, and that he prophesies of the new era which was to begin with the birth of Christ. And though, as Conington and others have pointed out, the picture of the Golden Age given in the poem is drawn immediately from Classical and not from Hebrew sources, yet there is no parallel in Classical poetry to that which is the leading idea of the poem, the coincidence of the commencement of this new era with the birth of a child whom a marvellous career awaited.

The poem begins with an invocation to the Sicilian Muses and with the declaration that, though the strain is still pastoral, yet it is to be in a higher mood, and worthy of the Consul to whom it is addressed. Then follows the announcement of the birth of a new era. The world after passing through a cycle of ages, each presided over by a special deity, had reached the last of the cycle, presided over by Apollo, and was about to return back to the Golden or Saturnian Age of peace and innocence, into which the human race was originally born. A new race of men was to spring from heaven. The first-born of this new stock was destined hereafter to be a partaker of the life of the gods and to 'rule over a world in peace with the virtues of his father.' Then follow the rural and pastoral images of the Golden Age, like those given in the first *Georgic* in the description of the early world before the reign of Jove. The full glory of the age should not be reached till this child should attain the maturity of manhood. In the meantime some traces of 'man's original sin' ('priscae vestigia fraudis') should still urge him to brave the dangers of the sea, to surround his cities with walls, and to plough the earth into furrows. There should be a second expedition of the Argonauts, and a new Achilles should be sent against another Troy. The romantic adventures of the heroic age were to precede the rest, innocence, and spontaneous abundance of the age of Saturn. Next the child is called upon to prepare himself for the 'magni honores'—the great offices of state which awaited him; and the poet prays that his own life and inspiration may be prolonged so far as to enable him to celebrate his career.

There seem to be no traces of imitation of Theocritus in this poem. The rhythm which in the other *Eclogues* reproduces the Theocritean cadences is in this more stately and uniform, recalling those of Catullus in his longest poem. The substance of the poem is quite unlike anything in the Sicilian idyl. Though this substance does not stand out in the clear light of reality, but is partially revealed through a haze of pastoral images and legendary associations, yet it is not altogether unmeaning. The anticipation of a new era was widely spread and vividly felt over the world; and this anticipation—the state of men's minds at and subsequent to the time when this poem was written—probably contributed to the acceptance of the great political and spiritual changes which awaited the world[35].

Two questions which have been much discussed in connexion with this poem remain to be noticed; (1) who is the child born in the consulship of Pollio of whom this marvel-lous career is predicted? (2) is it at all probable that Virgil, directly or indirectly, had any knowledge of the Messianic prophecies or ideas?

In answer to the first we may put aside at once the supposition that the prediction is made of the child who was born in that year to Octavianus and Scribonia. The words 'nascenti puero' are altogether inapplicable to the notorious and unfortunate Julia, who was the child of that marriage. If Virgil was sanguine enough to predict the sex of the child, we can hardly imagine him allowing the words to stand after his prediction had been falsified. We may equally dismiss the supposition that the child spoken of was the offspring of the marriage of Antony and Octavia. Not to mention other considerations adverse to this supposition[36], it would have been impossible for Virgil, the devoted partisan of Caesar, to pay this special compliment to Antony, even after he became so closely connected with his rival. There remains a third supposition, that the child spoken of is the son of Pollio, Asinius Gallus, who plays an important part in the reign of Tiberius. This last interpretation is supported by the authority of Asconius, who professed to have heard it from Asinius Gallus himself. The objection to this interpretation is that Virgil was not likely to assign to the child of one who, as compared with Octavianus and Antony, was only a secondary personage in public affairs, the position of 'future ruler of the world' and the function of being 'the regenerator of his age.' Still less could a poem bearing this meaning have been allowed to retain its place among Virgil's works after the ascendency of Augustus became undisputed. Further, the line

Cara deum suboles, magnum Iovis incrementum

(whatever may be its exact meaning[37]) appears an extreme exaggeration when specially applied to the actual son of a mortal father and mother. These difficulties have led some interpreters to suppose that the child spoken of is an ideal or imaginary representative of the future race. But if we look more closely at the poem, we find that the child is not really spoken of as the future regenerator of the age; he is merely the firstborn of the new race, which was to be nearer to the gods both in origin and in actual communion with them. Again, the words

Pacatumque reget patriis virtutibus orbem[38]

would not convey the same idea in the year 40 B.C. as they would ten or twenty years later. At the time when the poem was written the consulship was still the highest recognised position in the State. The Consuls for the year, nominally at least, wielded the whole power of the Empire. The words 'reget orbem' remain as a token that the Republic was not yet entirely extinct. The child is called upon to prepare himself for the great offices of State in the hope that he should in time hold the high place which was now held by his father. The words 'patriis virtutibus' imply that he is no ideal being, but the actual son of a well-known father. Virgil takes occasion in this poem to commemorate the attainment of the highest office by his patron, to celebrate the birth of the son born in the year of his consulship, and at the same time to express, by mystical and obscure allusions, the trust that the peace of Brundisium was the inauguration of that new era for which the hearts of men all over the world were longing.

In turning to the second question, discussed in connexion with this *Eclogue,* the great amount and recondite character of Virgil's learning, especially of that derived from Alexandrine sources, must be kept in view. Macrobius testifies to this in several places. Thus he writes, 'for this poet was learned with not only a minute conscientiousness, but even with a kind of reserve and mystery, so that he introduced into his works much knowledge the sources of which are difficult to discover[39].' In another place he speaks of those things, 'what he had introduced from the most recondite learning of the Greeks[40].' And again he says, 'this story Virgil has dug out from the most recondite Greek literature[41].' It is indeed most improbable that Virgil had a direct knowledge of the Septuagint. If he had this knowledge it would have shown itself by other allusions in other parts of his works. But it is quite possible that, through other channels of Alexandrine learning, the ideas and the language of Hebrew prophecy may have become indirectly known to him. One channel by which this may have reached him would be the new Sibylline prophecies, manufactured in the East and probably reflecting Jewish as well as other Oriental ideas, which poured into Rome after the old Sibylline books had perished in the burning of the Capitol during the first Civil War.

Still, admitting these possibilities, we are not called upon to go beyond classical sources for the general substance and idea of this poem. It has more in common with the myth in the Politicus of Plato than with the Prophecies of Isaiah. The state of the world at the time when the poem was written produced the longing for an era of restoration and a return to a lost ideal of innocence and happiness, and the wish became father to the thought.

There still remain the eighth and tenth *Eclogues* to be examined. The first, like the fourth, is associated with the name of Pollio, the second with that of Gallus. The date of the eighth is fixed to 39 B.C. by the victory of Pollio in Illyria and by his subsequent triumph over the Parthini. The words

> Accipe iussis
> Carmina coepta tuis[42]

testify to the personal influence under which Virgil wrote these poems. The title of 'Pharmaceutria,' by which the poem is known, indicates that Virgil professes to reproduce, in an Italian form, that passionate tale of city life which forms the subject of the second idyl of Theocritus. But while the subject and burden of the second of the two songs contained in this *Eclogue* are suggested by that idyl, the poem is very far from being a mere imitative reproduction of it.

Two shepherds, Damon and Alphesiboeus, meet in the early dawn—

> Cum ros in tenera pecori gratissimus herba[43],

(one of those touches of truthful description which reappear in the account of the pastoral occupations in *Georgic* iii). They each sing of incidents which may have been taken from actual life, or may have formed the subject of popular songs traditional among the peasantry of the district. In the first of these songs Damon gives vent to his despair in consequence of the marriage of his old love Nysa with his rival Mopsus. Though the shepherds who sing together bear the Greek names of Damon and Alphesiboeus, though they speak of Rhodope and Tmaros and Maenalus, of Orpheus and Arion, though expressions and lines are close translations, and one a mistranslation, from the Greek . . ., and though the mode by which the lover determines to end his sorrows,

> Praeceps aerii specula de montis in undas
> Deferar[44],

is more appropriate to a shepherd inhabiting the rocks over-hanging the Sicilian seas than to one dwelling in the plain of Mantua, yet both this song and the accompanying one sung by Alphesiboeus approach more nearly to the impersonal and dramatic representation of the Greek idyl than any of those already examined. The lines of most exquisite grace and tenderness in the poem,—lines which have been pronounced the finest in Virgil and the finest in Latin literature by Voltaire and Macaulay[45],—

> Saepibus in nostris parvam te roscida mala,
> Dux ego vester eram, vidi cum matre legentem:
> Alter ab undecimo tum me iam acceperat annus,
> Iam fragiles poteram ab terra contingere ramos:
> Ut vidi, ut perii, ut me malus abstulit error[46]—

are indeed close imitations of lines of similar beauty from the song of the Cyclops to Galatea. . . .

But they are so varied as to suggest a picture of ease and abundance among the orchards and rich cultivated land of Italy, instead of the free life and natural beauties of the Sicilian mountains. The descriptive touches suggesting the picture of the innocent romance of boyhood are also all Virgil's own.

The song of Alphesiboeus represents a wife endeavouring to recall her truant, though still faithful, Daphnis from the city to his home. Though some of the illustrations in this song also are Greek, yet it contains several natural references to rustic superstitions which were probably common to Greek and Italian peasants; and the fine simile at line 85 (of which the first hint is to be found in Lucretius[48]) suggests purely Italian associations. The final incident in the poem, 'Hylax in limine latrat' (though the name given to the dog is Greek), is a touch of natural life, such as does not often occur in the Eclogues. On the whole, Virgil seems here to have struck on a vein which it may be regretted that he did not work more thoroughly. If, as has been suggested by Mr. Symonds, in his account and translations of popular Tuscan poems, any of the *Eclogues* of Virgil are founded on primitive love-songs current among the peasantry of Italy, the songs of Damon and Alphesiboeus are those which we should fix on as being the artistic development of these native germs.

The tenth *Eclogue* was the last in order of composition, probably an after-thought written immediately before the final publication, or perhaps before the second edition, of the nine other poems. In this poem Virgil abandons the more realistic path on which he had entered in the eighth, and returns again to the vague fancies of the old pastoral lament for Daphnis, as it is sung in the first idyl of Theocritus. Nothing can be more remote from actual fact than the representation of Gallus—the active and ambitious soldier and man of affairs, at that time engaged in the defence of the coasts of Italy—dying among the mountains of Arcadia, in consequence of his desertion by Lycoris (a dancing-girl, and former mistress of Antony, whose real name was Cytheris), and wept for by the rocks and pine-woods of Maenalus and Lycaeus. Yet none of the poems is more rich in beauty, and grace, and happy turns of phrase. As the idealised expression of unfortunate love, this poem is of the same class as the second, and as the song of Damon in the eighth. That vein of modern romantic sentiment, already noticed in the second, the longing to escape from the ways of civilised life to the wild and lonely places of Nature, and to follow in imagination 'the homely, slighted shepherd's trade,' meets us also in the lines,

> Atque utinam ex vobis unus vestrique fuissem
> Aut custos gregis aut maturae vinitor uvae[49],—

and again in these,

> Certum est in silvis, inter spelaea ferarum
> Malle pati, tenerisque meos incidere amores
> Arboribus[50].

II.

RELATION OF THE *ECLOGUES* TO THE GREEK PASTORAL.

The review of the *Eclogues* in the order of their composition shows that the early art of Virgil, like the lyrical art of Horace, begins in imitation, and, after attaining command over the form, rhythm, and diction of the type of poetry which it reproduces, gradually assumes greater independence in the choice of subject and the mode of treatment. The susceptibility of Virgil's mind to the grace and musical sweetness of Theocritus gave the first impulse to the composition of the *Eclogues*; but this susceptibility was itself the result of a natural sympathy with the sentiment and motives of the Greek idyl, especially with the love of Nature and the passion of love. He found this province of art unappropriated. He revealed a new vein of Greek feeling unwrought by any of his countrymen. He gave another life to the beings, natural and supernatural, of ancient

pastoral song, and awoke in his native land the sound of a strain hitherto unheard by Italian ears. The form of the Greek idyl, whether in dialogue or monologue, suited his genius, as a vehicle for the lighter fancies of youth, and for half-revealing, half-concealing the pleasures and pains personal to himself, better than the forms of lyrical and elegiac poetry adopted by Catullus and his compeers. In the opening lines of the sixth *Eclogue,*

> Prima Syracosio dignata est ludere versu
> Nostra, neque erubuit silvas habitare Thalia[51],

Virgil acknowledges at once the source of his inspiration and the lowly position which his genius was willing to assume. He may have consoled himself for this abnegation of a higher ambition by the thought suggested in the lines addressed to the ideal poet and hero of his imagination—

> Nec te paeniteat pecoris, divine poeta,
> Et formosus ovis ad flumina pavit Adonis[52].

In order to understand the pastoral poetry of Virgil, both in its relation to a Greek ideal and in its original truth of feeling, it is necessary to remember the chief characteristics of its prototype in the age of Ptolemy Philadelphus of Alexandria and in the early years of the reign of Hiero of Syracuse. The pastoral poetry of Sicily was the latest creation of Greek genius, born after the nobler phases of religious and political life, and the epic, lyric, and dramatic poetry which arose out of them, had passed away. In ancient, as in modern times, the pastoral idyl, as an artistic branch of literature, has arisen, not in a simple age, living in unconscious harmony with Nature, but from the midst of a refined and luxurious, generally, too, a learned or rather bookish society, and has tried to give vent to the feelings of men weary of an artificial life and vaguely longing to breathe a freer air[53]. But there was in ancient times a primitive and popular, as well as a late and artistic pastoral. Of the primitive pastoral, springing out of rustic gatherings and festivals, or from lonely communion with Nature,

> Per loca pastorum deserta atque otia dia[54],

and transmitted, from generation to generation, in the mouth of the people, no fragment has been preserved. Yet traces of the existence of this kind of pastoral song, and of the music accompanying it, at a time antecedent to the composition of the Homeric poems, may be seen in the representation, on the Shield of Achilles, of the boy in the vineyard 'singing the beautiful song Linus,'—a representation which is purely idyllic,—and of the shepherds, in the Ambuscade, who appear τερπόμενοι συριγξι as they accompany their flocks. The author of the Iliad absorbed the spirit of this primitive poetry in the greater compass of his epic creation, as Shakspeare has absorbed the Elizabethan pastoral within the all-embracing compass of his representation. Much of the imagery of the Iliad, several incidents casually introduced in connexion with the names of obscure persons perishing in battle, some of the supernatural events glanced at, as of the meeting of Aphrodite with

Anchises while tending his herds on the spurs of Ida,—a subject of allusion also in the Sicilian idyl,—are of a pastoral character and origin. In the lines which spring up with a tender grace in the midst of the stern grandeur of the final conflict between Hector and Achilles. . . .

the familiar cadences as well as the sweetest sentiment of pastoral song may be recognised.

This primitive pastoral poetry may have been spread over all Greece and the islands of the Aegean, from the earliest settlements of the Hellenic race, or of that older branch of the family to which the name Pelasgic has been vaguely given, and may have lingered on the same in spirit, though with many variations in form and expression, among the peasantry and herdsmen of the mountain districts till a late period. But the earliest writer who is said to have adopted this native plant of the mountains and the woods, and to have trained it to assume some form of art, was Stesichorus of Himera, who flourished about the beginning of the sixth century B.C. But nothing more is heard of it till it revived again at Syracuse in the early part of the third century.

Some of the primitive modes of feeling which gave birth to the earliest pastoral song still survive, though in altered form, in this later Sicilian poetry. The song of the . . . herdsmen, like the song of the masked worshippers of Bacchus . . ., may be traced to that stage in the development of the higher races in which Nature was the chief object of worship and religious sympathy. Under the symbols of Linus, Daphnis, or Adonis, the country people of early times lamented the decay of the fresh beauty of spring, under the burning midsummer heat[56]. This primitive germ of serious feeling has perpetuated itself in that melancholy mood which runs through the pastoral poetry of all countries. From that tendency of the Greek imagination to give a human meaning to all that interested it, this dirge over the fading beauty of the early year soon assumed the form of a lament over the death of a young shepherd-poet, dear to gods and men, to the flocks, herds, and wild animals, to the rocks and mountains, among which he had lived. In the Daphnis of Theocritus, the human passion of love produces that blighting influence on the life of the shepherd which in the original myth was produced by the fierce heat of summer on the tender life of the year. A still later development of the myth appears in the lament over the extinction of youthful genius by early death. It is not in any poem of Theocritus, but in the 'Lament of Bion,'—the work of a later writer, apparently an Italian-Greek, . . . that we find the finest ancient specimen of this later development.[57] It is from this new form of the old dirge of Linus or Daphnis that the fancies and feelings of the ancient pastoral have been most happily adapted to modern poetry, as in the Lycidas, the Adonais, and the Thyrsis of English literature.

Another traditional theme of 'pastoral melancholy,' of which Theocritus makes use, is the unrequited love of the Cyclops for Galatea. This too had its origin in the

personification of natural objects[58]. But, unlike the song of Daphnis, the myth of which it was the expression was purely local, and confined to the shores of Sicily. It also illustrates the tendency of all pastoral song to find its chief human motive in the passion of love. While the original motive of the primitive lament for Daphnis or Linus was the unconscious sympathy of the human heart with Nature, the most prominent motive of artistic pastoral or idyllic poetry, from the 'Song of Songs' to the 'Hermann and Dorothea' and 'The Long Vacation Pastoral' of these later times, has been the passion of the human heart for the human object of its affection, blending with either an unconscious absorption in outward scenes or a refined contemplation of them[59].

But there is another very distinct mode of primitive feeling traceable in Theocritus, which dictates the good-humoured, often licentious, banter with which the shepherds encounter one another. As the pastoral monologue continued to betray the serious character of the Lament out of which it sprung, so this natural dialogue continued to bear traces of that old licence of the harvest-home and the vintage-season, which

Versibus alternis opprobria rustica fudit[60].

The 'lusit amabiliter' of Horace's lines, which soon became inapplicable to the biting and censorious Italian spirit, expresses happily the tone of the dialogue in the fourth and fifth Idyls of Theocritus, which Virgil attempts to reproduce in his third Eclogue. This source of rural poetry was known to the 'Ausonian husbandmen' as well as to the country people of Greece and Sicily: and its native force passed not only into the Greek pastoral idyl, but into the Sicilian comedy of Epicharmus and the old comedy of Athens, and, through a totally different channel, into Roman satire. There is, however, another form in which the pastoral dialogue appears both in Theocritus and Virgil, namely, of extemporaneous contests in song. Probably these more artistic contests and the award of prizes to the successful competitor had their origin in the bantering dialogue of the shepherds; as the tragic contests at the Dionysian festivals had their origin in the rivalry with which the masked votaries of Dionysus poured forth their extemporaneous verses, in sympathy with the sufferings of their god.

Such were the first rude utterances of the deeper as well as the gayer emotions of men, living in the happy security of the country districts or the 'otia dia' of the mountains in Greece, Sicily, and perhaps Southern Italy, which the art of Theocritus and his successors cast into artistic forms and measures suited to the taste of educated readers. How far, in the manner in which he accomplished this, Theocritus had been anticipated by 'the grave muse of Stesichorus,' and whether this wild product of the mountains was of a native Sicilian or an Hellenic stock, it is not possible to determine. A citizen of Syracuse, in the palmy days of Hiero, before there was any dream of Roman conquest; deeply susceptible of the beauty of his native island, but, like a Greek, seeing this beauty in relation to human associations; familiar with the songs and old traditions of the land, as well as with the fancies of earlier poets; living his life in friendly association with his literary compeers, such as the Alexandrine Aratus[61] and Nicias, the physician and poet[62],—he sought to people the familiar scenery of mountain, wood, brook, and sea-shore with an ideal race of shepherds, in whom the natural emotions and grotesque superstitions of actual herdsmen should be found in union with the refinement, the mythological lore, the keen sense of the beauty, not unmixed with the melancholy, of life, characteristic of a circle of poets and scholars enjoying their youth in untroubled and uneventful times. All his materials, old and new, assumed the shape of pictures from human life in combination with the representations of the sounds, sights, and living movement of Nature. The essential characteristic both of his pastoral Idyls and of those drawn from city-life, such as the second, fourteenth, and fifteenth, is what has been well called the 'disinterested objectivity[63]' of Greek art: and this is the chief note of their difference from Virgil's pastorals. Even where, as in the seventh, the poet introduces himself on the scene, he appears as one, and not the most important, of the personages on it. He does not draw attention to his own feelings or fortunes, only to his playful converse and rivalry in song with the young shepherd-poet Lycidas, 'with the bright laughing eye and the smile ever playing on his lip[64].'

It may be urged against these Idyls that, as compared with the best modern Idyls, in prose or verse, they are, for the most part, wanting in incident or adventure; and this charge is equally applicable to Virgil's pastorals. But there is always dramatic vivacity and consistency in the personages of Theocritus, and this cannot equally be said of those introduced into the *Eclogues.* It might be urged also against the representations of Theocritus, and still more against those of Virgil, that the 'vestigia ruris' have been too carefully obliterated. Yet, though not drawn immediately from life, this picture of Sicilian shepherds and peasants, possessed with the vivid belief in Pan and the Nymphs, singing the old dirge of the herdsman Daphnis among the mountain pastures, or the love-song of the Cyclops and Galatea on the rocks overhanging the Sicilian sea, or the song of Lityerses among the ripe corn-fields[65], challenging each other to compete in song or plying each other with careless jest, tending their flocks rather as a picturesque pastime than as a toilsome occupation, and living a life of free social enjoyment in the open air, was a genuine ideal of the Greek imagination, not, perhaps, too far removed from the actual reality.

Before the time of Virgil there had been no attempt to introduce this form of art into Italy. Though the germ of a rude rustic poetry existed in the 'Fescennine verses,' no connexion can be traced between them and the highly artificial pastoral of the Augustan Age. The *Eclogues* of Virgil are in form and even in substance a closer reproduction of a Greek original than any other branch of Latin literature, with the exception of the comedy of Terence.

The 'Lament of Daphnis,' the song of unrequited love, the bantering dialogues of the shepherds and their more formal contests in song, reappear in Latin tones and with some new associations of individual and national life, but in such a manner as to recall the memory of the Sicilian idyl rather than to suggest a new experience from life. And yet Virgil is not satisfied, like the authors of Latin comedy, with presenting to the imagination types of Greek life, Greek sentiment and manners, and Greek scenes. He desires not only to reproduce in new words and music the charm which had fascinated him in Theocritus, but to blend the actual feeling and experience of an Italian living in the Augustan Age with this ideal restored from a by-gone time. The result is something composite, neither purely Greek nor purely Italian; not altogether of the present time nor yet of a mythical foretime; but a blending of various elements of poetic association and actual experience, as in those landscapes of the Renaissance which combine aspects of real scenes with the suggestions of classical poetry, and introduce figures of the day in modern dress along with the fantastic shapes of mythological invention. The scenes and personages of the Eclogues are thus one stage further removed from actuality than those of the Greek pastoral. They do not reproduce, as Keats has done, the Greek ideal of rural life, and they do not create a purely Italian ideal. There was, indeed, latent in the Italian imagination an ideal of a homely rustic life, finding its happiness in the annual round of labour and in the blessing of a virtuous home, and that ideal Virgil loved to draw with 'magic hand;' but that was altogether unlike the ideal of the Greek imagination. The life of industry and happiness which Virgil glorifies in the *Georgics,*—that of the 'primitive, stout-hearted, and thrifty husbandmen' of Horace,—whose pride was in their 'glad harvests,' their 'trim fields,' their 'vineyards,' and in the use which they derived from their flocks, herds, and beehives, had nothing in common with that of the 'well-trimmed sunburnt shepherds' whom Greek fancy first created, and whom Keats has made live for us again, enjoying the fulness of actual existence in union with the dreams of an 'Elysian idleness[66].' Least of all could the pastoral life of Arcadia or Sicily have been like the habitual ways of men in the rich plains of Mantua. The district of Italy most like the scenes of the Greek idyl was Calabria, where, among the desolate forest-glades, the herds and flocks of some rich senator or eques were now tended by barbarous slaves, with whose daily existence the ideal glories of pastoral song were not likely to intermingle.

III.

It is easy for those who wish to depreciate the art of Virgil to point out very many instances of imitation and artificial treatment in the *Eclogues,* and to establish their manifest inferiority to the Greek idyl in direct truth and vividness of representation. They are not purely objective, like the Greek idyl, nor purely subjective, as the Latin elegy generally is. They are very much inferior to the Greek originals in dramatic power; and the idyl is really a branch of dramatic poetry. Like the pure drama, it depends on the power of living in the thoughts, situations, and feelings of beings quite distinct from the poet himself. Some of the *Eclogues,* those in which the passion of love and the Italian passion for the land are the motives, are dramatic in spirit, though the conception of the situation is not consistently maintained. But in most cases, where he is not merely imitative, the dramatic form is to Virgil as a kind of veil under which he may partially reveal what moved him most in connexion with his own personal fortunes, and may express his sympathies with literature, with outward nature, and with certain moods and sentiments of the human heart. It is not in virtue of the originality and consistency of their conception, but of their general truth of feeling and the perfection of the medium through which that feeling is conveyed, that those who admire the *Eclogues* must vindicate their claim to poetic honour.

The reserve with which all his personal relations are indicated, and the allusive way in which the story of his fortunes is told, are in keeping with the delicacy and modesty of Virgil's nature. He tells us nothing directly of his home-life or occupations, though his attachment to the scenes familiar to him from childhood is felt in the language with which Meliboeus felicitates Tityrus on the restitution of his land, and in that in which Moeris and Lycidas discourse together. We know of no actual Galatea or Amaryllis associated with the joy or the pain of his youth; though his subtle perception of the various moods of the passion of love can hardly be a mere poetic intuition, unenlightened by personal experience. The eminent men with whom he was brought into contact, Octavianus, Pollio, Varus, and Gallus, are not individualised; though the different feelings of reverential or loyal respect, of colder deference, or admiring enthusiasm, which they severally excited in him, can be clearly distinguished. In the undesigned revelation of himself, which every author makes in his writings, there are few indications of the religious and moral feeling and of the national sentiment which are among the principal elements in Virgil's maturer poems; but we find abundantly the evidence of a mind open to all tender and refined influences, free from every taint of envy or malice, serious and pensive, and finding its chief happiness in making the charm, which fascinated him in books, in Nature, and in life, heard in the deep and rich music of the language, of which he first drew out the full capabilities:—

> Saepe ego longos
> Cantando puerum memini me condere
> soles[67].

The *Eclogues* also present Virgil to us as not only a poet, but, as what he continued to be through all his life, a student of the writings of the past. Like Milton he was eminently a learned poet, and, like Milton, he knew the subtle alchemy by which the duller ore of learned allusion is transmuted into gold. The tales of the Greek mythology and the names of places famous in song or story act on his imagination, not so much through their own intrinsic interest, as through the associations of literature. It is under this reflex action that he recalls to memory the tales of Pasiphae, of Scylla and Nisus, of Tereus and Philomela;

introduces Orpheus, Amphion, and Linus as the ideal poets of pastoral song; and alludes to Hesiod, Euphorion, and Theocritus in the phrases 'the sage of Ascra,' 'the verse of Chalcis,' 'the Sicilian Shepherd.' It is in this spirit that he associates the musical accompaniment of his song with the names of Maenalus and Eurotas, of Rhodope and Ismarus; and that he speaks of bees and thyme as 'the bees and thyme of Hybla,' of doves as 'the Chaonian doves,' of vultures as 'the birds of Caucasus.' He also characterises objects by local epithets, suggestive rather of the associations of geographical science than of poetry. Thus he speaks of 'Ariusian wine,' of 'Cydonian arrows,' 'Cyrnean yews,' 'Assyrian spikenard,' and the like. The interest in physical enquiries appears in the allusion in Ecl. iii, 40,

> In medio duo signa Conon, etc.,

and in the rapid summary of the Epicurean theory of creation at vi. 31, etc.,

> Namque canebat uti magnum per inane coacta, etc.

In these last passages it is not so much by the scientific or philosophical speculations themselves, as by their literary treatment by former writers, that Virgil appears to be attracted. Perhaps the frequent recurrence of these localising epithets, where there is nothing in the context to call up any thought of the locality indicated, may appear to a modern reader an unfortunate result of his Alexandrine studies; yet the grace with which old poetic associations are evoked and new associations created by such lines as these,

> Tum canit, errantem Permessi ad flumina Gallum
> Aonas in montis ut duxerit una sororum,

or these,

> Omnia quae Phoebo quondam meditante beatus
> Audiit Eurotas, iussitque ediscere laurus,
> Ille canit[68],

attests the cumulative force which ancient names, identified with the poetic life of the world, gather in their transmission through the literatures of different ages and nations.

In the *Georgics* and *Aeneid,* as well as in the *Eclogues,* Virgil shows a great susceptibility to the beauty and power of Nature. But Nature presents different aspects and awakens a different class of feelings in these poems. In the *Eclogues* he shows a great openness and receptivity of mind, through which all the softer and more delicate influences of the outward world enter into and become part of his being. The 'molle atque facetum' of Horace denotes the yielding susceptibility[69] to outward influences, and the vivacity which gives them back in graceful forms. In the *Georgics,* the sense of the relation of Nature to human energy imparts greater nobleness to the conception. She appears there, not only in her majesty and beauty, but as endowed with a soul and will. She stands to man at first in the relation of an antagonist: but, by compliance with her conditions, he subdues her to his will, and finds in her at last a just and beneficent helpmate[70]. In the ***Eclogues*** she takes rather the form of an enchantress, who, by the charm of her outward mien and her freely-offered gifts, fascinates him into a life of indolent repose. If the one poem may in a sense be described as the 'glorification of labour,' the other might be described as the 'glorification of the *dolce far niente*' of Italian life. The natural objects described by Virgil are often indeed the same as those out of which the representation of Theocritus is composed; but in Theocritus the human figures are, after all, the prominent objects in the picture: the speakers in his dialogue, though not unconscious of the charm proceeding from the scenes in which they are placed, yet are not possessed by it; they do not lose their own being in the larger life of Nature environing them. Theocritus shows everywhere the social temperament of the Greeks. It is an Italian, not perhaps without something of the Celtic fibre in his composition, who utters his natural feelings in the lines,

> ibi haec incondita solus
> Montibus et silvis studio iactabat inani[71].

In Virgil's representation neither the scenes nor the human figures are so distinctly present to the eye; but there is diffused through it a subtle influence from the outward world, bringing man's nature into conformity with itself. The genius in modern times, which shows most of this yielding susceptibility to the softer aspects and motions of Nature, is that of Rousseau; but in the manner in which he gives way to this sentiment there is a want of restraint, a strain of excited feeling, suggestive of the contrast between this transient intoxication of happiness and the abiding unrest and misery of all his human relations. In reading Virgil there is no sense of any such jarring discord; yet it is rather as a pensive emotion, not unallied to melancholy, than as the joy of a sanguine temperament, that his susceptibility to outward impressions is made manifest.

The objects through which Nature exercises this spell are, as was said, much the same as those out of which the landscape of Theocritus is composed. Virgil, like Theocritus, enables us to feel the charm of 'the sparkling stream of fresh water,' of 'mossy fountains and grass softer than sleep,' of 'the cool shade of trees,' and of caves 'with the gadding vine o'ergrown.' The grace and tender hues of wild flowers—violets, poppies, narcissus, and hyacinth—and of fruits, such as the 'cerea pruna' and the 'tenera lanugine mala,'—the luxuriant vegetation clothing the rocks and the ideal mountain glades,—

> Ille latus niveum molli fultus hyacintho[72],—

the plants and trees,—osiers and hazels, ilex and beech,—the woods, and meadow-pastures, and rich orchards of his native district, have communicated the soul and secret of their being to the mellow tones of his language and the musical cadences of his verse. He makes us hear again, with a strange delight, the murmur of bees feeding on the willow hedge, the moan of turtle-doves from the high elm tree, the sound of the whispering south wind, of waves breaking on the shore, of rivers flowing down through rocky valleys, the song of the woodman plying his work, the voice of the divine poet chanting his strain. By a few simple words he calls up before our minds the genial luxuriance of spring, the freshness of early morning, the rest of all living things in the burning heat of noon, the stillness of evening, the gentle imperceptible motions of Nature, in the shooting up of the young alder-tree and in the gradual colouring of the grapes on the sunny hill-sides. If the labour of man is mentioned at all, it is in the form of some elegant accomplishment or picturesque task—pruning the vine or grafting the pear-tree, closing the streams that water the pastures, watching the flocks and herds feeding at their own will. The new era on which the world was about to enter is seen by his imagination, like the vision of some pastoral valley, half hidden, half glorified through a golden haze. The peculiar blessings anticipated in that era are the rest from labour, the spontaneous bounty of Nature, the peace that is to reign among the old enemies of the animal kingdom.

The human affections which mingle with these representations of Nature are the love of home, and the romantic sentiment, rather than the passion, of love. The common human feeling of the love of home Virgil realises more intensely from his love of the beauty associated with his own home. Many of the sayings of Tityrus and Meliboeus bear witness to the strong hold which their lands and flocks had on men of their class:—

> nos dulcia linquimus arva—
> ergo tua rura manebunt, Et tibi magna satis—
> Ille meas errare boves ut cernis—
> Spem gregis a, silice in nuda conixa reliquit—
> Ite meae, quondam felix pecus, ite capellae[73].

In the passage of the same ***Eclogue,*** from 68-79,

> En unquam patrios . . . salices carpetis amaras,

Virgil tells, in language of natural pathos and exquisite grace, of the poor man's sorrow in yielding his thatched hut, his well-trimmed fields, his corn crops, his pear-trees and his vines, the familiar sight of his goats feeding high up among the thickets of the rocks, to some rude soldier, incapable either of enjoying the charm or profiting by the richness of the land.

The three poems—the second, eighth, and tenth—of which love is the theme are all of a serious and plaintive cast. There are few touches in Virgil's art descriptive either of the happier or the lighter and more playful experiences of the passion, which are the common theme of Horace's Odes. Still less does he treat the subject in the style of Propertius and Ovid. The sentiment of Virgil is more like that of Tibullus; only Virgil gives utterance, though always in a dramatic form, to the real despair of unrequited affection (indigni amoris), while the tone of Tibullus is rather that of one yielding to the luxury of melancholy when in possession of all that his heart desires. They each give expression to that modern mood of passion, in which the heart longs to exchange the familiar life of civilisation for the rougher life of the fields, and to share some humble cottage and the daily occupations of peasant life with the beloved object[74]. In Virgil also there appears some anticipation of that longing for lonely communing with Nature in her wilder and more desolate aspects which we associate with romantic rather than with classical poetry.

Though, unlike all other Latin poets, Virgil avoids all reference to the sensual side of this passion, there is no ancient poet who has analysed and expressed, with equal truth and beauty and with such a chivalrous devotion, the fluctuations between hope and despair, the sense of personal unworthiness, the sweet memories, the heart-felt longings, the self-forgetful consideration and anxieties of an idealising affection. In such lines as these, expressing at once the sense of unworthiness and the rapid sinking of the heart from hope to despair—

> Rusticus es Corydon, nec munera curat Alexis[75],

and again—

> Tanquam haec sint nostri medicina furoris[76];

in the lines in which Damon traces back his love to its ideal source in early boyhood—

> Saepibus in nostris, etc.;

in the fine simile at viii. 85—

> Talis amor Daphnim, qualis cum fessa iuvencum, etc.;

in the tender thought of the dying Gallus for the mistress who had forsaken him—

> A, tibi ne teneras glacies secet aspera plantas[77],—

there is a delicate and subtle power of touch not unworthy of the master-hand which, with maturer art, delineated the queenly passion and despair of Dido.

The supreme excellence of Virgil's art consists in the perfect harmony between his feeling and the medium through which it is conveyed. The style of his longer poems has many varied excellences, in accordance with the varied character of the thought and sentiment which it is called on to express. But the strong and full volume of diction and rhythm and the complex harmonies of the Georgics would have been an inappropriate vehicle for the luxurious sentiment of the *Eclogues.* The attitude of the poet's mind in the composition of these earlier poems was that of a genial passiveness rather than that of creative activity. There are few poems of equal excellence in which so little use is made of that force of words which imparts new life to things. A few such expressions might be quoted, like that given by Wordsworth as 'an instance of a slight exertion of the faculty of imagination in the use of a single word'—

> Dumosa *pendere* procul de rupe videbo;

and we notice a similar exertion of the faculty in the line—

> Hic viridis tenera *praetexit* harundine ripam
> Mincius[78].

But this actively imaginative use of language seldom occurs in these poems. The general effect of the style is produced by the fulness of feeling, the sweetness or sonorousness of cadence, with which words, used in their familiar sense, are selected and combined. Such epithets as 'mollis,' 'lentus,' 'tener' are of frequent recurrence, yet the impression left by their use is not one of weakness, or of a satiating luxury of sentiment. The soft outlines and delicate bloom of Virgil's youthful style are as true emblems of health as the firmer fibre and richer colouring of his later diction. What an affluence of feeling, what a deep sense of the happiness of life, of the beauty of the world, of the glory of genius, is conveyed by the simple use of the words *fortunatus, formosus, divinus* in the lines—

> Fortunate senex, ergo tua rura manebunt—
> Nunc frondent silvae, nunc formosissimus annus—
> Formosi pecoris custos, formosior ipse—
> Tale tuum carmen nobis, divine poeta—
> Ut Linus haec illi divino carmine pastor.

The effect he produces by the sound and associations of proper names is like that produced by Milton through the same instrument. Thus, to take one instance out of many, how suggestive of some golden age of pastoral song are the following lines, vague and conventional though their actual application appears to be in the passage where they occur:—

> Non me carminibus vincet nec Thracius Orpheus,
> Nec Linus, huic mater quamvis atque huic pater adsit,
> Orphei Calliopea, Lino formosus Apollo.
> Pan etiam Arcadia mecum si indice certet,
> Pan etiam Arcadia dicat se iudice victum[79].

More even in his rhythm than in his diction does Virgil's superiority appear, not only over all the poets of his country, but perhaps over all other poets of past times, except Homer, Milton, and Shakspeare, in those passages in which his dramatic art admits of a richly musical cadence. Our ignorance of the exact pronunciation of Greek in the Alexandrian Age makes a comparison between the effect that would have been produced by the rhythm of Theocritus and the rhythm of the *Eclogues* in ancient times difficult or impossible. Yet it may be allowed to say this much, that if the rhythm of the *Eclogues* does not seem to us to attain to the natural and liquid flow of the Greek idyl, yet its tones are deeper, they seem to come from a stronger and richer source, than any which we can elicit from the Doric reed. Rarely has the soothing and reviving charm of the musical sounds of Nature and of the softer and grander harmonies of poetry been described and reproduced more effectively than in these lines:—

> Hinc tibi, quae semper, vicino ab limite saepes
> Hyblaeis apibus florem depasta salicti

Saepe levi somnum suadebit inire susurro;
Hinc alta sub rupe canet frondator ad auras;
Nec tamen interea raucae, tua cura, palumbes,
Nec gemere aeria cessabit turtur ab ulmo[80]:

and in these which suggest the thought of that restorative power of genius which a poet of the present day has happily ascribed to Wordsworth[81]:—

Tale tuum carmen nobis, divine poeta,
Quale sopor fessis in gramine, quale per aestum
Dulcis aquae saliente sitim restinguere rivo[82]:

and in these again, which give both true symbols and a true example of the 'deep-chested music' in which the poet gives utterance to the thought which has taken shape within his mind:—

Quae tibi, quae tali reddam pro carmine dona?
Nam neque me tantum venientis sibilus austri,
Nec percussa iuvant fluctu tam litora, nec quae
Saxosas inter decurrunt flumina valles[83].

The objections often urged against the poetical value of the *Eclogues* may be admitted. They are imitative in form. They do not reproduce scenes and characters from actual life, nor are they consistent creations of the imagination. They do not possess the interest arising from a contemplative insight into the hidden workings of Nature, nor from reflection on the problems of life. Their originality, their claim to be a representative work of genius, consists in their truth and unity of sentiment and tone. If it be said that the sentiment which they embody is but a languid and effeminate sentiment, the admiration of two great poets, of the most masculine type of genius that modern times have produced, is a sufficient answer to this reproach. The admiration of Milton is proved by the conception and workmanship of his 'Lycidas,' the most richly and continuously musical even among his creations. Of Wordsworth's admiration there is more than one testimony,—this, from the recently published Memoir of the daughter of his early friend and associate in poetry, perhaps the most direct: 'I am much pleased to see (writes S. Coleridge) how highly Mr. Wordsworth speaks of Virgil's style, and of his *Bucolics* which I have ever thought most graceful and tender. They are quite another thing from Theocritus, however they may be based on Theocritus[84].' The criticism which the same writer applies to 'Lycidas' suggests the true answer also to the objections urged against Virgil's originality. 'The best defence of Lycidas is not to defend the design of it at all, but to allege that the execution of it is perfect, the diction the *ne plus ultra* of grace and loveliness, and that the spirit of the whole is as original as if the poem contained no traces of the author's acquaintance with ancient pastoral poetry from Theocritus downwards.' To the names of these two poets we can now add the name of one of the most illustrious, and certainly one of the least effeminate, among the critics and men of letters whom this century has produced—Macaulay; who, after speaking of the *Aeneid* in one of his letters, adds this sentence, 'The *Georgics* pleased me better; the *Eclogues* best,—the second and tenth above all[85].'

The appreciation of Wordsworth is a certain touchstone of the genuineness of Virgil's feeling for Nature. It is true that the sentiment to which he gives expression in the *Eclogues* is only one, and not the most elevated, of the many modes in which the spirit of man responds to the forms and movement of the outward world. But the mood of the *Eclogues* is one most natural to man's spirit in the beautiful lands of Southern Europe. The freshness and softness of Italian scenes are present in the *Eclogues,* in the rich music of the Italian language, while it still retained the strength, fulness, and majesty of its tones. These poems are truly representative of Italy, not as a land of old civilisation, of historic renown, of great cities, of corn-crops, and vineyards,—'the mighty mother of fruits and men;'— but as a land of a soft and genial air, beautiful with the tender foliage and fresh flowers and blossoms of spring, and with the rich colouring of autumn; a land which has most attuned man's nature to the influences of music and of pictorial art. As a true and exquisite symbol of this vein of sentiment associated with Italy, the *Eclogues* hold a not unworthy place beside the greater work—the 'temple of solid marble'—which the maturer art of Virgil dedicated to the genius of his country, and beside the more composite but stately and massive monument which perpetuates the national glory of Rome.

Notes

1. 'I, the idle singer of a pastoral song, who in the boldness of youth made thee, O Tityrus, beneath the shade of the spreading beech, my theme.'

   The lines of Propertius—

   Tu canis umbrosi subter pineta Galaesi
       Thyrsin et attritis Daphnin harundinibus,

   might suggest the inference that the seventh was composed at the time when Virgil was residing in the neighbourhood of Tarentum. But, at the time when Propertius wrote, Virgil was engaged in the composition of the Aeneid, not of the Eclogues. The present 'canis' seems rather to mean that Virgil, while engaged with his Aeneid, was still conning over his old Eclogues. Yet he must have strayed 'subter pineta Galaesi' some time before the composition of the last Georgic. It has been remarked by Mr. Munro that the 'memini' in the line

   Namque sub Oebaliae memini me turribus arcis

   looks like the memory of a somewhat distant past. Could the villa of Siron have been in the neighbourhood of Tarentum? (a question originally suggested by Mr. Munro); may it have passed by gift or inheritance into the possession of Virgil, and was he in later life in the habit of going to it from time to time? or was the distance too great from Mantua for him to have transferred his family thither?

2. 'This taught me "the fair Alexis was loved by Corydon," this too taught me "whose is the flock? is it the flock of Meliboeus?" '

3. viii. 56. 12.

4. Ep. ad Att. i. 12.

5. Dr. Kennedy refers to no less than seventeen parallel passages from Theocritus, many of them being almost literal translations from the Greek poet.

6. 'Look, the steers are drawing home the uplifted ploughs.'

7. 'O that it would but please you to dwell with me among the "homely slighted" fields and lowly cottages, and to shoot the deer.'

8. 'The Gods too were dwellers in the woods, and Dardanian Paris. Leave Pallas to abide in the towers which she has built; let our chief delight be in the woods.'

9. Dr. Kennedy refers to twenty-seven parallels from Theocritus.

10. 'Pollio loves my song, though it is but a shepherd's song.' 'Pollio himself too is a poet.'

11. 'Who hates not Bavius may he be charmed with thy songs, O Maevius!'

12. 'Menalcas Vergilius hic intelligitur, qui obitum fratris sui Flacci deflet, vel, ut alii volunt, interfectionem Caesaris.' Comment. in Verg. Serviani (H. A. Lion, 1826).

13. See Conington's Introduction to this Eclogue.

14. 'No beast either tasted the river or touched a blade of grass.'

15. Compare M. Benoist's note on the passage.

16. 'Proximis diebus equorum greges, quos in traiciendo Rubicone flumine consecrarat ac vagos et sine custode dimiserat, comperit pertinacissime pabulo abstinere ubertimque flere.' Sueton. lib. i. c. 81.

17. 'As to Bacchus and to Ceres so to thee shall the husbandmen annually make their vows; thou too wilt call on them for their fulfilment.'

18. 'The star beneath which the harvest-fields should be glad in their corn-crops, and the grapes should gather a richer colour on the sunny hill-sides.'

19. 'Graft your pears, Daphnis: your fruits will be plucked by those who come after you.'

20. Kennedy.

21. 'Here the green Mincio fringes its bank with delicate reeds, and swarms of bees are buzzing from the sacred oak.'

22. 'This I remember, and that Thyrsis was beaten in the contest: from that time Corydon is all in all with us.'

23. Cf.

> Ergo *tua* rura manebunt—
> Ille *meas* errare boves—
> Multa *meis* exiret victima saeptis.

24. Candidior postquam tondenti barba cadebat—
Fortunate senex.

25. See Kennedy's note on the passage.

26. 'Though all your land is choked with barren stones or covered with marsh and sedge.'—P.

27. 'And larger shadows are falling from the lofty mountains.'

28. M. Benoist.

29. 'Shall some unfeeling soldier become the master of these fields, so carefully tilled, some rude stranger own these harvest-fields? see to what misery fellow-countrymen have been brought by civil strife!'

30. 'Now in defeat and sadness, since all things are the sport of chance.'

31. 'Me too the shepherds call a bard, but I give no ear to them; for as yet my strain seems far inferior to that of Varius and of Cinna, and to be as the cackling of a goose among tuneful swans.'

32. 'Varus, thy name provided only Mantua be spared to us.'

'Daphnis, why gazest thou on the old familiar risings of the constellations?'

33. 'And now you see the whole level plain [sea?] is calm and still.'

34. i. 496.

35. Compare Gaston Boissier, La Religion Romaine d'Auguste aux Antonins: 'Il y a pourtant un côté par lequel la quatrième églogue peut être rattachée à l'histoire du Christianisme; elle nous révèle un certain état des âmes qui n'a pas été inutile à ses rapides progrès. C'était une opinion accréditée alors que le monde épuisé touchait à une grande crise et qu'une révolution se préparait qui lui rendrait la jeunesse. . . . Il regnait alors partout une sorte de fermentation, d'attente inquiète et d'espérance sans limite. "Toutes les créatures soupirent," dit Saint Paul, "et sont dans le travail de l'enfantement." Le principal intérêt des vers de Virgile est de nous garder quelque souvenir de cette disposition des âmes.

36. Any child born of this marriage in the year 40 B. C. must have owed its birth, not to Antony, but to Marcellus, the former husband of Octavia.

37. The application of the words 'magnum Iovis incrementum' by the author of the Ciris (398) to Castor and Pollux suggests a doubt as to Mr. Munro's interpretation of the words, accepted by Dr. Kennedy; though at the same time there is nothing improbable in the supposition that Virgil gave a meaning to the words which was misunderstood by his imitator.

38. 'And will rule the world in peace with his father's virtues.'

39. Fuit enim hic poeta, ut scrupulose et anxie, ita dissimulanter et clanculo doctus, ut multa transtulerit quae, unde translata sint, difficile sit cognitu. Sat. v. 18.

40. Quae a penitissima Graecorum doctrina transtulisset. Ib. 22.

41. De Graecorum penitissimis literis hanc historiam eruit Maro. Ib. 19.

42. 'Receive a song undertaken at your command.'

43. 'When the dew on the tender blade is most grateful to the flock.'

44. 'I shall hurl myself headlong into the waves from the high mountain's crag.'

45. 'But I think that the finest lines in the Latin language are those five which begin—

Saepibus in nostris parvam te roscida mala.

I cannot tell you how they struck me. I was amused to find that Voltaire pronounces that passage to be the finest in Virgil.' Life and Letters of Lord Macaulay, vol. i. pp. 371, 372.

46. 'It was within our orchard I saw you, a child, with my mother gathering apples, and I was your guide: I had but then entered on my twelfth year, I could just reach from the ground the fragile branches: the moment I saw you how utterly lost I was, how borne astray by fatal passion.'

47. 'I loved you, maiden, when first you came with my mother wishing to gather hyacinths from the mountain, and I guided you on the way: and since I saw you, from that time, never after, not even yet, can I cease loving you; but you care not, no, by Zeus, not a whit.'

48. Compare 85-86 with Lucret. ii. 355, etc.:—

At mater viridis saltus orbata peragrans.

49. 'And would that I had been one of you, and had been either shepherd of your flock or the gatherer of the ripe grape.'

50. 'I am resolved rather to suffer among the woods, among the wild beasts' dens, and to carve my loves on the tender bark of the trees.'

51. 'First my Muse deigned lightly to sing in the Sicilian strain, and blushed not to dwell among the woods.'

52. 'Nor need you be ashamed of your flock, O Godlike poet; even fair Adonis once fed his sheep by the river-banks.'

53. Compare the following passage from one of the prose idyls of G. Sand: 'Depuis les bergers de Longus jusqu'à ceux de Trianon, la vie pastorale est un Éden parfumé où les âmes tourmentées et lassées du tumulte du monde ont essayé de se réfugier. L'art, ce grand flatteur, ce chercheur complaisant de consolations pour les gens trop heureux, a traversé une suite ininterrompue de *bergeries*. Et sous ce titre, *Histoire des bergeries*, j'ai souvent désiré de faire un livre d'érudition et de critique où j'aurais passé en revue tous ces différents rêves champêtres dont les hautes classes se sont nourries avec passion.' François le Champi.

54. 'Among the lonely haunts of the shepherds and the deep peace of Nature.'

55. 'One may not now hold converse with him from a tree or from a rock, like a maid and youth, as a maid and youth converse with one another.'

56. Compare the account of the origin of pastoral poetry in Müller's Literature of the Greeks.

57. 'But I attune the plaintive Ausonian melody.' Incertorum Idyll. I. 100-101. (Ed. Ahrens.)

58. Compare Symonds' Studies of Greek Poets, First Series, The Idyllists.

59. Wordsworth's great pastoral 'Michael' is a marked exception to this general statement. So, too, love can hardly be called the most prominent motive in Tennyson's 'Dora.'

60. 'Poured forth its rustic banter in responsive strains.'

61. Idyl vii. 97, vi. 2.

62. Idyl xi. 2-6, xiii. 2.

63. Preface to Poems by M. Arnold, First Series.

64. vii. 19, 20. . . .

65. x. 41. . . .

66.   'Next well-trimm'd
A crowd of shepherds, with as sunburnt looks
As may be read of in Arcadian books;
Such as sat listening round Apollo's pipe,
When the great deity, for earth too ripe,
Let his divinity o'erflowing die,
In music, through the vales of Thessaly.'

And again:—

'He seem'd,
To common lookers on, like one who dream'd
Of idleness in groves Elysian.'
Keats, Endymion.

67. 'Often, I remember, when a boy I used to pass in song the long summer days till sunset.'

68. 'Then he tells in song how Gallus as he strayed by the streams of Permessus was led by one of the sisters to the Aonian mount.'

'All those strains, which when attuned by Phoebus, Eurotas heard, enraptured, and bade his laurels learn by heart, he sings.'

69. Compare for this use of *mollis* in the sense of 'impressible' Cicero's description of his brother Quintus (Ep. ad Att. i. 17): 'Nam, quanta sit in Quinto fratre meo comitas, quanta iucunditas, quam mollis animus et ad accipiendam et ad deponendam iniuriam, nihil attinet me ad te, qui ea nosti, scribere.'

70. 'Fundit humo facilem victum *iustissima* tellus.'

71. 'There all alone he used to fling wildly to the mountains and the woods these unpremeditated words in unavailing longing.'

72. 'He, his snow-white side reposing on the tender hyacinth,—'

73. 'We leave the dear fields'—'Therefore you will still keep your fields, large enough for your desires'—'He allowed my herds to wander at their will, even as you see'—'Ah! the hope of all my flock, which she had just borne, she left on the bare flint pavement'—'Go on, my she-goats, once a happy flock, go on.'

74. This is the tone of the whole of the first Elegy of Tibullus, e.g.

> Ipse seram teneras maturo tempore vites
> Rusticus et facili grandia poma manu.
> Nec tamen interdum pudeat tenuisse bidentem,
> etc.

75. 'You are but a clown, Corydon, Alexis cares not for gifts.'

76. 'As if this could heal my madness.'

77. 'Ah! may the rough ice not cut thy tender feet.'

78. 'Shall I see you from afar hang from some bushy rock.'

> 'Here green Mincio forms a fringe of soft reeds along his bank.'

79. 'I shall not yield in song either to Thracian Orpheus or to Linus, though he be aided by his mother, he by his father, Orpheus by Calliope, Linus by the fair Apollo. Even Pan, should he strive with me with all Arcadia as umpire, even Pan would say that he was vanquished, with Arcadia as umpire.'

80. 'On this side, with its old familiar murmur, the hedge, your neighbour's boundary, on all the sweets of whose willow blossom the bees of Hybla have fed, will often gently woo you to sleep; on that from the foot of a high rock the song of the woodman will rise to the air; nor meanwhile will your darlings, the hoarse wood-pigeons, cease to coo, nor the turtle-dove to moan from the high elm-tree.'

81. Poems by Matthew Arnold. Memorial Verses:—

> 'He found us when the age had bound
> Our souls in its benumbing round,' etc.

82. 'Such charm is in thy song for us, O Godlike poet, as is to weary men the charm of deep sleep on the grass, as, in summer heat, it is to quench one's thirst in a sparkling brook of fresh water.'

83. 'What gifts shall I render to you, what gifts in recompense of such a strain: for neither the whisper of the coming south wind gives me such joy, nor the sound of shores beaten on by the wave, nor of rivers hurrying down through rocky glens.'

84. S. Coleridge's Memoirs, vol. ii. p. 411.

85. Life and Letters, vol. i. p. 371.

H. J. Rose (essay date 1942)

SOURCE: "*Molle atque facetum*" in *The "Eclogues" of Vergil*, University of California Press, 1942, pp. 24-44.

[*In the following essay, Rose reviews contemporary issues surrounding Vergil's* Eclogues, *commenting in particular on the criticism of Horace and on political and economic factors that may have influenced Vergil's poetry.*]

In trying to appreciate an ancient work, or any work not of our own age and country, it is often useful to discover what the critics said about it when it was new. It is our good fortune to have a contemporary mention of the **Eclogues** by no less a connoisseur than Horace, who says, in a passage mentioned at the end of the last chapter, that the Muses who delight in the country-side have granted to Vergil *molle atque facetum*. Since, in the comparatively small Latin vocabulary, a word is apt to have a confusing variety of meanings, or at least shades of meaning, we may begin by asking exactly what Horace meant by the epithets he applied to his friend's compositions. Certainly he did not mean that they were, or that their style was, soft and comical. *Mollis* can indeed mean "soft," that is to say, it can be used of sundry things which are so described in English, with reference to that quality to which our adjective refers. Vergil himself uses the word of grass, for instance; it is commonly enough used of a man who is what we call a "softy," generally with the further implication that he is rather nastily immoral.[1] But this is certainly not the only appropriate translation of the word. The legs of a thoroughbred colt are not soft, but rather hard and firm; yet Vergil again calls them *mollia*,[2] and the context makes it perfectly clear that he means "springy," "not stiff." If, then, a style is called *mollis*, it means, not that it is lacking in vigour, but that it is flexible, subtle, delicate. What *facetus* means we shall perhaps see most clearly if we look at its opposite, *inficetus*. This can mean "lacking in wittiness," for a good saying is *haud inficete dictum*, a thing uttered not without wit; *irridicule* can be used in much the same sense. But three good authors testify that this is far from exhausting the meaning. Cicero tells a story of a man who was neither *inficetus* nor uneducated, but nevertheless was outwitted by a subtle Syracusan.[3] He is manifestly emphasising the victim's shrewdness, not his power of making or seeing a joke. Catullus has a grievance against the taste of his age, which commonly compares a certain damsel, according to the poet afflicted with too big a nose, ill-shaped feet, eyes of rather indeterminate colour and coarse speech, with Lesbia (that is to say, Clodia), one of the most beautiful and fascinating women of the time.[4] His words are, *o saeclum insipiens et inficetum,* "O age devoid of taste and of perception." And, to go back from these moderns (for such they are) to the most ancient surviving well of Latin pure and undefiled, when Diniarchus, in Plautus,[5] sees that wily courtesan Phronesium for the first time after an absence of some length, she asks him why he is so *inficetus* as not to offer to kiss her; why, in modern phrase, he is such a boob. If therefore Vergil's poetry, in the **Bucolics,** has point and elegance, if it shows quick perception of what it would describe, it may be called *facetum* without our casting about to find jokes in it. Perhaps it may be said that the word comes fairly near meaning "humorous."

So much for what Horace thought of Vergil. Can a modern reader, supposing him to be tolerably well seen in the Latin tongue, that is to say, fairly well educated, and of passable abilities, *nec inficetus et satis litteratus,* like the man in Cicero's anecdote, honestly say that he finds in the pastoral poetry of our author the qualities of a flexible, delicate style and quick, rather humorous perception of a situation? If we would make trial, it happens that there are two of the poems which are peculiarly handy material for such research, in that they offer none but purely literary difficulties. To appreciate them, perhaps almost as fully as Vergil's contemporaries did, we do not need to solve the numerous really thorny problems which we shall have to face later on, but only to know something of the literature which he knew and to get rid of some monstrously bad criticism, too bad to be worth repeating or refuting if it did not clog the pages of a very popular edition of Vergil, that of John Conington.[6] This editor, in his preface to and notes on the second *Eclogue,* expresses himself in part as follows:

> A shepherd gives utterance to his love for a beautiful youth. . . . Parts of this *Eclogue* are closely modelled after the eleventh Idyl of Theocritus. . . . We should be glad [with Ribbeck] to believe it to be purely imaginary, though even then it is sufficiently degrading to Virgil [he then quotes some ancient scandal from the scholia, not worth mentioning even to rebut]. . . . The beeches (v. 3) and mountains (v. 5) . . . point to Sicily, not to Mantua, and Sicily is expressly mentioned in v. 21. . . . The strains of Corydon . . . are unpremeditated. . . . If Corydon is a slave, we must suppose with Keightley that, in falling into the Cyclops' language [i.e., in 19 sqq.] he is really thinking of the advantage he gets from having so much under his charge.

Of this precious critique it may be said that the first sentence, the statement that Sicily is mentioned, and the remark about the eleventh Idyll of Theokritos are true in fact. The rest well illustrates an important principle of criticism, that people who cannot appreciate poetry ought not to talk about it. This "degrading" effort happens to be one of the most exquisite and delicate offerings ever made to the Muses of the country-side; it is to the manners of the age, which the poet had no sufficient ground for ignoring, that we must attribute the choice of subject, a passion involving sexual inversion, then probably commoner than now and certainly more freely talked about. The object of Corydon's fancy is in any case a mere lay figure, who never appears on the scene at all; what matters is Corydon's feeling and the way he expresses it. The poet sets the scene for us in two lines:

> Corin the shepherd for Alexis burned,
> His master's minion; hopeless was his love.

The rest of the poem consists of the complaints which he uttered amid thick-growing beeches (line 3), which cast a deep shade; there was none to hear him except the woods and hills. Since, as we shall see later, there is little or no hilly country near Mantua and few or no beeches, which do not much love hot plains, it is pretty clear that Corydon's haunt is where one would expect a shepherd's to be, on one of the hill-pastures—of which more must be said in a later chapter, when we discuss, not so much where Vergil's father had his estate as what parts of the country the poet in his boyhood had opportunity to become acquainted with. For the present, all that is required is to suppose some region with hills and a certain amount of woodland in it. We may add, if the mention of the singer looking at his reflection in calm sea-water is to be taken literally, that it must not be far from the sea; but it will presently appear that this is a false clue.

The poem falls into a number of irregular stanzas, not marked off by any refrain nor keeping to a fixed number of lines. After the introduction of five verses, in which Vergil speaks in his own person to explain what it is all about, there are eight which describe the lover at noonday, five which contrast old loves with new, nine dealing with the Cyclops, six about the homely country-side, leading up to six more about Corydon's pipe and five concerning some wild kids which he has caught, then eleven which treat of the joys of the country. Now comes the awakening of the singer to his own folly; this is expressed in four lines, which are followed by a last appeal, in nine; and finally, five verses which tell of Corydon's resolve to mend his ways balance the five which brought him and his troubles before us at the beginning of the poem. Except that the Cyclops-song is roughly in the middle of the work, there is no very elaborate arrangement, in fact Vergil himself tells us that there is none. Corydon, he says (line 4), used to sing *haec incondita,* the disordered matter which follows. Dramatically, this is good, for who expects a sorely troubled rustic to produce, offhand, a masterpiece of balanced self-expression? Yet, for the dramatic monologue is a piece of art, the author must not plunge so far into ultra-realism as to make his work totally incoherent, and therefore uncouth and uninteresting. There are clearly defined limits to the imitation of human speech in art, whether the medium be play, poem, novel, or song. One can hear grunts and groans, half-finished sentences and phrases disconnected from what goes before and after, periods which start and never end, and all the vices of ill-trained or emotionally disordered speakers, to say nothing of singers, without either learning Latin or opening a book of verse. It needs but to walk abroad in any country and listen to the speech of its inhabitants. It is for the artist, whether in verse or prose, to make us catch what his more sensitive ears have already perceived, the music which sings behind and through the broken sounds of "real" life. And so Vergil subtly hints at a regular arrangement, blending the fits and starts of his shepherd's singing with the geometrically correct pattern which would lie at the back of a professional poet's or rhetorician's mind if he sat down to compose, on his own behalf, a plea to a hard-hearted love. At the back of his mind, and not on his page, unless he were a very uninspired hack; for as geometry, though an admirable basis for any visible scheme, whether it be the conventional designs of embroidery or the outlines of a great building, yet will not of itself give an artistically satisfactory shape unless the imagination of the artist supplements it, so such rhetorical devices as symmetry, indispensable to the artist in words, must rather lie concealed than appear, if he is to give us anything better than a cold and artificial utterance, uninstinct with the breath of life.

But let us look again at the opening verses. They are worth it, if only for a kind of sentimental value; for although it is probable that we still have a little of the poetry Vergil composed before he wrote the **Bucolics,** yet these are the very first which we are sure came from his pen.

> Formonsum pastor Corydon ardebat Alexim,
> delicias domini, nec quid speraret habebat.

The very sound of them, as of all good hexameters written in the two languages capable of them, is delightful to the ear. Long practice on Vergil's part must have gone to acquiring the power to fit together the words of his native speech into such perfect and smooth melody. And yet longer practice, several generations of it, had gone, before his first beginnings or even his birth, to the same task, from the days when Ennius set out to prove that this difficult Greek metre could be adapted to Latin and incidentally showed that he, small blame to him, did not yet quite know how. By the time of Catullus the Latins had learned, with many experiments and failures, how to write a good hexameter. Vergil was taking the further step of learning, and teaching, how to write a good group of hexameters, all of the same general pattern and yet no two exactly alike. But I must not stray too far into the intricacies of ancient metre, if only because I am myself no expert on the subject.[7] Let us rather consider the words our poet uses, and how he fits them together.

He is writing verse, and so his word-order is freer than that of prose, which in turn is freer than the order in English, for Latin has no grammatical meanings to express by the arrangement of its words; being inflected, it can entrust all that to the case-endings and verbal terminations, leaving the question which word should come first and what ones next to be settled by the more subtle rules of rhetoric. So Vergil begins with two words which serve as a kind of title to the whole poem, *formonsum pastor,* almost "Beauty and the Shepherd." He thus has said already that his shepherd did something which somehow affected or had relation to one more than commonly good to look upon. While giving the names of his two characters (he puts the shepherd's first, by the figure known as chiasmus), he tells us what the something was; Corydon was made in love with the beauty, *ardebat.* That, and not the prose *amabat.* Vergil has no desire to be elaborate here, but to tell us quite simply what subject he has chosen. As in the opening verses of the *Aeneid,* he is perfectly easy to understand. Here his perfect taste contrasts sharply with that of his imitator Statius, for example, who begins his *Thebaid* with two and a half clever lines which say no more than "I tell the story of the Theban Brothers," and then writes fifteen more to add "beginning with a mention of Oidipus."[8] But neither here nor there is Vergil prosaic in

his plainness. To write poetry it is necessary to know how to handle verse, as to compose music it is needful to have mastered harmony and other technicalities; and part of the lesson is the difference in phraseology and vocabulary between good verse and good prose. If prose happens to scan, that does not make it verse, but simply bad or at least inferior prose. There was once a mathematician who, to his own great annoyance when the error was pointed out to him, began a chapter of his treatise thus:

> No finite force, however great,
> Can stretch a string, however fine,
> Into a horizontal line
> Which shall be absolutely straight.

This, since it had the scansion and rime-system of a stanza of *In Memoriam,* obviously was not good prose, such as a scientific treatise deserves. But certainly it was not poetry, which does not deal in that kind of truth. I should hesitate also to say that it was verse, for it was not in English poetical diction. "Horizontal line" is a term of art, appropriate to a technical essay, and for that very reason inappropriate to verse. Vergil, by the time he wrote the *Eclogues,* knew when and how to leave the language of Latin prose for that kind of Latin poetical speech which suited his style and subject; *ardebat* was one bit of it, and another came in the next verse, *quid speraret* where prose would have said *quod;* "had not how to hope" for "had nothing to hope."

It is a pity that so many moderns, trying to run before they can walk, seem to despise such necessary learning when they set about composing poetry in their own tongues. I could give, but that the task would be somewhat tedious and invidious, examples, not from those pretenders to art who appear to prefer the promptings of their own untutored senses to the whole experience of the centuries of English poetry, but from writers of real merit who err unbecomingly from ignorance of just such elementary things as Vergil knows and observes in these two lines. But aesthetic criticism, unless very good, is very wearisome and it is more germane to the present subject to consider what manner of songs they were which Corydon sang love-lorn under his shady beeches.

He begins with a straightforward appeal to Alexis' pity and asks if his love would have him die: *mori me denique coges?* The source here, as so often in the poem, is Theokritos, who makes a disconsolate lover[9] ask a hard-hearted mistress if she would have him hang himself. Vergil, in adapting the phrase, shows that he knows how to do it, and makes the necessary alteration to fit a close rendering to the conventions of his own tongue. Greek can without offence use in verse the plain word for "hang", . . . Latin cannot; it belongs to prose to say *suspendio necare, laqueo uitam finire,* or the like. When it is absolutely necessary to speak of that way of putting an end to one's own or another's life, Vergil knows how to do it, or did by the time he composed the *Aeneid;* Queen Amata there[10]

> nodum informis leti trabe nectit ab alta.
> Bound to a beam the knot of hideous death.

But here it is not necessary, so he contents himself with the plain *mori,* which is as good in verse as in prose. Corydon goes on to borrow from another passage in Theokritos and combine it with a third. The language of the next two lines smacks, as it is meant to do, of a totally different noonday scene in the seventh Idyll, the Harvest Festival. There, Theokritos and some of his friends are gathering, on a hot day in late summer, at the estate of certain of their acquaintance in Kos. As he trudges along the dusty road under the noonday sun, Simichidas (that is, Theokritos) is asked by another wayfarer what he is doing out at such a time, "when even the lizard sleeps in the dyke." This is manifestly a country proverb for intense heat and, like many such sayings, contains a jocular exaggeration; my own experience of Greek and Italian weather does not include any day when the lizards found it too hot to sun themselves.[11] Vergil, then, gives us the Theokritean lizard.

> Now even cattle seek the cooling shade,
> Now even lizards hide beneath the thorn,
> While Thestylis, for reapers tired with heat,
> Pounds thyme and garlic in an odorous mess.

Corydon being away from roads and farmsteads in his lonely pasture, there are no dykes for the lizards to run into, so the poet makes them shelter under thorn-bushes. As to Thestylis, while I would not go so far as to measure a poet's excellence by the strength of the scents arising from his verses, I do think that the best artists in words know how to appear to all the senses through the devious channel of the ear. In the hot Italian noon, smells carry far, and the national fondness for strong and pungent herbs is not a thing of yesterday, nor the day before. But to return to Theokritos, whom we have left for a moment, since Thestylis and her salad-making are none of his invention, he puts into the mouth of a girl using love-magic by night a pretty piece of inverted "pathetic fallacy."

> Now sleep the waters and the storm-winds sleep,
> But not the cares that ravage my poor heart.[12]

Vergil takes the hint, and takes it after the manner of a great and a Mediterranean poet. The other period of calm and stillness is noonday, the hour of the siesta, which is no modern innovation, but part of classical usage.[13] In this heavy-scented time of sleep Corydon has no peace, as Theokritos' Simaitha has none:

> But in the glare, while still I track thy steps,
> With me cicalas make the bushes ring.

A few lines follow of contrast between this new love and the older ones, a sunburned country lad called Menalcas and a cross-grained girl named Amaryllis,[14] with a word of warning to Alexis not to put too much trust in his lovely white complexion, carefully sheltered of course from the sun, as was the manner of city beauties of both sexes. Alexis had, it would seem,

> a skin
> As clean and white as privet when it flowers,[15]

but Corydon reminds him that no one gathers privet-flowers, but prefers the dark *uaccinium,* whatever that may be:[16]

> alba ligustra cadunt, uaccinia nigra leguntur.

This bit of botanising morality over, we come to the most misunderstood thing in the poem. I cannot get the sweetness of it into English, but perhaps a translation will carry with it some slight remnant of the humour.

> Thou scorn'st me, askest not what man I be,
> How rich in herds, how wealthy in milk as white
> As snow; mine are the thousand lambs that roam
> Sicily's hills, and still my pails are full,
> In summer's heat and winter's cold the same.
> My songs are those that once Amphion sang,
> The Theban herdsman, for his cattle-call,
> On Attic Aracynthus. For my face,
> 'Tis none so ugly, for I saw it late
> Reflected off-shore in a windless sea.
> Judge thou; if mirrors lie not, I dare cope
> Even with Daphnis' self, that comely wight.

This passage contains a designed absurdity, which Vergil's learned readers (he did not write for the unlearned) were meant to notice, though the later commentators, Servius and the rest, did not and missed the joke entirely. Corydon has been at some pains to remember the name of Amphion and his upbringing among shepherds, and even to get him on the right hill with his herd;[17] Arakynthos is the name of some high ground in Boiotia, also of a mountain in Aitolia, which does not now concern us,[18] and its suffix shows that it is a very ancient name, older than the coming of the Greeks to the country. But the singer is led by association of sounds to think of and distort another famous Theban name, that of Aktaion, and so proudly brings out the fine-sounding Greek line

> Amphion Dircaeus in Actaeo Aracyntho,

thus putting the hill on the wrong side of the frontier, for *Actaeus* can only mean "Attic." For the rest, he ministers to his own self-respect by bringing himself and his doings into association partly with the sons of Zeus and Antiope, but still more with Polyphemos. He is for the moment not poor Corin the slave-herdsman, but the amorous giant, scorned, not by a brat from the city, but by Galateia the mermaid. The Sicilian hills are of course part of the setting and throw no light whatever on the scene of the poem, the thousand lambs are an improvement on the Theokritean Cyclops' flock, which had a thousand head altogether,[19] and the milk seems to be a poeticising of the original's cheese; for some reason, it does not seem to have been elegant to call cheese by its name in Augustan verse,[20] but no one minds in a Greek pastoral. The singer continues with another Cyclops-passage, this time from a less-known Idyll, the sixth, where the giant says,

> For truly even in looks I am not so bad as they make me out; indeed it was but t'other day that I peered into the sea, when it was calm, and to my judgement my

beard showed handsome and also my one eye, while from my teeth there came a glitter whiter than from Parian marble; but lest the evil eye should hurt me, I spat thrice into my bosom, as old Kotyttaris had taught me.

All this borrowing is but pastoral convention; Theokritos is a shepherd, so is Corydon, and one shepherd may be assumed to know another's verses, supposed to have been heard, not read.

But modern commentators have introduced new merriment into the lines, at least for those readers who have any feeling for literature and any power to see the fun lurking behind bad criticism, by their ridiculous assumption that Corydon is singing here in his own person and the consequent solemnity with which they inform us that a man of ordinary stature could hardly use the sea for a mirror and that Corydon is not in a position to own property on a large scale and is not, or should not be, in Sicily. Some day perhaps there will arise a critic who will take Victorian literature for his subject and interpret it through the eyes of A.D. 3000 or so. He will find, it may be, a passage in which one of the characters, in a drawing-room of the 'nineties, sings "I am the Bandalero," and will gravely take the novelist to task, pointing out that on page 63 he mentioned that the singer was a very honest tradesman and no bandit, while pages 123 and 258 make it clear that he had never been in Spain and was quite ignorant of Spanish. And the criticism will be quite as good as that on Vergil, or on Corydon, for choosing to sing here the song of the love-lorn Cyclops instead of describing naturalistically the feelings of an Italian herdsman. Instead of blaming an ancient author for doing, without elaborate explanations, what a modern perhaps would not do in like case, it is better to examine ancient literature a little more closely, including a poem which we know served Vergil as a model, the sixth Theokritean idyll, already mentioned. In that, two shepherd-boys have a friendly singing-match while their flocks rest at noon by a spring. Both of them sing of the Cyclops, one addressing him and teasing him about Galateia, the other assuming his part and singing his song for him. Whether or not real Sicilian shepherds were fond of ballads about their local monster, it is pastoral convention to suppose they were, and for my own part I am very ready to take Theokritos' word for a fact which he must have known if it was a fact, since I can see no sufficient reason why he should invent it if it was not. But be that as it may, once he had become a classic, anyone else writing about shepherds and their songs had his paramount authority for such a theme to put into their mouths, just as he had for expressing their songs and their conversation alike by hexameters. To quarrel with Vergil for following authority in this respect, still more to imagine that he is not following it but making his *pastor* speak of himself in this Gargantuan manner, is to show oneself incapable of understanding what a pastoral poet would be at, or at least to condemn him for writing in this vein at all; in which case, why be at the trouble of reading him?

Corydon goes on to praise the unkempt country-side, *sordida rura,* and here I think we have less of the learned

Vergil than of Vergil the country-bred boy. It is hardly the scholar so much as the rustic who knows the exact kind of plant from which to pluck a tough switch for driving a flock of kids. It was the *uiridis hibiscus,* which our botanists say is marsh mallow.[21] But it is worth looking at this passage a little closely to see how convention mingles with realism. This Greek-derived genre ought to have a Greek flavour; therefore the shepherds of Corydon's acquaintance do not worship any Italian deity such as Faunus or Inuus, but are devout followers of Pan. It is true that to the theologians of Vergil's day the Greek and the Italian gods were identical.

> Here in the woods we'll mimic in our song
> Pan, him who first conjoined with wax the reeds,
> Who cares for sheep and for the shepherd cares.

There follows a section, pretty but not very remarkable, for Vergil, on the joys of the country, especially its flowers and fruits. Now comes the awakening. Corydon reminds himself that he is of the country and could offer Alexis nothing that would really please him, or if he could, would be outbid by his master (who for the purposes of the poem has a Greek name, Iollas, like the rest). But, as he rouses himself to a sense of his own folly and consequent neglect of his work, there comes a half-humorous consolation in the shape of a last appeal.

> Whom do you fly, poor fool? the gods themselves
> And Dardan Paris in the woods have dwelt.
> Let Pallas have her towns, she founded them,
> The woods be all our joy. The raging lioness
> Follows the wolf, the wolf the playful kid,
> The kid the clover, each his own desire;
> So Corin for Alexis. Look, the ploughs
> Are lifted and the oxen drag them home,
> The sun descends, the shadows double long,
> Yet love consumes me; love no measure knows.
> Poor Corin, why so moonstruck? See, your vines
> Hang on their elms half-pruned. There's work to do;
> At least take withies, take a pliant reed,
> Weave thee a basket. This Alexis lost,
> Thou'lt find another will not be so coy.

Vergil is an Alexandrian on one side of his literary ancestry, and Alexandrians, when they quote or half-quote, do their reader the compliment of supposing that he knows the context of the quotation and can apply it if necessary. It is easy to do so here, for Corydon is simply giving us more of Polyphemos:[22]

> Eh, Cyclops, Cyclops, whither have thy wits wandered? If thou'ldst go and weave cheese-baskets and gather fodder to take to thy lambs, it were better sense in thee. Milk the cow that's at hand; why run after the one that flees? Thou'lt find another Galateia, belike, fairer than this one.

Having just said that gods and princes lived in the woods, that is to say, the untilled land used for pasture and forestry, Corydon once more adds his favourite giant, also of the "woods," being a herdsman like himself. Well, then; if the matter is looked at aright, is there not something fine in being a lovesick herdsman, like the great ones of fable, Apollo when he longed for Admetos' society, Paris while yet unrecognised of his royal kin, Polyphemos while he wooed Galateia? Come, come; things are not going so badly for a poor rustic if he is matched with gods, heroes, and giants in his very woes. Corydon goes away with something of a swagger, thanks to his music and his fancies, thinking of himself as somehow great and desirable, in the same class as the uncouth but mighty monster who, as some say, did after all win his Galateia and become by her the father of the whole race of Gauls.[23]

Compared with the second *Eclogue,* the third is slight and has less originality, yet it is not without a contribution of Vergil's own to this branch of poetry. Essentially, it is an adaptation of Theokritos' fifth Idyll, whereof a little, part of the opening quarrel between the herd-boys, was quoted in the last chapter. Menalcas and Damoetas meet, pass from rude jests to downright abuse of each other, and in the course of their dispute mention music, which makes one challenge the other to a contest then and there. There is a preliminary wrangle as to what the stake shall be; one wants to wager a heifer, the other dare not for fear of his parents, who always count the beasts at night. Finally they agree to stake a pair of carved wooden bowls. Palaemon, another herdsman, appears on the scene just as they need an umpire, and they begin to cap couplets very prettily, until Palaemon finally decides he cannot prefer either and the match is a draw. A later chapter will have more to say about the fashion of the contest; for the present we may note that, being the kind of imitator he is, Vergil is not content to follow one Theokritean model. He commences with the opening line of the third Idyll and ends with the drawn match of the sixth. He is not at his best in the more colloquial parts of the work, for Latin hexameters, pastoral or other, pay a price for their stateliness in that they cannot be quite natural, as the more flexible Greek can, without ceasing to be pleasing in sound and rhythm. Four men of great talent tried the hexameter for writing about everyday matters of life and conduct, and of these, Lucilius produced some of the worst specimens of Latin metre ever read or heard, but kept the naturalism of language to a greater degree than most of his imitators; Persius combined a designed ruggedness of metre with the most extraordinarily contorted style that has come down to us under the name of a respectable author; while Juvenal produced rather machine-made lines embodying rhetoric of the most effective, bitter, and completely artificial. Only Horace ever managed to be both natural and elegant, and his secret was born and died with him. Vergil had not that kind of genius. He could not write like Terence in a non-Terentian metre, nor, probably, would he have succeeded in those measures which Terence himself used. He gets away therefore from the slanging-match as soon as he decently can, to imitate yet another passage of Theokritos, the description of the cup in the first Idyll. He does not here translate the Greek passage nor imitate it closely, but uses it as a starting-point for giving us his own idea of a piece of artistry in wood by an imaginary craftsman. Soon after, when the umpire arrives to decide the match between

the shepherd-boys, Vergil again slips away from his immediate subject into three lines (not undramatic nor without significance, as shall presently be shown) of pure poetry. Palaemon speaks:

> Say on, for now soft grass provides our seat,
> The birthtime's coming for each field and tree,
> The woods in leaf, the year at its most fair.

To anyone who knows Italy, the picture is complete; the grass is fit to sit upon, as it is only in the cooler parts of the year or the country.[24] It is springtime.

The two lads now begin to sing against each other, one starting with two lines and the other answering with two of like style and subject. The matter of the forty-four verses which they sing varies from love to literature, and so to the troubles of countrymen (snakes, treacherous streams, burning heat), then back to love again, ending with a pair of riddles which are distinguished by the fact that no one hitherto has succeeded in solving them to the general satisfaction.[25] The literary references include one to Pollio, which we shall have occasion to deal with in a later chapter, and one to that famous couple Bavius and Mevius, poetasters so obscure that we should not know they ever existed but for their having annoyed Vergil and Horace, of whom the latter devoted a little poem to calling Mevius a "stinker" and genially wishing him ill luck on a voyage,[26] while the former here pairs them (it would indeed appear that they were close friends)[27] and remarks that he who does not hate the one is at liberty to love the other, but only a fool big enough to use foxes for draught-cattle or try to milk hegoats would do either.[28]

But the end of the poem contains a wholly original touch. Generally the umpire in these contests is a mere lay figure, at most giving the author's opinion on the songs of the competitors. Vergil's Palaemon suddenly comes to life— indeed he had given signs of it in his charming little description of the spring weather—and in a few lines (the best of the ancients liked their psychology and character-drawing brief and good) is sketched for us as a romantic and amatory poet, probably young, not much older than the singing shepherds themselves. His judgement is no more than a modest refusal to judge, and makes it clear that his mind has been busy at least as much with his own thoughts and desires as with what they have been singing.

> Non nostrum inter uos tantas componere lites;
> et uitula tu dignus et hic, et quisquis amores
> aut metuet dulcis aut experietur amaros.[29]

> So great a quarrel is not mine to end;
> Ye both deserve the heifer; so do all
> Who fear love's honey or who taste its gall.

The umpire's absence of mind is betrayed by two little points. In the first place, the fears and woes of lovers have hardly been mentioned, and love has by no means been the only theme. In the second, the heifer has not been wagered. Before Palaemon came up, the stake had been decided, and the offer to make it a heifer declined; he does not know what they are singing for, but merely assumes that so earnest a contest must be for a considerable prize. Then who is the third, indeterminate claimant, the person, "whoever he is," to render Vergil's perfect verse into very plain prose, "that either shall fear love in its sweetness or taste it in its bitterness"? The two competitors, after a pious couplet apiece, to Iuppiter and Apollo respectively, have started with the names of loves—Galatea, Amyntas, Delia. It is obvious enough that they are bragging of affairs which have no existence but in their own imaginations, for they are still very young, and no great credence can be placed in the sincerity of a passion which calls a mistress first Galatea and then Phyllis. Of love's bitterness neither has said or hinted anything. But Palaemon is of a different cast of mind, a kind of shepherd whose existence has been assumed at least since Theokritos wrote his third Idyll, the passionate lover. The convention, like many others, may well go back ultimately to truth and nature, but in any case it exists. As the serenader in Theokritos (if we may call that a serenade which is not sung in the evening) addresses a hard-hearted and unresponsive Amaryllis, so we may suppose Palaemon to have spent much thought and song over his love, whoever she may be, and it needs but a few notes of music to set his mind on that familiar theme once more. I much doubt if he has heard more than the amatory lines which came early in the contest, unless it be a passing *Phyllida amo ante alias,* "Phyllis is my chief love," from Menalcas. Therefore, when the singers pause, as they do unbidden, it dawns on the poor umpire that he has not really been listening, and is in no position to decide which has done better. So he hastily declares a draw, and assures them that they have sung enough:

> claudite iam riuos, pueri; sat prata biberunt.
> Shut off the waters, for the fields are moist.

No one, at this time of day, can be sure that he sees in Vergil all, or nearly all, that Horace saw and admired. On the contrary, it is probable that we miss many delicate points of language and allusion that were perfectly clear to him and to other educated contemporaries of the poet. But I think we may fairly claim to see those qualities which he mentions and which I have tried to point out. There is in these two poems, perhaps the simplest and least interesting of the ten, a power of passing easily from theme to theme and from mood to mood, from the desperate earnestness of Corydon's passion to the slightly ridiculous figure of Corydon himself; from the rough chaff of Damoetas and Menalcas to their dainty singing and from that again to the slight but vivid sketch of their umpire, with his love of poetry and beauty and his preoccupation with his own affairs. This may serve to show why Horace styled his friend's work *molle,* flexible. And as to the humour, surely that is present in works which handle with so light a touch matter over which it would be quite easy to grow sentimental and rhetorical, letting us see at once that Corydon's woes are a trifle absurd and that, for the moment, they are the most important things in the universe to Corydon. For it is the destiny of the little man that his affairs, however intensely he may feel them, still remain little in

comparison with the scheme of things and that to make them out important must always be just a shade absurd to the impartial observer. It is not snobbishness but sound judgement which lies behind the old precept of critics, that the proper subjects for tragedy are kings and princes, not common folk.

Now this sense of humour, a rare thing among Latins, which Vergil shows that he had, is nothing but a particular form of the sense of proportion, which is none too common in any people or age. That sense is put to an acid test in the next group of *Eclogues* we have now to examine. Vergil could see that his imaginary shepherds were not space-filling figures and became less, not more impressive when they tried to make themselves out to be such. Could he continue to see troubles and misfortunes in so sane a light when they were his own? Was he capable of realising that although he or his household might suffer, the world at large could not be expected to join in their complaints; in fact, that Publius Vergilius Maro, his father and his friends, might weigh little heavier in the scales of the world than a slave-herdsman, who might be very wretched, or very angry, and yet leave the district of Mantua generally content and prosperous? Such detachment needs, not merely native humour or sense of proportion, but more than a slight tinge of philosophy, inborn or acquired. Now Vergil had had a philosophic training, and, if the little poem which generally stands fifth in the *Catalepton* is really his, as many think, he had been an enthusiastic pupil. He was, or had been, an Epicurean, and Epicurus, like most of the later teachers and their followers, made it his chief task to liberate the mind from the disturbances which it would otherwise suffer in this mortal life. So Vergil, if indeed it was he, had thought when he looked for the reward of "a life set free from every care"[30] as a result of his studies under his teacher Siron. If we are to judge how he faced his share of earthly miseries, we must first make up our minds what exactly these were and then ask concerning his reaction to them. We of today, used as we became to two or three fresh crises every month till the last of them once more plunged Europe into open and declared hostilities, do not need much imagination to realise how easy it was for a man of Vergil's generation to fall a prey to what we inelegantly term "jitters," while Latin more plainly styled it *formido,* fear. Economic distress, again, is nothing new, although Vergil's word for it is *egestas,* and it was extremely common when Octavian, afterwards the Emperor Augustus, was fighting for his position and his supremacy. Both these evils seem to have come the poet's way, and he spoke his mind about them after his fashion. . . .

Notes

1. For example, Paris is *mollis* when he runs away from Diomedes (Horace, *carm.,* I, 15, 31); a lustful woman accuses Horace of being *mollis* (*epod.,* 12, 16), meaning that he is not a vigorous lover; *mollis inertia, epod.,* 14, 1, is unmanly idleness; *molles querelae* are womanish complaints, *carm.,* II, 9, 17; valiant soldiers are *non molles uiri, epod.,* 1, 10.

Catullus puts *mollis* alongside an even plainer word in lampooning Thallus, 25, 1, and examples in Martial are not far to seek, e.g., III, 73, 4.

2. *Georg.*, III, 76: mollia crura reponit, "puts his feet down springily."

3. Cicero, *de off.*, III, 58.

4. Catullus, 43.

5. Plautus, *Truc.*, 355. See further Excursus I, below.

6. I use the fifth ed., revised successively by Nettleship and Haverfield. Both these good scholars seem to have been withheld by mistaken piety from pruning the original editor's appallingly bad criticisms. For some good comments on the form of this Eclogue, see R. Maxa, *Die strophische Gliederung an der zweiten und zehnten Ekloge des Vergilius nachgewiesen,* Trebitsch, 1882.

7. For consideration of some curious features of Vergil's prosody, see W. F. J. Knight, *Accentual Symmetry in Vergil* (Oxford, Blackwell, 1939).

8. Statius, *Theb.*, I, 1-17.

9. Theokr., III, 9, απαγξασθαι με ποιησεις; (so, not ποιησεις.) Cf. in general E. Pfeiffer, *Virgils Bukolika* (Stuttgart, Kohlhammer, 1933).

10. *Aen.*, XII, 603.

11. Theokr., Id. VII, 22; see Rose in *C. R.*, XLI (1927), p. 100.

12. Theokr., Id. II, 38–39. . . .

13. See for instance Ovid, *Amores,* I, 5, 2.

14. Cf. Rose, *op. cit.,* p. 99.

15. Tennyson, *Walking to the Mail.* See, for the identification of botanical names in Vergil, J. Sergeaunt, *The Trees, Shrubs and Plants of Virgil* (Oxford, Blackwell, 1920); on pp. 67 sq. the author explains the meaning of *ligustra* here and cites the English parallel.

16. Sergeaunt, pp. 56 sqq.

17. Cf. Propertius, III, 15, 41-42: uictorque canebat/paeana Amphion rupe, Aracynthe, tua.

18. See Steph. Byzant., *s. u.* 'Αρα κυνθος, who cites Rhianos; Serv. on *Ecl.*, II, 24.

19. Theokr., Id. XI, 34.

20. Hence Vergil calls it *pressi copia lactis, Ecl.,* I, 81; contrast, e.g., Theokr., Id. V, 87; XI, 36.

21. Theokr., Id. VI, 34 sqq.

22. Sergeaunt, p. 54.

23. Theokr., Id. XI, 72 sqq.

24. Rose, *Handb. of Gk. Myth.,* pp. 39 sq., note 55. The story is of course quite late and artificial, but may have been known to Vergil.

25. See Excursus II, below.

26. The riddles are (lines 104-107):

D. Dic quibus in terris, et eris mihi magnus Apollo,
      tris pateat caeli spatium non amplius ulnas.
M. Dic quibus in terris inscripti nomina regum
      nascantur flores, et Phyllida solus habeto.

Servius gives two interpretations of the former riddle, one that it alludes to the tomb of a certain Caelius, luxuriosi cuiusdam, qui uenditis omnibus rebus et consumptis tantum modo sibi spatium reseruauit quod sepulchro sufficeret. This is obviously a piece of scholiast's invention, made to suit the occasion, and may safely be neglected. His other solution is that it means the famous well at Syene which was said to have the sun directly at its zenith at noon of the summer solstice, or simpliciter . . . cuiuslibet loci puteus, since the sky would show no more than three cubits wide from the bottom of it. This is yet more absurd, and a better than either is the modern guess (attributed in De la Rue's note to "Ciacconius et Cerdanus") that *caeli* here means *mundi* in the sense of the ritual pit, or rather pits, so called. Unfortunately we have no information of how wide they were, but it is quite possible that Vergil knew and that some of them, e.g., that dug in founding a city, were no wider than 4½ ft. Servius is much more plausible on the second riddle; the flowers are *hyacinthi,* and *nomina regum* is a rhetorical plural for *nomen regis,* the markings on the plant, by one explanation, spelling the name of Aias.

27. Hor., *epod.,* 10.

28. For refs., see my *Handb. of Lat. Lit.,* p. 345.

29. Lines 90-91: qui Bauium non odit, amet tua carmina, Meui,/atque idem iungat uolpes et mulgeat hircos. Servius glosses by faciat ea quae contra naturam sunt; the metaphors smack of country proverbs.

30. Simple though Vergil's language is, the lines have been erected into a crux by certain interpreters, ancient and modern, partly because *aut* and *haut* or *haud* tended to be confused in writing as they were in pronunciation, the *h* becoming silent in late Latin. Servius explains well enough: et tu et hic digni estis uitula et quicunque similis uestri est; nam supra unus dixerat "triste lupus stabulis, maturis frugibus imbres, arboribus uenti, nobis Amaryllidis irae" (80 sq.), item aliter, "dulce satis umor, depulsis arbutus haedis, lenta salix feto pecori, mihi solus Amyntas" (82 sq.), ad cuius amatoris similitudinem pertinet "aut metuet dulces," etc. But Filargirius writes amazing rubbish: si metuet dulces, experietur amaros, sin autem non metuet amaros, experietur dulces. He apparently read *haut* for the second *aut.* Hirtzel, following Graser, reads *haud* both times; I leave the honoured shades of these scholars the task of determining what, if anything, the lines may then be supposed to mean.

31. *Catal.,* 5, 10; for the reading, see chap. iv, note 38, end.

Excursus I

(Cf. Note 6)

The phrase *molle atque facetum* has a little literature of its own, ancient and modern, with the findings of which I am partly but not wholly in agreement. Setting aside commentators on Horace himself and on Vergil, we may begin with Quintilian, *inst. orat.,* VI, 3, 2, who says truly: facetum quoque non tantum circa ridicula opinor consistere, neque enim diceret Horatius facetum carminis genus natura concessum esse Vergilio. decoris hanc magis et excultae cuiusdam elegantiae appellationem puto. ideoque in epistula Cicero haec Bruti refert [the letter in question is lost save for this quotation] uerba; ne illi sunt pedes faceti ac deliciis [?] ingredienti molles; quod conuenit cum illo Horatiano, e.q.u. Brutus' acquaintance, that is, had not exactly witty feet, but a subtle and delicate way of walking, especially under the circumstances which the probably currupt *deliciis* is meant to indicate. Among moderns, the following have all had something to contribute. L. Bayard, in *Rev. de Philologie,* XXVIII (1904), No. 3, p. 213, takes both words as adjectival, agreeing with *epos* in the preceding line (Horace, *sat.,* i, 10, 43, after discussing the merits of Fundanus in comedy, Pollio in tragedy: forte epos acer/ut nemo Varius ducit; molle atque facetum e.q.s.), but admits that, even so, Horace refers or may refer to matter as well as style. A *molle epos* might be a verse or poem which treated of *molles,* or *mollia,* certainly. R. Pichon, *ibid.,* XXXII (1908), pp. 64 sq., adds that *mollis* is especially used by elegiac poets of their own works. Going into the matter more thoroughly, Professor C. N. Jackson (*Harvard Studies in Class. Phil.,* XXV, 1914, pp. 117-137), notes the use of both adjectives in rhetoric and concludes that both are appropriate to the elegance and delicacy of the *genus tenue* affected by the Atticising writers of the day, whereof Pollio was one. This is true, but may not at once be converted into the proposition that wherever a writer, especially a master of words like Horace, uses them of literature he means no more than that; the generic sense is not swallowed up by the specific and technical. Moreover, as M. B. Ogle shows (*Am. Four. Phil.,* XXXVII, 1916, pp. 327-332), *mollis* is used with a wider range of meaning, even in rhetoric. It was not the word his contemporaries would use of the rather harsh style of Pollio, and it is by no means employed only of the *genus tenue.* Agreeing on the whole with him, Charles Knapp (*ibid.,* XXXVIII, pp. 194-199) quotes with approval the explanation of Arthur Sidgwick and one or two others of *facetum* as "playful," which is not far from the meaning "humorous" which I incline to give it.

Excursus II

(Cf. Note 26)

I find that it is necessary to point out in more detail that Palaemon in *Ecl.,* III, 55-57, means spring and not summer, for by no means the worst of the writers on

Vergil, A. Klotz in *Neue Fahrb. f. das klass. Altertum,* XLV/XLVI (1920), p. 148, still insists that the latter season is meant. Let us analyse and interpret the lines closely. I have spoken of the first, dicite, quandoquidem in molli consedimus herba. The grass is soft, therefore the weather has not been hot for long; and the shepherd-boys are near home, 34, therefore they are not in a hill pasture; therefore they are in the lowlands and yet they can sit on the grassy ground in comfort and their flocks have apparently plenty to feed upon (that Aegon's ewes are milked twice in an hour, 5, is of course Menalcas' scandalous exaggeration, but it is not the sort of joke which could be made of beasts with a poor yield of milk; cf. 30, where a young cow has milk enough for two calves and two milk-pails over). 55, et nunc omnis ager, nunc omnis parturit arbos. *Parturit,* not *parit,* so the "birth-pangs of the sheath" (κάλυκος εν λοχευμασιν, Aesch., *Agam.,* 1392) are not yet come; in other words, everything is showing signs of growth, but nothing is mature yet. 56, nunc frondent siluae, the woods are leaving, nothing being said of the size of the leaves; nunc formosissimus annus, which in itself should be enough for anyone who has read the ancient authors; spring and no other season is the proverbially lovely time.

Bruno Snell (essay date 1953)

SOURCE: "Arcadia: The Discovery of a Spiritual Landscape" in *Virgil: A Collection of Critical Essays,* edited by Steele Commager, Prentice Hall, Inc., 1966, pp. 14-27.

[*In the essay below, originally published in 1953, Snell investigates Vergil's manipulation of the pastoral Arcadian setting in the* Eclogues, *contending that Vergil synthesized Theocritus's Arcadia with the mythological world.*]

Arcadia was discovered in the year 42 or 41 B.C. Not, of course, the Arcadia of which the encyclopedia says: 'The central alpine region of the Peloponnesus, limited off on all sides from the other areas of the peninsula by mountains, some of them very high. In the interior, numerous ridges divide the secetion into a number of small cantons.' This humdrum Arcadia had always been known; in fact it was regarded as the home of Pelasgus, the earliest man. But the Arcadia which the name suggests to the minds of most of us to-day is a different one; it is the land of shepherds and shepherdesses, the land of poetry and love, and its discoverer is Virgil. How he found it, we are able to tell in some detail, thanks to the researches of Ernst Kapp.[1] The historian Polybius who came from the humdrum Arcadia cherished a great affection for his country. Although there was not much of interest to be related of this land behind the hills, he could at least report (4.20) that the Arcadians were, from the days of their infancy onwards, accustomed to practice the art of singing, and that they displayed much eagerness in organizing musical contests. Virgil came across this passage when he was composing his shepherd songs, the ***Eclogues,*** and at once understood it to refer to the Arcadian shepherds, for Arcadia was shepherds' country and the home of Pan, the god of the herdsmen, inventor of the syrinx. And so Virgil located the lives and the poetic contests of his shepherds in Arcadia. 'You Arcadians,' he says (10.32), 'who are alone experienced in song.' He mentions two Arcadians 'who are equal in song, and equal to giving response in turn' (7.5). He remarks on mount Maenalus in Arcadia 'which ever hears the love songs of the shepherds and Pan blowing his pipe' (8.23). He calls upon Arcadia to judge a contest between the singers (4.58). The shepherds whom Virgil introduces in his earliest eclogue are not Arcadian but Sicilian (2.21): this setting comes to him from the idylls of Theocritus, the Hellenistic poet who served as the model for all Roman pastoral poetry. Since the shepherds of Theocritus, too, indulged in responsive singing and competitions, Virgil had no difficulty in linking them with the Arcadians of Polybius.

Theocritus who was born in Syracuse had written about the herdsmen of his own country. Meanwhile, however, Sicily had become a Roman province, and her shepherds had entered the service of the big Roman landlords. In this new capacity they had also made their way into Roman literature; witness Lucilius' satire on his trip to Sicily. But they could no longer be mistaken for the shepherds of song and love. Thus Virgil needed a new home for his herdsmen, a land far distant from the sordid realities of the present. Because, too, pastoral poetry did not mean to him what it had meant to Theocritus, he needed a far-away land overlaid with the golden haze of unreality. Theocritus had given a realistic and slightly ironical description of the herdsmen of his country engaged in their daily chores; Virgil regarded the life of the Theocritean shepherds as a sublime and inspired existence. If we look at the beginning of his earliest bucolic poem: 'The shepherd Corydon loved fair Alexis,' it has a different ring from anything comparable that Theocritus might have said. In Greek these names were hardened by daily usage; in Virgil they are borrowed words, cultured and strange, with a literary, an exotic flavour, like the names of the mythical heroes which Virgil had drawn from Greek poetry. The effect of this upon the persons of the shepherds was decisive. Later, when Virgil himself had become an example to be followed, the shepherds of European literature were called Daphnis and Amyntas, but they too were awkwardly out of place in the Cotswolds, or the Cornish heath. In the end, when Johann Heinrich Voss by-passed Virgil and re-established Theocritus as his model, he gave the protagonists of his idylls the good German peasant names Krischen and Lene.

Virgil, then, did not aspire to furnish a realistic portrayal of everyday life, but searched for a land which could harbour herdsmen named Corydon and Alexis, Meliboeus and Tityrus, a land which might be a fitting domicile for everything that seems to be implied in such poetic names. In the tenth Eclogue, the latest in date of writing, which more than any other pastoral piece by Virgil stresses the Arcadian milieu, the poet Gallus has been set down in Ar-

cady and there finds himself in the company of the gods and shepherds. The Roman god Silvanus and two Greeks, Apollo god of song and Pan the deity of the Arcadian herdsmen, express their sympathy with his unhappy love. How would this be possible in so near and familiar a setting as Sicily? This scene too has its precedent in Theocritus, but there (1.77ff.) the gods Hermes, Priapus, and Aphrodite are shown paying a visit to the mythical shepherd Daphnis, not just to an ordinary human, much less to an identifiable contemporary of the writer. Theocritus' scene is mythical, and he keeps that mythical atmosphere clear of any intrusions. In Virgil's Arcadia the currents of myth and empirical reality flow one into another; gods and modern men stage meetings in a manner which would have been repugnant to Greek poetry. In actual fact this half-way land is neither mythical nor empirical; to the Roman Virgil and his Roman public, Apollo and Pan convey even less of their divinity, as objects of genuine faith, than they had to Theocritus and his Hellenistic audience. Arcadia is not an area on the map, either; even the person of Gallus appears misty and unreal, which has not, of course, prevented the scholars from trying to penetrate through the mist and identify the historical Gallus.

The air of unreality which hangs over Virgil's poems is thus explained by the fact that he seeks to approximate the world of Theocritus and that of myth, and that therefore he manipulates the traditional mythology with a greater licence than would have been possible for a Greek. The tragedians of the fifth century, to be sure, had begun to elaborate the ancient tales and to interpret them anew, but they had nevertheless maintained the fiction that they were discussing events of the hoary past. Plato's inventions in the mythical genre are often no longer connected with the ancient motifs, but they are always profoundly significant tales, genuinely mythical in tenor and aim. Callimachus says that when he first put his writing-tablet on his knees, Apollo gave him some useful hints for his poetry. But that is obviously a joke; and when he reports that the lock of Queen Berenice was placed among the stars, he bases that on the belief of his time that a great man may after his death be received among the gods. But nobody, prior to Virgil, seriously shows men of the present in close contact, and on an equal footing, with divine beings.

When the early age, during which the Greeks had accepted myth as history, came to a close the tragic writers and the historians of the fifth century divorced the two fields from each other. Myth retired beyond the world of man, and though at first it retained its old function of providing a standard of explanation and interpretation for human experiences, tragedy turned it into a poetic counterpart of reality. With the emancipation of myth came two important changes. On the one hand the ancient heroes and events were interpreted realistically—the psychological approach to the myths is part of this trend—in order to render them more useful to men in their daily lives; and secondly new dramatic situations were invented to the end of adapting the old myths to the stage. Hellenistic poetry carried the psychological interpretation of mythical characters even further, and it made the setting more naturalistic than ever before; but as against this, it also discovered new aesthetic possibilities for the myths. From these up-to-date versions of the ancient tradition, poetry learned to turn its aesthetic energies into the glorification and embellishment of the objects of commonplace reality. In the end, Theocritus domesticated the Sicilian shepherds and made them acceptable to his sensitive art. Virgil, in a certain sense, set about reversing this order of events, and in fact he finally wound up restoring the grand form of the epic. The *Eclogues* contain the first indications of his role which was to exalt the realistic writing which served as his point of departure, *viz.* the idylls of Theocritus, by suffusing it with elements of myth. Myth and reality are thus once more joined together, albeit in a manner never before witnessed in Greece.

Virgil arranges the meeting between his friend Gallus and Pan and Apollo because Gallus is a poet. As a poet he is on excellent terms with the Arcadian shepherds; Virgil had transferred his shepherds to Arcadia because the inhabitants of that country, as Polybius had informed him, were especially well versed in song. The shepherds of Theocritus, too, delight in song; but the ancestry of the musical herdsman is older yet. To trace it all the way back, we must turn to the age before Homer, for on the shield of Achilles (*Il.* 18.525) we find shepherds rejoicing in the sound of the syrinx. We have already mentioned the fact that it was the Arcadian deity Pan who was responsible for the invention of this instrument. Bucolic poetry, also, is of an ancient vintage. It appears that, about the year 600 B.C., Stesichorus introduced it into the repertory of Greek literature, with a choral ode in which he told the story of Daphnis. Daphnis was loved by a nymph; but when, in a bout of drunkenness, he became unfaithful to her, he suffered the punishment reserved for him: he was blinded. This account is obviously based on a simple rustic tale, localized in the vicinity of Himera, the city where Stesichorus lived. In his version, as we might expect in a Greek poetic treatment, the folk-tale is changed into a divine myth, for Daphnis is said to be the son—or, according to others, the beloved—of Hermes, and he tends the cattle of Helios. Our information about the poem is, unfortunately, late and imperfect, but we know that an important section of it was a lament for Daphnis. From that time onward the shepherds have been in love, usually without hope of success; either they indulge in their own suffering, or they wring a poetic expression of sympathy from their friends. We cannot say for sure how Stesichorus formulated all this, but it may be supposed that he endowed the pastoral life with some of the subdued lustre which Homer allows to the figure of Eumaeus, the faithful swineherd of Odysseus. The familiar and selfsufficient world of the simple shepherd is rendered in a myth which, though evidently sprung from a folk-tale, is for all that no less real than the myths which tell of heroes and heroic deeds.

More than three hundred years later, Theocritus composes yet another lament for Daphnis. This time it is given out as a song of the Sicilian shepherd Tityrus (7.72), and again

as a composition of the herdsman Thyrsis (1.66). Theocritus takes some pains to present a realistic picture of the life led by Sicilian shepherds. But in one respect they are anything rather than country folk: their mood is a literary one. Theocritus engineers a kind of masquerade; he wishes us to recognize poets of his own circle behind the rustic disguise. He adopts the classic motif of the singing and playing shepherd, and develops the scope of the pastoral poem by voicing the literary themes of the day. All this is done in a spirit of good-natured jesting; the dissonance between the bucolic simplicity of the pasture and the literary refinement of the city is never completely resolved, nor was it ever intended to be, for the whole point of Theocritus' humour lies in this dissonance. In the lament for Daphnis we read: 'The trees mourned for him, those which grew along the Himera river, when he melted away like snow on mount Haemus or Athos or Rhodope or on the furthest Caucasus.' This is the speech of the literati, for it is not customary with shepherds to discuss Haemus or Athos, Rhodope or Caucasus; it is the grand style of tragedy.

This high-flown diction must not be compared with the Greek geographical nomenclature with which Horace, who is our best example for this technique, equips his poems. To a Roman ear his place names do not convey the parody of tragedy, but respect for a noble tradition. And that is the spirit in which Virgil purloined his characters from Theocritus. The Roman poets use these strange-sounding names, dignified, as they thought, by the Greek passages in which they had occurred, to add to the stateliness of their speech; for the Latin tongue has no poetic diction of its own. The names help to lift the writing to a higher plane of literary art. As far as the Romans were concerned, if we may venture a paradox, all these mountains lie in Arcadia, in the land of Corydon and Alexis, of Pan and Apollo. It would not be fair to suggest that in the Augustan period such places had already degenerated into a kind of scenic backdrop for a poetic stage which may be exchanged at will. But it is certain that they have nothing whatever to do with any real landscape outside the theatre, where you might find ordinary, nonfictional men.

When Theocritus has his shepherds enumerate these mountains, he creates roughly the same impression as when Menander puts his quotations from tragedy in the mouths of uneducated slaves. With deliberate irony he makes his Sicilian shepherds live above their intellectual means. But when Virgil read these passages and others like them, he accepted them in the spirit of the more solemn context from which they had originally come, as expressions of genuine feeling. The tension between the real and the literary world which Theocritus had exploited for its peculiar charms, is brought to nought, and everything shifts back to the even plane of an undifferentiated majesty.

In Theocritus, Daphnis is the shepherd from the myth of Stesichorus. In other works he is just an ordinary herdsman, like Tityrus or Corydon. But he is always either the one or the other. Virgil mentions him already in his earliest eclogue: there he is unquestionably the mythical shepherd (2.26). In two other passages (7.1 and 9.46) he is a common herdsman. But what is his identity in the fifth *Eclogue*? As in other bucolic poems, two shepherds, Menalcas and Mopsus, want to stage a singing contest. They sing of the death and apotheosis of Daphnis, i.e. apparently the Daphnis of the myth. But this Daphnis had been the friend of Menalcas and Mopsus (line 52); thus he also belongs to the immediate environment of the competing herdsmen. Now at the end of the poem we discover that Virgil is using one of the two men as a mask for his own person. Once Virgil had placed his shepherds in Arcadia, it seems, it was but a short step to blend the bucolic with the mythical. This transition was, of course, facilitated by the fact that Theocritus himself had used the figure of Daphnis in both capacities.

In Theocritus, as in Virgil, the shepherds are less concerned with their flocks than they are interested in poetry and love. In both writers, therefore, they are gifted with passion and intellect, but in different ways. Theocritus' herdsmen, notwithstanding their pastoral status, often prove to be urban intellectuals in disguise. Virgil's shepherds, on the other hand—and it is charming to follow the steady progress from ecologue to eclogue—become increasingly more delicate and sensitive: they become Arcadian shepherds. Theocritus, too, stands at a distance from his shepherds; being a man from the city, he looks down upon them partly with a feeling of superiority, partly with an open mind for the straight simplicity of their primitive life. The simplicity is more ideal than fact, and so his shepherds, in spite of all realism, remain fairly remote from the true life in the fields. But this remoteness is as it should be, for a genuine summons back to nature would silence the whole of pastoral poetry; as it turned out, that is exactly what happened in a later age. Above all, these shepherds are not really taken seriously. Their quarrels have something comical about them; how different from the harsh wrangling between Eumaeus and Melanthius in the *Odyssey!* The violent head-on conflicts which we find in tragedy, even between kings, do not exist in Theocritus, and Virgil goes even further in smoothing the differences. From Theocritus on the shepherds display a courtly behaviour, and this courtliness, or courtesy, remains true of all bucolic poetry. The rustic life is made palatable to good society by its acquisition of manners and taste; if there are any embarrassing features left, the poet neutralizes them by making them appear droll, by smiling at them. Virgil is even more intent than Theocritus on toning down the crudeness and coarseness of the shepherds; as a result, he has less occasion to feel superior to them. Furthermore, while endowing the herdsmen with good manners and delicate feelings, he also makes them more serious-minded. But their seriousness differs from that of a Eumaeus; they have no strength to stand up for their genuine interests, nor do they ever clash with one another in open conflict. They are no more conversant with the true elemental passions than the heroes of the *Aeneid* were to be. And it is significant that in those ages when Arcadian poetry was in

fashion, and when courtly manners were the order of the day, the *Aeneid* has always been more highly favoured than the *Iliad* or the *Odyssey.*

Virgil's Arcadia is ruled by tender feeling. His herdsmen lack the crudeness of the peasant life as well as the over-sophistication of the city. In their rural idyll the peaceful calm of the leisurely evening hours stands out more clearly than the labour for their daily bread, the cool shade is more real than the harshness of the elements, and the soft turf by the brook plays a larger role than the wild mountain crags. The herdsmen spend more time playing the pipe and singing their tunes than in the production of milk and cheese. All this is incipient in Theocritus, but the Alexandrian still shows some interest in realistic detail. Virgil has ceased to see anything but what is important to him: tenderness and warmth and delicacy of feeling. Arcadia knows no reckoning in numbers, no precise reasoning of any kind. There is only feeling, which suffuses everything with its glow; not a fierce or passionate feeling: even love is but a delicate desire, gentle and sad.

Virgil, the discoverer of Arcadia, did not set out to explore new lands. He was no adventurer of the spirit who listens to the call of foreign shores. With utmost modesty he admits that he is proud to have been chosen by the Muse to introduce the Theocritean pastoral among the Romans (6.1). It was not any wish to be an innovator or reformer which caused him to swerve off the path of Theocritus. We must assume that when in his reading of Theocritus he found the grotesque tale of Polyphemus who tried to find a cure for his love in singing, the figure of the Cyclops changed under his very eyes, while he was yet perusing the tale, and turned into a lonely shepherd who voices his longing (*Ecl.* 2). Theocritus says (11.12) that the herds of Polyphemus had to make their way home by themselves in the evenings, because the herdsman forgot all else over his singing. Virgil interprets this as a picture of the golden age when the flocks were able to return to the stables of their own accord, without any herdsman to look after them (4.21). Or again: Virgil has read that during the noon heat lizards sleep in the thornbush. He had found this in Theocritus, where someone expresses his amazement that another person is up and about during that hour, 'while even the lizards take their siesta' (7.22). Virgil has a shepherd who is unhappily in love sing as follows: 'While the flocks seek the cool shade and the lizards hide in the bushes, I must continually sing of my love' (2.8). Thus the sensible beasts have become the happy beasts. Theocritus concludes a jocular prayer to Pan (7.111) with these words: 'If you do not comply with my prayer, I hope you will pasture your flocks during the winter in icy Thrace on the Hebrus, and during the summer among the Ethiopians in the furthest south.' In Virgil, Gallus mourns (10.65ff.): 'Nor will my unhappy love subside if I drink from the Hebrus in mid-winter or if I plough through the snowfalls of the Thracian winter, nor if I pasture the sheep of the Ethiopians under the sign of Cancer (i.e. in mid-summer).' The drastic punishment threatened to the shepherd's god is transformed into the sorrows of the unhappy lover who roams through the whole wide world and cannot find a hardship extreme enough to free him from his tortures. These subtle changes are numerous; little by little, without drawing our attention to it, Virgil varies the Theocritean motifs. The transformation is so slight that it took a long time before it was noticed how far Virgil had progressed in his *Eclogues* beyond the pleasantries of the Hellenistic poet. He admired and acknowledged the work of Theocritus, he dwelt lovingly on his scenes; but because he read them with the eyes of the new classicistic age, he slowly came back to the classical Greek poetry, with its earnestness, its deep feeling, its drama. Virgil had not intended to be original; he merely re-moulded Theocritus in the image of what he considered to be characteristically Greek. This was the route by which Virgil discovered Arcadia: without searching for it, without proclaiming his arrival; and so we, for our part, have no easy time in discovering that it was he who discovered the land, and what its discovery means to us.

. . . . .

About six hundred years before Virgil, the early Greek lyrists had awoken to the fact that man has a *soul;* they were the first to discover certain features in the feelings of men which distinguished those feelings sharply from the functions of the physical organs, and which placed them at opposite poles from the realm of empirical reality. For the first time it was noticed that these feelings do not represent the intercession of a deity or some other similar reaction, but that they are a very personal matter, something that each individual experiences in his own peculiar fashion, and that originates from no other source but his own person. Further they had found out that different men may be united with one another through their feelings, that a number of separate people may harbour the same emotions, memories, or opinions. And finally they discovered that a feeling may be divided against itself, distraught with an internal tension; and this led to the notion that the soul has intensity, and a dimension of its own, *viz.* depth. Now everything that we have so far remarked about Virgil's Arcadian world may be summed up by saying that Virgil developed these three basic modes which the early lyric had ascribed to the soul, and interpreted them afresh.

Under Virgil's hands, the spontaneity of the soul becomes the swirling tide of the dream, the creative flux of poetic fancy. The feeling which transcends the individual and forges a link between many men becomes Virgil's longing for peace and his love for his country through which even the beasts and the trees and the mountains are welcomed as fellow-creatures. And finally, the dissonance and depth of the emotions unfold into the conscious suffering of the sensitive man, his awareness that his tender and vulnerable soul lies at the mercy of a harsh and cruel world.

Later on Virgil himself appears to have sensed the futility of pursuing further such an indulgence in the feelings; but the three functions of the soul which he had brought into the open: poetic reverie, unifying love, and sensitive suffering, point far into the future. It was not merely because

of his prophecy in the fourth *Eclogue* that Virgil was, in the Middle Ages, regarded as a pioneer of Christianity. His Arcadia is set half-way between myth and reality; it is also a no-man's land between two ages, an earthly beyond, a land of the soul yearning for its distant home in the past. However, in his later years Virgil avoided the regions discovered by him. For in his later poems he acquired a temper of severe manly restraint which led him to draw closer to the classical Greek expressions of feeling and thought; but many a trace of his earlier sensibility remained.

Along with his new understanding of the soul, Arcadia also furnished the poet with a radically new consciousness of his artistic role. Virgil, for his own person, was too modest to boast loudly of his achievement, but in his portrait of Gallus in the tenth *Eclogue* he gives us a general idea of his views on the special function of the poet. The reasons, he hints, why the poet takes his stand among the gods, and why he receives the sympathy of nature, is because his feelings are more profound than those of other men, and because therefore he suffers more grievously under the cruelties of the world. Virgil does not actually spell out these ideas which were to become so important in modern poetry, but even his hinting at them is new. At the beginning of the sixth *Eclogue* Virgil for once formulates a programme of poetic art, but, as is his manner, he is careful not to make too much of himself or his poetry. Following the traces of Callimachus, he refuses to have anything to do with the great epic—later, of course, he was to reverse himself—and he confines himself to the delicate pastime of brief compositions. But in this connexion he accidentally drops a remark which is quite unlike anything that Callimachus ever said; he expresses the hope that his lines, insignificant as their theme is, may be read by someone 'captured by love.' This sympathetic affection is the mark of the poet, and the poet seeks to transmit his compassion to his reader.

. . . . .

. . . Horace does not speak of Arcadia, but he too envisages a realm to which the poet alone has access and which is closed to ordinary mortals; a place where dignity of intellect, delicacy of soul and bodily beauty thrive and flourish. The poet who seeks this place is a stranger among men. This land in which the Roman poet finds the objects of his striving is the realm of Greek culture and literature. It follows, of course, that the Greek motifs lose their ancient contact with reality; the Muses cease to be real divinities, the priest is no longer a practising priest, the mystery cult is no longer a genuine worship, and the teacher has no actual disciples before him. Each image acquires a metaphorical meaning, and in this land of literary hopes everything, as in Arcadia, must be taken with a grain of salt. Myth and reality intrude upon each other; concrete existence gives way before significance. The heritage of the Greeks is turned into allegory, and literature is transformed into a kingdom of symbols.

This uncovers a deep cleavage between the factual and the significant. The concrete world of experience finds itself face to face with a new world of art. True, even in Greek literature allegory and symbols had not been unknown, but they had been innocuous and unproblematic by comparison. A Greek writer who speaks of Hephaestus may actually mean a fire. The evolution of that formula might roughly be sketched as follows. In an early period it was possible to say: 'Hephaestus destroyed a city,' in the firm belief that the god's fury was in the fire. Then came the enlightenment which taught that there were no gods, and that Hephaestus 'signified' fire, for only fire was real. In the same fashion it became possible to 'explain' all other gods. Finally there was the theory of poetry which stipulated that the writer must use a picturesque and dynamic style, and that it was more beautiful and more poetic to use the name Hephaestus rather than speak of fire. Rationalism on the one hand, poetic theory and the desire for embellishment on the other, were responsible for the metonymic use of the names of the gods.

These considerations prevailed also upon Virgil and Horace, but in one essential the Romans differed from the Greeks. A Greek poet, so long as he is a believer, recognizes a reality in the name; for one who has ceased to believe, the name becomes a sylistic device or merely poetic play. But the Romans employ these names to create their Arcadia, the land of the spirit and of poetry; without the names, the land could not exist. It is true that the names had already lost much of their original impact in Attic tragedy; since the myth is not related, but acted out or played, the gulf between reality and signification was apparent even then. The drama, that which is happening on the stage, leads us beyond its own limits to a spiritual meaning; it expounds a problem which cannot be expressed directly. But despite this, the outlines of the mythical figures do not vanish behind a mist of unreality; on the contrary, they stand in the very centre of a grimly tangible plot.

Another reason why the characters of Attic tragedy could never be mere allegories is that they were always accepted as real creatures of flesh and blood. Although the ancient myths are no longer enacted as if they were history pure and simple, and although the straightforward limitation of mythical events was gradually forsaken in favour of an added emphasis upon the intellectual and spiritual sides of the action, the dramatic figures remain with their feet firmly planted on the ground. They are no longer regarded as *real,* but every effort is directed at making them appear *possible.* And as the belief in the reality of the myth dwindled, poetry tried hard to preserve at least a semblance of reality by resorting to the devices of realism and psychology. Allegory, on the other hand, does not insist on this kind of semblance; within its realm, the function of a figure is only to convey one specific meaning. In Virgil the nymphs and the Muses, Pan and Apollo are very close to the level of allegory, for they embody the idyllic life of Arcadia, the peace which fills its pastures and the romantic poetry to which its shepherds are dedicated.

Thus the ancient gods are, so to speak, reduced to the form of *sigla:* they are deprived of their primeval mysteri-ous power, and all that is left to them is an ideality which no longer springs from religious awe but from literary erudition. They have taken on a Utopian quality, embodying the spiritual truths which are not to be found in this world. A similar change in the thinking concerning the gods is indicated in many examples of the classicistic painting and sculpture which flourished in Attica at the time of Virgil. We do not know enough about the Greek literature of this epoch to be able to tell to what extent Virgil was indebted to it in his allegorization of the gods. But what was least as important was this, that for the Romans the gods and the myths of the Greeks had never been real. They adopted them as part of their cultural heritage from Greek literature and art, and they found in them the world of the spirit which the Greeks had discovered. Among the Romans, therefore, these figures are emphasized chiefly for whatever meaning they may hold for the life of man; they are allegories in the real sense of the word, for they signify something entirely different from what they had originally meant. They are like loan words taken into another language, which are called upon to translate a strange legacy for the benefit of the heirs and their thought and feelings, if such a thing is possible in matters of the mind. The gods become allegories at the very moment when Greek literature gives birth to a literature of the world.

A similar development occurred also in the East. Allegorical interpretation helped Philo to incorporate Greek myth and Greek wisdom into Hellenistic Judaism, and Clement of Alexandria performed the same office for Christianity. Much was accepted, but the religious and philosophical core was rendered harmless by this reformulation. The world of the Greek spirit was, perforce, a strange in the cultures which absorbed it, and the allegorical interpretation was needed to permit the Greek heritage to be accepted by nations and ages whose beliefs were in many respects diametrically opposed to Greek thought.

The special importance of Virgil, which distinguishes his accomplishment from the Jewish and the Christian assimilation of Greek culture, and which places him squarely in the Roman tradition leading from Ennius to Catullus, is the fact that he uses the arts *viz.* poetry, to channel the Greek heritage into the body of Roman thought. But further than that, his **Eclogues** represent the first serious attempt in literature to mould the Greek motifs into self-contained forms of beauty whose reality lies within themselves. Thus art became 'symbol.' Comparable tendencies do not exist in Greek literature. At most we might establish a certain similarity with the myths of Plato; but even this last comparison serves only to stress the special quality of Virgil's achievement. Plato's myths, too, had been concerned with 'significance' rather than with reality. But they are not self-contained poetry; on the contrary, their objective is to illustrate something else. They refer to a specific argument which Plato would like to express rationally, but for which his language does not suffice. That is why Plato deprecates his myths and calls them mere play. In Greek literature this species of myth-making had no successors.

Arcadia was a land of symbols, far distant from the quarrels and the acrimony of the present. In this land the antique pagan world was permitted to live on without injury to anybody's feelings. Arcadia was so remote that it was no more in danger of clashing with the See of Rome or with the Holy Roman Empire than it had run afoul of the *Imperium Romanum* of Augustus. Only when Europe began to be dissatisfied with the goods handed down to her, and when she took thought upon her own spiritual substance, did Arcadia run into trouble. But that was also the time when the genuine Greece was restored to her rightful place.

Notes

"Arcadia: The Discovery of a Spiritual Landscape." From *The Discovery of the Mind* by Bruno Snell. Translated by T. G. Rosenmeyer. Copyright 1953 by the President and Fellows of Harvard College and Basil Blackwell & Mott, Ltd. Reprinted by permission of the Harvard University Press and Basil Blackwell & Mott, Ltd. The pages reprinted here are only part of a chapter entitled "Arcadia: The Discovery of a Spiritual Landscape."

  1. E. Panofsky, *'Et in Arcadia ego,' Festschrift E. Cassirer.* Cf. *Hermes,* LXXIII (1938), 242.1.

Charles Paul Segal (essay date 1965)

SOURCE: *"Tamen Catabitis, Arcades*—Exile and Arcadia in *Eclogues* One and Nine," *Arion,* Vol. IV, No. 2, Summer, 1965 pp. 237-66.

[*In the following essay, Segal studies the literary relationship between* Eclogues *One and Nine, emphasizing that Vergil's treatment of political issues in these poems is that of a poet rather than of a historian.*]

One of the difficulties hampering students of Vergil's *Eclogues* has been a certain loss of perspective about the relations between poetry and biography. While no one would deny that Vergil's writing of the *Eclogues* has some definite relation to certain political circumstances, that relation is one of a poet and not an historian. It is the ability to transform personal experience into larger, more intensely significant terms wherein lies the distinguishing quality of the poet's genius. The poet's experience of the "actuality" around him is, as other men's, rooted in the succession of historical events; but, if he chooses—or feels compelled—to make poetry of these events, it is because they supply him with profound insights into issues which often far transcend their historical source and may be (in fact, usually are) of a totally nonhistorical character.[1] The poet, then, transforms historical reality into poetic reality; and it is with this transformed reality that the study of poetry is properly concerned, however much it may be aided by historical or biographical information. This distinction, though fundamental, has often become obscured in recent decades of "scientific" scholarship,

though it has been restated sporadically by scholars of a rather more humanistic outlook, as for example by Plessis half a century ago:

> (*Les Bucoliques*) sont des oeuvres d'actualité—ce qui ne veut pas dire de circonstance,—et d'une actualité sentie par une des âmes les plus anxieuses et les plus belles qui ait jamais été; ce sont les tristesses et les rêves d'un grand coeur et d'une grande intelligence.[2]

Increasing numbers of scholars in recent years have abjured the "biographical fallacy" and its limitations; but the biographical approach still weighs heavily on students of the *Eclogues* and perhaps most heavily on students of *Eclogues* 1 and 9.[3] Vergil's farm—its location, confiscation, restoration—the identification of Tityrus or Meliboeus or Menalcas with Vergil, the chronological relation between the two poems, the ambiguous praise of Octavian (if indeed he is the *iuvenis* in *E.* 1) by the young poet— *audax iuventa,* "bold in his youth," as he says looking back on his poem a decade or so later (*Georg.* 4.565-66)—these are questions which have been discussed with such energy and subtlety that they have often (though by no means always) distracted scholars from approaching the two works as poetry. Furthermore, though scholars have examined the poetic qualities of each poem individually, studies of the relation between the two poems have all too often limited themselves to the "biographical" issues.

In the following pages I shall offer some detailed literary analysis of each poem separately, but my major concern will be the relation between the two poems and some of the larger implications of this relation in the light of the poetic character of the *Eclogues* considered as a unified work. This unity is, to be sure, of a looser kind than that found within a single poem. Yet these ten poems, written within the space of three years (if we can believe the biographical tradition) with their cross-references and recurrent characters, real and imaginary, are cast in a single mood and style. Indeed, it has been suggested that they may be the first book of single poems in Latin literature to have been put together with a conscious sense of the design and artistic unity of the whole.[4]

I

Eclogues 1 and 9 are obviously intended as pendants one to the other. Both involve exile from a peaceful, familiar world; and both develop a contrast (stronger and more pathetic in *E.* 1) between a shepherd facing exile and one who is still at rest within the pastoral world. Both too (in this like *E.* 6 and 10) end on the theme of rest and the fall of evening. Some deliberate verbal echoes make the connection even more explicit (though again the parallels provide no certain evidence for the chronological relation of the two poems). Most obviously, *E.* 9.50,

> Insere, Daphni, piros: carpent tua poma nepotes
>
> (Graft your pear-trees, Daphnis; your descendants will pluck the fruit)

recalls *E.* 1.73,

> Insere nunc, Meliboee, piros, pone ordine vitis

(Now, Meliboeus, graft your pear-trees; set your vines out in rows),

save that this latter sentence is bitterly ironical, while the former is more neutral in tone, though as will appear later, also not lacking in a certain pathos. Further, in *E.* 1.16-17 Meliboeus speaks of a foreboding of his disaster which he failed to recognize:

> Saepe malum hoc nobis, si mens non laeva fuisset,
> de caelo tactas memini praedicere quercus

(I remember, if my mind hadn't been turned awry, that oaks struck by lightning foretold this woe to us.)

In *E.* 9.14-16, at roughly the same point in the poem, Moeris too describes an omen, though one which he successfully recognized:

> Quod nisi me quacumque novas incidere lites
> ante sinistra cava monuisset ab ilice cornix,
> nec tuus hic Moeris nec viveret ipse Menalcas.

(But had not a raven from the hollow oak on my left hand warned me in advance to cut short somehow my new proceedings, neither your Moeris here nor Menalcas himself would be among the living.)

The difference between these two passages is symptomatic of general differences between the two poems. Though the disaster intimated by the omen of *E.* 9 makes that of *E.* 1 seem trivial by comparison, still the omen served its purpose. The warning was heeded and the disaster averted. Bad as things are, then, there still seems to be, in *E.* 9, some kind of favoring order. Hence one can still hope and look forward to better times:

> Carmina tum melius, cum venerit ipse, canemus

(We'll sing our songs better when he comes himself, *E.* 9.67.)

Eclogue 1, on the other hand, ends less positively. Meliboeus, the exiled shepherd, is left in far greater despair than his counterpart, Moeris, in *E.* 9. In *E.* 9 too the threat of dispossession by no means suppresses the shepherds' delight in song, whereas the situation hangs more oppressively over the characters of *E.* 1. In *E.* 9, in other words, the pastoral world, the remote and imaginative song-filled hills of Theocritus, can assert itself still. In *E.* 1 this world is clouded over far more by the intrusive realities of Roman politics.

Yet to whatever degree the two poems complement one another, both, taken individually and as a pair, present a leitmotif of the *Eclogues,* the interplay between the real and the imaginary, between the familiar, often troubled present and the distant, hope-filled future.

This mixture of contrasting elements is perhaps the major stylistic device of *E.* 1 and, as will be suggested more fully later, is in part responsible for its opening the collection. The first exchange at once sets the oppositions into motion: two speeches of five lines each, both beginning with a vocative (***Tityre,*** 1; ***O Meliboee,*** 6). The first speech complains of exile; the second exults in good fortune. The contrast of exile and settledness, however, is developed even within the first speech:

> Tityre, tu patulae recubans sub tegmine fagi
> silvestrem tenui musam meditaris avena:
> nos patriae finis et dulcia linquimus arva.
> nos patriam fugimus: tu, Tityre, lentus in umbra
> formosam resonare doces Amaryllida silvas.

(Tityrus, you, as you lie under the cover of a spreading beech, practise your forest muse with light oaten flute: we leave the borders of our country and our sweet fields. You, Tityrus, easeful in the shade, teach the woods to echo the fair Amaryllis, 1-5.)

Not only is there the pointed contrast, "You under a beech . . .; we in exile . . ." (lines 1 and 3), but also the carefully balanced *Tityre, tu* (1) . . . *tu, Tityre* (4) frames the statement of exile in the central portion, lines 3-4. With "Tityrus" in line 4, the last line and a half moves back into the pastoral peace, now lost to the speaker, of lines 1 and 2:

> tu, Tityre, lentus in umbra
> formosam resonare doces Amaryllida silvas.

This circular a-b-a movement in the first five lines is, in small, the pattern of the whole poem.[5] Thus from the good fortune of Tityrus (6-10) we move again to Meliboeus' misfortune (11-18), then back once more to Tityrus' success at Rome (19-25), with its ramifications both into the past (27-41) and the future (46-58, 59-63), then once more to Meliboeus' misfortune (64-78), and finally to Tityrus' promise of rest (79-84). This movement can be tabulated sketchily as follows:

1-5	a-b-a	Meliboeus' introduction
6-10	a	Tityrus' good fortune
11-18	b	Meliboeus' misfortunes
19-63	a	Emphasis on Tityrus' success and its background:
		1) 19-45: his past life leading up to his visit to Rome
		2) 46-58: Meliboeus' description of the good things Tityrus is to enjoy in the country (*Fortunate senex*)
		3) 59-63: Tityrus refers again to his success at Rome
64-78	b	Meliboeus' lament for his exile; *At nos hinc* (64) marks the contrast with what precedes
79-83	a	Tityrus' promise of rest. *Hic tamen* (79) answers *At nos hinc* (64).

The middle section is complex, and I make no attempt here at a complete analysis. The fact that Tityrus' good fortune is described by the dispossessed Meliboeus (*Fortunate senex,* "happy old that you are," 46) in the most "pastoral" part of the poem is a dramatic device which adds considerably to the pathos, for we see a future projection of Tityrus' pastoral life, with its untroubled continuities, through the eyes of one condemned to give up this life as he has known it in his own past.

Tityrus, on the contrary, has been deeply and favorably impressed by the city and tends to demean his rustic surroundings by comparison to it:

> Urbem quam dicunt Romam, Meliboee, putavi
> stultus ego huic nostrae similem . . .
> sic canibus catulos similis sic matribus haedos
> noram, sic parvis componere magna solebam.
> verum haec tantum alias inter caput extulit urbes
> quantum lenta solent inter viburna cupressi.

> (The city which they call Rome, Meliboeus, I thought in my foolishness to be like ours. . . . So did I know that puppies are like dogs and kids like mother goats, thus was I wont to compare great things with small. But this city lifts its head as far among other cities as cypresses are wont to do among the winding osiers, 19-24.)

There is a further pathetic irony here in that the terms of Tityrus' comparison, and especially his last line,

> quantum lenta solent inter viburna cupressi,

vaguely seem to recall Meliboeus' lament in the opening lines, and intensify in Meliboeus the awareness of the beauty of exactly that which Tityrus is depreciating; and thus his response is,

> Et quae tanta fuit Romam tibi causa videndi?

> (And what great reason did you have for seeing Rome? 26.)

There is a characteristic Vergilian delicacy and sensitivity, and a touch of humor too, in the *tanta* which effectively distinguishes the two men and the two situations. Tityrus, while demeaning the rustic world, unconsciously praises it; and Meliboeus, whose mind responds far more readily to the praise than the depreciation, can conceive of leaving it only under the compulsion of the weightiest reasons (*quae* tanta . . . *causa,* "what *so great* reason").[6]

Tityrus too has a more prosaic attitude than Meliboeus toward his rustic world. For him it is a place of work and hard-earned savings (*peculi,* 32) and frustrations (*pinguis et* ingratae *premeretur caseus urbi,* "and the cheese is pressed out for the *ungrateful* city," 34). The exile is far more prone to idealize what he must leave, and he dwells lovingly on the familiar features of his beloved country with lush adjectives which he seems scarcely able to refrain from applying to every noun. The bees are "Hyblaean," sleep is "soft," the rock is "lofty," the doves "hoarse," and in a single line (52) the founts "sacred" and the coolness "shaded."

The last two lines of the poem are again deep in the peace of the pastoral world:

> Et iam summa procul villarum culmina fumant
> maioresque cadunt altis de montibus umbrae

(And already from afar the tops of the houses send forth their smoke and longer shadows fall from the tall hills)

and thus mark a circular return, though with a heavier, more somber resonance, to the untroubled liquids of the first two lines.[7]

Within this large movement there are several related groups of contrasts. First, as already suggested, that between country and city. The city is, of course, Rome (19) and hence connotes all the threatening realities (*en quo discordia civis/ produxit miseros,* "To what a pass has discord brought the wretched citizens," 71-72) which are driving Meliboeus out of the pastoral world. *Civis* in 71, and *miles* in 70, are significant words in pointing up the realities which the *urbs* threatens; they would ordinarily have no place in a traditional pastoral setting.

The city-country antithesis carries with it another contrast of a somewhat more subtle nature, that is, a difference between simplicity and artificiality of language. All the descriptions of the country are put into the mouth of the exiled Meliboeus. His language, lavish of adjectives as it may be in 46-58, is nevertheless direct and straightforward, whereas Tityrus tends toward syntactical complexity (note the harsh and unnatural syntax of 27-30) and rhetorical exaggeration (see 7ff., *namque erit ille mihi semper deus* . . .; 22ff., *sic canibus catulos similis* . . .) which reaches its peak (or should one say nadir) in the inflated commonplaces and periodic structure of 59-63 (*Ante levesergo* . . . *quam nostro* . . .). It is not that Vergil had not quite completed his farewells to the *inanes* . . . *rhetorum ampullae* ("the empty jars of the rhetors," *Catalepton* 5), nor that "this verse [62], with its fortissimo in the dynamic movement of the poem, completes the breakthrough to the sublime."[8] Rather, Vergil, with a typically subtle humor, is using style to enhance the dramatic movement and the characterization. Tityrus' language can be attributed to the fact that he is, naturally, exultant. Yet it is perhaps also as if he has brought back from the city some of its complexity and artificiality. So too what is rhetorical artifice for Tityrus in 62 is bitter reality for Meliboeus in 64-66. Meliboeus, who has never been to the city but, because of the city and its wars, is being driven from his "sweet fields" (*dulcia arva,* 3) speaks with a directness and nobility that enhance the pathos of his situation. Simplicity of expression such as his is the natural vehicle for interpreting the simple beauty of the country. Meliboeus is the true poet, the one to describe the beauties of the country; Tityrus, whose mind seems as prosaic as his language, talks of savings and cheese. Yet he who appreciates this beauty and can respond to it and give it expression in its proper terms, he who possesses the true "forest muse" (*silvestrem musam*) with its "light oaten flute" (*tenui avena,* 2) is the one to be exiled.[9]

Through the stylistic differences in the speech of the two rustics also, city and the powerful "god" it contains are made even more remote from Meliboeus' world. They belong not only to a different geographical area, but also to a different verbal area, a mode of speech that is unfamiliar and distant. They thus appear as spiritually as well as spatially removed.

There is yet another important set of contrasts running throughout the *Eclogue:* the interplay between past and future. Meliboeus sees all his happiness as belonging to the past. His flock is *quondam felix,* "happy once" (74), while for the future he sees only darkness: "Shall I ever, a long time after (*longo post tempore*) look with wonder upon my native country . . . " (67-69); "I shall not in time afterward (*posthac*) see you . . ., my goats; no songs shall I sing" (75-77). Conversely he uses the same future tenses of Tityrus (*ergo tua rura manebunt,* "Your fields, then, will remain," 46), but his companion's future Meliboeus sees as unblemished happiness since he will stay in the country. Tityrus himself can regard as assured the calm link between past and future, for he has been told, "Pasture your oxen *as before,* my children" (*pascite* ut ante *boves, pueri,* 45). But for Meliboeus this link is broken, and he leaves behind his past happiness with his *patria.*

Yet just as Vergil ends the poem with the settled, not the exiled rustic, so in the concluding lines he leaves the complex movement from happy past to uncertain future for the calm certainty of the present. For this one night, at least, Meliboeus is promised rest: *Hic tamen hanc mecum poteras requiescere noctem* (79); and the poem ends with the same present-tense timelessness with which it began (cf. *sunt, fumant, cadunt,* 80-83; *recubans, meditaris, doces,* 1-2, 5).

Tityrus can still occupy the timeless present which is the heritage of every pastoral shepherd: action free equally from bondage to a past and from responsibility for future consequences and hence removed both from regret and from guilt. Action for Tityrus, then, is static, without results or limits, as Meliboeus unhappily points out in his opening lines (*recubans, meditaris, lentus, doces;* and the languour reaches also to the tree, the *patula fagus,* 1). But the present tenses used by Meliboeus of himself—*linquimus, fugimus*—only carry him farther away from Tityrus' happy world. And so the last lines of the poem, with the verbs of pastoral nonaction-in-action, are indeed a final attempt to regain peace, to reaffirm Arcady. But peace and Arcady belong now only to Tityrus.

Thus despite the temporary effort toward calm and rest the tensions between sadness and peace, settledness and dispossession are unresolved. Rest is promised, it is true, but exile is no less pressing. The morrow still awaits. This atmosphere of suspension amid contraries, of rest amid disturbance, sets the tone for the *Eclogues.* The momentary pause of these last lines creates the silence in which the collection can be entered. Yet the *temporary* duration of the silence is not forgotten, nor with it the sense of the effort required to create a world of peace and beauty apart from the surrounding threats of disturbance and violence.[10]

In such a world—the world before Actium—the poet is indeed an exile. He can respond to and express the beauty he can find in the world; yet he cannot claim this beauty as a stable and permanent possession. It is a precarious holding from which he may be all too easily dislodged.

II

Like *Eclogue* 1, the Ninth *Eclogue* is a dialogue between two shepherds, one dispossessed, the other apparently unthreatened by the troubles in the region. Yet there is a crucial difference. Lycidas, the unthreatened shepherd, makes a genuine attempt to console his friend. Unlike the self-centered Tityrus, his counterpart in *E.* 1, he does not simply receive congratulations on his good luck. In fact, the poem contains no reference to the happier fortune of Lycidas. Thus the contrast that is so strongly developed in *E.* 1 never fully materializes here. There is still some dramatic movement in the attempts of the rather enthusiastic and cheerful Lycidas to brighten the mood of his more somber and stolid friend. Yet Lycidas, though he is more sympathetic than Tityrus, is also less vivid. This lack of full characterization should not necessarily be regarded as a weakness in the poem (there has indeed been a tendency, unjustified, as I hope to show, to disparage the literary merits of *E.* 9);[11] it is probably a deliberate attempt on Vergil's part to restrict the dramatic element.

By so doing, Vergil helps diminish the reality of the entire situation and hence the intensity of the sense of loss. Measured against *E.* 1, this reduction is significant. The setting especially is not so clearly localized as in *E.* 1, with its explicit reference to Rome. Even lines 7-9 of *E.* 9, despite the claims of commentators hunting for Vergil's farm, present a fairly generalized description: hills sloping down gently, water, old beech trees; and, to confuse further any precise identification, the sea is in sight (note *aspice,* "behold," 57).[12] Also the relation of Moeris to Menalcas is left rather vague. It is presumably a master-servant relation, but it is never made quite clear whether Moeris is slave or free (contrast the emphasis on Tityrus' acquisition of his freedom in *E.* 1.27ff.). Then the fact that the loss of the farm primarily concerns a third person, the absent Menalcas, contributes to this same effect of rendering more remote the sense of disaster.

This lessening of the immediacy of the misfortune allows the poem to assume a more "literary" character than *E.* 1. The shepherds can take time to exchange songs, and they are not so crushed that there is a sense of incongruity between their singing and the darker mood created by the news of dispossession. In the same way the large number of translations from Theocritus which the poem contains and rather obtrusively exhibits reduces the dramatic immediacy and calls attention to the artificial, "literary" framework of the poem itself. There is thus a degree of poetic self-consciousness, heightened by the references back to the Fifth *Eclogue* in lines 19-20 (cf. *E.* 5.20 and 40), which is almost totally absent in *E.* 1. While the First *Eclogue,* then, attempts to present the situation in direct, dramatic form, the Ninth deflects attention to the intervening frame.

Paradoxically, the very beginning of the Ninth *Eclogue* is characterized by a greater dramatic vividness than that of the First. While *E.* 1 begins with the regretful fluidity and drawn out, almost sensuous melancholy of Meliboeus' lament,

> Tityre, tu patulae recubans sub tegmine fagi,

E. 9 begins abruptly with a question in an almost flippantly conversational style and in a short, choppy rhythm:

> Quo te, Moeri, pedes? an, quo via ducit, in urbem?

> (Where do your feet carry you, Moeris? Is it where the road leads, to the city?)

Vergil is translating almost literally from Theocritus' Seventh *Idyll,* after which the setting of the poem as a whole is modelled. But the verse of Theocritus occurs well along in his poem (VII.21); and Vergil has modified the tone considerably: . . .

> (Where are you heading on foot, Simichidas, at midday?)

Vergil's line is far more elliptical, and its rhythm more harsh (he has two spondees—excluding the final foot—to Theocritus' one, and has broken up the utter simplicity of the Theocritean movement by placing the vocative later in the line and by interrupting any easy balance between the two coordinate phrases with the parenthetical *quo via ducit*). There is nothing like the easy dactylic flow of Theocritus' final four feet or the limpid syntax of his whole line. The addition, *in urbem,* "to the city," never a good sign for a Vergilian rustic as we have seen from *E.* 1, also adds a certain suggestion of foreboding, or at least unpleasantness.

Vergil can translate Theocritus better than this when he chooses. Here he has deliberately roughened Theocritus' verse for his own purposes. Thus by announcing, as it were, in the first line both his source and his intention to differ from his source, he lays the foundation for a significant contrast between his poem and its Theocritean model.

The tone of this difference develops quickly in the following lines. Moeris' speech, like Lycidas' question, is excited, abrupt, not especially adorned by poetical felicities. The words seem to pour out without any order, as if he is too excited to organize his thoughts; and indeed his first words come about as close to suggesting incoherence as the formal hexameter permits:

> O Lycida, vivi pervenimus, advena nostri
> (quod numquam veriti sumus) ut possessor agelli
> diceret: 'haec mea sunt; veteres migrate coloni.' (2-4).

A somewhat exaggerated, yet justifiable, translation would punctuate with dashes:

> O Lycidas, we have lived to see—a foreigner—our own—a thing we never feared—that he should take

possession of our little plot and say, "This is mine; you old settlers, depart."[13]

Instructive again is the contrast with the formal, plaintive tone of Meliboeus in *E.* 1 with its circular movement and studied repetitions. Equally important is the contrast with the Theocritean original, for the questioner in Theocritus goes on to observe that it is no time to travel: even lizards and tree-frogs sleep (22-23); and his friend, he conjectures with a lyrical comment, is going to a banquet or a revel: "Ah, as you walk every stone sings as it strikes against your sandals" (. . . 25-26). He receives the reply, preceded by a gracious compliment about his own poetic superiority, that the friend, Simichidas, is going to a harvest-festival, the *Thalysia,* from which the poem derives its title in the ancient editions. The tone of Vergil's Moeris, however, is but one of several related differences: his journey has a different character and a different destination.

This tone, however, now changes in the reply of Lycidas in lines 9-10. Here the peaceful description of the country, with the reference to the old rustic traditions and sense of continuity in the old beech trees, *veteres, iam fracta cacumina, fagos* (9), introduces a note of quiet and stability which the poem is not to lose again. Thus even the reality of the loss of the farm to the rude arms of the soldier in Moeris' reply is tempered by the "literary" language which Moeris uses:

> sed carmina tantum
> nostra valent, Lycida, tela inter Martia quantum
> Chaonias dicunt aquila veniente columbas.

> (But our songs, Lycidas, have as much power amid the arms of Mars as they say the Chaonian doves have when the eagle comes, 11-13.)

The poetic proper adjectives and the contrived word order of line 13 (matched by a similar arrangement in line 15) distance the experience and remind the reader again of the poetic frame.[14] This frame obtrudes again even more strongly in the references to *Eclogue* V in 19-20, in the symmetrical quotations from Menalcas' songs in 23-25 and 27-29, in the two following songs of the shepherds themselves (39-43, 46-50), and in the allusions to the contemporary poets, Varius and Cinna, in line 35.

There is, it is true, a certain alternation, somewhat analogous to the movement in *E.* 1, between the pressing realities of the present and the realm of pastoral song. Most immediately, in each pair of songs the first is purely pastoral (so 23-25, 39-43), the second concerned with the political situation (27-29, 46-50). Vergil thus shifts quickly from the depths of the timeless pastoral world to Mantua and Rome of the present. Yet the fact that the references are parts of songs makes the shift less abrupt than would otherwise be the case; the "dissonance" is thus softened. Even the reference back to *E.* 1.73 in line 50 (*insere, Daphni, piros*) can here hardly carry with it the bitterness and irony of disappointment of that context, but occurs in a joyful song celebrating the beneficent star of Caesar. Hence the poem does not carry through the a-b-a alternation of *E.* 1. Instead the threatening realities of the introductory lines, though not entirely obliterated, are attenuated as the poem spins about itself its own world of pastoral song.

In its own terms, however, and with its difference of emphasis *E.* 9 contains as subtle a movement between reality and pastoral as *E.* 1. Much of this movement comes from Vergil's use of Theocritus. Since Theocritus VII is the most directly autobiographical of the *Idylls,* Vergil, by using it, may mean to indicate that he too is writing an autobiographical poem. The quotations from the Fifth *Eclogue* and the explicit reference to Mantua in line 27 confirm this suggestion.

At the same time, as the first line implies, Vergil is signaling deep differences between himself and his model, and these differences are made more pointed as the poem develops. Vergil translates from Theocritus' Third *Idyll* in lines 23-25 and returns to *Idyll* VII in 32ff., lines 33-34 being a close translation of Theocritus VII. 37-38:

> me quoque dicunt
> vatem pastores; sed non ego credulus illis

(The shepherds say that I too am a poet, but I am not inclined to believe them.) . . .

The next two lines (35-36) are a freer adaptation from Theocritus VII. 39-41. Yet in what directly precedes this five-line close imitation of his Greek model, Vergil marks a sharp contrast with Theocritus. Moeris in 27-29 has sung of the dangers of Mantua, "too near to poor Cremona," and then Lycidas utters a two-line blessing (30-31) as a prelude to further songs:

> Sic tua Cyrneas fugiant examina taxos,
> sic cytiso pastae distendant ubera vaccae,
>   incipe, si quid habes.

(So many your bee-swarms escape the Corsican yews, so may your cows, well-grazed, stretch full their udders: begin with what you have.)

The corresponding passage in Theocritus (VII. 31-34) is as follows: . . .

(This is the road for the Harvest Fesival, for our companions are making an offering-feast in honor of Demeter as the first-fruits of their bounty. For the goddess in rich measure filled their threshing floor to the full with good grain.)

In Vergil blessing alternates with disaster, and the first half of the blessing is itself a warning about sinister yews from remote Corsica. Rather than the unambiguous richness and exuberant fertility of Theocritus, then, Vergil presents a complex intermingling of hopefulness and danger. Characteristically too what good fortune Vergil does envisage refers to a remote and uncertain future; Theocritus' bounty is a tangible and established fact in the present.

In the two songs that follow (39-43, 46-50), as already noted, close imitation of Theocritus contrasts with the star of Caesar. Yet it is interesting that it is the troubled Moeris who sings the mythological themes of Hellenistic pastoral. The exiled shepherd has been silently meditating (*tacitus . . . mecum ipse voluto,* 37) on pastoral fancies about Galatea and the Cyclops. Moeris, even in the midst of his misfortunes, has forgotten neither pastoral song nor pastoral manners. So he grants his friends request, and with this rather gallant touch Vergil seems to assert a minor triumph of the poetic-pastoral spirit over the harsh facts of discord and force.

But later Moeris does remark sadly that he has forgotten all his songs (though he attributes his forgetfulness to age rather than to his present troubles: see 51ff.); and he then utters one of the most beautiful verses in the *Eclogues:*

> Saepe ego longos
> cantando puerum memini me condere soles

(I remember that as a boy I often laid long days to rest with singing, 51-52.)

The joy of poetry is looked on with the vague nostalgia of something past and lost. The phrase is Vergil's own, and is eminently suited to the complex tone of this *Eclogue.* But again Vergil may be intentionally drawing a contrast with Theocritean pastoral. The language seems to have been suggested by Theocritus XI, 39-40, that is from the same general context as Moeris' song in 39-43. In the Theocritus passage, the Cyclops boasts of his skill in song: . . .

(singing of you, my dear honey-apple, and myself together often late into the night.)

Vergil has taken the mythical, comic singer from his untroubled erotic context and made him a mortal facing age and sorrow in a disordered, violent world.

In keeping with the tone of *E.* 9, however, Vergil does not let this somber trait of Moeris go too far or dominate too much of the poem. He only touches on it here with a single fine stroke, and then has Lycidas try to coax him into song again. Lycidas' speech, his last in the poem, again draws heavily on Theocritus:

> Causando nostros in longum ducis amores.
> et nunc omne tibi stratum silet aequor, et omnes,
> aspice, ventosi ceciderunt murmuris aurae.

(By your excuses you only put off our desires. And now all the sea lies flat and silent, and look, all the breezes with their murmuring gusts have fallen, 56-58.)

Vergil's model, however, is a song, not direct speech, and a song of love, newly written by one of the rustic poets:

(Warm love of him burns me. And the halcyon-birds will lay to rest the waves and the sea and the south wind and the east wind which stirs up the bottom-most sea-weed—the halcyons who most of all birds are beloved by the grey-eyed Nereids and by all who have their prey from the sea. VII. 56-60.)

The original is not only a song of love, but passes quickly into the realm of myth and mythical beings like the Nereids. It comes too at about a third of the way through the poem. In Vergil the words are direct speech, have no mythological allusions, and come at the end of the poem. He thus again takes the graceful calm of Theocritus and overlays it with a suggestion of complexity and melancholy. He seems to be glancing too at another Theocritean context where the silence of the sea does carry somber, even tragic overtones, that is, Theocritus' Second *Idyll*, the *Pharmaceutria:* . . .

> (Behold, the sea grows silent, silent the winds; but silent not my pain within my breast. II. 38-39.)[15]

And Vergil may have learned something from the expansive view out into a calm, but remote and indifferent realm with which Theocritus ends this poem: . . .

> (Farewell, Moon-goddess of the brilliant throne, farewell you other stars, attendants following the chariot of still Night. II. 165-66.)

Within the framework of Vergil's own poem, then, his lines on the sea and the winds create a broad, quiet, more somber atmosphere after the conventional exchange of pastoral song—a hint at something remote, a more than human silence that seems to anticipate some of the mysterious and awesome nightfalls of the *Aeneid:*

> Et iam nox umida caelo
> praecipitat suadentque cadentia sidera somnos.
>
> (And now the damp night falls from the sky and the falling stars urge sleep, *Aen.* 2.8-9.)

or

> Iamque fere mediam caeli nox umida metam
> contigerat, placida laxabant membra quiete.
>
> (And now damp night had attained the mid-point of its goal in the sky, and peaceful limbs were being loosed in rest, *Aen.* 5.835-36.)[16]

This suggestion of a larger and darker perspective is deepended in the next two lines:

> hinc adeo media est nobis via; namque sepulcrum
> incipit apparere Bianoris.
>
> (This is the middle of our road; for the tomb of Bianor begins to appear.)

Again a close translation of the Seventh *Idyll:* . . .

> (And we did not yet reach the middle of our road, nor did the tomb of Brasilas appear to us, 10-11.)

Yet in Theocritus this passage comes at the very beginning of the poem to help create the setting and perhaps refers to a real place. Vergil uses it at the end of his poem in close conjunction with a later passage from *Idyll* VII, and (despite the ancient commentators) he probably has no real place in mind. He uses the tomb, after the solemn lines about the sea, to create a deeper mood of sadness, a reminder of death that is in keeping with the suggestions of melancholy in the poem, the vicissitudes of fortune (5) and the losses entailed by age (51). (Note too that Vergil's *sepulcrum* is a more sinister reminder of death than Theocritus' natural ςιμα.) He thus sounds a new, typically Vergilian note that will influence later conceptions of pastoral: Death too in Arcady, *Et in Arcadia ego.*[17]

Vergil closes his poem too on a note of suspension and vague hope. Lycidas, after his reference to the tomb in 59, suggests that they sing right where they are, amid the rich foliage of the pastoral setting:

> hic, ubi densas
> agricolae stringunt frondes, hic, Moeri, canamus.
>
> (Here, where the farmers trim the thick leaves, here, Moeris, let us sing, 60-61.)

But the timeless moment of pastoral is not for those who have such a journey as Moeris. Thus Lycidas—almost inadvertently, it would seem—recalls Moeris' destination and the pressing reality of the journey: *tamen veniemus in urbem* ("even so we shall come to the city," 62). His words, with their echo of *in urbem* of the first line, evoke again the awareness of exile and unrest. His next line too contains a mildly ominous element, also associated with travel: the fear of nightfall and rain:

> aut si nox pluviam ne colligat ante veremur,
> cantantes licet usque (minus via laedit) eamus.
>
> (Or, if we fear that night may first gather rain, we may go straight on singing—the road is less irksome thus, 63-64.)

The sinister, or at least unpleasant, suggestion—carried largely through the vivid *colligat*—appears even through the bright naiveté and hopeful playfulness of a Lycidas. Despite the generosity and cheeriness of Lycidas, whose touching simplicity in offering help and a song strikes a more genuine and pathetic note than Tityrus' offer in *E.* 1, his more experienced companion cannot accept: *Desine plura, puer* ("cease from further efforts, my boy," 66) Moeris replies. His *puer* brings out, sadly, the difference between the two shepherds, a bit like Meliboeus' closing *amaras,* "bitter," in *E.* 1.78: the youthful singer who will remain among the *densas frondes* of 60-61, and the older man, travelling reluctantly *in urbem.* Amid such contrasts songs must be put off, at least for the moment: *Carmina tum melius, cum venerit ipse, canemus* ("We'll sing our songs better when he comes himself," 67).

This uncertain, hesitant ending is again in the most marked contrast with Vergil's model, for Theocritus' poem ends with laughter (128, 156) and an elaborate and graceful enumeration of all the beauties that the pastoral world holds, including Nymphs and Polyphemus (128-57).

A portrait of Vergil.

Indeed Theocritus' final lines leave a picture of the benign fertility of the grain-goddess and a "mellow fruitfulness" that is almost Keatsian in its richness: . . .

(I wish I might fix in her grain-heap a huge winnowing-shovel while she laughs holding in either hand sheaves and poppies. VII. 155-57.)

Vergil thus creates a different kind of pastoral world, one which he subtly, but inevitably contrasts with that of his Greek predecessor. Theocritus' shepherd world is peaceful, happy, in close touch with the realm of myth; Vergil's is precarious and disturbed. The Roman poet, writing in the closing decades of the "Age of Agony," (as Toynbee has termed the period from about 300 to 31 B.C.) must come to closer grips with the realities of violence and disorder about him. He cannot so freely indulge in the exuberant richness that characterizes large parts of Theocritus' Seventh *Idyll,* and indeed nearly all the *Idylls.* Or, if he does turn to a beautiful and untroubled Arcady, he must come back, back to war-torn Italy, to Rome or to Mantua "too close to poor Cremona."

There is thus a divided tendency in Vergilian pastoral. On the one hand the pressures of the realities lead the poet to transform Theocritus' Sicily or Cos into a totally imaginary Arcadia, an Arcadia such as never existed in Greece or anywhere else. On the other hand, the poet cannot enter too far into his Arcady. Neither his purpose nor the pressing nature of the realities themselves will allow him. Hence he must check his song, resist the attraction which such an Arcady exerts: *Desine plura, puer, et quod nunc instat agamus* ("Cease from more singing, my lad, and let's attend to what is now at hand," *E.* 9.66). He might, of course, not have resisted; but then the *Eclogues* would lack the complexity of tone, the delicate mixture of beauty and sorrow that mark their poetic maturity and comprise half their beauty.

What has not often enough been made clear by those who emphasize the "realism" of Theocritus over against the dreamy unreality of Vergil is that even the "realistic" parts of Theocritus involve no actual break with his pastoral world. There is little discontinuity for the Greek poet between the erotically tinged realm of myth and the realm of "realistic" rusticity (also, usually, erotically tinged). In Theocritus' First *Idyll,* for instance, it is an easy and smooth movement from the song of Daphnis, dying of love, to the frolicsome female and lusty male goats of the shepherd in the last two lines. There is a certain contrast for an effect of pathos, it is true; but the rustics still stand partly in the mythical world, or at least the rustic "realities" are not at variance with the myth and do not disturb the frame into which the myth is set. For Vergil, however, there is a harsh discrepancy between the remote peace of pastoral Arcadia and the realities of the present, for these realities actually *do* threaten the pastoral world in a way in which Theocritus' touches of realism never do. For Theocritus the contrast between myth and "realism" may be amusing or pathetic, but it is never ominous or destructive.

The realm of myth for Theocritus too is much more present, much more an autonomous world than it is for Vergil. However vague and "unreal" Vergil's pastoral setting is, he has nothing that corresponds to the Polyphemus-Galatea *Idylls* or the Hylas *Idyll.* In works like *Idylls* I or VI or XI, where the myth is especially strong, Theocritus' rustics stand in some indefinable ground between the real and the imaginary, whereas Vergil's shepherds, however idealized, are always to some extent real people with real problems or sufferings. Theocritus, on the other hand, can dispense with the pastoral element almost entirely, as in *Idylls* II or XIV or XV. Here, in his treatment of love in a Greek town or his portrayal of middle-class life, Theocritus can be totally "realistic"—but he is not simultaneously pastoral. He can write *Idylls* which, properly speaking, are not bucolic at all. His range is wider than Vergil's, and this has led to an incorrect estimate of Theocritean and Vergilian "realism."

Most recently Snell has exaggerated Vergil's "dreaminess," his need for a "far-away land overlaid with the golden haze of unreality"[18] and has made of him "a nostalgic refugee from sombre realities."[19] Though such statements have some validity, they oversimplify Vergil's complexity. Vergil certainly longs for peace; yet he has a keen sense of the discrepancy, the "dissonance" (to use Snell's own term) between the longed-for serenity and the realities which prevent such hopes from being more than the shelter and rest offered for a single night, as in *E.* 1, or the hesitant glance toward the future, as at the end of *E.* 9. Not only is it *not* true of Vergil that "the tension between the real and literary world which Theocritus had exploited for its peculiar charms is brought to nought, and everything shifts back to the even plane of an undifferentiated majesty,"[20] but, on the contrary Vergil (at least in *E.* 9) actually uses Theocritus' pastoral settings as a foil for the disturbed and threatened world from which his shepherds are brusquely exiled.

It is, in fact, just because Vergil's pastoral world is totally an artificial creation that it is so threatened by the realities "outside." Vergil's Arcady, unlike Theocritus' Greek or Sicilian landscapes, comes into being by opposition to and removal from these realities, but Vergil does not forget that the realities are there. Thus, while another Vergilian scholar, Klingner, is justified in stressing that "for Vergil the world of Theocritus' shepherds has hardened into a pastoral art-world (Kunstwelt) enclosed within itself,"[21] it should be remembered that the price of the ideality of this artificial world is exactly its fragility:

> Hac te nos *fragili* donabimus ante cicuta

(First we shall present you with this fragile pipe, *E.* 5.85)

Vergil himself says of the instrument which sang *Eclogues* 2 and 3, two of the least trouble and most purely "pastoral" of the *Eclogues.*

Vergil's use of Theocritus should not, then, be looked upon as a mere exercise in translation for a poet with abundant leisure. It is rather in the nature of a creative borrowing and transformation by a poet who delights in allusion. The ancients themselves were aware of the extent to which Vergil deliberately modified his models. So, for example, Aulus Gellius:

> Sicuti nuperrime aput mensam cum legerentur utraque simul Bucolica Theocriti et Vergilii, animadvertimus reliquisse Vergilium quod Graece quidem mire quam suave est, verti autem neque debuit neque potuit. Sed enim quod substituit pro eo quod omiserat, non abest quin iucundius lepidiusque sit.

> (For example when just recently the Bucolics of both Theocritus and Vergil were both read together at table, we noted that Vergil left out something that was marvellously delightful in the Greek, but which he should not and could not have translated. But yet what he put in its place succeeds in being even more pleasing and graceful. *Noct. Att.* 9.4.4-5.)

Of modern critics, W. F. J. Knight has suggested an analogy with Pound's use of Propertius.[22] And elsewhere Knight remarks,

In the *Eclogues* Vergil used the particular past of the *Idylls* in order to vitalize and generalize his own particular experience. He is a good poet partly because he takes that method, the best and perhaps the only good method, to make experience artistic. Poets must, for some mysterious reason, place themselves in a true relation to world poetry, by fixing themselves where they belong in its stream.[23]

And Vergil's ability to use Theocritean passages in complex new ways is well illustrated by the Eighth *Eclogue,* where Vergil not only adapts several Theocritean *Idylls,* but within his first song deepens the seriousness and sadness of Damon's love-plaint by fusing the rustic banter of Theocritus III with the somberness and pathos of Theocritus I (the lament for Daphnis). This tendency to combine different elements into a new and rich synthesis has long been noted as a characteristic of Vergil's art and is already well pronounced in the *Eclogues,* perhaps most notably in the Sixth.[24] There is, as already suggested, a possible example of this technique in the Ninth *Eclogue* too in the lines on the sea (57-58) with the probable reminiscene of Theocritus II.

This tendency of Vergil suggests a further motive in his use of Theocritus VII. Theocritus' poem is not simply an autobiographical account, but is concerned primarily with poets and poetry. Hence in using it, Vergil may be suggesting that the farm and the dispossession, however vivid and distressing in themselves, are but parts of a larger issue, that is, the nature of pastoral poetry, and in a sense all poetry, in a time of violence and disruption. The conflict between Arcady and Rome (or Mantua) is not only a conflict between peaceful Theocritean pastoral and Vergilian lament, but also, and more generally, part of a larger and sempiternal tension between the creative independence of poetry and the demanding, often chaotic, realities of the external world. It is a conflict, then (and one that occurs throughout Augustan literature) between order and disorder, between man as creative agent and man as passive victim of circumstance, between the formative act of will and mind and the fortuitous succession of events that are meaningless in themselves and dissolve the meaning and coherence that still remain.

That Vergil in the *Eclogues* is aware of these tensions and often self-consciously aware of poetry in its autonomous, creative power is intimated in the Sixth *Eclogue* and perhaps to some extent in the Tenth also. The various quotations of the *Eclogues* from one another also point to this poetic self-consciousness. That poetry itself is a major concern in the Ninth *Eclogue* appears from the emphasis given to song and singing throughout. Yet "songs" are mentioned only after the *Eclogue* has been introduced by the non-poetic realities of expulsion and war. Lines 1-6 have the movement of prose (in so far as this is possible in Vergil) rather than of verse; and it is significantly only after Lycidas' beautiful description of the country in 7-10 that the theme of song and the power of song emerges: *omnia carminibus vestrum servasse Menalcan* ("I heard . . . that your Menalcas had saved all with his songs,"

10). Moeris, however, knows, sadly, of the weakness of song against force, and corrects his friend:

> Audieras, et fama fuit; sed carmina tantum
> nostra valent, Lycida, tela inter Martia quantum
> Chaonias dicunt aquila veniente columbas.

> (So you heard, and such was the tale. But our songs, Lycidas, have as much strength against the weapons of Mars as they say Chaonian doves have at the approach of the eagle. 11-13.)

Even so, the poetical coloring of this statement suggests that there is yet hope for poetry; and the two friends proceed to quote from Menalcas' songs and discuss their own poetic abilities with abundant references to words for song and singing like *carmen, canere, cantare* (see, e.g. 19, 21, 26, 33, 38, 44).[25] Yet Moeris, with his sober knowledge of the limitations of song reflects nostalgically on the time when he sang songs till sunset (52) and complains that he has now forgotten all his songs (*nunc oblita mihi tot carmina,* 53) and even has lost his voice. Lycidas, however, urges that they continue singing as they travel (*canamus,* 59; *cantantes . . . cantantes,* 64-65), but Moeris persists in his refusal and closes the poem with hope for songs in the future (*carmina,* 66).

The theme of song thus dominates the poem, but with a difference between the two singers. Moeris, the elder, has been more exposed to the realities which exist "outside" the realm of pastoral song. He has a sense of cruel forces in the world, of vicissitude and old age (note the parallel forms of expression, *quoniam fors omnia versat,* "because chance turns all things about," line 5, and *omnia fert aetas . . .,* "age carries off all things . . .," line 51). He knows too from experience how feeble song is against the violence of the world "outside" (11ff., and note the military image in *victi,* "conquered," line 5); and he knows how easily the capacity for song is lost (52f.). Indeed in his words and in his situation he is the reminder of that "fragility" of the Vergilian pastoral world.

There is a corresponding difference in the subjects chosen by two friends. Lycidas refers to Menalcas' song about Nymphs and flowers (19) and quotes a song of his about Theocritean shepherds at play (23-25). Moeris, on the contrary, quotes from Menalcas' song about the woes of Mantua (27-29). Then in the second pair of songs, Moeris quotes his own song about Galatea, while Lycidas quotes from Moeris' song in honor of the star of Caesar. Lycidas' songs (i.e those he chooses to quote from Menalcas and from Moeris, lines 23-25 and 39-43) are direct, simple, exuberant; they belong to the untroubled rustic world of Theocritus, from whom they are largely close translations. Moeris' song of 23-25, on the other hand, deals with harsh political realities. Vergil thus creates an opposition between two kinds of pastoral song, one belonging to the Hellenistic past, the other to the troubled present. It would be oversimple to identify Lycidas with Theocritus (or Theocritean pastoral) and Moeris with Vergil, for Moeris too, after all, does quote an old song of his own on Galatea,

dimly remembered though it is (39-43). What Vergil is perhaps suggesting, however, is that pastoral in his age must embrace the experiences of a Moeris as well as the gay enthusiasm of a Lycidas. His shepherd can no longer be simply a carefree singer but will know the insults of force, will have a sense of change and age, will be aware of the precarious fragility and vulnerability of song and the realms song can create.

It is perhaps for these reasons that the full realization of the pastoral form in Latin had to await Vergil, a poet with the technical skill to adapt Theocritean diction and rhythms into Latin, yet also with the depth of feeling and power of allusive fusion to remake the Hellenistic form into something expressive of the Roman *gravitas* and *dignitas.* Such a poet has (figuratively speaking) to reconcile Moeris and Lycidas, and this means to create a pastoral framework which can include also Rome and Mantua, wars and confiscations, a form in which the Greek feeling for pure beauty, for the formal qualities of image, rhythm, and sound for their own sake, can be fused with the Roman concern with the practical realities of administration, war, and empire and the sufferings they entail. Thus the eagerness and sunny flippancy of Lycidas (line 1) ripen into the deeper, more comprehensive experience and more complex hesitation of Moeris (lines 66-67). Or, to put it differently, the poet begins the Ninth *Eclogue* as a tentative Theocritus and ends it definitely, though delicately, as Vergil.

It is, however, perhaps because the realities of Rome can be kept in the background that the *Eclogues* succeed, within the limits of their intention and their form, more fully and unambiguously than does the *Aeneid* (which is not to say, of course, that they are greater). The small and intimate scale of the *Eclogues,* their personal tone and "literary" character enable the poet to keep firm control on the amount of "reality" and *Romanitas* that he need absorb into his poetry. When he is to attempt to absorb the totality of the Roman ideal into poetry, the results could not but be aesthetically less uniform and more controversial. But, as the ancients too realized, perfect evenness and freedom from flaws are not a final criterion of poetic greatness.[26]

III

The relation between the First and Ninth *Eclogues,* then, may be more significant than the fact that both concern the loss and restitution of a farm. Both poems, as has been seen, deal with the confrontation between a peaceful, undisturbed pastoral world and the hard political realities of the Roman present. In larger terms their theme is the problem of the writing of poetry, indeed the creation of anything beautiful, in an atmosphere of disruption and disorder. Hence the singer's loss of his songs recurs as an important subject at the end of both poems: *Carmina nulla canam* ("No songs shall I sing," *E.* 1.77); *Nunc oblita mihi tot carmina* ("Now I have forgotten so many songs," *E.* 9.53).

Of the many attempts to establish the chronological relation between the two poems, none have been decisive (though a strong tendency favors the priority of *E.* 9); and it is perhaps more fruitful and more in accord with Vergil's poetic intention to regard the poems as parallel in theme rather than sequential in time. So too Vergil's change of the names of his characters in the two works need not indicate, as has been claimed, a desire to plead his cause afresh or to intercede for both slave and free alike,[27] but may merely signify that he is treating different aspects of the same general theme. *Eclogues* One and Nine would thus span the collection (of *E.* 10 something will be said presently), again not necessarily, as has been suggested, because Vergil is trying to separate his personal troubles as far as possible from the triad, *E.* 4, 5, 6, in the center of the collection,[28] but rather because he thus frames the other poems, and especially the more purely "pastoral" *Eclogues* Two and Three and Seven and Eight, with a sense of the precariousness and threatened circumstances out of which such poetry is achieved, the difficulties from which is it wrested.[29] In this way too he colors the rest of the collection with the poignancy of beauty amid loss and sadness, the quality that so strongly predominates in *E.* 1 and 9.

There are reasons too why Vergil would have chosen *E.* 1 to begin the collection. Its position cannot be wholly accounted for by the explanation that it serves to dedicate the book to Octavian, for, as a host of commentators have noted, it offers as much criticism as praise of the young ruler (see especially lines 70ff.). One explanation can perhaps be found in the relation of the theme and tone of the poem to the pastoral framework of the *Eclogues* as a whole. Thus while concerned with the interplay between the imaginary and the real, the First *Eclogue* modulates with greater pathos than the Ninth from the beauty of the pastoral world to the disturbances in the poet's Italy. This pastoral beauty is seen with a heightened intensity precisely because it has to be left behind. Because of the "distancing" effects in the Ninth *Eclogue* discussed above, the pain of this loss is mitigated there, whereas the confrontation between pastoral and reality is sharper in *E.* 1 than in any other of the *Eclogues.* Perhaps, then, Vergil intended to begin with an emotionally involving situation and to reserve his more "intellectual" and more aesthetically selfconscious treatment of the same theme for the later place in the collection.

Yet at the same time the gentle note on which *E.* 1 begins and the circular, a-b-a movement of the introductory passage serve not only to present a microcosm of a characteristic movement in the *Eclogues,* but also to lead slowly and gradually into the pastoral world being opened, while lightly suggesting some of the complexities involved in the existence of that world.

The Ninth *Eclogue,* on the other hand, while beginning more harshly than the First, does not develop the threats of loss and exile so vividly. There is still a *scelus* (17), a sense of evil and disaster, but they remain further in the background than the *impius miles* of *E.* 1.70. The movement of *E.* 9 too, as befits a journey poem, is linear rather than circular; and the concluding lines make only a muted reference back to the disturbances at the beginning. This less pessimistic mood is again in keeping with the place of *E.* 9 in the collection, for it comes after the large constatements of order in the three central poems, *E.* 4, 5, and 6. Indeed not only does it quote from the Fifth *Eclogue,* but in the song about Caesar's star (46-50) expresses hope for a more beneficent order of things. The attitude toward Octavian seems more optimistic too; but regardless of any chronological development, Vergil seems to have created a deliberate counterpoise between the First and Ninth *Eclogues.* He thus introduces an element of movement into the collection, a movement from the temporary rest of a single night to a more assured and stable, if still indefinite order, possible now after the vision of the *magnus saeculorum ordo* in *E.* 4 and the larger themes, the *paulo maiora* (*E.* 4.1) of *Eclogues* Five and Six. In the Ninth *Eclogue,* though we return again to the "mixed" atmosphere of violence in pastoral Arcadia, something can be envisaged, if only in song and poetic vision (cf. *ecce Dionaei processit Caesaris astrum,* "Lo, the star of Caesar, descendant of Dione, has come forth," 47), that seemed impossibly remote in the despairing atmosphere of the first poem of the collection.

Eclogue Nine too has a certain calm, lacking in *E.* 1, which is fitting at the point where the collection draws to a close. It is less dramatically intense than that poem, but has a wider scope, as in the expansive lines on the sea (57-58). The characters, though less vivid, convey a larger sense of the general condition of human life (see lines 5 and 51). Since the threat of exile is less explicitly visualized, the two shepherds, threatened and unthreatened alike, can still communicate through the medium of pastoral song. Vergil thus creates a sense of aesthetic completeness, characteristic of the individual poems, in ending his collection in an atmosphere of greater calmness and breadth of view.

The calmer and larger tone of the Ninth *Eclogue* also helps prepare for the Tenth. This poem, like *E.* 1 and 9, is concerned with exile; but, as in *E.* 9, the experience is at a certain remove, indeed far less serious than in either of these two poems. The spontaneous sympathy which Lycidas feels for Moeris in *E.* 9—rather more than Meliboeus is able to evoke from Tityrus in *E.* 1—also leads into the sympathy that the poet and the whole of Arcadia feel for the deserted lover in *E.* 10. The development is a natural one within the collection, for after poems like *E.* 2, 6, or 8 the pastoral world appears as colored with a certain gentleness and tenderness. By *Eclogue* Ten it is clearly as Snell called it, "a spiritual landscape." Hence the poet can confidently claim, *Non canimus surdis, respondent omnia silvae* ("We sing not to things deaf; the forests echo back all," *E.* 10.8). Hence too the lament of the pastoral world over the fading lover (13ff.). There is a similar passage in the First *Eclogue* (38-39), but the contrast is instructive, for there the description is shorter (only one-and-one-half lines), and only trees and fountains are involved. In the Tenth *Eclogue* all of Arcadian nature, trees, two major mountains, the rustic folk, even the sheep (*stant et oves* circum, 16) weep for Gallus (note too that in *E.* 1 the pines and fountains do not weep for Tityrus; they simply call him back: *vocabant,* 39). Thus what is a pretty conceit in the First *Eclogue* becomes expanded in the Tenth to suggest an element of feeling deeply pervading the pastoral world.

This pastoral world of *E.* 10, then, gains a reality and autonomy of its own. It is an imaginative creation of the individual poet, but it has something of the large independence that tradition conferred on the myths of Theocritus. This world, then, is no longer threatened by the reality outside, but can in fact attract these "real" figures into its own framework and even console them in their griefs.[30] Gallus would himself become an Arcadian shepherd (50ff.), though there is a slightly humorous suggestion that he sticks a bit at the reality of the transformation (cf. *iam mihi per rupes videor,* 58).

Yet there is seriousness amid the humor too, for the welcoming of the exiled poet in a gentle Arcadia is the inverse of the theme of *E.* 1 where the restored shepherd has himself been affected by the artificiality of the city while the "authentic" poet-shepherd, the one whose language and sensibilities fit and enrich the pastoral world, is exiled. Recompense is thus made for the violence done to the pastoral folk of *E.* 1. The Gallus-episode serves to reinstate the worth both of the poet and of the Arcadian landscape in which he lives after the losses and indignities of *E.* 1 and 9. Sympathy replaces insensitivity, war yields to love (omnia vincit amor, *E.* 10.69; contrast *E.* 9.5, *nunc victi, tristes, quoniam fors omnia versat,* "Now defeated, saddened, because chance turns all things about"). The victory of love for Lycoris, with the poetic consequences it inspires, over "the mad love for war" (*insanus amor duri me Martis in armis/ tela inter media, E.* 10.44-45)[31] is a validation of poetry in a troubled world and cancels the ineffectuality of the poet against force and brutality in the Ninth *Eclogue* (cf. *tela inter Martia,* 9.12. The arms which once unjustly drove the poet-shepherd out of his peaceful haunts are now to be cast away by a warrior who would abandon Mars for a poetic Arcadia.

The end of *Eclogue* X provides another, and final, statement of reassurance to the threats of exile in *E.* 1 and 9. Gallus' exile is described in deliberately exaggerated rhetoric that recalls the tone of Tityrus in *E.* 1 (*E.* 10.56-58; cf. *E.* 1.59-63). But, as in the First *Eclogue* too, the wanderings to distant places are followed by the calm of nightfall and the placid regularity of shepherd life:

> Surgamus: solet esse gravis cantantibus umbra,
> iuniperi gravis umbra; nocet et frugibus umbrae.
> Ite domum saturae, venit Hesperus, ite capellae.

> (Let us rise; shade is wont to be harmful to singers, harmful the shade of the juniper; growing crops too are harmed by shadows. Go on homeward, full-fed, the Evening Star comes, go on my goats, *E.* 10.75-77.)

The echo of *E.* 1 is obvious and intentional. Yet here the "heavy shadow" follows directly upon a description of new growth in the spring:

> Gallo, cuius amor tantum mihi crescit in horas
> quantum vere novo viridis se subicit alnus

> (. . . Gallus for whom my love grows hour by hour as fast as a green alder shoots up when spring is fresh, *E.* 10.73-74);

and the goats are full-fed and are being driven *home.* The shepherd still has his goats and his *domus* to which to drive them. This shepherd-poet is far from the cry of Meliboeus in *E.* 1.74,

> Ite meae, quondam felix pecus, ite capellae.

> (Go on, my goats, once happy flock, go on.)

The prayer of *E.* 9.31,

> Sic cytiso pastae distendant ubera vaccae

> (Let the cows, grazed on clover, stretch full their udders)

is thus fulfilled, though in the most imaginary and least real setting of the *Eclogues.* And yet perhaps the poet who promises a time of better song (*E.* 9.67) has come.[32]

It is characteristic of the *Eclogues,* as should now be clear, that they should end with this mixture of spring and shadow, exile and home, unfaithful and faithful love (see *E.* 10.73). Yet the assurance of settledness and fullness in the last line of the collection, spoken by the poet *in propria persona* and thus bridging the gap between pastoral framework and reality, seems to answer the tentative note on which the Ninth *Eclogue* ended. In the Tenth *Eclogue,* not only the theme of song and exile, but also that of fertility and growth are given a final positive turn. Its conclusion, with the *saturae capellae,* is far closer to the richness and bounty of Demeter at the end of Theocritus VII, Vergil's model for *E.* 9. The assurance of settledness and fertility which could not be given there is given (though not unambiguously: there is still the *gravis umbra*) at the end of the whole collection. It is as if the Ninth *Eclogue* ends on a suspended cadence to which the Tenth finally gives a resolution, but still in a minor key.

On the whole, then, the last two poems are positive, optimistic, expansive; but they, and *Eclogue* I too, partake of the "mixed" quality characteristic of the *Eclogues* as a whole, the sense of joy amid sadness, beauty amid loss. The counterpoise between *Eclogues* 1 and 9 articulates this quality in terms of the movement and symmetry of the collection, spanning the whole with a suggestion of the tension between pastoral and reality and the larger conditions under which and in the midst of which this poetic world comes into being. That tension is given no easy or oversimplified resolution. The poet seems to wish, in *E.* 10, to make the final impression hopeful and positive. Yet exile still has a central place in the poem, and with it a sense of deliberate unreality, an element of wishfulness; and these themes, in their close relation to the contrasts and uncertainties of *E.* 1 and 9, evoke at the very end of the collection a quality of suspension, though hopeful and fruitful suspension, between fundamental contraries of human life.

Vergil's problem in adapting the untroubled limpidity of Theocritean pastoral for the Roman scene is analogous to that faced by other Roman poets trying to create things of beauty in times of war and disturbance. Lucretius prays to Venus to bring peace to Rome:

> Nam neque nos agere hoc patriai tempore iniquo
> possumus aequo animo
>
> (For we cannot work with calm spirit at a time of woe
> for our country, *De Rer. Nat.* 1.41-42.)

Horace too looks with admiration on a poet of the Greek past who, though "fierce in war," could yet sing, amid battles and dangers, of wine, song, and love (*Odes* 1.32.6ff.).

But Vergil, in balancing *E.* 1 by *E.* 9 and partially resolving the uncertainties of *E.* 9 in *E.* 10, affirms a hope and belief in order and beauty. Moeris' *carmina tum melius,* tentative as it is, is nevertheless a positive statement in the face of a negative world. Despite exile and disorder, still joy, beauty, and song predominate in the *Eclogues;* and in ending with *E.* 9 and 10 Vergil affirms a regenerative sense of life's continuities and possibilities, something of what Yeats, in another poem written in troubled times, spoke of as "gaiety transfiguring all that dread."[33] Vergil's "gaiety," however, is of a very mixed and complex nature; and it should be recalled that the *Aeneid* too, like *Eclogues* 1 and 9 a poem of exile and dispossession, ends with mixed triumph and shadows, but shadows of a far more sinister kind than those of the *Eclogues* (*vitaque cum gemitu fugit indignata sub umbras,* "with a groan his life fled in anger to the shadows [or, "to the shades"] below").[34] This sense of the sadness and losses of life, the Vergilian *lacrimae rerum,* already permeates the *Eclogues,* richly interwoven though they are with bucolic landscape and song. The presence of these "shadowy" elements, even in Arcady, is part of the complex greatness of Vergil's art. They are, indeed, essential to his, as to all, poetry, for they comprise that in the face of which poetry is almost always written, yet that which great poetry never forgets.[35]

Notes

1. Vergil's characteristic fusion of personal elements with larger themes in the *Eclogues* is stressed by F. Klingner, *Gnomon* 3 (1927) 581.

2. F. Plessis, in Plessis et Lejay, *Oeuvres de Virgile* (Paris 1913) xvii.

3. Biographical problems in *E.* 1 and 9 still receive a large share of the energy of Vergilian scholars, as can be seen from G. Duckworth's survey, "Recent Work on Vergil (1957-63)," *CW* 57 (1963-64) 198 and 200; see also the earlier survey (1940-56) in *CW* 51 (1958) 124. C. Vandersleyen, *LEC* 31 (1963) 266 has well protested, "Cette désolante explication

autobiographique est répandue dans la majorité des éditions, scolaires ou autres." The most recent study of the Ninth *Eclogue* also focuses largely (though not exclusively) on biographical and historical matters: G. Cipolla, "Political Audacity and Esotericism in the Ninth *Eclogue,*" *Acta Classica* 5 (1962) 48-57.

4. On the unity of the *Eclogues* see Klingner, *Gnomon* 3 (1927) 582, and, most recently, Brooks Otis, *Virgil* (Oxford, 1963) 128-43.

5. For a similar circular movement in the introductory portion of the poem, compare also the Eighth *Eclogue,* where the introduction, also of five lines, begins, *Pastorum Musam Damonis et Alphesiboei,* and ends (line 5), *Damonis Musam dicemus et Alphesiboei.*

6. The point of the *tanta* seems to be missed by G. Stégen in his discussion of the passage, "L'unité de la première Bucolique," *LEC* 12 (1943-44) 13-14. He refers the "so great reason" to Tityrus' leaving of Amaryllis who is mentioned twenty lines before(!) and again (by Meliboeus) some ten lines later. For the opposition of city and country, in favor of the country, see also *E.*2.60ff., esp., *Pallas quas condidit arces / ipsa colat; nobis placeant ante omnia silvae* ("Let Pallas Athene herself inhabit the citadels she has founded; but let woodlands please us before all else").

7. For a similar use of a circular movement compare also *E.*2, which both begins and ends with "shadows" (lines 3 and 67) and with the heat of passion (*ardebat,* 1; *urit,* 68) set against the peace and steadiness of nature and farm work (cf. 8-9, 10-11 with 63-65, 66-67, 70-72; also *at mecum raucis,* etc., 12-13, with *me tamen urit amor,* 68). Here, however, the circular form has its own special function, i.e., to suggest the hopeless continuity of Corydon's passion despite his rather vacillating efforts to cast it off. Compare too the theme of the disconsolate heifer in *E.*8: *immemor herbarum . . . iuvenca,* vs.2; *cum fessa iuvencum / . . . quaerendo bucula,* vss. 85ff.

8. F. Klingner, "Das erste Hirtengedicht Virgils," in *Römische Geisteswelt,* ed. 3 (Munich 1956) 307.

9. The contrast between the two shepherds, by far in favor of Meliboeus, has been stated by René Waltz in an essay which deserves more attention than it has received, "La Ire et la IXe Bucolique," *Rev. Belge de Philologie et d'Histoire* 6 (1927) 31-58. The contrast has recently been stressed again by L. A. MacKay, *Phoenix* 15 (1961) 157.

10. The tension between peace and disorder is brought out (though with some overstatement) by Vandersleyen (above, note 3) 270: "Ainsi par la confrontation entre les deux hommes, entre ce bonheur et malheur, le poème se charge progressivement d'une douleur qui éclate à la fin en

chagrin, colère, ironie amère. Est-ce là l'esprit d'une bergerie? Ou un remerciement, alors que le privilégié est ridicule et honteux de lui-même?" With Vandersleyen, I cannot agree with interpretations that make *E*.1 into a laudation of Octavian, as does Hanslik *WS* 68 (1955) 18-19.

11. E.g. Waltz (above, note 9) 51; Stégen, *LEC* 21 (1953) 334. *Contra:* Sellar, *Vergil* (Oxford 1897) 142.

12. A glance at Duckworth's survey, *CW* 57 (1963-64) 200, shows that the search for the country described in *E*.9 goes on apace.

13. On Moeris' incoherence see Waltz (above, note 9) 45.

14. Conington's view, in the introduction of his edition (ed. 3, London 1872, I 6-8), that Vergil's "literary" epithets like *Chaonias* are the result of his youthful bookishness and lack of experience of the world, thus needs strong qualification. Vergil uses such epithets often with dramatic intention (as in *E*.1) or with a touch of humor (as in *E*.2. 24, *Amphion Dircaeus in Actaeo Aracyntho*), or for the "distancing" effect conveyed here.

15. Vergil's adaptation of Theocritus II in *E*.8 helps support the possibility that he has that poem in mind here; at least he knew it well and admired it. The closing lines of Theocritus II seem to have impressed another of Vergil's contemporaries: see Tibullus 2.1.87-88.

16. For Vergil's early sensitivity to scenes of nightfall, the transitional, penumbral states he is to depict so often in the *Aeneid,* compare *E*.8.14, *Frigida vix caelo noctis decesserat umbra.*

17. On later treatments of this theme of death in Arcady see E. Panofsky, "*Et in Arcadia Ego:* Poussin and the Elegiac Tradition," in *Meaning in the Visual Arts* (New York, 1955) 297ff.

18. Bruno Snell, "Arcadia: The Discovery of a Spiritual Landscape," in *The Discovery of the Mind,* tr. T. Rosenmeyer (Cambridge, Mass. 1953) 282.

19. *Ibid.* 293.

20. *Ibid.,* 286-86. A different, and on the whole more satisfactory, view has been expressed recently by J. Heurgon, "Virgile, la poésie et la vérité," *L'Information littéraire* 10 (1958) 68-72 and esp. p. 69: "Les guerres civiles l'injustice des spoliations, l'angoisse générale s'imposent de plus en plus à lui. C'est ce progressif et irrésistible envahissement de son art par l'actualité, sous le voile de l'allégorie d'abord, mais parfois aussi directement exprimée, qui me paraît merveilleusement lisible dans la diversité des *Bucoliques.*" In fairness to Snell, however, it should be granted that he does, at one point (p. 292), qualify his position and speak of the "genuine political reality" which the *Eclogues* reflect and the "important political and historical function"

they exercised (on this latter point not all would agree). But Snell's overwhelming emphasis is in the opposite direction. Vergil's relation to historical realities in the *Eclogues* has been sensitively treated by Otis (above, note 4) 128ff, though his conclusions on *E*.1 and 9 differ from those reached here.

21. Klingner, *Gnomon* 3 (1927) 582.

22. W. F. Jackson Knight, *Roman Vergil* (London, 1945) 79.

23. *Ibid.,* 121.

24. For Vergil's synthesis of diverse elements in *E*.6 see the recent study by Zeph Stewart, "The Song of Silenus," *HSCP* 64 (1959) 170-205. For a good example of the ways in which Vergil can use different Theocritean contexts to modify the tone of an *Eclogue* see Klingner on *E*.2, *Gnomon* 3 (1927) 579-81.

25. Hanslik (above, note 10) 10-11 argues that the two songs, 39-43 and 46-50, are both songs of Menalcas and not of the two shepherds. But his argument is unconvincing, resting as it does on the assumption that whatever is translated from Theocritus (including lines 32-36) must belong to Menalcas (=Vergil); and he must give a forced and unnatural interpretation to line 55. Some scholars, however, while not going so far as Hanslik, have taken lines 31-36 as a quotation from a song of Menalcas and not part of Lycidas' own words: so H. J. Rose, *Mnemosyne* 7 (1954) 58-59. I find this assumption awkward for the movement of the dialogue (esp. in lines 32-33) and disturbing to the symmetry created by the balance of 21-23 and 27-29.

26. See, for instance, Ps.-Longinus, *De Sublimitate* 33-34, 36.

27. For these suggestions see Hahn, *TAPA* 75 (1944) 224-26.

28. *Ibid.,* 239-41.

29. Heurgon (above, note 20) 70 has suggested that *E*.9, at the end of the collection, serves as a farewell to older poetic forms and an invocation to the new ones to come. And he notes that Vergil's "farewells" are never abrupt and final, as *Catalepton* 5 shows.

30. L. Alfonsi, "Dalla II alla X Ecloga," *Aevum* 35 (1961) 193-98, has also pointed out some interesting parallels between the Second and Tenth *Eclogues,* suggesting that the Arcady that is tenuous and hesitant in *E*.2 is clear and strong in *E*.10. Thus in *E*.2. 28-30 the lover tentatively invites his beloved to the *sordida rura* and *humilis casas* of a rather lustreless pastoral life, whereas in *E*.10 the lover himself is eager to enter Arcadia and finds there not "lowly huts," but brightly colored flowers, cool springs, soft meadows (*E*.10. 35-43).

31. Whether *Martis* should go with *amor* or with *armis* is a little uncertain. Conington argues persuasively

for the connection with *amor,* and this seems to me the more natural reading, both for the word order and the sense. In either case the attitude toward war is not favorable, and it certainly comes out inferior to love, as line 69 makes unambiguously clear: *omnia vincit Amor.*

32. With *E.*9.31 compare *E.*10.30: *nec cytiso saturantur apes nec fronde capellae* ("nor are the bees sated on clover nor the goats on leaves"). But in *E.*10 it is love, not exile, which creates this effect, and this love is to be consoled and answered within the framework of the poem (lines 73-74):

> Gallo, cuius amor tantum mihi crescit in horas quantum vere novo viridis se subicit alnus
>
> (. . . Gallus, for whom my love grows hour by hour as fast as a green alder shoots up when spring is fresh.)

33. Yeats, "Lapis Lazuli," in *Last Poems* (1936-39). Indeed, the structure of Yeats' poem might be compared to that of the *Eclogues* as a whole. It begins with a sense of uncertainty and dissolution amid the threats of war ("I have heard that hysterical women say / They are sick of the palette and fiddle-bow, . . . "); and it ends with the reaffirmation of "gaiety," though with a complex mixture of sadness, age, decay in the "discoloration of the stone," the wrinkles in the Chinamen's eyes, the expectation of "mournful melodies":

One asks for mournful melodies;
Accomplished fingers begin to play.
Their eyes mid many wrinkles, their eyes,
Their ancient, glittering eyes, are gay.

(*The Collected Poems of W. B. Yeats,* New York, 1956, 293). The Yeatsian, and modern, restlessness, however, knows not the suspended bucolic peace that ends the *Eclogues.*

34. On a larger meaning in the "shadows" at the conclusion of *E.*1 (and, one should add, of *E.*10 too) see Elder's fine remarks in *HSCP* 65 (1961), unfortunately relegated to a footnote (p. 124, note 36):

> Consider the first Eclogue. Here Vergil probes, as he will in the *Aeneid,* the absorbing contemporary problem of the individual and social upheaval. The Eclogue offers no pragmatic answer; Tityrus is safe but Meliboeus is ruined. Yet the poem finally breathes out a peace and a harmony, not economic but emotional, and that is owing to the bucolic closing. The shadows of the oncoming evening and the mountains are regular and constant, and against them transitory man and his ephemeral problems are dwarfed.
>
> Peace and order are there, to be sure, and the regular cyclical movements of nature; but also the touch of sadness and uncertainty that goes with all things that end. Hence the melodious, but somber intimation at the conclusion of *E.*10,

gravis cantantibus umbra, / iuniperi gravis umbra. Panofsky (above, note 17) 300, speaks of this "vespertinal mixture of sadness and tranquillity" as "perhaps Virgil's most personal contribution to poetry."

35. I am indebted to Professor Charles Babcock, my colleague at the University of Pennsylvania, for a number of helpful criticisms and suggestions.

L. P. Wilkinson (essay date 1966)

SOURCE: "Virgil and the Evictions," *Hermes: Zeitschrift Für Klassiche Philologie,* Vol. 94, No. 3, July, 1966, pp. 320-24.

[*In the essay below, Wilkinson examines the relationship between the subject of* Eclogues *One and Nine and political events in Vergil's life. Wilkinson stresses that despite the influence of Vergil's personal situation (such as the threat of eviction of his family) on his writing, these* Eclogues *should not be read as straight allegories.*]

An apology is needed for returning to the question of the Ninth and First *Eclogues.* But it does seem that an intelligible story emerges if we interpret the poems in the light of pastoral convention and with the aid only of a few pieces of what seem really reliable external evidence, disregarding anything that may be based on conjecture by later commentators and biographers.

After Philippi, at the end of 42, it was agreed that Antony should go and pacify the East while Caesar Octavian remained in Italy to settle the veterans on confiscated land. In 41 trouble broke out between the Antonians and Caesarians leading to the Perusine War, which the Antonians lost early in 40. Antony's man Pollio, hitherto in charge of Cisalpine Gaul, then withdrew to Venetia, and the task of assigning the lands was handed over by Octavian to Alfenus Varus[1]. The duty of taxing such Transpadane townships as were exempted from confiscations was given to the poet-statesman Cornelius Gallus[2]. Cremona was one of the centres designated for confiscations, and detailed execution of this operation was in the hands of one Octavius Musa as *limitator.* In a note on Ecl. 9, 7-10 Servius Auctus says knowledgeably: "To this spot Octavius Musa had extended his surveying-poles, that is to say, through fifteen miles of Mantuan territory, since that of Cremona was insufficient." Whether (as Servius alleges) because Musa had a grudge against her, or simply for administrative convenience, Mantua was losing land next,

Mantua, vae, miserae nimium vicina Cremonae.

There was no general reprieve; for at G. 2, 198 Virgil refers to

qualem infelix amisit Mantua campum.

What can we learn about this affair from *Eclogue* 9? Moeris there represents the *veteres coloni* who are being either evicted ('*migrate*') or, as in his case, apparently still working the farm but paying produce to its new owner (1-6). Menalcas, a poet, has tried to intercede for them. He was rumoured to have largely succeeded, but local confusion and violence[3] were stronger than orders from a central authority; and in the new quarrel caused by the intercession both Moeris and Menalcas were lucky to have escaped with their lives (7-20). Lines 19-20 refer not to his actions but to the subjects of his poems. It is important to note that we are not told that Menalcas has himself lost any land, nor that he has any relationship to Moeris other than champion[4]. The whole passage could refer, as Servius supposed, to Musa's 15-mile strip.

At 27-29 we hear of a petition of Menalcas to Alfenus Varus bound up with a poem which is *necdum perfecta* and will only be finished if it succeeds:

> *Vare, tuum nomen, superet modo Mantua nobis, . . .*
> *cantantes sublime ferent ad sidera cycni.*

If only Mantua is spared the swans of song will bear his name to the skies. '*Mantua*' could naturally mean the city itself with its neighbourhood, as distinct from Mantuan territory such as Musa cut off, and the reference would be to a further stage in the confiscations. Servius auctus quotes on l. 10 a passage from a speech by 'Cornelius' (sc. Gallus) against Varus which is surely authentic and could come from Pollio's history of the civil war[5]: *cum iussus tria milia passus a muro in diversa[6] relinquere, vix octingentos passus aquae quae circumdata est admetireris reliquisti.* The text is not quite right: Kroll inserted a *cum* before *admetireris,* but perhaps the latter should be transferred to follow the initial *cum.* Anyway, the sense is clear[7]: "when you were assigning land, having been ordered to leave three miles in every direction from the wall, you scarcely left 800 paces of water which lie around it." This must refer to the lagoon which still surrounds Mantua on three sides. The intention had obviously been to leave the city something to live on, not largely water. And Gallus had a good motive, besides humanity or partiality, for opposing Varus' interpretation or encroachment: it gave him a smaller area of exempted municipium to tax.

So far I have said nothing of Virgil. But the poet has gone out of his way to indicate that Menalcas is he, as he did at 5, 85-87: ll. 19-20 are a direct reference to 5, 40, and ll. 23-25 and 39-43 are translations from Theocritus[8]. His departure may have been for Rome, to appeal at the highest level. Now if it is true that the Virgil home was at Pietole[9], *three miles* to the south-east of Mantua, then he was vitally concerned in this dispute, whereas in the earlier stages he had simply tried to use the influence he had acquired as a poet with influential people in order to help his countrymen. If Gallus prevailed, his land might be restored. This could well be the occasion of the anxiety expressed in Catalepton 8,

> *si quid de patria tristius audiero.*

By whom could Varus be *iussus?* Only by Octavian, whose overriding power is perhaps hinted at in the reference to his adoptive father at ll. 47-50[10]. Before whom could Gallus make a speech against Varus? Only before Octavian, and probably at Rome. *Hic illum vidi iuvenem.* And Octavian's verdict (translated into pastoral terms) was,

> *pascite, ut ante, boves, pueri; summittite tauros*[11].

Tityrus in 1 represents, as Leo saw[12], the reprieved peasants (in my submission those in the three-mile zone round Mantua), Meliboeus the unfortunates outside it. I agree with those who believe that there was only one eviction, or threat of eviction, of Virgil's family: that 1 is later than 9, but comes first in the collection as a compliment to Octavian, as ancient etiquette, if not modern also, would dictate.

But what about the scenery? That in 9, 7-10 does seem less conventional and idealised than the rest:

> *certe equidem audieram, qua se subducere colles*
> *incipiunt mollique iugum demittere clivo*
> *usque ad aquam et veteres, iam fracta cacumina, fagos*
> *omnia carminibus vestrum servasse Menalcan.*

"Indeed I had heard that from where the hills begin to fall and descend in a gentle slope, as far as the water and the old beech trees with their broken tops—all this your Menalcas had saved with his songs." If that is a real locality, it is nowhere near the city of Mantua; and all those excursions to Valeggio or Calvisano or Carpenedolo or Montaldo should be renamed 'In Quest of Moeris' Birthplace:' they have no bearing on that of Menalcas-Virgil[13]. And what about the *aequor* that *stratum silet* and l. 57? It is imported, as everyone knows, from Theocritus 2, 38, and is the sea, nowhere near Mantua. And the tomb of Bianor three lines later? It is introduced to remind us of Theocritus 7, 10, but the name comes, as has recently been perceived, from a Hellenistic epigram[14]. Similarly in 1 the swampy, pebbly patches on Tityrus' land (56-58) would suit the disputed land round the Mantuan lagoon; but those shadows that fall from the high hills in the last line were remembered from some other landscape. The poet simply wanted a peaceful evening close.

It must be accepted that these *Eclogues* are not straight allegories: they are Theocritean pastorals with occasional outcrops of reality. We must not expect the details all to fit. We may even have dust thrown in our eyes[15]. In his introduction to 7 Conington remarks: "The scenery is, as usual, confused. Arcadian shepherds are made to sing in the neighbourhood of the Mincius, while neither the ilex, the pine, the chestnut, nor the flocks of goats, seem to belong to Mantua." There is no need to suppose, with one scholar, that these shepherds are descended from Arcadians captured by Mummius; nor, with another, that because Gallus says in 10, 44-45 that he is a soldier on campaign, whereas elsewhere in the poem he appears to be in Arcadia, he must be holidaying there on leave.

Virgil, however relieved, was now in an embarrassing situation. Varus was presumably still in office. Mantua had been reprieved, so in a sense he owed him the swans' praises; but it had in fact been reprieved through Gallus. *Eclogue* 6 is his solution. He would use the famous prologue to Callimachus' Aitia as basis for a witty and elegant *recusatio*. He would recommend unspecified epic-style poets who would be more worthy of the task (cf. Horace's *recusatio* to Agrippa, c. 1, 6: *Scriberis Vario*). He had in fact been urged to write pastoral (*non iniussa cano*); and in any case, if he put Varus at the top of the page, any applause it earned would redound to his credit, so the debt was paid in a sense (9-12). And with a fulsome, empty compliment about Apollo and no further ado he turns to his pastoral. *Pergite, Pierides.*

This proves to have no connection at all with Varus; but whatever the significance of Silenus' repertoire of songs, it cannot be denied that it gives quite exceptional honour to Gallus, the only poet mentioned by name. This is true even if only lines 64-73 refer to him and there is no substance in the arguments of Franz Skutsch that the other subjects of Silenus' songs are taken also from works of his[1]. It was to Gallus that the debt of song was really owed, and it was paid both here and, with interest, in 10. *Neget quis carmina Gallo?*

Notes

1. Serv. auct. on Ecl. 6, 6 and 9, 27.

2. Serv. auct. on Ecl. 6, 14.

3. Cf. Appian 5, 12, 49ff.; Dio 48, 9, 4ff. *Undique totis usque adeo turbatur agris.* Ecl. 1, 11.

4. W. Kroll realised this, but his words have been little heeded. Rhein. Mus. 1909, pp. 50-53. *Nostri agelli* (2) simply means that of the *coloni, vestrum Menalcan* (10), your friend or champion. *Ipse* (67), though it does presumably refer to Menalcas, does not mean 'the master' here. The obvious interpretation after what has gone before is that when Menalcas comes he will be able to refresh their memory of the songs they have partly forgotten. But if *ipse* does mean 'the master', it must hint at Octavian, who will make all right again.

5. K. Büchner, P. Vergilius Maro RE. col. 30. R. SYME appears to overlook the evidence of this passage when he writes of Alfenus Varus: "Virgil dedicated to him the Sixth of his Eclogues; hence, in the Virgilian Lives and the scholiasts, the allegation that he was a land-commissioner." (The Roman Revolution, p. 235, n. 8.)

6. Peerlkamp for *indivisa*.

7. Or should be. Tenney Frank however (Vergil p. 125) disregards '*vix*' and translates "you included within the district . . .".

8. Probably not from completed Eclogues that have not come down to us, but analogous rather to the cases of Sherlock Holmes which are casually referred to but do not occur in the corpus. H. Oppermann (Hermes 67, 1932, pp. 202-203) rightly says that Lycidas also represents Virgil to the extent that it is he who at ll. 32-36 adapts Theocritus 7, 37-41, where the speaker, Simichidas, is Theocritus himself. But to say, as he does, that Moeris also represents Virgil, is to force the meaning of *carmina nostra,* which is simply "songs such as we sing".

9. The late XV century MSS. of the Vita Probiana say Andes was 'XXX' miles from Mantua. But Roman numerals are easily corrupted, and Egnatius' scarcely later. . . . Princeps of 1570 gives 'III'. The Vita Donatiana says "*abest a Mantua non procul*". If XXX were right, Virgil could hardly have called himself so emphatically a Mantuan. Pietole is the traditional place. How could it ever have maintained a claim to a man so famous in his lifetime if it had not had the support of truth embodied in common knowledge?

10. F. Klingner, Hermes 62, 1927, pp. 149ff.

11. 1, 42; 45.

12. Hermes 38, 1903, pp. 1ff.

13. A recent one, "Virgil's Home Revisited", by K. Wellesley, is described in the Proceedings of the Virgil Society, 1963-1964, pp. 36-43.

14. A. P. 7, 261; S. Tugwell, C. R. 1963, pp. 132-133. So much for Servius' imaginings. Similarly in 2 the name Alexis may be simply borrowed from an epigram by Meleager (A. P. 12, 127) about a beautiful boy, which comes next before a pastoral one by him about love for Daphnis; in which case what Suetonius and others tell us about a boy Alexander given to Virgil is probably fiction.

15. H. J. Rose's objection, "I dislike calling a favourite poet a gratuitous liar" is singularly inept (The Eclogues of Vergil, p. 64). His whole chapter on "The Poet and his Home" is strangely literal-minded. Contrast Conington's Introduction, pp. 9-17.

John B. Van Sickle (essay date 1967)

SOURCE: "The Unity of the *Eclogues*: Arcadian Forest, Theocritiean Trees," *Transactions and Proceedings of the American Philological Association*, 1967, Vol. 90, pp. 491-508.

[*In the essay that follows, Van Sickle analyzes the significance of Arcadia in Vergil's* Eclogues *and argues that it serves as a poetic symbol used to emphasize the unity of the work as a whole.*]

The idea of a *Liber Bucolicorum*, the principle of artistic unity by which the *Eclogues* form a book, is a kind of philosopher's stone of classical scholarship.[1] Accounts are legion and contradictory.[2] The book itself, however, closes with a representation of the unities of its making: to sit, to weave, and to love a poet (10.70-74). From the Arcadian vantage point of the tenth poem, the poet sees his own work as a whole and gives expression to his own recollective, assiduous, passionate self-consciousness in the symbol of Arcadia. The Arcadian is a key, offered by the poet, to the unity of the book.

The origin of the poetic symbol, Arcadia, is another philosopher's stone. Arcadian poetry has been sought in sources outside the *Eclogues* and also has been considered the invention of Virgil in them.[3] Prudently taking a middle course, Karl Büchner has suggested that Virgil made Arcadia the land of poetry because of the well established tradition that it was home of Pan. Büchner cites Meleager's oath by Pan the Arcadian and also Lucretius' treatment of Pan (4.524-94).[4] Surely also he should have adduced the Pan of the seventh *Idyll* of Theocritus (7.103-14) and above all the Pan of the first *Idyll*. He was an object of deference and present awe for the rustics (1.1-6, 15-19); but in the song Daphnis dying summoned him from Arcadia to inherit the singer's pipe (1.123-26). Without looking beyond Virgil's most familiar source we can find Arcadian material. The question of the origin of Arcadia as a poetic locus can thus be assimilated to the question of how Virgil used Theocritus. If we understood the one, we would understand the other as well.

This paper proposes, in short, to reformulate three familiar problems into one: the unity of the *Liber,* the origin of Arcadian poetry, and the Virgilian imitation of Theocritus. A new reading of Theocritus is also implicit in the enterprise, though we can give no more than hints of that here.

The familiar problems are symptoms of a fourth, more fundamental problem that is latent in recent studies of pastoral and that, once recognized and stated, will be well on its way to solution. Scholars have been finding statements of poetics piecemeal in various *Eclogues* and in *Idylls.* The tendency has been to speak of a poetics in, say, the first or seventh *Idyll* or in the ninth or fourth, sixth or seventh *Eclogue,* as if poetics could be the property of one or another poem. This is criticism by a principle of divide and conquer. In fact, every bucolic *Idyll* and every *Eclogue* contains a poetics, which is to say that it reflects on its own nature as poetry. Each poem reflects on its own peculiar way of shaping and knowing; some also reflect their relation to others and even a quality of the whole. Pastoral poetry is symbolist in the sense that, far from representing country matters, it uses country matters to represent a new kind of art, to mediate experience.[5] Pastoral is poetry in reduced circumstances, cut off from the public media and heroic mediators of other times. Its heroes are poets, with the significant exception of the fourth *Eclogue*; and through this momentarily expansive vision comes another, the discovery of Arcadia as a poetics of the whole. In order to read the *Eclogues,* then, it will be necessary and enough to look with new attentiveness and discrimination at the Arcadian elements in the book.

Arcadia is a poetic symbol, poetics of gradually realized, carefully proportioned, and deeply felt relations within and among poems. In the book, first it is a distant hope, then a fuller remembrance of past voices. It collects itself at last, circumstantially and visibly, into a poetic locus. Three poems, Four, Seven, and Ten, broach, enlarge, and perfect the idea. Set at equal intervals in the book, they establish a framework for the poetry of the others.

The fourth *Eclogue* begins with talk of going somewhat beyond the usual matter of Sicilian Muses (4.1-3), though the Sicilians take part in much of the poem. The furthest stretch of imagination in the fourth, however, is expressed as an ambition of the poet alone for a poetry such as would surpass even Pan, even if the singing match were held in Arcadia itself (4.53-59, contrast *Id.* 1.1-6). The poetic trajectory, from Sicilian toward Arcadian, foreshadows what the *Eclogues* as a whole accomplish.

In the seventh poem, a palpable Sicilian, Daphnis (7.1), had taken a seat easily if paradoxically on the banks of a north Italian river (7.13). In this purposefully mixed context, so reminiscent yet far from the sixth and eighth *Idylls* and representative of the gradual change of pastoral from Sicilian to Arcadian, the narrator is no longer the poet of the fourth and cohort of Sicilian Muses, but rather now a figure from an earlier *Eclogue.* He represents an internal memory within the book, and the voices he recollects are the first Arcadians.

Finally, in the tenth poem, Gallus dies in the Theocritean myth of a poet's death. Yet we hardly have to be reminded that Gallus is a rather different lover dying under new circumstances. In the first *Idyll,* after a cryptic reminder of Love's triumph (1.95-98), Daphnis called Pan to come from Arcadia to take the pipe (1.122-30). In the *Eclogue,* Pan and a motley company of Italians, Virgilians, and *hapax legomena*—the new Arcady—come of their own accord (10.19-26), like the he-goat to the place of song in the seventh poem (7.7, cf. 11), or the goats to the child in the incipient golden age of Four (4.21). The presence of Pan is a crucial element in the new, Arcadian reading of Theocritus.

That, in barest outline, is the Arcadian forest which Virgil fabricated from Theocritean wood: Sicilian toward Arcadia; Sicilian and Italian as a context for Arcadians; Gallus (Daphnis, Arethusa) among Arcadians. The fourth *Eclogue* first articulates a change of locus, while the unique manner of its construction effects the departure. The fourth is the most historicizing and public, most Catullan and Lucretian, said to be the least Theocritean of the *Eclogues.* We cannot treat all these matters here, but we shall consider one characteristic of the fourth *Eclogue* that raises questions about the nature of Arcadian poetry, about Virgil's relations to Theocritus, and about the poetry of Theocritus itself. Speaking of change and growth in poetry, the fourth *Eclogue* uses number and numerical symmetry so boldly that it poses a question about numerical composition in other—Theocritean and Virgilian—products of the Sicilian

Muses. Arcadian poetry, Virgil's imitation of Theocritus, appears to take numerical, as well as the more familiar, forms.

The structure of the fourth *Eclogue* is a function of the single number seven, a more exclusive principle than in other pastoral. It has seven sections, disposed symmetrically and corresponding to units of sense:[6] thus 3-7-7-(4 × 7)-7-7-4, for a total of 63 lines. Such a structure imposes itself, is meant to impose number as part of poetic experience, whether we should then think of poetry aspiring to music or to philosophy.[7] The poem deliberately breaks through to a new order of art, consonant with its new themes, raising a new question of order in the poetry left behind.

The fourth *Eclogue* speaks of leaving Sicilian norms; in fact among the *Idylls,* not to mention other *Eclogues,* we find nothing with quite the same numerical singleness. The second *Idyll* is Theocritus' most elaborately visible exercise in symmetries of number. After a proem of 16 lines, the incantations of the feverish girl fall into four-line stanzas, arranged by groups of three for a total of nine stanzas. Then her song of the cause of her passion falls into five-line stanzas, arranged in two groups of six for a total of twelve. The example of this paradox of more than usual order in a speech of more than usual agitation was not lost on the eighth *Eclogue,* with its Maenalian, Arcadian verses (8.21, cf. 68; 25, cf. 72; and so on). The symmetries of the third *Idyll,* a paraclausithyron, turn on a bold dissymetry (3.24).

One manner of symmetry in the fifth *Idyll,* the great contest, is immediately apparent and resembles that of the second *Idyll:* in the contest, each singer has fourteen catches; but a further mode of symmetry in the poem is less obvious. Komatas, who wins the singing match, has fourteen catches, plus a last word, in which he says that his rival is fond of quarrelling . . . (5.137). This echoes his earlier charge—in effect framing the contest—that the rival and former student loves to jeer . . . (5.77), while Komatas himself does not boast and all that he says is true. Their exchange (You're a babbler! No! I purvey truth! But you love to jeer.) occupies the exact center of the poem (5.74-77), so that the entire structure turns on a question of the love of truth versus love of strife.[8]

In the fifth *Idyll,* the truth-teller wins; truth also is a poetic touchstone in the seventh, where young Simichidas is hailed as a sprout of Zeus, fashioned all for truth (7.44). . . .

Truth conspicuously is absent from the *Eclogues,* though it might be expected where the third *Eclogue* imitates the form of the fifth *Idyll* (as we shall see in a moment), or where the fourth *Eclogue* translates the just cited praise of Simichidas in one of its most striking lines (4.49):[9]

> cara deum suboles, magnum Iovis incrementum.

If Virgil's child is made *for* any end, it would seem to be the *honores* mentioned in the line before, or else for grow-ing, as the epithets *suboles* and *incrementum* suggest: natural and political processes, not truth. Instead of a concrete term, ερνος (7.44), Virgil uses an abstract word in the separative pattern framing the god's name—*incrementum*—which refers to processes, instruments, and products of growth in the language of philosophy, linguistics, history, and agriculture—later too of rhetoric.[10] In the place of truth, Virgil authenticates his prophecy by reference to the utterances of the Parcae (4.46-47), *fata,* mere reflection thus of words—here an imitation of Catullus.[11]

Among the remaining *Idylls,* that one which our editions place fourth seems remarkably lacking in symmetry or number. A. S. F. Gow speaks of the "absence of restriction in the subject matter."[12] Gilbert Lawall, in an article called "Animal Loves and Human Loves," and now in his Coan pastoral book, speaks rather of "apparently random conversation."[13] He suggests that in fact "juxtaposition of polar types of erotic behavior produces both the poem's irony and its thematic coherence."[14] Mr. Lawall's proposal marks a considerable advance. He entertains as he instructs; and yet he concentrates on theme to the neglect of other, complementary modes of organization.

The fourth *Idyll* begins with two groups of 14 lines each, followed by a group of 14 plus one. It concludes with groups of six, eight, and six, making a total of 63 lines. Within the first three groups, form and content progress together. Talk gets started with the famous challenge, Ειπε μοι (4.1), that starts off 14 lines of strict stichomythy. This gives rise in turn to a two-line, then three-line strophic response as the new manager, Corydon, gradually gains confidence. He defends his practical capacities against a querulous critic who is nostalgic for what used to be. From this crescendo of self-justification (4.1-14, 15-28), Corydon rises in the third group to a climax. He vindicates his own skill at music in a nine-line spurt, the longest single stretch of speech in the poem. The critic melts. Corydon even ventures a snatch of song with the name of a town and an echo of Homeric language in line 32, which is the poem's exact center: praise of Croton and a recollection of "bonny Zacynthus" which is not integrated with the syntax of the rest.[15] Lawall observes that this *Idyll* lacks the song which forms a core in others.[16] In fact the fourth *Idyll* is engaged in poetic preliminaries, like the third, circumstantial, positioning, and testing, with a rustic prick of passion toward the end and only a hint of song at the center.[17]

Four of the *Eclogues* also place a crucial motif at the exact center. In the first *Eclogue,* it is the epiphany of the young god at Rome: *hic illum vidi iuvenem* (1.42). The second *Eclogue,* at the exact mid-point, displays a coveted poetic tool, *fistula,* invented by Pan, prominently set off as the first word in the line and framed within a five-line section by the name of Amyntas, who covets it (2.37). It is interesting that this poetic center of the poem is by no means the highest pitch of its art (cf. 2.45-55). The voices of lover and narrator do not quite yet coincide.

The more obvious symmetries of the third *Eclogue* point to the fifth *Idyll,* while a bold echo of the fourth *Idyll* introduces a run of testy, positioning talk. Again, transfer of control over material is at issue, as in *Idyll* 4. When the apparent dialectic finally resolves itself into mere responsion, a judge comes on the scene, ostensibly as in the fifth *Idyll.* But the Theocritean judge was a city man who broke into speech only after the contest (5.138). He was a woodcutter (5.64) who cut off song, declared a victor, and showed unseemly eagerness for the slice of the prize (5.140). We may suspect that he favored the singer who would sacrifice a tender *capretto* over the one whose prize would be a tough he-goat. Virgil's judge, by contrast, is a neighbor from the country, party to the desires of Camenae. He speaks both before and after the contest, acclaiming both singers, and any lover, worthy to win; making an affirmation more than a judgment. In keeping with these innovations, Virgil's rustics are less acrimonious from the start, turn quickly toward poetical responsion (3.28), and, once the contest begins, show skill at comprehensive variation only, though their Theocritean counterparts were contentious to the last (5.116-23, 142-43). Virgil's innovations altogether represent a symmetrical, incremental poetics.[18] The poem is preoccupied with moments when speech of different kinds begins: *dic mihi* (3.1) and *dicite,* spoken by the judge near the center (55), then *dic quibus . . . dic quibus* (104, 106), a mutual, dark hint at further speech.[19] At the exact center, the judge bases his invitation to the contest on the favorable analogy of nature's own production (3.56-57):

> et nunc omnis ager, nunc omnis parturit arbor,
> nunc frondent silvae, nunc formosissimus annus.

It is the season if not yet the decisive moment for new art.[20] Natural fecundity occasions facundity in a way unparalleled in Theocritus or the other *Eclogues,* though by very universality the third anticipates the confident language of poems Four, Five, and in a way also Six.[21] The Theocritean judge in the fifth *Idyll* spoke neither at the center nor on behalf of both poets, nor did he set poetry any such universal example; on the other hand, nature, not truth, appears at the center of the *Eclogue.*

One other *Eclogue* places an important motif in the exact center. It is clear that the ninth *Eclogue* moves counter to the seventh *Idyll,* taking singers toward the city and away from favorable conditions for song like those the Theocritean travellers were entering. Two singers flee the composite Sicilian, Italian locus, murmuring fragments of Italian, Sicilian songs and salvaging nothing else but two kids of dubious ownership.[22] Their master poet is absent; the disaster would appear total, but for the fact that he, though not they, will reappear in the Arcadia of the tenth *Eclogue.*[23] The ninth *Eclogue,* then, as if replying to the fortune and the structure of Tityrus in the first, sets a statement of poetics in the center. Young Lycidas, whose name and poetic principles recall the seventh *Idyll* (7.35-41), rejects an honorific title in poetry—*vatem,* "bard"—set at the beginning of line 34, emphasized like *fistula* before it. Singers may be compelled to repeat the journey to the city, but they reject a more ambitious, perhaps then implicitly Tityran, art.

The young god at Rome, pipe of Pan, conscious liaison with nature—all represent a new poetry, though the centering structure still recalls Theocritus. The fourth *Eclogue* makes change explicit, going to an extreme with the poetry of Rome, nature, and more elaborate number, broaching Arcadia in defiance of Pan. The eighth *Eclogue* offers a garland to the poetic, public man already honored in the third and fourth poems (8.6-13, cf. 3.84-89, 4.11-14); yet the Arcadian verses of Eight oppose their formal rigidity to interior turbulence and loss of the woods. Eight has been justly called a kind of caricature of the dream of Four.[24] The poem closes with an effort to force Daphnis from the city. In the ninth *Eclogue,* the effort of the eighth, *ab urbe* (8.110, etc.), collapses, giving way to *in urbem* (9.1), and yet Lycidas rejects poetic ambition, specifically the poetics of the first and fourth (*E.* 9.30-36 reaffirms the poetic limits of *Id.* 7.35-41, but *E.* 4.1, 49, reversed, exceeded them). In the seventh *Eclogue,* too, a withdrawal from public to interior, private concerns, Arcadian voices, took place. The Arcadian series, which began with a challenge to Pan, completes itself in the tenth poem with a reported epiphany of the god (10.26-27). Arcadia first appears on the crest of poetic ambition, in public language and innovating structure, 63 lines in contradiction of the seventh *Idyll.* It reappears detached from the public, but as a fuller poetic idea, in the seventh poem, 70 lines; and finally is a complete poetic locus, far from Sicily, Italy, or Rome, in the tenth poem, 77 lines. Seven is the numerical principle of the poem in which Arcadia first appears and it measures the growth of the idea in the Arcadian series. Progression by sevens carries on from the innovation of *Eclogue* 4 to represent the growth of a principled structure, Arcadia, the poetry book. Nothing so concerted took place among the *Idylls,* although the third and fourth amount to consecutive multiples of nine—54, 63: the passion and then the nostalgia for Amaryllis.

Scholars have been talking of a poetics in the middle of the Arcadian series, in *Eclogue* 7. It is agreed that the contest of Seven weighs two different conceptions of bucolic: but most recently the winner has been called Arcadian, *ipso facto* Virgilian, while the loser was said to be uncouth, realistic, Theocritean.[25] Such would be the Theocritus of the handbooks. Yet Virgil himself emphasized that both singers were Arcadians (7.4); and both sing in the mingled context of *Idyll* 6 and *Idyll* 8, while the winner has affinities with the seventh and the loser with the first *Idyll.* I would suggest therefore that the poem be taken more at its word. It says that there was a wish to recollect alternation in verse: *alternos . . . meminisse* (7.19). This alternation which the seventh *Eclogue* intends to recall must simply be that of the dialectic which runs through all the poems, from the polarity of Tityrus and Meliboeus to its final transformation into Gallus and Arcadia. The singers of the seventh poem must be Arcadians precisely because they do represent and recollect the polarities of other poems. Through memory of other poems, the poet's own revision of his own work, the seventh *Eclogue* makes an important step toward realization of Arcadia and the book. The judgment of the seventh prefigures the opposition and yet unity of Gallus and Arcadia in the tenth poem. At the same time, Theocritean associations of the contestants call attention to a polarity between the first and seventh *Idylls* and to the opposition between their echoes in the fifth *Eclogue,* and, further, between the ninth and tenth *Eclogues.*

The fourth *Eclogue* enunciates the terms of imitation and departure from Theocritus. The seventh *Eclogue* brings them into focus. If *Eclogue* 4 may be said to gainsay the seventh *Idyll,* the principle of the *Idyll* reasserts itself in *Eclogue* 5, but especially in *Eclogues* 7 and 9 (9.30-36), and in the Arcadian elements of *Eclogue* 10.

In *Eclogue* 7, the contest exemplifies two tendencies in the poetry of Virgil. The name of the loser, Thyrsis, suggests the bacchant's wand and recalls the singer's name in *Idyll* 1. Ambitious, expecting even to become a *vates,* he has as deities Priapus, Liber, and Jupiter, mentioned as the god of abundant rain (7.25-28, 33, 60, 58). The winner, Corydon, has a name that suggests the larks of the seventh *Idyll* (7.23) and the hazels of the first *Eclogue,* where Meliboeus assisted at the difficult birth of two kids (1.14). The poetic ambition of Corydon is circumspect; his deities are the nymphs, Phoebus, Delia (7.21-24, 29; cf. 61-64). On the hint of Corydon and Thyrsis, we prick out, retracing, a dialectic of Bacchus and Apollo through all the poems.

Thyrsis claims to be going to be a *vates* (7.28; cf. the refusal of 9.34). His language actually echoes the fourth *Eclogue,* as Servius observed (7.25, 27; 4.19, 49), so that his defeat implicates Four as well. He is a swelling poet who vows to erect a golden phallus in a modest garden: the effect is almost a parody of the rise of the golden race (7.36, 4.9). His energies also recall the Mopsus of the fifth poem, who pushed on from the familiar pastoral shade to a grotto (5.6), who was testy (5.9), competitive (5.15), somewhat crass—or perhaps one might say detached, esthetic, in his apprehension of poetry (5.13-15, 81-84)—and who was content to embroider on Daphnis as Theocritus left him, which is to say dead: a completed, closed tradition in literature. Thyrsis was the name of the singer of the first *Idyll.* In the *Eclogues* it also has further associations with the Dionysiac singer of the sixth and also then with Tityrus, of the first and sixth, with his equivocal *libertas* (1.27). Tityrus, Silenus, and Damon of the eighth poem, and Gallus of the sixth and tenth, are lovers of women, but not all as the Arcadians love.

On the other hand, Corydon has affinities with Menalcas of the third, fifth, second, ninth, and tenth poems. Menalcas composed at least the introduction to the second, placing the *fistula* in the center, and he took part in the third. In the fifth, he is more restrained than Mopsus, finer since for him poetry is a restorative (5.46); yet he declares his part in the second and third poems (5.86-87), and goes

beyond Theocritus to sing of Daphnis resurrected, surpassing the first *Idyll* with echoes of the seventh (*E.* 5.72-73; *Id.* 7. 71-73). Since his figure unifies the first half of the book, he will appear appropriately as an Arcadian in the tenth *Eclogue* (10.20).[26] Corydon's self-limiting poetics are consonant too with the rule of Apollo in *Eclogue* 6, directing and restraining Tityrus and Silenus (6.4-5, 82), while his poetic tool is still the *fistula* that Corydon offered in the second poem. In short, the contest initiates a train of associations and reflections that draws all the poems together.

So much was in the memory of Meliboeus. It has been said that he, not Tityrus, was the more poetic soul in the first *Eclogue.*[27] Yet Tityran *libertas,* with all its compromising, public connotations,[28] was clearly a condition both for the tranquillity and also for the energy and authority that a major creative enterprise demands. A Tityran, Roman, Dionysiac poetics grows through *Eclogues* 3, 4, and 5, mounting the challenge of a new Marsyas to Apollo; broaching the idea of Arcadia in Catullan, Lucretian language, over against Apollo, Calliope, even Pan (4.53-59)—Roman poetry over against Theocritus (*E.* 4.1, 49; *Id.* 7.37-44). These poems see a god who is not Pan (1.42, 5.64).

Apollo is reasserted in the sixth poem, with a Callimachean reaction to ambitious, public poetry (6.3-5). Apollo's famous tweak of Tityrus' ear has the effect of purging *libertas* of its public, too Roman connotations; it finds its full, natural expression in Silenus, limited only by time and by form (6.82-86). *Eclogue* 6 returns to the origins of poetry, to the pure dialectics of passion and form, as well as to a beginning of the book (1.2, 6.8). *Origo,* with its suggestion of etiology, is the poem's most important word. *Eclogue* 6 makes a shift to natural, interior energies, propagative after a run of what might be called propaganda.

The seventh *Eclogue* takes stock of rise and fall, alternation. In the sixth, Tityrus of the first poem reappeared and, freed of dependence on the city, sang a song far bolder than the didactic, echoic praise of Amaryllis he was said to be meditating when first sighted (1.1-5); thus *pergite Pierides* (6.13). His sensitive, poetical alternate, Meliboeus, returns in the seventh, not to distinguish between Virgil and some other poetry but between the expansionist and the recollective—which is the ultimately Arcadian—in Virgil himself. Artistic unification and conscious intent to recall are the poetics of the seventh poem, and of Arcadia. In the introduction to Seven, Corydon and Thyrsis had driven their herds together, both young, Arcadians both, and there was intention to recollect poetry. Unifying separate materials and newly sorting them out, remembering all and making distinctions within, is the process of this poem, symbolized by the apparent reference to a gathering of herds (7.2-3, cf. 19). It was a *certamen,* a means or a process of sifting out, making distinctions in poetics.

The *magnum Iovis incrementum* of the fourth *Eclogue* (4.49), which is to say the growth from Sicilian toward

Arcadian, required 63 lines. Then the *certamen . . . magnum* (7.16) takes place in 70 lines. The *extremus . . . labor* (10.1), that implies both unity and an end, has 77 lines. The fourth poem establishes seven as a principle of form; in the series, seven becomes the numerical token of Arcadia, one extreme in the dialectics of a new art, the Apollonian counter to some Dionysian element as yet unplumbed. In the book, the sixth *Eclogue* is the most Dionysian, and if it has yet to receive a satisfactory reading, this is because we are not readers *comme il faut,* not off in some perfect fit of love, as Virgil imagined his reader (6.9-10):

> . . . si quis tamen haec quoque, si quis
> captus amore leget . . .

whether it be love of poetry or of the singer (6.13-26). Number and Apollo are easier to study.

The postulate of number in pastoral has already given scandal to some. The erection of a golden Priapus in that modest garden (7.36) ought to give scandal of another sort—or the commerce of Silenus (6.26) or the traffic of Pasiphaë (6.52-60). The life of pastoral consists in maintaining a grasp of both extremes; for pastoral is like the etymological Pan of Plato's *Cratylus:* not only that it "declares and always moves all," . . ., so that it is rightly the poetry of the goatherd, . . ., but especially that it too, like the god who is speech or the brother of speech, is both false and true, smooth in its upper parts, rough and goat-like in its lower parts.[29]

We set out to theorize, to formulate the genesis of Arcadian from Theocritean in Virgilian pastoral. We postulate and we find evidence of unity, coherence, and dialectical consistency, a considerable and important enterprise in poetry. Yet our very position, positiveness, generates its contrary, demands a notice of the opposite if we are to be anything like readers of the *Eclogues.* The poems are keen on their own ambivalence, on the paradox of great in small, work as play, design in chance, the fortuitousness of contrivance, truth in a reflected image: *si numquam fallit imago* (2.27), *res est non parva* (3.54), *forte* (7.1), *mea seria ludo* (7.17), *pauca* (10.2), *maxima* (10.72), hints of slight reeds and more than Orphic powers of poetry.[30] The fourth *Eclogue,* like the seventh and tenth, is equivocal about itself and its poetic enterprise. At the beginning, *paulo maiora canamus* raises the question of what is in fact large or small, what constitutes change in poetry.[31] Interpreters have vacillated between excluding the fourth poem from pastoral altogether and finding ways to reduce and assimilate it to a humble pastoral convention. When Pope asserted that his four pastorals "comprehend all the subjects which the critics upon Theocritus and Virgil will allow to be fit for Pastoral," he meant to exclude much of the matter of poems Four and Six, though he imagined his shepherds in a kind of golden age (*Discourse on Pastoral Poetry*). Taken in the context of the entire book, the opening of Four poses a question, whether the Arcadian is a very slight or a very great change from the Sicilian,

whether this *paulo* is to be taken as descriptive, or prescriptive, or ironical understatement. Is birth itself a very great or a slight matter? The pastoral equivalent, or hint, of heroism perhaps? These are matters for a longer discourse. The fourth *Eclogue* poses the acute paradoxes of humility in high locations, the heroic brought low, one child gripping the whole cosmos (4.52), an indeterminate present moment controlling the entirety of historical and mythical future and past (5, 6, 8-9, 11-17).

A particular instance of the general paradox is the word *incrementum,* mentioned above. Itself abstract and prosaic, it is placed here in a separative pattern as old as Homer, forming a spondaic ending (the only one) in the forty-ninth verse of a poem constructed on the number seven, echoing and reversing a crucial poetic statement of Theocritus, part of a verse which Eduard Norden singled out for its great art in the midst of a very artful poem.[32] In the context, the word can hardly be called elevated, nor yet colloquial and prosaic; nor can one refuse to call it either. Contraries persist, will not simply cede or be reduced to one another. The matter is both *tenuis* and *non parva,* like the poetry of the other poems, both small and great, *rus* and *urbs.* The dialectics cannot be simplified without violence to what was meant to be both still and still moving (*E.* 10.70-77).

Love defeated the Dephnis of the first *Idyll,* a symbol of limit to the poetic grasp of passion. Priapus and Aphrodite came, equivocal comforters. Daphnis called on Pan in vain; he said goodbyes to Arethusa (*Id.* 1.117). Love also defeats Virgil's obstreperous poet; but now some comfort is to be had. At least the mortal discontent of Gallus becomes the eternal content of Arcadian song. The myth of poetry of the first *Idyll* passes into Arcadian dimensions; Arethusa returns from her exile. In the tenth *Eclogue,* the poetics of the seventh *Idyll* come to terms with the poetics of the first. The new formal circumstances, poetic feeling, promise a certain immortality in art.

Number and numerical symmetry have their importance in Virgil's reading of Theocritus and in the formation of the poetic book, but always in strict conformity with more apparent content. They blend easily into the shadows of the familiar trees. Yet, from the reader, numbers in pastoral invite a readiness to entertain opposites simultaneously, an awareness that every assertion will find its contrary in some other part of the whole. Arcadian number exacts a science, of the inner dialectics of poetry itself, whatever affinity one or another cipher may seem to show with some half-mythical figure of Sicily or of Croton.[33]

Notes

1. This study took impetus from an observation by Mr. David Kuhn on the usefulness of an idea of the whole when one is trying to grasp the separately elusive elements of a poem; the study kept constantly in mind a lucid expression of the idea of the *Liber* by Professor Wendell Clausen in "Callimachus and Latin Poetry," *GRBS* 5 (1964)

193; finally, in the face of a certain aporia—mutual contradiction among various studies of individual poems—it seemed necessary to attempt some sort of apperception of the whole, if only to understand the parts, as Dante puts it in the letter to Can Grande, dedicating the *Paradiso:* "volentes igitur aliqualem introductionem tradere de parte operis, oportet aliquam notitiam tradere de toto, cuius est pars."

2. For examples, Karl Büchner, *RE* 15A (1955) 1256-57, s.v. "Vergilius." If, with Clausen (above, note 1), we imagine "a certain amount of rewriting," the tangle of chronological arrangements of the Eclogues becomes more than ever illusory, while the arrangement in the book takes on importance as the product of the poet's *extremus labor.*

3. For a useful summary and dismissal of earlier proposals, see Günther Jachmann, "L'Arcadia come paesaggio bucolico," *Maia* 5 (1952) 161-67, first published as part of *Miscellanea Max Pohlenz* (1952).

4. Büchner (above, note 2) 1261-62; Jachmann (above, note 3) 170, suggests that even the mention of Arcadia in *E.* 4.58-59 implies traditional associations of Arcadia with poetry. The association with Pan and song at least is certain, suitable for what Virgil does with it but hardly anticipating him. For a more penetrating view of the relationship between *silvestris Musa* in Lucretius (4.589) and Virgil (*E.* 1.2), see Philip Damon, "Modes of Analogy in Ancient and Medieval Fiction," *UCPCP* 15 (1961) 281, 286. Cf. also Lucr. 5.1398 with *E.* 6.8, and contrast *E.* 6.8 with *E.* 1.2. Tityrus' second Muse is more ambitious after the expansion of *E.* 3, 4, and 5. We never hear a simple song of Amaryllis.

5. Interpreting a symbolist poem, C. M. Bowra, *The Heritage of Symbolism* (Schocken, New York, 1961; first publ. 1943) 31, writes of *Les Pas* by Valéry, "The steps belong not to a human mistress but to poetry, the poetic impulse, for which the poet waits." Mallarmé after all entitled *The Afternoon of a Faun* an Eclogue. Symbolism, however, is not a recurrent fashion but a perennial, half-hidden tradition in poetry. Every poem is about its own making. Poetry is both much more and less than the scholars style it. For "poetics" in pastoral, see notes 23 and 25, below.

6. For a sketch of the form and content of *E.* 4, see J. B. Van Sickle, "The Unnamed Child: A Reading of Virgil's Messianic Poem," *HSCP* 71 (1966) 349-52, Summary of Dissertation. Among other things, the lines that mention Arcadia and Pan each have seven words: ". . . etwas vom Zauberspruch," Büchner (above, note 2) 1202, line 48.

7. Given such attention to number on the part of the poet, it will not do to say with Professor E. L. Brown (*Numeri Vergiliani=Coll. Latomus* 63 [1963] 16), among others, that the first three lines of *E.* 4 "may be reserved without undermining the structure.

. . ." Mr. Brown himself does not choose to reserve them when, for example, he numbers the lines of the *Eclogues* all consecutively and finds that line 216 falls at the imitation of Aratus, *ab Iove principium* (3.60), and that *Pergite Pierides* (6.13) follows a second cycle of 216, or that *surget gens aurea* (4.9) coincides with consecutive line 276, another important Pythagorean number (Brown, p. 67). Between mentions of Jove at 3.60 and 4.49, just 100 lines elapse. Professor Otto Skutsch has pointed out to me that if we exclude 8.75, the extra refrain, then the lines of *Eclogue* 8 fall into three groups of 36 each, consisting of 36 and 36, the songs, and 36 of refrains and introduction. The songs themselves are composed of stanzas of 3×3 verses, 3×4, and 3×5, apparently a formal analogue to the enigmatic talk of distribution, *terna . . . triplici* (8.73). In the book as a whole, there are thus 828 verses, so that 5.85 is number 415 of the whole, the first line of the second half, the point at which Menalcas gives the retrospective pipe, recalling poems two and three, and Mopsus replies with the staff, foreboding new journeys. *Idyll* 1 is distributed into sections of 63 + 63 (+ 19 of refrain) + 7, and *Idyll* 4 has 63 lines.

17+T.P. 98

8. Cf. Plato, *Phaedo* 91A, for a distinction in modes of argument. . . . The nature of Theocritean truth may perhaps best be inferred from the instruction offered in the fifth *Idyll.*

9. Eduard Norden, *Die Geburt des Kindes* (Leipzig 1924) 129, calls *E.* 4.49 the richest in art of all the verses.

10. The earliest uses of *incrementum* include Cic. *De fin.* 2.88, moral philosophy, 45 B.C.; Varro, *De ling. Lat.* 8.17, about the same time, of changes in words (cf. Schanz-Hosius 1.161, 191); Cic. *De senec.,* about one year later, in a description of Cato's agricultural interests, first recorded use of the plural (*ThLL* wrongly cites Ovid, *M.* 3.103 as the first); Varro, *Res rust.* 2.4.19, of 37 B.C.; and cf. Livy 1.33.8, 5.54.4, 27.17.4, etc. On the origins and meanings of words in *-men* and *-mentum* see Jean Perrot, *Les dérivés latins en -men et -mentum* (Paris 1961). For an appreciation and partial summary of Perrot, J. W. Poultney, *AJP* 85 (1964) 206-9. On the relationship of an idea of *incrementum* to *E.* 4, see Van Sickle (above, note 6). *E.* 4.1, 49 reverses *Id.* 7.35-41, but then *E.* 7.25-28 implies reversal of *E.* 4, and *E.* 9.30-36 reaffirms *Id.* 7.35-41.

11. Catullus 64.327 etc., first noted by Macr. *Sat.* 6.1.41; studied briefly by Professor E. K. Rand, "Catullus and the Augustans," *HSCP* 17 (1906) 21; cited as requiring further study by Büchner (above, note 2) 1260, cf. 1206; treated by Van Sickle (above, note 6).

12. A. S. F. Gow, *Theocritus*[2] 2 (Cambridge 1952) 76.

13. G. W. Lawall, "Animal Loves and Human Loves," *RFIC* 94 (1966) 47, and *Theocritus' Coan Pastorals: A Poetry Book* (Cambridge, Mass., 1967) 42, where reference is made to the "seemingly uncontrolled, realistic flow of conversation."

14. Lawall (above, note 13) *RFIC* 94.50, and now in the *Pastoral Book,* 51.

15. In the *Pastoral Book* (above, note 13) 50, Lawall paraphrases Miss Wildberger, *Theokrit-Interpretationen* (Diss. Zürich 1955) 43-48, on "the gradual elevation of subject matter and tone, as the conversation moves away from the initial discussion of the flock and turns to the herdsmen's poetic and emotional interests. In this central part of the poem, the rustics are no longer merely commonplace figures drawn from the real countryside, but conscious artists whose interests extend beyond the horizons of their limited rustic world." Consciousness of art, of its gradations, powers, and limits, would seem to be more controlling even than this suggests. The wandering into distant, musical matters has its immediate analogue in the straying of the calves which follows: a symbolist device reflecting the movement of the language. The calves nibble tender shoots, and it takes shouting, harsh language to return them, the poem, to a balance.

16. Lawall (above, note 13) *RFIC* 94.45, *Pastoral Book* 42.

17. Lawall (above, note 13) *RFIC* 94.48, *Pastoral Book* 49, on the thorn in the foot as a rustic counterpart to Eros' shaft.

18. Caution must be exercised in speaking of the "gentler pastoral atmosphere diffused over the whole poem," which a recent writer attributes to *Idylls* 1 and 5. In One to be sure; but less true of Five or Four: Charles P. Segal, "Vergil's *Caelatum Opus,*" *AJP* 88 (1967) 296, see also 292 (comments on *E.* 3 that would describe *Idyll* 4 almost as well) and 281-99 (detailed treatment of the dialectical turn toward song of the *Eclogue's* first half).

19. Segal (above, note 18) 297-99 interprets the riddles in terms of other themes and alternations in the poem (cf. 281); he also observes the centering effect, 292. After the Sicilian, proto-Arcadian *E.* 2, *Camenae* (3.59) would seem to anticipate Italian, perhaps Roman, matters: the turn to Pollio at 3.84, and to Pollio and much else in 4.1-17. In *E.* 7, after the *recusatio* of 6.4-5, song will be a matter of volition, not love, and of Muses, not *Camenae* (7.19).

20. Professor Martin Ostwald pointed out to me that *nunc* (3.56) would be more generic, more diffuse than the incisively repeated adverb of time in *E.* 4.4, 6, 7 *et passim, iam.*

21. Not only Pollio, but Jove (3.60, 4.49) and the exotic balm, *amomum* (3.89, 4.25).

22. Damon (above, note 4) 289 speaks of 9.57 ff. as "the one instance of true pastoral singers addressing a silent, unresonant nature. . . . This is a terrain without echoes, one which wastes pastoral song as the *trivium* (3.26-27) does." Menalcas used to leaf over springs (9.20); now farmers are stripping the leaves (9.61). *Migrate* (9.4) recalls the exile of Meliboeus. I am happy to acknowledge the usefulness of several conversations on the *Eclogues* held in Rome with Professor Michael Putnam in the spring of 1964. He first brought to my attention, as I recall, the paradox of the displaced songs of *E.* 9.

23. Charles Segal, "Tamen Cantabitis, Arcades—Exile and Arcadia in Eclogues One and Nine," *Arion* 4 (1965) 255, observes that *Idyll* 7 "is not simply an autobiographical account, but is concerned primarily with poets and poetry. Hence in using it, Vergil may be suggesting that the farm and dispossessions, however vivid and distressing in themselves, are but parts of a larger issue, that is, the nature of pastoral poetry, and in a sense all poetry, in a time of violence and disruption." Segal moves well beyond the conventional impasse in studies of Virgil's land question (cf. note 2, above) and is consonant with the approach of a Lawall (note 13, above) to Theocritus. His particular interpretation of the ninth *Eclogue,* however, is far more optimistic than Damon's (note 22, above). In a sense, Segal takes the viewpoint of Lycidas, sanguine about the possibilities of song, anticipating the guarded optimism of *tamen cantabitis* (10.31), the Arcadian solace. Damon takes more the viewpoint of Moeris, the dismantling of the Italian, Sicilian locus.

24. Charles Fantazzi, "Virgilian Pastoral and Roman Love Poetry," *AJP* 87 (1966) 181; suggestive comments on the ironies of *E.* 6 and 10, p. 184.

25. "The suggestion has been made that in some of the Eclogues, again the Sixth and also the Seventh, Vergil is attempting to sketch his 'poetics' of pastoral or even his view of poetry in general." Segal (above, note 18) 279. Hellfried Dahlmann, "Zu Vergils siebentem Hirtengedicht," *Hermes* 94 (1966) 228-29, suggests that the contrast is between Virgilian and *derb, realistik* Theocritean.

26. Cf. above, note 7.

27. Segal (above, note 23) 241-43, with an especially nice touch in *tanta* (1.26), p. 241.

28. On the relationship of *Liber* and *Libertas,* see remarks and references in Robert J. Rowland, Jr., "Numismatic Propaganda under Cinna," *TAPA* 97 (1966) 417. See also Chap. II, "Political Catchwords," in Ronald Syme, *The Roman Revolution* (Oxford 1960).

29. Plato, *Crat.* 408C-D, translation by H. N. Fowler (Loeb Classical Library, 1953).

30. On the paradox of *forte* at the beginning of so carefully contrived a poem as Seven, E. E. Beyer, "Vergil: Eclogue 7—A Theory of Poetry," *AClass* 5 (1962) 39. Segal (above, note 23) 254, notes a

fragility in pastoral, represented in the instrument of *E*. 2 and 3 by Menalcas at 5.85. Not only fragile, but broken by the end: thus the *patulae . . . tegmine fagi* (1.2), the *densas, umbrosa cacumina, fagos* (2.4), have become the *veteres, iam fracta cacumina, fagos* of a disintegrating locus (9.9). Segal (p. 255) also notes the poet of the sixth *Eclogue* "aware of poetry in its autonomous creative power."

31. In Virgil's works, *paulo* occurs only here; *paulatim* (4.28) occurs also at *E*. 6.36, *G*. 1.134, 3.215, and seven times in the *Aeneid;* both are frequent in Lucretius, *paulo* 15 times, *paulatim* 23 times. B. Axelson, *Unpoetische Wörter* (Lund 1945) 95, comments: "Auch im Gebrauch von *paulo post (post paulo)* treffen Lukrez und Horaz zusammen: bei jenem steht es 6,1240, bei diesem an vier Stellen, von denen eine der Lyrik angehört (carm. 3, 20, 3); bei den anderen Dichtern [list p. 17] findet man es nicht." A note adds that *paulo ante* is more frequent in Lucr., occurs twice in Juv., elsewhere only at Cat. 66.51, Sil. 9.89, to which add Statius, *Th*. 6.756, 11.653; *paulo post* occurred also at Plaut. *Ps*. 380, *Tri*. 191, and in Cinna, *Zmyrna* ap. Serv. *G*. 1.288 (cf. *RE* 8.1227, line 32, and Cat. 64.269, 62.35 Schrader). *Paulo prius* occurs at Plaut. *Ci*. 546, *Men*. 681, 873, *Ps*. 896. Note the other comparatives with *paulo* collected by H. C. Gotoff, "On the Fourth Eclogue of Virgil," *Philologus* 111 (1967) 67, note 4; add also Lucr. 3.602, *ut gravior paulo possit dissolvere causa*. Ovid uses *paulo* four times, all with the comparative. It does not occur in Propertius or Lucan. *Paulum* occurs five times in Lucretius, twice in the *Aeneid* (3.597, 4.649), and at Cat. 38.7, 10.25 (cf. *paulo* at 68.131). In short, *paulo* is used in comedy, satire, and especially in Lucretius. Links between the language of comedy and bucolic hardly surprise: take only the example of Plaut. *Amph*. 197, 201-2, "ea nunc *meditabor* quo modo illi dicam . . . sed quo modo et verbis quibus me deceat fabularier, prius *ipse mecum* etiam volo hic *meditari*"; cf. *E*. 1.2, 6.8, 9.37 (and Lucr. 1.143). The relations, however, between Virgil and Lucretius are more complex, more direct and programmatic: see note 4, above; and B. Farrington, "Vergil and Lucretius," *AClass* 1 (1958) 45 ff.; G. Radke, "Aurea Funis," *Gymnasium* 63 (1956) 82-86; Van Sickle (above, note 6); and for an unsorted compendium of Lucretian tags in Virgil, W. A. Merrill, "Parallels and Coincidences in Lucretius and Virgil," *UCPCP* 3.3 (1918) 135-247. Among the phrases on which Virgil's use of Lucretius turns is *paulo maiora lacessunt* (Lucr. 2.137), in a crucial passage on the direct relationship between small and greater in nature, which permits analogical investigation of the invisible: cf. C. Bailey, *Lucretius* 1 (Oxford 1949) 58-59. *Paulo maiora* (*E*. 4.1) raises the question of small and great in

language; here the poet, not the atoms, exercises a *facultas:* poetry assumes for itself the natural power to make trees change (*silvae*, 4.3). For a comparably Orphic metaphor, *E*. 3.111, see Segal (above, note 18) 302. An invisible process in language, bucolic, is to make itself visible; it is to grow to get beyond the limits of words. Not everyone may understand the *incrementum* in the bucolic *silvae* proposed at the beginning (4.1-3); everyone can get the message of the mother and child, smile at the end (4.60). A smile is with the lips, yet beyond words. The very structure of the poem is, in this sense, self-denying, ironic. Attempts to recapture ironic tones in the language of the *Eclogues* are thus fundamental and useful (cf. suggestions by Fantazzi [above, note 24] 184). In particular, Gotoff (*Philologus* 111.67-68), supporting Deubner's perception of a light tone in *E*. 4.1-3, points to a real ambivalence of poetic language, and of the poet's attitude to his work. Yet, as it stands, Gotoff's reading of the fourth is as one-sided in its way as are the readings of the ninth mentioned above, notes 22 and 23.

32. Norden (above, note 9) 129, comments on the spondaic ending and unexampled parison; for *incrementum*, see also note 10, above. An older treatment of it by Tenney Frank, "*Magnum Iovis Incrementum*," *CP* 11 (1916) 334 ff., loses itself in dichotomies which the linguistic phenomenology of Perrot (above, note 10) has nicely resolved; words in *-mentum* mean both process, instrument, and product: both the middle terms and the end, sometimes also the principle.

33. Delivered in slightly shorter form December 28, 1967, at the ninety-ninth annual meeting of the American Philological Association, Boston, Massachusetts. I am particularly grateful to the Editor of the Association and to its anonymous referee for encouraging me to give a more telling formulation to these ideas. I am grateful too for the interest of several of the Virgilians who heard my paper. I have heeded the counsel of Professor J. P. Elder in not expanding the present version, for the sake of stating the thesis but with the understanding and expectation that development will be required. It has been my experience that working with the present principles one can easily expand, concentrating on individual poems or parts of poems, assimilating and reformulating the most diverse critical methods. This paper then is only meant as a starting point. If inveterate Virgilians point to the strands left loose, traces omitted, exaggerations, and ellipsis, the dialectic with them and the poems will be well on its way and the purpose of this study well served. But it has also been my experience that memory is all too fallible, time short, the essentials for a valid reading of the *Eclogues* and of the best contemporary poetry lacking: *omnia fert aetas, animum quoque*.

Eleanor Winsor Leach (essay date 1968)

SOURCE: "The Unity of *Eclogue* 6," *Latomus*, 1968, Vol. XXVII, No. 1, January-March, pp. 13-32.

[*In the essay below, Leach studies the Song of Silenus in the Sixth* Eclogue *and explores the principles of unity in its thematic elements and mythological language. Furthermore, Leach demonstrates how these uniting principles may be applied to the poem as a whole.*]

Principles of unity in *Eclogue* 6 have been sought on many different bases, but chiefly by investigation of the rationale governing the selection and arrangement of myths in the Song of Silenus[1]. Scholars have generally agreed that both the myths and Vergil's stylistic treatment of them recall aspects of Alexandrian poetic convention, and also that the use of such a series of myths goes beyond the limits of decorum in the pastoral form. Among recent explicators, Otto Skutsch considers the poem composed of legends popular in Alexandrian literature[2]; Zeph Stewart sees definite suggestions for a range of popular Alexandrian genres: didactic, theological, epyllion, tragedy and metamorphic poems[3], and J. P. Elder finds a compendium of bucolic themes supporting an introduction that has to do with Vergil's inspiration as a pastoral poet[4].

Although genre study can provide important insights into the poem, it does not seem to me to give a complete interpretation. The several theories I have mentioned all argue for a kind of topical continuity in the myths, but one in which we may still fail to see a coherence of verbal design. As Stewart remarked, an illuminating explanation of the poem must show its various elements—the myths, the introduction, the poetic initiation of Gallus on Mount Helicon—existing in a balanced unity[5]. To this I would add that explanation must go beyond simple relationships of subject matter in the myths and explore the cryptic, yet very precise, language in which they are presented. The reading I offer here seeks to discover principles of unity in the themes and language of the myths and to show how these principles extend to the poem as a whole.

The *Eclogue* centers about major topics of pastoral: man, nature and poetry. I shall study the interassociation of these topics under three heads: 1) a relationship between man and nature depicted in the myths and emphasized by thematic grouping and contrast and by the use of repeated verbal suggestions; 2) questions concerning pastoral poetry and nature as its subject which are developed in the introductory section of the poem; 3) a relationship between the poet and nature implied by the juxtaposition of the first two patterns and developed in the myth of Gallus on Helicon.

In recounting the myths of Silenus, the poet frequently reminds us that he is abstracting elements of a much longer song, one lasting from morning until sunset[6]. The effect of the reminders is chiefly to call attention to the highly selective manner of the mythological narration. Of the variety of actions or scenes potentially present in each myth, Vergil chooses only one or two to call to our attention. But such abbreviation tends to create precision, rather than vagueness of reference. The vast possibilities of meaning in the myths are subjected to the poet's own interpretation and the reader's attention is focused on a particular, limited aspect of each[7]. At times only one action is presented: the stones cast by Pyrrha, the girl wondering at the apples of the Hesperides. In other cases two or three actions are juxtaposed as when we hear of the theft and punishment of Prometheus or the feast of Philomela and the changed limbs of Tereus.

A useful comparison may be made between the technique of presentation here and some aspects of second and third style mythological landscape paintings. In many paintings a single action represents a story; yet is developed chiefly for its possibilities as a visual image. A monochrome Artemis and Acteon from Herculaneum that combines elements of sacral-idyllic painting with mythology[8] gives a symbolic rendering of a dramatic situation. A baetylus shrine in the center dominates the landscape. To the left a horned Acteon has turned away from the shrine, apparently in haste, while on the right Artemis gestures, seeming to call up two dogs. Acteon has been arrested at the shrine where he has come either to challenge or to violate the goddess[9]. The moment is one of transition between his guilty act and his punishment. Between the figures themselves, however, there is no real dramatic interchange. Their association is created by the surrounding details of the painting, by the shrine which stands between the two, representing their antagonism, and by the sacral-idyllic mood of the landscape which points up Acteon's tole as violator of divine sanctity and superiority.

The principal difference between the dramatic representation here and that we find in vase painting is of course the participation of the figures in a landscape in some manner related to the action itself. The use of setting and of iconographic detail create an interpretation, or in fact, force the spectator to create it for himself. The picture will seem clear or meaningless depending on the spectator's ability to associate the details.

A more complicated use of dramatic abstraction in mythological landscapes develops in some works of the third style. Peter von Blanckenhagen speaks of a type of «continous narrative» painting where «events separated in time are represented as occuring simultaneously at the same place in the same setting . . . where in the same setting one or more identical persons appear more than once»[10]. Among the most familiar examples of this type is the Polyphemus from Boscotrecase where the Cyclops serenades Galatea in the foreground while in the background he is stoning the ship of Ulysses[11]. In an interpretation of the myth of Acteon different from that mentioned above, one continuous landscape provides the background for three scenes: the hunter's viewing the goddess at her bath, her angry pursuit and finally the attack on Acteon by his own dogs[12]. As von Blanckenhagen has pointed out, such paintings make no attempt at logic of composition or narrative. Their settings are universalized, divorced from time and place. He interprets this development as something particularly Roman[13].

Although *Eclogue* six is much earlier than such paintings, it is analogous in its use of dramatic abstractions and perhaps also in its placing the task of interpretation on the reader[14]. In the Silenus Song, iconographic details define the myths: the comrades of Hylas at the spring, the daughters of Protois shaking imagined horns on their heads. A visual image, comparable to that of the paintings, is suggested and in some cases the image implies a landscape which itself figures in the dramatic action.

The importance of landscape as a unifying factor in the myths has been observed by Elder who remarks on the way that Vergil has given this part of the poem a pastoral coloring by consistent use of bucolic detail. He finds here, as in the other poems, a «pastoral background that remains constant, the trees streams and mountains giving . . . an ultimate emotional stability—the harmony against which each pastoral incident may be set and proportionately evaluated»[15]. This point is important, but might be both qualified and extended. Vergil creates his unity by eliciting the bucolic possibilities in each myth; yet he does not merely show a juxtaposition of man and nature. Nature is more than a background here; it is a part of the iconography of each myth, and appears in close inter-action with each subject. Thus it is seldom constant and stable, but a part of the shifting play of human emotions, representing in some cases the object of man's desires, in others his aversion. In several instances we find man leaving his human shape to take on one of the forms of nature. It is directly in this precise and dramatized presentation of the inter-action of man and nature that we must begin to seek the themes of the Silenus myths.

The first part of the song creates the landscape which is, in a sense, the setting for a continuous narrative of all the myths. Strikingly it neither includes man nor makes provision for his point of view. Vergil's choice of a scientific over a mythological description of the origins of the world gives a peculiarly impersonal quality to nature. Many scholars have observed that the material does not adhere to the doctrines of any one school of thought, that it is, in fact, a mixture of the cosmologies of Lucretian Epicureanism and of Empedocles[16]. Such a conflation makes the description suggestive of science in the broadest sense as a way of thinking implicitly different from myth[17]. Silenus shows natural forms arising from a coalescence of the elements, with each part of the world spontaneously taking its place within a general order[18]. There is emphasis on the inter-relationship of natural phenomena. Verbs that tend to personify natural forces provide a sence of action and response within nature (37-39)[19]:

iamque nouum terrae stupeant lucescere solem,
altius atque cadant summotis nubibus imbres;
incipiant siluae cum primum surgere . . .

A sense of spontaneous action suggests the presence of natural law as nature displays a coherence of its own, a coherence that excludes both man and the gods. The climax of the account leaves man conspicuously absent and we see only the animal creatures wandering through their new environment (40):

rara per ignaros errent animalia montis.

As Silenus continues, the objective landscape is peopled with human figures in a series of three legends drawn from early mythological history, often categorised as stories of the origins of man himself (41-42):

hinc lapides Pyrrhae iactos, Saturnia regna,
Caucasiasque refert uolucris furtumque Promethei.

As Servius first observed[20], these myths are not cited in chronological order. They may even seem contradictory for they are not all commonly found in the same accounts and provide three distinct ideas of the nature of mankind. The stones cast by Pyrrha show man as a creature of the physical world. The theft of Prometheus implies a divine creation and a divine nature, while the *Saturnia regna* has less to do with creation than a harmonious balance between man and his environment. Still, the two creation myths are not entirely opposite. The stones cast by Pyrrha imply a transformation of nature, an elevation of inanimate objects to the human level. Solitary man needed human companionship for nature alone was inadequate. The theft of Prometheus goes even further in suggesting man's need for something from the gods to raise him above other living creatures, while the punishment—the Caucasian vultures—calls to mind solitude amidst a wild, cruel nature. Both allusions show a separation between man and nature, and give images of human restlessness within the confines of a purely natural world.

The second and central allusion, the *Saturnia regna* is in apparent antithesis to those framing it, for the golden age implies man's active, although sentimental, desire for affinity with nature and a peaceful, harmonious acceptance of its limitations[21]. Its central position and juxtaposition with the other myths reminds us that no view of nature and man is absolute. Yet *Saturnia regna* itself is an ambiguous term, for it tends towards an ideal organization or government rather than a spontaneous life in nature. Instead of a more natural man, *Saturnia regna* suggests a more humanly oriented nature. Vergil's manner of reference makes all three myths capable of suggesting both the harmony and disharmony of life in the natural world.

An even greater distance between man and nature appears in the myth of Hylas. Although this allusion has been taken as a reference to man's first journey, the journey is not the point stressed. Here are elements of a developed landscape scene—one that was in fact to become popular in landscape painting[22]—a direct confrontation of man and nature. Hylas is a character who enters the natural world, yet Silenus does not mention the nymphs and the seduction, but only the spring that was the landmark of his fate and the grief of the comrades in their fruitless search. The lamenting cry, *Hyla, Hyla,* echoes along the shore. Hylas has vanished in a way that his baffled comrades do not understand and they are rendered helpless by a nature that poses barriers to knowledge and returns no answer save the echo of the human voice.

The legends of Pasiphae and of the daughters of Protois are structurally and thematically bound together. The opening comment is pertinent to both (45): *et fortunatam, si numquam armenta fuissent.* The *armenta* may recall the *animalia* of the creation scene. Pasiphae is a human being consciously seeking a closer bond with nature and frustrated by the distance between. She is at once compelled by animal instincts and restrained by her human form. Vergil's account centers about her pursuit of the bull, emphasizing the bafflement of the unhappy queen to whom nature can only be a source of discomfort. To the bull, however, nature is a source of pleasure. Vergil shows the animal's joy in its proper environment—the luxury of his soft hyacinth bed (53), his peaceful feeding in the shade (54) and his pursuit of cows from the herd (55). The queen's human form is brought before us in the words (47) *a, virgo infelix.* If this phrase is, as Servius tells us[23], an echo of the *Io* of Calvus, it makes a clear point. By repeating another poet's lament for a woman transformed into a cow, Vergil ironically suggests that Pasiphae is to be pitied because she would welcome just such a metamorphosis—a release of animal energy into its natural form. Being restrained, Pasiphae can only attempt to restrain in turn the life of the bull. She orders the nymphs to close the paths from the groves and meditates strategies to lure him home (55-60). Her desire for nature seeks to distort the ways of nature itself, as well as to overcome the natural law separating the human from the animal worlds. Intellectually the queen has already undergone a metamorphosis[24]; she has already transgressed that law, yet physical nature still poses a barrier to her desires.

A variation on the theme of intellectual metamorphosis appears when Vergil contrasts the frustration of Pasiphae with the humiliation of the daughters of Protois who believe they have been turned into cows. Fear and repugnance take the place of desire. We see them shaking the imaginary horns on their heads (51), fearing the loss of human identity in animal form. For them the assumption of such form is not freedom, but bondage, and they dread bending their necks to the yoke (50): *collo timuisset aratrum.* Thus the two legends, each containing elements of the grotesque, are complimentary in showing how human dignity demands the preservation of a distance between man and nature. In certain aspects of the natural world man may see an image of his baser self, his animal nature, and may desire or fear its ascendency over his rational being. Intellectual metamorphosis, the extreme form of these desires or fears, is to the spectator a kind of comic madness.

The myth of Atalanta is one of the most narrowly focused, for Vergil chooses only one detail, the reaction of the maiden seeing the golden apples (v. 61):

tum canit Hesperidum miratam mala puellam;

The appearance of the apples is already a traditional moment for poets alluding to Atalanta. Theocritus describes her seeing, her confusion and her love (3.40)[25]. . . .

Catullus also makes the apples, in themselves a traditional erotic symbol, represent a realization of desire (*C.* 2a)[26]:

tam gratumst mihi quam ferunt puellae
pernici aureolum fuisse malum,
quod zonam soluit diu ligatam.

Vergil's *miratam* seems capable of similar suggestions, but is developed and made specific by an addition of his own. His apples are not simply *mala aurea,* but *mala Hesperidum*[27]. They are apples from a magic garden, both natural and supernatural, and the *miratam* is directed towards this point. Atalanta is halted by the sight of something from outside of nature, which may at the same time represent a natural desire. Her wonder at the apples draws her towards capture and love. Here, as in the myth of Prometheus, we have the sense of man's exceeding the limitations of nature to gain a human end. But if we look forward to the conclusion of Atalanta's story, we find that once more the unusual effort ends in disaster.

The allusion to the sisters of Phaeton follows the pattern laid down by Pasiphae and the Proteids. Where metamorphosis had first been introduced as a state of mind, an illusion or madness, it now becomes a physical reality. The language emphasizes imprisonment and bitterness. Vergil's use of the phrase (62-63), *circumdat amarae/corticis,* makes the transformation less an escape from, or an allievation of grief, than a solidification of it into permanent form. The unhappy maidens do not act; they are helpless and passive. The verbs *circumdat* and *erigit* make the singer himself the agent of their transformation[28]. The bitterness is that of the human being whose emotion has betrayed him to an external force. *Erigit,* a word usually associated with some form of mental stimulation or renewal, even with cheering and consolation, seems ironic in this context,

All these myths have shown man on the borderline of the human and natural worlds. They suggest the twofold character of the human situation which includes both a desire to be natural or yield to nature and a striving to exceed the limitations imposed by the physical world. A turning towards nature seems alien to human dignity and freedom. It is this aspect of the theme that is stressed in the two final myths of Scylla and Philomela where metamorphosis is a punishment for crime[29]. Even before their transformation, these characters have sunk below the human level with deeds that sever them from the world of men. Vergil places less emphasis on the deeds than on their consequences. Changes of form confirm the alienation from mankind. Not only does the once beautiful Scylla become monstrous[30], but also she attacks the ships of Ulysses proving a danger to the human world. The transformed Philomela embodies the melancholy of a one-time human being condemned to animal form. She seeks out lonely places (80): *quo cursu deserta petiuerit,* and flies sadly before her former home (80-81): *quibus ante infelix sua tecta super uolitaverit alis.* The idea of man's exclusion from nature seen in earlier myths is ironically reversed here, as the character who has become a part of nature longs vainly to return to the human world.

Although Philomela's crime is the most extreme instance of subhuman conduct, the final words of the description suggest a theme prevalent in several of the myths: that of seeking or wandering. Philomela seeks out desert places. The comrades of Hylas seek him on the shore. The sisters of Phaeton have sought their brother. Ulysses, attacked by Scylla, is himself a wanderer. The condition of man in nature seems lacking in direction and certainty. In the myth of Pasiphae, wandering is most explicit and forms of *errare* occur twice. Pasiphae wanders in the mountains (52): *tu nunc in montibus erras,* and the bull himself leaves wandering footprints (57-58): *si qua forte ferant oculis sese obuia nostris / errabunda bouis uestigia.* Wandering is a condition natural to animals and the *tu nunc in montibus erras* explicitly recalls the earlier *rara per ignaros errent animalia montis,* the description of the animals in the newly formed world. Tracking down her hope for the fulfillment of animal desire, Pasiphae follows the bull into a condition of wandering, a condition unsuited to human beings but suggestive of the frustration of man looking for satisfaction in the natural world.

A second pattern of recurrent thematic suggestions centers about the idea of bondage or capture. Bondage is implied by Prometheus in the Caucasus. Atalanta is captured by her wonder. The sisters of Phaeton are surrounded by bark, and Scylla is girt about (*succincta*) by monsters. The daughters of Protois fear the yoke. In the myth of Pasiphae this theme is also overtly expressed. Pasiphae is captured by madness (47): *quae te dementia cepit,* and in turn seeks to capture the bull (58-59): *forsitan illum / aut herba captum uiridi.* Pasiphae is both wandering and in bondage, and this paradoxical condition leads to an interpretation of the series as a whole.

Looking backward we may see the scheme created by Vergil's abbreviation and abstraction. By selecting a dramatic moment for each myth and developing this moment through image and metaphor he has stressed the potentially thematic quality of the myths. On the basis of his abstractions he has grouped the myths so as to bring out their similarities and contrasts within a developing pattern of suggestion. An account of creation gives a sense of man's distance from nature; and the three allusions that follow show him seeking, amidst nature, an identity that belongs peculiarly to man. Close upon these come the myths that demonstrate a loss of human identity through emotional assimilation into the natural world. Then follow those where human characteristics are forfeited through crime. But interassociation is not limited to this grouping. Hylas and Phaeton suggest each other because both deal with grief for bereavement and the condition of the

bereaved in the natural world: in one case shut out from nature, in the other absorbed into natural form. Phaeton himself, like Prometheus, is a character who desires something beyond that offered by the limited natural world. The imagined metamorphosis of the daughters of Protois looks forward to the real metamorphosis of the sisters of Phaeton, Scylla and Philomela. Thus the abstractions show all the myths participating in one common problem of the confrontation between nature and man. The themes of wandering and bondage further enforce the sense of common participation. Consistently we are made aware of man's struggle to define his own place in his environment. Thus the scheme of Vergil's mythology exploits the simple assumption that man occupies a place higher than the rest of creation, yet may descend below his given level[31]. Man is not inevitably in conflict with the laws of nature; but his desires and impulses bring him up against nature's limitations and put him in bondage.

As we turn from the myths themselves to the framework of the poem, we may see that the ideas of capture, limitation and bondage have already been introduced. The two opening sections show a striking resemblence of pattern and theme. Both the dialogue between the Eclogue poet and Apollo and the capture of old Silenus by the shepherd boys are incidents where the poet accepts an injunction concerning his verse. In the first instance, Tityrus is restricted to a given mode of composition. In the second, Silenus is taken prisoner and bound for the sake of a song. The first section gives an oblique thematic statement which is spelled out by its literal restatement in the second: the binding of the poet. In verse 10 the captivity is transferred from poet to audience as Vergil speaks of a reader held by admiration of his verse: *si quis captus amore leget.* In the second section an audience is again captivated as the trees move their heads to the Silenus Song and the fauns and wild beasts dance in measure (27-28). The pattern will be repeated later with a different emphasis when Gallus is hailed by the Muses as the poet to inherit the nature-animating power of Hesiod and please Apollo with a celebration of the Grynean Grove.

The Callimachean *recusatio* of verses 1-12 must be read as a thematic statement and judged for its relevence to its context. I do not believe that its purpose is to express either Vergil's total rejection of epic or his intention of devoting himself to Callimachean verse[32]. Rather, it prepares for the investigation of pastoral poetry in *Eclogue* six itself by placing pastoral within a larger literary scheme. The echoes of the *Aetia* are not entirely straightforward, or at least do not merely repeat the points made there. Callimachus, in his introduction, defines a style that is itself one of the major aims of his work. He chooses a kind of poem susceptable to craft and finish, indeed one where these qualities may predominate. The metaphors he uses to describe poetic style—the thunder of epic, the poet's fat victim and his thin Muse, the small-voiced cicala and the braying of asses are clear[33], but not especially relevant to the subject matter of the *Aetia* itself. Vergil draws his literary terms directly from the pastoral context and speaks of subject as well as of style. The *pastor* who fattens his sheep gives the bucolic setting and iconography; the thinness of the verse suggests the limitation of the bucolic point of view. *Deductum carmen* is not in itself a literary goal, but the characteristic of a particular mode. Unlike the speaker in the *Aetia*, Tityrus has not chosen between two modes of writing but has rather threatened to transgress the boundaries of the mode in which he writes, to overstep a kind of natural law of poetry that dictates the province of the shepherd poet[34].

At the very outset, then, pastoral poetry is given a very limited, very literary definition. *Reges et proelia* are excluded. The poet seems isolated within a world of his own making and denied contact with any larger literary sphere. Furthermore, he must ask Varus also to accept the limitations of pastoral, to join with himself in a somewhat rarified milieu. The poet's humorous characterization of himself adds to the concept of pastoral limitation. The *Cynthius aurem uellit* and the somewhat mocking tone of the god's address suggest a brash young speaker somewhat in need of artistic discipline. Apollo's pull at the ear may remind us of the asses' ears the god gave Midas for his bad judgement in poetry.

Within this highly literary setting, pastoral has been described as a kind of play (1-2)[35]:

> *prima Syracosio dignata est ludere uersu*
> *nostra neque erubuit siluas habitare Thalia.*

The literary conference of god and poet is itself a game of sorts. In fact the poet seems somewhat akin to the bold Chromis and Mnasyllus who ask Silenus for a song. The sense of sophisticated poetic playfulness is thus carried over to the second section. The shepherd boys have been seeking Silenus for a long time and he has consistently eluded them (18-19): *nam saepe senex spe carminis ambo / luserat.* The capture is evidence that the game has at last been played right. The boys have surprised Silenus sleeping and have come provided with a sportive nymph. Silenus readily grants their success (24): *soluite me, pueri; satis est potuisse videri.* His song continues the spirit of the game.

The description of the song gives a stronger and more complicated meaning to *ludere* (27-28):

> *tum uero in numerum Faunosque ferasque uideres*
> *ludere, tum rigidas motare cacumina quercus.*

What before had been the limited and personal activity of the ***Eclogue*** poet is now the animated yet orderly response of nature to song. Song raises nature from its ordinary inamination and raises it to something nearer the human level[36]. The activity of the poet thus shifts from a self-contained world of literature and literary terms to the wider sphere of nature.

The capture of Silenus completes the definition of the poetic subject. Silenus, a character of rich and varied history in literature and art, is here an arch-figure of pastoral, combining the freedom and playfulness of a Theocritean shepherd with highly developed powers of song and articulate knowledge. He is also a didactic speaker. Vergil plays upon traditional legends of the binding of Silenus found in Greek mythology particularly in connection with King Midas[37]. But the binding has also a significance developed from its context here. Silenus who speaks the greater part of the poem becomes an intermediary between the literary world of the introduction and the natural world of the myths. In discovering Silenus the poet indicates that he is calling on nature to speak for him; the binding of Silenus is a binding of subject and poem.

In the course of his mythological song, Silenus creates a further association between nature and poetry. The adventure of Gallus on Helicon is parallel to the opening sections in that it also portrays a poet receiving commands for his verse. It would seem significant that Gallus himself is wandering when he approaches the River Permessus to be greeted by the Muses and led to the seat of Apollo (64-65):

> *tum canit errantem Permessi ad flumina Gallum*
> *Aonas in montis ut duxerit una sororum.*

In these verses *errantem* and *duxerit* assume almost opposite meanings. If *errare* represents the undirected condition of man in nature, *ducere* can be associated with the order and direction to be gained through art. *Deductum* is the word which has described the kind of verse suited to the shepherd poet. *Deducere* appears here as Linus speaks to Gallus describing the control over nature effected by Hesiod's poems (70-71): *ille solebat / cantando rigidas deducere montibus ornos.* As before in the passage concerning the Silenus Song (28), *rigidas* describes the trees that succumb to the power of the poet. The word implies a stiffness and unyielding quality in nature which is overcome by art. Such statements of the poet's power to alter or direct nature have often been read in association with Orphic beliefs in the divine, enchanting power of song[38]. I think these expressions need not be taken as entirely mystical or magical, nor do they refer entirely to the poet's effect on his hearers. Rather they are metaphors for the orderly way nature may be encompassed in verse. The order that each poet creates in his own poems leads to an orderly vision of nature as a whole.

If we compare the new myth of Gallus with the old myths surrounding it in the Silenus Song, we see a difference between the poet's association with nature and that of mankind. The adventure of Gallus on Helicon is in direct contrast to the frustrations depicted in the other myths. No unqualified myths of rebirth or renewal occur in the series; and this image of a poet's initiation—his assumption of a new intellectual identity—stands out sharply from its context. Gallus is changed from wanderer to poet; he gains a place of his own in nature and a control over the physical world which others have not achieved.

The topic of Gallus' new poem, the origins of the Grynean Grove, is itself suggestive. Like the investiture of a poet, the establishment of a divine sanctuary is a dynamic myth, one of order and harmony, rather than of futility and discord. Whether Gallus had already composed the poem, or only planned it; whether it was known only to Vergil, or to the reading public, seems to me somewhat inessential. The topic itself is most important here. Servius gives testimony to a poem of Euphorion on the same subject[39]. The Grove may well have been familiar enough for Vergil to suggest its salient characteristics by the mere use of the name. Pausanius praises the actual Grove for its variety of sweet smelling trees. His remarks suggest a kind of *locus amoenus*[40]—a paradise of nature created by the god, or even an art garden where nature was ordered by human design. The Grynean Grove must stand for an order surpassing that of ordinary nature, and is therefore capable of representing the achievement of poetry itself.

Within a carefully designed context of contrasts and repetitions, the poet has come to stand out as the person most capable of dealing with nature. Neither yielding nor opposing himself to the world in which he lives, he recreates it in an image of his own making. The poet is not, like man, in conflict with natural law, but rather he demonstrates the possibility of living in harmony with nature. First the master poets, Silenus and Hesiod, give life to inanimate objects. Through the agency of their singing we see not just man descending to the animal level, but nature rising to the human and taking on symptoms of order and design. The master poets are models for the Roman poets[41]. Just as Hesiod sets the pattern for Gallus, so does Silenus for the *Eclogue* poet. Hesiod and Gallus sing of nature and the gods; Silenus and the *Eclogue* poet of nature and man[42].

At the beginning the *Eclogue* poet had been in conflict with a law of poetry just as man conflicts with nature's laws. Being forced to accept his limitations, he demonstrates their value. Once he has accepted his subject, he shows that the poet's function is to speak of nature, to organize the world for man's understanding. He can at one time both satisfy and criticise human desires. The impasse of man and nature seen in the myths can only be broken by the poet whose bondage to nature differs from that of ordinary man. In making nature his subject, the poet rises above its limitations, gaining a freedom that in turn confers order and freedom on nature itself. Art is the chief approach of man to nature, the only means for making nature responsive to man.

In the first verses of the poem, the pastoral world seems, as we have noticed, very limited and isolated. As the poem develops, the boundaries of pastoral expand and it becomes the locus for a broad exploration of the nature of man. Pastoral is of course only one vehicle for the poet's speaking of nature. In mentioning Gallus, Vergil makes us aware of other courses than his own. But he shows also that pastoral has the capacity to present a satisfactory symbolic discourse encompassing all nature. This is the point towards which the *recusatio* is directed, the Eclogue poet's answer to his divine critic.

But the conclusion of the poem ironically brings back the limitations of the natural world. As the river Eurotas had once cherished the words of Apollo, so do the gods on Olympus wish for the continuation of the Silenus Song. There is no return to the limited literary world of pastoral seen at the beginning of the poem; instead pastoral, myth and nature blend into one larger world which is both the landscape and substance of the Silenus Song. But since this world is natural, Vesper moves steadily on, sending the cattle home from the field (84-86):

> *ille canit (pulsae referunt ad sidera ualles),*
> *cogere donec ouis stabulis numerumque referre*
> *iussit et inuito processit Vesper Olympo.*

The one end the song cannot accomplish is that of creating a timeless world. As the poet had earlier accepted his pastoral subject with its own limitations, now the song itself becomes subject to the limitations of the ordinary world. In a final confrontation of art and nature, nature has the last word. No matter how it may be transformed by the poet, the natural world preserves its identity and its independence subscribing the final boundary to the inclinations of man.

Notes

1. For summaries and evaluations of major interpretations of the song see Zeph Stewart, *The Song of Silenus H.S.C.Ph.* 64 (1959), p. 180-183, and E. De Saint-Denis, *Le chant de Silène à la lumière d'une découverte récente, Revue de Philologie* (1963), p. 23-35. To the material discussed in these should be added the perceptive commentary of Jacques Perret, *Virgile Les Bucoliques* (Paris, 1961), p. 67-76, and the important interpretation of Brooks OTIS, *Virgil. A Study in Civilized Poetry* (Oxford, 1963), p. 138-140. Both depart from the line of genre study that has characterized most recent work on the poem. Otis sees a chronological order in the series beginning with the Golden Age and fall and progressing through the Age of Heroes to the Iron Age. The poem is thus a history of man's decline and culminates in a series of violent, criminal *amores* punished by metamorphosis. Although I do not believe that the dominant plan of the entire series is historical, I agree with Otis on the importance of the thematic aspects of the myths. Perret, although he does not aim for a complete interpretation of the poem, lays stress on the importance of nature in the myths and my interpretations coincide with his at many points noted below.

2. *Zu Vergils Eklogen, Rh.M.* 99 (1956), p. 193-195.

3. *Op. cit.,* p. 183-199.

4. *non iniussa cano, H.S.C.Ph.* 65 (1961), p. 109-125.

5. *Op. cit.,* p. 1.

6. The series of transitional words (31: *namque canebat;* 42: *refert;* 43: *his adiungit* etc.) marking

divisions of topic within the song is usually taken to imply that Vergil intends his account of the Silenus Song as a mere summary of material. See e. g. Karl Büchner, *P. Vergilius Maro. der Dichter der Römer* (Stuttgart, 1961), p. 201, or Stewart, *op. cit.,* p. 1.

7. With very few exceptions, scholars have approached the myths purely as a series of references intended to evoke the reader's knowledge of the stories or else his knowledge of their association with some particular literary situation, e. g. Stewart, *op. cit.,* p. 179: "The effort is not so much to reproduce what Silenus sang as to give an account of the subject matter". Rose, *The Eclogues of Vergil* (California, 1942), p. 103-114, is one of the few who attempts thematic interpretation; but his theory, that the myths represent the interference of the gods in human affairs, is still dependent on interpolated material, rather than upon the language of the text itself.

8. For descriptions and comments see W.J. T. Peters, *Landscape in Romano-Campanian Mural Painting* (Assen, 1963), p. 73-74, and Peter H. von Blanckenhagen, *The Paintings from Boscotrecase, Mitteilungen des Deutschen Archeologischen Instituts, Römische Abteilung, Sechstes Ergänzungsheft* (Heidelberg, 1962), p. 46, note 68. Von Blanckenhagen dates the painting as a work of the second style while Peters sees elements of second and third style combined. In interpreting the composition I disagree with von Blanckenhagen in his opinion that the shrine is the true center of interest in the landscape and Artemis and Acteon are merely «staffage figures».

9. The version of the Acteon myth depicted here corresponds with Diodorus Siculus 4.81, an account roughly contemporary with the painting. Acteon is punished for boasting that his skill in hunting is greater that that of Artemis, or for an attempt to celebrate a marriage with the goddess or for both reasons. The first of these explanations goes back at least to EURIPIDES, *Bacchae,* 337 f.

10. *Narration in Hellenistic and Roman Art,* A.J.A., Series 2, Vol. 78 (1957), p. 78.

11. For description and analysis of this painting see von Blanckenhagen, *The Paintings from Boscotrecase,* p. 38-51 and esp. p. 41-42.

12. Dawson, *op. cit.,* p. 97-98, § 36 and § 37; also p. 118-119.

13. von Blanckenhagen, *Narration in Hellenistic and Roman Art,* p. 78-82; also *The Paintings from Boscotrecase,* p. 43.

14. The selection and grouping of subjects in the House of the Cryptoporticus and the House of the Epigrams (see PETERS, *op. cit.,* p. 24-27) suggest that Roman spectators may have expected to be puzzled by paintings and to use their ingenuity to explain the rationale of a group. A great many rooms or houses, especially those of the third and fourth styles contain subjects with some thematic relationship to each other.

15. *Op. cit.,* p. 118.

16. For discussion see Stewart, *op. cit.,* p. 184-185.

17. Vergil's choice of science over mythology is suggested by comparison of the Silenus Song with that of Orpheus in *Argonautica* 1. 496-512. De Saint-Denis, *op. cit.,* p. 26 and 38-39, believes that the genesis of the Silenus Song lies here and in the song of the bard, Demodocus in *Odyssey* 8. 266 ff. Undoubtedly these passages are important, but they are still very different in technique. The song of Orpheus is historically oriented, and although it is a summary or list of topics for the song, it nonetheless emphasizes the sequence and inter-relationship of the events told. De Saint-Denis likewise compares Vergil's Song of Iopas (*Aeneid* 1. 740-746), which also contains allusions to creation but again differs greatly in the style of reference. If the Silenus Song anticipates any part of Vergil's later work, I would suggest that it is the description of the legends on the shield of Aeneas (*Ae.* 8. 626 ff.) where again a selection of pictorial details creates and illuminates a developing theme.

18. Perret, *op. cit., ad* vs. 38, p. 71 comments: «en fait, le soleil, comme les nuages, s'éloigne per à peu de la terre à mesure que les éléments, se dissociant les uns des autres, tendent à occuper leur lieu naturel».

19. The text of the *Eclogues* is that edited by F. A. Hirtzel, Oxford, O.C.T., 1959.

20. *Servii Grammatici qui feruntur in Vergilii Bucolica et Georgica Commentarii,* ed. Georg Thilo (Leipzig, 1887), p. 71-72. Servius takes the series as a misguided attempt to present a chronological order and suggests that the *Saturnia regna* could be interpreted as the reign of Jove to preserve chronology.

21. Otis, *op. cit.,* p. 138, makes the *Saturnia regna* the keynote of the series. He finds in *Eclogue* 6 and its history of decline from the Golden Age a counter to *Eclogue* 4 with its prediction of a Golden Age in the future. I do not believe that the phrase *Saturnia regna,* balanced as it is by contrasting myths, occupies a position important enough to justify OTIS' reading. The displacement of chronology seems to me deliberate and important, aimed at puzzling the reader and causing him to seek an explanation.

22. For Hylas and the journey as an allusion to the Age of Heroes see OTIS, *op. cit.,* p. 138. The first journey would of course be a landmark in the decline of man. But the Hylas of Theocritus, *Idyl* 13 is not primarily associated with a journey, nor is the figure found in painting. See Dawson, *op. cit.,* p. 151-152.

23. *Ad loc.,* p. 74: *a, virgo infelix, herbis pasceris amaris.* Possibly Vergil's picture of the bull himself feeding on grass (53): *ilice sub nigra pallentis ruminat herbas,* is intended to continue the allusion.

24. The idea of intellectual metamorphosis in these myths was suggested to me by W. S. Anderson's study of the vocabulary of metamorphosis in Ovid, *Multiple Change in the Metamorphoses, T.A.P.A.* 94 (1963), p. 1-27.

25. The edition used is *Theocritus,* edited with a Translation and a Commentary, A. S. F. Gow (Cambridge, 1952).

26. The edition used is *C. Valerius Catullus,* ed. W. Kroll (Stuttgart, 1959).

27. *Mala Hesperidum:* Although Vergil probably was not the first to make the garden the source of the apples, the detail is not very common. It is given by the *scholia* on Theocritus 3.40 and Servius on *Aeneid* 3, 113 but not in any extant poet. C. Robert, *Hermes* 22 (1887), p. 450, conjectures that both *scholia* go back to a lost passage in Hesiod's *Eoae.*

28. Servius, *op. cit., ad loc.,* p. 76: *mira autem est canentis laus, ut quasi non factam rem cantare, sed ipse eam cantando facere videatur.*

29. OTIS, *op. cit.,* p. 138, thinks the passage is climactic because it represents the complete decline of man into *Amor indignus* toward which the whole series has been tending. That the section of the poem beginning with vs. 42 is chiefly concerned with the power of love is also the opinion of Herbert Holtorf, *P. Vergilius Maro. die Grösseren Gedichte, Band* I, *Einleitung, Bucolica* (Frieberg, 1959), p. 187, 193. My chief criticism is that *amor,* while it may be a sufficient description of the subject matter of the myths has little to do with Vergil's specific dramatization or language. Holtorf is not at all clear in his division of the poem. He does not attempt to explain the interruption of the ancient myths by the Gallus passage or to find a relationship between the Tereus-Scylla section and what precedes it.

30. The transformation of Scylla belongs, of course, to the myth of Scylla and Glaucus (see *Metamorphoses* 13, 398-14, 74). But this legend involves no real crime. Vergil would seem to have conflated two myths in order to include both a notable crime and a spectacular metamorphosis.

31. The principle is more of a *locus communis* than a matter of doctrine, e. g. Sallust, *Catilina,* 1; Cicero, *De Officiis,* 30. 105-106.

32. This is the most commonly held opinion concerning the meaning of the *recusatio.* The most recent statement to this point is Wendall Clausen, *Callimachus and Latin Poetry, G.R.B.S.* 5 (1964), p. 193 f. Clausen thinks that Vergil rejected the possibility of epic because of his own experience of and distaste for war. Clausen furthermore believes that these statements constitute an aesthetic credo for the entire *Eclogue Book,* arguing that all Vergil's pastoral is Callimachean. But for the Callimachean intentions of the Silenus Song, most critics seem to forget that Callimachus was a «water-drinker» and Vergil's Silenus is most explicitly drunk on wine!

33. *Callimachus. Aetia, Iambi, Hecale and Other Fragments,* C. A. Trypanis, trans., Loeb Classical Library, (Cambridge, 1958), p. 6-8. *Aetia,* 1. 20-24, 29-36.

34. I believe there is no need to consider, as readers since Servius have done, that the *reges et proelia* refer either to Vergil's epic plans or to an epic poem. Although the phrase certainly implies an heroic subject, it also looks back to *Eclogue* Four which incorporates such a subject. Here Vergil has taken liberties with the decorum of pastoral by creating a new and imaginary context, the *siluae . . . consule dignae.* Apollo's reprimand is a criticism of something already accomplished and available to the reader. The literary purpose of *reges et proelia* is to make pastoral less limited and more relevant to the historical world. This interpretation is proposed by Jean Hubaux, *Les thèmes bucoliques dans la poésie latine* (Brussels, 1930), p. 13-14, but has found few supporters.

35. *Ludere* is a common enough term in discussions of poetry, but its meaning is worth consideration. In an enlightening and suggestive article, *Ludus Poeticus, Les Études Classiques,* 4 (1935), p. 108 f., trans. in *Studies in Roman Literature, Language, Culture and Religion* (Leiden, 1956), p. 30-32, H. Wagenvoort proposes that the term need not always indicate mere frivolity in poetry. He argues that the idea of the *ludus* as a kind of training or practice may be extended to certain poems or kinds of poetry where the poet expresses his intention of developing his art in preparation for a greater work in the future. I believe that something of this sort is suggested here. Vergil has written his first pastorals in a Theocritean manner (*Syracosio*) and progressed, in *Eclogue* 4 to a more ambitious style of his own invention.

36. Perret, *op. cit.,* p. 68, sees such an inverse relationship between song and metamorphosis: «au lieu que par le chant humain on voit la nature s'exalter, arbres et bêtes soulevés par un noble ferveur (27-28), c'est ici l'humanité que se fige dans le végétal immobile et se perd dans l'épouvante diffuse de l'animal».

37. Servius, *op. cit., ad loc.,* p. 66, records the opinion that Vergil acquired the material from Theopompus. See Aelian, *V.H.,* 3.18. There Silenus is very much a nature deity and speaks of the topography and geography of the world. The binding and capture of the nature god and the demand for revelation are adapted by Ovid to the story of Numa's quest for Picus and Faunus on the Aventine (*Fasti* 3. 291 f.).

38. See esp. Marie Desport, *L'incantation virgilienne. Essai sur les mythes du poète enchanteur et leur influence dans l'œuvre de Virgile* (Bordeaux, 1952), p. 49 *et al.* De Saint-Denis, *op. cit.,* p. 35-40, argues that the chief associations are with Dionysus as the god of wine and of poetic inspiration. He finds a parallel for the scene of Silenus' capture in a

2nd-3rd century mosaic panel from a recently discovered house with a Dionysian scheme of decorations in Tunisia (L. Foucher, *Découvertes archéologiques à Thysdrus en 1960, Notes et documents de l'Institut d'archéologie de Tunis* (Tunis, 1961), p. 29, which shows a drunken Silenus being bound by three boys with a nymph looking on. De Saint-Denis conjectures that the prestige and influence of the Dionysian religion in 3rd century Tunis might be considered comparable to that which influenced Vergil in composing the Silenus Song. It does not, however, seem to me that the mosaic provides sufficient proof that the Dionysian element is to be considered as the chief unifying feature of the poem. The binding of Silenus is a common motif, here distinctly subordinated to and made to serve the pastoral theme.

39. *Op. cit., ad loc.,* p. 78.

40. Servius' description of the Grove, *op. cit., ad* vs. 72, p. 78, will also support this point: *ubi est locus arboribus multis, iunco, gramine, floribus uariis omni tempore uestitus, abundans etiam fontibus. . . .* Even more interesting is his citation of Varro to the effect that fetters were removed from those who entered the Grove and nailed to the trees. Perret, *op. cit.,* p. 74, thinks that Vergil has emphasized the «aspect champêtre» of the sanctuary by his choice of the words *nemus* and *lucus.*

41. Desports, *op. cit.,* p. 169, sees a kind of heirarchy of inspiration among the poets in the *Eclogue:* «. . . les chants de Silène et à la suite tous les chants de chacun des poètes énumérés, sont vraiment à considérer de ce point de vue, comme les échos du *carmen* divin».

42. Perret, *op. cit.,* p. 70, remarks, «Silène, c'est Tityre promu au rang d'un Génie».

Charles Segal (essay date 1969)

SOURCE: "Vergil's Sixth *Eclogue* and the Problem of Evil," *Proceedings: American Philological Association,* Vol. 100, 1969, pp. 407-35.

[*In the essay that follows, Segal analyzes the moral outlook of the poem and asserts that in the Sixth* Eclogue Vergil *uses the pastoral mode to point out a correlation between disorder in the universe and man's evil nature.*]

I

Eclogue 6 is one of Vergil's most ambitious and most difficult short poems.[1] Grand themes are its concern: passion, violence, cosmic and poetic creation, the relation between man and nature. No one formulation of the many subtle and complex relationships between these themes is likely to prove definitive, just as no one principle of unity for its bewildering exuberance of narrative material has emerged

as entirely satisfactory. "No one can feel confident of exhausting all the possibilities of this poem or of understanding all that Virgil intended: it is the original creation of a fertile poetic imagination."[2]

There has been a growing dissatisfaction with attempts to interpret the *Eclogue* in terms of external criteria: the work of Gallus, Vergil's relations to Callimachean poetics or to Alexandrian themes or to contemporary literary genres or works.[3] Recent interpreters like Otis, Klingner, and Mrs. Leach have concentrated more fully upon the moral and aesthetic attitudes which the poem implies,[4] have allowed a more flexible, less mechanical unity to the whole and especially to Silenus' song, and have recognized that the poem may be far more than a "document of Virgilian literary autobiography."[5] I propose to follow this line of approach, laying perhaps more stress than the above-mentioned scholars on the moral outlook implied in the poem, yet acknowledging that the poem's moral and aesthetic positions—the emphasis upon the creative power of poetry[6]—are inseparable. Not only does my interpretation posit a firm unity for the *Eclogue,* but it seeks to give the proem (1-12) a more integral part in that unity than most previous interpreters have done.

The entire corpus of Vergil's work involves a profound knowledge of and struggle with the reality of evil in the human psyche. Asking why history contains such suffering, the *Aeneid* finds a partial answer, at least, in the passions within man. From the *Eclogues* to the *Aeneid,* outward events and settings have a symbolical correspondence with the inner world of human emotional life; and the inner world is as much the subject of Vergil's poetry as the outer.[7] Juno, obstructress of a tranquil and stable order, is symbolically identified with these internal disorders and makes use of figures (like Allecto) who are as much symbols of the life of the soul as powerful agents in the external world.[8] The *Eclogues,* as Bruno Snell has argued,[9] go even further than the *Aeneid* in using the forms of the external world to create a symbolical landscape of the emotional life, a "spiritual landscape," in Snell's phrase. The emotions dealt with in the *Eclogues,* however, are not always so tender as Snell maintains. The sixth *Eclogue* especially casts into the terms of pastoral something of that correlation between disorder in the universe and evil within man which is so richly developed in the *Aeneid.*

One of Vergil's achievements in the sixth *Eclogue* is precisely the incorporation of these basic moral issues into his poetics and *vice versa.* Through his concern with the scope and character of creativity in pastoral (and by extension in all poetry), he seeks, as Mrs. Leach observes, "to present a satisfactory symbolic discourse encompassing all nature."[10]

II

The problem of evil is not foreign to the *Eclogues.* The idea of a *scelus,* a moral impurity infecting the whole Roman people, was much in the air (see *G.* 1.501-14, Horace, *Epod.* 7 and 16).[11] The political disorders of *E.* 1, the callous soldier of *E.* 9, death (*E.* 5), and above all the passion of love, are all tokens of the disturbing realities against and amid which the poet weaves his fragile symbolic refuge of art and love (see *E.* 10.71, *E.* 5.85).[12] The fourth *Eclogue* desiderates a visionary peace which will obliterate "the traces of our sin (*sceleris vestigia nostri,* 13) and free the world of fear (14). Yet even here, amid the bounty of the pacified nature of the *aurea aetas,* some traces of human sinfulness remain (*pauca tamen suberunt priscae vestigia fraudis,* 31).[13] Thus even in this hopeful mood Vergil qualifies any total optimism about human destiny. *Scelus* recurs in the ninth *Eclogue,* as the shocked pastoral singer recognizes that invaders from the world of war and politics will dispossess and even kill the helpless Arcadian: *heu cadit in quemquam tantum scelus?* (17). War, at the end of the first *Georgic,* reveals the *multae scelerum facies* (*G.* 1.506).

Like the *Aeneid,* the sixth *Eclogue* correlates internal and external disorder and fixes the source of evil within man. He can, like the poet-shepherd, Tityrus, or like the poet Gallus on Helicon, follow the "orders" (*non iniussa cano,* 9) of Apollo and receive homage from "Apollo's band" (*Phoebi chorus,* 66). Or, like Pasiphae, Scylla, Tereus, he can sink into bestial degradation which finds its external ratification in bestial metamorphosis.

While *Eclogue* 4, like the end of the first *Georgic,* projects the problem of evil upon the history and traditions of man or the Romans generally, *Eclogue* 6, like *Eclogue* 10, examines it within the framework of the private, individual life as writ large in mythical paradigms (Pasiphae, Scylla, Tereus). Yet the sixth *Eclogue* also raises the question of a fundamental flaw in human nature. The myths of lines 41-42 involve a constellation of ideas centering upon human perversity and the loss of a happy state because of human evil:

> hinc lapides Pyrrhae iactos, Saturnia regna,
> Caucasiasque refert volucris furtumque Promethei.

In the story of Pyrrha and her husband, Deucalion, Jupiter destroys the human race with a flood because he cannot endure man's evil ways. The stones (*lapides . . . iactos*) out of which the new race of men is created are, according to Ovid, a fitting aetiology for the hardness of his lot (*Met.* 1.414-15):

> inde genus durum sumus experiensque laborum
> et documenta damus qua simus origine nati.

The *Saturnia regna* of 41 are obviously connected with a happy time of innocence and purity lost in the harshness of a later time.[14] Prometheus in 41, though not necessarily connected with an evil inherent in man, is yet a reminder of an anthropomorphic cunning and pride refractory toward the divine order; and his tale is also connected with the bad character of the female half of the species (see Hesiod, *Erga* 59-82; *Theog.* 570-602). Even more important,

Prometheus is associated with the development of technology; and technology, as *Eclogue* 4 makes clear (see *E.* 4.18 and generally 18-45), accompanies the loss of the simple innocence of the Golden Age.[15] The three myths of 41-42, then, all form a cluster of ideas focusing on that antinomy between innocence and sinfulness which is part of the Golden-Age theme. Vergil has perhaps deliberately jumbled the chronology of the three episodes in order to make the reader think about the element they have in common: the flawed character of human existence and man's removal from any absolute purity of life or spirit.

These very concise allusions should not be pressed too hard. Yet combined with the amount of space devoted to Pasiphae and with the eschatological frame of the preceding two *Eclogues* (in *E.* 5 see especially 57-64), they indicate a recurrent concern with the moral problem of human nature. By including the myths of Hylas, Phaethon, and Tereus along with those of Pasiphae and Scylla, incidentally, Vergil goes beyond Hesiod's localization of evil in the woman: Vergil distributes it more equitably between both sexes.[16]

The first two poems of the *Eclogue Book* pair war (*E.* 1) and love (*E.* 2) as both manifestations and causes of evil and disorder. War plays a relatively minor part in *Eclogue* 6, but it is not entirely negligible. The Apolline warning against *reges et proelia* (3) may be more than a literary program,[17] if, as we have suggested, the moral and the aesthetic spheres are closely joined. War and love, kept separate in *Eclogues* 1 and 2, are first brought together, though haltingly, in *Eclogue* 6. *Eclogue* 10 will establish a still firmer connection, until, in the *Aeneid,* with its symbolical interplay between the political and psychological, external and internal realms, war and love are coordinate destroyers both of inward and outward order.

For a people destined *paci(s) imponere morem,* war represents the victory of chaos and unreason. *Bella, horrida bella* carry an especially ominous ring in the *Aeneid* (see 6.86, 7.41). Juno, exultant in the triumph of irrationality that she has engineered, bursts open the *geminae belli portae* (7.607-22) and lets in a mood of murderous violence that is not stilled even in the final outcome of the battles (12.945-52). Juno's minister, Allecto, with all her dark associations of the Underworld, is both the inspirer of inward *furor* and the inciter to war (7.324-26):

> luctificam Allecto dirarum ab sede dearum
> infernisque ciet tenebris, cui tristia bella
> iraeque insidiaeque et crimina noxia cordi.

Allecto's sister, Tisiphone, rages amid the futile slaughter and "empty wrath" of the poem's most tragic battle (10.755-61); but she also punishes the guilty souls in Tartarus' *durissima regna* (6.555, 571-72). In the fourth *Eclogue* the disappearance of war accompanies a confidence in the regeneration of human nature, in man's capacity for order and happiness. Universal peace is a distinguishing trait of the new moral order and a sign of the conquest of evil. The *puer* will reign over a world made peaceful by the virtues of his father (17).

The sixth **Eclogue,** in introducing war, sets it against two related opposites: the pastoral world and pastoral-poetic *amor. Tristia bella* in line 7 may later become something of a cliché, but here it still has considerable force. *Tristis* itself is a strong word in the **Eclogues.**[18] It is used again in connection with the horrors of war in *E.* 9.5: *nunc victi, tristes, quoniam fors omnia versat.*

Vergil places these *tristia bella* immediately against a line in which the language and careful word-order stress the delicacy, fragility, and contemplative peace of his poetic Arcadia (8):

agrestem tenui meditabor harundine Musam.

The echo of the opening lines of the collection (*E.* 1.1-2) suggests that Vergil is thinking of the **Eclogue Book** and his pastoral world as a whole. It also reminds us of the threats to Arcadian peace presented in that initial poem: *tu . . . silvestrem tenui musam meditaris avena: nos patriae finis et dulcia linquimus arva.* Yet in *E.* 6 Arcady is to win out over war. The Tityrus who in *E.* 1 escaped being exiled from Arcadia by making an unbucolic visit to the *urbs,* is here chosen to reject warlike themes. No urban *iuvenis* (*E.* 1.42), but Apollo himself will keep him within the realm of his *pinguis ovis.*

War and Arcadia, epic and pastoral, stand against one another in terms of content as well as style. Having framed their antithetical relation in lines 1-8, Vergil goes on to widen that antithesis by introducing poetic *amor.* If the reader, "caught by love" (*captus amore*), reads this poem, then "our tamarisks and every grove, Varus, will sing of you" (9-11). The *amor* of poetry serves both to create another opposition to war and to establish an antithesis with a different kind of *amor* later in the poem. Yet this *amor,* though it excludes the violence of war, does not necessarily exclude totally the violence of erotic passion (cf. Corydon in *E.* 2 and Gallus in *E.* 10). It thus hints at a dialectical union of the two poles of art which is to be explored more deeply in the interplay between Silenus and Apollo (see 13-30, 82-83, and below, sections III and V).

Poetry turns the tables on war in two ways. First, the language of *captus amore* uses a military metaphor (*captus*) for a most unmartial experience.[19] Second, pastoral incorporates the warrior. The pastoral world threatened by the warrior in *E.* 1 can now enclose the warrior Varus, metaphorically, amid its groves and make his name one of those songful echoes which the exiled Meliboeus of the first **Eclogue** finds such pain in leaving (*E.* 1.5).

At the same time Vergil recognizes that love and desire do not always lead to peaceful themes. Despite Tityrus' own Apolline call to the *deductum carmen,* there will be more than enough (*super*) of others who "desire" (*cupiant*) to sing of war (6-7). Presumably the reader who is *captus*

amore in Vergil's sense will not feel such "desires." Here too the poem intimates the divergent paths which love and desire may take.

Deepening and sharpening the opposition between pastoral and epic, Arcadia and Varus, enters the figure of Silenus (13). Mythical, grotesque, fantastic, he stands as far as possible from the flesh-and-blood, responsible Varus.[20] Not only is he an Alexandrian symbol of poetry, as O. Skutsch has pointed out;[21] he is also a drunken, amorous reveler, a sensualist and a follower of Dionysus.[22] As part of this opposition, the line which introduces him (13),

pergite, Pierides. Chromis et Mnasyllus in antro
Silenum . . . videre,

belongs fully to poetry (*Pierides*) and to bucolic levity. As a nature-god, Silenus' sphere is totally removed from the urban atmosphere where war and politics have their seat. His audience, Chromis, Mnasyllus, and Aegle, are doubly removed from Roman political realities by their associations with a mythicized nature and by their suggestive Greek names.[23]

If the ambiguous possibilities of love and poetry are hinted at in lines 6-10, they are fully developed in Silenus. He is an embodiment of the opposites which Vergilian poetry seeks to span.[24] Hence his song will embrace that array of diverse myths which has puzzled interpreters. Here too we should not try to reduce to a bare schematic simplicity what Vergil intended to stand as deliberate multiplicity.

Silenus is central to the poem's fusion of the aesthetic and moral realms. He is a poet whose song moves all nature in rhythmic harmony (27-28). Yet he is also a mythical figure who brings into focus the problematical quality of human nature. He is, according to tradition, part animal himself; yet he is possessed of supernatural powers and mysterious wisdom about life and death.[25] Pindar makes of him a sort of impassioned dancer.[26] His veins are full of Dionysiac spirit, in more than one sense (cf. *Iaccho,* 15; *gravis attrita . . . cantharus ansa,* 17).[27] Yet at the end his song is identified with that of Dionysus' opposite, Apollo (82-84).[28] He has obvious affinities with the natural world and its earthy appetites: witness his offer to Aegle (26) and his effect on the Fauns and wild beasts (27). Yet the subject of his first song is philosophical (31-40); and serious themes of both philosophical and historical import continue in the stories of Pyrrha, the *Saturnia regna,* and Prometheus (41-42), with their implications of didactic and theological poetry.[29]

The scene between Silenus and his captors forms a little drama illustrating his special relation to the energies of nature and his easy participation in its mythical life of rustic demigods. Chromis and Mnasyllus, as Servius (followed by Heyne) suggests, are Fauns or satyrs;[30] and hence they are plausible acquaintances of the Naiad, Aegle. *Pueri* (14) and *saepe* (19) emphasize the familiar terms on which they and Silenus stand. Aegle, "the shining one," is, as her name might suggest, "the most beautiful of the Naiads" (21). The young Fauns would bind, though hesitantly (*timidis*, 20), this mysterious figure; but they are warned off by the somewhat ominous reminder of his strange power: *satis est potuisse videri* (24): "It is enough to have seemed able (to bind me)."[31] The allusion to Silenus' sensual appetite in 26 clearly marks him as one of the gay crew of nature-spirits, figures close to the earth and fully endowed with spontaneous animal energies. Yet he is not merely a participant in nature's life. He also stands apart from nature and exerts a creative power over it, as the next lines (27-28) show. We have here a dichotomy particularly suggestive for the nature of poetry, but relevant equally to the nature of man.

Silenus gives an amusing twist to the rejection of *tristia bella* in the proem. Martial language figures in the attack upon him: *adgressi* (18), the chains (*vincula*), and the "bloody" (*sanguineis*, 22) mulberries with which the *pueri* paint his face. But naturally these warlike gestures are all play. Play is the appropriate way to approach such a figure, who is himself playful (*luserat*, 17). Playfulness of a sort also characterizes the Apolline *deductum carmen* of pastoral (*ludere versu*, 1). The language used of Silenus in 18-19 and 22 dramatically heightens the rejection of Varus' *tristia bella*: the attack on Silenus transforms war into its opposite, a bit of light horseplay appropriate to Arcady and its mythical characters. *Grandia* are stood on their heads. Yet there is an underlying seriousness, "Ernst im Spiel," as Klingner remarks of the entire Silenus-scene.[32] By neutralizing war (and the language of war, line 3) through play, poetry offers a restorative perspective in which it can survive the threats posed to it by the unplayful reality which appears in *Eclogues* 1 and 9.

Silenus will sing at length of the terrible passion of Pasiphae (45-60). Yet in his own person he handles love with a healthful frolicsomeness and an open naturalness far from any morbidity (cf. 26).[33] Like Vergil himself in the proem, he answers war (or mock-war) with song and love. The balanced phrasing of lines 25-26 presents song and love as equal, coordinate elements: *carmina vobis, / huic aliud mercedis erit*. Taken together, Silenus' two gifts stand in a balance of appetite and intellect, sense and spirit, which is, once again, both aesthetic and moral in its implications: it applies both to poetry and to the question of human nature.

The binding of Silenus and the extortion of a song, therefore, are on the one hand poetry's attempt to encompass that mysterious, magical realm where Silenus dwells, to fix its forms in song, to "capture" the essence of nature's movements, and ultimately to relate nature's vitality to art's. On the other hand, it is an attempt to confront and grasp intuitively the duality of human nature and seize through imagination and myth the basic forms of experience.[34] Silenus may be compared with Proteus in the fourth *Georgic*, also a deity to be bound, also located between man and nature and encompassing all experience (*G.* 4.387-414).[35]

As in the case of Proteus, approaching Silenus has its dangers: *solvite me pueri; satis est potuisse videri* (24): Behind the laughing face (23) lies the demonic otherness of nature, a realm to which men dare not abandon themselves fully. But Silenus, through his song, belongs both to humanity and to nature. He is, in a sense, the subject of his song as well as the singer, or, in Yeats' terms, both "the dancer" and "the dance."

Like his counterpart, Proteus, Silenus points to the elusiveness of the creative energies in ourselves, the Dionysiac in the midst of the Apollonian (cf. 82-84)—imagination, playful spontaneity, love—and to the shifting, iridescent quality in the experiences in which these energies are present. To touch these Dionysian energies and the sources in ourselves from which they spring, Vergil has, of necessity, recourse to a symbol: the mythical magic of a charmed *locus* removed from time and space (the only indications are *in antro* and *hesterno*), where Satyrs, Fauns, and Naiads drink wine, play, sing, make love.[36] This concern with the shifting quality of our experience and the duality in our nature upon which it is in part founded is perhaps another reason for the poem's emphasis upon metamorphosis. Silenus' realm, no more than Silenus himself, is not easily held firm; its essence is a kaleidoscopic intensity.

Not only human experience, but the natural world envisaged by the poem is full of movement and instability. The first part of Silenus' song (31-40) stresses the changes of state in nature. The soft becomes hard, the liquid elements become firm (33-36), and nothingness (cf. *magnum per inane*, 31) gives way to the solid matter of the present world. The effect of Silenus' singing is to change the clear, fixed relation between the animate and inanimate in favor of more fluid relationships; he makes the "stiff (*rigidas*) oaks move their tops" (28). He knows how things find their forms (*et rerum paulatim sumere formas*, 36). This mastery of the *rerum formas* applies to the elements of experience as well as to the elements of the physical world. Singing of the creation of the natural world both illustrates poetry creating a world and is a symbol of the encompassing power of poetic creativity. Poetry, like cosmogonic processes, gives form to reality. Silenus, standing between human and animal impulses, a playful dealer in love and war as well as in song, a singer both of nature and of myth, philosophy and love, is the archetype of the poet reaching out to give shape to all of reality. His active power over nature is continued in the active verbs which describe his song (*solatur*, 46; *erigit*, 63; and see note 47, below). Yet his art does not just order nature: it also invites nature to participation and shared joyous fusion (27-30).

The poem provides an analogue to the binding of Silenus which puts that action into perspective, namely the attempt of Pasiphae's Nymphs to close in the bull (55-56):

> claudite, Nymphae,
> Dictaeae Nymphae, nemorum iam claudite saltus.[37]

In the bull, symbol of nature's animal energies from Minoan times on, Pasiphae seeks to possess something of that power with which Silenus is in touch. The Dictaean Nymphs on whom she calls are kindred to Silenus' Fauns and Naiads. But, of course, she fails. Passion *per se* cannot make up for the spontaneous animal life of these nature spirits, nor does it give her a controlling intellectual order through which she could hold such energies within the frame of human life.[38] Instead her passion distorts her grasp on reality, on the relation between man and nature. Her Dictaean Nymphs thus become a part of her delusion rather than an indication of reconciling man and nature. She is too willing to abandon the human form. In this, she stands at the opposite extreme from the daughters of Proetus with whom she is unfavorably compared (48-51), for in one version of their myth they become mad because of their resistance to Dionysian rites.[39]

Silenus in a sense stands between Pasiphae and Apollo, comprehending both in his many-faceted nature. Thus his song is in touch with the earthiness of Fauns, wild beasts, trees; yet he is compared to Apollo and Orpheus (29-30). His *vincula* and the laughter at the *dolum* of his captors (23) contrast with the serious bondage and *furtum* of Prometheus (42), as his playful sexual proclivities are the lighter side of what emerges later in Pasiphae, Scylla, Tereus. Everything about him, as we first see him, is formless, slack, dissipated (14-17, where note *delapsa* and *pendebat*); yet his concern is with a creative ordering of experience. The contrast between his outward appearance and his power of song is itself an attempt to confront the Dionysian-Apollonian duality of his nature and to resolve what a recent critic has called "the pure dialectics of passion and form."[40] The rhythmic play (*in numerum ludere*) to which he moves the Fauns and beasts (27-28) expresses just this transcendence of the dichotomy between passion and form, animal energies and spirit. *Ludere* is a word which applies both to poetry and love.[41] Its poetic meaning occurs in the first line of the *Eclogue*, and both meanings are perhaps present in the allusive description of Silenus' past relation with his rustic attackers: *nam saepe senex spe carminis ambo luserat* (18-19). Such a being can elicit spirit from matter (27-28), but also knows of the violence in nature's processes (cf. *discludere*, 35; *stupeant*, 37). Communicative (albeit reluctantly, 13-26) of Apolline order, he is also a Dionysian participant in those experiences which efface the barriers between man and nature: wine (15-17) and love (26).

Later in the *Eclogue* a mortal poet is also given the power to move nature. Linus presents Hesiod's reed-pipe to Gallus with the explanation that Hesiod too could "by singing lead the stiff ash trees down the mountains": *cantando rigidas deducere montibus ornos* (71). *Rigidas . . . ornos* is a verbal and metrical echo of the *rigidas . . . quercus* of line 28. Yet there is a subtle difference. There is no mention here of the playing (*ludere*) of Fauns and wild beasts (27-28). *Deducere* too implies an element of direction and constraint absent from the simple *motare cacumina* of 28. Indeed *deducere* can even have the connotation of leading the trees *away* or *down from* their mountains, removing them from their natural setting.[42] The

Dionysian poet thus seems able to allow nature a greater measure of its inherent spontaneity, a greater freedom on its own terms, than the purely Apolline band on stately Helicon.

III

Love is an important motif in the *Eclogue*, extending from the proem (10) through the meeting with Silenus (26) to the song he sings and finally by implication to Apollo at the end (82-83). In love, as in Silenus himself, Vergil reveals contrasting possibilities and thus poses from a different point of view that complexity of experience which the poem seeks to confront.

The two extremes are the poetic *amor* of line 10 and the passion of Pasiphae (45-60). Pasiphae's tale receives both more space and a more dramatic coloring than any other single episode (e.g. the second-person address of 47, 52, 55-60).[43] This emphasis confers a special importance upon her. She is the fullest embodiment of the problematical side of human nature. Although Vergil's generalizing diction and the lyrical call to the Nymphs enable him to keep the tale within the distanced, imaginary frame of Silenus' song, her desire for union with the bull is the poem's most disturbing instance of the potential bestiality in man.

The word *amor* occurs only in line 10 and line 46. Art and animal passion, both forms of *amor*, are thus made to contrast. The one subordinates nature to human imagination, filling the groves with song; the other leads the human imagination to run riot in a lustful and deranged union with nature. Silenus unites the best of both realms. He joins song and love (25-26); and his healthy, playful love (cf. also *luserat*, 19) keeps an exquisite balance between the two extremes.

Amor is usually a negative force in the *Eclogues*.[44] In *Eclogue* 6, however, though the negative side preponderates, Vergil also lets us glimpse other possibilities, obviously in the *amor* of line 10, but also within the myths of Silenus' song.

The story of Hylas (43-44) alludes to a passion which balances Pasiphae's,[45] though neither Theocritus nor Vergil would regard the homosexual attachment, unlike Pasiphae's bestiality, as "unnatural." But through its connection with the Argonauts' expedition, it is also connected with the positive side of close male companionship, wherein, of course, erotic ties may play a part. If Vergil has intensified the emotional and lyrical side of the tale in using the repeated, melodious *Hyla, Hyla*, instead of Theocritus' more formal anaphora. . .[in] (*Idyll* 13.59-60), he has also laid greater stress on the human community by having the cry come from the sailors (*nautae*, 43). In Theocritus it is Heracles, alone in the woods, who shouts (13.58); and there is in fact a sharp and somewhat hostile division between the rest of the expedition and Heracles (cf. 13.69-75). The *nautae* of 43-44 are also to be connected with another group of marine adventurers, the *ti-*

midi nautae, victims of Scylla, with whom the singer commiserates in 77. In both cases we have a hint of the human bonds of fear and cooperation—not just erotic love—which may exist among men involved in a common enterprise and subject to the dangers of supernatural forces. In the Hylas episode, however, this humane companionship is left unfulfilled and helpless as the sailors' cries echo along the empty shore.[46] There is a strong contrast with the controlled and friendly aspect of nature which appears in the songful echoes of pastoral woods in lines 10-11 and 84.

The sisters of Phaethon are another partial corrective to Pasiphae's subhuman passion. They exemplify a sisterly rather than an erotic love, a strength of affection which makes them worthy of pity rather than reproach. Hence their love unites them with nature in a more positive way than Pasiphae's. The expression *solo proceras erigit alnos* (63) suggests life and creation.[47] There is even a sad, vague beauty in their metamorphosis: not only is the bark "bitter," but it is "the *moss* of bitter bark," *musco amarae corticis.* This expression is a lovely synecdoche. *Musco* is chosen not only for the sound and the association with water (cf. *muscosi fontes, E.* 7.45), but also for the suggestiveness of the genitival construction which appears to make the bark less real, stranger, even gentler. One is again reminded of that shifting between different tactile senses in 31-40. The metamorphosis is very different from the shocking transformation which Pasiphae desires, and it has a beauty to which Vergil, like Euripides before him (*Hipp.* 737-40), was highly sensitive, as his fine lines in the *Aeneid* show (10.189-90). Though the girls are surrounded by "bitter" bark, that "bitterness" also has associations with poetic creation and enduring life: the shepherd Linus, "of divine song," is crowned with "bitter parsley" only six lines later (68, where *amarus* also stands emphatically at the end of the verse).[48]

After the account of Gallus on Helicon, Silenus returns to the passionate and disastrous type of love in the Scylla and Tereus narratives (74-81). But the last tale of love to which the poem alludes is the story of Hyacinthus in 82-84:

> omnia quae Phoebo quondam meditante beatus
> audiit Eurotas iussitque ediscere lauros,
> ille canit (pulsae referunt ad sidera valles) . . .

Here Apollo himself is the lover, and his love for a mortal leads to a song which once more fruitfully bridges the gap between man and nature and repeats nature's response to Silenus in 27-28. Here too, as in line 10, love and poetry are joined to create an order which overlaps the dualities (man-nature, sense-spirit)of our world.[49] The fusion of Silenus' song with Apollo's in 82-84 is the ultimate statement of confidence in the power of art to unify experience. This confidence is affirmed by the active participation of nature: the valleys carry this plaint of death-tainted love to the remote stars. Celestial rhythms end the poem, but all the gods (not just Apollo) have been involved: *invito processit Vesper Olympo* (86).

In another way too poetry bridges dualities here at the end, for the ending joins the lofty personifications, Vesper and Olympus, with the humble pastoral task of driving home and tallying the sheep (85). *Numerumque referre* (85) recalls the songful echo, *referunt,* in the previous line (84), and also the *numerum* (="rhythm") with which the Fauns and beasts danced to Silenus' song in 27. Through these verbal parallels the prosaic terms of pastoral life are made to overlap with the wide-reaching metaphors of echoing nature and divine singers. Rather unexpectedly, the "sheep-pasturing" and the "slight song" of line 5 attain the full measure of dignity which the opening lines claimed for them. Even more, the earthy side of pastoral life seen in 5 and 85-86 has been transfigured through the Silenus episode of 13-30 and the scenes of 64-73 and 82-84. The shepherd's humble pastoral realm in the proem has been touched by the power of mythical singers and encounters with hallowed poets on sacred mountains. The rustic Muse whom the poet meditates in 8 gains both in dignity and solidity as we hear of Gallus being ushered into the Muses' presence (cf. 65, 69). As the poem goes on, the groves and tamarisks of lines 10-11 become increasingly a magical realm of Fauns, Naiads, and mountain Nymphs.

IV

Giving form to the formless, reconciling passion and order involve not only poetry and love, but also nature. Throughout the sixth *Eclogue* it is the natural world which stands in antithesis to man as the substance and the symbol of recalcitrant matter. The recurrent exclamations of compassion and the adjectives expressing or implying moral evaluation in Silenus' song define the distinctively human qualities of feeling and judging and thereby set into sharper relief the differences between man and nature. We may list here *fortunatam, a virgo infelix,* and *tam turpis* of Pasiphae (45, 47, 49), the richly connotative *amarae* of 62, the exclamatory *a timidos nautas* in 77, *infelix* again of Philomela in 81, and *beatus* in 82.

Vergil is careful to keep before us the concreteness and the multiplicity of the natural world. He attains this effect through the presentation of the power of the elements and the diversity of earth, sea, sun, forests in 31-39, through the sounds and suggestive phrasing of some of his descriptions of natural phenomena, like *summotis nubibus imbres* in 38 or *musco . . . amarae corticis* in 62-63, or the carefully juxtaposed adjectives of 53-54. He gives scrupulous attention to different kinds of trees, all enumerated in concrete detail (see 10, 22, 28, 54, 63, 71, 83).[50] Although nature, like almost everything else in the poem, becomes symbolical of the ramifying struggle between passion and order, Vergil also allows it to stand in its own right as the physical setting of our experiences.

He skilfully uses the "pathetic fallacy" to break through the reductive dichotomizing of man and nature. The trees move in response to song (27, 71), the mountains feel joy and wonder (*gaudet, miratur,* 29-30),[51] the river Eurotas is "happy" as it hears Apollo's song (82) and teaches the laurels (83). Yet the artificiality and conventionality of the device keep us aware that this deliberate humanization of nature is only a metaphor, a way of expressing the power of art. Vergil retains the complexity and the truth of our relation to the world in two ways. First, he keeps in the background the ungentled violence of nature which cannot be absorbed into the pathetic fallacy: the deserted shore of Hylas, Pasiphae's bull, Scylla's dangerous sea. Second, by his descriptions of the actual processes of nature (31-40) and the concrete particularity of its phenomena, he allows nature to resist total symbolification and enables it to keep its autonomy and its mystery.[52]

Like Silenus and *amor,* nature is also a focal point of fundamental antinomies. It has both negative and positive aspects. The forests (*silvae*) of line 2 form a place of Arcadian peace where the Muse does not blush to dwell. Related to this image of nature, which is really a metaphor for pastoral poetry and the atmosphere it both needs and creates, are the *agrestis Musa* of line 8 and the tamarisks (significantly *"our"* tamarisks) and the echoing grove of lines 10-11.

Yet forests can also reflect the elemental power of nature's processes and a realm less immediately amenable to the gentle Muse. The earth, when it "gapes in amaze" at the new sunlight (37), and the forests, when they "first begin to rise forth" (39), show a vital potency in nature which contrasts with the gentler landscape, the tamarisks and groves of 10-11 and the *deductum carmen* to which it belongs. So we have the *agrestis Musa* of 8 and the Grynean grove of Apolline song (73-74), yet also the *agri* which the maddened daughters of Proetus fill with their lowing (48) and the grove of Pasiphae's bull (55-56). The shore which resounds to Hylas' cry (43-44), the ominous "deep sea" (76) where Scylla preys on "frightened sailors" (contrast Mopsus' joy in the power of the sea in the preceding *Eclogue,* 5.82-84),[53] the "deserted places" traversed by the transformed Philomela (80), are all reminders of nature's vast and threatening power. The beginning of Silenus' song describes a *mundus* which is *tener* (34), "new" or "fresh." The adjective also connotes the delicacy and gentle beauty of the pastoral landscape where the down of apples, myrtle, rushes, grass, thickets, and trees may be *tener* (*E.* 2.51, 7.6, 7.12, 8.15, 10.7, 10.53). But this *tener mundus* comes into being with a force that awakens overpowering wonder (cf. *stupeant,* 37).

These glimpses of a non-pastoral nature are nevertheless incorporated into a pastoral song. Thus the modest self-limitation and self-deprecation in the proem prove to be a bit of playful, ironic understatement. Vergil here follows an amusing device common in the *recusatio* (e.g. Horace, *C.* 1.6). His *agrestis Musa* shows herself able, after all, to reach beyond her *deductum carmen* with its groves and tamarisks. Indeed not only the didactic verses of 31-40, but the entire *Eclogue* anticipates the *Georgics* in commanding a broad range of natural phenomena and appreciating nature's violence beside her pastoral charm.

In Silenus' song, as elsewhere in Latin poetry, contact with nature's mysterious power often takes the form of wandering.[54] Wandering in the mountains can be a sign of disorder, passion, potential violence.[55] The *rara animalia* wandering through *ignaros montis* in 40 belong to a world still in the process of being created and hence in some sense imperfect. It is "in the mountains" that the luckless Pasiphae "wanders" (52), while her bull's wandering tracks (*errabunda vestigia*) are to be found in the meadows (55-58). On the other hand, Gallus, "wandering to the streams of Permessus" (64), is led to the Muses' mountain, symbolical center of Apolline order and beauty. Why should the poet too be a "wanderer"? Perhaps Vergil means to suggest that poetry is akin to erotic passion in confronting (but overcoming) the threat of disorder and formlessness. Inspired poetry too, as the figure of Silenus implies, is in touch with nature's vital energies and animal force, but ultimately, unlike Pasiphae, contains the potential for bending them to its will (see 27-28, 71). Against the nameless mountains of the *rara animalia* (40) and Pasiphae (52) stand the mythical mountains connected with Orpheus, Apollo, the Muses: Parnassus, Rhodope, Ismarus in 29-30; the "Aonian mountains" (Helicon) in 65.

Though nature yields to the Apolline order of poetic form (27-28, 71, 82-84), it also has its own lessons to teach. It is not simply the utter negation of order. In this respect it shares the complexity of its poet, Silenus. The human Pasiphae is inflamed by a shameful and unnatural passion, while the bull's quiescence on the "pale grass" (53-54) stands almost as nature's reproach to her wild search (52). The bull is not even *captus amore* (10), but *herba captus viridi* (59). The effect of this animal's ruminatory peace is analogous to the contrast between the regular work on the land and Corydon's *dementia* at the end of the second *Eclogue* (67-72), a passage which, in fact, Vergil has in mind here (*quae te dementia cepit? E.* 2.69 and *E.* 6.47).[56] Nature's peace here reads a lesson to human passion, as poetic *amor* and the pastoral echoes do to man's delight in war and warlike poetry in the proem (6-11).

From Homer and Hesiod on, a bounteous and harmonious order of nature is a symbol and a proof of a larger moral order.[57] This symbolical significance of nature still has validity for Vergil. At a time when the civil wars—the symptom and expression of moral disorder—have interrupted work on the land, order, peace, and the regular cultivation of nature's goods are easily felt to go together. *E.* 4.18-45 makes just this correlation between moral, political, and natural order. To that set of analogies *Eclogue* 6 adds order brought through art, while Silenus' cosmogonic song (31-40) and Pasiphae's love expand and intensify the themes of natural and moral order to include nature's remoter processes and man's inner being.

V

It is significant that it should be Vesper, the personification of one of nature's rhythms, that ends the poem. He commanded (*iussit,* 86) the bringing in of the sheep and then "strode forth" (*processit*), though the gods were still held by the song: *invito processit Vesper Olympo* (86). *Processit,* like the "rising up" (*surgere,* 39) of the primal forests, is a reminder of nature's autonomous energies. The Olympians, the gods of light and the day, must give way, and a new power enters to lead in the realm of darkness which does not belong to them. Earlier Apollo had given his commands to the poet (*non iniussa cano,* 9), and the poet has commanded nature (27-28, 70-71). Now it is nature which commands man.

The poet stands in both an active and a passive relation to the world. He may move trees and animals to his rhythms; yet, as the double nature of Silenus and Gallus' wandering imply, he may also participate in her animal energies. The end of *Eclogue* 6, like the natural frame at the end of *Eclogues* 1 and 2, extends to him the possibility of receiving the boon of her beauty and regularity. The sheep here at the end evoke (as in *E.* 2) the fruitful bond which must exist between man and nature if man is to survive, both physically and spiritually.[58] At the same time the closing in of the sheep (*cogere . . . ovis stabulis,* 85) points back to the Nymphs' attempt to close in the bull (55-56). That effort, within the frame of Silenus' song and thus in the realm of art and imagination, belongs to a love which violates nature's laws. The shepherd's safe enclosure of his sheep, however, reflects an obedience to those laws in the tranquil round of daily labor and implies an objective reality to which imagination and art are ultimately subject.

Love, however, continues to be present at the end in the figure of Eurotas. He is chosen because the river Eurotas is the setting for the tale of Hyacinthus, and Apollo presumably sang this song to assuage his grief.[59] Like Vesper, Eurotas belongs to nature. Yet he also reflects that bridging of the dichotomy between human personality and the impersonality of nature with which the poem has been struggling. He too gave "commands" (*iussit,* 83). Yet his commands resemble not just those of Vesper, but those of the poets, Silenus, Orpheus, Hesiod: he bids the laurels to learn Apollo's song and proves again the harmony between art and nature, between human feeling and the material world.

As the poem's last two lines reflect a return to a harmonious relation to nature's laws, so the Eurotas reminds us of a kind of love that breaks through the antinomy of passion *versus* order. The Eurotas, scene of unhappy love, can be *beatus.* There is an obvious contrast with the *infelix* of Pasiphae and Philomela (47, 52, 81), which in turn measures the difference between Apolline and Pasiphaean love. The latter leaves only an infamous name; the former, though also tragic in its outcome, leaves the "soft hyacinth" (cf. 54 and Linus' flowers in 68)[60] and the beautiful song which makes the Eurotas "happy." But the "happy Eurotas" also implies some unresolved antitheses. Nature (here the personification of a landscape) can be "happy" as the lover (god or man) cannot; the echoing song brings joy, though it is the outpouring of grief. *Pulsae referunt ad sidera valles* (84) may suggest the indifference of nature's vast

spaces as well as possible sympathy. We may note once again the ambiguity of the "pathetic fallacy" in the poem pointed out above (p. 425).[61]

The rather abrupt and arbitrary allusion to the Eurotas and the story of Hyacinthus implies that Apollo, the symbol of poetic order, restraint (3-5), and beauty throughout the *Eclogue,* can also experience love and pain. Even the Apolline realm can be affected by *amor.* Poetry and love are thus once more associated in a positive sense as they were in the proem (10, *captus amore*). The order imposed by art is not stark and rigid, not out of touch with suffering.

The allusion to Apollo's love confirms in another way the identification of Silenus' song with Apollo's. The Dionysian satyr and the god of the orderly, intellectual aspect of art are identified, not opposed. Both have a common ground in a susceptibility to love (cf. 26). So the Apolline poet's "wandering in the mountains" (64-65) and the "bitter" parsley which crowns Linus (68) have affinities with the preceding tales of passion and suffering (52, 62), realities which the poet incorporates but holds in tension with his commanding power of form.[62]

It is Silenus, as we have seen, who is the chief representative of this freer, more flexible, more encompassing view of the order under which art and passion meet and grapple with one another. Hence it is appropriate that the song, with all its intensity and diversity of experience, shold be his. But by fusing Silenus' song with Apollo's and by hinting at Apollo's experience of love, Vergil deepens these responsive connections between art and passion, the ordering human mind and nature's unbound, wayward energies.

VI

In the light of the poem's confrontation of opposites we may look again at the puzzling appearance of Gallus. Gallus, writer of love-elegies, is potentially a representative of passion in its disordered aspect. It is in this function that he appears in *Eclogue* 10, and we must now briefly consider that poem's connection with *Eclogue* 6.

In *Eclogue* 10 love, in its violent invincibility, defeats the pastoral tranquillity for which Gallus longs (see *E.* 10.36-43). *Nunc insanus amor* of the next line (44) sets Arcadian peace sharply against the reality of passion. With this *insanus amor* are to be compared the other statements of love's power throughout the poem: *sollicitos amores* (6); *indigno . . . Gallus amore peribat* (10); *crudelis Amor* (29); *deus ille malis hominum mitescere discat* (61). Apollo, Pan, and Silvanus all appear, but to no avail. They recall the fanciful mythology of the Silenus scene of *Eclogue* 6, and Pan is painted by the "bloody berries" (*E.* 10.27), like Silenus (*E.* 6.22). The helplessness of Pan and Silvanus only underlines the defeat of the creative power of imagination and art which triumphed so exuberantly through Silenus in *Eclogue* 6.

Though Gallus imagines pastoral amours with a Phyllis or an Amyntas (38-41), his language is that of the disruptive passion of the Pasiphaean type (note *furor*, *E* 10.38). Even the quiet he thinks of has an erotic tinge in the first two words of *molliter ossa quiescant*, 33. His thoughts of a serene natural setting (*gelidi fontes, mollia prata, nemus*, 42-43) are vitiated by the vehemence of his emotional vocabulary in these same lines: *consumerer* (43) and *insanus amor* (44).[63]

The potential wildness of nature which appeared in Hylas' shore or Pasiphae's mountains or Philomela's *deserta* in *E.* 6 becomes much more tangible and ominous in *E.* 10. Now it engulfs not just remote mythical characters, but the "real," living Gallus (see *E.* 10.47-52, 55-56). Gallus will wander on the mountains hunting savage (*acris*) boars (56-57), and he will surround the peaceful Arcadian meadows with hunting dogs (*E.* 10.57; contrast the meadows of *E.* 6.53-56).

In using the violent pursuit of hunting to solace his love, Gallus reveals how far his restlessness stands from the peacefulness of an Arcadian romance. Hunting and love can go together, at least in imagination, for the regular figures of pastoral too (see *E.* 2.29, *E.* 3.75). But Gallus will hunt with a "Parthian bow" (*E.* 10.59). The epithet is more than just decoration. It marks another abrupt intrusion of an un-Arcadian reality, the presence of a foreign and brutal world with which Gallus is in closer touch than the shepherds. The Parthian bow is also a small example of the other threat, besides passionate love, to pastoral serenity: that is, war and politics. War and love, as we have seen, both have their place in *Eclogue* 6. But *Eclogue* 10 expands the negative power of both. Gallus, both a warrior and a lover, is doubly removed from the Heliconian poet led to Apollo's band in *E.* 6.63-73. Gallus' initiation into that Apolline realm in *E.* 6 is both an expression of confidence in the encompassing power of art in that poem and a measure of Gallus' defeat through *furor* in *E.* 10.

Yet Vergil does not end *Eclogue* 10 on an entirely negative note. After Gallus' capitulation *omnia vincit Amor: et nos cedamus Amori*, (*E* 10.69), Vergil, with a rare intrusion of the first person (*mihi*, 73), declares his own *amor* for his friend.[64] The growing (*crescit*, 73) of this love answers the growing of the trees into which the desperate Gallus carved the tale of his stubborn passion *crescent illae, crescetis, amores*, (*E* 10.54; contrast the *crescentem poetam*, to be adorned with ivy, in *E.* 7.25).[65] *Amor* in 73, unlike the disruptive, dispersive *amor* of Pasiphae or Gallus' *insanus amor*, has a creative, unifying force, like the *amor* of *E.* 6.10.

As in *Eclogue* 6, Vergil ends the tenth *Eclogue* with evening and with the humble pastoral task of driving home the flock (*E.* 10.76-77). Here, however, the remote mythical figures in the sixth *Eclogue*—Apollo, Eurotas, Olympus—are subordinated to the small, intimate details of personal life and personal affection. The little basket

woven of the slender hibiscus (*gracili fiscellam texit hibisco*) suggests the creative efforts of poetry and recalls the *deductum carmen* of *E.* 6,[66] as the humble goats at the end of *E.* 10 also recall Apollo's command about the sheep in *E.* 6.4-5. The *Pierides* are here too (*E.* 10.72), as in the other poem (*E.* 6.13). But the basket, symbol of poetry, makes creation a much humbler, yet also a more personal, more human, more accessible activity. The power lies not with mythical figures on Greek mountains, but in the hands of the "I" who speaks of his friend and "sits" (*sedet*) quietly at his work.

Here Vergil retreats from the lofty claims of *Eclogue* 6. But he holds to at least one part of the achievement of that poem, the bridging over of the gap between emotional intensity and artistic order. The woven basket, a sign of order and artistic "making," not only answers the violent *amor* which drives Gallus from Arcadia; it is followed by an offer of personal *amor* which grows with the alder in the new springtime (*E.* 10.73-74). This love, growing in the spring, brings together the poet's participation both in emotional life and in the rhythms of nature. One kind of *amor* can cut Gallus off from the peace of pastoral glades and founts; another *amor* can join the poet with his friend and with the freshly burgeoning green of vernal growth.

These alders recall another attempt to connect human emotion and nature. The alders of *Eclogue* 6 are the trees into which Phaethon's sisters are transformed (62-63). In this episode growth and movement are also present, though more faintly than in *E.* 10, as an answer to death: *solo proceras erigit alnos,E* 6.63; *viridis se subicit alnus, E* 10.74. In both passages a non-passionate, fraternal, or sisterly love is associated with a union with nature. The fact that Phaethon's sisters are usually transformed into poplars, not alders, enhances the possibility of a deliberate connection between the two passages.

Yet in the calmer, less Dionysian atmosphere of the end of *E.* 10 the poet will retain his poetic and human self-consciousness (cf. *poetam*, 70; *mihi*, 73), while still sharing in the warmth of affection associated with those trees in *E.* 6. But both the *amor* and the identification with nature's rhythms in *E.* 10.73-74 mark a greater concession to the realm of nature, feeling, matter. It is as if the lesson of Gallus' disruptive *amor* has brought the poet closer to a Silenus-like participation in nature than to Apolline-Orphic control over it.

At the same time this very openness of participation in nature raises the possibility that the poet may be more exposed to its dangers and to the mystery of its unfathomed power. The darkness which comes with the regular close of day can be harmful to singer and crops alike: *gravis cantantibus umbra, . . . nocent et frugibus umbrae* (75-76). At the close of *E.* 6, Olympus was unwilling to see the night descend, but there was no sense of a potential danger. Here nature, not art, has the upper hand.

Silenus' play with the Fauns and Naiad of *E.* 6 implied that *amor*, poetry, and participation in nature's life go together. But *E.* 10 is much less sanguine about the power of art to hold passion or nature at a safe distance. Both realities are much less amenable to enclosure in the frame of a Silenus' song, and the "singers" have a healthy appreciation of their subjection to nature (75). Yet the poet's little basket—to which nature, the hibiscus, contributes the material—marks a modest yet courageous gesture of artistic independence. Nature's forbidding desolation and the waves of human passion do not submerge the poet's capacity to realize beauty and love, albeit in little things. The poet of this *Eclogue,* nevertheless, less innocent and less hopeful about nature's power, knows that he dare not expose himself to night's *gravis umbra.*[67]

VII

To return to our starting point, *Eclogue* 6, like *Eclogues* 4 and 10, is concerned with the *sceleris vestigia nostri,* man's capacity for destructive passion in love and incidentally in war (*E.* 6.7). It knows of tragic passion, but incorporates it into the playful, controlling framework of a song sung by a grotesque character immersed in the fanciful world of Fauns and Naiads. In *E.* 10 the destructive forces within man, war and love, are in the ascendant; and Apollo—along with Silenus' mythical kindred, Silvanus and Pan—are helpless bystanders of passion's triumph (*E.* 10.21-27).

Eclogue 6 suggests an answer to the tension between order and passion in man by fusing them in the process of artistic creation and symbolically in the figure of Silenus. In *Eclogue* 10, however, the fusion fails. War and passion win out. Gallus, carried to Helicon in *E.* 6, falls a victim to *crudelis Amor* in 10.

This somber end to the *Eclogue Book* is a typically Vergilian acknowledgment of the complexities of existence and of the need for a "dialectical" response to them. Moving from the liberating buoyancy of Silenus' joyful spanning of sense and spirit to the irresistible harshness of *crudelis Amor,* Vergil refuses to dwell entirely in the world of the imagination. The refusal is already implicit in the presence of war and history in *Eclogues* 1, 4, 9, and passion in *Eclogues* 2, 6, 8.

This movement from *E.* 6 to *E.* 10 is itself, in small, a foreshadowing of the poet's development to the stern, tragic realities of the *Georgics* and the *Aeneid.* Yet the *amor* and the green alder at the end of *E.* 10, like the *captus amore* and the rising alders of *E.* 6.10 and 63, imply an ability to face the chaos of human existence without losing sight of the positive potential of human nature and human creativity. Not all emotion need be destructive, not all love selfish and unnatural.

If the defeat of Gallus foreshadows the disastrous *furor* of Orpheus in the fourth *Georgic* or Dido's passion and Aeneas' all too human violence in slaughtering Turnus; if the ominous *gravis umbra,* dangerous to singers, anticipates in its hint of nature's foreignness to man the savage Ciconian

matrons who tear the poet apart to vindicate the claims of nature, nevertheless the poet's personal declaration of love for his lost friend anticipates those redeeming moments of melancholy tenderness that illumine the dark sufferings of the *Aeneid:* Creusa at the end of II, Anchises and Marcellus in VI, Nisus and Euryalus in IX, Pallas and Lausus in X.

Notes

1. I shall refer to the following by author's name only: Carl Becker, "Virgils Eklogenbuch," *Hermes* 83 (1955) 314-49; Karl Büchner, "P. Vergilius Maro," *RE* 8A1 (1955) 1219-24 (on *E.*6): John Conington and Henry Nettleship, edd., *P. Vergili Maronis Opera, I*[4] (London 1881); J. P. Elder, "*Non Iniussa Cano:* Virgil's Sixth Eclogue," *HSCP* 65 (1961) 109-25; Charles Fantazzi, "Virgilian Pastoral and Roman Love Poetry," *AJP* 87 (1966) 171-91; G. Karl Galinsky, "Vergil's Second *Eclogue:* Its Theme and Relation to the *Eclogue* Book," *C & M* 26 (1965) 161-91; A. Hartmann, "Silenos und Satyros," *RE* 3A1 (1927) 35-53; Herbert Holtorf, *P. Vergilius Maro, Die grösseren Gedichten, I, Einleitung, Bucolica* (Freiburg/Munich 1959); Günther Jachmann, "Vergils sechste Ekloge," *Hermes* 58 (1923) 288-304; Friedrich Klingner, *Virgil, Bucolica, Georgica, Aeneis* (Zürich/Stuttgart 1967); Eleanor Winsor Leach, "The Unity of *Eclogue* 6," *Latomus* 27 (1968) 13-32; Brooks Otis, *Virgil* (Oxford 1963); Jacques Perret, *Virgile* (Paris 1959); H. J. Rose, *The Eclogues of Vergil* = "Sather Classical Lectures" 16 (Berkeley and Los Angeles 1942); E. de Saint-Denis, "Le chant de Silène à la lumière d'une découverte récente," *RPh* 37 (1963) 23-40; Otto Skutsch, "Zu Vergils Eklogen," *RhM* 99 (1959) 193-201; Bruno Snell, "Arcadia: The Discovery of a Spiritual Landscape," in *The Discovery of the Mind,* tr. T. G. Rosenmeyer (Cambridge, Mass. 1953) 281-309; Zeph Stewart, "The Song of Silenus," *HSCP* 64 (1959) 179-205; John B. Van Sickle, "The Unity of the *Eclogues:* Arcadian Forest, Theocritean Trees," *TAPA* 98 (1967) 491-508; Gordon Williams, *Tradition and Originality in Roman Poetry* (Oxford 1968); K. Witte, "Vergils sechste Ekloge und die Ciris," *Hermes* 57 (1922) 561-87. I wish to acknowledge a special debt of gratitude to my friend Professor John Van Sickle, whose detailed comments on this paper and scrupulous resistance to simplistic approaches to the *Eclogues* have been both a help and an example. I am especially indebted to his concept of dialectics in the poems, though I have not always interpreted the dialectical movement along lines with which he would agree.

2. Williams 249; it is worth repeating his quotation (246) from F. Leo, *Hermes* 37 (1902) 22: "Man wagt kaum mehr es laut zu sagen, aber ich glaube immer noch, wenn ich Vergil tractire, dass ich es mit einem Dichter zu thun habe."

3. For discussion and bibliography of the various views and especially those of Franz Skutsch, see

Jachmann 288-89, Rose 97 ff., Saint-Denis 20-35, Stewart 181-83.

4. Otis 137-39, Leach *passim*, Klingner 106-11. See also Williams 243-49, who takes "strange and tragic love" as "a unifying thread" (248), yet hedges on the question of whether one should look for any unity at all (245).

5. The phrase is Elder's (121), though his own approach goes beyond the biographical interpretation in a narrow sense.

6. See Büchner 1219 and 1223-24, Elder 111, Klingner 110, Saint-Denis 40, Van Sickle 504.

7. *Aen.* 1.92-101 and 198-209 are the familiar examples: see Victor Pöschl, *The Art of Vergil,* tr. Gerda Seligson (Ann Arbor 1962) 48-53 and *passim.*

8. For the symbolical fusion of inner and outer realms, soul and action, see Pöschl (above, note 7) 17-18; Otis 230-33, 276-77, 322-28; Francis A. Sullivan, S. J., "Virgil and the Mystery of Suffering," *AJP* 90 (1969) 168-71.

9. Snell, *passim,* especially 301-2, emphasizing Vergil's union of "poetic reverie, unifying love, and sensitive suffering" (301) and the Vergilian idea of the special sensitivity of the poet who "receives the sympathy of nature . . . because his feelings are more profound than those of other men, and because therefore he suffers more grievously under the cruelties of the world" (302).

10. Leach 31; Klingner 109 also points out the *Eclogue's* concern with "etwas Allumfassendes."

11. See Otis 139: "The dark *amores* and *metamorphoses* of 6 are . . . symbolic of the moral decline (scelus) of the 'iron age' through which Rome had just passed."

12. Perret 64 speaks of "la fragilité de l'univers arcadien." See also my essay, "*Tamen Cantabitis, Arcades*—Exile and Arcadia in *Eclogues* One and Nine," *Arion* 4 (1965) 254-56; Van Sickle 505, note 30.

13. Otis 139 stresses "the inverse relation of *Eclogues* 4 and 6," though I think he oversimplifies the relation for the sake of his schematic symmetry: *scelus* by no means dominates *E.* 6; and the Pasiphae episode, though important, should not be exaggerated out of all proportion to the rest of the poem (see below, Section III). We should not forget the presence of Apollo along with the Dionysian Silenus: see Van Sickle 502-5 and below, note 40.

14. For the theme of the *Saturnia regna* see Becker 321, Klingner 107, Leach 19, and Otis 138-39. One should recall in this context *Aen.* 6.791-94, 7.45-49, 8.324-27, and 11.252-54. On the first three of these passages see my remarks in *Arion* 5 (1966) 49-50, and most recently R. J. Rowland, *Latomus* 27 (1968) 832-42 with the bibliography cited in note 2, p. 832.

15. See Jachmann 293; Aeschyl. *PV* 436-506. Many of the arts of civilization listed in *E.* 4.18-45 belong, of course, in the culture-histories with which Prometheus is associated, notably sailing (*PV* 467-68) and the domestication of animals (*PV* 462-66). Agriculture and the city, though not specifically attributed to Prometheus, usually have a place in such lists; Soph. *Antig.* 335-60; Pl. *Protag.* 322 AD. For possible influence of the Aeschylean Prometheus figure on the *Eclogues* (somewhat straining the evidence) see William Berg, "Daphnis and Prometheus," *TAPA* 96 (1965) 15-20.

16. See Witte 571-72, who compares Theocr. *Id.* 13.64-71 and *E.* 6.47 and 52.

17. Skutsch 193; Wendell Clausen, "Callimachus and Latin Poetry," *GRBS* 5 (1964 193-95. See the valuable reservations of Leach 26-27, with notes 1 and 3, p. 26. Clausen, however, also observes that Vergil's refusal to write about war "was not merely esthetic, it was also (as the reminiscence of the first Eclogue intimates) moral" (194).

18. In addition to *E.* 9.5 see *E.* 2.14 (irae), *E.* 3.80 (lupus), *E.* 10.31 (the suffering Gallus).

19. Elder 112 calls attention to *amor* in a similar context in Lucret. 1.924-25, *amorem/Musarum quo nunc instinctus.* Cf. also *G.* 2.476 and 3.291-92. If Vergil had this passage in mind, the change from *instinctus* to *captus* is a typically Vergilian toning down of Lucretian violence. Snell 302 stresses the peculiarly Vergilian (and un-Callimachean) emotionality implied in the phrase: "This sympathetic affection is the mark of the poet, and the poet seeks to transmit his compassion to his reader." Van Sickle 505 notes the possible ambiguity of the *amor* of *E.* 6.10. In the light of the attitude toward war through the *Eclogues* one may wonder if *tristia condere bella* does not play on the double sense of *condere,* viz. "compose" and "put away": cf. *E.* 9.52 and Holtorf *ad loc.*

20. See Büchner 1220: "Übermutiger Scherz . . . und laszive Andeutung . . . spielen in diesem Stück, das aus dem Vollen schöpft, wie sonst nirgends in den Eklogen eine Rolle."

21. Skutsch 194.

22. For Silenus' connections with Dionysus see Hartmann 39 and 43; James A. Notopoulos, "Silenus the Scientist," *CJ* 62 (1966-67) 308-9.

23. Klingner 106 observes the mythical and unreal quality of the setting. On the effect of such names in the *Eclogues* see also Snell 306.

24. See my essay, "Vergil's *Caelatum Opus:* An Interpretation of the Third *Eclogue,*" *AJP* 88 (1967) 300-4, 307-8.

25. E.g. Cic. *Tusc. Disp.* 1.48.114; [Plut.] *Cons. ad Apoll.* 27 (115B). For the complexity of Silenus see Hartmann 40 ff., esp. 43: "Weit entfernt von der

rohen und lächerlichen Figur, die man später ihn gern machen lässt, ist er ein sehr ernst genommener Gott, dem tiefste Weisheit und Erfahrung eignet, der Musik und Tanz liebt" (43). Also Servius on *E.* 6.13 and Conington's introductory note; Klingner 111, Saint-Denis 37-39, Stewart 197, Holtorf on *E.* 6.14 (p. 190), and Notopoulos (above, note 22) 308-9. The name of Tityrus also has something in common with satyrs, as appears in the lexicographical equation, *satyroi-tityroi-tragoi:* see Hartmann 52.

26. Pindar, frag. 156 Snell[3] = 142 Bowra (Pausan. 3.25.2). . . . See also Lucret. 4.580-89.

27. Servius on line 17 notes *attrita ansa, frequenti scilicet potu.* See also the Berne scholia *ad loc.*

28. It is now generally agreed that 82-84 mark the identification of Silenus' song with Apollo's, not another item in Silenus' song as F. Skutsch and Leo had held: see Witte 572 and Stewart 196.

29. See Stewart 186-88.

30. Most modern scholars seem to assume that Chromis and Mnasyllus are human shepherds. Yet their long-continued familiarity (cf. *saepe,* 18) with Silenus, their easy association with a Naiad, the liberties they take with Silenus himself tell against this view. It is true that in Theopompus' *Thaumasia* it is shepherds who capture Silenus (cf. Servius on line 13 and 26 and Aelian, *VH* 3.18). But that tale is only a loose parallel to Vergil's, and Vergil's freedom in transforming his originals is well known. The presence of sheep in 85 is also inconclusive. Mortals ran a risk from *seeing* figures like Silenus, and with the present question is therefore connected the interpretation of line 24, for which see the next note. For fuller discussion see my forthcoming paper, "Two Fauns and a Naiad? (Virgil, *Ed.* VI, 13-26)," *AJP* 92 (1971).

31. The two possibilities are given by Servius *ad loc.*: (1) "It is enough for me to have been able to be seen," and (2) "It is enough for you to have seemed able (to bind me)." Servius also notes that (1) implies that the attackers must be men to whom Silenus would usually be invisible. This interpretation involves a contradiction (of which Servius seems unaware) with his previous identification (on 13 and 14) of the *pueri* as Satyrs. Conington arrives at no solution, though he points to *videre* in 14 as favoring (1). This point, however, is not necessarily valid, for the specialness of "seeing" Silenus would seem to contradict the frequent association between Silenus and his attackers. Further, if the emphasis in 14 and 24 were on seeing, one would expect the active voice in 24. *Potuisse* could also be taken absolutely (as in *Aen.* 5.231), but this would not substantially change the meaning of (2).

32. Klingner 111.

33. In Pindar, frag. 156 (above, note 26), he is "the Naiad's husband". . . .

34. For a different interpretation of the binding-motif see Leach 24-25.

35. See Klingner 106.

36. One might compare Hermann Hesse's use of the Dionysian figure of Pablo (a mysterious jazz-player) and his "magisches Theater" ("Eintritt nur für Verrückte, kostet den Verstand") to explore (far more morbidly) this area of experience in *Der Steppenwolf.*

37. For the attribution of the lines to Pasiphae see Servius *ad loc.* On the scene see Leach 20-21.

38. It is interesting that where Pasiphae returns in the *Aeneid* there is a not dissimilar contrast between the creative, encompassing order of the artist, his pity, and his mastery of darkness and the maze on the one hand (*Aen.* 6.28-30), and the queen's bestial *crudelis amor,* the *Veneris monimenta nefandae* (*Aen.* 6.23-26) on the other.

39. Apollodorus 2.2.2; but this version of the myth has been doubted: see G. Radke, "Proitides," *RE* 23.1 (1957) 118-19, 123.

40. Van Sickle 504, who also goes on to assert (505) that *E.* 6 is "the most Dionysian" of the *Eclogues.* From another point of view (cf. the proem and Gallus' "Dichterweihe") it is also the most Apollonian: this too is part of the "dialectic." For the importance of Apollo in the poem see Becker 317-18, Elder 115-16, Williams 249.

41. For *ludere* see Leach 27 with note 1. For its combination of erotic and literary meaning cf. Catull, 2.2, 2.9 and 50.2, 50.5. Poem 50 probably exploits the double sense.

42. Holtorf *ad loc.* (p. 197), however, explains *deducere* as leading "zum Tanz nach dem Takt des Flötenspiels," but offers no evidence. For a different interpretation see Leach 28-29.

43. See Stewart 179, 189-90.

44. E.g. (in addition to *E.* 10) *E.* 2.68, 3.101, 8.18 and 47.

45. See Witte, cited above, note 16.

46. See Leach 20.

47. Stewart 191-92 tries (implausibly) to find a connection with "the *activity* created uniquely by the dramatist" (192). To Leach 22, "*Erigit,* a word usually associated with some form of mental stimulation or renewal, even with cheering and consolation, seems ironic in this context." I agree about the "renewal" or "cheering," but not about the irony.

48. On the repetition see Leach 22. For the suggestive connotations of *amarus* see *E.* 1.77, 3.110, 7.41 and Segal (above, note 24) 306. Perhaps *Doris amara* in *E.* 10.5 anticipates the tone of sadness and defeat in that poem.

49. For a fuller discussion of the ending see below, Section v.

50. See Elder 118. Cf. also the contest of trees in *E.* 7.61-68.

51. See *E.* 8.3, where the lynxes are *stupefactae* at the shepherds' song.

52. For a similar point on the bees of *G.* 4 see R. D. Williams, "Virgil," *G & R, New Surveys in the Classics* 1 (1967) 22.

53. Cf. also the quiet beauty of the calm sea (if that is the meaning of *aequor*) in *E.* 9.57-58, though there too the dangerous violence of sea is in the background: *insani feriant sine litora fluctus* (43).

54. See Lucret. 1.926; Verg. *G.* 3.291-93. For the theme of wandering generally in *E.* 6 see Elder 118-19, Leach 28-29.

55. Cf. *E.* 8.41, *me malus abstulit error.* The story of Hylas too suggests wandering: cf. Theocr. *Id.* 13.66-71. Note too the dangerous wandering in remote places in Ovid's *Metamorphoses:* 1.479, 3.25, 3.175, 3.370, 4.292-95.

56. See Büchner 1221, Galinsky 178.

57. Homer, *Od.* 19.109-14; Hesiod, *Erga* 225-47.

58. For the "overarching frame" of "bucolic elements" in *E.* 6 see Elder 117-18, with note 36 on p. 124; also Fantazzi 190-91. On the ending of *E.* 2 see Eleanor Winsor Leach, "Nature and Art in Vergil's Second *Eclogue,*" *AJP* 87 (1966) 442-45.

59. See Williams 247.

60. It may be that the hyacinth in 54 is meant to help prepare for the allusion to the Hyacinthus myth at the end. *E.* 3 seems to use this kind of anticipation (lines 63 and 106-7): see Segal (above, note 24) 297-98.

61. *Beatus* occurs only here in the *Eclogues* and only twice in the *Aeneid,* both in emphatic emotional contexts stressing an impossible happiness or a tension between suffering and happiness: *o terque quaterque beati,* 1.94; *sedesque beatos* of the Elysian fields, 6.639. Both in this latter passage and in Horace's *beata arva* (*Epod.* 16.41-42) the word carries associations of an innocent joy far from the world's trouble or the ordinary state of human existence, but a joy quite remote from present reality. On *E.* 6.82-83 Galinsky 178 remarks, "But the desire for *beatitudo* clashes strongly with the actual subjects of Apollo's and Silenus' songs, i.e. the *infelices* and *indigni amores* which are described in gruesome detail."

62. "Wonder" (*mirari*) may be inspired in the realms of both art (30, Orpheus) and love (61, Atalanta).

63. See Fantazzi 183-84 and Perret 64-65, who see in Gallus' defeat the "décomposition de l'univers arcadien" (64): "Mais l'amour est le plus fort, Gallus s'en va, la poésie n'a pu sauver l'un des

meilleurs de ses fidèles et pour lui l'Arcadie désormais n'est plus qu'un rêve" (65). Snell 296 underestimates the irony and bitterness in the passage when he speaks of its "sentimental sensuality."

64. The interpretation of *E.* 10.73-74 as referring to "Gallus' love for Lycoris" recently suggested by R. R. Dyer, *CP* 64 (1969) 233-34, seems to me unconvincing, though his remarks on Vergil's rejection of escapism are valuable and interesting.

65. On *E.* 7.25 see Van Sickle 502-3.

66. On the *fiscella* Fantazzi 184 remarks, "The key word is *gracili*, symbolic of his *carmen deductum.*"

67. It is part of the deliberate tension at the end of the *Eclogue Book,* however, that these goats are *saturae* and have a *domus* (i.e. unlike *E.* 1). For this positive aspect of the passage see Segal (above, note 12) 261-62, which should now be balanced by the interpretation offered in the present essay.

Michael C. J. Putnam (essay date 1970)

SOURCE: An introduction to *Virgil's Pastoral Art: Studies in the "Eclogues,"* Princeton University Press, 1970, pp. 3-19.

[*In the essay below, Putnam discusses some of the major critical issues surrounding Vergil's* Eclogues, *arguing that one of the most appealing and pertinent aspects of the collection is Vergil's effort to identify the role of the individual within a restrictive society.*]

The notion of Virgil as gentle poet of simple charm has been slow to die.[1] We accept melancholy as the poet's dominant characteristic, yet we assume its incorporation in a stance which is poised, reserved, aloof—"classical," in a word. Though evil continues to scheme and life remains charged with passions, though man be forced into a not always kindly dialogue with nature, his fellow creatures, and himself, Virgil somehow manages (we are assured) to bathe all suffering in a magic glow which reconciles opposites and leaves a sense of virtue and justice triumphant. The ten poems which comprise Virgil's first major work, the *Eclogues,* have been most subjected to this devitalizing approach. Since the publication of Horace's first book of *Satires* a few years after the *Eclogues* were completed, readers have been schooled to characterize Virgil's work—in the words of his great contemporary—as *molle atque facetum,* smooth and elegant.[2] We presume the judgment applies to content as well as to the rhetoric of expression.

The *Eclogues* are pastorals, and poetry of this form, perhaps more than any other kind of poetry, stands open to easy abuse. It is, by convention, a fantasy; a countryside with singing shepherds and their loves, with heroes like Daphnis (once human, now divine), with epiphanic gods and demi-gods. But Virgil's is no rugged, bleak, literal Arcadia. The closest he comes to projecting his dream upon a real landscape is in the seventh eclogue where the banks of his beloved Mincius offer the hospitable setting for a contest. Even there, however, the shepherds are twice styled *Arcades,* not to shatter the spell; so it is easy to see how the *Eclogues* can be labeled "escapist" verses, witnesses of responsibilities evaded and of studied withdrawal from the pressures of society into a "rustic," simple life.

Other definitions accommodate an allied, nostalgic yearning for the distant in space or time, for a situation of stable perfection, far removed from anything odd or evil, tragic or transitory, a situation impossible to achieve but inspirational or mesmeric to contemplate. I am referring not to the many different shapes the pastoral myth may take but to formal poetry which assumes a deliberately bucolic guise.[3] The history of pastoral poetry from Theocritus through the Renaissance to Milton and Arnold shows that its use as a vehicle for ideas, for social comment, for "involvement" while maintaining a detached pose, is the exception rather than the rule. Especially in the Renaissance it is the exceptions like Spenser who, because they resisted easy satire, kept vital the best aspects of what was for more than fifteen hundred years a highly creative tradition.[4]

Virgil's *Eclogues* are the first, and in many ways the greatest, example of pastoral poetry used to convey a message as well as to delight. Nevertheless certain misconceptions about them, some of which are superficial, persist. Though filled with problems which we still cannot solve, the *Eclogues* are not veiled allegories whose mysterious references to contemporary affairs in the fourth and third decades of the last century before Christ cannot be understood today.[5] Virgil does use disguises—the first eclogue offers a notable instance in the young god living at Rome—and understatement is the essence of his art. However, when a clue is necessary—for example, in the third and fourth poems the mention of the soldier and man of letters Pollio—it is usually forthcoming.

The *Eclogues* are no more mere variations on Theocritean themes than they are veiled allegories. It is true that the relationship between the Alexandrian master and his Roman disciple is an intricate one: Virgil has often absorbed the matter and wording of his predecessor.[6] But a close analysis of the parallels reveals that Theocritus was only a stepping-stone for Virgil's new approach, which pays little attention to Theocritus' ethical and aesthetic ideas. In Theocritus the city still represents civilization and society complements rather than challenges nature. The pains of love to which Theocritus' shepherds submit are pleasantly ephemeral when compared to the horror which the bucolic life faces in some of the *Eclogues.* Even in the "lighter" eclogues Virgil expands upon his master. Compare *Eclogue* 2 with its model in Theocritus, *Idyl* 11, a lovesong of the cyclops Polyphemus to the sea nymph Galatea. Juxtaposition brings out a twofold meaning in Virgil's work. There is a "rhetorical" side in which the poet proves, with engag-

ing humor, how one must *not* sing if he is to succeed as a lover. Such *incondita,* such rude uncouthness as Corydon mouths—and the deprecatory word is common in Cicero's vocabulary of oratorical criticism[7]—can scarcely effect the desired result. Yet a distinct implication in the shepherd's words confirms that nature postulates an unswerving rationale whereas man's emotions defy logic and ruin the harmony with his surroundings, which is one justification of the shepherd's lot. In *Idyl* 11, Polyphemus apparently loses Galatea, but in *Eclogue* 2, Corydon's lack of success causes him to regain a higher and tougher reasoning.

The structural interrelationship of the ten poems is also still debated. Since poems 3 and 7 are amoebean, or poems 5 and 8 have two long, separate songs, one common argument runs that we are meant by Virgil to view them in pairs. But the superficial resemblances which abound among these poems are no defense of their quality as literature and should not receive undue stress. The seventyh eclogue may have technical similarities with the third; its force largely results from conjunction with poems 6 and 8. That the application of any system of balances to the *Eclogues* as a group cannot help but project one or more poems for focal consideration[8] and that the number of differing proposals is considerable is reasonable evidence that none in particular fulfills the poet's intention. It is more economical to argue that he would have wished us to read the poems in the order the manuscripts assign them, watching the ideas progress and interact from one poem to the next in a culminating design.

One reason for the *Eclogues'* having gained the epithet "escapist" derives from a more basic misinterpretation. Only a trite reading can see in these poems the delineation of a "pastoral" way of life in its literal, agrarian sense—as if they were pieces written to distract the citified Roman from his urban cares or, to put it more romantically (and borrow a traditional distinction), as if they described some more lasting, model value to be found in "emotional" rural man than in the practical city-dweller. In this formulation the first is somehow associated with intelligence, the second with matter; the one, an inhabitant in a "sophisticated," private nirvana, the other, mired in the slough of vulgar reality. The *Eclogues,* however, are not an obscure espousal of an Emersonian triumph of mind over artifice.

This is not to deny the hold of the actual countryside on the imagination of the Roman people, indeed on its most important poets. Rural landscape did provide a necessary foil to the elaborateness and difficulties of city life. As the responsibilities of empire grew, the countryside came more and more to symbolize simplicity and other evaporating virtues of a once essentially agricultural populace.[9]

Certainly this moral and intellectual dialogue between city and country is a topic of Latin literature at least from the time of Lucilius on.[10] It is a constant theme in the works of Cicero. At the opening of *De Oratore* (I. 24), for instance, Crassus, spokesman for the great orator in the subsequent dialogue, withdraws from the press of Roman political life to Tusculum for the sake of "collecting" himself (*quasi conligendi sui causa*). Yet however much Cicero, philosopher and litterateur, depends on the country for the quiet of renewal, Cicero, advocate and statesman, cherishes, indeed requires, the bustle of the forum.

There is no doubt on which side of the fence Catullus stands: *rusticitas* in all its forms is anathema. He, too, has a villa which lovingly receives him after a bout of flu (*Carmen* 44), but its location near Tibur was a matter of humorous concern to him because it reflected on his social standing and intellectual attitudes (lines 2-4):

> nam te esse Tiburtem autumant, quibus non est
> cordi Catullum laedere; at quibus cordi est,
> quovis Sabinum pignore esse contendunt, . . .

> For those who do not wish to harm Catullus affirm that you are Tiburtine; those who do, maintain on any terms that you are Sabine.

Catullus' detractors, he tells us, put his villa in the Sabine country and, accordingly, accuse master and house of boorishness. If, on the other hand, it is near enough to Tibur (and Rome) to earn the epithet *suburbana,* then Catullus is happy. The villa is civilized, like himself.

Lucretius can even go so far as to satirize the constant flitting back and forth between city and villa in which the well-to-do Roman indulges (*De Rerum Natura* 3, lines 1053-1075). There is no question here of any higher, curative value in country life: the bored Roman is only seeking forgetfulness through change. This restless ennui would not be such a besetting trial, the Epicurean poet claims, if men could analyze their burdens and, other concerns put aside, devote themselves to learning "the nature of things."

On the contrary, the countryside for Virgil is only in a secondary sense to be viewed either literally or as a garden of Eden. His shepherds are no symbols of youth and innocence, dwelling in a paradise in danger of being lost to that epitome of vice and crime, the city. Rather "pastoral," for Virgil, has significance on a still deeper level: it means, at least during this decade in his career, the life of the imagination and the poet's concerned search for freedom to order experience. The landscape and its inhabitants are a realization in tangible form of the poetic mind at work. The shepherds are his voices. Their debates are his thoughts on poetry and life in the process of formulation. This is the sense in which "pastoral" will be used in the pages which follow.

The poet and his fictitious world, the creator and the created, uninvolved with reality as they may at first seem, are, in Virgil's view of bucolic poetry, open to the challenges any writer of poetry must face from a sometimes narrow, often alien milieu in which he must exist. In this regard the ***Eclogues*** have as much in common with fifth-century tragedy as with Theocritus. Not only is Virgil writing of the spiritual world of the artist, he is emphasizing the need for preserving individual freedom if the highest human values are to survive.

If pastoral poetry delineates the imagination at work, it depends upon a concomitant personal liberty to create in an atmosphere of integrity and order. Virgil evokes the challenges of the complex world of power to his shepherds' retreat not to suggest escape from the battle of life or to depict a charming image of evasion into a magical golden age. His purpose is to show what is at stake in Rome if the life of the imagination loses, and what could be gained if the two opposing conceptions of "pastoral" and power, poetry and history, were to live in harmony. That the notion is idealistic does not detract from the force of either those poems which claim it as true or their pessimistic counterparts which acknowledge the vanity of the search.

Part of the appeal and pertinence of the ***Eclogues*** lies in following the poet's search to define the place and status of the individual in an increasingly intricate and more restrictive society, victimized by civil disturbance for almost a hundred years. Virgil is the observer of a people in transition, whose old institutions were decaying but whose power, by astute employment of political and technological acumen, not to speak of military strength, was unparalleled in ancient civilization. This tension forced upon Virgil a question the varying answers to which were to become one of the intellectual concerns of the Augustan literary scene, a question which, though it is allied to the conflict of *physis* and *nomos* in fifth-century Greek thought, remains one of the few original formulations of the Roman mind. What is the relationship of society and "nature," of the institutions which impose an apparent order on life and the landscape which, at the opposite extreme, has come to symbolize freedom from such restraints as well as, paradoxically, a higher form of morality?

The one instance of such an implied comparison usually cited as an example from Greek literature—Socrates' choice of the banks of the Ilissus instead of the city of Athens itself as a setting for discussion in the *Phaedrus*[11]—is a far cry, say, from Horace's admonition to Maecenas to abandon the *fumum et opes strepitumque Romae,* the smoke and commercialism and noise of Rome, for the simplicity of the Sabine farm. This reflects, in part, a basic difference between Socratic and Stoic ethics. For the Stoics, the wise and just man, far from accepting his soul as a microcosm of the state and participating in civic life accordingly, should seek an order beyond mere political convention and detach himself from *Realien* to achieve morality and wisdom. In Horace's specific case the countryside offers a chance for the integrity of poetry as well. Horace's prayer is, to him, the only way to sanity as well as the only way to remain a poet. For Socrates, lover of his polis, to withdraw from the city is an act of whimsy which can scarcely endure for any length of time: "Country spots and trees will not teach me a thing. Men in the city do" (*Phaedrus* 230d).

Dr. Johnson, according to Boswell, would have agreed: "Our conversation turned upon living in the country, which Johnson, whose melancholy mind required the dissipation of quick successive variety, had habituated himself to consider as a kind of mental imprisonment. 'Yet, Sir (said I), there are many people who are content to live in the country.' Johnson: 'Sir, it is in the intellectual world as in the physical world; we are told by natural philosophers that a body is at rest in the place that is fit for it; they who are content to live in the country are *fit* for the country.'" Or, as he says elsewhere, "When a man is tired of London he is tired of life." The Johnsonian manner is amusing and typical of the eighteenth century. Yet the glorification of the city is the other side of the coin from the bucolic mode and anticipates, paradoxically (for Johnson was no lover of "vulgarity"), the succeeding century's search to free the proletariat, the urban mob, from the shackles which, according to Marx and Engels, had long held it.

But Horace and Virgil were in no sense "unurbane" or unaware that their lives were closely involved with the affairs of Rome, however far away their thoughts might flee. As the republic changed to empire, the pressure of society—indeed the artificiality imposed on life by society as it grew—expanded to such a point that the poets reacted against it. They reversed the mode of thinking we have seen in Cicero, Lucretius, and Catullus and returned to what was partially a traditional stance. One must, however, emphasize again that the countryside of Virgil's *Eclogues* is not to be interpreted objectively as the habitat of woolly sheep and piping shepherds. Nor is it the territory worked by the sturdy ploughman, that primitive nobleman, outdistanced by culture albeit representative of a Saturnian age long past. Virgil's landscape takes on virtually the opposite of the rustic, though morally upright, role it ordinarily plays as foil to the cultured grace of the metropolis. Even in a poem such as *Eclogue* 2, which seems at first to deal with the traditional dichotomy, the levels of meaning are still more complex.

In part the *Eclogues* are meditations on the position of the human personality, always caught in the turmoil of conflicting values and attempting to make "nature" meaningful, to create a rationale for life. They pose for the thoughtful reader many of the same problems as the tragedies of Shakespeare, and demand that he ponder the place of traditional ethical values in a fluctuating, disordered world subject to the necessities of time and death. In some poems the matter is treated gently and the poet withdraws through the lightness of the particular aspect under discussion (*Eclogues* 2 and 3) or the imaginative virtuosity which emblazons his theme (*Eclogue* 4). In other, more matter of fact poems the tone borders on despair in the realization that politics and morality are rarely reconcilable or in contemplation of the poet's apparently losing battle against society and history.

Even Tityrus' seemingly ideal happiness in the first eclogue leaves the reader wondering: What about Meliboeus? Is that god who can dispose of things physical and spiritual with something approaching unfair nonchalance really so divine? Will the monolithic state ever understand the plight, not to say rights, of the loser? Can the position of Tityrus be called perfect when it is created and bestowed by a higher power, or stable when Tityrus can allow himself to make only a passing and ineffectual bow to the suffering of Meliboeus? Can callousness or even indifference toward another's grief be a possible characteristic of a true singer of songs, pastoral idyls though they be? Tityrus is Virgil's symbolic victim before his time of that harmful, even evil, aspect of Romanticism which depends upon "a severance of mind from world, soul from circumstance, human inwardness from external condition."[12]

Too often in the criticism of Latin literature, a flatly literal interpretation of poetry does the poet the gravest disservice. To see Virgil as Tityrus alone, the happy shepherd-bard, beloved by Rome, with his land restored, is to burden Virgil with a false piece of common criticism: that the poet is himself involved in only one part of his poem while the other part is merely a convenient foil for his own felicity. We tend to decide in advance what we think Virgil wants to do—to perform his first act of homage to Octavian—rather than to consider objectively what he accomplishes.

The opposite view, which sees the figure of Tityrus as pure artifice, entirely false to reality, unresponding and aloof to the tragedy of life, is perhaps too bitter and severe—though we may remember Nietzsche's dictum: "We have art in order not to perish of truth." Nevertheless *Eclogues* 1 and 9 are poems which almost "make pessimism seem a hopeful evasion."[13] Yet such is the poet's mastery of the art of restraint that his strongest thoughts are conveyed in an atmosphere of spiritual generosity and external quiet.

The *Eclogues* postulate the search for an order which is only rarely attained but is, nevertheless, a prerequisite for happiness. Lack of order can be caused by unrequited love, by death, by some indefinable outside force inimical to the bucolic "retreat," by the violent pressures of political reality. The search for reconciliation between these adverse elements and the pastoral dream is a basic theme in the *Eclogues.* An idealistic vision such as *Eclogue* 4 can propose such an exalted union. Poetry itself—the magic incantation of song or the power of disciplined verse—can sometimes harmonize opposites, but although the poet in his own person may try his luck, the result is often irrational passion or terror. Finally, the poet may be forced to acknowledge in himself the tense union of reason and emotion which is his inheritance from Orpheus.

Here, too, Theocritus is only partially a prototype. We often sense that the Alexandrian poet aims to define the power of verse as well as to scrutinize the poet's motivation to sing. Nevertheless, in the *Idyls* there seems an almost deliberate unconcern with deep issues, as if the poet believed that the chief value of his verse was to entertain, to attract his readers by beauty of setting or richness of sound. The *Eclogues* are not poems that flee from life, diverting, artificial masquerades for "nature," soothing antidotes to urban elaborateness. Virgil's poetry is no ritual aimed at turning "complex into simple," but rather one of deep involvement in issues just as important now as they were in Rome in the decade after Caesar's assassination.

Similar discussions of the relationship of the individual to society and of man to nature, of the world of institutions to a world which parallels Virgil's conception of the poet and his landscape, are not unknown in American literature. In the nineteenth century, in *Walden, Huckleberry Finn,* or Melville's *Typee* (which fabricates and then destroys a perfect pastoral dream), these discussions regularly take the form of the claims which a society grown increasingly more machine-oriented and industrialized makes upon a quasi-idealized agricultural existence of oneness with nature. In the twentieth century Frost is one champion of individual man's experiences, feelings, desires—for good or evil, or purely for self-knowledge—against the increasing threat of impersonal, fragmentizing scientific schemata which reduce humanity and its purposes to little more than abstractions. Yet even nature herself, for Frost as for Virgil, is not without menace.

In the Rome of the last half of the first century B.C. the steady expansion of city and empire forced similar considerations upon the two chief poets and their colleagues. How is the individual to survive—or the poet to create—when his freedom remains unconfirmed? What of a government which relies on force (or the possible use of force) and appeals to the populace with hollow slogans, while materialistic goals more and more displace humane values as the yardstick to measure achievement? The answers which Horace and Virgil regularly supply are as damning of the present as ominous for the future. We might summarize this side of the *Eclogues* as "social commentary," a poetry of ideas dealing with the writer and mankind at large, the confrontation of the essentially stable life of the free imagination and the forces of history, be they represented by an urban Alexis (*Eclogue* 2) or by the grandest progress of the ages (*Eclogue* 4).

There is another kindred aspect to the *Eclogues*: the collection is also an informal *ars poetica* which seeks a broadened definition of pastoral as a form, often by bringing it into conjunction with other poetic modes. We are made to examine the appropriate setting for song and the proprieties of expression as well as to contemplate contents of far greater variety than in the *Idyls* of Theocritus.

In the sixth eclogue the figure of Silenus and the songs he sings illustrate well the added dimensions of Virgilian pastoral poetry: while serving as the promulgator of novelty in bucolic song, he is also poetry itself. The drunken Silenus, part god, part animal, is omniscient; he is an emblem of knowledge and of inspiration, both of which are prime necessities for the poet at work but of no value without the discipline of expression. Just as he must be physically bound by his garlands before he can sing, so too the content of poetry must first be confined by form—infused by madness, yet subjected to craft—before it can

become a true *carmen,* which enchants by mere utterance and moves the tangible with the spiritual. He is a poetic Proteus who from his chains shapes themes of varied sorts to charm his listeners and creations as well as to "free" himself.

Silenus' songs, which Virgil quotes only in summary fashion, embrace one basic topic in different patterns. Amorphous and disordered nature is fashioned and confined by the singer's words. With his *carmen* he "soothes" the stricken Pasiphaë and with verse controls her madness, which is a complete reversal of life's natural processes. Then, turning directly to poetry per se, he initiates Gallus, former devotee of an "errant" type of verse, into a possibly loftier realm of poetry than elegy. Once purged of direct emotional involvement with his theme, Gallus can sing of *origines* and define through poetry the world of experience and knowledge. All these songs Apollo approves and reiterates, pastoral, unbacchic god though he is.

Both sides of the *Eclogues,* exploring the form of pastoral poetry and the meaning of "pastoral" life in general, meet most directly in the ninth and tenth poems. The first of these poems asks and answers a question never before directly posed in the *Eclogues,* though the reader has been subtly prepared for it: Assuming that the happiness of nature is an essential backdrop for song, how can poetry be written under such conditions as presently prevail in Mantua, a mirror for Italy? When soldiers (and the politicians behind them) impose themselves on the poet's land, not only is freedom lost but the ability to create departs as well.

The tenth eclogue changes the perspective but not the theme. This time the challenge to "pastoral" comes not from armed might but from the person of Gallus, who is not only an historical figure, a soldier and statesman of repute, but also the writer of subjective love elegy, a genre of poetry whose axioms threaten those of the pastoral to the core. Virgil presents him as lovesick, in an almost conventional bucolic setting, craving relief first in death and then in acceptance by the company of shepherds. His reorientation out of the countryside back to the world of elegiac love, where to die is to delight in living, comes ironically, though not unexpectedly. Whatever his reasons (beginning with the disharmony in reality), Virgil's own stand does not survive unscathed. This time the loss to the bucolic life is, if anything, more disastrous than the destruction of the landscape. Now the poet himself, the imaginer of the whole fabric, instead of being forced to leave in search of a way to return (as in *Eclogue* 9), abandons the shepherd-poet's life of his own volition.

Yet, at the end of the tenth eclogue Virgil is far from denying the validity of his work; rather, he admits the necessity of moving on to another genre of writing, more suitable to his maturing outlook. If in the *Georgics,* which follow, Virgil appears to embrace a more practical subject and approach, the poetry itself, instead of negating the ideas of the *Eclogues,* carefully reaffirms their force while expanding their horizon. The *Georgics* discuss the obstructions nature puts in the path of man, forcing upon him the necessity of trial and hardship to make life viable. If the actual death of the poet is adumbrated in *Eclogue* 9 and his disavowal of bucolic poetry stressed at the conclusion of 10, the myth of Orpheus, which virtually ends *Georgic* 4, treats the same topic in a new guise. Human emotion again destroys the ideal. It kills love and the poet, and ruins the possibility of poetry, though the farmer's existence itself is renewed.

The *Aeneid* is the culmination of the sequence. It, too, starts, as the *Eclogues* at first seem to do, as poetry of un-involvement. In this case the hero's commitment is necessary only to an ideal mission. Allegiance to fate's progress precludes immediate submission to suffering or emotion, but gradually Aeneas is forced to confront the humanity which is at first easier to ignore. The supposedly simple heroism of establishing an allegorical model for the greatness of a future empire becomes a much more real struggle entailing carnage and violence which the hero must take part in as well as cause. Finally the power struggle centers on a defeated opponent who should be spared but is not, and emotion once more triumphs over reason.

The basic problems the *Aeneid* explores—the confrontation of history and the individual, of progress and freedom, of practical action and idealistic pose, of passion and poetry, to name only a few areas of concern—are all suggested to the observant reader not many lines after the start of the first eclogue. In their search for meaning in human life, the *Eclogues* are in the profoundest sense ethical poems. They do not so much deny "progress" as aver that society can only survive if the moral quality of each of its members is preserved and fortified. Even following the "shepherd's life" man may be subject to the vagaries and pressures of existence, to love and to death. He may yearn by nature for that very social fabric which contains the seeds of his undoing, but there is an immutable element of grandeur within him—call it what you will, the soul, or poetry, or heroism—which cannot be suppressed, much less denied. This forces him to break away from the society which he has helped to create and seek what the existentialists would term his own essence with its challenging union of flesh and spirit, formed by, yet rising above, social *mores.*

But the fifth and fourth eclogues are visions which claim that this ideal reconciliation between man and society through poetry is possible. The former asserts that Daphnis, poetshepherd whose presence is essential to the landscape, though claimed by death, is nevertheless raised to the stature of divinity. Thence he can bless a pastoral world whose processes have been regularized by his apotheosis. The fourth has a still more idealistic notion. It affirms that the value of history lies precisely in those decisive moments which, by assertion of the superhuman, allow us to see beyond the prison of ourselves as creatures of society to a vista of timeless beauty. *Virtus,* as the word

is used in the fourth eclogue, has its common double sense: it is literally that aspect of heroism which suffers present violence for future peace, that creates (or recreates) spiritual order through physical action. It also symbolizes that power to initiate an era of perfect morality in which mankind is victimized by no crime (*scelus*). Human nature is envisioned by Virgil above the struggles that derange existence, even above the labor necessary to exist.

Yet the fantasy of the fourth eclogue, by its very unreality, conjures up its opposite. Such a poetic dream, by denying life the drama of striving for the ideal, becomes ineffectual, if fascinating, banter—perhaps deliberately so. By imagining life as it is not, the poet destroys not only suffering but that heroism which makes of suffering an aesthetic as well as a moral act. This division was very much with Virgil in all his works. Nevertheless by accepting Gallus' world of history and the turmoil of love at the end of *Eclogue* 10, and by emphasizing not the courage of an idealistic, triumphant Aeneas but the anguish of his beaten rival, Turnus, at the conclusion of the *Aeneid,* Virgil sides, as he does from the start of *Eclogue* 1, with troubled humanity. The quest for the ideal has no happy conclusion except in the poet's fancy.

Notes

1. A writer in the *Times Literary Supplement* of August 23, 1963 (p. 640) remarks: "The charm, and *significance,* of the *Eclogues* lies . . . in their tenderness and in their feeling for the countryside, the qualities which were later to flower into the Georgics" (italics mine).

2. Horace *Sat.* 1. 10. 44.

3. For a suggestive treatment of bucolic elements in works which do not stay strictly within the pastoral convention, see William Empson, *Some Versions of Pastoral* (London, 1935).

4. On the importance and achievement of pastoral poetry in the Renaissance, see Hallett Smith, *Elizabethan Poetry* (Cambridge, Mass., 1952), pp. 1-63, esp. 41.

5. The allegorical approach is taken by Leon Herrmann (*Les masques et les visages dans les Bucoliques de Virgile* [Brussels, 1930]) and, more recently, in a series of articles by J. J. H. Savage (*TAPA* 91 [1960]: 353-75 and *TAPA* 94 [1963]: 248-67). See the just strictures on this method of criticism by H. J. Rose, *The Eclogues of Vergil* (Berkeley, 1942), pp. 71ff.

6. The influence of Theocritus on the *Eclogues* has been much discussed, though a reappraisal is long overdue. See especially G. Rohde, "De Vergili Eclogarum forma et indole" (Ph.D. diss., University of Marburg, Berlin, 1925) and the review of it by Friedrich Klingner, *Gnomon* 3 (1927): 576-83. Klingner's chapter "Virgil" in *L'influence grecque sur la poésie latine de Catulle à Ovide,* Entretiens II (Geneva: Fondation Hardt, 1956), pp. 131-55, is of

great value. See also his *Römische Geisteswelt* (Munich, 1961), p. 265.

7. See below, chap. 2, notes 3 and 5.

8. See, for instance, Brooks Otis, *Virgil: A Study in Civilized Poetry* (Oxford, 1963), chap. 4, "The Young Virgil." Otis sees *Eclogue* 5 receiving particular emphasis from the book's structure. Cf. Carl Becker, "Virgils Eklogenbuch," *Hermes* 83 (1955): 314-49, esp. 320ff.

9. See Viktor Pöschl, "Horaz und die Politik," *Sitz. Heid.*, Abhandlung 4 (1956): 14 and 17ff.

10. See chap. 2, n. 2.

11. On the *Phaedrus* and pastoral tradition, see Clyde Murley, "Plato's *Phaedrus* and Theocritean Pastoral," *TAPA* 71 (1940): 281-95; Adam Parry, "Landscape in Greek Poetry," *Yale Classical Studies* 15 (1957): 3-29; C. P. Segal, "Nature and the World of Man in Greek Literature," *Arion* 2 (1963): 45ff.

12. Erich Heller, *The Artist's Journey into the Interior* (New York, 1965), p. 103, summarizes Hegel's diagnosis of his age.

13. The phrase is that of Randall Jarrell, talking of Robert Frost ("The Other Frost" in *Poetry and the Age* [New York, 1955], p. 27), a poet who shares much in common with Virgil and whose power, until recent decades, has been equally misinterpreted. Frost once remarked that he "first heard the speaking voice in poetry in Virgil's *Eclogues*" (see R. A. Brower, *The Poetry of Robert Frost* [New York, 1963], pp. 156-57).

Abbreviations Used in the Notes

AJP	*American Journal of Philology*
Cal. Pub. in Class. Phil.	University of California Publications in Classical Philology
CJ	*Classical Journal*
CP	*Classical Philology*
CQ	*Classical Quarterly*
CR	*Classical Review*
CW	*Classical World*
HSCP	*Harvard Studies in Classical Philology*
JRS	*Journal of Roman Studies*
Journ. War. and Court. Inst.	*Journal of the Warburg* and Courtauld Institutes
Mem. Am. Aca. Rome	*Memoirs of the American Academy in Rome*
P.-W. Pauly-Wissowa-Kroll	*Realencyclopädie der classischen Altertumswissenschaft*
REL	*Revue des Études Latines*
REA	*Revue des Études Anciennes*
RhM	Rheinisches Museum für Philologie
Sitz. Heid.	Sitzungsberichte der Heidelberger Akademie der Wissenschaften, Philos.-Hist. Klasse
TAPA	*Transactions and Proceedings of the American Philological Association*
WS	Wiener Studien

R. W. Garson (essay date 1971)

SOURCE: "Theocritean Elements in Virgil's *Eclogues*," *The Classical Quarterly*, 1971, New Series, Vol. XXI, No. 1, May, pp. 188-203.

[*In the following essay, Garson focuses on* Eclogues *2, 3, 5, 7, and 8, examining their poetics as well as their Theocritean elements.*]

Much of the early scholarship on Virgilian borrowings from Theocritus offered mere lists of parallel passages and, where criticism was attempted at all, the *Eclogues* often attracted such uncomplimentary labels as 'cento' or 'pastiche'. In more recent scholarship the tendency to concentrate on insoluble problems and arithmetical correspondences lingers and, while some critical works of the sixties are characterized by a welcome upsurge in sensitivity, one occasionally suspects that Virgil has had attributed to him concepts which are two millennia ahead of his time. To redress the balance, the following pages adhere to the text of Virgil and aim at being fairly conservative. Despite the volume of literature on the *Eclogues,* ample scope remains for differing interpretations, for the filling in of details and for a more methodical approach to the specific subject of borrowings from Theocritus. These are the lines along which it is hoped now to contribute, but it will sometimes be necessary briefly to re-state points already made by others in order to present a reasonably comprehensive picture. The accent in this article is on the mechanics of Virgilian composition, and *Eclogues* 2, 3, 5, 7, and 8, in which Theocritean elements are all-important, will be treated in detail. Where there is a meaningful parallel or contrast, occasional observations about echoes from Theocritus in *Eclogues* 1, 9, and 10 appear in footnotes.

The Polyphemus idylls are the most obvious source of the second eclogue. Echoes occur in the opening words of the lament (cf. *Ec.* 2. 6 and *Id.* 11. 19); in the lover's boasts about his material wealth (cf. *Ec.* 2. 19-22 and *Id.* 11. 34-7), about his musical accomplishments (cf. *Ec.* 2. 23-4 and *Id.* 11. 38-40), and about his physical appearance (cf. *Ec.* 2. 25-7 and *Id.* 6. 34-8). Both lovers invite their beloved to share life together (cf. *Ec.* 2. 28-34 and *Id.* 11. 42-9 and 63-6); offer gifts of animals (cf. *Ec.* 2. 40-2 and *Id.* 11. 40-1) and flowers (cf. *Ec.* 2. 45-55 and *Id.* 11. 56-9); and, finally realizing their madness, they seem to recover their reason (cf. *Ec.* 2. 69-73 and *Id.* 11. 72-6). Yet, with all these correspondences, Virgil's basic conception of this poem of lamentation and wooing is totally different from Theocritus', and he contrives to make even his most literal renderings of the Greek subservient to his different design.

Corydon's literary ancestor is, in the deepest sense, Simaetha, not Polyphemus. It is only in the second idyll that

Theocritus portrays a serious and irresistible passion in which poet and reader alike are involved. Polyphemus in the eleventh idyll serves as a παραδειγμα to Theocritus, Nicias, and the reader. He is the living proof that love, even ορθαι μανιαι, may be assuaged by song. He is regarded with detachment all round. Occasional sympathy is tempered with amusement at the incongruity of his suit. He is always the monster, and he understands his situation no better at the end of the poem than at the beginning. Corydon, like Simaetha, is presented directly to the reader. His psychic contortions, like hers, illustrate no evident moral. They are traced by the poet for their own sake. There is no grotesqueness about Corydon's appearance or his being. He is an ordinary man suffering, and the sensitive reader will suffer with him. The second eclogue, like the second idyll, is almost a drama of an all-consuming passion, whose futility is realized but not heeded. Yet Simaetha differs from Corydon in that she is hopeful at the beginning. She passes from hope to despair, from acts of magic to bring Delphis back, to a bitter recollection of past joys and to an acceptance of her defeat. Polyphemus, of course, is hopeful throughout. He sings looking towards the sea, from which he expects Galatea to emerge. His boasts and ruses are directed towards a very tangible result. But Corydon has no real hope at any stage—*nec quid speraret habebat* (2). All the while he is wooing a distant beloved; his only communion is with Nature (3-5), and when his fancy, ever more impassioned, raises him to hope (esp. 51-5), his sudden awareness of his own inadequacy shatters his brief illusion (56-9).

It is a mark of Virgil's ingenuity as a craftsman that, with all these contrasts, he has been able to use so much of the eleventh idyll, which may be regarded as the *leitmotiv*. It supplies the opening and closing strains of Corydon's song as well as substantial sections of the middle. But the very first echo underlines the difference between the two poems: ωλευκα Γαλατεια (19), an acknowledgment of Galatea's beauty, which is the prize to be won, *o crudelis Alexi* (6), the despairing cry of a man slighted in love. Polyphemus praises the appearance of the fawns he is keeping for Galatea—πτσας μαννοφρως (41). Corydon in *praeterea duo nec tuta mihi ualle reperti / capreoli . . .* (40-1) adds the point that he risked his life to obtain the gift for Alexis. Polyphemus says that if only he could swim he would bring Galatea snowdrops or poppies, and he apologizes clumsily for not being able to bring them together, as they flower in different seasons (56-9).[1] The emotional climax of Virgil's poem is reached where Corydon lovingly describes the fruit he fancies he will bring Alexis, and the flowers he will arrange for him. In this section Virgil concentrates his poetic devices—the pregnant use of *honos,* the address to the bays and the myrtle, which he sees in his mind's eye as already arranged in the basket so as to give Alexis most pleasure (note the proleptic use of *proxima* in 54), the sweetness of *sic positae quoniam suauis miscetis odores* (55), which comes so soon after *mollia luteola pingit uaccinia calta* (50)—a uniquely beautiful impression of texture and colour.

Hamlet is no less serious a play because Polonius and others provide comic relief. Scholars have been signally humourless in not seeing Corydon's three boasts (about his wealth, his musical accomplishments, and his beauty) as being comic relief in an essentially sombre poem. Virgil often wrote ατρεμας ςεςαρως in the *Eclogues.* There is no reason to doubt the truth of Polyphemus' boast that he tends a thousand head of cattle (*Id.* 11. 34), or that he is outstandingly good at piping (38). Even his claim to attractiveness in Damoetas' song (6. 34-8) is a subjective one and sincerely expressed. The humour, which is tinged with pathos, lies in Polyphemus' failure to realize that Galatea cannot be won over by these attributes. Virgil's adaptations of the above passages at *Ec.* 2. 19-27 has more often than not drawn grim comment of the following nature: Corydon is speaking as though his master's flocks belonged to him; Virgil is mistaken in placing Aracynthus in Attica; the sea cannot act as a mirror—Corydon must have gone to a rock-pool. But surely the point is that in his hopeless soliloquy Corydon allowed himself the luxury and comfort of fanciful exaggeration, even untruth. One is meant to smile at the incongruity of any one, especially Corydon, having a flock so vast that its female lambs alone number one thousand. Or that an unlettered shepherd should not only associate his musical skill with that of Zeus' son Amphion, who actually built the walls of Thebes by the power of his music, but even utter a neoteric line like *Amphion Dircaeus in Actaeo Aracyntho,* complete with Greek hiatus and doubly learned allusion in *Dircaeus.*[2] Amid such incongruity the misuse of *Actaeo* is more likely to be Corydon's than Virgil's. Finally, Daphnis was the ideal shepherd, and so Corydon's claim to equal him in beauty was unutterably extravagant. Bearing this in mind, we do not need to send him off to a rock-pool to see his face. If he says he saw it in the unruffled sea, let us take the location of his mirror only as seriously as the boast itself.[3]

Touches of humour are not confined to these echoes of Polyphemus. Corydon's strains are described as *incondita* ('artless') in line 4, yet Virgil, the budding poet, knew full well that his learned readers would not fail to notice and appreciate the elaborate construction of the poem—its ordered progression of thought as opposed to Polyphemus' rambling soliloquy, its attunement of sound and sense, its formal balance,[4] its inherent antitheses of theme.[5] Another touch of humour is a pun in line 18. When Virgil writes *uaccinia nigra leguntur* he is echoing . . . *Id.* 10. 29, referring to violets and hyacinths, but λεγονται in this context is much more likely to mean 'are accounted' than 'are gathered'.

The Polyphemus echo concluding the second eclogue (69-73: cf. *Id.* 11. 72-6) is troublesome. The Theocritean version is relatively straightforward, as Polyphemus must recover his sanity and, moreover, do so by means of song in order to fit in with the lesson Theocritus is offering Nicias. In answer to the possible objection that the change of tone is, none the less, too sudden and not psychologically motivated, one could seek refuge in the supposition that

Polyphemus is only trying a ruse in order to whet Galatea's appetite. In the Virgilian poem the change of feeling is, if anything, more sudden. Various suggestions have been made in order to explain it, e.g. that Virgil was still fumbling in his art and a slave to the Theocritean tradition; that he was seeking to illustrate the same point as Theocritus, namely that singing cures lovers; that Corydon, the experienced lover (see lines 14-15), would readily come to the conclusion that there were lots of fish in the sea; that Corydon returns to weaving baskets out of loyalty to the countryside which he loves so much. These theories vary in their degree of implausibility. It is here suggested, very tentatively, that Corydon may be indulging in self-deception. At line 17 Corydon believes that he can overcome his devotion to Alexis, and at 43-4 he thinks of turning to Thestylis, but the sequel, especially 51-5, 58-9 and 68, proves that he has underestimated Alexis' hold over him. The most natural explanation would be that in the last lines of the poem Corydon has regressed into self-deception, which would be in keeping with the rapidly changing moods of the last third of the poem. The reader is, then, left to imagine that this self-deception will again give way to a realization of hopeless love. The cycle will continue. The painful drama will be re-enacted innumerable times—*assidue ueniebat* (4).

When Corydon invites Alexis to come and live with him and share his pursuits (28-34), one naturally thinks of Polyphemus' invitations to Galatea (*Id.* 11. 42-9 and 63-6), even though the details of the invitations must of necessity be different. Polyphemus is inviting Galatea to give up her life in the sea for what he depicts as the greater comfort of life on land, while Corydon even at this stage of his soliloquy suspects that Alexis would require greater sophistication than life in the country could offer. The connotation of *sordida rura* and *humilis . . . casas* would differ in Corydon's eyes and Alexis'. In developing the idea of this great gulf between the two Virgil almost certainly had the twentieth idyll in mind. It opens with a city girl's insolent speech of rejection to a cowherd (2-10). . . . He in return reflects that in the country he is found desirable . . . (30-1), and he uses a contemptuous neuter . . . (31), of Eunica who rejects him. He goes on to give examples from mythology of loves enjoyed by gods in the woodland (34-41), and he taunts Eunica bitterly . . . (42-3). The main difference in the handling of the theme by Virgil is that the action takes place only in Corydon's mind. After imagining so lovingly all the rustic gifts he would give Alexis, suddenly he becomes aware that he himself, along with his gifts, is inadequate for Alexis—*rusticus es, Corydon* (56). *Rusticus* means 'countryman' to Corydon, 'boor' to Alexis. Corydon then uses an argument similar to that of the cowherd in the twentieth idyll to prove the value of the country, namely that the gods have dwelt there (60-1), but he does so more briefly, more in sorrow than in anger. And with a quiet dignity he reasserts his loyalty to the countryside—*Pallas quas condidit arces / ipsa colat; nobis placeant ante omnia siluae* (61-2).

Intimately linked with the town/country antithesis is that of white skin resulting from life in the city and the swarthy skin of country folk. In Theocritus' tenth idyll Bucaeus sings of Bombyca's charms: while others call her αλιοκανοτον, he finds her μελιχλωρον (27); then he points out that violets and hyacinths, which are dark, are particularly sought after for garlands. Virgil has taken this theme and adapted it to the antithetical pattern of his poem: *quamuis ille niger, quamuis tu candidus esses?* (16), and *alba ligustra cadunt, uaccinia nigra leguntur* (18). It is, also, fitted into his recurrent theme of competition, especially between lovers. Here Corydon compares the swarthy Menalcas favourably with the white Alexis. Elsewhere there is rivalry or implied rivalry between Iollas and Corydon for Alexis, Daphnis and Corydon for superior beauty, Amyntas and Corydon for Damoetas' pipe, Thestylis and Alexis for the two goats, Alexis and 'another Alexis' for Corydon's love. An obvious difference between Bucaeus' words and Corydon's is that the former are a tribute, whereas the latter are a warning. In this connection it is worth pointing to *Id.* 23. 28-32, where a desperate lover warns the boy he loves that his beauty will fade, like that of flowers. . . .The finished product in the second eclogue is evidently a fusion of the two passages.

Immediately after Bucaeus' tribute Theocritus introduces the following simile: α αιξ ταν κτιϛον, λυκος τον αιγα διωκει, / αγαρ*alpha;νος τωροτρον αγα δ' επι τιν μεμνημαι (10. 30-1). Virgil seems to copy this quite closely: *torua leaena lupum sequitur, lupus ipse capellam, / florentem cytisum sequitur lasciua capella, / te Corydon, o Alexi: trahit sua quemque uoluptas* (2. 63-5). However, his alterations are noteworthy. He has introduced true symmetry in sense (cf. Theocritus' scheme AB, CA, DE and Virgil's AB, BC, CD). He has made the picture more vivid by the addition of epithets. He has eliminated the contrast inherent in Theocritus' simile (i.e. the crane follows after the plough, *but* I am mad over you). Virgil is concerned not with differing degrees of feeling, but rather with its naturalness: *trahit sua quemque uoluptas*. Corydon has just sworn allegiance to the country, and his emotions, like those of the beasts around him, are irresistible. The simile is thus adapted to illustrate the gulf between the unspoiled rustic and the sophisticated city-dweller. It is at the next stage of his poem that Virgil passes more specifically to the intensity of Corydon's feelings by means of the antithesis of sunset and blazing love, and this leads to the equation of love and madness (69 and cf. Theocritus' μεμαυνημαι at 10. 31 as well as 11. 72). In lines 60-9 Virgil has in turn adapted themes from *Idylls* 20, 10, 2, and 11, and Corydon has passed from calling Alexis *demens* for misprizing the country, to regarding his own passion for Alexis as *dementia*.

We have already observed the double use of the stillness/turmoil contrast (*Ec.* 2. 8-13 and 66-8). Each antithesis singly was suggested by *Id.* 2. 38-40, though Virgil's details are his own. The double occurrence gives the poem a better balance of form as well as emphasizing the continuity of Corydon's passion. It is, further, interesting to note that while the sunset motif serves to bring several eclogues, including the last, to a neat conclusion, Virgil has here superimposed on this more conventional use the refinements of formal and thematic antithesis. Finally, one of the details of the first antithesis—*nunc uiridis etiam occultant spineta lacertos* (9) recalls [the passage at] (*Id.* 7. 22). It is likely that Virgil is here hinting at a further contrast, namely that between the light-hearted walk to the harvest festival[6] and Corydon's frenzied quest for Alexis. The use of echoes from the third idyll, a trivial serenade which lacks any depth of feeling, is similarly pointed (cf. *Ec.* 2. 7 and *Id.* 3. 9; *Ec.* 2. 43-4 and *Id.* 3. 35-6).

Antithesis plays a part not only within given poems but also outside them. In turning from the second to the third eclogue the reader passes from a sorrowful monologue relieved by occasional humour to a light-hearted singing contest at the fringes of which lie hints of Virgil's more serious bent. The most obvious source of **Eclogue** 3 is Theocritus' fifth idyll. Both poems are in the form of an amoebaean contest in couplets preceded by abuse and followed by an umpire's verdict, and the number of verbal borrowings is very great indeed. However, in substituting the good-humoured banter of Menalcas and Damoetas for Comatas' and Lacon's expressions of deep animosity, Virgil has made a happy poem out of an idyll which leaves a distinctly unpleasant after-taste. Presumably in the cause of bucolic realism Theocritus makes Comatas allude to homosexual acts between himself and Lacon in quite specific terms. Both before the contest (5. 41-2) and in the course of it (5. 116-17) he gloats over the discomfort he has caused Lacon. Virgil's *nouimus et qui te transuersa tuentibus hircis / et quo—sed faciles Nymphae risere—sacello* (3. 8-9) is infinitely more delicate, with its aposiopesis probably suggested by *Id.* 1. 105, and since the act did not involve the protagonists of the poem there is no legacy of resentment as in the Greek version. Instead, we have the charming touch of the hegoats, those sexually incontinent animals, looking askance, and the nymphs laughing indulgently over the profanation of a holy place. Similarly, Virgil has altered the accusations of theft and envy which he has taken over from his Greek model. The fifth idyll begins with Comatas accusing Lacon of stealing his goatskin, and Lacon countering that Comatas stole his pipe. Much less conspicuously in Virgil's poem (3. 17-18) Menalcas claims that he saw Damoetas sneaking up on Damon's goat.[7] At *Id.* 5. 12-13 Comatas uses strong language of Lacon's feeling of envy towards himself, whereas at *Ec.* 3. 14-15 Daphnis, who does not appear in the poem, is the object of Menalcas' alleged envy.[8] It is significant, too, that Virgil dispenses with the prolonged wrangling over the choice of a spot for the contest (cf. *Id.* 5. 45-61). These lines contain some enchanting details in themselves, but as nothing seems to please both contestants, the feeling of well-being which they might otherwise have created is destroyed. Virgil simply makes Palaemon the umpire, who has been chosen without bickering (cf. *Id.* 5. 63), describe the surroundings with such loving enthusiasm that the reader cannot but be affected by it: *in molli consedimus herba / et nunc omnis ager, nunc omnis parturit arbos, / nunc frondent siluae, nunc formosissimus annus* (55-7). Virgil has set the stage by translating the

minutiae of several Theocritean descriptions into more general terms.[9] The beauty of the whole countryside and of the season, so succinctly described, is in keeping with the happiness of the occasion. It is noteworthy, too, that Palaemon praises both contestants at the end and refuses to rate one more highly than the other, whereas in *Id.* 5. 141-4 Comatas mocks his defeated rival.

As Virgil has eliminated and compressed so much from the introduction to *Idyll* 5, he supplements it with themes from *Idylls* 4, 8, and 1. The opening lines of the third eclogue echo those of *Idyll* 4 so closely[10] that one must assume that Virgil is throwing his one real innovation—*cuium*—into relief. He is too conscious, too Augustan an artist to allow himself at all times the greater naturalism of Theocritus, or to rival the easy flow of *Idyll* 4, with its rambling dialogue. But *cuium,* an uncommon lapse into real rusticity of language,[11] serves as a keynote to the reader, who is then left to supply other provincialisms in his own imagination while enjoying a poem of Augustan polish. Several other themes taken over from the fourth idyll are significantly altered: the flock in **Eclogue** 3 is neglected because Aegon is away making love (3-4),[12] and love is a recurrent theme in this poem, whereas in Theocritus Aegon's only love is for a victory in athletics (*Id.* 4. 27). The bull at *Id.* 4. 20 is thin through neglect, whereas in Virgil he is wasting away through being in love (*Ec.* 3. 100-1), and incidentally he has turned up within the actual amoebaean contest. Another theme from *Idyll* 4, that of excessive milking, is exaggerated by Virgil for comic effect . . . , but the pathetic possibilities are exploited as well: *et sucus pecori et lac subducitur agnis* (6). A similar exaggeration with heightened emotional overtones occurs where the stakes are discussed. . . .

From *Id.* 1. 27-60 Virgil borrows the idea of describing a cup[13] and indeed some of the decoration is similar: cf. *Ec.* 3. 38-9 and 45 and *Id.* 1. 27-31. (For the fact that the cup has not been used cf. *Ec.* 3. 43 and *Id.* 1. 59-60.) There are several possible justifications for the length of Theocritus' description: he was an Alexandrian; he was influenced by the epic tradition (cf. Achilles' shield in *Iliad* 18); he wanted a counterweight to Thyrsis' song. But Virgil was intent on not straying too far from his subject, and so the representations within his cups take up only a few lines (40-2 and 46). Instead of Theocritus' sheer delight in description for its own sake, description full of charm and human interest, we find the quintessence of Virgil's thought at this time: natural science and agriculture, which were soon to preoccupy him in the **Georgics;** song and its emotive power, a theme recurrent in the **Eclogues.**[14] It is hardly surprising that Virgil had pruned his Theocritean model of its obscenity and extremes of vituperation before introducing so solemn a note, a note which is later echoed in Damoetas' opening couplet on the pervasiveness of Jupiter.[15] Menalcas' answering couplet (62-3) reintroduces the bucolic tone, but it is worth noticing that Virgil succeeds in retaining some rustic simplicity even when he adumbrates the most profound themes. In line 40 Menalcas is made to forget the name of one of the scientists, and in 48

Damoetas compares his cups unfavourably with his heifer, a comparison which leads very neatly to the 'comic' lines 49-53.

Reference has already been made to two delightful touches of characterization: Menalcas being a little vain over his attractiveness to Neaera (4), and his deliberate misunderstanding of Damoetas (49). But the most memorable characterization in this poem is of Palaemon. In *Idyll 5* the umpire Morson shows no colourfulness of character beyond asking Comatas for a piece of the lamb he has awarded him (140). Palaemon, however, is a poet *manqué,* depicted with some humour: he shows himself most sensitive to the joys of nature (55-7), and his rhetorical anaphorae are charmingly incongruous on the greensward; his skilful Romanization of Μονοαων θ', αι αειδον αομειβαιμεναι (*Il.* 1. 604) in *amant alterna Camenae* (59) must have been close to Virgil's heart. His closing remarks show his versatility in metaphor: *tantas componere lites* (108) and *claudite iam riuos* (111). And he could not have predicted what trouble he would cause scholars with his cryptic and not altogether relevant lines on sweet and bitter love (109-10). Had he just been carried away by his own thoughts, so that he was not listening? The gently humorous Virgil apparently chose to keep his readers wondering.

Even within the amoebaean contest Virgil introduces fleeting but memorable touches of characterization which are not present in his model. At 3. 64-5 he adopts the theme of pelting with apples from *Id.* 5. 88-9. The strength of the Theocritean passage lies in the onomatopoeic and inviting ποππυλι•οςδει. Virgil does not seek to rival this, but with somewhat greater subtlety he makes Galatea hide behind the willows only after she has been seen—perhaps the most charming illustration of the adjective *lasciua* in Latin literature. When Damoetas and Menalcas sing of the presents they have for their darlings we are reminded of Theocritean passages (cf. *Ec.* 3. 68-9 and *Id.* 5. 96-7; *Ec.* 3. 70-1 and *Id.* 3. 10-11). But Comatas' description of his present is factual and dull, whereas Damoetas chooses his words most carefully to emphasize the trouble he has been to (especially *parta, ipse,* and *aëriae*). The answering couplet, likewise, is much more vivid than its original. Although δεκα μαλα have become *aurea mala decem,* Menalcas pretends to disparage his gift in *quod potui.* The question arises, also, whether Virgil intended a pun in *aurea,* since αυριον occurs nearby in the Greek.

From the examples immediately above it emerges that Virgil could take couplets from two different poems and make them responsive. Similarly, the balancing couplets at *Ec.* 3. 80-3 owe something to three unrelated passages (*Id.* 8. 57-9; ib. 76-8; 9. 31-2), which Virgil has drawn together and disciplined in structure, while using original details. Also, in *mella fluant illi, ferat et rubus asper amomum* (3. 89) Virgil has combined two elements which occur in balancing couplets in his model (cf. *Id.* 5. 125/126).

We have noticed incidentally how Virgil has arranged his matter so that the singing match arises logically and

naturally from Menalcas' accusation of theft (3. 17-18). The placing of *non tu in triuiis, indocte, solebas / stridenti miserum stipula disperdere carmen?* (3. 26-7 and cf. *Id.* 5. 6-7) is, likewise, superior in Virgil. These disparaging remarks about Damoetas' musical ability immediately precede the challenge to the contest, whereas in Theocritus Comatas' equivalent comment is just part of the general abuse. Another change in Virgil is his incorporation into the actual amoebaean contest of themes from the surrounding dialogue in Theocritus: cf. the 'wide berth' motif in *Ec.* 3. 92-9 and *Id.* 5. 1-4, and note that from Comatas' exultation over his victory (*Id.* 5. 146) Virgil has taken the detail of washing goats (97), which is integrated most ingeniously into the remodelled 'wide berth' theme. Finally, Virgil has extended the love motif so that it comes close to unifying the poem. Apart from the conventional preoccupation with love in the amoebaean contest, Virgil has introduced the Aegon-Neaera-Menalcas triangle (3-4), the amorous bull (100-1), and the romantic Palaemon (109-10). By a clever shift in the meaning of *amare* (84 and 88) Virgil has taken the opportunity of glorifying Pollio and vilifying Bavius and Maevius.[16]

The emphasis in this treatment of *Eclogue 3* has been on its decorum, its wit, its flashes of inspiration. Alongside these qualities one should recognize the calculated and painstaking rearrangement of Theocritean motifs essential to this poem whose 'simplicity' could so easily beguile.

One's interpretation of Theocritean adaptation in *Eclogue 5* will depend on whether one believes the poem is about Daphnis *per se* or about Caesar. Virgil's innovations would obviously be more daring in the latter case. To the arguments so often repeated on either side nothing new can be added here beyond recording a vote firmly on the side of allegory. To deny allegory because of some factual discrepancies seems a trifle insensitive to the political and emotional atmosphere in which Virgil wrote, the pattern of his work, and the nature of poetry in general, but as doubts will always linger, this treatment will be confined to an examination of parallel passages, and will disregard the new dimension which Virgil almost certainly meant to give his poem through allegory.

After a study of *Eclogues 2* and *3*, Virgil's greater independence of Theocritus in *5* is very marked. A fair proportion of the similarities are in ideas rather than verbal reminiscences. *Eclogue 5* is amoebaean in the sense that there is balance of form and theme, but the songs of Daphnis' death and deification are not presented within the framework of a competition; there is no rivalry or abuse, only the courteous exchange of compliments and gifts. A similar atmosphere prevails in *Idylls* 1, 6, and 7. *Idyll 1* begins with an exchange of compliments about their musical skill between Thyrsis and the goatherd, and this leads ultimately to Thyrsis' song about Daphnis. In the opening lines Thyrsis likens the goatherd's piping to the whispering of a pine tree (*Id.* 1. 1-3), and the goatherd likens Thyrsis' singing to a plashing stream (7-8). The corresponding sections in the fifth eclogue occur after the respective songs of Mopsus and Menalcas. Menalcas praises not the mere sound of Mopsus' song, but rather its refreshing effect on the soul. The beauty of its presentation and feeling has transcended its sorrowful subject, and hence the simile of refreshment (*Ec.* 5. 45-7) is a compliment in the most profound sense. In the Virgilian passage alone human emotions are brought to the forefront, and the similarity of idea between το καταχος / . . . καταλεεβεται υψον νδωρ and *dulcis aquae saliente . . . riuo* is almost incidental. It is likely that Virgil had in his mind also *Id.* 12. 8-9 where Theocritus compares his eagerness to be with his boy-love to the eagerness of a traveller to be under a shady oak when the sun is scorching. Mopsus' praise of Menalcas' song (*Ec.* 5. 82-4) does concentrate on sound, and it combines ideas from Thyrsis' and the goatherd's expressions of praise. . . .

Compliments over songs are common enough in bucolic poetry, but the praise of Mopsus at *Ec.* 5. 16-18, which owes something to Theocritus in form (see below), arises from a situation which Virgil himself invented with wit and delicacy. Menalcas, under-estimating his young companion's sensitivity in the matter, has mentioned Amyntas' claim to sing as well as he does (8). Mopsus' annoyance is very evident in line 9, and it still rankles at 15, after which Menalcas, presumably sorry about his *faux pas,* feels constrained to humour him in the following simile: *lenta salix quantum pallenti cedit oliuae, / puniceis humilis quantum saliunca rosetis, / iudicio nostro tantum tibi cedit Amyntas.* The closest parallel in Theocritus is *Id.* 5. 92-5, where Comatas and Lacon each disparage the other's choice in love, with some obscurity. One should compare also *Id.* 12. 3-8 where the simile, likewise in a love context, involves an infelicitous juxtaposition of measures of difference and an absolute quantity. Virgil has eliminated the obscurity of the one passage and the imperfect logic of the other, and the details are mainly original in a simile which forms a neat conclusion to the delicate social situation invented by Virgil.[17]

Mopsus' song is in effect a continuation of Thyrsis' in *Idyll* 1. The nymphs, who were absent while Daphnis was dying and who, by implication, might have saved him, are now foremost among the mourners (cf. *Id.* 1. 66-9 and *Ec.* 5. 20-1); the animals which lamented while Daphnis was dying continue to mourn and lament after his death (cf. *Id.* 1. 71-5 and *Ec.* 5. 24-8). The reversal of nature which Daphnis called for, perhaps figuratively, in his last words is a *fait accompli* in Mopsus' song, however different the details (cf. *Id.* 1. 132-6 and *Ec.* 5. 34-9).[18] And Virgil had the subtlety to detect the lapidary style of.. . .(*Id.* 1. 120-1) and to transform it into Daphnis' epitaph (*Ec.* 5. 43-4). His addition of *hinc usque ad sidera notus* is a hint of the deification which follows in Menalcas' answering song.[19]

Menalcas' song owes nothing significant to Theocritus. The hearty giving of gifts after it has Theocritean parallels (cf. *Idylls* 6. 43-4 and 7. 128-9), but Menalcas' mention that the pipe taught him '*formosum Corydon ardebat Alexis*' and '*cuium pecus? an Meliboei?*' (86-7) is a purely Virgilian touch. It emphasizes the unity of the collection of poems, and Virgil is at the same time indulging in a little quiet self-flattery.

The seventh eclogue has been treated as a problem poem. Great ingenuity has been expended on rival theories to explain the victory of Corydon in the amoebaean contest. From these some interesting facts, especially in connection with Thyrsis' alleged metrical flaws, have come to light, but serious doubts must remain whether Virgil intended his readers to take his poem so seriously. Even if he did, arguing about the reason or reasons for Corydon's victory is at best enlightened guesswork, whereas the view that Virgil meant to delight and amuse his readers is not open to doubt. The strength of the poem lies in its formal excellence, its characterization, and its delicate wit, which so often springs from incongruity. And this strength is not to be found in Virgil's models.

At first glance **Eclogue** 7 may seem to be markedly Theocritean.[20] The introduction is a fusion of the opening lines of *Idylls* 6 and 8 . . .; there is a narrator, as in *Idyll* 9; the amoebaean contest is in quatrains, as in *Idyll* 8; its main themes are the Theocritean ones of love and nature, and there are specific echoes which may seem a little pale (cf. *Ec.* 7. 37-8 and *Id.* 11. 20-1; *Ec.* 7. 45 and *Idylls* 8. 37, 5. 51, 15. 125).

It is after the introduction of Corydon and Thyrsis that Virgil shows his originality and wit. Meliboeus explains how he came to judge the contest. It all happened by chance, because of a he-goat which had strayed to the place where Corydon and Thyrsis were about to sing. In the contest of *Idyll* 8 Menalcas humorously addresses a he-goat as ταν λευκαν αιγων ανερ. (49), which Virgil echoes in *uir gregis ipse caper* (*Ec.* 7. 7). However, there is additional point here, as the implication is that an animal of such eminence should have known better than to lose the way. Furthermore, this one mock-heroic phrase which Virgil has borrowed from Theocritus blends with the tone of the ensuing narrative, or perhaps that tone was even suggested by the phrase. After the straying of the goat, Daphnis (deified?) appears like a *deus ex machina* (note the vivid construction *deerrauerat; atque . . . aspicio*), utters a prophecy about the salvation of Meliboeus' flock, and instructs him, in effect, to judge the singing match.[21] Meliboeus is in a quandary because of his obligation towards his flock, and Virgil's description of his thought process is engagingly ponderous: *quid facerem? neque ego Alcippen nec Phyllida habebam / depulsos a lacte domi quae clauderet agnos, / et certamen erat, Corydon cum Thyrside, magnum. / posthabui tamen illorum mea seria ludo* (14-17). After this resolution of Meliboeus' inner conflict, the actual singing match is introduced in a markedly spondaic rhythm.

Corydon's epithet for the Muses in his opening quatrain is *Libethrides,* alluding to a fountain in Macedonia with which the Muses were occasionally associated. To regard this as a vulgar display of learning on Virgil's part is to underestimate him grossly. The poet is aiming at incongruity in order to amuse. After the errant goat, the elevation of the pastoral genre, and the shock of finding himself by the Mincius, the reader should be in the mood for a goatherd of incredible erudition. In *paruus /* . . . *Micon* (29-30) the same Corydon is Virgil's mouthpiece for an etymological pun involving the Doric form μικκος. But the great novelty in this eclogue, which is not foreshadowed in Theocritus or in Virgil's other amoebaean poems, is the starkly contrasted characterization of the contestants in the actual songs. Corydon is modest and self-effacing—witness his generous tribute to Codrus (21-4)—while Thyrsis has an opinion of himself which is belied both by Meliboeus' verdict and by occasional imperfections in his improvisations. Virgil depicts the extreme nature of his conceit with humour: *crescentem* . . . *poetam* (25), *uati* . . . *futuro* (28). His exaggerated promise of a golden statue of Priapus, whom he has addressed with some condescension (33-6), is entirely in character. He has a great gift for unpleasant details (41-4), and from his final quatrain (65-8) it appears that his love is less unconditional, less tender than Corydon's. Virgil has sketched two characters in miniature, with indulgence and good humour. In this he has given the amoebaean form a new dimension.

Finally, some details deserve brief consideration. Thyrsis' sketch of a domestic interior in winter (49-52) is modelled on *Idd.* 11. 51 and 9. 19-21, but Virgil's actual simile in *hic tantum Boreae curamus frigora quantum / aut numerum lupus aut torrentia flumina ripas* owes no detail to εχω δετοι ονωδ' ωσον εραν / χεαματος ενωδος καρυων αμυλοιο παροντος. In view of the rustic mentality of Thyrsis in *Eclogue* 7 and Menalcas in *Idyll* 9, we need not linger over the logical flaws in the similes which have been pointed out by hardened classicists: the cold is an evil against which Thyrsis and Menalcas must protect themselves, whereas a wolf is not on the defensive, and nuts are a pleasure to be forgone by the toothless, not an evil. Perhaps it is more to the point to observe that Theocritus' simile has a quaint charm which is absent in the Virgilian one. Thyrsis' inspiration is here at a low ebb. Were he invariably accomplished as a poet, then the insolent boast of his opening quatrain might appear to be justified, and Meliboeus could turn out another Palaemon, unable to decide between the contestants. If Virgil intends us to be in the least serious about the relative merits of the two contestants, Thyrsis' simile is the one obvious place in which he betrays his inferiority. Otherwise, Virgil has given him an ample talent. One need only compare *Id.* 8. 41-8 with *Ec.* 7. 53-60 to see how Thyrsis transforms a fairly conventional conceit by the refinement of chiasmus, or consider his masterly capping of Corydon's *hedera formosior alba* (38) with *proiecta uilior alga* (42).

Eclogue 7 ends with a colourful phrase from the lips of Meliboeus. Instead of the factual κυκ τοντω πρατος παρα ποιμεοσι Δαφνις εγεντο (*Id.* 8. 92) we have *ex illo Corydon Corydon est tempore nobis* (*Ec.* 7. 70). Corydon has come into his own, he has become a symbol of excellence

in Meliboeus' eyes. And Virgil is juggling with words. The sound recalls *a, Corydon, Corydon* (*Ec.* 2. 69), but the grammar and, happily, the situation for Corydon are very different.

If *Eclogue* 2 is akin to the Simaetha idyll, 8 is its direct descendant. Broadly speaking, the first part of *Idyll* 2 consists of Simaetha's incantations to get Delphis back and the second of her lament and her recollections of her blighted love. Each part has its own refrain. In *Eclogue* 8 Virgil has taken up the themes of incantation on the one hand and lament and recollection on the other, but he has reversed the order and put them into separate amoebaean songs with refrains.

Damon's song,[22] like the second part of *Idyll* 2, is introspective and wholly serious, being a lament over a frustrated passion, with recollections of a happier past. But whereas scholars look to the genre of mime for the sources of the second idyll, in the case of *Eclogue* 8 one must consider both epic and tragedy as the genres with which Virgil has sought to ennoble what he culled from Theocritus. Virgil's intention of writing a monumental poem is evident in its opening where the wonderment of all Nature is framed between two similar lines with an identical ponderous rhythm: *Pastorum Musam Damonis et Alphesiboei, / immemor herbarum quos est mirata iuuenca / certantis, quorum stupefactae carmine lynces, / et mutata suos requierunt flumina cursus, / Damonis Musam dicemus et Alphesiboei*. And in the immediate introduction to Damon's song there is a blend of epic and pastoral features: *Frigida uix caelo noctis discesserat umbra, / cum ros in tenera pecori gratissimus herba: / incumbens tereti Damon sic coepit oliuae* (14-16). Finally, while the idea at 43-5 that Amor has no natural mother but was born of Tmaros or Rhodope or the distant Garamantes may owe something superficially to *Idylls* 3. 15-16 and 7. 76-7, one is reminded most forcibly of *Il.* 16. 33 f., where Patroclus says rocks and sea are Achilles' mother.

Among other tributes to Pollio, Virgil praises his accomplishments as a writer of tragedy (*Ec.* 8. 10), and it is probable that tragic themes are introduced into this poem partly as a compliment to him. However that may be, the eighth eclogue undoubtedly gains in profundity thanks to these themes. Nysa is characterized by υβρις (32, 35, and 19-20, the last implying that she broke solemn vows). *Me malus abstulit error* (41) is reminiscent of the blind infatuation of such tragic heroes as Ajax. Both Damon and Ajax recognize their *error,* and take their lives in consequence of it. The cruelty of Amor is not treated in a superficial Alexandrian way, but the seriousness of Virgil's treatment of it may even recall *Antigone* 781 f. And, however unrealistically for a shepherd, Damon uses Medea as an example of a human being overpowered by love, and he questions whether Man or God is responsible for evil: *saeuus Amor docuit natorum sanguine matrem / commaculare manus; crudelis tu quoque, mater: / crudelis mater magis, an puer improbus ille? / improbus ille puer; crudelis tu quoque, mater* (47-50). These lines, so often condemned for their unloveliness, not only touch on the problem at the heart of so many Greek tragedies but, on a personal level, convey the feeling of one distraught, a man who has through wishful thinking come close to clearing his faithless love of blame, but who at the last moment cannot do it entirely.

Woven into the fabric of this poem are hints of Theocritus' *Liebestod* idylls (1 and 23), but the differences are marked. The emphasis in *Idyll* 1 is on Daphnis' death, not his love, while Virgil concentrates on Damon's love, using the suicide motif only as a kind of frame (20 and 58-60). However, Virgil twice adapts the reversal of nature idea from *Id.* 1. 132-6. Each use has its own justification, and together they lend the poem a formal unity. Nysa's marriage to Mopsus provokes from Damon the embittered outburst *iungentur iam grypes equis, aeuoque sequenti / cum canibus timidi uenient ad pocula dammae* (27-8). At this stage of his lament Damon is stressing the grotesqueness of the union,[23] and Virgil's choice of griffins to mate with mares is particularly apt, as griffins themselves are half lion and half eagle. In ταϛ κυναϛ ωλαφοϛ ελκοι Theocritus has presented a reversal of nature in its most literal sense, i.e. the attacker has become the attacked, but Virgil has in *cum canibus timidi uenient ad pocula dammae* adapted his source to the idea of an unlikely union. The change of grammatical mood, too, is noteworthy. Daphnis' words in *Idyll* 1 have been differently interpreted: he says either that if even he is to die anything can happen or, according to the rival interpretation, that since he is dying he does not care what happens. The reversal of nature is in the optative. However, Damon represents Nysa's marriage as a brutal fact and, in a world already so rotten, he says, grotesque unions will continue to take place. Virgil has attuned his matter to a mood of utter disillusionment.[24] The dying words of Daphnis reappear just before Damon's suicide (52-8). Here some of the alterations are slight. Virgil's subjunctive is equivalent to Theocritus' optative. . . . It is Virgil's progression of thought from this last example that gives the adaptation his individual stamp. The addition of *sit Tityrus Orpheus* leads naturally in the next line to a recurrence of the 'emotive power of song' theme from 2-4, and also neatly introduces a contrast between land and sea which is elaborated on two planes: the next reversal of nature is *omnia vel medium fiat mare*,[25] and Damon is about to forsake land for sea: *uiuite siluae: / praeceps aërii specula de montis in undas / deferar* (58-60).

Damon describes his suicide as his last gift to Nysa (60), just as the lover at *Id.* 23. 21 offers his halter as a gift to the boy who has spurned his love, but otherwise Damon's song has nothing in common with this shallow and unattractive idyll. One must compare, if only to dismiss, *Id.* 3. 25-7, where the threat of the unhappy lover to jump from a rock is not followed up at all, and even the last words of the poem in which he says he will lie down where he has fallen and let the wolves eat him should probably be taken no more seriously. His passion is totally lacking in depth. The whole spirit of his serenade to Amaryllis is different from that of Damon's solitary lament.[26] It is from the third

idyll, also, that Virgil has taken *nunc scio quid sit Amor* . . . (43 and cf. *Id.* 3. 15-16), but we have already observed how Virgil has altered and developed the remarks about the parentage of Amor into something wholly his own, with epic and tragic overtones. In addition, Virgil has deepened the significance of *nunc*. In Theocritus νον is fairly otiose. The only hint of better days occurs in τι μ' ονκετι . . . / . . . καλειϛ (6-7), whereas in *Eclogue* 8 the passage comes just after a beautiful recollection of the first meeting with Nysa. *Nunc* marks the contrast between earlier hope and present despair. Damon's recollection of his first meeting with Nysa (37-40) clearly echoes Polyphemus remembering how he first saw Galatea (*Id.* 11. 25-7), but Virgil is describing the beginning of young love: *paruam te . . . / . . . uidi . . . / alter ab undecimo tum me iam accep erat annus, / iam fragilis poteram a terra contingere ramos.* The conspicuous elisions may represent Damon's youthful hesitation. Damon's love has been nurtured hopefully over the years, whereas nothing indicates that Polyphemus was at an impressionable age when he met Galatea, that the meeting was other than a recent one, or that he ever had grounds for hope. There is a difference, too, in the lovers' explanation of their rejection (cf. *Ec.* 8. 32-5 and *Id.* 11. 30-3). While echoing Polyphemus slightly, Damon says with bitterness that Nysa is haughty and impious, she despises not just his appearance but his whole way of life. The assonance and alliteration of gloomy sounds in this part of Damon's lament widens the gulf between him and the comic, pathetic, grotesque giant.[27]

The emotional pitch of Damon's song is consistently high. By way of contrast Alphesiboeus' song seems to be deliberately drained of emotion. The incantations, unlike Simaetha's, are not interrupted by passionate outbursts. The suicide of Damon contrasts with the happy ending of Alphesiboeus' song where the incantations have their effect and Daphnis comes home. (At the end of *Idyll* 2 Simaetha is still alone and resigned to her lot.) Acts of sympathetic magic are taken over wholesale from *Idyll* 2, with few alterations significant in a literary study: cf. *Ec.* 8. 73-8 and *Id.* 2. 2 (wool); *Ec.* 8. 82 and *Id.* 2. 18, 23-6, 33 (cereals and bay-leaves); *Ec.* 8. 91-3 and *Id.* 2. 53-4 (clothes of the beloved); *Ec.* 8. 95-6 and *Id.* 2. 59-62 (herbs). The instruction about throwing ashes into the stream without turning round (*Ec.* 8. 101-2) comes from Tirosias' speech at *Id.* 24. 93-6. Virgil has elaborated. . . . [it] into *limus ut hic durescit, et haec ut cera liquescit / uno eodemque igni, sic nostro Daphnis amore* (*Ec.* 8. 80-1). We need not linger over the symbolic significance of the clay, which scholars have interpreted variously. The important point is that Virgil has introduced an antithesis with a jingle which is characteristic of such rituals in real life.

Two more radical alterations concern the setting of the poem and its refrain. It is presumably to blend his poem with the rest of the collection that Virgil has transferred his action from the city to a rural décor. Even the eclogues with the loftiest tone and not specifically rural themes are studiously integrated into the collection: *Ec.* 4. 3 *si canimus siluas, siluae sint consule dignae,* and the various instances of life in the Golden Age are set in the country; and the actual setting in which Silenus sings in *Eclogue* 6 is purely rural. In the refrain of Alphesiboeus' song Virgil has, significantly, substituted *carmina* for ιυγξ. Although we may distinguish between *carmen* in the sense of 'poem' or 'song' on the one hand and 'incantation' on the other, to a Roman the meanings merged. Thus Virgil's choice of *carmina* in the refrain (cf. 69-71) is in keeping with the 'emotive power of song' theme recurrent throughout the Eclogues.[28]

Virgil's equivalent of Theocritus' ιππομανες simile (*Id.* 2. 48-50) is the simile of the heifer at *Ec.* 8. 85-9. Owing something to Lucretius 2. 355-66, this passage is remarkable for its pathos and sympathy as well as its evocative natural description. Finally, in producing his own counterpart of Theocritus' macabre section about Hecate (*Id.* 2. 12-14) at 97-9, Virgil has altered the details completely and included a Roman allusion, as the charming away of crops was specifically prohibited in the Twelve Tables.

The above alterations do not destroy one's impression that as a whole Alphesiboeus' song is remarkably like a replica of Simaetha's incantations without her emotional turmoil. But if it had been as deeply felt and as complex in structure as Damon's song the contrast would have been destroyed and the eighth eclogue would have been overloaded. This seems to be the most plausible explanation why Virgil was, for once, content to be almost blatantly Theocritean.

Notes

1. The reader is taken even further away from the romance that lay behind the original thought by an ironic reference which Theocritus chooses to make to Polyphemus' subsequent encounter with Odysseus (61).

2. The epithet refers to the killing of Dirce by Amphion, and also geographically to Thebes, near which Dirce became a fountain.

3. The extravagance of the boast is actually more akin to *Id.* 20. 19-27 (probably not by Theocritus) than to anything said by Polyphemus.

4. 5 lines of introduction, 13 lines of lament, 37 lines of wooing, 13 lines of lament, 5 lines of supposed renunciation.

5. The siesta at noon/Corydon's frenzied activity; the setting of the sun/the blazing of Corydon's passion; town/country; white skin/dark skin; hyacinths/marigolds, etc. The first two contrasts were suggested in general idea by *Id.* 2. 38-40, of which there is a very close imitation at *Ec.* 9. 57-8. Rather interestingly, this latter passage involves no contrast at all, as the stillness of nature is used by Lycidas only as a reason for sitting down to sing.

6. The setting of the ninth eclogue is clearly based on that of Theocritus' οαλνοςια, but the sorrow of the

dispossessed and the convulsions of the state are in stark contrast to the pleasant diversions of Simichidas and his companions. Compare *Ec.* 9. 1 and *Id.* 7. 21; *Ec.* 9. 32-6 and *Id.* 7. 37-41; *Ec.* 9. 59-60 and *Id.* 7. 10-11 for close imitations in this poem.

7. Virgil has not only toned down *Id.* 5. 1-4, but has actually used the idea to help his poem structurally. Damoetas retorts that Damon was withholding the goat which he, Damoetas, had won in a singing match, and when Menalcas doubts whether this were possible, Damoetas proposes the competition which is the main point of the poem. The Greek version has no such neat transition from abuse to song.

8. In his own way Virgil, too, uses strong language. . . .

9. Cf. *Ec.* 1. 51-8, where Virgil reproduces many individual details from *Id.* 7. 131-46 and acknowledges his Theocritean legacy by the addition of *Hyblaeis* (54). But Virgil's tone is, again, different. The Theocritean passage is pure description, bringing a happy poem to a fitting close, while in the first eclogue Menalcas is wistfully alluding to the joys that await Tityrus, but not him. Virgil has thus imbued the passage with intense emotion as well as integrating it into what is essentially a political poem.

10. Cf. *Dic mihi, Damoeta, cuium pecus? an Meliboei? / Non, uerum Aegonis; nuper mihi tradidit Aegon* and Ειπε μοι, ωΚορνδων, τινος αι βοες;να Φιλυνδα; / ονκ, αλλ' Αιγωνος βοςκειν δε μοι αντας Εδωκεν. Another very close imitation, at *Ec.* 9. 23-5 (cf. *Id.* 3. 3-5), may be explained as follows: the various snatches from Menalcas' poetry are representative of different facets of Virgil's art. *Ec.* 9. 23-5 symbolizes Virgil still finding his feet, while the second Theocritean echo (cf. *Ec.* 9. 39-43 and *Id.* 11. 42-9) shows him as being much more emancipated from his model. The address to Varus (*Ec.* 9. 27-9) represents the Italian elements as well as the personal and political ones in the *Eclogues,* while the final quotation from Menalcas' works (*Ec.* 9. 46-50) blends pastoral and Roman elements together.

11. *Cuium* occurs in comedy, and it is worth drawing attention also to lines 49-53, which have a comic flavour in language, in Menalcas' deliberate misunderstanding of Damoetas' remarks, and in Palaemon's incredibly opportune arrival. *Quin age, si quid habes* is actually an echo from a discarded section of *Id.* 5 concerning the talkativeness of Comatas. At *Id.* 5. 78 is an expression of impatience, whereas Virgil's echo of it begins Damoetas' answer to Menalcas' charge that he is seeking to avoid the contest.

12. Virgil introduces an interesting complication by making Aegon and Menalcas rivals for Neaera. Menalcas' *ac ne me sibi praeferat illa ueretur*

shows a rather delightful self-confidence, which may even be a compensation for defeat.

13. The naming of the craftsman at *Ec.* 3. 37 is, however, suggested by *Id.* 5. 105.

14. e.g. 8. 2-4, but the power of song is illustrated most graphically in *Eclogue* 9. where Lycidas' and Moeris' utter despondency about their dispossession and the upheaval in the state is dispelled by their loving recollection of Menalcas' poetry.

15. Although Theocritus' sycophantic seventeenth idyll begins Ἐκ Διος αρχωμεσθα, Virgil here plainly harks back to the opening lines of Aratus' *Phaenomena*. . . . Ironically, the young Virgil could hardly have known that this hint of Stoicism in the *Eclogues* foreshadowed in part the spirit of his third great work.

16. For contemporary literary allusions in bucolic poetry Virgil had a precedent in *Id.* 7. 39-41 and 45-8.

17. *Ec.* 5. 1-19 is much more than a mere fusion of Theocritus and Virgil. *Tu maior; tibi me est aequum parere, Menalca* (4) could be spoken by one of Socrates' interlocutors, and the decorous tone of the conversation which takes place as the two men are walking along together in such pleasant surroundings is reminiscent of the philosophical dialogue in general. Such an introduction adds great dignity to Virgil's poem, whether it is meant as a tribute to Caesar or not.

18. Formally, *Ec.* 10 owes more to *Id.* 1 than does Mopsus' song: cf. *Ec.* 10. -12 and *Id* 1 66-9; *Ec.* 10. 18 and *Id.* 1. 109; *Ec.* 10. 19-30 and *Id.* 1. 77-85. Gallus, like Daphnis, is wasting away through love, and all Nature is in sympathy with him. Virgil's daring manifests itself in putting Gallus, the soldier-poet, into a bucolic setting. The Virgilian poem alone has considerable psychological complexity. The reader follows the stages of Gallus' struggle against the realities of his life, how he tries hard, but vainly, to fit into the dream-like world which Virgil has created for him.

19. The only point at which Mopsus' song echoes Theocritus outside Thyrsis' song is 32-4. Here the construction reflects *Idylls* 8. 79-80 and 18. 29-31, but the details are different without being very novel.

20. The fact that two of the sources, *Idylls* 8 and 9, are nowadays generally considered spurious is here irrelevant.

21. Daphnis' words contain a surprise for the reader as well. The two 'Arcadians' turn out to be Arcadians only in spirit, worthy disciples of Pan. They are seated by Virgil's own Mincius! It is not that Virgil is reckless of geography, or that Corydon and Thyrsis are descended from slaves brought from Arcadia, as some have seriously suggested. Virgil has gently misled his readers, who should take the hint and not be too humourless about the rest of the poem.

22. It is quite likely that Damon is not singing in his own person, but it is convenient to call the lover Damon.

23. A little later, however, his mood has changed and he exclaims with bitter irony that she got the husband she deserved (32).

24. Cf. *Ec.* 1. 59-63, where Virgil gives the reversal of nature theme yet another original twist. Tityrus in fact says that all nature will be topsy-turvy before he forgets Octavian, i.e. he will never forget him. The individual details are Virgil's own, and he has given the passage an appropriately political flavour by referring to Rome's enemies and the boundaries of the Roman Empire. Moreover, the hypothetical, or rather impossible, migrations of Tityrus' lines are immediately matched by the very real ones gloomily foreshadowed by Meliboeus in his reply.

25. The theory that Virgil misunderstood παντα δ' Εναλλα (or αναλλα) γενοιτο is now, happily, unfashionable. Scholars suggest with rather greater plausibility that the *sound* of the Greek made Virgil think of the sea.

26. A similar distinction was drawn above between Polyphemus' song in *Id.* 11 and Corydon's in *Ec.* 2.

27. It is interesting that Damon's song contains only one obvious verbal reminiscence of Simaetha's lament with which it has so much in common in tone and subject-matter. . . . Virgil's daring linguistic innovation in *ut . . ., ut . . ., ut . . .* presupposes his readers' acquaintance with the Greek idiom in his models. Also, his hiatus is clearly inspired by the one at the same point of the second Theocritus passage. However, this hiatus together with the preceding heavy elision gives Virgil's line a unique emotional quality. Finally, note how Virgil's line, [and] especially the introduction of *error*, act as a bridge between the preceding romantic passage and the following epic/tragic one.

28. In Damon's refrain Virgil's remodelling a αρχετε βουκολικας, Μοιςαι, παλιν αρχετ' from *Idyll* 1 as *incipe Maenalios mecum, mea tibia, uersus* looks forward especially to *Eclogue* 10, with its dream-like setting in Arcadia.

Gordon Williams (essay date 1974)

SOURCE: "A Version of Pastoral: Virgil, *Eclogue* 4" in *Quality and Pleasure in Latin Poetry*, edited by Tony Woodman and David West, Cambridge University Press, 1974, pp. 31-47.

[In the essay below, Williams offers a line-by-line analysis of Eclogue *4, contending that the poem's meaning is linked to its historical significance: it is concerned primarily with the establishment of peace in the Roman world, the end of civil war, and the onset of a new era.]*

Sicelides Musae, paulo maiora canamus:
non omnis arbusta iuuant humilesque myricae—
si canimus siluas, siluae sint consule dignae.

Vltima Cumaei uenit iam carminis aetas:
magnus ab integro saeclorum nascitur ordo.
iam redit et uirgo, redeunt Saturnia regna:
iam noua progenies caelo demittitur alto.
tu modo nascenti puero, quo ferrea primum
desinet ac toto surget gens aurea mundo,
casta faue Lucina: tuus iam regnat Apollo.

(teque adeo decus hoc aeui, te consule, inibit,
Pollio, et incipient magni procedere menses;
te duce, si qua manent sceleris uestigia nostri,
inrita perpetua soluent formidine terras.)

ille deum uitam accipiet diuisque uidebit
permixtos heroas et ipse uidebitur illis,
pacatumque reget patriis uirtutibus orbem.

at tibi prima, puer, nullo munuscula cultu
errantis hederas passim cum baccare tellus
mixtaque ridenti colocasia fundet acantho.
ipsae lacte domum referent distenta capellae
ubera, nec magnos metuent armenta leones.
ipsa tibi blandos fundent cunabula flores.
occidet et serpens, et fallax herba ueneni
occidet; Assyrium uulgo nascetur amomum.

at simul heroum laudes et facta parentis
iam legere et quae sit poteris cognoscere uirtus,
molli paulatim flauescet campus arista
incultisque rubens pendebit sentibus uua
et durae quercus sudabunt roscida mella.
pauca tamen suberunt priscae uestigia fraudis,
quae temptare Thetim ratibus, quae cingere muris
oppida, quae iubeant telluri infindere sulcos;
alter erit tum Tiphys et altera quae uehat Argo
delectos heroas, erunt etiam altera bella
atque iterum ad Troiam magnus mittetur Achilles.

hinc, ubi iam firmata uirum te fecerit aetas,
cedet et ipse mari uector, nec nautica pinus
mutabit merces; omnis feret omnia tellus—
non rastros patietur humus, non uinea falcem,
robustus quoque iam tauris iuga soluet arator.
nec uarios discet mentiri lana colores,
ipse sed in pratis aries iam suaue rubenti
murice, iam croceo mutabit uellera luto;
sponte sua sandyx pascentis uestiet agnos.

'Talia saecla' suis dixerunt 'currite' fusis
concordes stabili fatorum numine Parcae.
adgredere o magnos (aderit iam tempus) honores,
cara deum suboles, magnum Iouis incrementum!
aspice conuexo nutantem pondere mundum,
terrasque tractusque maris caelumque profundum;
aspice, uenturo laetentur ut omnia saeclo!

(o mihi tum longae maneat pars ultima uitae,
spiritus et quantum sat erit tua dicere facta!
non me carminibus uincet nec Thracius Orpheus
nec Linus, huic mater quamuis atque huic pater adsit,
Orphei Calliopea, Lino formosus Apollo.

Pan etiam, Arcadia mecum si iudice certet,
Pan etiam Arcadia dicat se iudice uictum.)

incipe, parue puer, risu cognoscere matrem
(matri longa decem tulerunt fastidia menses),
incipe, parue puer: qui non risere parenti,
nec deus hunc mensa, dea nec dignata cubili est.

1-3 The poet begins with a prayer for inspiration to the Muses whom he deliberately calls 'Sicilian' to designate Theocritus[1] as his model; this emphasis is expanded in the next three words—the theme is to be grander than any normal pastoral theme. This elevation is further explained in the next two lines by symbolizing pastoral poetry in a common feature of its landscape as described by Theocritus, *myricae* 'tamarisks'.[2] The word *humiles* here not only describes the shrub but also suggests that pastoral themes normally lack elevation.[3] The climax of the opening is reached with *consule*: the poet intends to address a Roman consul, therefore the subject-matter (*siluae*) must be grander than usual. The tone is not apologetic, but excited.

4-7 The tone deepens as the poet utters a solemn prophecy. This is marked by the parallelism of each of two pairs of line-long sentences. In the first (4-5), each line is framed by adjective and noun in agreement (*ultima . . . aetas; magnus . . . ordo*),[4] and the second line (5) expands and explains the first. 'The last age of the Sibylline prophecy has come' is portentous (with precise symmetry) and riddling; the poet says nothing more of this Sibylline prophecy, but his words refer it to the famous Italian Sibyl[5] and assume the reader's understanding of that reference.[6] When the poet says the age 'has come', he is, as will become clear, slightly anticipating: the age will actually begin with the birth of the child, to be mentioned in lines 8-9. The phrase *magnus saeclorum ordo* is ambiguous since there is no definite article in Latin, and it could mean either 'the great cycle of ages' or 'a great series of centuries';[7] the former interpretation is ruled out by line 4 since the 'last age' is clearly identical with the 'Golden Age' of the poem.[8] This means that the common interpretation of *magnus ordo* as referring to the Stoic concept of a *Magnus Annus*[9] is mistaken: that would involve a repetition of the series of 'Ages',[10] and contradict the sense of *ultima aetas*. The Sibyl's prediction is of a final age that will be ideal and will last for ever; *magnus* (5) is used in an emotive, not a descriptive, way.[11] So the lines (4-5) mean: 'The final age of the Sibyl's prophecy has come; a grand succession of centuries is beginning from a completely new start.'

The second pair of lines (6-7) is linked by anaphora of *iam* and makes precise what was meant by (5) *ab integro*. The Virgin is returning to earth: this is Justice, called Virgin because she was identified with the constellation Virgo . . ., having been placed there when she left degenerate men in the Age of Bronze.[12] Also the age of Saturn is returning: by this was meant the original Golden Age, identified as the age of Saturn by Virgil.[13] This line has a particularly artistic shape, since the repetition of the verb (*redit . . . redeunt*) can function as a repetition of *et,* and the structure is equivalent to the prose sentence *et Virgo et Saturnia regna redeunt.*[14] The prophecy reaches its climax and becomes most specific in line 7. Here *nova progenies* means 'new race of men', a meaning which becomes obvious if the reader thinks of the Ages of Men as described by Hesiod and Aratus, since the ages were treated by both poets in terms of the men who lived in them, and since Hesiod spoke specifically of each age of men being successively created and destroyed by Zeus. The language reflects the traditional account of the Ages of Men. There is now a pause and change of direction.

8-10 The poet turns aside into a prayer. This break comes after the momentous words *caelo demittitur alto,* and allows the poet not only to give an oblique explanation of *nova progenies,* but also to introduce an astonishing new assertion. A boy is being born and the disappearance of 'iron' men and the rise of 'golden' men are directly[15] related to his birth. The future tenses here are simple and absolutely authoritative. So the poet calls on the goddess of child birth (who is Diana—or Artemis—in one of her aspects) to assist at the birth, and adds, by way of encouragement, that her brother Apollo 'is in control' (*regnat*). The form of the words need not imply an ascendancy of Apollo at the expense of other deities;[16] they can express a fact relative only to the immediate situation.[17] There are several sides to this. In one way the assertion refers to the Sibylline oracle, for which Apollo (as god of prophecy and especially the god who controlled the Sibyl) was the ultimate authority. But the confident future tenses of the poet suggest superior knowledge. Here it is relevant that the break and change of direction between lines 7 and 8 show that the birth of the child was not part of the original oracle but is being added by the poet. This is underlined by the mention of Apollo here since the poet is unlikely to be imagining that there was any reference to Apollo in the oracle which Apollo had himself inspired and, as it were, dictated to the Sibyl.[18] The implication is rather that Apollo has revealed something to the poet that was not mentioned in the oracle,[19] and that the poet suddenly realizes, with Apollo's help, that not only was the oracle true but that the birth of the child is intimately connected with the fulfilment of the oracle. It is because of this that he can assure Diana 'your brother now is in control'; he means by this both that the oracle is coming true and also that the poet is himself personally being inspired by Apollo. For the birth of the child (as will become clear) is associated with the recent Peace of Brundisium[20] (its effects are treated as still in the future) which the poet goes on now to mention in the following parenthesis (11-14); and, beyond the parenthesis, the poet expounds further miracles connected with the child which can only have come to him by Apollo's revelation. So (10) *tuus iam regnat Apollo* functions dramatically (as it were) as an encouragement to Diana, but poetically to the reader as an indication of the poet's source for his assertions here. That is, the 'control' of Apollo is evidenced by the conception of the child, by the Peace of Brundisium and by Apollo's further revelations to the poet. The control of Apollo may also express the important concept that, civil

war being now over, the arts of civilization (which were Apollo's concern) will now be practised without hindrance.

Something of Virgil's meaning here can be illustrated by a poem which was clearly influenced by *Eclogue* 4, that is Tibullus 2. 5. There Apollo is asked to attend at his temple on the Palatine, where Augustus had deposited the Sibylline books, for the installation of the new *quindecimuir,* Messalinus. Apollo is invoked as wearing laurels of triumph (5); this refers to the battle of Actium and points to the idea that Apollo not only foretells the future but also, in some degree, sees that his predictions are carried out. His control of the future is emphasized (11-16) and especially (15-16) *te duce Romanos numquam frustrata Sibylla | abdita quae senis fata canit pedibus.* At a later stage in the poem (71-8) Tibullus lists the portents connected with the murder of Julius Caesar and the last stages of the civil war; then (79) he says that all these were in the past, and calls on Apollo who is now *mitis* to sink prodigies in the sea and to produce an omen for a new age (80-2). Here, quite clearly, the prodigies and the events portended by them are treated as interchangeable and Apollo's actions will be effective not only in foreshadowing the future but also in actually bringing it to realization. It is this way of thinking, by which Apollo is regarded as responsible for the future which he foresees, that Virgil expresses in saying *tuus iam regnat Apollo;* and *regnat* expresses the same idea as Tibullus in (15) *te duce.*

11-14 A parenthesis[21] here adds a further address and connects the miracle with concrete events on earth. This glorious age[22] will begin in Pollio's consulship and the great months will commence their course. Here (12) *magnus* has the same emotive function as in line 5 and it likewise has no hint of the Stoic Great Year about it. The phrase *magni menses* can only naturally refer to the period of a pregnancy and the line is taken up at the end of the poem by (61) *matri longa decem tulerunt fastidia menses.* The implication of these two lines (11-12), as a parenthesis following on the mention of the child and of the child's connexion with the coming of (9) *gens aurea,* is that a child has been conceived in Pollio's consulship and that future generations will date the beginning of the glorious age by saying *consule Pollione.* But the next two lines assign a much more active role to Pollio and culminate in an impressive prophecy (14): Pollio will lead the Roman people in rendering harmless (*inrita*) all traces of sin[23] and so relieve the world from its never-ending fear. Both Horace and Virgil constantly refer to the civil war which tore Rome and Italy apart almost continuously for over half a century from about 90 B.C. as 'sin' (*scelus*).[24] Here there is a clear reference to the part which Pollio played in bringing about the Peace of Brundisium in September 40 B.C.[25] This address to a mere individual human being (after a goddess) is cleverly managed in a parenthesis, as the poet turns aside for a moment from his grand theme, motivated by the mention of the child's birth; these four lines also serve to establish the entire historical setting for the poem.

15-17 The poet prophesies that the child will live as if he were a god on earth[26] and will meet with gods and heroes face to face on earth—thus bringing back a feature of the Golden Age whose loss was explicitly regretted by Catullus (64. 384ff.).[27] Finally, the child will rule with inherited virtues a world made peaceful.[28] This prophecy connects with the poet's words to Lucina (8-10), and, just as it is implied that the poet's prophetic authority is there derived from Lucina's brother Apollo, so here in 15-17 the poet relies on the same prophetic source.[29] This section reaches its climax and end with an impressive line (17) framed between adjective and noun in agreement.[30]

18-45 The next section of the poem (18-45) is divided into three parts. Here the poet switches direction again and apostrophizes the still unborn infant. The contrast in (18) *at tibi prima* means that what has just been said (15-17) was looking further into the future, under Apollo's guidance, than what is now to be said. The poet here describes the Golden Age in nature.

(i) 18-25 The earth will, without cultivation (a traditional feature of the Golden Age), produce gifts for the child[31]—a series of plants with medicinal or cosmetic functions (18-20); pastoral poetry is particularly fond of the names of plants; their sound and strangeness here create one of the specific effects of pastoral poetry[32] and mark the move away from the elevated prophetic style of the last section. Of their own accord (*ipsae*) goats will bring back udders distended with milk: this detail mirrors two features of the Golden Age, its plenty and the absence of work (a goatherd is not needed). A detail follows (22) which belongs to another feature of the Golden Age: men were vegetarians then. This is a widespread feature of descriptions of the Golden Age;[33] only Plato in *Politicus* 271d-e adds the further, logically related, concept that men and animals lived together in harmony so that there was 'no savagery nor eatings of one another, nor was there war nor dissension at all'. It is not that lions did not exist then, but that they were not carnivores. The next detail (23) is introduced by a sense of *ipsa* which differs from that of (21) *ipsae:*[34] 'his very cradle will produce sweet flowers'—this detail is unparalleled in literature before Virgil's time.[35] There follow (24-5) the deaths of snakes and poisonous plants and the growing of the scented Assyrian balsam everywhere. No writer before Virgil says that snakes did not exist in the Golden Age, but in **Georgics** 1. 129 he asserts that god put poison into snakes at a later stage. To destroy them (and poisonous plants) is the one act of violence in the production of the new Golden Age.[36] This section ends (25) with a clause framed between adjective and noun,[37] and notable for its musical sounds.

(ii) 26-36 The child is now depicted as of an age to read, and he reads the favourite themes of Romans, their own great past history;[38] from this he will learn what *uirtus* is. This child has another advantage: he can read of his own father's great deeds (26 *facta parentis*). Once he reaches this age, further features of the Golden Age will appear: (28) corn will grow of its own accord[39] (another 'framed'

line); grapes (29) will grow, without cultivation, on thornbushes (a 'golden' line);[40] and (30) honey will sweat from oaks.[41] These three lines (28-30) are remarkable for their variation of a basic two nouns with adjectives and a verb (28 has an adverb instead of one adjective) into three different patterns. Now (31-3) comes a warning, a chilling of enthusiasm and a slowing down of the tempo of change, in the form of a tricolon crescendo (see above, p. 5 and n. 5) with anaphora of *quae*. Traces of the old sin (*priscae vestigia fraudis*)[42] will however remain, and these will prolong habits of seafaring,[43] of walling cities (for protection) and of ploughing. All of these were characteristic features of the Iron Age. Then, in another tricolon crescendo (with *alter . . . et altera . . . ; erunt etiam altera . . .*) the leading characteristic of the Iron Age is exemplified—war; but here, with mention of the Argo and its helmsman Tiphys and the Argonauts and finally with mention of Achilles and the expedition to Troy, war appears in its heroic form against external enemies (*iusta bella* as Romans would have said) and not as the shameful civil war of line 31. Here, in the mention of the Argonauts, there is another recall of Catullus 64, and, of course, most of all in the prominence given to Achilles in the expedition to Troy.[44]

(iii) 37-45 Now (37) the child is pictured as a full-grown man, and the poet foresees that not only will sailing cease (38), but all seaborne commerce (38-9). The reason is (39) that the earth will everywhere produce everything (that man needs), so that exchange of products will be unnecessary. Then two lines (40-1) specify that this will involve man in no labour: no violence will be done to soil or trees or ploughingoxen.[45] Line 40 is chiastic in form, and 41 concludes the thought with another 'framed' line. These two lines (40-1) also form a tricolon crescendo, with the negatives taken up by the positive *soluet* in 41. Here again is another distinct reminiscence of Catullus 64.[46] There follows a fantastic idea, expressed in complex and difficult language (42-5): dyeing, a deceitful and laborious process, will no longer be necessary—sheep in the fields will grow purple and yellow and scarlet fleeces. The unusual words and the ornate expression of the three colours attempt to achieve something of the same exotic effect in pastoral poetry as the naming of rare plants,[47] but the idea is extravagant, even silly, and it is not surprising that it is found nowhere else in Classical literature. The shaping of the lines is particularly artistic: first (42) a line-long general statement, which is a 'framed' line;[48] then the subject of the next clause is stated (43) *ipse sed in pratis aries* and the sentence is executed in the form of a dicolon with anaphora of *iam* and the verb postponed to the second colon;[49] then the whole section is closed (45) with a solemn statement in asyndeton (i.e. without a co-ordinating word such as *et*), commencing with the authoritative *sponte sua* and a notable triple alliteration,[50] and conveying the sense of an unanswerable assertion. Virgil has here lavished his art on an idea which he perhaps sensed would not carry poetic conviction.

46-47 There is a pause and the poet records that 'the Fates, who speak in concord the fixed will of Destiny, said to their spindles "May times like that arrive quickly" '. The word *talis* is often used in Latin poetry to look back over, and sum up, a section of poetic composition.[51] Here there would be no point in making the Fates say this to their spindles unless they had themselves at some time spoken the prophecy in 18-45. This is simply the poet's way of expressing the idea that in 18-45 he has merely been repeating the prophecy of the Fates. In fact, were it not for the introductory particle (18) *at,* it would be possible to print 18-45 in inverted commas as being the actual speech of the Fates. The purpose of the poet's taking over the exposition of the prophecy was to enable him to dominate the poem in the form of an address to the unborn child from line 18 to the end, since the Fates (as in Catullus 64) would only deliver the prophecy to the parents (not to the child who *ex hypothesi* was not yet conceived). Here is another obvious reference to Catullus 64. Catullus seems to have invented the idea that the Parcae spoke the prophecy about Achilles at the wedding of Peleus and Thetis.[52] Their prophecy there is lengthy (323-81) and is marked by the recurrent refrain *currite ducentes subtegmina, currite, fusi.* The fact that in Virgil the prophecy concerns the birth and growth to maturity of a child (as in Catullus) together with the fact of Virgil's constant reference to Catullus 64 can only mean that the reader is to understand for himself that in Virgil too the prophecy of the Fates was made on the occasion of a wedding. This is underlined by the tense of (46) *dixerunt* which is the only true aorist in the poem (in 4 *uenit* is a true perfect) and which consequently refers to a specific occasion in the past. The contrast between the prophecies in Catullus and Virgil could not be more extreme; that of Catullus is extremely pessimistic, that of Virgil wildly optimistic.

THE MEANING AND STRUCTURE OF 18-47

In other writers Golden Ages were magical times: they existed, they ceased to exist, but one could not possibly imagine a Golden Age gradually coming into being, growing little by little, and no writer before Virgil conceived such a picture. But Virgil has divided the Golden Age into three instalments, as it were, to be handed out at the birth of the child, at his reaching the age of education, and finally at his coming of age as a man. He had the further idea that there should be an intimate connexion between the child's birth and the beginning of the Golden Age. There were two serious difficulties here: (i) the actual establishment of a sympathetic connexion between the child and the New Age; (ii) the devising of some mechanism for slowing down the coming of the Golden Age. Both aims were realized by incorporating among the traditional elements of Golden Ages elements that were quite novel. In 18-25 the novel element is the poet's capacity to address the boy and assert that the new Age would do certain things specifically for him. One of these is the otherwise unheard of flowering of his cradle, and this line (23) is placed in such a position that it breaks up a series of traditional features which could not be linked intimately with the child. The other—the concept of the earth rejoicing at this birth and giving him presents *nullo cultu,* of its own accord (18-20)—has two important analogies in

earlier literature. In *Idyll* 17. 64ff. Theocritus (Virgil's pastoral model) describes how the personified island of Cos rejoiced at the birth of Ptolemy and invoked blessings on him. In this, however, Theocritus was inspired by a more significant predecessor: in the *Homeric Hymn to Apollo* (61ff.) Delos takes an active interest in the birth of Apollo, prophesies about him and hopes for future honours from him. This motif was taken up by Callimachus in his hymn to Delos (4. 260-74). This connexion with Apollo is significant in view of the part that Apollo plays in this *Eclogue.* This god was firmly in the forefront of the poet's mind.

In 26-36, the novel element is the mechanism for slowing down the Golden Age, (31) *pauca tamen suberunt priscae vestigia fraudis,* and allowing specific elements of the Iron Age to remain particularly that of war—but the wars to come are symbolized in terms of the great heroic wars of the past. To anyone looking round the world in 40 B.C. it was clear that war could not immediately end—to look no further the shameful and dangerous defeat of the Roman army under Crassus in 53 B.C. was still unavenged—but it would no longer be disgraceful civil war. The slowing down also allows the elements of ploughing and seafaring to last on and be negated in the third instalment. But there (37-45) it was not sufficient for the poet simply to negate elements that had already been mentioned, and so he invented the fantastic idea of the sheep grazing varicoloured in the fields as a new and positive element.

This whole section of the poem is clearly the real basis to its claim to be pastoral in genre, and it is also the point where virgil devoted his whole art to combine the details of the Sibylline oracle (the traditional concept of a Golden Age) and his own new inspiration (the theme of the birth of a politically significant child); in this grand conception he tried to weld these themes into a unity, without complete success.

48-63[53] That this should probably be regarded as a single paragraph is indicated by the related imperatives (48) *adgredere* and (60) *incipe.* The address to the child in 48-9 is solemn and high-flown: this is shown not only by the honorific titles that fill line 49, but also by the use of *o* with the imperative in 48, which is always elevated and emotional.[54] The time indication (to become in 60ff. the subject of the poet's impatience), which looks forward over the three periods of the child's growth, is neatly subordinated in a parenthesis. The *magnos honores* which the child is urged to enter upon are those which the poet has described particularly in the three stages of 18-45. On the other hand, the vocative phrases in 49 refer particularly to the poet's revelation (derived from Apollo) in 15-17; the child is *cara deum suboles* 'a cherished descendant of gods', and this phrase is then expanded with the extraordinary *magnum Iouis incrementum.* The meaning here must be that the child is an 'ally', or a 'reinforcement' of Iuppiter,[55] somewhat as Thucydides uses the corresponding Greek word αυξησις in 1. 69. 4 . . . ('alone failing to stop the reinforcement of your enemies as it is just beginning but only when it is on the point of doubling'). Virgil's use of *incrementum* here is without real parallel in Latin, but Cicero *De Finibus* 2. 88 (*qui bonum omne in uirtute ponit, is potest dicere perfici beatam uitam perfectione uirtutis; negat summo bono afferre incrementum diem*) and Juvenal 14. 259 (*incrementa domus*) come close to it. It anticipates ideas that Horace and Virgil were later to express about Augustus:[56] for example, Horace, *Odes* 1. 12. 49-52:

> gentis humanae pater atque custos
> orte Saturno, tibi cura magni
> Caesaris fatis data: tu secundo
> Caesare regnes.

Augustus is there regarded as Iuppiter's right-hand man, his vice-gerent on earth. The child in *Ecl.* 4. 49 is Iuppiter's *incrementum* in that sense.

Now (50-2), by way of encouragement, the poet calls on the child to see how the whole universe anticipates his coming.[57] 'The whole universe, with its arched weight (*conuexo . . . pondere* i.e. the sky), is trembling.' Then the poet expands the word *mundus* into its constituent parts: the land, the tracts of the sea and the depth of heaven. The trembling of the world (*nutare*) here does not signify imminent collapse, but mirrors the traditional reaction of nature to the epiphany of a god[58]—for example, the phenomena which Callimachus describes (*Hymn to Apollo* 2. 1-8) as Apollo is about to appear in his temple: 'How the laurel branch of Apollo quivers! How the whole shrine trembles! Away, away all sinful persons. Now indeed Phoebus knocks at the door with his fair foot. Look: don't you see? The Delian palm-tree suddenly swayed . . . gently; the swan in the sky sings sweetly. Of their own accord now let the bolts of the gates swing back, now too the locks. The god is now not far off. Young men, prepare for the song and for the dance.' Virgil makes the whole universe move in anticipation, and then (52) calls on the child to see 'how everything is rejoicing at the prospect of the age to come'. Here the 'framed' sentence *uenturo . . . saeclo* brings the idea to an impressive conclusion.

Now (53-9), with a slight pause (signified by asyndeton and change of direction), the poet in parenthesis muses—mostly to himself, though still formally addressing his thoughts to the child (indicated only in 54 *tua*). He thinks what a wonderful subject for poetry will be the child's life and deeds; and he wishes (53) that 'the final part of a long life may last out' for him—he means, may his life be long and its last part (when the child has grown up) be long enough[59]—and that he may have enough *spiritus*[60] (which means both poetic inspiration and also the capacity to express it) to sing of the child's deeds. When Virgil mentions *tua dicere facta* he is thinking of a different genre of poetry, as when he says to Pollio in *Ecl.* 8. 7-8 *en erit umquam | ille dies mihi cum liceat tua dicere facta?* and at the beginning of *Ecl.* 6 he regrets that Apollo stopped him (3) *cum canerem reges et proelia* and then consoles Varus with the words (6-7) *namque super tibi erunt qui dicere laudes, | Vare, tuas cupiant et tristia condere bella.* In us-

ing such language Virgil is always thinking of epic poetry, and it may well be that in such passages he was expressing a real personal ambition. But caution is needed, since these passages are related to the form of *recusatio* which Augustan poets used as an oblique way of expressing such praises, while at the same time declaring themselves incapable, or else postponing them (as in *Ecl.* 4. 54) to an indefinite future.[61] This possibility is underlined by the highly formalized series of comparisons into which the poet now launches himself. The first (55-7) amounts to saying that neither Orpheus nor Linus will outdo him; and the second (58-9) to saying that he will defeat even Pan. The poets or musicians (the concepts were conventionally interchangeable) which the poet thinks of are partly pastoral—Linus appears as a shepherd in *Ecl.* 6. 67 and Pan is the god of the pan-pipes and of the region which Virgil was the first to use as a setting for pastoral poetry;[62] but Orpheus is not particularly pastoral. Antiquity and distinction were the real reasons for choosing Orpheus and Linus; and Pan was chosen not just for his relevance to this pastoral poet, but because he gave ground for an utterance of a particularly Theocritean pattern at a point where Virgil's pastoral model was being left far behind. In fact, it looks as if Virgil in lines 55-9 deliberately employed some characteristic conventions of pastoral poetry. Patterned phrases, with symmetrical elements of repetition are a characteristic feature of Theocritus' poetry.[63] Virgil also uses these patterns in his *Eclogues,* but in a much more restrained way. The structure of 55-7, where *non me carminibus uincet* is followed by three parallel clauses in which the subject is successively expanded, has some similarity in literary motivation to Theocritus, *Idyll* 16. 3-4: . . .

> *The Muses are goddesses and, as goddesses, they sing of gods;*
> *but we are mortals here and, as mortals, let us sing of mortals.*

The Virgilian structure is more sophisticated, but what both have in common is the interest in giving the patterning of verbal structures priority over the actual thought which has to be expressed. This motive can be seen in various passages of the *Eclogues:* for instance, 6. 9-12; 7. 1-5; 8. 22-4; 8. 47-50; 8. 52-6. It can be no coincidence that this motive operates in Virgil most strongly at the beginnings of poems and in particularly formal passages of song. The motive reaches a climax, however, in *Eclogue* 4. 58-9, and to this there are clear Theocritean analogies:[64] for example *Idyll* 1. 120-1: . . .

> *I am that Daphnis who here herded his cows; the Daphnis who*
> *here watered his bulls and heifers.*

or *Idyll* 11. 22-3: . . .

> *You come right near to me whenever sweet sleep subdues me and*
> *you go straight away whenever sweet sleep releases me.*

The only real analogy in the *Eclogues* to *Ecl.* 4. 58-9 is 6. 29-30:

> nec tantum Phoebo gaudet Parnasia rupes,
> nec tantum Rhodope miratur et Ismarus Orphea.

The stylistic motive in *Eclogue* 4. 55-9 must be that, at this point, where the poet looks forward to a different form of poetic composition and a new subject-matter, he casts his thought in the most characteristically pastoral style—a feature which also serves to underline the element of *recusatio* here (i.e. this really is a pastoral poet who is expressing this wish and one who is still imprisoned within the pastoral form). The reader is not unjustified in feeling that the poet is here anxious to assert his pastoral identity in a poem which has risen so far above the traditional genre.

Now (60-4) the poet appeals again to the child really to hurry up and be born, though he puts this in the form of a request to recognize his mother with a smile and discreetly expresses in a parenthesis the idea that his mother has carried him long enough (the line directly recalls line 12). He urgently repeats the request, and adds (62-3) the warning that if a child does not smile on his mother,[65] then no god will invite him to his table nor goddess to her bed. In this he thinks mainly of Hercules, the hero who was reckoned among the great benefactors of mankind and who was admitted to heaven and given Hebe in marriage.[66] But the second element of the warning (which ends the poem) also recalls Anchises who was considered by Venus worthy of her bed and who thereby founded the Julian line (which issued most recently in Julius Caesar and Octavian). The patterning of the language in the last sentence conceals a lightness of touch that is at the opposite extreme from the solemnity of the poem's opening (in 3ff.).

The 'Meaning' of the Poem

The clue lies in the historical background. After the battle of Philippi in 42 B.C.,[67] Antony, the senior partner, sent Octavian back with the veterans due for retirement to Italy, while he himself went to the Near East. Octavian's task was the highly dangerous one of pensioning off the veterans in the only way then known to the Romans, i.e. by confiscating land and settling them on it.[68] This led—as no doubt Antony anticipated—to fierce civil war in Italy. A key figure in all this was Gaius Asinius Pollio who had been a close friend of Julius Caesar, but who had no taste for civil war and had only joined Caesar out of friendship (see Cicero, *Ad Fam.* 10. 31). After the murder of Caesar in 44 B.C., his natural allegiance lay with Antony. He had in 43 B.C. been designated to the consulship for 40 B.C., but during the civil wars over Octavian's resettlement of veterans in 41/40 B.C. he played a very ambiguous part (he was, and remained all his life, a foe to Octavian). However, when Antony came to Italy in September 40 B.C. and there seemed a strong likelihood of civil war breaking out again on a large scale between Antony and Octavian, Pollio was instrumental in bringing both men to the conference table in October 40 B.C. at which they arranged the Peace of

Brundisium, agreeing to divide the Roman empire virtually between them, with Octavian taking Italy and the West, and Antony the East—and at the same time marrying Octavian's sister, Octavia.

This was the point at which *Eclogue* 4 was composed: peace in the Roman world—i.e. the cessation of civil war—seemed assured and Virgil felt inspired to interpret this as the beginning of a new age. No doubt the Sibylline oracle, declaring this to be the beginning of a new Golden Age, was a reality. But the additional concept of a child whose birth was to mark the beginning of the age was Virgil's. The only real analogy which Virgil had for a poem of this sort in a pastoral collection was Theocritus, *Idyll* 17. There the centre of the poem (53-120) is occupied with the praises of the son of Ptolemy and Berenice; the happiness of the couple occupies the poet and is led up to by the portrait of Ptolemy Soter in heaven, carousing with Alexander the Great and Herakles; then Herakles' happiness with Hebe leads to the marital bliss of Ptolemy and Berenice. The poem finally ends with the marriage of Ptolemy Philadelphus to his sister. Virgil owed to this poem the themes of the birth of a child of great promise, the feasting in the presence of the gods, and the happiness of Herakles.

What is remarkable in Virgil's poem is that there is no indication of the child's identity. There are however two themes which converge on this. (i) There is a great series of references to Catullus 64, culminating in the mention of the *Parcae* (46-7). Catullus' poem is about the marriage of Peleus and Thetis, and a large proportion of it concentrates on the prophecy of the *Parcae* about the child of the wedding, Achilles: it is a most pessimistic prophecy and culminates in that break between divine and human which meant the gods no longer appeared on earth. Virgil's poem moves in the opposite direction: it is highly optimistic and it foresees a new intermingling of gods and men (15-17). At the same time, the clear references to Catullus 64, and particularly the entrance of the *Parcae*, imply a wedding. (ii) The number of references which Virgil makes to the child clearly suggest a divine origin and relationship (15-16, 49, 62-3), and also nominate him as a future ruler of the Roman world (17). Only one family in Rome at the time could be designated in these terms (especially in view of the hint at Anchises in 63): that was the Julian, whose most recent representative, Julius Caesar, had been officially deified in January 42 B.C.

Now it would have been grossly tactless for Virgil, in the context of the Peace of Brundisium, to designate Antony's putative son (he would be the son of Octavia, sister of Octavian, and a member of the Julian family) as the future—and favoured—ruler of the world. But, by an odd coincidence, probably only weeks before the Peace of Brundisium, Octavian himself had married Scribonia, the sister-in-law of Sextus Pompeius, an adherent of Antony, and a desperate enemy of Octavian.[69] Virgil seems to have made use of this unique situation to concentrate his poetic attention on the child of a marriage which had Julian (and so divine) connexions in such a way that he said nothing of the marriage itself, much less of the actual parents. Either marriage could be meant,[70] and in the atmosphere of peace and concord decision was unnecessary. The reminiscences of Catullus 64 were enough for the imaginative reader—so Virgil hoped.[71]

The poem is astonishingly ambitious, and in its imaginative grasp it shows the hallmark of that mind which in *Aeneid* 6 was to weld Greek conceptions of the Underworld with the history of Rome. This capacity for association of ideas was Virgil's greatest strength, the fertile amalgam of Greek and Roman into an imaginative unity. In *Eclogue* 4 there are elements of fantasy and exaggeration (the varicoloured sheep, for instance) which suggest a youthful genius somewhat over-reaching itself, but, by any standard, this is great poetry on the grand scale.[72]

Notes

1. Theocritus was born in Sicily, though later he probably lived in Cos and Alexandria. On him see also above, p. 2 n. 1.

2. Tamarisks . . . are a prominent feature of the landscape at the beginning of *Idyll* 1 (line 13) and Virgil's use of this Greek word here underlines the connexion with Theocritus (though Romans, in fact, also, as often, used the Greek term as the botanical name: cf. Pliny, *N.H.* 13. 116; 24. 67). The word *arbusta* is a generic term for 'forested region'.

3. Virgil often uses the basic symbolism which equates 'writing pastoral poetry' with 'being a shepherd' (see especially *Ecl.* 10 and G. Williams (1968), 233-9). From this, various symbolic details are deduced whereby objects in the pastoral landscape or situation represent aspects of the poet's subject-matter.

4. On this pattern see Pearce (1966), 140-71, 298-320. This pattern is referred to below as the 'framed' line.

5. At least ten Sibyls were known and listed by Varro (*Res Diuinae* in Lactantius, *Inst.* 1. 6. 8-12), but for Romans the Sibyl of Cumae was supreme. From her originated the Sibylline Books which were consulted, on order of the Senate, by the *quindecimuiri* (these books were burnt in the Capitol fire of 83 B.C. and a new collection made; there was further pruning by Augustus some time after 12 B.C.—Suet. *Aug.* 31. 1). It seems, however, that the Sibyl from time to time produced oracles on consultation (like the Delphic Oracle) and it is to one of these, and not to the official Books, that Virgil refers. See Latte (1960), 160-1. A selection of the later (largely Jewish and Christian inspired) Sibylline oracles is conveniently edited with a good introduction, translation and notes by Kurfess (1951).

6. This does not mean that Virgil counted on his reader's knowing the actual oracle (the poet reveals its contents in the poem) but only the nature and authority of such oracles.

7. Cf. *Aeneid* 7. 44 *maior rerum mihi nascitur ordo* 'a grander series of events is opening before me'. The sense is that of Horace, *Odes* 3. 30. 4-5 *innumerabilis | annorum series et fuga temporum* 'the unnumbered series of years and the flight of ages'.

8. *ultima aetas* cannot mean 'the end of the present age' when qualified by *Cumaei carminis,* and *uenit* cannot mean 'has come and gone'. What Virgil means is a final age which is really a repeat of the first age of the world.

9. The 'Great Year' of the Stoics was just one of several theories of cycles in the history of the universe: on one calculation the cycle lasted 291,400, on another 12,954, years; it ended with a conflagration of the world and then the process started again. For the various schemes and their variations see van der Waerden (1952), 129-55. The concept has no relevance to *Ecl.* 4 since Virgil envisages no repetition of the ages again, but only a final age which repeats the first (see previous note).

10. The idea of five ages of the world goes back to Hesiod, *Works and Days* 109ff. The ages were Golden, Silver, Bronze, Heroic, and Iron. The ancient commentator Servius here speaks of ten ages . . . *saecula per metalla diuisit; dixit etiam quis quo saeculo imperaret, et Solem ultimum, id est decimum, uoluit.* Censorinus, *De Die Natali* 17. 6 speaks of an Etruscan system of ten *saecula,* and cf. the story of Servius on *Ecl.* 9. 46 *sed Vulcanius aruspex in contione dixit cometen esse qui significaret exitum noni saeculi et ingressum decimi; sed quod inuitis diis secreta rerum pronuntiaret statim se esse moriturum: et nondum finita oratione in ipsa contione concidit. hoc etiam Augustus in libro secundo de memoria uitae suae complexus est.* No doubt Augustus recognized good propaganda when he saw it, but this 'oracle' belonged to July 44 B.C. The reason for regarding such systems of ages as irrelevant to *Ecl.* 4 is that Virgil goes on to use the scheme of Hesiod and Aratus. For the same reason, speculations based on supposed Pythagorean doctrines are disregarded here: for them see Carcopino (1930), 57ff. Servius on *Ecl.* 4 imagines a repetition of the ages, and, for that reason (see n. 9), his view is disregarded.

11. As often by Virgil with *magnus* and *ingens* (see Austin (1955) on *Aeneid* 4. 89).

12. This version of the legend is that of Aratus (*c.* 315-240 B.C.) in his *Phaenomena* 96-136, where he describes Justice finally leaving the earth in the Age of Bronze. In Hesiod Αἰδώς and Νέεσις leave earth in the Age of Iron.

13. For Hesiod (*Works* 111) it had been the time of Kronos. But for Virgil's view cf. *Georg.* 2. 538

aureus hanc uitam in terris Saturnus agebat, and for Augustus as the founder of the new Golden Age, *Aen.* 6. 792ff.

14. Cf. e.g. *Aeneid 7. 327 odit et ipse pater Pluton, odere sorores | Tartareae monstrum.* See Conington (1963) ad loc.

15. That is the point which is emphasized in (8) *primum.*

16. Any such assertion about Apollo by a poet in this period would be implausible. In the *Aeneid* Apollo is mentioned more than any god except Iuppiter, but he is not an active god, with the single exception of his intervention at *Aeneid* 9. 638ff. to congratulate Ascanius and dissuade him from further fighting, but even this has a strong element of prophecy in it and was doubtless inspired by the fact that Augustus regarded Apollo as his own personal protecting deity. Apollo's function throughout the *Aeneid* is to deliver prophecies not to initiate action. See Bailey (1935), 163-72.

17. The ancient commentator Servius asserts that the Sibylline prophecy made the last age the age of the sun, but this is a mere guess and 40 B.C. is too early a date to assume an identification of Apollo with the sun in Roman literature (see Fontenrose (1939), 439ff.). Servius' weakness is shown by his quoting Horace even on 46-7, and never referring to Catullus 64. Apollo was the favourite god of Octavian (Augustus), but again this connexion belongs to a later period (probably the battle of Actium in 31 B.C. was decisive), and anyway such a partisan connexion is alien to the general political impartiality of this poem. But one has an uneasy sense with Virgil that his ideas are not readily exhausted or explained. See further note 71 below. Norden (1924) has a most ingenious theory about the position of 1 January (when consuls entered on office) as midway between two festivals of the sun, but it relies on oriental evidence and is quite unconvincing.

18. It is worth noticing that Apollo is never mentioned by name in Delphic oracles unless some directions for the observance of his cult are needed. An outstanding example of this is the oracle given to Thera, ordering the foundation of Cyrene, quoted in a short form by Herodotus 4. 150 and a longer form by Diodorus Siculus 8. 29 ('king Phoebus Apollo sends you . . . Phoebus Apollo guides you'). Otherwise Zeus, Pallas Athene etc. are mentioned in the oracles as the activists. It is less important that Apollo is not named in the later Sibylline oracles (see n. 5 above).

19. Such a revelation would be the most natural to imagine for a poet from the god of poetry and prophecy.

20. See pp. 36 and 44-6, above.

21. That this is to be seen as a parenthesis is clearly shown by the force of (11) *adeo* ('what is more', cf.

e.g. *Aeneid* 11. 369 where also a subordinate expansion rather than a fact of parallel weight is added) together with the fact that (15) *ille* immediately takes up the reference to the child in 8-10.

22. Literally 'this glory consisting in an age' (cf. 24 *herba ueneni*); on this genitive see L-H-S 62ff. The phrase cannot mean 'the child' ('this glory of the age') for which *inibit* would be an implausible verb, though perfectly suited to the beginning of a temporal age.

23. The form *si qua . . . uestigia . . .* is merely indefinite ('all traces that exist') and does not throw doubt on the existence of such traces.

24. Cf. e.g. Horace, *Odes* 1. 2. 29; 35. 33.

25. See p. 44, above.

26. For *deum uitam accipiet* cf. Terence, *Heaut.* 693 *deorum uitam apti sumus.*

27. The connexion with Catullus 64 will be seen to be very important to the understanding of *Ecl.* 4. This situation particularly mirrors the time when the gods regularly came among men as Catullus describes it in 64. 386 *nondum spreta pietate* and when it was not the case that (398) *iustitiamque omnes cupida de mente fugarunt* (and cf. 406). These were virtues which Apollo, guardian of law and order, especially upheld. On this aspect of Apollo, see e.g. Guthrie (1950), 183ff.

28. This is probably the meaning rather than 'a world made peaceful by the bravery of his father' because the peace implied seems to be the peace that will come particularly from cessation of civil war (cf. 13-14 and 31), and it is this that is important rather than the wars implied in 34-6. At this period wars against external enemies were actually desirable as a means of expiating the shame of civil war: see Nisbet-Hubbard (1970) on *Odes* 1. 2. 51.

29. It is relevant here to remember that in most of the tradition about Achilles it was Apollo who, at the wedding of Peleus and Thetis, delivered the prophecy about the (as yet unconceived) hero's future: *Iliad* 24. 62-3, Aeschylus fr. 284a Mette, Plato *Republic* 383B. Catullus varied that in poem 64.

30. See note 4, above.

31. See further p. 39, above.

32. On the flora of Theocritus see e.g. Lindsell (1936), 78ff.; and for Virgil's see Sargeaunt (1920).

33. For descriptions of the Golden Age see Lovejoy and Boas (1935), 24ff., 145ff., and 156ff.

34. A re-arrangement of lines with 23 transposed to follow 20 (designed to produce four lines directed to the child, followed by four lines devoted to the traditional Golden Age) is mistaken since not only are the differing senses of *ipse* then made to follow

one another immediately and (23) *fundent flores* to follow (20) *fundet acantho,* but also the clear intention of Virgil is defeated (see above, p. 39).

35. See further p. 39, above.

36. Nicander (Alexandrian poet of second century B.C.) in *Theriaca* 8ff. quotes Hesiod for the view that snakes sprang from the spilt blood of the Titans—implying an age when they did not exist. But, of course, once they do exist, they can only be killed off.

37. See note 4, above.

38. Cf. Cicero's description of 'heroic lays': *Brutus* 75 *atque utinam exstarent illa carmina quae multis saeculis ante suam aetatem in epulis esse cantitata a singulis conuiuis de clarorum uirorum laudibus in Originibus scriptum reliquit Cato.* Cf. *Tusculan Disputations* 4. 3, and Varro apud Nonium 77. 2.

39. This spontaneity of growth is clearly implied from the context, since there would be no point in mentioning corn otherwise.

40. On the so-called 'golden' line, see Norden (1926), 393ff. and Wilkinson (1963), 215-16.

41. Cf. Seneca *Epistle* 84. 3-4 *de illis non satis constat utrum sucum ex floribus ducant qui protinus mel sit, an quae collegerunt in hunc saporem mixtura quadam et proprietate spiritus sui mutent. quibusdam enim placet non faciendi mellis scientiam esse illis, sed colligendi.* Aristotle (*Hist. An.* 5. 22) and Pliny (*N.H.* 11. 30) express the common ancient belief that honey dropped as a kind of dew from heaven. Only Seneca expresses doubts. Virgil here means that the work of bees will not be needed to collect it.

42. This is analogous to (13) *sceleris uestigia nostri. fraus* is the basic untrustworthiness of behaviour which in *Georgics* 1. 502 (*Laomedonteae luimus periuria Troiae*) Virgil traces to an origin in the building of Troy when Laomedon cheated Apollo and Neptune of their agreed payment. This is, once again, a reference to the shame of civil war; citizens should trust and respect one another. (See further above, p. 52.)

43. Horace treats this as a sin, a basic transgression of God's ordinance, in *Odes* 1. 3. 23-4 *si tamen impiae | non tangenda rates transiliunt uada:* see Nisbet-Hubbard (1970) ad loc.

44. Catullus 64. 1-10—especially (4) *cum lecti iuuenes = delectos heroas,* and 338 *nascetur uobis Achilles.*

45. This idea is conveyed particularly by (40) *patietur* and (41) *robustus.*

46. Catullus 64. 38-42

  rura colit nemo, mollescunt colla iuuencis,
  non humilis curuis purgatur uinea rastris,
  non glaebam prono conuellit uomere taurus,
  non falx attenuat frondatorum arboris umbram:
  squalida desertis rubigo infertur aratris.

47. See p. 36, above.

48. See note 4, above.

49. This is technically the απο]κοινον position, when a word which is common to two clauses and required in each is postponed to the second of them.

50. The -*s* sounds are continued in 46-7.

51. See Fraenkel (1962), 261.

52. See G. Williams (1968), 226-8 and Bramble (1970), 26ff.

53. I have made a break in the exposition between 47 and 48 because it is convenient—the content of 46-7 belongs closely with that of 18-45. But this obscures a feature of *Eclogue* 4. It seems to be composed in units of seven lines, subdivided into four and three. So the poem opens with three lines and ends with four. The fourteen lines 4-17 are composed in units of three and four (4-7, 8-10, 11-14 and 15-17). Virgil, in the *Eclogues,* avoids any obvious arithmetical balances (for instance, *Ecl.* 1 opens with two speeches of five lines each and ends with speeches of five, fifteen and five lines respectively, but the balance is not carried further; *Eclogue* 10 opens and closes with sections of eight lines each). In *Eclogue* 4 the central prophecy occupies twenty-eight lines, divided into units of eight, eleven and nine lines each. Since the wishes of 53-7 form a unit of seven lines, the poet probably viewed 46-52 as a unit of composition in which, as it were, he joined the Parcae in their wish for a speedy approach of the Golden Age. On the numbers, see Skutsch (1969), 158.

54. See especially Fraenkel (1957), 242 n. 1.

55. The other possible meaning 'the germ of a (future) Iuppiter' is impossible in the context since the child is clearly not in itself a god and the equation of an emperor with Iuppiter is out of the question in 40 B.C.

56. See Nisbet-Hubbard (1970) ad loc. and G. Williams (1968), 161 and 441.

57. The elevation of these lines is increased by two Greek metrical features: the spondaic ending of 49, and the lengthening in arsis of (51) *terrasqué tractusque.* See Maas (1962), 59 and 76, and Norden (1926), 438, and 451f.

58. This rules out the interpretation which would take *conuexo nutantem mundo* as an adjectival description of *mundum* and *mundum* as standing in a simple series with the nouns in 51 which would all then be taken up in (52) *omnia.* In that interpretation *nutantem* could only suggest a collapsing world.

59. Virgil was 30 when he was writing this poem.

60. Roman writers were inclined to avoid final -*s* followed immediately by initial *s*-. So, instead of writing *spiritus et quantus . . .,* Virgil has compressed this structure: *spiritus et (tantus)*

quantum (*eius spiritus*) *sat erit . . .* For the avoidance of the above-mentioned clash of -*s,* see Löfstedt (1933), Chapter 5, 'Zum Gebrauch von *quis* und *qui*'.

61. On the literary form of *recusatio* see Wimmel (1960), and G. Williams (1968), 46f. and 'Index' s.v.

62. On Virgil's invention of Arcadia as an ideal pastoral region and the setting for bucolic poetry, see Snell (1953), Chapter 13, 'Arcadia: The Discovery of a Spiritual Landscape', pp. 281-309.

63. See, most conveniently, Dover (1971), xiv-l.

64. For the origin of these patterns in non-literary songs and ritual compositions see Merkelbach (1956), 97-133 (esp. 117ff.).

65. The MSS here uniformly provide *cui non risere parentes.* This gives inadequate sense since nothing is then required of the child and since it necessitates understanding (60) *risu cognoscere matrem* most implausibly as 'recognize your mother by *her* smile'. Pliny (*N.H.* 7. 72) asserts that only of Zoroaster was it recorded that he smiled on the day of his birth (and that his brain throbbed so violently as to shake off a hand placed on his head—a sign of his future wisdom). Censorinus, *De Die Natali* 11. 7 asserts that babies never smile before the fortieth day. Quintilian, *Inst. Orat.* 9. 3. 8 says '*qui non risere parentes, | nec deus hunc mensa, dea nec dignata cubili est:* ex illis enim "qui non risere", hic, quem non dignata.' Clearly his MS of Virgil read *qui,* and *parentes* is corrupt and easily emended to *parenti* (Bonnell)—the dative corresponds syntactically to *ad*+acc. in Catullus 61. 219 *dulce rideat ad patrem.* The shift from *qui* (pl.) to *hunc* (sing.) is a Greek rather than Latin syntactical feature; examples in Latin normally place the singular first (see L-H-S 432f.). But Greek syntactical usages were one means which late Republican and Augustan poets used to construct a poetic language, particularly Horace and Virgil (compare the Greek metrical features in 49ff.—see note 57, above). For Greek examples, see K-G 1. 87. On the corruption, see especially Maas (1958), 36f.

66. See particularly Homer, *Odyssey* 11. 602-3 . . . 'among the immortal gods, he enjoys himself in banqueting and has for wife trim-ankled Hebe'. But it is even more relevant (see pp. 44f.) to remark that a picture of Herakles' bliss in heaven (feasting and Hebe) is prominent in Theocritus, *Idyll* 17. 20-33.

67. On the details see Syme (1952), chs. 15 and 16.

68. See Brunt (1962), 69-86.

69. The marriage was a purely political move, intended to conciliate Pompeius, and it failed both as politics and as a marriage. Within a year followed the birth of Julia, divorce, and a new pact with Pompeius at Puteoli.

70. That the children of both marriages turned out to be girls does not affect the issue—prophecy cannot be corrected and, when darkly poetic, need not be withdrawn.

71. Yet it is not surprising that the poem was misunderstood from a time soon after it was composed. It was the poem's sheer difficulty that enabled Pollio's son, C. Asinius Gallus, to make the absurd claim to Asconius (Servius on *Ecl.* 4. 11) that he was the designated child. However, the possibility that Asinius Gallus was also intending a leg-pull cannot be ignored.

72. My thanks are due to Mr J. H. Simon for helpful criticism and advice.

Bibliography

A fair idea of older views on *Ecl.* 4 can be gained from Mayor-Warde Fowler-Conway (1907). A very useful survey of more recent views on the poem is given by Büchner (1955), 175-93 (this is a separate printing of Büchner's article on Virgil in Pauly-Wissowa). Still worth reading for its wide learning—and in spite of its 'orientalizing' interpretation—is Norden (1924). By far the best work on *Ecl.* 4 has been done by Jachmann (1952), 13-62 (there is a shortened version in Jachmann (1952*a*), 37-62). Little is added to the actual understanding of *Ecl.* 4 by Becker (1955), 328-41 or by Klingner (1967), 68-82. Of commentaries, the most useful is Conington-Nettleship (1963), though this was largely based on Heyne-Wagner (1830-1) which is still worth consulting. For a treatment of *Ecl.* 4 in the context of similar poetic techniques, see G. Williams (1968), 274-85.

Abbreviations

Note. Standard works of reference and titles of periodicals are abbreviated as follows under list A. Scholarly discussions and commentaries are listed under B and throughout the book are referred to by author's name, date, and page number only. E.g. 'Brink (1965), 7-8' is a reference to pages 7-8 of Brink, C. O. (1965). *On Reading a Horatian Satire.* Sydney.

AJP	*American Journal of Philology*
CIL	*Corpus Inscriptionum Latinarum,* Berlin, 1862-
CLE	*Carmina Latina Epigraphica,* Leipzig, 1895-1926
CM	*Classica et Mediaevalia*
CP	*Classical Philology*
CQ	*Classical Quarterly*
CR	*Classical Review*
Daremberg-Saglio	Daremberg, C.-Saglio, E. *Dictionnaire des Antiquités Grecques et Romaines,* Paris, 1897-1919
GR	*Greece and Rome*
GRBS	*Greek, Roman and Byzantine Studies*
Gymn.	*Gymnasium*

H	*Hermes*
HSCP	*Harvard Studies in Classical Philology*
IG	*Inscriptiones Graecae,* Berlin, 1873-1939
JHS	*Journal of Hellenic Studies*
JRS	*Journal of Roman Studies*
K-G Kühner, R.-Gerth, B.	*Ausführliche Grammatik der griechischen Sprache.* II. *Satzlehre,* 3rd edn., Hanover-Leipzig, 1898-1904
L-H-S Leumann, M.-Hofmann, J. B.-Szantyr, A.	*Lateinische Grammatik.* II. *Syntax und Stilistik,* Munich, 1965
L & S Lewis, C. T. and Short, C.	*Latin Dictionary,* Oxford, 1897
MH	*Museum Helveticum*
Mnem.	*Mnemosyne*
OCD	*Oxford Classical Dictionary,* 2nd edn., Oxford, 1970
OCT	Oxford Classical Texts
OLD	*Oxford Latin Dictionary,* Oxford, 1968-
PCA	*Proceedings of the Classical Association*
PCPS	*Proceedings of the Cambridge Philological Society*
PMLA	*Publications of the Modern Language Association of America*
PLM	*Poetae Latini Minores,* ed. Baehrens, Leipzig, 1879-86
Pauly-Wissowa	*Paulys Real-Encyclopädie der classischen Altertumswissenschaft,* ed. G. Wissowa et al., Stuttgart, 1893-
Philol.	*Philologus*
REL	*Revue des Études Latines*
RM	*Rheinisches Museum*
TAPA	*Transactions of the American Philological Association*
TLL	*Thesaurus Linguae Latinae,* Leipzig, 1900-
WS	*Wiener Studien*
Walde-Hofmann	Walde, A.-Hofmann, J. B. *Lateinisches Etymologisches Wörterbuch,* repr. Heidelberg, 1965

Robert Coleman (essay date 1977)

SOURCE: An introduction to *Vergil: "Eclogues",* Cambridge University Press, 1977, pp. 1-40.

[*In the following essay, Coleman identifies elements of Theocritus's pastoral poetry that would later influence Vergil and discusses the chronology and arrangement of the* Eclogues. *Coleman concludes his overview of the* Eclogues *by observing that although Vergil's range of themes is somewhat conventional, his details are almost entirely original, and his poetic technique is mature.*]

1. THE PASTORAL BEFORE VERGIL

The pastoral myth is the creation of a highly civilized urban sensibility. It is a reaction against certain aspects of the culture and material environment of the city: *Musa illa rustica et pastoralis non forum modo uerum ipsam etiam urbem reformidat* (Quint. 10.1.55). In his longing for a simple innocence and carefree spontaneity that he has lost urban man looks to the country and its way of life, which he knows only as an outsider and from a distance, and creates out of it a myth embodying the ideals that he seeks. This idealization of the rustic life is well portrayed by Shakespeare in the Duke's speech in *As You Like It* 2.1 and the King's soliloquy in *Henry the Sixth, pt 3* 2.5. The tendency of the upper classes to idealize certain aspects of urban proletarian life, which in modern times has occasionally taken over a similar role, was not unknown even in antiquity (see Athenaeus 12.536e).

The pastoral conception, like the romantic 'return to nature' with which it is often contrasted, is informed throughout by the sophisticated sensibility that produced it. Its illusion consists 'in exposing only the best side of a shepherd's life and in concealing its miseries'.[1] It conjures up a pretty, fictional world into which one may escape from the real world now and then in imagination; it is not a programme for the reform or conversion of that world. There is thus little room for the realistic portrayal of country life. For this we must look not to the pastorals of Theocritus or Pope but to the poetry of true countrymen like Hesiod or George Crabbe, whose *Village* in fact contains an explicit protest against the pastoral tradition.

Although there are references to shepherds' music-making as early as Homer (*Iliad* 18.525-6), the earliest pastoral poetry in Greek literature is the work of the third-century Syracusan Theocritus. The only predecessors mentioned by ancient authors are the mythical Sicilians Diomus and Daphnis.[2] The Theocritean scholiasts' accounts of the origins of the genre in popular cult hymns to Artemis—complete with aetiological fables[3]—are highly implausible when one considers the predominantly secular character of much of the earliest pastoral and the very minor part played by the chaste goddess of the hunt in the devotional life of Arcady[4] in comparison with Pan, Apollo, Hermes and Priapus, the patrons of country life and music, and the nymphs and muses, who inspire country song. Some modern scholars have detected in the epigrams of Theocritus' contemporary Anyte of Tegea hints of an earlier Peloponnesian school of pastoral writing. But such pastoral motifs as appear occasionally in her poetry (e.g. *A.P.* 9.313, *Plan.* 228) are a common feature of Hellenistic epigram (e.g. *A.P.* 9.823, *Plan.* 12).

While Theocritus may be credited with inventing the pastoral, it is only in the work of his successors Moschus and Bion that it emerges as a distinctive genre, to become established in Latin in the work of Vergil, Calpurnius, the anonymous author of the two Einsiedeln Eclogues and Nemesianus. The pastorals of Theocritus in fact form a loosely knit group within the collection of thirty Idylls[5] that have been traditionally attributed to him. Nevertheless they established definitively much of the formal and thematic character of the later pastoral tradition.

The short dramatic form—sometimes a dialogue, complete in itself (4) or combined with a singing display (5, 10, also 7, where it is given a narrative framework), sometimes a reported monologue (3, 11)—is also found in the urban idylls (2, 15). It clearly owes much to that other specifically Sicilian invention, the mime, which is represented for us by the meagre fragments of the fifth-century Epicharmus and Sophron and by the *Mimiamboi* of Theocritus' contemporary Herodas. The ancient references to the mime however give no hint of pastoral motifs. The only attested parallels are with Theocritus' urban idylls: the magic rites of *Id.* 2 and a fragment of Sophron (Page *Greek literary papyri* 1.328ff.), the Syracusan women at the Adonis-festival in *Id.* 15 and Herodas *Mim.* 4.

The singing competition, which is one of the recurrent forms in the genre, seems to be a stylized derivative of actual country music-making. The test of wits involved in the amoebaean contest (*Idd.* 5, 6, 8, 9), with its requirement that the second singer must match the themes or figures employed by the first, is widely paralleled in folk culture. The use of refrains (*Idd.* 1, 2), a familiar device in folk song, is probably also popular in origin.

The language of the herdsmen's conversation, though vivid and animated, is on the whole refined, reflecting the urbanity of their creator. They even show, occasionally, some surprising pieces of literary erudition; e.g. *Id.* 3.40-51, where the goatherd is admittedly showing off, and 5.150, where Morson clearly is not. There are colloquial touches, it is true, notably in *Idd.* 4, 5 and 10, though not on the scale of the urban mime *Id.* 14 or of the *Mimiamboi* of Herodas, where the sustained colloquialism brings a coarse verisimilitude to the low urban world that he patronizingly depicts. Even so the coarse language of *Id.* 4 was explicitly condemned by the seventeenth-century critics, Rapin and Fontenelle.[6]

The Doric dialect, which Theocritus established for Greek pastoral, is often praised for its naturalness and simplicity. Dryden in his *Dedication to the Pastorals* (*Works* ed. Scott-Saintsbury 12, 323-4) even declares that 'the boorish dialect of Theocritus has a secret charm in it which the Roman language cannot imitate'. But that dialect is in fact a highly artificial synthesis of Doric forms belonging to different districts and periods with occasional Ionic and even Aeolic usages. In this respect it is like all Greek literary dialects, including Herodas' Ionic. Its affinities are not primarily with any spoken dialect but with literary Doric, as exemplified in choral lyric poetry from Alcman and Stesichorus onwards.[7] To the stylized evocation of Sicilian or Coan rusticity is thus added a lyric dimension appropriate to the dream-like world of the pastoral. The association of literary genres with distinct dialects of the language—usually those of their earliest exponents—was a notable, perhaps unique, feature of classical Greek literature.[8] Attempts to recapture something of the effect of the Doric of Greek pastoral in other languages—whether by translators or imitators—have for the most part proved disastrous. Samuel Johnson's censure (*Rambler* no. 37, 1750) on

Spenser's *Shepheardes calendar* for its medley of 'obsolete terms and rustic words', 'a mangled dialect which no human being could have spoken', could equally well be applied to Theocritus. Indeed Dryden (*op. cit.* 325) believed Spenser to have 'exactly imitated the Doric of Theocritus'. Johnson's comment illustrates the great difference between the linguistic conventions that were acceptable within the two literary traditions.

More surprisingly, Theocritus adopted for both his pastoral and other Idylls[9] not the iambic metre traditionally associated with dialogue in the drama and the mime but the dactylic hexameter, which was long established in the higher literary genres of epic, cult-hymn and didactic poetry, as represented among Theocritus' contemporaries by Apollonius' *Argonautica*, Callimachus' *Hymns* and Aratus' *Phaenomena* respectively. Indeed *Id.* 22 is in the form of a cult-hymn and 13, 24, 25 are short occasional narrative poems on subjects from heroic mythology of the kind favoured by Callimachus and his associates. That Theocritus belonged to this circle is indicated by *Id.* 7, where Lycidas after praising Philitas and 'Sicelidas' expresses some very Callimachean sentiments on poetry (39-48), and the songs of both Lycidas and Simichidas (52-89, 96-127) have more in common with Hellenistic erotic poetry than with pastoral. The poem is in fact a literary manifesto. Indeed the Idylls as a whole can be seen as another manifestation of the development of literary forms *katà leptón* 'on a small scale'—to use Callimachus' own phrase (*Aet.* fr. 1.11Pf.)—in conscious reaction against full-scale epic writing. The pastoral was always *katà leptón*: Theocritus' longest pastoral (*Id.* 7) has 157 lines, Vergil's (*Ecl.* 3) 111 lines, Calpurnius' (*Ecl.* 4) 169 lines. The hexameter became the regular metre of Greek and Latin pastoral,[10] and in the anonymous *Lament for Bion* (71-84) not only is Bion accorded a status equal to Homer but the themes of pastoral are extolled in rivalry to those of traditional epic:

> 'Both poets were the favourites of fountains; one drank from the spring of Pegasus, the other took his drink from Arethusa. The former sang of Tyndareus' fair daughter and the mighty son of Thetis and Menelaus son of Atreus; but the theme of this poet's music was not wars and tears but Pan. With the clear voice of the herdsman he sang as he pastured his herds, he fashioned pipes and milked the placid cows; he taught the delights of boys' kisses, nursed Eros in his arms and roused Aphrodite herself.'

The attractions of the countryside to disillusioned urban man were of course recognized in earlier Greek literature, e.g. Eur. *Hipp.* 73-87, Plato *Phdr.* 230d, where Socrates expressly rejects them. The Bacchants' cult represented a temporary periodic revolt against the constraints of civilization, but its orgiastic flights were to wild nature, not to the inhabited countryside. Nevertheless their *thíasos* did confer upon initiates a sense of belonging for a time to a community set apart and—when the rites were over—a serene and joyous feeling of being in sympathetic communion with nature, which have much in common with the mood of the herdsmen in Arcady. But in the classical city-state town and country were closely in contact, and it is not till the growth of the large metropolitan complexes of the Hellenistic period that they were sufficiently dissociated to admit the idealization of rustic life that characterizes the pastoral. In the generations immediately preceding Theocritus the longing for a lost simplicity and naturalness had found expression in the Cynic philosophy. Although Cynicism has at first sight little in common with pastoral, they both share a rejection of civilized constraints on natural behaviour and an acceptance of anarchy in human society. An even closer affinity with pastoral can be found in the philosophy of Theocritus' older contemporary Epicurus, who preached 'tranquillity' and *ataraxía,* 'freedom from disturbance', and with his disciples withdrew from the world into the idyllic seclusion and frugal simplicity of 'the garden'. In Seneca's definition of Epicurean *uoluptas* (*Ben.* 4.13.1) the phrases *sub densa umbra latitare* and *intra hortorum latebram* recall the secluded *otium* of the pastoral 'green shade'. It may not be coincidental that when Vergil forsook philosophy for literature, he passed from the idyllic world of Siro's Epicurean *hortus* to that of pastoral poetry.

The literary tradition provides evidence for the survival of an older, mythological concept that is important in the formation of the pastoral. In Euripides' description of the Maenads in repose (*Ba.* 704-11) and in Lucretius' setting for the Epicurean life of primitive man (5.1379-96) there are details that belong to traditional accounts of the Golden Age. Many mythological traditions preserve a belief that in the remote past, before the invention of agriculture, the use of metals and the building of cities and ships, men lived in an age of peaceful anarchy and innocent ease, sustained by the spontaneous fruits of the earth. The Golden Age first appears in Greek literature in Hesiod's *Works and days* 109-19. Most of its characteristic features are familiar to English readers from Gonzalo's commonwealth in Shakespeare *Tempest* 2.1. Varro *R.* 2.1.4-5 cites Dicaearchus for the view that the Golden Age was succeeded by a pastoral culture, when men first tamed animals but had not yet learnt the corrupting habits of commerce and city life.[11] Hence the idealized picture of the herdsman's life in the pastoral easily incorporated features of the Golden Age myth, and Donatus could justly assert that *illud erit probabilissimum bucolicum carmen originem ducere a priscis temporibus, quibus uita pastoralis exercita est et ideo uelut aurei saeculi speciem in huiusmodi personarum simplicitate cognosci* (*Vit. Verg.* 240-4).[12]

But the myth of the pastoral is brought close to the present day. For although the poems are often set in the past, it always seems a recent past, so that we have the persistent illusion of a world that is permanently 'there', timeless and unchanging. Moreover, it is often given a geographical location—Sicily, South Italy, or Cos in Greek pastoral, Arcadia in Vergil's later pastorals and in much of the subsequent history of the genre. In this way it is related to the real world but in a way that is so vague in its specification and so remote from the environment of the reading

public as to be immune to the intrusion of grimmer realities from the more accessible countryside. In more recent times Utopias have generally been situated *in* the world but at a safe distance: the Indies or Ceylon in sixteenth- and seventeenth-century European literature, the South Sea Islands in the eighteenth and nineteenth. Sicily and South Italy were often disrupted by war in Theocritus' own time (cf. *Id.* 16.76-97), but they were a long way from readers in Cos or Alexandria.

The pastoral landscape is always idyllic. The herdsmen may sometimes speak of the excesses of summer heat and winter cold but the prevailing season seems always to be early summer or spring 'the fairest season of the year' (*Ecl.* 3.57), and the immediate setting always a *locus amoenus* with shady rocks and leafy trees rustling in the breeze, the sound of cicadas and bees among the shrubs, a cool spring and a stream flowing through lush flowery meadows. The delights of shade in summer heat were familiar enough to ordinary countrymen; *circiter meridianos aestus,* says Varro (*R.* 2.2.11) in his account of the herdsman's day, *dum deferuescant, sub umbriferas rupes et arbores patulas subigunt* [sc. *greges*] *quoad refrigeratur.* The *locus amoenus* itself as a literary theme has a long history from Homer onwards. It is always an inhabited landscape,[13] a setting for the activity or repose of gods and men, but one which like the Golden Age has a dream-like quality that sets it apart from the ordinary world of experience. Three instances will suffice to illustrate its functional range. Homer's idyllic account of Calypso's island (*Od.* 5.63-84) is contrasted with the picture of the homesick Odysseus alone on the shore, weeping as he gazes out over the sea. In *O.C.* 668-92 the Sophoclean chorus extol the serene beauty of Colonus, where the wandering Oedipus is destined at last to find peace and a refuge from the world. Ovid's exquisite account of Diana's bathing-place (*M.* 3.155-64) serves to heighten the subsequent pathos of Actaeon's unwitting intrusion.[14]

In the pastoral there are few passages of extended landscape description: the picture is built up gradually from details scattered incidentally in the course of the poem. But the evocation of the *locus amoenus* here too is never gratuitous. It provides the appropriate setting for making music, e.g. *Idd.* 1.12-14, 5.31-4. Even the most elaborate Theocritean landscape (*Id.* 7.135-46), though it forms the setting for a harvest celebration, comes at the end of a singing contest.[15] We are often made aware—at the beginning or end of a poem, in the incidental dialogue, even (as in *Id.* 5) within the formal songs themselves—of the workaday world of the herdsmen apart from their music-making. Nevertheless music occupies a central place in Arcadian life; it is the social activity to which the herdsmen instinctively turn whenever they gather together with their flocks in the cool shade; it is their chief, almost their only, artistic pursuit. For the carved cup in *Id.* 1 is an import (56-8), the cups in *Ecl.* 3 the work of Alcimedon (37, 44), whose name is otherwise unknown to pastoral. The pastoral herdsman in his ideal landscape is *ex officio* a poet and the traditional image of the poet as shepherd

(Hes. *Th.* 22-3) is now reversed. It is very un-Arcadian of Meliboeus in Calpurnius *Ecl.* 4.19-28 to reprimand Corydon for neglecting his rustic tasks in order to make music.

The formal songs of the herdsmen are dominated by three themes—the beauties and comforts of the countryside, the pleasures of music and the joys and sorrows of love. All three are brought together in various combinations in the singing contest of *Id.* 8.

The representation of a sympathetic correspondence between external nature and the events for which it provides the setting is of course widespread in ancient literature; e.g. the opening scene of [Aesch.] *P.V.,* Soph. *Phil.* 1453-68, and Vergil *A.* 4.160-72. The sympathetic bond that links the Arcadian landscape, its inhabitants and their music is often noted:

'Pleasant is the whisper of the pine tree over there beside the spring, friend goatherd, and pleasant too is your piping' (*Id.* 1.1-3).

It gives added point to a characteristic pastoral figure, the *rustic analogy:*

'Cicada is dear to cicada, ant to ant and hawk to hawk, but to me it is the Muse and Song' (*Id.* 9.31-2).

Nature-comparisons are of course common in Greek literature from Homer onwards; but the accumulation of parallels and the homeliness of some of the detail—both illustrated in this example—suggest that the figure may have affiliations with popular poetry. Much more important: the Arcadian symbiosis provides an appropriate context for the *sympathy figure,* in which surrounding nature is portrayed as reflecting the emotions and moods of its human inhabitants:

'Everywhere that Nais roams there is spring and pastures, everywhere milk flows forth from the udders and the young are nourished. But if ever she departs, the cattle and the cattle-herd alike waste away' (*Id.* 8.45-8).

The 'fallacy' of the figure, which is explicitly remarked in Nemesianus' *Ecl.* 2 (44-52, after 27-36), may be intended to show the naivety of the herdsmen. But it is found in other poetic genres. In erotic poetry a complex version of it appears as early as Ibycus (fr. 286P *ap.* Athen. 13.601b). The 'Where'er you walk' variant of it, illustrated just now, recalls a motif traditionally associated with the blessings conferred by a god or goddess (e.g. Callim. *H.* 3.129-35). In the pastoral itself it becomes so stylized as to rule out any suggestion of the singers' naivety.

The concept of love in the pastoral seems at times crude and superficial: a relationship that is almost wholly sensual, casually entered into with partners of both sexes (for like the lyric and elegiac traditions of erotic poetry the pastoral accepted bisexuality as normal and natural) and no less casually terminated. In *Id.* 4.38-44 Battus is easily consoled for the death of his Amaryllis, and the easy

promiscuity displayed in the coarse exchanges of *Id.* 5 recurs even in the charming *Id.* 27, whose form and mood, if not its outcome, has much in common incidentally with the mediaeval *pastourelle.* Where a lover's constancy is depicted, it is usually in terms of the pain and sorrow that it causes: a discordant note in the idyllic world of Arcady.

The rejected goatherd of *Id.* 3 is a ludicrous and comic figure, as he sings his futile serenade outside Amaryllis' cave. The poem is a parody of the *paraklausíthuron* 'the address to the closed door', which belongs to the comic and elegiac tradition (e.g. Aristoph. *Eccl.* 952ff., Plaut. *Curc.* 147ff., Callim. *A.P.* 5.23, Tib. 1.2.5-14), and exposes the essential absurdity of the slighted suitor's predicament. In *Id.* 20 by contrast the rejected goatherd is vaunting and vindictive. In *Id.* 7 Lycidas' address to Ageanax is in the form of a *propemptikón* or 'farewell poem' familiar from the elegiac and lyric genres; e.g. Callim. fr. 400 Pf., Prop. 1.8, Hor. *C.* 1.3. It is lightened by thoughts of the boy's joyous home-coming but the good wishes are strictly conditional. The competing song from Simichidas is about Aratus' unrequited love for the boy Philinus.

The most famous of Theocritus' love-poems is *Id.* 11, an exquisite blend of the comic and pathetic. Polyphemus' playful affair with Galatea was the subject of the singing competition in *Id.* 6, but now the Cyclops' emotions are far more deeply engaged; the monster shepherd is mellowed, his grosser physical and mental characteristics purged away; he has become an Arcadian and love has inspired him to undreamt-of powers of Arcadian song. His serenade to the sea-nymph is offered by Theocritus to his physician-friend as a model of the 'medicine of the Muses', by which the disappointed lover can soothe his sorrow. Theocritus' finest study of rejected love, *Id.* 2, is not in the pastoral genre. So it is the singing Cyclops, already portrayed in a dithyramb of Philoxenus (Plut. *Mor.* 622c), who now becomes the pastoral exemplar of the rejected lover; as in Bion fr. 16, [Bion] 2.1-3 (cf. Callim. *A.P.* 12.150).

The consolations of music in Arcady were to become a permanent theme of later pastoral. So too was the alienation of the lover, which is the antithesis of the sympathetic relation between man and idyllic nature in Arcady. It is hinted at here in the Cyclops' neglect of the flocks in which he takes such pride, and more fully elaborated in the preceding Idyll. For in *Id.* 10 Bucaeus' alienation is two-fold: his 'starveling love' (57) for Bombyca has distracted him from the work of the harvest, and the love-song that he sings to cure the affliction is, as his friend points out, a high-flown piece quite unfitted for his station. The homely edifying verses that Milon offers as a model, reminiscent of the closing pages of Hesiod's *Works and Days,* come dangerously close, like old Canthus' song in Calp. *Ecl.* 5, to exploding the fragile illusion of Arcady. It may however be no accident that the context here is agricultural, not pastoral, and Bucaeus' status as 'a working man who toils in the sun', stressed at the beginning and end, mark him off from the Arcadian herdsmen. The lover's dissociation from the normal pattern of life and the inspiration to music that his passion brings him certainly provide a link with the elegiac tradition; cf. Prop. 1.1.6, 2.1.4.

Erotic themes are even more prominent in the fragments of Theocritus' successors, and Bion proclaims explicitly (fr. 9)

> 'if ever a man sings who has not love in his soul, the Muses slink away and refuse to instruct him; but if anyone whose mind is stirred by Eros makes sweet music, then they all come thronging to him in a great rush'.

This is the voice of Hellenistic epigram rather than pastoral, and a number of the fragments find their closest parallels in the Anthology: the poet's encounter with Eros (Bion fr. 3 and 10) and the character-sketches of the malicious young god (Mosch. *Id.* 1, and his epigram, *Plan.* 200, Bion fr. 13 and 14), though they have their precedent in the fable of Cupid and the Bees, [Th.] *Id.* 19, have much more in common with the sequence of epigrams in *A.P.* 5 beginning with Meleager's 176 and 177.[16] The address to Hesperus in Bion fr. 11 belongs with the 'nocturnal serenade'—or *kômos*-epigrams, in particular Meleager *A.P.* 5.191. Unless the surviving extracts are wholly untypical, it seems that both Moschus and Bion intensified the Theocritean bias towards the exploration of the pains and sorrows of love, a universal literary theme to be sure but one that finds an especially poignant context in the idyllic world of Arcady.

The other melancholy note in the pastoral is that of untimely death. The extinction of youthful promise like the sorrows of love is a perennial motif of folk-literature. In the traditional mythology it is linked symbolically with the cycle of nature's brief season of fertile beauty through such figures as Attis, Linus and Adonis. The link is already implicit in Homer's comparison of the dying Gorgythion to a poppy bent by the spring winds (*Il.* 8.306-7). But in the pastoral this theme finds an appropriately pathetic setting. The pastoral landscape is depicted at its fairest season and peopled by herdsmen and women in the flower of their youth. In fact older characters rarely intrude and are never in the foreground: e.g. the absent Aegon (*Id.* 4.4), the old fisherman on the cup (*Id.* 1.39). Moreover traditional mythology had filled the countryside with monuments to the pathos of love and the extinction of youth in the metamorphoses of Daphne, Syrinx, Hyacinthus, Adonis. . . . These are seldom explicitly alluded to in pastoral; e.g. Mosch. fr. 3 (Alpheus and Arethusa), Bion fr. 1, *Lament for Bion* 37-43; but they provided for the reader brought up in the mythological tradition of literature resonances that the pastoral poet could tacitly exploit.

The two themes of the sorrows of love and untimely death come together in one of Theocritus' finest poems, *Id.* 1, where Thyrsis sings a dirge for the master poet and herdsman Daphnis. The precise circumstances of Daphnis' suffering are not made explicit. (In *Id.* 7.72-7 it is the love of

Xenea that causes his death.) But his status as a pastoral *hero*[17] is underlined by his Promethean silence at the advent of the three deities, the Hippolytan defiance of his final taunts to Aphrodite and the fact that all nature mourns for him.

In Bion's *Lament for Adonis* the pastoral colour and some of its characteristic figures are employed, as in Theocritus' *Hylas* (*Id.* 13), on a subject from traditional mythology; but, characteristically, attention is concentrated less on the image of the dead shepherd, pathetically drawn though it is, than on the grief of the love-stricken goddess. Bion fr. 1 suggests that the death of Hyacinthus may have been treated similarly in that poem. In the anonymous *Lament for Bion* the theme finds yet a further dimension, applied as it is to the death of a real person. A long tradition was thus initiated, which lasted into the nineteenth century, with Shelley's *Adonais* and Arnold's *Thyrsis;* but in the Hellenistic exemplar the fact that the dead poet is a pastoralist enables the pastoral colour and the imagery of nature in mourning, elaborated superbly from hints in *Id.* 1, to be sustained with a homogeneity that is uniquely appropriate. The analogy between the brevity of nature's beauty and the fragility of human life is here broken, once and for all:

> 'Alas, when the mallows die away in our gardens and the green parsley and exuberant dill with its curly leaves, they live and grow again for another year; but we men, tall and strong as we are and wise too, once we are dead, lie there in the hollowed earth unhearing, in a long sleep that has no end and no awakening' (99-104).

Pastoral consolation is thus darkened by a note of sombre pessimism that was to have its definitive utterance in Horace's spring Odes (*C.* 1.4, 4.7).

With Theocritus the range of pure pastoral had been defined in its form, figures and subject matter. The melancholy vein that has characterized the whole European tradition is already there in the sorrows of love—most finely depicted in *Idd.* 10 and 11—and of untimely death—in *Id.* 1. In *Id.* 10 the setting is already subtly widened beyond the strictly pastoral way of life in a manner that Vergil was to exploit far more boldly. In *Id.* 7 the genre is brought into relation with other modes of poetic creation and the literary controversies in which Theocritus and his friends were involved, but in a manner that risks turning the pastoral setting into a mere framework for other forms of poetry—as it has already become in the fragment of 'Myrson and Lycidas' ([Bion] 2: *The Epithalamium of Achilles and Deidameia*). The extension of the genre to traditional mythological subjects, as in Bion's *Adonis* and Moschus' *Europa,* whose opening is rich in pastoral colour, can be recognized as a specifically Hellenistic development, without significant influences in later pastoral literature. But the *Lament for Bion* and the prevalence of erotic themes in the post-Theocritean pastoral both provide integral features of the tradition. It is against this background that we must attempt to place the Eclogues of Vergil.

2. The Chronology and Arrangement of the *Eclogues*

Greek pastoral poetry was known to Vergil and contemporary Latin poets chiefly from the collected edition published in the first half of the first century B.C. by Artemidorus, who was probably the authority for the Theocritean canon of ten bucolic idylls.[18] There is, however, no evidence for any Latin pastoral poetry before Vergil. If Valerius Messalla wrote pastorals, [V.] *Catal.* 9.13-20 indicates that they must have been in Greek; Pliny's reference to a Catullan *incantamentorum amatoria imitatio* (*Nat.* 28.19) gives no indication of genre; the bucolic ingredients in other genres, e.g. Porcius' epigram cited by Aulus Gellius (*N.A.* 19.9) and certain poems of the *Appendix Vergiliana*, have adequate precedents in Hellenistic elegiac poetry.

The natural inference from the words addressed to Pollio in *Ecl.* 8 *a te principium, tibi desinam*, can be set beside the explicit statement in the Servian *Vita* 24-5 *tunc ei proposuit Pollio ut carmen bucolicum scriberet, quod eum constat triennio scripsisse et emendasse*, which in its context is unlikely to refer to just one *carmen*, e.g. *Ecl.* 2 or 8. It was Pollio who suggested to Vergil that he try his hand at pastoral, having been impressed no doubt by the promise of his earlier poetry.[19]

The ancient *testimonia* concerning the date of the Eclogues are somewhat ambiguous and inconsistent. Thus besides *Vit.* 24-5 (cited above) Serv. *Buc. prooem.* 3.26-7 *sane sciendum Vergilium XXVIII annorum scripsisse bucolica*, Don. *Vit.* 89-90 *Bucolica triennio, Georgica VII, Aeneida XI perfecit annis;* and from the commentary attributed to Probus *scripsit Bucolica annos natus VIII et XX Theocritum secutus, Georgica Hesiodum et Varronem* (323.13-14) and *eum, ut Asconius Pedianus dicit, XXVIII annos natum Bucolica edidisse* (329.6-7). Relevant too is Servius' remark *quae* [sc. *eclogae*] *licet decem sint, incertum tamen est quo ordine scriptae sint* (*Buc.* prooem. 3.15-16). Two clues can however be salvaged from all this: the importance of the poet's twenty-ninth year, viz. the year beginning 15 October 42 B.C., and the period of three years that is mentioned by both Servius and Donatus. As at least three of the poems, 6, 8, and 10, are in their present form manifestly later than 42-41 B.C., we may infer that in this year Vergil either began writing the Eclogues or more likely published the first of them. For it is reasonable to suppose that the poems were first published individually or in pairs, each with a title and a dedication. Neither the titles given by Donatus (*Vit.* 306ff.: *Tityrus, Alexis, Palaemon, Pollio, Daphnis, Varus* or *Silenus, Corydon, Damon* or *pharmaceutria, Moeris, Gallus*) nor those recorded in the manuscript tradition and noted in the apparatus to each poem can be authenticated; but the dedications of some at least are certain: 4 and 8 to Pollio, 6 to Varus, 10 to Gallus. This piecemeal publication of the **Bucolica** accounts perhaps for the alternative name **Eclogae:** each poem was an *ekloge* 'excerpt, extract' from a projected whole. Part of the confusion in the *testimonia* may be due to the use

of **Bucolica** in two different senses: individual 'pastoral poems' and 'the pastoral poems' as a collected group. The latter meaning is certain in the Donatus and first 'Probus' passages. The three year period takes us to October 39 B.C. The significance of this date will appear shortly.

Apart from the *testimonia* we have three criteria for dating.

The first is by references in the poems to external events. Thus the occasion of *Ecl.* 4 is Pollio's consulship. The miraculous sequence of events that is to begin in his year of office is spoken of in the future tense, but this does not guarantee a date before 40 B.C.; ancient poets like modern ones were not averse from producing their occasional verses after the occasions that they purport to herald. A publication date in late 41 or 40 B.C. is therefore equally possible. Similarly the dedication of *Ecl.* 8 looks forward to Pollio's triumphal return from his Macedonian proconsulate and so provides a notional date in the late summer of 39 B.C. But again the actual date may be later. The allusion to Varus' campaigning in *Ecl.* 6 must be to his proconsular service in 38 (he was consul in the preceding year); and that takes us beyond the *triennium* mentioned by the ancient authorities.

Some of the external allusions are disputable. Thus the publication of *Ecl.* 5 must be placed after July 42 B.C. only if (as is maintained on pp. 28-9 and in the commentary) it was connected with the first celebration of Julius Caesar's birthday with full divine honours. Other allusions are now irrecoverable: for instance the date of Pollio's *noua carmina* (3.86), of Gallus' aetiological poem (6.72-3) or his love affair with Cytheris (10 passim). Even *Ecl.* 1 and 9, concerned with the aftermath of the land-confiscations, cannot be accurately placed; for although the resettlement of veterans that necessitated the evictions was begun by the triumvirs late in 42 B.C. after the battle of Philippi, it continued right through the thirties. The reference to Varus and Mantua in 9 point to a notional date in 42-40 B.C., but there is no such clue in the other poem.

The first criterion enables us at best to place Eclogues 5, 4, 8 and 6, in that order, within the period 42 B.C. to 38 or a little later.

Cross-references and echoes between Eclogues provide a second dating criterion. Thus 5.85-7 reveals that 2 and 3 were already published, otherwise the allusion to them would be not only pointless but unintelligible. The oblique reference to the theme of 5 at 9.46-50 likewise presupposes the reader's familiarity with the former poem. Indeed Menalcas' fragments in 9.23-5 etc. would lose much of their impact if most of the other Eclogues had not already been published. Again the probable connection between 8.97-9 and 9.54 is the more effective if the former passage was the earlier. By contrast the much-discussed links between 3.89 and 4.25, 30 and between 1.74 and 9.50 cannot by themselves be used to establish priority one way or the other, and the echoes in 10 from 2 and 8 add nothing to our knowledge of the relative chronology of these two poems.

The second criterion, combined with the first, suggests an order 2, 3, 5, 4, 8, 9, 6, 10 (with the possibility that 9 preceded 8).

Lastly there is the stylistic criterion. Inevitably subjective impressions enter at this point and the time-span of the whole collection is too short for the application of objective statistical checks. Moreover such distinctive features as can be plotted—like the relatively high incidence of spondaic rhythm in *Ecl.* 4 or of fourth-foot homodynes and contracted perfect forms of the verb in *Ecl.* 6—are more likely to be connected with the thematic individuality of the poems in which they occur than with their chronological location.

Of more importance is Vergil's changing relationship to Greek pastoral. Here too caution is needed; for so little survives of post-Theocritean Greek pastoral that apparent innovations by the Latin poet may have had more precedent than we are aware. So far as Theocritus is concerned a 'spectrum' of *imitatio* can be observed both at the level of whole poems and in terms of local detail. 2, 3, 7 and 8 stand formally or thematically within the Theocritean tradition; 5, 10 and 9 employ setting and motifs from Theocritus, but in new contexts or in association with new material; 1, 4 and 6 are original compositions with few essential traces of Theocritean influence. As for local detail: many lines of *Ecl.* 3 are little more than paraphrases of Theocritus; but a freer more original mode of adaptation is revealed for instance in the description of the cups in 3.35-48, the recollection of the first falling in love in 8.37-41 and the visitation of the gods in 10.21-30; and a distinctively Vergilian handling of conventional figures is to be found in the rustic analogies of 5.16-18, 45-7, 82-4, the sympathy figure in 7.53-60 and the *locus amoenus* of 1.51-8. Lastly we find in all the poems details that are entirely without Theocritean precedent.

The pattern of Vergilian *imitatio* is in fact very complex and cannot be neatly reconciled with the chronology suggested by the other criteria; there is far more of Theocritus for example in 8 than in 4, and we may have to reckon here with the reworking of earlier compositions. Nevertheless it is broadly true that poems which can be shown on other evidence to be late exhibit a bolder, more independent treatment of such Theocritean material as they employ. Taking Eclogues that are comparable in form or subject matter, we can detect in 1, 7 and 8 signs of greater maturity both of conception and composition than in their partners 9, 3 and 2 respectively.

The third criterion gives no ground for revising the order proposed earlier; but it does support the location of 7 in the latter half of the series and 1 in the latest group, along with 6 and 10.

Taking together the phrase *a te principium* in 8.11, the tribute to Pollio in 3.84-7 and the ancient tradition concerning the motivation of *Ecl.* 2, which is discussed in the final note on this poem, we may conclude that certainly the second Eclogue and probably also the third were dedicated explicitly to Pollio. From 45 B.C. Pollio was in Hispania Ulterior, whence he returned in 42 or 41 to take charge of Gallia Cisalpina on Antony's behalf. His return from Spain would have provided an appropriate occasion for Vergil to present him with the first-fruits of his patronage. So the publication of *Ecl.* 2 and 3 can be assigned to 42-41 B.C., when the poet was *XXVIII annos natus*. The words *tibi desinam* also in 8.11 suggest that this poem, dedicated again to Pollio on the occasion of his triumphal return in 39 B.C., was intended to complete Vergil's Pastoral *œuvre*. To date this would have comprised a pair of Eclogues on the pains and perils of love, both homosexual (2) and heterosexual (8), a pair on political themes, 5 and 4, and the contest-poem 3. To these we can surely add 7, the other contest-poem, on the assumption that 7 and 8 were intended to form a complementary pair to 3 and 2 and published close to each other in 39 B.C. The **Bucolica** that Vergil *triennio perfecit* were thus 2, 3, 5, 4, 7 and 8. With minor revisions to the earlier ones (Servius' *emendasse*) these could all have been published in a collected edition towards the end of 39 B.C. and dedicated to Pollio. They form a nicely varied set of pastorals and the chronological order also provides a neat chiastic arrangement of forms and themes for the whole group.

If a Theocritean Bucolic corpus of ten idylls was already accepted, it is likely that Vergil had the idea of a decad of Eclogues in mind from the start. However, even if the Pollio group were not actually published as a collection, the implication of 8.11 is that he had put aside any such idea, at any rate until new sources of inspiration for pastoral invention could be found. In the event some of his most novel and important work in the genre was to come; for it is probable that 9 and 1, certain that 6 and 10 belong to the years after 39 B.C.

It is not known at what date all ten Eclogues were republished as a single book; but the early years of the Principate seem the most likely period. There is no reason to doubt that the order of the poems in that edition was the one that is observed consistently in the manuscript tradition, or that Vergil himself intended it to have some significance. What that significance was seems already to have eluded the ancient commentators: *naturalem consertumque ordinem nullum esse certissimum est* (Don. *Vit.* 322-3). In recent years the question has been much discussed. Arithmetical explanations have been especially in favour, ranging from fantastic structural analogues with 'Bucolic chapels' and Neo-Pythagorean number-symbolism, through the calculation of 'Golden sections', to more sober ingenuities concerning 'Symmetry and sense'. There is little agreement among the scholars who choose this kind of approach, and the firm numerical facts are hardly sensational, e.g. that 2 and 8 together have almost the same number of lines (182 or 183) as 3 and 7 (181), which may be deliberate, or that 4 and 6 together have almost the same number (149) as 1 and 9 (150), which is probably coincidental. The discussion that follows is on altogether different lines.

Clearly the Pollio group forms the core of the book: 2, 3, 5, 4, 7, 8. The four poems published subsequently form two pairs: 9 and 1 on the effects of the land confiscations, 6 and 10 on Gallus and poetry. *Ecl.* 10 is explicitly the end-piece of the collection. A straight chronological arrangement would probably have given 2, 3, 5, 4, 7, 8, 9, 1, 6, 10, or something very similar. But if the Pollio group was kept intact and its chiastic arrangement of complementary pairs continued, with the earlier poem preceding in each instance, the order would have been 6, 9, 2, 3, 5, 4, 7, 8, 1, 10, with the two pairs of conventional pastorals, 2 and 3, 7, and 8 alternating with the three pairs of more original poems, 6 and 9, 5 and 4, 10 and 1, and the political Eclogues 5 and 4 in central position. The prominent position of 6 and 10 would reflect both the influence of Gallus on Vergil's literary ideas at the time when these two Eclogues were published and the personal esteem in which Vergil held him. The opinion reported by Servius, *alii primam illam uolunt 'prima Syracosio'* (**Buc** prooem., 3.19-20; cf. Don. *Vit.* 324-5), which is usually taken as a silly inference from the first word of the sixth Eclogue, may ultimately reflect Vergil's intention for the first decad edition.

It seems clear that Ovid (*A.* 1.15.25) and Calpurnius (4.62-3) knew *Tityrus* as the first poem of the **Bucolica**. But the implications of *G.* 4.565-6, *carmina qui lusi pastorum audaxque iuuenta,* | *Tityre, te patulae cecini sub tegmine fagi,* are much less certain. We do not know the date of this coda to the Georgics, and in any case the reference may be not to the Eclogues as a whole but specifically to *Ecl.* 1. It is not difficult however to see why *Ecl.* 6 was not retained in first position. It would have been aesthetically somewhat disconcerting to begin the collection with its least pastoral member. The Eclogue is dedicated to a minor patron who on the evidence of 9.27 had in the event done little to earn the poet's gratitude. Moreover, if the final edition came out in the early Augustan period, it would not have seemed inappropriate to promote to a prominent position the one Eclogue in which the Princeps himself appears; *deus nobis haec otia fecit* would now have a significance far beyond its immediate context in the poem. If that edition postdated Gallus' public disgrace and suicide in 26 B.C., then the political motive would have acquired a more sinister urgency.

The demotion of 6 and the concomitant transposition of 1 and 9 (if indeed they were not already in this order) entailed adjustments to the pattern of the book. With 10 now taking on the status of an epilogue to the chiastically ordered group 1, 2, 3, 5, 4, 7, 8, 9, the obvious place for 6 was in the centre of 1-9, between 5 and 4. Instead Vergil chose, somewhat surprisingly, to place it before 7 and to reverse the order of 5 and 4 (assuming that they were not already in this order). Now to have left 5, 4, 6 in that order would have spoiled the chiastic symmetry, since 5 and 6 cannot on any interpretation be paired together like 3 and 7, 2 and 8; but it would have left the Messianic Eclogue in central position, a fine Augustan gesture from the poet who was to write, if he had not already written,

of *Augustus Caesar* as founder of the new *aurea . . . saecula* (*A.* 6.792-3). The arrangement finally adopted detaches 4 from its original thematic counterpart 5 and sets it in a new relationship with 6—Sibyl's prophecy balanced by Silenus' song—leaving 5 centrally placed within the chiastic group, and incidentally in a new relationship with the concluding 10, comparable to that of 4 with 6. The effect of placing 5 centrally and after 4 rather than before it is to place the emphasis on the vaguer, less extravagant, statement of political optimism, which may reflect the poet's feelings towards the Augustan Golden Age after the persecution of his friend Gallus.

Something of the pattern discernible in the Pollio group of six has indeed survived into the final edition of ten. The impressively ranging sequence of themes—poetic manifestos, the dispossessions, the pains and perils of love, the conventional topics of pastoral singing contests, political tributes and aspirations, and then back again—has been truncated, to be sure, but at least the pattern of formal variation remains. First the odd-numbered poems: 1 and 9 are conversation-pieces, 3 and 7 singing competitions introduced by conversation, 5 a conversation enclosing a pair of balanced songs. Among the even poems: in 8 a brief scene-setting leads to a competition in the form of two balanced songs, in 2 it is followed by a monologue, 6 and 10 have a narrative scene leading to a monologue, 4 has a brief proem followed by a monologue in the poet's own person. While the even-numbered poems are thus more varied in form, the general distinction holds throughout: in contrast to the other five they are all non-conversational. Indeed this formal criterion, which was clearly important in the general arrangement, may have determined the final order of 4, 5, 6 after 6 had been demoted.

Much of this discussion has of necessity been speculative. Many readers of the **Eclogues** would no doubt prefer, given the impossibility of definitive answers, to leave questions of both chronology and arrangement unexplored. Yet arguments about the order in which the poems were written are closely bound up with our views of what Vergil was attempting to do with the pastoral genre and how his conception of it developed as he wrote. Furthermore a poet's decisions about the arrangement of his book are an integral part of the creative process itself, even if only a minor one. Hence in grappling with both questions we are continually brought back to various aspects of the poems and their interrelationships, some of which will be taken up in the concluding section. This is perhaps the chief justification of the enquiry.

3. VERGIL'S ACHIEVEMENT AS A PASTORAL POET

The reader who comes to the **Eclogues** direct from Theocritus immediately recognizes much that is familiar, and we have already noticed some of the modes of Vergilian *imitatio* (p. 17). Yet the conventional figures and motifs are often treated with an originality of detail and a care for their integration into the new contexts that is both striking and effective. Thus, for instance, the rustic analogy (p. 9), which in 2.63-5 still retains much of its Theocritean naivety, becomes in its recurrent variations at 5.16-18, 45-7, 82-4 a vehicle for asserting the pastoral integrity of the poem. Similarly with the sympathy figure (p. 9). In 1.38-9 the image of Tityrus' farm mourning his departure grows naturally out of the preceding lines, in which the signs of neglect resulting from his absence are realistically depicted. Again at 7.53-60 the 'Where'er you walk' variant of the figure has been transformed by Vergil into a subtle and evocative conceit, reminiscent—like much else in the poem—of Hellenistic epigram at its best.

The conventional singing competition appears in two of the poems. The first of them, *Ecl.* 3, is in many places little more than a pastiche of Theocritean reminiscences. The original details, though significant for the direction that Vergil's concept of the genre was already taking, are either obscure—like the symbolic figures on the cups and the related pair of riddles at the end—or else clumsy—like the abrupt intrusion of Pollio and contemporary literary controversy into the songs of the two herdsmen. By contrast Vergil reverts in *Ecl.* 7 to a purer, more homogeneous pastoral conception. The range of themes—rustic piety, delight in the countryside and its music, the pleasures and sorrows of country love—is entirely conventional. But the detail is almost. . .original, the technique is mature and the choice of quatrains rather than couplets enables each theme to be elaborated more fully. Moreover Vergil manages subtly to characterize the two singers through the songs that he assigns to them. In fact this highly wrought poem stands as one of the finest essays in pure pastoral ever written.

An important innovation in *Ecl.* 7 is the description of the two singers as *Arcades*. The mythical character of their Arcady is indicated by its setting here (7.13) beside the Mantuan river Mincio: it represents a synthesis of the conventional pastoral myth, certain traditions about Arcadia (see 7.4n.), and Vergil's own view of the Italian countryside and its way of life, coloured by the memories of his own boyhood home in Cisalpine Gaul. The definitive presentment of this Arcady occurs only in the last pastoral that he wrote, *Ecl.* 10, whence it was mediated by way of Sannazaro's *Arcadia* (1504) to the Renaissance exponents of the genre.

As in Theocritus, the very full picture that we get of the idealized landscape is built up gradually by descriptive details scattered through each poem. At first sight it is remarkably consistent in the two poets. In the foreground meadows grazed by goats, sheep or cattle, with flowers and shrubs humming with bees, nearby springs and rivers lined with willows and marsh-reeds, hollow rocks and shady trees to provide shelter from the heat, in the branches above the rustle of the breeze and the throaty cooing of pigeons and doves; not far off are orchards, vines and ploughed fields—here Vergil widens the Golden Age landscape of the pastoral to incorporate more of the real countryside—and in the near distance wooded hills,

sometimes a tract of open water—specifically the sea in 2.26—and further away a market town. That the poet of the *Georgics,* born and brought up in the farming region of Mantua, depended for any of this on the writings of his distinguished Syracusan predecessor passes all belief. The details of the scene right down to the flowers and trees that are named belong not to exotic places evoking magical landscapes but to the familiar Italian countryside. In Vergil's *locus amoenus* as in so much else the Theocritean convention has been revitalized and enriched by personal experience and observation of the world about him.

The few passages of detailed description are all contextually significant, but in ways that go far beyond Theocritus. Meliboeus' description of Tityrus' farm (1.51-8) as a *locus amoenus* is contrasted emphatically with his brutally realistic account of the place a few lines earlier (1.47-8). But the intervening couplet, recalling the hazards that await him in exile, reveals the significance of the contrast. To one deprived even the familiar scene of the humblest farm takes on the aura of Arcady.

The same contrast is to be found as early as *Ecl.* 2, where Corydon describes in detail (46-55) the gift of flowers and fruits that the Nymphs will bring to Alexis, if by some chance he deigns to descend to the *sordida rura* (28). It is a rich complex of sensuous imagery: colour, scent and texture. But it is entirely the product of his imagination - for the ingredients could never be in season together - and its significance lies, like Meliboeus' *locus amoenus,* in its revelation of the power of the humble countryside to inspire in its inhabitants a truly Arcadian vision, one which in the end no alien townsman can fully share.

Intimations of the real countryside and its routines occur in Theocritus of course, especially before and after the interludes of song. But they are more numerous and wideranging in Vergil. Thus, in addition to Theocritean details like the dangers to the flocks (3.94-9) and the basketwork (2.72), there are references to ploughing and sowing (2.66, 5.36) and pruning (9.61), swineherding (10.19), marketing (1.34-5) and even the technicalities of animal husbandry (1.45). Hunting too figures more prominently in the *Eclogues* than in the Idylls (2.29, 3.75, 5.60-1, 7.29-30). References to Italian religion, e.g. the *Ambarualia* in 3.76, Pales and Ceres in 5.35, 79, Fauni in 6.27, Silvanus in 10.24, are less remarkable, as are the riddles in 3.104-7, a rustic detail without precedent nevertheless in extant pastoral. Calpurnius adds to the Italian colour by including for instance the finger-game and the deities Flora and Pomona in his *Ecl.* 2.25-33. Even socio-legal concepts, which are distinctly foreign to pure pastoral, are introduced in the Eclogues—citizen and slave status (1.32, 71), formal marriage (8.29-30), the rights of *possessio* (9.3). Some of these details, to be sure, have a particular contextual relevance, but this in itself indicates the widening of the range of the genre. We can certainly reconstruct far more of the conditions of ordinary life in the country from the *Eclogues* than we ever could from the Idylls.

The herdsmen, as in most subsequent pastoral, still have Greek names. To Vergil's contemporaries, familiar with the *latifundia* of the Italian countryside, which were heavily dependent upon slave-labour from the Greek-speaking world, this would not have seemed remote from reality. Yet Meliboeus in *Ecl.* 1 and Menalcas in *Ecl.* 9 seem to be Roman citizens, and the retention of the Greek names here is a device for integrating them fully into the pastoral fiction. Indeed the retention of the Greek case forms *Alexi, Daphnin, Amaryllida* etc. throughout the Eclogues intensifies the Greek colour. As in Theocritus, it is not easy to determine the precise status of individual herdsmen: some may be slaves, others hired farm-hands, others again small-holders. However where social status is relevant to the dramatic situation of the poem it is usually clarified, as with Tityrus and Meliboeus in *Ecl.* 1, Corydon and Alexis in *Ecl.* 2. Donatus' observation (*Vit.* 215-18) that cattleherds take precedence over shepherds, shepherds over goatherds—swineherds do not even merit a mention—certainly applies to the real countryside, where the type of stock grazed reflects the quality of the land. However apart from the fact that, as in Theocritus, the prestigious Daphnis is always a cattleherd and Tityrus generally in a position of subservience to the other characters, there seems to be no particular hierarchy among the herdsmen. Some of Vergil's herdsmen graze a variety of animals, for instance Tityrus (1), Meliboeus (7); and even when they are explicitly associated with one kind—Mopsus (5) and Corydon (7) have goats, Menalcas (3) and Thyrsis (7) sheep, Damoetas (3) cattle—this hardly ever excludes the possibility of diversification, nor is it implied that one kind of herdsman is superior to another. Indeed goats and sheep, not cattle, appear in the Golden Age imagery of *Ecl.* 4 and Vergil's choice of the goatherd's role for himself in *Ecl.* 10, though it may be a suggestion of humility (as Servius believed), is more likely to mark the difference between the poet and Gallus in their commitment to Arcadian life.

The fact that Corydon is a Mantuan goatherd in *Ecl.* 7 and a Sicilian herdsman grazing principally sheep in *Ecl.* 2 raises specifically a more general question: how far can we expect to see connections between characters in different poems who bear the same name? Certainly the two gentle Corydons have much in common and 7.37-40 seems a deliberate, if oblique, invitation to associate them. Amaryllis too is consistently portrayed throughout, and it is possible, as with some of the other characters, to compose a biographical sketch of her. She is pretty (1.5), quick-tempered (2.14, 3.81), an efficient housewife (1.30), not unfamiliar with the occult (8.77), fancied by Corydon (2.52), Damoetas (3.81), Lycidas and Menalcas (or Moeris, 9.22), but she settled for security with old Tityrus (1.5, 30). Again the subservient role assigned to Tityrus elsewhere is clearly relevant to his situation in *Ecl.* 1; and the possibility that in Moeris' words at 9.54 we are meant to recall the Moeris of 8.97-8 adds to the pathos of the former context. On the other hand the Meliboei of 3.1 and 7.9 seem irrelevant to the Meliboeus of *Ecl.* 1, and Daphnis can hardly be the same person in 5.56-7 as in 9.46. On the whole it seems that with the exception of Menalcas (see pp. 29, 31) there is, as in Theocritus, nothing much to

be gained (or for that matter lost) from a general assumption that the recurrence of the same name is significant.

Latin had of course no literary dialects. So in an effort to reproduce something of the effect of Theocritus' Doric Vergil puts into the mouths of his herdsmen colloquial and archaic forms and idioms redolent of rural dialects. Whether he went as far as introducing rustic spellings like *hedus* for *haedus* is very doubtful; for although such forms are often attested in our manuscripts of the poems, they may reflect late Latin pronunciation rather than the rusticity of the classical period. The colloquialisms that do occur come chiefly in conversations or in those parts of the formal songs that concern practical husbandry. It is likely that ancient purists objected, as Boileau and Pope did later, to such linguistic realism as being beneath the dignity of the genre; and it can hardly be coincidental that colloquialism is prominent in all three parodies of the Eclogues cited in Donatus' *Vita* (174-7) and Servius (on 5.36). However such details do not seem to have affected Horace's assessment of the general tone of the *Eclogues* as being *molle atque facetum* 'delicate and witty' (*S.* 1.10.44). The two epithets probably refer to style rather than matter, and are notoriously difficult to translate.[20] They clearly imply a register far removed from that of epic (cf. Prop. 2.1.2, 41); which is indeed the point of the phrase in Horace's own context. The combination of Latin rusticity with Greek colour, produced by the frequency of Greek proper names complete with Greek case forms, is the linguistic counterpart of the blend of Greek myth and Latin reality that is the distinctive characteristic of the *Eclogues*.

Molle atque facetum would serve as a description of the personal poetry of Catullus or the Hellenistic epigrammatists. Indeed the affinities between the Greek pastoral and elegiac treatment of erotic themes were taken up and explored further by Vergil in the *Eclogues*. As in Theocritus and his successors, the emphasis is again on the sorrows of constant love, set against a background of more carefree bisexual promiscuity.

Ecl. 2, the lament of Corydon, has many echoes of Greek pastoral—the comic serenader of *Id.* 3, the angry goatherd of *Id.* 20, the alienated reaper of *Id.* 10 and above all the love-sick Polyphemus of *Id.* 11. The formative influence of Meleager's Alexis epigram (*A.P.* 12.127) is seen in the homosexuality of the poem and the conceit that it exploits in the contrast between the transient heat of the midday sun and the unabating fires of frustrated passion. Moreover Vergil has added to the situation a successful rival, Iollas, the *dives amator* familiar from Augustan elegy. Out of this material he is able to create a more complex human character, whose abrupt changes of mood—between longing and brutal self-awareness—bring a dramatic movement to the shepherd's monologue. Like the lovers of Roman elegy Corydon is more preoccupied with the pains of his love than with the praises of the beloved, and is at once a comic and a pathetic figure. In fact here in this elegiac pastoral we have the true prototype of the Passionate Shepherd of the later pastoral tradition.

In *Ecl.* 8 we are presented with a study in the contrasting reactions of lovers to infidelity, real or imagined. Formally the carefully balanced songs of Damon and Alphesiboeus represent a *contaminatio* of motifs taken from the first two idylls of Theocritus. Damon's goatherd, who has been jilted by Nysa, reveals all the passivity of Corydon in *Ecl.* 2, but with none of the turbulent fluctuations of mood; and his grief, intensified by the memory of their first meeting—a brilliant adaptation of a scene from *Id.* 11—leads not to the day-dreaming resignation that we saw in *Ecl.* 2 or to the defiant martyrdom of Theocritus' Daphnis but to suicidal despair. In Alphesiboeus' song, a pastoral adaptation of one of Theocritus' urban idylls, the girl, suspecting her absent lover's infidelity, resorts to the *carmina* of magic to bring him back. Unlike the goatherd she is positive and determined, and in a passage inspired by Lucretius, which subtly exposes her own vulnerability, she looks forward to the triumphal conclusion of her arts. There is here perhaps an implied *praeceptum amoris:* to the forsaken lover resourceful boldness may accomplish more than the application of the 'Muses' medicine'.

Finally in *Ecl.* 10 the theme of *sollicitus amor* appears in relation to an historical person; Vergil's friend and fellow-poet Cornelius Gallus is depicted languishing in Arcady. The opening scene recalls the setting of Daphnis' death in *Id.* 1, but Gallus' address to the Arcadians is wholly new to pastoral. Gallus longs to have escaped from his troubles by becoming an Arcadian; yet his commitment is half-hearted. His conception of Arcady is dominated by the image of its abundant and varied love-life and the pleasures of hunting. No suggestion here of tending the flocks and pastures. Indeed some of the details of his monologue (10.44-9, 53-4) recall non-pastoral motifs from elegy. Like Corydon in *Ecl.* 2—and the comparison is reinforced by several echoes of that poem—he experiences abrupt changes of mood; his yearning to escape to Arcady leads to a desire to share its delights with the faithless Lycoris. His conclusion, *omnia uincit Amor, et nos cedamus Amori,* takes us back in this the latest of all the ***Eclogues*** to the resignation of the rejected lover, which was the theme of the earliest of them.

The Vergilian treatment of love in these three poems is more complex, its melancholy more distinctively elegiac than in Theocritus, and it is not surprising that Propertius and Ovid recognized in the Eclogues a kindred voice (*Eleg.* 2.34.67ff., *Tr.* 2.537-8). Nevertheless, if we apply Johnson's criterion of true pastoral as a 'poem in which any action or passion is represented by its effects on a country life' it must be admitted that in Vergil, as in Theocritus and even more in later pastoral, the rustic setting is but a masque for the presentment of a generalized study of the *chagrins d'amour.* Only in *Ecl.* 2 is the rustic voice essential to the conception of the lover's suffering.

The presence of Gallus in *Ecl.* 10 brings us to another feature of Vergilian pastoral: the concern to relate the mythical world directly and explicitly to contemporary reality. The precedents were there in *Id.* 7 and the *Lament for Bion.* As early as *Ecl.* 3 we can see an attempt to extend it in the explicit reference to Pollio, Bavius and Mevius. Apart from the dedication of *Ecl.* 6 (Varus), historical characters are introduced in their own names also in *Ecl.* 4 (Pollio), 6 and 10 (Gallus) and 9 (Varus, Varius and Cinna); and *iuuenem* in 1.42 clearly alludes to Octavian. So Vergil did not scruple to break the pastoral illusion when it suited his purpose. But it must be admitted that, apart from Pollio in *Ecl.* 4 and Gallus in *Ecl.* 10, who are portrayed in a way that is not inorganic to the mythical context, these unassimilated intrusions of real persons are awkward and disconcerting. Johnson's comment on *Ecl.* 6 is very much to the point: after conceding that it 'rises to the dignity of philosophic sentiment and heroic poetry' he concludes that 'since the compliment paid to Gallus fixes the transaction to his own time, the fiction of Silenus seems injudicious' (*The Adventurer* no. 92, 22 Sept. 1753).

A different mode of allusion appears as early as *Ecl.* 5. Like *Ecl.* 8 it contains a pair of equally balanced and thematically complementary songs: on the death and deification of Daphnis. In contrast to the other *retractationes* of the Daphnis-motif in 8.17-61 and 10.9-30 the erotic context of Daphnis' death in *Id.* 1 has been removed and the apotheosis of Daphnis added. Vergil has in fact gone back beyond Theocritus to the original Daphnis, the Sicilian rustic hero, and used the myth of his death and deification to allude to recent history, paying a poetic tribute to Julius Caesar and proclaiming in pastoral imagery his own political sympathies. In *Ecl.* 8 he was to bring together the treatment of erotic themes from urban and pastoral idylls of Theocritus. In *Ecl.*5 he introduced the political themes of *Idd.* 16 and 17 into the pastoral genre. The image of the ruler as shepherd of his people is as old as Homer (*Iliad* 2.243). Pastoral precedent for panegyric on the death of an historical person existed in the *Lament for Bion.* The further step that Vergil has taken is a small one, but it was decisive. For it opened the way to the employment of pastoral in the praise of princes, which appears already in the eulogies of Nero in *Einsiedeln Ecl.* 1 and Calpurnius *Ecl.* 1 and 4, and in the Renaissance provided a precedent for converting the genre into elaborate allegory, to the eventual impoverishment of its distinctive character. In *Ecl.* 5 the technique is allusive rather than allegorical. All the detail is organic to the pastoral myth; it is only in the poem taken as a whole and read in its historical context that we can see that it is more than a variation on the traditional pastoral theme. The representation of Vergil and Caesar through the pastoral figures of Menalcas and Daphnis assimilates them to the Arcadian world[21] in a way that Pollio, Varus and the rest never are; the retention of their historical names marks them off as outsiders, not necessarily hostile but intruders nonetheless from the historical world beyond the myth.

Menalcas' song reflects the optimism inspired by the Julian comet, which had appeared in the heavens in the summer of 44 B.C. These hopes for a new era of peace and prosperity, reiterated in 9.46-50, also inspired a far more original pastoral. *Ecl.* 4 is based upon the contrapuntal elaboration of two powerful apocalyptic images, the miraculous birth of a Wonder-Child and the return of nature's Golden Age.

As we have already observed, the Golden Age had close links with the pastoral myth; but Vergil seems to have been the first poet to conceive the *Saturnia regna* not as belonging exclusively to the irrecoverable past but as something destined to return to the earth in the future. Here we can detect the influence of cyclic conceptions of history like the *magnus annus,* which is in fact alluded to in the opening thematic exposition. The image of the Child, easily associated with the primaeval innocence of the Golden Age and the pastoral, seems to have had a prominent role in many myth-ritual patterns relating to the annual rebirth of the seasons. As an apocalyptic figure it belongs to Near Eastern culture and is most familiar to us from the prophetic verses of the Book of Isaiah, which Christians have always interpreted as foretelling the birth of Jesus. St Augustine likewise identified Vergil's Child here, and *Ecl.* 4, combining with the pastoralism of the Gospels, as represented in Luk. 2.8, 15.4, Joh. 10.11 (cf. Heb. 13.20), 21.16, established Messianism as a theme for Christian pastoral. Vergil himself probably took the image of the Child from Sibylline oracle, to which allusion is made explicitly in the opening exposition of the poem, and saw the imaginative possibilities of combining it with ingredients of the Hesiodic Golden Age to form a new kind of pastoral poem. The hopes for peace in time of crisis that had been expressed by Theocritus in the non-pastoral context of *Id.* 16.88ff. are thus incorporated into the thematic range of this most pacific of all poetic genres.

Fifteen years or so later, in *A.* 6.791-7, Vergil purported to see the fulfilment of the prophesied Golden Age in the principate of Augustus. But when the Eclogue was published, few could have dreamt that the struggle for power between the triumvirs would end as it did. In 40 B.C. the immediate future looked dark indeed, and it is not surprising that the optimism of the poem is qualified, at its centre, by the prediction of heroic wars still to come.

One of the legacies of continuing civil war was the upheavals throughout Italy caused by the confiscation of land for the resettlement of veterans from the victorious armies. The dispossessions began late in 42 B.C., after Philippi, and continued until after Actium. Their effects on the Italian countryside are the subject of the next two poems.

Both are conversation-pieces. In *Ecl.* 9 Lycidas and Moeris meet on the way to town—the situation vaguely recalls *Id.* 7. Moeris' former master, the poet Menalcas, has lost his land and gone away, leaving him in reluctant service—perhaps as a hired farm-hand—to the new absentee landlord. On their way the two men sing snatches of Menalcas' poetry, and the contrast between Lycidas' eagerness to sing and Moeris' growing reluctance brings out the more intimate relationship of the latter to the departed poet. The fragments—on themes of Theocritean pastoral, on Varus and Mantua and on Daphnis and the Julian

comet—clearly allude to the range of styles and subject matter found in the Eclogues themselves. So we may conclude that, as in *Ecl.* 5, Menalcas represents Vergil.[22] There is perhaps a touch of presumption in the tribute that he thus obliquely pays to himself; but it is set in the context of the impotence of poetry in times of civil strife, the protest against which becomes explicit in lines 11-13. By adopting the pastoral mask of Menalcas he is able not only to identify himself with the pastoral scene that he has created but also to generalize his own misfortunes. In the same way the pastoral figures of Lycidas and Moeris serve to typify the harsh effects of the dispossessions in breaking up old friendships and associations. The sadness of the two herdsmen must have been repeated many times up and down Italy.

The first Eclogue, one of the finest poems in the language, is a study of the contrasting fortunes and temperaments of two typical Italian countrymen. The ageing slave Tityrus, threatened by the evictions with the loss of his one hope of gaining freedom, has secured both his land and his freedom by joining in the protest march to Rome. Octavian, the *iuuenis* of line 42, has conceded the demonstrators' requests and is rewarded by the promise of divine honours. Meliboeus, apparently a Roman citizen, has been evicted but has done nothing to help himself. As in *Ecl.* 8 there is the same contrast between the gentle, passive sufferer and the more resourceful and determined character. Meliboeus, who has all the finest poetry of the Eclogue, is wistful as he goes off into exile, and his envy, not marred by any bitterness towards his friend, gives way to anger only at the thought of the barbarian usurper on his land. Tityrus' success has made him complacent and hard, insensitive to others' plight, and it is only at the end—with his offer of a night's hospitality—that the Arcadian values of sympathy and friendship are reasserted.

From *Ecl.* 9 it is clear that Vergil like Meliboeus had known the pain of eviction. But although the loss of his ancestral land at Mantua must have affected him deeply, he could at least rely on powerful friends to secure material compensation. In these two poems, then, he is less concerned with his own personal troubles than with the plight of his fellow-countrymen in rural Italy, the recent disruption of that peace on which the prosperity of farmers and of the arts alike depends, and the grim reminder that such things were at the mercy of dynasts and generals. Through the refined verses of the two Eclogues we catch the authentic voice of the countryman, modulated with a sympathetic understanding that is far removed from the patronizing urbanity of most pastoral poets before or since.

Vergil saw in the myth of Arcady not just a pretty *divertissement* for those disaffected citizens who were refined enough to appreciate it but an embodiment of certain moral ideals that he could himself identify closely with the real countryside: a simple way of life, contentment with little, delight in natural beauty, homely piety, friendship and hospitality, devotion to poetry and to peace. If the longing for a lost organic culture is, as some modern theorists have claimed, implicit in the pastoral concept, it was Vergil who developed and exploited this potentiality, to make the genre a vehicle for positive moral criticism of the urban society of his own day. Hence the truth of the Renaissance view, as represented for instance by George Puttenham in *The Arte of English poesie* (1589), 1.18: 'These *Eglogues* came after to containe and enforme morall discipline for the Amendment of man's behauiour . . .'

Throughout the *Eclogues* the city represents a constant threat to Arcadian values: in *Ecl.* 2 the urban Alexis despises Corydon's humble passion and simple rustic life, in *Ecl.* 8 it is the city that threatens to deprive the girl of her lover, in *Ecl.* 9 the city is the goal of Moeris' distasteful journey, in *Ecl.* 1 the *ingrata urbs* preys on farmers in peace and has them at its mercy in time of war. The antithesis of rural and urban life provides a further link with the Golden Age myth, and the walled cities are symptoms of *priscae uestigia fraudis* in 4.31-3. Within the pastoral itself the countryman's hostility towards the city, taken from the real world, is the ideological counterpart to the idealized view of the country that is urbanely exhibited in the orthodox genre itself. In earlier pastoral the very existence of towns seems to have been ignored nor is antagonism to towns an explicit theme of later classical pastoral. On the contrary in Calp. *Ecl.* 7 the countryman Lycotas is reprimanded for neglecting the delights that the city has to offer. But the antithesis of town and country, which was important in Horace's moralizing (e.g. *C.* 3.29, *Ep.* 1.10), became an important ingredient in the Renaissance tradition of the pastoral, where it was enriched by the mediaeval *pastourelle* and by the '*Nature* v. *Nurture*' topos.

The moral criticism borne by the antithesis was elaborated and deepened by Vergil himself in the *Georgics* (especially 2.467ff.). The Arcadian *otium* of the Theocritean tradition is there counterpoised by the Hesiodic doctrine of *labor*. Hard and soft primitivism are thus brought together and the idea of a sympathetic bond between man and his natural environment is underpinned not by the Epicurean *securitas* of the pastoral but by a more distinctly Stoic creed. It is carried through even into the idyllic homeliness of Evander's Arcadian settlement in *Aeneid* 8, which is exhibited as a model to the contemporary Augustan metropolis.

The notion that pastoral *otium* and rustic *labor* are complementary, that the ideals of Arcady are attainable only to those who accept the humble round of work in the country, is already there in the *Eclogues*. Corydon's eulogy of the music of Pan and his imaginative rhapsody on the fruits of his land go with his acceptance of the *sordida . . . rura* and *humilis . . . casas*. The disconsolateness of Gallus who seeks only *otium* in Arcady is set against the homely picture of the Arcadian herdsmen themselves (10.19-20) and the concluding image of the Arcadian poet plaiting baskets even while he sings. Within this synthesis of myth and reality the linguistic blend of exoticism and realism mentioned earlier (pp. 24-6) finds its appropriate context.

Yet the fine balance of myth and reality on which Vergilian pastoral depends was too delicate to remain for long undisturbed. The introduction of allusions to contemporary history opened the way to the presentment of situations that have little to do with the country. The identification of Menalcas with Vergil in *Ecl.* 5 and 9 became the cue for commentators to hunt for politicians and poets in all the characters of the *Eclogues*. Servius is representative: *aliquibus locis per allegoriam agit gratias Augusto uel aliis nobilibus, quorum fauore amissum agrum recepit. in qua re tantum dissentit a Theocrito; ille enim ubique simplex est, hic necessitate compulsus aliquibus locis miscet figuras quas perite plerumque etiam ex Theocriti uersibus facit, quos ab illo dictos constat esse simpliciter* (**Buc.** prooem. 2.17ff. cf. Don. *Vit.* 294ff.). It is significant that there are no such allegorizing speculations in the *scholia* to Theocritus. This tradition of Vergilian exegesis, which is illustrated in Servius' note on *Ecl.* 1.39, was reinforced by mediaeval and Hermetic traditions of allegorizing, in which special importance was assigned to the *arcana significatio* of shepherd names and the obscure symbolism of every detail in the setting and landscape. From Petrarch and Boccaccio onwards pastoral became a recognized vehicle for social, political and ecclesiastical controversy. The shepherds' cloak conceals not a countryman but a prelate or courtier or even some allegorical abstraction. The descriptive details of the rustic setting, the conversations and songs of its inhabitants have become an elaborate code to be cracked by the ingenious reader. The range of themes of course was greatly extended in other ways. New settings appeared in the piscatory and venatory Eclogues, new subjects included autobiographical fragments and the deaths of friends and relatives, state occasions such as royal birthdays and funerals, invasions and armistices, religious devotions to Christ and the Mother of God, and especially ecclesiastical and theological controversy with moral allegorizing. Johnson's strictures on Milton in this respect (*Lives of the English poets,* ed. Hill, 1.163-5) are well known. There was some fine poetry still, both in Latin and in vernacular pastoral, not least by Milton himself; but the fragile integrity of the genre had been almost totally surrendered. Only perhaps in the treatment of the lover's misfortunes, equally elaborated with allegory and symbolism in the hands of Sannazaro or Sidney, can we see anything essential to the original Theocritean genre surviving. For much of Renaissance pastoral the rustic setting often seems merely a pretty frame for alien material.

Here too Vergil provided something of a precedent with one of his latest pastorals, the enigmatic *Ecl.* 6. The charming bucolic mime in the first part of the poem is the setting for the decidedly un-Arcadian song that the monster Silenus sings to the shepherd boys. After a cosmogony the recital passes, like Ovid's *Metamorphoses,* to a series of myths concerned in the main with disastrous love-affairs and sensational transformations. It is true that we can interpret the lusty satyr's recital as the portrayal of love in both its creative and destructive aspects; for there is an erotic undertone to the whole poem, from the opening reference to the reader *captus amore* to the closing image of the singing Phoebus. But this is a tenuous link indeed with the pastoral eroticism of *Ecl.* 2, 8 and 10.

In fact the style of the recital, like its content, recalls the tradition not of pastoral but of neoteric narrative: elliptical, allusive, picturesque and subjective. It is therefore no surprise to find already in the opening dedication to Varus an echo from the prologue to Callimachus' *Aetia*. The *Eclogue* is Vergil's counterpart to *Id.* 7: a manifesto of poetic principles expounded obliquely in an appropriate poetic form. Silenus' song asserts the universality of poetry: science and mythology alike are its province, 'things that are true' and 'fictions that are just like fact', to quote the Muses' commission to Hesiod. For Vergil himself this conception was associated specifically with the neoteric movement and Gallus, whose Hesiodic initiation makes an abrupt intrusion into the mythological sequence of Silenus' song.

This view of the universality of poetry recalls the symbolic figures of Orpheus and the astronomers in *Ecl.* 3. It points forward to the exquisite blend of science and mythology that Vergil was to achieve in that most Alexandrian and yet most Italian of didactic poems, the *Georgics. Ecl.* 6 reveals the direction in which his thoughts were turning even before his pastoral *œuvre* was complete and so stands somewhat apart from the rest of the collection, even more than 4 and 10, which Donatus (*Vita* 302-3) also excludes from those that are *proprie bucolica*. But like 4 it is surely not unrelated to the particular synthesis of myth and reality that characterizes Vergil's conception of pastoral. The bucolic frame to Silenus' song is after all more significant than it is in the anonymous *Achilles and Deidameia* ([Bion] 2) of Greek pastoral or in Calpurnius' first Eclogue in praise of Nero.

In the *Eclogues* Vergil had explored ways of extending the pastoral that nevertheless preserved and even deepened its essential character. He had developed the theme of *solliciti amores* in directions that brought out the affinities of the genre with the elegiac tradition; he had brought the Arcadian myth into closer relation with the realities of country life and used it as a model by which to criticize the moral values of the world in which he lived, while at the same time enriching the vision of pure pastoral itself. In making the impersonal myth of Arcady the vehicle for an intense, if oblique, form of personal poetry he—far more than Theocritus—can be deemed the father of European pastoral. He might well have disowned much of his progeny, in particular those works that claimed to find their precedent in the Eclogues but for all their undoubted poetic qualities emptied the genre of its essential character and lacked his own passionate commitment to country life. But he could justly take pride in what he himself had achieved in the genre. Moreover the popular success of the poems was instantaneous: *Bucolica* eo successu edidit ut in scaena quoque per cantores crebro pronuntiarentur (Don. *Vit.* 90f.; cf. Tac. *Dial.* 13.2, Serv.ad *Ecl.* 6.11), and they became a classic text for study in the schools. At the end of the

Georgics Vergil contrasts Octavian's achievements in politics and war with his own cloistered devotion to the Muses:

> . . . illo Vergilium me tempore dulcis alebat
> Parthenope studiis florentem ignobilis oti,
> carmina qui lusi pastorum audaxque iuuenta,
> Tityre, te patulae cecini sub tegmine fagi.

The modest humility of the contrast is ironical, coming from the poet who had so eloquently championed Arcadian peace against the discord of *tela Martia;* and the irony is underlined by the allusion to *Ecl.* 1. Octavian is dead; he has gone the way of Ozymandias, King of Kings. But Vergil lives, and a precious part of that life is this little book written 'in the boldness of youth', which contains some of the finest and most original pastoral poetry ever written.

Notes

1. Alexander Pope *Discourse on pastoral poetry* (1709) §5, reproducing the view of Fontenelle and other continental theorists.

2. Athen. 14.619a-b and Diod. 4.84, Aelian *V.H.* 10.18.

3. See *Scholia in Theocritum Vetera* (Wendel) 1-13 and for the corresponding Latin accounts 13-22.

4. 'Arcady' is used for the setting of the pastoral myth throughout this introduction, though it is not found in this sense before Vergil. See *Ecl.* 7.4n.

5. The Greek word *eidúllion* 'a little scene' 'a miniature form (of poetry)'—the precise meaning is obscure—does not occur before Pliny (*Ep.* 4.14.9). Of the twelve pastoral Idylls (1, 3-11, 20, 27) only the first ten were included in the Pastoral canon known to Servius (*Buc. prooem.* 3.21). Two of the ten (8, 9) together with 20 and 27 are nowadays generally acknowledged to be post-Theocritean.

6. Cf. Boileau's censure of the pastoral idiom of Ronsard who 'abject en son langage | fait parler ses bergers comme on parle au village' (*L'Art poétique* 2.17-18) - a judgement which Theocritus would not perhaps have been much inclined to dissent from.

7. Elsewhere in the Idylls it is used for the mime of *The fishermen* (21), urban mimes (2, 14, 15), heroic and mythological pieces (18, 19, 26) and erotic narrative (23). Of these 19, 21, 23 are post-Theocritean. The use of Doric in 18 and 26 may be intended to relate these poems to the treatment of such themes in choral lyric. Both Moschus (*Europa*) and Bion (*Adonis*) employed Doric in mythological poems.

8. Hence the choice of dialects in the non-pastoral Idylls is not whimsical. The Ionic of the two heroic poems (22, 25) relates them to the tradition of epic narrative and the 'Homeric' hymn. In *Id.* 12 the same dialect places the theme in the tradition of Ionian elegy and epigram. In *Id.* 13 the Doricized Ionic may be intended to give pastoral colour to the

myth; in *Id.* 24 and the two patronage poems (16, 17) it contributes an appropriate Pindaric colour to the 'epic' contexts. The Aeolic of *Idd.* 28-30 evokes the personal and especially erotic character of Aeolian lyric.

9. Except 8, which is partly in elegiacs, and 28-30, in Aeolic metres.

10. Quintilian, while noting the distinctively pastoral mood of Theocritus' verses, places him among the Hellenistic epic and didactic poets (10.1.55; cf. 'Longinus' *Sublim.* 33). Servius however assigns the pastoral to the *humile genus* (*Buc. prooem.* 1.16-2.5; cf. Hermog. *Id.* 2.3), clearly distinguishing the Eclogues from the *grandiloquus character* of the *Aeneid*.

11. In Hebrew mythology similarly the pastoral stage intervenes between the expulsion from the Garden and the building of cities: Abel 'the feeder of sheep' is murdered by his brother Cain 'the tiller of the ground', who subsequently builds the first city (Genesis 2 and 4.2, 8, 17).

12. Cf. Pope's definition of the pastoral (*Discourse* §5), 'an image of what they call the Golden Age; so that we are not to describe our shepherds as shepherds at this day really are, but as they may be conceived then to have been; when the best of men follow'd the employment'.

13. Praise of the countryside ultimately became a poetic common-place (cf. Persius *Sat.* 1.70-1) and its ingredients codified in the rhetorical schools (see Libanius 1.517, §200). However the description of natural beauty as an independent self-contained poetic subject is perhaps not found before Tiberianus' *Amnis* and Asmenius' *Adeste Musae*.

14. To these may be added Plato *Phdr.* 229-30 and Lucr. 5.1379-96 referred to earlier.

15. Music-making in the country is a common theme in Hellenistic epigram; e.g. Plato *App. Plan.* 13, Nicaenetus *ap.* Athen. 15.673b, Meleager *A.P.* 9.363.

16. The relative chronology of the examples here, as elsewhere, is less important for our purpose than the occurrence of the theme in the two separate genres.

17. For his prowess as musician and cattleherd see *Idd.* 5.80, 8.81-7 and *A.P.* 9.433. In *Idd.* 6, 8, 9, 27 he appears as a typical Arcadian. Both Diodorus and Aelian (see p. 1 n. 2) make him the inventor of pastoral. See *Ecl.* 5.20n.

18. Cf. *A.P.* 9.205, 434 with Serv. *Buc. Prooem.* 3.21.

19. Some of which is probably preserved in the *Appendix Vergiliana*, e.g. *Catal.* 5 and 7.

20. *mollis* is associated with *perlucens* 'translucent', *tener* and *flexibilis* 'supple' (e.g. Cic. *Brut.* 274) and contrasted with *durus, fortis; facetus* associated with *elegans* (ib. 292) and *urbanus* (Cic. *de Or.* 1.159), contrasted with *grauis, seuerus,*

21. Mopsus too must represent in pastoral terms, if not a specific fellow-poet, then at least a type of those whose Caesarian sympathies caused them to mourn the dictator's death.

22. The identification in both Eclogues poses in a particularly acute form the question raised on p. 25. Can we avoid associating this Menalcas with the Menalcas of *Ecl.* 3, of 2.15 and 10.20, even though Vergil has there given us no comparable clues to identification? Ought we to?

Paul Alpers (essay date 1979)

SOURCE: "*Eclogue* 1: An Introduction to Virgilian Pastoral" in *The Singer of the "Eclogues": A Study of Virgilian Pastoral*, University of California Press, 1979, pp. 65-95.

[*In the essay below, Alpers presents a detailed analysis of Vergil's* Eclogue *One and maintains that the poem suspends potential conflicts, thereby achieving a certain harmony.*]

I

Virgil's first *eclogue* is a problematic poem, yet it has always been felt to be a representative pastoral. It is perhaps too neat to say that it is representative because problematic, and yet no less an authority than Sidney feels something of the sort: "Is it then the Pastoral poem which is misliked? . . . Is the poor pipe disdained, which sometime out of Meliboeus' mouth can show the misery of people under hard lords or ravening soldiers? And again, by Tityrus, what blessedness is derived to them that lie lowest from the goodness of them that sit highest."[1] Sidney assumes both that the poem is an exemplary pastoral and that it somehow takes care of the potential contradiction in attitude between Meliboeus and Tityrus. Sidney makes it easy for himself by not remarking that the "hard" and "good" lords in this case are one and the same. Even so, I think his sense of the poem is right—that it holds potential conflicts in suspension and that its particular kind of harmony is of the essence of what makes it a pastoral. So too are the ways this harmony is achieved. As the poem is suspended between Meliboeus' and Tityrus' sense of life, so too is it suspended between dramatic and lyric. Its doubleness in this respect fully explains (and can be thought to justify) the indecisiveness, in the critical tradition, over which mode pastoral should be assigned to.[2]

Eclogue 1 is a dialogue between two friends who formerly shared a way of life, but whose destinies are now diametrically opposed. Meliboeus has had his farm expropriated and given to a veteran of Octavian's armies, while Tityrus is able to enjoy the ease that one expects to be the lot of every (literary) shepherd. Meliboeus speaks first:

> Tityre, tu patulae recubans sub tegmine fagi
> silvestrem tenui musam meditaris avena;

nos patriae finis et dulcia linquimus arva.
nos patriam fugimus; tu, Tityre, lentus in umbra
formosam resonare doces Amaryllida silvas.

(1-5)

You, Tityrus, under the spreading, sheltering beech,
Tune woodland musings on a delicate reed;
We flee our country's borders, our sweet fields,
Abandon home; you, lazing in the shade,
Make woods resound with lovely Amaryllis.

These lines contain all the issues of the poem and raise all the critical questions about it. We observe, first, the idyllic portrayal of Tityrus, and it is this, no doubt, that made these lines as famous once as "To be or not to be" or "April is the cruelest month." But we also observe that Tityrus' bliss is set off against Meliboeus' exile, and the problems of the poem lie in the way we evaluate this contrast. It is indubitably there, but how do we take it in? On the one hand, we can appeal to the dominant impression of the lines and to their formal symmetry (*tu, Tityre,* in line 4), and say that Tityrus' pastoral happiness encloses or contains Meliboeus' lot. On the other hand, we can compare, to Tityrus' disadvantage, the scope and quality of the juxtaposed ways of life—Tityrus' singing love songs in the shade, as opposed to Meliboeus' concern for fields and *patria.*

Both ways of looking at these lines find support in the poem as a whole. Meliboeus' poetry—both his imaginings of Tityrus' bliss and his accounts of his own suffering—dominates the poem for many readers. His words, grounded in distress, have a resonance not found in Tityrus' more naive speeches. Formally, too, Meliboeus comes to dominate the poem: the second half is largely given over to two of his speeches, the longest and most intensely felt of the eclogue. Yet the last word belongs to Tityrus, whose response to Meliboeus' farewell to his flock and fields is so rich in its effect that it has become, for many readers, the hallmark of Virgilian pastoral:

Hic tamen hanc mecum poteras requiescere noctem
fronde super viridi: sunt nobis mitia poma,
castaneae molles et pressi copia lactis;
et iam summa procul villarum culmina fumant,
maioresque cadunt altis de montibus umbrae.

(79-83)

Still, you could take your rest with me tonight,
Couched on green leaves: there will be apples ripe,
Soft roasted chestnuts, plenty of pressed cheese.
Already rooftops in the distance smoke,
And lofty hills let fall their lengthening shade.

It is these lines that prompted Panofsky to say, in a memorable passage: "In Virgil's ideal Arcady human suffering and superhumanly perfect surroundings create a dissonance. This dissonance, once felt, had to be resolved, and it was resolved in that vespertinal mixture of sadness and tranquillity which is perhaps Virgil's most personal contribution to poetry. With only slight exaggeration one might say that he 'discovered' the evening."[3] To the extent that we feel this sort of power in these lines, we will agree that because of them "the sense of opposites, the union of polarities in tension, changes into a centered, relaxed, static unity."[4] We note the formal balance with the opening speech (also five lines), the return to the shadows that create the environment of pastoral well-being, and we see that "the circular movement in the first five lines is, in small, the pattern of the whole poem."[5]

These divergent readings reflect differing views of the nature of speech, dialogue, and human encounter in the poem; it is these that will most concern us, and, I hope, most reward our investigation. But we must first pause to observe that there is a corresponding divergence of interpretation (which is to say, our interpretation of Virgil's interpretation) of the political and social situation with which the poem deals. After the battle of Philippi (42 B.C.), Octavian's and Antony's veterans were rewarded with land—seized, of course, from farmers like Meliboeus. Expropriations took place in Mantuan territory; according to ancient commentators on the *Eclogues,* Virgil's farm was spared only because of Octavian's intervention. Tityrus' devotion to the *deus* to whom he owes his happy life was therefore taken as Virgil's expression of gratitude to Octavian: hence the traditional identification, beginning with Servius and unquestioned in the Renaissance, of Virgil and Tityrus. Though this story is difficult to reconstruct in detail and evidence for it comes entirely from the *Eclogues* and ancient commentaries, some aspects of it cannot be dismissed. The eclogue certainly refers to the expropriations, and Tityrus' *deus,* who is later identified as a young man in Rome, must be Octavian.[6] But if we must recognize that Tityrus' gratitude is praise of Octavian, we must equally acknowledge that Meliboeus' fate exposes the human consequences of the expropriations and that his bitter lament is, as Servius said, wounding to the man responsible for them:

impius haec tam culta novalia miles habebit,
barbarus has segetes. en quo discordia civis
produxit miseros: his nos consevimus agros!

(70-72)

Think of these fields in a soldier's cruel hands!
These crops for foreigners! See how discord leaves
Countrymen wretched: for *them* we've tilled and
sown![7]

It is difficult to reconcile these unequivocal words with the view of Octavian expressed through Tityrus. It is not surprising that the two critics to whom English-speaking students of the *Eclogues* will turn first take diametrically opposed views of the political point of this poem. For Brooks Otis, it is a celebration of Julio-Augustan themes and reveals the possibilities of peace and order under the future Augustus.[8] For Michael Putnam, it is severe and pessimistic, revealing how destructive is tyranny to human freedom and the life of the imagination.[9]

It sounds as if what we have here is a debate between Meliboeus' point of view and Tityrus' point of view. But putting it that way misses the precise nature of the exchange, because it treats it as essentially dramatic in mode, a contention (in our minds, for it does not exist in theirs) between the two characters. In fact, the question is precisely whether and to what extent the eclogue is dramatic. The "pessimistic" interpreters, who are in the ascendant these days, emphasize the dramatic aspect of the poem. That is, they view it as a representation of real characters in a real situation, and they take the center of interest to be the way the characters deal with that situation and with each other. To read the poem dramatically means more than taking Meliboeus' experience and speeches at face value, and more even than comparing them with Tityrus' in respect to fullness of experience, felt seriousness, and the like. It also puts the exchange between the two men in a certain light: where Meliboeus is intensely responsive to Tityrus' happiness, while trying to avoid personal bitterness or envy, Tityrus throughout the poem seems insensitive to Meliboeus' plight. The most striking instance occurs after Meliboeus' intoxicating evocation of the rural music that will surround Tityrus. Tityrus responds with some strong poetry of his own:

> Ante leves ergo pascentur in aethere cervi
> et freta destituent nudos in litore piscis,
> ante pererratis amborum finibus exsul
> aut Ararim Parthus bibet aut Germania Tigrim,
> quam nostro illius labatur pectore vultus.
>
> (59-63)

> Sooner light-footed stags will graze in air,
> The waves will strand their fish bare on the shore;
> Sooner in exile, roaming frontiers unknown,
> Will Gauls and Persians drink each other's streams,
> Than shall *his* features slip out of our hearts.

What is striking about these *adynata* (the rhetorical term for such a catalogue of impossibilities) is that, though they appear impossible to Tityrus, they are all too real for Meliboeus. His flock is hungry, he and it are being forced out of their element, he has left newborn lambs stranded on bare rock, and, most important, he too is condemned to wander in exile. The abundant verbal connections with Meliboeus' speeches make it beyond question that Virgil meant us to see these ironies, and they will be felt powerfully to just the extent that Tityrus' lines seem to be a spontaneous overflow of powerful feelings. One can well understand why many critics feel the ironies redound upon Tityrus here and identify the reader's stance with Meliboeus' final speech, which begins with a foreboding vision of his exile (a conscious response to Tityrus' *adynaton*) and contains the heartfelt farewell to his fields and flock.

Critics who do not accept reading the poem from Meliboeus' point of view do not dispute the facts about the speakers, their experiences, the power of their speeches, and the nature of their exchanges. But they seek to interpret all these in an essentially nondramatic way. In the most subtle and convincing of such readings, Tityrus' *adynata* are interpreted as a breakthrough to the sublime *for the whole poem;* the ironies are to be referred not to the

speakers and their relations, but to the situation as a whole and the tensions inherent in it.[10] By the same token, the final lines are taken as a powerful conclusion to the poem as a whole; they are attributed, so to speak, to Virgil, rather than to Tityrus. (Critics who read the poem dramatically, on the other hand, try to cut these lines down to Tityrus' size.)[11] The critical debates about the poem, then, are essentially debates about its mode—that is, they concern not only the nature of its strategies and devices, but also our relation to them and the attitudes and meanings implicit in them.

II

The nondramatic aspect of Virgil's poetry is very evident in the opening lines, both in the formal symmetry of the speech as a whole and in the perfection and richness of the lines. The second and fifth lines in particular, with their fullness of meaning and atmosphere, have an air of defining pastoral song in general, and thus seem quite detached from a particular speaker in a particular situation. But as soon as we go on to Tityrus' reply, we realize that the poem has a dramatic aspect:

> O Meliboee, deus nobis haec otia fecit.
> namque erit ille mihi semper deus, illius aram
> saepe tener nostris ab ovilibus imbuet agnus.
> ille meas errare boves, ut cernis, et ipsum
> ludere quae vellem calamo permisit agresti.
>
> (6-10)

> O Melibee, a god grants us this peace—
> A god to me forever, upon whose altar
> A young lamb from our folds will often bleed.
> He has allowed, you see, my herds to wander
> And me to play as I will on shepherd's pipes.

There is a good deal more circumstance connected with "this peace" than we could possibly have imagined from Meliboeus' speech—the dependence on a god, the sacrifices promised to him, the very fact that Tityrus is a real herdsman and not simply a singer in a landscape. The indication of real circumstances carries with it a sense of real time: instead of the "timeless" present tense of Meliboeus' speech, we have here the promise of future acts and remembrances in gratitude for a condition that is due to a past action.[12] Furthermore, Tityrus is self-conscious about himself (redefining "a god" as "a god to me") and about his situation (pointing to it as separate with *ut cernis,* "as you see"). And Tityrus' sense of his happiness is different from Meliboeus': he includes the fact that his herds can wander at will and he describes his singing in terms that are much less grand than Meliboeus'.

The dramatic aspect of this opening exchange is especially clear when we compare the opening of Theocritus' first idyll:

> *Thyrsis.* Sweet is the whispering music of yonder pine that sings
> Over the water-brooks, and sweet the melody of your pipe,

Dear goatherd. After Pan, the second prize you'll bear
away.
If he should take the hornèd goat, the she-goat shall
you win:
But if he choose the she-goat for his meed, to you
shall fall
The kid; and dainty is kid's flesh, till you begin to
milk.
Goatherd. Sweeter, oh shepherd, is your song than the
melodious fall
Of yonder stream that from on high gushes down the
rock.
If it chance that the Muses take the young ewe for
their gift,
Then your reward will be the stall-fed lamb; but
should they choose
To take the lamb, then yours shall be the sheep for
second prize.

This exchange is much more symmetrical than Virgil's. As
the translation indicates, each speech begins with two lines
comparing the other herdsman's music to nature's and
concludes with three lines (each set structured in the same
way) promising a gift to honor a song. The translation
does not indicate more intimate symmetries, such as the
fact that the major word for nature's music falls in exactly
the same position in each speech (*melisdetai*, in line 2;
kataleibetai, in line 8), and that the word *geras*, prize, falls
in the exact middle of each of the three-line passages
about the gifts. These formal symmetries perfectly convey
the atmosphere of this meeting and the attitude of the
herdsmen. They do not mirror each other (there are later
indications that they have individual circumstances and
histories), but they do perfectly understand each other and
their situations, and they can therefore exchange speeches,
just as they propose to exchange songs and gifts. The
change Virgil has wrought can be seen in the way he uses
Theocritus' device of beginning the second speech with
the same word or formula as the first. When the goatherd
repeats Thyrsis' "Sweet is the *x*" formula, the primary motive is formal responsiveness, in the spirit of equal
exchange. But Tityrus' *O Meliboee*, though it formally
answers to *Tityre, tu,* is said with full dramatic intensity: it
is responsive to Meliboeus' evocation of Tityrus' bliss and
it begins Tityrus' expression of his feeling of gratitude.

Yet we can look at this matter in quite a different way. The
traditional comparison of Theocritus and Virgil would
make Theocritus the more dramatic, on the grounds of his
being more realistic and concrete. We can see the reasons
for this view in the opening lines of each poem, in which
the singer is set in the midst of nature and its music. Here
we must quote Theocritus in Greek:

> Hadu ti to *psithurisma* kai ha pitus, aipole, tēna,
> ha poti tais pagaisi, *melisdetai,* hadu de kai tu
> *surisdes:* meta Pana to deuteron athlon apoisē.

The grammar is beautifully expressive here. By superim-
posing two coordinating devices (roughly, supplying a
"both-and" for both the repeated "sweet" and the subjects
of the verbs),[13] the sentence suggests the harmony between
the music of man and nature, but keeps their separation
clear: quite literally they are coordinated, not directly
responsive to each other. We are thus not encouraged to
read too much into the personifications that render the
music of the pine, especially since the third of the musical
words here (italicized in the quotation), used of the goatherd, unequivocally refers to human music making. In
both meaning and effect, the lines have a lovely discretion
and lucidity. The major word in each line literally "makes
music," and the three words are linked by similarities of
sound. But syntax, meaning, and disposition of the words
keep these meanings and effects from spilling over and
dominating either the courteous address or the sketching
in of the setting (*ha poti tais pagaisi,* "by the brooks").
Even in so conspicuously musical a passage, we see how
just it is to say that "music as an affective bond between
man and man and between man and nature need not be
thunderous. In the pastoral, it is the small and brittle sound
that Theocritus characterizes as 'dry,' *kapyros,* and which
is best produced on the reed pipe."[14]

When we turn to Virgil from Theocritus' dry lucidity, we
can well understand the traditional comparison of the two
poets. As opposed to the directness of *surisdes,* "you are
piping" (a verb cognate with *surinx,* a pipe), the phrase
musam meditaris is generalized and open-ended. *Meditor*
means "meditate, consider, etc." with a transferred sense
of "exercise one's self in." It can be used of literary
composition, but usually the object is perfectly clear. Thus
Horace, just before he meets the bore, describes himself
nescio quid meditans nugarum, "musing over some
(poetic) trifle or other" (*Sat.* 1.9.2). Creatures, human or
divine, are not characteristic objects of *meditor.* Editors
therefore tell us to take *musam* as "poem," and cite Lucretius: *Fistula silvestrem ne cesset fundere musam* ("so that
the pipe ceases not to pour forth woodland music").[15] But
the clarity of the rest of that sentence makes it easy to
supply the transferred sense of *musam,* the more so as the
whole passage concerns the way men attribute physical
echoes to the presence of gods. What is distinctive about
Virgil's phrase, compared with these other examples, is
that neither word gives a concrete sense or secure "prose"
meaning, so that we are immediately involved in interpretation, accommodation, suggestion. The phrase might well
be called vague, were it not that it combines general
obviousness with a suggestiveness that always rewards
investigation—for example, the sustaining of the literal
idea of a muse, an inspiring female, when we learn that
the lovely Amaryllis is the subject of Tityrus' song. (We
might note that these objections and justifications are ones
we associate with Milton, who of course anglicized this
phrase in *Lycidas.*) The same point might be made about
the sound effects. Where Theocritus' lines, as has often
been noted, imitate the sound of the reed-pipe,[16] the
m-sounds of Virgil's phrase seem "pure" verbal music,
Tennysonian if you will. But again the effect is not left
vague, for it is given substance by line 5, where sylvan
music is defined as the echo of human song. We now see
the three elements attuned by the letter *m* in distinct relations to each other: you teach (*meditaris*) the woods

(*silvestrem*) to echo Amaryllis (*musam*). But though these elements are now structured, we can believe in the echoing song because of their union in the grammar and sound of the earlier phrase.

I would suggest "pregnant" as the opposite of "vague" in speaking of such phrases. As W. J. Knight has said, "compression into density of meaning is the main principle of Vergil's expression."[17] Just as the aural and grammatical union of *musam* and *meditaris* makes us take in and interpret suggestions of sound and meaning, so the phrase *tenui avena* is "impregnated" by the sentence in which it occurs. Literally, the adjective and noun mean "a thin oaten stalk," the latter metonymic for a shepherd's reed-pipe; we would translate "on a thin reed," if the verb were like Theocritus' "you are piping." But the rest of the line makes us take the ablative as a very general "by means of." Moreover, *tenuis* is not simply a physical term, but has a range of metaphoric meanings—"slight," "trifling," "low" in both stylistic and social senses (hence "humble" in both senses relevant to pastoral poetry).[18] Because these meanings are already "in" the word, Virgil can count on ease of communication and at the same time richness of meaning for the reader who pauses to inspect and meditate (again the analogy with Milton suggests itself). We note that the one unequivocally concrete word, *avena,* is the last in the line. By such verbal tactics does the oaten flute become a symbolic instrument.

The Virgilian pregnancy of line and phrase is due to a fusion of what we have identified as dramatic and nondramatic elements in his poetic speech. We ought not to lose sight of either aspect. It is perhaps not so vital to recognize that Meliboeus' resonant last line, general and detached from him as it seems, is (as the rest of the eclogue shows) very much in character. But if we do not hear the personal inflection in *dulcia,* "sweet," as an epithet of *arva,* "fields" (and we hear it because of the meaning and movement of the line),[19] we will fall into the mistake of flatly identifying Meliboeus' usages and sensibility with Virgil's. On the other hand, we cannot refer all fullness of meaning to dramatic realities. The pregnancy of *lentus in umbra* comes from its fusing natural and human meanings. This is the first such fusion in the poem; given the way the phrase is produced, the effect is of giving a single formula to grasp, serve as a motto for, the harmony between man and nature rendered by lines 1 and 2.[20]

If Meliboeus' lines seem in the first instance to be general, Tityrus' response seems dramatic in both tone and substance. But his lines emerge with a fullness that answers Meliboeus'. This is obvious in *deus nobis haec otia fecit* ("a god has granted us this peace"), but phrases are equally pregnant when the voice itself is less resonant. *Ille meas errare boves* ("he [has allowed] my cattle to wander") has a very down-to-earth meaning—the shepherd's gratitude at his flock's being able to wander and graze. At the same time, the freedom of movement suggests to us a spiritual freedom: Tityrus is free of the care that Meliboeus feels and that determines his movement of

purposeful flight. Tityrus can care for his flock without feeling care. Meliboeus' next speech, which presents precisely the opposite situation, may be thought to respond and bear witness to the pregnancy of phrase here. Similarly *ludere* (given prominence by its place in the line) has all the range of meaning the English "play" would have, and in such a context *quae vellem* ("what I want") takes on general force. Hence this last line of Tityrus' speech is not simply a character's statement of feeling and experience, but serves as a definition of rural music that answers (in another adaptation of Theocritean symmetry) to Meliboeus' concluding line. The writing here, though less resonant than in Meliboeus' speech, is just as interesting and suggestive. Given the importance of Tityrus' herd and sheepfold in his account of his happiness, his final word *agresti* ("of the fields") takes on general significance, especially when we see how it answers to and differs from Meliboeus' *silvestrem* ("of the woods"). The problematic relation between freedom and dependency, already evident in Tityrus' account, appears pointedly, though not ostentatiously, in the *quae vellem . . . permisit* ("what I wish . . . has allowed") of the final line. Hence, though we might say that the final lines, by themselves, render two versions of rural music, the speeches as wholes offer two versions of pastoral.

III

Virgil's presentation of "versions of pastoral" depends on a dramaturgy that exists, like his rhetoric, on a middle ground between dramatic and nondramatic. In the usual summary of the first half of the poem, Meliboeus asks Tityrus to tell who his beneficent god is; Tityrus, however, avoids satisfying this natural request until he is backed into speaking of the young man in Rome, at the exact midpoint of the poem. Critics hostile to Tityrus have a field day here, finding him evasive, insensitive, aimlessly garrulous, and what not. Again the defense involves a nondramatic interpretation of dramatic facts: Klingner argues that Meliboeus' pursuit of the question and Tityrus' evasion of the answer are meant to create, in the mind of the reader, a tension that produces the revelations of the poem and underlies its harmonies.[21] This argument still assumes that dramatic purposes and tensions, though transformed, are present in full force.

But despite much dramatic responsiveness and utterance, the reader will find little in the way of forward-looking energies, purposes, or resolutions—little, that is, in the way of plot. Meliboeus' answer to Tityrus' first speech is a lament over the state of the countryside and his own flock: he responds directly to the main elements of Tityrus' speech and only asks about the god at the end, in the manner of an afterthought. Tityrus' response to this question is a little speech about Rome, which he says far exceeded his rustic knowledge of and expectation about cities. As Michael Putnam suggests, praise of Rome does not really evade the question.[22] It only seems to if we expect a direct answer, in the manner of realistic dialogue, and therefore feel blocked by Tityrus' delivery of a small set piece. But both the opening exchange and Meliboeus' speech, with its pathetic vignette of his flock (lines 12-15), suggest that set pieces are precisely what we can expect to find in this poem. This is of course true in the second half of the eclogue, which consists of Meliboeus' two great speeches, alternating with Tityrus' *adynata* and his final invitation to the evening meal. It is equally true of the "dialogue" that leads to the revelation of the young god:

M.

Et quae tanta fuit Romam tibi causa videndi?

T.

Libertas, quae sera tamen respexit inertem,
candidior postquam tondenti barba cadebat,
respexit tamen et longo post tempore venit,
postquam nos Amaryllis habet, Galatea reliquit.
namque (fatebor enim) dum me Galatea tenebat,
nec spes libertatis erat nec cura peculi.
quamvis multa meis exiret victima saeptis,
pinguis et ingratae premeretur caseus urbi,
non umquam gravis aere domum mihi dextra redibat.

M.

Mirabar quid maesta deos, Amarylli, vocares,
cui pendere sua patereris in arbore poma;
Tityrus hinc aberat. ipsae te, Tityre, pinus,
ipsi te fontes, ipsa haec arbusta vocabant.

T.

Quid facerem? neque servitio me exire licebat
nec tam praesentis alibi cognoscere divos.
hic illum vidi iuvenem, Meliboee, quotannis
bis senos cui nostra dies altaria fumant.
hic mihi responsum primus dedit ille petenti:
"pascite ut ante boves, pueri; summittite tauros."

(26-45)

M.

And what so made you want to visit Rome?

T.

Freedom, though late, looked kindly on this sluggard,

After my beard hung whitened for the shears;
Looked kind at last and came, long overdue.
This was when Amaryllis took me over
From Galatea, under whom I had
No care of property nor hope of freedom.
Though many a victim went forth from my folds
And rich cheese for the thankless town was pressed,
Never did hands come home heavy with coins.

M.

I wondered, maiden, why you called the gods,
Grieved and left apples hanging on the tree;
Tityrus was away. The pines, O Tityrus,
The streams, these very orchards called for you.

T.

What could I do? not leave my servitude
Nor meet such favorable gods elsewhere.
Here, Melibee, I saw that noble youth
For whom our altars smoke twelve times a year.

He gave his suppliant this oracle:
"Graze cattle as before, lads, breed your bulls."

Each piece begins with a dramatic response, but in each case—Meliboeus' as well as Tityrus'—there is generated a set piece with its own distinctive rhetoric.

What we have seen supports Rosenmeyer's account of the unity of pastoral poems:

In Theocritus and Virgil the net effect of the structure, however complex, runs counter to Aristotle's recommendations. There is no single curve, no anticipation of a dramatic development. . . . Symmetrization absorbs all structural instincts. One analogy that might throw some light on what Theocritus does is that of the suite or a similar musical form of successive units. . . . Almost every Theocritean or Virgilian pastoral is best analyzed as a loose combination of independent elements.[23]

"Loose combination" is an overstatement for *Eclogue* 1, and Rosenmeyer underrates the dramatic aspects of poems like this. But what is important, for the moment, is to be aware of the speeches as "independent elements." Tityrus' apparently digressive speech about freedom makes sense when we read it as an independent presentation of his own circumstances and history. It exists not for dramatic ends (Tityrus' or Virgil's) but for purposes of collocation and comparison with similar speeches of Meliboeus. Tityrus' account of his past enslavement, in all senses, is a narrative of ordinary pastoral unhappiness, which, now resolved, is set over against the exceptional distress of Meliboeus, whose deeper anguish corresponds to drastic, irremediable circumstances. Tityrus' narrative is made representative by its range and economy: it includes the various frustrations of age, social status, mistakes in love, the small farmer's normal activities, and the mysteries of one's own motives. To see Tityrus this way, as an individual assessing his own history and situation, makes him someone truly to be compared with Meliboeus, rather than a mere foil for him. Rosenmeyer well suggests the way we compare, but do not adjudicate between the two men. By the same token, our judgment of the young Octavian is mediated by the fact, powerfully impressed by the poem, that the same historical situation affects two men so diversely.

The static, undramatic view of the poem, though not wholly adequate, at least enables us to avoid some misleading commonplaces about it. By not thinking of dramatic encounter, in which the present absorbs us, we can see that Virgil does not contrast Tityrus' unmitigated present bliss with Meliboeus' unmitigated woe. The comparison is rather between two experiences of unhappiness and its modes of resolution and acceptance. We can also see how wrong it is to think that Tityrus views his life the way Meliboeus does.[24] As Charles Segal points out, he "has a more prosaic attitude than Meliboeus toward his rustic world. For him it is a place of work and hard-earned savings (*peculi,* 32) and frustrations. . . . The exile is far more prone to idealize what he must leave, and he dwells lovingly on the familiar features of his beloved country with lush adjectives which he seems scarcely able to refrain from applying to every noun."[25] This comparison holds true for Tityrus' most intense expressions of feeling. His gratitude to his *deus* characteristically takes the form of the periodic sacrifices that were so important a part of Roman domestic and rural life. Meliboeus' motto for Tityrus' life may be *formosam resonare doces Amaryllida silvas.* Tityrus' own motto is not a piece of his own poetry at all, but the young god's *responsum* (a word used of oracles or replies to suppliants): *Pascite ut ante boves, pueri; summittite tauros* ("Graze cattle as before, lads, breed your bulls").

Yet too neat a separation will not do. Let us now try to bring the shepherds together in ways that are true to the poem. Compare the following:

> Vrbem quam dicunt Romam, Meliboee, putavi
> stultus ego huic nostrae similem, quo saepe solemus
> pastores ovium teneros depellere fetus.
>
> (19-21)

> The city they call Rome, my Melibee,
> I like a fool thought like our own, where shepherds
> Drive down the new-weaned offspring of their sheep.
> Fortunate senex, ergo tua rura manebunt
> et tibi magna satis, quamvis lapis omnia nudus
> limosoque palus obducat pascua iunco.
> non insueta gravis temptabunt pabula fetas,
> nec mala vicini pecoris contagia laedent.
>
> (46-50)

> Lucky old man! your lands will then remain
> Yours and enough for you, although bare rock
> And slimy marsh reeds overspread the fields.
> Strange forage won't invade your heavy ewes,
> Nor foul diseases from a neighbor's flock.

We can see the familiar contrasts here. Tityrus speaks of his limited horizons in his homey way and with his usual confidence that life goes on. Meliboeus' rather melodramatic imaginings express both his finer sensibility and his greater suffering. And yet certain likenesses are evident. Both men speak energetically, as if fully engaged in their own experiences and the life around them. Furthermore, that life is the same, the raising of and caring for flocks. And from the sense of full engagement comes Virgil's characteristic pregnancy of phrase. The density of *pastores ovium teneros depellere fetus* ("Drive down the new-weaned offspring of their sheep") comes from the double relation of the genitive *ovium* ("of sheep") with *pastores* ("shepherds") and then with *fetus* ("offspring"); from the suggestive relation of *teneros* ("delicate, tender, young") to the shepherds' care of the sheep and to their naiveté (cf. *pueri,* "lads"); and most importantly from the phrase *depellere fetus,* which here refers to driving the young sheep to market, but which, as a phrase by itself, means "to wean" (i.e. remove from the breast). In this fine example of the way a great poet extends language, Virgil suggests, in a completely unsentimental way, the herdsman's

continual round of breeding, raising, and selling stock. A different, but equally powerful, density of phrase occurs in Meliboeus' *non insueta gravis temptabunt pabula fetas* ("Strange forage will not tempt-infect-assail your heavy ewes"). *Gravis* (lit., "heavy") *fetas* means both "pregnant ewes" and "sick ewes," with a suggestion of "sick lambs."[26] The ambiguity and the line as a whole convey Meliboeus' sense of doom about raising a flock: one might think he cannot help seeing Tityrus' state in the light of his own. Yet the good meaning of the phrase and of the sentence is essential, for they bring out that Tityrus' life is normal, at least in the sense of valuable, and that what has happened to Meliboeus is something gone wrong.

There are dramatic energies in these speeches, but they go into self-assessment, self-expression, and self-assertion. Their end seems more lyric than dramatic, as if each shepherd were primarily concerned to express his experience and his sense of the world. And yet, as we have just seen, the two men assume the same life and values. As opposed to what we find in Theocritus' *Idyll* 7 or any number of Renaissance pastorals, the speakers here do not come from different worlds. Rather, their versions of pastoral express divergent relations to, experiences of, histories within the same life. And yet to each shepherd his experience and history *are* "the world," his version of pastoral *is* "the pastoral." The peculiar poetics of the eclogue, somewhere between drama and lyric, is Virgil's means of displaying the relations in man's condition between "solidarity of plight and diversity of state."[27]

IV

Virgil's profound understanding of these relations emerges in the second half of the eclogue, which begins with Meliboeus' vision of Tityrus' future life. His speech continues, after the lines just quoted, with the most famous piece of pastoralism in the poem:

> fortunate senex, hic inter flumina nota
> et fontis sacros frigus captabis opacum;
> hinc tibi, quae semper, vicino ab limite saepes
> Hyblaeis apibus florem depasta salicti
> saepe levi somnum suadebit inire susurro;
> hinc alta sub rupe canet frondator ad auras,
> nec tamen interea raucae, tua cura, palumbes
> nec gemere aëria cessabit turtur ab ulmo.
>
> (51-58)

> Lucky old man! here by familiar streams
> And hallowed springs you'll seek out cooling shade.
> Here for you always, bees from the neighboring hedge,
> Feeding on willow blossoms, will allure
> To slumber soft with their sweet murmurings.
> The hillside pruner will serenade the air;
> Nor will the throaty pigeons, your dear care,
> Nor turtledoves cease moaning in the elms.

The first two lines are a beautiful example of the density of Virgil's writing. Commentators frequently note how much in character (really "in situation") these words are: to be among *familiar* rivers is now, for Meliboeus, the hallmark of happiness. But dramatic propriety is only part, not the whole, of poetic force here. Familiar streams are an aspect of an ideal scene for anyone, not only for exiles, and *fontis sacros* is primarily a general phrase, not tied (though appropriate) to Meliboeus. The springs are sacred not because the exile longs for them, but because, as Servius says, they are dedicated to local deities. We have the seeds here not of a romantic "Exile's Song" but of Horace's poem on the fountain Bandusia (*Odes* 3.13), one of the masterpieces of secure, "at home" poetry. Meliboeus' particular situation enables him to bear witness to general truths and sentiments. It is appropriate to give an eighteenth-century cast to our praise here, for the third of these noun-adjective pairs, *frigus opacum,* is Augustan in the English sense. But Virgil's lines are free of what critics called the frigidity of such formulas. Virgil not only gauges the progression from particular to general (and dramatic to nondramatic) in the three phrases, he also animates the last with the active desiring of *captabis* ("you will seek out") and with the suggestive relations of *frigus* ("coolness") to *fontis sacros.* Hence, when we come to *opacum,* the last word in the line and the only one of these adjectives separated from its noun, we are reading actively, prepared to ask, "What kind of coolness?" and hence to feel a concrete, specifying force in "shady." Precisely what makes such phrases "frigid" in neoclassical verse is that only the formulaic and static character is imitated. It is revealing that the only way we now have to translate this phrase into English is to reverse noun and adjective and say "cooling shade."

If these two lines are Augustan, the rest of the passage might be called Tennysonian. We can understand why the man who wrote of "the moan of doves in immemorial elms / And murmur of innumerable bees" was called the English Virgil. But it is unjust to Virgil to think of him simply as the Roman Tennyson. Here, as in the first two lines, we find obvious effects deeply grounded and beautifully gauged. The neighboring hedge fed upon by bees is the exact antithesis of Meliboeus' vision, four lines earlier, of strange foods afflicting the cattle and of diseases spreading from neighboring herds. But to see that Meliboeus' version of pastoral reflects his sense of reality is not to discount it: quite the reverse, by displaying its source in experience and feeling, Virgil makes us take it seriously.

Here again we must remember that these speeches are not purely dramatic. One would not speak here of a reversal of feeling in Meliboeus, because his whole speech is very much a set piece, consisting of contrasted negative and positive visions, each introduced by *fortunate senex* ("lucky old man"). Both the way the contrasting vignettes are produced—with the speaker disappearing into fully imagined scenes—and the neatness and obviousness of the contrast encourage us to take in and compare these lines as general modes of pastoral and antipastoral, just as the physical distresses and pleasures they envisage are certainly common to us all. Thus, when a critic like Snell assumes that Virgil is speaking here, the appropriate correction is not to say, "No, Meliboeus is," but rather to

define the connections that exist in this poem and mode between what is individual and what is common in experience and expression. The two aspects are completely fused in the final lines of this speech. For all its atmosphere, it is not a fairyland—rather an exquisitely benign version of real life as it is assumed to be throughout the eclogue. The trimming of leaves (the task of the *frondator*) occurred at various seasons, for various practical purposes; doves were normal on Roman farms, and they are a *cura* ("care") both as animals to be tended and as objects of particular affection. The loveliness of the scene is due to the fact that all creatures in it are singing; but here, as opposed to the sleep-inducing bees, there is a human singer, and the birds' songs are actually or potentially sad.[28] Thus what Meliboeus imagines as pastoral bliss is not the land of the lotus-eaters, but the transformation of normal labor, concern, and unhappiness into song. The idyllic atmosphere very much reflects Meliboeus' version of pastoral, and yet the transformations he envisages can be applied to Tityrus' experience and taken as a definition of the enterprise of the whole poem.

Meliboeus' speech makes a good text for "sentimental" or romantic theories of pastoral, because it presents the songs into which experience is transformed as nature's. Despite the presence of the *frondator,* man is unquestionably dominated by nature if we look to imagery alone. But other aspects of the speech put man in the center of nature's music. He is always present as an auditor: when not explicitly invoked in words like *suadebit* ("will persuade") and *tua cura* ("your care"), he is implicitly present in sensory and auditory effects and in acts of interpretation, comparison, and discrimination.[29] And intensity of listening here produces song of a quite unexpected kind. For it is in response to this speech that Tityrus utters his *adynata:*

> Ante leves ergo pascentur in aethere cervi
> et freta destituent nudos in litore piscis,
> ante pererratis amborum finibus exsul
> aut Ararim Parthus bibet aut Germania Tigrim,
> quam nostro illius labatur pectore vultus.
>
> (59-63)

> Sooner light-footed stags will graze in air,
> The waves will strand their fish bare on the shore;
> Sooner in exile, roaming frontiers unknown,
> Will Gauls and Persians drink each other's streams,
> Than shall *his* features slip out of our hearts.

From the *ergo* of the first line and the unaccustomed grandeur of his speech, it is clear that Tityrus is responding to the intensity that we ourselves have felt in Meliboeus' evocation of his life.

Tityrus' intensity of feeling seems natural at this point, but the form of its expression is very problematic. Why did Virgil make him so obviously subject to the charges of self-satisfaction and self-involvement? The particular problem, it seems to me, is to explain why Tityrus speaks in so elevated a way. For what offends readers here is not his limited horizons in themselves, but the self-assertion implicit in the rhetorical device that equates "my world" and "the world" and crowns all with the assumption that the coherence of the world depends on the shepherd's remembering his benefactor. Man and his speech are back in the center with a vengeance, but the diversity of critical views of the passage shows how uncertain we are about how such poetry speaks to or for us—a particularly interesting dilemma, since everyone knows how to take the lines that prompt the speech.

Tityrus' *adynata* ("impossibilities") are a special form of inventory, a term we shall use, following Rosenmeyer,[30] to include all serial listing. No pastoral convention is more familiar, but this is due to Virgil's influence. When we look for this convention in Theocritus, we discover that it occurs infrequently and that with one notable exception it is not used for elevated expression. The inventories that strike the modern reader as the genuine article are in two idylls now thought to be spurious.[31] If we leave these aside, we find that all but one of Theocritus' inventories are uttered by conspicuously rustic speakers.[32] That Virgil understood the device this way is indicated by his using it for Tityrus' explanation of his rustic failure to understand what Rome is like:

> sic canibus catulos similis, sic matribus haedos
> noram, sic parvis componere magna solebam.
>
> (22-23)

> Pups are like dogs, kids are like mother goats
> I knew, and thus compared great things and small.

Yet forty lines later Tityrus is given an inventory, the source of which is the one exception to the Theocritean rule—the final boast of the dying Daphnis:

> Bear violets henceforth, ye brambles, and ye thistles too,
> And upon boughs of juniper let fair narcissus bloom;
> Let all things be confounded; let the pine-tree put forth figs,
> Since Daphnis lies dying! Let the stag tear the hounds,
> And screech-owls from the hills contend in song with nightingales.
>
> (*Idyll* 1.132-36)

This is genuinely heroic self-assertion, by the one figure in Theocritus' pastorals who can sustain such claims about himself. Virgil unquestionably wants us to hear these accents and to recognize that his humble shepherd is now speaking like Theocritus' godlike man. This context is suggested not only by Tityrus' rhetoric but also by Meliboeus' earlier words, recalling his absence from the country: *ipsae te, Tityre, pinus, / ipsi te fontes, ipsa haec arbusta vocabant* ("the pines, O Tityrus, / The streams, these very orchards called for you"). Putnam is surely right to say that with these words—very puzzling in their context—Meliboeus sees Tityrus as "a Daphnis figure, one of the semi-divine creatures upon whose well-being the landscape depends."[33] When he utters his *adynata*, twenty

lines later, Tityrus takes on the role of Daphnis that he appears to Meliboeus, much more than to himself, to play.

Two main purposes seem to me at work here. First, by turning rustic speech into a form of heroic assertion, Virgil makes explicit what we have called the lyric tendency in the eclogue—the sense of oneself and one's experience filling the world, in some sense being the world. "Lyricism" in this sense need not be heroic. Meliboeus has just given a lovely pastoral emblem of it in his phrase *canet frondator ad auras* ("the pruner will sing to the airs"). Normal singing goes out to the world in all the ways suggested by the divergent interpretations of *ad auras*.[34] When Tityrus responds to this emblem with a speech in Daphnis' mode, Virgil makes explicit what he saw as a deep puzzle in the pastoral ideal of self-sufficiency in the midst of one's world. This puzzle is beautifully stated in Meliboeus' first description: *formosam resonare doces Amaryllida silvas* ("you teach [the] woods to resound lovely Amaryllis"). In imagining Tityrus at the center of his world, do we emphasize his creative powers ("you teach") or his receptivity to nature's echoes? Is his poetry dependent on his mistress or is it he who, in proclaiming her, in a sense makes her *formosam* ("lovely")? In this line these polarities are held in suspension. The point is that Virgil seems to have felt that "pure" pastoral receptivity and diffidence had in it the seeds of heroic separateness and self-assertion. In the other eclogues, it is precisely the twin forces of love and song that prompt the shepherd to self-consciousness and thus to self-assertion.

Ironic, indeed, for love seeks union, and Theocritean pastoral envisages "music as an affective bond between man and man and between man and nature."[35] But irony tends to compose itself in pastoral: much of the elusiveness of the mode is that we do not know how to pursue and resolve ironic recognitions that seem to be offered (think of Marvell). With Tityrus' *adynata*, it is not enough to perceive self-assertion and its attendant dilemmas. Extraordinarily, even mysteriously, these lines bear witness to the bonds that exist between the two shepherds. For in giving vent to his intense gratitude, what one critic calls his exultation,[36] Tityrus sings Meliboeus' song for him. It is not a question of being or meaning to be selfish. It is simply the fact that Tityrus' self-expression leads him to imagine Meliboeus' world and to adopt a heroic mode that seems much more natural in Meliboeus' circumstances than in his own. (Theocritus' Daphnis is heroic precisely to the extent of his defiant isolation from the pastoral world). Exactly the same thing has happened in the preceding speech. There, too, strong self-expression produces intense poetry; but Meliboeus' imaginings are of Tityrus' world, and the song produced is in a mode more appropriate to Tityrus. Each shepherd responds to the other with poetry that is self-expressive but that also reaches out to, speaks and sings for, the other.

Meliboeus' reply shows that this is the right way to regard—we should indeed say "hear"—Tityrus' speech:

> At nos hinc alii sitientis ibimus Afros,

pars Scythiam et rapidum cretae veniemus Oaxen
et penitus toto divisos orbe Britannos.

(64-66)

Ah, but we others leave for thirsty lands—
Africa, Scythia, or Oxus' chalky waves,
Or Britain, wholly cut off from the world.

These words are usually taken as a truthful view of Meliboeus' future which rebukes Tityrus' rhetoric. A juster account is given by a critic who certainly cannot be accused of favoring Tityrus:

> Excited by the lyricism of Meliboeus, Tityrus tries to begin at the same pitch. But he lapses into his customary pomposity and carries it, this time, to absurdity. . . . Tityrus unwittingly uses rhetoric—a most unfortunate rhetoric. Meliboeus resumes his speech again. But, strangely enough, carried away by the grandiloquence of his interlocutor, he begins with an exaggeration that seems rather out of place in his mouth. . . . This is the only lapse of taste in the poem, and it is a pardonable one, the grief of Meliboeus excusing his exaggerations.[37]

Waltz does not like what he sees, and therefore apologizes for Meliboeus, but I think he sees what is there. Tityrus gives Meliboeus his own voice here. Indeed, where Tityrus envisaged exile as drinking from foreign rivers, Meliboeus foresees not being able to drink at all. No one likes to accuse a refugee of being melodramatic; but is there not a good deal, if not of self-pity, then of self-dramatization in Meliboeus' envisaging his going off to a place totally cut off from the rest of the world? Once again we do not want to reduce the line to its dramatic aspects—only to recognize that what holds for Tityrus holds for Meliboeus as well: here, as everywhere, these shepherds bear witness to wider experience and general truths out of the particular pressures of their characters and situations. Certainly Meliboeus has a strong sense of his own presence here. He moves from these lines to frank self-dramatization:

en umquam patrios longo post tempore finis
pauperis et tuguri congestum caespite culmen,
post aliquot, mea regna, videns mirabor aristas?
impius haec tam culta novalia miles habebit,
barbarus has segetes. en quo discordia civis
produxit miseros: his nos consevimus agros!
insere nunc, Meliboee, piros, pone ordine vitis.

(67-73)

Shall I ever again, within my country's borders,
With wonder see a turf-heaped cottage roof,
My realm, at last, some modest ears of grain?
Think of these fields in a soldier's cruel hands!
These crops for foreigners! See how discord leaves
Countrymen wretched: for *them* we've tilled and sown!
Go graft your pear trees, Melibee, plant your vines!

At this point we might feel that we have reached the parting of the ways that is in store for the shepherds. Meliboeus seems genuinely isolated here. Taken by themselves,

his nos consevimus agros ("for them we have sown fields") and the preceding *en* ("Lo!" ironic) could be directed either to sympathetic listeners or, in more bitter and defiant indignation, to himself. The last line confirms the more self-enclosed reading, and its ironic echo of the oracular injunction to Tityrus seems to mark, even if Meliboeus is not conscious of it, a true separation of the two men. Yet an extraordinary final movement in the poem brings them together again. Meliboeus' speech concludes:

ite meae, felix quondam pecus, ite capellae.
non ego vos posthac viridi proiectus in antro
dumosa pendere procul de rupe videbo;
carmina nulla canam; non me pascente, capellae,
florentem cytisum et salices carpetis amaras.

(74-78)

Go now, my goats; once happy flock, move on.
No more shall I, stretched out in a cavern green,
Watch you, far off, on brambly hillsides hang.
I'll sing no songs, nor shepherd you when you
Browse on the flowering shrubs and bitter willows.

The first line repeats the rhetorical pattern of *insere nunc, Meliboee* ("[Go] graft now, Melibee"), but the bitterness now involves sorrow for his flock and not anger and resentment about himself. It would be nice to say that Meliboeus turns to something outside himself, but it is not so simple as that. The repetition of an ironic command and the general self-dramatization show how much Meliboeus continues in his earlier vein: one might even say that as he looks back to an unrecoverable past, nostalgia locks him even more within himself. And yet though separate, he is not unreachable. His nostalgia, if it is that, is not self-dramatizing in the invidious sense. Where we might expect him to use subjunctives ("Would that. . .") or past tenses ("Once I . . ."), we find him speaking of himself in simple futures, expressing a fine balance of recognition, regret, resolution. Fittingly, at the end of this poem, there is a beautiful poise between lyric and dramatic address. Meliboeus is not talking to any human auditor here, but he is not simply talking to himself. There is a corresponding suspension of the dichotomy between "my world" and "the world." Much of the force of these lines comes from the rendering of pastoral vignettes in the manner of Meliboeus' earlier speeches. The line about the goats hanging from the rock—which Wordsworth used to illustrate the creative powers of the imagination[38]—has a poetic presence that is not wholly controlled by the *non ego . . . videbo* ("I will not see") that frames it. The last line consists of a distinct descriptive item in the manner of Theocritus; and though it is true, as is often pointed out, that Meliboeus' last word is *amaras* ("bitter"), there is a double perspective that Servius notes: "bitter to our taste, for they are sweet to the goats."[39]

If Meliboeus is enclosed in memory, what he remembers is a full and concrete world that Tityrus still inhabits. Hence, though his speech is not addressed to anyone, a listener can respond to it:

Hic tamen hanc mecum poteras requiescere noctem

fronde super viridi: sunt nobis mitia poma,
castaneae molles et pressi copia lactis;
et iam summa procul villarum culmina fumant,
maioresque cadunt altis de montibus umbrae.

(79-83)

Still, you could take your rest with me tonight,
Couched on green leaves: there will be apples ripe,
Soft roasted chestnuts, plenty of pressed cheese.
Already rooftops in the distance smoke,
And lofty hills let fall their lengthening shade.

This invitation makes explicit that the two shepherds still share a world. Tityrus makes actual what Meliboeus had made imaginatively present—the concrete goods of food and drink, the green couch, the lovely distant sight by which the shepherd locates himself in his world. And if Meliboeus' speech already belies, to some extent, his *carmina nulla canam* ("No songs I'll sing"), Tityrus' response makes these too actual, by its exploitation of the verbal music that to this point has been a characteristic of Meliboeus' speeches. Not only does this final exchange bring the poem full circle, ending as it began, with responsive five-line speeches; the speeches are, if anything, more alike and responsive to each other, hence more like Theocritus, than the opening exchange. If the pressures toward heroic self-assertion enabled Meliboeus and Tityrus to sing each other's songs, what underlies this possibility is the mode these shepherds share.

Notes

1. Sir Philip Sidney, *An Apology for Poetry,* ed. Geoffrey Shepherd (London, 1965), p. 116.

2. Those interested in this problem can begin to explore it by means of the remarks and references in Thomas G. Rosenmeyer, *The Green Cabinet* (Berkeley and Los Angeles, 1969), pp. 3-5.

3. Erwin Panofsky, "*Et in Arcadia Ego:* Poussin and the Elegiac Tradition," in *Meaning in the Visual Arts* (Garden City, N.Y.: Anchor Books, 1955), p. 300.

4. Friedrich Klingner, "Das Erste Hirtengedicht Virgils," in *Römische Geisteswelt,* 4th ed. (Munich, 1961), pp. 325-326.

5. Charles Paul Segal, "*Tamen Cantabitis, Arcades:* Exile and Arcadia in *Eclogues One* and *Nine,*" *Arion* 4 (1965), 240.

6. Octavian was in his mid-twenties when the *Eclogues* were written (42-38 B.C.; there is much uncertainty about the dates). The lines (quoted in the text) about the *barbarus miles* ("foreign soldier") who will possess Meliboeus' lands are the most direct evidence that the widespread disturbance in the fields, to which Meliboeus refers earlier (lines 11-12), are the expropriations. Cf. also the reference to the woes of Mantua in *Ecl.* 9 (lines 27-28), which has many connections with *Ecl.* 1. Finally, cf. the opening lines of *Ecl.* 6, in which Tityrus is unequivocally Virgil's poetic pseudonym.

7. Of *impius,* Servius says, "Here Virgil has sharply criticized Octavian; nevertheless he has followed truth: for by carrying arms and conquering others, a soldier is heedless of human feeling" ("hic Vergilius Octavianum Augustum laesit; tamen secutus est veritatem: nam miles portando arma et vincendo alios pietatem praetermittit"). Servius was a fourth-century grammarian who wrote a commentary on Virgil's works—the most extensive ancient commentary we have and full of every sort of interest. The standard modern edition (to be superseded, it is hoped, by the long-delayed Harvard edition) is that of G. Thilo and H. Hagen (1881-1887), of which the commentary on the *Bucolics* and *Georgics* is vol. 3, part 1. I quote from Thilo-Hagen, but the reader will find Servius' commentary in some form or other (see below, n. 19) in almost any sixteenth- or seventeenth-century edition of Virgil and in many eighteenth-century editions.

8. *Virgil: A Study in Civilized Poetry* (Oxford, 1964), ch. 4.

9. *Virgil's Pastoral Art* (Princeton, 1970), Introduction and ch. 1.

10. Klingner, p. 325.

11. See Putnam, p. 67; Perret's commentary on the lines; and Eleanor Winsor Leach, *Vergil's "Eclogues": Landscapes of Experience* (Ithaca, N.Y., 1974), pp. 137-138. Since the publication of *Virgil's Pastoral Art,* Putnam shifted his emphasis and discussed the lines as a conclusion that contains the ambiguities of the whole poem. "Virgil's First Eclogue: Poetics of Enclosure," *Ramus* 4 (1975), 167, 180-181.

12. *Fecit* and *permisit* are surely to be regarded as true perfects—actions completed shortly before or in present time and denoting an accomplished state. Thus in Greek, which unlike Latin has separate forms for perfect and aorist (simple past action), one would use the perfect to say "I am in prison." Archimedes' "Eureka!" is the perfect of "to find," and means not simply "I found it" (aorist) but "I have found it (and it is found)."

13. I owe this point to Dover, who points out, in his commentary, that "*kai . . . kai* [both . . . and] is superimposed on *hadu . . . hadu de* [sweet . . . and sweet]."

14. Rosenmeyer, p. 147.

15. *De Rerum Natura* 4.589; trans. Cyril Bailey (Oxford, 1910).

16. See Rosenmeyer, pp. 152-153.

17. *Roman Vergil* (Harmondsworth, Middlesex, 1966), p. 239.

18. Cf. Servius' comment: "a straw, a stalk, on which rustics commonly make music . . . however, by saying 'tenui avena,' he secretly indicates the

humble style which he uses in bucolics" ("*Tenui avena* culmo, stipula, unde rustici plerumque cantare consuerunt . . . dicendo autem 'tenui avena,' stili genus humilis latenter ostendit, quo, ut supra dictum est, in bucolicis utitur"). See also Peter L. Smith, "Vergil's *Avena* and the Pipes of Pastoral Poetry," *Transactions of the American Philological Association* 101 (1970), 497-510. The scholarly detail and analysis in this article in effect fill out what is suggested in Servius' comment—that Virgil's purpose, in Smith's words, "is to invent in his First *Eclogue* a personal and literary musical instrument, an instrument that may symbolize the creative process of pastoral composition without violating musical commonsense" (p. 507).

19. Cf. the observation in Servius Danielis (the enlarged Servian commentary, so-called because first published by Pierre Daniel in 1600): "*Et dulcia arva* because his own land seems sweet to everyone, for not every delightful thing is called sweet" ("unicuique propria terra dulcis sibi videtur, nec enim omnis res delectationem habens dulcis appellatur").

20. *Patulus* in line 1 means "spreading" and could also be used to render the first word of Wordsworth's line, "Open unto the fields, and to the sky"; it seems not to be used of the postures of human beings. *Lentus* has very full human extensions of its two main physical meanings, pliant or tough (as of the shrubs in line 25 of this eclogue) and sluggish or immovable. As a moral term used of Tityrus, we might translate "easy-going." But the real point is that it is hard to find a one-word equivalent, and the attention (and diverse meanings) given by lexicographers and commentators shows that a good deal of ad hoc interpretation is required. A typical Virgilian usage, then—apparently vague, but full of harmonious possibilities. Note that there is a dramatic element here, which may affect our interpretation of the word. If we think of Meliboeus simply calling Tityrus *lentus,* we might ask whether he uses a word that can have pejorative meanings (e.g., "sluggish"), as if unconsciously or covertly to express his resentment. But if we look at the whole line and the contrast between "you, Tityrus" and "us," the contrast with the act of fleeing suggests that Meliboeus invokes the word for its suggestion of slowness and immovability in (for him) good senses.

21. Klingner, pp. 321-324.

22. See his discussion of the lines, pp. 32-36.

23. P. 47.

24. Note that even in an account of the poem that tries not to exaggerate its idyllicism, the summary of Tityrus' experience is based entirely on Meliboeus' speeches: "Tityrus is spared the deprivations and anxieties associated with both the city and the wilderness. . . . His mind is cultivated and his

instincts are gratified. Living in an oasis of rural pleasure, he enjoys the best of both worlds—the sophisticated order of art and the simple spontaneity of nature." Leo Marx, *The Machine in the Garden* (New York, 1964), p. 22. More hostile critics fill their commentaries with remarks like Putnam's about Tityrus' "sheltered search for shallow perfection within the myth" or his invidious comparison: "Meliboeus is worried about the land itself. No mythical Amaryllis mesmerizes his leisured attention" (pp. 39, 22). But of course no such thing claims Tityrus' attention. In his account, the praise of Amaryllis is that she does not drain his purse. Coleman's note on *peculi* (line 32) brings out how realistic the word and its implications are.

25. P. 241. Even so, two pages later we find Segal saying, "Tityrus can still occupy the timeless present which is the heritage of every pastoral shepherd" (p. 243).

26. The noun *feta* means "a female animal that is pregnant or has just given birth," from the adjective *fetus, -a, -um. Fetus, -ūs,* a masculine noun, means "offspring, brood" (as in line 21). "Sick offspring" would be "gravis . . . fetus."

27. Christopher Burney in *Solitary Confinement,* an account of his wartime imprisonment by the Nazis. Quoted in Frank Kermode, *The Sense of an Ending* (New York, 1967), p. 157.

28. *Gemere* characteristically includes the idea of mourning, lamenting; presumably for this reason Servius remarks that here it means "sing: properly of the dove" (canere: proprie de turture"). Tennyson's "moan" gives the force in this context and the desired overtones. *Raucus* ("hoarse") can be harsh and unglamorous. Ovid uses it of asses, frogs, magpies, apes; and in the poets it is often used of trumpets and other metallic sounds of battle.

29. Cf. Perret's comment: "Scenery according to Theocritus 7.135-142, but composed (*huc, hinc, hinc*), reduced in detail, changed to produce a unique impression in which moral components dominate (*nota, sacros, semper, suadebit, cura*)." On the difference between Theocritus' appeal to the pleasures of smell and taste and Virgil's dwelling on pure sound, see Viktor Pöschl, *Die Hirtendichtung Virgils* (Heildelberg, 1964), pp. 46-48. For a brief and penetrating account of Virgil's transformation of Theocritean settings, see Klingner's short essay, "Bukolische Landschaft," in *Virgil* (Zürich, 1967), pp. 60-66.

30. P. 257.

31. *Idylls* 8.57-60, 76-80, and 9.7-8, 31-35. From his having imitated both these idylls (especially 8), it would seem that Virgil thought they were genuine. Their authenticity is doubted now because of the quality of the verse. For details, see Gow's edition. Cf. Dover's comment on the problem of

authenticity: "There was a tendency throughout antiquity to ascribe to a famous poet works which had a generic resemblance to his but were in fact by lesser-known poets; the same tendency operated recklessly and notoriously in the ascription of speeches to orators" (p. xviii).

32. *Idylls* 5.92-95 and 136-137; 10.28-31; 11.20-21.

33. P. 41.

34. The two leading Victorian commentators, Conington and Page, say, respectively, "fill the air with his song" and "his song seems wafted on the breeze." (Cf. the remarks that follow about the way pastoral song holds assertion and receptivity in suspension.) Putnam says the pruner "sends his words toward the breezes of heaven" (p. 50). All these renderings are quite justified; a glance at Lewis and Short or the Oxford Latin Dictionary will persuade the reader that there is no one "correct" translation of the phrase.

35. Rosenmeyer, p. 147.

36. Segal, p. 242.

37. René Waltz, "La Ire et la IXe Bucolique," *Revue Belge de Philologie et d'Histoire* 6 (1927), 36. This article compares the two shepherds, much to the disadvantage of Tityrus.

38. Preface to the Edition of 1815, in *Poetical Works,* ed. E. de Selincourt, vol. 2 (Oxford, 1944), p. 436.

39. "*Amaras* quantum ad nostrum saporem; nam capris dulces sunt." Servius notes a similar double perspective in his gloss on *gemere* (line 58), "mourn," which means simply "to sing" for the doves (above, n. 28). Cf. the beautiful use of *amarus* in *Ecl.* 6.62-68 and the discussion by Charles Segal, "Vergil's Sixth *Eclogue* and the Problem of Evil," *Transactions of the American Philological Association* 100 (1969), 423.

Abbreviations

The following editors and commentators are referred to, in both text and footnotes, by their last names:

Cartault   A. Cartault, *Étude sur les Bucoliques de Virgile* (Paris, 1897)

Coleman   Vergil, *Eclogues,* ed. Robert Coleman (Cambridge, 1977)

Conington   *The Works of Virgil,* with a commentary by John Conington and Henry Nettleship, vol. 1: *Eclogues and Georgics,* 5th ed., rev. F. Haverfield (London, 1898)

Dover   Theocritus, *Select Poems,* ed. K. J. Dover (London, 1971)

Gow   A. S. F. Gow, *Theocritus,* edited with a translation and commentary, 2 vols. (Cambridge, 1950; revised, 1952)

Martyn   John Martyn, *The Bucolicks of Virgil,* with an English translation and notes (4th ed., Oxford, 1820)

Page   *P. Vergili Maronis Bucolica et Georgica,* ed. T. E. Page (London, 1898)

Perret   Virgil, *Les Bucoliques,* ed. Jacques Perret (Paris, 1961)

Servius   *Servii Grammatici qui feruntur in Vergilii Bucolica et Georgica Commentarii,* ed. Georgius Thilo (Leipzig, 1887)

FURTHER READING

Bibliography

Briggs, Jr., W. W. "A Bibliography of Virgil's *Eclogues* (1927-1977)." *Principat,* edited by Wolfgang Haase, pp. 1267-1357. Berlin: Walter de Gruyter, 1981.

> Extensive bibliography listing published text and commentaries; translations in seventeen languages; indices; manuscripts; general studies; sources; individual *Eclogues*; contemporary and later ancient authors; Medieval, Renaissance, and modern authors; and textual criticism.

Criticism

Berg, William. *Early Virgil.* London: The Athlone Press, 1974, 222 p.

> Includes the text and translation of Vergil's *Eclogues,* as well as interpretation and criticism of the individual poems.

Currie, H. MacL. "The Third *Eclogue* and the Roman Comic Spirit." *Mnemosyne* XXIX, No. 4 (1976): 411-20.

> Analyzes the use of the conundrum, or riddle, within the poem, observing that the use of such devices was common in the Italian comic tradition.

Galinskiy, G. Karl. "Vergil's Second *Eclogue*: Its Theme and Relation to the *Eclogue* Book." *Classica et Mediaevalia: Revue Danoise De Philologie et D'Histoire* XXVI, No. 1-2 (1965): 161-91.

> Maintains that none of the *Eclogues* is "typical," and examines the theme, structure, and relation of the second *Eclogue* to its Theocritean counterpart.

Kidd, D. A. "Imitation in the Tenth *Eclogue*." *Bulletin of the Institute of Classical Studies* 11, No. 9 (1964): 54-64.

> Examines the imitative nature of the poem, arguing that the imitation is quite developed, subtle, and complex, and that the pattern of imitation is different in each of the four parts of the poem.

Leach, Eleanor Winsor. *Vergil's "Eclogues": Landscapes of Experience*. Ithaca: Cornell University Press, 1974, 281 p.

> Book–length study of the poems, focusing on the Roman view of the pastoral, symbolism in the first *Eclogue,* characterization in the rustic poems, and the use of prophecy within the poems.

Lee, Guy. "A Reading of Virgil's Fifth *Eclogue*." *Proceedings of the Cambridge Philological Society*, No. 203 (1977): 62-70.

> Analyzes characterization and dramatic progression within the poem.

Nisbet, R. G. M. "Virgil's Fourth *Eclogue*: Easterners and Westerners." *Bulletin of the Institute of Classical Studies*, No. 25 (1978): 59-78.

> Examines the analogies between religions of the East and Western tradition.

Otis, Brooks. "The Young Virgil." In *Virgil: A Study in Civilized Poetry*, pp. 97-143. Oxford: Clarendon Press, 1963.

> Offers an overview of Vergil's early works and the sources from which he may have drawn to compose such poetry.

Rudd, Niall. "Architecture: Theories about Virgil's *Eclogues*." In *Lines of Enquiry: Studies in Latin Poetry,* pp. 119-44. Cambridge: Cambridge University Press, 1976.

> Studies the structure of the *Eclogues* as a whole, rather than focusing on the structure of the individual poems.

Segal, Charles Paul. "Vergil's *Caelatum Opus*: An Interpretation of the Third *Eclogue*." *American Journal of Philology* LXXXVIII, No. 3 (1967): 279-308.

> Examines the third *Eclogue* and argues that it is not a "pure and simple" pastoral, but that in it Vergil highlights the limits of the pastoral form.

Wormell, D. E. W. "The Originality of the *Eclogues*: *Sic Paruis Componere Magna Solebam.*" In *Virgil,* edited by D. R. Dudley, pp. 1-26. London: Routledge and Kegan Paul, 1969.

> Studies the relationship between Theocritus's *Idylls* and Vergil's *Eclogues,* stating that the debt Vergil owes Theocritus is "almost incalculable."

Additional coverage of Vergil's life and career is contained in the following source published by the Gale Group: *Poetry Criticism,* **Vol. 12.**

William of Palerne

Fourteenth-century English romance.

INTRODUCTION

William of Palerne, an English translation of the late twelfth-century French romance, *Le Roman de Guillaume de Palerne*, was commissioned circa 1350 by Humphrey de Bohun, Earl of Hereford. Nothing is known about William, the poet who translated *Guillaume de Palerne* for de Bohun, and just as little is known of the author of the original French poem. The story contains common folklore motifs, including the transformation of a man into a werewolf. Critics have examined these motifs, as well as the plot, setting, and style of both versions of the poem; from such analyses some scholars have attempted to draw conclusions about the authors of both the French and English versions of the poems, as well as about the poets' methods of composition.

TEXTUAL HISTORY

The story is extant in three original forms: a French poem in octosyllabic couplets, an English alliterative poem, and a French prose romance dating from the sixteenth century. Little is known regarding the origins of the French verse *Guillaume de Palerne*. The poem is believed to have been completed around the end of the twelfth century. Many scholars concur that the French poet based the romance on several Italian legends or sources. From evidence within the poem, it has been concluded that the romance was written for the Countess Yolande, the eldest daughter of Baldwin IV, Count of Hainault and Alice of Namur. References within *William of Palerne* reveal that it was translated into English from the French verse circa 1350, at the behest of Humphrey de Bohun, Earl of Hereford, who died in 1361. The English author is noted for having been quite faithful to the French original.

PLOT AND MAJOR CHARACTERS

The poem traces the adventures of two princes. One is Prince Alphouns, heir to the Spanish crown, who as a youth was transformed by his stepmother into a werewolf; the other is William, Prince of Apulia and Sicily. When William's evil uncle, in an effort to become heir to the crown, attempts to have young William murdered, the little boy is rescued by the werewolf (Alphouns). Throughout William's life, he is followed and guided by the werewolf. William is eventually taken under the wing of the Roman emperor, and falls in love with the emperor's daughter, Melior. The two run off together and are led by the werewolf back to Sicily. Finding his family under attack by the Spaniards, William goes to war and conquers his enemies. Meanwhile, Alphouns is restored by his stepmother to his human form. The story ends with the marriage of Alphouns to William's sister, Florence, and William to Melior. Additionally, William is elected to the emperor's throne following the death of his father-in-law.

MAJOR THEMES

William of Palerne is filled with common folklore motifs and themes, such as animal transformations, and various occult occurrences. The themes of love and marriage, as well as separation and restoration—elements commonly found in earlier romances and folktales—are examined in *William of Palerne*. The poet's treatment of love and marriage, which has been described as light-hearted and playful, plays a greater role in the poem than in earlier romances. Warfare is a major issue in the poem, and while elements of battle are depicted graphically, as in other medieval romances, the treatment of warfare is less gruesome than in other contemporary poems.

CRITICAL RECEPTION

Many scholars have analyzed *William of Palerne* strictly in terms of the limited facts regarding its textual history, while others have compared the French version to its later English counterpart. Still others study the adaptation of contemporary legends and folktales within the romance. Frederick Madden discusses the history of the extant French and English manuscripts, and presents the pertinent biographical backgrounds of the patrons for whom both the French and English poems were composed. Walter W. Skeat praises Madden's edition of the poem, commenting that Madden is one of the first editors to present a strict and literal interpretation of the text. Skeat also offers a brief synopsis of the plot of *William of Palerne*. Kate Watkins Tibbals, in her study of the romance, observes that while the author of the English poem remained faithful to the French original, the English poet increased the poetic merits of the romance through description, characterization, and humor. Furthermore, Tibbals suggests that the werewolf, rather than William, is the true hero of the story. Tibbals goes on to assess the significance of the magical elements within the poem, the most notable of which is the transformation of a man into a werewolf. Irene Pettit McKeehan, on the other hand, views William as the story's hero. McKeehan describes the plot similarities between *Guillaume de Palerne* and a number of other French and Celtic tales. McKeehan maintains that the story also bears resemblances to contemporary history, and that the compiler tailored the story to appeal to Countess Yolande (his patroness) and her court. Similarly, Charles W. Dunn agrees that the poet attempted to write a story designed to be of special interest to his patroness. In particular, Dunn argues, the story's Italian setting was especially suited to the Countess and her circle, because it was "both familiar and fantastic." Dunn also discusses elements commonly found in contemporary legends—such as love, slaughter and warfare, and "wonder-elements," including magic and prophecy—and discusses the poet's adaptation of these legends and his treatment of these elements in *Guillaume de Palerne*. Like Dunn, G. H. V. Bunt asserts that the poem's setting is of particular importance. Bunt states that the author's descriptions of the setting display an extensive knowledge of the geography of Southern Italy and Sicily. Along with McKeehan, Bunt takes notice of the historical aspects of the poem, which would have been recognized by the poem's original (French) audience. Bunt notes that such historical associations must have seemed extremely remote to the English audience of the fourteenth-century *William of Palerne*. Additionally, Bunt discusses the plot and structure of the poem and comments on other critics' similar analyses, registering disagreement with Tibbals' assessment that Alphouns the werewolf is the hero of the story.

PRINCIPAL WORKS

Principal English Edition

The Ancient English Romance of William and the Werwolf (edited by Frederick Madden) 1832

CRITICISM

Frederick Madden (essay date 1832)

SOURCE: An introduction to *The Ancient English Romance of William and the Werwolf*, Burt Franklin, 1832, pp. i-xvii.

[*In the essay below, Madden reviews the circumstances surrounding the composition of* William of Palerne, *discussing in particular the likely date of composition, the patron for whom this translation of the French poem* Guillaume de Palerne *was written, and what is known about the origins of* Guillaume de Palerne.]

The **Romance of William and the Werwolf,** contained in the present volume, is printed from an unique Ms.

preserved in the library of King's College, Cambridge, and its literary history renders it of more than common interest to the poetical antiquary. It is to the memorable Rowleian controversy we are indebted for the first notice of this poem in its English dress. In that singular dispute, in which Jacob Bryant, Fellow of King's College, and the Rev. Jeremiah Milles, D. D. Dean of Exeter, so notably distinguished themselves in defence of the pseudo-Rowley and his writings, the former, by a piece of good fortune, stumbled on the Romance, and, still more fortunately for us, resolved to force it into his service in support of the antiquity of Chatterton's forgeries. Accordingly, in his "Observations," 8vo. Lond. 1781. pp. 14-23. he gives a short account of the poem, with a few extracts from it. His argument tends to prove it written in a provincial dialect, and for this purpose he produces a list of words, which he pronounces of a local nature. But however profound Bryant may have been as a classic scholar, he possessed very little, or rather, no knowledge of the formation or genius of the old English language. Indeed, his attempt to prove Chatterton's poetry the production of the 15th century, is quite sufficient to acquit him of any such pretensions. The consequence is natural. Nearly all the words considered by him provincial, are to be met with in every other writer of the period, and even those of rarer occurrence are for the most part, found in the Scottish alliterative Romances of the same century.[1] But the citations made by Bryant from this Ms. were sufficient at a somewhat later period to attract the attention of the kennel of 'black-letter hounds' then in full cry after the pothooks of Shakspeare's prompter's book, and George Steevens, I believe, applied for permission to inspect it. The volume was then in the hands of Dr. Glynne, Senior Fellow of King's College, who, like Bryant, was a sturdy Rowleian,[2] and he, fancying that an examination of the book might not assist the claims of Rowley to originality, very prudently locked the treasure up, and there it slumbered till it was once more brought to light by the Rev. C. H. Hartshorne, about the year 1824.[3] By permission of the Provost, about 560. lines of the commencement were copied, and they form a portion of a volume intitled "Ancient Metrical Tales," published in 1829. 8vo. pp. 256-287. Of the inaccuracy of this transcript I shall say nothing, as it will sufficiently appear by comparison with the text now printed.

Having thus briefly stated the mode in which this Ms. became known to the public, the next point of inquiry will be the author of the poem in its present shape; and here, I regret to add, no information can be gained. All we know on the subject is derived from the writer himself, who tells us, he translated it from the French at the command of Humphrey de Bohun, Earl of Hereford. These are his words, at the end of the first *fytte* or passus:

> Thus passed is the first pas of this pris tale,
> And ze that loven and lyken to listen ani more,
> Alle wizth on hol hert to the heiz king of hevene,
> Preieth a pater noster prively this time,
> *For the hend Erl of Herford, sir Humfray de Bowne,*
> *The king Edwardes newe, at Glouster that ligges,*

For he of Frensche this fayre tale ferst dede translate,
In ese of Englysch men, in Englysch speche.

—f. 3.

And at the end of the poem, in similar but in fuller terms:

But faire frendes, for Goddes love, and for zour own
mensk,
Ze that liken in love swiche thinges to here,
Preizeth for that gode Lord that gart this do make,
The hende Erl of Hereford, Humfray de Boune;
The gode king Edwardes douzter was his dere moder;
He let make this mater in this maner speche,
For hem that knowe no Frensche, ne never under-
sto[nd]:
Biddith that blisful burn that bouzt us on the rode,
And to his moder Marie, of mercy that is welle,
Zif the Lord god lif, whil he in erthe lenges,
And whan he wendes of this world, welthe withoute
ende,
To lenge in that liking joye, that lesteth ever more.

—f. 82.

It has been the more necessary to quote these passages at
length, in order to correct the absurd mistakes of Bryant,
who, not understanding the phrases, "at Glouseter that *lig-*
ges," and "ferst *dede* translate," nor the import of the line
"Zif the Lord god lif," &c. has supposed, first, that the
Earl himself had made a prior translation to the one before
us, and secondly, that he was dead and buried at Gloucester, when the second version was undertaken! It is scarcely
necessary to point out, that the words "ferst *dede* translate,"
only mean first *caused* to be translated, and are strictly
synonymous with "*gart* this do make," and "*let* make."
Then, as to the Earl's lying dead at Gloucester, the Poet
can have no such meaning, for at the conclusion of the
Romance he begs his hearers to pray to God and the Virgin
to give the Earl 'good life,' and after his decease, eternal
felicity. The line simply means, resident or dwelling at
Gloucester,[4] and although the term *to ligge* was in
subsequent times more often used in the sense understood
by Bryant, yet there is no reason, in the above instance, to
depart from its original and obvious meaning.

The nobleman thus alluded to was the sixth Earl of Hereford of the name of Bohun, and third son of Humphrey de
Bohun, fourth Earl of Hereford, and Elizabeth Plantagenet,
seventh daughter of King Edward the First; consequently
he was nephew to King Edward the Second, as intimated
in the poem, and first cousin to King Edward the Third.
He succeeded to the earldom at the age of twenty-four, on
the death of his brother John without issue, 20th Jan.
1335-6. and died, unmarried, 15th Oct. 1361.[5] We are,
therefore, enabled to fix the date of the composition of the
English Romance with sufficient accuracy, nor shall we
greatly err, if we refer it to the year 1350. This will agree
extremely well with the scanty notices transmitted to us of
De Bohun's life, which, like most of those relating to the
belted barons of this chivalric period, are chiefly of a
military character.[6] Yet it may be doubted whether, as a
soldier, the Earl of Hereford was at any time distinguished,

and whether he may not have been confounded by Froissart with his brother, the Earl of Northampton. And this
conjecture corresponds with the instrument preserved in
Rymer,[7] dated 12th June, 1338. by which the King ratifies
Humphrey de Bohun's resignation of his hereditary office
of Constable of England, in favor of his brother, "*tam ob*
corporis sui inbecillitatem, quàm propter infirmitatem diu-
turnam qua detinetur, ad officium Constabulariæ exercen-
dum," &c. We may, therefore, with great probability
conclude, that the Earl's weak state of bodily health
exempted him from taking an active part in the warfare of
the time, although he might have assisted the King with
his counsels. To the same cause we may doubtless ascribe
that love for literature which induced him to cause the
Romance of William and the Werwolf to be translated
from the French,—not, as is evident, for his own use,
since French was then the language of the Court, but for
the benefit of those persons of the middle class, to whom
the French language was unknown. By the influence of a
similar motive we possess the translations made by Robert
of Brunne at the commencement of this century:

"Not for the lerid bot the lewed,
For tho that in this land wonn,
That the Latyn no Frankys conn,
For to haf solace and gamen,
In felawschip whanne thai sitt samen."[8]

Higden's testimony to the prevalence of French in the
education of gentlemen's children at that period is very
precise, and it became so much the fashion towards the
middle of the century, that a proverb was made of inferior
persons who attempted to imitate the practice of the higher
classes: "Jack wold be a gentylman yf he coude speke
Frensshe."[9] Trevisa adds, that "this was moche used tofore
the grete deth [1349] but syth it is somdele chaunged;"
which was, doubtless, accelerated by the Act passed in
1362. ordering all pleadings to be in the English tongue,
and much more by the popular compositions of Gower,
Chaucer, and the author of Piers Plouhman. From all these
circumstances it would seem most probable that the work
was executed after the Earl's return from France in 1349.
between which year and his second expedition in 1359. he
appears to have resided on his estates. That this style of
composition was much admired and encouraged in
England during the 14th century is apparent from the alliterative Romances still extant of the period. But it is very
seldom we are indulged with the names of the persons by
whom or for whom these poems were written, and in that
respect, the present poem becomes more intitled to notice,
from its introducing us to a nobleman, whose claims to
biography are so very feeble, and who would never
otherwise have been known as a patron of literature.

The history, however, of the Romance does not conclude
here. We must next trace it in its original form; and here,
also, we shall find some circumstances which render it
worthy of attention. The origin and progress of French
poesy, both of the Trouvères and Troubadours, have been
successfully illustrated by Fauchet, Roquefort,[10] De la Rue,
Raynouard, and others, but, more particularly, by the

authors of the *Histoire Litteraire de la France.* From these authorities we know that many Romances were composed by the Norman poets previous to the year 1200. which subsequently became the text books of the English versifiers of the 14th century. Most of these were founded on the two great sources of fiction throughout Europe; the exploits of Charlemagne and his *Douze Pairs,* and of Arthur and the Knights of the Round Table, amplified from the fictitious histories of Turpin and Geoffry of Monmouth. The chief exceptions to this cycle of poetry at the period we are treating of, are the Romances of Havelok, Horn, Benoit's Guerre de Troie, Garin le Loherain, Alexander, Athys et Porfilias, Florimond, Gerard de Rousillon, and, perhaps, some few others composed by Raoul de Houdanc, and Thiebaut de Mailli, all of which come under the class of *Romans mixtes.* Among these also we are intitled to place our **Romance of William and the Werwolf,** the title of which in the original, is, *Roman de Guillaume de Palerne.* The popularity of this singular tale, (which one would suppose was formed on some Italian tradition, picked up by the Norman adventurers in Apulia and Sicily) must have been considerable, since in the ancient inventories of the libraries of the Dukes of Burgundy, taken in 1467. and 1487. we find no less than three copies of it.[11] At present, the catalogues of Mss. in England have been searched in vain for the poem, and in France, on a similar inquiry being made, only *one* copy has been discovered, preserved in the Bibliothèque de l'Arsenal, at Paris,[12] and, to all appearance, is the same Ms. which was formerly at Brussels.[13] By the obliging attention of M. Van Praet, the distinguished Librarian of the Bibliothèque Royale, the Editor is enabled to give some account of this unique volume. It is a vellum Ms. of a small folio size, consisting of 157. leaves, and written in double columns of 31. lines each, towards the close of the thirteenth century. It contains the *Roman d'Escouffle* (fol. 1-77.) and the *Roman du Guillaume de Palerne.* The latter commences thus:

> Nus ne se doit celer ne taire,
> S'il set chose q^i doie plaire,
> K'il ne le desponde en apert,
> Car bñ repont son sens et pert,
> Q' nel despont apertement,
> En la presence de la gent:
> Por ce ne voel mon sens repondre,
> Q' tot li mauuais puissent fondre,
> Et cil q^i me vaurront entendre,
> I puissent sens et bñ aprendre;
> Car sens celés, q^i n'est oïs,
> Est autresi, ce m'est auis,
> Com maint tresor enfermé sont,
> Q' nului bñ ne preu ne font,
> Tant comme il soient si enclos,
> Aut' si est de sens repos;
> Pur ce ne voel le mien celer,
> Ancois me plaist a raconter,
> Selonc mon sens et mon memoire,
> Le fait d'une ancienne estoire,
> Q' en Puille iadis avint,
> A un roi q^i la terre tint.

> Li rois Embrons fu apelés,
> Mult par fu grans sa poestés, *etc.*

And ends in the following manner:

> Del roi Guill' et de sa mere,
> De ses enfans et de son geurre, (?)
> De son empire et de son regne,
> Trait li estoires ci a fin.
> Cil q^i tos iors fu et sans fin
> Sera, et pardoune briement,
> Il gart *la contesse Yolent,*
> La bonne dame, la loial,
> Et il descort son cors de mal.
> *Cest liure fist diter et faire,*
> *Et de Latin en Roumans traire.*
> Proions dieu por la bonne dam[e]
> Qñ bon repos en mete l'ame,
> Et il nous doinst ce deseruir,
> Q^a boine fin puissons venir. Amen.

> *Explicit li Roumans de Guilliaume de Palerne.*

The lady here referred to can be no other than Yoland, eldest daughter of Baldwin IV. Count of Hainault, and Alice of Namur. She was married, 1st. to Yves, or Yvon, Count of Soissons, surnamed *le Viel,* who is characterised by an old Chronicler as a nobleman "de grande largesse, et sage sur tous les Barons de France."[14] On his death, without issue, which took place in 1177. she married, secondly, Hugh Candavene IV. Count of St. Paul, by whom she had two daughters, the eldest of which carried the title into the family of Chastillon. By the union of Judith, daughter of Charles the Bold, with Baldwin I. Count of Flanders, the Countess Yoland claimed descent from the blood of Charlemagne, and by the marriage of her brother Baldwin the Courageous with Margaret of Alsace, heiress of Flanders and Artois, she became aunt to Baldwin VI. Count of Hainault and Flanders, who in 1204. was elected Emperor of Constantinople,[15] and to Isabel of Hainault, who, in 1180. shared the throne of Philip Augustus, King of France. Such was the splendid alliance of the lady to whom our poem owes its origin. In accordance with the prevailing taste of the age, we find the Counts of Hainault and Flanders distinguished patrons of poesy. Chrestien de Troyes is said to have dedicated several of his Romances to Philip of Alsace, Count of Flanders, who died in 1191.[16] and Baldwin V. Count of Hainault, having found at Sens, in Burgundy, a Ms. of the Life of Charlemagne, gave the work at his death [1195.] to his sister Yoland (the same lady above mentioned), who caused it to be translated into French prose.[17] We have once more to lament that the author of our original (most probably, a native of Artois,) should have concealed his name, but the time of its composition may be assigned between 1178. the probable date of her marriage with the Count of St. Paul, and the year 1200. The Count died at Constantinople before 1206. and Yoland did not, in all probability, survive him long. She was, certainly, alive in 1202. as appears from an instrument in Du Chesne. This Romance may therefore be ranked among the earliest of those composed at the close of the 12th century, and it is surprising it should have been overlooked by Roquefort and the Benedictines.

At a much later period, apparently, at the beginning of the 16th century, this poem was converted into French prose. Three editions of it are known to book-collectors; the first printed at Paris, by Nicolas Bonfons, 4to. *litt. goth.*[18] the second at Lyons, 1552. by Olivier Arnoult, 4to.[19] and a third at the same place (probably a re-print) by the widow of Louis Coste, *s. a.* about 1634. The 'traducteur,' in a short preface, tells us he obtained the original by gift of a friend, and finding the language to be "romant antique rimoyé, en sorte non intelligible ne lisible," he turned it into modern French, with some additions of his own, for the assistance of those who might wish to read it: "Car en icelle lisant," he adds, "pourra l'on veoir plusieurs faictz d'armes, d'amours, & fortunes innumerables, & choses admirables, q' aduindret au preux & vaillant cheualier Guillaume de Palerne, duquel l'histoire port le nom." He afterwards adverts to the Countess Yoland, and her nephew Baldwin, Emperor of Constantinople, who was slain by the infidels at the siege of Adrianople, in 1205. And adds: "Pour l'hõneur de laquelle, & de si haut empereur, pouuõs facilement accroistre les choses au present liure contenues." Whether the story will appear quite so credible at the present day is rather questionable. The French bibliographers are silent as to the author of this prose version, and Dr. Dibdin's sagacity seems to have failed him here. But at the end of the volume is an acrostic of twelve lines, the first letters of which form the name of *Pierre Durand*, who, no doubt, is the compiler. Any further information respecting him I have been unable to obtain, unless he is the same with the Pierre Durand, Bailli of Nogent le Rotrou, en Perche, mentioned by La Croix du Maine, who adds, that he was an excellent Latin poet, and composed many inedited verses both in Latin and French.[20] No notice is supplied of the period at which he lived. It was, most likely, from this prose translation, that the imperfect analysis of the Romance was borrowed, printed in the *Nouvelle Bibliothèque des Romans*, tom. ii. pp. 41-68. 12mo. Par. an. vi. [1808.] where it is placed in the class of "Romans de Féerie," although professedly extracted from a Ms. of the 14th century.

By the assistance of Durand's version we are enabled to judge of the accuracy of the English versifier, since they both translate from the same text, and it is surprising how closely the latter has adhered to his original. Another advantage gained from it is to supply the *hiatus* which, unfortunately, occur in the English poem. To avoid the prolixity of the prose author, the substance of the passages wanting, is here annexed:

> "There was formerly a King of Sicily, named Ebron, who was also Duke of Calabria and Lord of Apulia; rich and powerful above all other princes of his time. He married Felixe, daughter of the Emperor of Greece, and not long after their union, they were blessed with a son named William, the hero of the present story. The infant was intrusted to the care of two sage and prudent ladies, named Gloriande and Esglantine, who were chosen to superintend his nurture and education. But the brother of King Ebron, foreseeing that his succession to the throne would be now impeded, soon formed a resolution to destroy the boy, and, by means of

> promises and bribes so wrought on the governesses, that they at length consented to a plan by which both the Prince and the King were to be put to death. At that time the Court was held at the noble city of Palerne, [Palermo] adjoining to which was a spacious garden, abounding with flowers and fruits, in which the King was often accustomed to take his recreation. But one day, when Ebrons was walking here, accompanied by the Queen and the Prince, (then about four years old) attended by the two governesses, an event took place which turned all their joy into the deepest consternation and grief. For, whilst the King's brother and the two ladies were holding a secret conference how to carry their project into execution, a huge werwolf, with open jaws and bristled mane, suddenly rushed forth from a thicket, at which the ladies were so terrified, that they swooned away, and the rest fled, leaving the child alone, who was immediately carried off, without injury, by the beast. The King ordered pursuit to be made, but in vain, for the swiftness of the animal soon enabled him to distance his pursuers; to the great distress of the monarch and his court. The werwolf bore the child away to a place of safety, and thence, pursuing his course night and day, at length conveyed him to a forest, not far from the city of Rome, where he remained some time, taking care to provide what was necessary for his sustenance; and having dug a deep pit, and strewed it with herbs and grass for William to sleep on, the beast was accustomed to fondle the boy with his paws in the same manner a nurse would have done."

Here commences the English Romance, which, with the exception of a folio (or 72 lines) missing between ff. 6-7. proceeds regularly to the end. This second defect occurs at the close of the Emperor's speech to his daughter Melior, p. 16. and the text again begins with Melior's reproaches to herself for loving William. What intervenes may be easily supplied, even from fancy, but in the prose Romance we read as follows:

> "The Emperor's daughter received the infant, which proved of so gentle a disposition, that it seemed to have been bred at court all its life time. It was soon clothed in dresses of silk and velvet, and became the play-thing of the fair Melior. 'Et alors,' says the writer, 'le faisoit mout beau veoir: car en toute la court ny auoit si bel enfant que luy, ne si aduenant. Sobre estoit en son manger & boire, facilemens fut apprins à seruir les dames à tables; à tous ieux, & à deuiser & à dire ioyeuses sornetes à tous propos.' But, above all, William studied how best to serve his lady and mistress Melior, whom he loved above every one else. As he advanced in age he began to share in the chivalrous exercises of the time; to bear arms, ride on the great horse, and practice various feats of strength, all for the love of Melior, his 'mie;' and so great a favorite was he with all the ladies and demoiselles, that Melior heard of nothing but his praises. The Emperor, too, was so fond of William, as to keep him constantly by his side. In the meantime, the Princess would often withdraw to her chamber to dwell secretly on the personal attractions and graceful demeanor of William, and was at length so pierced by love's keen arrow, that she could not refrain from sighing, and desiring to hold him in her arms. But then again, considering with herself, that a lady of her noble birth ought not to bestow her affec-

tion on any one but a Knight of her own rank, she often vainly endeavoured to drive William from her thoughts."

The remaining part of *la belle Melior's* soliloquy will be found in our poem, and the translation is sufficiently *naïve* to be interesting even to those who may, in general, despise the simple language of our old Romances.

The tradition developed in this story, and which forms its chief feature, namely, the transformation of a human being into a wolf, but still retaining many of the attributes of his nature, has been so learnedly and ably discussed by the author of the Letter annexed to the present remarks, as to render any additional illustration unnecessary. But it may not be improper here to suggest, that the belief in this notion in the southern provinces of Europe may have been partly derived through the medium of the Northmen, among whom, as appears from various authorities, it was very general. A curious story of a *were-bear* in Rolf Kraka's Saga is quoted by Sir Walter Scott,[21] which has some slight features of resemblance with our werwolf, and it is singular, that this metamorphosis should have been accomplished by striking the person transformed with a glove of *wolf-skin.* In the *Volsunga Saga,* also, cap. 12. we read of the similar change of Sigmund and Siufroth into wolves.[22] In general, the transformation was supposed to be accomplished, as in our Romance, by the aid of certain magical unguents.[23] With regard to the supposed form of these werwolves, and whether they differed from those of natural wolves, I have searched many writers, without much success, but Boguet informs us, that in 1521. three sorcerers were executed, who confessed they had often become *Loupsgaroux,* and killed many persons. A painting was made to commemorate the fact, in which these werwolves were each represented with a knife in his right paw. This picture, we are told, was preserved in the church of the Jacobins, at Pouligny,[24] in Burgundy, One distinctive mark, however, of a werwolf is said to have been the absence of a tail,[25] yet this does not seem to correspond with the vulgar notions on the subject, since in the wooden cut prefixed to the prologue of the prose translation of this Romance (which, for its curiosity, has been transferred to the title-page of the present volume) representing the werwolf carrying off the infant Prince of Palermo, there certainly appears a tail of due proportions.

On the style in which this poem is written, and its peculiarities of language, it is needless to dwell long. The history of our alliterative poetry has already been illustrated by Percy, Warton, and Conybeare, and the principle on which it was composed, even to so late a date as the middle of the 16th century, is sufficiently known.[26] The lines in the poem consist of an indeterminate number of syllables, from eleven to thirteen, but sometimes more or less, which, like Piers Plouhman, and other compositions of this class, may be divided into distichs, at the cæsural pause, so as to give them the Saxonic character on which they all are formed. Thus, for instance:

> Hit bi *f*el in that *f*orest,
>   there *f*ast by side,

Ther *w*oned a *w*el old cherl,
     that *w*as a couherde,
That *f*ele winterres in that *f*orest,
     *f*ayre had kepud, &c.

It adds, however, to the value of this Romance, that we have in it the earliest specimen of unrimed alliterative metre yet discovered; for of the other pieces of this kind extant, there is not one which may not be placed subsequent to Piers Plouhman, composed after the year 1362.[27] It is also matter of satisfaction to be able to fix the date of this work prior to the period which produced such writers as Gower and Chaucer. We can now trace the English language step by step from the year 1300. since the writings of Robert of Gloucester, Robert of Brunne, Robert Davies, William of Shoreham,[28] Robert Rolle, and Laurence Minot, lead us up to the precise period when our poem was composed, and which forms the connecting link with Langland and the subsequent writers. Without deciding with Bryant, that our Romance betrays very distinctly a provincial dialect, we may accede to his conjecture of its author being, probably, a native of Gloucestershire, or an adjoining country; although the orthography by no means betrays that decided western pronunciation which characterises the poems ascribed to Robert of Gloucester. Of his ability as a poet we ought on the whole to form a favorable judgement; and when we consider the fetters imposed on him by the metre he adopts, and by the closeness of his translation, we may readily forgive the repetitions he abounds in, as well as the somewhat tedious minuteness of his narrative. There are some lines, such for instance these:

> And than so throli thouztes thurlen myn herte,
> That I ne wot in the world where it bi comse;

and again,

> So many maner minstracie at that mariage were,
> That whan thei made here menstracie eche man wende
> That heven hastili and erthe schuld hurtel to gader;

which would seem to mark the author capable of better things. But the poet shall plead his own apology, in some lines at the close of the Romance:

> In thise wise hath William al his werke ended,
> As fully as the Frensche fully wold aske,
> And as his witte him wold serve, thouzh it were febul;
> *But thouzh the metur be nouzt made at eche mannes paye,*
> *Wite him nouzt that it wrouzt, he wold have do beter*
> *Zif is witte in eny weizes wold him have served.*

It would seem from this, as if the alliterative form of alexandrine verse had not yet become popular, and was, in fact, but lately introduced. It is worth observing also, that the number of French words here introduced, will serve to exonerate Chaucer from the charge made against him of debasing the English language by Gallicisms. Such a remark could only have come from one ignorant of what early English literature owes to our continental neighbours.

There are some minuter details respecting the grammatical construction of the poem, which perhaps deserve notice, such as the use of the present tense for the past, as *askes, arise, bere, seweth*, &c. for *asked, arose, bore, sewede*, &c. the use of the singular for the plural, (if, indeed, it be not a contracted form of the plural, which I am inclined to believe, like *childer* from *childeren*,) in the instances of *daie, dede, burgeys, bere*, &c. for *daies, dedes, burgeyses, beres*, &c. but the fact is, these are not peculiarities, but authorised by usage, and many similar forms are retained, even at present, in familiar conversation, particularly among the lower classes.

It only remains to give a brief description of the Ms. from which the present poem has been transcribed. It is a moderate sized folio, written on vellum soon after the middle of the 14th century, and consisting of 130. folios, 82. of which are occupied by the Romance. A quire is wanting at the commencement, and a single leaf shortly after. The text is disposed in single columns, of 36. lines in a page, and the writing is in a remarkably distinct, but rather thick and inelegant letter, with small blue and red initials. . . .

At the conclusion of the Romance, f. 82. b. is written in a hand of the early part of the 16th century as follows: "Praye we all to that heaven kinge that made all ye worlde off nowght to perdō the solle of hūmfray boune, that was erlle of herfo^rd, for hys grete dylygens & peyns takynge to translate thys boke owt off freynsche in to englys; to ye entent to kepe youythe from ydellnes [he] hathe sete furthe thys goodly story, wher apon we showld bestou o^r tym apon the holy day, & suche other tymes when we haue lytle o^r nothynge a doyng elles, & in so doynge ye may put awey all ydell thowghtes & pensyffnes [of] hart, for the wyche traueyll pray we all to that heuy kynge to graunt hym eternall lyf for hys good wyll." The rest of the volume is occupied by a portion of the Metrical Lives of the Saints, composed in the reign of Edward the First, and written in a different and rather earlier hand. The lives are those of *Judas, Pilatus, Seint Marie Egiptiak, Seint Alphe, Seint George, Seint Dunston, Seint Aldelme, and Seint Austyn.* There are several other perfect copies of these curious legends in existence. With respect to the history of this Ms. volume before it was presented to King's College library I could gain no information, nor even the name of the donor. There are several names scribbled on the margins, but all of a late period, and of no importance.

The Romance has been printed, as nearly as possible, in exact accordance with the Ms. and not the slightest liberty has been taken, either with the punctuation or orthography. It is, in short, as near a facsimile of the original, as could be imitated by typography. But for the convenience of those unacquainted with the mode of contracting words in old MSS. a list of the abbreviations is placed at the end of these remarks. The Glossary has been compiled with much care, and rendered as comprehensive as possible, but with all due regard to avoid unnecessary prolixity. Only those words are illustrated which appeared absolutely to require it: it being deemed in other cases sufficient to mark the immediate derivation of the term.

The Editor, in conclusion, has to express his thanks to the Rev. George Thackeray, D.D. Provost of King's College, for his permission to copy the Ms. and also to Martin Thackeray, Esq. M. A. Vice Provost, John Heath, Esq. M. A. Dean, and George Crauford Heath, Esq. M. A. Bursar of the College, for their very obliging attentions during the residence made among them.

Notes

1. Bryant's blunders in explaining these words are marvellous. A few instances, which may be compared with the Glossary at the end of this volume, will serve to shew how little he understood the subject. Thus, he interprets *arnd*, around, *bourde*, a public house, or shop, *bretages*, bridges, *kud*, good, *kinne*, can, *maid*, madam, *welt*, held, *warder*, further, *boggeslyche*, boyishly! Many are also copied so incorrectly that they can scarcely be recognised, as *eni* for *em*, *asthis* for *aschis*, *gemlych* for *gamlyche*, *kevily* for *kenely*, *komchaunce* for *konichaunce*, *wlouke* for *wlonke*, *satheli* for *scathli*, *neege* for *neize*, *henden* for *hiezeden*, *feyful* for *feizful*, *wyeth* for *wyez*, *fayte* for *fayre*, *path* for *paye*. And yet this is the man who pretended to judge of Chatterton's forgeries, and even correct them by his own notions of Rowley's fancied original. We may truly apply to him some of the precious lines he wastes his commentary on:

   > "Wordes wythoute sense fulle groffyngelye he twynes,
   > Cotteynge hys storie off as wythe a sheere;
   > Waytes monthes on nothynge, & hys storie donne,
   > Ne moe you from ytte kenne, than gyf you neere begonne."

   p. 69. *Ed. Tyrwh.*

2. Dr. Glynne bequeathed to the British Museum the original parchments fabricated by Chatterton, which now remain a 'damning proof,' were any wanted, of the imposture. They present a series of the most contemptible and clumsy forgeries. Mss. Add. 5766. A. B. C. Alas, for the shade of Rowley!

3. Weber has, indeed, pointed it out as one of those Romances worthy of publication, but he never saw the Ms. itself. See Metr. Rom. Introd. p. lxviii.

4. In the 21 Edw. 3. Humphrey de Bohun, Earl of Hereford, obtained the royal license to embattle his Manor-Houses in the Counties of Gloucester, Essex, Middlesex, and Wiltshire. In the former of these only one mansion is mentioned, that of Whitenhurst, or Wheatenhurst, situated about eight miles south from Gloucester, and it is very probable that this is the spot alluded to in general terms by the Poet. We know moreover, that the Earl was not buried at Gloucester, but at the Augustine Friars, in London, which he had himself re-edified in 1354. See Dugdale, Baron. 1. 184. Rudder's Gloucest. p. 813. and Stowe's Survey, p. 185.

5. Dugd. Baron. 1. 184. Milles, p. 1072.

6. In 1337. he was entrusted with the guard of the important garrison of Perth in Scotland. (Dugd.

Baron. 1. 184.) Three years afterwards he is said to have taken a part, together with his warlike brother, William de Bohun, Earl of Northampton, in the battle of the Sluys, fought in the King's presence, (Froissart, by Lord Berners, f. 30. Ed. 1525.) and commemorated by Laurence Minot, a contemporary poet. The next year, 1341. we meet with him in the magnificent feast and jousts held by the King at London in honor of the Countess of Salisbury—the same to whom the noble Order of the Garter is said to owe its origin, (Froissart, f. 46.) In 1342. he was ordered to provide forty men of arms and sixty archers for the King's service in Britanny, and to attend the Council at London, to treat concerning their wages. (Dugd. Baron. 1. 184.) In 1346. he accompanied the King into France to relieve the town of Aguillon, then besieged by the French, (Froissart, f. 59. b.) but it is not stated by our historians whether he was present at the famous battle of Cressy, fought shortly after. In 1359. he again attended the King on a similar expedition, (Froissart, f. 100.) and nothing further is recorded of him till his death, which took place two years afterwards.

7. Vol. v. p. 52.

8. Prol. to Chron. ap. Hearne, Pref. p. xcvi.

9. Descr. of Brit. c. 15. Ed. 1515. *Jul. Notary.*

10. When speaking of our English Romances Roquefort is by no means to be relied on. Thus, describing the English *Kyng Horn,* he says it was composed in the 8th or 9th century. He then confounds it with the Frankish fragment of Hildebrand and Hathubrand, published by Eckard, and takes Ritson to task, for saying that the French text was the original; who would not, he writes, have committed such an error, if he had consulted Ms. Harl. 2253. where the Romance exists in Anglo-Saxon!!! The reply is easy. The copy of Kyng Horn in the Harleian Ms. was written about the year 1300. and it was from this very Ms. Ritson published his text. The Editor of the present volume was fortunate enough to discover another copy of Kyng Horn in the Bodleian, of the same age, which, in many respects, gives preferable readings. M. Roquefort goes on to call the Auchinleck Ms. a collection of *French* poetry, &c. See his Dissertation "*De l'état de la Poésie Françoise dans les xii. et xiii. siecles.*" 8vo. Par. 1815. pp. 48. 49.

11. See a curious volume, intitled "Bibliothèque Protypographique." 4to. Paris, 1830. pp. 199. 302. 323.

12. Marked *Belles Lettres,* 178.

13. See the work just cited, p. 323. It is there called of the *fourteenth* century.

14. Du Chesne, Hist. de la Maison de Chastillon, fol. Par. 1621. *Preuves,* p. 33.

15. The author of the analysis of this Romance, in the *Nouv. Bibl. des Romans,* t. ii. p. 41. who copies

from the printed prose version, hereafter to be noticed, makes a singular mistake, by confounding the Countess of St. Paul with Yoland, sister of the Emperor Baldwin, and wife of Peter de Courteney, who was subsequently, in her right, Emperor of Constantinople, and died in 1221. He says also, that the Countess Yoland found the Romance among the papers of her nephew after his death [1205.] but this is a mere invention of the writer himself, and contradicted by the original text.

16. Hist. Litt. de la France, XIII. 193.

17. Ib. XIII. 386. Fauchet, Recueil de l'Origine de la Langue Françoise, fol. Par. 1581. p. 34.

18. Copies of this exist in the British Museum, and in Mr. Douce's library. In the former is a note in the hand-writing of Ritson, who supposes it to have proceeded from the press of Nicholas, the *father* of John Bonfons, whose *son* Nicholas printed from about 1550 to 1590. The title is as follows: "*L'Histoire du noble preux & vaillant Cheualier Guillaume de Palerne. Et de la belle Melior. Lequel Guillaume de Palerne fut filz du Roy de Cecille. Et par fortune & merueilleuse auenture deuint vacher. Et finablement fut Empereur de Rome, souz la conduicte dun Loupgaroux filz au Roy Despagne.*" The text is accompanied with wood-cuts. This volume is noticed both by Du Verdier, t. iv. p. 169. Ed. Juvigny, and Bibl. des Romans, t. ii. p. 245. but neither of these writers mention the author.

19. See Dr. Dibdin's Tour, vol. ii. p. 337. who describes a copy of this, and the later edition, in the Bibliothèque de l'Arsenal.

20. Bibl. Françoises, tom. ii. p. 272. ed. 1772. He is said also to have had an *œnigma* or rebus in the front of his house, which seems to indicate the same taste which prompted the composition of the acrostic cited above.

21. Border Minstr. ii. 110. Ed. 1803.

22. Biörner's Kämpa-Dæter, fol. 1737.

23. See *Discours des Sorciers,* par Henry Boguet, 12mo. Lyon, 1608. 2de ed. pp. 363. 369. Verstegan's *Restitution of decayed intelligence,* 4to. Antv. 1605. p. 237. Jamieson's Dictionary, in v. *Warwolf,* and Nynauld's treatise *De la Lycanthropie,* 8vo. Par. 1625. where several of these ointments are described.

24. Boguet, p. 341. Wierus de *Præstigiis,* lib. v. c. 10.

25. Boguet, pp. 340. 361.

26. See Essay in the Relics of English Poetry, vol. ii. Warton's Hist. of Engl. Poetry, vol. ii. §. 10. 8vo. ed. Whitaker's Introductory Discourse to Piers Plouhman, and Conybeare's Essay on Anglo-Saxon Metre, prefixed to the Illustrations of Anglo-Saxon Poetry, 8vo. Lond. 1826.

27. Mr. Conybeare is certainly mistaken in assigning the Romances of Sir Gawayn and Alexander to the 13th century, as I shall endeavour to shew in another place.

28. The poems of this writer, who flourished from 1320 to 1340. are preserved in an unique Ms. belonging to Alexander Henderson, Esq. of Edinburgh, who intends, at some period or other, giving them to the public.

Walter W. Skeat (essay date 1867)

SOURCE: An introduction to *The Romance of William of Palerne,* N. Trübner and Co., 1867, pp. i-v.

[*In the following essay, Skeat praises Frederick Madden's edition of* William of Palerne *for its "strict and literal accuracy," and offers a brief outline of the story.*]

1. The "Extra Series" of the publications of the Early English Text Society, of which this is the first volume, is intended to be supplementary to the ordinary series in such a way as to expedite the printing of the whole quantity of work to be printed. It has been proposed that it shall be reserved entirely for reprints and re-editions, and this rule will in general be adhered to. At the same time, a little laxity of definition must be allowed as to what constitutes a *reprint.* Thus, the editions of "Piers Plowman" (Text A) and of "Pierce the Ploughmans Crede," being entirely new, and from entirely new sources, have been issued with the ordinary Series, though both have been edited before more than once; whilst, on the other hand, more than a thousand lines, never before printed, have purposely been included in the present volume, as belonging to the same date, and as having been written by the same author as the rest.

2. Of the two poems here printed, it is the former that has been edited before, in a volume of which the title is— **"*The Ancient English Romance of William and the Werwolf;*** edited from an unique copy in King's College Library, Cambridge; with an introduction and glossary. By Frederick Madden, Esq., F.R.S., F.S.A., M.R.S.L., Assistant-Keeper of the MSS. in the British Museum. London: printed by William Nicol, Shakspeare-Press. MDC-CCXXXII." It forms one of the "Roxburghe Club" series, and only a limited number of copies were printed.

'The thorough excellence of both the text and glossary of this edition is known to all who have had the opportunity of access to it, and it has always ranked as a contribution of great importance to our knowledge of Early English literature. Sir F. Madden justly claims to have been one of the first editors who insisted on the necessity of strict and literal accuracy, and it is impossible to say how much we owe to him, directly and indirectly. His edition is, in fact, almost a facsimile of the MS., being printed in black-letter, and with all the contractions of the original, a table of these being added to explain them to the reader. A copy of it having been provided for my use, it was sent to the printer, after I had expanded all the contractions by the use of italic letters, numbered the lines, inserted marks of punctuation, and added side-notes. Had the proof-sheets been corrected by this only, the volume would have contained no error of importance; but I judged it to be due to Sir F. Madden and to subscribers to make it absolutely correct (as I hope it now is, in the text at least,) by reading the proof-sheets with the MS. itself, to which I had ready access through the kindness of Mr Bradshaw, Fellow of King's College, and our University Librarian.[1] I have also added a few words within square brackets where there are obvious omissions; they are chiefly taken from Sir F. Madden's notes. As his glossary contained references to the *pages,* and our object is to have references to the *lines* of the poem, I have re-written it entirely, incorporating with it the more difficult words in the fragment of "Alisaunder." For the sidenotes, most of the notes at the end, and indeed for the whole volume in its present state, I am altogether responsible; but I consider it as no little gain that Sir F. Madden, with very great kindness, has looked over the revises of the whole work, and I am much indebted to him for his suggestions. The glossary is, of course, copied from his almost wholly; but to some illustrative notes that are left entirely in his own words I have drawn special attention by attaching to them the letter "—M." He has also permitted the reprinting of his preface to the former edition, and of his note on the word "Werwolf" (with fresh additions).

3. We are also under great obligations to M. Michelant, of the Bibliothèque Impériale at Paris. To him we owe the transcript of a considerable portion of the beginning of the French version of the poem, enabling me to supply the missing portions of the English version at pp. 1-6 and 19-23, and further to compare the French with the English throughout the first 500 lines; some of the results of which comparison will be found in the "Notes." He even did more; for he secured for us the accuracy of the portions printed by comparing the proof-sheets with the MS. Bibl. de L'Arsenal, *Belles Lettres,* 178, from which his transcript was made.

THE STORY.

Most of the details of the story can be gathered from the "Index of Names" at the end of the volume, and from the head-lines and side-notes, but a *brief* sketch of it may be acceptable.

Embrons, King of Apulia, by his wife Felice, daughter of the Emperor of Greece, had a fair son named William. The brother of Embrons, wishing to be heir to the throne, bribed two ladies, Gloriande and Acelone, to murder the child. But at this very time, as the child was at play (at Palermo), a wild wolf caught him up, ran off with him, swam the Straits of Messina, and carried him away to a forest near Rome, not injuring, but taking great care of him. But while the wolf went to get some food for him, the child was found by a cowherd, who took him home and adopted him. (Now you must know that the wolf was not a true wolf, but a *werwolf* or *man-wolf;* he had once been Alphouns, eldest son of the King of Spain, and heir to the crown of Spain. His stepmother Braunde, wishing her son Braundinis to be the heir, enchanted him so that he became a werwolf.) One day the Emperor of Rome, going out a-hunting, lost his way, and met with the boy William, with whom he was much pleased, and took the child from the cowherd behind him on his horse to Rome, and committed him to the care of his own daughter Melior, to be her page. William, growing up beloved by *everybody,* attracted, as might have been expected, the love of Melior in particular; who, in a long but amusing soliloquy, concludes that, though she is degrading herself to think upon a foundling, she finds it harder still *not* to think of him, and seeks the advice of her dear friend Alisaundrine, a daughter of the Duke of Lombardy. This young damsel bids her be at ease, and, having some slight knowledge of witchcraft, causes William to dream of Melior, and to fall in love with her hopelessly. All his consolation is to sit in Melior's garden, and he considers himself sufficiently fed by gazing at her window the whole day. Worn out by this, he falls asleep there, and is found by the two ladies, and, by Alisaundrine's devices, the young couple are soon betrothed; but it has to be kept a great secret, lest the emperor should come to hear of it. About this time the emperor's lands are invaded by the Duke of Saxony. William, knighted for the occasion, is, by his prowess, the chief instrument of the invader's defeat; a defeat which the duke takes so much to heart that he shortly dies of grief. The emperor thanks and praises William greatly, very much to his daughter's delight. But the next circumstance is untoward enough. The Emperor of Greece (who be it remembered, is William's grandfather) sends an embassy, headed by Lord Roachas, to ask the hand of Melior for his son Partenedon. The emperor at once accepts the proposal, and the Emperor of Greece and Prince Partenedon set out for Rome. William falls ill at the news, but is soon recovered by the expressions of devoted constancy which he receives from Melior. The Greeks arrive at Rome, and great preparations are made; what is to be done? Melior and William consult their unfailing friend Alisaundrine, who, not knowing what else to do, steals the skins of two white bears from the royal kitchen, sews her friends up in them, and lets them out by a postern-gate from Melior's garden, and bids them a sad farewell. But they had been observed; for a Greek, walking in this garden, had seen, to his great astonishment, two bears walking off on their hind legs, and tells his companions of his adventure, for which he is well laughed at, nothing more being thought of it at the time. The lovers hurry away till they find a den, wherein they conceal themselves, but fear to die of hunger. In this strait the werwolf finds them, and brings them sodden beef and two flasks of wine, having robbed two men whom he met carrying them. Meanwhile, great are the preparations for the wedding, which is to take place at St Peter's church. But at the last moment, *where is the bride?* The Emperor of Rome, frantic with rage, questions Alisaundrine, who evades his questions, but at last avows her conviction that, if *William* cannot be found, neither will *Melior.* William is indeed missing, and the Greek's story about the two white bears is at once understood, and a hue and cry is raised after them. They are not found, and the Greeks return to

their own country. The lovers, still disguised as bears, and guided and fed by the werwolf, flee to Benevento, where they are nearly caught, but escape by the werwolf's help. Finding their disguise is known, they dress up as a hart and hind, and at last, after a strange adventure at Reggio, cross the Straits of Messina to Palermo, the werwolf still guiding them. Palermo is in a state of siege. King Embrons is dead, and Felice is queen, but is hard pressed by the Spaniards, as the King of Spain has asked the hand of her daughter Florence (William's sister) for his son Braundinis, and, on her refusal, has come to enforce his claim. Queen Felice has a dream of happy omen, and, perceiving the hart and hind, dresses herself also in a hind's skin, and goes to meet them, welcoming them and offering them protection, if William will deliver her from the Spaniards. Rejoiced at this, William, on Embrons' horse, and with a werwolf painted on his shield, performs marvels, and takes both the King and Prince of Spain prisoners, never to be released till the wicked Queen Braunde shall disenchant the werwolf. She is sent for, and arrives, and reverses the charm, restoring Alphouns to his right shape, for which she is pardoned; and the Prince Alphouns receives great praises for his kindness to William, it being now seen that he did but steal him away to save his life from the plots of King Embrons's brother. By way of further reward, he is to marry Florence, and William is, of course, to marry Melior. William sends a message to this effect to Melior's father, who, for joy to hear that she is alive, promises to come to the wedding, and to bring Alisaundrine with him. At the same time the Emperor of Greece, Queen Felice's father, sends Partenedon his son to Palermo to help the queen against the Spaniards; but the prince is not a little chagrined at finding that he has come to see Melior, whom he once wooed, and whom he lost at the last moment, married to the husband of her own choice. Seeing no help for it, however, he submits as well as he can. But there is another disappointed suitor, Prince Braundinis; can nothing be done for him? It is at once arranged that he can marry Alisaundrine, and the triple wedding of William and Melior, Alphouns and Florence, Braundinis and Alisaundrine, is celebrated in one day; after which, Partenedon returns to Greece, and the Spaniards return to Spain. The Emperor of Rome dying, William is elected to succeed him as emperor, and is crowned at Rome; and Alphouns, his steadfast friend, who has become King of Spain on his father's death, is present at the joyful ceremony. And thus the Queen of Palermo lived to see her dream come true, that her right arm reached over Rome and her left arm lay over Spain; for her son was the emperor of the former country, and her daughter queen of the latter; nor was the kind cowherd forgotten, for his adopted son gave him an earldom, and brought him out of his care and poverty.

It ought to be remarked that the curious fancies about the enchantment of Alphouns into a werwolf, and the dressing up of William and Melior, firstly in the skins of two white bears and afterwards in the skins of a hart and a hind, as also the wearing of a hind's skin by the Queen of Palermo, form the true groundwork of the story, and no doubt, at the time, attracted most attention. To a modern reader this part of the narrative becomes tedious, and one wonders why the disguises were kept on so long. But as a whole, the story is well told, and the translator must have been a man of much poetic power, as he has considerably improved upon his original. For further remarks upon him, see Sir F. Madden's preface, and the "Introduction to Alisaunder." . . .

Notes

1. May not some of the alleged difficulty of the study of Old English be fairly attributed to the shameful inaccuracy of some of the texts? The portion of *William and the Werwolf* printed by Hartshorne is, in places, simply inexplicable.

Kate Watkins Tibbals (essay date 1903)

SOURCE: "Elements of Magic in the *Romance of William of Palerne*," in *Modern Philology*, Vol. 1, No. 2, October, 1903, pp. 355-37.

[*In the following essay, Tibbals briefly discusses the textual history of* William of Palerne *and analyzes the nature and significance of the story's magical incidents, including animal transformations and prophetic dreams.*]

About the year 1350, at the command of Sir Humphrey Bohun, the French *Roman de Guillaume de Palerne* was translated into English by one William, of whom we know nothing but this name. The translator was unusually faithful to his original, omitting nothing essential and making no important addition; though he greatly increased the poetic merit of the whole by adding, here and there, some bit of description or character portrayal, as unusual in the romances of the fourteenth century as the fresh humor which is William's undying charm.

Of the origin of the French *Roman* we know nothing. Sir F. Madden in his preface to the first modern edition of the English poem[1] makes the suggestion that the story was founded "on some Italian tradition picked up by the Norman adventurers in Apulia and Sicily;" thus taking for granted that in the French poem[2] of the last quarter of the twelfth century we have the earliest version of this delightful and unusual little romance.

It would seem necessary, before turning to the discussion of the subject of this paper, to give a brief synopsis of the story embodied in both versions of the romance. Short portions of the first part of the English version are missing, so that it is necessary to supply the corresponding parts from the French. As the stories are identical, however, in all other parts, it is both safe and easy to use the original version.

Although William of Palerne bears the title rôle in this romance, he is not, in my opinion, the real hero of the story. Alphouns, the Werwolf, who does, in fact, appear in the second title of the English poem, is undoubtedly its most interesting, indeed its central, character. His story is briefly as follows: His father was the king of Spain, a just and kindly man. At Alphouns's birth his mother died, and in course of time the king married again. The new queen was a woman renowned for her occult wisdom and the power of her magic charms. She seemed, for a time, merely indifferent to the boy Alphouns; but, after the birth of a son, she grew jealous on his behalf and determined to remove the king's elder son from her boy's path to the throne. By means of a magic salve and charms she transformed Alphouns, therefore, to a werwolf, who, realizing his plight, very naturally rushed at the queen—

And hent her so hetterly to have hire astrangled
Þat hire deth was nei dit to deme þe soþe.[3]

At her cries he fled, and thus began his many years of wandering, in his strange disguise.

One day Alphouns came to Sicily, and there discovered that the baby heir to the throne, William of Palerne, was about to be slain at the command of his wicked uncles. He seized the child, bore him across to Italy, and at last left him in the care of a kindly cowherd living near Rome.

For seven years the little William, always watched from a distance by his rescuer, lived happily with his foster parents. Then the werwolf, thinking it time his protégé should be advanced and educated, led the emperor of Rome, whom he found opportunely hunting in the forest, to the spot where William was tending his kine. Charmed with the unusual beauty of the boy, the emperor took him home and placed him under the care of his little daughter, Melior. The two, growing up together—always, though they knew it not, under the eye of the "witty werwolf"— not unnaturally fell in love, and, at last, upon the eve of a projected marriage between Melior and a Greek prince, ran away together, disguised by their clever little friend Alexandrine as two white bears.

Upon their arrival in the forest, the werwolf claimed them as his charge, and led the lovers—quite unconscious of his maneuvers—back to Sicily, William's native land. After many adventures and hair-breadth escapes from the eager pursuit, the pair reached the island, constantly guided, provided for, and consoled by their four-footed friend. Finding his mother and sister besieged by the king of Spain, William, without knowledge of his relationship to them, at once espoused their cause, and, with a werwolf as device upon his shield, overthrew all that opposed him and reduced the king, not only to subjection, but to imprisonment.

Alphouns, the werwolf, who had meanwhile been absent, now reappeared and by his curious motions and obeisances before his father, the king of Spain, led him to think of his lost son and the rumors concerning his transformation into a werwolf. His stepmother, the queen, being promptly summoned, aroused a murderous rage in Alphouns, who was with difficulty restrained by William from rushing upon her at once. In terror, she confessed her guilt and her present readiness to make amends; retired with the werwolf, now quieted, and by means of a ring tied with a red thread about his neck, and the usual charms, restored him to humanity in the shape of a naked man. The story ends with the marriage of Alphouns to William's sister, Florence, of William to Melior, of the clever Alexandrine to Alphouns's half-brother, Braundins; the return of all to their homes; and, finally, the election of William, after the death of his father-in-law, to the empire of Rome.

Apart from its literary excellence, the characteristic which distinguishes this romance, as outlined above, and gives it a place all its own among the non-cyclic romances, is the great prominence it gives (1) to the element of magic, especially as expressed in the transformations of men into animals, and (2) to the influence of prophetic dreams. No less than five dreams, bearing directly upon the story and influencing its development, are related at length. Two of these are caused by the magic of the witch-like Alexandrine, to promote the love affair of William and Melior.[4] Two are prophetic of immediately ensuing events, the one leading to the escape of William and Melior from their pursuers, the other acquainting them with events occurring at a distance,[5] and the fifth, that of the queen of Palerne, longest and most elaborate of all, foretells, not only the coming of William and Melior in their second disguise as deer, and William's conquest of her enemies, but her son's final triumph as emperor of Rome.

More interesting than the dreams, however, are the three cases of men's transformation into animals presented in this poem: the change of Alphouns into a werwolf, the change of William and Melior into white bears, and their and the queen's final change into deer. It is true, the last two metamorphoses mentioned are spoken of in the poem merely as disguises: William and Melior, determined to escape together for the sake of their love, appeal to the crafty Alexandrine to aid them in their departure. Alexandrine, having procured two white bearskins from the kitchen, sews up the lovers in the skins and sends them off on all fours.[6]

From this time until they change their disguise, William and Melior are most frequently mentioned by the poet as "the beres," and he seems throughout to lose consciousness of the fact that they had not actually undergone transformation.[7] The change from human to bear-nature was almost as common, especially in Germanic countries, as that to wolf-nature, as witness the Berserker of Scandinavia. A popular tradition of the sort, in which the transformation has been rationalized and Christianized (by the introduction of the devil!) is found in Grimm's "Bearskin" Tale 101—where "Bearskin" hardly retains any human characteristics during his seven years' compact with the Evil One. In this instance, as in that of the chief transformation in our poem, the werwolf, the man does not partake the character of the animal whose shape he assumes, but retains the better part of his human mind.

Having become notorious as bears, William and Melior, led always by the ready wisdom of their wolf-friend, reject the telltale white skins and assume those of a hart and hind, provided for them by Alphouns.[8] This would seem to be mere repetition in another form and hardly worth remark, were it not for a curious bit of additional detail which appears to corroborate the theory that the disguises of this poem must have been, in some earlier form of the story, actual animal transformations. This additional bit of evidence consists in the account of how the queen of Palerne, having seen the hart and hind in her garden, and having learned, through her dream, that these were to be her deliverers, herself put on a *deerskin* before going down to meet them.[9] Of course, this may be merely the elaboration of the poet, but it seems rather to bear the marks of early tradition. For why should the queen, if perfectly sure that the strangers were actual human beings, merely clothed in deerskins, not go to meet them in her proper costume? It seems an unanswerable question. If, on the other hand, the lovers were actually transformed into deer, they would very naturally be afraid of a human queen, but quite unaffrighted by one of the same form as themselves. To primitive conceptions it was perfectly natural that the queen should herself become a deer, in assuming the deerskin, in order the better to parley with her deer-transformed guests. The fact, too, that transformations into the forms of animals or birds were, from the earliest times, often accomplished for the sake of speed falls in with this theory.[10] Strength, represented by the bears, and speed, represented by the deer, were both necessary to bring the lovers, William and Melior, from Rome to their asylum in Sicily, and to enable them to escape the vigilant pursuit and the manifold dangers of their journey.

Whether William, Melior, and the queen were or were not originally transformed into the creatures whose skins they wore, however, we have an actual transformation here which forms the central interest of the story for students today, as it doubtless did for the less analytical readers on whose account it was first set down in French and English. The werwolf, Alphouns, is, as I have said above, without doubt the real hero of the romance, combining in himself most strangely the characteristics of victim and *dens ex machinâ,* of wild beast and guardian angel.

Mr. Kirby F. Smith, in "An Historical Study of the Werwolf in Literature,"[11] mentions the *Lai de Bisclavret* and two other *lais* closely connected with it, as the only stories of the "constitutional werwolf" in which the author is on the side of the werwolf and enlists the sympathy of the reader on his behalf. We have in William a yet more conspicuous example of the glorification of the man-beast. His type is that of those involuntarily transformed; but, even among stories of such guiltless victims, sympathy on the part of the author is exceedingly rare.

It will have been seen in the synopsis of the story, not only that the attitude of the author is very unusual, but that the character of the werwolf himself is almost unprecedented. In only two instances does Alphouns show a resemblance in nature to the traditional werwolf: in his two meetings with the step-mother who transformed him. The ferocity and thirst for blood and the horrible gruesomeness which are the traits of the man-wolf from time immemorial are entirely absent here. He is most often spoken of as the "witty werwolf," and even when deeds of violence would be perfectly natural, as in stealing food for William and Melior, he harms no one. He rushes not upon a man "wip a rude roring," but lets him escape unhurt save for a grisly fright. "His wit welt he euer," in the full sense that not only could he reason and calculate with a man's mind, but he could feel with a man's heart. He was, in fact, no more truly transformed than William and Melior when they donned the bearskins as a disguise. And it may be added here that the unusual rationalization and humanization of the acknowledged magic change from man to werwolf is an additional argument in favor of the bear- and deerskin changes being originally actual transformations also.

This unusual characterization of the werwolf might arise from one of two causes; either directly from the influence of the author of the French romance, or from the late form of the story as it came to him. Since we have nothing earlier than the French version, and since our English poem is a direct translation of that, it is impossible actually to decide between these alternatives. It seems more probable, however, since the whole plot of the story as we have it hinges on the character of the werwolf, that wherever the poet found it, he found it in substantially its present shape. Of course, it is easy to imagine that, in an earlier form of the tradition, the theft of William by the werwolf had no other motive than the satisfaction of the latter's hunger, and that the child was afterward rescued by the cowherd with whom he passed his boyhood. If, as I have suggested, the earlier story had really transformed the lovers into bears, they would then be fitting companions for a werwolf and their journeyings together were not unnatural. In the dearth of facts, however, it is only possible to say that the character of the werwolf would of itself be sufficient to stamp this story as very late, and it is impossible to do more than guess at its primitive form.

Let us turn, now, to a discussion of the various classes of werwolves and to the place of Alphouns among them. I shall first consider three general types of werwolf-transformations—for it is by their transformations that the classes are distinguished—and then try to show that the widely spread and various stories of swan-transformations can be placed in corresponding categories.

Mr. Kirby Smith, in his article on the werwolf, to which I have already had occasion to refer, makes two general divisions under which the werwolf stories that have come down to us from all ages can be grouped; these are the "voluntary," or "constitutional," werwolf, and the "werwolf by magic." The distinction between the two is sharply drawn, but no possibility of a connection is considered. For the purposes of this paper it would seem better to make three divisions, all more or less connected, yet each

clearly distinct. Before describing them, however, I must state the fact that the use of magic charms and ointments which often accompanies one or other method of animal transformation is not in any way distinctive of these methods, but belongs to the general province of folk-magic, and will not therefore be more particularly considered here. In every instance of transformation, as here in the case of Alphouns, the charms and ointments have probably been added at a late date, after a sophisticated system of magic had been developed.

To return: the first of my three types is that so ably discussed by Mr. Kirby Smith—the constitutional type, or werwolf-by-nature. Here the change from man-form to wolf-form is purely voluntary[12] and occurs either at the option of the wolf-man or at fixed time intervals. The only condition necessary to the change is the removal of the man's clothes when he desires to become wolf, and his resumption of the same clothes to become man. Here the wolf-nature is distinctly predominant, and, as Mr. Smith says, the man is looked upon as "a demoniac wolf in disguise, a flimsy disguise which he may throw off at any moment." The best illustrations of this type are: the "Freedman's Tale" in Petronius, *Satire 61,* and the *Lai de Bisclavret* by Marie de France, both quoted by Mr. Kirby Smith. In the former a freedman sees a soldier, a friend of his, suddenly stop at a lonely place in the road, remove his clothes, emit a howl, and rush off into the woods in the form of a wolf. Later the freedman hears that a ravenous wolf has been among the cattle of another friend and has received a severe cut in the neck. On returning to the soldier's lodging, his friend finds him lying bathed in blood which pours from a great gash in his neck. The conclusion is evident: the man is a voluntary,[13] constitutional werwolf, and an object of horror ever after.

In Marie's *lai* a husband is guilty of frequent and mysterious absences from home, recurring at regular intervals. His wife, evidently acquainted with the habits of werwolves, having wormed from him the admission that he possesses the hated dual nature, begs him to tell her where he hides his clothes. After much hesitation he reveals the secret hiding-place, and to his sorrow. For when next the desire for transformation comes upon him, his wife follows him, steals his clothes, and leaves him powerless to regain his human shape. Afterward, by the intervention of King Arthur, he is restored and his unfaithful wife punished.[14]

The second method of transformation is that called "Teutonic" in Mr. Smith's article. The process is just the reverse of the former one. A man becomes a werwolf by putting on a "wolf-shirt"—or later a wolfskin girdle—and returns to human shape by removing it. Here, as in the first type, the change is usually voluntary, and occurs at either regular or irregular intervals.[15] It is usually periodic, the periods often connected with the number nine. In this type the human nature, on the whole, predominates, even though, as in the case related in the *Volsunga Saga* (chaps. 5-8), the werwolves are wolves for longer periods than they are men. Mr. Smith quotes this latter story. Sigmund and Sinfiötli "fared forth into the forest after spoil; and they came upon a house, and two men with great gold rings were sleeping therein. They were at the time free from a great ill, for wolf-shirts were hanging upon the wall above them; every tenth day they might get out of those shirts." Sigmund and Sinfiötli, having put on the shirts, found themselves unable to return to human form, and rushing forth into the forest, gave themselves up to ravage and murder for the prescribed nine days. Then they returned, burned the skins, and so relieved themselves and the king's sons of the fatal temptation to lead the wolf-life.

An Armenian story, into which later religious ideas have been introduced, shows the same fundamental characteristics. A woman, for her sins, is condemned to wander seven years as a wolf. A spirit robes her in wolf-clothes, which arouse in her wolf-appetites. She devours first her own children and those of her relatives, then the children of strangers. She rages only at night. When morning comes, she returns to her human shape and carefully conceals her wolfskin. Hertz says that this legend is so closely related to European, especially Slavic, werwolf legends that it almost seems as if it must have wandered into Armenia from Russia or Greece.[16]

The third type of transformation is distinguished from the first two by the fact that, in the large majority of cases, it is brought about by the power of some person other than the werwolf, and against his will. The change both to and from the wolf-form is accomplished by means of a ring or necklace, *i. e.,* a magic circle, usually of gold. It is not periodic, therefore, and frequently the man, once transformed, remains wolf to his death. A good illustration of this method is a story taken from the German-Jewish *Maase Buch.*[17] In this story a rabbi sees one day a curious-looking weasel with a large gold ring in its mouth. He captures the weasel, obtains the ring, and finds it to be a magic talisman capable of granting his wishes. All this he tells his wife, but keeps the ring from her. At last, and of course, she discovers the ring and gains possession of it. In revenge, probably, for her goodman's lack of confidence in her, she promptly uses the powers of the captured ring to turn him into a wolf. He leaps out of the window and makes for the forest. The erewhile harmless rabbi now becomes a pest to the entire neighborhood, killing the cattle, threatening men's lives, and ravaging as no mere wolf could ravage. The king sets a price on his head, and a famous knight starts out to take him. When he reaches the depths of the forest he meets the wolf and struggles with it. Almost overcome, he resorts to prayer, and the wolf falls fawning at his feet. The knight having obtained the promised prize, the wolf remains with him till, one snowy day, he discovers the beast *writing Hebrew* with his paw on the snow. He hurries back to town, secures the king, and returns to the forest, where the wolf is awaiting him, his whole story scratched out upon the ground. The wicked wife is, of course, sought at once and the ring procured. When it has been placed upon the paw of the

wolf, the witnesses see a wolf no longer, but the man restored to his humanity.

In this third division—of involuntary werwolves—must be placed our werwolf, Alphouns, who, though apparently made werwolf by magic salves only, no ring being mentioned, is restored to human form through a combination of ring and necklace.

> A noynment anon sche made: of so grete strengþe
> bi enchaunmens of charmes: þat euil chaunche hire tide,
> þat whan þat womman þer-wit: hadde þat worþi child
> ones wel an-oynted þe child: wel al a-bowte
> he wex to a werwolf witly þer-after
> al þe making of man so mysse hadde he schaped.[18]

But at the last, when compelled to redress the wrong she had committed:

> þan raut sche forþ a ring: a rich and a nobul.
> þe ston þat þeron was stit was of so stif vertu
> þat neuer man upon mold: mit it him on haue
> ne schuld he with wicchecraft be wicched neuer-more
> . . .
> þat riche ring ful redily with a red silk þrede
> þe quen bond als bliue a-boute þe wolwes necke.
> seþe feiþli of a forcer a fair bok sche raut.
> & radde þeron redli riþt a long while
> so þat sche made him to man,[19]

a naked man, as almost all werwolves seem to become when freed from the wolf-nature.

Of course, there are endless combinations of these types with each other and with other methods of magic, as shown by the salve and the magic book in **William.** All probably represent some confusion or combination of stories, and all are comparatively late. Even the story of Sigmund and Sinfiötli, one of the earliest of the Teutonic tales of werwolves that have come down to us, may be a combination of Types II and III, since it is expressly stated that the men who lay asleep with the wolf-shirts hanging above them had "great gold rings" on their fingers. Again, we have a combination of Type I, the constitutional werwolf, with the ring type, III, in the *Lai de Mélion,* where the hero removes his clothes, but must also be touched with his magic ring before he can assume werwolf shape, and touched with it again before he can return to human form.[20]

It was in trying to fix the position of Alphouns among his werwolf brethren that I was led to make the foregoing distinctions, with the results that shall be summed up later on. Having settled the predominating types of werwolves, in the three chief divisions that I have described and illustrated, I was struck with the fact (hinted by Mr. Kirby Smith in a general statement that the Scandinavians worked out a complete theory of transformations—but not in any way developed or illustrated by him) that the swan-transformation stories and legends, which, in various forms, are interwoven in the romances of the Middle Ages, would fall into exactly parallel classes—even including that first class which Mr. Kirby Smith makes *sui generis* and quite unparalleled in literature or legend.

Under the first method of transformation come the stories recorded by Grimm that represent the folk-tales corresponding to the "Schwann-Ritter Saga." In these the children who have become swans must put on *shirts* to become human children again. The mere throwing of the human garments about them transforms them at once to human shape. The detail that, in most cases, the shirts are required to be of a special sorf, made after a magic formula—as in the story where the small sister must weave the shirts of nettles gathered by night in a churchyard, and must neither speak nor laugh during the seven years of the weaving—all this is mere late addition of folk-magic, designed to heighten the effect of the tale.[21]

In the second category fall the legends of the swan maidens, the valkyrie, who for the sake of speed assume the swan-mantles for which they are specially distinguished. One of the most charming of the stories about them is that into which Wayland has also been introduced.[22] Wayland, following a hind that appears suddenly before him, is led to a fountain in the midst of the forest. Presently to this fountain come three swans (another version says three doves), who transform themselves into beautiful women by the removal of their swan-mantles, or clothes, and, leaving these on shore, step into the fountain to bathe. Wayland possesses himself of their garments, and so has the maidens in his power. In the one story he lets two of the swans escape, keeping the third for his wife; in the other, the "Volundarkvida," where he is joined by his two brothers, each takes one and forces her to marry him. The point of the story lies in the fact that the moment the swan-mantles are removed their owners become human, and they cannot possibly resume their bird-forms without regaining and assuming the mantles.

In one of the swan-boy legends, also, the boys return to their swan-shapes by means of swan-shirts which they have removed to become human. In this case, since the boys are enchanted, they can remove their feather-clothing only at fixed intervals—during the night—and are compelled to resume it, even against their wills, at daybreak.[23]

But the method of transformation that is most frequently used in the versions of the swan-knight story is that third method that depends upon the magic circle of gold, in this case represented by a necklace. The six little boys, all born at one time in the forest, excite the envy of the wicked queen, their grandmother, by the gold necklaces found upon their necks. When the necklaces are stolen from them, all become swans, and remain in that form until, years afterward, the necklaces are restored. The one little swan-boy whose necklace has been melted up, and the magic thus destroyed, never becomes human.[24] In one swan-maiden story also the maiden's necklace is mentioned, and though it is not directly connected with the transformation, in some older version it is altogether probable that it figured more prominently.

Perhaps the last-named story would stand best as a combined type, like some of the *Märchen* of the swan-children, where the boys, transformed by their wicked grandmother, can be brought back to their rightful shape only through the shirts woven by the little sister whose necklace is mentioned as her most precious possession. Since no adequate reason appears to explain why the little girl did not become a swan with her brothers, perhaps it is not too presumptuous to assume that here, as in the more elaborate romance versions of the story, the necklace proved an effective charm to keep its owner human.

We have seen, then, that both werwolf stories and swan stories—the best-known and most widespread examples of the human-animal transformation idea—may be grouped in three general classes. The first class accomplishes its transformation simply by the removal of human clothes, and by the resumption of these same clothes. A dual nature is presupposed. Ordinarily there is no fixed time at which the metamorphosis takes place. The change is usually voluntary. The man becomes wolf when and where he pleases, and returns to the human shape when his wolf-passions are appeased. The swan-boys, on the other hand, have been cursed with the swan-shape and cannot return to their true form at will. The wolf story, in this instance, is probably the more primitive. Definite time limits, such as are imposed in the "Lai de Bisclavret," are probably a later addition also.[25]

The second class comprises the transformations by means of the skins of animal or bird—when the skins assumed are removed their wearers return to human shape. The change may be voluntary or involuntary; forced upon the man by a curse, or assumed at his own discretion and for a special purpose. The human nature here is uppermost, as is the animal nature in the first class, the power to transform it lying, as before, in the clothes assumed. Here the change is more frequently periodic than not, as we saw in the case of the swan-children who were boys by night, swans by day, and in that of the *Sigmund* story, where the periods were nine days long.

Lastly, the third class covers all those legends in which voluntary—or involuntary—change to wolf or swan is caused by the use of a magic circle of gold—ring or necklace—with or without accompanying charms.

What, now, is the relative age of these three classes of transformations? Undoubtedly, Class I, in its *oldest* form a purely voluntary constitutional type,[26] in which only the removal and resumption of human clothes are necessary to accomplish the change of shape, is the most ancient.[27] For, in the first place, it is the simplest in device, thus agreeing with the principle that, the farther back we go, the simpler do beliefs and legends become; the older they are, the less are they burdened with detail. Again, it shows a primitive belief in the weakness of the division between man and the lower animals, and in the ease with which the line may be crossed by one and the other. Finally, it is not only the simplest, but the most perfect expression of the underlying idea, in at least all the werwolf transformation stories, of the duality existing in the very nature of the man-wolf; that duality which, more than all his acts of ferocity while in the wolf-form, has rendered him an object of hatred and grisly horror from the oldest times until now.

The relative ages of the second and third types are harder to determine. The magic-circle type is not necessarily the latest. For this idea of a magic circle is very ancient. Possibly this, once a general formula for changes of all kinds, may have come to be used for changes in form and nature between man and animals as early as the use of the actual skins of animals—or earlier. On the face of it, however, the use of the skins of the birds or animals themselves appears more primitive. It is a case of the appearance making the man: as, in the first type, one puts on human clothes to become human, so, in the second, one puts on animal clothes, and with them the nature and attributes represented by them in the popular imagination. As Mr. Kirby Smith says:[28] "The reasoning is simple and clear to the primitive mind—put on the wolf-shape, you become wolf." In the same way, assume the feathers of a swan, you are swan—with, of course, traces of the original nature remaining. A later age, with its more sophisticated ideas of magic, finds insufficient causation in the old stories, and the most widely used instrument of its magic, the *ring,* is introduced as a result.

The primitive form of the werwolf stories which group themselves in classes I and II, as compared with that of those in Class III, corroborates the belief in the comparative lateness of the latter. Moreover, in the case of the swan-series, we find the *Märchen* and folk-tales going into Classes I and II with, if anything, only a trace of the ring idea; while the romances, in all cases less primitive, group themselves in Class III.

The werwolf story embodied in **William of Palerne,** therefore, falls into what is probably the least primitive class of transformations, and its nearest parallel is found in the romance of the swan-knights. The fact that the ring, in Alphouns's case, is not used as a ring upon the finger, but is suspended by a cord about his neck, makes him the more nearly akin to the knights whose necklaces were necessary to their lives as men. Their stories in general, too, are similar. Like them, he suffered from the wrath of a witch in his father's household; like them, he wandered far and wide in his transformed shape; like them, he performed services of kindness wherever he went; and, like them, was finally restored to humanity through the golden circle. Though inhabiting a form which carried with it suggestions of wickedness and horror beyond expression, he seems to me fully worthy to stand in our affections side by side with those darlings of romance.

Notes

Note.—A transformation analogous to a combination of Classes I and II of the werwolf transformations has been pointed out to me by Professor F. I. Carpenter in Straparo-

la's *Nights* (English edition, Vol. I, pp. 58-64). The story is as follows: Galeotto, king of Anglia, had a very beautiful wife named Ersilia. Their union was perfect but for one thing—the lack of children. One day Ersilia fell asleep in the forest, and while she slept three fairies came and blessed her. One said she should never fear, and should have a son. The second endowed this son with great gifts of mind and character. The third said he should be born in the shape of a pig, and should retain that form until he had thrice wedded a beautiful maiden.

In process of time the prince was born. Great was the horror of king and queen when they beheld his shape. His mother loved him, however, and he was allowed to run at will over the palace, oven after wallowing in the mud of the street. One human gift he possessed—that of speech.

When the pig-prince had attained to years of manhood, he came one day to his mother and demanded a wife; and so violent did he become, when his request was refused, that the king and queen were forced to consider some means of agreeing to his demand.

There was a poor widow in the country who had three beautiful daughters. Her they summoned and asked the oldest of the girls for their son. Reluctantly the mother conseuted. The daughter was brought to the palace and wedded to the pig-prince. But at night, when she saw him come in covered with mud, she plotted with herself how to kill him. He heard her whispered words, and rushing upon her slew her in her bed.

Some time after he again demanded a wife. The widow's second daughter, who had married him, like her older sister, in the hope of murdering him and succeeding to his wealth, met with the first wife's fate.

Once more Prince Pig demanded a spouse, and this time so violently that the queen went trembling to the widow to beg the hand of her third and youngest daughter for her terrible son. Gladly and humbly the young girl consented. With great gentleness and show of affection she called the prince to her and bade him lie on a fold of her gorgeous bridal gown. With patience she awaited his return at night, and lovingly summoned him to her side. What was her astonishment to see him strip off the loathsome hide of the pig and stand before her a radiantly beautiful naked prince. By day he continued for some time to assume the pigskin, by night his human form. At last, however, he was freed from the charm, and king, queen, and people rejoiced in his release.

Here we see indicated several characteristic points of the general transformation formula: (1) The prince possesses the dual nature, for while he retains the swine-shape he has the swinish desires of wallowing and gluttony. (2) He has certain murderous instincts which ally him with the werwolves, though in this instance justified as self-defense. (3) After his marriage with the youngest daughter he can assume or remove the skin at will—a trait of the transformations under Type II. (4) His animal shape is the result of a curse laid upon his mother previous to his birth—a common circumstance among the stories under Type I. On the whole, his is a combination of Types I and II.

The gift of speech is not generally granted to transformed men while in their animal or bird shapes; e. g., Alphouns communicates with William and Melior only by signs, the Jewish wolf by writing.

No doubt many other sporadic examples of transformation into the shapes of various animals could be adduced. Those given above, however, seem sufficient to establish the theory of three distinct yet interconnected types, under which may be grouped parallel stories at least from the swan and werwolf series of legends.

1. Quoted in the Introduction to the Early English Text Society edition, Extra Series I, p. xiv.

2. Société des Anciens Textes Français, ed. H. Michelant, 1876.

3. Ll. 150, 151.

4. Ll. 657-77, 862-70.

5. Ll. 2293-2313, 3104-7.

6. Ll. 1686-1744.

7. See l. 2401 and elsewhere.

8. Ll. 2574-96.

9. Ll. 3059-71, 3110-19.

10. Cf. the story of the Swedish soldier Afzelius, Umgewitter, 2, 361, quoted by Mr. K. F. Smith, "The Werwolf," p. 23, note; also, p. 25. The gods of Scandinavia use the power of transformation "for the purpose of making rapid journeys."

11. *Publications of Modern Language Association*, New Series, Vol. II (1894).

12. "Voluntary" in the sense that, whether the change be periodic or not, *desire* for the change always procedes. The *wish* may recur at regular intervals, but, the nature of the man being twofold, the wish always precedes the act. Cf. *Lai de Bisclavret*.

13. See note on preceding page.

14. See, in connection with this *lai*, the interesting article of Professor G. L. Kittredge appended to his recent edition of "Arthur and Gorlagon," a Latin version of a Welsh-Irish werwolf tale. The four versions of *The Werwolf's Tale* with which he deals all belong to the "constitutional" type with more or less admixture of later magic (*Harvard Studies and Notes in Philology and Literature*, Vol. VIII, pp. 149 ff.).

15. In these stories, however, it is taken for granted that *whoever* puts on the "wolf-shirt" will become wolf, while in the case of the first class the gift of change, depending on a dual nature, is purely personal.

16. W. Hertz, *Der Werwolf*, p. 27.

17. Earliest known edition, Basel, 1602; quoted by Reinhold Kohler in the Introduction to the "Lais de Marie de France." *Bibliotheca Normanica,* Vol. III, pp. lxxix, lxxx.

18. *William of Palerne*, E. E. T. S. Ex. Sor., I, ll. 136-41.

19. *Op. cit.,* ll. 4424-34.

20. See Introduction by R. Kohler to "Lais de Marie de France—*Bisclavret*," *Bibliotheca Normanica,* Vol. III, pp. lxxvi-lxxviii.

21. See Brüder Grimm, *Kinder- und Hausmärchen* (Berlin, 1870), Tale 49, p. 191. Compare Hans Andersen, "The White Swans;" also Grimm. Tale 9, p. 37, "Die zwölf Brüdof"—a similar story.

22. See "Friedrich von Schwaben" and "Volundarkvida," quoted by Schofield, "The Lays of Graelent and Lanval," *Publications of Modern Language Association*, New Series, Vol. VIII (1900), pp. 134, 135.

23. *Kinder- und Hausmärchen*, Tale 49, p. 193.

24. In English, *The Romance of the Chevalere Assigne*, ed. H. H. Gibbs, Early English Text Society, Extra Series 6, 1868; prose version, *Helyas Knight of the Swan*, printed by Robert Copland early in the sixteenth century, ed. Thoms, 1858. The earliest version of the story known to exist is in the Latin romance by the monk Jean de Haute Seille (Johannes de Alta Silva), entitled *Dolopathos sive de Rege et Septem Sapientibus*, twelfth century, ed. Oesterley, 1873. There are several French versions, the first directly from *Dolopathos* by the poet Herbert, twelfth century, "Naissance du Chevalier au Cygue," ed. in the *Publications of the Modern Language Association*, Vol. IV (1889); *Chanson du Chevalier au Cygne et de Godefroy de Bouillion* (so-called *Elie* version), ed. Hippeau (Paris, 1874), etc. Cf. Wagner's *Lohengrin* for modern treatment of the story.

25. Cf. Kirby Smith.

26. In many versions coming under this type the change is due to a curse, inherited or incurred by the man himself, and so is *involuntary,* occurring periodically at definite intervals of time. But in the *most ancient* form of the legend the change would seem to have depended on the man's own will, and so may be classed as purely voluntary. Cf. Kirby Smith, as before.

27. Cf. Kirby Smith, "The Werwolf," pp. 39, 40.

28. "The Werwolf," p. 40.

Irene Pettit McKeehan (essay date 1926)

SOURCE: "*Guillaume de Palerne*: A Medieval 'Best Seller'," *PMLA*, Vol. 41, No. 4, December, 1926, pp. 785-809.

[*In the following essay, McKeehan focuses on the plot of* Guillaume de Palerne. *McKeehan discusses the numerous similarities between this story and several other tales, particularly* Floriante et Florete, *a French romance written circa 1300,* Cormac Mac Art, *an Irish tale about a prince raised by a wolf, and the* Lai de Melion, *a "Celtic Werwolf Tale." McKeehan also investigates the elements of the story that were likely to have increased its popularity among contemporary audiences.*]

So many things about the Middle Ages seem strange to the modern reader that it is easy to over-emphasize the differences between the points of view and the methods of medieval and of modern writers. Especially is this true of the writers of fiction. We seldom get more than a brief glimpse of the medieval fiction-writer, specifically the author of medieval romances, actually at work; for example, when we find Chrétien de Troyes using the old book from the cathedral library at Beauvais in the composition of *Cligès*. Generally we have only the finished product on the one hand, and on the other hand, "sources" of various kinds, folk-tale or saga or classical story. Where the relation between the finished product and the source is close and obvious, as in such romances as *Sir. Amadas* and *Sir Isumbras*, the mere identification of the source reveals the method of the writer: he found an attractive old story and retold it, adding such embellishments as his audience would probably like. Nothing could be simpler. But the writers of the more courtly and sophisticated romances were not mere redactors; they were authors, in very much the same sense as the modern novelist is an author. And like most modern novelists, they showed their inventive powers, not often in finding new material, but usually in making recombinations of old material. They sometimes had the advantage over the present would-be producer of "best sellers" in writing for specific courtly groups presided over by single leaders of taste. It was therefore relatively easy to discover what their public wanted. Thus Chrétien wrote his *Chevalier de la Charrette* to satisfy Marie de Champagne, though it seems not to have been exactly in accordance with his own ethical standards.

What differentiated the medieval fiction-writer most sharply, however, from his modern successor was the fact that in such a case as that just mentioned, which may be regarded as typical, the reaction of his public was immediate and apparent to himself, probably even while his work was in process of composition; for it is surely reasonable to suppose that the long, rambling romances of the twelfth and thirteenth centuries were composed piecemeal as well as read in sections to their courtly audiences. The writer could test the predilections of his readers—or hearers—by a particular type of incident or method of treatment in the first part of his story and repeat or avoid it in the latter part according as it succeeded, or failed to please them. Above all, from what we know of those medieval groups of high-born ladies and their attendant courtiers, their interest in courtly love, in problems of conduct, in the glorification of heroic prowess, in parallels and comparisons and *debats*, it must be evident that one of the criteria by which the success of a romance could be measured was the amount of interesting conversation aroused by it. The writer of a medieval "best seller"—that is, of a piece of fiction definitely designed to provide what the reading public of those days wanted—would be inclined to produce something that would provoke discussion.

In a recent attempt to analyze the romance of *Guillaume de Palerne,* my own conception of the methods and motives of such medieval writers became much clearer, and the conclusions derived from this analysis may perhaps be of wider application than appears at first sight.

THE EXTANT VERSIONS AND THE ORIGINAL FORM

The romance of *Guillaume de Palerne* is extant in three versions:

(1) A French poem in octosyllabic couplets, which is generally regarded as the original form of the romance, though some doubt has been expressed on this point. At any rate, it dates from near the time of probable composition—the concluding years of the twelfth century.[1]

(2) An English alliterative poem, which can be dated pretty definitely as "1350, or soon after" by its references to Humphrey de Bohun, Earl of Hereford.[2]

(3) A French prose romance extant in several editions of the sixteenth century. So far as I know, this version has not been reprinted and is not available in this country. Sir Frederick Madden, who evidently examined it, says that the English text is closer to the French prose than to the metrical version. Later writers have apparently accepted this statement without attempting to verify it or to discover the details in which the two French forms differ. M. Michelant, the editor of the French verse romance, discusses the language and format of the various prose editions with no reference to their content.[3] Professor Max Kaluza has made a detailed analysis of the relations of the English and the French texts, *Englische Studien,* IV, 197-274; most of the differences may be accounted for by the exigencies of translation, the change in metrical form, adaptation to a middle-class audience, and the English author's greater power of visualization.[4]

There has been considerable difference of opinion as to the genesis of this romance, the merit of which is rather greater than has been generally recognized. Professor Wells writes:

> Just what is the ultimate source of the story, is uncertain. The werwolf motive was known among Romans, Scandinavians, and Celts. The title of the romance and the names of the cities referred to, seem to point to Italy and to support the ascription of the French poem to a Latin source, composed perhaps in Italy or in Sicily. The love-matter between the hero and the heroine is derived from later Greek romance . . . , and its treatment gives to the story much of the atmosphere of the Greek tales.

Gaston Paris classifies the story as an old Celtic *conte*, carried into Sicily by the Normans and localized there. He comments on the fact that some details in the Norman chronicles of Sicily seem to have a Scandinavian origin and to go back to the time before the Normans came into southern Europe; the disguise of William and Melior as white bears and perhaps some other matters might be thus accounted for.[5] Ten Brink is in substantial accord with this view.[6] Körting regards the story as of Germanic origin on account particularly of the werwolf motive, but believes that before it came into the hands of the French poet it had received a Byzantine working-over. Probably, he says, the tale was brought by the Normans into Italy, and there received the southern romantic decoration.[7] These general remarks constitute about the sum total hitherto of scholarly attention to the sources of *Guillaume de Palerne,* with the exception of some discussion as to its possible relation to the Celtic Werwolf Tale, which will be noted later.

Such hypotheses seem to imply that the romance has a single source and that the writer is, in a way, a mere redactor. My own hypothesis is that the romance is a composite, put together by the author of the original French poem from several different sources and treated in such a way as to appeal directly to the immediate interests of the Countess Yolande, for whom it was written, and her court circle.[8]

The plot of the romance according to the English version will serve for the French as well. Moreover, the running marginal outline in the E.E.T.S. edition greatly facilitates the identification of subject-matter. There are two or three fairly noticeable differences in the plots, one of which will be commented on later. The following is the summary of the story, as given by Wells (*op. cit.,* pp. 19, 20):

> The English MS. is defective at the beginning. From the French one learns that William is son of a King of Apulia, Sicily, Palermo, and other lands. His uncle plots to poison the child. A werwolf, who in his childhood has been enchanted by his stepmother, the Queen of Spain, saves the boy by carrying him off and fostering him. One day (and here the English begins), William is found and carried home by a cowherd. Childless, the peasant and his wife adopt the boy, whom they come to love dearly. Attracted by his appearance, the Emperor of Rome takes the youth under his patronage. His daughter, Melior, and the boy fall in love. Through Alesaundrine, the girl companion of Melior, who acts as go-between, the lovers are brought together and long enjoy each other in secret. William exhibits great prowess in battle in Saxony and in Lombardy. Marriage is arranged between Melior and the Emperor of Greece. The lovers flee, sewed in bearskins. In the forest, the werwolf supplies them with food, and misleads their pursuers; finally, he guides them into Sicily, clothed as hart and hind. There they find [Alphonse, the werwolf's][9] half-brother and his father, the King of Spain, [waging war upon the widowed Queen, William's mother, and her daughter]. William overcomes the Spaniards, and acts for the Queen in the stead of her lost son. Ultimately, he captures the King of Spain and his son. Learning from the King of the enchantment of the werwolf, William compels the Queen to undo her magic. The restored Alphonse reveals the identity and the past history of William. William and Melior are wedded. Alphonse marries William's sister. Alesaundrine is advantageously matched. William becomes Emperor of Rome, and rewards his foster-parents.

A careful analysis shows the romance to be composed of the following elements:

A. Nucleus: the story of a lost prince, who, as a "fair unknown," falls in love with an emperor's daughter, rescues his mother from an enemy, and is eventually restored to his rights.

B. The old folk-tale of the wolf's fosterling, very widespread and in western Europe at least as old as the story of Romulus and Remus. (*B* may have been joined to *A* before the latter came into the hands of the author.)

C. The Celtic Werwolf Tale analyzed by Professor Kittredge,[10] in a very much modified form, owing to the influence of *B* and *D,* but showing striking resemblances in detail to the version in the *Lai de Melion.*[11]

D. A selection and a treatment of names, localities, and incidents such as to suggest persons and events of considerable contemporary importance and of special interest to the author's immediate audience.

A. The Nucleus of the Story

In the French romance we find the following statements: (vv. 18-22) 'It pleased me to tell, according to my understanding and memory, the facts of an ancient story (*estoire*) which happened in Apulia to a king who held the land.' (vv. 9649-52) 'Of King William and of his mother, of his children and of his race, of his empire and of his reign treats the *estoire* here at the end.' (vv. 9658-60) 'This book he caused to write and make and turn from Latin into *roumans,* praying God for the good lady,' etc. Though the claim of a Latin original is so common in the earlier romances as to seem almost like a convention, it is known in a number of specific cases that the claim is well-founded, and there is no good reason for doubting the truth of it here. A Latin *estoire* emanating from Sicily or southern Italy would naturally exhibit those Byzantine, "Late Greek," or oriental qualities that various scholars have discovered in *Guillaume de Palerne.*[12] Also, if it were produced by or for the Norman ruling class, the emphasis on fighting and the war-like character of the hero, which differentiate it sharply from such typical Byzantine or oriental romances as *Floris and Blauncheflur,* would be accounted for.[13]

I shall give evidence later to show that the purpose of the author obliged him either to find and use a Sicilian story or to locate in Sicily a story having some other origin. In this case I believe that he found the story already placed in the proper environment, for the only other well-known romance with a definitely Sicilian setting has a plot show-ing marked similarities to that of *Guillaume de Palerne*.[14]

Floriant et Florete is extant in a unique MS. of the 14th century at Newbattle Abbey and was edited by Francisque Michel for the Roxburghe Club in 1870. So far as I have been able to discover, its resemblances to *Guillaume de Palerne* have never been noted, though Gaston Paris classes them together as old Celtic *contes* carried into Sicily by the Normans and localized there.[15] The failure to observe the likeness in the main plots of the two stories is probably due to the unlikeness in their fairy-tale embel-lishments, which to the modern reader are much the most interesting elements in these romances. *Floriant et Florete* (*F*) in its present form and perhaps in its general character is later than *Guillaume* (*G*), but there has probably been no borrowing on either side. If my hypothesis is correct, both represent literary composites built up around a nucleus, a fairly simple story of courtly love and war, originally attached to a legendary Sicilian prince.

The resemblances follow:

(1) Floriant and William are both sons of a King of Apulia or Sicily. (2) A wicked steward forms a conspiracy against Floriant's father, kills him, and usurps his throne. In *G.* the conspiracy is directed against William himself by a wicked uncle, who immediately disappears from the story. (3) Floriant is a posthumous child, born in a forest while his mother is fleeing from the usurper; he is carried off by the fairy Morgain to save him from his enemies, is brought up in ignorance of his birth, but trained in arms and courtesy. William, at the age of four, is carried off by a friendly werwolf to save him from his enemies, is nurtured in a forest, brought up in ignorance of his birth, but trained in arms and courtesy. (4) In both stories, the mother, who survives, believes her son to be dead. In *F.* the steward-usurper seeks to marry her, and besieges her in Monreale. In *G.* the queen has a daughter. The King of Spain seeks the daughter as a wife for his son and, being refused, besieges the queen and the princess in Palermo. Here the fact that no reason is given why the Spanish prince is an undesirable suitor spoils the motivation in *G.* (5) In both stories, the son comes to the rescue of his mother. In *G.* he is brought by the werwolf; in *F.* he is sent by the fairy, Morgain. (6) In *F.* the hero fights a single combat with the steward and defeats and slays him. In *G.* the hero fights with and kills the steward of the King of Spain for no particular reason except the chance of battle. (7) In *F.* the fairy reveals the son's origin; in *G.* the werwolf does so. (8) In *F.* the hero falls in love with the daughter of the Greek emperor, who is aiding the steward against the queen. In *G.* the hero falls in love with the daughter of the Roman emperor, who has befriended him, and the Greek emperor is represented as his rival. (9) In both romances, the lovers are brought together in a garden by the confidante and companion of the princess. (10) In both, the father of the princess becomes reconciled and accepts the hero as his heir; the hero becomes emperor. (11) In *F.* the hero and heroine after marriage wander in disguise in

search of adventures. In *G.* the disguise and the wander-ings occur before marriage.

It will be seen from the preceding analysis that the main stories of the two romances, in spite of their substantial resemblance, contain several minor differences, these dif-ferences tending to produce better coherence and motiva-tion in *F.* than in *G.* I shall endeavor to show later—in section *D*—that the author of *G.* probably changed the incidents in his source in order to suggest contemporary events and persons.

This nucleus constitutes a kind of common-stock romance of courtly love and war. Resemblances in it to *Tristan* have already been noted by Professors Brandl and Gröber.[16] In the *Histoire littéraire de la France*, the romance of *Floriant et Florete* is analyzed in detail to show its borrow-ings from other romances, though no mention is made of any likeness to *Guillaume de Palerne*.[17] Further compari-sons might be made with *Percival*, with *Cligés*,[18] with *Le Bel Inconnu*, and with other romances, but it is hardly necessary to prove that the material in the central plot, which I have called the "nucleus," is composed of the sort of story-stuff that medieval readers of romance wanted. There is just one question here: If, as Professor Schofield says, the chief hero of *Guillaume de Palerne* is the wer-wolf,[19] it is scarcely conceivable that there should have been no werwolf in the original nucleus. But is the wer-wolf the hero? Out of 5540 lines extant in the English ver-sion, only 1913 are connected in any way with the story of Alphons. Even the addition of the missing introduction, which in the French version contains some account of Al-phons, would not materially alter the proportions. The werwolf disappears completely while William is with the cowherd (vv. 160-211); while he is at the Emperor's court (vv. 224-1836); while the lovers are being introduced into the castle at Palermo (vv. 2856-3480); while the fighting is taking place at Palermo (vv. 3513-4009). Between lines 4767 and 5174, Alphons gets two lines about his marriage to William's sister. The last 100 lines and the first 85 of the French poem are devoted entirely to William. Only 52 lines in the English romance are occupied with the independent adventures of the werwolf. A hero is not thus subordinated to another and so often and completely lost sight of in medieval romance.

B. THE WOLF'S FOSTERLING

Though I am convinced that the werwolf story was not a part of the nucleus of *Guillaume de Palerne*, the striking resemblance between the first part of *Floriant et Florete* and the old Irish tale of the birth of Cormac Mac Art[20] suggests that the story of the wolf's fosterling may have been in the original source and may have put into the author's head the happy notion of combining it with the Celtic Werwolf Tale—his final version, as will be indicated, retaining several of the features of the wolf's fosterling motive. An analysis of the introductory portions of *Cormàc Mac Art* (*C*) and of *Floriant et Florete* (*F*) follows:

(1) In both *C.* and *F.* the father has been killed, and the mother is on her way to seek refuge at the house of a loyal

friend of her husband. (2) The queen is seized with the pains of childbirth on her journey; in *F,* in a forest, in *C.* in an undescribed locality, but obviously of a similar kind. (3) In *C.* she is accompanied by one servant, in *F.* by four. (4) In *C.* the mother goes to sleep, leaving the child in the keeping of the maid, who also falls asleep. Similar incidents in *F.* are less probable, because the negligence of four servants at once seems extraordinary. (5) In *C.* the child is carried off by a she-wolf; in *F.* by Morgain la Fay.

It seems unreasonable to account for these detailed resemblances as merely accidental. Yet one can hardly say that they prove the presence of the wolf motive in the nucleus out of which both *Floriant et Florete* and *Guillaume de Palerne* were composed. The marked likenesses, however, in the latter to typical instances of the wolf's fosterling tale can be shown by a comparison between *Guillaume de Palerne, Cormac Mac Art,* Herodotus's account of the birth of Cyrus, the well-known legend of Romulus and Remus, the stories of Amargenus and Albeus from old Irish saints' legends, and the Middle High German romance of *Wolfdieterich.*[21]

(1) Of the seven boys, Cyrus and William alone are of legitimate birth. (2) Cyrus, Romulus, Amargenus, and Albeus are delivered over by a king to a servant in order to be killed; they are exposed instead. Wolfdieterich is placed in a hedge by his mother's direction in order to conceal his birth from his grandfather until an opportunity can be found to send him to his father. William and Cormac are not exposed, but are simply left unguarded, one in a garden, the other in a forest; both have powerful enemies. (3) Romulus, Amargenus, Albeus, and Cormac are each found by a she-wolf and suckled and cared for in her den. A bitch is substituted as the foster-mother of Cyrus. A male wolf finds Wolfdieterich and takes him to the den where its mate and cubs are; nothing is said about the child's nourishment. William, who is not a new-born infant, but a child of four years, is kidnapped for benevolent purposes by a male werwolf, who keeps the boy in a forest den, cherishes him tenderly, and provides him with food. (4) Romulus is found in one version by a cowherd, in another by a swineherd, Cyrus by a cowherd, William by a cowherd, Amargenus by swineherds, Albeus and Cormac by men whose status and occupations are not specified, Wolfdieterich by his own grandfather and a hunting party. The stories of William and of the Irish Albeus here resemble each other closely. In each a man finds the child in the wolf's den while the wolf is out searching for food. The wolf, returning and being greatly distressed over the loss of its charge, follows the man. Albeus's foster-mother catches up with him, and he sends her home in grief. William's guardian, being a "witty werwolf," when he sees the child in the arms of the cowherd's wife, comprehends at a glance that she can give his charge better care than he can, and departs, reasonably satisfied. (5) Romulus, Cyrus, and William are reared by the herds who find them. Amargenus remains with the wolf, and is not found until grown. The man who takes Albeus, true to the Celtic institution of fosterage, entrusts the boy to the care

of "certain Britons" to be nurtured. Cormac and Wolfdieterich are almost immediately identified and returned to their mothers. All except Albeus are said to have been unusually beautiful. (6) All these heroes except the saint, Albeus, are of royal descent, and all except the saint's ancestor, Amargenus, come into their kingdoms and attain great power and glory.

(7) Only in three of the tales, the Celtic stories of Cormac and of Albeus and that of William, is there any future association of the wolf and the hero. When Cormac goes to the court of the High King at Tara, he is accompanied by the wolf-cubs that were brought up with him, and, we are told, "The reason for that great esteem which Cormac bore to wolves was that wolves had fostered him." After Albeus has attained maturity and sainthood, there is organized in that territory a great hunting party against the wolves. One female wolf runs to the place where Albeus is and, when the horsemen pursue her, puts her head into the folds of the saint's robe. He saves her life and that of her whelps. William likewise saves from would-be slayers the life of his "witty werwolf," who, like Cormac's wolf-cubs, aids the hero in his undertakings. The scene in the legend of Albeus in which the she-wolf seeks and finds safety at the hands of the saint bears a general resemblance, not only to the incident in *Guillaume de Palerne,* but also to the somewhat similar incident in the romantic versions of the Celtic Werwolf Tale, the *Lai de Melion,* Marie de France's *Bisclavret,* and the Latin romance of *Arthur and Gorlagon.*[22]

From this analysis it seems evident that the author of *Guillaume de Palerne* either found the wolf's fosterling story already connected with his original source or inserted the parts of it that he wished to use. The differences between the version in the romance and the normal folk-tale version are fundamentally due to the fact that the child William is four years old instead of a new-born babe; that, therefore, he does not need to be suckled; that the author is thus permitted to change the wolf-mother into a male werwolf and to introduce the fascinating ingredients of the Celtic Werwolf Tale. Personally I feel that this latter possibility would not have occurred to him, had there been no wolf in the original nucleus. A reason for changing the infant into a four-year-old boy will appear in *D.*

C. The Celtic Werwolf Tale

The fact that the author of *Guillaume de Palerne* did use the Celtic Werwolf Tale and that he used it in the form in which it is found in the *Lai de Melion* will now be established; the evidence is, I think, conclusive. Professor Kittredge, in the article already referred to, appends the following note:

> In *Guillaume de Palerne* the guardian and constant helper of the hero and heroine is a Spanish prince, who has been changed into a wolf by the magic power of his stepmother. The enchanted prince's interview with his father (vv. 7207ff. . . . .) reminds one of that between the Werewolf and his father-in-law in our tale,

and there are other resemblances (see vv. 7629ff., 7731ff., 7759ff.). There may or may not be some connection between *Guillaume de Palerne* and *The Werewolf's Tale*. Paris (*Litt. franc. au Moyen Age*, §67) inclines to the affirmative; Ahlström (*Studier i den fornfranska Lais-Litteraturen*, p. 81) and Warnke (*Lais*, 2nd ed., p. civ) oppose.[23]

The passages cited by Professor Kittredge deal with the werwolf's attack on his stepmother, with her use of the ring in restoring him to human form, and with his nakedness and provision with clothing. It will be shown that the resemblances are closer and more numerous than have hitherto been noted.

The various versions of the Celtic Werwolf Tale which Professor Kittredge analyzes are four in number: (1) Marie de France's *Bisclavret*, referred to in the following analysis as *B;* (2) the Latin romance of *Arthur and Gorlagon*, referred to as *A;* (3) an Irish folk-tale retold by Professor Kittredge, referred to as *I;* (4) the *Lai de Melion*, extant in the Picard dialect and by an unknown author, referred to as *M*. *Guillaume de Palerne* will be designated as *G*.[24]

The comparison which follows shows the resemblance between the last-named romance and the four stories analyzed by Professor Kittredge, particularly between *Guillaume de Palerne* and *Melion:*

(1) In *A, B, I,* and *M* the woman responsible for the transformation of the hero into a werwolf is his wife; in *G* she is his stepmother. This is the greatest difference between our romance and the other versions, and is probably due to the fact that, as will be shown later, the author desired to marry Alphons to William's sister. In *A, B,* and *I* the woman has no supernatural power; in *M* she retains a kind of fairy nature, in *G* she is a magician. The methods of transformation and restoration are unlike in the four tales; but in *M* the hero is both transformed and restored with the aid of a ring having two jewels, while in *G* the restoration alone is made by means of a ring with a stone of "stif vertu" in it (v. 4424).

(2) In *A, I, M,* and *G* the hero after transformation leaves his own country and goes to another. In *I* no motive is given for his departure; in *A* and *G* he goes to escape pursuit and death; in *M* he follows his wife to secure redress. In *M* and *A* the journey is traced; in *G* it is not traced, though M. Michelant's statement (*op. cit.*, p. viii) that the werwolf immediately after his transformation takes his course across Europe to Sicily in order to watch over the life of the young prince whom he saves from peril is not accurate. The French text (vv. 326-40) says that he arrived in Apulia after many travails and pains, and remained there two years before he heard of the conspiracy against William.

(3) In *A, I, M,* and *G* the werwolf at one time makes a voyage in a ship.

(4) There is a stag hunt in *A, M,* and *G*. In *A* the werwolf pursues and brings down a stag at the command of the king who has saved his life. In *M* the hero shows his wife how to transform him into a wolf in order to hunt and kill a stag for her. In *G* the werwolf pursues a stag in order to entice the emperor to find William; later he pursues and kills a hart and a hind to obtain their skins for William and Melior. (Note the doubling up of the incident in *G;* it is typical of the author and helps to confirm the imitative nature of his work. Miss Hibbard comments on this characteristic, *op. cit.*, p. 221.)

(5) In all versions the werwolf seeks favor and release from a king. In *A* the king is his brother; in *B* and *M* his liege lord; in *G* his father. In *I* there is no special connection between the hero and the king. In *A, B,* and *I* the wolf seeks the protection of the king while he is being hunted by the king's men; in *M* and *G* the wolf goes to the hall where the king is sitting, as a guest in *M*, as a prisoner in *G*, of the ruler of the country. In *A, M,* and *G* the wolf kisses the king's feet. In *M* immediately afterwards the werwolf sees the squire who had helped his wife and rushes upon him. The men in the hall interfere and would have slain the beast if Arthur had not prevented them by saying that it was his wolf and he would protect it. In *G* the men in the hall start to attack the wolf without any reason except that according to the English writer they are "savage" men (v. 4022). William interferes and declares that he will kill any man who harms "that beast" (v. 4033).

(6) In *A, I,* and *M* the wolf commits depredations; in *A* and *M* he kills men. In *B* there is no mention of depredations. In *G* except for hunting wild animals in the forest to provide clothing and food for the lovers, he shows no wolfishness of nature. He frightens men to get bread and wine from them, but does no harm.

(7) In *B, M,* and *G* the werwolf attacks and tries to kill a person or persons responsible for his transformation: in *B* his wife and her lover at separate times; in *M* the squire who helped his wife; in *G* the stepmother who transformed him. In *G* the attack occurs twice, once just after the transformation, once just before the restoration, which is the place of the occurrence in *M* and of the attack on the wife in *B*. (Note again in *G* the doubling up of an effective incident.)

(8) In *A, B, I,* and *M* the king takes the wolf home and treats him as a pet. William's treatment of Alphons is slightly parallel. In *B* and *M* the wolf never leaves the king and sleeps in his bedchamber. In *G* just before the restoration, though nothing has been said of this before, we are told that the werwolf was in William's chamber and had been there in bliss by night and day since the messengers had gone after the queen (vv. 4328-4331).

(9) In *A* the king says that the wolf has human intelligence, "illum humanum sensum habere" (*Arthur and Gorlagon*, p. 159); in *B* the king says that the wolf has the sense of a man, "Ele a sen d'ume" (v. 154), "Ceste beste a entente e sen" (v. 158); in the English version of *G*, William says of the werwolf to the King of Spain, "He has man's mind more than we both" (v. 4123), in the French version (vv. 7345, 7346),

Autant a il *sens et memore,*
Com j'ai on plus, et plus encore;

in *M* the same phrase is used (vv. 219, 220):

Mais ne porquant se leus estoit,
Sens et memore d'ome avoit.

(10) In *B* the clothes which are to restore the werwolf to his own form are placed before him, but he does not touch them. An old man suggests that he is ashamed to remove his beast's hide in their presence and advises privacy. The wolf and the clothes are therefore taken to a private chamber, where the wolf transforms himself. In *M* Arthur, by Gawain's advice, takes the wolf into a private chamber and restores him to his human form. In *G* the queen, without advice or discussion, takes the werwolf into a private chamber and restores him; he is naked and ashamed. The queen sends him to bathe, and William gives him clothes (vv. 4421-4478).

So much for the comparison between *Guillaume de Palerne* and the four versions of the Celtic Werwolf Tale; but between *Guillaume* and *Melion* there are further resemblances.

(1) What is perhaps the most conclusive parallel has not been noted, because no one has thought—apparently—of comparing *M* with the English **William of Palerne.** In *M* (vv. 221-250) the werwolf, seeking to reach Ireland, hides on board a ship and is carried across the sea. When the ship reaches port, he jumps ashore, is struck at and hit by one of the crew, but escapes. In the English romance, when the wolf, the hart, and the hind seek to cross the straits from Italy to Sicily, the three disguised animals hide themselves among the casks of wine on a ship about to sail. When it reaches the opposite shore, the werwolf jumps out, is struck at by one of the crew, is hit, but escapes. All the men except one ship-boy pursue the wolf. When the hart and the hind appear in their turn and jump overboard, the boy strikes at the hind and knocks her, down, but she escapes by the help of the hart without any injury. (vv. 2729-84) Now there is evident borrowing here, and that the writer of **William** borrowed from *Melion* rather than *vice versa* is indicated by the obvious repetition of the incident in **William**—the third instance already noted of the double use of an effective bit of business by our author. In the French poetic version the narrative of the crossing (vv. 4561 ff) is much briefer than in the English, and the characteristic duplication does not occur.[25] It is, of course, open to the critic to say that the English translator added the story, but he did not add anything else of that kind; and it seems more probable that the original writer borrowed that particular incident along with other material from the *lai* of *Melion* than that the Englishman a century and a half later should have chanced to hit upon the same source for further embellishment. What is needed, of course, is an examination of the French prose text to discover whether this is one of the particulars in which it more closely resembles the English than the French poem.

(2) A minor resemblance occurs between the transformation scene in *M* (vv. 543-70), where Arthur weeps for pity, and the transformation scene in *G,* where everybody—apparently—weeps for "love, tenderness, and pity." (vv. 7716, 7717.) The tendency of the author of *G* to "improve" on his source is again displayed.

(3) A further parallel between *G,* vv. 3886 ff., and *M,* vv. 283 ff., is especially interesting because in *G* it is of no great use to the plot and may be regarded as a mere embellishment. Melion, the werwolf, has gathered about him a band of ten other wolves, with which he has ravaged the countryside. Being worn out in the morning, they seek rest and seclusion in a wood on a little hill near Dublin; the surrounding country is all open and level. A peasant sees them there asleep and takes the tidings to the king, who organizes a hunt in order to exterminate the wolves. His daughter, Melion's wife, accompanies him to see the sport. Eventually the other wolves are killed, but Melion escapes. In *Guillaume,* William and Melior, disguised as white bears, are being conducted through Italy to Sicily by the werwolf. They have been traveling by night through the woods and sleeping by day. At dawn in the neighborhood of Beneventum they arrive, worn out by their night's journey, at a place where the land is a great treeless plain except for one little hill. They take refuge in a quarry on this hill and fall asleep. Workmen, who find them there, report the fact to the governor of Beneventum, who organizes a hunt and takes with him his son, a child, to see the bears. At the critical moment the werwolf snatches up the child and runs off with him, thus leading the entire company in pursuit and giving the lovers a chance to escape. When he thinks that they are safe, he drops the boy unhurt and, making a wide circuit, rejoins them. It is evident that the presence of the king's daughter at the hunt in *Melion* is a vital part of the story, while the presence of the governor's son at the hunt in *Guillaume* is unessential, though it gives the author another opportunity to repeat an effective incident—in this case, the abduction of a child by a friendly wolf in full view of a large group of people. The narratives of the two hunts are not only parallel in subject-matter, but present some noteworthy verbal resemblances, as will be seen from the following quotations:

(*Melion,* vv. 283ff.)
Une nuit orent mont erré,
Traveillié furent et pené,
En un bois joste Duveline
Sor un tertre les la marine.
Li bois estoit les une plaigne,
Tot environ ot grant campaigne.
(*Guillaume,* vv. 3886-87)
Mais les forest lor sont faillies,
N'i voient se champaigne non.
Regardé ont lés un grant tertre. (3896)
Et il estoient as plains chans.(3902)
Traveillié furent et lassé, (3921-2)
Car cele nuit ont plus erré.

This phraseology, added to the other parallels already noted, suggests that the author of *Guillaume de Palerne* was writing with a copy of the *Lai de Melion* or of the original of the *Lai* before him. Certainly there can be no room for doubt that he wove into his romance large parts of a version of the Celtic Werwolf Tale closely resembling that which appears in the *Lai*.

D. CONTEMPORARY ALLUSIONS

As has already been noted,[26] *Guillaume de Palerne* is addressed to a Countess Yolande, whom Sir Frederick Madden identified as the daughter of Baldwin IV, Count of Hainault, the wife of the Comte de St. Pol. This identification becomes almost certain when one discovers how close is the connection between the "local color" of the romance and the contemporary adventures of Yolande's husband.

In the *Itinerarium Regis Ricardi* are several references to the Count of St. Paul.[27] On the Octave of Easter, 1191, he arrived in Palestine in the train of Philip Augustus. He did not, however, return to France with Philip. It seems evident that he was one of the French knights who, attracted by the superior prowess and financial resources of the English king, transferred their services from Philip to Richard.[28] At any rate, he is mentioned several times as fighting under the immediate command of Richard, in close association with the Earl of Leicester. His valor and success are commented on by the English chronicler at a point where, besides the count, Richard alone is praised.

Since he arrived in Palestine with Philip, he must have left Sicily with Philip; in other words, he was in Sicily during the autumn and winter of 1190-91, along with the rest of the French and English crusaders. This fact alone is sufficient to account for the romancer's use of Sicily as a setting for his story.

But what was going on in Sicily during those months? A brief summary will indicate the resemblance between the actual historical events of which the Comte de St. Pol was a spectator and the fictitious events recounted for his wife's entertainment by the author of *Guillaume de Palerne*.[29]

William the Good, King of Sicily, or, as he is called by the chronicler, of Apulia—the same title given to William of Palerne's father—had died in November, 1189. His widow, Joanna, was Richard's sister. Upon the death of her husband without issue, Tancred, an illegitimate son of Roger I and cousin of William, took possession of the throne and also of the person and property of his predecessor's widow, whom he kept in custody at Palermo. When Richard and Philip landed in Sicily almost a year later, the former sent envoys to Tancred to demand his sister and her dowry. Finding Tancred willing to restore Joanna, but reluctant about the dowry, Richard attacked and took by assault the city of Messina.[30] This was an unanswerable argument, and Tancred yielded completely. He not only accepted Richard's terms, but negotiated a marriage between his own daughter and Arthur of Brittany. Soon after this friendly compact had been arranged, Eleanor, Richard's mother, accompanied by his betrothed, Beren-

garia of Navarre, arrived at Reggio. Richard met them there, and took them across the straits to Messina. Eleanor soon returned to Normandy. Berengaria and Joanna accompanied the crusaders to Palestine, Richard and Berengaria being married on the way at Cyprus. There was a good deal of friction between Philip and Richard over the marriage, as Philip alleged a previous contract with his sister.

In *Guillaume de Palerne,* a prince, called 'the kuddest knight known in this world,' is found in Sicily, accompanied by his betrothed; he comes to the rescue of his mother and sister, who are besieged in Palermo by an unfriendly, but not particularly obnoxious king; he fights with distinguished success; the fighting ends with a friendly compact and a group of advantageous marriages. At or near the time of the romance, the husband of the lady for whom it was intended was serving in Palestine under 'the kuddest knight known in this world,' Richard Coeur-de-Lion. The year before both king and count had been in Sicily; Richard had met there his betrothed and his mother, his devotion to whom was well known; he had rescued his sister, held in custody at Palermo; he had fought successfully against the unfriendly king who had control of her; the fighting had been terminated by a friendly compact and an advantageous marriage contract; the hero himself had been married shortly afterwards.

The resemblances between contemporary history and the romance are obvious. That there are noticeable differences is of no importance, for I have no intention of arguing that the author of *Guillaume de Palerne* was retelling that history. He simply chose and retold an old story which would serve to suggest the situation and events uppermost in the minds of his auditors. Apparently, however, he made some alterations in his source in order to increase its likeness to the historical facts. It will be remembered that in *Floriant et Florete,* the mother of the hero is wooed and besieged by the usurper and rescued by her son; the introduction into *Guillaume de Palerne* of the unnecessary and almost invisible sister, which rather spoils the motivation of the story, may be accounted for by the relations between Richard and Joanna.

The names chosen by the romance-writer for his principal characters are such as would attract interested attention. *Guillaume de Palerne,* the title, would call to mind instantly the recently dead and much lamented William the Good, King of Sicily and Apulia, one of the noblest of medieval sovereigns, whom Dante more than a century later placed in the eye of the eagle in Paradise along with David, Trajan, Hezekiah, Constantine, and Rhipeus the Trojan.[31]

The name of the werwolf, Alphons, is naturally appropriate for the son of a King of Spain. It is curious that the author should have used that title, for there was not then, nor had there been for some centuries, any such political entity as Spain. He may have deliberately created an ambiguity of suggestion as between the two living princes,

Alfonso II of Aragon and Alfonso VIII of Castile. Both were closely associated with Richard.[32] The former was a great king, just, firm, religious, surnamed the Chaste. He spent much of his time in southern France, where he had great possessions contiguous to those which Richard governed before his accession to the English throne; he was in alliance with Richard in several local wars. Like Richard, he was a patron of literature, and is said to have introduced the "gaie science" south of the Pyrenees. He married the sister of Alfonso of Castile, towards whom, though his natural rival, he behaved with great magnanimity. Both had been boy-kings, the Aragonese seven years older than the Castilian. Their mutual helpfulness, their connection as brothers-in-law, and their relative ages suggest the relations between Alphons and William in the romance.

Alfonso VIII of Castile married Richard's sister, even as the Alphons of the story marries the sister of William. He also was an intelligent and successful ruler, one of the best of Castilian kings. But the interesting thing about him is an event of his early life, so astonishingly like the opening incident in *Guillaume de Palerne* that the resemblance can scarcely be accidental. Sancho of Castile died in 1159, leaving as his heir his four-year-old son, Alfonso VIII. Sancho's brother, Ferdinand of Leon, seized several of the Castilian cities and demanded that Alfonso's guardian, Manrique de Lara, should bring the child to an appointed place to do homage to himself as king. When the little prince was brought by Manrique into the assembly, he began to cry. Being taken outside to be pacified, he was snatched up by an adherent of the Laras, who carried him off on a swift horse to a place of safety and concealment. Search was made for him in vain. Manrique managed to escape the wrath of Ferdinand, and in the war which followed succeeded in enthroning the rightful heir. One of the principal events in this war was the successful resistance of Alfonso's capital, Toledo, against the besieging forces of Ferdinand. All this happened thirty years before the probable date of *Guillaume de Palerne,* but such a dramatic story is not likely to be soon forgotten, especially while its central personage is still alive and of great prominence. The author's desire to remind his readers of this picturesque incident would easily account for the otherwise unaccountable changes that he introduced into the normal wolf's fosterling story: the use of the wicked uncle, from whose plots the boy is rescued and who immediately disappears from the tale; the substitution of a child of four—Alfonso's exact age—for the new-born infant; the employment of a male werwolf as the agent of the abduction and his benevolent motive; the seizure of the child in broad daylight in the presence of the court instead of in the usual concealed fashion.

CONCLUSION

In addition to the narrative elements dealt with in the preceding paragraphs, the French romance is, as Miss Hibbard remarks, "impregnated with the doctrines of *l'amour courtois* . . . constantly analyzes the emotions and emphasizes the agonies of love-sickness and the joys of lovers in one another's company." It is "full of formal speeches . . . and marked by occasional allegorical tendencies, especially in the consideration of love."[33] The natural tendency of such material to stimulate conversation in the Countess Yolande's courtly circle is too obvious to need further comment.

But would not the other parts of the curious conglomerate revealed by our analysis have the same effect? The present tendency among scholars to pull to pieces medieval romances in order to find sources and analogues and historical or other *raisons d'être* is of comparatively recent date. Nevertheless, if we put ourselves in the places of the original audience of such a courtly composite as *Guillaume de Palerne,* I think we shall discover that their natural psychological reaction would bear a strange resemblance to that of the modern scholar, though their methods of approach would, of course, be quite different.

Leaving out of consideration their perennial interest in the problems of courtly love, they would find abundance of opportunity for discussion along the following lines:

(1) The comparison of the new romance with other romances. The medieval reader—and in this respect he resembled the modern reader more than is usually supposed—had no great desire for novelty of plot. He enjoyed the same situations indefinitely repeated, but, if he were at all sophisticated, he must have noted with delight ingenious variations in the treatment of stock motives. The resemblances and differences between *Guillaume de Palerne* and the romances with which it has been compared in modern times were surely far more interesting to the Countess Yolande and her ladies than they can be to us.

(2) The discovery and identification of familiar folk-lore embedded in the narrative. The abundant use of folk-tales by the writers of romances proves not only their own knowledge of them, but also the knowledge and interest of their audiences. It is absurd to assume that the medieval author could not have invented or found in real life new, or at any rate fresh, incidents and situations. As a matter of fact, some invention of that sort does occur in medieval literature. But the readers of the time obviously liked to recognize the story-stuff of the folk dressed up in courtly fashion. And the recognition must have given greater delight when it was not too easy. Folk-tales frequently appear in romances in rather bewildering contaminations and combinations. Must we suppose that they came into the writer's hands thus corrupted? Or may he not have deliberately altered them and put them together for the greater enjoyment of his more ingenious readers? It is surely no illegitimate exercise of the historical imagination to picture the Countess Yolande's circle delightedly discovering in *Guillaume de Palerne* both the Celtic Werwolf Tale and the story of the wolf's fosterling, by whatever names they may have known them.

(3) The recognition of contemporary or pseudo-contemporary allusions. I should like to emphasize

particularly the second of the two adjectives, *pseudo-contemporary*. The analysis of the historical references in *Guillaume de Palerne* given in section D of this paper may have impressed the reader as too confused to be convincing; suggestions pointing to William of Sicily, to Richard and his mother and his sister and his betrothed, to Tancred, and to the two Alfonsos criss-cross one another in every direction. But—to run the risk of being as paradoxical as Bishop Warburton—it is the confusion that proves my point. Granted that the author aimed to stimulate conversation, what could more obviously accomplish his purpose than to suggest several possible identifications, each one of them a little dubious? Resemblances and differences, not identities, lead to discussion.

At the beginning of this analysis of *Guillaume de Palerne* I remarked that conclusions drawn from it might be of fairly wide application. I should like to make just one such application myself—a small contribution to the much-agitated question, "What is the *Parlement of Foules?*" It has been suggested and re-suggested that the poem was intended to celebrate a possible betrothal or a wedding, Richard's or John of Gaunt's daughter's, and various identifications have been proposed for the suitors and have been discredited, and great names have been involved in the controversy.[34] Now, if my theory is correct, one of the author's purposes when he produced the poem was to arouse just such a controversy, though he could hardly have expected it to be still alive five hundred years after his death. To provoke discussion it would be worth while to make several different explanations easily possible and no one of them really accurate.

At any rate, whether these side-remarks on *The Parlement of Foules* are appropriate or not, the main aim of the medieval as of the modern writer of "best sellers" was to interest his readers—in the case of the former, a very limited and special group—and the methods by which he sought to appeal to their temporary or permanent interests may be well seen by the study of such an obviously derivative and imitative composite as *Guillaume de Palerne.*

Notes

1. Ed. by H. Michelant, *Soc. des anciens Textes français,* 1876; MS. in the Bibliothèque de l'Arsenal. Cf. John Edwin Wells, *Manual of the Writings in Middle English,* 1916, p. 19; also Introd. by Sir Frederick Madden in work cited below; Laura A. Hibbard, *Medieval Romance in England,* 1924, p. 214.

2. Wells, *op. cit.,* p. 19. The poem is in *King's Coll. Camb. MS.* 13. defective at the beginning, and has been edited by Sir Frederick Madden for the Roxburghe Club (1832) and by W. W. Skeat for the *EETS* (Ext. Ser., I, 1867). I have not seen the Roxburghe Club edition, but Professor Skeat reprints Sir Frederick Madden's valuable introduction. There is also extant a fragment of an English prose version, Herrig's *Archiv,* CXVII, 318 ff.

3. Michelant, *op. cit.,* pp. xviii-xxi. Madden, unfortunately, did not have first-hand acquaintance with the French verse romance; cf. *EETS,* ed., p. xvii,

4. Professor Wells' remark that "the English romance shows in details extraordinary independence of the extant French poetical version," though literally true—with the possible exception of the word "extraordinary"—might be misleading; for in all essential particulars, the stories are identical.

5. Gaston Paris, "La Sicile dans la litterature française du moyen age," *Romania,* V, 109.

6. Bernhard Ten Brink, *Geschichte der englischen Literatur,* Strassburg, 1899, I, 389-91.

7. Gustav Körting, *Grundriss der Geschichte der englischen Literatur,* 1893, ¶91. See summary of discussion of origin by Miss Hibbard, *op. cit.,* pp. 217 ff.

8. Sir Frederick Madden's identification of the Countess Yolande, mentioned in the French text, as the daughter of Baldwin IV, Count of Hainault, is generally accepted and in this paper is taken as proved.

9. Professor Wells prints "William's," but this is an obvious error.

10. *Arthur and Gorlagon,* [Harvard] *Stud. and Notes,* VIII, 149-275.

11. *Zsf. für Rom. Phil.,* VI (1882), 94 ff., ed. by W. Horak. Miss Hibbard, *op. cit.,* p. 220, writes: "Although only the more obvious parallels of incident and character have been touched on here, it seems sufficiently clear that the author of *Guillaume de Palerne* was familiar with the particular story of which *Bisclavret* and *Melion* were independent derivations." Evidence will be given later to show the probable dependence of *Guillaume* on *Melion* or on a version closely resembling the extant text of the latter.

12. Michelant, *op. cit.,* p. xx; G. Paris, *La Litterature française au moyen age,* Paris, 1914, ¶¶ 51, 52; Wells, *loc. cit.;* Körting, *op. cit.,* ¶91. This would also account for the accurate references in the romance to Sicilian localities, Hibbard, *op. cit.,* p. 220, though the author's knowledge might have been derived directly or indirectly from the Countess Yolande's husband; cf. D *infra.*

13. In the English *William of Palerne,* which in this respect does not differ essentially from the French, one eighth of the entire poem is taken up with actual accounts of battles.

14. Hue de Rotelande's *Ipomedon* is located principally in Apulia and Calabria. It is obviously a "courtly composite," as Professor Wells calls it (p. 148). Curiously enough, it has one prominent incident in common with both *Guillaume de Palerne* and *Floriant et Florete:* the attempt to force a princess

into marriage by besieging her in her castle and her rescue by a knight, who is a "fair unknown." This is, however, a very frequently recurring incident.

15. *Op. cit., Romania,* V, 111.

16. Alois Brandl in Paul's *Grundriss der germanischen Philologie,* II, Pt. 1, 660-61; Gustav Gröber, *Grundriss der romanischen Philologie,* II, Pt. 1, 529-30. Brandl's statement that William and Melior are bound together by means of a "Zaubertrank" is inaccurate; Gröber's comparison of the part played by the wolf to the part played by the dog in *Tristan* is decidedly misleading.

17. XXVIII, 139-79.

18. M. Lot-Borodine, *La femme et l'amour au XIIe siècle d'après les poèmes de Chrétien de Troyes,* Paris, 1909, p. 247.

19. Schofield, *English Literature from the Norman Conquest to Chaucer,* London, 1914, p. 312. Miss Hibbard makes a similar statement, *op. cit.,* p. 217.

20. Standish H. O'Grady, *Sylva Gadelica, A Collection of Tales in Irish,* 2 vols., London and Edin., 1892, II, 286 ff.

21. Herodotus, Book I, ¶'s 107 ff.; Plutarch's *Lives,* ed. by Bernadotte Perrin, *Loeb Library,* 1919-21, I, 97 ff.; Carolus Plummer, *Vitae Sanctorum Hiberniae,* 2 vols., Oxford, 1910, I, 65 ff., and I, 46 ff.; *Der grosse Wolfdieterich,* hrsg. von Adolf Holtzmann, Heidelberg, 1875. To avoid awkwardness, the story of Romulus and Remus is referred to as that of Romulus.

22. *William of Palerne,* ll. 4010 ff.; *Melion,* ll. 407 ff.; *Die Lais der Marie de France,* hrsg. von Karl Warnke, 2 vols., Halle, 1885, *Bisclavret,* pp. 75 ff., vv. 135 ff.; *Arthur and Gorlagon,* ed. by Kittredge, *Harv. Studies and Notes,* VIII, 149 ff., p. 159.

23. *Arthur and Gorlagon,* p. 184, note 2.

24. See notes 11 and 22 for citations of these works. Professor Kittredge discusses all of these except *G* and shows their common provenience. There are two extant MSS. of the *Lai de Melion,* both in the Picard dialect, one of the late 13th, the other of the late 14th, century. Concerning them Professor Kittredge writes (p. 198): "Neither presents a perfect text, and the Picard version may therefore be put back some time. Probably it is not much later than Marie herself. . . . Though Marie wrote her Lais about 1180, there is no MS. earlier than the second half of the 13th century." I have assumed, on Mr. Kittredge's authority, as well as on other grounds, that *Melion* antedates *Guillaume.*

25. This duplication of incidents is so characteristic of the French author that it affords a real argument for the theory that the boat episode was in the original version. Another notable duplication—or "triplication"—is found in his use of animal disguises. Having discovered apparently that the

transformation of a man into a wolf is intensely interesting, he proceeds to disguise his lovers, first as white bears, and later as a hart and a hind. There seems to be some uncertainty even in the author's mind as to whether William and Melior are temporarily changed into animals or merely put on the skins of animals. On the whole, their behavior seems to indicate that the transformation is complete. The change is entirely under their own control, and is accomplished merely by putting on the animal-skins; whereas Alphons is under enchantment, from which he is powerless to escape. Both conditions are abundantly paralleled in folk-lore from all parts of the world. Cf. Wilhelm Hertz, *Die Werwolf,* Stuttgart, 1862 (this is the most valuable book on the subject); also Caroline Taylor Stewart, "The Origin of the Werwolf Superstition," *Univ. of Missouri Studies, Soc. Science Series,* II, no. 3, 1909; Kirby F. Smith, "An Historical Study of the Werwolf in Literature," *PMLA,* IX (1894), 1-42 (largely indebted to Hertz), etc.; for a bibliography on the subject, see George F. Black, "A List of Books relating to Lycanthropy," *N. Y. Pub. Lib. Bulletin* 23, 1919, pp. 811-15.

26. See above, note 8.

27. *Chronicles and Memorials of the Reign of Richard I,* 2 vols., ed. by Wm. Stubbs, *Rolls Series,* 1864, Vol. I, *Itinerarium Peregrinorum et Gesta Regis Ricardi, auctore, ut videtur, Ricardo, Canonico Sanctae Trinitatis Londiniensis.* Dated by the editor, p. lxx, as probably between 1200 and 1220. References to the Count of St. Paul are on pp. 213, 257, 258, 292, 293, 298.

28. Of course, he may have held lands from Richard; I have not been able to discover his feudal relations, but his original appearance with Philip implies that he was the vassal of the French, rather than of the English, king.

29. The account is drawn from the *Itinerarium Ricardi,* pp. 146 ff. and from the article on Richard I in the *Dict. of Nat. Biog.*

30. Accounts differ as to the details. The author of the *Itinerarium* states that the attack on Messina took place as a result of a quarrel between Richard and the citizens, and that the demand on Tancred was not made until the spoils of the city were in Richard's hands to offer in exchange for Joanna's dowry; cf. pp. 154 ff.

31. *Paradiso,* XX, 62.

32. Cf. article on Richard I in *Dict. of Nat. Biog.* by T. A. Archer. The detailed information about Alfonso II of Aragon is taken from Rousseau St. Hilaire, *Histoire d'Espagne,* Paris, 1844, Vol. IV, Book X, Chap. II; that about Alfonso VIII of Castile from the same work and volume, Book X, Chap. I.

33. *Op. cit.,* p. 214.

34. Professor Manly and Professor Emerson especially. See Wells' *Manual,* pp. 871, 1028, 1143, for

references to controversial articles on the interpretation of the poem. A remark made in class by Mr. Manly on the ease with which the suitors could be identified with different persons started me on this particular line of thought.

Charles W. Dunn (essay date 1960)

SOURCE: "From Legend to Romance," in *The Foundling and the Werwolf: A Literary-Historical Study of* Guillaume de Palerne, University of Toronto Press, 1960, pp. 125-39.

[*In the following essay, Dunn focuses on the setting and plot of* Guillaume de Palerne. *Dunn comments on the author's adaptation of Sicilian source legends into the French romance.*]

Now that we have established the probability that *Guillaume* derives its setting from geographical facts and its plot from national Sicilian legends, we are in a position to analyse the romancer's methods by asking how he obtained his material, why it appealed to him, and how he converted it into romance.

The use of a Sicilian setting and legend by a writer in the service of a countess from Hainaut may be readily explained by the close contact preserved between France and the Kingdom of the Two Sicilies during the period of Norman and Hohenstaufen rule. Crusaders, adventurers, diplomats, clerics, and merchants all contributed to the circulation in France, even as far north as Flanders (and Hainaut within the Holy Roman Empire), of oral and written reports concerning the fabulous Kingdom of the South.[1] Some of the chronicles already mentioned demonstrate the general interest taken by northerners in Sicilian affairs, and an impression of the intimate contacts possible between Countess Yolande's entourage and a land which she herself had presumably never visited can be gleaned from the following chronologically arranged list of events, miscellaneous though they are.

In 1151 Beatrice of Rethel, who was daughter of the Count of Rethel and related to the counts of Flanders, became the third wife of King Roger of Sicily and in 1154 bore him Constance, later Queen of Sicily.[2]

Peter of Blois joined a band of 37 travellers led by Stephen, son of the Count of Perche, which reached Palermo in 1166. He was appointed preceptor to the young King William II, but because of a rebellion against Stephen of Perche, two years later he returned most willingly to France, where he recorded in his letters his tumultuous experiences at the royal court.[3]

When Henry VI left Germany in 1185 for Milan, where on January 27, 1186, he married Constance, the heir apparent to the Sicilian throne, he was accompanied by Philip of Alsace, Count of Flanders, the brother-in-law of Baldwin V.[4]

Constance of Sicily supported her French kinsmen after her marriage, interceding in 1188 on behalf of Yolande's brother, Count Baldwin V, and in 1192 on behalf of Albert, Count of Rethel, the kinsman and ally of Count Baldwin VI of Hainaut.[5]

On the Third Crusade (1189-92) the French forces under Philip Augustus, sailing from Genoa to Palestine, reached the Straits of Messina just after the death of King William II and the election of King Tancred;[6] and, as Miss McKeehan points out, Hugh of Saint-Pol, Countess Yolande's husband, who was with them, may have landed on Sicily;[7] and, it may be added, he undoubtedly had a clerk at his disposal.[8]

In view of the romancer's detailed references to Sicily and southern Italy, it is tempting to argue that he had personally visited his *mise en scène* during this crusade. His description of the devastation of Apulia recalls the fact that when Philip Augustus' forces returned in 1191 from their crusade, they found that Emperor Henry VI had laid Campania waste.[9] His special reference to the imperial rights over the papal city of Benevento may reflect a firsthand knowledge of the fact that the emperor had just granted the city new privileges in June of 1191, four months before the French visited it on their way to Rome.[10]

But the description of the siege of Palermo and especially the statement that the invaders had killed off most of the animals in the park recalls the later events of 1194, when Henry VI attacked Palermo and slaughtered the beasts in the Royal Park to feed his troops.[11] The romancer may have been present at this occasion, for Flanders was subject to the emperor and sent him ships to aid him in his conquest.[12]

Baldwin VI, in common with his father before him, supported the Hohenstaufen emperors and enjoyed their favours.[13] He must have been well acquainted with the attempts to defeat the election of both Tancred and William III as Sicilian kings. Hence the story which, according to the prose *Guillaume,* Baldwin obtained for the romancer was perhaps a Romulus ecotype vindicating the Hohenstaufen claims to the Sicilian throne. But, since the poet does not seem to have attempted to preserve any political propaganda in his use of the Romulus Type, some legend which favoured the Norman cause may just as well have provided suitable material for his romance.

If the poet had lived nearer to the source of his plot, his inclination might then have been to refer the legend more specifically to historical figures, in the same way, for instance, that Gautier of Tournai dealt with the local traditions of Hainaut in *Gilles de Chyn.*[14] But the chief appeal of the legend for the romancer obviously lay in its wonder-elements; in it the poet saw fresh narrative material which he could turn to his own advantage. He did not think of the rescue of a royal child by a werwolf as proof of a divine providence guiding the destiny of a national hero but rather as a marvel which would delight those in search of romance.

It is difficult to know what estimate one may make of the credulity of the poet's audience. The twelfth century witnessed in western Europe a vigorous growth of intellectualism, it is true; but even an emperor so enlightened and inquiring as Frederick II did not entirely succeed in throwing off the beliefs inherited from the Dark Ages; and the ladies of fashion for whom *Guillaume* was written, though perhaps also intellectually curious, certainly never attained an enlightenment comparable to that of the ruler who came to be called the *stupor mundi*. Andreas Capellanus, for instance, complains of their superstitious practices:

> . . . there is not a woman living in this world, not even the empress or the queen, who does not waste her whole life on auguries and the various practitioners of divination, as the heathen do, and so long as she lives she persists in this credulousness and sins without measure again and again with the art of astrology. Indeed, no woman does anything without considering the proper day and hour for beginning it and without inaugurating it with incantations. They will not marry, or hold funeral rites for the dead, or start their sowing, or move into a new house, or begin anything else without consulting this feminine augury and having their actions approved by these witches.[15]

It seems likely, then, that the romancer's marvels were readily acceptable and that, for his audience, suspension of disbelief was an effortless gesture.

Similar considerations presumably lay behind the poet's development of the Sicilian setting. He must have sensed the potential appeal inherent in a portrayal of the exotic splendour of the royal gardens, the sumptuous palace, and the thronging harbour of Palermo. For his northern audience, the warm south was an enchanted country, exercising then somewhat the same fascination which Goethe six centuries later was to ascribe to the land where the citrons bloom; and the romancer knew how to utilize this charm.

Nothing could better reveal the nature of poetic creation than a comparison between the French romancer's dispassionate adaptation of Sicilian legend and the violently partisan literature composed by residents in the south who were directly involved in the national crises of the Kingdom of the Two Sicilies. For instance, the Tacitus of Sicily, Hugo Falcandus, himself a strong opponent of the Hohenstaufen claims, crystallizes in his eloquent prose all the foreboding felt by a once peaceful country on the eve of its invasion by Henry VI. Shortly after the death (1189) of his royal pupil King William II, he wrote:

> I had resolved, . . . once the harsh winter had been mellowed by the benignancy of a milder breeze, to write you something cheering and pleasant which could be dedicated to you as a first offering of the awakening spring. But now that I have heard the news of the king's death and have begun to think over and foresee in my own mind how great a calamity this reversal of events might bring about and how much the deep quiet of the realm would either be shattered by the uproar of an enemy invasion or disturbed by the grave unrest of civil rebellions, then in my consternation of mind I

have abruptly given up my attempt; and, retuning my lyre for lament, I have felt more inclined to compose doleful melodies and a lugubrious song of lamentations. . . . Indeed, just as it is difficult to restrain a child from mourning after the death of his nurse, so, I admit, I cannot hold back my tears, I cannot pass over in silence or record with dry eyes the desolation of Sicily, which has nurtured, reared, and raised me, taking me kindly to her most beloved breast.

> Already I seem to see the disorderly files of barbarians breaking in wherever their onrush carries them, and the opulent cities and the lands which have blossomed under a lasting peace being shaken with horror, desolated by slaughter, laid waste by pillage, and defiled by lust. . . . For the Teutonic frenzy, which is born of an innate madness, stimulated by rapacity, and aggravated by lust, can neither be controlled by reason, nor deflected by compassion, nor awed by religion.[16]

Peter of Eboli, on the other hand, a violent advocate of the Hohenstaufen cause, scornfully mocks "little Tancred" (Tancredulus), Henry's Norman rival. His invective, perhaps inartistic in its excesses, at times reaches truly great satiric heights. The phrase he applies to Tancred, for instance, "Embrion infelix et detestabile monstrum" (Unhappy embryo and detestable monstrosity, v. 208), condenses within the confines of a single hexameter an astonishingly suggestive characterization of the hated pretender to the throne. The extreme sycophancy pervading his encomium of Henry VI is best illustrated by a brief excerpt of his breathless elegiacs, to which an English translation can hardly do justice:

> Felix nostra dies nec ea felicior ulla,
>   Lecior aut locuples a Salomone fuit.
> Evomuit serpens virus sub fauce repostum
>   Aruit in vires mesta cicuta suas.
> Nec sonipes griphes nec oves assueta luporum
>   Ora timent: ut ovis stat lupus inter oves.
> Una fonte bibunt, eadem pascuntur et arva
>   Bos, leo, grus, aquila, sus, canis, ursus, aper.
> Non erit in nostris, moveat qui bella, diebus;
>   Amodo perpetue tempora pacis erunt,
> Nulla manent hodie veteris vestigia fraudis,
>   Qua tancridinus polluit error humum,
> Ipsaque transibant derisi tempora regis.
>   Nam meus Augustus solus et unus erit,
> Unus amor, commune bonum, rex omnibus unus,
>   Unus sol, unus pastor et una fides.[17]

(Fortunate is our day, nor was there ever any such from the time of Solomon more fortunate or happy or prosperous. The serpent has voided the venom from under his jaws; the hemlock, mowed down, is sapped of its power. Those of the sounding hooves, no longer fear the familiar jaws of the griffons, nor the sheep the jaws of the wolves; like a sheep the wolf stands among sheep. The cow, the lion, the crane, the eagle, the pig, the hound, the bear, the boar drink from one spring and crop the same fields. There will be no one in our time who will wage war; instead there will be an era of perpetual peace. No traces of the old guile remain today by which the Tancredine delusion prevailed over the land; those times of the ridiculous king have passed away. For my Augustus will be the one and only, the one love, the common good, the one king for all, one sun, one shepherd, and one faith.)

The author of *Guillaume,* remote from such political stresses, ignores the possibilities of propaganda offered by tales of the Romulus Type. The romance becomes in his hands, to translate Myrrha Lot-Borodine's phrase, "a courtly idyll encased in an adventure story."[18] The conflicts of the plot are produced through no fault in the protagonists but by the unrestrained lust for power exhibited in differing degrees by the various villains—Guillaume's uncle, Queen Brande, the Duke of Saxony, the King of Spain, and Brandin.

In the world which the romance portrays, not only do the good and the innocent blissfully surmount the schemes of the ambitious, but even the evil escape punishment. The poet's faith in the potency of goodness and the bounty of human forgiveness is remarkably sanguine. When the rebellious Duke of Saxony is captured, the Emperor of Rome spares his life, and the duke dies from grief over his own pride (2415-32). After Queen Brande repents for having transformed Alphonse and disenchants him, there is not even any suggestion that she might deserve punishment; and, although Alphonse rebukes his father for having tried to force Florence into marriage with Brandin, the invading king remarks that everything will be restored (8055-63) and apparently feels that his revelation of Guillaume's identity will be sufficient recompense to the Queen of Sicily for all the loss her lands have suffered from the Spaniards. The treacherous Gloriande and Acelone are spared by Guillaume and allowed to enter "the hermitage" (8393-5).[19]

By contrast, fairy stories, even those circulating in the most enlightened countries, traditionally allow that the evil-doer shall be killed; and certainly during the Middle Ages in the real world of fact, a culprit was invariably made to suffer, often much beyond his deserts. Henry VI's treatment of the Norman-Sicilian conspirators in their second uprising (1197) against the Hohenstaufen forces illustrates the measures actually employed in the twelfth century by a ruler intent on preserving his power. The hostages whom Henry had previously sent to Germany after the conspiracy of 1194 he ordered to be blinded. Those who were arrested in Sicily suffered a variety of fates: some were drowned, some severed with the saw, some covered with pitch and burned, and some pinned out upon the ground with pointed stakes; and Queen Constance, as the penalty for her complicity in the conspiracy against her husband, was forced to watch the punishment of the lord of Castrogiovanni, the leader of the rebellion, while the executioners nailed a molten-red crown of metal upon his head. Yet as Toeche points out, Henry's contemporaries saw in this violent revenge only an expedient punishment. Arnold of Lübeck unexcitedly remarks that Henry "had the good fortune to capture his opponents and exact a deserved vengeance upon them."[20] Such firmness was indeed advocated by the emperor's tutor, Geoffrey of Viterbo, as the proper means of preserving peace in the realm.[21]

When we have mentioned both the marvellous and the idyllic in *Guillaume,* we have by no means exhausted the ingredients of the romance produced by the poet from the raw materials of plot and setting. George Saintsbury has suggested that romance is compounded of all three of Dante's touchstones of poetic material—religion, love, and war—*salus, venus,* and *virtus.*[22] All three features are certainly important in *Guillaume,* and each is developed by the romancer in the way established by his predecessors. He not only borrows details from Chrétien de Troyes[23] and Marie de France;[24] he perpetuates their spirit.

The preponderance of *virtus* in *Guillaume* may seem to be somewhat out of keeping with what has been said about the idyllic nature of the romance. Certainly the poet's descriptions of the Roman campaign against the Saxons and of Guillaume's three sorties against the besieging Spaniards abound with the noise and colour of battle: trumpets, horns, and tabors (1838-41), banners, ensigns, lances, pennons, swords, helmets, shields, mailed haubercs, and war-horses (1882-8). In the heat of combat, "brains, entrails, and bowels are spread over the field" (1908-9), and horses wander at large, riderless, with saddles reversed, trailing broken reins between their hooves (1934-40). Death comes violently and vividly. Heads are severed, and the ground is covered with blood (2030-1) and blackening bodies (2033). Guillaume with one blow cuts through a helmet and splits open the head, throat, chest, and spine of his adversary (2058-62). A Spanish horseman runs his lance through a Sicilian, point, stock, and pennon (5761); and he in turn is hewed down by Guillaume, so that his lifeless body falls from the saddle and his helmet rolls over the sand (5801).

Zingarelli has remarked that such descriptions are in language and imagery reminiscent of the *Chanson de Roland,*[25] and McKeehan has suggested a Norman influence behind the emphasis upon warfare.[26] We might add as further examples the historical works of the Norman chroniclers, who, as Chalandon has pointed out, are even more interested in individual combat than in the outcome of battle;[27] and, in a different sphere of art, the scenes of carnage on the Bayeux Tapestry. But in the twelfth century the fascination of slaughter was not limited to one locality in western Europe. The miniatures in Peter of Eboli's *De rebus siculis,* for instance, reflect exactly the same taste in southern Italy. In one battle-scene, the artist (probably Peter himself) is not satisfied merely to depict warriors falling severed in battle; with dogged realism he includes in the illustration a carter leading two oxen which are dragging a large two-wheeled cart laden with dismembered trunks, limbs, and heads, to be thrown into the river.[28] The author of *Guillaume,* it should be noted, hardly proceeds to such grotesque extremes. Pity softens his picture.

To be sure, the romancer, like his contemporaries, does not shun bloodshed, and he highly admires the prowess of his hero. In describing the part played by Guillaume in the battle against the Saxons, he writes:

> Au brant d'acier tex cox lore done
> Que tos les fent et decopone;

Fiert et ocit et acravente,
Les vis desor les mors adente;
Comme sanglers lor livre estal.
Diex, quel baron et quel vassal!

(2209-14)

(With sword of steel such blows he gives them that he
hacks and hews them all. He strikes and kills and shatters; the living upon the dead he hurls. Like a boar he
charges at them. Lord God, what a baron, what a
vassal!)

Yet he does not forget the tragedy of slaughter:

Diex! tex frans hom i pert la vie,
Dont grans deus fu et grant dolors
A lor amis . . .

(1910-12)

(Lord God! So many a bold man lost his life there, for
whom his friends felt sorrow and great grief . . .)

Nor does he overlook the grief even of the villains in the
romance. When the Spaniards ride out for their second attack on Palermo and see the field of the previous day's
battle under the light of the morning sun, the poet writes:

. . . grant duel faisoient
De lor amis qu'iluec gisoient,
Voient tant hiaume a or luisant
Et tant vassal souvin gisant
Et tant espiel et tante lance
Et tante bele connaissance.

(6067-72)

(They greatly mourned for their friends who were lying
there, so many a helmet of shining gold they saw, so
many a spear, so many a lance, so many a beautiful
coat-of-arms.)

Under the heading of *salus,* one would characterize the
romancer as being both pious and moral, though not
moralistic. The good characters in *Guillaume* all exhibit
decorously Christian behaviour. Consequently, prayers
play an important part in the unfolding of the romance, as
they do in other writings of this period.[29] The Emperor of
Rome prays that God will not permit the disloyalty of the
Duke of Saxony to prosper (1954-68). Alexandrine utters a
moving prayer that God will aid Guillaume and Melior in
their escape from Rome.

"Hé! vrais dous peres Jhesu Cris,
Rois sor tos rois poesteis,
Vraie paterne, omnipotent,
Biau sire Diex, si vraiement
Com ciel et terre et tout formas,
Et en la vierge t'aombras
Et preis incarnation,
Sire, par sainte anoncion,
Et forme d'ome et char humaine,
Et garesis en la balaine
Jonas qu'ele avoit englouti,
Si voir, sire, par ta merci
Ces dous enfans gart et deffent

D'anui, de mal et de torment,
Et remet en prosperité,
Sire, par ta sainte bonté."

(3129-44)

("O, true, kind Father of Jesus Christ, King empowered
above all kings, true Parent, omnipotent, good Lord
God, you truly formed heaven and earth and all things
and were created in the Virgin and incarnated, Lord, by
the holy annunciation, and took the form of man and
human flesh, and protected Jonah in the whale which
swallowed him, then, Lord, indeed by your mercy guard
and defend these sweet children from harm, from evil,
and from suffering, and restore them, Lord, to prosperity by your holy goodness.")

The Queen of Sicily and her daughter likewise pray for
protection from the Spanish invaders (4505-27); and the
queen, as we have seen, seeks guidance from her priest.
Similarly, Guillaume and Melior invariably refer their acts
to God's approval (4922, 4928, 5861, 6532, etc.).

The poet ingeniously contrives, moreover, to prevent the
paganism of the wonder-elements from clashing with the
Christianity of his good characters. To realize what dangerous ground it is that the poet traverses, we have only to
remember that in the version of *The Pseudo-Turpin*
acquired by Baldwin VI, necromancy is classified as an
adulterine art whose textbook is labelled *Death of the
Soul.*[30]

Thus, when the Queen of Sicily, disguised as a hart, ac-
costs Guillaume, he answers the speaking animal with all
the pious caution of Horatio addressing King Hamlet's
ghost:

. . . "Je te conjur,
Beste, de par le roi du mont,
Se de par lui paroles dont,
Ne se c'est autres esperites,
Ne qui ce est que vos me dites,
Ne se par toi i arons mal."

(5214-19)

(. . . "I conjure you, animal, by the King of the World,
whether your words are of Him or of some other spirit,
or what it is that you tell me, or whether we shall be
harmed by you.")

Likewise, when Moses the priest interprets the queen's
dreams, he recognizes the aid of God (4803-4, 4883-6)
and does not in any way take on the character of magician. Alexandrine the confidante, who plays a role in many
respects identical with that of the Greek necromancer Thessala in Chrétien de Troyes' *Cligès,* also retains an unsul-
lied character and at the end of the adventure is therefore
fit to become the wife of a prince. She promises Melior a
herb which will cure her love-sickness (1086-92). In Thessala's hands this remedy would certainly have been a magical aphrodisiac (Motif D 1355.2).[31] But, although Melior
seems to believe in the herb (1100-1104, 1352-3), the poet
makes it clear that Alexandrine is only subtly encouraging

her mistress to confess her ailment, the nature of which she has already guessed (1078-9, 1093-9).

Again, in *Cligès,* when Thessala the confidante aids the hero and heroine to escape, she resorts to magic:

> Mes Thessala qui les an mainne,
> Les conduit si seüremant
> Par art et par anchantemant,
> Que il n'ont crieme ne peor
> De tot l'esforz l'anpereor.
>
> (6660-4)

(But Thessala, who leads them away, guides them so securely by art and enchantment that they know neither worry nor fear despite all the forces of the emperor.)

Alexandrine, on the other hand, uses only her ingenuity and recommends the use of bearskin disguise;[32] and the werwolf who completes the escape does not taint his character by resorting to the black arts, even though he himself is enchanted. Indeed, the poet remarks as the fugitives near Palermo that Christ has been aiding them (4551).

The sorcery of Queen Brande, on the other hand, is openly condemned by the poet:

> Mult sot la dame engien et mal;
> Sorceries et ingremance.
> Avoit mult apris de s'enfance.
>
> (286-8)

(Much the lady knew of malice and of evil; from her childhood she had learned much of sorceries and necromancy.)

When she appears before the tribunal at Palermo, the usually temperate Guillaume threatens that, if she does not confess, she will be burned to death and her ashes scattered to the winds (7664-5), presumably a time-honoured method for the disposal of witches.

The good characters in *Guillaume* are not only pious but moral. The humble cowherd does not hesitate, even in the presence of the Emperor of Rome, to admonish his foster-son (546-81), following the best literary tradition of the Speculum Principis.[33] The emperor advises both his daughter and Alexandrine on how to behave as the wives of kings (9019-36, 9067-76); the Queen of Sicily gives similar counsel to her daughter (9504-20); and the poet enumerates Guillaume's virtues on three occasions (360-85, 726-816, 9611-21). The essence of the morality advocated in all these passages is courtesy, the courtesy which acts without pride towards the powerful and the weak, the rich and the poor, alike. In this way the poet not only reminds us of the *salus* of his characters but also counterbalances their *virtus,* the quality so strongly overemphasized in the *chansons de geste.*

It is, however, in the poet's treatment of love that he, in common with the other romancers of his age, makes the most influential contribution to the development of literature. Because of works such as *Guillaume* the latter part of the twelfth-century may be said to mark a turning point in the history of the narrative art. The audiences of this period probably resented Virgil's insensitivity in allowing Aeneas to prefer the founding of Rome to the love of Dido; they may even have come to regret the *jongleur*'s brusque treatment of Aude in the *Chanson de Roland;* but with the advent of the romancers they no longer had cause to reproach the poets for neglecting love.

In *Guillaume, venus* shares equal place with *salus* and *virtus.* Even in the midst of battle the poet does not forget the heroine's anxiety for her lover (2453-2523, 7037-50). How this element of love entered the literature of the period is a problem beyond the scope of the present investigation. Suffice it to remark that the treatment in *Guillaume* does not coincide entirely with the system of courtly love expounded by Andreas Capellanus so highly favoured by the aristocrats of northern France, for the romancer completely ignores Andreas' cardinal rule that love cannot exist between married people.[34] Here is no sophisticated problem of illicit love. An unknown young prince falls in love with a princess, discovers his identity, marries her, and lives happily ever after.

In most respects, the poet follows contemporary convention.[35] Melior feels melancholy before she realizes that she is in love with Guillaume and then berates her heart and eyes for troubling her peace; and when Guillaume in turns falls in love with her, he can neither eat nor sleep but pines away.

In his treatment of love the author of *Guillaume* mingles the same light-hearted playfulness which in the twelfth century is represented at its best by a romance such as Chrétien de Troyes' *Ivain.* This type of humour, foreshadowed by the mock seriousness of Ovid's lyrics and culminating in the tragicomic genius of Chaucer's *Troilus and Criseyde,* transcends the conventionality of *Guillaume* and makes the romance seem something much more than a curious specimen of an extinct literary species. In scope the humour varies from the ludicrous to the subtle. Guillaume, in his agony of longing, dreams that he is embracing Melior and awakens to find that what he holds in his arms is his pillow (1118-68).[36] Melior pretends not to know what ails Guillaume until Alexandrine tells her that he will die unless he can have her love; and when Melior hears what she has longed for, she innocently remarks to her go-between:

> "Je ne voudroie pas de lui
> Estre homecide ne d'autrui,
> Ne pecheresse en tel maniere;
> Por vos et por vostre proiere
> Et por lui qu'en tel peril voi,
> N'ains qu'il ensi muire por moi,
> Moi et m'amor li otroi toute."
>
> (1691-7)

("I shouldn't wish to be his murderer or anyone else's and a sinner in such a manner; for you and your entreaty and for him whom I see in such peril, rather than that he should thus die on my account, I grant myself and my love to him entire.")

When Guillaume once more relapses into misery after Melior's betrothal to Partenidon, Melior risks public criticism by going to see him; as the result of her visit he reappears at court cured of his mysterious malady, and the poet slyly remarks:

> Mult par en est li pules liés;
> Bien sevent tuit ceste novele
> Que gari l'a la damoisele,
> Et dient tuit que mult est sage,
> Quant garir set de tel malage.
>
> (2882-6)

(The people are greatly delighted; they all have learned the news that the young lady has cured him, and they all say that she is very wise in knowing how to cure such an ailment.)

In his graceful treatment of *salus, venus,* and *virtus,* the nameless poet obviously learned much from Chrétien de Troyes. He does not, it is true, achieve any greater literary subtlety than his master, nor does he introduce any new element into the *genre* of romance established by Chrétien. Yet he was more than a mere imitator. The measure of his success is suggested by the fact that his work, like Chrétien's, was perpetuated in the mainstream of European fiction by later translators.

Presumably the chief appeal of *Guillaume* lay in those elements which have formed the core of this investigation, namely the plot and the setting. The plot is traditional and age-old and, to a comparative folklorist, even trite; but this very fact may partly explain its perennial charm. The wondrous tale of an animal's nursling has been repeatedly adapted into myth and legend and romance because it has always seemed satisfying. This ancient literary invention is, as it were, too appealing to fall into oblivion and is in its transmuted forms ever capable of exciting its audience anew.

The setting of *Guillaume,* on the other hand, is specific, immediate, and unique and is especially suited to the romancer's aristocratic patroness and her circle. More real to French crusading families than Chrétien's never-never land of Caerleon, it was for them, at one and the same time, both familiar and fantastic. They had seen or heard enough of Sicily, Apulia, and Calabria to recognize the scenery of the romance as something resembling a known realm, and yet their familiarity was not sufficient to dispel their awe for the storied marvels of the enchanted South.

Notes

1. For northern Frenchmen in Sicily, see G. Paris, "La Sicile"; Diehl, *Palerme,* p. 63; Haskins, *Studies in the History of Mediaeval Science,* pp. 188-9; and Antonio de Stefano, *La cultura in Sicilia nel periodo normanno* (Palermo, 1938), pp. 59-71.

Concerning reports of Sicily circulated outside, see Schlauch, "Literary Exchange," and Evelyn Jamison, "The Sicilian Norman Kingdom in the Mind of Anglo-Norman Contemporaries," *Proceedings of the British Academy,* XXIV (1938), 237-85.

2. Petrus de Ebulo, *De rebus siculis,* ed. Rota, p. 8n. (line 32).

3. Chalandon, *Histoire,* II, 320-1, 346.

4. Toeche, *Kaiser Heinrich,* pp. 53, 637.

5. *Ibid.,* pp. 100, 220.

6. The route is marked in Shepherd, *Historical Atlas,* pp. 70-1.

7. McKeehan, "*Guillaume* a Best Seller," p. 803.

8. Two letters written by Hugh of Saint-Pol and eight letters by his nephew Baldwin VI survive from the Fourth Crusade (1202-4). Dom Brial suggests in "Hugues Camp-D'Avenne, Comte de Saint-Paul; et Jean de Noyon," and "Baudouin, Comte de Flandre et de Hainaut, puis Empereur de Constantinople," *Histoire littéraire de la France,* XVI (Paris, 1824), 490-4 and 521-8 respectively, that the actual writer may have been Baldwin VI's chronicler Jean de Noyon, Bishop of Soissons (who died in 1204). Baldwin maintained his cultural contacts with France to the very end of his life. In 1205, through Pope Innocent III, he appealed to the masters and scholars of Paris "to come to Greece [i.e., Constantinople] and strive to reform the study of letters there." *Chartularium universitatis Parisiensis,* ed. H. Denifle and E. Chatelain (Paris, 1889-97), I, 63; the editors' identification, p. 63 n. 1, with "Balduinus I (1204-1237)" seems to be wrong.

9. See p. 82 above, and cf. "Chronici ab Ottone Frisingensi conscripti continuatio auctore . . . Ottone S. Blasii monacho," ed. Roger Wilmans, *Monumenta Germaniae historica, Scriptorum,* XX (Hanover, 1868), p. 323 (chap. 37).

10. *The Chronicle of the Reigns of Henry II. and Richard I.,* ed. W. Stubbs ("Rolls Series," 49) (London, 1867), II, 227. See also p. 82 above.

11. *Chronici ab Ottone . . . continuatio,* p. 325 (chap. 40). Cf. pp. 49-50 above.

12. Petrus de Ebulo, *De rebus siculis,* plate L (p. 100) and v. 1132 (p. 150).

13. Toeche, *Kaiser Heinrich,* pp. 50, 100, 308, 479, 600, 606.

14. Gautier de Tournay, *L'Histore de Gille de Chyn,* ed. Edwin B. Place ("Northwestern University Studies in the Humanities," No. 7) (Evanston and Chicago, 1941), pp. 5-11.

15. Andreas Capellanus, *The Art of Courtly Love,* tr. Parry, pp. 208-9.

16. Ugo Falcando, *La historia e la epistola,* pp. 169, 170 (quotation translated from Latin original).

Evelyn Jamison, *Admiral Eugenius of Sicily* (London, 1957), identifies Falcandus as the Eugenius who became Admiral in 1190 and died *ca.* 1202-3.

17. Petrus de Ebulo, "De rebus siculis," p. 198, vv. 1523-38.

18. Myrrha Lot-Borodine, *Le Roman idyllique au moyen âge* (Paris, 1913), p. 265.

19. See further the comments on *Guillaume* in F. C. Riedel, *Crime and Punishment in the Old French Romances* (New York, 1938), pp. 6, 107-8, 109-10, 112, 115.

20. Arnoldus abbas Lubecensis, "Chronica," V, xxvi, ed. Baron Lappenberg in *Monumenta Germaniae historica,* ed. Georg H. Pertz, *Scriptorum,* XXI (Hanover 1869), 203.

21. Toeche, *Kaiser Heinrich,* pp. 455-6.

22. George Saintsbury, "Romance," *Encyclopaedia Britannica* (14th ed.; London and New York, 1929), XIX, 425 *d.* Though he does not name Dante, he is presumably reinterpreting the three topics described in the *De vulgare eloquentia,* II, ii, 5; II, iv, 6, as the proper subjects of poetry. See also Margaret A. Gist, *Love and War in the Middle English Romances* (Philadelphia, 1947), pp. 29, 39, 43, 65, 73, 120 n. 34, 126.

23. Possible borrowings or echoes have already been mentioned above, pp. 27 n. 6, 44, 68, 71, 74, and 113. Besides these and the parallels still to be mentioned in this chapter, two others may be mentioned. Chretien's *Cligès,* v. 315, may have suggested *Guillaume,* vv. 2577-8; and *Cligès,* vv. 6430-2, *Guillaume,* vv. 2088-9.

24. See pp. 26, 30 n. 11, 62 n. 60 and 117.

25. Zingarelli, "Il 'Guillaume,'" pp. 260-1.

26. McKeehan, "*Guillaume* a Best Seller," p. 790.

27. Chalandon, *Histoire,* I, 91-2.

28. Petrus de Ebulo, "De rebus siculis," plate XXIX.

29. Cf. Sister Marie Pierre Koch, *An Analysis of the Long Prayers in Old French Literature* (Washington, D.C., 1940); *Guillaume* is not included.

30. *The Pseudo-Turpin,* p. 94.

31. It seems to become so in *William* (vv. 633-9, 643-6, 797-802) under the less subtle treatment of the English poet, who likewise attributes William's dream to Alexandrine's sorcery (vv. 653-8), although the dream occurs naturally in *Guillaume* (vv. 1118-24).

32. It is possible that the escape by disguise represents the romancer's rationalization of a common folktale motif, the supernatural transformation of the fugitive into animal form in order to evade capture. (See the "Motifs not in *Guillaume*" listed above, D531, D642.3, D671.) The non-supernatural counterpart,

K521.1, *Escape by dressing in animal (bird) skin,* is, however, well attested in folk literature, and might just as well have suggested the device to the poet. Those who see Byzantine influence in *Guillaume* might cite the instance in *Daphnis and Chloe* when Dorcon lies in wait for Chloe wearing a wolfskin and is attacked by the sheep-dogs, who mistake him for a real wolf (I, xx-xxii). Such use of an isolated folklore motif to establish specific literary influence would, however, be hazardous.

33. For a historical survey of this theme see Born's introduction to Desiderius Erasmus, *The Education of a Christian Prince,* tr. Lester K. Born ("Records of Civilization Sources and Studies," XXVII) (New York, 1936), pp. 44-130.

34. Andreas Capellanus, *The Art of Courtly Love,* tr. Parry, pp. 107, 156, 184. The author explicitly rejects the doctrine, however, in the last chapter of his peculiarly ambiguous work (p. 196).

35. See Lot-Borodine, *Le Roman idyllique,* pp. 233-65; Sarah F. Barrow, *The Medieval Society Romances* (New York, 1924), pp. 14, 16, 33, 115; Donnell van de Voort, *Love and Marriage in the English Medieval Romances* (Nashville, Tennessee, 1938), pp. 116-17; and Gist, *Love and War,* as cited above p. 131 n. 22.

36. Lot-Borodine in *Le Roman idyllique,* p. 249 n. 1, points out that this feature is probably inspired by a passage in the *Roman d'Enéas* which was derived in turn, as Edmond Faral has shown (in his *Recherches sur les sources latines des contes et romans courtois du moyen âge* [Paris, 1913], pp. 137-8), from Ovid. The facetious tone of *Guillaume* is lacking, however, in the two sources.

Thorlac Turville-Petre (essay date 1974)

SOURCE: "Humphrey de Bohun and *William of Palerne,*" *Neuphilologische Mitteilungen,* Vol. LXXV, No. 2, 1974, pp. 250-52.

[*In the following essay, Turville-Petre maintains that* William of Palerne *likely was composed prior to 1361 at the command of Humphrey de Bohun for members of his retinue, who resided at two neighboring manors.*]

That Humphrey de Bohun, Earl of Hereford and Essex, commissioned the alliterative poem **William of Palerne** at some date before 1361 is one of the few ascertainable facts about the social background of the poems of the Alliterative Revival.[1] Since, as a result, so much importance is accorded to this one nugget of information, the position is worth investigating a little more closely.

The earl's estates, like those of most great lords of his time, were scattered over a wide area, from the Welsh marches to Essex,[2] but it is on his estates in the South

West Midlands that we should concentrate our attention, for examination of the dialect of *William of Palerne* shows that it was in this general area that the poem was composed.[3] The Inquisition into the lands held by Humphrey at his death in 1361[4] records that he held three manors in Gloucestershire, all situated within a few miles of the county town itself. Southam lies to the north east of Gloucester, and Haresfield and Wheatenhurst (now Whitminster) are situated close to one another to the south of the town. This pair of manors is particularly interesting, and the recently-published volume of *The Victoria History of the Counties of England*[5] gives several details of them which are relevant here. About Wheatenhurst we are told that 'the earls had no under-tenant in Wheatenhurst, which was one of their demesne manors. . . . It was recorded as a chief house with a courtyard in 1336.' (pp. 291-3). This manor-house was one of those which Humprey obtained licence to crenellate in 1347.[6] Haresfield, too, was a manor of some importance to the Earls of Hereford. The second Earl had stocked the park with sixteen deer in 1251, and there were deer there in the sixteenth century. In 1318 a private chapel was built on the manor.[7]

The evidence suggests that the Earl of Hereford with his retinue would have made periodic visits to these two neighbouring manors, perhaps while he was on his way to one of his four castles with their surrounding estates in the Welsh marches—Caldicot, Brecon, Hay and Huntingdon. Caldicot, on the Severn estuary, lies only about thirty miles from Gloucester, and was apparently a fairly large castle.[8] Unfortunately, very little is known about Humphrey's life, for it seems that a prolonged infirmity kept him, like his elder brother John, out of the public eye.[9] Probably he spent much of his time at his castle of Pleshy in Essex, where he died.[10] A reference to Gloucester in *William of Palerne* was previously taken to mean that Humphrey resided thereabouts:

> Preieth a pater noster priuely þis time
> For þe hend erl of herford, sir humfray de bowne,
> Þe king edwardes newe, at glouseter þat ligges.

(164-6)

Recently, however, it has been maintained[11] that the line refers rather to the magnificent tomb of Edward II at what is now Gloucester Cathedral, and this interpretation is very probable. Humphrey was not, at any rate, as intimately involved in the affairs of the West as some of his ancestors, such as the second Earl of Hereford who fought against the Welsh, was justice itinerant for Gloucestershire, Worcestershire and Herefordshire,[12] and was buried just outside Gloucester at Lanthony Abbey, of which the earls were patrons.[13] We should remember in this connection that *William of Palerne* was not written principally (if at all) for Humphrey's cars, but 'for hem þat knowe no frensche' (5533)—presumably members of the earl's retinue established in the West Midlands. Some fifty of Humprey's associates and household servants—ranging from 'frere William de Monkeland n're confessour' to 'Davy q'est Barber et Ewer'—are remembered in his will.[14]

It is likely that the author of the poem, who identifies himself merely as 'William' (5521), was also a member of Humphrey's household at Haresfield and Wheatenhurst, or conceivably he may have been an Austin canon at Lanthony, writing at the behest of the Abbey's patron. For a small house Lanthony possessed a very large library of some five hundred books, although the catalogue drawn up at the beginning of the fourteenth century and later revised[15] lists nothing that might have inspired the writer of this most romantic of alliterative poems.

Notes

1. See *William of Palerne*, ed. W. W. Skeat, E.E.T.S. E.S. 1 (1867), ll. 165-8 and 5529-33.

2. See G. A. Holmes, *The Estates of the Higher Nobility in Fourteenth-Century England* (Cambridge, 1957), pp. 19-25.

3. See J. P. Oakden, *Alliterative Poetry in Middle English,* vol. i (Manchester, 1930), pp. 55-8.

4. *Calendar of Inquisitions Post Mortem,* vol. xi, no. 485.

5. *A History of the County of Gloucester,* vol. x (Oxford, 1972). For Haresfield see pp. 188 ff., and for Wheatenhurst pp. 289 ff. For Southam, which the Bohuns held of the Bishop of Worcester, see ibid., vol. viii (1968), pp. 9 ff.

6. *The Complete Peerage,* vol. vi, p. 472.

7. *A History of the County of Gloucester,* vol. x, pp. 189-91.

8. Brief descriptions of Caldicot and the other Bohun castles in Wales are given by A. H. A. Hogg and D. J. C. King, 'Masonry Castles in Wales and the Marches', *Archaeologia Cambrensis,* cxvi (1967), 71 ff.

9. Both John and Humphrey resigned the hereditary office of Constable of England on the grounds of infirmity. For John see *The Complete Peerage,* vol. vi, p. 471, and for Humphrey see Madden's remarks reprinted in the introduction to *William of Palerne,* pp. xi f.

10. *The Complete Peerage,* vol. vi, p. 472.

11. By C. W. Dunn in *A Manual of the Writings in Middle English,* fasc. i, ed. J. B. Severs (New Haven, 1967), p. 36.

12. *The Dictionary of National Biography,* vol. ii, p. 770.

13. For an account of the dealings between the Earls of Hereford and Lanthony Abbey see J. N. Langston, 'Priors of Lanthony by Gloucester', *Transactions of the Bristol and Gloucestershire Archaeological Society,* lxiii (1942), 1-144.

14. Printed in J. Nichols, *A Collection of All the Wills, now Known to be Extant, of the Kings and Queens of England* (London, 1780), pp. 44-56.

15. Printed and analysed by T. W. Williams, 'Gloucestershire Mediaeval Libraries', *Trans. Bristol & Glos. Arch. Soc.*, xxxi (1908), 139-78. Many of the Lanthony manuscripts are now in the Lambeth Palace Library.

G. H. V. Bunt (essay date 1985)

SOURCE: "The Story," in William of Palerne: *An Alliterative Romance*, Groningen, 1985, pp. 93-108.

[*In the following essay, Bunt studies the structure, setting, historical background, and magical elements in* William of Palerne.]

1. Since the first three leaves of the Ms. are lost, we are dependent on the French *Guillaume de Palerne* for the opening episodes of the story, which are, however, recapitulated later in our English poem.

The French poem, then, tells us that king Embron of Sicily and his queen Felise have a four-year-old son, Guillaume, who is entrusted for instruction to two Greek ladies, Gloriande and Acelone. The king's brother, who wishes to gain the throne for himself, bribes the ladies to poison Guillaume and his father. However, while the king, the queen and Guillaume are in the royal park, a large wolf takes the child in his mouth and runs off with it. A pursuit is fruitless; the wolf swims across the Strait of Messina with the little prince and escapes. The wolf goes with the child to a forest in the vicinity of Rome, where he hides the child in a cave and takes care of it. At this point the English text begins.

While the werwolf is away, a cowherd's dog finds William and frightens him. The cowherd hears the dog's barking and the child's cries, finds William and takes him home. He and his wife adopt William as their son (1-79). When the werwolf returns, he finds William gone, but soon discovers him in the cowherd's house. Seeing that he is well looked after, the werwolf departs contented (80-108). The werwolf is in reality a Spanish prince, whose stepmother has transformed him so that her own son may succeed to the throne (109-160). The audience is invited to say a paternoster for the poet's patron (161-170). William becomes a cowherd and an able huntsman. He has many friends, to whom he gives generous gifts (170-197). One day the emperor of Rome loses his way while hunting a boar and becomes separated from his company. A werwolf races past, pursuing a hart. The emperor follows them and comes upon William. He is struck by the boy's beauty and asks him to call his father. The cowherd reluctantly obeys the emperor's summons, and explains that he has found William dressed in rich clothes. The emperor wants to take the boy with him to court. Before they depart, the cowherd admonishes his fosterson on the proper behaviour at court. William sends greetings to his friends and his fostermother, who is very sad over the loss of the boy (198-384). The

emperor arrives in Rome with William, but refuses to tell anyone how he has come by the child. He entrusts him to the care of his daughter Melior (385-432).

At this point another leaf is lost. The French poem here tells of William's popularity at the imperial court. Melior falls in love with him and debates within herself.

When the text of the English poem resumes, Melior is musing upon her lovesickness, and hesitates over whether to blame her heart or her eyes, but decides to follow the dictates of her heart and to love William. She cannot, however, tell him of her love (433-570). Her cousin and confidante Alisaundrine, noting Melior's distress, offers her help, and Melior reveals her problem (571-628). Alisaundrine promises a herb which will cure Melior's disease. By her magic arts she causes William to dream that Melior comes to him at night and offers her love. When he awakes he is only clutching his pillow. He tells himself he is deluded and presumptuous to think that Melior would love a mere foundling (629-730). However, love continues to torment William. He spends his days sitting under a tree in the palace garden staring at Melior's window. One day he falls asleep there (731-794). Melior asks whether Alisaundrine has found the herb yet. She replies that they might find comfort in the garden. She knows that William is there and leads Melior to him. Alisaundrine causes William to dream that Melior hands him a rose which cures all his suffering. He wakes up and is greeted by Melior as *leve lemman*. At Alisaundrine's request he describes his ailment to her, but refuses to explain himself further. Melior thinks to herself that she is suffering from the same illness as William, but dare not reveal herself. Alisaundrine tells William that she understands his illness, and he implores her help. Alisaundrine calls on Melior to accept William as her lover, and she promises herself to him (795-1001). They embrace and make love; Alisaundrine passes the time gathering flowers. When evening comes she tells the lovers to part. They enjoy each other's love in secret for three years (1002-1066).

The rebellious duke of Saxony is attacking the emperor's realm; the emperor summons an army to fight him. William is knighted and given the command of eighty princes' sons who are knighted with him. The emperor's council advise him to fight the duke (1067-1117). The duke challenges the emperor to battle. When their forces meet, the duke's army proves the stronger. William overhears the emperor's prayer for help, and exhorts his own men to attack. William slays six great nobles. The duke rallies his army, and William is captured and brought before the duke, but his followers rescue him (1118-1229). William renews the attack and captures the duke. The Saxons are routed and many nobles are taken prisoner. They are brought before the emperor's council and made to do homage. Peace is thus restored, but the duke grieves at the result of his pride, dies and is buried honourably (1230-1325). The imperial army returns home. Melior receives the news of her lover's prowess and his wounds. With her maidens she sets out to welcome her father and William, and invites him to her room. With the help of Alisaundrine William and Melior are able to keep their love secret (1326-1415).

The emperor is holding a feast at Easter, when thirty Greek barons arrive and ask Melior in marriage for the son of the Greek emperor. The emperor and his council agree to this request and the wedding day is fixed for midsummer (1416-1475). When William learns of Melior's betrothal he falls ill. The emperor visits him and grieves to see him in such suffering. Melior and Alisaundrine also visit William and inquire after the cause of his illness. William reproaches Melior for breaking her pledge to him; she replies that she does not feel bound by her father's promises, and that she will be his for ever. On hearing this, William speedily recovers and returns to court (1476-1588). A Greek delegation arrives in Rome for the wedding and is received with due ceremony (1589-1637). William again reproaches Melior for deluding him, but she replies that she will keep her promise to him, and suggests that they elope. Alisaundrine suggests that they disguise themselves in bearskins. She brings two white bearskins from the kitchen, sews the lovers up in them, and escorts them out of the palace (1638-1764). In the garden they are seen by a Greek, who runs away in terror, and tells his companions of his adventure (1765-1784). William and Melior rest in a den under a hollow oak. The problem of food and drink arises, and they decide to live on the fruits that they find in the woods. However, the werwolf knows all about their plight. He robs food from a passing churl and brings it to the lovers (1785-1880). Realising that they need drink, the werwolf then robs a clerk of two flagons of wine. They are guided by the werwolf (1881-1929). In Rome preparations are made for the wedding, but Melior does not appear. The emperor sends a baron to her chamber and then goes himself. When she does not answer his calling, he becomes enraged. Alisaundrine tells him that she has lost Melior's favour; Melior had heard that Greek wives were shut up in a tower, and for this reason she would not be married to a Greek. She was in love with William, and Alisaundrine had reproached her for this. The emperor finds Melior's room empty, and Alisaundrine tells him she must have eloped with William. The emperor sends men to find William at his lodging, but to their relief they do not find him (1930-2095). The emperor informs the Greek emperor of what has happened; the Greek emperor accepts his apologies and advises him to order a thorough search for the runaway pair. The search is, however, in vain (2096-2154). The Greek who saw the disguised William and Melior in the garden now tells the two emperors of his experience. A search is made with bloodhounds for the two white bears. They are in great danger, but the werwolf succeeds in luring the hounds away from them. The Greeks return home. The werwolf guides the lovers to the borders of Apulia (2155-2214). They find themselves in open country near Benevento, and hide in a quarry. A party of quarrymen start work in the quarry; one has seen the bears and goes to town to tell the provost. The provost comes with a large crowd to catch the bears. William and Melior wake up, and Melior relates her dream. When they realise that they are about to be caught, William tells Melior to take off her disguise so that her life shall be spared, but she refuses to leave William. The werwolf abducts the provost's little son, and thus lures the pursuers away from the quarry (2215-2400). William and Melior pray for the safety of the werwolf. They take off their now useless bearskins, and leave the quarry undisguised. They find shelter in a forest, where the werwolf provides them with food and drink (2401-2518). They overhear a debate between two colliers; one hopes to catch the white bears and win the reward, the other sympathises with the runaway lovers (2519-2567). The werwolf kills a hart and a hind and signals to William and Melior to put on the skins. In this new disguise they travel towards Sicily (2568-2617).

The country here is laid waste as the result of a war. William's father, king of Sicily, is dead, and his mother rules the kingdom. The Spanish king wants her daughter as wife for his son, the werwolf's half-brother, but she has refused the match, and he is now besieging Palermo. The situation is nearly hopeless for the besieged. The queen has sent for help to her father, the emperor of Greece, but no help has come so far (2618-2712). William and Melior, guided by the werwolf, reach Reggio; the werwolf finds a ship which they board. They cross to Sicily, where the werwolf leaps overboard. He receives a blow from one of the sailors. The sailors pursue him, leaving their ship in the charge of a 'barelegged bold boy' (2713-2767). The hart and the hind leave their shelter on board the ship to go ashore, but the frightened boy hits Melior in the neck. William wants to punish the boy, but Melior, who is unhurt, dissuades him (2768-2829). The werwolf guides the lovers to Palermo, where they hide in the palace garden near the queen's window (2830-2855). The besieged queen dreams that a werwolf and two white bears, who change into deer, help her and her daughter against a large number of animals. The hart imprisons the leaders of the attacking animals. She then finds herself in a tower of her castle; her right arm reaches over Rome and her left arm lies over Spain. The priest Moses interprets her dream (2856-2968). The queen sees the hart and the hind in the garden, but is unable to hear what they say. She asks her knights not to surrender to the besiegers. She then disguises herself as a hind, and, attended by a maiden, goes out into the garden to make contact with the deer. She overhears their conversation; Melior has had a dream, which William feels portends good. They see the disguised queen, who makes herself known, and asks their help against the besiegers, promising William full powers. The three enter the palace (2969-3192). William and Melior are bathed and clothed. William adopts a werwolf as his cognizance. King Ebrouns' horse recognises William as his rightful master (3193-3260). The steward of Spain attacks the city. William arms himself and rides to battle on king Ebrouns' horse. The queen and her daughter admire William's appearance, but Melior fears they may take him away from her. William exhorts the knights and rides out with 400 men. He slays the steward; a general battle follows, in which William kills the steward's nephew and makes many prisoners (3261-3474). William and Melior, while sitting with the queen at her window, see the werwolf, who seems to be asking for mercy. The queen is reminded of her lost son. William rejects the idea that he might be the queen's son (3475-3527). The son of the king of Spain undertakes to avenge the steward and his nephew. In the ensuing battle William takes the king's son prisoner and hands him over to the queen (3528-3666). The queen is again reminded of her lost son. William reproaches her for her tears: she will never get her son back. They again see the werwolf in the park (3667-3730). The Spanish king threatens to punish his men for allowing his son to be captured, but is brought to reason by his knights. He vows to avenge his son and to hang William. The dead of the previous battle are buried. In the new battle Meliadus slays numerous Sicilians and wounds William, but is eventually killed by him. The Spanish king sees William approach and rallies his troops, but when William is victorious, he flees. William overtakes him and captures the king and many nobles. He hands them over to the queen, who again makes William effective lord of Palermo (3731-3961). The Spanish king is led into hall, where he asks to see his son. They confess their guilt and offer to make amends. Suddenly the werwolf enters the hall, kneels before the king and disappears. William prevents his men from harming the werwolf. The Spanish king, by William's order, tells of the disappearance of his son by his first marriage, and of the rumours that his second wife had transformed him into a werwolf. William demands that the Spanish queen be summoned to disenchant the werwolf (3962-4150). The Spanish king sends messengers to fetch his wife. They arrive in Spain and inform the queen of the outcome of the war. She agrees to accompany them to Sicily (4151-4283). The queen of Spain arrives in Palermo. The werwolf has been accommodated in William's chamber. When the queen is in hall, he rushes in and attacks her, but William restrains him and promises disenchantment (4284-4374). The Spanish queen asks the werwolf's forgiveness. She takes him into a private room, and with the help of a ring with a protective stone and a book she restores him to human form. The disenchanted werwolf, Alphouns, is ashamed of his nakedness. He wishes to receive the order of knighthood and his knightly array at William's hands (4375-4474). William, accompanied by Melior, the queen and her daughter, goes in to Alphouns, but does not recognise him. Alphouns makes himself known. He falls in love with the queen's daughter. In hall he is welcomed by all present. He reveals William's true identity and recalls his adventures. He has abducted the child William to save him from a plot against his life by his uncle and his two nurses. His revelations are greeted with great joy. Alphouns reminisces about his adventures with the eloped lovers. William thanks him for all he has done for himself and for Melior. Alphouns asks for the hand of his sister in return, which is immediately granted (4475-4766). The two nurses implore William's mercy and are granted their lives. They retire to a hermitage (4767-4806).

William sends messengers to Rome to invite the emperor to his wedding with Melior. The emperor travels to Palermo, accompanied by Alisaundrine (4807-4922). The Greek fleet has arrived to help the queen of Sicily against her Spanish attackers; the fleet is led by the queen's brother Partenedon. He is annoyed to hear of the intended wedding of William and Melior, but is forced to accept the situation (4923-4989). A marriage is arranged between Alisaundrine and Braundnis, Alphouns' half-brother. The next day the triple wedding takes place with great ceremony; the festivities last a month (4990-5076). After the festivities, Partenedon is the first to take leave. At home he reports his experiences to his father, who takes a lighter view than his son. The emperor of Rome admonishes Melior and Alisaundrine before departing. Then the Spanish king with his wife and his two sons take their leave. William and Alphouns promise each other assistance in case of war. The king of Spain abdicates in favour of Alphouns (5077-5233). William restores order in his kingdom and introduces good laws. He and Melior are greatly loved (5234-5249). A message arrives that the emperor of Rome has died; William is asked to succeed him. William invites Alphouns to his coronation. They are overjoyed to meet again. Together they travel to Rome, where the pope crowns William emperor. William summons the cowherd and rewards him richly. The leave-taking after the festivities is again described elaborately (5250-5467). William travels through his empire. He is a good ruler and much loved. He and Melior have two sons: one later succeeds his father as emperor, the other as king of Calabria and Apulia (5468-5520).

In his epilogue the poet, who names himself as William, apologies for the defects of his poem, and calls upon his audience to pray for his patron (5521-5540).

> 2. Simms (1969:xix) finds a four-part structure in the poem:
>
> > 1. William's youth in the forest and in Rome (3-1415).
> >
> > 2. The great escape with the adventures on the road to Sicily (1416-2855).
> >
> > 3. The war against the Spaniards (2856-3961).
> >
> > 4. The revelations and revels which follow William's victory (3962-5540).

Such a subdivision of the poem has its undoubted attractions from the point of view of narrative structure. There are indeed large initials at the beginning of each of these sections, but also at numerous other points; and there are no very clear breaks in the text at the places indicated. In fact, three of the first lines of these proposed subsections contain anaphoric words which refer to an antecedent in the final lines of the preceding section, which makes it unlikely that these points mark the beginning and end of instalments for public recitation.

The only clear evidence of a subdivision of the poem is in line 161, which tells the audience that *þus passed is þe first pas of þis pris tale.* Nowhere else is the word *pas,* which recalls the *passus* of *Piers Plowman* and *The Wars of Alexander,* used in our poem. If we count the lost three leaves which once contained the opening sections and estimate the number of lines on them at 216 (the first quire has 36 lines to the page), the *first pas* must have had something like 376 lines. But we look in vain for evidence of a division into passus of approximately this length. We do find the narrative punctuated with transitional lines and sequences of lines saying 'now we cease to tell of X, and begin to speak of Y', but these occur at irregular intervals and probably have a purely local connective function rather than a structural one. We must conclude that, apart from ll. 161-9, there are no obvious points at which the poem might have been interrupted.

3. The story of **William of Palerne** evidently contains a fair number of elements that are familiar in romance and folktale. As in many English romances, the overall pattern is what Wittig (1978) terms 'separation-restoration', with the 'love-marriage' pattern embedded into it. Both patterns, in fact, occur twice: separation-restoration in the story of William and in that of Alphouns, the werwolf; the love-marriage pattern is found in its variant form 'love-threatened marriage-rescue-marriage' in the story of William and Melior, whereas in the case of William's sister Florence the first 'type-episode', love, is treated very briefly and in a somewhat aberrant position. The pattern seems to be introduced here mainly to allow William to fulfil his destined rôle by delivering his mother from her enemies and winning back his lost inheritance through his knightly prowess. This second instance of the love-marriage pattern is also less well motivated: while Melior is given good reasons for not wanting to marry her Greek suitor, no reason is given for the refusal of the Sicilian queen and her daughter to accept the suit of the heir to the Spanish throne.

On a lower level, that of the episode or the scene, we also find much that belongs to the staple of medieval romance. Frequent 'type-episodes' and 'type-scenes' (the terms are Wittig's) which are represented in **William of Palerne** are expulsion of the hero, kidnapping, adoption, love, single combat, threat of a marriage, disguise, recognition, restoration, marriage, etc.; several of these are used more than once, such as expulsion of the hero, kidnapping, adoption, threat of a marriage, etc.

The individual motifs in **William of Palerne,** or rather in its French source, have been studied thoroughly by Charles Dunn, who gives a full list (1960: 19-23) with references to Thompson's *Motif-Index* (Thompson 1955-58), but not, naturally, to Gerald Bordman's *Motif-Index of the English Metrical Romances* of 1963. Although Wittig's criticism of the motif approach to the romances as too atomistic is certainly justified (1978:59, 195), Dunn's list enables us to recognise the close affinities between stories such as ours and the folk-tale.

While the plot of **William of Palerne** is certainly made up from commonplace materials, there is much in the story

and in its treatment by the poet that is highly distinctive. In what follows we shall briefly discuss the Sicilian setting, possible historical backgrounds, the magical element and the disguises. We should, however, also note the ample attention given to meetings and leave-takings, festive ceremonial and ritual, and to religious observances. The tone is genuinely and sincerely pious, but the ritualistic manner in which these scenes are handled, often in highly formulaic language, also gives an impression of stemming from a need to say and do 'the right thing'; the narrative style comes to function, as Wittig puts it (1978:45), 'as a powerful social force which supports, reinforces and perpetuates the social beliefs and customs held by the culture'.

4. Sicily is used as a setting in several medieval French and English romances[1]. But in no other romance is such knowledge displayed of the geography of Southern Italy and Sicily. It has been supposed[2] that the author of the French *Guillaume de Palerne* must have known these parts from personal observation. In the ME adaptation, many of the place-names (Far, Messina, Santa Maria della Scalla, Cefalù), much of the description of Palermo and other geographical details are omitted, but what remains of the geographical data is still accurate by modern standards.

Sicily[3] was much in the forefront of European attention in the 12th century. Having been conquered by the Saracens from the Byzantine Empire during the 9th century, it was wrested from them in the 11th century by Norman war bands led by the sons of Tancred de Hauteville, among whom Robert Guiscard was the most prominent. Robert's nephew Roger was crowned king of Sicily in Palermo Cathedral in 1130; his kingdom consisted of Sicily and the mainland provinces of Apulia and Calabria, which had been conquered from Byzantium. Roger was succeeded by his son William I, nicknamed the Bad (1154-66), who married Margaret of Navarre, and by his grandson William II the Good (1166-89), who was married to Joanna, sister of Richard the Lionhearted. After the death of William II, Tancred, an illegitimate son of a brother of William I, seized the throne; he reigned as king from 1190 to 1194, and was succeeded by his baby son William III. The island was then conquered by another claimant, the emperor Henry VI, son of Frederick Barbarossa, who was married to Constance, daughter of king Roger and aunt of William II. Henry died in 1197 and Constance the next year, leaving an infant son, Frederick II, who had been born in Palermo. Frederick took the government into his own hands in 1208 and reigned as emperor and king until his death in 1250.

There are, therefore, certain parallels between the history of Sicily and the story of **William of Palerne:** two kings named William (or three if we count the unfortunate boy king William III), although neither William I nor his son married an emperor's daughter, and a union of the Sicilian and imperial thrones.

Nor are these the only parallels between fable and historical fact. As McKeehan (1926) points out, in 1159 Alphonse VIII, then four years old, succeeded his father as king of Castile; but his uncle seized power and demanded homage of his young nephew, who, however, was snatched away by loyal adherents and, after a civil war, placed on the throne. Alphonse later married Leonor, another sister of Richard the Lionhearted. These events might have provided a clue for the abduction story as well as for the Spanish connection in our romance. Nothing is known of a Spanish attempt to control Sicily until 1282, after the Sicilian Vespers, when king Peter of Aragon became king of Sicily; but he did not fight to obtain his throne[4]. A Spanish conquest took place in 1392. Both these dates are, of course, too late for our purpose.

According to McKeehan, the hero of *Guillaume de Palerne* is created in the likeness of William the Good of Sicily, Alphouns[5] in that of Alfonso II of Aragon or Alfonso VIII of Castile. The two Spanish kings were brothers-in-law, and both were associated with Richard the Lionhearted. Dunn wisely does not attempt such an identification. He seeks the origin of the story in propagandistic legends which were purposefully circulated to promote the political aims of the Hauteville kings of Sicily or their Hohenstaufen successors[6].

This hypothesis seems plausible, if incapable of verification. But the historical parallels remain vague, and to the English audience of the mid-fourteenth century they must have been quite remote. To them Sicily must have been a faraway land torn by protracted wars which attracted adventurers from many countries. Sicily's Norman past and the contacts with England that existed in Norman times may still have been remembered, but the island can hardly have called up such immediate associations as it did for Countess Yolent and her circle round the year 1200.

A rôle of some importance is also played by the Byzantine Greeks. Melior's unwelcome fiancé is a Greek prince, the heir to the imperial throne. The basileus is also the father of the queen of Sicily, and sends her a fleet to help her against her Spanish enemies, although it does not arrive until after the war is over. Some prominence is also given to Partenedon's feelings when he attends the wedding of his former betrothed. No historical parallels can be found for these elements in the narrative. There was no queen of Sicily who was the daughter of the Byzantine emperor; nor was the Byzantine fleet ever strong enough to be of any help against the queen's enemies. The rôle that the Greeks play is slightly comic; their military aid comes when it is no longer needed, and their prince's marriage is thwarted by the unwillingness of the intended bride. Yet these comic aspects are not really elaborated, and nowhere are the Greeks held up to ridicule, as they are frequently in other sources. This state of affairs accords well with the findings of dr B. Ebels-Hoving (1971), who points out that the many Greeks who figure in the French *romans* cannot be said to embody a clearly definable attitude towards Byzantium.

Since the French source was written for a patroness who through her husband and her nephew was closely con-cerned in the conquest of Constantinople in 1204 (see above, ch. 4), the absence of any reference to this historic event in a romance in which the Greek empire plays a rôle is striking. It may be considered an argument, if not a very strong one, for assigning to the French *Guillaume* a date before 1204.

5. The belief in werwolves has given rise to a considerable body of literature, which it is impossible to catalogue or to summarise here. The most immediately relevant publications on the subject are the two letters by Algernon Herbert to Lord Cawdor, the President of the Roxburghe Club, which are printed in Madden's edition, as well as Hertz (1862), Smith (1894), Tibbals (1903-4), Kittredge (1903), Stewart (1909), McKeehan (1926) and Dunn (1960); what follows here is heavily dependent on these authorities.

The belief in the transformation of human beings into wolves is known in many cultures. The transformation, usually of a temporary nature, could occur voluntarily, by removing human clothing or putting on a wolfskin or a girdle made of wolfskin, but it could also be the result of a compelling curse or spell. In werwolf stories Tibbals (1903-4) distinguishes (1) the constitutional werwolf, whose transformation to wolf-shape occurs as it were spontaneously after the removal of human clothes, and can be ended by the simple resumption of the clothes; (2) the 'Teutonic' werwolf, who is transformed by putting on a wolfskin or a wolfskin girdle, and becomes man again by removing it; and (3) the magically transformed werwolf, who, unlike the two other types, cannot assume wolf shape and human form at will, but is under the compulsion of some other power, a necklace, a ring, a curse or a spell. Tibbals adds that these types often occur in combined form, as in the *Lai de Melion* (see below). As Dunn notes (1960:117), in many tales the werwolf takes on a more ravenous nature than that of the wolf itself, and lives by the slaughter of animals. But we also find werwolves whose favourite diet is human flesh; thus Marie de France writes, in the opening lines of her *Bisclavret*:

> *Garualf, ceo est beste salvage:*
> *Tant cum il est en cele rage,*
> *Hummes devure, grant mal fait,*
> *Es granz forez converse e vait.*
>
> (9-12)

(The werwolf is a savage beast; while it is in this rage[7], it devours men and does much harm; it lives and walks in the great forests.)

Algernon Herbert (in Madden 1832:15-16) says that werwolves delight in eating children, especially girls, and that they distinguish themselves from 'natural' wolves by the lack of a tail. Whether this is a general characteristic of werwolves, he does not say; it does not occur in **William of Palerne,** its French source, or in any of the other tales discussed in this chapter.

Werwolves were often regarded with fear and horror, and actively persecuted both in story and in actual life. Herbert and Hertz (1862) cite several cases of werwolf trials and of men executed as werwolves. ***William of Palerne,*** however, belongs to a group of tales in which a werwolf is treated sympathetically. Kittredge (1903) gives the Latin story of *Arthur and Gorlagon* and several examples of werwolf tales from Wales, Brittany and Ireland in which the protagonist is transformed under the compulsion of a spell. We also find the werwolf treated sympathetically in Marie de France's *Bisclavret* and in the anonymous early 13th-century *Lai de Melion*[8].

In *Bisclavret,* the hero is a baron whose wife is distressed by his weekly three-day absences. One day she wrings from him the secret that during these absences he is a werwolf. He takes off his clothes, which he hides in a secret place; if he does not recover them, he is doomed to remain a werwolf forever. The wicked wife also wheedles the secret of the hiding-place of the clothes out of him, and instructs her lover to remove them, promising that she will become his mistress. With her husband thus got out of the way, she marries her lover. One day the king's hounds, having hunted the werwolf Bisclavret down, are about to tear him to pieces, when Bisclavret implores the king's mercy. The king concludes he must have a human mind, and takes him under his protection. At a feast he suddenly attacks his wife's new husband. On a later occasion, he bites his wife's nose off. On a wise councillor's advice, the king interrogates the wife under torture, and she confesses her crime. She is made to return the clothes and they are laid before Bisclavret, who, however, refuses to put them on. The wise councillor suggests that he is ashamed and that he should be taken to a private room to put on the clothes and become man again. So it happens, and Bisclavret is found asleep in the king's bed. The wife is exiled; several of her daughters are born without noses.

A very similar story, probably dependent on Marie's *Lai,* is included in the 14th-century *Roman du Renart Contrefait,* where the protagonist's name is Biclarel.

Melion is considerably longer than *Bisclavret* and less well told. The story is given an Arthurian setting. Its hero is a young knight, highly esteemed at court, who make a foolish vow after which the ladies at court refuse to speak to him. When Melion hears this he falls into a great sadness. King Arthur sends him to a distant castle to forget his grief. One day while hunting he comes upon a richly dressed maiden who declares that she has come from Ireland to find him, because she has loved him for a long time. Melion and the lady are speedily married and live happily for three years. During a hunting party Melion and his wife come upon a huge stag. She declares she will never eat again unless she has a piece of that stag. Melion hands her a ring with a white and a red stone. She is to touch his head with the white stone once he has undressed; he will be turned into a wolf and he will bring her the stag. He begs her to guard his clothes well, since unless he is touched again with the other stone, he must remain a werwolf forever. The wife, however, departs for Dublin, where her father is king, attended by a squire whom she

soon marries. When Melion realises that his wife has betrayed him, he determines to pursue her. He hides himself in a ship, where he receives a blow when leaping overboard. In Ireland he lives in the forests, ravaging the country with a band of ten wolves, and killing even men and women. The king pursues them and kills all the wolves except Melion. Meanwhile, Arthur arrives in Ireland to conclude peace. Melion recognises him and implores his mercy. Arthur is moved by the wolf's human actions and claims him as his own. At a feast in Dublin Melion attacks the squire who accompanied his wife back to Ireland. The squire is made to confess the truth, and the king's daughter is persuaded to give Arthur the magic ring. Gawain insists that Melion should be taken to a private room to be touched with the ring, so that he need not be ashamed in front of the company. Melion is restored to human shape and is given rich clothing. Arthur dissuades him from punishing his faithless wife, but he consigns her to the devil before leaving home with Arthur, adding that one should never believe what any woman says.

There is a striking number of details that ***William of Palerne*** has in common with *Bisclavret* and *Melion,* such as the werwolf imploring the king's mercy, the king's conclusion that the werwolf has a human mind, the king taking the werwolf under his protection, the werwolf's attack on the person whom he holds responsible for his sad condition, the forced confession, the disenchantment in a private room, the nakedness and the shame of the werwolf after disenchantment. In *Bisclavret* and in ***William,*** but not in *Melion,* the disenchanted werwolf lies in bed; and *Melion* has in common with ***William,*** but not with *Bisclavret,* the werwolf's crossing by boat, the blow that he receives when leaping overboard, and the rich clothing given him after disenchantment. But the differences are even more striking. The werwolf in ***William*** lacks the ferocity of the transformed heroes of the two *lais;* he is ferocious only when he twice attacks his wicked stepmother (145-55, 4339-74). ***William*** does not contain the motif of the faithless wife, but makes a stepmother responsible for the werwolf's condition; and it employs a number of important motifs that are absent in the two French poems.

In ***William*** only does the werwolf act out the traditional rôle of the wolf as 'baby-snatcher'[9] when he abducts the four-year-old William and later the son of the provost of Benevento. Dunn (1960:113) quotes Bartholomeus Anglicus' *De Proprietatibus Rerum* on the delight that wolves take in stealing boys and eating them[10], and we have already cited Herbert, who notes a similar motif. Our werwolf's motives are, however, entirely noble, and he treats the abducted children with great care so as not to harm them.

Another important and widespread motif associated with wolves is that of the Wolf's Fosterling. Dunn (1960:86-111) gives a detailed discussion of this motif as combined with that of the Fair Unknown, and labels the type of tale which contains this combination, after its best-known manifestation in the legend of the foundation of Rome, the

Romulus Type. Dunn notes that the Romulus Type is not common in folktale, but is best represented in romance, legend and myth; in addition to that of Romulus and Remus, he cites legends about Sargon, Cyrus, Zoroaster and Wolfdietrich.

A third ubiquitous motif which is also prominent in our poem is that of the Helpful Animal. The werwolf saves William from his uncle's plot by abducting him, he engineers his discovery by the emperor and faithfully aids the eloped lovers, attending to their needs and rescuing them from manifold dangers. Dunn (1960:19-20) refers us to ten motif-numbers in Thompson's *Index* which are relevant here.

Tibbals (1903-4) and Hibbard (1924:217) argue that the real hero of our story is not William, but Alphouns, and that the werwolf story is central to its plot. McKeehan (1926), however, rightly rejects this view. However important a rôle the werwolf may play, it is the story of William which forms the nucleus of the romance; he is constantly 'on the stage', whereas the werwolf remains in the background during long stretches of the narrative.

6. William and Melior escape from the Roman imperial court disguised as white bears; later they discard the bearskins and don deerskins provided by the werwolf. When they have arrived at Palermo, and the queen of Sicily sets out to make contact with the disguised lovers, she also dons a deerskin; but the poet no more than vaguely hints at her reasons for assuming this disguise. As Dunn (1960:24) emphasises, the animal skins remain disguises which the personages can put on and take off at will; they do not actually transform them into bears or deer, although the poem often refers to the disguised lovers as *þe beres* or *þe hert* and *þe hinde*. Tibbals (1903-4) argues that the disguises are a kind of rationalised transformations, and that in earlier, more 'primitive', versions of the story they must have been actual transformations. In support of Tibbals' hypothesis we might cite a story referred to in Chevalier (1965:163, *s.v. cerf*), that St Patrick changed himself and his companions into deer to escape the traps set for them by a king. It remains strange, however, that the same romance should contain both an actual transformation and a rationalised one. Although, as Simms has pointed out, the werwolf transformation and the disguises, as well as several of the dreams in which personages in the story are represented by animals, are thematically related in that they exemplify the loss of human form and are concerned with human and bestial nature, it seems better to regard disguise and transformation as distinct narrative motifs each with their own history[11].

Kane (1951:51) considers the bearskin disguise 'an offence against simple physical probability so outrageous that by comparison with it even the benevolent werewolf . . . seems credible and acceptable', and argues that it is 'hard to swallow' precisely because it is not a supernatural marvel but a merely physical improbability. Yet the bearskin disguise seems less unconvincing than the deer disguises, whose physical improbability is even more glaring. However, we may doubt whether the medieval and early modern audiences of the various versions of the story would have responded in the same way. To them disguise was a familiar narrative motif, although disguise in animal skins is admittedly less frequent. They may have been more readily prepared to accept the story on its own terms than modern critics or readers can be. Moreover, that a bearskin disguise is not altogether so improbable as Kane makes it out to be, is shown by a remarkable incident which was reported in the Dutch daily press late in December 1981. Children had told the police that they had seen a large bear in Hackney Marshes near London. A thorough search by the police remained fruitless; but the next day a man telephoned *The Sun* to say that he had dressed himself in a bearskin suit by way of a practical joke.

The choice of bear and deer skins is reasonably well motivated. Alisaundrine considers bears most similar to man (1694) and most *grisli* (1687); and deer are the most likely large animals that a werwolf might, with some willing suspension of disbelief, be believed to kill. It seems somewhat less likely, however, that bearskins should be present in a kitchen, and the presence of *white* bearskins is even more difficult to accept. Perhaps the colour white is here a reminiscence of the priestly, druidical and magical associations of this colour in the Celtic world (Chevalier 1969: 109, *s.v. blanc*).

Kane (1951:52) considers the possibility that the poet's sense of the ridiculous is responsible for his acceptance of the animal disguises. But it is not the animal disguises as such that provoke mirth in the poem (1725-44, 3110-92), but the thematically important contrast between the ferocious animal appearance and the gentle humanity of the characters who adopt the disguise[12].

7. Two of our poem's personages possess magical skills, queen Braunde of Spain and Melior's confidante Alisaundrine. The queen is *a worchipful ladi* (115), but in her youth she had learned *miche schame* (117), because she was well versed in *wicchecraft* and *nigramauncy* (118-20). The king's second wife, she attempts to secure the succession for her own son by getting rid of her stepson. Her magical actions are described in unusual detail. She prepares an ointment *bi enchaunmens of charmes* (136-7) and anoints the child so that he is transformed into a werwolf. The narrator condemns her action in no uncertain terms: when she thinks of how sad it is that her own son will never succeed to be king, she does so *as a mix* (125), and when she prepares the magic ointment he curses her: *þat evel chaunche hire tide!* (137). Yet, in spite of her wicked crafts and her atrocious crime against her stepson, she retains the dignity that befits her royal station. The messengers who bring her the summons to come to Palermo to disenchant the werwolf address her with due respect, although they lapse into *þou / þe / þi* when referring to her witchcraft and her transformation of Alphouns, and when reporting William's threats (4248-65). She obeys

with a good grace, and promptly travels to Sicily to undo her earlier crime. In Sicily she is again received with due ceremony. After the werwolf's attack, she shows herself repentant and confesses her misdeed (4387-4403). She finally restores the werwolf to human form with the help of a ring with a magical stone which protects the wearer against witchcraft, poison and an unsuitable marriage. The ring is hung round the werwolf's neck, but in order to effect the disenchantment, she also needs a long reading from a book of magic.

When she has disenchanted her stepson, she shows sensitivity and tact towards Alphouns in a situation full of embarrassment. She fully understands his shame about his nakedness, and makes arrangements for him to be clothed ceremonially in knightly garments. We may conclude that she is not utterly depraved, but an erring woman who has misused her dangerous and morally reprehensible skill, and who, when forced by circumstances, acknowledges her sin and makes every effort to undo its effects.

Alisaundrine's magical arts, on the other hand, are used only to bring the lovers together. She herself speaks of a *craft þat ich kan* (635) through which she will cure her mistress Melior, if she can find a certain *grece* (636). The poet-narrator tells us a little later that she knew much *of charmes and of chantemens to schewe harde castis* (654), but nowhere does he use such terms as *nigramauncy* or *wicchecraft* to refer to Alisaundrine's magical skills. Her *craft* enables her to cause William to dream that Melior visits him in his room and asks for his love (655 ff.), and later, that Melior comes to him in the garden and offers him a rose (862-6). These are Alisaundrine's only magical actions; the *grece* that she needs to cure Melior is not a literal herb[13]), but, as becomes clear to us through later more or less oblique references (799 ff., 1030), stands for William's love. But her craft also gives her remarkable powers of foresight and enables her to know in advance that she and Melior will meet William in the palace garden (813-15).

Alisaundrine's magical arts have been given her by the English adapter; in the French poem she is merely, what she is also in the English version, a faithful confidante, with more practical shrewdness than her mistress, and always actively concerned for the happiness and the safety of William and Melior. It is remarkable that although procuring and matchmaking are among the activities usually associated with witches, and although she is given magical skills, the poet never speaks of her as a witch; on the contrary, she is wholly good, and in the end she is rewarded, although her own wishes have not been consulted in the matter, with a princely marriage.

Notes

1. For French examples, see Dunn (1960:84-5). In English we have *Ipomedon, Robert of Sicily, The Three Kings' Sons* and *Roswall and Lillian*. The story of the 14th-century Dutch play of *Esmoreit* is also set in Sicily.

2. See Dunn (1960:39-85), who gives a detailed study of the setting of the story of the French poem.

3. The following historical synopsis is derived from Mack Smith (1968), Norwich (1970) and Dunn (1960); see also Bezzola (1958-63).

4. More possible parallels are discussed by Dunn (1960).

5. Alfonso was a frequent name in the various royal houses of Spain.

6. In a short article published in 1948, Dunn called attention to a sculpture in the cloister of Monreale Cathedral, which might be interpreted as representing William and his guardian werwolf.

7. Marie clearly regards the *rage* of the werwolf, during which he eats men, as a temporary state.

8. I quote from the edition of Marie de France's *Lais* by Ewert (1944); the older edition by Warnke (1885) is also still valuable. For *Melion* I have used Grimes (1928); a more recent edition is in Tobin (1976).

9. Abducting animals may belong to many other species, such as lions, griffins, apes, etc.

10. In Trevisa's translation (ed. Seymour *et al.* 1975), lib. XVIII, cap. lxxi, *He is ful hardy and loueþ wel to play wiþ a childe. If he may take him he sleeþ him afterward and eteþ him atte laste.* Aristotle is cited as authority.

11. See also Dunn (1960:136 footnote), who cites Thompson's motif K 521.1.

12. On the absurdity of the disguises and the poet's humorous treatment of the theme, see also Mehl (1967:206).

13. Kooper (forthcoming), partly following Simms (1969), points out its 'plainly sexual connotations', which ll. 637-41 make quite unmistakable. Note also William's shame when Alisaundrine slily inquires whether Melior has got the herb (1035).

FURTHER READING

Criticism

Dunn, Charles W. "*Guillaume de Palerne* and Monreale Sculpture." *Mediaeval Studies* X (1948): 215-16.

> Discusses a sculpture group, carved circa 1174-1189, on the capitals of the Benedictine cloister of Monreale Cathedral. One of the sculptures resembles a legend upon which *Guillaume de Palerne* may be based.

Foster, Edward E. and Gail Gilman. "The Text of *William of Palerne*." *Neuphilologische Mitteilungen* LXXIV, No. 3 (1973): 480-95.

Analyzes various editions of the text of *William of Palerne*, including that of Walter W. Skeat, and proposes a number of emendations.

Nicholson, Edward W. B. "An Unknown English Prose-Version of 'William of Parlene.'" *The Academy* 43, No. 1088 (11 March 1893): 223.

States that a fragment of an English prose version of *William of Palerne,* printed circa 1520, has been discovered.

Zoroaster
628 B.C.?-551 B.C.?

(Also known as Zarathustra.) Founder of the Persian-Iranian national religion and hymn writer.

INTRODUCTION

As the founder of what has been described as either a qualified monotheistic or a dualistic religion, Zoroaster and his doctrines stood in stark contrast to the polytheism of the contemporary Indo-Iranian religious traditions that surrounded him. The hymns of praise he composed, known as the *Gathas,* may have been either dictated by him or transcribed by his disciples. From his *Gathas* developed a religious tradition and scriptures that eventually took a form very different from what Zoroaster originally conceived. The Avesta—which includes Zoroaster's *Gathas* as well as commentary and other scriptures—became the text of Zoroastrians and, in its later editions, known as the Younger or Later Avesta, preached a ritualistic polytheism. Zoroastrian practice subsequently reverted to a dualistic theology. Modern practitioners of the faith are torn between orthodoxy and a purist reform movement advocating a strict return to the *Gathas* as the basis of faithful worship.

BIOGRAPHICAL INFORMATION

Extremely little is known about Zoroaster's life. His birth and death dates are conjecture based on assumption and late Zoroastrian tradition, which date Zoroaster 258 years before Alexander the Great. It has been suggested that this date refers to the year Zoroaster converted King Vishtaspa, when, as tradition has it, Zoroaster was forty-two years old. Just as little is known about where Zoroaster was born and lived, although many scholars agree that he lived and taught in eastern Iran, and linguistic evidence appears to support this contention.

MAJOR WORKS

Zoroaster's *Gathas,* critics believe, dates from about the seventh century B.C. The earliest manuscripts of the Avesta, which contains the *Gathas,* date from the thirteenth century, although the majority of extant manuscripts date from the seventeenth century. In seventeen metrical stanzas, sixteen of which are attributed to Zoroaster, the prophet presents anthems of divine praise. The hymns are arranged into five groups, based on meter. The god worshiped by Zoroaster in the *Gathas* is known as Ahura Mazdah, who is identified with a number of emanations or

entities, including a Holy Spirit and a Fiendish Spirit, drawn respectively to Truth and Falsehood. It is the close identification of Ahura Mazdah and the Holy Spirit, as well as the opposition between Ahura Mazdah and Angra Mainyu, the spirit of falsehood and evil, that have led to Zoroastrianism's being described as a dualistic religion. Additionally, the Later Avesta translated the Gathic and Avestic dialects of the earlier texts into the middle Persian dialect, Pahlavi, and the names of Ahura Mazdah and Angra Mainyu were replaced with Ormuzd and Ahriman. Conflict between the two was emphasized, which again contributed to the characterization of Zoroastrianism as dualistic in nature. Other elements of Zoroastrian doctrine include the bestowing of free will on humanity by Ahura Mazdah and man's subsequent responsibility for his own fate, as well as the use of fire as the symbol of truth.

CRITICAL RECEPTION

Critical analyses of Zoroastrianism in general and of the *Gathas* in particular have focused largely on the nature of the faith as originally outlined by Zoroaster in the *Gathas* and on the development of the faith into its later and modern forms. John W. Waterhouse details the way the Avesta was compiled, beginning with the *Gathas* and the writings of the faithful who immediately followed Zoroaster, through the layers of editing, elaboration, and commentary on these earlier writings. Waterhouse also discusses the structure of the *Gathas* and the Avesta. R. C. Zaehner surveys what little is known about Zoroaster's life and briefly discusses the influence of Zoroastrianism on Judaism, noting that in both faiths there exists a system of rewards and punishments for man's behavior, and an afterlife filled with either "bliss" or "woe" reserved for good and evil people. Zaehner then goes on to examine the primary characteristics of Zoroaster's doctrines. Like Zaehner, Richard N. Frye reviews the controversy over the dates affixed to Zoroaster's life and death. Frye comments on the differences between Zoroaster's message and the ancient beliefs out of which the faith arose. Additionally, Frye observes that Zoroaster's *Gathas* influenced the development of the epic tradition in Iran. Many critics study the way in which the beliefs of Zoroastrianism progressed from the faith professed by Zoroaster in the *Gathas* to the way it was presented in the Later Avesta. Ilya Gershevitch traces this development, demonstrating how the monotheistic/dualistic religion found in the *Gathas* was later practiced as a form of pagan polytheism, but then reverted to a system of belief in two deities, God and the devil. Gershevitch maintains that the Younger Avesta, which contains this mixture of monotheism, dualism, and polytheism, should be interpreted not as a religious system, but as an anthology of Old Iranian cults and folklore. Like Gershevitch, Cyrus R. Pangborn's main interest is in the evolution of Zoroastrianism. Pangborn studies in particular the transition from Zoroaster's qualified monotheism to the ritualistic polytheism of the Later Avesta and to the subsequent practice of theological dualism. Jal Dastur Cursetji Pavry similarly outlines the development of the religion of Zoroastrianism, but focuses on the style and structure of the *Gathas*. Noting that the language Zoroaster uses is archaic and quite different from that used in the rest of the Avesta, Pavry goes on to describe the style of the *Gathas* as "exceedingly lofty," and the ideas expressed there as abstract in nature. George G. Cameron likewise studies the literary elements of the *Gathas*, examining Zoroaster's use of metaphor. Explaining that Zoroaster's references to the cow, pasturage, and herdsmen have been interpreted literally by followers and critics, Cameron argues that such references should be viewed as figures of speech, in the same way that Christian texts employ the shepherd/flock metaphor to refer to Christ and his followers.

PRINCIPAL WORKS

Gathas (hymns) 7th century B.C.

Principal English Translations

The Gathas (translated by J. H. Moulton in *Early Zoroastrianism*) 1913

CRITICISM

Jal Dastur Cursetji Pavry (essay date 1929)

SOURCE: An introduction to *The Zoroastrian Doctrine of a Future Life: From Death to the Individual Judgement*, second edition, 1929. Reprint AMS Press, 1965, pp. 1-8.

[*In the following essay, originally published in 1929, Pavry discusses the form and style of Zoroaster's* Gathas *and observes that according to Zoroaster's doctrines, salvation is achieved through faith and works.*]

> *Yōi mōi ahmāi səraošəm dan čayascā*
> *upā.jimən haurvātā aməṛətātā vanhəuš*
> *mainyəuš šyaoθanāiš.*
>
> —GĀTHĀ USHTAVAITĪ, Ys. 45. 5.

ZARATHUSHTRA'S MESSAGE OF IMMORTALITY.

'All those who will give hearing for Me unto this one (the Prophet) will come unto Salvation and Immortality through the works of the Good Spirit'—such was the promise given by Ahura Mazdāh to those who accepted the Religion of Zarathushtra, the Prophet of Ancient Iran, and such were the words in which the Supreme Deity vouchsafed the revelation to him. Divinely inspired and strongly convinced of his own mission, the Prophet (*maθran*) delivered his message (*dūtya*) to mankind nearly three thousand years ago. It was a message full of hope for the future. It throbbed with a pious expectation of a world perfected in the present life and to be realized in all its fulness in the world beyond. We can understand the echo which it found in the heart of the folk when he appeared as the spiritual leader (*ratav*) of Old Iran in the bygone ages of history. Nor has its ringing truth been forgotten today.

Zarathushtra's pre-eminent concern with the bearing of eschatology on conduct can easily be seen from a study of the **Gāthās.** Faith and works form the foundation of the doctrine of salvation in the religion of Ancient Iran. A belief in the freedom of the will, in the acknowledgment of man's ability to choose the right or to choose the wrong, and in his consequent responsibility to his Creator, lies at the basis of the moral and ethical system of the Zoroastrian religion, which above all emphasizes the existence of the two warring principles of Good and Evil, Light and Darkness. To guide man to the choice of right, and thus to assure his gaining eternal salvation, was the very purpose of Zarathushtra's mission upon earth.

The very words 'Salvation' (*haurvatāt*), or the essence of wholesome completeness in a spiritual sense—that personified 'saving health' with all the connotation of the term as used in Christianity—and 'Immortality' (*amərətāt*) in the life eternal have already struck this note. Not this world alone, which the Prophet sought to improve through his teachings, but the outlook for a world regenerate, made perfect and renewed (*fərašəm kərənāun ahūm, fərašōtəma,* etc.), formed the burden of his *Gāthās*, 'Hymns' or 'Psalms.' He visualized all this as the sovereign rule, dominion, and power, 'the Kingdom' (*xšaθra*) to come, when mankind, regenerate and individually judged, should bring to pass the final Renovation (*frašōkrti*) of the world. As a 'Savior,' or, perhaps more literally, as 'He who will be the Benefactor' (*saošyant*), Zarathushtra came forward with his message of endless hope and cheerful optimism, which has never failed to animate the hearts of his followers. It may be that in later times the religion which he founded looked forward to the fulfilment of his prophetic view through the appearance in successive millenniums of three Saoshyants spiritually born of his seed, and in many other points gave more concrete form to his ideal conceptions; but, as we study the sources, from his own words preserved in the *Gāthās,* the *ipsissima verba* of the Prophet, down through the centuries, we shall always find the belief in the future life and the heavenly world present as one of the main currents in Zoroastrain thought.

The sources in general.

The sacred writings of the Zoroastrian Faith, from the earliest texts to the latest works that deal with the Religion, bear abundant witness to what has been stated above, as will be shown in the course of the following investigation. The examination is naturally based upon the texts comprised in the Avestan canon itself, and upon the traditional literature in Pahlavi as developed in Sasanian times and afterwards, supplemented later by the religious writings in Parsi-Persian.

It were to be wished that we had some material to add from the Old Persian inscriptions of the Achaemenian Kings, since these monuments in stone present records which are most nearly akin to the Avesta in religion and language.[1] We do not find in them, however, any mention of a future life; the blessings which are prayed for and the imprecations which are invoked are purely of a temporal character.[2] The absence of specific reference to the life hereafter may be due perhaps to the official character of these records (*haⁿdugā*) and to their limited extent.

The silence of these official records would not be so significant if we felt assured that we could accept as corroborative testimony certain references made by Greek writers to the religious beliefs of the Achaemenian rulers,[3]

but these do not concern this particular part of our study and are reserved for treatment later.

It is clear in any case, however, that the later Greek authors were acquainted with the doctrine of the Frashōkereti,[4] but since again these references relate rather to eschatology proper than to the immediate fate of the soul, they may simply be mentioned here, but reserved for presentation elsewhere. Laying aside such classical evidences, we may now turn to the direct Zoroastrian sources themselves, beginning with the *Gāthās.*

The Gathas.

The *Gāthās,* as being the oldest part of the Avesta and embodying the veritable words of Zarathushtra (seventh century B.C. or earlier),[5] naturally form the starting-point from which to proceed in our research. These *Gāthās,* 'hymns, psalms,' are akin to the verses of the Vedic bards. They contain the teachings of the Prophet, summed up in metrical stanzas which he composed as a nucleus of his discourses.[6] These anthems of divine praise are always spoken of as 'the Holy *Gāthās*' (*gāθa ašaonīš*) from an early date (cf. for example, Ys. 55. 1). Their language is more archaic and somewhat different from that used elsewhere in the Avesta. The style of expression is exceedingly lofty, and the ideas are prevailingly abstract in character, so that the interpretation of some of the passages affords great difficulty.

The *Gāthās,*[7] comprising seventeen hymns in all, are arranged in five groups, the *Gāthā Ahunavaitī* (Ys. 28-34), *Ushtavaitī* (Ys. 43-46), *Spentā Mainyū* (Ys. 47-50), *Vohukhshathrā* (Ys. 51), and *Vahishtōishti* (Ys. 53). This grouping as a pentad is based on the scheme of the meters employed; we have no knowledge, however, of what the original order of the seventeen may have been. In any case, their importance is recognized by their position as the very center of the whole Yasna.

Between the first two of these Gāthic groups is interpolated the so-called Yasna Haptanghāiti, or 'Yasna of the Seven Chapters' (Ys. 35-42). Its language is as archaic as that of the *Gāthās,* but the form of composition is almost entirely prose. In age these 'Seven Chapters' would rank next after the *Gāthās,* but their special contents yield little if anything for the purpose of our present investigation.

The Later Avesta.

Though the *Gāthās* are preponderantly eschatological in character, they deal much more with principles than with details. The later Avestan texts, sometimes termed the Younger Avesta, consequently serve to develop the picture outlined in those older documents. The Later Avesta, or remaining portion of the sacred canon so far as extant,[8] may be classified, according to the commonly adopted arrangement, into the following divisions, or books. First in order comes the Yasna, 'sacrifice, worship,' the chief liturgical work of the sacred canon. It consists principally of ascriptions of praise and prayer, and, together with the

Gāthās and the Yasna Haptanghāiti, it comprises seventy-two chapters. Then comes the Visprat (or Vīspered, as it is sometimes called), the book of invocations and offerings to 'all the lords' (Av. *vīspe ratavō*). It consists of additions to portions of the Yasna, which it resembles in language and in form, and comprises twenty-four chapters. Third in order come the Yashts (Av. *yešti,* 'worship by laudation'), consisting of twenty-one hymns in praise of various divinities or 'worshipful ones' (Av. *yazata*). Together with these Yashts may be grouped certain minor texts, consisting of brief prayers and constituting what is called the Khvartak Apastāk (or Khorda Avesta). The last book of the sacred canon is the Vidēvdāt (or the Vendīdād, as it is commonly known), 'law against the demons,' a priestly code in twenty-two chapters. Besides the above texts there are a number of fragments, which are pieces surviving from the other Nasks, or divisions of the Avesta, no longer extant. The most important of these fragments, in the present connection, are those from the Hadhōkht Nask, and what is generally known as the Vishtāsp Yasht. Of minor importance are the Avestan quotations contained in the Nīrangastān, the Aogemadaēchā, and the Vicharkart i Dēnīk.

Although the books of the Later Avesta differ greatly in theme and style, they may be regarded in general as contemporaneous with the Achaemenian rule (B.C. 558-323) in Persia, although some portions may belong to the succeeding centuries.

THE PAHLAVI LITERATURE.

The subject of our study is developed further in the Pahlavi books, which belong mainly to the Sasanian period (A.D. 226-651), when Zoroastrianism enjoyed both material prosperity and a spiritual revival.

The Pahlavi literature[9] may here be conveniently divided into two classes. First, Pahlavi translations (or versions) of the Avestan texts, intermingled with Pahlavi commentary. The work of translating the scriptures into the current idiom may already have begun during the latter part of the Parthian period. (B.C. 250-A.D. 226), and must have been completed at the latest during the reign of Shahpuhar II (A.D. 309-380), when the final revision of the Avestan texts was made by Āturpāt i Mahraspandān. Second, independent Pahlavi treatises on matters connected with religion. The importance of these latter Pahlavi texts can hardly be overestimated. They often preserve old material no longer extant in its Avestan form, and thus supplement the lacunae in the earlier doctrinal scheme, besides elaborating and adding to the data already found in the Avesta. It may be noted further that some of these Pahlavi works were either completed, though begun earlier, or written in their entirety during the rule of the Abbasids (A.D. 749-847), after the downfall of the Sasanian Empire. Additions seem to have been made to some Pahlavi works as late as the end of the eleventh century.

Among these independent Pahlavi treatises the most important for our investigation are (1) the Bundahishn,[10]

'creation of the beginning,' or 'original creation,' a sort of Iranian Genesis and Revelation, based upon the old Dāmdāt Nask of the Avesta; (2) the Dēnkart, 'acts of the religion,' an encyclopaedia of Zoroastrianism; (3) the Artāk Vīrāz Nāmak, 'book of Saint Vīrāz,' or a Dantesque vision of Heaven and Hell; (4) the Dātastān i Dēnīk, 'religious ordinances or opinions,' together with (5) the Pahlavi Rivāyat accompanying this theological treatise; (6) the Dātastān i Mēnūk i Khrat, 'ordinances of the Spirit of Wisdom'; (7) the Shāyist nē-Shāyist, 'the proper and the improper'; and (8) the Shkand-vimānīk Vichār, 'doubt-dispelling expositions.' Of minor importance for our purpose, and seldom cited, are (9) the Handarz i Āturpāt i Mahraspandān, 'admonitions of Āturpāt, son of Mahraspand'; (10) the Handarz i Hōsrav i Kavātān, 'admonitions of Hōsrav, son of Kavāt'; (11) the Ganj i Shāhīkān, 'treasure of the royal depository,' a book of good counsel, containing gems of wisdom; and finally (12) the Vichītakīhā i Zātsparam, 'selections of Zātsparam.'

THE PARSI-PERSIAN WRITINGS.

In surveying the literary material we must include the priestly writings of later times (dating after the eleventh century), the so-called Modern-Persian Zoroastrian literature of the Parsis.[11] The principal and doubtless earliest book among these is the prose Sad Dar, a treatise on 'a hundred subjects' connected with the Parsi religion. There exist two metrical versions of the Sad Dar, known as 'the short-meter version' (composed in 1496) and 'the long-meter version' (composed in 1605). The exact date of the writing of the prose Sad Dar has not yet been ascertained, but we can safely conjecture that it was already a very old book when the metrical versions were composed.[12] The second in order is the Sad Dar Bundahish, or the 'Bundahish of a hundred chapters' (composed some time before 1528), detailing in a hundred sections the chief customs and religious laws of the Parsis.[13] Both these treatises are very often quoted in the later Persian Rivāyats, or collections of religious traditions (compiled between the years 1478 and 1773 A.D.).[14] The most important of these latter writings, which stand third in order both as regards age and as regards contents, is the Rivāyat of Dārāb Hormazdyār. It may be noted that it is the most complete and systematically arranged among the so-called classified Rivāyats. It was compiled in A.D. 1679, and a Gujarati version of it was made by the author at a later date.

PRESENT-DAY CEREMONIES.

Further light may be thrown on the whole subject by the discussions added here and there to bring out the significance of certain of Zarathushtra's tenets which are observed today by the Parsis in their ceremonies connected with the dead, and which give assurance of life eternal in Paradise to the faithful who follow the religion of Zarathushtra, the Prophet of Ancient Iran.

NOTE ON THE TRANSCRIPTION OF IRANIAN WORDS

The system here adopted for the scientific transliteration of Avestan, Pahlavi, and Modern Persian words is substantially that employed by various scholars in the *Grundriss der iranischen Philologie* and in particular by Bartholomae in his *Altiranisches Wörterbuch* (see especially his introduction, page 23).

This exact mode of transcription is used to represent Iranian words when quoted from the texts translated by the author or when adduced in the footnotes. In these cases the words are printed in italics. In order to facilitate pronunciation, a slightly different method of transcription is followed when Iranian proper names and titles of books occur in continuous English text and are printed in roman type (š being represented by *sh*, č by *ch*, etc.).

Two points are particularly to be noted in connection with the transliteration of Pahlavi. First, the titles of Pahlavi works are uniformly given in the old Pahlavi form rather than in a form inclining to Modern Persian (e.g. *Vičarkart i Dēnīk* instead of *Vijirkard i Dēnīg*). Secondly, the Huzvārish words occurring in the Pahlavi text are invariably replaced (in accordance with the principles enunciated by Bartholomae in *Indogermanische Forschungen*, vol. 38, page 39) by the Pāzand equivalents which those wordforms were intended to represent.

Notes

1. See Clemen, *Nachrichten pers. Religion,* p. 54-94; cf. further Jackson in *GIrPh.* 2. 687-693, and also Gray in *ERE.* 1. 69-73.

2. For example, the Behistan inscription of Darius, col. 4. 54-59: 'may Auramazdā be thy friend (*dauštā*) and thy family be numerous, and mayest thou live long (*dargam jīvā*). . . . (But, if wicked,) may Auramazdā be thy smiter (*jaⁿtā*) and there be no family to thee.' Cf. also Bh. col. 4. 73-80.

3. Cf., for example, the words of Prexaspes as recorded by Herodotus (3.62), see Clemen, *op. cit.* p. 123; or again the speech placed on the lips of the dying Cyrus the Great by Xenophon in the *Cyropaedia* (8. 7. 17-24), see Clemen, *op. cit.* p. 89.

4. Among such references would be Theopompus (flourished B.C. 338) as quoted by Diogenes Laertius (flourished c. A.D. 210), *Prooem.* 6, 9; Plutarch (c. A.D. 46-120), *Isis and Osiris,* ch. 47; Aeneas of Gaza (flourished at the beginning of the sixth century), *Theophrastus,* 77; also others. Cf. Jackson in *GIrPh.* 2. 684; Clemen, *op. cit.* p. 123, 128-131, 167-169, 215; also Moulton, *EZ.* p. 415-417.

5. For views regarding the much-discussed question of the date of Zarathushtra see Jackson, *Zoroaster, the Prophet of Ancient Iran,* p. 150-178 (New York, 1899), who makes a strong case in favor of accepting the date that stands in the Parsi tradition, namely B.C. 660—583. So also Meillet, *Trois conférences sur les Gāthā* (Paris, 1925), p. 21-32. Hertel, in a recent monograph, *Die Zeit Zoroasters* (Leipzing, 1924), advances arguments in support of a still later date, according to which (p. 47)

Zarathushtra must have been alive in 522 B.C. and probably after that date also. Charpentier, in *BSOS.* (London, 1925), 3. 747-755, refutes this 'new theory' and is in favor of a much earlier date, namely (p. 754) 'somewhere in the neighborhood of 1000-900 B.C.—or perhaps even somewhat earlier.' This he holds 'with Eduard Meyer, Andreas, Clemen, Bartholomae, and others.' See especially Bartholomae, *Zarathuštra's Leben und Lehre,* p. 10-11 (Heidelberg, 1924), and compare Geldner in *Encyclopaedia Britannica,* 11th ed., 21. 246, but particularly 28. 1041.

6. The theory that the Gāthās presuppose a frame-work of prose no longer extant is mentioned by Jackson, *Av. Grammar,* introd. p. 18; see also Geldner in *GIrPh.* 2. 29; Bartholomae, *Die Gatha's des Awesta,* introd. p. 4-5; and cf. especially Meillet, *Trois Conférences sur les Gāthā,* p. 39-52.

7. For a detailed description of the contents, arrangement, extent, and character of the Gāthās and the Later Avesta, see Geldner, 'Awestalitterature,' in *GIrPh.* 2. 1-53.

8. See above, page 4, note 7.

9. For a detailed description of the extent and character of the Pahlavi literature and the later Parsi-Persian writings, see West, 'Pahlavi Literature,' in *GIrPh.* 2. 75-129.

10. There exist two recensions of the Bundahishn, one Indian and the other Iranian; see below, page 12, note 16.

11. See above, page 6, note 9.

12. For additional details as to this book, see below, page 18.

13. For further remarks, see below, page 18.

14. See also below, page 19, note 48.

Abbreviations and Symbols

Bh. Behistan inscription of Darius. . . .

BSOS. Bulletin of the School of Oriental Studies, London Institution. . . .

Enc. Brit. Encyclopaedia Britannica. . . .

ERE. Encyclopaedia of Religion and Ethics, ed. Hastings. . . .

EZ. Early Zoroastrianism (Moulton) . . .

GIrPh. Grundriss der iranischen Philologie. . . .

Bibliography

. . . Clemen, Carl. Die griechischen und lateinischen Nachrichten über die persische Religion. Giessen, 1920. . . .

Geldner, Karl F. Article 'Zoroaster.' In *Encyclopaedia Britannica,* 11th ed., vol. 28, p. 1039-1043. . . .

Gray, Louis H. Article 'Life and Death (Iranian).' In *ERE.* 8. 37. . . .

Jackson A. V. Williams. Die iranische Religion. In *GIrPh.* 2. 612-708, Strassburg, 1903. Pages 683-687. . . .

Meillet, A. Trois Conférences sur les Gâthâ de l'Avesta. Paris, 1925. (*Annales du Musée Guimet, Bibliothèque de Vulgarisation,* vol. 44.) . . .

Moulton, J. H. Early Zoroastrianism. London, 1913. Pages 154-181. . . .

John W. Waterhouse (essay date 1934)

SOURCE: "The Scriptures of Zoroastrianism" in *Zoroastrianism,* Epworth Press, 1934, pp. 42-56.

[*In the essay below, Waterhouse examines the process by which the Avesta, including Zoroaster's* Gathas, *was compiled and discusses the structure of each.*]

The discovery of the key to the understanding of the Avesta, the Bible of the Parsis, is a romantic story. In the year 1754, a young Frenchman, Anquetil du Perron, saw a few pages of a manuscript in an unknown Oriental tongue, in a library at Paris. His interest and curiosity were so awakened that he determined at all costs to decipher the writing. He thereupon joined the French East India Company as a ranker, and embarked on a ship bound for Bombay, the centre of the Parsi community in India. After a hazardous journey, he reached his destination, and the French authorities honoured his purpose by releasing him from duty, and by granting him a certain amount of support. Although at first du Perron could find no one to teach him the language, eventually, through bribing an erudite priest, or Dastur, he acquired the requisite knowledge for his task, and also secured nearly two hundred manuscripts. The Parsis were very suspicious of the intruder, and he had to return to France to do his work of translation. This occupied du Perron ten years, but in the year 1771 he was able to publish a volume which he called *Zend-Avesta, Ouvrage de Zoroastre.* That this title was misleading will be shown later, but du Perron had rendered magnificent pioneer service to Iranian scholarship. The reception given in Europe, however, to his work was by no means favourable, as the Persian scholars of the day, such as Sir William Jones, did not believe in a separate Avestan dialect, which was postulated by du Perron.

Although the discoverer was right in his assumption, the translation he then made cannot now be relied upon, as it contains many inaccuracies and reflects in parts his somewhat credulous disposition. Nevertheless, it was to be expected that du Perron's work would be inaccurate as the Parsis themselves knew the translation of their own Books only through the medium of a disused language, Pahlavi. The verbal traditions, however, that du Perron had received from his Parsi instructor were of great reliability. Many of the names of ancient Persian deities, hitherto unknown,

were revealed, and most valuable light was thrown on old customs and ceremonial. But the authorities decried du Perron's work as a hoax, and naturally it was pointed out that the contents of the Avesta to a large extent did not accord with what was known of the teaching of Zoroaster. The lack of resemblance between the Avestan language and modern Persian was held to be sufficient reason for denying the genuineness of what du Perron had produced. Although du Perron's work gained some credence in France, the general opinion of European scholarship was hostile to it.

Some fifty years later, another Frenchman, Eugene Burnouf, who believed in the so-called Avestan tongue, carried out further research into the philology of the language, and corrected many of du Perron's obvious mistakes. Burnouf did valuable work on the grammatical side, but did little to sift the manuscripts before him as to relative importance in matter of date or doctrine. It was, moreover, not yet realized that the **Gathas** were the only likely relics of the writings of Zoroaster himself. But Burnouf had made possible the work of many subsequent investigators such as Bopp, the grammarian, Brockhaus, the lexicographer, and Westergaard, who published a monumental compendium of the Parsi religion and literature. These and many others have presented to us through their researches both in Sanskrit and Pahlavi, a fairly reliable text of the Avesta. Perhaps the most comprehensive translation yet undertaken, however, is that by James Darmesteter and L. H. Mills, in the *Sacred Books of the East.* But this translation cannot be taken as final, as much has been added to the knowledge of the language since the work was undertaken. Of course, previous to the discoveries of du Perron, Europe had not been without Persian Books of great antiquity, but few could be understood. The statements of Greek and Roman writers concerning Zoroastrianism had been collated, and Thomas Hyde, a famous Oxford scholar of the early eighteenth century, had published a 'magnum opus' on the subject,[1] but it did not show much knowledge of the original sources.

Although the expression Zend Avesta is widely found, and was used originally by du Perron, it is not an accurate description of the Bible of the Persians, as the term means 'commentary on the Avesta.' The derivation of the term 'Avesta' is uncertain. It is possibly akin to 'Veda,' i.e. Knowledge, 'vista' being the past participle of the Sanskrit root 'vid,' to know. More generally it is taken as coming from an ancient Avestan form 'upasta' which means 'the original text,' or 'scriptures.' Since Zend means 'commentary,' Avesta, simply, is the better title. As we now have it, the Avesta is only a fragment—though substantial at that—of a much greater literature, a great deal of which, some say two thirds, has been either lost or destroyed. A very small amount belongs to the period of the Prophet himself, though Pliny attributed to him two million verses. Zoroaster's output may well have been considerably greater than the **Gathas:** such an estimate as

Pliny's, though of course absurd, affords, however, some indication of the immense labours of the followers of the Prophet.

The contents of the Avesta represent a long period of diverse development, and there are few religious Books in the world which present so many literary problems to the investigator. The original Avesta is said to have consisted of twenty one Nasks, or volumes, one for each word of the Ahuna Vairya formula (See ch. 1). These were divided into three sections, each of seven groups, containing an encyclopaedic account of Zoroastrian history, devotion and science. The 'science' was chiefly of an astronomical and astrological character. The Avesta was at first jealously guarded, and copies were preserved in the chief Fire Temples. The ravages of Alexander the Great (B.C. 330), however, were responsible for the loss and dislocation of a large number of Persian manuscripts, the nature of which can now be ascertained only through the evidence of those Books, such as the Dinkart, which contains summaries and quotations from the missing material. Diodorus the historian records that when Alexander burnt Persepolis, he put to death some of the leading scholars who lived there, and their manuscripts perished with them, as the Achaemenian stronghold was the repository of many Persian archives. The Arsacid king Valkhash (c. second century B.C.)[2] was probably the first to inaugurate a collation of the various scattered manuscripts, and also caused many oral traditions of Zoroastrianism to be committed to writing. But it is doubtful whether the priests of those times could compose in the same language as the original Avesta. It was not until Sassanian days (third and fourth centuries A.D.) that a comprehensive collection of Books was made. The first Sassanian monarch, Ardashir-i-Papakan, (226-240), by the help of his high priest, Tansar, produced a text of the Pahlavi writings. Shahpur I (A.D. 241-272) and Shahpur II (A.D. 309-380) were instrumental in gathering further texts from different parts of India and the Roman Empire. Adarbad Maraspand, the prime minister of Shahpur II, made an arrangement of all the resultant discoveries, and a Canon of Scripture was announced.

This Canon of Parsi scripture includes all that survives in an extinct language, Avestan, which few Oriental scholars can understand. In fact, very few Parsis know it, and many of the Zoroastrian priests of the present day are compelled to recite their sacred Books in words utterly meaningless both to them and to their listeners. The modern translations of the Avesta, accepted by the Parsis, are in part most inaccurate, and certain stereotyped and traditional interpretations are now accepted without question. The later Pahlavi writings have, for instance, seriously changed the names of many of the old religious terms of Persia, and the Pahlavi translations of the Avesta do scant justice to the greatness of the finer passages, especially in the *Gathas.* One result has been that Darmesteter's translation of the *Gathas,* founded largely on the Pahlavi, is rendered practically useless, as the translator did not rely on the Gathic Avestan, the only true text. Incidentally, Darmesteter relegated the whole Avesta to the period of the

Neo-Platonic literature, as he considered the religious allegories of the *Gathas* to resemble those of Philo. His argument was that, before the Greeks, there had been practically no philosophical development—a very hazardous hypothesis. Carnoy has aptly suggested that Darmesteter's mistake was due to his identifying ethical abstractions with philosophical concepts. That many of the writings are the product of activity in the Christian era will not be disputed, but the *Gathas,* Yashts and Vendidad are among the documents of far earlier origin. It is extremely difficult to assign dates to many parts of the Avesta, and sometimes the only reliable evidence that can be so used is internal. The style and metre of the contents are rough indication of the period to which they belong. Many of the texts, however, are corrupt. An exception to this is the text of the *Gathas.* The conclusion is that the Gathas were regarded as especially sacred, and have suffered little from editors. This strengthens our hypothesis that they represent the actual teaching of the great Prophet. In the later Books textual alterations abound, together with obvious blunders and intentional scribal glosses.

We have in the Avesta a library of Books which extends, like our own Bible, over a period of a thousand years. But revelation, in the Avesta, does not culminate at the end of the period as it does in our own Bible: generally speaking, the finest Avestan works are the earliest chronologically. The process of compilation of the Avesta was roughly as follows. The sayings of the Prophet and those who immediately followed him were the first to be recorded, and are found in a dialect called 'Gathic Avestan.' These records were then edited and elaborated by successive generations, who used practically the same language. In process of time there was necessitated a new explanation of the original sayings. This was supplied in a similar dialect, known to us as 'Younger Avestan,' and was called Zend. After another lapse of time, the old sayings and the commentary on them were looked upon as one, and equally sacred. But since the various forms of the Avestan language had become obsolete, another Zend was made on the extant scriptures, in Pahlavi, which was the ordinary tongue of Persia during the Sassanian era.

Finally, there was the Pazand, or re-exposition of the whole lot. When Zend is spoken of as a language to-day, Pahlavi is usually meant, because the Zend language, if ever it existed as a separate tongue, has dropped out of use. Originally the term Avesta was used only of the writings of the Prophet and those who were closely associated with the early propagation of the faith. Later on, a wider significance was adopted, to include the commentaries, and because of the increasing difficulty of sifting the wheat from the chaff, all the traditional writings became adorned with the same halo of sanctity. It was not generally known what was from Zoroaster and what was not, and there was no doctrine of degrees of inspiration. The ancient Greek and Roman writers, as well as the Persians themselves, ascribed a great deal that was obviously not Zoroaster's to his authorship. Just in the same way, Moses was long accredited with the account of his own death! The difficulties involved in the theory that Zoroaster was responsible for the bulk of the Avesta were overcome by the assumption that the Nasks were dictated to the Prophet, as they stand, through divine revelation. Thus chronological obstacles were neatly swept away, as God could dictate words and phrases appropriate to a generation to come, and was not limited to the vocabulary or thought-forms of Zoroaster.

There is no statement in the earliest Persian Books as to who transcribed the narrative of the experiences or message of Zoroaster. Unlike Muhammad, the Prophet of Iran does not seem to have been commanded to publish the visions he had received. It is possible that Zoroaster himself wrote nothing, but that his friends and disciples transcribed his sayings; parallels to this may be found in the composition of the Christian Gospels and the Vedic hymns. But there is an atmosphere of personal reminiscence in the *Gathas* which would suggest that the Prophet at least dictated some of the Yasnas. The oral tradition which is manifest in many portions of the Avesta is responsible for a certain amount of inaccuracy. Haug thinks that the majority of the Parsi scriptures were written down when their language was unintelligible to the scribes. Various additions to the manuscripts were made by the high priests in particular. In later days it was believed that the high priests, who claimed to be in the succession of Zoroaster, were given inspiration to interpret his mind without fail, and had authority to add to his writings. This may partly account for the tradition that Zoroaster was responsible for the whole of the Avesta.

The languages and dialects of the Avesta, which have been outlined, are all inter-related. The Avestan, in which the majority of the Books is written, is a very rich tongue, making especially effective usage of compound words which add colour and charm to the narrative. It belongs to the Aryan family of languages, and consequently has affinities with Greek, Latin, Sanskrit and Teutonic forms. Of these, it is perhaps closest to Sanskrit, as it is merely a different dialect of the Sanskrit in which the Vedic books are found. Haug maintains that the two dialects are as close as, for example, the Ionic and Doric dialects of Greek: 'As the Ionians, Dorians, Aetolians, &c., were different tribes of the Greek nation, whose general name was *Hellenes,* so the ancient Brahmans and Parsis were two tribes of the nation which is called *Aryas* both in the Veda and Zend-Avesta; the former may be compared with the Ionians, and the latter with the Dorians. . . . There can be no doubt that classical Sanskrit was formed long after the separation of the Iranians from the Hindus.'[3]

As to the relationship between the two main Avestan dialects there is considerable dispute. It is difficult even to prove that Pahlavi is less ancient than the Gathic, as the latter may just have been a tongue spoken in a different part of Iran. But grammatically, the Gathic is more primitive, and the bulk of evidence favours its greater antiquity. Unfortunately, we have not much knowledge of the grammar of either dialect, and since the original forms of many words are now beyond recall, any translation is bound to be inadequate. Because of this, we have to pardon the great variations in the rendering of the Avesta, which are at times at least disconcerting. When the translations of Moulton, Darmesteter, Haug and Spiegel, for instance, are compared, it is sometimes quite a task to recognize the same passage so variously translated! The available texts have, moreover, presented the greater difficulty to the translators in as much as many of the Parsis care little for the sense of the words in their scriptures, and are content if they are able to recite them.

In the Pahlavic sections of the Avesta, translation has been found easier, especially as there is a modern form of Pahlavi spoken to-day. The ancient form contained a number of Semitic words which had been incorporated during the period when Israel had close contacts with Persia; to which period reference will be made later. Modern Pahlavi, however, has assimilated Arabic forms to the general exclusion of the Semitic. A great need is for modern Parsi scholars to produce a critical edition of their own scriptures; too long have they relied on the researches of Europeans and Americans. It is reported that the Dasturs of Bombay are attempting this task, and it is to be hoped that their labours will bear quick fruition. Since the Great War, and the untimely death of James Hope Moulton, there has been very little work attempted in the realm of Iranian studies.

It now remains to describe and discuss briefly the contents of the extant Avesta, with some reference to the so-called 'deutero-canonical' literature. The Avesta proper contains the Yasna and *Gathas,* the Yashts, the Visperad, the Vendidad and a number of smaller Books and fragments. The *Gathas* are the most important part of the Yasna. They have been described as 'metrical sermons' and contain most of what is known of the teaching of Zoroaster himself. Their metre is not of a nature that lends itself to translation in English verse, and it is unfortunate that the remoteness of many of the Gathic allusions and the inadequacy of any rendering of them have put these remarkable poems out of the reach of the general reader, together with the rest of Persian poetry. There has, alas, been only one Persian poem which has made special appeal to the West—the *Rubáiyát* of Omar Khayyám. But this was largely due to the wonderful translation of Edward Fitz Gerald. Says Moulton: 'Would Omar have been heard of in English literary circles had (say) Carey translated him?'[4] But Omar comes from a period very different from that which is our present concern, for the date of the *Gathas* is something like three thousand years ago. Considering this vast age, it is more than remarkable that such fine literature, nobler by far than the later Avesta, should find birth in a primitive civilization. There is more colour and movement in the language of the *Gathas* than in the somewhat conventional phraseology of the subsequent Books, and the strong personality of the Prophet outstands through all these poems that tell the story of his ministry. Although their language is obscure, and the text mutilated, there remains, as Söderblom remarks, 'a notable sureness of style. Comparison with the Veda hymns of the earlier period leads us to suppose that the art of verse was highly developed even in Indo-Iranian times before the eastward bound Aryans had been split between India and Iran. Zarathushtra or his friends were able to move in this heavy, artificial armour, so to speak, and these queer, twisted, complicated, and abstruse expressions. From these complicated verses and stanzas we can picture a very early and simple civilization, and a burning prophetic zeal.'⁵ We need to remind ourselves that a simple civilization often may produce great poetry. Examples of this abound in the Old Testament, whilst Arab farmers and shepherds have shown no small poetic gifts.

The metre of the *Gathas* is very different from that of the later Avesta: Moulton likens it to that of *Hiawatha,* as it is also octosyllabic. One *Gatha,* however, is in prose. This is the Yasna haptanghaiti, or **Seven Chapter Gatha,** a collection of prayers addressed not only to Ahura, but to his surrounding Spirits (the Amesha Spentas) and the genii of the elements. In style and in doctrine this *Gatha* differs greatly from the others; it is later, and represents the trend of the faith after the death of the Prophet. The old Nature deities which Zoroaster had banished, here return, though Ahura Mazdah is still supreme. A parallel process which may be observed in the early history of Christianity: some of the dethroned pagan gods returned as Christian saints, with scarcely a change of name. Later still, when Zoroastrianism came under Magian influence, yet more banished deities were restored.

In all, the *Gathas* are seventeen hymns, or poems, and their arrangement is according to their metres, of which there are five. The first word in each section determines their name. The Ahuna Vairya formula, which has previously been referred to, is also appended to the *Gathas,* together with a few other passages especially suitable for repetition, such as the Ashem Vohu, a proverbial saying to the effect that Right rights itself.

The Yasna, of which the *Gathas* are a part, has seventy two chapters, and is a liturgical compendium meant to be used in connexion with the ceremonies connected with the drinking of the Haoma plant. There are three divisions in this Book: invocations, hymns and commentary. Some of these hymns are known as Yashts, and are dedicated to Angels. But there is also a separate Book of Yashts, comprised of twenty one poems of praise. Chief among the Angels, or Yazatas, are Mithra, Anahita and Sraosha. Some of these Yashts are very fine literature, but they are most unequal in merit. It is likely that many belong to the Achaemenian period, though they incorporate and adapt earlier material for purposes of worship under later conditions. The Visperad is included in the Yasna, and is a series of disconnected invocations to many deities—thus by derivation its name means 'to all the lords.' It personifies many of the heavenly bodies. The Vendidad means 'law against the demons,' and is a late Book dating from about the second century B.C. Many early legends are recorded in this work, such as the story of Yima, the Persian Noah. The story is also told of the temptation of Zoroaster to

worship the Daevas. Three chapters are devoted to instructions as to the way in which true Zoroastrians treat their dogs—as dogs are regarded as sacred creatures among the Parsis. There is also a list given of things clean and unclean, as touching ceremonial, and methods of avoiding defilement are specified in detail. This strange Book is mainly cast in dialogue form, the Prophet asking questions and receiving answers of Ahura. The above works, with the addition of various small fragments, complete the contents of the Avesta proper.

The deutero-canonical literature is written in 'Middle Persian,' or Pahlavi, which was the language of Persia between about the third century B.C. and the ninth century A.D. These Pahlavi writings are an attempt to explain the Avesta which, together with the Zend, is attributed to Zoroaster himself. By this time the Prophet had become regarded as a supernatural being, and his teaching was neglected while his person was exalted. The Dinkart, composed about the ninth century A.D., is a summary and exposition of the Avestan texts and Zend known to the author, who by his quotations exhibits knowledge of a greater number of Avestan Books than we now possess. It is a huge volume of over a thousand pages, although the first two treatises are lost: among the remaining contents is a very fanciful life of the Prophet. The Bundahish and the Zartusht Namah are two later Books, written in Persian, subsequent to the invasion of Islam. The latter bears the date of A.D. 1277, yet purports to give accurate information of the details of the life of Zoroaster. The Bundahish, probably of somewhat earlier date than the Zartusht Namah, is a kind of 'Enquire within upon Everything' concerning medieval Zoroastrianism. Among the host of less important Pahlavi Books, only two need here be mentioned—the Arda-Viraf and the Dadistan-i-Dinik. The former is an interesting sixth century account of the nature of Heaven and Hell, and the latter a series of questions put to a ninth-century priest, together with his answers. These deuterocanonical Books form what is known as the Kordah, or little, Avesta. Modern Persian translations of this Kordah Avesta have been published, and are of some use in determining the meaning of words that are obscure in the Pahlavi, but often they paraphrase rather than translate literally.

There are no manuscripts of the Avesta earlier than the thirteenth century A.D., the majority belong to the seventeenth. Not only did the old manuscripts suffer mutilation from Alexander the Great, for the Muhammadans also destroyed many Zoroastrian Books. The Quran was offered as a substitute for the Avesta, at the point of the sword. Although many faithful Zoroastrians refused to accept it, others acquiesced on the ground that many of the doctrines of the Avesta were also to be found in the Quran. A certain number of Persian religious ceremonies were allowed by the Moslem conquerors, and some of the old Fire Temples remained. But the glory of Persia had departed.

Notes

1. Entitled *Historia Religionis veterum Persarum eorumque Magorum.* Published A.D. 1700.

2. It is not certain which of the three kings who bore this name was responsible for the work.

3. *Essays on the Religion of the Parsis,* pp. 69-70.

4. *Early Religious Poetry of Persia,* p. 2.

5. *The Living God,* pp. 187-8.

R. C. Zaehner (essay date 1961)

SOURCE: "The Prophet" in *The Dawn and Twilight of Zoroastrianism,* G. P. Putnam's Sons, 1961, pp. 33-61.

[*In the essay that follows, Zaehner offers an overview of Zoroaster's life and his spiritual doctrines, as outlined in the* Gathas.]

HIS PLACE AND DATE

The traditional date the Zoroastrians assign to their Prophet is '258 years before Alexander', and for the Persian or Iranian the name 'Alexander' can only have meant the sack of Persepolis, the extinction of the Achaemenian Empire, and the death of the last of the kings of kings, Darius III. This occurred in 330 BC, and Zoroaster's date would then be 588 BC, and this date we may take to refer to the initial success of his prophetic mission which consisted in the conversion of King Vishtāspa when Zoroaster was forty years old.[1] Since he is traditionally said to have lived seventy-seven years, we will not be far wrong in dating him at 628-551 BC. It seems also to be generally agreed that the Prophet's sphere of operation in which his message was proclaimed was ancient Chorasmia—an area comprising, perhaps, what is now Persian Khorasan, Western Afghanistan, and the Turkmen Republic of the U.S.S.R.[2] There is, however, evidence to show that Zoroaster was not a native of these lands, for he himself complains to his God that he is persecuted in his homeland and asks him to what land he shall flee.[3] Ultimately he found refuge with King Vishtāspa who was, according to Henning, the last paramount chief of a Chorasmian confederation finally overthrown by Cyrus. The only place in the Avesta which is brought into connexion with Zoroaster is Raghā (the classical Rhages and modern Ray, now a suburb of Tehran) which is described as 'Zarathushtrian'.[4] It is then rather more than possible that Zoroaster was a native of Rhages in Media and that he fled from there to Chorasmia where he finally found a patron in Vishtāspa. Yet even at the court of this prince, it would appear, he found no rest, for there are constant references to continuing hostile action on the part of his enemies even after he was assured of the royal protection.

The Economic and Political Background

The moral dualism between *Asha* and *Druj,* Truth and the Lie, Righteousness and Unrighteousness, which is so characteristic of the *Gāthās,* can be seen as a universalization of a concrete political and social situation in which a peaceful pastoral and cattle-breeding population was constantly threatened by the inroads of fierce nomadic tribes. To these latter Zoroaster habitually refers as the *dregvants* or *drvants,* the 'followers of the Lie', whereas his own supporters are the *ashavans,* the 'followers of Truth or Righteousness'. The 'Lie', however, which both in the *Gāthās,* in the later Avesta, and the much later Pahlavi books, is the term used to represent the very principle of evil—Angra Mainyu or Ahriman, the 'Evil' or 'Aggressive Spirit' being only its leading personification—is not only the opponent and denial of *Asha* or abstract truth: much more essentially, in the *Gāthās* at least, it is predatory aggression against, or subversion of, good government and a peaceful agricultural and pastoral order. 'This do I ask thee, Lord,' the Prophet asks his God, 'What retribution will there be for him who would secure the kingdom (political power) for the follower of the Lie, for the evil-doer who cannot earn a livelihood except by doing violence to the husbandman's herds and men, though they have not provoked him (*adrujyantō,* lit. "not lying to or harming him')."[5] The nomad is the aggressor and the word used to represent and, to some extent, to personify his aggressive impulse, is *Aēshma,* 'violence' or 'fury', from a root *aēsh-* meaning 'to rush forward' or 'violent movement'.[6] This violence is directed against both men and cattle, the latter being sought after not only as booty but as sacrificial victims. The plight of the ox, indeed, which finds itself defenceless in a world of violence, forms the subject-matter of a whole *Gāthā.* Its soul appeals in anguish to Ahura Mazdāh, the 'Wise Lord', who is also for Zoroaster the one true God and to the 'Bounteous Immortals' (*amesha spentas*) who at once surround him and are yet inseparable from him in that they are his most characteristic attributes.

'For whom did ye create me?' the soul of the ox demands. 'Who was it that fashioned me? Violence, fury, cruelty, frightfulness, and might hem me in. No other husbandman have I but you; so assign me good grazing lands.[7]

To this Ahura Mazdāh replies:

> 'None has been found to be thy master and to judge concerning thee in accordance with Righteousness; for the Creator fashioned thee for the herdsman and the husbandman. In agreement with Righteousness did the Wise Lord create for the ox the sacred formula of the oblation of fat[8] and for parched(?) men [did he], bounteous in his ordinances, [create] milk.'[9]

This answer seems far from satisfactory to the soul of the ox who replies: 'Whom hast thou from among men, who, being well disposed to us[10] (the ox and the cow) would take care of us?' 'This man [alone] have I found here,' the Wise Lord replies, 'who has given ear to [my] ordinances, Zarathushtra of Spitama's lineage.'

Now what is the significance of this singular dialogue? The soul of the ox complains that it has become the object of violence and rapine, and this despite the fact that it has or believes it has divine protectors ('No other husbandman have I but you'). Yet, far from comforting it, the Wise Lord replies that no one exists who can be its master or pass judgement concerning it according to Righteousness, for the Wise Lord himself in agreement with Righteousness had created for it 'the sacred formula of the oblation of fat' whereas its milk was to assuage the thirst of men. This is as much as to say that in the original dispensation the bovine species was destined not only to nourish man with its milk but also to serve as a sacrificial victim. This Ahura Mazdāh had decreed 'in agreement with Asha', that is, Righteousness or Truth.

Now of all the 'Bounteous Immortals'[11] who surround and partake of the nature of Ahura Mazdāh, Asha alone is of demonstrably Indo-Iranian origin, that is to say, as a major religious concept it is common to both the earliest stratum of Indian religion found in the *Rig-Veda* and to the Avesta. *Vohu Manah,* the 'Good Mind', on the other hand, is a purely Iranian concept and is probably an invention of the Prophet Zoroaster himself. So it is that the soul of the ox asks whether no man exists who would take care of cattle *in accordance with the Good Mind.*[12] Such a man, Ahura Mazdāh replies, is to be found in Zoroaster.

This would seem to indicate that the Prophet did not regard himself as 'doing away with the law and the prophets' that preceded him *in toto,* rather he was adding a new dimension to the old religion in so far as it was represented by Ahura Mazdāh (if indeed he existed before his time) and Asha. Hence he continues to refer to his own followers as *asha-vans,* 'followers of Truth or Righteousness' and to his opponents as *dreg-vans,* 'followers of the Lie', that principle which violates the natural order.

Now it is obvious from the **Gāthās** that Zoroaster met with very stiff opposition from the civil and ecclesiastical authorities when once he had proclaimed his mission. The soul of the ox, when it learns that the powers above have entrusted it to him, cries out in genuine dismay and barely concealed derision: 'What, am I to be satisfied with a protector who has no power, with the word of a feeble man, I who crave [a protector] who exercises his sovereignty at will?'[13] Will a man ever exist who will give him [effectual] aid with his hands?'[14] Zoroaster too was conscious of his weakness and of how formidable the opposition to his teaching was: he complains of being persecuted by his own community because he is master of only a few cattle and men[15] whereas his enemy is stronger than he.[16]

Once, however, he becomes confident of the patronage of King Vishtāspa his tone changes and he sets himself up as the judge between the two parties:

> 'Remembering your laws we proclaim words to which those who cleave to the laws of the Lie and lay waste the worldly goods of the [followers of] Truth, will not listen, [words] most good, forsooth, to those who have given their hearts to Mazdāh. Though, maybe, the bet-

ter path to choose may not be plain for all to see, yet will I face you all, for Ahura Mazdāh recognizes [me as] judge between the two parties, for it is we who live in accordance with Truth.'[17]

TRUTH AND THE LIE

The Prophet knew no spirit of compromise and, as prophets do, he saw things very much in black and white. On the one hand stood Asha—Truth and Righteousness—on the other the Druj—the Lie, Wickedness, and Disorder. This was not a matter on which compromise was possible: it was literally a matter of life and death, for he promised to bring as 'an offering the life of his own body, the first-fruits of his good mind and deeds to Mazdāh and to the Truth. Through these are his hearkening (*s(e)raosha*) [to the Word] and his Kingdom (*khshathra*).'[18] For him the issue is crystal clear and the battle is on.

There would seem to be little doubt that an actual state of war existed between the two parties, Zoroaster and his patron Vishtāspa standing on the one side and the so-called followers of the Lie, many of whom he mentions by name, on the other; for not only does the Prophet forbid his followers to have any contact with the 'followers of the Lie',[19] but he also asks his God directly to which of the two opposing *armies* he will give the victory.[20] Like Muhammad, Zoroaster relied on the sword to enforce the efficacy of his prophetic word.

'A true enemy of the follower of the Lie and a powerful support of the follower of Truth':[21] that is how Zoroaster describes himself. There can be no question of compromise with what the Prophet considers to be evil: the enemy must be either vanquished or converted. 'He who, by word or thought or with his hands, works evil to the follower of the Lie or converts his comrade to the good, such a man does the will of the Wise Lord and pleases him well.'[22]

Now who were these followers of the Lie whom Zoroaster so vigorously attacks? Primarily they were worshippers of the *daēvas,* a word that, in Zoroastrianism, comes to mean simply 'demon'. Originally, however, the *daēvas* were not demons, they were a class of gods that were common to the Indians and Iranians alike. This is made certain by the fact that in the *Rig-Veda* in India two classes of deity are distinguished, the *asuras* and the *devas,* the former being more remote from man and the latter being closer to him. In the *Rig-Veda* the greatest of the *asuras* is Varuna, the protector of Truth, who is the guardian of the moral law, whereas the greatest of the *devas* is Indra, the war-god of the Aryans, who is the very personification of victorious might and who is not at all concerned with the moral order. The fate of the two classes of deity was very different in India and Iran; for whereas, in India, the *asuras* in the course of time sank to the rank of demon, in Iran it was the *daēvas* (= *devas*) who met with the same dismal fate, largely as a result of the direct onslaught that Zoroaster unleashed against them.

The leaders of Zoroaster's opponents, the followers of the Lie as he calls them, are usually called *kavis* and *kara-*

pans. It has generally been assumed that the latter were a priestly caste, and the word itself has been shown to mean 'mumbler',[23] a reference, presumably, to the recitation of a traditional liturgy. The former term *kavi*, however, is not so clear, for it seems to have a quite different meaning in the Indian and the Iranian traditions. In India the word means a composer of hymns, but in the **Gāthās** Zoroaster uses the word not only to denote the leaders of his opponents but also as an epithet of his own patron Vishtāspa. Moreover, in the later Avesta the word is used to mean 'ruler' or 'king' and is regularly applied to the legendary kings of Iran, and the same development is maintained in the later languages. Despite the Indian evidence, then, it would appear that the *kavis* (of whom Zoroaster's patron was one) were local rulers who in the normal course of events would be supporters of the old religion which Zoroaster attacked. His enemies, then, were the established civil and religious authorities which supported the ancient national religion.

What this religion was is made fairly clear by Zoroaster's own attacks on it.

THE TRADITIONAL RELIGION

That it is a traditional religion he is attacking is made quite clear by the fact that it is Yima, the first man according to the ancient Iranian tradition, whom he singles out for especial abuse. 'Among those sinners,' he says, 'was Yima, the son of Vivahvant, for so have we heard, who, to please our men, gave them portions of the flesh of the ox to eat. As to these, O Mazdāh, I leave the decision to thee(?).'[24] Zoroaster is here attacking a practice said to have been instituted by Yima who was both in the Indian and Iranian tradition[25] the first man, and which must therefore have been a national institution. Yima's crime would seem to have been not so much that he had introduced meat-eating among his people as that he had slaughtered cattle in sacrifice to the ancient gods. This sacrifice would appear to have been associated with the equally ancient rite of the consumption of the fermented juice of the Haoma plant which appears to have been associated with ritual intoxication.[26] 'When wilt thou strike down this filthy drunkenness,' the Prophet exclaims, 'with which the priests (*karapans*) evilly delude [the people] as do the wicked rulers of the provinces in [full] consciousness [of what they do].'[27] More strangely Yima and his co-religionists are accused not only of laying waste the pasture lands but of declaring that the sun and the ox were 'the worst things to see'.[28] This seems very odd indeed since Yima himself was almost certainly a solar figure, and there seems no ready explanation for so extraordinary an accusation except that the rite alleged to have been instituted by Yima consisted of the ritual slaughter of a bull or cow in a sunless place or at night. This is so strikingly similar to the Mithraic mysteries which were later to be practised in the Roman Empire and which were certainly of Iranian origin, that scholars have maintained that these rites were performed in honour of Mithra. We shall have to consider this view when we come to deal with the god Mithra as he appears in the Avesta.

From the passage we have been discussing, however, it would seem clear that Zoroaster is attacking a traditional cult in which a bull was slaughtered at night or in a sunless place in honour of the *daēvas*: this rite was accompanied by another in which the juice of the Haoma plant was extracted and ritually consumed. This juice must have been fermented and was certainly intoxicating. What is strange, however, is that already in the later Avesta the Haoma rite had become central to the Zoroastrian liturgy itself, and the whole of the later liturgy shows that in its original form animal sacrifice must have been prominent. So in *Yasna* 11, which forms part of the liturgy dedicated to Haoma, both the ox and Haoma are represented as complaining of being illused; but the ox does not, as one might expect, complain of being slaughtered but merely accuses the priest of not distributing its sacrificial flesh equitably, while Haoma complains that the priest withholds from him the jaw, tongue, and left eye of the sacrificial animal which had been allotted to him by his father, Ahura Mazdāh.

This, indeed, is one of the most puzzling aspects of early Zoroastrianism, for the whole liturgy of the *Yasna* (of which the **Gāthās** of the Prophet form part) centres round the Haoma rite, one form of which was certainly condemned by Zoroaster, and it is clear that although the rite as performed in later times did not involve animal sacrifice, it certainly did so in its earliest form, for among the offerings mentioned are both the 'beneficent ox' and the 'living ox'. In the historical development of the ritual the 'living ox' was represented by milk, but in its original form it seems clear that an ox must actually have been immolated in sacrifice. How such a radical distortion of the Prophet's express wishes can have come about we shall shortly have to discuss when we come to deal with the later Avesta. For the moment it is sufficient to note that the so-called 'followers of the Lie' must have been worshippers of the traditional gods whose liturgy included the slaughter of an ox and the consumption of the fermented juice of the Haoma plant. Zoroaster sees himself as a prophet sent by God not only to proclaim a new doctrine but also to reform ritual practices claiming immemorial antiquity.

What this traditional religion was is fairly clear in its broad outlines both from the later Avesta into which much of the earlier 'paganism' has been readmitted, and from the parallel religion of the *Rig-Veda* in India which was never subjected to any radical reform. In the *Rig-Veda*, as we have seen, two types of deity were recognized, the *asuras* and the *devas*—the former being more remote and more directly concerned with the right ordering of the cosmos, the latter being nearer to man, more active, and more nearly associated with the victorious advance of the Aryan tribes then swarming into India. So too in Iran these two types of deity must have existed side by side before the Zoroastrian reform, and it is amply clear from the **Gāthās** themselves that the *daēvas* (= the Indian *devas*) were considered by Zoroaster to be no gods at all but maleficent powers who refused to do the will of the Wise Lord. Further evidence of this is supplied by the later

Avesta where we find some of these demons' names, and these names correspond exactly to the names of some of the most prominent gods of the *Rig-Veda*. Thus the most popular of all the Rig-Vedic gods, Indra, the patron war-god of the Aryans, turns up in the later Avesta as a demon. So too we meet with Saurva corresponding to the Indian Śarva or Rudra, the most sinister of the Vedic gods who was later to be known as Śiva, and Nāñhaithya corresponding to the two Nāsatyas or Aśvins of the Vedic texts. Never, however, does Zoroaster attack the other class of deity, the *ahuras* (= the Indian *asuras*), and yet he, pointedly perhaps, refrains from mentioning any of them by name. It would, however, not be true to say that he ignores their existence, for he twice speaks of *ahuras* or 'lords' in the plural,[29] thereby indicating that he had not, at least at the time when the two hymns in question were composed, entirely rejected the *ahuras* existing alongside his own supreme God, Ahura Mazdāh, the Wise Lord. It is, however, fair to say that he found them inconsistent with his own religion and therefore studiously avoided mentioning them by name.

Zoroaster's world-view is rooted in the actual conditions of his time. From the old religion he takes over the antithesis—already attested in the *Rig-Veda*—of Truth (*asha*) and the Lie (*druj*), and in this respect his religion may be called an ethical dualism, but, unlike the *Rig-Veda*, he thrusts this fundamental antagonism right into the forefront of his religious teaching. He does not, however, start from any abstract principle, he starts from the concrete situation as it faced him in Eastern Iran. On the one side he found a settled pastoral and agricultural community devoted to the tilling of the soil and the raising of cattle, on the other he found a predatory, marauding tribal society which destroyed both cattle and men, and which was a menace to any settled way of life. Their gods were like unto them: never were they good rulers, delivering over, as they did, the ox to Fury (*aēshma*)[30] instead of providing it with good pasture.

In his war against the 'followers of the Lie' Zoroaster neither offers nor seeks a compromise: for him his opponents are evil incarnate, and they are to be treated as such. In an astonishing passage he says: 'Whether a man dispose of much or little wealth, he should show kindness(?) to the follower of Truth, but should be evil to the follower of the Lie,'[31] for the man 'who is most good to the follower of the Lie is himself a follower of the Lie'.[32] There can, then, be no question of loving your enemies because they embody the Lie, and so long as they do so, they are evil creatures to whom no mercy should be shown. So in his colloquy with the Good Mind[33] Zoroaster describes himself as a 'true enemy of the follower of the Lie' and a 'strong support of the follower of Truth'.[34] The Prophet, however, did not believe that the followers of the Lie were necessarily irretrievably damned, for every man is free to choose between the two parties for himself. So long as they persist in adhering to what he considers to be a false religion they must be attacked, but the possibility of conversion is always at the back of his mind. 'He who

by word or thought or with his hands works evil to the follower of the Lie or converts his comrade to the good, such a man does the will of Ahura Mazdāh and pleases him well.'[35] His ultimate aim, indeed, is not merely to make war on the followers of the Lie, but rather to convert them and all men to the new religion he proclaimed.[36]

FREE WILL

Zoroastrianism is the religion of free will *par excellence*. Each man is faced sooner or later with making his choice between Truth and the Lie—the true religion which the Prophet claimed had been revealed to him and the false religion which his contemporaries had inherited from their forebears. Zoroaster, however, projected this basic opposition between Truth and the Lie which he saw working itself out here and now on earth on to the purely spiritual sphere: on all levels were the two principles opposed, and so he came to see that the whole cosmos, both material and spiritual, was shot through with this fundamental tension: over against a transcendental Good Mind stood the Evil Mind, over against the Bounteous Spirit the Evil or Destructive Spirit, over against Right-Mindedness Pride and so on; and on every level a choice had to be made, Ahura Mazdāh, the Wise Lord, himself not being exempt.

On the lowest level the ox has freedom to choose between the good husbandman and the man who is no husbandman, and 'of the two it chose the husbandman who would tend it, a master who follows Truth and cultivates(?) the Good Mind; no share in the good news shall the man who is no husbandman have, however much he strive.'[37] The free choice which is the privilege even of the animal kingdom was God's free gift to his creatures at the very beginning of existence, for 'in the beginning, O Mazdāh, by thy mind didst thou create for us material forms (*gaēthā*) and consciences and rational wills (*khratu*), for thou didst establish corporeal life—deeds and doctrines that men might thereby make their choices in freedom of will.'[38] The choice that must be made is ultimately always that between Truth and the Lie. 'For our choice,' the Prophet says, 'Truth has been presented for our own benefit, but to the [false] teacher the Lie for his own undoing.'[39] Thus though there is no doubt at all in Zoroaster's mind that Truth is exclusively on his side, he realizes that the freedom of the will entails freedom to make the wrong choice, freedom, that is, to err; and it is interesting that the word *varena* which in Avestan means 'free choice' comes, in its Pahlavi form *varan*, to mean 'heresy'—an exact parallel to the development of the Greek word *hairesis* in Christianity. 'Both he who speaks true and he who speaks falsely, both the wise and the fool, raise their voices in accordance with [what is in their] hearts and minds.'[40] Both parties are entitled to proclaim their doctrines and there would seem to be no obvious way of deciding which doctrines is true unless some universally accepted authority is recognized. This difficulty was fully apparent to Zoroaster for he asks of his God who is really a follower of the Truth and who a follower of the Lie,[41] thereby conceding that his enemies may have been sincere in holding their false views. To solve the difficulty and because he sincerely saw himself as a prophet of God, he claimed such authority for himself and set himself up as judge between the two parties. 'Though,' he says, 'maybe, the better path to choose may not be plain for all to see, yet will I face you all, for the Wise Lord recognizes [me as] judge between the two parties, for it is we who live in accordance with Truth.'[42]

It is in this capacity of judge, perhaps, that Zoroaster in *Yasna* 30 summons all men to make the great decision. 'Hear with your ears,' he prophesies, 'behold with mind all clear the two choices between which you must decide, each man [deciding] for his own self, [each man] knowing how it will appear (?) to us at the [time of] great crisis.'[43] With these words he introduces the myth of the primeval choice that the two Spirits whom he calls 'twins' had to make at the beginning of time:

> 'In the beginning those two Spirits who are the well-endowed(?) twins were known as the one good and the other evil, in thought, word, and deed. Between them the wise chose rightly, not so the fools. And when these Spirits met they established in the beginning life and death that in the end the followers of the Lie should meet with the worst existence, but the followers of Truth with the Best Mind. Of these two Spirits he who was of the Lie chose to do the worst things; but the Most Holy Spirit, clothed in rugged heaven, [chose] Truth as did [all] who sought with zeal to do the pleasure of the Wise Lord by [doing] good works. Between the two the *daēvas* did not choose rightly; for, as they deliberated, delusion overcame them so that they chose the most Evil Mind. Then did they, with one accord, rush headlong unto Fury that they might thereby extinguish(?) the existence of mortal men.'[44]

THE TWO SPIRITS

It is impossible to say whether this myth of the two twins was original to Zoroaster himself or whether he was reformulating a more ancient myth in accordance with his own ideology. In the myth, however, he projects the concrete situation he saw on earth—where the followers of the Lie represented destructive forces hostile to physical life, and the followers of Truth the life-conserving and life-enhancing forces—on to the spiritual world. Here the basic duality of Truth and Falsehood, Righteousness and Wickedness, Order and Disorder are personified in a pair of Primal Twins whom he calls the Bounteous or Holy Spirit—for the word *spenta* usually translated as 'holy' implies increase and abundance—and the Destructive or Evil Spirit (*Angra Mainyu*, the later Ahriman), the one the bringer of life and the other the author of death. These two Spirits stand over against each other, irreconcilably opposed to each other in a total contradiction.

'I will speak out,' the Prophet proclaims, 'concerning the two Spirits of whom, at the beginning of existence, the Holier thus spoke to him who is Evil: "Neither our thoughts, nor our teachings, nor our wills, nor our choices, nor our words, nor our deeds, nor our consciences, nor yet our souls agree."'[45]

In the *Gāthās* the Holy or Bounteous Spirit is not identical with Ahura Mazdāh, the Wise Lord, who is also the supreme God, but is only an aspect of him, one of his 'sons'. But even Ahura Mazdāh himself must make his choice between Truth and the Lie, between good and evil. In a strange passage in which both men and *daēvas* are represented as making supplication at the divine court Zoroaster says:

> 'Family, and village, and tribe, and you *daēvas* too, like me, sought to rejoice the Wise Lord [saying]: "Let us be thy messengers that we may keep at bay those who hate thee." To them did the Wise Lord, united with the Good Mind and in close companionship with bright Truth, make answer from his Kingdom: "Holy and good Right-Mindedness do we choose: let it be ours."'[46]

So does God himself make the choice that all must make between good and evil. United with the Good Mind and in close companionship with Truth or Righteousness, God chooses the good and utterly condemns the old religion which he identifies with evil.

> 'But you, you *daēvas*,' he exclaims, 'and whosoever multiplies his sacrifice to you, are all the seed of the Evil Mind, the Lie, and Pride; doubtful(?) are your deeds for which ye are famed throughout the seventh part of the earth. For ye have so devised it that men who do what is worst should thrive [as if they were] favoured by the "gods" (*daēvas*)—men who depart from the Good Mind and break away from the will of the Wise Lord and from Truth. So would you defraud man of the good life and immortality even as the Evil Spirit [defrauded you], you *daēvas*, through his Evil Mind—a deed by which, with evil words, he promised dominion to the followers of the Lie.'[47]

So does the Wise Lord unequivocally condemn the old religion and take the part of Truth which he identifies with Zoroaster's reform.

ZOROASTER AND HIS GOD

Zoroaster, on his side, saw himself as a prophet and a visionary. He was also a priest[48] and therefore, presumably, must originally have been connected with the earlier cult which he was later to condemn. He saw himself as a prophet speaking to God and hearkening to his word. He is 'the Prophet who raises his voice in veneration, the friend of Truth'[49] and God's friend.[50] His relationship to his God is not one of servility, rather he asks his help—the kind of help that a friend grants to a friend.[51] His mission was foreordained, for he was chosen by God 'in the beginning',[52] and he claims to have seen him in a vision which transported him back in time to the beginning of the world. 'Then, Mazdāh, did I realize that thou wast holy when I saw thee in the beginning, at the birth of existence, when thou didst ordain a [just] requital for deeds and words, an evil lot for evil [done] and a good one for a good [deed]: by thy virtue [shall all this come to pass] at the last turning-point of creation.'[53] Repeatedly he asks to see his God and the entities associated with him.[54] 'When will I see thee in Truth, and the Good Mind, and the path [that leads] to the Wise Lord, the most mighty, [the path that is] to hearken [to his word]?'[55] The word *sraosha* which we have translated as 'to hearken' and which is usually translated as 'obedience' or 'discipline' probably originally meant the Prophet's relationship to God, the one hearing and obeying the divine message, the other hearkening to the prayers of his prophet. Although Sraosha, the genius of hearing and obeying, was later to become more fully personalized and anthropomorphized than almost any other deity, surviving right down into Islamic times as Surūsh, the messenger of God sometimes identified with the angel Gabriel, yet the original meaning of his name was never wholly lost, for the Pahlavi translators often render it with the Pahlavi word *nighōshishn* meaning 'listening' or 'hearkening'; and this meaning of the Avestan word too can still be detected in *Yasna* 56.1 in the phrase 'May the listening to [the word of] the Wise Lord be present here'. Thus Zoroaster not only sees his God, he also hears the words he speaks. This 'hearing' of God's voice he expresses in the most concrete possible imagery: he asks God to speak to him 'with the tongue of his mouth'.[56] He hears God and he sees him, and seeing him knows him as he is in Truth: 'Now have I seen him with my eyes, knowing him in Truth to be the Wise Lord of the Good Mind and of [good] deeds and words.'[57] Zoroaster realizes the holiness of God not by thought or concentration but by a direct vision of his goodness, truth, and eternity. 'Then did I understand in my mind,' he confesses, 'that thou art the ancient, thou the [ever] young, the father of the Good Mind, when I comprehended thee with my eyes—[thee], the very creator of Truth, Lord of [all] creation in thy works.'[58] For the Prophet this vision is self-authenticating: he has *seen* God as the holy and good, as the eternal, the primeval being who is yet ever young, the first and the last, and the origin of all goodness: he sees him with his eyes and grasps him with his mind. It is, if you like, an intellectual vision of God's holiness. 'Then did I realize that thou wast holy, Wise Lord . . .' is the refrain that runs throughout *Yasna* 43: it is an intensely personal *experience* of the reality of God's goodness.

The Avestan word we have translated as 'holy' is *spenta*, but we might equally translate 'bounteous'. The Pahlavi translators render the word by the Pahlavi equivalent *abh-zōnīk*, an adjective derived from *abhzōn* ('increase'). Holiness, for Zoroaster, also meant abundance, growth, and health. The divine nature is seen as an overwhelming giving of self, as superabundant life both in the spiritual and the material realm; for Zoroastrianism is in all its phases a religion that enthusiastically and thankfully accepts and blesses all the good things of *this* world as well as those of the next: indeed, in the *Gāthās*, the work of the Prophet himself, it is often exceedingly difficult to decide whether he is referring to a concrete situation here on earth or whether he is speaking of the last things.

THE BOUNTEOUS IMMORTALS

God is *spenta*: he is holy and he gives abundance. Ahura Mazdāh, however, the Wise Lord, is not identical with *Spenta Mainyu,* the Holy Spirit, who, as we have seen, is the eternal antagonist of the Evil or Destructive Spirit 'who chose to do the worst things'. The relationship between the Holy Spirit and those other entities that are close to the Wise Lord is not easy to define. Very soon after the Prophet's death these 'entities' were drawn into a closed system, forming a heptad of so-called *amesha spentas,* 'Holy' or 'Bounteous Immortals'. Ahura Mazdāh, the Wise Lord, came to be identified with the Holy Spirit, though nowhere in the *Gāthās* is such an identification made, and beside him were six abstractions, all of which figure prominently in the *Gāthās*—the Good Mind, Truth or Righteousness (*asha*), Right-Mindedness (*ārmaiti*), the Kingdom, Wholeness, and Immortality. In the *Gāthās* Ahura Mazdāh is spoken of as the father of the Holy Spirit,[59] as he is the father of Truth,[60] the Good Mind,[61] and Right-Mindedness;[62] but paternity in God is not to be understood in any crude sense, for he is also said simply to have *created* Truth or Righteousness by an act of will (*khratu*). Zoroaster's idea of paternity in God, then, is very like its Christian counterpart: Holy Spirit, Good Mind, Truth, and Right-Mindedness are thought into existence by the Wise Lord who is the supreme Being. Of these various entities the Holy Spirit, Truth, and the Good Mind stand nearest to God and are rightly regarded as his hypostases. Right-Mindedness, on the other hand, is rather the attitude of man towards God, it is an attitude of humility, the opposite of pride,[63] while the Kingdom, though it is an essential attribute of Ahura Mazdāh, being his by right, may on occasion be usurped by the followers of the Lie.[64] Wholeness and Immortality are indeed attributes of God, but in Zoroaster's thought they are also regarded as being primarily his gifts to man.[65] Indeed, of the 'Bounteous Immortals' only the Holy Spirit is exclusively appropriated to God: the others belong to God by nature but can be and are bestowed on man if he lives according to Truth. So intimately are the spiritual and material worlds connected that very soon after the Prophet's death each of the Bounteous Immortals came to be identified with physical 'elements'—the Good Mind with cattle, Truth with fire, the Kingdom with metals, Right-Mindedness with the earth, Wholeness with water, and Immortality with plants. This linking up of the spiritual with the material world in so concrete and apparently arbitrary a manner seems to date back to Zoroaster himself. Already in the *Gāthās,* Ārmaiti or Right-Mindedness seems to have been identified with the earth, for it is said to have been created as a pasturage for the ox[66] and plants are made to grow for it,[67] whereas in *Yasna* 51.7 Wholeness and Immortality seem to be equated with water and plants.[68] Moreover, already in the *Gāthās,* fire is a symbol of Truth and has its power,[69] while the Good Mind is closely connected with cattle.

Yet in Zoroaster's thought all this is subsidiary: the Bounteous Immortals are primarily aspects of God, but aspects in which man too can share. Wholeness and Immortality are pre-eminently the divine qualities which the Wise Lord bestows on the followers of Truth, and it is the Good Mind which unites man to God[70] and, so to speak, activates Righteousness in him; and it is through Righteousness or Truth that the just man treads the paths of the Good Mind.[71] Yet it is quite impossible to assign any definite role to these Bounteous Immortals in the *Gāthās:* they are little more than the agencies through which God acts. The Good Mind is simply God's mind, though this does not prevent man from participating in it. Truth is what it is because it is God's creation, and he himself is not only *spenta,* 'holy' or 'bounteous', he is also *asha-van* 'truth-ful'.[72] That the Bounteous Immortals were not conceived of by Zoroaster as having an existence separate from God seems to be shown by the fact that God usually appears as the agent and his various divine operations take place *through* one of the Bounteous Immortals, and it is for this reason that, grammatically, they so frequently appear in the instrumental case. Typical of the way in which Zoroaster sees God and his Bounteous Immortals in mutual interdependence is the following stanza: 'May the Wise Lord give us Wholeness and Immortality through the Holy Spirit and the Best Mind, through deeds and words [that are] in accordance with Truth, and through the Kingdom and Right-Mindedness.'[73]

Here all the Bounteous Immortals appear together—two being God's direct gift to man—Wholeness and Immortality, the other five being the instruments through which he operates. This 'instrumental' role of the Bounteous Immortals can perhaps be better understood if we compare it to the formulae of Christian prayer. Christianity too is a monotheistic religion, but its God is not an absolutely pure monad but a Trinity: so the ending of a well-known Catholic prayer is *per eumdem Dominum nostrum Jesum Christum Filium tuum, qui tecum vivit et regnat in unitate Spiritus Sancti Deus per omnia saecula saeculorum*— 'through the same Jesus Christ, thy Son, our Lord, who liveth and reigneth with thee, in the unity of the Holy Spirit, God, world without end.' Man prays to God through Christ just as God creates through the same Christ, his Son and pre-existent Word. So, too, in Zoroastrianism, it is through the Good Mind that God communes with man, and through the Holy Spirit that he creates, both the Good Mind and the Holy Spirit being his 'sons'. He also reigns in virtue of the Kingdom which is his by right in union with the Holy Spirit, and his reign lasts for ever and ever because he is possessed of Wholeness and Immortality.

It is true that there are traces of a specific relationship between Right-Mindedness and the earth, and between Wholeness and Immortality and water and plants in the *Gāthās* themselves, but this is because Zoroaster saw the spiritual and material worlds as being the opposite poles of a unitary whole intimately linked together. The link is only weakened with the appearance of the Lie and its most illustrious representative, Angra Mainyu, the Destructive Spirit, who first introduces death into the world. In the later tradition man is the earthly counterpart of Ahura Mazdāh himself, the ox of the Good Mind, fire of Truth, the earth of Right-Mindedness, water and plants of Wholeness and Immortality. None of this does violence to the Prophet's own thought, for physical life in its perfection is the mirror of the divine life: earth and water which give rise to plants, plants which provide fodder for cattle, and cattle which furnish both milk and meat to man are all part of the universal life-process, of the universal natural harmony that is only marred by the violence and corruption introduced by the Lie. But since the Lie is with us and is likely to remain with us as long as the world lasts, man needs weapons with which to defend himself, he needs the metals which are the earthly counterpart of the Kingdom, but which, like the Kingdom itself, can be filched from him and used against him by his enemies. Finally there is the fire which Zoroaster made the centre of his cultus[74] because in its power to destroy darkness it is the symbol of Truth itself whose brilliance too destroys the darkness of error.

Very much has been written on the 'origin' of the Bounteous Immortals, and the mere fact that scholars are in such total disagreement on this subject only goes to show that we know nothing certainly. Asha who is Truth, Righteousness, and Order, we also know in the *Rig-Veda* as *Rta;* and we can therefore be certain that the concept is inherited from Indo-Iranian times, as is its opposition to the Lie. In the case of the Kingdom (*khshathra*), Wholeness, and Immortality, it would seem rather futile to look round for an origin at all since these are concepts that are common to almost all religions. As to the Good Mind and Right-Mindedness, these would seem to be further and more specific elaborations of the basic antithesis between Truth and the Lie that gives its especial flavour to Zoroastrianism. Over against the Good Mind is set the Evil Mind,[75] just as the Holy Spirit on a yet higher level is opposed to the Destructive Spirit. There is, however, this difference: the Holy Spirit is conceived of as being totally divine whereas the Good Mind, though divine and of divine provenance, can be shared by man, and it is this selfsame Good Mind which envelops the Prophet when he comes to the realization of the holiness of God;[76] and it is the Good Mind whom he consults[77] and with whom he seeks union.[78] Similarly Ārmaiti, Right-Mindedness, is opposed to Tarō-maiti or Pairimaiti, 'pride'. Right-Mindedness, then, is predominantly a human excellence, and because this is so, it is Right-Mindedness rather than Truth that the Wise Lord chooses when he himself is required to make his irrevocable choice between truth and falsehood; for Truth and the Good Mind are his from all eternity whereas Right-Mindedness is rather the right and fitting response of man to the Good Mind of God in accordance with Truth.

It would, then, seem quite likely that both the Good Mind and Right-Mindedness on the one hand and their opposites, the Evil Mind and 'perverted-mindedness' or 'pride', are concepts developed by Zoroaster to fill out the overall picture of the great antagonism between Truth and Lie he had inherited from his forebears. That Zoroaster felt himself to be especially close to the Good Mind seems clear from the following passages. In *Yasna* 29 where the soul of the ox complains of ill-treatment at the hands of the 'followers of the Lie', neither Truth nor the Wise Lord himself can or will grant the ox a protector. On the contrary: 'In agreement with Righteousness did the Wise

Lord create for the ox the sacred formula of the oblation of fat and for parched(?) men [did he], bounteous in his ordinances, [create] milk.'⁷⁹ The soul of the ox, then, appeals directly to the Good Mind and in return the latter appoints Zoroaster as his protector. Thus the Good Mind is represented as modifying an eternal ordinance promulgated by the supreme Being and his Truth, but he does this not of himself but at the behest of Ahura Mazdāh himself, who chooses him as his vehicle of prophecy through which he inspires him not indeed to abrogate his ordinances but to reform what in them had been corrupted. Similarly in what is perhaps the most personal of all the revelations vouchsafed to Zoroaster it is the Good Mind who envelops him and asks him who he is and what his credentials are. 'Who art thou? Whose son art thou? By what token wilt thou appoint a day that I may question thee concerning thy worldly goods and thy self?'⁸⁰ To this the Prophet replies: 'First I am Zarathushtra, a true enemy of the follower of the Lie as far as lies within my power, then a powerful support for the follower of Truth.' Thus it is to the Good Mind that Zoroaster confesses himself to be a genuine follower of Truth, and again it is through him that he establishes the fire as the centre of his cult. There is then good reason to suppose that the Good Mind at least was a personal invention of Zoroaster's—the Good Mind which was the manifestation of the divine mind to him personally.

It should not, however, be supposed that the modification of an age-old ordinance of the Wise Lord and his Truth by the Good Mind indicates any tension within the personality of the divine heptad, for Truth and the Good Mind are always represented as being intimately united:⁸¹ the Good Mind is merely the more active partner, the agency through which God prefers to reveal himself to Zoroaster. Both are intimately associated with the supreme Being, and Professor Duchesne-Guillemin is quite right to refer to the three combined as the divine 'Triad'. Truth and the Good Mind are inseparably united to Ahura Mazdāh in a way that the other Bounteous Immortals are not.

The very originality of Zoroaster's conception of these divine entities which surround his God has disconcerted scholars ever since the Avesta was discovered. The theories that have been elucubrated to explain them in fact explain nothing at all and are scarcely worth even a cursory notice. They have been likened to the Ādityas of early Indian mythology despite the fact that not one single name is common to the two groups; or, because their number is seven, they have been likened to the Babylonian planetary system with which they have nothing whatever in common. More recently the distinguished French scholar, Georges Dumézil, has seen in them the representatives of the 'three functions' into which, he maintains, all Indo-European society was divided—Truth and the Good Mind representing what he calls the function of sovereignty, the Kingdom representing the warrior function, and Wholeness and Immortality representing the pastoral and agricultural activity of the peasant. This hypothesis, though not wholly implausible, really explains nothing, and it is

further vitiated by the parallels that Dumézil and his disciples attempt to draw between Zoroaster's Bounteous Immortals and specific Vedic deities: the parallels are not parallel at all. The defenders of this latest fashion, quite undaunted by the fact that none of the Zoroastrian 'entities' correspond in name with the Vedic deities they are supposed to resemble or by the fact that their nature and function are quite different, seem indifferent to the acknowledged fact that the *Asha*—Truth and Righteousness and Cosmic Order—of the *Gāthās* corresponds most exactly, in etymology and in function, to the *Rta* of the *Rig-Veda*. This, at least, can safely be said to form part of a common Indo-Iranian heritage, and, for lack of any evidence to the contrary, we must suppose that the other 'entities' were developed from very rudimentary beginnings by Zoroaster since they are only faintly adumbrated in the *Veda*. The Prophet's originality may be disconcerting, but it is none the less real for that. That his thought was indeed profoundly original becomes glaringly obvious once we compare his *Gāthās* both with the hymns of the *Rig-Veda* and with the later Avesta. The parallels between these latter two are unmistakable: in the *Gāthās* we are in a totally different religious world. Both the *Rig-Veda* and the later Avesta are frankly polytheistic or—if one prefers the more ambiguous phrase—henotheistic, whereas in the *Gāthās* we meet with a pure monotheism that not only has the stamp of a profoundly experienced revelation but also gives the impression of having been deeply thought out.

God and the Two Spirits

Yet, just how far are we justified in describing the religion of the *Gāthās* as being an ethical monotheism? Earlier in this chapter we had occasion to quote two crucial passages depicting the eternal antagonism that exists between the twin Spirits, Spenta Mainyu and Angra Mainyu, the Holy Spirit and the Destructive Spirit. Whence did the Destructive Spirit arise? The answer would seem to be clear enough, for the two Spirits are explicitly said to be twins, and we learn from *Yasna* 47.2-3 that the Wise Lord is the father of the Holy Spirit. In that case he must be the father of the Destructive Spirit too—a conception that has recently been described as 'absolutely absurd in the mental framework of the *Gāthās*'.⁸² In actual fact the logical conclusion we are bound to draw from our texts, namely, that Ahura Mazdāh is the father of the Destructive as well as of the Holy Spirit is only 'absurd' if we persist in judging Zoroaster's own teaching by the standards of a very much later dualist orthodoxy: and there are very good reasons for refusing to do this. First it is undeniable that in many respects as, for example, in the matter of animal sacrifice the later tradition grossly distorts the Prophet's teaching. Secondly, the later tradition identified Ahura Mazdāh, the Wise Lord, with the Holy Spirit, whereas the *Gāthās* ascribe paternity of the Holy Spirit to the Wise Lord. Thirdly, the later tradition assimilates the Wise Lord, now identical with the Holy Spirit, to light and the Destructive Spirit to darkness, whereas the *Gāthās* declare that the Wise Lord creates both light and darkness.⁸³ Lastly, the later tradition is divided on the interpretation of the stanzas in question; for the rigid dualism of late Sussanian orthodoxy did not hold the field alone. Orthodoxy, indeed, maintained a rigorously dualist position—there were two eternal distinct and separate principles of good and evil, the good principle being Ahura Mazdāh whom tradition had erroneously identified with the Holy Spirit. Zurvanite heterodoxy, however, drew the obvious conclusion from the Gāthic text that describes the two Spirits as twins and argued that, if they were twins, then they must have had a common father. Since Ahura Mazdāh was already identified with the Holy Spirit, he could no longer be considered to be the latter's father. So, for reasons that are obscure, they made the two Spirits the sons of *Zrvan Akarana* or Infinite Time. Yet another sect maintained that the Evil Spirit arose from a single evil thought of the supreme Being. Since, then, two sects among the later Zoroastrians themselves interpreted this stanza (*Yasna* 30.3) as meaning that the Evil Spirit derived from God himself, it seems a trifle wayward to condemn such a notion out of hand in the case of the Prophet himself.

All that we can say is that, by describing the two Spirits as 'twins', Zoroaster implied that the Evil Spirit too must derive from God, but he differs from the later Sassanian orthodoxy in that, for him, the Evil or Destructive Spirit is not an evil substance—he is evil by choice. Like Lucifer he '*chooses* to do the worst things'; he is not forced to do so either by God or by any inner compulsion of his own nature: the misery he brings upon himself and upon his followers is entirely his own fault and will inevitably lead to his destruction.

THE TWO SPIRITS IN THE DEAD SEA SCROLLS

An almost exact parallel to this solution of the problem of evil is to be found in the *Manual of Discipline,* perhaps the most interesting document of the Dead Sea sect of Qumrān. That Judaism was deeply influenced by Zoroastrianism during and after the Babylonian captivity can scarcely be questioned, and the extraordinary likeness between the Dead Sea text and the Gāthic conception of the nature and origin of evil, as we understand it, would seem to point to direct borrowing on the Jewish side. According to the account given in the *Manual of Discipline* God:

> 'created man to have dominion over the world and made for him two spirits, that he might walk by them until the appointed time of his visitation; they are the spirits of truth and of error. In the abode of light are the origins of truth, and from the source of darkness are the origins of error. . . . And by the angel of darkness is the straying of all the sons of righteousness . . . and all the spirits of his lot try to make the sons of light stumble; but the God of Israel and his angel of truth have helped all the sons of light. For he created the spirits of light and of darkness, and upon them he founded every work and upon their ways every service. One of the spirits God loves for all ages of eternity, and with all its deeds he is pleased for ever; as for the other, he abhors its company, and all its ways he hates for ever.'[84]

Here, in a Jewish setting, we have an exact parallel to the attitude of Ahura Mazdāh to the Holy and Destructive Spirits. Like the Jewish God, Ahura Mazdāh abhors the company of the Destructive Spirit, and 'all its ways he hates for ever'; but his hatred is based on rather more rational grounds than is his Jewish counterpart's, for he did not create the Evil Spirit evil: he only becomes such by choice. Yet though there seems to be no valid reason for doubting the Wise Lord's paternity of the Destructive Spirit, repulsive though such an idea may have seemed to a later orthodoxy, it cannot be denied that there is a basic dualism underlying the Prophet's monotheism; but it is not the dualism between the Holy Spirit and the Destructive Spirit who are what they are by their free choice, but between Truth and the Lie, that is, the twin objects of all choice. Zoroaster does tell us indirectly how the Destructive Spirit came into existence and how and why he went wrong; he does not tell us how the Lie originated but leaves us rather to infer that it was there from the beginning. This dualism is basic to all his teaching, and it is this one idea, which he took over from his Indo-Iranian heritage, that he developed and expanded as the cornerstone of the new religion. His followers who elaborated the later orthodoxy merely systematized a doctrine that was already there.

Yet, though Zoroaster's whole vision of the cosmos is dominated by this mortal antagonism between Truth and the Lie, Ahura Mazdāh, the Wise Lord, stands above and beyond them, wholly committed though he is to the side of Truth. In the **Gāthās** the Destructive Spirit does not presume to set himself up as a principle independent of and antagonistic to the supreme God: he is content to measure his strength against the Holy Spirit which emanates from God yet is not God. The *daēvas* too, those ancient gods who had been dethroned, perhaps by Zoroaster himself, do not forget their divine origin, for, by asking the Wise Lord that they may still be allowed to be his messengers, they show that they too acknowledge him as supreme Lord.

> 'Family, and village, and tribe, and you *daēvas* too, like me, sought to rejoice the Wise Lord [saying]; "Let us be thy messengers that we may keep at bay those who hate thee." To them did the Wise Lord, united with the Good Mind and in close companionship with bright Truth, make answer from his kingdom: "Holy and good Right-Mindedness do we choose: let it be ours."'[85]

Here we are allowed a glimpse of the old order: the dethroned *daēvas* appeal to the God whom they too acknowledge as supreme, against the new authority claimed by the Prophet Zoroaster. Plainly the followers of the old religion did not lightly acquiesce in being dubbed 'followers of the Lie', for they too must have claimed to be *ashavans,* 'followers of the Truth'; and Zoroaster himself seems to be aware of this, for he exclaims:

> 'This I ask thee, Lord: answer me truly. Which of those whom I consult is the follower of Truth and which the follower of the Lie? On which side is the aggressor (*angra*)? [Is it I?] or is he the aggressor, the follower of

the Lie, who seeks to thwart thy bounty (*savah*)? How do things stand? Surely it is he, not those near me, that must be held to be the aggressor.'[86]

So it would seem that Ahura Mazdāh, the Wise Lord, was recognized as the supreme Being by the worshippers of the *daēvas* themselves, and these are rebuked for not taking pains to associate with Truth and for not consulting with the Good Mind, the inference being perhaps that though they may have claimed to be 'followers of Truth', this was not apparent from their behaviour. In accusing them of not consulting with the Good Mind, however, Zoroaster contrasts them with himself, for his very claim to prophethood is based on the close communion with the Wise Lord he experiences through the Good Mind.

The essence of Zoroaster's reform would appear to be that he immensely raised the stature of Ahura Mazdāh, seeing in him not merely the 'greatest and best of the gods' but the sole creator and preserver of the universe, omnipotent and omniscient Lord. We have seen that he is called the 'father' of the Holy Spirit and the Good Mind, of Truth and Right-Mindedness, but these entities are not brought into being by any crassly physical act of generation, they are thought into existence as eternal attributes of God himself. Truth, for instance, is created by God's will or wisdom (*khratu*)[87] and it is by Truth that he maintains his own Good Mind. Again at the beginning of existence God *thinks*, 'Let the wide spaces be filled with lights',[88] and it is so. Again it is by thought, that is, by the Good Mind operating within him, that Zoroaster comes to the realization that God is the eternal, the ancient and the ever new;[89] and it is by the Good Mind, the exteriorization of the divine thought, that the world is brought into existence, 'by [his] mind, in the beginning, [he] fashioned forth corporeal things, consciences, and wills, [he] created bodily life, and deeds and doctrines among which men could freely make their choices'.[90] Man's free will, then, so passionately insisted on in the **Gāthās,** is also a direct creation of God's, his deliberate plan for humanity.

THE HOLINESS OF GOD

In *Yasna* 43 Zoroaster adopts the refrain 'Then did I realize that thou wast holy when . . .', and it will repay us to see in what he considers this holiness and bounty to consist. First he realizes God's holiness when he receives the Good Mind from his hand which holds the destinies of both good and evil men; secondly when he 'sees' him 'at the birth of existence' deal out their lots of weal and woe to good and bad and when he sees him pass judgement at the end of time; thirdly, when at the urgent behest of the Good Mind, he makes his confession of faith and resolves to be a 'true enemy of the follower of the Lie and a powerful support to the follower of Truth'; fourthly when, once more impelled by the Good Mind, he vows to venerate the fire as the symbol of Truth; fifthly when he first hears God's words, puts aside all trust in men, and resolves to do whatever God tells him is best; sixthly when he glimpses eternal life in God's Kingdom which is his alone to grant or withhold; seventhly, when his 'silent thought'

teaches him not to attempt to curry favour with the followers of the Lie who pretend that evil men are good.

Zoroaster, then, recognizes God's holiness first in the act of revelation itself which is transmitted to him through the illumination he receives from the Good Mind, secondly in the content of that revelation. And the content is this: that God is just and that he will judge men according to their good and evil deeds; that evil which is the Lie exists and must be fought; that Truth exists and is to be reverenced in the sacred fire; that God is to be obeyed and that no trust is to be put in men; that God will reward whom he will with eternal life; and lastly that it is wicked to dress up evil in the garb of good. In short, God is a just judge.

GOD, THE SOLE CREATOR

God is judge; and he is the creator of all things,[91] both spiritual and material, and since he thinks all things into existence, his creation is *ex nihilo*. He is omnipotent for he 'rules at will',[92] that is to say, though his Holy Spirit may be pitted against the Destructive Spirit, this happens by his will and consent. His being is in no way circumscribed by the forces of evil as it is in later Zoroastrianism: and it is he who will judge all men according to their deeds in the last days. God's creative activity is magnificently portrayed in a series of rhetorical questions that go to make up the bulk of *Yasna* 44:

'This I ask thee, Lord: answer me truly. Who is the primeval, the father of Truth through [generation and] birth? Who appointed their paths to the sun and stars? Who but thou is it through whom the moon waxes and wanes? This would I know, O Wise One, and other things besides.

'This I ask thee, Lord: answer me truly. Who set the earth below and the sky [above] so that it does not fall? Who the waters and the plants? Who yoked swift steeds to wind and clouds? Who, O Wise One, is the creator of the Good Mind?

'This I ask thee, Lord: answer me truly. What goodly craftsman made light and darkness? What goodly craftsman sleep and wakefulness? Who made morning, noon, and night to make the wise man mindful of his task?

'This I ask thee, Lord: answer me truly. Is the message I proclaim really true? Will Right-Mindedness [among men] support Truth by its deeds? Hast thou illumined (lit. taught) thy Kingdom with the Good Mind? For whom didst thou fashion the pregnant cow that brings prosperity?

'This I ask thee, Lord: answer me truly. Who created Right-Mindedness venerable with the Kingdom? Who made the son dutiful(?) in his soul to his father? Recognizing thee by these [signs] as the creator of all things through thy Holy Spirit, I [go to] help thee.'[93]

God, then, is the creator of all things, both spiritual and material, and he is the creator of free will. Man, then, enjoys an awful responsibility for his own actions, and though he will be judged by God, it is really he who automatically condemns or saves himself by his evil or good deeds. This is made amply clear in the following passage: 'At the last, glory will be the portion(?) of the man who adheres to a follower of Truth. A long age of darkness, foul food, and cries of woe—to such an existence will your own consciences lead you because of your own deeds, ye followers of the Lie.'[94]

Yet though man earns his own heaven and his own hell by his own good and evil deeds, it is Ahura Mazdāh who passes judgement[95] or this judgement is delegated to Sraosha;[96] for Sraosha is not only man's hearkening to the word of God, he is also God's all-hearing ear which nothing escapes; and so it is that in the later Avesta Sraosha becomes God's chosen instrument for the chastising of the *daēvas* and all evil men.

POST MORTEM JUDGEMENT

In later Zoroastrianism there is both an individual judgement at death and a universal ordeal by fire and molten metal at the end of time. Both ideas are present in embryo in the *Gāthās.* The individual soul is required to cross the 'Bridge of the Requiter' where those who have performed good works will receive a just return for their righteousness (*asha*) and the kingdom by their good mind.[97] Here, as so often in the *Gāthās,* we cannot be certain whether 'righteousness' and 'good mind' refer to the divine entities which are hypostases of the Wise Lord or to the righteousness and good thoughts of individual men. The underlying idea, however, would appear to be that when the good man crosses the Bridge of the Requiter the righteousness and good thoughts that had accompanied him on earth are united with substantial Righteousness and Truth and with the Good Mind of God which are themselves the source of all earthly goodness and truth. This thought is elsewhere expressed as union with the Good Mind.[98]

The good man's guide across the bridge is Zoroaster himself. He leads the souls of his followers across the dreaded Bridge and conducts them into the House of the Good Mind[99] where they will come face to face with their creator who dwells together with Truth and that same Good Mind.[100] The wicked meet with a very different fate: 'their souls and consciences trouble them when they come to the Bridge of the Requiter, guests for all eternity in the House of the Lie'.[101]

The Bridge of the Requiter at which the soul is judged figures prominently in the later tradition.[102] On it the deeds of the soul are weighed in the balance of Rashnu, the just judge *par excellence* who is himself the Requiter,[103] and the gods Mithra and Sraosha assist him. This was probably the traditional picture as it existed before the Zoroastrian reform, and, if this is so, it shows how great the Prophet's zeal on behalf of Ahura Mazdāh, whom he regarded as the one true God who could brook no rival, was, for in the *Gāthās* it is not Rashnu nor even Sraosha who had been accepted into the Prophet's system, but Ahura Mazdāh himself who is the Requiter and judge of pure and impure alike.[104]

HEAVEN AND HELL

Heaven and hell are variously described in the *Gāthās;* they are the best[105] and the worst[106] existences, and these quite unlocalized conceptions of the future life survive in the Persian language today: *behesht,* heaven, meaning originally simply 'the best', and *dūzakh* meaning 'a wretched existence'. That the 'best' existence is regarded as being on a mental and spiritual level is shown by the fact that the opposite of the worst existence is not simply the best existence but the best Mind.[107] Similarly heaven and hell are the House of the Good Mind[108] and the house of the Worst Mind,[109] or, more typically, the House of Song[110] and the House of the Lie.[111] Unlike Muhammad, Zoroaster does not describe the joys of heaven in physical terms; the blessed attain to 'long life', that is, presumably, eternal life and the Kingdom of the Good Mind;[112] they will be blessed with ease and benefit[113] and will be possessed of Wholeness and Immortality, God's supreme gifts to the faithful.

Oddly enough, the torments of hell are more fully described than the joys of heaven. The damned will be oppressed with discomfort and torments,[114] condemned to 'a long age of darkness, foul food, and cries of woe'.[115] Unlike later Zoroastrianism in which the souls of the damned are released in the last days, the Prophet seems to have regarded the torments of the damned as being eternal, for whereas the souls of the just will be granted immortality, the souls of the damned will be tormented in perpetuity (*utayūtā*).[116]

INFLUENCE ON JUDAISM

Zoroaster's doctrine of rewards and punishments, of an eternity of bliss and an eternity of woe allotted to good and evil men in another life beyond the grave is so strikingly similar to Christian teaching that we cannot fail to ask whether here at least there is not a direct influence at work. The answer is surely 'Yes', for the similarities are so great and the historical context so neatly apposite that it would be carrying scepticism altogether too far to refuse to draw the obvious conclusion. The case for a Judaeo-Christian dependence on Zoroastrianism in its purely eschatological thinking is quite different and not at all convincing, for apart from a few hints in the *Gāthās* which we shall shortly be considering and a short passage in *Yasht* 19.89-90 in which a deathless existence in body and soul at the end of time is affirmed, we have no evidence as to what eschatological ideas the Zoroastrians had in the last four centuries before Christ. The eschatologies of the Pahlavi books, though agreeing in their broad outlines, differ very considerably in detail and emphasis; they do not correspond at all closely to the eschatological writings of the inter-testamentary period nor to those of St Paul and the Apocalypse of St John. They do, however, agree that there will be a general resurrection of body as well as soul, but this idea would be the natural corollary to the survival of the soul as a moral entity, once that had been accepted, since both Jew and Zoroastrian regarded soul and body as being two aspects, ultimately inseparable, of the one human personality. We cannot say with any certainty whether the Jews borrowed from the Zoroastrians or the Zoroastrians from the Jews or whether either in fact borrowed from the other.

The case of rewards and punishments, heaven and hell, however, is very different; for the theory of a direct Zoroastrian influence on post-exilic Judaism does explain the sudden abandonment on the part of the Jews of the old idea of *Sheol,* a shadowy and depersonalized existence which is the lot of all men irrespective of what they had done on earth, and the sudden adoption, at precisely the time when the exiled Jews made contact with the Medes and Persians, of the Iranian Prophet's teaching concerning the afterlife. Thus it is Daniel, allegedly the minister of 'Darius the Mede', who first speaks clearly of everlasting life and eternal punishment. 'Many of them that sleep in the dust of the earth,' he writes, 'shall awake, some to everlasting life, and some to shame and everlasting contempt.'[117]

Thus from the moment that the Jews first made contact with the Iranians they took over the typical Zoroastrian doctrine of an individual afterlife in which rewards are to be enjoyed and punishments endured. This Zoroastrian hope gained ever surer ground during the intertestamentary period, and by the time of Christ it was upheld by the Pharisees, whose very name some scholars have interpreted as meaning 'Persian', that is, the sect most open to Persian influence. So, too, the idea of a bodily resurrection at the end of time was probably original to Zoroastrianism, however it arose among the Jews, for the seeds of the later eschatology are already present in the *Gāthās.*

THE 'SECOND EXISTENCE'

In later Zoroastrianism there is a well-defined eschatology: at the end of time the Saoshyans or 'Saviour' will come to renew all existence. He will raise the bodies of the dead and unite them with their souls, there will be a mighty conflagration, and all men will have to wade through a stream of molten metal which will seem like warm milk to the just and be in very truth what it is to the wicked. The sins of the damned are, however, purged away in this terrible ordeal and all creation returns to its Maker in joy. The ideas from which this eschatology developed are present in the *Gāthās* but not systematically worked out; moreover there is no looking forward to a time when the damned will be released from hell.

It would seem that Zoroaster first looked forward to himself 'reforming' existence here on earth, and that only later was the coming of God's Kingdom indefinitely postponed. So in *Yasna* 34.6 he asks God for a sign which will be 'the total transformation of *this existence*'[118] here and now, and begs him to make existence 'most excellent' (*ferasha*)[119]—again apparently here and now. Even clearer is his prayer that it may be '*we* who make existence most excellent'.[120] Similarly the Saoshyans in the *Gāthās* is no

eschatological figure but Zoroaster himself. This seems to be certainly so in *Yasna* 48.9 and 45.11 whereas in *Yasna* 53.2, the only *Gāthā* composed after Zoroaster's death, the 'religion of the Saoshyans' which Ahura inaugurated must be the religion of Zoroaster. Again, when the word is used in the plural[121] it probably refers to Zoroaster and his earthly allies, although this cannot be regarded as absolutely certain.

Yet alongside a belief that the world was to be made anew here and now by the Prophet, there was also a belief in 'last things'—a 'second existence'[122] at the end of time when all things will be re-created in perfection. Then 'at the last turning-point of existence'[123] the evil will be allotted their final doom and the just their eternal reward. The judgement will be in the form of an ordeal by fire and molten metal; and here again we almost certainly have another example of that interpenetration of the two worlds—the material and the spiritual—which is so characteristic of Zoroaster's thought, for the trial by ordeal certainly refers to an ordeal to which the Prophet himself must have submitted in order to prove the truth of his message as well as to an eschatological ordeal which will decide the lot of the two parties for ever and ever.[124] This fire it is which allots portions of weal and woe to the two sides[125] both here on earth and at the final reckoning.

The Zoroastrians have always been known as fire-worshippers and have, not unnaturally, resented this appellation; but it is quite clear that the Prophet himself revered this element 'which possesses the power of Truth'.[126] Its association with the Wise Lord is, however, far less apparent in the *Gāthās* than it is in the later Avesta where it is habitually called his son, but 'his' fire is indeed bestowed on Zoroaster along with the Good Mind as his special protector, and it is through this fire that he will make Righteousness to thrive at the expense of the followers of the Lie.[127]

Zoroaster's own eschatology is not identical with the more familiar eschatology of the later Avesta and the Pahlavi books. The Saoshyans is not yet an eschatological figure and the *Frashkart* or Final Rehabilitation of existence is only very vaguely adumbrated in the *Gāthās,* for it is Zoroaster himself who will make existence *frasha,* that is, 'excellent'. In the *Gāthās* there appears an individual judgement at death when souls are judged at the Bridge of the Requiter and a final universal ordeal by fire when the two parties are allotted their eternal destinies of weal and woe. This is in marked contrast to the later doctrine in which there is one individual judgement only: the final eschatological ordeal is not in any sense a judgement but a purgation by molten metal in which the sins of the damned are burned away. By this final purification they are made fit for eternal life and eternal joy.

SUMMARY OF DOCTRINE

The main doctrines preached by the Prophet Zoroaster can, then, be summed up as follows:

(1) There is a supreme God who is creator of all things both spiritual and material. He thinks his creation into existence by his Holy Spirit: he is holy and righteous, and by holiness are also understood creativeness, productivity, bounty, and generosity. He is surrounded by six other entities of which he is said to be the father and creator. Three can be said to be inseparable from his own essence—the Holy Spirit through which he creates, the Good Mind, and Truth. He dwells in his Kingdom, which means, no doubt, that he is absolute Lord of all that he has created—a kingdom which is now marred by the onslaughts of evil but which will be restored to its purity in the last days. Wholeness and Immortality, too, are inseparable from his essence, but they are also the reward he promises to those who do his will in Right-Mindedness. This last 'entity' or virtue is common to God and man and represents a right relationship between the two. God, the Wise Lord, stands beyond the reach of the powers of evil.

(2) The world as we know it is divided between Truth and the Lie. Truth is created by the Wise Lord or is his 'son'. About the origin of the Lie the Prophet is mute. This dualism between these two opposite poles, these two alternatives offered to the free choices of men, is basic to Zoroaster's thought; and although there are dim parallels to it in the sister tradition of India, nowhere in that civilization are they so tremendously and so uniquely emphasized.

(3) The creatures of the Wise Lord are created free—free to choose between Truth and the Lie. This applies as much to spiritual beings as it does to man. So Angra Mainyu, the Destructive Spirit, described surprisingly as the twin brother of the Holy Spirit, 'chooses to do the worst things'. This he does of his own free will as do the *daēvas,* the ancient gods whom, on account of the violence associated with their worship, Zoroaster considered to be evil powers.

(4) Since the will of man is entirely free, he is himself responsible for his ultimate fate. By good deeds he earns an eternal reward: Wholeness and Immortality are his. The evil-doer too is condemned by his own conscience as well as by a just God to the eternal pains of hell, the 'worst existence'.

(5) The outward symbol of Truth is the fire; and it is the fire-altar that becomes the centre of the Zoroastrian cult. It is by an ordeal of fire and molten metal that the Prophet vindicates the truth of his message, and it is by fire and molten metal that all humanity will be judged in the last days.

These would appear to be the salient doctrines taught in the **Gāthās.** Characteristic for the whole teaching is the word *savah,* 'benefit' or 'increase'. The word is used both for prosperity on earth and for the joys of heaven. Zoroaster is the Prophet of life, and of life ever more abounding.

Notes

1. This agrees with Theodore bar Kônai who gives Zoroaster's date (sc. his birth) as 628 BC. See Zaehner, ZZD, p. 442.

2. See W. B. Henning, *Zoroaster, Politician or Witch-Doctor?*, pp. 42ff.

3. Y. 46.1.

4. Ibid., 19.18.

5. Ibid., 31.15.

6. Ibid., 29.1,2: 30.6: 44.20: 48.7,12: 49.4.

7. Ibid., 29.1.

8. *mānthrem āzūtōish: mānthra*—means 'sacred word'. Āzūiti is plainly akin to Vedic *āhuti*—'oblation', but in the later Avesta it comes to mean 'fat' and is so translated into Pahlavi (*charpīh*), or, as Bartholomae rightly says 'solid food in contrast to liquid'. Nyberg's translation (*Religionen des alten Iran,* p. 197) is merely perverse.

9. Y. 29.6-7.

10. *Vohū manañhā,* 'in accordance with good mind, or the Good Mind.' See p. 46.

11. See pp. 45-50.

12. See n. 10.

13. *Ishā-khshathrīm:* to '*aēsh-,* 'to be powerful', on the analogy of *vasō-khshathra.*

14. Y. 29.9.

15. Ibid., 46.1-2.

16. Ibid., 34.8.

17. Ibid., 31.1-2.

18. Ibid., 33.14.

19. Ibid., 49.3.

20. Ibid., 44.15.

21. Ibid., 43.8.

22. Ibid., 33.2.

23. W. B. Henning, *Zoroaster, Politician or Witch-Doctor?*, p. 45.

24. Y. 32.8. Humbach's translation of this passage is totally different.

25. In India he becomes the lord of the dead.

26. Y. 32.14.

27. Ibid., 48.10.

28. See pp. 126-44.

29. Y. 30.9:31.4.

30. Ibid., 44.20.

31. Ibid., 47.4.

32. Ibid., 46.6.

33. See p. 54.

34. Y. 43.8.

35. Ibid., 33.2.

36. Ibid., 31.3.

37. Ibid., 31.10.

38. Ibid., 31.11.

39. Ibid., 49.3.

40. Ibid., 31.12.

41. Ibid., 44.12.

42. Ibid., 31.2.

43. Ibid., 30.2.

44. Ibid., 30.3-6.

45. Ibid., 45.2.

46. Ibid., 32.1-2.

47. Ibid., 32.3-5.

48. Ibid., 33.6.

49. Ibid., 50.6.

50. Ibid., 44.2.

51. Ibid., 46.2.

52. Ibid., 44.11.

53. Ibid., 43.5.

54. Ibid., 33.6-7.

55. Ibid., 28.5.

56. Ibid., 31.3.

57. Ibid., 45.8.

58. Y. 31.8.

59. Ibid., 47.2-3.

60. Ibid., 44.3: 47.2.

61. Ibid., 45.4: 31.8.

62. Ibid., 45.4.

63. Ibid., 60.5: cf. 33.4.

64. Ibid., 31.15.

65. Ibid., 33.8: 34.1: 45.5, etc.

66. Ibid., 47.3.

67. Ibid., 48.6.

68. Ibid., 34.11.

69. Ibid., 43.4.

70. Ibid., 28.4: 46.12: 49.3.

71. Ibid., 34.12.

72. Ibid., 46.9.

73. Ibid., 47.1.

74. Ibid., 43.9.

75. Ibid., 32.2-3: 47.5.

76. Ibid., 43.7.

77. Ibid., 45.6.

78. See p. 46.

79. See p. 34.

80. Y. 43.7.

81. e.g. Y. 45.9.

82. Ugo Bianchi, *Zamān i Ohrmazd,* Turin, 1958, p. 82.

83. See p. 55.

84. Millar Burrows, *The Dead Sea Scrolls,* New York, 1956, p. 374.

85. Y. 32.1-2.

86. Ibid., 44.12.

87. Ibid., 31.7.

88. Ibid.

89. Ibid., 31.8.

90. Ibid., 31.11.

91. Ibid., 44.7.

92. Y. 43.1.

93. Ibid., 44.3-7.

94. Ibid., 31.20.

95. Ibid., 30.11: 45.9.

96. Ibid., 43.12.

97. Ibid., 46.10.

98. Ibid., 46.12: 49.3,5.

99. Ibid., 32.15.

100. Ibid., 44.9.

101. Ibid., 46.11.

102. See pp. 302-4.

103. PR. 48.66. Cf. BSOAS, xvii, pp. 246-7.

104. Y. 46.17.

105. Ibid., 44.2.

106. Ibid., 30.4.

107. Ibid.

108. Ibid., 32.15.

109. Ibid., 32.13.

110. Ibid., 51.15.

111. Ibid., 51.14.

112. Ibid., 33.5.

113. Ibid., 30.11: 43.12.

114. Ibid., 30.11.

115. Ibid., 31.20.

116. Ibid., 45.7.

117. Daniel 12.2.

118. Y. 34.6.

119. Ibid., 34.15.

120. Ibid., 30.9.

121. Ibid., 34.13: 46.3: 48.12.

122. Ibid., 45.1.

123. Ibid., 51.6.

124. Ibid., 51.9.

125. Ibid., 31.19.

126. Ibid., 43.4: 34.4.

127. Ibid., 46.7.

Abbreviations

A²H. Inscription of Artaxerxes II at Hamadan.

AVN. *Artāy Virāf Nāmak.*

BSOAS. *Bulletin of the School of Oriental and African Studies.*

Clemen, Fontes. *Fontes historiae religionis persicae.*

DB. Inscription of Darius I at Bīsitūn.

Dd. *Dātastān i dēnīk.*

DkM. *Dēnkart,* ed. Madan.

DN. Inscription of Darius I at Naqsh-i Rustam.

DP. Inscription of Darius I at Persepolis.

DS. Inscription of Darius I at Susa.

GB. *Greater Bundahishn.*

MKh. *Mēnōk i Khrat.*

Murūj. [Mas'ūdī], *Murūj al-dhahab.*

Ny. *Nyāyishn.*

Phl. Pahlavi.

PR. Pahlavi *Rivāyats.*

PT. *Pahlavi Texts.*

RV. *Rig-Veda.*

ShGV. *Shikand-Gumānīk Vichār.*

TM. [R. C. Zaehner] *The Teachings of the Magi.*

Vd. *Vidēvdāt.*

XP. Inscription of Xerxes at Persepolis.

Y. *Yasna.*

Yt. *Yasht.*

ZKhA. *Zand i Khwartak Apastāk.*

Zs. *Selections of Zātspram.*

ZZD. [R. C. Zaehner] *Zurvan, A Zoroastrian Dilemma.*

Richard N. Frye (essay date 1963)

SOURCE: "Iranian Traditions" in *The Heritage of Persia,* World Publishing Company, 1963, pp. 15-52.

[*In the following excerpt, Frye reviews the controversy surrounding the dating of Zoroaster and his scriptures, outlines the differences between Zoroaster's teachings and other ancient beliefs, and comments on the influence of Zoroaster on the development of the Iranian epic tradition.*]

ZOROASTER AND HIS MESSAGE

Zarathushtra, or Zoroaster, as the Greeks called him, presents many problems, and it is discouraging that after so many years of research we do not know when or where he lived or even precisely his teachings. One may marshal the evidence and conclude that he was not one thing or did not live at a certain period, but positive information about the prophet and his time is conspicuous by its absence. Let us attempt to gather material relating to him, trying to group the less uncertain data first, and finally coming to some tentative conclusions.

It is highly probable that Zarathushtra is not a figment of the imagination and that he did exist. Arguments that he was created to match prophets in other religions, or that the Avesta was a late forgery, are really unacceptable and we only need to follow history to refute them. The form of his name is also plausible among the names one would expect in an ancient society somewhere in Iran. The name Zarathushtra might be explained as 'he who can handle camels', although other etymologies have been proposed. In the Avesta we learn about his clan of Spitama and the closely related family of Haechataspa, indeed about his daughter and friends, and from the later Middle Persian commentaries we even learn the names of his father and mother. None of this, however, helps us with the *history* of Zoroaster, especially his time and place. We must turn primarily to the **Gathas**, presumably the words of the prophet, and to later sources and general considerations, to aid us in placing Zoroaster in history and geography.

To determine the date of Zoroaster we have no historical data to help us, and we can only say that most probably he lived before the Achaemenid empire. To further determine the time we should look at the evidence of the **Gathas**, Greek sources, and later Zoroastrian tradition subdivided into the tradition of the Pahlavi books and the tradition as found in Islamic sources. These we should try to bring into harmony, or at least we should come to a probable estimate of his dates from all of them.

The **Gathas**, 'verses or poems', were undoubtedly preserved by memory for centuries before being written down. The seventeen verses or five groups of verses, known collectively as **Gatha,** belong together by virtue of similarity in metre and archaic language. Certain features of the language of the **Gathas** and of the Younger Avesta as well are more archaic than corresponding features in Vedic Sanskrit, but this, of course, does not mean that the **Gathas** are therefore older in time than the Rig Veda, since as a parallel in Altaic languages modern Mongolian in many features is 'more archaic' than the oldest Turkish, and Arabic is in the same relation to Hebrew.

Greek sources are not encouraging either. Xanthos of Lydia, the oldest source (fifth century BC) places Zoroaster

600 (or 6,000) years before Xerxes, and other Greek authors are more extravagant. From the classical sources we gain no precision at all, only that Zoroaster lived in great antiquity. Obviously they had no accurate knowledge of his history, but we should explain even this lack. Some of the sources which give numbers in the thousands can be explained as reflecting an Iranian mythical world age number—an eschatological doctrine. Did the Greeks reproduce this, or other extreme dates on Zoroaster, because the Persians fooled them, either intentionally or because they themselves believed it, or was Zoroaster so removed from the West in time or space that a myth about him was all that was known? If the Persians tried to fool the Greeks, then how is it that no indication of the real state of affairs leaked out to the Greeks, and why did the Persians try to fool the Greeks? In answer to the first question, it is unlikely that the Persians could keep true information from the Greeks, and if they did try, it can hardly be explained as pure perversity or a desire to sanctify Zoroaster by a hoary age. What then is the conclusion to draw from the Greek sources? One probably could say that the Greeks got their information from Persians who themselves did not know the date of Zoroaster. From the Greek sources, a date of, say, 1,000 BC might seem a shade more reasonable for Zoroaster than 600 BC, but this is speculative. The burden of bringing more evidence seems to rest on Iranian sources, or the Zoroastrian tradition.

Since the chronology of the ancient Near East before the Achaemenids is mostly based on the Egyptian king lists and anything outside the hieroglyphic-cuneiform cultural areas is hardly datable, it follows that the non-literary Iranians could not be expected to have a chronology of Zoroaster unless they kept genealogical lists like the Hebrews, which apparently was not the case. It would not be unreasonable to assume that the ancient Iranians, even shortly after Zoroaster's death, could not place him chronologically, at least in relation to any of the great events occurring in Mesopotamia or possibly even in western Iran. But later Zoroastrian tradition, followed by Islamic authors such as al-Bīrūnī, gives a precise date for Zoroaster, 258 years before Alexander the Great. Many scholars have rejected this date, while others have accepted it as genuine. Recently an impressive attempt was made to substantiate the date based on the reasonable assumption that the followers of Zoroaster counted the years from a significant moment in the life of the prophet, and when 258 years had passed in the era of Zoroaster, a great calamity occurred, the death of Darius, the last Achaemenid king and the accession to power of Alexander the Great. This would mean 258 years subtracted from 330 BC or 588 BC for the year one of reckoning on the part of Zoroaster's followers. It is interesting to observe that the dating of Buddha is apparently secured in a similar manner by reference to later traditions assigning events in Buddha's life to so many years before the reign of Aśoka. But actually it is only a later tradition and based on an assumed date of the Buddha rather than on Aśoka. One need not be reminded that the date 588 BC, which may have

been the date Zoroaster converted King Vishtaspa, when tradition says the prophet was forty-two years old, is based on a number of assumptions which might be criticised. Further tradition says the prophet was seventy-seven when he died, so if one prefers fixed historical dates for Zoroaster based upon reasonable *assumptions* and late Zoroastrian *traditions,* then 628-551 BC is the best theory we have. Otherwise, one may prefer to believe that the date is about the eighth or seventh century BC but not determined. If we could find evidence from outside the Zoroastrian tradition, which tradition assumes that the Zoroastrians had a clear 'era' reckoning from the time of the prophet, until Alexander so shocked them that they changed their outlook to date their prophet so many years before Alexander, then it would be easier to accept a more precise date for Zoroaster.

It is true that the number 258 is curious, hardly apocalyptic or fitting into an eschatological system. Yet the negative reckoning, so many years before Alexander, presupposes the existence of an era of reckoning from some event in Zoroaster's life by his followers. As far as we know the Seleucid era was the first dating by a fixed year which was widely accepted. On the other hand, the followers of Zoroaster may have been well ahead of their time in adopting an 'era of Zoroaster', counting from the date of his conversion of Vishtaspa, possible echoes of which may survive in the Pahlavi book *Bundahishn* (ed. Anklesaria 240.1) where an era of the 'acceptance of the religion' (*padīriftan-i dēn*) is implied. The *Bundahishn,* of course, was written over 1,200 years after Alexander, but the mere fact that the apocryphal reign of Vishtaspa is said to have lasted for ninety years after the 'acceptance of religion' is a point, together with the number 258, in favour of a 'Zoroastrian era'. Needless to say, we are still much in the dark.

The homeland of Zoroaster has also raised great controversies which are by no means all resolved. Most scholars now agree that he lived and taught in eastern Iran. Late Zoroastrian tradition placed the prophet in Azerbaijan, but the geographical horizon of the Avesta is limited to eastern Iran, and the transfer of his activities to western Iran at a later date can be explained by political circumstances. It is true that one may fit the *mythical* geography of the Avesta with the homeland of *Airyāna Vaējah,* into Azerbaijan, or for that matter elsewhere in Iran, but the geographical picture of the Avesta is not very helpful. One may say, however, that the legends and stories about Zoroaster's activities, not his birth, seem to be more specific when localised in the east than the stories localised in the west. For example, the story of the planting of a cypress tree in Kishmar in Khurasan to commemorate the conversion of Vishtaspa is old and widespread. Another tradition has him born in Raga, mediaeval Rayy, near Tehran, with a *hegira* to the east where he converts Vishtaspa. Furthermore, there is no apparent reason why Zoroaster should be moved to the east if in fact he lived in the west, while the reverse is more plausible since eastern Iran was subjected to invasion from Central Asia many times and was lost to Iranian rule for long periods. There is a Zoroastrian tradition that the prophet was killed in Bactria, but other traditions place his activity elsewhere in the east. One may guess that he was active in the Herat area with connections south to Seistan, east to Bactria (Balkh) and north to Merv.

Linguistic evidence too would tend to place the prophet in eastern Iran. Historically, one would expect that the Avesta, with its mythology and heroic epic features blending into the general eastern Iranian sagas which we shall shortly discuss, would be composed in a language close to that spoken in the Aryan homeland. That homeland may have been in Transoxiana, or even more to the south in the Herat area. Just as the Indians wherever they went in the subcontinent preserved the Vedic hymns in the old traditional language no matter what changes happened in their various dialects, so the Iranians wherever they went on the Iranian plateau preserved theogonies to Mithra and other Aryan gods. I suggest that the Iranian tribes of Persians, Medes and others, at the time of their wandering to their later homes, recited hymns to the gods similar in content and *language,* which was the language of the old homeland *Airyāna Vaējah.* The tribes which went to western Iran gave their tongues to the indigenous population of Elamites, Hurrians or the like, and consequently their dialects began to lose distinctions of grammatical gender and a general breakdown of the languages started. Before this happened, however, a prophet appeared in the east preaching in an archaising, conservative idiom of the dialect possibly of the Herat area, the language of the **Gathas.** This sounded more lofty and authoritative than the Avestan idiom used everywhere by 'priests' praying to Mithra, Ardvisura or other deities. Later when Zoroaster's teachings spread all over Iran other priests simply attached his hymns in the Gathic dialect to the common hymns in Avestan. This probably happened under the Achaemenids, and we shall discuss this later.

To return to the two languages, or better characterised as dialects, Gathic and Avestan, the former the language of the **Gathas,** the latter the tongue of the 'Young Avesta', they would best fit into the area between the central deserts and the mountains of Afghanistan. Since the contents of the Younger Avesta have connections with the eastern Iranian epic traditions, we may say that in content as well as language, both parts of the Avesta point to eastern Iran. This does not mean, however, that the hymns of the Younger Avesta were only recited or sung in eastern Iran. Indeed parts of the Younger Avesta, particularly the Vendidad or Videvdat 'the anti-demonic law', may well have been composed in western Iran by the Magi, who seem to have been the priests of the Medes and later of all western Iranians. If this be true then the Magi may have known the Avestan language before Zoroaster. The Magi were probably influenced in ritual and practices by the indigenous population and by the ancient cultures of Mesopotamia while their counterparts in the east, the *zaotars,* remained truer to Aryan practices. But this is turning away from Zoroaster himself. Before turning to the historical, or better, epical milieu of eastern Iran at the time of Zoroaster, something should be said about his life and teachings.

We have said that Zoroaster does not appear in a vacuum, for we learn about his family, friends and enemies from the Avesta and from later Zoroastrian tradition.[32] Furthermore, as we shall shortly see, the prophet is placed among the epical, pre-historical kings of eastern Iran in an orderly picture of this pre-literary period in the sagas of the people. Because of this order, much, or even most of it may be historical, but we do not know. The age of Zoroaster seems to correspond with the phenomenological characterisation of an age when the gods have descended upon earth bringing an end to mythology, and the beginning of epic, the heroic age of Iran. The family and relations of Zoroaster need not detain us beyond the remark that the names are in general what one would expect in ancient, eastern Iran, though any royal connections among the ancestors of the prophet are suspicious and I for one do not believe them.

Zoroaster was probably a priest of the old Aryan religion, for he calls himself a *zaotar* (Indian *hotar*) in the **Gathas** (Yasna 33.6). Since he retained this ancient word and did not give it a bad sense, one may suppose he retained the old institution of the Aryan 'priest' in his new religion. He also retained the old poetic form, for the metre of his **Gathas** is similar to that of the Vedas. He further exalted the concept of *asha,* 'truth', the *rta* of India, and further used words in the same sense as in the Vedas. But Zoroaster is more; he is a prophet who preaches a new gospel not accepted by his own people. We obtain glimpses of opposition to him and then the prophet's *hegira* and chilly reception elsewhere (Yasna 51.12), and finally his acceptance by Kavi Vishtaspa and the success of his preaching. So Zoroaster was a prophet who found favour not at home but among others. In what way did his message differ from ancient beliefs and customs?

One difference between the **Gathas** and the Rig Veda is the different relation between the worshipper (this is Zoroaster himself in the **Gathas**) and the deity. The familiar tone of the **Gathas** strikes one at once, especially in Yasna 44 where the verses begin, 'I ask you, tell me truly oh Ahura (Mazda)'. The deity is like a partner in discourse with the prophet, and this is new with Zoroaster. His followers too are not neglected, so one senses a possible social base for Zoroaster's preaching. Whether one can distinguish between the followers of Zoroaster as peaceful shepherds with flocks of cattle and his enemies as fierce nomads who steal and slaughter the cattle of their foes is perhaps reading too much into the words of Zoroaster. What stands out in the teaching of the prophet is the dualism of Good and Evil and the great importance of man as an arbiter between them. Whether he raised his dualism as a protest against existing monotheism is uncertain, but most people would agree that he was first and foremost a prophet with high ethical ideals and persuasive ideas. With which ideas did Zoroaster move the hearts of his contemporaries? Study of the **Gathas** led the latest translator to the following remarks.[33]

> 'He took over belief in the Ahuras from his predecessors. It is likely he transformed that belief; perhaps even created the name Ahura Mazda and interpreted

the Ahuras as personifications of the qualities of Ahura Mazda. But it was hardly possible with such theological discussion to set an entire people in religious motion. The favoured position of *asha*, which was also honoured by Zoroaster's opponents, is not new, nor is veneration of the cow, which Zoroaster already had ascribed to Fryana, the mythical ancestor of Kavi Vishtaspa. Perhaps even the dualism in substantial points had already been worked out by Zoroaster's predecessors. What is then the distinctive concept which Zoroaster brought out above all the cow-centred Magi and Brahmins, and which made him one of the great world founders of a religion? It is really the knowledge of the directly imminent beginning of the last epoch of the world, in which Good and Evil would be separated from one another, which he gave to mankind. It is the knowledge that it lies in every individual's hand to participate in the extirpation of Falsehood and in the establishing of the kingdom of God, before whom all men devoted to the pastoral life are equal, and so to re-establish the milk flowing paradise on earth.'

Zoroaster's teachings must have made a great impression on his followers so that they memorised his sayings and passed them on to their children. There may have been prose explanations of the concise verses of Zoroaster like the commentaries on the sayings of Buddha, but unfortunately these Gathic commentaries have not survived, which makes our present understanding of the **Gathas** very difficult. Yet the power and intensity of feeling in the verses may be sensed even in translation, as for example Yasna 44.3-4:

> This do I ask Thee, Oh Lord, tell me truly;
> Who is the creator, the first father of Righteousness?
> Who laid down the path of the sun and stars?
> Who is it through whom the moon now waxes now wanes?
> All this and more do I wish to know, Oh Wise One.
> This do I ask thee, Oh Lord, tell me truly;
> Who holds the earth below and the sky as well
> from falling? Who (created) the waters and the plants?
> Who harnesses the (two) coursers to wind and clouds?
> Who, oh Wise One, is the creator of Good Mind?

SAGAS OF THE EAST

The Persians are a people with an epic tradition which is surely very old. There are many problems in tracing the legends in the New Persian *Shahname*, or book of kings, back to Parthian, Achaemenian or Aryan times, and the changes or layers in various stories throughout the ages are almost impossibly difficult to determine. One may, however, come to some general conclusions which would serve to clarify the role of the epic in pre-Islamic Iran.

Mythology is intimately bound up with the beginning of epic literature, for the former is concerned with the acts of the gods, and the latter with the heroic deeds of men. Just as later bards wove various stories of different dates with little regard to chronology into a unified epic, so the earlier priests recited hymns to the gods, and they, or associates, composed stories about the gods. As in the mythology of

Japan where the descendants of the Sun goddess came to earth and ruled it, so in ancient Egypt and elsewhere the rulers are of divine origin. One may suppose that the undivided Aryans had a mythology but not yet an epic. After the separation of Indians and Iranians the new contacts of both, the former in the subcontinent and the latter in western Iran and Mesopotamia, may well have changed the outlooks of these people, now in more settled, more secure surroundings, to a more prosaic or pragmatic *Weltanschauung* which the heroic life which engenders epics lacked. In one place, however, the Aryan homeland, conditions propitious to the development of the epic continued. I suggest that circumstances and milieu were more favourable to the flowering of the epic in eastern Iran and Central Asia than elsewhere in the area covered by Iranians. It is inherently probable that the Iranians wherever they went had a common mythology, for even with the Indians there are parallel myths and names, such as the Iranian Yima and Indian Yama, an earthly first king or king of the dead, Iranian Thraetaona, Indian Traitaná, and others. Now it may well be, as some scholars have argued, that a common Indo-European eschatology engendered common stories and motifs in the later oral literature of some of the daughter languages, but few of these languages have an epic tradition. Persian is one and the *Shahname* is recited by countless people even today. The beginning of an epic tradition in Iran probably coincided with the appearance of the prophet Zoroaster which event surely influenced the later development of the epic. If there had been no Zoroaster the epic might have developed as in India or among the Germanic peoples, or it might have died out under the rule in Iran of the Greeks or later the Arabs. If Zoroaster had appeared about the time of Christ and had been so willed he might have destroyed the old mythology and the epic with it. These are all 'ifs' and one may suppose that Zoroaster appeared at a time and place which almost insured his inclusion in a developing epic. For the Iranian epic, as found in the *Shahname* and other variations of it, can be said at least to be in harmony with the Zoroastrian religion as it developed, if it were not actually 'Zoroastrianised', as is most likely.

Much has been written about the place of origin of local epic traditions or of various motifs in an all-Iranian epic tradition. This has led to a general conclusion about the Iranian epic, that it is really composed of two epic traditions, but there is some difference about the classification or nomenclature of these two traditions. One scholar called them the mythical tradition and the tradition of the eastern Iranian rulers, or the 'religious' and the 'national' traditions.[34] Another postulates a 'Zoroastrian' and a 'nomadic' epic tradition.[35] The main problem here, I believe, is the different history of the epic in eastern and western Iran and its accretion by the addition of various local cycles. I have already proposed that all Iranians had a common mythology but not a common epic, at least not until the rule of the eastern Parthians spread over all of Iran. There is no evidence that stories of the eastern rulers or *kavis* were sung or recited in western Iran under the Achaemenids. Presumably there were local 'epics' about the ancestors of local rulers, but the inclusion of Zoroaster in the particular cycle of the *kavis* of eastern Iran probably helped to make that cycle the basis for the earlier part of the all-Iranian epic of later times. Furthermore, the stories of the eastern *kavis* may well have been more exciting and more heroic than others elsewhere, for any epic is primarily concerned with heroic deeds, religion being secondary.

One may suppose then that the Iranian epic was basically an eastern cycle of stories, the 'legendary' ancient history of eastern Iran with the prophet Zoroaster included in it as part of that history. There may have been stories in western Iran similar to some in the east in the time of the Achaemenids, such as the love story of Zariadres and Odatis, told by the Greek, Charles of Mytilene, but this proves nothing about the borrowing of motifs from east by west. Generally speaking, unless proper names can be traced as borrowed forms, the possibility of a common heritage or parallel development of story themes must always be present. One scholar has convincingly shown that the Kayanian cycle stories were not generally known everywhere in Iran until the Parthians spread them and the Sasanians collected them and recorded them.[36] Of course, it is very difficult to follow the changes in stories and adaptations from other sources; for example, the attempts of Christensen to attach the Rustam stories in Seistan to the feudal lords of the Suren family and the Godarz tales to the Karen family, both in Parthian times, are plausible but cannot be proved.[37] In any case, we may say that the eastern Iranian Kayanian heroic cycle is the main source for the later all-Iranian epic. Since Zoroaster belonged to the Kayanian milieu the Zoroastrian religious leaders adopted the cycle as part of their lore or ancient history. While one may postulate a religious epic cycle and a national, or secular epic cycle, they are so intermingled later that the *Shahname* could be regarded as both the secular and religious history of the Zoroastrian religion by a Zoroastrian priest in recent times. Obviously the priests were not the only persons who kept the epic alive. Bards and minstrels entertained rulers and aristocracy by reciting epics down the ages. If one is concerned with literature, religion plays an insignificant role in the epic, but if one studies religion then contrariwise the tales are unimportant. That epics existed outside the purview of Zoroastrianism is indicated by an independent cycle, that of the Scythians, represented in a modern form by the legends of the Iranian Ossetes in the north Caucasus. Apparently these Iranians were untouched by Zoroastrianism, for there is no parallel word for 'demon, evil spirit', *dev,* which exists in other Iranian languages. One may consider their Nart tales as an epic and undoubtedly there were other cycles no longer existent. We will return to the epic when discussing the Parthians and Sasanians, but the next matter for consideration here is the historical material in the stories of the Kayanids and other ancient heroes of Iran. . . .

Notes

1. A. Meillet, *Linguistique historique et linguistique générale* (Paris, 1921), 15.

2. Cf. J. Pokorny, *Indogermanisches Etymologisches Wörterbuch* (Bern, 1959), 15.

3. *Ibid.,* 62.

4. A. Meillet, 'La religion indo-européenne', in *op. cit.,* 323-334. The following remarks follow Meillet to whose general conclusions I, for the most part, subscribe.

5. J. Vendryes, 'Correspondances entre l'indo-iranien et l'italo-celtique', *Mémoires de la société de linguistique,* 20 (Paris, 1918), 272.

6. Meillet, *op. cit.,* 323.

7. The best summary of Dumézil's position can be found in his *L'idéologie tripartite des Indo-Européens* (Brussels, 1958).

8. E.g. S. Wikander, 'Germanische und Indo-Iranische Eschatologie', *Kairos, Zeitschrift für Religionswissenschaft,* 2 (1960), 83; 'Från Bråvalla till Kurukshetra', *Arkiv för Nordisk Filologi,* 75 (1960), 183; A. V. Ström, 'Das indogermanische Erbe in den Urzeit- und Endzeitschilderungen des Edda-Liedes Voluspa', *Akten des X. Internationalen Kongresses für die Geschichte der Religionen* (Marburg, 1961).

9. E.g. M. Molé, 'La structure du premier chapitre du Vidēvdāt', *Journal Asiatique* (1951), 283, and J. Duchesne-Guillemin, *The Western Response to Zoroaster* (Oxford, 1958).

10. G. Redard in *Kratylos,* I (1956), 144.

11. J. Hertel, *Die Methode der arischen Forschung* (Leipzig, 1926).

12. The Hittite and Assyrian records are sometimes confusing in their nomenclature, for 'Hurrian' and 'Mitanni', as well as other designations, seem to be used interchangeably. See now P. Thieme, 'The Aryan Gods of the Mitanni Treaties', *Journal of the American Oriental Society,* 80 (1960), 301–317.

13. Cf. M. Mayrhofer, 'Zu den arischen Sprachresten in Vorderasien', *Die Sprache,* 5 (1959), 77-95. Corresponding forms for 'one' would be: Aryan **aika,* Ur-Iranian **aika,* Indian *eka.* I propose another line of descent for Avestan and Old Persian from Indo-European **oiuo,* Aryan **aiva,* with a *ka* ending in Old Persian. But **aiva-ka*>Middle Persian *ēvak*>New Persian *yak* is another problem; perhaps a more direct descent **aika*>*yak,* as Avestan *aēxa*>*yax* 'ice' is to be preferred. Varuna presents difficulties, but both 'Ur-Iranian' and Aryan forms would be from **var-,* as an Avestan reconstruction **vouruna* would parallel Avestan *vouru*-<Ur-Iranian **varu-* 'wide'. Cf. E. P. Hamp, 'Varuna and the suffix -*una*', *Indo-Iranian Journal,* 4 (1960), 64. Cf. now Thieme (above) 301.

14. Of course we may have a dialect division in Indo-European both **oiqo* and **oiuo* influencing the later developments. We follow here Brugmann and

the *Indo-European-*Aryan hypothesis although it may require revision.

15. We are concerned here with the cultural-historical data to be gained from the sources rather than with the philological exegesis of the texts or linguistic questions of vocabulary, grammar or syntax.

16. Indicated by Sanskrit *krsi-* 'agriculture', Avestan *karšu-*, as well as other relevant words. We have suggested above that the Aryans were Indo-Europeans who became nomadic and then reverted to pastoralists-agriculturists when they arrived at their new homes. The other alternative would place the separation of the Aryans from the other Indo-Europeans just at the beginning of their acquaintance with agriculture, which would explain the different agricultural words in Indo-Iranian from other Indo-European languages.

17. Cf. R. N. Frye, *'Georges Dumézil and the translators of the Avesta'*, *Numen*, 7 (1960), 161 foll.

18. Pokorny, *op. cit.* 184.

19. Cf. W. Rau, *Staat und Gesellschaft im alten Indien* (Wiesbaden, 1957), 17.

20. H. Ljungberg, *Hur Kristendom kom till Sverige* (Stockholm, 1946), 27.

21. P. Thieme, *Mitra and Aryaman* (New Haven, Connecticut, 1957), 59, 61.

22. Translation after K. Geldner, *Der Rig-Veda*, 3 (Cambridge, Massachusetts, 1951), 384; text ed. T. Aufrecht 2 (Bonn, 1877) 445. Geldner's translation of the third line above by *'den gleichgewillten (Gegenstand des) Preises, die Keule'*, is somewhat over-poetic.

23. H. Berger, *'Die Burushaski-Lehnwörter in der Zigeunersprache'*, *Indo-Iranian Journal*, 3 (1959), 17. Also *Munchener Studien zur Sprachwissenschaft*, 9 (1956), 4 foll.

24. I do not accept the theory that the Brahuis are a group of Dravidians who migrated from the Deccan to Makran in historic times.

25. For example, the Aryan dipthong ai is preserved in Avestan, while in Vedic Indian it became *e*. Cf. A. Meillet, *'Sur le texte de l'Avesta'*, *Journal Asiatique* (1920), 187 foll., and, *Mémoires de la société de linguistique*, 18 (Paris, 1913), 377.

26. The classical sources are conveniently assembled in A. V. W. Jackson, *Zoroaster* (New York, 1898), 152-157. Cf. C. Clemen, *Die griechischen und lateinischen Nachrichten über die persische Religion* (Giessen, 1920).

27. As explained in many modern writings, for example, in H. S. Nyberg, *Die Religionen des alten Iran* (Liepzig, 1938), 28.

28. Sources in Jackson, *op. cit.*, 157.

29. The date 258 is considered apocalyptic by Nyberg, *op. cit.*, 33-34, and historical by E. Herzfeld, *Zoroaster*, I (Princeton, 1947), chapter one.

30. W. B. Henning, *Zoroaster* (Oxford, 1951), 41.

31. Cf. O. Klima, *'The Date of Zoroaster'*, *Archiv Orientální* 27 (Prague, 1959), 558. On p. 564 he proposes the date of Zoroaster as 784-707 BC.

32. Cf. Jackson, *op. cit.*, 19-22.

33. H. Humbach, *Die Gathas des Zarathustra*, I (Heidelberg, 1959), 74.

34. A. Christensen in *Handbuch der Altertums-Wissenschaft, Kulturgeschichte des alten Orients*, Dritter Abschnitt, Erste Lieferung (Munich, 1933), 217, and his *Les Kayanides* (Copenhagen, 1932), 69.

35. I. Gershevitch in E. B. Ceadel, *Literatures of the East* (London, 1953), 56.

36. M. Boyce, *'Zariadres and Zarēr'*, *Bulletin of the School of Oriental and African Studies*, 17 (London, 1955), 474.

37. A. Christenson, *Les Kayanides* (Copenhagen, 1932), 138. . . .

Bibliography

The fundamental old work on Indo-European philology is still the five-volume comparative grammar by Karl Brugmann, which has appeared in many editions and in a French translation. It is, of course, much in need of revision but nothing has yet replaced it. The Indo-European comparative dictionary is by P. Walde and J. Pokorny (Berlin, 1928 foll.), in 3 vols. with a revision of it by Pokorny entitled *Indogermanisches Etymologisches Wörterbuch* (Bern, 1959). Needless to say, scholars do not agree on many of its etymologies. This is not the place to list contributions to Indo-European philology by A. Meillet, E. Benveniste, J. Kurylowicz and many others, for ample bibliographies may be found in such journals as *Kratylos, Indogermanisches Jahrbuch and Linguistic Bibliography*. A good survey of the question of an Indo-European *Ursprache*, homeland and culture may be found in the article of A. Scherer, *'Indogermanische Altertumskunde (seit 1940)'*, *Kratylos*, 1 (1956).

The Indo-Europeans in the ancient Near East have been discussed many times, and the latest account by P. Thieme in *Journal of the American Oriental Society*, 80 (1960), came to my attention after my text was written. It is a good survey of relevant problems.

On Zoroaster one need only add to Zaehner's exhaustive bibliography the book of W. Hinz, *Zarathustra* (Stuttgart, 1961), which contains a new translation of the Gathas.

Regarding the pre-Islamic epic literature of Iran and the East-Iranian sagas the article by Mary Boyce in the volume on literature of the *Handbuch der Orientalistik*, ed. B. Spuler (Leiden, 1963), will be the best survey available. For a shorter survey see the article on 'Iranian Literature', by I. Gershevitch in E. B. Ceadel, *Literatures of the East* (London, 1953). The classic study on Firdosi's *Shahname* is by T. Noeldeke in the *Grundriss der iranischen Philologie,* 2 (Strassburg, 1904). This may be supplemented by the small book of A. Christensen, *Les gestes des rois dans les traditions de l'Iran antique* (Paris, 1936). A guide to Pahlavi literature is found in the book of J. Tavadia, *Die mittelpersische Sprache und Literatur der Zarathustrier* (Leipzig, 1956).

The book *Saka-Studien* by J. Junge (Leipzig, 1939) is a useful survey of ancient north-eastern Iran but it must be used with caution. The monumental but outdated studies of F. Spiegel, *Eranische Altertumskunde,* 3 vols. (Leipzig, 1871-1878), and W. Geiger, *Ostiranische Kultur in Alterthum* (Erlangen, 1882) still may be used to orient oneself with profit.

The social structure of the ancient Iranians is discussed by E. Benveniste in '*Les classes sociales dans la tradition avestique*', *Journal Asiatique,* 116-134 (1932). The book by A. A. Mazahéri, *La famille iranienne aux temps ante-islamiques* (Paris, 1938), contains much material, but is to be used with care. Much interesting work has been done by Soviet scholars on ancient class structure and slavery. See various papers presented at the twenty-fifth International Congress of Orientalists in Moscow, 1960, published as separate pamphlets, and also to appear in the general proceedings, especially the articles '*Indoiranische Kastengliederung bei den Skythen*', by E. Grantovskii, '*Foreign Slaves on the Estates of the Achaemenid Kings*', by M. Dandamayer and '*Quelques nouvelles observations sur les documents elamites de Persepolis*' by V. O. Tyurin.

Ilya Gershevitch (essay date 1964)

SOURCE: "Zoroaster's Own Contribution," *Journal of Near Eastern Studies,* Vol. XXIII, No. 1, January, 1964, pp. 12-38.

[*In the essay below, Gershevitch investigates the nature of the discrepancies between the doctrines Zoroaster puts forth in the* Gathas *and those beliefs attributed to him in the Later Avesta.*]

I. THE THREE VERSIONS OF ZOROASTER'S DOCTRINE

Zoroaster's own verses, the **Gathas,** which may be dated to the first half of the sixth century B.C., form only a small part of the scripture that goes under the name of the Avesta. The difference between the doctrine which Zoroaster states or implies in the **Gathas** and the doctrine which is attributed to him in the remainder of the scripture has long attracted attention. To avoid confusion it is convenient to refer to the religion of the **Gathas** as "Zarathuštrianism" and to the doctrine of the Younger Avestan texts as "Zarathuštricism." The term "Zoroastrianism" may then be

reserved for the form which the doctrine takes in the much later, Sasanian, period.[1]

In the **Gathas** Zoroaster reveals himself as a monotheist in that he worships one god only, Ahura Mazdāh. He is, however, also a dualist, because he assumes the existence of two aboriginal principles, Truth and Falsehood. The common denominator of these two apparently irreconcilable viewpoints is in Zoroaster's system Truth. For Truth is one of the organs, aspects, or emanations of Ahura Mazdāh through which the god acts and becomes accessible. Two religions, therefore, appear to have been syncretized by the prophet: a monotheism centered in a god of whom Truth is an emanation, and a dualism in which Truth is primordial.[2]

The prophet himself refers to God's aspects or emanations by expressions which we may translate as "Entities" (cf. below, p. 17), but in the post-Gathic parts of the Avesta they are called *Aməša Spəntas,* that is, "Holy Immortals."[3] One of these Immortals, in fact the chief one, since he is God's creative organ, is *Spənta Mainyu,* the "Holy Spirit" (cf. *AHM,* pp. 11 f., 165 f.). This Spirit sometimes appears in the **Gathas** in the company of *Angra Mainyu,* the later *Ahriman,* or "Fiendish Spirit." A profound disagreement separates the two, which arises from the different choice they have made. The Fiendish Spirit, says Zarathuštra, chose to do evil, thus siding with Falsehood, while the Holy Spirit chose Truth (*Yasna* 30.5). This choice is the prototype of the choice which faces each man as he decides between following the path of Truth or that of Falsehood.

While in one Gathic passage (*Yasna* 47.3) Zarathuštra refers to God as the "father" of the Holy Spirit, in another (*Yasna* 30.3) he describes the Holy and the Fiendish Spirits as "twins."[4] The conclusion that the Fiendish Spirit, too, was an emanation of Ahura Mazdāh's is unavoidable.[5] But we need not go so far as to assume that Zarathuštra imagined the Devil as having directly issued from God. Rather, since free will, too, is a basic tenet of Zarathuštrianism, we may think of the "childbirth" implied in the idea of twinship as having consisted in the emanation by God of undifferentiated "spirit," which only at the emergence of free will split into two "twin" Spirits of opposite allegiance. Truth alone being, in addition to a primordial principle, also an aspect of Ahura Mazdāh, the fact that the Fiendish Spirit had chosen Falsehood would all but obliterate his original connection with God. It would follow that the names "Holy" and "Fiendish" of the two Spirits did not in the prophet's view pre-exist the choice which they made, but accrued to either as a result of it.

The different election of the two Spirits contained the seed of a clash. But, as we gather from the much later, Zoroastrian, texts, conflict could not take place in a purely spiritual state. This is presumably why the Gathic myth reports no struggle, or even bitterness, between the two Spirits, but only hints at a struggle to come. To bring about conflict—a desirable aim, since only through conflict could either Spirit hope to prevail over the other—life, death, and after-life had to be created, mainly, we may take it, in regard to Man, who would serve as champion, battleground, and prize. This thought Zarathuštra expressed in the following words: "In order that they might meet (in battle), the two Spirits first created[6] life and not-life (i.e. the Holy Spirit created life, the Fiendish not-life), and established[6] how ultimately existence will be: (that) of the owners of Falsehood (will be) very bad, but the owner of Truth (will) have the best dwelling" (*Yasna* 30.4).[7]

Although in conformity with their common origin both Spirits are seen in *Yasna* 30.4 to have been "creators,"[8] only the Holy Spirit acts as *God's* creative organ. In this capacity he is frequently mentioned in the Gathas, while the Fiendish Spirit, having through his election ceased to be an organ of God's, receives no further attention from the poet.

In one Gathic passage (*Yasna* 44.7) we are clearly told that it is through the Holy Spirit that God created everything. Nevertheless it is God, not the Holy Spirit, who dominates the Gathic scene. God did not have to choose between Truth and Falsehood, like the two Spirits, because Truth, inasmuch as it is not only an aboriginal principle but also one of God's aspects, is part of God and belongs to his definition. God thus stands outside the struggle which is waged between the forces of Truth and Falsehood. His only intervention consists in revealing to Zarathuštra the responsibility which rests on mankind: the support which each man lends to the side he has chosen will add permanent strength to it; in the long run, therefore, the acts of man will weigh the scales in favor of the one side or the other.[9]

It will thus be seen that Zarathuštra's dualistic attitude hinges exclusively on his postulate of the two principles, Truth and Falsehood. The two Spirits have no independent dualist status. They merely react to a pre-existing dualism.

So much for the **Gathas.** The composition of the bulk of the Younger Avestan texts appears to have begun more than a century after Zarathuštra's death, towards the last quarter of the fifth century B.C. (cf. below, p. 28). In the Younger Avestan texts the monotheism of the **Gathas** is strangely contaminated with what has been called a "pagan" polytheism. Beside Ahura Mazdāh numerous other gods are worshiped, Mithra, Anāhitā, Vrthraghna, Tištrya, Vayu, etc. There are passages in the hymns to these gods in which Ahura Mazdāh himself is represented as worshiping them. This polytheistic attitude is of course a travesty of Zarathuštra's intentions, even though the pious authors expressly ascribe it to him. In the Younger Avesta even statements which flatly contradict the prophet's own doctrine are blandly introduced with the prefatory remark: "Thus said Ahura Mazdāh to Zarathuštra," as if the authors meant to forestall any objections to what they were about to state.

Where the dualist doctrine is concerned, however, the authors of the Younger Avesta conform fairly closely to Zarathuštra's teachings. They still distinguish between the followers of Truth and the followers of Falsehood and range the Fiendish Spirit as an Archdemon with the latter. The Holy Spirit, on the other hand, is not very prominent in the Younger Avesta. He now bears the epithet "creator" (*Yašt* 10.143), like Ahura Mazdāh himself, so that one might almost expect him to become absorbed and replaced by Ahura Mazdāh. Of such an absorption, however, there is no indication in the scripture, except perhaps in the last chapter of the *Vendidad*, a late Younger Avestan book which was composed in post-Achaemenian times. This chapter relates that the Fiendish Spirit created against Ahura Mazdāh 99,999 diseases, to rid himself of which the god engaged the services of a number of genii. With this one exception, whenever the opposite number of the Fiendish Spirit is mentioned in the Younger Avesta, he is, as in the **Gathas,** the Holy Spirit and not God himself.[10]

The situation is very different in the late Zoroastrian books of the ninth century A.D., which are written no longer in the Avestan language but in Middle Persian. These books reflect in the main the views of the Zoroastrian Church at the time when Zoroastrianism occupied the position of official state religion under the Sasanian kings of Persia (A.D. 226-642). At this stage the doctrine appears in a simplified form. The pagan polytheism of the Younger Avestan, Zarathuštric scripture, has been virtually abandoned: the once powerful rivals of Ahura Mazdāh, such as Mithra, Vərəthraghna, Vayu, etc., have been reduced to little more than genii or angels surviving as Avestan reminiscences. In addition, the complications arising in the **Gathas** from a simultaneous belief in a monotheism centered in Ahura Mazdāh, on the one hand, and a dualism of two opposing principles, Truth and Falsehood, on the other, have been eliminated. In the place of Falsehood now stands the Fiendish Spirit, in the place of Truth, God himself. Zoroaster's religion has become an uncompromising dualism, in which two aboriginal deities, Ohrmazd and Ahriman, God and the Devil, face each other and contend for ultimate victory.

This simple formulation, so familiar to all, presents an interesting problem. Who was responsible for it, since neither the Zarathuštrian **Gathas** nor the Zarathuštric Younger Avesta can be regarded as its direct source?[11] The circumstances in which this un-Avestan doctrine came to be imputed to Zoroaster deserve to be investigated.

At this point we must remember that it is not among the Sasanian Zoroastrian priests that the formula Ohrmazd *versus* Ahriman makes its first appearance. From a fragment of the περι φιλοσοφιας of Aristotle we learn that already in the fourth century B.C., while part of the Younger Avestan scripture was still being composed, the Magi preached the existence of two principles . . . referred to as Spirits . . . , one of whom, the good one, was called Ὠρομέσδης, the other, evil, Ἀρειμένιος.[12]

Aristotle and his circle were greatly interested in the teachings of the Magi. They would not have been slow to appreciate the significance of a dualism based on the opposition of Truth and Falsehood, as Zoroaster had preached it. If nevertheless the fourth-century philosophers thought that the essence of the Magian doctrine consisted in the opposition of Oromasdes and Areimanios, it is clear that the Magi professed a dualist doctrine which considerably differed from that of the Avesta.

Now, it is true that the περι φιλοσοφιας attributes the formula Oromasdes *versus* Areimanios to the Magi, not to Zoroaster. Several considerations, however, suggest that the Magi were teaching this formula in the name of Zoroaster. That this was so at a later stage is known from Plutarch's attribution of the formula to "Zoroaster the Magus,"[13] and from the fact that with the Sasanian Zoroastrians the formula passed as the essence of the prophet's doctrine. But even in the beginning of the fourth century B.C. or at the end of the fifth, the Magi could hardly have given out the doctrine implied in the formula except by referring it to Zoroaster. For this doctrine is quite unrelated to the information which Herodotus had collected on the Persian and Magian religion.[14] It is unbelievable that, had the Magi identified themselves with this arresting doctrine by the middle of the fifth century, it would have failed to come to the notice of Herodotus. The absence of the formula from Herodotus' detailed account, and the presence of it alone in the περι φιλοσοφιας fragment as a succinct description of Magian thought, necessitate the assumption that the Magi changed their outlook at some time within the second half of the fifth century. The most likely reason for such a change would be the adoption on the part of the Magi of Zoroaster as their prophet. This is only another way of saying that up to the middle, at least, of the fifth century the Magi were not Zoroastrians, but in the first half of the fourth century they were.

II. Darius and Xerxes

We are thus using a well-known fact, namely the appearance in the fourth century of the formula Oromasdes *versus* Areimanios, as a new argument in support of a conclusion which can also be reached on the strength of two other considerations. One is that Herodotus' description of the Persian and Magian religion lacks all reference not only to the formula but even to the Zarathuštrian premises out of which the formula appears to have been developed.[15] One cannot therefore argue that the Magi were orthodox Zarathuštrians before they adopted the heterodox formula.

The other consideration is, that while in the Achaemenian inscriptions Darius I (522-486 B.C.) and Xerxes (486-465) name only Ahura Mazdāh as their god, Artaxerxes II (405-359) proclaims himself as worshiping Ahura Mazdāh, Mithra, and Anāhitā, and Artaxerxes III (359-338) invokes both Ahura Mazdāh and Mithra. It is generally thought that the religion of the Achaemenids from Artaxerxes II onwards must have been similar to the Zarathuštricism of the Younger Avesta, if not identical with it. At any rate, there can be little doubt that a relation existed between the change from the religious attitude of Darius and Xerxes to that of Artaxerxes II on the one hand, and the change from the monotheism of the Gathas to the polytheism of the Younger Avesta on the other. This relation, and the relevance it may have to the date of the conversion of the Magi, we must try to ascertain, but not without first attempting to define as closely as possible the religious attitude of Darius, Xerxes, and Artaxerxes I (465-425).

The inscriptions of Darius leave no doubt that his religion was a monotheism centered in Ahura Mazdāh. It is true that Darius occasionally refers to Ahura Mazdāh as "the greatest of the gods" and frequently invokes Ahura Mazdāh with the gods," which formula is replaced in one inscription (Persepolis, *d*) by "Ahura Mazdāh with all the gods." But such collective reference to "gods" is generally taken to reflect not a polytheistic attitude on the king's part but his tolerance of the numerous gods other than his own who were worshiped within his vast empire.

I believe we can be a little more precise. There is evidence which can be interpreted to the effect that Darius was tolerant enough towards the foreign, non-Iranian gods, but not altogether towards Ahura Mazdāh's Iranian rivals. The wording "Ahura Mazdāh with (all) the gods" does not yet appear in the Behistun inscription, the first which Darius dictated. In it we find, instead the wording "Ahura Mazdāh bore me aid, and the other gods who are."[16] In translating this expression the Elamite translator added to the name of Ahura Mazdāh the explanation "the god of the Iranians."[17] It seems reasonable to infer that in his opinion at least, the "other gods who are" were not Iranian. If this inference is correct, he must have had reasons to think that Darius held no brief for any "other" Iranian god that he, the translator, knew of,[18] including, of course, Mithra,[19] of whose existence the translator cannot have been unaware.

At all events, Darius's exclusive attribution of his success to Ahura Mazdāh, the fact that on the eve of his murder of Gaumāta he "prays"[20] to Ahura Mazdāh alone, and his almost Gathic statement that "Ahura Mazdāh is mine, I am Ahura Mazdāh's" (Susa, *k*), leave no room for doubt that he was a monotheist. Since in addition he speaks of "Falsehood" (*Drauga*) as if it were a personification of the principle whose opposition to "Truth" constitutes the basis of Zarathuštra's dualism,[21] I agree with those scholars who consider Darius to have been a follower of Zarathuštra.

It has often been argued against this view that Darius mentions neither Zarathuštra nor the Aməša Spəntas.[22] The latter, it will be remembered, play a prominent role in the Gathas as the seven Aspects of Ahura Mazdāh. They are called "Holy Immortals" in the Younger Avesta, but Zarathuštra, who mentions them collectively only on two occasions, has a different way of referring to them. In one passage (*Yasna* 51.22) he describes them by the phrase "those who have been and are," in the other (the *Yeňhē Hātγm* prayer) by the plural of the present participle of the verb "to be," which requires the translation "those who are, the being ones," cf. *AHM*, p. 164 f.[23] It is on the strength of this definition that modern scholars sometimes refer to the Holy Immortals as "Entities."

The objection that Zarathuštra and the Aməša Spəntas are not mentioned by Darius has, of course, no probative value, since in inscriptions of a political character there was no necessity to refer to either. In fact, however, I believe that Darius does refer to the Aməša Spəntas, and we shall see later (p. 28) that the Greek rendering of Zarathuštra's name as "Zoroaster" makes it at least likely that Darius was familiar with the prophet's name.

To take the Aməša Spəntas first, we have noted in the Behistun inscription Darius's wording "Ahura Mazdāh bore me aid, and the other gods who are," which strangely differs from the formula he used in his later inscriptions, "Ahura Mazdāh with (all) the gods." Even assuming that by the time Darius used the second formula he really meant to refer to foreign gods, can one be sure that he employed the earlier formula with the same intention? As the puzzling relative clause "who are (*or* exist)" has not yet been explained,[24] I venture to suggest that it was prompted by Zarathuštra's definition of the Aməša Spəntas as "Entities."[25] If this interpretation is acceptable, it will remove the last doubt that the definition of Ahura Mazdāh which Darius carried in his mind was the one which Zarathuštra had given.

The manifestation of Ahura Mazdāh in seven Aspects or "Shapes," as the Younger Avesta calls them (*Yašt* 13.81), is no less enigmatic a notion than the Christian Trinity. If the expression "gods who are" refers to the Aməša Spəntas, it is a fair assumption that only initiates of genuine Zarathuštrianism would understand it correctly. It would therefore be only natural for the Elamite translator to assume, and indicate to his compatriots, that by "the other gods who are" the king meant the gods of Elam, Babylonia, Egypt, etc. Foreigners probably placed the same interpretation on Darius's usual formula "Ahura Mazdāh with (*hadā*) the gods." If they were right, one would have to interpret this phrase as a curious abbreviation of "Ahura Mazdāh with all the gods," which is in fact the wording Darius used in the Persepolis *d* inscription. The phrase could, however, stand for "Ahura Mazdāh with the gods-who-are (viz. the Amša Spntas),"[26] in which case the adjective "all" in Persepolis *d* would be pleonastic.[27]

As far as Xerxes is concerned, he clearly followed or tried to follow in his father's steps in religious matters. He, too, only worships Ahura Mazdāh but frequently invokes for protection "Ahura Mazdāh with the gods," as Darius had done. In addition, Xerxes claims to have destroyed a "temple of the *daiva*'s,"[28] that is, of certain gods collectively so described, whom Zarathuštra had singled out for disapproval.

It has been argued, however, that Xerxes cannot have been a Zarathuštrian (or Zarathuštricist), because for him the word *artāvan* had a different meaning than for the prophet.[29] In considering this argument it will be of help to bear in mind that, from all accounts and on the evidence of the inscriptions, Xerxes lagged considerably behind Darius in intellectual power and curiosity. Provided both

took an interest in Zarathuštrianism, one would expect Darius not only to have applied his mind more intensely to it because he was the first to promote it over other beliefs, but also to have penetrated more deeply into its meaning than his son would be able to do. In particular, Darius would have been able to cope more easily than Xerxes with a difficulty which any ancient Iranian confronted with Zarathuštra's terminology was bound to meet, namely the re-interpretation implied in the prophet's utterances of certain pan-Iranian religious terms. We have already credited Darius with understanding and approving of what Zarathuštra had meant by "those who are." What Xerxes thought on this point we have no means of telling; but he certainly shows no knowledge of the new meaning which the prophet had given to the term *artāvan*, while Darius, I suspect, does.

The word *Arta*, "Truth", of which *artāvan* is a derivative, represents a basic religious notion which the ancient Persians, like the Eastern-Iranian speakers of Avestan, had inherited from Indo-Iranian times. The seat of Truth is located according to the Rig Veda in the other world, and the Younger Avesta has preserved the pre-Zarathuštrian belief that "the souls of the dead dwell in the radiant quarters of Truth" (*Yasna* 16.7). Accordingly before Zoroaster's time the adjective *artāvan*, which literally means "one who has acquired Truth," must have been used by all Iranian speakers in the sense of "one who has gained Paradise, one of the blessed dead." The other-worldly connotation of *artāvan* is not only attested in the "Daiva" inscription of Xerxes, but is attributed by Greek lexicographers to the grecized form of the world, αρταιοι, and is presupposed by the meanings "demon" of Khwarazmian *arδāw,* and "spirit, genius" of Ossetic (*i*)*dāwag*[30] (cf. *AHM*, pp. 155, 321).

For Zarathuštra, however, Truth and the state of grace it held out were within reach of the faithful already in *this* life. Accordingly in the prophet's terminology *artāvan* (or rather, as he pronounced the word, *ašāvan*) denoted additionally a *living* person "who had gained possession of, and was consequently acting in accordance in the Behistun inscription (column V, 19 f., 34 f.) seem to require a restoration which would show that Darius was aware of Zarathuštra's extension of the meaning of *artāvan*. Xerxes, on the other hand, incurious about the refinements of Zarathuštra's doctrine, continued to use *artāvan* in the sense in which it had been generally accepted from times immemorial.[31]

The same tendency of Xerxes to continue in the rut of traditional Old Persian religious parlance shows itself in his association of *Arta*, "Truth," with the age-old term *brazman*, "rite" (the etymological and factual equivalent of Vedic *bráhman*[32]), a term which is conspicuously absent from the Avesta.

Xerxes thus appears to have been a Zarathuštrian in intention. But he was not sufficiently versed in Zarathuštrian terminology to be aware of all the instances where the prophet had discarded a pan-Iranian religious word or invested one with a new meaning.

III. ARTAXERXES I AND THE CALENDAR

While the inscriptions of Darius and at least the Daiva inscription of Xerxes bear the stamp of a personal style, those of Xerxes' successors have little individuality. Apart from a few innovations in the substance matter, such as the mention of Mithra and Anāhitā as protective deities by Artaxerxes II, they merely reproduce the wording of earlier texts. This lack of a personal stamp suggests that the later inscriptions were not dictated by the kings themselves but were drafted at their command, or even at the request of mere builders or goldsmiths, by scribes whose initiative rarely extended beyond copying existing inscriptions.

That the dependence of the later inscriptions on wording coined by Darius is due to their being copy-work, and not to a persistence of Darius's words in the memory of his royal successors, may also be inferred from the absence in them of sentences and phrases which Darius had used only in the inscriptions of Behistun and Naqš-i Rustam: these inscriptions were placed too high for would-be imitators to be able to read and copy them.

The reason why no Achaemenian king later than Xerxes insisted on having his own words inscribed was presumably that, as a result of the Aramaic language and writing having become the chief means of written communication, the scribes had lost familiarity with the letters and spelling conventions of the Old Persian cuneiform script and could not be expected to do more than to slightly adapt existing patterns to new needs. Even within these limits the scribes were apt to fall back on Aramaic spelling conventions, cf. Appendix IV, p. 33.

It is with these considerations in mind that we must evaluate the religious references which are found in the few inscriptions of Artaxerxes I (465-425 B.C.) and Darius II (424-405). These references consist of the following three formulas, which Darius I and Xerxes had abundantly used: "A great god is Ahura Mazdāh" (Artaxerxes I), "Ahura Mazdāh with the gods" (Darius II), and "by the will of Ahura Mazdāh" (Artaxerxes I and Darius II).

That such formulas need not in the case of Artaxerxes I and Darius II imply the same monotheistic attitude as is vouchsafed by additional statements in the inscriptions of Darius I and Xerxes, can be seen from the fact that under Artaxerxes II (405-359) the third formula is used, and under Artaxerxes III (359-338) the first, each in an inscription where a few lines later Mithra and Anāhitā, respectively Mithra alone, are invoked in addition to Ahura Mazdāh.

The inscriptional evidence, therefore, although it requires us to suppose that Artaxerxes I and Darius II continued to worship Ahura Mazdāh, does not exclude that their religious attitude may have been closer to that of Artaxerxes II than to the monotheism of Xerxes. There is in fact reason to think that by the year 441 Artaxerxes I had come to support, though not necessarily to practice, a polytheism which closely resembled the one of the Younger Avestan scripture.

The year 441 has emerged from S. H. Taquizadeh's calculations (*Old Iranian Calendars,* pp. 13, 33, and *passim*) as the most likely date at which the so-called "Zoroastrian" calendar was introduced as civil calendar throughout the empire. Such a step could not have been taken unless the Great King had approved of the religious implications of the calendar.

The calendar is called "Zoroastrian" by modern scholars because it was used by the authors or some of the authors of the Younger Avesta. In the scripture each day of the month and each month of the year has a religious name. Divinities honored by the names include Ahura Mazdāh,[33] six "Holy Immortals," Mithra, Anāhitā,[33] Tištrya, Fire, the Fravašis,[34] Sun, Moon, Sky, Earth, Wind, the Soul of the Cow, the Religion, Discipline, Reward, in short, most of the deities of the Zarathuštric religion, with the notable exception of Haoma (cf. below, p. 26, n. 43).

Although apart from the Avesta no source belonging to the Achaemenid period mentions this calendar, its appearance in later times both in Sogdiana and Chorasmia in the East, and in Armenia and Cappadocia in the West, leaves no doubt that it had been in general use as a civil calendar before the Achaemenian empire broke up. We may note, however, that while the Cappadocian month-names fully agree with the Avestan ones, whose Persian equivalents are still used today, some of the Armenian, Chorasmian, and Sogdian months have names which differ from their Avestan counterparts.

The chronological system of the "Zoroastrian" calendar as attested in all sources has been shown by Taquizadeh to have been the result of a reform of an earlier religious calendar which we shall henceforth call the "unreformed" one. The latter may have been instituted in about 510 B.C., and was used until 441 beside the Old Persian civil calendar which we find in the Behistun inscription of Darius and the Elamite tablets of Persepolis. The date of therefrom, 441, must also have been the date of the official promotion of the religious calendar to civil use. Thereafter the Old Persian civil calendar was presumably abandoned.

While the Old Persian civil calendar as used by Darius followed a Babylonian pattern, the unreformed religious calendar must have been modeled on the Egyptian calendar with its vague year of twelve months of thirty days each and a yearly intercalation of five days. The reform of 441 consisted of two measures: the vague year of the unreformed calendar was changed into a fixed year by means of a new intercalation system; and the beginning of the year was set near the vernal equinox. One result of these measures was that the month which in Avestan is called "(the month of) the Fravašis," having come to fall at the beginning of spring in 441, remained the first month of the year ever after.

At the time when the unreformed religious calendar was instituted, the first month of the year must have borne the name of the Iranian chief god. The apparently illogical fact that in the reformed, "Zoroastrian," calendar the month dedicated to "the Creator" occupies the tenth place is easily explained within Taquizadeh's scheme by the shift of position which all months had to undergo when the month of the Fravašis became the first. But this convincing explanation necessarily implies that the month which after the reform became the tenth was dedicated to "the Creator" also before the reform.

Were the names of the other months of the "Zoroastrian" calendar, in particular the "pagan" ones, also taken over from the unreformed calendar? If they were, we could reasonably conclude that the Zarathuštric-looking polytheism which is attested for a later period in the inscriptions of Artaxerxes II, had received the official recognition of the Court not later than 441. If on the other hand the "pagan" month-names of the "Zoroastrian" calendar replaced names of the unreformed calendar which belonged exclusively to the Gathic-looking Mazdāh-worship of Darius,[35] we shall have to consider two alternatives: either the replacement was part of the reform, in which case we would again be driven to the conclusion stated in the preceding sentence; or it took place at some later date within the Achaemenid period. The odds are heavily in favor of the first alternative.

For, once the new civil calendar had been promulgated throughout the empire, its promulgators would scarcely revoke part of its terminology and thus cause much inconvenience and confusion in the imperial administration, unless they had very strong reasons for doing so.[36] Such reasons, in the given case, could only have been religious. But it is difficult to see why even Artaxerxes II or Artaxerxes III, who more than any other Achaemenid king display in their inscriptions a religious attitude which agrees with the one implied by the "Zoroastrian" calendar names, should have felt that a Gathic-looking calendar would be unrepresentative of their religion. Do not both kings, despite their polytheism accord pride of place to Ahura Mazdāh, as do the authors of the Younger Avestan scripture? And as the latter, despite their polytheism, call themselves Mazdayasnians, that is, "worshippers of Mazdāh," would not the two kings consider themselves as faithful Mazdayasnians as Darius had been? A Gathic-looking set of month-names, we may surmise, would therefore have seemed to the two kings as venerably archaic and authentic, as the Gathas themselves must have seemed to the Younger Avestan authors, and as little in need of "modernization" as were the Gathas in the eyes of Zarathuštra's polytheistic epigones.

Thus we reach the conclusion that, whatever may have been the relation between the month-names of the reformed and the unreformed calendar, one of which at least, "the Creator," was the same in both, the reformed calendar was characterized already in 441 B.C. by the month-names, and presumably also the day-names, which we know from the Younger Avesta.[37]

IV. Artaxerxes I and Zarathustricism

On first consideration one might think that the adoption of the "Zoroastrian" calendar under Artaxerxes I means that this king had by 441 B.C. embraced or at least approved of the Zarathuštric religion of the Younger Avesta, which the calendar names would in this case faithfully reflect.[38]

And yet, a basic question remains to be asked. Artaxerxes I could not have been influenced by the Zarathuštric religion unless this religion was there to influence him. But this religion, in the form in which it appears in the Younger Avesta, is in fact a perversion of Zarathuštra's original message. For such a perversion to be not only tolerated but actually enjoined by the Eastern Iranian Church which Zarathuštra had founded, a strong incentive must have come into being. Can we discover such an incentive before the introduction by Artaxerxes I of a polytheistic civil calendar? If not—and the answer has so far been "no"—would we be justified in reversing the tables and assuming that, far from the king having been influenced by the Zarathuštric religion, it was he who by his acknowledgement of the pagan gods brought this religion into being?

While the carefully balanced structure of Zarathuštra's original doctrine is pleasing even to our sophisticated minds, one may well wonder as to who may ever have derived satisfaction from the bewildering contradictions of the Younger Avesta, in which monotheism, dualism, and polytheism are all preached simultaneously. The lack of appeal of this scripture is illustrated by the fact that, when Zoroastrianism re-emerges from the dark ages in Sasanian Iran, its priests regard the sacred texts of the Avesta with affectionate veneration, translate them into the Middle Persian language, and write commentaries on them, but in fact preach the very different Magian version of the doctrine.

Nevertheless, it will be said, the mixed scripture did exist; however contradictory its "system," must there not have been at some time people who approved of it as it stands?

The answer, to my mind, is that the religious mixture of the Younger Avesta is precisely what it appears to be: not a single religion which anyone would defend as a system, but a sum, an agglomeration, of different creeds to which different communities were attached in the fifth century in the distant Eastern Iranian homeland of the Avesta.

Thus viewed the Avesta is not the religious nightmare which it is sometimes, and pardonably, treated by religious historians. As far as the religious data which it preserves are concerned, the Avesta may be regarded simply as a record of cults, an anthology, as it were, of Old Iranian religious lore. It transcends, however, the character of an anthology, in that it is pervaded and held together by the pious fiction that the whole of it was revealed by Ahura Mazdāh to Zoroaster.

It is in this fiction that we can recognize the wood through the maze of trees. If the purpose of the authors of the

Younger Avesta had been to provide an attractive syncretism of existing beliefs, their failure to avoid glaring contradictions would be incomprehensible. But if their intention was to restate existing beliefs for the sole purpose of claiming that Zoroaster had recommended them all, the motley assortment presented by the scripture ceases to be surprising. As a "proof" of Zoroaster's sponsorship of all the Iranian cults that are mentioned in it, the Younger Avestan scripture makes perfect sense.

On the other hand, for a pious fiction of this kind to take shape and gain acceptance, there must have existed a strong motive, the time must have been ripe, the conditions favorable. So long as the Great Kings gave official recognition to Ahura Mazdāh alone it is very unlikely that the Eastern Iranian Zarathuštrian priests would claim that their prophet had approved of the pagan gods whose worship he had in fact prescribed. But a powerful motive and a favorable climate of opinion for advancing such a claim would come into being from the moment an Achaemenian ruler had publicly stated that the pagan gods were as worthy of worship as Ahura Mazdāh. The introduction in 441 of the polytheistic civil calendar amounts to a public statement to this effect, the earliest to our knowledge. At that date, therefore, the calendar names were more likely a premonition than an echo of the mixed, Younger Avestan, scripture.

V. THE MAGI

If the Zarathuštric religion of the Younger Avesta was not the source of the polytheistic calendar names or, more generally, the stimulus for the recognition and eventual adoption of polytheism by the royal House, what else may have been the source or stimulus? To answer this question we must try to reach a closer definition than Herodotus provides of the religious data which he quotes.

The Iranian gods whom the Persians worshiped according to Herodotus, are "Zeus," Mithra, Anāhitā,[39] the Sun, the Moon, the Earth, Fire, Water, and the Winds. All these divinities are also objects of worship in the Younger Avesta and duly appear among the calendar names. The probability is that on the soil of Western Iran the same variety of cults existed as in the Eastern Iranian homeland of the Avesta. Yet in Western Iran only one priesthood is known to have officiated: the Magi.

To all the gods mentioned, the Persians are said by Herodotus to have offered sacrifice; but, Herodotus adds, "without a Magus it is not lawful for them to offer sacrifice" (i.132). This statement permits the hypothesis that the Magi were qualified and expected to minister in the service of any of a number of different gods worshiped by different people in Persis. Now Darius, we know, worshiped Ahura Mazdāh. We also know that at the time of his accession he had a grudge against the Magi. The manner in which he settled it does not suggest that the Magi were the priests of *his* religion: his first concern after obtaining the throne was to order a slaughter of Magi.

Year after year the anniversary of this slaughter remained an occasion of great celebrations.[40] Nevertheless, from all accounts, the position of the Magi at the Achaemenian court, at any rate from Xerxes onwards, remained unchallenged, and this despite the fact that the Magi did not hold the religion of their rulers in such high regard that it should be brought to the notice of Herodotus.

That the Magi might not initially have greatly cared for the Zarathuštrian Ahura Mazdāh is understandable. As far as we can tell, this modified version of the pan-Iranian god Ahura (cf. n. 1) was introduced in Western Iran by Darius after he had accepted the substance of Zarathuštra's message.[41] Like most long-established priesthoods, the Magi were probably inclined to be conservative and would not lightly accept a new form of worship. If the new form were introduced by a king they hated and feared, this would commend it even less to their affection. But the Magi could hardly afford openly to flout the one god cherished by Darius and Xerxes and to refuse to serve him. Rather we may suppose that the reason why they were allowed to become again the priests of the Court was that, despite their resentment, they had agreed to officiate in the Zarathuštrian service of Ahura Mazdāh, along with their service on behalf of the polytheistic communities whose priests they had been for centuries.

How then would the mind of a Magian priest appear? Eclectic in the extreme, we may suppose, as far as the Iranian gods were concerned. The Magi would be, not the representatives of one particular religion, but technical experts of worship, professional priests who, equipped with barsman twigs and all the paraphernalia of a meticulous ritual, would conduct the service of any Iranian god to whom an employer willing to pay them should wish to render homage.

Such an interpretation would also account for the fact that Herodotus has not really anything to say about the Magian religion. It would appear that there *was* no Magian religion before the Magi became Zoroastrians. The peculiarities of Magian behavior could be observed only in the minutiae of ritual or purification, such as their mode of disposing of the dead or their zeal for destroying animals which they considered impure, both of which Herodotus duly noted.

If the Magi were a professional priesthood to whom Zarathuštrianism was merely one of the forms of religion in which they ministered against payment, much as a professional musician earns his living by performing the works of different composers, then we are in a better position to understand why Zoroaster and his doctrine remained unnoticed by the Greeks for such a long time. The Greeks relied for information on the Magi and for the Magi of the first six or seven decades of the fifth century Zarathuštrianism need not have meant more than an idiosyncratic treatment of the age-old Ahura, whom *they* continued to regard, within the pantheon of the non-Zarathuštrian gods whom they continued to serve on behalf of the majority of their Persian employers, as an approximate equivalent of the Greek Zeus. If the information we read in Herodotus was provided by a Magus, the latter may well have felt that by mentioning Ahura (="Zeus") first, he had taken sufficient account of the special regard in which the god was held by the Great Kings.

Although the Magi must have become thoroughly familiar with the terminology Zarathuštrianism, their eclectic upbringing would prevent them for a long time from penetrating to the core of the prophet's doctrine. Not being prepared to revere Ahura Mazdāh as sole god, they would be unable to appreciate the inner necessity of the complicated relationship, possibly even to understand the relationship itself, which Zarathuštra had been led logically to envisage, between Truth, Ahura Mazdāh, the Holy Immortals, and the two Spirits. What presumably the Magi understood and liked best in Zarathuštrianism was its condemnation of the Daivas, which agreed with their own exorcistic bent and which they may have associated with the Gathic account of the incompatibility of the two Spirits (cf. below, p. 30).

But if by the second or third decade of the long reign of Artaxerxes I the Magi had become perfectly reconciled with Zarathuštrianism, within the limits of their understanding of it, and without surrendering to it the cults in which they had officiated for centuries, the members of the royal house would also be due for a change of heart. The effect of allowing, over a period of several decades, the spiritual as well as to some extent the political affairs of the State to be handled by a priesthood which served with professional impartiality both the King's god and many others, could hardly have been but to loosen the monotheistic exclusiveness on which Darius had insisted. The resulting laxness can be seen at an advanced stage in the invocation by Artaxerxes II of Mithra and Anāhitā beside Ahura Mazdāh. The introduction in 441 of a polytheistic civil calendar may mark its beginning.

Here then lies the answer I would suggest to the question we posed at the beginning of this chapter: the stimulus for the adoption by the royal house of a polytheism which looks Avestic was provided by the consistently eclectic attitude of the Magi.

VI. The Scripture

Let us now return to the "Zoroastrian" calendar. Shortly before 441 B.C., the year of its inception, the Great King and his advisers, among whom Magian opinion was no doubt represented, must have decided to introduce a reform of the civil calendar, as part of which the numbers until then assigned to the days of the month were to be replaced with names, and new names were to be given to the months. As the new calendar was intended to replace also the old, "unreformed," religious calendar, it was decided that the names of days and months should all be religious. At least one name, "the Creator," was taken from the "unreformed" calendar. Of the other names we cannot tell whether they had been used as calendar terms before. The

result, at any rate, was a calendar whose names were representative not of one cult only but of all the main cults in which the Magi officiated as professional priests. Even though the lion's share of the names belongs to Zarathuštrianism, the religion of the royal house, it would be misleading, with reference to the year 441, to describe such a calendar as "Zoroastrian." Being a selective index of the Magian repertory, a more appropriate term for it would be "Magian."[42]

In due course the new civil calendar would reach the Zarathuštrian communities of the homeland of the Avesta, in faraway Eastern Iran, and enter into daily use with them. Inevitably, however, its names would mean more to them than merely a new device for distinguishing days and months. The names, insofar as they belonged to a civil calendar, would constantly remind Zarathuštrians that important concessions had officially been made to cults other than their own. In the days of Darius and Xerxes the Eastern Iranian Zarathuštrians were no doubt aware that their sole god, Ahura Mazdāh, was also the sole god of the Great King. After the year 441, however, it would become increasingly clear to them that the religious climate of the Court had changed. The calendar provided, as it were, a summary of what the Court had officially come to regard as the national religious patrimony.

We now encounter the incentive I alluded to earlier . . . , for the Eastern Zarathuštrian Church to take the initiative and to produce a new scripture. The fact that the Great King himself was prepared to countenance non-Zarathuštrian beliefs would lend them respectability even in the eyes of Zarathuštrian priests. Zarathuštrianism *per se,* with its exclusive worship of Ahura Mazdāh, was obviously on the decline at Court, perhaps also in Eastern Iran. To cling to it alone, against the trend of the time, would have meant for the Zarathuštrian priesthood connivance at its own extinction. But the Zarathuštrian Church had two invaluable assets by which it could try to insure its survival. One was the prestige of its founder, whose fame was growing the more he receded into legendary antiquity. As that fame grew, the legends must have grown, and with them the possibility of attributing to Zoroaster views he had never held. By a masterstroke of priestly wisdom, if this is how things happened, the Zarathuštrian Church claimed that the national religious patrimony now sanctioned by the Court was not a mere co-existence of unconnected or loosely connected beliefs but had a hitherto unperceived unity, in that Zoroaster himself had preached it all.

There may be more than one way in which a determined Church might attempt to substantiate such a claim. But the most effective would undoubtedly be, to produce a scripture that proved it. Here the second asset of the Zarathuštrian priests would come into its own: the fact that they already had a scripture consisting of Zarathuštra's own words, as well as the skill, accruing to them from the literary tradition of which they were the heirs,[43] to engage in creative literary activity on a large scale. A readily acceptable excuse for adding to their existing scripture would be, that what was now being composed and given scriptural status was what Zarathuštra had taught but failed to embody in verses. Accordingly the late disciples of Zarathuštra could set to work with a good conscience and provide a scripture for the motley religious patrimony of which the Magi had been in charge. All they had to do was to inform themselves of the contents of the hymns and liturgies of the various cults concerned and compose new texts in which these contents were presented as part of Ahura Mazdāh's revelation to Zarathuštra.

Thus, by an intense literary effort, the Zarathuštrian priests, whom we may now call Zarathuštric, transformed the eclectic standpoint of the Magi into a system purporting to be Zarathuštra's. The logical weakness of the system would not concern them. This was not a case of thinking out what would persuade, but merely of reproducing, elaborating, and combining what everyone, from the Great King downward, was ready to accept. The success fully justified the effort. By producing a new, all-embracing scripture which exploited to the full the propandistic value of Zarathuštra's authority, the priestly authors turned the narrowly denominational character of their Church into a truly pan-Iranian one and ensured the survival of Zoroastrianism on a national scale down to the conquest of Islam and, on a more limited scale, down to the present day.

Supposing this to have been the course of events, what would be the reaction of the Magi? Whereas in early Achaemenian times there does not seem to have existed a single, definable religion that could be called Magian, the scripture of which the Magi now came to hear presented the whole of the Magian repertory as a single, pan-Iranian religion, such as could properly only be called "Magian" but in fact claimed to be "Zarathuštrian." Had the Magi fought this claim on the ground that they had had no share in the composition of the scripture and were scarcely mentioned in it,[44] they would merely have cut their own flesh. For if they did not even know that the cults in which they were officiating had all been founded by the greatest of all sages, what excuse would they have had for continuing in their ministry?

The only sensible reaction of the Magi would have been to accept the claim and to acknowledge Zoroaster as their prophet. We are on safe ground in assuming that this is precisely what they did. For the later sources show that the Magi appropriated Zoroaster altogether: the prevalent opinion expressed in Greek texts is that Zoroaster was a Persian or a Mede, and the Sasanian Zoroastrian writers not only regard Media as Zoroaster's homeland but locate in Media a number of Avestan toponyms which, according to the geographical horizon of the scripture, must in fact have belonged to Eastern Iran.[45] It is clear that this misleading information emanated from the Magi; and that the most suitable occasion for their inventing it would be at the time when they felt impelled to claim that they, and

not the Eastern Iranian Zarathuštrian (or Zarathuštric) priests, were the true heirs and custodians of Zoroaster's doctrine.

If our reconstruction of the course of events is correct, the composition of the new Zarathuštric scripture will have begun soon after the year 441. The adoption by the Magi of Zoroaster as their prophet may have followed within the next two decades. From then onwards something which could be called a Magian doctrine took shape and became known to the Greeks before the middle of the fourth century, while the prophet's name, once the Magi began to take a personal interest in him, reached the Greeks already at the beginning of the fourth century.[46]

It reached them at first, however—and this has so far been insufficiently appreciated—not in its Median form *Zaratuštra, which was to reappear, slightly altered, as *Zarduŝt* in Sasanian Persia, nor in its Avestan form *Zaraθ-uŝtra*, but in the characteristically Old Persian form *Zarauŝtra which the Greeks, because of the prophet's alleged preoccupation with astrology, transformed into Ζωρο-άϛτηρ by popular association with their own word for "star. . . ."[47]

The unmistakably Persian origin of the name *Zoroaster* seems to me to confirm that the original sponsors of the prophet in Western Iran, and his sole supporters for a number of decades, were not the Median-speaking Magi, but an influential group of Persians. On whose initiative this group adhered to the prophet's doctrine is a question to which the religious purport of the Darius inscriptions supplies a reasonably clear answer.

By the time the Magi took control over Western Iranian Zoroastrian affairs, their own Median form of the prophet's name could no longer prevail over the one which had gained currency in Europe: the name Zoroaster is still with us as an indictment, as it were, of the slowness with which the Magi embraced the cause of the prophet.[48]

Conversely, the fact that the Sasanian Zoroastrian priests used neither the Avestan nor the Persian form of the prophet's name but the Median one confirms that these priests were not called "Magi" for nothing.[49] Their using this title, their referring to the prophet as "Zarduŝt," their preaching a doctrine based on the formula Ohrmazd *versus* Ahriman, are all clear indications that although these priests were by then and remained the sole custodians of the Avestan scripture, they were the direct heirs, not of the Avestan Zarathuštric tradition, but of the Magian tradition as it had crystallized in the fourth century B.C.

VII. THE MAGI AND THE SCRIPTURE

At the beginning of this article we saw that the Holy Spirit is in the Gathas Ahura Mazdāh's creative Aspect and is referred to as "Creator" in the Younger Avesta (*Yašt* 10.143), where conversely Ahura Mazdāh, in his capacity of creator, is often addressed as "Holiest Spirit" (*Yašt* 8.10, 10.73, etc.). This terminology may seem almost to invite the inference that God and the Holy Spirit are identical, from which it would follow easily that the opponent of the Fiendish Spirit must have been Ahura Mazdāh himself, and only a little less easily that the Fiendish Spirit was as primordial as God. Yet, logical, or fairly logical, as it might have been to deduce the formula Oromasdes *versus* Areimanios from the position as it is stated in the Avesta, such a step was neither taken by the authors of the scripture in Achaemenian times nor explicitly approved in Avestan texts that were added to the scripture in post-Achaemenian times.

There is, it is true, the last chapter of the post-Achaemenian Vendidad, where Ahura Mazdāh himself faces the Fiendish Spirit (see above, p. 14). But it is a far cry from the 99,999 diseases with which the Fiendish Spirit infects the god in that chapter to the integrated design of a cosmic conflict resulting from the primordial co-existence of Ohrmazd and Ahriman, as it is outlined in the Middle Persian books and presupposed by the two αρχαι of the περι φιλοσοφιας. Had the authors of the Vendidad approved of this design, it would be hard to understand why it is not prominently displayed in this "Book against the Demons"—which is what "Vendidad" means—for which it would have made an admirable framework.

We may then say that in Achaemenian times the Zarathuš-tric priests, who probably continued adding to the scripture until the collapse of the empire, either did not learn of the Magian formula or deliberately ignored it as a heresy. The authors of the Vendidad, on the other hand, who can hardly have been unaware of the formula, probably regarded it as a heresy but were nevertheless somewhat affected by it in their outlook.

That the formula Oromasdes *versus* Areimanios was in fact a heresy is obvious from its absence from the oldest Avestan texts. That it was an original and elegant heresy is also undeniable. Nevertheless originality and elegance are hardly qualities we have reason to associate with the Magi. Once the Magi had adopted the great sage as their prophet, it seems to me that, far from wishing to be different, they would be likely to try hard to conform to his message. But to conform to it they would have to understand it. And to understand it, at a time when Zoroaster's own Avestic epigones were crediting him with the very views he had condemned, they had only one guide to turn to: the **Gathas.**

Zarathuštra's **Gathas** today count among the most difficult products of world literature. This is not merely because we are so remote from them. The conciseness of the wording, the ambiguity of the inflectional endings, the abundance of technical terms that do not recur even in the Younger Avesta, the apparent attempt to depict by means of the word order obscure sequences of thought, all these are factors which must have made the **Gathas** extremely difficult to understand at all times. In addition, it must be realized that there was a considerable language-barrier between the ancient Persians and the speakers of the Avestan language. The difference between Median and Avestan must have been less great, but a difference undoubtedly existed.

A portrait of Zoroaster.

I said earlier that Darius appears to have accepted the *substance* of Zarathuštrianism (above, p. 24). It is unlikely that much more than the main drift of this subtly balanced doctrine could have been apprehended by a foreigner, as Darius was in respect to Zarathuštra. But if our reading of the relevant hints in the Darius inscriptions is correct, Darius understood the principles of the faith far better than anyone else in antiquity of whom we have any record, apart, of course, from Zarathuštra himself. In any effort to inform himself of the message of the alloglot prophet, Darius would have been favored by an opportunity forever denied to those who after him endeavored to understand the **Gathas**: his chronological nearness to Zarathuštra. In Darius's youth and early manhood, at a mere two or three decades from the death of the prophet (v. Henning, *Zoroaster,* 41), the possibility still existed for Persians or Medes to have the Gathas explained to them by men who had known Zarathuštra, provided that one of those concerned was bilingual. By the middle of the fifth century such opportunities had vanished, not only in Western Iran but also in the homeland of the scripture. Even the authors of the Younger Avesta, who must have known the text of the

Gathas by heart, had only an imperfect understanding of their contents.[50]

How much less is it to be expected that the Magi who, if our theory is correct, never claimed to be Zoroastrians until the bold bid of the Eastern Zarathuštrian Church compelled them to do so, would belatedly extract from the *Gathas* the correct details of the prophet's theology. Their new approach to Zoroaster's doctrine would be conditioned by their old one. We need not assume that, because the Magi for a long time failed to identify themselves with Zarathuštrianism, they had not formed their own views of it quite early. And if it is true that they had missed the essence of the prophet's message to such an extent that they saw no objection to serving both his religion and other cults, then we need not be surprised if they misinterpreted his message in respect of the identity of the protagonists of his dualism. It may have been, at a wild guess, in the context of the Daiva-worship proscribed by Xerxes, that the Magi came to the conclusion that Zarathuštra's Fiendish Spirit was the aboriginal chief of all demons, the "daivic" counterpart of Ahura Mazdāh.[51] There is nothing to show that Xerxes, if confronted with such a view, would have been in a position to refute it. What is more, we need not expect that such a misapprehension would have shocked Western Zarathuštrians nearly as much as it would shock us. What mattered most to them, witness Darius, was the exclusive worship of Ahura Mazdāh and the rejection of the principle "Falsehood" which the Fiendish Spirit had chosen. Zarathuštrians who conceived of the prophet's message in such simple, practical terms, would scarcely give much thought to the implications of a replacement of the name "Falsehood" by "Fiendish Spirit."

By the time the Magi adopted Zoroaster as their prophet and the *Gathas* as their guide to his meaning, these difficult poems could no longer act as a corrective of the Magian dualist formula. Their obscure wording might just as well have been thought by the Magi to confirm it. More than that, even if the formula had not yet been evolved by the Magi, they could at this late stage deduce it from the *Gathas* themselves, without realizing that they were misrepresenting the prophet's views. For although Truth is in the *Gathas* an aboriginal principle distinct from God, and the two Spirits are emanations of God's, both Truth and the Holy Spirit are identical with Ahura Mazdāh insofar as not only the Holy Spirit, but also Truth, is an aspect of his (cf. above, n. 3). The Magi could therefore hold in perfect good faith that in Zoroaster's opinion "Truth" and "Holy Spirit" were no more than parts of the definition of the aboriginal δαιμων Ahura Mazdāh. With such a premise it would be difficult to avoid the fallacy that the Gathic "Falsehood" was, like "Truth," a mere aspect of an aboriginal δαιμων, for whose role the Fiendish Spirit must have seemed to the Magi to have been ideally cast.

Considering the odds against them, the Magi did very well. The simple and arresting formula Oromasdes *versus* Areimanios, by which they replaced the complicated situa-

tion of the *Gathas,* may have been misleading and heretical. But it was destined to exert a far greater and more lasting appeal than Zoroaster's own rarefied doctrine. Moreover, the Magi deserve credit for having understood and transmitted to posterity Zoroaster's emphasis on the dignity of man as a free agent, on whose recognition of Truth and consequent support the very cause of God depends.[52] This moral teaching is, after all, what would matter much more to ordinary men and women than the niceties of the relationship between God, the two Spirits, the Immortals, and Truth. It is no doubt the satisfying insistence on the intelligence and trustworthiness of man which more than anything else has enabled Zoroastrianism to remain a living religion to this day.

To the student of Iranian civilization, however, the merit of the Magi lies not so much in what they made of Zoroaster's doctrine, as in the fact that, by adopting Zoroastrianism, they ensured the preservation down to the present day of its Avestan scripture. Without this scripture the bright dawn of Iranian thought would be hidden from us. Much of it, indeed, is still unclear, after nearly two centuries of study. But the scripture is with us, and it is for us to make the best of this Magi-sent opportunity. In the present article I have really only attempted to show where Zoroaster's own contribution does *not* lie. A close study of the *Gathas,* however, permits, even at the present stage of imperfect understanding, an analysis of certain ingredients of his doctrine as belonging to earlier, Indo-Iranian thought, while other religious elements appear for the first time in the *Gathas*. It is thus possible, to some extent, to discern where Zarathuštra innovated, where he took over notions we can trace elsewhere, and even where he expounded ideas which cannot be traced anywhere else but of which nevertheless he is unlikely to have been the inventor.

Our purpose here has been the more modest one of trying to account historically for two drastic and more or less contemporaneous innovations on Zoroaster's doctrine, the one represented by the Younger Avesta, and the other inherent in the formula Oromasdes *versus* Areimanios; and to suggest reasons why either innovation was presented not as such, but as Zoroaster's own contribution.

APPENDICES

I

The introduction of the term "Zarathuštricism" is intended as an improvement on H. Lommel's and my own earlier terminology, according to which "Zarathuštrianism" denotes the prophet's own doctrine, and "Zoroastrianism" both its Younger Avestan and its Sasanian modifications. The objection to applying the term "Zoroastrianism" to the Younger Avesta (except when precision does not matter) is that its authors called the prophet "Zarathuštra," not "Zoroaster," while the ancient Greeks, who called him "Zoroaster" (see above, p. 28) never learnt to know the Younger Avestan form of the doctrine. What the Greeks believed to have been Zoroaster's teaching is substantially the version we find centuries later in the Sasanian books. It is therefore to this version alone that the term "Zoroastrianism" should strictly speaking be applied.

II

The details of the "twin" passage, *Yasna* 30.3, are controversial, but all translators except one agree that in it the dual *ymā,* "twins," refers to the dual *mainyū,* "the two Spirits." The divergent view is W. Lentz's (*A Locust's Leg, Studies in Honour of S. H. Taquizadeh,* [1962], pp. 132 f.), whose translation, however, defeats itself: one has only to remove the explanatory parentheses to discover, even through the disguise of the English wording, that the two duals belong together. In my view the verse should be translated as follows:

> *aṯ tā mainyū paouruyē yā yəmā x^vafnā asrvātəm*
> *manahičā vačahičā šyaoθanōi hī vahyō akəmčā*
> *ɑsčā hudɑnhō ərəš vīšyātā nōiṯ duždɑnhō*

"Firstly the two twin Spirits [*lit.* the two Spirits who (are) twins] were revealed (to me), each-endowed-with-own-wish (= free will). Their (*hī*) two ways-of-thinking, ways-of-speaking, and ways-of-acting are (respectively) the better and the bad. And between these two (ways-of-thinking, etc.) it is the wise, not the fools, who choose correctly." This means taking *hī* as a general dual form of the enclitic pronoun, comparable in its multivalence to Vedic *sīm,* and *x^va-fna* as a nominative dual, comparable in formation and meaning to Skt. *sva-cchanda,* "following one's own will or pleasure," and displaying, in conditions of compound reduction (cf. Av. *ərədva-fšna-*), the base **fan-* which is known from Khot. (*pa-, us-)phan-,* "to be pleased," and Oss. *fændon,* "wish" (see H. W. Bailey, *Trans. Philol. Soc.* [1956], p. 121, and M. J. Dresden, *Trans. Amer. Philos. Soc.,* XLV [1955], 478, *b*). However, since *x^vafna-* occurs elsewhere in the sense of "sleep; dream," there remains the possibility that the first line means: "At first the two twin Spirits were revealed (to me) through a vision."

Since Av. *paouruya-,* "first," is never used as a noun, its adverbial locative *paouruyē* should not be translated "in the beginning," as is usually done, but "at first, firstly." This would always have been understood, had not the first line of *Yasna* 45.2 obscured the issue: *aṯ fravaxšyā anhəuš mainyū paouruyē* literally means: "I shall mention firstly of the world the two Spirits," that is: "I shall mention the two Spirits before I mention anything else that belongs to the world." Here the normal construction of the adj. *paouruya-* with the partitive genitive (cf. *Yasna* 57.2: "Sraoša . . . who (is) the first of Mazdāh's creation [= the first out of all the creatures of Mazdāh's]") has been transferred to the adverb *paouruyē.*

III

To import the formula Oromasdes *versus* Areimanios into the Gathas one would have to assume that (1) the two Spirits were unrelated, and (2) the Holy Spirit was identical with Ahura Mazdāh.

The first assumption would require an evasion of the prime meaning of the word "twin," to which indeed Lommel, *Die Religion Zarathustras,* pp. 27 f., took recourse, on the ground that unless one did so the prophet's doctrine would be marred by the "unthinkable" contradictions which he lists on pp. 26 ff. These contradictions, however, are all of Lommel's own making, as they only arise from the unwarranted supposition that if the two Spirits were real twins, their father would have been in Zoroaster's opinion not Ahura Mazdāh but Zurvan.

The second assumption is so firmly refuted by *Yasna* 47 (as even Lommel grudgingly admits on p. 20, lines 12-20), that not even a comparison, not made by Lommel, of *Yasna* 30.5, where Zoroaster describes the Holy Spirit as "being clad in the most steadfast skies," with the Younger Avestan statement that "Ahura Mazdāh wears the sky as a dress" (*Yašt* 13.3), can reduce its improbability. Being clad in the sky, to judge from the similar attribute of having the sun as eye, which the Younger Avestan Ahura Mazdāh (cf. *Yasna* 1.11, 3.13, etc.) and the Vedic Varuna have in common, was probably a characteristic already of the Indo-Iranian god Asura (on whom cf. above, p. 12, n. 1). By transferring the heavenly garment to the chief son of God, Zoroaster would indirectly maintain its traditional association with Ahura and yet remain true to his conception of God as being devoid of naturalistic or anthropomorphic traits.

We may note in this connection that the dual deity which the Indo-Iranian Asura formed together with Mitra may also have been thought of as being clad in the sky, since its Younger Avestan representative, Mithra-Ahura, is invoked in association with the heavenly luminaries (*Yašt* 10.145), while its Vedic descendant, Mitrā-Varuṇā, has, like Āsura Varuṇā alone, the sun as its eye. See below, Appendix IX.

IV

It need hardly be stressed that even after the conquest by Darius of Hinduš, Iranian Mithraists worshiped the *Iranian* Mithra, and not the Old Indian Mitra. The occasional spelling *Mitra* in the inscriptions of Artaxerxes II is not due to borrowing from "Indic," as R. G. Kent has it (*Old Persian,* p. 9, end of §9), but betrays the influence of the Aramaic spelling *MTR* of Miθra's name. The scribe who prepared the cuneiform draft for Artaxerxes II's stonemasons would normally be employed to write in Aramaic. When so engaged, he would have frequent occasion to write *MTR* as part of Iranian theophoric proper names such as the attested *MTRDT* and *MTRWHŠT* of the papyri. The awkward form *paradayadā-* (written *pa-ra-da-ya-da-a-*), . . . in an inscription of Artaxerxes II is similarly best explained as a mere transposition into cuneiform characters of the Aramaic spelling **PRDYD'* of OPers. **paridaidā-.*

V

It does not seem to have been adequately realized how closely Darius's personified *Drauga* agrees with the personified form which Zarathuštra's *Drug* ("Falsehood") sometimes assumes in the **Gathas** (cf. E. Benveniste, *The Persian Religion*. p. 36). According to Darius it was Drauga who "made the countries rebellious inasmuch as these (rebel leaders) deceived the people" (Beh. Inscr. IV, 34), and Drauga "comes" to a country as do hostile armies and famine (Persepolis, *d*). According to Zarathuštra the wicked "destroy the creatures (*or* property) of Truth by the commands of Drug" (*Yasna* 31.1), Drug can be "removed from ourselves" (*Yasna* 44.13), a wicked man is "a son of Drug" (*Yasna* 51.10, cf. *AHM*, p. 169), and Drug should be "placed into the hands of Truth" (*Yasna* 30.8, 44.14). If Zarathuštra had been asked to name a supernatural instigator of mutiny among men he would certainly, on the evidence of the **Gathas,** have named Drug and not the Fiendish Spirit who in the Gathas entertains no relations with men. That Darius and Zarathuštra use slightly different though etymologically very closely related words for what each of them treats as a proper name meaning "falsehood" is of course no argument for denying the identity of the two personifications. Old Persian and Avestan also have slightly different words where the meanings "brick" (*išti-: ištya-*), "daughter" (**duxθrī-: duγδar-*, v. Benveniste, *BSL* 1951, 22), "eye" (*čaša-: čašman-*), and others, are concerned.

VI

There may be a connection, overlooked hitherto, between the usual Avestan designation of Ahura Mazdāh's Aspects as "Immortals," and Zarathuštra's definition of them as "those who have been and are," since this definition can be understood as an equivalent of "those who never cease to be." One may consider two possibilities: either the term "Immortals" was introduced by Zarathuštra's disciples as a simplification of the definition given by the prophet, or, more likely (cf. *AHM*, p. 165), the prophet's definition represents his metaphysical elaboration of the term "Immortals," the latter having been either coined or inherited by him. It should be borne in mind that in ordinary Iranian parlance the "Holy Immortals" are the "elements," in which meaning the term may have been used before Zarathuštra's time (cf. *AHM*, p. 10).

VII

It would be highly irregular if, in the sentence "Ahura Mazdāh bore me aid, and the other gods who are," the Old Persian relative pronoun were used in the sense of "whoever they," or "as many as." King and Thompson translated "and the other gods, (all) that there are." This is certainly permissible, since the later formula "with the gods" has a variant "with all the gods"; but the assumption that "all" was implied still fails to account for the addition of the relative clause "who are." That a metaphysical definition, such as the one of Yahwe in Exod. 3: 14 ("I am He who is" in E. Schild's convincing translation, *Vetus Testamentum*, IV [1954], 296 ff., to which Mr. J. V. Kinnier Wilson obligingly drew my attention), would have been offered by Darius of gods other than his own, can be safely excluded. Upon enquiry as to whether Darius's

wording could be a calque of a Semitic phrase meaning "God X and all the other gods," Mr. Kinnier Wilson very kindly sent me the following note: "Akkadian could say *ilū mala bašû* (as *The Epic of Creation*, V, 106) 'the gods, as many as there are,' or *ilū gimiršun* (*ibid.*, III, 130), meaning the same thing. Akkadian certainly has no formula equivalent to 'god X and the other gods who are,' or even (and this may be important to you) to 'god X and all the other gods,' because in the latter instance the word 'other' (which is quite rare in Akkadian) would not be expressed. I cannot quote an example, but to express this idea it would be quite natural for Akkadian to write simply 'god X and all the gods,' using one of the phrases given above. In fact, in the line in question [see above, p. 17, n. 18], the word *šanūtum* 'other,' strikes me as being very probably 'translation Akkadian,' in which case the whole phrase need not have been a native expression at all."

VIII (SEE P. 18, N. 29)

R. C. Zaehner's doubts as to the correctness of the usual translation of OPers. *daiva-dāna-* by "daiva-temple *or* sanctuary" (*The Dawn and Twilight of Zoroastrianis'm* [1961], pp. 159, 331) are unfounded. The word has its expected counterpart in **baga-dāna-*, "god-temple, altar, sanctuary," which survives in Armenian, Bactrian, and Sogdian, as well as, indirectly, in the name of the town of Baghdad; see W. B. Henning, *BSOAS*, XVIII (1956), 367, who refers *inter alia* to Sogdian [*c*]*xwδ-βγδ'nyy*, "the temple of the Jews = synagogue." The difficulty raised by Zaehner, viz. that *-dāna-* normally means "receptacle" (from the base *dhā-*), which, as he says, "seems a very odd way of referring to a temple," can be overcome by an analysis of the word in these two compounds as a derivative of the base *dam-*, "to build" (cf. *Asia Major*, New Series, II, 136), with the expected meaning, "building, house, structure": *dāna-* (IE **dmHno-*) would then stand to *dmāna-*, "house," (IE **dmeHno-*), as Av. *gata-* (IE **gʷmto-*) stands to OPers. *gmata-* (IE **gʷmeto-*).

IX (SEE P. 24, N. 40)

It has long been realized that in calling the Persian Aphrodite Μιτραν (i. 131), Herodotus confused Anāhitā with Mithra. If the fault was his and not of his informants, it would seem that not only had he failed to record the name of the Persian Aphrodite, but the notes which he brought back did not contain a clear statement on the function of Mithra, as an individual god, either. The latter deficiency would hardly have occurred, had his informants told him that they regarded Mithra as the Persian sun-god (cf. E. Benveniste, *The Persian Religion*, p. 27), as indeed Mithra scarcely was at such an early period (cf. *AHM*, pp. 38, 41 f.). What Herodotus might have been told is that the Persians worshiped a god of the sky who was sometimes referred to as *Ahura* (this being the un-Zarathuštrianized Iranian descendant of the Indo-Iranian *Asura*, see above, p. 12, n. 1) and sometimes as *Mithra-Ahura*. The latter, dual, deity, being the equivalent of the Vedic *Mitrā-Varuṇā* and the Younger Avestan *Mithra-Ahura*, can confidently be supposed to have been worshiped by the Persians from the earliest times, even though it is named in Western sources only from Plutarch onwards, as Μεσορομέσδης and Μιθρας 'Ωρομέσδης (cf. *AHM*, pp 4 f., 44 ff., 320, bottom). We have seen in the last paragraph of Appendix III that this dual deity, like Ahura alone, may have been thought of as being clad in the sky.

If then Herodotus says that the Persians call the whole circuit of the sky "Zeus" . . . and "Zeus" is his rendering of Ahura, we may surmise that his notes also contained a reference to *Μιτραν Δια as the dual deity of the sky. Being unfamiliar with this Indo-Iranian type of dual deity and consequently finding himself at a loss, back at home, to understand what the name Μιτρας was doing in front of what he had written down as "Zeus," and noticing, moreover, the vacancy in his notes for the Persian name of Aphrodite, he filled the vacancy with the redundant Μιτρας, possibly under the misapprehension that the juxtaposition *Μιτραν Διαν referred to "Zeus" and his (Persian) spouse. On this assumption, a confirmation that Mithra had indeed been described to Herodotus as Ahura's partner in the rule of the sky may be found in the specification, in the passage in question, of Aphrodite as "Urania": "In addition, they learned from the Assyrians and Arabians to worship Urania. Aphrodite is called Mylitta by the Assyrians, Alilat by the Arabians, Mitra by the Persians."

X

There is no reference to the Magi in the extant books of the Avesta, with the possible exception of the hapax *moγu.biš-*. Even if this compound meant "hater of the Magi," as Bartholomae and Schaeder (*OLZ* [1940], 376 f.) thought, it would hardly have been quoted by the Magi and should not be quoted by us, as a proof that the composition of the Younger Avestan scripture, far from having taken the Magi by surprise, was wholly or partly the work of Magian priests. E. Benveniste, *Les Mages dans l'ancien Iran,* pp. 18 ff., has attractively argued that the term *magu-* denoted a particular social class in the proto-Iranian language, and continued to do so in Avestan. One might then suppose that in Media this social class became the priestly caste, so that the Persians, if within their own class distinction the term *magu-* had fallen into disuse, would know the word in no other sense than that of "a member of the Median priestly caste." At all events the absence of Media and Persis from the lists of countries quoted in the Younger Avesta (cf. Appendix XI) suffices to refute the theory that the Magi were its authors. As to R. C. Zaehner's hypothesis that "the sacerdotal caste of the Magi was distinct from the Median tribe of the same name" (*Dawn and Twilight,* pp. 163 f.), this rests on a supposed identity of meaning between Old Persian *magu-* and Gathic Avestan *magavan-*. Even if this identity were granted, the absence of the term *magavan-* from the Younger Avesta would still militate against the identification of its authors with the Magi.

XI

It is invariably assumed that the country which in the Younger Avesta is called "the Zarathuštrian Raγa" is identical with the country Raga which Darius defines as being in Media, the medieval Rai. This assumption ill agrees not only with the absence of any reference to Media in the Avesta but also with the place which Raγa occupies in the relevant part of the list of countries in the first chapter of the Vendidad. There the succession is: *Harax-ᵛaitī* (Arachosia)—*Haētumant* (Hilmand)—*Raγa*—*Čaxra* (possibly the Ghazna region)—*Varəna* (Buner, see W. B. Henning, *BSOAS,* XII [1947], 52 f.)—*Hapta Həndu* ("the Seven Rivers," that is, the *Sapta Sindhavas* of the Rig Veda, which included the Punjab), cf. A. Christensen, *Le premier chapitre du Vendidad,* pp. 36-54. The use of identical toponyms in different parts of Iran was common at all times. Suffice it to refer to the eastern mountain *Harā Bərəz* of the Avesta (cf. also Khotanese *Haraysä,* H. W. Bailey, *Khotanese Texts IV,* 12), "across which the sun comes forth" (*Yašt* 10.118), against the western *Alburz,* or to the Avestan country *Nisāya,* which is described as lying "between Margiana and Bactria," against the country *Nisāya* "in Media" of the Behistun inscription. Such homonymity is natural with descriptive toponyms: *Harā Bərəz* means "high watchpost" (Av. *har-* "to watch," cf. *Yašt* 10.51), *Nisāya,* "region of settlements," *Raγa,* "plain, hillside," etc. (cf. W. B. Henning, *BSOS,* X, 95, sect. 5, and W. Eilers, *Archiv Orientální,* XXII [1954], 301). The difference in the inflection of *Ragā* in Old Persian (ablative *Ragāyā*) and Avestan (ablative *Rajōit*) should also not be lost sight of. As the Avestan Raγa had been Zarathuštra's see (cf. *AHM,* p. 265), the homonymity of the two regions was bound to encourage the belief among Western Iranians of later generations that the scene of the prophet's activity had been in Media. We, by contrast, shall be more inclined to find the eastern location of the prophet's see confirmed by the consideration that the Gathic variant of the clearly Eastern Iranian Avestan language may well have been the vernacular of the "Zarathuštrian Raγa."

XII

I assume with Benveniste, *The Persian Religion,* p. 16, that "it is in Plato, in the *First Alcibiades* (I, 121), the authenticity of which has been wrongly contested (written about 390 B.C.) that appears the first definite mention of the name of Zoroaster in Greece," cf. Bidez and Cumont, *op. cit.,* vol. II, 21 f. The reference to Zoroaster which Diogenes Laertius attributes to Herodotus' contemporary, Xanthus of Lydia, is of doubtful authenticity, cf. Bidez and Cumont, *op. cit.,* vol. II, 9, top, and J. Marquart, *Philologus,* Suppl. VI, 531, 608, n. 353, end. The emigrated Magi . . . of Lydia, who would have been the most likely informants of Xanthus, were in any case scarcely Zoroastrians, as they seem to have been especially connected with the cult of Anāhitā (*ibid.,* p. 5). To them, and generally to the μαγουσαιοι of Asia Minor, Zoroaster need have been no more than a legendary sage of great eminence. The alleged Xanthus quotation therefore makes sense at least insofar as the μαγουσαιοι were quite likely the source of the phantastic chronology (however cleverly linked with World-year speculation) according to which Zoroaster was placed at 6000 years before either Plato (thus Pliny, who probably wrongly attributed this information to Eudoxus of Cnidus, see *ibid.,* vol. I, 12, n. 1, II, 11, n. 5, and above, p. 15, n. 13), or the expedition of Xerxes (thus the alleged Xanthus quotation, cf. *ibid.,* vol. II, 8, n. 4). The Zoroastrian Magi, by contrast, were well acquainted with the date of Zoroaster, to judge from a tradition preserved by the Sasanian Zoroastrian priests, according to which 258 years had been counted from that date until the beginning of Alexander's rule over Iran in 330 B.C. (see W. B. Henning, *Zoroaster,* p. 40).

XIII

The discovery in the Twenties of the Middle Parthian form of the prophet's name, *Zar(a)hušt,* which goes back to the Avestan form *Zaraθuštra,* seemed to confirm Bartholomae's view (*Gdr. d. Ir. Phil.,* I, 1, p. 39) that Ζωροάστηρ was a rendering of an Iranian pronunciation *Zarahuštra,* cf. W. B. Henning, *Deutsche Literaturzeitung* (1932), 830. However, while the change of intervocalic θ to *h* is the rule in Middle Parthian, its taking place in this name at the Old Iranian period would be unparalleled. Already Hübschmann, *Zeitschr. f. vgl. Sprachf.,* XXVI (1883), 604, concluded from the Old Persian form of Darius's name, *Dāraya-va(h)uš,* which goes back to an earlier *Dārayat-vahuš,* that the proper Old Persian equivalent of Avestan *Zaraθ-uštra* (itself a secondary development from *Zarat-uštra*) would have been *Zara-uštra,* which form he regarded as the source of Greek Ζωροάστηρ. Since *Zarah-uštra* is a phonologically improbable form in any Old Iranian language, while *Zara-uštra* is predictable in Old Persian, we must reutrn to Hübschmann's explanation.

That *Zara-uštra* was not also the Median form of the prophet's name appears from the Middle and Modern Persian form *Zarduŝt* (in Manichean Middle Persian *Zard-ruŝt* < *Zardurŝt* [whence by dissimilation Zoroastrian Middle Persian *Zarduxŝt*] < *Zarduŝtr*), which can only have had as Old Iranian antecedent *Zarat-uštra.* As the last form disagrees both with OPers. *Zara-uštra* and Av. *Zaraθ-uštra,* we must conclude that it was Median. We thus incidentally recover a detail hitherto unnoticed of Median phonology: the preservation without change of a proto-Iranian postvocalic *t* at the end of first compound terms, and therefore, presumably, of any final postvocalic *t.*

The original meaning of the name may have been "camel-driver," see H. W. Bailey, *Trans. Philol. Soc.* (1953), 40 f. For the contamination with Greek αστήρ cf. Bidez and Cumont, *op. cit.,* vol. I, 6, and Henning, *loc. cit.*

Notes

Revised text of a lecture delivered at the Oriental Institute of the University of Chicago on 18 May, 1961. Several paragraphs have been replaced by references to my book, *The Avestan Hymn to Mithra,* here abbreviated as *AHM.* I have, however, abandoned the reconstruction proposed in that book, of an Avestan divine name * (*Ahura*) *Vouruna.* Whatever I wrote about the god * *Vouruna* should be understood as applying to a god called simply *Ahura.* This

means a return to A. Hillebrandt's derivation of both the Iranian *Ahura* (who partly survived in Zoroaster's *Ahura Mazdāh*) and the Vedic *Asura* (who was generally referred to by his epithet *Varuna*) from an Indo-Iranian god whose name was *Asura* without further qualification: see *WZKM,* XIII (1899), 320, *ZII,* IV, 212, and his *Vedische Mythologie* (2d ed., 1929), II, 9; cf. also P. Thieme, *JAOS* (1960), 308 f. Hillebrandt's theory accounts better than any other for the co-existence of a close resemblance on the one hand, and a basic difference on the other, between the Avestan *Ahura Mazdāh* and the Vedic *Āsura Varuna,* cf. *AHM,* pp. 44 f., 321. A further divergence from *AHM,* which arises from an observation of F. B. J. Kuipers (see n. 30), will be found below, pp. 18 ff.

1. See Appendix I, p. 32.

2. On the dual role of Truth in Zoroaster's system cf. *AHM,* p. 45 f. One may conjecture that the two components of the name of Zoroaster's god reflect the two religious systems which the prophet had syncretized, one in which a chief god, Ahura, guarded primordial Truth against primordial Falsehood, the other in which a sole god, Mazdah, had Truth as one of his aspects or emanations.

3. On the name "Immortal" see Appendix VI, p. 34. I retain here the usual translation "holy" of *spənta-,* although the meaning of the adjective would be better rendered by a term conveying the idea of increase, such as "incremental."

4. The Gathic "twin" passage is discussed in Appendix II, p. 32.

5. See Appendix III, p. 33.

6. For clarity's sake I translate *dazdē* twice, since its meaning is both "created" and "established."

7. I agree with Humbach's interpretation of the third line and of the verb for "to meet" as implying hostility (*ZDMG* [1957], p. 369). His rejection of the traditional understanding of *dazdē* as 3rd dual perf. is, however, unjustified and makes nonsense of the first two lines. Av. *dazdē* stands to Ved. *dadhāte* as Av. *daiδītm* to Ved. *adadhātām,* the reduced grade of *ā* being in the first case zero, in the second *ī.* The meaning is precisely the one which Humbach thinks the form should have, but denies it: "sie schufen für sich" (i.e. the two Spirits created respectively, each to further his own aim, life and not-life, paradise and hell). The 3rd dual middle *jasaētəm* may be injunctive or optative.

8. Cf. the Younger Avestan statement that "the two Spirits, the Holy and the Fiendish, created the creation" (*Yasna* 57.17, *Yašt* 13.76).

9. Cf. W. B. Henning, *Zoroaster,* p. 46. To the Gathic passages that illustrate the prophet's missionary aim, *Yasna* 28.1 may be added in the following revised translation:

ahyā yāsā nəmanhā ustānazastō rafəδrahyā
manyəuš mazdā pourvīm spəntahyā ašā vīspng

šyaoānā
vanhəuš xratūm mananhō yā xšnəvīšā gəušča
  urvānəm

"I appeal firstly, O Mazdāh, with hands outstretched in prayer, to all (men) of (= who side with) the Holy Spirit with (= and) Truth, for actions of support of him (*ahyā*, viz. the Holy Spirit) with whom I am anxious to satisfy the will of (the Holy Immortal called) Good Mind, and the Soul of the Cow."

Here the meaning of *xratu-* approaches that of "injunction," which is attested for a much later period in Armenian *xrat*, Middle Pers. *xrd* (see W. B. Henning, *Trans. Philol. Soc.* [1944], p. 114), and Khotanese *grra, grata* (see H. W. Bailey, *BSOAS,* X [1942], 901).

10. Between the Gathas and the Younger Avesta proper lies a group of seven brief texts known as the "Yasna of the Seven Chapters," which may be as early as the sixth century. They contain no dualistic statements but are rich in polytheistic ones. Their authors worship not only Ahura Mazdāh and his Aspects but also fire, the waters, wind, earth and sky, the Haoma-plant, the souls of animals and pious people, a mythical donkey, cornfields, cross-roads, and much else. The great gods of the Younger Avesta, however, such as Anāhitā, Tištrya, Vərəthraghna, Vayu, do not appear in these texts; neither does Mithra, unless he is to be identified with the unnamed "Protector" of *Yasna* 42.2 (cf. *AHM,* pp. 54 ff.). What therefore makes the Seven Chapters less un-Zarathuštrian than the texts we have called Zarathuštric, is that apart from a possible half-hearted concession to Mithra, their authors did not admit as objects of worship any personal gods acting in rivalry with Ahura Mazdāh and detracting from his omnipotence.

11. On the incompatibility of this formulation with statements found in the Gathas cf. Appendix III, p. 33.

12. See J. Bidez and F. Cumont, *Les Mages Hellénisés,* II, 9, 67²⁶. Aristotle (384-322 B.C.) wrote the περι φιλοσοφιας after Plato's death (347 B.C.), at the same time as part of the first book of the *Metaphysics,* see W. Jaeger (transl. R. Robinson), *Aristotle,* p. 128. As the above information on the Magian doctrine is credited by Diogenes Laertius both to Aristotle and to Plato's friend Eudoxus of Cnidus (408-355 B.C.), who was an expert in Oriental lore, it is likely that Aristotle learned it from Eudoxus.

13. See Bidez and Cumont, *op. cit.,* Vol. II, 71.

14. See C. Clemen, *Fontes historiae religionis persicae,* pp. 3-16, especially 5-7.

15. See E. Benveniste, *The Persian Religion,* pp. 25 ff. The religion described by Herodotus can be defined *grosso modo* as the residue obtainable by subtracting the Zarathuštrian elements from the Zarathuštricism of the Younger Avesta. Even after the subtraction, however, an important difference remains, in that Herodotus not only does not mention Haoma, but expressly states (i. 132) that the Persians "pour no libations" (although, according to Book VII. 43, the Magi did, at least to the Trojan *artāvan's*). Cf. also below, p. 24 and, on Haoma, n. 43.

16. Old Persian version, col. IV, lines 60 f., 62 f.

17. Elamite version, col. III, lines 77 f., 78 f. In the Akkadian version (lines 103 f.) there is a gap after "Ahura Mazdāh bore me aid, and the other gods [. . .]," cf. Appendix VII, p. 34.

18. The gloss does not, of course, exclude the possibility that the expression "the other gods who are" may allude to Iranian gods that had not come to the notice of the Elamite translator. This is in fact what I believe to be the case. See below.

19. Cf. Appendix IV, p. 33.

20. *Auramazdām patiyāvahyaiy,* Beh. Inscr. i, 55, "I prayed to Ahura Mazdāh." Kent translated "I besought help of A. M.," but cf. W. B. Henning, *ZII,* IX, 174, line 8, and the Akkadian translation (line 22) *us-sal-la* (see Benedict and von Voigtlander, *JCS,* X [1956], 4).

21. See Appendix V, p. 34.

22. To a further argument, viz. that Darius fails to mention the Fiendish Spirit, Appendix V may serve as answer.

23. See Appendix VI, p. 34.

24. See Appendix VII, p. 34.

25. For Darius's use of the word "other" in this connection, note the Younger Avestan expression "Ahura Mazdāh and the other Aməša Spəntas," cf. *AHM,* p. 12, n. The Younger Avestan word for "god," *yazata-,* is applied to the Aməša Spəntas in *Visprat* 8.1 and 9.4.

26. Cf. Zarathuštra's wording in *Yasna* 50.4: "I worship you (plur. *ad sensum*), Ahura Mazdāh, with (*hadā*) [the three Aməša Spəntas called] Truth, Best Mind, and Power."

27. Cf. the phrase "all the Aməša Spəntas" in the Seven Chapters (*Yasna* 42.6), where "all" is clearly pleonastic.

28. See Appendix VIII, p. 35.

29. Cf. F. B. J. Kuiper, *Indo-Iranian Journal,* IV (1960), 185 f., who rightly points out that the sense in which Xerxes uses *artāvan* must go back to Indo-Iranian times (as I had failed to realize in *AHM,* pp. 153-55), but draws in my opinion the wrong conclusion.

30. Provided, of course, that Oss. (*i*)*dāwag* does go back to *artāwa-ka-,* see *BSOAS,* XVII (1955), 483-84. The alternative explanations of (*i*)*dāwag,* as

proposed by G. Dumézil, V. I. Abayev, H. W. Bailey (cf. *Hommages à Georges Dumézil* (1960), pp. 7, 11), and E. Benveniste (*Études sur la langue ossète,* p. 133), fail to satisfy me. I remain convinced that this is a religious term of substance, like the *izad* (from *yazata-,* "god") with which it is constantly associated in Ossetic literature, and that, as in the case of Sogdian *xatu* (see *AHM,* pp. 240 f., 329) a phonetically acceptable paper etymology will not by itself suffice to account for it. A derivation from *vitāwa(ka)-,* as Abayev proposes, meets in any case a serious obstacle in the unsuitable meaning of Sogdian *witāw-,* "to endure, persevere," as was pointed out already in *BSOAS,* XVII, 484, n. 1. The realization that the restriction of *artāvan* to the dead is a pre-Zarathuštrian notion makes it unnecessary to see in the Oss. *(i)dāwag*'s any Zoroastrian influence, and thus disposes at least of the conceptual objection which has been raised against my interpretation of these spirits.

31. Xerxes' statement runs: "The man who . . . worships Ahura Mazdāh . . . will become both *šiyāta* (= happy) while living, and *artāvan* (= one who has acquired Truth) when dead." The translation of the Darius passage as restored in *AHM,* p. 250 f., reads: "Whoso worships Ahura Mazdāh [, Truth]h will fo[rever] be [his,] both (while he is) alive and (after he is) dead." Here everything hinges on the restored word [*arta*]*m,* "[Trut]h," whose *m* is merely an inflectional ending that is applicable to a large number of other nouns as well. The attested Old Persian abstract noun corresponding to the adjective *šiyāta* in the Xerxes passage, is *šiyātiš* (nom. sg.), "happiness," which suits neither the gap nor the legible *m.* If one insists on the restoration "[happines]s," an Old Persian synonym of *šiyātiš* of suitable length and ending will have to be invented, in which case the use which one would be forced to attribute to Darius of a different word for "happiness" from the one Xerxes had in mind, would be a valid objection to any restoration that would produce such a meaning.

32. See W. B. Henning, *Trans. Philol. Soc.* (1944), pp. 108 f., 117.

33. Ahura Mazdāh and Anāhitā are not referred to in the calendar by these names, but respectively as *Dąθušō,* lit. "the Creator," and *Apam,* lit. "the Waters" (of which Anāhitā was the goddess).

34. These twelve divinities account for the names of the months, but they also occur as day-names.

35. Names, that is, to choose from the day-names of the Younger Avestan "Zoroastrian" calendar, such as "Discipline" (Av. *Sraošahe*), "Reward" (Av. *Ašōiš*), or "(Soul of the) Cow" (Av. *Guš (urvanō)*).

36. In some provinces with strong traditions of their own, such as Sogdiana, the terminology introduced by the central government need in any case not always have prevailed in every detail over the existing local calendar names.

37. The above discussion and conclusion are offered as an attempt to close the loophole which I had felt obliged to leave in *AHM,* p. 18, n.

38. Cf. J. Duchesne-Guillemin, *The Western Response to Zoroaster,* p. 54 f., who infers from the calendar names that Artaxerxes I was a "Zoroastrian," without, however, drawing a distinction, vital in the present context, between Zarathuštrianism and Zarathuštricism.

39. See Appendix IX, p. 35.

40. See W. B. Henning, *JRAS* (1944), 133 ff.

41. The circumstances in which Darius may have embraced Zarathuštrianism have been considered in *AHM,* p. 15 f. The picture would be somewhat different if the first Achaemenian convert to Zarathuštrianism were Cyrus, as has been suggested by W. Hinz, *Zarathustra,* pp. 146-52.

42. The definition of the calendar as "Magian" agrees with the fact that Haoma's name appears neither among the calendar names nor in Herodotus (cf. above, p. 16, n. 16), whose description, moreover, of the part played by worshiper and Magus at the sacrifice (i. 132) shows that no Haoma ritual was involved. Zarathuštric priests, by contrast, if the selection of the Younger Avestan calendar names had been left to them, would scarcely have failed to include the patron-god of their own class, whom they regarded as the divine priest of Ahura Mazdāh (*Yašt* 10.89 f.) to whom Ahura Mazdāh himself had entrusted the Mazdayasnian Religion (*Yasna* 9.26).

43. This tradition, of which the surviving "Yasna of the Seven Chapters" (see above, n. 11) affords us a glimpse, must have arisen in response to the need for simpler scriptural texts than the Gathas, on a level with the hymns and liturgies which the priests of the pagan Eastern Iranian communities continued to recite. These priests, like the Magi in the West, cannot readily be credited with a traditional literary skill in the second half of the fifth century. The texts which they recited had in all probability been composed centuries earlier, and the only effort required by the priests consisted in memorizing them. It should be understood, incidentally, that the terms "scripture," "texts," "literary activity," etc., are a mere *pis aller* in the present context, as the Avesta had scarcely as yet been committed to writing in the fifth century.

44. See Appendix X, p. 36.

45. See Appendix XI, p. 37.

46. See Appendix XII, p. 37.

47. See Appendix XIII, p. 38.

48. It was scarcely from a Magian source that Hecataios of Abdera elicited towards the end of the fourth century B.C. the Avestan name of the prophet . . . and the true country of his activity, Aryana Vaējahh . . . the homeland of the Avesta, see Bidez and

Cumont, *op. cit.,* vol. II, 30 f. This information was ignored by the Greeks, no doubt because they believed the Magian version to be more authoritative.

49. Even 780 years after Darius had referred to Gaumāta as "a Magian man" (*martiya maguš,* Behistun I, 36), Šāpūr I in his Great Inscription at Naqš-i Rustam still called his priests *mgw GBR'.* . . .

50. Cf. Yašt 5.94, 9.25 f., 16.6, and the crude and deficient account of Zarathuštra's achievement in *Yašt* 13.88 ff., where one looks in vain for the essential tenets of the Gathas, let alone for an echo of the prophet's lofty vision of God's designs and man's destiny.

51. That the Magi may have been led to such a conclusion by acquaintance with the dualistic religion of the "Harrānians" is a possibility which, in view of Hildegard Lewy's most stimulating article on the subject (*The Locust's Leg, Studies in honour of S. H. Taqizadeh* (1962), pp. 139 ff.), deserves to be borne in mind.

52. Although the Iranian Manichees of the third century A.D. no longer had the technical term *arta* for Zarathuštra's Truth, they were still aware of what had mattered more than anything else to the prophet. In the words of a Parthian Manichean hymn-writer, "Zarhušt descended to the kingdom of Pārs, and showed truth (*rāštēft*)" ('*wsxt zrhwšt 'w p'rs šhrd'ryft 'wš nm'd r'štyft,* Andreas-Henning, *Mitteliranische Manichaica,* III, *SPAW* [1934], 879, lines 19 ff.).

George G. Cameron (essay date 1968)

SOURCE: "Zoroaster the Herdsman," *Indo-Iranian Journal,* Vol. X, No. 4, 1968, pp. 261-81.

[*In the essay below, Cameron argues that Zoroaster's many references to the cow, pasturage, and herdsmen in the* Gathas *should be read as metaphors, rather than be taken literally—as they often have been by followers and scholars alike.*]

The message of the prophet Zoroaster would have made strong appeal to those people in any era of time who, in the morass of polytheism, were searching for new approaches toward deity. He taught that there was a single god whom all men should recognize and worship since He, who was present at the beginning and would still be present at the end of time, represented the best in all life. He proclaimed that there was open to every man a free choice for good or evil, and that every man must make that choice. And he was confident that the reign of the righteousness of his Wise Lord would ultimately triumph on earth as of course it was supreme in heaven. That such lofty sentiments should be expressed by a prophet whose career had ended before the middle of the sixth century B.C. is an astonishing fact of history.[1]

Interspersed among these profound statements, however, are a surprising number of specific references to that very earthy animal, the milch cow. "How", he beseeches the Wise Lord, "is he who desires the cow to obtain it, together with good pasturage for it?"[2] He says of God, "Thou art the father of the Holy Spirit which has created for us the cow, the source of good fortune, and which has also created the spirit of Devotion for the pasturage of the cow."[3] He declares that Righteousness was the "creator of the cow"[4] and then asks God to bestow on him those acts of the Holy Spirit which will enable him to satisfy both Good Thought and the soul of the cow.[5] He avers that God, as the creator of the cow, gave it "a free path towards the herdsman (husband-man) or the non-herdsman; then between the two it chose for itself the (cattle-) tending herdsman as a just master". This statement seems to assert that the cow is free to choose between a proper herder and no herder at all; if it is wise and intelligent it will choose the herdsman—and live; if it is stupid and witless it will select as master someone who is not a herdsman—and die. The passage apparently concludes with the truly astonishing declaration that "the man who is not a herdsman, despite his striving, may have no share in the good news"—that is, he may not share in Zoroaster's own message![6]

The very number of similar references to the cow or ox, its pasturage, and its herdsmen (who are sometimes irreverently dubbed "cowboys" by modern scholars) is itself impressive. Of the sixteen *Gathas* ("Songs") believed to stem directly from the prophet, fourteen contain at least one such allusion; and as if to compensate for the omission in the other two, one whole *Gatha* has been understood to be a play or drama in which two of the principal characters are the "soul of the ox" (or cow) and the "creator" of that soul.[7]

Many other like allusions will be touched on below; I will here draw attention only to two passages which seem to be glaringly inconsistent. In referring to those rewards which the righteous will obtain in the future life, Zoroaster proclaims that men of the faith will secure "a cow and an ox and all that they desire through Good Mind."[8] Yet curiously enough when he himself asks deity for the mundane reward due him for his own activity on God's behalf it is not for cattle, or the land in which to pasture them, or the food with which to nourish them that he makes request; instead, his humble prayer is for "Ten mares, with a stallion, and a camel—which were promised to me, O Wise one."[9] Although this seeming inconsistency has been remarked upon, the conclusions drawn have not affected the prevailing view of the economic and social milieu within which the prophet Zoroaster is believed to have proclaimed his faith.

Almost universally, Zoroaster's auditors have been presumed to be primarily cattle breeders, and such a statement as "The care and preservation of cattle is a central feature of the Zoroastrian doctrine"[10] is repeated, with only minor variations, in most of the modern essays concerned with the prophet's teachings.[11] Once, indeed, there was even a question whether agriculture was known to and practised by those auditors,[12] but happily the problem has been so resolved that one of the latest—and best—interpreters has been able to define Zoroaster's milieu as follows:

> On the one side he found a settled pastoral and agricultural community devoted to the tilling of the soil and the raising of cattle, on the other he found a predatory, marauding tribal society which destroyed both cattle and men, and which was a menace to any settled way of life. Their gods were like unto them: never were they good rulers, delivering over, as they did, the ox to Fury (*aēshma*) instead of providing it with good pasture.[13]

So it is that the majority still hold to the view that Zoroaster's audience consisted predominantly of cattle herdsmen and that a major function of his mission was to preserve and protect cattle; as one fine scholar puts it, "On its positive, practical side, this is Zoroaster's doctrine: *The ox, as the source of life, must be made to survive.*"[14] Confronted by this near-perfect unanimity of opinion, one is compelled to consider it extremely odd that Zoroaster, who was seeking to found a new faith, should declare that "one who is not a herdsman, despite his striving, shall not share in (my) good news" or that there should be an inconsistency between his promises of heavenly rewards for his followers ("a cow and an ox, and all that they desire") and his own request simply for "ten mares, with a stallion and a camel".

Is it not possible, however, that many of the prophet's explicit statements regarding the cow and its pasturage may be figures of speech which, if we fail to understand them correctly, can continue to be stumbling blocks to a fuller interpretation of his message? If we interpret them literally must we not admit that his teachings were a curious combination of superficiality and profundity, of the sublime and the ridiculous? Or may we not accept at face value the depth of his sentiments and clear away our own misunderstandings of his many allusions to the barnyard cow?

It is my belief that the respect approaching sanctification which the prophet appears to have for cattle, the honor he seems to bestow on cattle breeders, and his apparent insistence on good pastures for the cow and ox can by no means be explained on the basis of the social and economic practices of his auditors. What seems to have been overlooked is that no portion of his homeland, the Iranian plateau, could now or ever have accommodated a peasant economy founded exclusively or even primarily on cattle culture. In addition to the ever-present sheep and goats, a few cattle, there are, of course, and probably always have been: cows to provide some milk and *māst,* and oxen to serve as draft animals for cart and plow; but the sparse

vegetation that, throughout all known history, has always prevailed in Iran emphatically precludes an assumption that cattle raising could have been the sole or even the major occupation of the prophet's intended converts.[15]

Nor can his statements respecting the preservation ("sanctity") of cattle reflect an age-old concept held by Indo-European-speaking-peoples everywhere and Indo-Aryans in particular. It is of course true that the number of cattle possessed constituted the measure of wealth, the standard of value, among Homeric Greeks, Romans, Anglo-Saxons, Germans, and Hindus in India; but surely conceptions of wealth and those of holiness are wholly separate and distinct! It is even possible that the sanctity of the ox and cow in India originated, not with the Indo-European Aryans, but with the indigenous inhabitants among whom they penetrated![16]

Furthermore, it is wholly unlikely that Zoroaster's statements regarding the preservation of "cattle" can be based substantially on the opposition accorded him by members of some other religious faith who practiced animal sacrifice in connection with ritual drunkenness and the Haoma cult. It is quite true that the prophet appears to condemn both practices when he denounces cruelty to the "cow", when he quotes his adversaries as saying "Let the ox which sets afire (the deity) from whom death flees (an epithet of Haoma) . . . be slain", and when he damns ritual drunkenness in the strongest possible terms.[17] Yet herein lies one of the most puzzling aspects of Zoroastrianism in the form it adopted almost immediately after the founder's death: the whole liturgy not only centered around the Haoma rite but also did in fact involve the immolation of cattle—a feature which only subsequently was discarded![18] The task of explaining this seeming radical distortion of the prophet's views has led to a number of ingenious efforts on the part of modern scholars; perhaps all such may be discarded if we understand Zoroaster's references to cattle and their pasturage in the way he meant them to be understood.

One who looks objectively at the historical personnage Zoroaster, and dispassionately at his precepts, finds it quite impossible to believe that he, who sought to win all men to his single deity, would admit to the faith only those who raised cattle or were concerned with their pasturage, and that he would deny that faith—which to him had universal value—to such people as tradesmen, potters, carpenters, metal workers, or even city dwellers, who were non-herdsmen. Surely we who read his words, "The non-herdsman, despite his striving, shall have no share in the good news" do him a grave injustice if we interpret him to mean that even the best of men, obedient to the Wise Lord in thought, word, and deed, cannot share in the triumph of the faith unless he buys a cow and tenderly nourishes it. Such an interpretation could only lead logically to the conclusion—surely anathema to Zoroaster—that a great landowner with thousands of cattle on his acreage, despite his low measure of faith and failure to perform good works, merited a greater reward in heaven as on earth than a simple, devoted peasant who had but one or two animals (or none!) on his meagre holdings. By the same token Zoroaster's own earthly reward would be but a pittance, for he himself declares, "I have few cattle!"[19]

If, however, we recognize that his **Gathas** teem with figures of speech which would appeal to all auditors whether or not they lived on the fringes of a nomadic or a semi-nomadic world, we may gain a deeper insight into his basic message. Let us then make the following assumptions. When he speaks of "cattle" he is speaking of God's "flock"; if men but believed in the new faith they constituted the flock of Ahura Mazda, and Zoroaster himself was leading them to a new and richer life much as a shepherd guides his flock to greener pastures. But—and this was a vital part of his teachings—it was not enough for a man to believe: merely to become a *member* of the flock; he, too, must become an active proponent of God's will, must himself, in thought, word, and deed, become a *herdsman* of the deity's "flock".

So it was that in his preaching Zoroaster would be using metaphors which brought these ideas to expression in concrete terms. To repeat, most of his allusions to cattle would apply not merely to a herd of kine, but to the flock of God; his references to pasturage would pertain not to the open Iranian fields sparse with grain, but to the way of life of believers in God; when he speaks of shepherds he would mean not the herdsmen of the cow and the ox, but those who lead God's fold or who are active in His work; and when he points to nourishment he would be alluding not to the fattening of the draft ox or the milch cow, but to that heavenly sustenance—our and his Holy Spirit—which descends on all men of good will.

That Zoroaster should employ such figures of speech should occasion no surprise whatever; have great religious thinkers not always done so? Does not the Psalmist aver, "Know ye that Yahweh, He is God; it is He that hath made us, and we are His. We are His people, and the sheep of His pasture"?[20] Did not the Second Isaiah say of God, "He will lead His flock like a shepherd, He will gather the lambs in His arm and carry them in His bosom and will gently lead those that have their young"?[21] Do we not remember that Jesus said, "Fear not, little flock, for it is your Father's good pleasure to give you the kingdom",[22] and that Peter urged the elders of the church to "Tend the flock of God that is among you"?[23] Even in more ancient times the same metaphorical expression was in fashion. The Sumerian Lugal-zaggisi prayed that he might always be the "shepherd at the head of the flock", Gudea asserted that he was chosen by his god to be the "true shepherd of the land", and later Babylonian and Assyrian kings freely assumed such a title.[24] Also in Egypt the pharaoh or the god Re is called the "shepherd of the land" and men are said to be the "cattle of god".[25] Zoroaster's manner of speaking then, is not new to the Near Eastern or Western world; the wonder is only that his allusions have for so long a time been interpreted literally and so misunderstood!

Cattle, of course, played then as in more recent days a part in the life of the inhabitants. It is but natural, therefore,

that some few of the prophet's references to the cow should have no metaphorical significance whatsoever. "Ahura Mazda made the cattle, the water, and the plants", he says, and prays that He will "cause both cattle and men to prosper",[26] much as the author of Genesis relates, "And God said, let the earth bring forth living creatures after their kind: cattle and creeping things and beasts of the earth after their kind."[27] Such allusions, obviously, may be understood and interpreted literally.

Not so, however, the host of other references to the cow and ox, to cattle pasturing and herding. In them we find the prophet making allusion to objects and institutions with which he and his hearers were familiar in the course of their daily existence, and turning them into parables which could illustrate his ethical and religious concepts. A too literal interpretation of his metaphors may blind us to some of his most profound utterances and so lead us to make a travesty of his teachings.

It nevertheless is a sad but demonstrable fact that Zoroaster's own immediate followers misunderstood those same allusions; though seeking to retain his inspiration, they made—as he did not—a semi-sacred animal of the barnyard cow. These successors, earnest but unimaginative, sought to achieve a religious doctrine which would combine Zoroaster's teachings with a ritualistic religion known to their forefathers for centuries. Ostensibly as Zoroastrians, they reinstituted sacrificial rites involving the cow, and superstitious customs of all types which had been ignored or repudiated by the founder of their faith.[28] His allusions, literally interpreted, fitted effortlessly into their eclectic doctrines, and the prophet's **Gathas,** which were never intended for ritualistic purposes, were recited at the very sacrifices which the prophet abhorred.

Thus it was that there arose, seemingly as an integral part of Zoroaster's doctrine, a number of beliefs and teachings regarding the cow, the ox, and their pasturage that were wholly at variance with the prophet's will and intentions. This, indeed, was bitter mockery—but is it not a universal fault that men, blind to the vision of a great leader and incapable of understanding his inspiration, should misinterpret his message and thereby pervert his doctrine? We are reminded of Jesus' sad plaint, "Have I been so long time with you, and dost thou not know me?"[29]

Secure in the knowledge that Zoroaster's references are to be understood as metaphors or figures of speech, we may now see that they illuminate rather than obscure his meaning and that the earthy terms familiar to his auditors dramatize his ethical and religious thoughts. Valiantly endeavoring to fulfill the role of "shepherd", he announces that he has tried to "keep wantonness from the household, wickedness from the community, oppression from the tribe, and 'Worst Thought' from the 'pasture of the cattle'".[30] Like any honest caretaker, he doubted his own adequacy and, perplexed, besought his God to tell him how he should protect the "flock": "What help can my soul expect from anyone? In whom can I put my trust as a protector for my 'cattle', or in whom for myself . . . except in Righteousness, in Thee O Wise Lord, and in the Best Mind?"[31] In a passage insisting on Ahura Mazda's creative powers he still wonders about the message he is delivering and about his own persuasive abilities among men: "This I ask Thee, O Lord: answer me truly. Is the message I proclaim really true? . . . For whom hast Thou fashioned the 'pregnant cow' that brings prosperity?"[32] When both he and his few adherents were in danger he uttered a sweeping condemnation of "liars, infamous and of repellent deeds, who prevent the promoter of Righteousness from fostering the 'cattle'",[33] and gave assurance to his followers that there would be grievous punishments inflicted on that individual who "found his living only in outrage to the 'cattle and men of the herdsmen'".[34] The righteous members of the productive flock, however, should have their reward: "This precious gift, O Wise One, you shall give for the action of Good Thought to all those who are in the community of the 'cattle,' (namely) Your good doctrine . . . which makes the community prosper".[35]

The rewards to be obtained by the faithful is the subject of a spirited declaration: "Whoever for me, Zoroaster, will bring to pass according to Righteousness that which I most wish for, to him as a reward shall come 'a cow and an ox' and all that he desires."[36] If this passage be interpreted literally the "gift" is singularly inadequate, for the grant of a solitary cow and ox, even if the recipient were a poor peasant, could hardly be considered "all that he desired" among assumed cattle-raising peoples. That earthly blessings should accrue to the righteous man was of course to be expected; but surely, in this context, the prophet is only saying that he who adheres to the message preached by him and who becomes an active proponent of the Wise Lord shall obtain great return: a hearing among men who will themselves propagate the faith.

At one stage in his ministry the prophet's fortunes were at low ebb. Thrust out from family and community, he turned to God with the plaintive query: "How can I, O Lord, assure myself of Thy favor?" and, aware of the cause of his banishment, expressed it in concrete terms: "I know why I am impotent, O Wise One: mine are few 'cattle' and I possess few men."[37] Misled by a literal interpretation of this declaration, students of the Gathas have actually debated whether his lack of cattle was itself responsible for the few adherents he had gained, or whether he simply possessed few cattle and also lacked friends.[38] The grounds for any such dispute disappears with the recognition that the two terms, "cattle" and "men" are, in fact synonyms and that Zoroaster's weakness and consequent flight stemmed from the absence of influential supporters—that is, a worthy flock—who could lend him assistance. Immediately after this quoted confession to the deity appears a plea which was intended to clarify the allusion to cattle: "Attend to it, O Lord, and give me the support which friend grants to friend"; the prophet knew as well as we that God's active help comes through men and their allegiance to the faith, not through the bovine species. A similar thought is brought to expression in a passage filled with doubts about his own ability. With reference to himself he beseeches God, "How is he to obtain the 'cattle' which bring prosperity—he who desires it, together with its 'pasture'?" As though it were an afterthought, he continues with an explanation of what he means by 'cattle': they are "those who, among the many that behold the sun, live uprightly according to Righteousness."[39]

The passages just referred to illustrate a homely truth that he who reads the *Gathas* will soon understand. In expressing his religious convictions and his prayers, in voicing condemnations of the wicked and blessings upon the righteous, Zoroaster often introduces his theme by stating it in metaphorical terms having reference to the cow or ox, to cattle herding, cattle pasturage, and the like. Immediately afterwards, he develops the theme; this time, however, his thought is offered in more concrete terms which refer to the relationship of God to man, of man to God, or of man to man. There is thus a twofold presentation: one abstract and metaphorical, which we may call the introduction, and one concrete, which may be known as the sequel or the continuation; but the thought in both parts is identical. Without the continuation it would perhaps too often be easy and self-deluding merely to substitute 'God's flock' for the prosaic word "cattle" and thus subjectively to read into the Gathas religious values comfortable to us in the twentieth century but not intended or envisioned by the prophet two thousand five hundred years ago. But when there lies before us the continuation with its concrete application of the abstract situation, no further misinterpretation is possible.

One such passage, already frequently referred to, appears in the second of two *Gathas* which have been aptly named "The *Gathas* of the Choice" because they describe the free path that is open to man to choose for good or ill. Translated, the passage reads:

> Thine was Devotion. Thine also was the Spirit as creator of the ox,
> O Wise One, when Thou didst give the ox a free path towards the herdsman or the non-herdsman.
> Then between the two it chose for itself the (cattle-)tending herdsman as a just master, a farmer(?) of Good Mind.
> He who is no herdsman, despite his striving, O Wise One, shall have no share in the good news.[40]

This, to be sure, is abstract; the continuation demonstrates that it is merely metaphorical:

> At the beginning of time, O Wise One, by Thy Mind Thou didst for us create material forms and consciences and (rational) wills,
> For Thou didst establish corporeal things. (Thou didst also create)
> Deeds and words whereby one may exercise choice by one's own free will.
> Ever since, man may lift up his voice—the man of false words as well as the man of true words, the wise as well as the fool—
> Each according to his own heart and mind.

Here it is clearly not the cow which has free choice, but man; the choice lies not between a herdsman or a non-herdsman by *cattle* but between the acceptance of God or the denial of Him by *man*. In the continuation, mankind's "material forms, consciences, and wills" correspond to "ox" or "cattle" in the preceding metaphor; every man has been given by God the option of becoming a member of His flock or not, and in this option man may decide freely.

But—and here Zoroaster propounds a thought unknown to his predecessors—choosing to follow God's way of life as taught by a good 'herdsman' is not, in itself, enough; sheep may follow a shepherd blindly, cattle a herdsman because they sense that he guides them wisely and knows what serves their best interests. Every convert, insists Zoroaster, must himself become a "worker in the vineyard", as a later religious leader put it. No man, says the prophet, may rest assured of future bliss unless he too, in thought and action, works diligently for the good of the believing community, becomes himself a herdsman of the flock. Otherwise, said he, "Despite his striving, he who is not a 'herdsman' may not share in the good news."

Another sequence of thought appears in a **Gatha** which has been called the "**Gatha** of Dominion" because the prophet besieges deity with a number of searching questions regarding His kingdom on earth as in heaven and, more specifically, regarding Zoroaster's own ability as a 'shepherd' to bring about that Kingdom. One of his questions reads, "Shall the 'herdsman' of good will and upright deeds receive, through Righteousness, the 'cow'?" The answer, following almost immediately, reveals that the gift to be bestowed upon the shepherd of the flock—in this instance, Zoroaster—is not the earthly cow but divine blessings; here we read; "The Wise Lord, through His power, appoints what is better than good to him who is attentive to His will."[41]

As a deeply religious man, Zoroaster felt that he had been summoned by God to carry his mission to men. He thought himself unworthy, but knew that the deity would lend assistance. Desperately in need of his message was man, God's creation. Such thoughts are embodied in a prayer which figuratively calls man the "soul of the cow": "With hands outstretched in prayer toward men possessed of the Holy Spirit and of Righteousness, O Wise One, I will first ask You for those acts in support of him (the Holy Spirit) whereby I may bring satisfaction both to the will of Good Mind and to the 'soul of the cow'."[42] As though to clarify this figurative expression he almost immediately seems to say that he seeks the good things of both worlds—that of the body and that of the mind—"by which one may transport his friend into felicity".[43]

Understandably, as said, to his contemporaries such symbolic allusions to cattle, shepherding, pasturage, and nourishment would make strong appeal. They reach their maximum effectiveness in a **Gatha** which has long been recognized to be a drama or play in which many of the stage directions have been written directly into the text.

The dramatis personae in inverse order of their appearance, seem to be first, the prophet Zoroaster; second, Ahura Mazda's helpers or "entities"; third, the "creator of the ox"—that is, the Wise Lord himself; and fourth, the "soul of the ox"—that is, the souls of mankind, sometimes also alluded to as the "soul of the milk-producing cow". Thus two of the characters bear figurative names, and throughout the play there are many allusions which seem to have abstract reference to their earthly activities. Once the significance of these allusions has become apparent, however, there is little need to replace the figurative terms except when they do violence to twentieth century religious idioms. The **Gatha** reads as follows:[44]

Stage Direction. To You (O Wise One) did the "soul of the ox" complain:

"Who made me? For whom did you create me? Fury and violence, cruelty, frightfulness, and tyranny oppress me! I have no other 'herdsman' than You; then make known to me good 'pastures'!"

Stage Direction. Then the "Creator of the Ox" asked of Righteousness:

"Have you a judge for the 'cow', that you may provide it with both 'pasture' and zealous care? Whom did you appoint to be its master, who will drive off the malevolent who bring about fury?"

Stage Direction. Then Righteousness replied, without enmity toward the 'ox':[45]

"There is . . . no way of knowing (in advance?) how the powerful will act toward the weak. But that man is the strongest of beings to whose aid I come when he calls! It is the Wise One who can best proclaim plans carried out by false gods and men in the past, or plans that will be carried out in the future; He, the Lord, will decide; let His will be done!"

Stage Direction. Then with hands outstretched we pray to the Lord, we two, my ('ox') soul and the 'soul of the milch cow,' urging the Wise One who alone can command:

"Can neither the right-living man nor his 'shepherd' live in the midst of the wicked who surround him?"

Stage Direction. Then spoke the Wise Lord Himself, He who understands prayers in His own soul:

"No master has, then, been found, no judge to act in accordance with Righteousness, even though the Creator made *you* (i.e., mankind) to become a 'herdsman'!"

Stage Direction omitted. (The "soul of the cow"(?) questions:)

"Then did the Wise Lord, in agreement with Righteousness, create for the 'cow' (merely) a formula involving an offering of fat, although He, bounteous in his ordinances, (created) milk for thirsty men?[46] Whom hast Thou from among men who, in accordance with Good Mind, may take care of us?"

Stage Direction omitted. (Ahura Mazda answers:)

"I know only this one: Zoroaster, of Spitama's lineage. He is the only one who has heard Our teachings. He wishes, with Wisdom, to recite hymns dedicated to US and to Righteousness; sweetness of speech shall be given to him'."

Stage Direction. Then moaned the 'soul of the ox':

"(To think) that I must be content to have as my protector the ineffectual word of an impotent man when I long for one who exercises his sovereignty at will! Will there ever be one who will give strong-handed help? Then do You O Lord, with Righteousness and Good Mind, grant that he should have strength and Dominion so that he may obtain good dwellings and security for them! O Wise One, I have recognized Thee as the first provider of these! Where are Righteousness, Good Mind, and Dominion? Admit me, together with (that is, as) mankind, to the great gift, O Wise One! To our aid now, O Lord! May we have a part in Your bounty!"

The bounty or reward that righteous men could expect from God would come, Zoroaster believed and taught, in both this world and the next. He himself expected tangible profits during his lifetime: mares, a stallion, and a camel;[47] but such things were, he knew, merely an earnest of things to come. Though fervent believers and active "shepherds" could hope to receive in the present existence a dominion "rich in pasture" together with "all the good things of life that have been, are, or will be" and the "wonders of Best Mind and the joy of long life all his days",[48] greater rewards were still in store: whoever does his utmost for the righteous and labors diligently on behalf of God's "cattle" will ultimately be in the "pasture" of Righteousness and of Good Mind regardless of the social stratum to which he belonged![49]

Not all men, of course, approved Zoroaster's preaching. Some gave active opposition to him personally; others, by cunning and violence, sought to hinder the spread of his message perhaps because it threatened their vested interests. Against such men the prophet inveighed forcefully and repeatedly: they were decimating or making to suffer God's "cattle", destroying its "pastures", and harming its "herdsmen". The metaphorical use of such terms in this context is peculiarly apt, for the traditional religion which he was attempting to replace seems to have involved the sacrifice of a bull or cow and the ritual drinking of the intoxicating *haoma*. Since the prophet's new faith denied the efficacy of the old sacrificial cults,[50] his pronouncements against the sacrifice of the ox or cow—that is, the destruction of God's "flock",—were a two-edged sword.[51] Said he:

> That man does indeed destroy the doctrine who speaks of the 'ox' and the sun as though they were the worst things the eye can behold,
> Who makes men of purity become men of evil deeds, And who lays waste God's 'pasture' by taking up arms against the righteous.
> Truly evil men destroy life who, allegedly as lords and ladies, divert the righteous from Best Thought (And so) deprive them of their proper inheritance.

Let them beware:

> The Wise Lord has condemned those who take the life of the 'ox' with ecstatic cries![52]

Such men, in Zoroaster's view, were leaders of the older cult, the *karapans*, who (he claimed) preferred money or possessions to righteousness or the ministry of men. They and their like bent all their will and effort to crush Zoroaster, whose "wealth" they sought.[53] In the coming dominion they would have that "wealth",—but in Hell! And there with them would be all others who failed to heed the inspired message![54] The punishment was just; for such men of their own volition served false gods and, says Zoroaster: "Have false gods ever been good masters? This I ask of those who . . . in their cult, take part with *karapans* and the *usigs* to give the 'ox' over to violence!"[55]

In two additional references Zoroaster alludes to the fate of these same evil men, and in both the destiny in store is identical: they are to be consigned to the "House of Evil" or the "Dwelling of the Lie". It is doubtful, however, if two passages dealing with the same subject in the whole of the prophet's **Gathas** could more dramatically demonstrate his metaphorical terminology. One utterance reads:[56]

> The *karapans* do not obey the statutes and just rules concerning 'pasturage';
> They destroy the 'cow' by their deeds and doctrines.
> Such judgment shall, at the end, consign them to the House of the Lie!

Here the accusation is specific: the leaders have ignored the divinely inspired prophetic ordinances regarding "pasturage" and brought suffering to "cattle".

The second passage sheds welcome light on Zoroaster's meaning:[57]

> The *karapans* and *kavis* have subdued *mankind* to the yoke of their dominion
> In order to destroy life by evil deeds.
> They shall be tortured by their own souls and consciences
> When they come to the 'Bridge of the Requiter' (to be) inmates forever in the Dwelling of the Lie!

Here the symbolism is gone. It is not the cow which has been maltreated, but mankind which has been exposed to evil deeds. The parallelism is complete; but in the one instance the prophet's allusion, though no doubt clear to his contemporary auditors, has been obscure to us; in the other, the forceful message of the "herdsman" Zoroaster, prophet of old Iran, is vivid even in the twentieth century.

Notes

1. This essay was initially one of a series of lectures on "Zoroaster and his World" which, in 1953, was delivered at Oberlin College in the "Haskell Lectures on Old Testament Studies". It has received only the slightest of revisions, but in its earlier form was read by Jacques Duchesne-Guillemin; see his

The Western Response to Zoroaster (1958), p. 104. The entire series of lectures was accepted for publication by a university press in 1958, and subsequently I learned that one of the readers who recommended publication was Professor Wolfgang Lentz. Late in the same year, however, I decided to withhold publication until I could include a modern translation of all of Zoroaster's Gathas; the latter task, unhappily, remains unfinished. I know only too well how difficult it is to understand and to translate the Gathas of Zoroaster, and how full of obscurities they are. It is perhaps particularly dangerous for one who lays no claim to being essentially an Iranian-language specialist to cite (even from far better authorities) as many translations of various passages as are here presented. I realize also (as Professor F. B. J. Kuiper first pointed out to me when, in the summer of 1965, I suggested to him briefly and orally the interpretations here proposed) that I have taken no account of the prominent role which the cow plays in the Vedas (see, however, the article of W. P. Schmid cited, under the year 1958, in n. 11 below); perhaps one might even suggest that Zoroaster may have emphasized the cow and cattle herding because he was dimly aware of some very old—and pre-Zoroastrian—myth involving this animal, the outlines of which had long since been lost; yet see also the comments in n. 51 below. Thus it may be that certain deficiencies of mine or a number of inadequacies of translation are of such serious nature that they vitiate a part of the "argument". I am encouraged to publish, nevertheless, in the hope that a substantial part of the residue will remain valid, and also in the belief (so aptly phrased by Duchesne-Guillemin in the concluding sentence of his book noted above) that "The West has not said its last word on Zoroaster." For the most recent interpretation of Zoroaster's message, with an excellent annotated bibliography to all earlier literature, see R. C. Zaehner, *The Dawn and Twilight of Zoroastrianism* (London, 1961). Recent translations of the Gathas are: J. Duchesne-Guillemin, *Zoroastre* (Paris, 1948) and *The Hymns of Zoroaster* (London, 1952); Helmut Humbach, *Die Gathas des Zarathustra* (Heidelberg, 1959); and Walther Hinz, *Zarathustra* (1961), pp. 161 ff.-The most common abbreviations employed throughout are:

AAWL: Abhandlungen der Akademie der Wissenschaften und der Literatur in Mainz, Geistes- und sozialwissenschaftliche Klasse, Wiesbaden.

Bartholomae, *AiW:* Christian Bartholomae, *Altiranisches Wörterbuch* (Strassburg, 1904).

BSOS: Bulletin of the School of Oriental and African Studies, University of London.

Duchesne-Guillemin, *Hymns:* see above.

Herzfeld, *ZW:* Ernst Herzfeld, *Zoroaster and His World,* 2 vols. (Princeton, 1947).

Humbach, *Die Gathas:* see above.

JRAS: Journal of the Royal Asiatic Society.

Meillet, *Trois conf.:* A. Meillet, *Trois conférences sur les Gâthâ de l'Avesta (= Annales du Musée Guimet, Bibliothèque de Vulgarisation,* Tome 44) (1925).

Moulton, *EZ:* James Hope Moulton, *Early Zoroastrianism* (London, 1913).

NAWG: Nachrichten von der Akademie der Wissenschaften in Göttingen, Philologisch-historische Klasse, Göttingen.

Nyberg, *Religionen:* H. S. Nyberg, *Die Religionen des alten Iran (= Mitteilungen der Vorderasiatisch-aegyptischen Gesellschaft,* Band 43) (Leipzig, 1938).

Smith, *Studies:* Maria Wilkins Smith, *Studies in the Syntax of the Gathas of Zarathushtra (= Language Dissertations,* published by the Linguistic Society of America, No. IV) (1929).

Ys.: Yasna

Zaehner, *Dawn:* see above.

ZDMG: Zeitschrift der deutschen Morgenländischen Gesellschaft.

2. Ys. 50:2. Moulton, *EZ,* p. 382 n. 7 observes that both Bartholomae and Geldner understood this to be a reward in the future life.

3. Ys. 47:3. Cf. Wolfgang Lentz in *Donum Natalicum H. S. Nyberg Oblatum* (1954), pp. 42 ff.

4. Ys. 46:9; note, however Humbach's translation *ad loc.*

5. Ys. 28:1.

6. Ys. 31:9-10. On the translation, cf. Duchesne-Guillemin, *Zoroastre,* p. 296a, after Nyberg, *Religionen,* p. 210 n. 2 and Moulton, *EZ,* p. 353; also Zaehner, *Dawn,* p. 41 and Humbach, *Die Gathas,* I, 90 f.; contrast, however, Herzfeld, *ZW,* pp. 170 and 580. The translation of Andreas-Wackernagel in *NAWG,* 1911, p. 21 makes Ahura Mazda the subject: "then He chose for them—of these two—the cattle-tending peasant as a just master"; see, however, Smith, *Studies,* p. 77 n. 1 to verse 10.—On the word here translated "good news", Moulton, *EZ,* p. 353 n. 5 remarked that in meaning as in etymology it is like Greek *Euaggelion.* Nyberg, *Religionen,* p. 210 n. proposes that "it corresponds to what we understand by 'rites', since it has to do with memories or traditions". Herzfeld, *ZW,* pp. 580 f., argued for "division of profits" or "settling of accounts." Cf. also Duchesne-Guillemin, *Zoroastre,* p. 296a: "*la bonne Souvenance* (des Immortels)".

7. Ys. 29; see below, pp. 277 ff.

8. Ys. 46:19. This passage, always troublesome, was particularly so ("rätselhaft") to H. Lommel in

NAWG, 1934, Fachgruppe III, pp. 114 f.; Humbach, *Die Gathas,* I, 135 translates simply "zwei Milchkühe", whereas Nyberg, *Religionen,* p. 197 thought of a pregnant cow and an ox".

9. Ys. 44:18. On the last words of the stanza see Gershevitch, *JRAS,* 1952, p. 177 and *The Avestan Hymn to Mithra* (1959), p. 201, but contrast Humbach, *Die Gathas,* II, 100.

10. Said Bartholomae, "Die Pflege und Schonung des Rinds . . . steht in Mittelpunkt der zarathushtrischen Lehre", *AiW* (1904), p. 509; a similar view is expressed in his *Zarathuštra's Leben und Lehre* (1919), pp. 14* ff.

11. From the beginning of the scientific study of the entire Avesta there has been remarkable uniformity in the scholarly acceptance of this notion which, in large part, stems from the respect approaching sanctification of the *gav-* visible in the Later Avesta. Few authors (and even those only recently) have expressed doubt about the intent of the prophet's allusions, and a considerable body of literature has been devoted to the similarity of his teachings in this regard with the alleged holiness of the cow among the Indo-Aryans in India (on which see below) and to the prophet's residence among cattle-tending nomads who knew little or nothing of agriculture. Some of the more pertinent observations by many of the foremost Gathic scholars are here subsumed in chronological order (see also the previous note).

1882. Wilhelm Geiger. This great pioneer first demonstrated conclusively that Zoroaster must have lived in northeastern Iran. However, after describing briefly the poor quality and meager number of cattle presently to be found in that area he then concluded with a sweeping generalization which should long since have been suspect but which set the pattern for nearly all subsequent authorities: "Beim altiranischen Volke wären die Verhältnisse nach den Bemerkungen des Awesta wesentlich andere gewesen. Nach ihnen müsste man annehmen, dass damals die Rinderzucht unverhältnismässig mehr beliebt und verbreitet war, als die Zucht des Kleinviehs. Schafe und Ziegen werden nur gelegentlich erwähnt, ohne dass die Texte sich weiter bei ihnen aufhalten. Die Kuh dagegen spielt in allen Teilen des Awesta, in den ältesten wie in den jüngsten, eine sehr wichtige Rolle und man wusste ihre Vorzüge zu würdigen und anzuerkennen." (*Ostiranische Kultur im Altertum,* p. 344).

1911. K. F. Geldner. "The devil-worshippers, at their sacrifices, slay the ox; and this the *daēvas* favor, for they are foes to the cattle and to cattle breeding and friends to those who work ill to the cow. In Zoroaster's eyes this is an abomination: for the cow is a gift of Ormazd to man, and the religion of Mazda protects the sacred animals. It is the religion of the settled grazier and the peasant, while the ruder *daēva*-cult holds its ground among the uncivilized nomadic tribes." (*Encyclopedia Britannica,* 11th ed., Vol. 28, p. 1042a, s.v. "Zoroaster")

1912. J. H. Moulton rather carefully avoided the subject in his Hibbert Lectures, yet on p. 303 of *EZ* appears this comment: "The Ox-Soul (and the) Ox-Creator represent the world of animal life entrusted to the diligent husbandman." Elsewhere (pp. 382 n. 7, 385 n. 2) he follows Bartholomae and Geldner in explaining the gift of "pregnant cows" as referring perhaps to the reward in the future life: "Bartholomae . . . notes that one who makes cattle and pasture the source of good fortune here cannot conceive of Paradise without it."

1920. Raffaele Pettazzoni. "The mission of the prophet, religious as it was at the beginning, had also to become civil in character; . . . every utterance concerning Ahura Mazda, accompanied by the praise of beef cattle, was intended to put an end to robberies and the devastations of them, to promote increased care, labor of the field, and a milder condition of life on their behalf." (*La Religione di Zarathustra,* 1920, p. 88).

1922. M. N. Dhalla. The great Parsi scholar unconsciously wavers. Once he interprets the term "herding" literally: "The Creator points to (Zoroaster) as the ideal protector of the kine"; however he then explains the term to mean husbandry (but only husbandry) in general, as when "Ahura Mazda . . . created his prophet for the support and care of the tillers of the land" (*Zoroastrian Civilization,* p. 143; see also his *History of Zoroastrianism,* 1938, pp. 45 ff.; for both explanations Dhalla cites Ys. 29:6).

1925. A. Meillet. The "soul of cattle represents the entire bovine species"; a translation "cow" or "ox" is inadequate, for the context demands inclusion of both male and female sexes! (*Trois conf.,* pp. 43-44 and 47).

1930. H. Lommel. "It is well known with what deep and significant piety Zarathustra has determined the position of the cow and its nurture in the religious world of thought" (*Oriental Studies in Honour of C. E. Pavry,* p. 284); see also his *Die Religion Zarathustras* (1930), pp. 123-26 and 246-50; also *NAWG,* 1935, Fachgruppe III, pp. 138 f. [esp. pp. 149,157 "das Heil"].

1933. Arthur Christensen. "The peasant-farmer was designated as *vāstrya* (derived from *vāstra,* pasture), or as *fšuyant,* cattle herder. But we should not conclude from these titles that agriculture—in contrast to cattle herding—was without significance; for cattle were employed in plowing. The peasant owned property, felt a strong attachment for his home and possessions, and put himself and his animals under the protection of the gods. His desires for the blessings of peace were connected with the possession of a good home and fine grazing lands." (*Die Iranier,* p. 219)

1938. H. S. Nyberg. "Zarathustra battles *for* a normal reception of the divine power of the cow through the drinking of milk and *against* a ritualistic, ecstatic appropriation of that power through wild, sacrificial orgies; *for* the claim of the earth to possess the heavenly power of the cow's urine and *against* the wasting of this heavenly gift through the slaughter of bulls; *for* the inviolability of the soul of the beast and *against* murderous attacks on its divine life" (*Religionen,* p. 200).

1947. Ernst Herzfeld. Some vacillation is apparent. He says, for example, that "the ox is in Zoroaster's figurative speech the symbol of the peasant" (*ZW,* p. 347), but he also understands Avestan *vāstrya-*("herdsman") and similar terms to mean the "peasantry, . . . man of the pasture, especially of large cattle" or "cowboys" (*ibid.,* pp. 126, 196 f., 344-47, 579-81); he then translates the associated words as "'cattle-pasture,' figurative for neat-herds and shepherds" (*ibid.,* p. 245).

1948. J. Duchesne-Guillemin. See the quotation from *Zoroastre* cited below at n. 14. In the new preface to the English translation of part of this work (*Hymns* [1952], pp. 5 f.), the same author expresses regret that the "latest Parsee interpreter of the Gāthās refuses, for reasons of piety, to admit that such a trivial thing as cattle-raising could be mentioned in sacred hymns".

It is unfortunate, in my view, that more attention has not been paid to the approved Parsi interpretation of the "ox-soul" of Ys. 28 and Ys. 29—yet even this has been limited chiefly to this particular actor. Cf. Smith, *Studies,* § 84, citing E. S. D. Bharucha, *A Brief Sketch of the Zoroastrian Religion and Customs,* 2nd ed. (1903), p. 48: "(The ox-soul is) the whole living world personified as a cow." Cf. also F. A. Bode and P. Nanavutty, *Songs of Zarathushtra* (1952), p. 43 n.: "(The ox-soul is the) symbol of the whole of Creation and all living things." Contrast, however, the views of M. N. Dhalla cited above under the year 1922.

1950. J. C. Tavadia. This fine scholar recognized "human beings, the people at large" in the "Ox-Soul" of Yasnas 28 and 29, yet even for him "people were then at the pastoral stage of civilization, and the ox formed the basis of the whole economic life." See his *Indo-Iranian Studies,* I (= *Viśva-Bharati Studies,* No. 10) (1950), p. 51, and *Indo-Iranian Studies,* II (= *Viśva-Bharati Studies,* No. 15) (1952), pp. 28 and 35 f. He also suggested the metaphoric use of *gav-* as the "Quell des Lebendigen" in Ys. 47:3; see *ZDMG,* 103 [n.f. 28; 1953], p. 323 n. 11 and p. 338.

1954. Wolfgang Lentz. Tavadia's views were at first cautiously then (happily) more enthusiastically endorsed by Lentz in his monograph on "Yasna 28" in *AAWL,* 1954, No. 16. On pp. 975-78 (57-60), Lentz briefly insists, among other things, that there is at least a 50

possibility that such terms as "cow" (Rind) were used metaphorically by Zoroaster; that the Yasna which he translates is devoted to purely spiritual matters, and not to such mundane affairs as cattle herding (or tribal organization); and that references in other Yasnas (cited, however, are only Yasnas 29 and 47:3) may also be explained metaphorically. Cf. also his brief remark in *Orient. Suec.,* 3 (1954), p. 42.

1958. Wolfgang P. Schmid. In a highly significant article on "Die Kuh auf der Weide" (*Indogermanische Forschungen,* 64, 1958-59, 1-12) Schmid successfully presents Rigvedic parallels to a number of Gathic utterances in order to demonstrate the metaphorical usage of such terms as "cow", "ox", and "pasture". We must welcome this forward-looking approach, but I personally am unimpressed by Schmid's conclusion that the "cow" represents a "Symbol der Dichtung" or poetical composition.

1959. Helmut Humbach. This author accepts Lentz' argument that certain common or frequently appearing words in the Gathas have significances other than those implied by their "etymological bases" (*Die Gathas,* I, 61 f.). Subsequently (*ibid.,* p. 72) he almost seems to promote the views promulgated in this article. In all its occurrences (except in Ys. 53:4), he says, the word *vāstrya* "herdsman" is to be understood "as a religious expression in general for the adherent of Zoroaster's *pastoral religion*—that is, for one who, independently of his social position as warrior or priest, has resolved to dedicate himself to the service of the *cow as Ahura Mazda*" (italics mine).

While welcoming these statements I seriously doubt the validity of the concept that Zoroaster's was a "Hirtenreligion" or that the cow or ox represented the Wise Lord; I also regret that even these notions do not come to expression in either the translations or the paraphrases which the learned author presents.

1961. Walther Hinz. When, during my residence at the University of Göttingen in 1956-57, I presented my views to this scholar, I found him even then in at least partial agreement. He has now offered his own interpretation (*Zarathustra,* pp. 69 f.): that for Zoroaster's concept of "the cow" one or more of three distinct "layers" of meaning may be involved: (1) the mundane or earthy animal; (2) all living species ("creatures") of the animal world; and (3) the flock of "believing or wishing-to-believe humanity, to whom Zoroaster was sent as shepherd."

It is gratifying to see that Zoroaster's concepts need no longer be restricted to the literal interpretation of the words he uses.

12. See, e.g., H. Lommel, "War Zarathustra ein Bauer?", *Zeitschrift für vergleichende Sprachforschung,* 58 (1931), 248 ff., esp. 254-57, and cf. Christensen's comment cited in the previous note.

13. Zaehner, *Dawn* (1961), p. 40.

14. Duchesne-Guillemin, *Zoroastre* (1948), p. 153. ("Telle est en effet, dans sa partie positive, pratique, la doctrine de Zarathustra: *il faut faire vivre le bœuf, source de vie*") (italics his).

15. This is true whether we visualize Zoroaster as having lived in any part of the plateau—in the northeast, north, or northwest—unless, of course, we postulate beyond all reason and knowledge a climatic shift of such dimensions as would change once-fertile grasslands into the comparatively barren areas familiar to us in the twentieth century and to Arabs in the eighth, and even in that event cattle culture will have played a comparatively small part in the economic life. For those unacquainted with the northeastern portion of the Iranian plateau today, perusal of the Human Relations Area Files on Afghanistan, Khorasan, Tadzhikistan (embracing the former regions of Bokhara and Turkestan), Turkmenistan, etc. can be most revealing; there will be found such eye-witness statements as "goats and sheep are exclusively the main herds"; "livestock raising is based on the yak, sheep, and goats"; "villages of tents and huts, with a few cows and horses running with the black goats common to these districts"; and the enlightening statement that "almost every household keeps poultry, and perhaps a cow".—For data regarding the possibility of a drastic climatic shift (or lack of it!) in our area since early historic times see the excellent discussion by Hans Bobek, "Klima und Landschaft Irans in vor- und frühgeschichtlicher Zeit" in *Geographischer Jahresbericht aus Österreich,* XXV (1953/54), 1ff., especially pp. 28ff. See also K. W. Butzer in *Erdkunde,* XI (1957), pp. 21 ff. and especially p. 30; C. E. P. Brooks, *Climate Through the Ages,* rev. ed., (1949), pp. 318 ff.; R. C. F. Schomberg, *Geographical Journal* (London), LXXII (1928), 357; and the chapter on "Climate and Prehistoric Man in the Eastern Mediterranean" by Herbert E. Wright, Jr., in Robert J. Braidwood and Bruce Howe, *Prehistoric Investigations in Iraqi Kurdistan* (Oriental Institute, *Studies in Ancient Oriental Civilization,* No. 31) (Chicago, 1960), pp. 71 ff., especially pp. 96 f.

16. For the view that the Indo-Europeans in general and Indo-Iranians in particular held the cow to be a sacred animal see, e.g., the quotation from Geiger cited above under n. 11; Gordon Childe, *The Aryans* (1926), pp. 82 ff.; A. B. Keith in *Cambridge History of India,* I (1922), 99 ff.; V. M. Apte, *The Vedic Age* (*The History and Culture of the Indian People,* eds. R. C. Majumdar and A. D. Pusalker) (1951), pp. 393 ff., 457ff., 520ff. It is, however, a well-recognized fact that the Rigvedic Indians were

a nation of beef-eaters; see Keith, *loc. cit.;* George Dunbar, *History of India* (1936), pp. 9ff.; V. A. Smith, *The Oxford History of India,* 3rd rev. ed. (1958), p. 52; also P. V. Kane, *History of Dharmaśāstra* (= Government Oriental Series, Class B, No. 6), II, Part II (1941), pp. 772 ff. Furthermore, several scholars have suggested that it was not before the time of the Upanishads (after 800 B. C.) that the cow was viewed as a sacred (i.e. more than a highly prized) animal in India. It is therefore not surprising that many of these scholars suggest that its sanctity originated, not with the Indo-European Aryans but with the indigenous inhabitants among whom they penetrated; cf. S. K. Chatterji, *The Vedic Age* (see above), pp. 161 ff.; W. H. Moreland and A. C. Chatterjee, *A Short History of India,* 3rd ed. (1953), pp. 30 f.; and especially Heinrich Zimmer, *Philosophies of India,* ed. Joseph Campbell (1956), pp. 184 f., 59 ff., 217 ff., 306, and *passim.*

17. See Ys. 32:14, following Zaehner, *Dawn,* p. 84 (note, however, the interpretation of Humbach, *Die Gathas, ad loc.*) and Ys. 48:10.

18. See Zaehner, *Dawn,* pp. 38 f. and 84 ff.

19. Ys. 46:2.

20. Psalm 100:3

21. Isaiah 40:11.

22. Luke 12:32.

23. I Peter 5:2-3.

24. See the references cited in C. J. Gadd, *Ideas of Divine Rule in the Ancient East* (1948), pp. 38 f.

25. W. Spiegelberg, *Zeitschrift für Aegyptische Sprache,* 64 (1929), 89 f. and Fritz Hintze, *ibid.,* Vol. 78 (1943), 55f.

26. Ys. 51:7 and 45:9. The latter citation, however, is probably also metaphorical; as Benveniste observed in *BSOS,* 8 (1935-37), 405 ff., and in *Les infinitifs avestiques* (1935), p. 46 (see also Herzfeld, *ZW,* p. 527), the Avestan words *pasūš vīrng* constitute a *dvandva* almost identical to Ovid's *pecudēs virōsque;* see below on n. 34.

27. Genesis 1:24.

28. Cf. Meillet, *Trois conf.* (1925), pp. 17 f.; Bartholomae, *Zarathustra's Leben und Lehre* (1924), pp. 4 ff.; Zaehner, *Dawn,* pp. 77 ff.

29. John 14:9.

30. Ys. 33:4.

31. Ys. 50:1.

32. Ys. 44:6, with translation following Zaehner, *Dawn,* p. 55. In passing, it may be noted that nearly all translators of the post-Zoroastrian Ahuna-vairya prayer (Ys. 27:13) once had Zoroaster named as "herdsman to the poor"; cf., e.g. Fritz Wolff, *Avesta* (1910), p. 66; Benveniste, *Indo-Iranian Journal,* I

(1957), 77 ff. Recent translations, however, confer the title of "herdsman" upon Ahura Mazda himself; see Gershevitch, *The Avestan Hymn to Mithra* (1959), 328 f.; Humbach, *Die Gathas,* II, 98 f.; Duchesne-Guillemin, *Indo-Iranian Journal,* II (1958), 66 ff. Contrast, however, W. Hinz, *Indo-Iranian Journal,* IV (1960), 154 ff.

33. Ys. 46:4, with translation following Duchesne-Guillemin.

34. Ys. 31:15; cf. also Ys. 51:14. The presence of the connective "and" in Ys. 31:15 here cited might at first glance appear to eliminate the possibility of an equivalence of meaning between "cattle" and "men", and the same conclusion might be drawn about the passage in Ys. 46:2 which, as we have seen, reads "Mine are few cattle and I possess few men." Hindu grammarians, however, gave the name *dvandva* "pair" to a usage in which two or more words (most commonly nouns) which have a coordinated construction are sometimes combined into compounds; cf. W. D. Whitney, *Sanskrit Grammar* (1941), § 1252 ff., and cf. above under n. 26. The usage is not, indeed, limited to Indo-European; the particle *wa-* is thus sometimes similarly employed in Arabic and its equivalent in other Semitic languages; see, e.g., W. Wright, *A Grammar of the Arabic Language,* 3rd ed. (1951), II, § 183; Gesenius-Kautzsch, *Hebräische Grammatik,* 26th ed. (1896), § 141*e.* In this context, one is reminded of Bartholomae's comment about the *dvandva* in *AiW,* p. 575*a*, n. 3, rephrased by H. Reichelt in *Awestisches Elementarbuch* (1909), p. 222: "Das *cā* verknüpft in diesen Fällen nicht die beiden Duale untereinander, sondern beide zusammen als ein Glied mit einem oder mehreren Andern."

35. Ys. 34:14; cf. Humbach, *Die Gathas,* I, 47.

36. Ys. 46:19; cf. Nyberg, *Religionen,* p. 197 and above, n. 8.

37. Ys. 46:2; on the connective *cā* here also, see above nn. 26 and 34.

38. Cf. Smith, *Studies,* p. 122 n. *ad loc.;* Duchesne-Guillemin, *Hymns,* p. 74; Nyberg, *Religionen,* p. 195.

39. Ys. 50:2.

40. Ys. 31:9-12; the translation follows closely that of Zaehner, *Dawn,* p. 41. On the word "farmer" see Bailey, *BSOS,* 7 (1933-35), 275 f.; Bartholomae, *AiW,* p. 1029, proposed "conducive to"; Herzfeld, *ZW,* pp. 169 ff. suggested "herald" (cf. also Nyberg, *Religionen,* p. 210 n. 2); Zaehner, *Dawn,* p. 41, translates "who cultivates(?)"; and Humbach (*Die Gathas,* II, 27, to whom the word was "ganz unklar") translates "Genosse".

41. Ys. 51:6.

42. Ys. 28:1. The translation follows Gershevitch, *JNES,* XXIII (1964), 14 n.; for a different translation cf. Humbach, *Die Gathas,* I, 76 and II, 8 and 98.

43. So Humbach (*Die Gathas,* I, 76; cf. also II, 8) translates Ys. 28:2c; contrast, however, Lentz, *AAWL,* No. 16 (1954), pp. 931ff. and Gershevitch, *The Avestan Hymn to Mithra,* p. 296*a.*

44. On Yasna 29 (in addition to the translations of Humbach, Duchesne-Guillemin, and Moulton) see also Walther Hinz, *Zarathustra* (1961), pp. 59 ff. and 168 f.; A. Meillet, *Trois conf.* (1925), pp. 44 ff. (but cf. Tavadia, *ZDMG,* 100 [n. f. 25; 1950], 205ff.); H. Lommel, *ZII,* 10 (1935), pp. 96ff.; Benveniste, *Journal asiatique,* 1938, pp. 538 f.; Nyberg, *Religionen* (1938), pp. 101 ff. and 196 ff.; Dumézil, *Naissances d'archanges* (1945), pp. 119 ff.

The translation here tentatively offered owes much to each of these and, while making no pretense to originality, is offered simply in an attempt to show that my interpretation of the figurative terms applies also to this particular Gatha.

The characters in the drama have been much in dispute. Most scholars have taken the "Ox-soul" literally, though frequently pointing out that "cattle" in general (including both male and female animals) must be intended; see, e.g., Humbach, *Die Gathas,* II, 12. However, Dhalla equated it with Ahura Mazda (*Zoroastrian Theology,* 1914, pp. 44 and 110 f.), Nyberg with both "a heavenly being" which comprised "the ox and the pregnant cow" and also the cattle on the earth below (*Religionen,* pp. 196 f.), and Moulton declared it to be a "quasi-angelic figure which, with the Ox-creator, represents the world of animal life entrusted to the diligent husbandman" (*EZ,* p. 303 and p. 346, n. 6). M. W. Smith, after citing Bharucha's interpretation of "Ox-Soul" as "the whole living world personified as a cow" (see above, n. 11; this, of course, is the approved Parsi tradition), suggests a restriction so that the cow or herd be understood in this Gatha to be "the representative of the pastoral community only"—a pregnant thought; elsewhere, Smith understood Avestan *gav-* to refer "specifically to the cow" (*Studies,* pp. 58 and Notes to Yss. 31:9; 34:14; and 48:6).

The "Ox-creator" (*guš tašan*) has been identified generally with Ahura Mazda (as in Dhalla, *loc. cit.;* Smith, *Studies,* § 70), but also with "a genius representing Mithra" (Moulton, *Early Religious Poetry,* 1911, p. 91 and *EZ,* p. 347 n. 1) and with "a special creator of a type well known elsewhere in primitive religions" (Nyberg, *Religionen,* p. 101). Humbach, *Die Gathas,* II, 14, suggests that it appears as one of the "ahurischen Qualitäten des Ahura Mazda".

45. Cf. P. Thieme *apud* Fr. Altheim in *Paideuma,* 3, Heft 6/7 (1949), 276, and I. Gershevitch in *JRAS,* 1952, pp. 174 f., but see also Humbach, *Die Gathas,* II, 98.

46. Some of the words of Ys. 29:7 are obscure and have given rise to such irrational explanations as ox urine

being used in the fertilizing of pastures; see, e.g. Nyberg, *Religionen,* pp. 197 ff. and contrast Herzfeld, *ZW,* pp. 357 f.; Gershevitch, *JRAS,* 1952, p. 178, and especially Zaehner, *Dawn,* p. 34.

47. Ys. 44:18.

48. Yasnas 48:11, 33:10, 43:1-2.

49. Ys. 33:3.

50. Cf. Zaehner, *Dawn,* pp. 36 ff.

51. The prophet's opposition to a ritual sacrifice of cattle (accompanied by drunkenness) may have been the very reason for his choice of the word "ox" (and "cow") to represent "flock, followers, adherents", etc. His word was *gav-* "the ox" rather than some word for those sheep or goats which, I maintain, will have constituted the main herds for his northeastern Iranian "shepherds" or "herdsmen". To "small cattle" he makes no reference whatsoever, perhaps because they were not sacrificed in the observance of the religion he was attempting to displace. Contrast the involved way by which Zaehner (*Dawn,* pp. 84ff.) endeavors to explain the prophet's condemnation of animal sacrifice and the cult of Haoma with the adoption of both by his earliest disciples.

52. Ys. 32:10-12*b;* cf. especially Zaehner, *Dawn,* p. 84.

53. Ys. 32:13 f.

54. Ys. 32:12*c*-13; cf. Ys. 46:4.

55. Ys. 44:20.

56. Ys. 51:14.

57. Ys. 46:11.

Mary Boyce (essay date 1975)

SOURCE: "Iconoclasm among the Zoroastrians" in *Christianity, Judaism, and Other Greco-Roman Cults,* Part Four, edited by Jacob Neusner, E. J. Brill, 1975, pp. 93-111.

[*In the essay below, Boyce examines the way in which the veneration of fire, which served an important role in Zoroaster's teachings, was transformed by his followers to a ritual temple cult.*]

The iconoclastic movement in Christianity has been carefully studied, as has Islamic iconomachy, but the origins of both still present problems; and in investigating these consideration should certainly be given to the fact that Zoroastrianism, ancient and until the 9th century A.D. immensely influential, had an iconoclastic movement which preceded both, and which may well have played a part in inspiring them. Zoroastrian iconoclasm has been ignored for various reasons. The history of the faith is poorly documented for all periods before the 17th century A.D., and has to be pieced together (as far as this is at all possible) from sparse and diverse sources. It is easy,

therefore, to overlook whole strands in its composition. Moreover, the assumption that the cult of temple fires was original to it, and remained its sole form of public worship, has obscured this particular issue. That such an assumption has been generally made is in itself a tribute to the success of the Zoroastrian iconoclasts, who triumphed so completely that in the end fire was the sole icon in the temples of their faith, and they and their coreligionists became known to the world at large simply as 'fire-worshippers'.

The fact is that, though veneration of fire is very ancient among the Iranians, and was of supreme importance in Zoroaster's teachings, the cult of *temple* fires appears to have been unknown in early Zoroastrianism.[1] Indo-Iranian religion had taken shape during millennia of nomadic wanderings on the Central Asian steppes, and its cult was therefore materially very simple, without temples, altars or statues. The Iranians, like the Vedic Indians, held tenaciously to this tradition. The essence of Zoroastrian devotional life was worship of Ahura Mazdā, the Creator, in the presence of his own creations, namely the sky, water, earth, plants, animals, man and fire. The last, held to be the all-pervading element which gave life and warmth to the rest, was represented visibly both by the sun on high and by fire on the domestic hearth, which from time immemorial was tended with reverent care and never allowed to go out. In Zoroaster's teachings fire was linked with Aša, the *yazata* of righteousness and good order; and his followers were enjoined to pray either at their hearths or in the open, turned towards the sun, so that they had fire always before them to help fix their thoughts on righteousness.

This tradition of worship under the sky or in the home was continued evidently during the early Achaemenian period. The great sanctuary at Zela in Asia Minor, founded, it is said, in thanksgiving in the 6th century B.C., consisted of an artificial mound raised on the plain so that men could go up to offer their veneration there;[2] and at Pasargadae two massive plinths still stand in the open, one with steps leading up it; and it has been suggested that these were built so that the king, mounting upon the one, could fix his eyes on fire set on the other and thus pray in fitting manner before a great assembly.[3] Still in the mid-5th century B.C. Herodotus records that 'as to the usages of the Persians . . . it is not their custom to make and set up statues and temples and altars'.[4] Instead they climbed high into the mountains to offer sacrifice there. The Western Iranians were exposed, however, to strong influences from their alien subjects and neighbours—Elamites, Babylonians, Assyrians, Mannai and others—all of whom used statues and altars in their worship. Near Hamadan, in Medean territory, a curious tower-like structure has been excavated, thought to belong to the 8th century B.C., and in it was found an altar, about waist-high, with broad, stepped top and shallow bowl, in which fire was evidently sometimes kindled, for traces of burning remain.[5] Moreover, in the carvvings set above the tombs of Darius the Great and his descendants each king is represented as standing on a three-stepped dais, facing fire burning on a three-stepped 'altar'.[6] In the light both of Herodotus' report, and the absence of temple ruins at Pasargadae and Persepolis,[7] it is possible that these 'altars' bore occasional fires only (like, perhaps, the second plinth at Pasargadae), placed upon them for the public performance of royal acts of devotion. (Such 'altars', called simply 'fire-holders',[8] are still to be found in the outer rooms of all old fire temples in the Yazdī area.) Later usage suggests that such fires were either kindled when needed, or created from embers brought from the nearest hearth fire. Another possibility is that each fire upon a funerary monument was the king's personal fire, that is, his hearth fire, elevated thus to burn in a manner fitting to royal dignity, and dying when he died.

The oldest temple ruin as yet to be found in Zoroastrian Persia is one excavated at the Achaemenian capital of Susa.[9] This has been attributed, on the evidence of architectural detail, to the reign of Artaxerxes II Memnon (404-359)—the very monarch who is reported to have imposed an image-cult generally upon his subjects.[10] He was much attached, we are told, to Anaïtis, an alien fertility goddess whose cult had already been adopted by Western Iranians at the time when Herodotus wrote. She had become assimilated, it seems, to the Iranian river-goddess *Harahvatī Arədvī Sūrā,[11] who came to be known thereafter as Arədvī Sūrā Anāhita; and at some point in his long reign Artaxerxes is said to have given orders that statues to her should be erected in many of the chief places of his empire, including Medean Ecbatana (Hamadan), at or near Persepolis itself,[12] and in Bactria in the remote north-east, a noted Zoroastrian stronghold. The cult thus dictatorially established was fostered evidently with the utmost lavishness. Verses in the hymn to Ardvī Sūrā Anāhita are held to describe one such statue, and they present the goddess as wearing golden shoes and earrings, a precious necklace and jewel-encrusted mantle, with a radiate crown upon her head.[13] Splendid temples were evidently built to house these costly images, and later that at Ecbatana (tiled, it is said, with silver and with gold-plated columns) was ruthlessly plundered for its wealth by Macedonian soldiery.[14]

The king's power was absolute in Achaemenian Persia; and it is natural that there should have been men, both priest and lay, who were ready to bow to Artaxerxes' will and do their utmost to please him. The verses incorporated in Arədvī's hymn illustrate this conformity; and possibly the Persian word for image, *uzdaēsa (Middle Persian uzdēs) was coined at this time to justify the new cult. It seems to mean, like Greek εἰκον, a 'showing forth, representation';[15] and perhaps in evolving it Zoroastrian iconophils sought to characterize their new images as a semblance of the divine only, in whose presence men should pray in order to direct their thoughts to what lay beyond, rather than idols, to be worshipped for themselves. Yet however scholar-priests of the royal party may have argued the matter, the introduction of an image cult must have shocked the orthodox profoundly; for by it a man-

made statue was substituted for the living icon of fire, the creation of Ahura Mazdā, which had been enjoined as *qibla* by the prophet himself.[16] There was, moreover, a serious doctrinal consideration involved. Zoroastrian theologians taught that originally Ahura Mazdā had made his creation in spirit-form only, *mēnōgīhā* as it was expressed in Middle Persian.[17] His Adversary, Anra Mainyu, countered with an evil creation, also intangible; and thereafter Ahura Mazdā by a mighty exertion of power enabled his *mēnōg* creation to 'put on appearances', that is, to take physical (*gētīg*) forms.[18] This second stage was beyond Anra Mainyu's capacity, and so the powers of evil have no material bodies of their own, but steal shapes to inhabit in the furtherance of wickedness. To the orthodox, therefore, an image maker was guilty both of impiety, in seeking to perform the act of creation himself (the prerogative of God the Creator), and also of rash folly, since he had fashioned an empty form which a *daēva* or evil being could enter to misappropriate the worship intended for the divinity, and grow stronger thereby. Hence in surviving Zoroastrian works temples with statues in them are referred to as the 'abode of *dēvs*' (*nišēmag ī dēwān*),[19] and the term 'image worship' (*uzdēs-parastagīh*) has for a synonym 'demon worship' (*dēwīzagīh*).[20]

In these circumstances one can safely assume that an impulse towards iconoclasm sprang into being among Zoroastrians with the setting up of the first statues to Arədvī Sūrā Anāhita in the 4th century B.C.; and there may well have been unsung martyrs then in this cause. Royal patronage brought it about, however, that the image cult was firmly implanted; and the energies of the orthodox seem to have been turned therefore into another channel, that of instituting the veneration of fire, the true Zoroastrian icon, as a rival temple cult. The origin of the movement cannot be closely dated; but since temple fires were still unknown, it seems, in the mid-5th century, but were widely attested after the downfall of the Achaemenians—all across their former dominions from Parthia to Asia Minor (then no longer an Iranian possession), it is a reasonable assumption that the cult was instituted in late Achaemenian times, probably very soon after that of images.[21] It appears, therefore, that whereas at the beginning of the Achaemenian period the Zoroastrians had no sacred buildings for public worship, by the end of it they had temples of two kinds, the one sheltering images, the other sacred fires.

This state of affairs evidently continued all through the Parthian period. Strabo records that in his day the Persians in Cappadocia maintained both 'holy places of the Persian gods', and also fire-sanctuaries, *pyraithoi*.[22] In the latter, he says, stood altars bearing a great heap of ashes, on which the fire was kept ever alight; and in connection with one of the former he speaks of a wooden image, which on occasion was carried in procession. It appears, not surprisingly, that the Iranians had different names for these two kinds of shrines. The Parthians themselves seem to have called fire-temples *ātarōšan,* a word meaning perhaps 'place of burning fire',[23] and known from Armenian *atrušan* (for Armenia was steeped in the Zoroastrian culture of the

Arsacids). A shrine to a *yazata* or divinity was called a *bagin,* a term derived from older *bagina,* and meaning '(a place) belonging to the gods'.[24] This term occurs in Sogdian as *faγn* 'temple'; and as a Parthian loanword in Armenian it was used in the singular for an altar set before an image (as in the phrase 'to the altar of Anāhīt's image' *bagnin anahatakan patkerin*[25]), and in the plural for a temple.[26] *Bagnapet* (another Parthian loanword in Armenian) was the title of the chief priest of such a temple, and has its equivalents in other Middle Iranian languages (MPersian *bašnbed,* Sogdian *faγnpat*),[27] and is attested at Mathurā as *bakanapati.*[28] Wherever details occur, they show this group of words to have been associated with the cult of images, not fires. Thus in a Manichaean Middle Persian fragment there is a reference to *uzdēsān, bašn-bedān* 'images (and) masters of image-temples',[29] and a Sogdian text contains a description of golden images, jewel-adorned, within a *faγn.*[30] The words *bagin, bagnapet,* or their equivalents, are not attested in later Zoroastrian usage, and presumably they ceased to be current when the iconoclastic movement finally triumphed during the Sasanian epoch.

In Seleucid and early Parthian times, strong Hellenic influences in Iran must have encouraged an increased use of statues by the Zoroastrians. For these periods, as for the Achaemenian epoch, there is pitifully little internal evidence, and most data derive from lands on the borders of the Parthian Empire. In Zoroastrian Armenia, for instance, we learn that there were temples 'where is sculptured . . . Aramazd';[31] and in others stood Anāhīt's image.[32] There was a famous golden statue of this *yazat* at Erez, which was carried off by one of Mark Antony's soldiers in 36 B.C.;[33] and there are references to offerings made to her there.[34] Strabo writes of statues to Anāhīt in Cappadocia also, and possibly to Vohu Manah.[35] The temple in Ecbatana, built, it seems, to house one of the Anāhitā statues set up by Artaxerxes II, was pillaged by the Seleucid Antiochus III in 209 B.C.;[36] but thereafter it was restored once more, for Isidore of Charax records that sacrifices were continually offered there in his own day (sometime, that is, between 27 B.C. and A.D. 77).[37] In Armenia statues are further recorded to Mihr (Mithra),[38] Tīr[39] and Vahaghn (Vərəthraghna, *yazata* of Victory).[40] The Greeks equated the last-named with their own Herakles, whose cult-name, Kallinikos, 'Victorious' must have helped the identification.[41] The Iranian Vahaghn/Varahrān was patron-divinity of travellers; and beside the ancient highway which passes by Bisutun, near Hamadan, there is a little shrine to Herakles Kallinikos, with a carving in high relief of the god, and an inscription in both Greek and Aramaic, showing the meeting of the two cultures, Hellenic and Iranian.[42] The inscription tells that the shrine was made in the year 164 of the Seleucid era.

A number of other Herakles shrines and statues are known from Parthian Iran,[43] and the god is generally shown naked in the Greek style. The Iranians, with their long tradition of worship without images, had not even by this time, it is evident, created an iconography of their own. The first

Anaïtis/Anāhitā statues of the Achaemenian period were presumably Semitic in inspiration; and subsequently the Armenians declared that all their icons were made by Greeks, 'for no one in Armenia knew how to make statues'.[44] A fine bronze head of a goddess has been found near Erzinjan, which is thought to be from a statue, larger than life-size, of Anāhīt,[45] and this is certainly indistinguishable from a Greek Aphrodite. The work subsequently of zealous Christians in Armenia, and ardent iconoclasts in Iran itself has insured that very little of such statuary survives. The evidence of the Parthian coins, and those of the Kushans in the east, as well as of the sculptures of Nimrud Dagh in Armenia, combines to show, however, that in the post-Hellenic period the Iranians grew accustomed to having the *yazatas* of their faith identified with gods of the Greek pantheon, and represented plastically in the same way; and the archaeological and literary evidence attests that there were shrines where these representations took the form of cult-images, within the framework of Zoroastrian worship.

The use of images seems to have become widespread during the Parthian period in the home also. Thus Josephus tells how the widow of a Parthian nobleman, having been made captive, 'took along the ancestral images of the gods belonging to her husband and herself—for it is the custom among all the people in that country to have objects of worship in their houses and to take them along when going abroad . . . '.[46] At first, he says, she performed the due rites before these secretly, so they were evidently small objects, which could be honoured unobtrusively. How reliable Josephus is in his statement that possession of such household images was general there is no means of testing; but there is archaeological and literary evidence to show that, under Hellenistic influence, images came to be used in the universally popular cult of the dead. Excavations in Old Nisa,[47] the ancestral capital of the Arsacids, have uncovered two halls in which were many statues of men and women in Parthian dress, some larger than life-size, others small. These were made of clay, painted, and realistically modelled; and it is suggested that the halls in which they stood were shrines where rituals for the souls of the dead were performed, the statues being fashioned in honour of individuals to receive the offerings. Greek influence is apparent in the craftsmanship, and was presumably responsible for inspiring the practice. The use of images in the cult of the dead is recorded also in Zoroastrian Armenia;[48] and it appears to be attested in the remains of a shrine at Shami, a village of Khuzistan in south-western Iran.[49] Here there came to light in the 1930's a damaged but still splendid statue in bronze, life-sized, of a nobleman wearing Parthian dress.[50] Excavation of the mound where it had lain uncovered a brick platform which had apparently been partly roofed over to protect cult images—for the remains of other statues were found there, in bronze and marble, some big, some small, as at Nisa.[51] There was also a square imagebase, and before it a small, elegant altar of Hellenic type.[52] All the statues had been broken into pieces, and the shrine itself burnt over them. Whether this was the work of iconoclasts, or simply the result of local feuding, there is no means of knowing; but the fact that the custom of making images of the dead was wholly unknown in later times shows that this too must have roused the wrath of those opposed to icons, and so in course of time have been suppressed. The practice was possibly considered a little less wicked than that of making images for the divine beings, since such statues were no more than reproductions of the physical forms which men had once possessed. Nevertheless the departed soul belongs wholly to the *mēnōg* state, and to fashion anew a physical form for it, before the Last Judgment and the resurrection of the body, may well have been held by the orthodox to be both impious and rash (again as creating an empty abode for *dēvs*). There was also the potentially corrupting power of all icons to attract worship to themselves, as is indicated by the epithet by which Agathangelos stigmatised the Zoroastrians of Armenia, *urvapast* 'soul-worshippers'.[53] St. Gregory alludes moreover to their habit of prostrating themselves before the images of the dead.[54]

If the cult of images increased during the Parthian period, so too, evidently, did the rival one of sacred fires; so much so that when Ardašīr Pāpakān overthrew the Arsacids and established the Sasanian Empire, in about A.D. 224, one of his first acts was to suppress the many fires which had been founded by local rulers,[55] since these evidently provided a cultic focus for dynastic claims. Subsequent developments show, however, that this was a purely political measure, for Ardašīr and his successors distinguished themselves both by founding many new sacred fires, and by giving full support to the iconoclastic movement, which now became triumphant. It seems likely that this movement had already begun to gather strength in the latter part of the Arsacid period, though the indications are necessarily slight. Valakhš (Vologeses) I (c. A.D. 51-80) replaced representations of *yazads* on the reverse of his coins with a burning fire; and if he was also the Valakhš who commanded his subjects to gather up and preserve the Zoroastrian holy works, he may well have been moved to do this through well-instructed orthodoxy.[56] The Parthian Empire was, however, a loosely-knit confederacy rather than a firmly controlled state, and whatever position the later Arsacids themselves took up in this controversial matter, there is no evidence that they sought to impose a uniformity of observance on their Zoroastrian subjects throughout the land.

This, however, is what their successors, the Sasanians, did. It is probable that the Persian priests, favoured naturally by the new Persian dynasty, were burning to show that they were superior in zeal and orthodoxy to the Parthian priesthood which had so long had the chief voice in the community. They attacked heresy, set up an inquisition to deal with nonconformists and apostates, and (it seems) took stern measures to root out the cult of images, replacing this wherever possible with that of fires. Greek influence had been as strong, however, in Persia as in Parthia, and the rockcarvings of the Sasanians show that these monarchs made no objection to representation as such of the *yazads* of their faith.[57] Thus in the investiture-scenes of

Ardašīr I Ohrmazd is portrayed as a noble bearded figure in Persian dress, with turreted crown and *barsom*-rods in his left hand;[58] and Varahrān appears, as in Parthian days, as a naked Herakles with club.[59] In the rock-carvings of later kings are shown Mihr with radiate crown,[60] and Anāhīd holding a tilted jug from which the waters flow.[61] Such representations were set even on the walls of fire temples, in painting, or stucco in high relief;[62] for portrayals of this kind evidently did not offend Zoroastrian iconoclasts as did free-standing images. Presumably, not being fully-fashioned forms or objects of cult, they were not regarded as potential homes for *dēvs*, nor yet as presumptuous imitations of the works of God.[63]

The indications are, however, that, with regard to free-standing images, the Sasanians were active iconoclasts before ever they rose to imperial power. The family had the hereditary care of a great temple to Anāhīd at Istakhr (a town lying between Achaemenian Pasargadae and Persepolis, which was to become their dynastic capital). This temple was probably an ancient foundation, and evidently it housed originally a statue to the *yazad*, for the Muslim historian Mas'ūdī learnt in the 9th century A.D. that it had once been an 'idol temple', but that the idols had been removed and fire installed in their place.[64] Tabari (who drew on Sasanian sources) calls the Istakhr temple 'the temple of the fire of Anāhīd';[65] and the destruction of the statue there probably took place before Ardašīr seized power, or at the latest during the first decades of his dynasty's rule, for his grand-daughter, the Queen of queens of his son Šābuhr I, bore the name Ādur-Anāhīd 'Anāhīd of the Fire',[66] being named evidently for the patron *yazad* of the family. It is quite possible that the Istakhr image was the first of Anāhīd's statues to be overthrown; and thereafter, it seems, the divinity as she was venerated at this shrine was known by the distinctive appellation 'Anāhīd of the Fire'. (Other shrines to her were naturally made by springs and streams, and the name Āb-Nāhīd, '(A)nāhīd of the Water' is still commonly given to girls by Zoroastrians of the Yazdi area, in the north of Pars.[67]) It is unlikely that it will ever be possible to date at all closely the establishment of the Istakhr fire; but the probability seems that in general the active phase of Zoroastrian iconoclasm had its beginnings in the first century A.D., at a time when Hellenic influences were waning and there appears to have been a stirring of orthodox zeal in Parthian overlord and Persian vassal alike.

That Ardašīr's forbears were already convinced iconoclasts is suggested also by the fact that this king is known to have begun the destruction of images during his campaigns of conquest—although again we are dependent for evidence on the border-land of Armenia. Here he is said, on mastering the country, to have shattered statues of the dead, and to have set a sacred fire in the temple of Ohrmazd at Pakaran[68] (presumably in place of the image there). Even at this relatively late period only scraps of evidence survive for tracing developments within Iran itself; and in the main we hear more about the positive encouragement given by the kings and their chief priests to the founding of sacred fires than we do of the overthrow of images. Throughout the Sasanian period, it seems, the propaganda was broadcast that 'the Varahrān fire represents goodness, and images are its adversary' (*ātakhš ī warahrān wehīh, ud uzdēs pityārag*);[69] and whereas, as we have seen, the image shrine was characterized as 'the abode of *dēvs*', the 'house of fire' was called 'the abode of *yazads*', and it was said that the divine beings gathered there thrice daily (at the times when the devout should say their prayers in the presence of sun or fire), leaving gifts of 'virtue and righteousness'.[70] One of the most active founders of sacred fires during the early years of the dynasty was the priest Kirdēr, who held office during five reigns, and rose to great power and wealth. In his inscriptions he lays proud claim to founding many Varahrān fires, a work, he says, of benefit to Ohrmazd and the *yazads,* whereby water, fire and cattle were also deeply satisfied;[71] and he further states that he had brought it about that 'images were destroyed and the haunts of demons laid waste, and the place and abode of the *yazads* [i.e. fire sanctuaries] were established' (*uzdēs gugānīh ud gilistag ī dēwān wišōbīh ud yazdān gāh ud nišēm āgīriy*).[72]

Despite the strength of the Sasanian monarchy, and the zeal from the outset of the Persian priests, many generations evidently lived and died before the long-established use of images was wholly suppressed. Thus of the two relevant cases recorded in the Sasanian law-book (the *Mādigān ī Hazār Dādestān*) one took place as late as the 6th century A.D., during the reign of Khosrau Anōširvān (531-579).[73] The two men concerned in it, named Kaka and Ādurtōhm, owned a piece of land in common on which they had 'a house as an image-shrine' (*khānag pad uzdēsčār*). The priests ordered the image to be removed from it, and set in its place an Ādurōg. This was a sacred fire of a minor grade, which could be tended by a layman with the same rites and respect as a household fire.[74] After this fire had burnt for a while in the former *uzdēsčār* (evidently to drive out the *dēvs* and purify the place) the *Dīvān ī Kerdagān* or Ministry of (Religious) Works was prepared to take it back into its own keeping—for plainly the maintenance of even the humblest fire, with its need for fuel and regular tending, was more costly than that of a statue, and could not safely be imposed on the unwilling. However, the two men petitioned to be allowed to keep the fire, undertaking to endow it with the land on which the image-shrine had stood; and they built it a fitting sanctuary, in which it was installed with due ceremony. In the other recorded case (which has no indication of date) a judge had had an image removed from an image-shrine (*uzdēs kadag*), and later a man other than the original owner of the shrine installed an Ādurōg there.[75] These cases show that a law must have been passed under the Sasanians forbidding the veneration of images, although there is no suggestion that those involved were punished except by the removal of the statue. When it was not possible (for expense or other reasons) to replace it by a sacred fire there must have been a grave sense of loss for the worshippers, and a danger to faith; but the priestly iconoclasts stated firmly that 'when the worship of images

is ended, little departs with it of belief in the spiritual beings' ([*ka*] *uzdēs parastišnīh be absīhēd, mēnōg warrawišnīh andak abāg be šawēd*).[76] The resulting patterns of public worship can still be seen today in Yazd and its surrounding villages. There each place has its fire temple or temples, and also shrines to individual *yazads,* notably Mihr, Bahrām (Vərəthraghna), Tīr, Āštād and Srōš. These shrines are regularly visited by the devout, who go there to pray, to take solemn vows, or to make acts of contrition or thanksgiving to the divinity concerned; and on the feast day of the *yazad* a communal act of worship is performed. But these shrines are empty, except for a pillar on which fire is kindled on each separate occasion. Incense is burnt, candles are lit, and other offerings are made; but there is no icon now at whose feet to lay them, the *yazad* being once more present only as an invisible spirit, as in the early days of the faith—though the alien practice of building a shrine for him, a **bagin* or **bašn,* has thus persisted.[77]

Although there is the law-case to show that the image cult had not been entirely eradicated everywhere even by the 6th century, nevertheless iconoclasm must have won its main victories long before then. Ardašīr I is known to have imposed a number of new measures on the Zoroastrians who had come under his rule, and to have waded through blood to enforce them;[78] and the likelihood is that the law against images was one of these, for the iconoclastic campaign must have been begun early in the Sasanian period for the image cult to be so thoroughly obliterated that hardly any reference to it was made by Muslim historians (several of whom were themselves Persians of Zoroastrian stock). When one of them does mention that once there were images in Zoroastrian shrines, it is only to speak of this as something very remote and far-off.[79] A faint survival of the old icon cult seems to have persisted, however, in the Yazdī region, in connection with the worship of the much-loved Mihr; for in some Muslim villages there the face of the sun-god with radiate crown is still embroidered in traditional designs.[80] Since, however, the Arabs know the sun as female, the moon as male, this portrait is called that of Khorshīd Khānom, the 'Lady Sun'. Such pictures would not, it is clear, have offended the Zoroastrian iconoclasts; but they are wholly in breach of later Muslim edicts on the subject, and thus illustrate the stubbornness of the devotion to icons, once their use had become thoroughly established in Persia.

Although the Zoroastrian iconoclasts were victorious in the end, their battle had evidently been hard-fought and prolonged, lasting over 800 years and probably indeed longer, for it is likely that much controversy preceded the edict by which Artaxerxes II imposed an image cult on the whole community. The iconophils had the initial advantage of support from the all-powerful throne; and the cult had a strong stimulus subsequently from the inspiration provided by Greek craftsmen, who created works of noble beauty. Yet fire is itself one of the most beautiful of icons, and to pray in its presence was to follow the example of the prophet, as well as to maintain an age-old tradition of Iranian worship—considerations which gave orthodoxy the strength to triumph in the end. During the long struggle which it had to wage, however, its theological weapons must have become well sharpened and its doctrines ever more clearly defined. Throughout the period of controversy Zoroastrianism was temporally immensely powerful, as the state religion of three successive empires; and it had moreover the authority conferred by lofty ethical teachings and a clearly defined dogmatic system.[81] Its influence is already acknowledged in the transmission to other faiths of fundamental doctrines concerning the existence of God and the Evil One, the individual and last judgments, resurrection of the body, and life everlasting; and it would be strange if it had not contributed also to the debate on the propriety of making representations of the divine, which was a problem that exercised the minds of Greek philosophers and Jewish prophets, the early Buddhists, Christian priests and Muslim theologians. Controversy raged about this matter, in fact, over the whole area at whose centre lies Iran; and it is only the existence of so many blank pages in Zoroastrian history that has prevented the realisation that it was a burning issue for the Zoroastrians also.

The question of direct influence is naturally one which can only be approached with great caution; but it seems probable that it was exerted on at least two faiths, Christianity and Islam. In the case of the former, Armenia provided a channel for the transmission of Zoroastrian ideas. Under the Parthians, and governed by a cadet branch of the royal Arsacid family, this country had been predominantly Zoroastrian by profession, and the fact that the image cult was well established there means that the iconoclasts had abundant occasion to raise their voices, even if in vain. In A.D. 301, not long after the overthrow of the Arsacids, the Armenian king Tiridates III embraced Christianity (partly, it is thought, out of hostility to the Sasanian regime); and there ensued a general overthrowing of Zoroastrian images and a setting up of Christian ones instead. The Armenian Christian church never officially opposed the veneration of images;[82] but it is very likely that earlier controversy on this matter (stimulated by Ardašīr's ruthless iconoclasm) continued among the Christians of the land,[83] whose links were now westward with Byzantium, where Christian iconoclasm was subsequently to spring into being.[84] Meantime Islam had been born, whose followers in its early years showed no aversion to representational art.[85] It was only in the 9th century A.D., when through massive conversions, Iran had come to play a leading part in the Muslim community, that Islamic doctrines took shape in this respect; and their bases—usurpation of the prerogative of the Creator, the wickedness of making shapes to be inhabited by evil powers—are precisely those which appear to have been established centuries earlier by Zoroastrian divines. The Muslim theologians carried their own laws to a logical extreme in forbidding any representations whatsoever. For the Zoroastrian, however, moderation is a virtue, and the Persians evidently kept their own iconoclasm, though strictly enforced, within well-defined bounds.[86] This limitation was also no doubt due to the fact that they, like the Christian iconoclasts, had a long tradition of the use of images to contend against, and could

only win their war by fighting it intensively on a narrower front. Within the Iranian community it seems to have been the Persians who both instituted the image cult and finally brought it to an end; but during the intervening centuries it evidently affected the Zoroastrians far and wide.

Notes

1. This was argued forcefully by S. Wikander, *Feuerpriester in Kleinasien und Iran,* Lund 1946, 56 ff.; but he obscured a sound case by postulating that a temple cult of ever-burning fire had existed independently of Zoroastrianism and before that faith arose (a supposition unsupported by evidence); and that this cult was adopted into Zoroastrianism in the 4th century B.C. as a part of the worship of Ardvī Sūrā Anāhitā. Since this divinity is a *yazatā* of water, the unlikelihood of such a supposition was apparent. [Note: the Avestan term *yazata,* fem. *yazatā,* Middle Iranian *yazat/yazad,* 'being worthy of worship' is kept throughout this article rather than being rendered by some imperfect equivalent which would obscure the characteristic Zoroastrian doctrine that all beneficent divine beings were created by Ahura Mazdā (who in the beginning alone was), in order to help and serve him in his task of redeeming the world. Having been created, they are to be worshipped in their own right, although always as subordinate to him. The Zoroastrian *yazata* is thus both more than an angel, and different in his station from the independent god of a pagan pantheon.]

2. See Strabo, XI.8.4.512.

3. See D. Stronach, 'Urartian and Achaemenian tower temples', *JNES* 26, 1967, 287; for a detailed account of the plinths see Stronach, *Iran* III, 1965, 24-27 with Pl. VII.

4. I.131.

5. See M. Roaf and D. Stronach, 'Tepe Nūsh-i Jān, 1970: second interim report', *Iran* XI, 1973, 132-38 with Pl. VI-VIII. The shallowness of the bowl in the altar top makes it impossible that ever-burning fire should have been maintained there, for this requires a deep bowl of hot ashes to sustain it. The excavators, although acknowledging this fact, nevertheless call the altar a 'fire altar', and the building containing it a 'fire temple'.

6. These carvings are superbly reproduced by E. F. Schmidt, *Persepolis* III, Chicago 1970.

7. The so-called *Frātadāra temple by Persepolis, attributed by G. Widengren (*Die Religionen Irans,* Stuttgart 1965, 131, 358) to the Achaemenian period, is in fact later. See, with full bibliography, K. Schippmann, *Die iranischen Feuerheiligtümer,* Berlin 1971, 177-85.

8. Either *āδokhš* (the old Zoroastrian term), or *kalak,* a common Persian word for 'brazier'.

9. See M. Dieulafoy, *L'acropole de Suse,* Paris 1893, 411 ff.; K. Erdmann, *Das iranische Feuerheiligtum,*

Leipzig 1941, 15-16; Schippmann, *op. cit.,* 266-74.—The term 'Persia' is used throughout the present article in its restricted meaning of Pārs (the present Iranian province of Fārs).

10. Berossus, fragment apud Agathias II.24, Dindorf, *Historici graeci minores,* II.221; Clemens Alexandrinus, *Protrepticus,* V. 65.3. On the form of the goddess' name there see Wikander, *Feuerpriester,* 61 n. 2.

11. See H. Lommel, 'Anahita-Sarasvati' *Asiatica, Festschrift F. Weller,* Leipzig 1954, 405-413.

12. On the force of the phrase εν επρσαις (in the citations from Berossus) see G. Hoffmann, *Auszüge aus syrischen Akten persischer Märtyrer,* Leipzig 1880, repr. Liechtenstein 1966, 137; Wikander, *op. cit.,* 65. If a statue to the goddess were in fact erected at Persepolis itself, this would again pose a problem with the lack of identifiable temple ruins there; but perhaps it was the famous temple to Anāhitā at Istakhr nearby (a site still unexcavated) which was founded by Artaxerxes. On this temple see further below.

13. *Yašt* 5.126-8. It has been suggested that it was 'Anāhitā' with her eight-rayed crown who was represented on the coins of Demetrius I of Bactria, see P. Gardner, *Catalogue of coins in the British Museum: Greek and Scythic kings of Bactria and India,* 1886, Pl. III. 1; W. W. Tarn, *The Greeks in Bactria and India,* 115, cf. 135.

14. Polybius X.27. On this incident see E. R. Bevan, *The House of Seleucus,* London 1902, repr. 1969, II 18.

15. From the root 'show', Skt. *diś-,* Av. *daēs-,* which occurs with the same preverb in Khotanese *uysdīśś-* 'expound, declare', see R. Emmerick, *Saka Grammatical Studies,* London 1968, 16. Since the existence of a Zoroastrian image-cult was not formerly recognized, it used to be held that Persian *uzdēs* meant 'heathen idol', and the word was accordingly understood to derive from the base *daēs-* 'form, shape', and was interpreted as 'out-form', i.e. 'monstrous thing'. See P. Horn, *Grundriss der neupersischen Etymologie,* Strassburg 1893, 295; W. B. Henning, *ZII,* IX, 1933, 225.15; H. S. Nyberg, *Hilfsbuch des Pehlevi,* Uppsala 1931, II, 230.

16. Cf. his words in one of his own hymns, *Yasna* 43.9; 'Then indeed at the gift of veneration to thy fire truly shall I think of righteousness (*aša-*) to the utmost of my power'.

17. Zoroastrian theological utterances survive only in works compiled in the Sasanian period; but these clearly had a long tradition behind them, going back in essentials to the teachings of the prophet himself, see H. Lommel, *Die Religion Zarathustras nach dem Awesta dargestellt,* Tübingen 1930, passim; H. S. Nyberg, *Die Religionen des alten Iran,* deutsch von H. H. Schaeder, Leipzig 1938, Ch. 8.

18. *Dādestān ī dīnīg* (ed. T. D. Anklesaria) Purs. XXX. 5; text with transl. by H. W. Bailey, *Zoroastrian problems in the ninth-century books,* Oxford 1943, 112. On *mēnōg/gētīg* see most recently S. Shaked, 'The notions *mēnōg* and *gētīg* in the Pahlavi texts and their relation to eschatology', *Acta Orientalia* XXXIII, 1971, 59-107.

19. See *Zand ī Vohuman Yašt* (ed. and transl. by B. T. Anklesaria) VII. 37 (where the text has the late form *uzdēstčār* for 'image shrine'). On similar beliefs among neo-Platonists and Christians see E. Bevan, *Holy Images,* London 1940, 91-3. They are strongly held also by Muslims.

20. Contrast *Pahl. Vd.* I 9 with *Iranian Bundahišn* (ed. T. D. Anklesaria), 206.15.

21. The dating is that suggested by Wikander, *op. cit.,* although his interpretation of the development is different.

22. XV.3.14. That Strabo made this distinction has been stressed by O. Reuther, *A survey of Persian art* (ed. A. U. Pope), I, 1938, 559; A. Godard, *Athār-é Irān* III, 1938, 19.

23. See Wikander, *op. cit.,* 98, 219; E. Benveniste, *JA,* 1964, 57.

24. See W. B. Henning, *BSOS,* VIII, 1936, 583-5; *BSOAS,* XXVIII, 1965, 250 f.

25. See apud M.-L. Chaumont, *JA,* 1965, 174.

26. See H. Hübschmann, *Armenische Grammatik,* I 114.85.

27. See Henning, *BSOAS,* XII, 1948, 602 n. 3.

28. See H. W. Bailey, *BSOAS,* XIV, 1952, 420 f.

29. See F. C. Andreas-W. Henning, *Mitteliranische Manichaica aus Chinesisch-Turkestan* II (*SPAW,* Phil.-hist. Klass, VII, 1933), 311 (M 219 R 17-18).

30. See Henning, *BSOS,* VIII, 1936, 584-5 (M 5731 = T II D 117b V 11 ff.).

31. See S. der Nersessian, 'Une apologie des images du septième siècle', *Byzantion,* XVII, 1944-5, 63, and cf. Agathangelos, CIX.133 (V. Langlois, I 167).

32. Nersessian, *art. cit.,* 64.

33. Pliny, *Natural History,* XXIII.4.24.

34. See the passages brought together by M.-L. Chaumont, *JA,* 1965, 167-81.

35. XV.3.15.

36. Polybius X.27 (see above, n. 14).

37. *Parthian Stations,* 6.

38. Agathangelos, CX.134 (Langlois, I 168).

39. See most recently W. Eilers, *Semiramis* (Sb. Österreichische Ak. der Wissenschaften, 274 Bd., 2 Abh.), Vienna 1971, 43-4.

40. See G. Dumézil, *RHR,* CXVII, 1938, 152-69; J. de Menasce, *RHR,* CXXXIII, 1948, 1-18; E.

Benveniste, *The Persian religion according to the chief Greek texts,* Paris 1929, 64-6. The identity of the Iranian divinity of whom a wooden statue existed at a Cappadocian shrine, and to whom Strabo (XV. 3.14) refers as 'Omanos', remains doubtful. He is widely taken to be Vohu Manah, but this is by no means certain.

41. There are a number of traces of the worship of this popular Greek god in Iranian territory, and small terracotta figurines of him have been found in abundance in the ruins of Seleucia on the Tigris, see W. von Ingen, *Figurines from Seleucia on the Tigris,* Ann Arbor 1939, 106-8 with pl. XVIII.

42. For the Greek inscription see L. Robert, *Gnomon,* XXXV, 1963, 76. For knowledge of the (unfinished) Aramaic version I am indebted to the kindness of my colleague, Dr. A. D. H. Bivar. The Iranians still at this time used Aramaic for written records and documents, as under the Achaemenians.

43. For the statues see R. N. Frye, *The heritage of Persia,* London 1962, 156, with Pl. 68-71, and 87 (from Commagene). For the shrine at Masjed-i Suleiman in Khuzistan see R. Ghirshman, *Comptes rendus de l'Académie des Inscriptions et Belles-Lettres,* 1969, 493, Schippmann, *Feuerheiligtümer,* 249; and for that on Mt. Karafto in East Kurdistan Aurel Stein, *Old Routes of Western Iran,* London 1940, 324-46. Herakles is equated with Varahrān in the monument on Nimrud Dagh.

44. See Nersessian, *Byzantion* XVII, 75.

45. See M. H. Ananikian, *Armenian Mythology,* Boston 1925, Pl. III opp. p. 26.

46. *Antiquities,* XVIII.344.

47. See the reports by V. Masson, G. A. Pugachenkova and G. A. Koshelenko, detailed references apud G. Frumkin, *Archaeology in Soviet Central Asia* (*Handbuch der Orientalistik* VII. ed. J. E. van Lohuizen-de Leeuw), Leiden 1970, 144-6.

48. See, e.g., Moses Khorenaci, II.40 (Langlois II 101).

49. On this site, with references to earlier literature, see Schippmann, *Feuerheiligtümer,* 227 ff. As it is unique in character among known Iranian sanctuaries, there are naturally divergent opinions about the cult to which it was devoted.

50. See Aurel Stein, *Old routes of Western Iran,* 130-2.

51. See A. Godard. "Les statues parthes de Shami', *Athār-é Īrā* II, 1937, 285-305.

52. See Stein, *op. cit.,* 154.

53. See Ananikian, *Arm. Mythology,* 94.

54. See Nersessian, *Byzantion* XVII, 61.

55. See the *Tansar Nāme* (*Letter of Tansar*), ed. M. Minovi, Tehran 1932, 22, transl. M. Boyce, Rome 1968, 47.

56. The absurd but often repeated statement that there was no such thing as Zoroastrian orthodoxy before the Sasanians is a tribute to the propaganda of the Sasanian priesthood, who to increase their own authority attributed confusion and ignorance to their predecessors. See in more detail Boyce, *A history of Zoroastrianism* (*Handbuch der Orientalistik,* I, ed. B. Spuler), Leiden, Vol. II, Ch. 3 (in the press).

57. See W. Hinz, *Altiranische Funde und Forschungen,* Berlin 1969, for admirable photographs of these carvings.

58. See ibid., p. 123 ff. with plates 57, 60.

59. See ibid., p. 123 with Plates 57, 59.

60. See, e.g., E. Herzfeld, *Am Tor von Asien,* Berlin 1920, Pl. XXIX; A. U. Pope (ed.), *Survey of Persian art,* Pl. 160b.

61. See Herzfeld, op. cit., 92-3, with Pl. XLIV; Pope, *Survey,* Pl. 160 a. Anāhīd is also represented in the investiture scene of Narseh at Naqš-i Rustam, see Pope, *Survey,* Pl. 157b.

62. See the description of wall-carvings in the ruins of the great fire temple at Istakhr given by Mas'ūdī, *Les Prairies d'Or* § 1403 (ed. Ch. Pellat, Vol. II, Paris 1965). The walls of the 'palace' besides the fire temple on the Kūh-i Khwāja in Seistān were richly decorated with paintings, which included representations, in Hellenistic style, of divine beings; for descriptions and bibliography see Schippmann, *Feuerheiligtümer,* 57-70. Even more strikingly, fragments of human figures, life-size or a little larger, and in very high relief, belonging, it seems, to a stucco frieze, were found within what was probably the fire-sanctuary itself (room PD) at Takht-i Suleiman, see D. Huff, *Iran* IX, 1971, 181-182, and further Boyce, *A History of Zoroastrianism,* II. Ch. 4.

63. On the apparent anomaly of the setting up of royal cult-statues by the Sasanians themselves see Boyce, *op. cit.,* II, Ch. 3.

64. Loc. cit. He states that 'the queen Humāy, daughter of Bahman, son of Isfandiyār' was responsible for removing the images and transforming the shrine into a fire temple; but this transposing of the event into the legendary past is naturally not to be taken seriously, for the Zoroastrians (who have no historical tradition) tend to connect anything remote in time with the Kayanian dynasty who helped the prophet establish the faith.

65. This is rendered by Nöldeke (*Tabarī,* 17) a little freely as 'the fire temple of Anāhīd'.

66. See Šābuhr's Parthian inscription on the *Ka'ba-yi Zardušt,* l. 18. (His marriage with his daughter was a highly meritorious one according to the ancient Zoroastrian law of *xvaētvadatha.*)

67. See J. S. Sorushian, *Farhang-e Behdinān,* Tehran 1956, 201 (under *Āb-Nahīr*).

68. Moses Khorenaci, II.77 (Langlois II 119).

69. *Dīnkard,* ed. D. M. Madan, Bombay 1911, 551.13-15. The term *pityārag* is a theological one, meaning something evil brought into being by Ahriman in deliberate opposition to something good created by Ohrmazd.—A number of Pahlavi passages concerning *uzdēs* were collected by A. V. W. Jackson, 'Allusions in Pahlavi literature to the abomination of idol-worship', *Sir Jamsetjee Jejeebhoy Madressa Jubilee Vol.,* ed. J. J. Modi, Bombay 1914, 274-85.

70. *Sāyest nē-šāyest* (ed. F. M. Kotwal, Copenhagen 1969) XX.1.

71. *Ka'ba-yi Zardušt* ll. 9, 10 (facsimile ed. by W. B. Henning, *Corpus Inscriptionum Iranicarum,* Part III, Vol. II, Portfolio III (London 1963), Pl. LXXII-LXXV; transcription and translation by Ph. Gignoux, *JA,* 1968, 394-5.

72. KKZl. 10; facsimile, Pl. LXXII, LXXIII; translation, Gignoux, loc. cit. On the verbal construction (with imperfect passives) see W. B. Henning, *Handbuch der Orientalistik* I (ed. B. Spuler), IV.1, 102.

73. *Mādigān ī Hazār Dādestan,* Part II (ed. T. D. Anklesaria) Bombay 1912, 37.2-8; transl. J. de Menasce, *Feux et fondations pieuses dans le droit sassanide,* Paris 1966, 25; Boyce, *BSOAS,* XXXI, 1968, 63-4 (both then assuming that the case involved infidel idol-worshippers).

74. See Boyce, 'On the sacred fires of the Zoroastrians', *BSOAS* XXXI, 1968, 52-68; 'On the Zoroastrian temple cult of fire', *JAOS,* (in the press).

75. *MHD,* Part II, ed. J. J. Modi, Poona 1901, 94.3-6; transl. Menasce, *op. cit.,* 31; Boyce, *BSOAS,* XXXI, 64. The Middle Persian term *uzdēs kadag,* lit. 'image house', corresponds exactly to MP. *ātakhš kadag* (Pers. *āteš kade*) 'fire house', one of the standard names for a fire temple.

76. *Dīnkard,* ed. Madan, 553.16-17; cf. ibid., 551.17-19.

77. Partly, probably, to secure a measure of immunity for them from violation, the Zoroastrians have come to call these shrines by Muslim terms, i.e. Pīr-i Mihrīzed etc., or generally, *ma'bad.* Although the fire temples have all been rebuilt, some very pleasingly, since the second half of the 19th century, as have certain much-loved mountain shrines (places of general pilgrimage), the village sanctuaries mostly remain as they were during the years of oppression, humble mud-brick buildings given their aura of sanctity only through the devotions of centuries which have been paid there. Their inconspicuousness has meant that their existence has hitherto been largely overlooked by non-Zoroastrians.

78. See *Tansar Name,* text 14, transl. 39.

79. E.g. Mas'ūdī, *loc. cit.* (nn. 62, 64, above).

80. For knowledge of this I am indebted to the kindness of Khanom Ferangis Shahrokh, who has a striking collection of such old embroideries.

81. The writer finds it impossible to agree with those scholars who interpret this great faith as the product of compromise and confusion. On the contrary, the fundamental doctrines taught by Zoroaster appear to have been maintained with admirable strictness by his followers down to the 19th century, when the sudden impact of European ideas and modern science had a cataclysmic effect on their theology.

82. See S. der Nersessian, *Byzantion* XVII, 67, with n. 37.

83. Later in the 4th century there was some return to Zoroastrianism, and Faustus of Byzantium (transl. Langlois I 295) relates that 'a number of statues . . . were erected which were openly venerated'.

84. For some recent studies in this field see G. B. Ladner, 'The concept of the image in the Greek fathers and the Byzantine iconoclastic controversy', *Dumbarton Oaks Papers,* VII, 1953, 1-33; E. Kitzinger, 'The cult of images before iconoclasm', ibid., VIII, 1954, 85-150; M. V. Anastos, 'The ethical theory of images formulated by the iconoclasts', ibid., 155-160; A. Grabar, *L'iconoclasme byzantin, dossier archéologique,* Paris 1957. (I am grateful to Miss Helen Potamianos for kindly drawing my attention to these.)

85. See E. C. Dodd, 'The image of the word; notes on the religious iconography of Islam', *Berytus* XVIII, 1969, 35-61.

86. In general it was sculpture in the round which roused the wrath of iconoclasts; but whereas the Zoroastrians showed toleration for religious carvings in high relief, Christians after them were opposed to these also (see Bevan, *Holy Images,* 148).

Cyrus R. Pangborn (essay date 1983)

SOURCE: "Scriptures and Doctrines" in *Zoroastrianism: A Beleaguered Faith,* Advent Books, 1983, pp. 13-49.

[*In the following essay, Pangborn analyzes the development of Zoroastrianism from the qualified monotheism of Zoroaster's Gathas, through the ritual polytheism of the Later Avesta, to the controversy between the purist reform movement and the orthodoxy of modern Zoroastrianism.*]

We have now identified the Zoroastrians and those composing their largest single—and, in recent times, modestly dispersed—community, the Parsis. Meanwhile, little has been said about the substance of the faith which, after all, enough people having embraced it, sets Zoroastrians apart as a distinctive religious community. This substance, composed initially of the beliefs and convictions of the prophet Zoroaster but also of both older and later ideas added by his followers, found expression in Scripture, the *Avesta,* the composite work that became for subsequent generations the principal source of their inspiration, renewal, and regulation. We will look for the moment at the theology which has evolved from it, together with doctrines of man and his destiny, leaving for later the ideas that inform the cultus and define morality.

ZOROASTER AND HIS *GATHAS*

The religion of Zoroaster before he sought its reformation was Indo-Iranian religion, a version of a body of religious beliefs that had been held by the large Indo-European multi-tribal community in general before various groupings within it migrated elsewhere—as to Iran—from the steppes of Asia. The early Vedic religion of those who went India-ward was a comparable modification of the older religion affected by a different experience. A significant central core of the older belief and practice, however, may be verified as having survived for a long time with but little change before Zoroaster undertook its criticism and revision in Iran.

Common to both Iranian and Indian versions of the earlier religion were numerous deities personifying the forces and vitalities of nature, their functions differing according to whether they were powers operating within the immediate environment and the human community or in the more distant reaches of the sky or cosmos. The name of a deity might change slightly and be different in Iran from what it was in India because of the evolution of languages, but many names remained the same. In any event, it is clear that it was customary in both traditions to classify the deities as either *ahuras* (the Vedic *asuras*) or *daevas* (the Vedic *devas*). Both classes apparently comprised deities benevolent and good as well as those malevolent and destructive.

How Zoroaster assayed that *Weltanschauung* (world view) is revealed in his **Gathas.** These are prayer-hymns he composed in poetic form to distill and enshrine, in language both memorable and memorizable, the record of his spiritual journey. Only five of them (comprised of 17 chapters in all) have survived, yet these suffice for reconstructing the main lines of his thought and the decisive events of his life.[1]

His theology is shown to have developed from the way in which he treated the traditional dual classification of the deities. Of the ahuras, we hear of only one *supreme* deity worthy of worship, Ahura (Lord). He then linked with that title another one, *Mazda* (Wisdom), a word already familiar in Iran. There may have been precedent for this association, but we do not know for sure. In any case, whether he used one or the other alone, or the two together—sometimes in one order and sometimes in reverse—he meant that there is only one who is really the supremely good God, Ahura Mazda. It may seem curious that nowhere (in the **Gathas** we possess) did he deny the existence of other ahuras, but he mentioned none by name; and it was to one deity only that he ascribed *all* positive attributes, thus marking his system as perhaps a henotheism or, alternatively, a qualified monotheism.

His treatment of the daevas was likewise and uniquely his own. He saw them as the deities worshipped by the lawless, marauding nomads of the society. Their wills were one—to do evil. The semi-settled, pastoral tribesmen should worship deity only of the ahura type. If they then attended in any way at all to the daevas as well, they might not be honoring or adoring the daevas, but they were implying respect for their powers by entreating and placating them with sacrifices in order to ward off the evil they could do. The word of Zoroaster to one and all was that to pay either type of heed to the daevas was false religion. They were not true gods; they were the Evil Spirit (*Angra Mainyu*) and the hosts of evil who had sprung from his Evil Mind (*Aka Manah*). They were not to be honored, even by placation; they were to be fought, relentlessly, and all their evil intentions brought to naught.

The rest of Zoroaster's thought flows with reasonable consistency from these presuppositions. Ahura Mazda's Bounteous Spirit, *Spenta Mainyu,* is that aspect or "son" who is creative of life and the good in life. To say that this is God's Spirit is to affirm that his goodness or righteousness is his primary and all-encompassing attribute, with other qualities subsumed as further distinguishing traits. He is thus the eternal enemy of Angra Mainyu, the Evil Spirit. Whether, however, to regard Ahura Mazda and Spenta Mainyu as alternative terms for God or to think of Ahura Mazda as Spenta Mainyu's "creator" is a disputed question. Yasna 30:3 refers to two primordial "twin spirits," one of which would be Ahura Mazda (Spenta Mainyu) and the other, Angra Mainyu. This would be ethical, theological dualism. Yasna 47:3, on the other hand, by referring to Ahura Mazda as the good spirit's father, has led to the idea that Ahura Mazda created both spirits and gave them freedom of choice, after which one chose good and the other, evil.[2]

Associated with God are the attributes (or other entities) which Zoroaster in some measure personified and referred to as Good Mind (*Vohu Manah*), Truth or Righteousness (*Asha*), Good Power or the Kingdom of God (*Khshathra*), Right-Mindedness or Devotion (*Armaiti*), Wholeness or Perfection (*Haurvatat*), and Immortality (*Ameretat*). By right aspiration and obedience, man may participate in or conform his life to the first four of these qualities of God. The last two, Perfection and Immortality, cannot be won by man; they are bestowed by God as gifts to those who seek the other qualities. These six, together with the Bounteous Spirit, have been called since early post-Gathic times the Bountiful Immortals (*Amesha Spentas*). We know that the names of some of them were already familiar. But opinion is divided as to Zoroaster's precise intention. He may have been declaring that some familiar ahuras were actually only abstract attributes of God without separate existence. Equally plausible is the possibility that he meant merely to subordinate old ahuras to God by saying he was their creator and adding moral dimension to their character.

The ambiguity exists probably because Zoroaster's theological interest was subordinated to his preoccupation with the existential reality of evil, its threat to the quality of life, and the inescapability of struggle if evil was to be overcome by good. His theology, in its positive aspects, went little further than to provide a divine source and authority for his vision of the good life. The reality of evil demanded that there be a correlative postulate of a transcendent ground for it as well. The ground is Angra Mainyu, the Evil Spirit, who together with his Evil Mind (Aka Manah) and ally in wickedness, the Lie (*Druj*) do all in their power to subvert the righteous works of Spenta Mainyu, Vohu Manah, and Asha. Zoroaster's scheme of opposites, however, stops essentially right there, its incompleteness strongly suggesting that evangelism for the good life was more important to him than theological tidiness.

The concern Zoroaster had for man was grounded on the importance he understood him as having in the divine plan. Of all the creatures God placed in the world that he created, man alone is made to be God's ally. Thus, like the twin spirits of the spiritual realm, he possesses free will. If he chooses rightly and accepts his divinely intended role, he will conform his mind to that of Vohu Manah and his will to Asha. His rewards will be the gifts of wholeness (Haurvatat: well-being, health) and immortality (Ameretat). Everything that is the opposite of such boons will be his if he responds to the promptings of the Evil Spirit and his hosts, and becomes a participant with them in the battle they are waging at every level of God's spiritual and earthly creation.

Another chapter explains the specific duties of all persons who choose the good. Suffice it to say here that if these duties are accepted and the war against evil is fought bravely, Zoroaster envisaged a world made perfect in a final consummation, a final judgment that will bring an end to time and an eternal resolution of the conflict between good and evil. Zoroaster and his loyal followers will be entrusted with the perfecting of the world. Ahura Mazda, through (or supported by) Truth (Asha), Good Mind (Vohu Manah), and Devotion (Armaiti), will preside over the final resolution and judge the souls of men. The test is one of passing through fire and molten metal. Good men will pass through unscathed and even be purified by the ordeal but evil men will be unmasked and unmercifully seared. The lot of the good men will be eternal felicity with Ahura Mazda in his Kingdom of Righteousness, but for evil men, irrevocable doom.

The Theology of the Later Avesta

The Zoroastrianism of the Later Avesta is recognizable as having continuity with the Gathic picture of Zoroaster's reform. But there was change. Even if the substance of the religion was not so much altered as supplemented, this in itself wrought change in spirit or emphasis. The transition was effected in two stages.

The "*Gatha* of the Seven Chapters," a composition in Gathic prose that post-dates Zoroaster and reflects a change

of situation for his reforming religion, represents the first stage of the transition. Zoroaster's reform, even if finally successful in eastern Iran, did not immediately establish itself in the west. If it was to survive among the variations on Indo-Iranian religion in the provinces, its voice could not be Zoroaster's zealously exclusive one but had to be the more tolerant one of accommodation.

The "*Gatha* of the Seven Chapters" (Yasna Haptanghaiti: Yasnas 35-41) and Yasna 42 indicate that the adjustment was made. Ahura Mazda retained his primacy but in association with other lords (ahuras), known by name and enjoying a marked degree of autonomy. His own nature as pure spirit was materially diluted by speaking of his having the sun for his body. A new genre of feminine powers (*gena*) rated notice as the waters of earth. Old Iranian religion's fravashis, the pre-existent prototypal souls of all men born and to be born on earth, were mentioned for the first time since Zoroaster passed them over in silence. And the concreteness of *Haoma* was back. As a self-immolating god associated with sacrifice in the ancient cult, Haoma had been—and now was again—worshipped with intoxicating libations extracted from some plant and with the flesh of bulls or cows in ways which Zoroaster—without suppressing the cult altogether—had censured for profligacy. The teaching of Zoroaster was not forgotten, but much of the ancient religion he had so significantly reformed—in part, by ignoring it—was making a bid for re-affirmation.

The transition was completed by Zoroastrian athravans of the Achaemenid age. Their post-Gathic works, composing the so-called Later Avesta, tell us what they thought and practiced as "catholic Zoroastrianism."[3]

The several Avestan sections are not altogether representative of the same tendencies, but they are not contradictory—nor of such diversity as to prevent our making an economical summary of their general direction. Thus, the Yasna (the incorporated *Gathas* excepted) consists of invocations and miscellaneous prayers containing long lists of deities to be honored and whose aid or blessing was sought. As the text for a ritual that was in many respects pre-Zoroastrian, it had for a main purpose "the continuance, strengthening, and purifying of the material world of the good creation . . ." and "its daily performance . . . [*was*] essential."[4] Clearly, the implication is that every creation of God has been given a sacred vitality or life of its own and that it ebbs away or can be destroyed by evil if it is not ritually renewed day by day. This is not the same thing as regarding all that God has created as simply good and deserving of care and respect from man. On the contrary, it is the sacralization of material goods; they participate in sacredness because the "life" they possess flows into them from the deities whose function is their care and protection. But whence comes that vitality or potency which the deities have to spare? The answer seems obvious: from the offerings man makes as part of the rituals conducted by the priests. It can hardly be an accident that the six Bountiful Immortals (excluding the Bounteous Spirit) have feast-days honoring them, nor that one of them, Immortality, is offered fruit; and another, Good Mind, as the patron of cattle, is offered milk. Thus we come full cycle, the lesser deities (or the angels—*Yazatas*—if preferred; it is the same) invest the entities of the material world with their own life or vitality so that offerings of them can in turn be made to the deities for the renewing of their powers. Then the deities can renew every day the vitalities they had shared with material things in the first place.

That the Yasna alone is sufficient evidence for characterizing the late Avestan theology as polytheistic is not really in much dispute among present-day scholars. What is at issue is whether the Later Avesta was as much of a departure from primitive Zoroastrianism as an earlier generation of scholars supposed, and thus, also, whether Zoroaster was less of an ethical monotheist—or dualist—than they presumed. Suffice it to say that, historically, when polytheistic and ritualistic tendencies are in the ascendency in a religion, the definition of goodness and righteousness as cultic punctiliousness and correctness has also prospered at the expense of their definition as moral character and ethical conduct. Now, what Zoroaster is known to have said in the *Gathas* that did survive shows far more concern for condemning the ritual practices of which he disapproved than for prescribing those he approved, and far more concern for moral character and ethical conduct than for righteousness defined as the correct performance of a plethora of detailed and complex rituals. Again and again, he enjoined certain attitudes—right aspiration, right commitment, and discriminating wisdom—and not the mechanics of ritual as the marks of both acceptable worship and the moral life. There is therefore considerable plausibility for the presumption—and here it is better to speak of tendencies than of fixed positions—that Zoroaster tended toward ethical monotheism—or dualism—and the Later Avesta toward a ritualistic polytheism, in which case as regards both direction and spirit the two differed significantly.[5]

The Visparad supplements the Yasna and only confirms its temper by lengthily "spinning out"[6]—as Geldner put it—the Yasna's liturgy for the six seasonal holidays (*Gahambars*) and their accompanying feasts. The Yashts, however, together with the Khordeh Avesta, dispel all doubt that the late Avestan religion differed from Zoroaster's, for there really seems no way of denying that the *Avesta* made his economy in theology a casualty of inflation. Unlike the Yasna where many divinities are addressed at once, the Yashts invoke them one at a time and capture our attention by the prominence they give to three ancient deities and to the fravashis.

Mithra, in the old Iranian religion, had been a junior, but essentially equal, partner of that ahura whom Zoroaster singled out as being light and truth and then exalted as the one Wise Lord, Ahura Mazda. But in the *Gathas,* he is not even mentioned. That is why attention is attracted by his reappearance in the Yashts as Ahura Mazda's creation or son, a deity upholding justice by insisting upon the sanctity

of contract and treaty, and waging relentless war against all who invent lies or hold *him* in contempt. He was also understood as possessing the creating and preserving functions of the Bounteous Spirit (Spenta Mainyu), the theological consequence of which is the conflation of Ahura Mazda and his Bountiful Spirit (as in Yasna 30:3). Thus catholic Zoroastrianism supported the ethical dualism of opposing Angra Mainyu directly to Ahura Mazda.

The goddess *Anahita* was another familiar ahura of Indo-Iranian religion who, as "Lady of the Waters"—waters upon which the Iranian's dependence was measured by their scarcity—found her independent authority over water restored in the Yashts. She, too, received no mention in the Gathas of Zoroaster, the association of waters *there* having been with Wholeness (the Bountiful Immortal, Haurvatat) and thus with Ahura Mazda himself, whose gift they were as boon to man.

Verethraghna, as a god of war and victory, owed his recall from the limbo of Gathic silence to the place the Yashts give him as Mithra's agent in the war against violators of contracts and all enemies of the Good Mazdayasnian Religion in general. There is much that can be said about him, but it is enough for us to note that in being accommodated to Zoroastrianism, he was not shorn of the propensity for ruthlessness. His unhesitating destruction of enemies, which in the Yashts was made respectable, betokens a spirit at odds with that of Zoroaster, who sought first the conversion of his opponents and only after failing treated the unpersuaded as enemies and outcasts.[7]

Nothing in the Yashts having to do with the rehabilitation of some by-then half-starved gods, however, is as astounding as their recovery of functions that made even Ahura Mazda dependent upon them in the areas of their competence. The violence done to Zoroaster's theology was theoretically mitigated by crediting Ahura Mazda with the creation of the deities, but his divine supremacy was placed in jeopardy at the same time by the notion that in creating Mithra, in particular, he made him to be as worthy of veneration as he was himself. Ahura Mazda gave to him the task of protecting the whole material world as well as of vanquishing all daevic and human enemies. A house was built for him in heaven where even Ahura Mazda worships him. His portfolio bulged as he took on the assignments of protecting cattle, of granting men's pleas for sons, and of lighting the world by day after scourging the powers of evil through the night.[8] Anahita was less successful in accruing prerogatives, but it was she whom Ahura Mazda needed to persuade Zoroaster that he should adopt and preach the Good Religion,[9] and but for the fravashis, Ahura Mazda confessed that the human race could not have survived or his creation have been defended against its total domination by the Lie.[10]

This is perhaps as much as we need to say to understand the main tendencies of Zoroastrianism from its rise with the prophet to its "time of troubles" that began with Alexander's victory over Persia. The monotheistic *direction* of

Zoroaster's theology was seriously compromised by a return to popularity for gods obscured if not banished by his reform. This accommodation was achieved by ascribing their creation to Ahura Mazda and calling them yazatas (angels of various ranks including the Bountiful Immortals as a highest echelon of archangels). But the yazatas, for all of that, were *de facto* deities—cherished values and functions divinized and personified (or, if it be preferred, *re*-divinized and *re*-personified).[11] And one may speak all one wants to of catholic Zoroastrianism's retention of the Wise Lord's primacy in its theology,[12] but it was an empty honor if Ahura Mazda had to *ask* the help of his own spiritual creatures, even as having only one's title left was degrading to those Bountiful Immortals who found lesser angels absorbing their functions and then, as ranking gods, gaining ascendancy over them.[13] And yet, lest concern for theological tidiness be allowed to obscure the point and value of the changes wrought, it should be allowed that in all probability the willingness of Zoroaster's successors to try to be all things to all men may have saved the religion for posterity. It was a time, after all, not of reform-supporting Vishtaspas, but of Achaemenid kings whose interest in religion was in using it to justify their rule. A religion less eclectic and more capable of a critical stance toward both the social order and rival religious options might have marched straight into oblivion, taking both Zoroaster and his **Gathas** with it.

THE THEOLOGY OF THE SASANID AND POST-SASANID ERA

The task of re-collecting and collating the fragments of the *Avesta* not entirely forgotten between 330 B.C. and the Sasanid restoration of indigenous Persian rule in the 3rd century A.D. was difficult only in a logistical sense. The more difficult problem was the theological one of deciding (*a*) what the reconstituted *Avesta* meant, and (*b*) whether the Avestan theology was adequate or due for re-interpretation and revision in order to render it defensible in an age of more intellectual ferment.

The ferment was the result of Persia's association with other cultures during the course of its rise, fall, and domination by others. Because of success as well as exigency, Iranian thought became aware of Greek philosophies, Judaism, and Christianity, and of sects intending to improve upon one or another, or all, of these major traditions. It is tempting, because it was at least a disputatious if not an exciting intellectual age, to describe and analyze these currents of thought in detail. But the temptation must be resisted, principally because our concern is with what went into the making of contemporary Zoroastrianism and not with what was discarded or fought off along the way. Manichaeanism and the Mazdakite heresy, as noted earlier, languished in Persia or died out completely after their leaders were martyred, the former surviving mainly as a threat to Christian orthodoxy in lands to the west. Zurvanism, a movement that attempted to counter theological dualism by making Zurvan, as Infinite Time, the father of both Ahura Mazda and Angra Mainyu, failed so completely

that the Pahlavi tracts could be written without making a single direct reference to the controversies Zurvanism had generated.

The religion then, that emerged as the result of the literary and theological efforts of an age extending from the 3rd through the 9th century A.D. (and probably into the 11th) had these several features:

1. The language in which it was couched was Pahlavi, a name for a dialect of Middle Persian that Zoroastrians used and that is therefore sometimes called Zoroastrian Middle Persian. The remnants of the *Avesta* as gathered together during the reigns of Sasanian kings were in the Gathic and Avestan dialects. The Pahlavi writers translated all of this material into their language, with the exception of some of the Yashts, and wrote their own tracts in which they described the content of much of the *Avesta* for which they had no remembered text. They also preserved in this way an enormous amount of myth and legend that had become the popular form of the religion of the pious and beleaguered faithful.

Names and terms employed during this period remained the same in the rituals because their texts were almost entirely from the *Avesta*. But in the tracts recounting and interpreting the history and theology of the tradition, the Pahlavi words were sufficiently different in many instances that confusion may be avoided if the more important ones are cited. Thus, Ohrmazd = Ahura Mazda, Spena Menu = Spenta Mainyu, Ahriman = Angra Mainyu, Amahraspands = Amesha Spentas, Yazads = Yazatas, and Zaratusht = Zarathushtra (Zoroaster).

2. The formal and finally dominant theological dualism was a reformed version of catholic Zoroastrianism. The old Iranian gods rehabilitated in the Later Avesta were again forced into retreat and regarded at most as spirits subservient to God. However, the coalescence of God and his Bounteous Spirit, implied in catholic Zoroastrianism, was reaffirmed, so that Ahriman remained directly opposed to Ohrmazd.[14] Neither of the two was without the trait of finitude, but the dualism was made at least provisional rather than permanent by believing in God's final triumph and Ahriman's defeat. The Yazads, including the Amahraspands (Bountiful Immortals), were given back functions they had lost to rival deities, but allowed a status no higher than that of created and subordinate angels.

This is not to say that exponents of a more monotheistic doctrine of God as the only creator—even of Ahriman—did not attempt to hold out against the dualists, but the Pahlavi tracts, by not even mentioning the minority position, make it clear that dualism became orthodoxy.

3. The dualistic dogma of the theologians, however, was not bread for the lay remnant of believers in Muslim Persia. Their sustenance was myth and legend, and this too, the Pahlavi tractarians were willing to preserve and magnify. Reference has been made earlier to old Indo-

Iranian and Persian notions about the origins of the world and the prehistorical eras linking beginnings to the known and literate era of the Median and Persian empires. The *Avesta* refers, although but briefly, to these in passages of the legal section, the Videvdat, and also initiates the process of idealizing Zoroaster that ends in idolizing him. For the Later Avesta, he had been the first ideal man, the first to master God's law, and the one man on earth worthy—after his death—of homage in the form of prayers and sacrifices. But this was only the beginning. There are no religions that have not at some stage in their history mythologized one or more of their founders and prophets by identifying them primarily with a divine hierarchy, and by giving them the role of revealing to men the nature of the divine realm and how they may relate to it. Zoroastrianism is no exception. Fancy had had free play for five pre-Sasanid centuries when the task of preserving the religion had subordinated theological creativity. And the Pahlavi tractarians were as ready to pay court to these proliferating myths and legends in the corpus of the faith as they were to justify the religion with their dualistic theology.[15]

There were three principal subjects upon which such imaginative thought expanded. The first was Zoroaster himself. His birth was foreordained, his conception miraculous and his delivery attended by archangels. Throughout his childhood and until he won final acceptance for his religion at Vishtaspa's court, repeated threats were made upon his life by demons and wicked men, but from all of these he was miraculously rescued.

A second subject upon which imagination played was the "cast" of the spiritual realm. On Ohrmazd's side, the Bounteous Immortals were valued less for their representation of abstract virtues than for their guardianship of six parts of creation.[16] We learn that each of them, as well as Ohrmazd, had three Yazads (Av. Yazatas—angels) as aides, some of whom—e.g., Mihr (Av. Mithra), Srosh (Av. Sraosha), and Rashn (Av. Rashnu)—had ranked as deities in the Later Avesta. Many were now named who before had been nameless—which did not in any way diminish the ranks of the un-named! Functions also changed in many instances and care for the living and their welfare in this world gave ground to concern that the faithful might fare well in the next world. The Frawahrs (Av. fravashis) were also re-conceived. Quantitatively, they were diminished in number, since only earthly creatures—and not every heavenly being as well, including even Ohrmazd, as in the Later Avesta—were thought to have such prototypal souls. But more obvious was an inconsistency that emerged in thinking about their nature. As some of the earliest creations of Ohrmazd, the Frawahrs were throught to descend to earth, each to become the soul of a new-born person. At death, the soul of the good and faithful man would return to its earlier heavenly abode, but descend for every feast day commemorated to the dead, to bless the living who honored it properly or to curse irrevocably those who did not. It is this conflation of the Frawahr and soul that introduced confusion. For dualistic orthodoxy,

God's creations were good by nature, and it was not difficult to conflate the Frawahr with the soul of the person choosing to be good. But what of the case of the good Frawahr finding itself the soul of the person choosing evil? The conflation was then impossible, and the Frawahrs of evil men only could be considered, quite inconsistently, as "doubles" who leave their counterpart souls at the Bridge of Judgment and re-ascend to their appointed stations in the heavenly realm, while the evil souls go to hell until the final judgment and resurrection at the end of earthly time. In short, the confusion in the Pahlavi tracts consists in suggesting that the Frawahr and soul of a sinner are alike in essence but separable in nature, whereas the Frawahr of a good person becomes conceptually conflated with his soul. The consequence is that on feast days when an ancestor's presence and blessing are sought, only the Frawahr of a sinful ancestor can answer the call, but what is invoked in the case of a good ancestor can be either his Frawahr or his soul in the thought that they are one and the same anyway.[17]

So much for dualism's account of Ohrmazd's good spiritual creations. The other half of the story treats Ahriman and his evil ones. It is a half which has two parts. One deals with Ahriman's spiritual allies. Here again, we find the cast of characters imaginatively inflated. And—since reason is not a primary tool of theological construction when its task is preempted by fancy—the role pattern is far from tidy. The principal feature of the pattern, however, is that for every one of Ohrmazd's spiritual creatures, Ahriman conjured up an opposing demon of equivalent rank and power, each having its own minidemons as aides and all of them together charged with tempting man to embrace every vice for which there could possibly be an opposing virtue.

The half of the myth that is Ahriman's story has as its other part what he did (and does) to God's world. He is described as not content to oppose and corrupt God's work, as in the Gathas, but as having balanced every good creation of God with an evil one of his own. Much of this is presaged in the Later Avesta (in both the Yashts and the Videvdat), but the Pahlavi literature was even more starkly dualistic; there, every difficulty met by man in the natural order—whether radical threat or mere inconvenience—owes its ontological existence to Ahriman. Thus, as just one example, the darkness which God gave to man as his time for sleep and renewal, but which could be misused by wrongdoers as cover for theft or murder, was transferred from the good to the evil order and understood to be evil not by its corruption in use but in it svery nature. Dualism, then, was not only one pair of ontological opposites—Ohrmazd *vs* Ahriman—but many: light *vs* darkness, truth *vs* false-hood, Zoroastrians who wear the identifying shirt and girdle *vs* those who do not, ritual purity *vs* pollution, life *vs* death, health *vs* disease, good creatures *vs* noxious creatures, life *vs* smoke, rain *vs* drought, summer *vs* winter, south *vs* north, and of course heaven *vs* hell.

The third subject upon which the imagination played in the Pahlavi period was the destiny of man and the eschatological future, including the epochs during which saviors appear, a final universal judgment, the glorious renovation of creation, and the nature of Best Existence (Paradise, for which the Pahlavi term was *Vahishta Ahu*). With this subject, as with that of the beginnings of things, soaring fancies did not encounter limits, for they dealt with drama directed from and ultimately played out on the stage of the spiritual realm, and there, where the mundane and limiting realities of this world did not apply, anything was possible. The Pahlavi tracts show that full advantage was taken of the freedom to speculate in an age when defensive Zoroastrians found tasteless sustenance in reason and restraint, because they needed, as compensation for earthly trials, the sweeter viands of their visionary paradise to come.

There could hardly have been a question asked for which imagination did not conjure up a detailed and specific answer. The reader intrigued by the curios of a credulous age can examine them for himself,[18] but the concrete materialization of the spiritual realm that was involved cannot be entirely passed over on that account. The exact location of the Bridge of Judgment was cited. The anxieties of the soul of a deceased person during the three days that pass before the Bridge is reached were described. Angels ready at the Bridge to judge and then to condemn or aid were identified and named. The exact weight of good deeds as compared with that of evil deeds, which decided whether the soul's destiny was heaven or hell, was exactly determined; for those whose deeds were in exact balance, there was an intermediate place (*Hamistagan*) where the souls would wait without undue suffering until the day of resurrection. Hell (*Achishta Anghu*), it was averred, lay deep within the earth below the Bridge. The soul consigned to it went to one of four levels according to the amount of torture his degree of wickedness deserved, and the punishment was made to fit the crime. Heaven too had its four levels, and while each accorded its own degree of felicity, no soul's station afforded less bliss than that enjoyed by angels; and ambrosia, the angels' own food, was the food of all.

A rough sketch of the "choreography" for all this fateful dance of souls had been provided in the Later Avesta, especially by the Yashts and the Videvdat. The outline for the last Judgment and subsequent Renovation was there as well. The Pahlavists only filled it in by defining times, locating places, identifying old and many new members of the production crew, naming names, and describing the process by which evil souls as well as good ones would finally be gathered into God's perfected and everlasting Kingdom.

Zoroaster had spoken of himself and his followers—whether present or future is uncertain—as the saviors (*saoshyants*) who were God's agents in helping men make ready for a final consummation. The Later Avesta had named three successive saviors, only the last one of whom was cited as a direct descendant of Zoroaster and given Saoshyant as a name. It was he who would be born, in the "supernatural manner" of a "superman", to a "virgin" immaculately impregnated by seed of Zoroaster that had been preserved and "watched over by ninety-nine thousand nine hundred and ninety-nine Fravashis."[19]

Finally, there is the scenario elaborated by the Pahlavists, especially in the *Denkard* and the *Bundahishn* tracts. All three *soshyos* (Av. saoshyants), of whom the last is named *Soshyo* (or *Soshyans*) are to be immaculately conceived by virgins at intervals of a thousand years, to combat the evils of their respective periods and to move the good creation nearer to perfection than they found it. During each successive millennium, evil will lose some of its power and dominion until, finally, during a 57-year period of Soshyans' activity, perfection itself will be achieved—one token of which will be that men then living will need no material food, yet be vitally alive.[20]

The end will be near when all the dead are resurrected, given new material bodies, and re-judged in exact conformity with the judgments rendered when they died. A few persons will have been so evil that they crossed over into the demons' camp and will perish with them. Otherwise, the resurrected dead will join the then-living in passing through a flood of molten metal. This will be felt as an agonizing ordeal only by the wicked among the dead, but they have purgation of their sins and release from hell as compensation.

The seared world can now be renovated and made the eternal habitation for mankind. Families will be reunited, but there will no longer be birth or death. Those who died as adults will possess the vitalities of the age of 40, while whose who died as youths will remain as though they are but 15.[21] With the earth thus repopulated, the time will have come for a final confrontation with Ahriman. All his creations except darkness will be destroyed. He alone will survive in his own darkness, forever impotent, completely dissociated from the Kingdom of Ohrmazd. The world that Ahriman can no longer touch is Paradise, and all mankind will live by the spirit, needing neither material food nor drink.[22]

It would seem that the vision of last things grew the brighter as the light of theology faded. Texts dating from the 10th through the 14th centuries reveal the confusion engendered by a sectarianism that dualism did not wholly obliterate. But for the most part, they treat of ritual traditions and, like the later *Rivayats* that answered questions posed by the Parsis, say little about theology and then only by implication. One of Dhalla's sub-headings is apt: "Almost every vestige of Iranian scholarship perishes."[23] The case might be put differently. The more theological dualism was gilded with legend and myth, the more decisively the locus of the struggle between good and evil was shifted from the hearts and wills of men to an external arena where the antagonists were angelic and demonic forces and men were only partisans of the opposing teams. Religion, morally speaking, had become a spectator sport. Or, returning to Dhalla for an analogy, "The sacred fire, kindled by the holy prophet in the remote past, was still there, . . . [but] only smouldering in ashes upon the altar."[24]

THEOLOGY TODAY

The task of making sense of, and explaining to others, the structure and content of contemporary Zoroastrian theology is at once both difficult and easy. Difficult, because—unlike history which has after all happened and can be sifted again and again by its students until *some* measure of agreement can be reached as regards its essential lineaments—the present is the age of the living who take sides and whose thinking is or may be changing as the result of confrontations between parties (internal stimuli) or of either the desire or the necessity to come to terms with society, itself a changing thing (external forces). No analyst can ever be confident, therefore, that he has read aright all of his data, impressions, and suppositions, for all the parts that make up the picture his analysis is constructing may be shifting in place and importance as he works. Much less, we might add, can the analyst be sure that he is excluding his own bias from his understanding and interpretation. For the wish to enforce custom or to effect change is hard to nullify when dealing with the malleable present—and more difficult to detect than historical revisionism.

Nonetheless, the task may also be easy, or at least—because the subject is Zoroastrianism—reasonably manageable. For while, as Boyce remarks, "the present position of Zoroastrianism is complex", as a religion it "is characterized by immense conservatism," so that "essentially and in details . . . the later religion is unchanged from that of ancient Iran."[25] Moulton, were he still living to follow up his first (and only) *on-site* study of Zoroastrianism, would surely have to add a fervent Amen. He would say, at the least, that essentially and in most details the religion has not changed since he studied it 60 years ago.[26]

We may start by appropriating Boyce's typology for assaying the theological spectrum, and hope that it will also be useful when we come to every other topic treated by subsequent chapters. She notes first—and not without reason, as we shall see—the orthodox group, together with those of Ilm-e-Khshnoom whose esoteric sectarian views are designed somewhat curiously to defend orthodoxy rather than challenge it. The second major group represents the reform movement. Besides these, there are the "nominal believers" whose beliefs are vague and imprecise but still inclusive of the notion that a few principal rites are efficacious in gaining the divine favor; and "finally, agnostics and atheists" who retain their Zoroastrian connection by blood if not religion and are given by their prior wish or permission, or their families', the last rites when they die.[27] Obviously, neither nominal believers nor non-believers have anything to contribute to theological discussion even if by their presence and numbers they represent factors of great importance for the religion as a whole, especially as regards its present disposition and its

potential for survival. This leaves the othodox and reform positions as the only ones to consider, *vis-a-vis* theology—though there are differences within each group which make it impossible to describe either one as neatly uniform.

Unfortunately, all too little clarity is gained by finding that there are only two groups, with or without sub-groups, whose views are at issue. The reason is that neither Zoroastrians in general nor the Parsis in particular have concerned themselves enough with theology *per se* to make the theological vocation attractive and compelling to the best minds of any recent generation. As both Moulton and Boyce have observed, although half a century apart, the community makes almost no provision for religious instruction or the systematic teaching of doctrine. Moulton, for his part, lamented that a deficiency in "the critical faculty" made the imminent appearance of theological genius quite unlikely, while Boyce points to the concern with "the practice of religion" as, by implication, so preoccupying that theology is inevitably given short shrift.[28] One way of saying this is that ritual practice—i.e., the cultus (Boyce's "practice of religion")—defines theology, and that it is not the other way around. But the cultus of Zoroastrianism is a composite construction from the early periods in the religion's development, the parts and rationales of which have never been made consistent and coherent by the ordering principles of a single theology. The theological enterprise is never, therefore, given a position of priority, but is used to explain or justify now-this, now-that ritual practice or its reform according to whichever of several hoary ideals the particular apologist chooses as his norm. The results for theology are chiefly obscurantism, contradictions, and a babble of tongues. But enough of reasons (or excuses) for postponing the attempt to say what is believed, however problematical that belief may prove to be.

As a preliminary remark, it may be said that most contemporary exponents of the tradition, whether orthodox or reformist, are in greater or lesser measure reverting to the *Avesta* and its two languages, Gathic and Avestan, for their vocabulary of essential religious terms, and allowing the Pahlavi (Middle Persian) forms to fall gradually into disuse. There are at least two reasons for this. One is that, after all, the texts for the entire cultus are in the languages of the *Avesta,* the only exceptions being some short and supplementary benedictory prayers in Pazand, a post-Pahlavi dialect, and, similarly, the "sermonic" portions of such ceremonies as weddings. Surely it makes sense, if all the technical terms for theological discourse are drawn from languages already "dead" anyway, that economy should be effected by choosing the forms found in the languages they actually use for their treasured rituals. A second reason for this trend is more theological because it is related to a trend in theology *per se.* This is the trend that consists of looking backward to the original deposit of prophetic revelation and early development of the religion for "a pristine purity" not compromised or sullied by later accretions of inferior doctrine or by tendencies to remythologize the religion. Again, there is sense—if the most defensible foundations of the faith are, indeed, to be found in the earliest traditions—in supposing that they may be expounded more understandably if the technical terms used in their original expression are not exchanged for later and no less archaic derivations. Behind both of these reasons may be noted also the need felt by both orthodoxy and reform to counter with persuasive argument the criticism of non-Zoroastrian monotheists.

That having been said, however, the case seems to be that the reformers are the more purist than the orthodox in their effort to ground the religion in its "primitive truths." That is to say, reform is willing to prune away not only the imaginative excesses of the Pahlavi age but to question any portion of the Later Avesta found at odds with what Zoroaster said in his **Gathas.** Orthodoxy refuses to go that far because of all things that might be given up, the traditional cultus is not one of them. And since the Later Avesta provides most of the material for the liturgical texts as well as theological mandates for the rituals, the orthodox are perforce required to invest a great effort in interpretation of the Later Avesta in order to answer criticism from within and without. Then if the interpretation itself remains unconvincing, all that is left—for to concede more is unthinkable—is to fall back on tangential arguments for which they assume an *a priori* validity.

One such argument—already alluded to in the Introduction—is that age is a criterion for determining the truth-value of doctrine. Reform has its own scattered exponents of this notion, but in returning to primitive Zoroastrianism, the majority is content to accept for Zoroaster the approximate dates suggested by historians uninterested in theological apologetics. If they employ the argument of age at all, it is the age of Zoroaster and not the Later Avesta that concerns them, and any of the 2nd or early 1st millennium suggestions is an early enough date to have such truth-value as age is alleged to guarantee. Orthodoxy, however, seems more united in its position, that of being determined to identify the age of Zoroaster as that of about 8,000 years ago. Some of its polemicists go further, asserting that authentic "Mazdayasnism—Mazda-worshipping religion—began several thousands of years before Zarathushtra." Thus there was truth before *his* time, and his mission was not that of a founder of a new religion or a reformer of age-old error, but one of restoring "pristine purity" to Mazdayasni religion by ridding it of "the evil of devayasni. . . ."[29] Another apologist is even more precise in his dating. "As per my humble research," he writes, "our revered Prophet was born on [the day of] *Roz Hormazd, Mah Fravardin . . . 6,325 years before Christ,* most probably at dawn." For him, the idea that there had been an earlier age of pure theological truth is reinforced by noting that science as well, "the art of the Magi Priests, had reached its zenith: [for in those days] people could fly in the air . . . [and] fire could be summoned to our kitchen as and when desired (electric installation), etc." The Golden Age, however, deteriorated because "the Scientists of those hoary days" were able to put their knowledge to evil use as well as good. They "could stop the rains at any

time; destroy a whole city in minutes (atomic explosion), and so on." Together with "continuous wars and rumours of war and murder . . ." the evils of the age required the advent of Zoroaster if ancient truth was to be proclaimed afresh and men's feet turned once more toward the path of righteousness.[30] This is clearly a rare instance of unfettered imagination, as is also, probably, the case of the reformist priest who is convinced that Zoroaster was predestined to be born on New Year's Day as a sign of the *cosmic* significance of his advent.

Such doubtful claims aside, the ardency with which all parties maintain their positions goes far to explain why the task of reducing orthodox theology to clear and succinct statement has its difficulties. Consider, as example, the orthodox objective of retaining all that *can be* by *some* means retained. This is not the *organizing* principle that would be provided by, say, the ideals of rational coherence and a more rigorously scientific historicity. It should occasion no surprise, therefore, if students of the religion find an obscurantism, however unintended, that permits of different understandings of what they read or are told. The opinion of Boyce, for example, is that the orthodox perpetuate the theological dualism of the Later Avesta and the Pahlavi tracts, according to which Angra Mainyu has his own independent existence.[31] But Dhalla who, given his strictures against traditionalism, can hardly be rated an orthodox apologist was clearly of different mind, when he wrote in the 1930s that "we hardly ever find even at this day *any* learned Parsi priest or layman marshalling arguments in vindication of the [theologically dualistic] doctrine."[32] (emphasis added.)

The contemporary work, *Zoroastrianism,*[33] written by Masani for English speaking non-Parsi readers, illustrates the problem one has in deciding what is thought by the orthodox who, so far, have retained their control of the institutions of their religion. It is Masani's contention that the religion is a monotheism because there is no spirit opposing Ahura Mazda that equals him in power. To be sure, there is evil in the world, but it is a principle not devised by Ahura Mazda; and thus to speak of Angra Mainyu as a spiritual being is merely metaphor. Yet Spenta Mainyu's existence as God's created and subordinate good Spirit is affirmed, along with the view that the Gathas say evil is opposed directly to Spenta Mainyu rather than Ahura Mazda. Thus when Masani needs to prove that Ahura Mazda is untainted by any connection with or responsibility for evil, he posits an *independent* (but otherwise unspecified) origin for evil as a *principle*. But when he wishes to establish Ahura Mazda's supremacy as proof that the religion is a monotheism in its theology, he appeals to Zoroaster, alleging that for him Angra Mainyu was the rebellious one of Ahura Mazda's Twin Spirits. There is also an unresolved discrepancy in Masani's explanations of the divine hierarchy. When he stresses the unity of God, he treats the Amesha Spentas and the Yazatas as his *attributes,* but when his purpose is to deny that there is worship of material fire and water, he says that only the *spirits* in such elements are worshipped.[34]

Current tracts published by orthodox authors for circulation among Parsis, and notes taken on interviews with orthodox priests, indicate that Masani has represented orthodoxy with reasonable fidelity. There is no budging from the claim that the religion is a monotheism, but beyond that—in accounting for evil and in defining Ahura Mazda's spiritual "creations"—there are no positions that all the orthodox accept. Nor does any one theorist seem to take a single internally consistent position. Thus Dabu has written that Angra Mainyu is "one of the twins created by God," "the destructive and ephemeral principle of Cosmos," "the destroyer . . . [who] is not in revolt against God, but does unpleasant work assigned to him," the divinely appointed "agent . . . [who] is permitted to deceive and test all souls . . . causing death and destruction of form, until the world is ripe for immortality. . . ."[35] Satan would appear here to be the subverter of the "spirit and matter, Life and Form" that are the results of God's self-manifestation, yet Dabu says also that "wickedness is due to that part in man which we have derived during the evolutionary process from our material nature, and the body with an animal ancestry."[36] The difficulties are obvious. If life and form are divine manifestations, then material nature should not be, itself, the source of evil. But if having a material nature is the reason for men's wickedness, then is Satan needed as an agent? And if Satan is doing work that God has assigned to him, how do we reconcile that, on the one hand, with the idea that God is in no way responsible for evil, and on the other hand, with the notion that an agent attempting to thwart God's will is nevertheless not really God's adversary?

The two principal views among the orthodox about the Amesha Spentas are that they are attributes (aspects) of God or his creations with independent assigned functions, but there is little concern to decide the matter one way or the other. There is more evident certainty, however, that the Yazatas (angels) at the next lower level of the spiritual hierarchy are individual spiritual entities who hear and respond to the prayers addressed to them. The reason for the greater certainty on this issue is not readily perceived. Perhaps it is because the principal prayers of the liturgies are addressed to the Yazatas and the one thing on which orthodoxy is unified is that the traditional rituals must be preserved unchanged in order to be efficacious. In any case, the orthodox are driven on that account alone to regard the liturgical portions of the Later Avesta as having a scriptural authority equal to that of the Gathas. They do not, however, pay heed to the Pahlavists' imaginative multiplication of the angelic and demonic personnel of the spiritual realm. With respect also to doctrines about life after death and eschatology, views are determined by the Avestan texts rather than the Pahlavi tracts. Therefore, the only divinities associated with death and affirmed in doctrine are four Yazatas that figure prominently in the funeral liturgies, and while it is possible to find an occasional believer in the Pahlavists' positive identification and dating of the epochal saviors, the tendency is away from literalism. The "sons" of Zoroaster, says Dabu, can be taken "in an allegorical sense" as "more great mes-

sengers from God" for whom there is need "from time to time"; and as for the end time, it "must be far away," for "the universe does not progress with leaps and bounds . . . [but only by] slow natural evolution . . . to bring about the destined Utopia."[37]

The one group among the orthodox possessing a unique and unifying ideology for defending traditionalism and its core of ritualism is a sect called Ilm-e-Khshnoom. Its lineage is not easily traced, but it appears to represent an effort to free Zoroastrianism from explicit alliance with late 19th century Theosophy by providing the religion with its own body of occult wisdom and esoteric interpretation of history and doctrine. Its interests resemble those also of an occult ascetic mysticism known to have attracted some Persian Zoroastrians in the post-Pahlavi era who were very probably influenced by Muslim mystics. Evidence is lacking, however, for direct descendancy on the part of Ilm-e-Khshnoom from this strain of mysticism, either doctrinally or institutionally.

The sect has virtually no structure of organization, but is constituted of the few priests and laymen who are willing to devote time to writing and to leading and attending discussion group meetings. The "master" to whose teaching these contemporary sectarians look for their Khshnoom (Enlightenment) was the late Behramshah Naoroji Shroff of Surat in Gujarat. He is alleged to have been taught the real truths of the religion during the 1870's in an Iranian mountain fastness where "Master-souls" and their followers had hid from the Muslim conquerors of the 7th century. There, from the chief master, he learned about the evolution of the cosmos, the temporal duration of which is supposed to span four great eons divided into 64 eras, each of 81,000 years; about Zoroaster's having known the truth because of his atunement to the music of the heavenly spheres and of how his followers had to translate his divine songs into earthly human language if ordinary people were to understand them; and how the preservers of the ancient lore are protected from unwanted discovery by an invisible talismanic barrier of miraculously repelling power.

Shroff is supposed to have remained in Iran only three and a half years (or until about 1880), when he returned to India to lead an exemplary Parsi life apparently conventional in all respects except one—he had been given a miraculous liquid that enabled him to turn copper into gold as insurance against having to pursue any occupation other than that of the savant. Yet he remained uncommunicative until about 1910 when he is said to have overcome a reluctance to share with others the secrets in his possession.[38]

A major objective of the sect is the reinterpretation of the rituals. Every artifact and action has a deeper hidden meaning than any provided by exoteric explanation. It is not enough to say that the consecrated urine of a pure white bull owes its current usage in purification rites to the fact that the urine of the cow "was believed by the ancient

Zoroastrians to possess disinfecting properties,"[39] that feeding the temple fires with sandalwood stems from ancient regard for aromatic substances as symbols of divine power,[40] or that the sacred shirt (*sudreh*) worn by the initiated Zoroastrian has in addition to meanings for its separate parts the general value of being "a symbol that reminds one of purity of life and righteousness."[41] On the contrary, according to occult interpretation, "the liquid passed by cows and bulls alone possesses the special purifying property because the 'plexus,' the receptive centre (of magnetic current) operating on the urinary organs of cows and bulls is under the influence of Jupiter." Unconsecrated, the urine "remains pure for 72 hours from the time it is passed." But as *Nirang*—that is, as urine consecrated "through the elaborate holy ceremony of 'Nirang-din,' [it] does not turn putrid for several years . . ." and so has the power when administered to the body every morning to counteract the "invisible microbes" that, in one's sleep, "envelop the human body and impair the *Khoreh* (aura)."[42] Similarly, the sandalwood becomes more than an analogical or metaphorical symbol. According to Chiniwalla, the greater the quantity of sandalwood that is burned, the greater the "manthric" activity of the fire upon which the very existence of our "Eternal and Temporary Universes" depends.[43] As for the sudreh, it shares with a girdle (*kusti*) in possessing "certain talismanic qualities which act . . . as a magical protective mechanism in times of crisis.[44]

The ultimate authority for this body of wisdom rests upon the knowledge that Zoroaster himself possessed it, for he was not a mortal man but an angel—the deputy of the Yazad, Sraosha—"sent to this world endowed with great powers and . . . the knowledge of all ages."[45] Moreover, it is maintained that all of Zoroaster's revelations as translated into human language were saved and hidden in a talismanically-protected place. Hence there is a whole *Avesta* which only the "Master-souls" have known in its entirety and which serves as the source for corrections and additions to the fragmentary remnants known by the uninitiated majority of Zoroastrians.

A principal objective that such speculation serves is, as already stated, the defense of the whole cultus in as traditional and unmodified a form as possible. If every rite, and every liturgical text for every rite, are vehicles for invisible powers that illuminate, heal, protect from harm, and eventually transform mortality into immortality, then tampering with any part of the cultus is obviously unthinkable. Thus the sect serves to reinforce the orthodox theology of a pluralistic spiritual hierarchy as found in the liturgical texts from the *Avesta*. Beyond that, however, the sect embraces a doctrine of radical spirit-*vs*-matter dualism which the mainstream tradition has always subordinated and given only minor place in the total doctrinal system. That is to say, it is true that the Videvdat discloses an ancient revulsion toward some aspects of the material world—such as dead and decaying bodies, or creatures that poison or threaten in some way other material creations useful to man—and that much of this revulsion

has not been dissipated even in a scientifically more sophisticated age. But the doctrine is that if matter is "noxious," it has been made so by corrupters either demonic or human. Evil is therefore the consequence of devotion to lies and of actions that are immoral. But matter, in essence, is held to be the good creation of God whose intentions for it in the divine scheme of things were wholly wise and pure. Correlatively, the remedy for its corruption in the eschatological future is the world's renovation—its renewal or return to an originally perfect state.

The praise reserved for the purely spiritual and the disparagement of any material embodiment reflect a sectarian doctrinal position metaphysically irreconcilable with that of the orthodox majority, however complete the agreement that exists on retention of the traditional cultus. Several of the sect's propositions make the distinction clear. Behind and above everything is "*Ahu*, the Absolute One in Oneness, the Supreme Deity over Ohrmazd and Ahriman."[46] From this One, a spiritual cosmos emanated, with various levels of spirituality for spiritual beings of different grades. Souls deficient in divine knowledge are relegated from the 8th and lowest heaven to the material planetary realm where the more recalcitrant of them become embodied according to "the *law of Infoldment of Spirit into Matter* . . ., [and] go through the *rounds of birth and death* . . . till Emancipation is gained . . . [by the reverse process of] Unfoldment of Spirit from Matter. . . .[47] We hear of enlightenment for those who become adept in their responsiveness to spiritual vibrations, of pure matter being only fiery essence as contrasted with the concrete gross matter of our empirical experience, of immortality rather than resurrection or renewal, and the reunion of our "Divine Sparks" with the 'Divine Flame." This is none other than a philosophically monistic resolution of a dualism that is regarded as only apparent or provisional. When the process of manifestation, emanation, descent (of spirit into matter) ceases, then the reverse process of re-absorption begins. Its philosophical affinity is with Hindu Vedanta, but its fascination with mysteries makes it nearer kin to ancient astrological lore, Gnosticism, Jewish Cabala, and Theosophy.

There is little way of measuring the influence of occult doctrines such as those propounded by Ilm-e-Khshnoom. Many random impressions coalesce, however, to suggest that very few Parsis are theologically affected.[48] Nor are the few themselves particularly influential. If they are given a hearing by others, the reason is not credibility of doctrine but appreciation on the part of the orthodox for support of cultic traditionalism.

Any other sectarian divisions among Zoroastrians are based upon different calendars and comment upon them may be left to the chapter on the cultus. If there is any correlation between the calendar issue and metaphysics or theology, it is provided more by coincidence than design. That is to say, the same Parsis who believe in accommodating the ecclesiastical calendar to a contemporary secular one are likely to be reformers by temperament and thus ready to discuss new trends of thought in any area of religious thought.

As for reformers in general, they constitute a movement and are not identified as a sect. The priests among them are few, largely because most priests have an understandably vested interest in preserving the social and professional prerogatives which traditionalism underwrites. The reformers are therefore mainly laymen divided—how unevenly no one knows—between those who are aggressive and articulate and those who, finding that reformist agitation arouses only discussion but not change, settle for perfunctory observance of a few obligations that sustain their nominal membership in the Parsi community.

We have already noted that systematic theology is not a major interest of Parsis, but that they attend to it if and when they feel the need of disavowing polytheism. In this respect, reformers and most of the orthodox are similar, as they are also in making essentially non-theological issues their principal concerns. But when they do undertake to "do theology," they differ in that the reformers are the more radical of the two parties in their reductionism. The orthodox, professing monotheism, are prepared to repudiate the theological dualism and mythopoeic excesses of Sasanian orthodoxy, but they have trouble—as we have seen—in handling the theological implications of the Later Avesta because it provides the liturgies for a sacrosanct cultus. There are some who do re-interpret the divinities to whom prayers are addressed, by denying the need to be literal and saying that the divinities merely symbolize the attributes and powers of one God. But for many, the lack of training in theology makes a venture into speculative thinking too hazardous to contemplate. The result is a re-affirmation of the literal existence of the divinities combined with insistence that their monotheism is not thereby qualified because one God created them and made them his subordinates.

The reformers are more reductionist because they are ready to reform the cultus and on that account find it unnecessary to defend the Later Avesta as authoritative for contemporary Zoroastrianism. Their common maxim is "Back to the *Gathas.*" This modern impulse thus to go back to "primitive" Zoroastrianism is probably to be associated with the founding in 1851 of the *Rahnumae Mazdayasnan Sabha,* a society that has sought "to dissuade Parsis from superstitious and un-Zoroastrian beliefs and to present to them the teachings of the Prophet Zarathushtra in their original and pure form."[49] Further impetus was given to reform when the K.R. Cama Oriental Institute was founded in Bombay in 1916. While the Institute's objective was not reform but the promotion of scholary inquiry, the results have certainly aided the cause of reform by indirection—that is, by supplying reformers with knowledge of how Zoroastrian traditions in particular evolved and with criteria for distinguishing between their historical and mythopoeic elements. Today, neither the Sabha nor the Institute (where, since its founding, the

Sabha has centered its educational activities) serves as a vigorous generator of reformist sentiment, but their legacy has been the diffusion of such sentiment among many individual members of the Parsi community.

The theological element of this legacy is characterized by what has become a basic aim of reform: the establishment of the claim that Zoroaster's own theology—and the theology that should therefore be normative—was a clear-cut monotheism. The first corollary is that the Gathas are *the* authoritative Scripture, so that all Later Avestan writings have their value determined by whether they accord with or depart from Gathic conceptions. A second corollary is that any doubt allowed by the Gathas as to whether the Bounteous Spirit and the Bountiful Immortals are attributes of God or other divinities he has created is resolved by insisting that they are the former—as Dhalla says, "pure abstractions, etherealized moral concepts, symbolic ideals, abstract figures."[50] As God's attributes and states of perfection, they constitute the ideals after which man should pattern his own life in order that he may be worthy of God's benefactions and of admission to the "Abode of good mind," the "House of Song," the Kingdom of God.

The avoidance of polytheism or theological dualism is not complete, however, until it is shown that Angra Mainyu as well is not a spirit of God's creation or a rival deity. The reform position taken by many is that the evil one of the "Twin Spirits" is to be understood as a simple admission of the fact that evil must exist since men choose it. There does seem to be no question but that the Gathas posit human freedom and regard righteousness as an empty concept unless man makes it his ideal or way of life *by choice*. It then follows by logical necessity that man may choose its opposite. And if that is so, then God did not create a separate spirit and give him an evil nature, or foreordain his choice to be evil; rather, he allowed the possibility of evil as the condition of there being any meaning for goodness. There is no cosmic spiritual entity that is Angra Mainyu. "He" is simply the spirit in which people act who live by lies, violence, and wrath. According to one reformer, the Devil and his hosts were, for Zoroaster, the priests of his time who "put the fear of the Devil and demons in men and induced them into ceremonies to scare these away."[51] Dastur Bode sees Zoroaster as solving the problem of evil by declaring that "evil is not an entity or a being: it is only the twin mentality and relativity in the human mind."[52]

One area of doctrine about which reformers say very little is that of eschatology. One may infer that the speculative imagination is not kindled by hope of a future kingdom of righteousness if the prospect is that there will be no then-living Zoroastrians to aid in its inauguration. Lay reformers are preoccupied with trying to initiate change in traditional practices which they believe are the causes of the community's declining numbers. This leaves theological reflection to the priests among whom there are but a few of reform temper. Among these few, Dastur Bode is probably the most published spokesman, and he spares but a few paragraphs for eschatology in writings otherwise devoted to commending Zoroastrianism as a religion for modern man. His vision is one of a final judgment, the annihilation of all evil by ordeal, and a new everlasting heaven and earth. "Zarathushtra's message," he writes in succinct condensation of his eschatological doctrine, "is full of hope, optimism and cheer; the ultimate triumph of good and transmutation of evil into good are assured."[53]

Until that time, the reform view of human destiny is that the souls of the deceased may be safely left to the mercies of God who, if good, is also just. No demons need be frightened away or angels implored to guarantee safe passage of departed souls to the bar of judgment. That being the case, the polytheism of the funeral liturgies can be declared archaic and the rites be understood as having only the functions of honoring the dead and comforting the mourners.

Zoroastrian doctrine is obviously not one systematized and generally approved body of theological and philosophical tenets but several sets of tenets for each of which the claim is made that it represents early and therefore normative Zoroastrianism. "Early," in its turn, can mean either Zoroaster's Gathic doctrines or the doctrines of the whole *Avesta*. Lack of agreement, however, is not necessarily ennervating. A religion *can* be the more vital the more vigorously its ideological bases are debated. The problem is that the community lacks the leadership able by training or motivated by desire (1) to winnow appealing and viable theological insights from the chaff of many accretions, (2) to explain and interpret the salvaged insights for successive generations, and (3) to submit the insights repeatedly to the tests which knowledge acquired from any quarter may pose.

The present situation is that there are the priests trained mainly in the proper conduct of ritual and recitation of the liturgical texts. They are unprepared to engage in theological construction. Then there are the scholars, some of them priests and others laymen, who have pursued studies in history, philology and philosophy. They have the tools requisite for advanced theological reflection, but few if any are wiiing to enter the arena of debate where they would be distracted and diverted from objective research. Unfortunately, the few who are willing seem unaware of their need to engage, additionally, in comparative, phenomenological, and sociological studies of religion if they aspire to become credible apologists rather than educated partisans. A narrow-gauge education, however "advanced," cannot provide the perspectives necessary to appreciate Zoroaster's existential situation. Like all great prophets, Zoroaster was dealing with an immediate and preoccupying crisis. To do so decisively and successfully required addressing himself only to the questions and issues it involved and to answering only the questions thus raised. The task of fitting any prophet's thought into a total *Weltanschauung* that itself might have to be restructured to accommodate the new prophetic insight has always devolved upon his followers. This was the case

with Zoroaster but it has not been understood by his followers, with the consequence that they impute to him one or another set of final answers to ultimate ontological questions when his one overriding concern was the moral crisis of his time. By then proceeding to regard their respective versions of his allegedly "total" system as eternally valid and immutable, they cut the nerve of that fresh inquiry which alone would bespeak fidelity to the prophet's spirit.

The climate of the last quarter of the century is thus not significantly different from that of half a century ago when Moulton found the Parsis anxious to preserve understanding of the aims and symbolism of their ceremonies but given to "credulity at one end, almost complete denial at the other . . ."[54] as regards systematic theology. Believers themselves are not lacking awareness of need for a fresh burst of theological creativity, but rites and customs are their overriding concerns in the 20th century. The same can be said of the Iranis and Westerners, though there is a difference. Those outside of India are having perforce to make their first order of business that of meeting the challenge of adjusting their practices and making them functional within societies which they have had no share (or early share) in shaping. They are meeting this challenge willingly and with reasonable concord. It may be their youth who, when the task is well along, may turn to the long-languishing discipline of theology and effect its renewal. The Parsis have their own way of responding to the pressures exerted by their more familiar but nevertheless changing society. It is to talk and wait, and wait and talk—which, because it is a way that postpones action also prevents moving on to other business. One would guess that it is not to the Parsis, therefore, that the new theologians are likely in any immediate future to be born.

Notes

1. The language of the Gathas we know only as Gathic because they are the only literature employing it that has been preserved. How many such hymns Zoroaster composed and were memorized by the priests of the Achaemenid period will never be known, for the five were all that were recalled or found when the Sasanids undertook the reconstruction of the *Avesta* in the original and for translation into the Pahlavi language. Even the five could be only imperfectly translated because Gathic had already become archaic before the priests supplemented the Gathas with their own compositions in Avestan—another language the name for which we are obliged again to borrow from the term denoting the literature itself, i.e., the *Avesta*. Progress has been made, in modern times, in decoding elements of the Gathas that baffled the Pahlavi translators; yet obscurities still remain. The translators were somewhat more successful with the Avestan language, inasmuch as it more nearly resembled both the Old Persian which supplanted it and their own Pahlavi or Middle Persian into which the Old Persian had evolved by Sasanian times.

It will be helpful at this point to list the divisions of the reconstructed *Avesta*—the present canon representing only about one-fourth of the 21 Books (*Nasks*) which are believed to have composed the *Avesta* of Achaemenid times:

1. The *Yasna,* of 72 chapters (*Has*), incorporating the 5 Gathas (17 of the chapters) and one later Gatha, the Gatha of the Seven Chapters (*Haptanghaiti*) that is not ascribed to Zoroaster. Prayers used in the worship of many deities, with some prominence given in the non-Gathic material to *Haoma,* the worship of whom was involved in all the many liturgical rites that included the use of the intoxicating or hallucinatory juice of the Haoma plant.

2. The *Visparad,* of 23 chapters (*Kardas*) supplementing the Yasna. Invocations to angels used especially at 6 seasonal festivals called *gahambars.*

3. The *Videvdat* (or, as often corrupted, *Vendidad*), of 22 chapters (*Fargards*), preserving the 21st and only completely salvaged Nask. A legal and liturgical book, "against demons," consisting of regulations for avoiding, punishing, and atoning for evil, notably pollution. A work which Karl F. Geldner, in 1904, called "the Leviticus of the Parsis"—a phrase so apt that it has become common property by frequent usage.

4. The *Yashts,* 21 invocations to divinities of various ranks, but especially angels, for whom days of the month are named.

5. The *Khordeh Avesta,* or "Little Avesta," often combined with the Yashts in one manuscript, and intended for priests' and laymen's use or for services attended by laymen. Principal parts are prayers (*Nyaishes*) to address to the Sun. (*Mihr,* the light of the Sun), Moon, Water and Fire; prayers to the genii presiding over the five divisions (*Gahs*) of each day; invocations to the genii of the 30 days of the month (*Siroze*); "words of blessing" (*Afringans*) for several purposes but notably to honor the dead and their souls. The only part of the *Avesta* using *Pazand,* a special liturgical version of *Pahlavi,* as well as Avestan.

2. Students of the religion, unable to agree on a resolution of the difference between such passages, are consequently also without agreement on what to call Zoroaster's theology. If he believed in only one Ahura Mazda with attributes, he was a monotheist (Zaehner's position in *Dawn and Twilight,* 50). If he believed that Ahura Mazda created other deities as aides, his system was essentially a polytheism or perhaps a henotheism (the term used by Boyce in "Zoroaster the Priest," *Bulletin of the School of Oriental and African Studies,* Vol. XXXIII, Part 1 (University of London 1970), text and footnote 83, p. 36 (hereafter cited as *BSO AS*) and in her *History of Zoroastrianism,* Vol. I, pp. 192-203.) But suppose that Yasna 30: 3, with its reference to the twin spirits means exactly what it seems to mean; in that case, his system is an ethical, theological dualism. Simple dualism becomes a dualistic polytheism, however, if aides of spiritual nature are granted to each of the two protagonists. James W. Boyd and Donald A. Crosby in a sense combine two views. They find Zoroaster saying that when historical time began, there were already the two primordial spirits, but that in the course of their struggle, Ahura Mazda will prove to be the wise and powerful victor over the ignorant and artless Angra Mainyu. What began as a dualism will, when Angra Mainyu is annihilated, have become a monotheism! Boyd and Crosby, however, nowhere discuss the status of the Amesha Spentas or their opposite numbers. See their "Is Zoroastrianism Dualistic Or Monotheistic?" in JAAR, XLVII/4, (1979), 539-555.

3. *Athravan* was the generic word for priest used in the Avestan texts. It was related to *atar*—i.e., fire, the veneration of which was a Pan-Iranian phenomenon. See Dhalla, *History,* p. 129. "Catholic Zoroastrianism" is Zaehner's term, *op. cit.,* p. 81. See pp. 79 ff. for explication of the difference between "catholic Zoroastrianism" and the prophet's "primitive Zoroastrianism."

4. Boyce, *BSO AS,* XXXIII, I (1970), 24.

5. Objectors to some part or all of this conclusion come from many quarters. Many Zoroastrians, stung by accusations that their religion is an outright polytheism, find the Gathas strictly monotheistic and are not satisfied with saying that Zoroaster "tended" toward monotheism. The priests, too—most of whom lack higher education in theology—have learned to affirm Zoroaster's monotheism; yet with few exceptions, they grant the Amesha Spentas and the Yazatas the status of subordinate deities—and this without any awareness of contradiction.

Zaehner and Boyce typify the marked difference there can be among scholars. Though Zaehner sees radical discontinuity between the "pure monotheism" of the prophet's Gathas and the unabashed polytheism of the Later Avesta, Boyce finds in both a fairly consistent "henotheism." The difference, for her, would be that Zoroaster's Gathic views are metaphysically the more exalted and his system of thought deepened by thorough-going ethicization.

It would seem that the "monotheists" may err in expecting the first real critic of an ancient polytheism to make the gigantic leap to pure monotheism all at once. At the same time, an argument such as that of Boyce distinctly underestimates the measure in which a prophet's lofty ideals are inevitably and necessarily made more concrete and common when less charismatic disciples fall heir to the task of making the faith succeed with the masses.

6. Karl F. Geldner, "Avesta Literature," *Avesta, Pahlavi, and Ancient Persian Studies,* in honor of

the late Shamo-ul-Ulama Dastur Peshotanji Sanjana, First Series, ed. by Karl J. Trubner and Otto Harassowitz (Strassburg, 1904), p. 8.

7. Yasna 44.

8. See especially Yasht 10.

9. Yasht 5.

10. Yasht 13.

11. We should add to those mentioned: Haoma, the plant-god, son of Ahura Mazda (Yasna 11), whose repeated immolation bestows immortality upon the worshippers of Mithra (Yasht 10, the hymn specifically honoring Haoma) so that he becomes, in effect, the usurper of the function of the Bountiful Immortal, Ameretat; Sraosha (the state of being obedient for Zoroaster) who in the later tradition is clearly a yazata type of deity rather confusedly conceived as both exercising some of the same essential functions as Mithra (*e.g.,* routing evil and protecting good men on earth) and as exercising these only *for* Mithra as his subordinate (Yashts 11, 12, and 10); Rashnu, another associate of Mithra whose functions overlap with his as confusedly as do those of Sraosha (Yasht 10).

12. This is Boyce's tack when, in minimizing the difference between the religion of Zoroaster and that of the Later Avesta, she says, "All religious acts in Zoroastrianism are, however, first devoted to Ahura Mazda, whatever the dedication of the particular service [for which the *Avesta* provides the liturgical text]" (*BSO AS,* XXXIII, I [1970], p. 36). But pious genuflection can be made with or without a sense of actual dependence. There are other instances as well of Boyce's inattention to the necessity of having to distinguish, from time to time, between formal theory and what *de facto* practice indicates is functioning belief.

13. As Moulton—who *did* distinguish, perhaps too puristically, between theory and practice—remarked, "The monotheistic theology is preserved, but it can hardly be said that monotheistic religion remains" (*The Treasure of the Magi,* p. 100).

14. For the dualist argument, Dhalla has pointed us to the Pahlavi tracts, chiefly the *Shikand Gumanik Vijar, Zatsparam, Dadistan-i Denik.* and *Bundahishn* (as translated in *Sacred Books of the East*). These agreed that God could not be father of both the Good Spirit and the Evil Spirit without becoming responsible for evil. Ahriman, then, had to be an independent being co-existent and at least temporally co-equal with Ohrmazd. In the end, of course, Ahriman would be vanquished and annihilated. These ideas explain why the Bounteous Spirit was subsumed in Ohrmazd; there was no logical need for him in a theology that pitted the devil directly against God (Dhalla, *History,* pp. 384-397).

15. An instance of expanding the mythological and legendary content of belief is a tract named for its author, *Arda Viraf.* It is a visionary's account of what he experienced in visiting both heaven and hell during a week-long trance.

16. Man and animals, fire, metal, earth, water, and plants. See the "roster" of the Amesha Spentas, above, p. 16, with which this list of guardian functions may be aligned. It may be noted that *reference* to the Bounteous Spirit did not entirely disappear when dualistic theology made his position superfluous, but his functions became so much those of *Vohuman* (Av. Vohu Manah, Good Mind) that there was nothing he could do that Vohuman could not do just as well.

17. The confusion persists in the Parsi community although those who have become good students of their own religion have gone back to the Avestan view of the eternal distinction between fravashis and souls. This may clarify a point in theology but, as we will see later, the amount of attention ritually bestowed on both fravashis and souls at the time of death and thereafter for as long as the dead are held in memory has prompted reformers among those students to treat ancestor-worship as a pejorative term and to accuse the orthodox of perpetuating forms that render the religion of more use to the dead than to the living.

18. See the Pahlavi works in English translation, in *Sacred Books of the East,* or Dhalla's organized description of their eschatology, *op. cit.,* pp. 407-433.

19. Dhalla, *op. cit.,* p. 289. Persons familiar with the Christian doctrine of Jesus' virgin birth, and inclined to regard it as original and unique, have this Zoroastrian doctrine—already several hundred years old when Jesus was born—to take account of. They will find it relevant to read available studies of the diffusion of ideas among Middle Eastern cultures during the centuries of first Persian and then Greek imperial rule.

20. A part of this doctrine is that Soshyans will have the aid of a number of remembered heroes of the faith. Given immortality for their bodies when they departed from the world, they will return to help in the restoration of the world to its original state of perfection. It is a notion which, as we will see, is important to Zoroastrians of the sect, Ilm-e-Khshnoom.

21. The age of 15, in pre-modern Zoroastrian times, was the rough equivalent of 20 or 21 in our more literate and technological cultures—i.e., in terms of entry into vocation, marriage, and social responsibility. Knowing that it was the same, of course, throughout the Middle East should give students a clue to understanding why Muslims took over this same motif of ages for resurrected believers when they borrowed the schematic outline of Pahlavist Zoroastrian eschatology as a general framework for their own doctrines of the last judgement and the end of history.

22. For those who are curious to know if the great Renovation will occur in their lifetime, the answer is No! Moulton used the dating derived by E.W. West from the Pahlavi texts to place the first soshyant in the 4th century A.D. and the second in the 14th century. The date suggested for the third, Soshyans, is A.D. 2398 See Moulton, *op. cit.,* p. 105.

23. Dhalla, *op. cit.,* p. 440.

24. *Ibid.,* p. 445.

25. Boyce, "Zoroastrianism," *HR* II, pp. 233 and 211.

26. See Moulton, *op. cit.* It was one of the sources I put over for perusal until I completed my first visit of investigation. Despite the frankness of Moulton's bias—he was pejorative in treating Zoroastrianism and unabashedly apologetic as a Christian—I found his principal observations strikingly identical to my own. It seemed in fact, that either his book had been mistakenly pre-dated by more than 50 years or he had placed the religion in a time capsule before he left for me to discover intact and unchanged a half-century later.

27. Boyce, "Zoroastrianism," *HR* II, pp. 233-234.

28. See Moulton, *op. cit.,* pp. 171 and 173, and Boyce, *ibid.,* p. 230. A paucity of theologians, however, should not prompt the inference that there are no critical scholars among Zoroastrians of the modern period. But with regard to this, see my observations later in this chapter.

29. Ervad Dr. M. D. Karkhanavala, B.A., M.Sc., M.S., Ph.D., "Parsis, be true Mazdayasni-Zarathoshtis," in *Memorial Volume,* Golden Jubilee of the Memorial Column at Sanjan 1920-1971 and The Birth Centenary of Late Mr. Jehangirji Jamshedji Vimadalal, ed. N. E. Turel and Prof. K.C. Sheriar (Bombay: Bombay Zoroastrian Jashan Committee, 1971), p. 94.

30. Behram D. Pithawala, "Era of Lord Zarathushtra—As deciphered from the letters in his Holy Name," *Memorial Volume, ibid.,* pp. 177-178. Internal evidence indicates the author's agreement with the esoteric beliefs of Ilm-e-Khshnoom.

31. See Boyce, "Zoroastrianism," *HR II,* p. 230.

32. Dhalla, *op. cit.,* p. 489.

33. Rustom Masani, *Zoroastrianism* (USA: The Macmillan Company, 1968).

34. *Ibid.,* pp. 48 and 64.

35. Khurshed S. Dabu, *Message of Zarathushtra* (2nd ed.; Bombay: The New Book Co., Private Ltd., 1959), pp. 20-21. The author, from 1948 to 1977 the Dastur (High Priest) of Wadiaji Atesh-Beheram, Parsi Fire-Temple of Bombay, re-affirmed these theological views in an interview on November 19, 1971, when he was the eldest of Bombay's Parsi priests in active service.

36. *Ibid.,* pp. 23-26.

37. Dabu, *A Hand-Book of Information on Zoroastrianism* (Bombay: P.N. Mehta Educational Trust, 1969), pp. 47-48 (hereafter cited as *Hand-Book*).

38. A confidant was Framroze Sorabji Chiniwalla, who attempted to explain the doctrine with exquisite confusion, in *Essential Origins of Zoroastrianism, Some Glimpses of the Mazdayasni Zarathoshti Daen in its Original Native Light of Khshnoom* (Bombay: The Parsi Vegetarian and Temperance Society of Bombay, 1942).

39. Jivanji Jamshedji Modi, *The Religious Ceremonies and Customs of the Parsees* (Bombay: British India Press, 1922), p. 67 (hereafter cited as *RCCP*).

40. See *ibid.,* p. 321.

41. *Ibid.,* p. 183.

42. P.N. Tavaria, "Khshnoom: 'Nirang'", *Parsiana,* April 1967, pp. 24-25.

43. See Chiniwalla, *op. cit.,* pp. 224-225.

44. Naigamwalla, *Zarathushtra's Glorious Faith, op. cit.,* p. 129.

45. Tavaria, "Khshnoom," *Parsiana,* February 1966, p. 25. The reader should not be surprised to learn that Zoroaster's body was not a mortal one but "of solid aura . . . lustrous and transparent." The corollary is that he could not have been martyred by another mortal but was attacked by Satan himself whose body he shattered. ". . . the Prophet's luminous body elements were [then] dispersed and drawn back to their respective ethereal regions above . . . ," but such was the shock of the attack upon him that had he "allowed it to strike against the earth, it (earth) would have been pulvarized [sic]" (p. 26).

46. Tavaria, "Khshnoom: Numerological Expression," *Parsiana,* November 1966, p. 23.

47. Tavaria, "Talismanic 81,000," *Parsiana,* May 1966, p. 25.

48. Chiniwalla's work is now out of print, and *Parsi Avaz,* an eight-page Gujarati weekly devoted to propagating the cult, ceased publication in July 1974, its circulation having fallen from 3000 when it was founded in 1947 to 600 at the end. Whether the new bimonthly, *Dini Avaz,* launched in December 1975, will attract its predecessor's lost subscribers remains to be seen. As re *Parsi Avaz,* see Pervin Mahoney, "The Sound of Silence," *Parsiana,* June-July 1974, p. 23; and for a brief account of the new publication and the interest in new classes, Sanober Marker, "Dini Avaz," *Parsiana,* February 1976, p. 31.

49. Jehangir M. Ranina, "We Parsis," *Parsiana,* February 1969, p. 7.

50. Dhalla, *op. cit.,* p. 39.

51. Dara J.D. Cama, *We Parsis, Our Prophet, and Our Priests* (Bombay, 1966), p. 11. Cama, a Bombay

real estate agent, is a lay reformer more sharp-tongued than most in his criticism of traditionalism.

52. Framroze A. Bode, "Religion and Modern Man," a Reprint from *Dipanjali,* June 1967, New Delhi, p. 4 (of reprint). Dastur Bode, one of the few reformist priests of Bombay at midcentury, has in recent years lived part-time in California, lecturing and performing outer ceremonies there as in Bombay. Although as sympathetic to Vedanta as Dastur Dabu to Theosophy, his interest lies in relating the religion adaptively to contemporary need, whereas Dabu emphasizes mainly the importance of preserving traditions intact.

53. *Ibid.*

54. Moulton, *op. cit.,* p. 170.

FURTHER READING

Criticism

Afnan, Ruhi Muhsen. *Zoroaster's Influence on Greek Thought.* New York, N.Y.: Philosophical Library, 1965, 436 p.
  Analysis of the degree to which Zoroaster and his doctrines influenced the thinking of various Greek philosophers and schools of philosophical thought, including the Milesian school; the Orphic and Pythagorean mystics; the Eleatics; Heraclitus; Protagoras; Socrates; and Plato.

Boyce, Mary. *A History of Zoroastrianism.* Leiden: E. J. Brill, 1975, 347 p.
  Historical analysis of the religious background from which Zoroastrianism arose; Zoroaster and his doctrines; and the "prehistoric period" of faith.

Carter, George William. *Zoroastrianism and Judaism.* New York, N.Y.: AMS Press, 1918, 116 p.
  Studies the way in which Zoroaster and his spiritual doctrines influenced Judaism's conception of deity, heaven, morals and ethics, and the afterlife.

Dawson, Miles Menander. *The Ethical Religion of Zoroaster.* New York, N.Y.: AMS Press, 1931, 271 p.
  Discussion of Zoroaster's teachings as an ancient and "most accurate" ethical code of conduct.

Insler, S. *The Gathas of Zarathustra.* Leiden: E. J. Brill, 1975, 387 p.
  Offers an introduction to Zoroaster's *Gathas*; a translation of the text; commentary on the text; and a glossary to the *Gathas.*

Jackson, A. V. Williams. *Zoroaster: The Prophet of Ancient Iran.* New York, N.Y.: Macmillan, 1899, 314 p.
  Reviews what is known about Zoroaster's life and recounts the legends of his birth that sprung up after Zoroaster's death; discusses events contemporary with Zoroaster's life; and surveys the beliefs of Zoroaster as presented in the *Gathas.*

Klima, Otakar. "The Date of Zoroaster." *Archiv Orientalni* 27, No. 4 (1959): 556-64.
  Examines possible sources of dating Zoroaster's life that lie outside Zoroastrian tradition.

Moulton, James Hope. *Early Zoroastrianism.* London, 1913, 463 p.
  Contains a modern English translation of the *Gathas* as well as commentaries on Zoroaster's doctrines and the development of the religion.

How to Use This Index

The main references

Calvino, Italo
    1923-1985 .... **CLC 5, 8, 11, 22, 33, 39,**
                                      73; SSC 3

---

list all author entries in the following Gale Literary Criticism series:

BLC = *Black Literature Criticism*
CLC = *Contemporary Literary Criticism*
CLR = *Children's Literature Review*
CMLC = *Classical and Medieval Literature Criticism*
DA = *DISCovering Authors*
DAB = *DISCovering Authors: British*
DAC = *DISCovering Authors: Canadian*
DAM = *DISCovering Authors: Modules*
      DRAM: Dramatists Module; *MST: Most-Studied Authors Module;*
      MULT: Multicultural Authors Module; *NOV: Novelists Module;*
      POET: Poets Module; *POP: Popular Fiction and Genre Authors Module*
DC = *Drama Criticism*
HLC = *Hispanic Literature Criticism*
LC = *Literature Criticism from 1400 to 1800*
NNAL = *Native North American Literature*
NCLC = *Nineteenth-Century Literature Criticism*
PC = *Poetry Criticism*
SSC = *Short Story Criticism*
TCLC = *Twentieth-Century Literary Criticism*
WLC = *World Literature Criticism, 1500 to the Present*

The cross-references

See also CANR 23; CA 85-88;
obituary CA116

---

list all author entries in the following Gale biographical and literary sources:

AAYA = *Authors & Artists for Young Adults*
AITN = *Authors in the News*
BEST = *Bestsellers*
BW = *Black Writers*
CA = *Contemporary Authors*
CAAS = *Contemporary Authors Autobiography Series*
CABS = *Contemporary Authors Bibliographical Series*
CANR = *Contemporary Authors New Revision Series*
CAP = *Contemporary Authors Permanent Series*
CDALB = *Concise Dictionary of American Literary Biography*
CDBLB = *Concise Dictionary of British Literary Biography*
DLB = *Dictionary of Literary Biography*
DLBD = *Dictionary of Literary Biography Documentary Series*
DLBY = *Dictionary of Literary Biography Yearbook*
HW = *Hispanic Writers*
JRDA = *Junior DISCovering Authors*
MAICYA = *Major Authors and Illustrators for Children and Young Adults*
MTCW = *Major 20th-Century Writers*
SAAS = *Something about the Author Autobiography Series*
SATA = *Something about the Author*
YABC = *Yesterday's Authors of Books for Children*

Literary Criticism Series
Cumulative Author Index

Anderson, Jessica (Margaret) Queale 1916-
CLC **37**
See also CA 9-12R; CANR 4, 62

Anderson, Jon (Victor) 1940- CLC **9; DAM POET**
See also CA 25-28R; CANR 20

Anderson, Lindsay (Gordon) 1923-1994 CLC **20**
See also CA 125; 128; 146; CANR 77

Anderson, Maxwell 1888-1959 TCLC **2; DAM DRAM**
See also CA 105; 152; DLB 7; MTCW 2

Anderson, Poul (William) 1926- CLC **15**
See also AAYA 5, 34; CA 1-4R, 181; CAAE 181; CAAS 2; CANR 2, 15, 34, 64; CLR 58; DLB 8; INT CANR-15; MTCW 1, 2; SATA 90; SATA-Brief 39; SATA-Essay 106

Anderson, Robert (Woodruff) 1917- CLC **23; DAM DRAM**
See also AITN 1; CA 21-24R; CANR 32; DLB 7

Anderson, Sherwood 1876-1941 TCLC **1, 10, 24; DA; DAB; DAC; DAM MST, NOV; SSC 1; WLC**
See also AAYA 30; CA 104; 121; CANR 61; CDALB 1917-1929; DA3; DLB 4, 9, 86; DLBD 1; MTCW 1, 2

Andier, Pierre
See Desnos, Robert

Andouard
See Giraudoux, (Hippolyte) Jean

Andrade, Carlos Drummond de CLC **18**
See also Drummond de Andrade, Carlos

Andrade, Mario de 1893-1945 TCLC **43**

Andreae, Johann V(alentin) 1586-1654 LC **32**
See also DLB 164

Andreas-Salome, Lou 1861-1937 TCLC **56**
See also CA 178; DLB 66

Andress, Lesley
See Sanders, Lawrence

Andrewes, Lancelot 1555-1626 LC **5**
See also DLB 151, 172

Andrews, Cicily Fairfield
See West, Rebecca

Andrews, Elton V.
See Pohl, Frederik

Andreyev, Leonid (Nikolaevich) 1871-1919
TCLC **3**
See also CA 104; 185

Andric, Ivo 1892-1975 CLC **8; SSC 36**
See also CA 81-84; 57-60; CANR 43, 60; DLB 147; MTCW 1

Androvar
See Prado (Calvo), Pedro

Angelique, Pierre
See Bataille, Georges

Angell, Roger 1920- CLC **26**
See also CA 57-60; CANR 13, 44, 70; DLB 171, 185

Angelou, Maya 1928- CLC **12, 35, 64, 77; BLC 1; DA; DAB; DAC; DAM MST, MULT, POET, POP; WLCS**
See also AAYA 7, 20; BW 2, 3; CA 65-68; CANR 19, 42, 65; CDALBS; CLR 53; DA3; DLB 38; MTCW 1, 2; SATA 49

Anna Comnena 1083-1153 CMLC **25**

Annensky, Innokenty (Fyodorovich)
1856-1909 TCLC **14**
See also CA 110; 155

Annunzio, Gabriele d'
See D'Annunzio, Gabriele

Anodos
See Coleridge, Mary E(lizabeth)

Anon, Charles Robert
See Pessoa, Fernando (Antonio Nogueira)

Anouilh, Jean (Marie Lucien Pierre)
1910-1987 CLC **1, 3, 8, 13, 40, 50; DAM DRAM; DC 8**
See also CA 17-20R; 123; CANR 32; MTCW 1, 2

Anthony, Florence
See Ai

Anthony, John
See Ciardi, John (Anthony)

Anthony, Peter
See Shaffer, Anthony (Joshua); Shaffer, Peter (Levin)

Anthony, Piers 1934- CLC **35; DAM POP**
See also AAYA 11; CA 21-24R; CANR 28, 56, 73; DLB 8; MTCW 1, 2; SAAS 22; SATA 84

Anthony, Susan B(rownell) 1916-1991 TCLC **84**
See also CA 89-92; 134

Antoine, Marc
See Proust, (Valentin-Louis-George-Eugene-) Marcel

Antoninus, Brother
See Everson, William (Oliver)

Antonioni, Michelangelo 1912- CLC **20**
See also CA 73-76; CANR 45, 77

Antschel, Paul 1920-1970
See Celan, Paul
See also CA 85-88; CANR 33, 61; MTCW 1

Anwar, Chairil 1922-1949 TCLC **22**
See also CA 121

Anzaldua, Gloria 1942-
See also CA 175; DLB 122; HLCS 1

Apess, William 1798-1839(?) NCLC **73; DAM MULT**
See also DLB 175; NNAL

Apollinaire, Guillaume 1880-1918 TCLC **3, 8, 51; DAM POET; PC 7**
See also Kostrowitzki, Wilhelm Apollinaris de
See also CA 152; MTCW 1

Appelfeld, Aharon 1932- CLC **23, 47**
See also CA 112; 133; CANR 86

Apple, Max (Isaac) 1941- CLC **9, 33**
See also CA 81-84; CANR 19, 54; DLB 130

Appleman, Philip (Dean) 1926- CLC **51**
See also CA 13-16R; CAAS 18; CANR 6, 29, 56

Appleton, Lawrence
See Lovecraft, H(oward) P(hillips)

Apteryx
See Eliot, T(homas) S(tearns)

Apuleius, (Lucius Madaurensis)
125(?)-175(?) CMLC **1**
See also DLB 211

Aquin, Hubert 1929-1977 CLC **15**
See also CA 105; DLB 53

Aquinas, Thomas 1224(?)-1274 CMLC **33**
See also DLB 115

Aragon, Louis 1897-1982 CLC **3, 22; DAM NOV, POET**
See also CA 69-72; 108; CANR 28, 71; DLB 72; MTCW 1, 2

Arany, Janos 1817-1882 NCLC **34**

Aranyos, Kakay
See Mikszath, Kalman

Arbuthnot, John 1667-1735 LC **1**
See also DLB 101

Archer, Herbert Winslow
See Mencken, H(enry) L(ouis)

Archer, Jeffrey (Howard) 1940- CLC **28; DAM POP**
See also AAYA 16; BEST 89:3; CA 77-80; CANR 22, 52; DA3; INT CANR-22

Archer, Jules 1915- CLC **12**
See also CA 9-12R; CANR 6, 69; SAAS 5; SATA 4, 85

Archer, Lee
See Ellison, Harlan (Jay)

Arden, John 1930- CLC **6, 13, 15; DAM DRAM**
See also CA 13-16R; CAAS 4; CANR 31, 65, 67; DLB 13; MTCW 1

Arenas, Reinaldo 1943-1990 CLC **41; DAM MULT; HLC 1**
See also CA 124; 128; 133; CANR 73; DLB 145; HW 1; MTCW 1

Arendt, Hannah 1906-1975 CLC **66, 98**
See also CA 17-20R; 61-64; CANR 26, 60; MTCW 1, 2

Aretino, Pietro 1492-1556 LC **12**

Arghezi, Tudor 1880-1967 CLC **80**
See also Theodorescu, Ion N.
See also CA 167

Arguedas, Jose Maria 1911-1969 CLC **10, 18; HLCS 1**
See also CA 89-92; CANR 73; DLB 113; HW 1

Argueta, Manlio 1936- CLC **31**
See also CA 131; CANR 73; DLB 145; HW 1

Arias, Ron(ald Francis) 1941-
See also CA 131; CANR 81; DAM MULT; DLB 82; HLC 1; HW 1, 2; MTCW 2

Ariosto, Ludovico 1474-1533 LC **6**

Aristides
See Epstein, Joseph

Aristophanes 450B.C.-385B.C. CMLC **4; DA; DAB; DAC; DAM DRAM, MST; DC 2; WLCS**
See also DA3; DLB 176

Aristotle 384B.C.-322B.C. CMLC **31; DA; DAB; DAC; DAM MST; WLCS**
See also DA3; DLB 176

Arlt, Roberto (Godofredo Christophersen)
1900-1942 TCLC **29; DAM MULT; HLC 1**
See also CA 123; 131; CANR 67; HW 1, 2

Armah, Ayi Kwei 1939- CLC **5, 33; BLC 1; DAM MULT, POET**
See also BW 1; CA 61-64; CANR 21, 64; DLB 117; MTCW 1

Armatrading, Joan 1950- CLC **17**
See also CA 114; 186

Arnette, Robert
See Silverberg, Robert

Arnim, Achim von (Ludwig Joachim von Arnim) 1781-1831 NCLC **5; SSC 29**
See also DLB 90

Arnim, Bettina von 1785-1859 NCLC **38**
See also DLB 90

Arnold, Matthew 1822-1888 NCLC **6, 29; DA; DAB; DAC; DAM MST, POET; PC 5; WLC**
See also CDBLB 1832-1890; DLB 32, 57

Arnold, Thomas 1795-1842 NCLC **18**
See also DLB 55

Arnow, Harriette (Louisa) Simpson
1908-1986 CLC **2, 7, 18**
See also CA 9-12R; 118; CANR 14; DLB 6; MTCW 1, 2; SATA 42; SATA-Obit 47

Arouet, Francois-Marie
See Voltaire

Arp, Hans
See Arp, Jean

Arp, Jean 1887-1966 CLC **5**
See also CA 81-84; 25-28R; CANR 42, 77

Arrabal
See Arrabal, Fernando

Arrabal, Fernando 1932- CLC **2, 9, 18, 58**
See also CA 9-12R; CANR 15

Arreola, Juan Jose 1918- SSC **38; DAM MULT; HLC 1**
See also CA 113; 131; CANR 81; DLB 113; HW 1, 2

Arrick, Fran CLC **30**

See also Gaberman, Judie Angell

Artaud, Antonin (Marie Joseph) 1896-1948
TCLC 3, 36; DAM DRAM
See also CA 104; 149; DA3; MTCW 1

Arthur, Ruth M(abel) 1905-1979 **CLC 12**
See also CA 9-12R; 85-88; CANR 4; SATA
7, 26

Artsybashev, Mikhail (Petrovich) 1878-1927
TCLC 31
See also CA 170

Arundel, Honor (Morfydd) 1919-1973 **CLC
17**
See also CA 21-22; 41-44R; CAP 2; CLR
35; SATA 4; SATA-Obit 24

Arzner, Dorothy 1897-1979 **CLC 98**

Asch, Sholem 1880-1957 **TCLC 3**
See also CA 105

Ash, Shalom
See Asch, Sholem

Ashbery, John (Lawrence) 1927- **CLC 2, 3,
4, 6, 9, 13, 15, 25, 41, 77, 125; DAM
POET; PC 26**
See also CA 5-8R; CANR 9, 37, 66; DA3;
DLB 5, 165; DLBY 81; INT CANR-9;
MTCW 1, 2

Ashdown, Clifford
See Freeman, R(ichard) Austin

Ashe, Gordon
See Creasey, John

Ashton-Warner, Sylvia (Constance)
1908-1984 **CLC 19**
See also CA 69-72; 112; CANR 29; MTCW
1, 2

Asimov, Isaac 1920-1992 **CLC 1, 3, 9, 19, 26,
76, 92; DAM POP**
See also AAYA 13; BEST 90:2; CA 1-4R;
137; CANR 2, 19, 36, 60; CLR 12; DA3;
DLB 8; DLBY 92; INT CANR-19; JRDA;
MAICYA; MTCW 1, 2; SATA 1, 26, 74

Assis, Joaquim Maria Machado de
See Machado de Assis, Joaquim Maria

Astley, Thea (Beatrice May) 1925- **CLC 41**
See also CA 65-68; CANR 11, 43, 78

Aston, James
See White, T(erence) H(anbury)

Asturias, Miguel Angel 1899-1974 **CLC 3, 8,
13; DAM MULT, NOV; HLC 1**
See also CA 25-28; 49-52; CANR 32; CAP
2; DA3; DLB 113; HW 1; MTCW 1, 2

Atares, Carlos Saura
See Saura (Atares), Carlos

Atheling, William
See Pound, Ezra (Weston Loomis)

Atheling, William, Jr.
See Blish, James (Benjamin)

Atherton, Gertrude (Franklin Horn)
1857-1948 **TCLC 2**
See also CA 104; 155; DLB 9, 78, 186

Atherton, Lucius
See Masters, Edgar Lee

Atkins, Jack
See Harris, Mark

Atkinson, Kate CLC 99
See also CA 166

Attaway, William (Alexander) 1911-1986
CLC 92; BLC 1; DAM MULT
See also BW 2, 3; CA 143; CANR 82; DLB
76

Atticus
See Fleming, Ian (Lancaster); Wilson,
(Thomas) Woodrow

Atwood, Margaret (Eleanor) 1939- **CLC 2, 3,
4, 8, 13, 15, 25, 44, 84; DA; DAB; DAC;
DAM MST, NOV, POET; PC 8; SSC 2;
WLC**
See also AAYA 12; BEST 89:2; CA 49-52;
CANR 3, 24, 33, 59; DA3; DLB 53; INT
CANR-24; MTCW 1, 2; SATA 50

Aubigny, Pierre d'
See Mencken, H(enry) L(ouis)

Aubin, Penelope 1685-1731(?) **LC 9**
See also DLB 39

Auchincloss, Louis (Stanton) 1917- **CLC 4, 6,
9, 18, 45; DAM NOV; SSC 22**
See also CA 1-4R; CANR 6, 29, 55, 87;
DLB 2; DLBY 80; INT CANR-29;
MTCW 1

Auden, W(ystan) H(ugh) 1907-1973 **CLC 1,
2, 3, 4, 6, 9, 11, 14, 43; DA; DAB; DAC;
DAM DRAM, MST, POET; PC 1; WLC**
See also AAYA 18; CA 9-12R; 45-48;
CANR 5, 61; CDBLB 1914-1945; DA3;
DLB 10, 20; MTCW 1, 2

Audiberti, Jacques 1900-1965 **CLC 38; DAM
DRAM**
See also CA 25-28R

Audubon, John James 1785-1851 **NCLC 47**

Auel, Jean M(arie) 1936- **CLC 31, 107; DAM
POP**
See also AAYA 7; BEST 90:4; CA 103;
CANR 21, 64; DA3; INT CANR-21;
SATA 91

Auerbach, Erich 1892-1957 **TCLC 43**
See also CA 118; 155

Augier, Emile 1820-1889 **NCLC 31**
See also DLB 192

August, John
See De Voto, Bernard (Augustine)

Augustine 354-430 **CMLC 6; DA; DAB;
DAC; DAM MST; WLCS**
See also DA3; DLB 115

Aurelius
See Bourne, Randolph S(illiman)

Aurobindo, Sri
See Ghose, Aurabinda

Austen, Jane 1775-1817 **NCLC 1, 13, 19, 33,
51, 81; DA; DAB; DAC; DAM MST,
NOV; WLC**
See also AAYA 19; CDBLB 1789-1832;
DA3; DLB 116

Auster, Paul 1947- **CLC 47, 131**
See also CA 69-72; CANR 23, 52, 75; DA3;
MTCW 1

Austin, Frank
See Faust, Frederick (Schiller)

Austin, Mary (Hunter) 1868-1934 **TCLC 25**
See also CA 109; 178; DLB 9, 78, 206, 221

Averroes 1126-1198 **CMLC 7**
See also DLB 115

Avicenna 980-1037 **CMLC 16**
See also DLB 115

Avison, Margaret 1918- **CLC 2, 4, 97; DAC;
DAM POET**
See also CA 17-20R; DLB 53; MTCW 1

Axton, David
See Koontz, Dean R(ay)

Ayckbourn, Alan 1939- **CLC 5, 8, 18, 33, 74;
DAB; DAM DRAM**
See also CA 21-24R; CANR 31, 59; DLB
13; MTCW 1, 2

Aydy, Catherine
See Tennant, Emma (Christina)

Ayme, Marcel (Andre) 1902-1967 **CLC 11**
See also CA 89-92; CANR 67; CLR 25;
DLB 72; SATA 91

Ayrton, Michael 1921-1975 **CLC 7**
See also CA 5-8R; 61-64; CANR 9, 21

Azorin CLC 11
See also Martinez Ruiz, Jose

Azuela, Mariano 1873-1952 **TCLC 3; DAM
MULT; HLC 1**
See also CA 104; 131; CANR 81; HW 1, 2;
MTCW 1, 2

Baastad, Babbis Friis
See Friis-Baastad, Babbis Ellinor

Bab
See Gilbert, W(illiam) S(chwenck)

Babbis, Eleanor
See Friis-Baastad, Babbis Ellinor

Babel, Isaac
See Babel, Isaak (Emmanuilovich)

Babel, Isaak (Emmanuilovich) 1894-1941(?)
TCLC 2, 13; SSC 16
See also CA 104; 155; MTCW 1

Babits, Mihaly 1883-1941 **TCLC 14**
See also CA 114

Babur 1483-1530 **LC 18**

Baca, Jimmy Santiago 1952-
See also CA 131; CANR 81, 90; DAM
MULT; DLB 122; HLC 1; HW 1, 2

Bacchelli, Riccardo 1891-1985 **CLC 19**
See also CA 29-32R; 117

Bach, Richard (David) 1936- **CLC 14; DAM
NOV, POP**
See also AITN 1; BEST 89:2; CA 9-12R;
CANR 18; MTCW 1; SATA 13

Bachman, Richard
See King, Stephen (Edwin)

Bachmann, Ingeborg 1926-1973 **CLC 69**
See also CA 93-96; 45-48; CANR 69; DLB
85

Bacon, Francis 1561-1626 **LC 18, 32**
See also CDBLB Before 1660; DLB 151

Bacon, Roger 1214(?)-1292 **CMLC 14**
See also DLB 115

Bacovia, George TCLC 24
See also Vasiliu, Gheorghe
See also DLB 220

Badanes, Jerome 1937- **CLC 59**

Bagehot, Walter 1826-1877 **NCLC 10**
See also DLB 55

Bagnold, Enid 1889-1981 **CLC 25; DAM
DRAM**
See also CA 5-8R; 103; CANR 5, 40; DLB
13, 160, 191; MAICYA; SATA 1, 25

Bagritsky, Eduard 1895-1934 **TCLC 60**

Bagrjana, Elisaveta
See Belcheva, Elisaveta

Bagryana, Elisaveta 1893-1991 **CLC 10**
See also Belcheva, Elisaveta
See also CA 178; DLB 147

Bailey, Paul 1937- **CLC 45**
See also CA 21-24R; CANR 16, 62; DLB
14

Baillie, Joanna 1762-1851 **NCLC 71**
See also DLB 93

Bainbridge, Beryl (Margaret) 1934- **CLC 4,
5, 8, 10, 14, 18, 22, 62, 130; DAM NOV**
See also CA 21-24R; CANR 24, 55, 75, 88;
DLB 14; MTCW 1, 2

Baker, Elliott 1922- **CLC 8**
See also CA 45-48; CANR 2, 63

Baker, Jean H. TCLC 3, 10
See also Russell, George William

Baker, Nicholson 1957- **CLC 61; DAM POP**
See also CA 135; CANR 63; DA3

Baker, Ray Stannard 1870-1946 **TCLC 47**
See also CA 118

Baker, Russell (Wayne) 1925- **CLC 31**
See also BEST 89:4; CA 57-60; CANR 11,
41, 59; MTCW 1, 2

Bakhtin, M.
See Bakhtin, Mikhail Mikhailovich

Bakhtin, M. M.
See Bakhtin, Mikhail Mikhailovich

Bakhtin, Mikhail
See Bakhtin, Mikhail Mikhailovich

Bakhtin, Mikhail Mikhailovich 1895-1975
CLC 83
See also CA 128; 113

Bakshi, Ralph 1938(?)- **CLC 26**
See also CA 112; 138

Bakunin, Mikhail (Alexandrovich)
1814-1876 **NCLC 25, 58**

Baldwin, James (Arthur) 1924-1987 **CLC 1,**

2, 3, 4, 5, 8, 13, 15, 17, 42, 50, 67, 90,
127; BLC 1; DA; DAB; DAC; DAM
MST, MULT, NOV, POP; DC 1; SSC
10, 33; WLC
See also AAYA 4, 34; BW 1; CA 1-4R; 124;
CABS 1; CANR 3, 24; CDALB 1941-
1968; DA3; DLB 2, 7, 33; DLBY 87;
MTCW 1, 2; SATA 9; SATA-Obit 54

Ballard, J(ames) G(raham) 1930- **CLC 3, 6,
14, 36; DAM NOV, POP; SSC 1**
See also AAYA 3; CA 5-8R; CANR 15, 39,
65; DA3; DLB 14, 207; MTCW 1, 2;
SATA 93

Balmont, Konstantin (Dmitriyevich)
1867-1943 **TCLC 11**
See also CA 109; 155

Baltausis, Vincas
See Mikszath, Kalman

Balzac, Honore de 1799-1850 **NCLC 5, 35,
53; DA; DAB; DAC; DAM MST, NOV;
SSC 5; WLC**
See also DA3; DLB 119

Bambara, Toni Cade 1939-1995 **CLC 19, 88;
BLC 1; DA; DAC; DAM MST, MULT;
SSC 35; WLCS**
See also AAYA 5; BW 2, 3; CA 29-32R;
150; CANR 24, 49, 81; CDALBS; DA3;
DLB 38; MTCW 1, 2; SATA 112

Bamdad, A.
See Shamlu, Ahmad

Banat, D. R.
See Bradbury, Ray (Douglas)

Bancroft, Laura
See Baum, L(yman) Frank

Banim, John 1798-1842 **NCLC 13**
See also DLB 116, 158, 159

Banim, Michael 1796-1874 **NCLC 13**
See also DLB 158, 159

Banjo, The
See Paterson, A(ndrew) B(arton)

Banks, Iain
See Banks, Iain M(enzies)

Banks, Iain M(enzies) 1954- **CLC 34**
See also CA 123; 128; CANR 61; DLB 194;
INT 128

Banks, Lynne Reid CLC 23
See also Reid Banks, Lynne
See also AAYA 6

Banks, Russell 1940- **CLC 37, 72**
See also CA 65-68; CAAS 15; CANR 19,
52, 73; DLB 130

Banville, John 1945- **CLC 46, 118**
See also CA 117; 128; DLB 14; INT 128

Banville, Theodore (Faullain) de 1832-1891
NCLC 9

Baraka, Amiri 1934- **CLC 1, 2, 3, 5, 10, 14,
33, 115; BLC 1; DA; DAC; DAM MST,
MULT, POET, POP; DC 6; PC 4;
WLCS**
See also Jones, LeRoi
See also BW 2, 3; CA 21-24R; CABS 3;
CANR 27, 38, 61; CDALB 1941-1968;
DA3; DLB 5, 7, 16, 38; DLBD 8; MTCW
1, 2

Barbauld, Anna Laetitia 1743-1825 **NCLC
50**
See also DLB 107, 109, 142, 158

Barbellion, W. N. P. TCLC 24
See also Cummings, Bruce F(rederick)

Barbera, Jack (Vincent) 1945- **CLC 44**
See also CA 110; CANR 45

Barbey d'Aurevilly, Jules Amedee 1808-1889
NCLC 1; SSC 17
See also DLB 119

Barbour, John c. 1316-1395 **CMLC 33**
See also DLB 146

Barbusse, Henri 1873-1935 **TCLC 5**
See also CA 105; 154; DLB 65

Barclay, Bill
See Moorcock, Michael (John)

Barclay, William Ewert
See Moorcock, Michael (John)

Barea, Arturo 1897-1957 **TCLC 14**
See also CA 111

Barfoot, Joan 1946- **CLC 18**
See also CA 105

Barham, Richard Harris 1788-1845 **NCLC
77**
See also DLB 159

Baring, Maurice 1874-1945 **TCLC 8**
See also CA 105; 168; DLB 34

Baring-Gould, Sabine 1834-1924 **TCLC 88**
See also DLB 156, 190

Barker, Clive 1952- **CLC 52; DAM POP**
See also AAYA 10; BEST 90:3; CA 121;
129; CANR 71; DA3; INT 129; MTCW
1, 2

Barker, George Granville 1913-1991 **CLC 8,
48; DAM POET**
See also CA 9-12R; 135; CANR 7, 38; DLB
20; MTCW 1

Barker, Harley Granville
See Granville-Barker, Harley
See also DLB 10

Barker, Howard 1946- **CLC 37**
See also CA 102; DLB 13

Barker, Jane 1652-1732 **LC 42**

Barker, Pat(ricia) 1943- **CLC 32, 94**
See also CA 117; 122; CANR 50; INT 122

Barlach, Ernst (Heinrich) 1870-1938 **TCLC
84**
See also CA 178; DLB 56, 118

Barlow, Joel 1754-1812 **NCLC 23**
See also DLB 37

Barnard, Mary (Ethel) 1909- **CLC 48**
See also CA 21-22; CAP 2

Barnes, Djuna 1892-1982 **CLC 3, 4, 8, 11, 29,
127; SSC 3**
See also CA 9-12R; 107; CANR 16, 55;
DLB 4, 9, 45; MTCW 1, 2

Barnes, Julian (Patrick) 1946- **CLC 42; DAB**
See also CA 102; CANR 19, 54; DLB 194;
DLBY 93; MTCW 1

Barnes, Peter 1931- **CLC 5, 56**
See also CA 65-68; CAAS 12; CANR 33,
34, 64; DLB 13; MTCW 1

Barnes, William 1801-1886 **NCLC 75**
See also DLB 32

Baroja (y Nessi), Pio 1872-1956 **TCLC 8;
HLC 1**
See also CA 104

Baron, David
See Pinter, Harold

Baron Corvo
See Rolfe, Frederick (William Serafino
Austin Lewis Mary)

Barondess, Sue K(aufman) 1926-1977 **CLC 8**
See also Kaufman, Sue
See also CA 1-4R; 69-72; CANR 1

Baron de Teive
See Pessoa, Fernando (Antonio Nogueira)

Baroness Von S.
See Zangwill, Israel

Barres, (Auguste-) Maurice 1862-1923 **TCLC
47**
See also CA 164; DLB 123

Barreto, Afonso Henrique de Lima
See Lima Barreto, Afonso Henrique de

Barrett, (Roger) Syd 1946- **CLC 35**

Barrett, William (Christopher) 1913-1992
CLC 27
See also CA 13-16R; 139; CANR 11, 67;
INT CANR-11

Barrie, J(ames) M(atthew) 1860-1937 **TCLC
2; DAB; DAM DRAM**

See also CA 104; 136; CANR 77; CDBLB
1890-1914; CLR 16; DA3; DLB 10, 141,
156; MAICYA; MTCW 1; SATA 100;
YABC 1

Barrington, Michael
See Moorcock, Michael (John)

Barrol, Grady
See Bograd, Larry

Barry, Mike
See Malzberg, Barry N(athaniel)

Barry, Philip 1896-1949 **TCLC 11**
See also CA 109; DLB 7

Bart, Andre Schwarz
See Schwarz-Bart, Andre

Barth, John (Simmons) 1930- **CLC 1, 2, 3, 5,
7, 9, 10, 14, 27, 51, 89; DAM NOV; SSC
10**
See also AITN 1, 2; CA 1-4R; CABS 1;
CANR 5, 23, 49, 64; DLB 2; MTCW 1

Barthelme, Donald 1931-1989 **CLC 1, 2, 3, 5,
6, 8, 13, 23, 46, 59, 115; DAM NOV;
SSC 2**
See also CA 21-24R; 129; CANR 20, 58;
DA3; DLB 2; DLBY 80, 89; MTCW 1, 2;
SATA 7; SATA-Obit 62

Barthelme, Frederick 1943- **CLC 36, 117**
See also CA 114; 122; CANR 77; DLBY
85; INT 122

Barthes, Roland (Gerard) 1915-1980 **CLC
24, 83**
See also CA 130; 97-100; CANR 66;
MTCW 1, 2

Barzun, Jacques (Martin) 1907- **CLC 51**
See also CA 61-64; CANR 22

Bashevis, Isaac
See Singer, Isaac Bashevis

Bashkirtseff, Marie 1859-1884 **NCLC 27**

Basho
See Matsuo Basho

Basil of Caesaria c. 330-379 **CMLC 35**

Bass, Kingsley B., Jr.
See Bullins, Ed

Bass, Rick 1958- **CLC 79**
See also CA 126; CANR 53; DLB 212

Bassani, Giorgio 1916- **CLC 9**
See also CA 65-68; CANR 33; DLB 128,
177; MTCW 1

Bastos, Augusto (Antonio) Roa
See Roa Bastos, Augusto (Antonio)

Bataille, Georges 1897-1962 **CLC 29**
See also CA 101; 89-92

Bates, H(erbert) E(rnest) 1905-1974 **CLC 46;
DAB; DAM POP; SSC 10**
See also CA 93-96; 45-48; CANR 34; DA3;
DLB 162, 191; MTCW 1, 2

Bauchart
See Camus, Albert

Baudelaire, Charles 1821-1867 **NCLC 6, 29,
55; DA; DAB; DAC; DAM MST,
POET; PC 1; SSC 18; WLC**
See also DA3

Baudrillard, Jean 1929- **CLC 60**

Baum, L(yman) Frank 1856-1919 **TCLC 7**
See also CA 108; 133; CLR 15; DLB 22;
JRDA; MAICYA; MTCW 1, 2; SATA 18,
100

Baum, Louis F.
See Baum, L(yman) Frank

Baumbach, Jonathan 1933- **CLC 6, 23**
See also CA 13-16R; CAAS 5; CANR 12,
66; DLBY 80; INT CANR-12; MTCW 1

Bausch, Richard (Carl) 1945- **CLC 51**
See also CA 101; CAAS 14; CANR 43, 61,
87; DLB 130

Baxter, Charles (Morley) 1947- **CLC 45, 78;
DAM POP**
See also CA 57-60; CANR 40, 64; DLB
130; MTCW 2

See also AAYA 10; CA 69-72; CANR 11,
42, 79; JRDA; SAAS 4; SATA 41, 87;
SATA-Brief 27

Bennett, Louise (Simone) 1919- **CLC 28;**
BLC 1; DAM MULT
See also BW 2, 3; CA 151; DLB 117

Benson, E(dward) F(rederic) 1867-1940
TCLC 27
See also CA 114; 157; DLB 135, 153

Benson, Jackson J. 1930- **CLC 34**
See also CA 25-28R; DLB 111

Benson, Sally 1900-1972 **CLC 17**
See also CA 19-20; 37-40R; CAP 1; SATA
1, 35; SATA-Obit 27

Benson, Stella 1892-1933 **TCLC 17**
See also CA 117; 155; DLB 36, 162

Bentham, Jeremy 1748-1832 **NCLC 38**
See also DLB 107, 158

Bentley, E(dmund) C(lerihew) 1875-1956
TCLC 12
See also CA 108; DLB 70

Bentley, Eric (Russell) 1916- **CLC 24**
See also CA 5-8R; CANR 6, 67; INT
CANR-6

Beranger, Pierre Jean de 1780-1857 **NCLC
34**

Berdyaev, Nicolas
See Berdyaev, Nikolai (Aleksandrovich)

Berdyaev, Nikolai (Aleksandrovich)
1874-1948 **TCLC 67**
See also CA 120; 157

Berdyayev, Nikolai (Aleksandrovich)
See Berdyaev, Nikolai (Aleksandrovich)

Berendt, John (Lawrence) 1939- **CLC 86**
See also CA 146; CANR 75; DA3; MTCW
1

Beresford, J(ohn) D(avys) 1873-1947 **TCLC
81**
See also CA 112; 155; DLB 162, 178, 197

Bergelson, David 1884-1952 **TCLC 81**

Berger, Colonel
See Malraux, (Georges-)Andre

Berger, John (Peter) 1926- **CLC 2, 19**
See also CA 81-84; CANR 51, 78; DLB 14,
207

Berger, Melvin H. 1927- **CLC 12**
See also CA 5-8R; CANR 4; CLR 32;
SAAS 2; SATA 5, 88

Berger, Thomas (Louis) 1924- **CLC 3, 5, 8,
11, 18, 38; DAM NOV**
See also CA 1-4R; CANR 5, 28, 51; DLB
2; DLBY 80; INT CANR-28; MTCW 1, 2

Bergman, (Ernst) Ingmar 1918- **CLC 16, 72**
See also CA 81-84; CANR 33, 70; MTCW
2

Bergson, Henri(-Louis) 1859-1941 **TCLC 32**
See also CA 164

Bergstein, Eleanor 1938- **CLC 4**
See also CA 53-56; CANR 5

Berkoff, Steven 1937- **CLC 56**
See also CA 104; CANR 72

Bermant, Chaim (Icyk) 1929- **CLC 40**
See also CA 57-60; CANR 6, 31, 57

Bern, Victoria
See Fisher, M(ary) F(rances) K(ennedy)

Bernanos, (Paul Louis) Georges 1888-1948
TCLC 3
See also CA 104; 130; DLB 72

Bernard, April 1956- **CLC 59**
See also CA 131

Berne, Victoria
See Fisher, M(ary) F(rances) K(ennedy)

Bernhard, Thomas 1931-1989 **CLC 3, 32, 61**
See also CA 85-88; 127; CANR 32, 57;
DLB 85, 124; MTCW 1

Bernhardt, Sarah (Henriette Rosine)
1844-1923 **TCLC 75**
See also CA 157

Berriault, Gina 1926-1999 **CLC 54, 109; SSC
30**
See also CA 116; 129; 185; CANR 66; DLB
130

Berrigan, Daniel 1921- **CLC 4**
See also CA 33-36R; CAAS 1; CANR 11,
43, 78; DLB 5

Berrigan, Edmund Joseph Michael, Jr.
1934-1983
See Berrigan, Ted
See also CA 61-64; 110; CANR 14

Berrigan, Ted CLC 37
See also Berrigan, Edmund Joseph Michael,
Jr.
See also DLB 5, 169

Berry, Charles Edward Anderson 1931-
See Berry, Chuck
See also CA 115

Berry, Chuck CLC 17
See also Berry, Charles Edward Anderson

Berry, Jonas
See Ashbery, John (Lawrence)

Berry, Wendell (Erdman) 1934- **CLC 4, 6, 8,
27, 46; DAM POET; PC 28**
See also AITN 1; CA 73-76; CANR 50, 73;
DLB 5, 6; MTCW 1

Berryman, John 1914-1972 **CLC 1, 2, 3, 4, 6,
8, 10, 13, 25, 62; DAM POET**
See also CA 13-16; 33-36R; CABS 2;
CANR 35; CAP 1; CDALB 1941-1968;
DLB 48; MTCW 1, 2

Bertolucci, Bernardo 1940- **CLC 16**
See also CA 106

Berton, Pierre (Francis Demarigny) 1920-
CLC 104
See also CA 1-4R; CANR 2, 56; DLB 68;
SATA 99

Bertrand, Aloysius 1807-1841 **NCLC 31**

Bertran de Born c. 1140-1215 **CMLC 5**

Besant, Annie (Wood) 1847-1933 **TCLC 9**
See also CA 105; 185

Bessie, Alvah 1904-1985 **CLC 23**
See also CA 5-8R; 116; CANR 2, 80; DLB
26

Bethlen, T. D.
See Silverberg, Robert

Beti, Mongo CLC 27; BLC 1; DAM MULT
See also Biyidi, Alexandre
See also CANR 79

Betjeman, John 1906-1984 **CLC 2, 6, 10, 34,
43; DAB; DAM MST, POET**
See also CA 9-12R; 112; CANR 33, 56;
CDBLB 1945-1960; DA3; DLB 20;
DLBY 84; MTCW 1, 2

Bettelheim, Bruno 1903-1990 **CLC 79**
See also CA 81-84; 131; CANR 23, 61;
DA3; MTCW 1, 2

Betti, Ugo 1892-1953 **TCLC 5**
See also CA 104; 155

Betts, Doris (Waugh) 1932- **CLC 3, 6, 28**
See also CA 13-16R; CANR 9, 66, 77;
DLBY 82; INT CANR-9

Bevan, Alistair
See Roberts, Keith (John Kingston)

Bey, Pilaff
See Douglas, (George) Norman

Bialik, Chaim Nachman 1873-1934 **TCLC 25**
See also CA 170

Bickerstaff, Isaac
See Swift, Jonathan

Bidart, Frank 1939- **CLC 33**
See also CA 140

Bienek, Horst 1930- **CLC 7, 11**
See also CA 73-76; DLB 75

Bierce, Ambrose (Gwinett) 1842-1914(?)
**TCLC 1, 7, 44; DA; DAC; DAM MST;
SSC 9; WLC**

See also CA 104; 139; CANR 78; CDALB
1865-1917; DA3; DLB 11, 12, 23, 71, 74,
186

Biggers, Earl Derr 1884-1933 **TCLC 65**
See also CA 108; 153

Billings, Josh
See Shaw, Henry Wheeler

Billington, (Lady) Rachel (Mary) 1942- **CLC
43**
See also AITN 2; CA 33-36R; CANR 44

Binyon, T(imothy) J(ohn) 1936- **CLC 34**
See also CA 111; CANR 28

Bion 335B.C.-245B.C. **CMLC 39**

Bioy Casares, Adolfo 1914-1999 **CLC 4, 8,
13, 88; DAM MULT; HLC 1; SSC 17**
See also CA 29-32R; 177; CANR 19, 43,
66; DLB 113; HW 1, 2; MTCW 1, 2

Bird, Cordwainer
See Ellison, Harlan (Jay)

Bird, Robert Montgomery 1806-1854 **NCLC
1**
See also DLB 202

Birkerts, Sven 1951- **CLC 116**
See also CA 128; 133; 176; CAAE 176;
CAAS 29; INT 133

Birney, (Alfred) Earle 1904-1995 **CLC 1, 4,
6, 11; DAC; DAM MST, POET**
See also CA 1-4R; CANR 5, 20; DLB 88;
MTCW 1

Biruni, al 973-1048(?) **CMLC 28**

Bishop, Elizabeth 1911-1979 **CLC 1, 4, 9, 13,
15, 32; DA; DAC; DAM MST, POET;
PC 3**
See also CA 5-8R; 89-92; CABS 2; CANR
26, 61; CDALB 1968-1988; DA3; DLB
5, 169; MTCW 1, 2; SATA-Obit 24

Bishop, John 1935- **CLC 10**
See also CA 105

Bissett, Bill 1939- **CLC 18; PC 14**
See also CA 69-72; CAAS 19; CANR 15;
DLB 53; MTCW 1

Bissoondath, Neil (Devindra) 1955- **CLC 120;
DAC**
See also CA 136

Bitov, Andrei (Georgievich) 1937- **CLC 57**
See also CA 142

Biyidi, Alexandre 1932-
See Beti, Mongo
See also BW 1, 3; CA 114; 124; CANR 81;
DA3; MTCW 1, 2

Bjarme, Brynjolf
See Ibsen, Henrik (Johan)

Bjoernson, Bjoernstjerne (Martinius)
1832-1910 **TCLC 7, 37**
See also CA 104

Black, Robert
See Holdstock, Robert P.

Blackburn, Paul 1926-1971 **CLC 9, 43**
See also CA 81-84; 33-36R; CANR 34;
DLB 16; DLBY 81

Black Elk 1863-1950 **TCLC 33; DAM MULT**
See also CA 144; MTCW 1; NNAL

Black Hobart
See Sanders, (James) Ed(ward)

Blacklin, Malcolm
See Chambers, Aidan

Blackmore, R(ichard) D(oddridge)
1825-1900 **TCLC 27**
See also CA 120; DLB 18

Blackmur, R(ichard) P(almer) 1904-1965
CLC 2, 24
See also CA 11-12; 25-28R; CANR 71;
CAP 1; DLB 63

Black Tarantula
See Acker, Kathy

Blackwood, Algernon (Henry) 1869-1951
TCLC 5
See also CA 105; 150; DLB 153, 156, 178

Bowles, Paul (Frederick) 1910-1999 **CLC 1, 2, 19, 53; SSC 3**
See also CA 1-4R; 186; CAAS 1; CANR 1, 19, 50, 75; DA3; DLB 5, 6; MTCW 1, 2

Box, Edgar
See Vidal, Gore

Boyd, Nancy
See Millay, Edna St. Vincent

Boyd, William 1952- **CLC 28, 53, 70**
See also CA 114; 120; CANR 51, 71

Boyle, Kay 1902-1992 **CLC 1, 5, 19, 58, 121; SSC 5**
See also CA 13-16R; 140; CAAS 1; CANR 29, 61; DLB 4, 9, 48, 86; DLBY 93; MTCW 1, 2

Boyle, Mark
See Kienzle, William X(avier)

Boyle, Patrick 1905-1982 **CLC 19**
See also CA 127

Boyle, T. C. 1948-
See Boyle, T(homas) Coraghessan

Boyle, T(homas) Coraghessan 1948- **CLC 36, 55, 90; DAM POP; SSC 16**
See also BEST 90:4; CA 120; CANR 44, 76, 89; DA3; DLBY 86; MTCW 2

Boz
See Dickens, Charles (John Huffam)

Brackenridge, Hugh Henry 1748-1816 **NCLC 7**
See also DLB 11, 37

Bradbury, Edward P.
See Moorcock, Michael (John)
See also MTCW 2

Bradbury, Malcolm (Stanley) 1932- **CLC 32, 61; DAM NOV**
See also CA 1-4R; CANR 1, 33, 91; DA3; DLB 14, 207; MTCW 1, 2

Bradbury, Ray (Douglas) 1920- **CLC 1, 3, 10, 15, 42, 98; DA; DAB; DAC; DAM MST, NOV, POP; SSC 29; WLC**
See also AAYA 15; AITN 1, 2; CA 1-4R; CANR 2, 30, 75; CDALB 1968-1988; DA3; DLB 2, 8; MTCW 1, 2; SATA 11, 64

Bradford, Gamaliel 1863-1932 **TCLC 36**
See also CA 160; DLB 17

Bradley, David (Henry), Jr. 1950- **CLC 23, 118; BLC 1; DAM MULT**
See also BW 1, 3; CA 104; CANR 26, 81; DLB 33

Bradley, John Ed(mund, Jr.) 1958- **CLC 55**
See also CA 139

Bradley, Marion Zimmer 1930-1999 **CLC 30; DAM POP**
See also AAYA 9; CA 57-60; 185; CAAS 10; CANR 7, 31, 51, 75; DA3; DLB 8; MTCW 1, 2; SATA 90; SATA-Obit 116

Bradstreet, Anne 1612(?)-1672 **LC 4, 30; DA; DAC; DAM MST, POET; PC 10**
See also CDALB 1640-1865; DA3; DLB 24

Brady, Joan 1939- **CLC 86**
See also CA 141

Bragg, Melvyn 1939- **CLC 10**
See also BEST 89:3; CA 57-60; CANR 10, 48, 89; DLB 14

Brahe, Tycho 1546-1601 **LC 45**

Braine, John (Gerard) 1922-1986 **CLC 1, 3, 41**
See also CA 1-4R; 120; CANR 1, 33; CD-BLB 1945-1960; DLB 15; DLBY 86; MTCW 1

Bramah, Ernest 1868-1942 **TCLC 72**
See also CA 156; DLB 70

Brammer, William 1930(?)-1978 **CLC 31**
See also CA 77-80

Brancati, Vitaliano 1907-1954 **TCLC 12**
See also CA 109

Brancato, Robin F(idler) 1936- **CLC 35**

See also AAYA 9; CA 69-72; CANR 11, 45; CLR 32; JRDA; SAAS 9; SATA 97

Brand, Max
See Faust, Frederick (Schiller)

Brand, Millen 1906-1980 **CLC 7**
See also CA 21-24R; 97-100; CANR 72

Branden, Barbara CLC 44
See also CA 148

Brandes, Georg (Morris Cohen) 1842-1927 **TCLC 10**
See also CA 105

Brandys, Kazimierz 1916- **CLC 62**

Branley, Franklyn M(ansfield) 1915- **CLC 21**
See also CA 33-36R; CANR 14, 39; CLR 13; MAICYA; SAAS 16; SATA 4, 68

Brathwaite, Edward (Kamau) 1930- **CLC 11; BLCS; DAM POET**
See also BW 2, 3; CA 25-28R; CANR 11, 26, 47; DLB 125

Brautigan, Richard (Gary) 1935-1984 **CLC 1, 3, 5, 9, 12, 34, 42; DAM NOV**
See also CA 53-56; 113; CANR 34; DA3; DLB 2, 5, 206; DLBY 80, 84; MTCW 1; SATA 56

Brave Bird, Mary 1953-
See Crow Dog, Mary (Ellen)
See also NNAL

Braverman, Kate 1950- **CLC 67**
See also CA 89-92

Brecht, (Eugen) Bertolt (Friedrich) 1898-1956 **TCLC 1, 6, 13, 35; DA; DAB; DAC; DAM DRAM, MST; DC 3; WLC**
See also CA 104; 133; CANR 62; DA3; DLB 56, 124; MTCW 1, 2

Brecht, Eugen Berthold Friedrich
See Brecht, (Eugen) Bertolt (Friedrich)

Bremer, Fredrika 1801-1865 **NCLC 11**

Brennan, Christopher John 1870-1932 **TCLC 17**
See also CA 117

Brennan, Maeve 1917-1993 **CLC 5**
See also CA 81-84; CANR 72

Brent, Linda
See Jacobs, Harriet A(nn)

Brentano, Clemens (Maria) 1778-1842 **NCLC 1**
See also DLB 90

Brent of Bin Bin
See Franklin, (Stella Maria Sarah) Miles (Lampe)

Brenton, Howard 1942- **CLC 31**
See also CA 69-72; CANR 33, 67; DLB 13; MTCW 1

Breslin, James 1930-1996
See Breslin, Jimmy
See also CA 73-76; CANR 31, 75; DAM NOV; MTCW 1, 2

Breslin, Jimmy CLC 4, 43
See also Breslin, James
See also AITN 1; DLB 185; MTCW 2

Bresson, Robert 1901- **CLC 16**
See also CA 110; CANR 49

Breton, Andre 1896-1966 **CLC 2, 9, 15, 54; PC 15**
See also CA 19-20; 25-28R; CANR 40, 60; CAP 2; DLB 65; MTCW 1, 2

Breytenbach, Breyten 1939(?)- **CLC 23, 37, 126; DAM POET**
See also CA 113; 129; CANR 61

Bridgers, Sue Ellen 1942- **CLC 26**
See also AAYA 8; CA 65-68; CANR 11, 36; CLR 18; DLB 52; JRDA; MAICYA; SAAS 1; SATA 22, 90; SATA-Essay 109

Bridges, Robert (Seymour) 1844-1930 **TCLC 1; DAM POET; PC 28**
See also CA 104; 152; CDBLB 1890-1914; DLB 19, 98

Bridie, James TCLC 3

See also Mavor, Osborne Henry
See also DLB 10

Brin, David 1950- **CLC 34**
See also AAYA 21; CA 102; CANR 24, 70; INT CANR-24; SATA 65

Brink, Andre (Philippus) 1935- **CLC 18, 36, 106**
See also CA 104; CANR 39, 62; INT 103; MTCW 1, 2

Brinsmead, H(esba) F(ay) 1922- **CLC 21**
See also CA 21-24R; CANR 10; CLR 47; MAICYA; SAAS 5; SATA 18, 78

Brittain, Vera (Mary) 1893(?)-1970 **CLC 23**
See also CA 13-16; 25-28R; CANR 58; CAP 1; DLB 191; MTCW 1, 2

Broch, Hermann 1886-1951 **TCLC 20**
See also CA 117; DLB 85, 124

Brock, Rose
See Hansen, Joseph

Brodkey, Harold (Roy) 1930-1996 **CLC 56**
See also CA 111; 151; CANR 71; DLB 130

Brodskii, Iosif
See Brodsky, Joseph

Brodsky, Iosif Alexandrovich 1940-1996
See Brodsky, Joseph
See also AITN 1; CA 41-44R; 151; CANR 37; DAM POET; DA3; MTCW 1, 2

Brodsky, Joseph 1940-1996 **CLC 4, 6, 13, 36, 100; PC 9**
See also Brodskii, Iosif; Brodsky, Iosif Alexandrovich
See also MTCW 1

Brodsky, Michael (Mark) 1948- **CLC 19**
See also CA 102; CANR 18, 41, 58

Bromell, Henry 1947- **CLC 5**
See also CA 53-56; CANR 9

Bromfield, Louis (Brucker) 1896-1956 **TCLC 11**
See also CA 107; 155; DLB 4, 9, 86

Broner, E(sther) M(asserman) 1930- **CLC 19**
See also CA 17-20R; CANR 8, 25, 72; DLB 28

Bronk, William (M.) 1918-1999 **CLC 10**
See also CA 89-92; 177; CANR 23; DLB 165

Bronstein, Lev Davidovich
See Trotsky, Leon

Bronte, Anne 1820-1849 **NCLC 4, 71**
See also DA3; DLB 21, 199

Bronte, Charlotte 1816-1855 **NCLC 3, 8, 33, 58; DA; DAB; DAC; DAM MST, NOV; WLC**
See also AAYA 17; CDBLB 1832-1890; DA3; DLB 21, 159, 199

Bronte, Emily (Jane) 1818-1848 **NCLC 16, 35; DA; DAB; DAC; DAM MST, NOV, POET; PC 8; WLC**
See also AAYA 17; CDBLB 1832-1890; DA3; DLB 21, 32, 199

Brooke, Frances 1724-1789 **LC 6, 48**
See also DLB 39, 99

Brooke, Henry 1703(?)-1783 **LC 1**
See also DLB 39

Brooke, Rupert (Chawner) 1887-1915 **TCLC 2, 7; DA; DAB; DAC; DAM MST, POET; PC 24; WLC**
See also CA 104; 132; CANR 61; CDBLB 1914-1945; DLB 19; MTCW 1, 2

Brooke-Haven, P.
See Wodehouse, P(elham) G(renville)

Brooke-Rose, Christine 1926(?)- **CLC 40**
See also CA 13-16R; CANR 58; DLB 14

Brookner, Anita 1928- **CLC 32, 34, 51; DAB; DAM POP**
See also CA 114; 120; CANR 37, 56, 87; DA3; DLB 194; DLBY 87; MTCW 1, 2

Brooks, Cleanth 1906-1994 **CLC 24, 86, 110**

See also CA 17-20R; 145; CANR 33, 35; DLB 63; DLBY 94; INT CANR-35; MTCW 1, 2

Brooks, George
See Baum, L(yman) Frank

Brooks, Gwendolyn 1917- **CLC 1, 2, 4, 5, 15, 49, 125; BLC 1; DA; DAC; DAM MST, MULT, POET; PC 7; WLC**
See also AAYA 20; AITN 1; BW 2, 3; CA 1-4R; CANR 1, 27, 52, 75; CDALB 1941-1968; CLR 27; DA3; DLB 5, 76, 165; MTCW 1, 2; SATA 6

Brooks, Mel CLC 12
See also Kaminsky, Melvin
See also AAYA 13; DLB 26

Brooks, Peter 1938- **CLC 34**
See also CA 45-48; CANR 1

Brooks, Van Wyck 1886-1963 **CLC 29**
See also CA 1-4R; CANR 6; DLB 45, 63, 103

Brophy, Brigid (Antonia) 1929-1995 **CLC 6, 11, 29, 105**
See also CA 5-8R; 149; CAAS 4; CANR 25, 53; DA3; DLB 14; MTCW 1, 2

Brosman, Catharine Savage 1934- **CLC 9**
See also CA 61-64; CANR 21, 46

Brossard, Nicole 1943- **CLC 115**
See also CA 122; CAAS 16; DLB 53

Brother Antoninus
See Everson, William (Oliver)

The Brothers Quay
See Quay, Stephen; Quay, Timothy

Broughton, T(homas) Alan 1936- **CLC 19**
See also CA 45-48; CANR 2, 23, 48

Broumas, Olga 1949- **CLC 10, 73**
See also CA 85-88; CANR 20, 69

Brown, Alan 1950- **CLC 99**
See also CA 156

Brown, Charles Brockden 1771-1810 **NCLC 22, 74**
See also CDALB 1640-1865; DLB 37, 59, 73

Brown, Christy 1932-1981 **CLC 63**
See also CA 105; 104; CANR 72; DLB 14

Brown, Claude 1937- **CLC 30; BLC 1; DAM MULT**
See also AAYA 7; BW 1, 3; CA 73-76; CANR 81

Brown, Dee (Alexander) 1908- **CLC 18, 47; DAM POP**
See also AAYA 30; CA 13-16R; CAAS 6; CANR 11, 45, 60; DA3; DLBY 80; MTCW 1, 2; SATA 5, 110

Brown, George
See Wertmueller, Lina

Brown, George Douglas 1869-1902 **TCLC 28**
See also CA 162

Brown, George Mackay 1921-1996 **CLC 5, 48, 100**
See also CA 21-24R; 151; CAAS 6; CANR 12, 37, 67; DLB 14, 27, 139; MTCW 1; SATA 35

Brown, (William) Larry 1951- **CLC 73**
See also CA 130; 134; INT 133

Brown, Moses
See Barrett, William (Christopher)

Brown, Rita Mae 1944- **CLC 18, 43, 79; DAM NOV, POP**
See also CA 45-48; CANR 2, 11, 35, 62; DA3; INT CANR-11; MTCW 1, 2

Brown, Roderick (Langmere) Haig-
See Haig-Brown, Roderick (Langmere)

Brown, Rosellen 1939- **CLC 32**
See also CA 77-80; CAAS 10; CANR 14, 44

Brown, Sterling Allen 1901-1989 **CLC 1, 23, 59; BLC 1; DAM MULT, POET**
See also BW 1, 3; CA 85-88; 127; CANR 26; DA3; DLB 48, 51, 63; MTCW 1, 2

Brown, Will
See Ainsworth, William Harrison

Brown, William Wells 1813-1884 **NCLC 2; BLC 1; DAM MULT; DC 1**
See also DLB 3, 50

Browne, (Clyde) Jackson 1948(?)- **CLC 21**
See also CA 120

Browning, Elizabeth Barrett 1806-1861 **NCLC 1, 16, 61, 66; DA; DAB; DAC; DAM MST, POET; PC 6; WLC**
See also CDBLB 1832-1890; DA3; DLB 32, 199

Browning, Robert 1812-1889 **NCLC 19, 79; DA; DAB; DAC; DAM MST, POET; PC 2; WLCS**
See also CDBLB 1832-1890; DA3; DLB 32, 163; YABC 1

Browning, Tod 1882-1962 **CLC 16**
See also CA 141; 117

Brownson, Orestes Augustus 1803-1876 **NCLC 50**
See also DLB 1, 59, 73

Bruccoli, Matthew J(oseph) 1931- **CLC 34**
See also CA 9-12R; CANR 7, 87; DLB 103

Bruce, Lenny CLC 21
See also Schneider, Leonard Alfred

Bruin, John
See Brutus, Dennis

Brulard, Henri
See Stendhal

Brulls, Christian
See Simenon, Georges (Jacques Christian)

Brunner, John (Kilian Houston) 1934-1995 **CLC 8, 10; DAM POP**
See also CA 1-4R; 149; CAAS 8; CANR 2, 37; MTCW 1, 2

Bruno, Giordano 1548-1600 **LC 27**

Brutus, Dennis 1924- **CLC 43; BLC 1; DAM MULT, POET; PC 24**
See also BW 2, 3; CA 49-52; CAAS 14; CANR 2, 27, 42, 81; DLB 117

Bryan, C(ourtlandt) D(ixon) B(arnes) 1936- **CLC 29**
See also CA 73-76; CANR 13, 68; DLB 185; INT CANR-13

Bryan, Michael
See Moore, Brian

Bryant, William Cullen 1794-1878 **NCLC 6, 46; DA; DAB; DAC; DAM MST, POET; PC 20**
See also CDALB 1640-1865; DLB 3, 43, 59, 189

Bryusov, Valery Yakovlevich 1873-1924 **TCLC 10**
See also CA 107; 155

Buchan, John 1875-1940 **TCLC 41; DAB; DAM POP**
See also CA 108; 145; DLB 34, 70, 156; MTCW 1; YABC 2

Buchanan, George 1506-1582 **LC 4**
See also DLB 152

Buchheim, Lothar-Guenther 1918- **CLC 6**
See also CA 85-88

Buchner, (Karl) Georg 1813-1837 **NCLC 26**

Buchwald, Art(hur) 1925- **CLC 33**
See also AITN 1; CA 5-8R; CANR 21, 67; MTCW 1, 2; SATA 10

Buck, Pearl S(ydenstricker) 1892-1973 **CLC 7, 11, 18, 127; DA; DAB; DAC; DAM MST, NOV**
See also AITN 1; CA 1-4R; 41-44R; CANR 1, 34; CDALBS; DA3; DLB 9, 102; MTCW 1, 2; SATA 1, 25

Buckler, Ernest 1908-1984 **CLC 13; DAC; DAM MST**
See also CA 11-12; 114; CAP 1; DLB 68; SATA 47

Buckley, Vincent (Thomas) 1925-1988 **CLC 57**

See also CA 101

Buckley, William F(rank), Jr. 1925- **CLC 7, 18, 37; DAM POP**
See also AITN 1; CA 1-4R; CANR 1, 24, 53; DA3; DLB 137; DLBY 80; INT CANR-24; MTCW 1, 2

Buechner, (Carl) Frederick 1926- **CLC 2, 4, 6, 9; DAM NOV**
See also CA 13-16R; CANR 11, 39, 64; DLBY 80; INT CANR-11; MTCW 1, 2

Buell, John (Edward) 1927- **CLC 10**
See also CA 1-4R; CANR 71; DLB 53

Buero Vallejo, Antonio 1916- **CLC 15, 46**
See also CA 106; CANR 24, 49, 75; HW 1; MTCW 1, 2

Bufalino, Gesualdo 1920(?)- **CLC 74**
See also DLB 196

Bugayev, Boris Nikolayevich 1880-1934 **TCLC 7; PC 11**
See also Bely, Andrey
See also CA 104; 165; MTCW 1

Bukowski, Charles 1920-1994 **CLC 2, 5, 9, 41, 82, 108; DAM NOV, POET; PC 18**
See also CA 17-20R; 144; CANR 40, 62; DA3; DLB 5, 130, 169; MTCW 1, 2

Bulgakov, Mikhail (Afanas'evich) 1891-1940 **TCLC 2, 16; DAM DRAM, NOV; SSC 18**
See also CA 105; 152

Bulgya, Alexander Alexandrovich 1901-1956 **TCLC 53**
See also Fadeyev, Alexander
See also CA 117; 181

Bullins, Ed 1935- **CLC 1, 5, 7; BLC 1; DAM DRAM, MULT; DC 6**
See also BW 2, 3; CA 49-52; CAAS 16; CANR 24, 46, 73; DLB 7, 38; MTCW 1, 2

Bulwer-Lytton, Edward (George Earle Lytton) 1803-1873 **NCLC 1, 45**
See also DLB 21

Bunin, Ivan Alexeyevich 1870-1953 **TCLC 6; SSC 5**
See also CA 104

Bunting, Basil 1900-1985 **CLC 10, 39, 47; DAM POET**
See also CA 53-56; 115; CANR 7; DLB 20

Bunuel, Luis 1900-1983 **CLC 16, 80; DAM MULT; HLC 1**
See also CA 101; 110; CANR 32, 77; HW 1

Bunyan, John 1628-1688 **LC 4; DA; DAB; DAC; DAM MST; WLC**
See also CDBLB 1660-1789; DLB 39

Burckhardt, Jacob (Christoph) 1818-1897 **NCLC 49**

Burford, Eleanor
See Hibbert, Eleanor Alice Burford

Burgess, Anthony CLC 1, 2, 4, 5, 8, 10, 13, 15, 22, 40, 62, 81, 94; DAB
See also Wilson, John (Anthony) Burgess
See also AAYA 25; AITN 1; CDBLB 1960 to Present; DLB 14, 194; DLBY 98; MTCW 1

Burke, Edmund 1729(?)-1797 **LC 7, 36; DA; DAB; DAC; DAM MST; WLC**
See also DA3; DLB 104

Burke, Kenneth (Duva) 1897-1993 **CLC 2, 24**
See also CA 5-8R; 143; CANR 39, 74; DLB 45, 63; MTCW 1, 2

Burke, Leda
See Garnett, David

Burke, Ralph
See Silverberg, Robert

Burke, Thomas 1886-1945 **TCLC 63**
See also CA 113; 155; DLB 197

Burney, Fanny 1752-1840 **NCLC 12, 54, 81**
See also DLB 39

Burns, Robert 1759-1796 **LC 3, 29, 40; DA; DAB; DAC; DAM MST, POET; PC 6; WLC**
See also CDBLB 1789-1832; DA3; DLB 109

Burns, Tex
See L'Amour, Louis (Dearborn)

Burnshaw, Stanley 1906- **CLC 3, 13, 44**
See also CA 9-12R; DLB 48; DLBY 97

Burr, Anne 1937- **CLC 6**
See also CA 25-28R

Burroughs, Edgar Rice 1875-1950 **TCLC 2, 32; DAM NOV**
See also AAYA 11; CA 104; 132; DA3; DLB 8; MTCW 1, 2; SATA 41

Burroughs, William S(eward) 1914-1997
CLC 1, 2, 5, 15, 22, 42, 75, 109; DA; DAB; DAC; DAM MST, NOV, POP; WLC
See also AITN 2; CA 9-12R; 160; CANR 20, 52; DA3; DLB 2, 8, 16, 152; DLBY 81, 97; MTCW 1, 2

Burton, SirRichard F(rancis) 1821-1890
NCLC 42
See also DLB 55, 166, 184

Busch, Frederick 1941- **CLC 7, 10, 18, 47**
See also CA 33-36R; CAAS 1; CANR 45, 73; DLB 6

Bush, Ronald 1946- **CLC 34**
See also CA 136

Bustos, F(rancisco)
See Borges, Jorge Luis

Bustos Domecq, H(onorio)
See Bioy Casares, Adolfo; Borges, Jorge Luis

Butler, Octavia E(stelle) 1947- **CLC 38, 121; BLCS; DAM MULT, POP**
See also AAYA 18; BW 2, 3; CA 73-76; CANR 12, 24, 38, 73; CLR 65; DA3; DLB 33; MTCW 1, 2; SATA 84

Butler, Robert Olen (Jr.) 1945- **CLC 81; DAM POP**
See also CA 112; CANR 66; DLB 173; INT 112; MTCW 1

Butler, Samuel 1612-1680 **LC 16, 43**
See also DLB 101, 126

Butler, Samuel 1835-1902 **TCLC 1, 33; DA; DAB; DAC; DAM MST, NOV; WLC**
See also CA 143; CDBLB 1890-1914; DA3; DLB 18, 57, 174

Butler, Walter C.
See Faust, Frederick (Schiller)

Butor, Michel (Marie Francois) 1926- **CLC 1, 3, 8, 11, 15**
See also CA 9-12R; CANR 33, 66; DLB 83; MTCW 1, 2

Butts, Mary 1892(?)-1937 **TCLC 77**
See also CA 148

Buzo, Alexander (John) 1944- **CLC 61**
See also CA 97-100; CANR 17, 39, 69

Buzzati, Dino 1906-1972 **CLC 36**
See also CA 160; 33-36R; DLB 177

Byars, Betsy (Cromer) 1928- **CLC 35**
See also AAYA 19; CA 33-36R, 183; CAAE 183; CANR 18, 36, 57; CLR 1, 16; DLB 52; INT CANR-18; JRDA; MAICYA; MTCW 1; SAAS 1; SATA 4, 46, 80; SATA-Essay 108

Byatt, A(ntonia) S(usan Drabble) 1936- **CLC 19, 65; DAM NOV, POP**
See also CA 13-16R; CANR 13, 33, 50, 75; DA3; DLB 14, 194; MTCW 1, 2

Byrne, David 1952- **CLC 26**
See also CA 127

Byrne, John Keyes 1926-
See Leonard, Hugh
See also CA 102; CANR 78; INT 102

Byron, George Gordon (Noel) 1788-1824
NCLC 2, 12; DA; DAB; DAC; DAM MST, POET; PC 16; WLC
See also CDBLB 1789-1832; DA3; DLB 96, 110

Byron, Robert 1905-1941 **TCLC 67**
See also CA 160; DLB 195

C. 3. 3.
See Wilde, Oscar (Fingal O'Flahertie Wills)

Caballero, Fernan 1796-1877 **NCLC 10**

Cabell, Branch
See Cabell, James Branch

Cabell, James Branch 1879-1958 **TCLC 6**
See also CA 105; 152; DLB 9, 78; MTCW 1

Cable, George Washington 1844-1925 **TCLC 4; SSC 4**
See also CA 104; 155; DLB 12, 74; DLBD 13

Cabral de Melo Neto, Joao 1920- **CLC 76; DAM MULT**
See also CA 151

Cabrera Infante, G(uillermo) 1929- **CLC 5, 25, 45, 120; DAM MULT; HLC 1; SSC 39**
See also CA 85-88; CANR 29, 65; DA3; DLB 113; HW 1, 2; MTCW 1, 2

Cade, Toni
See Bambara, Toni Cade

Cadmus and Harmonia
See Buchan, John

Caedmon fl. 658-680 **CMLC 7**
See also DLB 146

Caeiro, Alberto
See Pessoa, Fernando (Antonio Nogueira)

Cage, John (Milton, Jr.) 1912-1992 **CLC 41**
See also CA 13-16R; 169; CANR 9, 78; DLB 193; INT CANR-9

Cahan, Abraham 1860-1951 **TCLC 71**
See also CA 108; 154; DLB 9, 25, 28

Cain, G.
See Cabrera Infante, G(uillermo)

Cain, Guillermo
See Cabrera Infante, G(uillermo)

Cain, James M(allahan) 1892-1977 **CLC 3, 11, 28**
See also AITN 1; CA 17-20R; 73-76; CANR 8, 34, 61; MTCW 1

Caine, Hall 1853-1931 **TCLC 97**

Caine, Mark
See Raphael, Frederic (Michael)

Calasso, Roberto 1941- **CLC 81**
See also CA 143; CANR 89

Calderon de la Barca, Pedro 1600-1681 **LC 23; DC 3; HLCS 1**

Caldwell, Erskine (Preston) 1903-1987 **CLC 1, 8, 14, 50, 60; DAM NOV; SSC 19**
See also AITN 1; CA 1-4R; 121; CAAS 1; CANR 2, 33; DA3; DLB 9, 86; MTCW 1, 2

Caldwell, (Janet Miriam) Taylor (Holland) 1900-1985 **CLC 2, 28, 39; DAM NOV, POP**
See also CA 5-8R; 116; CANR 5; DA3; DLBD 17

Calhoun, John Caldwell 1782-1850 **NCLC 15**
See also DLB 3

Calisher, Hortense 1911- **CLC 2, 4, 8, 38; DAM NOV; SSC 15**
See also CA 1-4R; CANR 1, 22, 67; DA3; DLB 2; INT CANR-22; MTCW 1, 2

Callaghan, Morley Edward 1903-1990 **CLC 3, 14, 41, 65; DAC; DAM MST**
See also CA 9-12R; 132; CANR 33, 73; DLB 68; MTCW 1, 2

Callimachus c. 305B.C.-c. 240B.C. **CMLC 18**
See also DLB 176

Calvin, John 1509-1564 **LC 37**

Calvino, Italo 1923-1985 **CLC 5, 8, 11, 22, 33, 39, 73; DAM NOV; SSC 3**

See also CA 85-88; 116; CANR 23, 61; DLB 196; MTCW 1, 2

Cameron, Carey 1952- **CLC 59**
See also CA 135

Cameron, Peter 1959- **CLC 44**
See also CA 125; CANR 50

Camoens, Luis Vaz de 1524(?)-1580
See also HLCS 1

Camoes, Luis de 1524(?)-1580
See also HLCS 1

Campana, Dino 1885-1932 **TCLC 20**
See also CA 117; DLB 114

Campanella, Tommaso 1568-1639 **LC 32**

Campbell, John W(ood, Jr.) 1910-1971 **CLC 32**
See also CA 21-22; 29-32R; CANR 34; CAP 2; DLB 8; MTCW 1

Campbell, Joseph 1904-1987 **CLC 69**
See also AAYA 3; BEST 89:2; CA 1-4R; 124; CANR 3, 28, 61; DA3; MTCW 1, 2

Campbell, Maria 1940- **CLC 85; DAC**
See also CA 102; CANR 54; NNAL

Campbell, (John) Ramsey 1946- **CLC 42; SSC 19**
See also CA 57-60; CANR 7; INT CANR-7

Campbell, (Ignatius) Roy (Dunnachie) 1901-1957 **TCLC 5**
See also CA 104; 155; DLB 20; MTCW 2

Campbell, Thomas 1777-1844 **NCLC 19**
See also DLB 93; 144

Campbell, Wilfred **TCLC 9**
See also Campbell, William

Campbell, William 1858(?)-1918
See Campbell, Wilfred
See also CA 106; DLB 92

Campion, Jane **CLC 95**
See also AAYA 33; CA 138; CANR 87

Camus, Albert 1913-1960 **CLC 1, 2, 4, 9, 11, 14, 32, 63, 69, 124; DA; DAB; DAC; DAM DRAM, MST, NOV; DC 2; SSC 9; WLC**
See also CA 89-92; DA3; DLB 72; MTCW 1, 2

Canby, Vincent 1924- **CLC 13**
See also CA 81-84

Cancale
See Desnos, Robert

Canetti, Elias 1905-1994 **CLC 3, 14, 25, 75, 86**
See also CA 21-24R; 146; CANR 23, 61, 79; DA3; DLB 85, 124; MTCW 1, 2

Canfield, Dorothea F.
See Fisher, Dorothy (Frances) Canfield

Canfield, Dorothea Frances
See Fisher, Dorothy (Frances) Canfield

Canfield, Dorothy
See Fisher, Dorothy (Frances) Canfield

Canin, Ethan 1960- **CLC 55**
See also CA 131; 135

Cannon, Curt
See Hunter, Evan

Cao, Lan 1961- **CLC 109**
See also CA 165

Cape, Judith
See Page, P(atricia) K(athleen)

Capek, Karel 1890-1938 **TCLC 6, 37; DA; DAB; DAC; DAM DRAM, MST, NOV; DC 1; SSC 36; WLC**
See also CA 104; 140; DA3; MTCW 1

Capote, Truman 1924-1984 **CLC 1, 3, 8, 13, 19, 34, 38, 58; DA; DAB; DAC; DAM MST, NOV, POP; SSC 2; WLC**
See also CA 5-8R; 113; CANR 18, 62; CDALB 1941-1968; DA3; DLB 2, 185; DLBY 80, 84; MTCW 1, 2; SATA 91

Capra, Frank 1897-1991 **CLC 16**
See also CA 61-64; 135

Caputo, Philip 1941- **CLC 32**

Churchill, Charles 1731-1764 **LC 3**
See also DLB 109

Chute, Carolyn 1947- **CLC 39**
See also CA 123

Ciardi, John (Anthony) 1916-1986 **CLC 10, 40, 44, 129; DAM POET**
See also CA 5-8R; 118; CAAS 2; CANR 5, 33; CLR 19; DLB 5; DLBY 86; INT CANR-5; MAICYA; MTCW 1, 2; SAAS 26; SATA 1, 65; SATA-Obit 46

Cicero, Marcus Tullius 106B.C.-43B.C. **CMLC 3**
See also DLB 211

Cimino, Michael 1943- **CLC 16**
See also CA 105

Cioran, E(mil) M. 1911-1995 **CLC 64**
See also CA 25-28R; 149; CANR 91; DLB 220

Cisneros, Sandra 1954- **CLC 69, 118; DAM MULT; HLC 1; SSC 32**
See also AAYA 9; CA 131; CANR 64; DA3; DLB 122, 152; HW 1, 2; MTCW 2

Cixous, Helene 1937- **CLC 92**
See also CA 126; CANR 55; DLB 83; MTCW 1, 2

Clair, Rene CLC 20
See also Chomette, Rene Lucien

Clampitt, Amy 1920-1994 **CLC 32; PC 19**
See also CA 110; 146; CANR 29, 79; DLB 105

Clancy, Thomas L., Jr. 1947-
See Clancy, Tom
See also CA 125; 131; CANR 62; DA3; INT 131; MTCW 1, 2

Clancy, Tom CLC 45, 112; DAM NOV, POP
See Clancy, Thomas L., Jr.
See also AAYA 9; BEST 89:1, 90:1; MTCW 2

Clare, John 1793-1864 **NCLC 9, 86; DAB; DAM POET; PC 23**
See also DLB 55, 96

Clarin
See Alas (y Urena), Leopoldo (Enrique Garcia)

Clark, Al C.
See Goines, Donald

Clark, (Robert) Brian 1932- **CLC 29**
See also CA 41-44R; CANR 67

Clark, Curt
See Westlake, Donald E(dwin)

Clark, Eleanor 1913-1996 **CLC 5, 19**
See also CA 9-12R; 151; CANR 41; DLB 6

Clark, J. P.
See Clark Bekedermo, J(ohnson) P(epper)
See also DLB 117

Clark, John Pepper
See Clark Bekedermo, J(ohnson) P(epper)

Clark, M. R.
See Clark, Mavis Thorpe

Clark, Mavis Thorpe 1909- **CLC 12**
See also CA 57-60; CANR 8, 37; CLR 30; MAICYA; SAAS 5; SATA 8, 74

Clark, Walter Van Tilburg 1909-1971 **CLC 28**
See also CA 9-12R; 33-36R; CANR 63; DLB 9, 206; SATA 8

Clark Bekedermo, J(ohnson) P(epper) 1935- **CLC 38; BLC 1; DAM DRAM, MULT; DC 5**
See also Clark, J. P.
See also BW 1; CA 65-68; CANR 16, 72; MTCW 1

Clarke, Arthur C(harles) 1917- **CLC 1, 4, 13, 18, 35; DAM POP; SSC 3**
See also AAYA 4, 33; CA 1-4R; CANR 2, 28, 55, 74; DA3; JRDA; MAICYA; MTCW 1, 2; SATA 13, 70, 115

Clarke, Austin 1896-1974 **CLC 6, 9; DAM POET**

See also CA 29-32; 49-52; CAP 2; DLB 10, 20

Clarke, Austin C(hesterfield) 1934- **CLC 8, 53; BLC 1; DAC; DAM MULT**
See also BW 1; CA 25-28R; CAAS 16; CANR 14, 32, 68; DLB 53, 125

Clarke, Gillian 1937- **CLC 61**
See also CA 106; DLB 40

Clarke, Marcus (Andrew Hislop) 1846-1881 **NCLC 19**

Clarke, Shirley 1925- **CLC 16**

Clash, The
See Headon, (Nicky) Topper; Jones, Mick; Simonon, Paul; Strummer, Joe

Claudel, Paul (Louis Charles Marie) 1868-1955 **TCLC 2, 10**
See also CA 104; 165; DLB 192

Claudius, Matthias 1740-1815 **NCLC 75**
See also DLB 97

Clavell, James (duMaresq) 1925-1994 **CLC 6, 25, 87; DAM NOV, POP**
See also CA 25-28R; 146; CANR 26, 48; DA3; MTCW 1, 2

Cleaver, (Leroy) Eldridge 1935-1998 **CLC 30, 119; BLC 1; DAM MULT**
See also BW 1, 3; CA 21-24R; 167; CANR 16, 75; DA3; MTCW 2

Cleese, John (Marwood) 1939- **CLC 21**
See also Monty Python
See also CA 112; 116; CANR 35; MTCW 1

Cleishbotham, Jebediah
See Scott, Walter

Cleland, John 1710-1789 **LC 2, 48**
See also DLB 39

Clemens, Samuel Langhorne 1835-1910
See Twain, Mark
See also CA 104; 135; CDALB 1865-1917; DA; DAB; DAC; DAM MST, NOV; DA3; DLB 11, 12, 23, 64, 74, 186, 189; JRDA; MAICYA; SATA 100; YABC 2

Cleophil
See Congreve, William

Clerihew, E.
See Bentley, E(dmund) C(lerihew)

Clerk, N. W.
See Lewis, C(live) S(taples)

Cliff, Jimmy CLC 21
See also Chambers, James

Cliff, Michelle 1946- **CLC 120; BLCS**
See also BW 2; CA 116; CANR 39, 72; DLB 157

Clifton, (Thelma) Lucille 1936- **CLC 19, 66; BLC 1; DAM MULT, POET; PC 17**
See also BW 2, 3; CA 49-52; CANR 2, 24, 42, 76; CLR 5; DA3; DLB 5, 41; MAICYA; MTCW 1, 2; SATA 20, 69

Clinton, Dirk
See Silverberg, Robert

Clough, Arthur Hugh 1819-1861 **NCLC 27**
See also DLB 32

Clutha, Janet Paterson Frame 1924-
See Frame, Janet
See also CA 1-4R; CANR 2, 36, 76; MTCW 1, 2

Clyne, Terence
See Blatty, William Peter

Cobalt, Martin
See Mayne, William (James Carter)

Cobb, Irvin S(hrewsbury) 1876-1944 **TCLC 77**
See also CA 175; DLB 11, 25, 86

Cobbett, William 1763-1835 **NCLC 49**
See also DLB 43, 107, 158

Coburn, D(onald) L(ee) 1938- **CLC 10**
See also CA 89-92

Cocteau, Jean (Maurice Eugene Clement) 1889-1963 **CLC 1, 8, 15, 16, 43; DA; DAB; DAC; DAM DRAM, MST, NOV; WLC**

See also CA 25-28; CANR 40; CAP 2; DA3; DLB 65; MTCW 1, 2

Codrescu, Andrei 1946- **CLC 46, 121; DAM POET**
See also CA 33-36R; CAAS 19; CANR 13, 34, 53, 76; DA3; MTCW 2

Coe, Max
See Bourne, Randolph S(illiman)

Coe, Tucker
See Westlake, Donald E(dwin)

Coen, Ethan 1958- **CLC 108**
See also CA 126; CANR 85

Coen, Joel 1955- **CLC 108**
See also CA 126

The Coen Brothers
See Coen, Ethan; Coen, Joel

Coetzee, J(ohn) M(ichael) 1940- **CLC 23, 33, 66, 117; DAM NOV**
See also CA 77-80; CANR 41, 54, 74; DA3; MTCW 1, 2

Coffey, Brian
See Koontz, Dean R(ay)

Coffin, Robert P(eter) Tristram 1892-1955 **TCLC 95**
See also CA 123; 169; DLB 45

Cohan, George M(ichael) 1878-1942 **TCLC 60**
See also CA 157

Cohen, Arthur A(llen) 1928-1986 **CLC 7, 31**
See also CA 1-4R; 120; CANR 1, 17, 42; DLB 28

Cohen, Leonard (Norman) 1934- **CLC 3, 38; DAC; DAM MST**
See also CA 21-24R; CANR 14, 69; DLB 53; MTCW 1

Cohen, Matt 1942- **CLC 19; DAC**
See also CA 61-64; CAAS 18; CANR 40; DLB 53

Cohen-Solal, Annie 19(?)- **CLC 50**

Colegate, Isabel 1931- **CLC 36**
See also CA 17-20R; CANR 8, 22, 74; DLB 14; INT CANR-22; MTCW 1

Coleman, Emmett
See Reed, Ishmael

Coleridge, M. E.
See Coleridge, Mary E(lizabeth)

Coleridge, Mary E(lizabeth) 1861-1907 **TCLC 73**
See also CA 116; 166; DLB 19, 98

Coleridge, Samuel Taylor 1772-1834 **NCLC 9, 54; DA; DAB; DAC; DAM MST, POET; PC 11; WLC**
See also CDBLB 1789-1832; DA3; DLB 93, 107

Coleridge, Sara 1802-1852 **NCLC 31**
See also DLB 199

Coles, Don 1928- **CLC 46**
See also CA 115; CANR 38

Coles, Robert (Martin) 1929- **CLC 108**
See also CA 45-48; CANR 3, 32, 66, 70; INT CANR-32; SATA 23

Colette, (Sidonie-Gabrielle) 1873-1954 **TCLC 1, 5, 16; DAM NOV; SSC 10**
See also CA 104; 131; DA3; DLB 65; MTCW 1, 2

Collett, (Jacobine) Camilla (Wergeland) 1813-1895 **NCLC 22**

Collier, Christopher 1930- **CLC 30**
See also AAYA 13; CA 33-36R; CANR 13, 33; JRDA; MAICYA; SATA 16, 70

Collier, James L(incoln) 1928- **CLC 30; DAM POP**
See also AAYA 13; CA 9-12R; CANR 4, 33, 60; CLR 3; JRDA; MAICYA; SAAS 21; SATA 8, 70

Collier, Jeremy 1650-1726 **LC 6**

Collier, John 1901-1980 **SSC 19**
See also CA 65-68; 97-100; CANR 10; DLB 77

Collingwood, R(obin) G(eorge) 1889(?)-1943
TCLC 67
See also CA 117; 155
Collins, Hunt
See Hunter, Evan
Collins, Linda 1931- **CLC 44**
See also CA 125
Collins, (William) Wilkie 1824-1889 **NCLC 1, 18**
See also CDBLB 1832-1890; DLB 18, 70, 159
Collins, William 1721-1759 **LC 4, 40; DAM POET**
See also DLB 109
Collodi, Carlo 1826-1890 **NCLC 54**
See also Lorenzini, Carlo
See also CLR 5
Colman, George 1732-1794
See Glassco, John
Colt, Winchester Remington
See Hubbard, L(afayette) Ron(ald)
Colter, Cyrus 1910- **CLC 58**
See also BW 1; CA 65-68; CANR 10, 66; DLB 33
Colton, James
See Hansen, Joseph
Colum, Padraic 1881-1972 **CLC 28**
See also CA 73-76; 33-36R; CANR 35; CLR 36; MAICYA; MTCW 1; SATA 15
Colvin, James
See Moorcock, Michael (John)
Colwin, Laurie (E.) 1944-1992 **CLC 5, 13, 23, 84**
See also CA 89-92; 139; CANR 20, 46; DLBY 80; MTCW 1
Comfort, Alex(ander) 1920- **CLC 7; DAM POP**
See also CA 1-4R; CANR 1, 45; MTCW 1
Comfort, Montgomery
See Campbell, (John) Ramsey
Compton-Burnett, I(vy) 1884(?)-1969 **CLC 1, 3, 10, 15, 34; DAM NOV**
See also CA 1-4R; 25-28R; CANR 4; DLB 36; MTCW 1
Comstock, Anthony 1844-1915 **TCLC 13**
See also CA 110; 169
Comte, Auguste 1798-1857 **NCLC 54**
Conan Doyle, Arthur
See Doyle, Arthur Conan
Conde (Abellan), Carmen 1901-
See also CA 177; DLB 108; HLCS 1; HW 2
Conde, Maryse 1937- **CLC 52, 92; BLCS; DAM MULT**
See also BW 2, 3; CA 110; CANR 30, 53, 76; MTCW 1
Condillac, Etienne Bonnot de 1714-1780 **LC 26**
Condon, Richard (Thomas) 1915-1996 **CLC 4, 6, 8, 10, 45, 100; DAM NOV**
See also BEST 90:3; CA 1-4R; 151; CAAS 1; CANR 2, 23; INT CANR-23; MTCW 1, 2
Confucius 551B.C.-479B.C. **CMLC 19; DA; DAB; DAC; DAM MST; WLCS**
See also DA3
Congreve, William 1670-1729 **LC 5, 21; DA; DAB; DAC; DAM DRAM, MST, POET; DC 2; WLC**
See also CDBLB 1660-1789; DLB 39, 84
Connell, Evan S(helby), Jr. 1924- **CLC 4, 6, 45; DAM NOV**
See also AAYA 7; CA 1-4R; CAAS 2; CANR 2, 39, 76; DLB 2; DLBY 81; MTCW 1, 2
Connelly, Marc(us Cook) 1890-1980 **CLC 7**
See also CA 85-88; 102; CANR 30; DLB 7; DLBY 80; SATA-Obit 25
Connor, Ralph TCLC 31

See also Gordon, Charles William
See also DLB 92
Conrad, Joseph 1857-1924 **TCLC 1, 6, 13, 25, 43, 57; DA; DAB; DAC; DAM MST, NOV; SSC 9; WLC**
See also AAYA 26; CA 104; 131; CANR 60; CDBLB 1890-1914; DA3; DLB 10, 34, 98, 156; MTCW 1, 2; SATA 27
Conrad, Robert Arnold
See Hart, Moss
Conroy, Pat
See Conroy, (Donald) Pat(rick)
See also MTCW 2
Conroy, (Donald) Pat(rick) 1945- **CLC 30, 74; DAM NOV, POP**
See also Conroy, Pat
See also AAYA 8; AITN 1; CA 85-88; CANR 24, 53; DA3; DLB 6; MTCW 1
Constant (de Rebecque), (Henri) Benjamin 1767-1830 **NCLC 6**
See also DLB 119
Conybeare, Charles Augustus
See Eliot, T(homas) S(tearns)
Cook, Michael 1933- **CLC 58**
See also CA 93-96; CANR 68; DLB 53
Cook, Robin 1940- **CLC 14; DAM POP**
See also AAYA 32; BEST 90:2; CA 108; 111; CANR 41, 90; DA3; INT 111
Cook, Roy
See Silverberg, Robert
Cooke, Elizabeth 1948- **CLC 55**
See also CA 129
Cooke, John Esten 1830-1886 **NCLC 5**
See also DLB 3
Cooke, John Estes
See Baum, L(yman) Frank
Cooke, M. E.
See Creasey, John
Cooke, Margaret
See Creasey, John
Cook-Lynn, Elizabeth 1930- **CLC 93; DAM MULT**
See also CA 133; DLB 175; NNAL
Cooney, Ray CLC 62
Cooper, Douglas 1960- **CLC 86**
Cooper, Henry St. John
See Creasey, John
Cooper, J(oan) California (?)- **CLC 56; DAM MULT**
See also AAYA 12; BW 1; CA 125; CANR 55; DLB 212
Cooper, James Fenimore 1789-1851 **NCLC 1, 27, 54**
See also AAYA 22; CDALB 1640-1865; DA3; DLB 3; SATA 19
Coover, Robert (Lowell) 1932- **CLC 3, 7, 15, 32, 46, 87; DAM NOV; SSC 15**
See also CA 45-48; CANR 3, 37, 58; DLB 2; DLBY 81; MTCW 1, 2
Copeland, Stewart (Armstrong) 1952- **CLC 26**
Copernicus, Nicolaus 1473-1543 **LC 45**
Coppard, A(lfred) E(dgar) 1878-1957 **TCLC 5; SSC 21**
See also CA 114; 167; DLB 162; YABC 1
Coppee, Francois 1842-1908 **TCLC 25**
See also CA 170
Coppola, Francis Ford 1939- **CLC 16, 126**
See also CA 77-80; CANR 40, 78; DLB 44
Corbiere, Tristan 1845-1875 **NCLC 43**
Corcoran, Barbara 1911- **CLC 17**
See also AAYA 14; CA 21-24R; CAAS 2; CANR 11, 28, 48; CLR 50; DLB 52; JRDA; SAAS 20; SATA 3, 77
Cordelier, Maurice
See Giraudoux, (Hippolyte) Jean
Corelli, Marie 1855-1924 **TCLC 51**
See also Mackey, Mary

See also DLB 34, 156
Corman, Cid 1924- **CLC 9**
See also Corman, Sidney
See also CAAS 2; DLB 5, 193
Corman, Sidney 1924-
See Corman, Cid
See also CA 85-88; CANR 44; DAM POET
Cormier, Robert (Edmund) 1925- **CLC 12, 30; DA; DAB; DAC; DAM MST, NOV**
See also AAYA 3, 19; CA 1-4R; CANR 5, 23, 76; CDALB 1968-1988; CLR 12, 55; DLB 52; INT CANR-23; JRDA; MAI-CYA; MTCW 1, 2; SATA 10, 45, 83
Corn, Alfred (DeWitt III) 1943- **CLC 33**
See also CA 179; CAAE 179; CAAS 25; CANR 44; DLB 120; DLBY 80
Corneille, Pierre 1606-1684 **LC 28; DAB; DAM MST**
Cornwell, David (John Moore) 1931- **CLC 9, 15; DAM POP**
See also le Carre, John
See also CA 5-8R; CANR 13, 33, 59; DA3; MTCW 1, 2
Corso, (Nunzio) Gregory 1930- **CLC 1, 11**
See also CA 5-8R; CANR 41, 76; DA3; DLB 5, 16; MTCW 1, 2
Cortazar, Julio 1914-1984 **CLC 2, 3, 5, 10, 13, 15, 33, 34, 92; DAM MULT, NOV; HLC 1; SSC 7**
See also CA 21-24R; CANR 12, 32, 81; DA3; DLB 113; HW 1, 2; MTCW 1, 2
CORTES, HERNAN 1484-1547 **LC 31**
Corvinus, Jakob
See Raabe, Wilhelm (Karl)
Corwin, Cecil
See Kornbluth, C(yril) M.
Cosic, Dobrica 1921- **CLC 14**
See also CA 122; 138; DLB 181
Costain, Thomas B(ertram) 1885-1965 **CLC 30**
See also CA 5-8R; 25-28R; DLB 9
Costantini, Humberto 1924(?)-1987 **CLC 49**
See also CA 131; 122; HW 1
Costello, Elvis 1955- **CLC 21**
Costenoble, Philostene
See Ghelderode, Michel de
Cotes, Cecil V.
See Duncan, Sara Jeannette
Cotter, Joseph Seamon Sr. 1861-1949 **TCLC 28; BLC 1; DAM MULT**
See also BW 1; CA 124; DLB 50
Couch, Arthur Thomas Quiller
See Quiller-Couch, SirArthur (Thomas)
Coulton, James
See Hansen, Joseph
Couperus, Louis (Marie Anne) 1863-1923 **TCLC 15**
See also CA 115
Coupland, Douglas 1961- **CLC 85; DAC; DAM POP**
See also AAYA 34; CA 142; CANR 57, 90
Court, Wesli
See Turco, Lewis (Putnam)
Courtenay, Bryce 1933- **CLC 59**
See also CA 138
Courtney, Robert
See Ellison, Harlan (Jay)
Cousteau, Jacques-Yves 1910-1997 **CLC 30**
See also CA 65-68; 159; CANR 15, 67; MTCW 1; SATA 38, 98
Coventry, Francis 1725-1754 **LC 46**
Cowan, Peter (Walkinshaw) 1914- **SSC 28**
See also CA 21-24R; CANR 9, 25, 50, 83
Coward, Noel (Peirce) 1899-1973 **CLC 1, 9, 29, 51; DAM DRAM**
See also AITN 1; CA 17-18; 41-44R; CANR 35; CAP 2; CDBLB 1914-1945; DA3; DLB 10; MTCW 1, 2

Cowley, Abraham 1618-1667 **LC 43**
See also DLB 131, 151

Cowley, Malcolm 1898-1989 **CLC 39**
See also CA 5-8R; 128; CANR 3, 55; DLB 4, 48; DLBY 81, 89; MTCW 1, 2

Cowper, William 1731-1800 **NCLC 8; DAM POET**
See also DA3; DLB 104, 109

Cox, William Trevor 1928- **CLC 9, 14, 71; DAM NOV**
See also Trevor, William
See also CA 9-12R; CANR 4, 37, 55, 76; DLB 14; INT CANR-37; MTCW 1, 2

Coyne, P. J.
See Masters, Hilary

Cozzens, James Gould 1903-1978 **CLC 1, 4, 11, 92**
See also CA 9-12R; 81-84; CANR 19; CDALB 1941-1968; DLB 9; DLBD 2; DLBY 84, 97; MTCW 1, 2

Crabbe, George 1754-1832 **NCLC 26**
See also DLB 93

Craddock, Charles Egbert
See Murfree, Mary Noailles

Craig, A. A.
See Anderson, Poul (William)

Craik, Dinah Maria (Mulock) 1826-1887 **NCLC 38**
See also DLB 35, 163; MAICYA; SATA 34

Cram, Ralph Adams 1863-1942 **TCLC 45**
See also CA 160

Crane, (Harold) Hart 1899-1932 **TCLC 2, 5, 80; DA; DAB; DAC; DAM MST, POET; PC 3; WLC**
See also CA 104; 127; CDALB 1917-1929; DA3; DLB 4, 48; MTCW 1, 2

Crane, R(onald) S(almon) 1886-1967 **CLC 27**
See also CA 85-88; DLB 63

Crane, Stephen (Townley) 1871-1900 **TCLC 11, 17, 32; DA; DAB; DAC; DAM MST, NOV, POET; SSC 7; WLC**
See also AAYA 21; CA 109; 140; CANR 84; CDALB 1865-1917; DA3; DLB 12, 54, 78; YABC 2

Cranshaw, Stanley
See Fisher, Dorothy (Frances) Canfield

Crase, Douglas 1944- **CLC 58**
See also CA 106

Crashaw, Richard 1612(?)-1649 **LC 24**
See also DLB 126

Craven, Margaret 1901-1980 **CLC 17; DAC**
See also CA 103

Crawford, F(rancis) Marion 1854-1909 **TCLC 10**
See also CA 107; 168; DLB 71

Crawford, Isabella Valancy 1850-1887 **NCLC 12**
See also DLB 92

Crayon, Geoffrey
See Irving, Washington

Creasey, John 1908-1973 **CLC 11**
See also CA 5-8R; 41-44R; CANR 8, 59; DLB 77; MTCW 1

Crebillon, Claude Prosper Jolyot de (fils) 1707-1777 **LC 1, 28**

Credo
See Creasey, John

Credo, Alvaro J. de
See Prado (Calvo), Pedro

Creeley, Robert (White) 1926- **CLC 1, 2, 4, 8, 11, 15, 36, 78; DAM POET**
See also CA 1-4R; CAAS 10; CANR 23, 43, 89; DA3; DLB 5, 16, 169; DLBD 17; MTCW 1, 2

Crews, Harry (Eugene) 1935- **CLC 6, 23, 49**
See also AITN 1; CA 25-28R; CANR 20, 57; DA3; DLB 6, 143, 185; MTCW 1, 2

Crichton, (John) Michael 1942- **CLC 2, 6,**

54, 90; **DAM NOV, POP**
See also AAYA 10; AITN 2; CA 25-28R; CANR 13, 40, 54, 76; DA3; DLBY 81; INT CANR-13; JRDA; MTCW 1, 2; SATA 9, 88

Crispin, Edmund CLC 22
See also Montgomery, (Robert) Bruce
See also DLB 87

Cristofer, Michael 1945(?)- **CLC 28; DAM DRAM**
See also CA 110; 152; DLB 7

Croce, Benedetto 1866-1952 **TCLC 37**
See also CA 120; 155

Crockett, David 1786-1836 **NCLC 8**
See also DLB 3, 11

Crockett, Davy
See Crockett, David

Crofts, Freeman Wills 1879-1957 **TCLC 55**
See also CA 115; DLB 77

Croker, John Wilson 1780-1857 **NCLC 10**
See also DLB 110

Crommelynck, Fernand 1885-1970 **CLC 75**
See also CA 89-92

Cromwell, Oliver 1599-1658 **LC 43**

Cronin, A(rchibald) J(oseph) 1896-1981 **CLC 32**
See also CA 1-4R; 102; CANR 5; DLB 191; SATA 47; SATA-Obit 25

Cross, Amanda
See Heilbrun, Carolyn G(old)

Crothers, Rachel 1878(?)-1958 **TCLC 19**
See also CA 113; DLB 7

Croves, Hal
See Traven, B.

Crow Dog, Mary (Ellen) (?)- **CLC 93**
See also Brave Bird, Mary
See also CA 154

Crowfield, Christopher
See Stowe, Harriet (Elizabeth) Beecher

Crowley, Aleister TCLC 7
See also Crowley, Edward Alexander

Crowley, Edward Alexander 1875-1947
See Crowley, Aleister
See also CA 104

Crowley, John 1942- **CLC 57**
See also CA 61-64; CANR 43; DLBY 82; SATA 65

Crud
See Crumb, R(obert)

Crumarums
See Crumb, R(obert)

Crumb, R(obert) 1943- **CLC 17**
See also CA 106

Crumbum
See Crumb, R(obert)

Crumski
See Crumb, R(obert)

Crum the Bum
See Crumb, R(obert)

Crunk
See Crumb, R(obert)

Crustt
See Crumb, R(obert)

Cruz, Victor Hernandez 1949-
See also BW 2; CA 65-68; CAAS 17; CANR 14, 32, 74; DAM MULT, POET; DLB 41; HLC 1; HW 1, 2; MTCW 1

Cryer, Gretchen (Kiger) 1935- **CLC 21**
See also CA 114; 123

Csath, Geza 1887-1919 **TCLC 13**
See also CA 111

Cudlip, David R(ockwell) 1933- **CLC 34**
See also CA 177

Cullen, Countee 1903-1946 **TCLC 4, 37; BLC 1; DA; DAC; DAM MST, MULT, POET; PC 20; WLCS**

See also BW 1; CA 108; 124; CDALB 1917-1929; DA3; DLB 4, 48, 51; MTCW 1, 2; SATA 18

Cum, R.
See Crumb, R(obert)

Cummings, Bruce F(rederick) 1889-1919
See Barbellion, W. N. P.
See also CA 123

Cummings, E(dward) E(stlin) 1894-1962 **CLC 1, 3, 8, 12, 15, 68; DA; DAB; DAC; DAM MST, POET; PC 5; WLC**
See also CA 73-76; CANR 31; CDALB 1929-1941; DA3; DLB 4, 48; MTCW 1, 2

Cunha, Euclides (Rodrigues Pimenta) da 1866-1909 **TCLC 24**
See also CA 123

Cunningham, E. V.
See Fast, Howard (Melvin)

Cunningham, J(ames) V(incent) 1911-1985 **CLC 3, 31**
See also CA 1-4R; 115; CANR 1, 72; DLB 5

Cunningham, Julia (Woolfolk) 1916- **CLC 12**
See also CA 9-12R; CANR 4, 19, 36; JRDA; MAICYA; SAAS 2; SATA 1, 26

Cunningham, Michael 1952- **CLC 34**
See also CA 136

Cunninghame Graham, R. B.
See Cunninghame Graham, Robert (Gallnigad) Bontine

Cunninghame Graham, Robert (Gallnigad) Bontine 1852-1936 **TCLC 19**
See also Graham, R(obert) B(ontine) Cunninghame
See also CA 119; 184; DLB 98

Currie, Ellen 19(?)- **CLC 44**

Curtin, Philip
See Lowndes, Marie Adelaide (Belloc)

Curtis, Price
See Ellison, Harlan (Jay)

Cutrate, Joe
See Spiegelman, Art

Cynewulf c. 770-c. 840 **CMLC 23**

Czaczkes, Shmuel Yosef
See Agnon, S(hmuel) Y(osef Halevi)

Dabrowska, Maria (Szumska) 1889-1965 **CLC 15**
See also CA 106

Dabydeen, David 1955- **CLC 34**
See also BW 1; CA 125; CANR 56

Dacey, Philip 1939- **CLC 51**
See also CA 37-40R; CAAS 17; CANR 14, 32, 64; DLB 105

Dagerman, Stig (Halvard) 1923-1954 **TCLC 17**
See also CA 117; 155

Dahl, Roald 1916-1990 **CLC 1, 6, 18, 79; DAB; DAC; DAM MST, NOV, POP**
See also AAYA 15; CA 1-4R; 133; CANR 6, 32, 37, 62; CLR 1, 7, 41; DA3; DLB 139; JRDA; MAICYA; MTCW 1, 2; SATA 1, 26, 73; SATA-Obit 65

Dahlberg, Edward 1900-1977 **CLC 1, 7, 14**
See also CA 9-12R; 69-72; CANR 31, 62; DLB 48; MTCW 1

Daitch, Susan 1954- **CLC 103**
See also CA 161

Dale, Colin TCLC 18
See also Lawrence, T(homas) E(dward)

Dale, George E.
See Asimov, Isaac

Dalton, Roque 1935-1975
See also HLCS 1; HW 2

Daly, Elizabeth 1878-1967 **CLC 52**
See also CA 23-24; 25-28R; CANR 60; CAP 2

Daly, Maureen 1921- **CLC 17**

Dubus, Andre 1936-1999 **CLC 13, 36, 97; SSC 15**
See also CA 21-24R; 177; CANR 17; DLB 130; INT CANR-17

Duca Minimo
See D'Annunzio, Gabriele

Ducharme, Rejean 1941- **CLC 74**
See also CA 165; DLB 60

Duclos, Charles Pinot 1704-1772 **LC 1**

Dudek, Louis 1918- **CLC 11, 19**
See also CA 45-48; CAAS 14; CANR 1; DLB 88

Duerrenmatt, Friedrich 1921-1990 **CLC 1, 4, 8, 11, 15, 43, 102; DAM DRAM**
See also CA 17-20R; CANR 33; DLB 69, 124; MTCW 1, 2

Duffy, Bruce 1953(?)- **CLC 50**
See also CA 172

Duffy, Maureen 1933- **CLC 37**
See also CA 25-28R; CANR 33, 68; DLB 14; MTCW 1

Dugan, Alan 1923- **CLC 2, 6**
See also CA 81-84; DLB 5

du Gard, Roger Martin
See Martin du Gard, Roger

Duhamel, Georges 1884-1966 **CLC 8**
See also CA 81-84; 25-28R; CANR 35; DLB 65; MTCW 1

Dujardin, Edouard (Emile Louis) 1861-1949 **TCLC 13**
See also CA 109; DLB 123

Dulles, John Foster 1888-1959 **TCLC 72**
See also CA 115; 149

Dumas, Alexandre (pere)
See Dumas, Alexandre (Davy de la Pailleterie)

Dumas, Alexandre (Davy de la Pailleterie) 1802-1870 **NCLC 11, 71; DA; DAB; DAC; DAM MST, NOV; WLC**
See also DA3; DLB 119, 192; SATA 18

Dumas, Alexandre (fils) 1824-1895 **NCLC 71; DC 1**
See also AAYA 22; DLB 192

Dumas, Claudine
See Malzberg, Barry N(athaniel)

Dumas, Henry L. 1934-1968 **CLC 6, 62**
See also BW 1; CA 85-88; DLB 41

du Maurier, Daphne 1907-1989 **CLC 6, 11, 59; DAB; DAC; DAM MST, POP; SSC 18**
See also CA 5-8R; 128; CANR 6, 55; DA3; DLB 191; MTCW 1, 2; SATA 27; SATA-Obit 60

Du Maurier, George 1834-1896 **NCLC 86**
See also DLB 153, 178

Dunbar, Paul Laurence 1872-1906 **TCLC 2, 12; BLC 1; DA; DAC; DAM MST, MULT, POET; PC 5; SSC 8; WLC**
See also BW 1, 3; CA 104; 124; CANR 79; CDALB 1865-1917; DA3; DLB 50, 54, 78; SATA 34

Dunbar, William 1460(?)-1530(?) **LC 20**
See also DLB 132, 146

Duncan, Dora Angela
See Duncan, Isadora

Duncan, Isadora 1877(?)-1927 **TCLC 68**
See also CA 118; 149

Duncan, Lois 1934- **CLC 26**
See also AAYA 4, 34; CA 1-4R; CANR 2, 23, 36; CLR 29; JRDA; MAICYA; SAAS 2; SATA 1, 36, 75

Duncan, Robert (Edward) 1919-1988 **CLC 1, 2, 4, 7, 15, 41, 55; DAM POET; PC 2**
See also CA 9-12R; 124; CANR 28, 62; DLB 5, 16, 193; MTCW 1, 2

Duncan, Sara Jeannette 1861-1922 **TCLC 60**
See also CA 157; DLB 92

Dunlap, William 1766-1839 **NCLC 2**
See also DLB 30, 37, 59

Dunn, Douglas (Eaglesham) 1942- **CLC 6, 40**
See also CA 45-48; CANR 2, 33; DLB 40; MTCW 1

Dunn, Katherine (Karen) 1945- **CLC 71**
See also CA 33-36R; CANR 72; MTCW 1

Dunn, Stephen 1939- **CLC 36**
See also CA 33-36R; CANR 12, 48, 53; DLB 105

Dunne, Finley Peter 1867-1936 **TCLC 28**
See also CA 108; 178; DLB 11, 23

Dunne, John Gregory 1932- **CLC 28**
See also CA 25-28R; CANR 14, 50; DLBY 80

Dunsany, Edward John Moreton Drax Plunkett 1878-1957
See Dunsany, Lord
See also CA 104; 148; DLB 10; MTCW 1

Dunsany, Lord **TCLC 2, 59**
See also Dunsany, Edward John Moreton Drax Plunkett
See also DLB 77, 153, 156

du Perry, Jean
See Simenon, Georges (Jacques Christian)

Durang, Christopher (Ferdinand) 1949- **CLC 27, 38**
See also CA 105; CANR 50, 76; MTCW 1

Duras, Marguerite 1914-1996 **CLC 3, 6, 11, 20, 34, 40, 68, 100; SSC 40**
See also CA 25-28R; 151; CANR 50; DLB 83; MTCW 1, 2

Durban, (Rosa) Pam 1947- **CLC 39**
See also CA 123

Durcan, Paul 1944- **CLC 43, 70; DAM POET**
See also CA 134

Durkheim, Emile 1858-1917 **TCLC 55**

Durrell, Lawrence (George) 1912-1990 **CLC 1, 4, 6, 8, 13, 27, 41; DAM NOV**
See also CA 9-12R; 132; CANR 40, 77; CDBLB 1945-1960; DLB 15, 27, 204; DLBY 90; MTCW 1, 2

Durrenmatt, Friedrich
See Duerrenmatt, Friedrich

Dutt, Toru 1856-1877 **NCLC 29**

Dwight, Timothy 1752-1817 **NCLC 13**
See also DLB 37

Dworkin, Andrea 1946- **CLC 43**
See also CA 77-80; CAAS 21; CANR 16, 39, 76; INT CANR-16; MTCW 1, 2

Dwyer, Deanna
See Koontz, Dean R(ay)

Dwyer, K. R.
See Koontz, Dean R(ay)

Dwyer, Thomas A. 1923- **CLC 114**
See also CA 115

Dye, Richard
See De Voto, Bernard (Augustine)

Dylan, Bob 1941- **CLC 3, 4, 6, 12, 77**
See also CA 41-44R; DLB 16

E. V. L.
See Lucas, E(dward) V(errall)

Eagleton, Terence (Francis) 1943- **CLC 132**
See also Eagleton, Terry
See also CA 57-60; CANR 7, 23, 68; MTCW 1, 2

Eagleton, Terry **CLC 63**
See also Eagleton, Terence (Francis)
See also MTCW 1

Early, Jack
See Scoppettone, Sandra

East, Michael
See West, Morris L(anglo)

Eastaway, Edward
See Thomas, (Philip) Edward

Eastlake, William (Derry) 1917-1997 **CLC 8**
See also CA 5-8R; 158; CAAS 1; CANR 5, 63; DLB 6, 206; INT CANR-5

Eastman, Charles A(lexander) 1858-1939 **TCLC 55; DAM MULT**
See also CA 179; CANR 91; DLB 175; NNAL; YABC 1

Eberhart, Richard (Ghormley) 1904- **CLC 3, 11, 19, 56; DAM POET**
See also CA 1-4R; CANR 2; CDALB 1941-1968; DLB 48; MTCW 1

Eberstadt, Fernanda 1960- **CLC 39**
See also CA 136; CANR 69

Echegaray (y Eizaguirre), Jose (Maria Waldo) 1832-1916 **TCLC 4; HLCS 1**
See also CA 104; CANR 32; HW 1; MTCW 1

Echeverria, (Jose) Esteban (Antonino) 1805-1851 **NCLC 18**

Echo
See Proust, (Valentin-Louis-George-Eugene-) Marcel

Eckert, Allan W. 1931- **CLC 17**
See also AAYA 18; CA 13-16R; CANR 14, 45; INT CANR-14; SAAS 21; SATA 29, 91; SATA-Brief 27

Eckhart, Meister 1260(?)-1328(?) **CMLC 9**
See also DLB 115

Eckmar, F. R.
See de Hartog, Jan

Eco, Umberto 1932- **CLC 28, 60; DAM NOV, POP**
See also BEST 90:1; CA 77-80; CANR 12, 33, 55; DA3; DLB 196; MTCW 1, 2

Eddison, E(ric) R(ucker) 1882-1945 **TCLC 15**
See also CA 109; 156

Eddy, Mary (Ann Morse) Baker 1821-1910 **TCLC 71**
See also CA 113; 174

Edel, (Joseph) Leon 1907-1997 **CLC 29, 34**
See also CA 1-4R; 161; CANR 1, 22; DLB 103; INT CANR-22

Eden, Emily 1797-1869 **NCLC 10**

Edgar, David 1948- **CLC 42; DAM DRAM**
See also CA 57-60; CANR 12, 61; DLB 13; MTCW 1

Edgerton, Clyde (Carlyle) 1944- **CLC 39**
See also AAYA 17; CA 118; 134; CANR 64; INT 134

Edgeworth, Maria 1768-1849 **NCLC 1, 51**
See also DLB 116, 159, 163; SATA 21

Edmonds, Paul
See Kuttner, Henry

Edmonds, Walter D(umaux) 1903-1998 **CLC 35**
See also CA 5-8R; CANR 2; DLB 9; MAICYA; SAAS 4; SATA 1, 27; SATA-Obit 99

Edmondson, Wallace
See Ellison, Harlan (Jay)

Edson, Russell **CLC 13**
See also CA 33-36R

Edwards, Bronwen Elizabeth
See Rose, Wendy

Edwards, G(erald) B(asil) 1899-1976 **CLC 25**
See also CA 110

Edwards, Gus 1939- **CLC 43**
See also CA 108; INT 108

Edwards, Jonathan 1703-1758 **LC 7, 54; DA; DAC; DAM MST**
See also DLB 24

Efron, Marina Ivanovna Tsvetaeva
See Tsvetaeva (Efron), Marina (Ivanovna)

Ehle, John (Marsden, Jr.) 1925- **CLC 27**
See also CA 9-12R

Ehrenbourg, Ilya (Grigoryevich)
See Ehrenburg, Ilya (Grigoryevich)

Ehrenburg, Ilya (Grigoryevich) 1891-1967 **CLC 18, 34, 62**
See also CA 102; 25-28R

Ehrenburg, Ilyo (Grigoryevich)
See Ehrenburg, Ilya (Grigoryevich)
Ehrenreich, Barbara 1941- **CLC 110**
See also BEST 90:4; CA 73-76; CANR 16, 37, 62; MTCW 1, 2
Eich, Guenter 1907-1972 **CLC 15**
See also CA 111; 93-96; DLB 69, 124
Eichendorff, Joseph Freiherr von 1788-1857 **NCLC 8**
See also DLB 90
Eigner, Larry CLC 9
See also Eigner, Laurence (Joel)
See also CAAS 23; DLB 5
Eigner, Laurence (Joel) 1927-1996
See Eigner, Larry
See also CA 9-12R; 151; CANR 6, 84; DLB 193
Einstein, Albert 1879-1955 **TCLC 65**
See also CA 121; 133; MTCW 1, 2
Eiseley, Loren Corey 1907-1977 **CLC 7**
See also AAYA 5; CA 1-4R; 73-76; CANR 6; DLBD 17
Eisenstadt, Jill 1963- **CLC 50**
See also CA 140
Eisenstein, Sergei (Mikhailovich) 1898-1948 **TCLC 57**
See also CA 114; 149
Eisner, Simon
See Kornbluth, C(yril) M.
Ekeloef, (Bengt) Gunnar 1907-1968 **CLC 27; DAM POET; PC 23**
See also CA 123; 25-28R
Ekelof, (Bengt) Gunnar
See Ekeloef, (Bengt) Gunnar
Ekelund, Vilhelm 1880-1949 **TCLC 75**
Ekwensi, C. O. D.
See Ekwensi, Cyprian (Odiatu Duaka)
Ekwensi, Cyprian (Odiatu Duaka) 1921- **CLC 4; BLC 1; DAM MULT**
See also BW 2, 3; CA 29-32R; CANR 18, 42, 74; DLB 117; MTCW 1, 2; SATA 66
Elaine TCLC 18
See also Leverson, Ada
El Crummo
See Crumb, R(obert)
Elder, Lonne III 1931-1996 **DC 8**
See also BLC 1; BW 1, 3; CA 81-84; 152; CANR 25; DAM MULT; DLB 7, 38, 44
Eleanor of Aquitaine 1122-1204 **CMLC 39**
Elia
See Lamb, Charles
Eliade, Mircea 1907-1986 **CLC 19**
See also CA 65-68; 119; CANR 30, 62; DLB 220; MTCW 1
Eliot, A. D.
See Jewett, (Theodora) Sarah Orne
Eliot, Alice
See Jewett, (Theodora) Sarah Orne
Eliot, Dan
See Silverberg, Robert
Eliot, George 1819-1880 **NCLC 4, 13, 23, 41, 49; DA; DAB; DAC; DAM MST, NOV; PC 20; WLC**
See also CDBLB 1832-1890; DA3; DLB 21, 35, 55
Eliot, John 1604-1690 **LC 5**
See also DLB 24
Eliot, T(homas) S(tearns) 1888-1965 **CLC 1, 2, 3, 6, 9, 10, 13, 15, 24, 34, 41, 55, 57, 113; DA; DAB; DAC; DAM DRAM, MST, POET; PC 5; WLC**
See also AAYA 28; CA 5-8R; 25-28R; CANR 41; CDALB 1929-1941; DA3; DLB 7, 10, 45, 63; DLBY 88; MTCW 1, 2
Elizabeth 1866-1941 **TCLC 41**
Elkin, Stanley L(awrence) 1930-1995 **CLC 4,**

6, 9, 14, 27, 51, 91; **DAM NOV, POP; SSC 12**
See also CA 9-12R; 148; CANR 8, 46; DLB 2, 28; DLBY 80; INT CANR-8; MTCW 1, 2
Elledge, Scott CLC 34
Elliot, Don
See Silverberg, Robert
Elliott, Don
See Silverberg, Robert
Elliott, George P(aul) 1918-1980 **CLC 2**
See also CA 1-4R; 97-100; CANR 2
Elliott, Janice 1931- **CLC 47**
See also CA 13-16R; CANR 8, 29, 84; DLB 14
Elliott, Sumner Locke 1917-1991 **CLC 38**
See also CA 5-8R; 134; CANR 2, 21
Elliott, William
See Bradbury, Ray (Douglas)
Ellis, A. E. CLC 7
Ellis, Alice Thomas CLC 40
See also Haycraft, Anna (Margaret)
See also DLB 194; MTCW 1
Ellis, Bret Easton 1964- **CLC 39, 71, 117; DAM POP**
See also AAYA 2; CA 118; 123; CANR 51, 74; DA3; INT 123; MTCW 1
Ellis, (Henry) Havelock 1859-1939 **TCLC 14**
See also CA 109; 169; DLB 190
Ellis, Landon
See Ellison, Harlan (Jay)
Ellis, Trey 1962- **CLC 55**
See also CA 146
Ellison, Harlan (Jay) 1934- **CLC 1, 13, 42; DAM POP; SSC 14**
See also AAYA 29; CA 5-8R; CANR 5, 46; DLB 8; INT CANR-5; MTCW 1, 2
Ellison, Ralph (Waldo) 1914-1994 **CLC 1, 3, 11, 54, 86, 114; BLC 1; DA; DAB; DAC; DAM MST, MULT, NOV; SSC 26; WLC**
See also AAYA 19; BW 1, 3; CA 9-12R; 145; CANR 24, 53; CDALB 1941-1968; DA3; DLB 2, 76; DLBY 94; MTCW 1, 2
Ellmann, Lucy (Elizabeth) 1956- **CLC 61**
See also CA 128
Ellmann, Richard (David) 1918-1987 **CLC 50**
See also BEST 89:2; CA 1-4R; 122; CANR 2, 28, 61; DLB 103; DLBY 87; MTCW 1, 2
Elman, Richard (Martin) 1934-1997 **CLC 19**
See also CA 17-20R; 163; CAAS 3; CANR 47
Elron
See Hubbard, L(afayette) Ron(ald)
Eluard, Paul TCLC 7, 41
See also Grindel, Eugene
Elyot, Sir Thomas 1490(?)-1546 **LC 11**
Elytis, Odysseus 1911-1996 **CLC 15, 49, 100; DAM POET; PC 21**
See also CA 102; 151; MTCW 1, 2
Emecheta, (Florence Onye) Buchi 1944- **CLC 14, 48, 128; BLC 2; DAM MULT**
See also BW 2, 3; CA 81-84; CANR 27, 81; DA3; DLB 117; MTCW 1, 2; SATA 66
Emerson, Mary Moody 1774-1863 **NCLC 66**
Emerson, Ralph Waldo 1803-1882 **NCLC 1, 38; DA; DAB; DAC; DAM MST, POET; PC 18; WLC**
See also CDALB 1640-1865; DA3; DLB 1, 59, 73, 223
Eminescu, Mihail 1850-1889 **NCLC 33**
Empson, William 1906-1984 **CLC 3, 8, 19, 33, 34**
See also CA 17-20R; 112; CANR 31, 61; DLB 20; MTCW 1, 2
Enchi, Fumiko (Ueda) 1905-1986 **CLC 31**

See also CA 129; 121; DLB 182
Ende, Michael (Andreas Helmuth) 1929-1995 **CLC 31**
See also CA 118; 124; 149; CANR 36; CLR 14; DLB 75; MAICYA; SATA 61; SATA-Brief 42; SATA-Obit 86
Endo, Shusaku 1923-1996 **CLC 7, 14, 19, 54, 99; DAM NOV**
See also CA 29-32R; 153; CANR 21, 54; DA3; DLB 182; MTCW 1, 2
Engel, Marian 1933-1985 **CLC 36**
See also CA 25-28R; CANR 12; DLB 53; INT CANR-12
Engelhardt, Frederick
See Hubbard, L(afayette) Ron(ald)
Engels, Friedrich 1820-1895 **NCLC 85**
See also DLB 129
Enright, D(ennis) J(oseph) 1920- **CLC 4, 8, 31**
See also CA 1-4R; CANR 1, 42, 83; DLB 27; SATA 25
Enzensberger, Hans Magnus 1929- **CLC 43; PC 28**
See also CA 116; 119
Ephron, Nora 1941- **CLC 17, 31**
See also AITN 2; CA 65-68; CANR 12, 39, 83
Epicurus 341B.C.-270B.C. **CMLC 21**
See also DLB 176
Epsilon
See Betjeman, John
Epstein, Daniel Mark 1948- **CLC 7**
See also CA 49-52; CANR 2, 53, 90
Epstein, Jacob 1956- **CLC 19**
See also CA 114
Epstein, Jean 1897-1953 **TCLC 92**
Epstein, Joseph 1937- **CLC 39**
See also CA 112; 119; CANR 50, 65
Epstein, Leslie 1938- **CLC 27**
See also CA 73-76; CAAS 12; CANR 23, 69
Equiano, Olaudah 1745(?)-1797 **LC 16; BLC 2; DAM MULT**
See also DLB 37, 50
ER TCLC 33
See also CA 160; DLB 85
Erasmus, Desiderius 1469(?)-1536 **LC 16**
Erdman, Paul E(mil) 1932- **CLC 25**
See also AITN 1; CA 61-64; CANR 13, 43, 84
Erdrich, Louise 1954- **CLC 39, 54, 120; DAM MULT, NOV, POP**
See also AAYA 10; BEST 89:1; CA 114; CANR 41, 62; CDALBS; DA3; DLB 152, 175, 206; MTCW 1; NNAL; SATA 94
Erenburg, Ilya (Grigoryevich)
See Ehrenburg, Ilya (Grigoryevich)
Erickson, Stephen Michael 1950-
See Erickson, Steve
See also CA 129
Erickson, Steve 1950- **CLC 64**
See also Erickson, Stephen Michael
See also CANR 60, 68
Ericson, Walter
See Fast, Howard (Melvin)
Eriksson, Buntel
See Bergman, (Ernst) Ingmar
Ernaux, Annie 1940- **CLC 88**
See also CA 147
Erskine, John 1879-1951 **TCLC 84**
See also CA 112; 159; DLB 9, 102
Eschenbach, Wolfram von
See Wolfram von Eschenbach
Eseki, Bruno
See Mphahlele, Ezekiel
Esenin, Sergei (Alexandrovich) 1895-1925 **TCLC 4**
See also CA 104

Eshleman, Clayton 1935- **CLC 7**
See also CA 33-36R; CAAS 6; DLB 5

Espriella, Don Manuel Alvarez
See Southey, Robert

Espriu, Salvador 1913-1985 **CLC 9**
See also CA 154; 115; DLB 134

Espronceda, Jose de 1808-1842 **NCLC 39**

Esquivel, Laura 1951(?)-
See also AAYA 29; CA 143; CANR 68;
DA3; HLCS 1; MTCW 1

Esse, James
See Stephens, James

Esterbrook, Tom
See Hubbard, L(afayette) Ron(ald)

Estleman, Loren D. 1952- **CLC 48; DAM
NOV, POP**
See also AAYA 27; CA 85-88; CANR 27,
74; DA3; INT CANR-27; MTCW 1, 2

Euclid 306B.C.-283B.C. **CMLC 25**

Eugenides, Jeffrey 1960(?)- **CLC 81**
See also CA 144

Euripides c. 485B.C.-406B.C. **CMLC 23; DA;
DAB; DAC; DAM DRAM, MST; DC 4;
WLCS**
See also DA3; DLB 176

Evan, Evin
See Faust, Frederick (Schiller)

Evans, Caradoc 1878-1945 **TCLC 85**

Evans, Evan
See Faust, Frederick (Schiller)

Evans, Marian
See Eliot, George

Evans, Mary Ann
See Eliot, George

Evarts, Esther
See Benson, Sally

Everett, Percival L. 1956- **CLC 57**
See also BW 2; CA 129

Everson, R(onald) G(ilmour) 1903- **CLC 27**
See also CA 17-20R; DLB 88

Everson, William (Oliver) 1912-1994 **CLC 1,
5, 14**
See also CA 9-12R; 145; CANR 20; DLB
212; MTCW 1

Evtushenko, Evgenii Aleksandrovich
See Yevtushenko, Yevgeny (Alexandrovich)

Ewart, Gavin (Buchanan) 1916-1995 **CLC
13, 46**
See also CA 89-92; 150; CANR 17, 46;
DLB 40; MTCW 1

Ewers, Hanns Heinz 1871-1943 **TCLC 12**
See also CA 109; 149

Ewing, Frederick R.
See Sturgeon, Theodore (Hamilton)

Exley, Frederick (Earl) 1929-1992 **CLC 6, 11**
See also AITN 2; CA 81-84; 138; DLB 143;
DLBY 81

Eynhardt, Guillermo
See Quiroga, Horacio (Sylvestre)

Ezekiel, Nissim 1924- **CLC 61**
See also CA 61-64

Ezekiel, Tish O'Dowd 1943- **CLC 34**
See also CA 129

Fadeyev, A.
See Bulgya, Alexander Alexandrovich

Fadeyev, Alexander TCLC 53
See also Bulgya, Alexander Alexandrovich

Fagen, Donald 1948- **CLC 26**

Fainzilberg, Ilya Arnoldovich 1897-1937
See Ilf, Ilya
See also CA 120; 165

Fair, Ronald L. 1932- **CLC 18**
See also BW 1; CA 69-72; CANR 25; DLB
33

Fairbairn, Roger
See Carr, John Dickson

Fairbairns, Zoe (Ann) 1948- **CLC 32**
See also CA 103; CANR 21, 85

Falco, Gian
See Papini, Giovanni

Falconer, James
See Kirkup, James

Falconer, Kenneth
See Kornbluth, C(yril) M.

Falkland, Samuel
See Heijermans, Herman

Fallaci, Oriana 1930- **CLC 11, 110**
See also CA 77-80; CANR 15, 58; MTCW
1

Faludy, George 1913- **CLC 42**
See also CA 21-24R

Faludy, Gyoergy
See Faludy, George

Fanon, Frantz 1925-1961 **CLC 74; BLC 2;
DAM MULT**
See also BW 1; CA 116; 89-92

Fanshawe, Ann 1625-1680 **LC 11**

Fante, John (Thomas) 1911-1983 **CLC 60**
See also CA 69-72; 109; CANR 23; DLB
130; DLBY 83

Farah, Nuruddin 1945- **CLC 53; BLC 2;
DAM MULT**
See also BW 2, 3; CA 106; CANR 81; DLB
125

Fargue, Leon-Paul 1876(?)-1947 **TCLC 11**
See also CA 109

Farigoule, Louis
See Romains, Jules

Farina, Richard 1936(?)-1966 **CLC 9**
See also CA 81-84; 25-28R

Farley, Walter (Lorimer) 1915-1989 **CLC 17**
See also CA 17-20R; CANR 8, 29, 84; DLB
22; JRDA; MAICYA; SATA 2, 43

Farmer, Philip Jose 1918- **CLC 1, 19**
See also AAYA 28; CA 1-4R; CANR 4, 35;
DLB 8; MTCW 1; SATA 93

Farquhar, George 1677-1707 **LC 21; DAM
DRAM**
See also DLB 84

Farrell, J(ames) G(ordon) 1935-1979 **CLC 6**
See also CA 73-76; 89-92; CANR 36; DLB
14; MTCW 1

Farrell, James T(homas) 1904-1979 **CLC 1,
4, 8, 11, 66; SSC 28**
See also CA 5-8R; 89-92; CANR 9, 61;
DLB 4, 9, 86; DLBD 2; MTCW 1, 2

Farren, Richard J.
See Betjeman, John

Farren, Richard M.
See Betjeman, John

Fassbinder, Rainer Werner 1946-1982 **CLC
20**
See also CA 93-96; 106; CANR 31

Fast, Howard (Melvin) 1914- **CLC 23, 131;
DAM NOV**
See also AAYA 16; CA 1-4R, 181; CAAE
181; CAAS 18; CANR 1, 33, 54, 75; DLB
9; INT CANR-33; MTCW 1; SATA 7;
SATA-Essay 107

Faulcon, Robert
See Holdstock, Robert P.

Faulkner, William (Cuthbert) 1897-1962
**CLC 1, 3, 6, 8, 9, 11, 14, 18, 28, 52, 68;
DA; DAB; DAC; DAM MST, NOV;
SSC 1, 35; WLC**
See also AAYA 7; CA 81-84; CANR 33;
CDALB 1929-1941; DA3; DLB 9, 11, 44,
102; DLBD 2; DLBY 86, 97; MTCW 1, 2

Fauset, Jessie Redmon 1884(?)-1961 **CLC 19,
54; BLC 2; DAM MULT**
See also BW 1; CA 109; CANR 83; DLB
51

Faust, Frederick (Schiller) 1892-1944(?)
TCLC 49; DAM POP
See also CA 108; 152

Faust, Irvin 1924- **CLC 8**
See also CA 33-36R; CANR 28, 67; DLB
2, 28; DLBY 80

Fawkes, Guy
See Benchley, Robert (Charles)

Fearing, Kenneth (Flexner) 1902-1961 **CLC
51**
See also CA 93-96; CANR 59; DLB 9

Fecamps, Elise
See Creasey, John

Federman, Raymond 1928- **CLC 6, 47**
See also CA 17-20R; CAAS 8; CANR 10,
43, 83; DLBY 80

Federspiel, J(uerg) F. 1931- **CLC 42**
See also CA 146

Feiffer, Jules (Ralph) 1929- **CLC 2, 8, 64;
DAM DRAM**
See also AAYA 3; CA 17-20R; CANR 30,
59; DLB 7, 44; INT CANR-30; MTCW
1; SATA 8, 61, 111

Feige, Hermann Albert Otto Maximilian
See Traven, B.

Feinberg, David B. 1956-1994 **CLC 59**
See also CA 135; 147

Feinstein, Elaine 1930- **CLC 36**
See also CA 69-72; CAAS 1; CANR 31,
68; DLB 14, 40; MTCW 1

Feldman, Irving (Mordecai) 1928- **CLC 7**
See also CA 1-4R; CANR 1; DLB 169

Felix-Tchicaya, Gerald
See Tchicaya, Gerald Felix

Fellini, Federico 1920-1993 **CLC 16, 85**
See also CA 65-68; 143; CANR 33

Felsen, Henry Gregor 1916-1995 **CLC 17**
See also CA 1-4R; 180; CANR 1; SAAS 2;
SATA 1

Fenno, Jack
See Calisher, Hortense

Fenollosa, Ernest (Francisco) 1853-1908
TCLC 91

Fenton, James Martin 1949- **CLC 32**
See also CA 102; DLB 40

Ferber, Edna 1887-1968 **CLC 18, 93**
See also AITN 1; CA 5-8R; 25-28R; CANR
68; DLB 9, 28, 86; MTCW 1, 2; SATA 7

Ferguson, Helen
See Kavan, Anna

Ferguson, Samuel 1810-1886 **NCLC 33**
See also DLB 32

Fergusson, Robert 1750-1774 **LC 29**
See also DLB 109

Ferling, Lawrence
See Ferlinghetti, Lawrence (Monsanto)

Ferlinghetti, Lawrence (Monsanto) 1919(?)-
**CLC 2, 6, 10, 27, 111; DAM POET; PC
1**
See also CA 5-8R; CANR 3, 41, 73;
CDALB 1941-1968; DA3; DLB 5, 16;
MTCW 1, 2

Fern, Fanny 1811-1872
See Parton, Sara Payson Willis

Fernandez, Vicente Garcia Huidobro
See Huidobro Fernandez, Vicente Garcia

Ferre, Rosario 1942- **SSC 36; HLCS 1**
See also CA 131; CANR 55, 81; DLB 145;
HW 1, 2; MTCW 1

Ferrer, Gabriel (Francisco Victor) Miro
See Miro (Ferrer), Gabriel (Francisco
Victor)

Ferrier, Susan (Edmonstone) 1782-1854
NCLC 8
See also DLB 116

Ferrigno, Robert 1948(?)- **CLC 65**
See also CA 140

Ferron, Jacques 1921-1985 **CLC 94; DAC**
See also CA 117; 129; DLB 60

Feuchtwanger, Lion 1884-1958 **TCLC 3**
See also CA 104; DLB 66

Feuillet, Octave 1821-1890 **NCLC 45**

See also DLB 192

Feydeau, Georges (Leon Jules Marie)
1862-1921 **TCLC 22; DAM DRAM**
See also CA 113; 152; CANR 84; DLB 192

Fichte, Johann Gottlieb 1762-1814 **NCLC 62**
See also DLB 90

Ficino, Marsilio 1433-1499 **LC 12**

Fiedeler, Hans
See Doeblin, Alfred

Fiedler, Leslie A(aron) 1917- **CLC 4, 13, 24**
See also CA 9-12R; CANR 7, 63; DLB 28, 67; MTCW 1, 2

Field, Andrew 1938- **CLC 44**
See also CA 97-100; CANR 25

Field, Eugene 1850-1895 **NCLC 3**
See also DLB 23, 42, 140; DLBD 13; MAI-CYA; SATA 16

Field, Gans T.
See Wellman, Manly Wade

Field, Michael 1915-1971 **TCLC 43**
See also CA 29-32R

Field, Peter
See Hobson, Laura Z(ametkin)

Fielding, Henry 1707-1754 **LC 1, 46; DA; DAB; DAC; DAM DRAM, MST, NOV; WLC**
See also CDBLB 1660-1789; DA3; DLB 39, 84, 101

Fielding, Sarah 1710-1768 **LC 1, 44**
See also DLB 39

Fields, W. C. 1880-1946 **TCLC 80**
See also DLB 44

Fierstein, Harvey (Forbes) 1954- **CLC 33; DAM DRAM, POP**
See also CA 123; 129; DA3

Figes, Eva 1932- **CLC 31**
See also CA 53-56; CANR 4, 44, 83; DLB 14

Finch, Anne 1661-1720 **LC 3; PC 21**
See also DLB 95

Finch, Robert (Duer Claydon) 1900- **CLC 18**
See also CA 57-60; CANR 9, 24, 49; DLB 88

Findley, Timothy 1930- **CLC 27, 102; DAC; DAM MST**
See also CA 25-28R; CANR 12, 42, 69; DLB 53

Fink, William
See Mencken, H(enry) L(ouis)

Firbank, Louis 1942-
See Reed, Lou
See also CA 117

Firbank, (Arthur Annesley) Ronald
1886-1926 **TCLC 1**
See also CA 104; 177; DLB 36

Fisher, Dorothy (Frances) Canfield
1879-1958 **TCLC 87**
See also CA 114; 136; CANR 80; DLB 9, 102; MAICYA; YABC 1

Fisher, M(ary) F(rances) K(ennedy)
1908-1992 **CLC 76, 87**
See also CA 77-80; 138; CANR 44; MTCW 1

Fisher, Roy 1930- **CLC 25**
See also CA 81-84; CAAS 10; CANR 16; DLB 40

Fisher, Rudolph 1897-1934 **TCLC 11; BLC 2; DAM MULT; SSC 25**
See also BW 1, 3; CA 107; 124; CANR 80; DLB 51, 102

Fisher, Vardis (Alvero) 1895-1968 **CLC 7**
See also CA 5-8R; 25-28R; CANR 68; DLB 9, 206

Fiske, Tarleton
See Bloch, Robert (Albert)

Fitch, Clarke
See Sinclair, Upton (Beall)

Fitch, John IV
See Cormier, Robert (Edmund)

Fitzgerald, Captain Hugh
See Baum, L(yman) Frank

FitzGerald, Edward 1809-1883 **NCLC 9**
See also DLB 32

Fitzgerald, F(rancis) Scott (Key) 1896-1940
TCLC 1, 6, 14, 28, 55; DA; DAB; DAC; DAM MST, NOV; SSC 6, 31; WLC
See also AAYA 24; AITN 1; CA 110; 123; CDALB 1917-1929; DA3; DLB 4, 9, 86; DLBD 1, 15, 16; DLBY 81, 96; MTCW 1, 2

Fitzgerald, Penelope 1916-2000 **CLC 19, 51, 61**
See also CA 85-88; CAAS 10; CANR 56, 86; DLB 14, 194; MTCW 2

Fitzgerald, Robert (Stuart) 1910-1985 **CLC 39**
See also CA 1-4R; 114; CANR 1; DLBY 80

FitzGerald, Robert D(avid) 1902-1987 **CLC 19**
See also CA 17-20R

Fitzgerald, Zelda (Sayre) 1900-1948 **TCLC 52**
See also CA 117; 126; DLBY 84

Flanagan, Thomas (James Bonner) 1923- **CLC 25, 52**
See also CA 108; CANR 55; DLBY 80; INT 108; MTCW 1

Flaubert, Gustave 1821-1880 **NCLC 2, 10, 19, 62, 66; DA; DAB; DAC; DAM MST, NOV; SSC 11; WLC**
See also DA3; DLB 119

Flecker, Herman Elroy
See Flecker, (Herman) James Elroy

Flecker, (Herman) James Elroy 1884-1915 **TCLC 43**
See also CA 109; 150; DLB 10, 19

Fleming, Ian (Lancaster) 1908-1964 **CLC 3, 30; DAM POP**
See also AAYA 26; CA 5-8R; CANR 59; CDBLB 1945-1960; DA3; DLB 87, 201; MTCW 1, 2; SATA 9

Fleming, Thomas (James) 1927- **CLC 37**
See also CA 5-8R; CANR 10; INT CANR-10; SATA 8

Fletcher, John 1579-1625 **LC 33; DC 6**
See also CDBLB Before 1660; DLB 58

Fletcher, John Gould 1886-1950 **TCLC 35**
See also CA 107; 167; DLB 4, 45

Fleur, Paul
See Pohl, Frederik

Flooglebuckle, Al
See Spiegelman, Art

Flying Officer X
See Bates, H(erbert) E(rnest)

Fo, Dario 1926- **CLC 32, 109; DAM DRAM; DC 10**
See also CA 116; 128; CANR 68; DA3; DLBY 97; MTCW 1, 2

Fogarty, Jonathan Titulescu Esq.
See Farrell, James T(homas)

Follett, Ken(neth Martin) 1949- **CLC 18; DAM NOV, POP**
See also AAYA 6; BEST 89:4; CA 81-84; CANR 13, 33, 54; DA3; DLB 87; DLBY 81; INT CANR-33; MTCW 1

Fontane, Theodor 1819-1898 **NCLC 26**
See also DLB 129

Foote, Horton 1916- **CLC 51, 91; DAM DRAM**
See also CA 73-76; CANR 34, 51; DA3; DLB 26; INT CANR-34

Foote, Shelby 1916- **CLC 75; DAM NOV, POP**
See also CA 5-8R; CANR 3, 45, 74; DA3; DLB 2, 17; MTCW 2

Forbes, Esther 1891-1967 **CLC 12**
See also AAYA 17; CA 13-14; 25-28R; CAP 1; CLR 27; DLB 22; JRDA; MAICYA; SATA 2, 100

Forche, Carolyn (Louise) 1950- **CLC 25, 83, 86; DAM POET; PC 10**
See also CA 109; 117; CANR 50, 74; DA3; DLB 5, 193; INT 117; MTCW 1

Ford, Elbur
See Hibbert, Eleanor Alice Burford

Ford, Ford Madox 1873-1939 **TCLC 1, 15, 39, 57; DAM NOV**
See also CA 104; 132; CANR 74; CDBLB 1914-1945; DA3; DLB 162; MTCW 1, 2

Ford, Henry 1863-1947 **TCLC 73**
See also CA 115; 148

Ford, John 1586-(?) **DC 8**
See also CDBLB Before 1660; DAM DRAM; DA3; DLB 58

Ford, John 1895-1973 **CLC 16**
See also CA 45-48

Ford, Richard 1944- **CLC 46, 99**
See also CA 69-72; CANR 11, 47, 86; MTCW 1

Ford, Webster
See Masters, Edgar Lee

Foreman, Richard 1937- **CLC 50**
See also CA 65-68; CANR 32, 63

Forester, C(ecil) S(cott) 1899-1966 **CLC 35**
See also CA 73-76; 25-28R; CANR 83; DLB 191; SATA 13

Forez
See Mauriac, Francois (Charles)

Forman, James Douglas 1932- **CLC 21**
See also AAYA 17; CA 9-12R; CANR 4, 19, 42; JRDA; MAICYA; SATA 8, 70

Fornes, Maria Irene 1930- **CLC 39, 61; DC 10; HLCS 1**
See also CA 25-28R; CANR 28, 81; DLB 7; HW 1, 2; INT CANR-28; MTCW 1

Forrest, Leon (Richard) 1937-1997 **CLC 4; BLCS**
See also BW 2; CA 89-92; 162; CAAS 7; CANR 25, 52, 87; DLB 33

Forster, E(dward) M(organ) 1879-1970 **CLC 1, 2, 3, 4, 9, 10, 13, 15, 22, 45, 77; DA; DAB; DAC; DAM MST, NOV; SSC 27; WLC**
See also AAYA 2; CA 13-14; 25-28R; CANR 45; CAP 1; CDBLB 1914-1945; DA3; DLB 34, 98, 162, 178, 195; DLBD 10; MTCW 1, 2; SATA 57

Forster, John 1812-1876 **NCLC 11**
See also DLB 144, 184

Forsyth, Frederick 1938- **CLC 2, 5, 36; DAM NOV, POP**
See also BEST 89:4; CA 85-88; CANR 38, 62; DLB 87; MTCW 1, 2

Forten, Charlotte L. TCLC 16; BLC 2
See also Grimke, Charlotte L(ottie) Forten
See also DLB 50

Foscolo, Ugo 1778-1827 **NCLC 8**

Fosse, Bob CLC 20
See also Fosse, Robert Louis

Fosse, Robert Louis 1927-1987
See Fosse, Bob
See also CA 110; 123

Foster, Stephen Collins 1826-1864 **NCLC 26**

Foucault, Michel 1926-1984 **CLC 31, 34, 69**
See also CA 105; 113; CANR 34; MTCW 1, 2

Fouque, Friedrich (Heinrich Karl) de la Motte 1777-1843 **NCLC 2**
See also DLB 90

Fourier, Charles 1772-1837 **NCLC 51**

Fournier, Pierre 1916- **CLC 11**
See also Gascar, Pierre
See also CA 89-92; CANR 16, 40

Fowles, John (Philip) 1926- **CLC 1, 2, 3, 4, 6,**

9, 10, 15, 33, 87; DAB; DAC; DAM MST; SSC 33
See also CA 5-8R; CANR 25, 71; CDBLB 1960 to Present; DA3; DLB 14, 139, 207; MTCW 1, 2; SATA 22

Fox, Paula 1923- **CLC 2, 8, 121**
See also AAYA 3; CA 73-76; CANR 20, 36, 62; CLR 1, 44; DLB 52; JRDA; MAI-CYA; MTCW 1; SATA 17, 60

Fox, William Price (Jr.) 1926- **CLC 22**
See also CA 17-20R; CAAS 19; CANR 11; DLB 2; DLBY 81

Foxe, John 1516(?)-1587 **LC 14**
See also DLB 132

Frame, Janet 1924- **CLC 2, 3, 6, 22, 66, 96; SSC 29**
See also Clutha, Janet Paterson Frame

France, Anatole TCLC 9
See also Thibault, Jacques Anatole Francois
See also DLB 123; MTCW 1

Francis, Claude 19(?)- **CLC 50**

Francis, Dick 1920- **CLC 2, 22, 42, 102; DAM POP**
See also AAYA 5, 21; BEST 89:3; CA 5-8R; CANR 9, 42, 68; CDBLB 1960 to Present; DA3; DLB 87; INT CANR-9; MTCW 1, 2

Francis, Robert (Churchill) 1901-1987 **CLC 15**
See also CA 1-4R; 123; CANR 1

Frank, Anne(lies Marie) 1929-1945 **TCLC 17; DA; DAB; DAC; DAM MST; WLC**
See also AAYA 12; CA 113; 133; CANR 68; DA3; MTCW 1, 2; SATA 87; SATA-Brief 42

Frank, Bruno 1887-1945 **TCLC 81**
See also DLB 118

Frank, Elizabeth 1945- **CLC 39**
See also CA 121; 126; CANR 78; INT 126

Frankl, Viktor E(mil) 1905-1997 **CLC 93**
See also CA 65-68; 161

Franklin, Benjamin
See Hasek, Jaroslav (Matej Frantisek)

Franklin, Benjamin 1706-1790 **LC 25; DA; DAB; DAC; DAM MST; WLCS**
See also CDALB 1640-1865; DA3; DLB 24, 43, 73

Franklin, (Stella Maria Sarah) Miles (Lampe) 1879-1954 **TCLC 7**
See also CA 104; 164

Fraser, (Lady) Antonia (Pakenham) 1932- **CLC 32, 107**
See also CA 85-88; CANR 44, 65; MTCW 1, 2; SATA-Brief 32

Fraser, George MacDonald 1925- **CLC 7**
See also CA 45-48, 180; CAAE 180; CANR 2, 48, 74; MTCW 1

Fraser, Sylvia 1935- **CLC 64**
See also CA 45-48; CANR 1, 16, 60

Frayn, Michael 1933- **CLC 3, 7, 31, 47; DAM DRAM, NOV**
See also CA 5-8R; CANR 30, 69; DLB 13, 14, 194; MTCW 1, 2

Fraze, Candida (Merrill) 1945- **CLC 50**
See also CA 126

Frazer, J(ames) G(eorge) 1854-1941 **TCLC 32**
See also CA 118

Frazer, Robert Caine
See Creasey, John

Frazer, Sir James George
See Frazer, J(ames) G(eorge)

Frazier, Charles 1950- **CLC 109**
See also CA 161

Frazier, Ian 1951- **CLC 46**
See also CA 130; CANR 54

Frederic, Harold 1856-1898 **NCLC 10**
See also DLB 12, 23; DLBD 13

Frederick, John
See Faust, Frederick (Schiller)

Frederick the Great 1712-1786 **LC 14**

Fredro, Aleksander 1793-1876 **NCLC 8**

Freeling, Nicolas 1927- **CLC 38**
See also CA 49-52; CAAS 12; CANR 1, 17, 50, 84; DLB 87

Freeman, Douglas Southall 1886-1953 **TCLC 11**
See also CA 109; DLB 17; DLBD 17

Freeman, Judith 1946- **CLC 55**
See also CA 148

Freeman, Mary E(leanor) Wilkins 1852-1930 **TCLC 9; SSC 1**
See also CA 106; 177; DLB 12, 78, 221

Freeman, R(ichard) Austin 1862-1943 **TCLC 21**
See also CA 113; CANR 84; DLB 70

French, Albert 1943- **CLC 86**
See also BW 3; CA 167

French, Marilyn 1929- **CLC 10, 18, 60; DAM DRAM, NOV, POP**
See also CA 69-72; CANR 3, 31; INT CANR-31; MTCW 1, 2

French, Paul
See Asimov, Isaac

Freneau, Philip Morin 1752-1832 **NCLC 1**
See also DLB 37, 43

Freud, Sigmund 1856-1939 **TCLC 52**
See also CA 115; 133; CANR 69; MTCW 1, 2

Friedan, Betty (Naomi) 1921- **CLC 74**
See also CA 65-68; CANR 18, 45, 74; MTCW 1, 2

Friedlander, Saul 1932- **CLC 90**
See also CA 117; 130; CANR 72

Friedman, B(ernard) H(arper) 1926- **CLC 7**
See also CA 1-4R; CANR 3, 48

Friedman, Bruce Jay 1930- **CLC 3, 5, 56**
See also CA 9-12R; CANR 25, 52; DLB 2, 28; INT CANR-25

Friel, Brian 1929- **CLC 5, 42, 59, 115; DC 8**
See also CA 21-24R; CANR 33, 69; DLB 13; MTCW 1

Friis-Baastad, Babbis Ellinor 1921-1970 **CLC 12**
See also CA 17-20R; 134; SATA 7

Frisch, Max (Rudolf) 1911-1991 **CLC 3, 9, 14, 18, 32, 44; DAM DRAM, NOV**
See also CA 85-88; 134; CANR 32, 74; DLB 69, 124; MTCW 1, 2

Fromentin, Eugene (Samuel Auguste) 1820-1876 **NCLC 10**
See also DLB 123

Frost, Frederick
See Faust, Frederick (Schiller)

Frost, Robert (Lee) 1874-1963 **CLC 1, 3, 4, 9, 10, 13, 15, 26, 34, 44; DA; DAB; DAC; DAM MST, POET; PC 1; WLC**
See also AAYA 21; CA 89-92; CANR 33; CDALB 1917-1929; DA3; DLB 54; DLBD 7; MTCW 1, 2; SATA 14

Froude, James Anthony 1818-1894 **NCLC 43**
See also DLB 18, 57, 144

Froy, Herald
See Waterhouse, Keith (Spencer)

Fry, Christopher 1907- **CLC 2, 10, 14; DAM DRAM**
See also CA 17-20R; CAAS 23; CANR 9, 30, 74; DLB 13; MTCW 1, 2; SATA 66

Frye, (Herman) Northrop 1912-1991 **CLC 24, 70**
See also CA 5-8R; 133; CANR 8, 37; DLB 67, 68; MTCW 1, 2

Fuchs, Daniel 1909-1993 **CLC 8, 22**
See also CA 81-84; 142; CAAS 5; CANR 40; DLB 9, 26, 28; DLBY 93

Fuchs, Daniel 1934- **CLC 34**
See also CA 37-40R; CANR 14, 48

Fuentes, Carlos 1928- **CLC 3, 8, 10, 13, 22, 41, 60, 113; DA; DAB; DAC; DAM MST, MULT, NOV; HLC 1; SSC 24; WLC**
See also AAYA 4; AITN 2; CA 69-72; CANR 10, 32, 68; DA3; DLB 113; HW 1, 2; MTCW 1, 2

Fuentes, Gregorio Lopez y
See Lopez y Fuentes, Gregorio

Fuertes, Gloria 1918- **PC 27**
See also CA 178; 180; DLB 108; HW 2; SATA 115

Fugard, (Harold) Athol 1932- **CLC 5, 9, 14, 25, 40, 80; DAM DRAM; DC 3**
See also AAYA 17; CA 85-88; CANR 32, 54; MTCW 1

Fugard, Sheila 1932- **CLC 48**
See also CA 125

Fukuyama, Francis 1952- **CLC 131**
See also CA 140; CANR 72

Fuller, Charles (H., Jr.) 1939- **CLC 25; BLC 2; DAM DRAM, MULT; DC 1**
See also BW 2; CA 108; 112; CANR 87; DLB 38; INT 112; MTCW 1

Fuller, John (Leopold) 1937- **CLC 62**
See also CA 21-24R; CANR 9, 44; DLB 40

Fuller, Margaret NCLC 5, 50
See also Fuller, Sarah Margaret

Fuller, Roy (Broadbent) 1912-1991 **CLC 4, 28**
See also CA 5-8R; 135; CAAS 10; CANR 53, 83; DLB 15, 20; SATA 87

Fuller, Sarah Margaret 1810-1850
See Fuller, Margaret
See also CDALB 1640-1865; DLB 1, 59, 73, 83, 223

Fulton, Alice 1952- **CLC 52**
See also CA 116; CANR 57, 88; DLB 193

Furphy, Joseph 1843-1912 **TCLC 25**
See also CA 163

Fussell, Paul 1924- **CLC 74**
See also BEST 90:1; CA 17-20R; CANR 8, 21, 35, 69; INT CANR-21; MTCW 1, 2

Futabatei, Shimei 1864-1909 **TCLC 44**
See also CA 162; DLB 180

Futrelle, Jacques 1875-1912 **TCLC 19**
See also CA 113; 155

Gaboriau, Emile 1835-1873 **NCLC 14**

Gadda, Carlo Emilio 1893-1973 **CLC 11**
See also CA 89-92; DLB 177

Gaddis, William 1922-1998 **CLC 1, 3, 6, 8, 10, 19, 43, 86**
See also CA 17-20R; 172; CANR 21, 48; DLB 2; MTCW 1, 2

Gage, Walter
See Inge, William (Motter)

Gaines, Ernest J(ames) 1933- **CLC 3, 11, 18, 86; BLC 2; DAM MULT**
See also AAYA 18; AITN 1; BW 2, 3; CA 9-12R; CANR 6, 24, 42, 75; CDALB 1968-1988; CLR 62; DA3; DLB 2, 33, 152; DLBY 80; MTCW 1, 2; SATA 86

Gaitskill, Mary 1954- **CLC 69**
See also CA 128; CANR 61

Galdos, Benito Perez
See Perez Galdos, Benito

Gale, Zona 1874-1938 **TCLC 7; DAM DRAM**
See also CA 105; 153; CANR 84; DLB 9, 78

Galeano, Eduardo (Hughes) 1940- **CLC 72; HLCS 1**
See also CA 29-32R; CANR 13, 32; HW 1

Galiano, Juan Valera y Alcala
See Valera y Alcala-Galiano, Juan

Galilei, Galileo 1546-1642 **LC 45**

Gallagher, Tess 1943- **CLC 18, 63; DAM POET; PC 9**
See also CA 106; DLB 212

Gallant, Mavis 1922- **CLC 7, 18, 38; DAC; DAM MST; SSC 5**
See also CA 69-72; CANR 29, 69; DLB 53; MTCW 1, 2

Gallant, Roy A(rthur) 1924- **CLC 17**
See also CA 5-8R; CANR 4, 29, 54; CLR 30; MAICYA; SATA 4, 68, 110

Gallico, Paul (William) 1897-1976 **CLC 2**
See also AITN 1; CA 5-8R; 69-72; CANR 23; DLB 9, 171; MAICYA; SATA 13

Gallo, Max Louis 1932- **CLC 95**
See also CA 85-88

Gallois, Lucien
See Desnos, Robert

Gallup, Ralph
See Whitemore, Hugh (John)

Galsworthy, John 1867-1933 **TCLC 1, 45; DA; DAB; DAC; DAM DRAM, MST, NOV; SSC 22; WLC**
See also CA 104; 141; CANR 75; CDBLB 1890-1914; DA3; DLB 10, 34, 98, 162; DLBD 16; MTCW 1

Galt, John 1779-1839 **NCLC 1**
See also DLB 99, 116, 159

Galvin, James 1951- **CLC 38**
See also CA 108; CANR 26

Gamboa, Federico 1864-1939 **TCLC 36**
See also CA 167; HW 2

Gandhi, M. K.
See Gandhi, Mohandas Karamchand

Gandhi, Mahatma
See Gandhi, Mohandas Karamchand

Gandhi, Mohandas Karamchand 1869-1948 **TCLC 59; DAM MULT**
See also CA 121; 132; DA3; MTCW 1, 2

Gann, Ernest Kellogg 1910-1991 **CLC 23**
See also AITN 1; CA 1-4R; 136; CANR 1, 83

Garber, Eric 1943(?)-
See Holleran, Andrew
See also CANR 89

Garcia, Cristina 1958- **CLC 76**
See also CA 141; CANR 73; HW 2

Garcia Lorca, Federico 1898-1936 **TCLC 1, 7, 49; DA; DAB; DAC; DAM DRAM, MST, MULT, POET; DC 2; HLC 2; PC 3; WLC**
See also Lorca, Federico Garcia
See also CA 104; 131; CANR 81; DA3; DLB 108; HW 1, 2; MTCW 1, 2

Garcia Marquez, Gabriel (Jose) 1928- **CLC 2, 3, 8, 10, 15, 27, 47, 55, 68; DA; DAB; DAC; DAM MST, MULT, NOV, POP; HLC 1; SSC 8; WLC**
See also Marquez, Gabriel (Jose) Garcia
See also AAYA 3, 33; BEST 89:1, 90:4; CA 33-36R; CANR 10, 28, 50, 75, 82; DA3; DLB 113; HW 1, 2; MTCW 1, 2

Garcilaso de la Vega, El Inca 1503-1536
See also HLCS 1

Gard, Janice
See Latham, Jean Lee

Gard, Roger Martin du
See Martin du Gard, Roger

Gardam, Jane 1928- **CLC 43**
See also CA 49-52; CANR 2, 18, 33, 54; CLR 12; DLB 14, 161; MAICYA; MTCW 1; SAAS 9; SATA 39, 76; SATA-Brief 28

Gardner, Herb(ert) 1934- **CLC 44**
See also CA 149

Gardner, John (Champlin), Jr. 1933-1982 **CLC 2, 3, 5, 7, 8, 10, 18, 28, 34; DAM NOV, POP; SSC 7**
See also AITN 1; CA 65-68; 107; CANR 33, 73; CDALBS; DA3; DLB 2; DLBY 82; MTCW 1; SATA 40; SATA-Obit 31

Gardner, John (Edmund) 1926- **CLC 30; DAM POP**
See also CA 103; CANR 15, 69; MTCW 1

Gardner, Miriam
See Bradley, Marion Zimmer

Gardner, Noel
See Kuttner, Henry

Gardons, S. S.
See Snodgrass, W(illiam) D(e Witt)

Garfield, Leon 1921-1996 **CLC 12**
See also AAYA 8; CA 17-20R; 152; CANR 38, 41, 78; CLR 21; DLB 161; JRDA; MAICYA; SATA 1, 32, 76; SATA-Obit 90

Garland, (Hannibal) Hamlin 1860-1940 **TCLC 3; SSC 18**
See also CA 104; DLB 12, 71, 78, 186

Garneau, (Hector de) Saint-Denys 1912-1943 **TCLC 13**
See also CA 111; DLB 88

Garner, Alan 1934- **CLC 17; DAB; DAM POP**
See also AAYA 18; CA 73-76, 178; CAAE 178; CANR 15, 64; CLR 20; DLB 161; MAICYA; MTCW 1, 2; SATA 18, 69; SATA-Essay 108

Garner, Hugh 1913-1979 **CLC 13**
See also CA 69-72; CANR 31; DLB 68

Garnett, David 1892-1981 **CLC 3**
See also CA 5-8R; 103; CANR 17, 79; DLB 34; MTCW 2

Garos, Stephanie
See Katz, Steve

Garrett, George (Palmer) 1929- **CLC 3, 11, 51; SSC 30**
See also CA 1-4R; CAAS 5; CANR 1, 42, 67; DLB 2, 5, 130, 152; DLBY 83

Garrick, David 1717-1779 **LC 15; DAM DRAM**
See also DLB 84

Garrigue, Jean 1914-1972 **CLC 2, 8**
See also CA 5-8R; 37-40R; CANR 20

Garrison, Frederick
See Sinclair, Upton (Beall)

Garro, Elena 1920(?)-1998
See also CA 131; 169; DLB 145; HLCS 1; HW 1

Garth, Will
See Hamilton, Edmond; Kuttner, Henry

Garvey, Marcus (Moziah, Jr.) 1887-1940 **TCLC 41; BLC 2; DAM MULT**
See also BW 1; CA 120; 124; CANR 79

Gary, Romain CLC 25
See also Kacew, Romain
See also DLB 83

Gascar, Pierre CLC 11
See also Fournier, Pierre

Gascoyne, David (Emery) 1916- **CLC 45**
See also CA 65-68; CANR 10, 28, 54; DLB 20; MTCW 1

Gaskell, Elizabeth Cleghorn 1810-1865 **NCLC 70; DAB; DAM MST; SSC 25**
See also CDBLB 1832-1890; DLB 21, 144, 159

Gass, William H(oward) 1924- **CLC 1, 2, 8, 11, 15, 39, 132; SSC 12**
See also CA 17-20R; CANR 30, 71; DLB 2; MTCW 1, 2

Gassendi, Pierre 1592-1655 **LC 54**

Gasset, Jose Ortega y
See Ortega y Gasset, Jose

Gates, Henry Louis, Jr. 1950- **CLC 65; BLCS; DAM MULT**
See also BW 2, 3; CA 109; CANR 25, 53, 75; DA3; DLB 67; MTCW 1

Gautier, Theophile 1811-1872 **NCLC 1, 59; DAM POET; PC 18; SSC 20**
See also DLB 119

Gawsworth, John
See Bates, H(erbert) E(rnest)

Gay, John 1685-1732 **LC 49; DAM DRAM**
See also DLB 84, 95

Gay, Oliver
See Gogarty, Oliver St. John

Gaye, Marvin (Penze) 1939-1984 **CLC 26**
See also CA 112

Gebler, Carlo (Ernest) 1954- **CLC 39**
See also CA 119; 133

Gee, Maggie (Mary) 1948- **CLC 57**
See also CA 130; DLB 207

Gee, Maurice (Gough) 1931- **CLC 29**
See also CA 97-100; CANR 67; CLR 56; SATA 46, 101

Gelbart, Larry (Simon) 1923- **CLC 21, 61**
See also CA 73-76; CANR 45

Gelber, Jack 1932- **CLC 1, 6, 14, 79**
See also CA 1-4R; CANR 2; DLB 7

Gellhorn, Martha (Ellis) 1908-1998 **CLC 14, 60**
See also CA 77-80; 164; CANR 44; DLBY 82, 98

Genet, Jean 1910-1986 **CLC 1, 2, 5, 10, 14, 44, 46; DAM DRAM**
See also CA 13-16R; CANR 18; DA3; DLB 72; DLBY 86; MTCW 1, 2

Gent, Peter 1942- **CLC 29**
See also AITN 1; CA 89-92; DLBY 82

Gentile, Giovanni 1875-1944 **TCLC 96**
See also CA 119

Gentlewoman in New England, A
See Bradstreet, Anne

Gentlewoman in Those Parts, A
See Bradstreet, Anne

George, Jean Craighead 1919- **CLC 35**
See also AAYA 8; CA 5-8R; CANR 25; CLR 1; DLB 52; JRDA; MAICYA; SATA 2, 68

George, Stefan (Anton) 1868-1933 **TCLC 2, 14**
See also CA 104

Georges, Georges Martin
See Simenon, Georges (Jacques Christian)

Gerhardi, William Alexander
See Gerhardie, William Alexander

Gerhardie, William Alexander 1895-1977 **CLC 5**
See also CA 25-28R; 73-76; CANR 18; DLB 36

Gerstler, Amy 1956- **CLC 70**
See also CA 146

Gertler, T. CLC 34
See also CA 116; 121; INT 121

Ghalib NCLC 39, 78
See also Ghalib, Hsadullah Khan

Ghalib, Hsadullah Khan 1797-1869
See Ghalib
See also DAM POET

Ghelderode, Michel de 1898-1962 **CLC 6, 11; DAM DRAM**
See also CA 85-88; CANR 40, 77

Ghiselin, Brewster 1903- **CLC 23**
See also CA 13-16R; CAAS 10; CANR 13

Ghose, Aurabinda 1872-1950 **TCLC 63**
See also CA 163

Ghose, Zulfikar 1935- **CLC 42**
See also CA 65-68; CANR 67

Ghosh, Amitav 1956- **CLC 44**
See also CA 147; CANR 80

Giacosa, Giuseppe 1847-1906 **TCLC 7**
See also CA 104

Gibb, Lee
See Waterhouse, Keith (Spencer)

Gibbon, Lewis Grassic TCLC 4
See also Mitchell, James Leslie

Gibbons, Kaye 1960- **CLC 50, 88; DAM POP**
See also AAYA 34; CA 151; CANR 75; DA3; MTCW 1; SATA 117

Gibran, Kahlil 1883-1931 **TCLC 1, 9; DAM POET, POP; PC 9**
See also CA 104; 150; DA3; MTCW 2

Gordon, Adam Lindsay 1833-1870 **NCLC 21**
Gordon, Caroline 1895-1981 **CLC 6, 13, 29, 83; SSC 15**
    See also CA 11-12; 103; CANR 36; CAP 1; DLB 4, 9, 102; DLBD 17; DLBY 81; MTCW 1, 2
Gordon, Charles William 1860-1937
    See Connor, Ralph
    See also CA 109
Gordon, Mary (Catherine) 1949- **CLC 13, 22, 128**
    See also CA 102; CANR 44; DLB 6; DLBY 81; INT 102; MTCW 1
Gordon, N. J.
    See Bosman, Herman Charles
Gordon, Sol 1923- **CLC 26**
    See also CA 53-56; CANR 4; SATA 11
Gordone, Charles 1925-1995 **CLC 1, 4; DAM DRAM; DC 8**
    See also BW 1, 3; CA 93-96; 180; 150; CAAE 180; CANR 55; DLB 7; INT 93-96; MTCW 1
Gore, Catherine 1800-1861 **NCLC 65**
    See also DLB 116
Gorenko, Anna Andreevna
    See Akhmatova, Anna
Gorky, Maxim 1868-1936 **TCLC 8; DAB; SSC 28; WLC**
    See also Peshkov, Alexei Maximovich
    See also MTCW 2
Goryan, Sirak
    See Saroyan, William
Gosse, Edmund (William) 1849-1928 **TCLC 28**
    See also CA 117; DLB 57, 144, 184
Gotlieb, Phyllis Fay (Bloom) 1926- **CLC 18**
    See also CA 13-16R; CANR 7; DLB 88
Gottesman, S. D.
    See Kornbluth, C(yril) M.; Pohl, Frederik
Gottfried von Strassburg fl. c. 1210- **CMLC 10**
    See also DLB 138
Gould, Lois CLC 4, 10
    See also CA 77-80; CANR 29; MTCW 1
Gourmont, Remy (-Marie-Charles) de 1858-1915 **TCLC 17**
    See also CA 109; 150; MTCW 2
Govier, Katherine 1948- **CLC 51**
    See also CA 101; CANR 18, 40
Goyen, (Charles) William 1915-1983 **CLC 5, 8, 14, 40**
    See also AITN 2; CA 5-8R; 110; CANR 6, 71; DLB 2; DLBY 83; INT CANR-6
Goytisolo, Juan 1931- **CLC 5, 10, 23; DAM MULT; HLC 1**
    See also CA 85-88; CANR 32, 61; HW 1, 2; MTCW 1, 2
Gozzano, Guido 1883-1916 **PC 10**
    See also CA 154; DLB 114
Gozzi, (Conte) Carlo 1720-1806 **NCLC 23**
Grabbe, Christian Dietrich 1801-1836 **NCLC 2**
    See also DLB 133
Grace, Patricia Frances 1937- **CLC 56**
    See also CA 176
Gracian y Morales, Baltasar 1601-1658 **LC 15**
Gracq, Julien CLC 11, 48
    See also Poirier, Louis
    See also DLB 83
Grade, Chaim 1910-1982 **CLC 10**
    See also CA 93-96; 107
Graduate of Oxford, A
    See Ruskin, John
Grafton, Garth
    See Duncan, Sara Jeannette

Graham, John
    See Phillips, David Graham
Graham, Jorie 1951- **CLC 48, 118**
    See also CA 111; CANR 63; DLB 120
Graham, R(obert) B(ontine) Cunninghame
    See Cunninghame Graham, Robert (Gallnigad) Bontine
    See also DLB 98, 135, 174
Graham, Robert
    See Haldeman, Joe (William)
Graham, Tom
    See Lewis, (Harry) Sinclair
Graham, W(illiam) S(ydney) 1918-1986 **CLC 29**
    See also CA 73-76; 118; DLB 20
Graham, Winston (Mawdsley) 1910- **CLC 23**
    See also CA 49-52; CANR 2, 22, 45, 66; DLB 77
Grahame, Kenneth 1859-1932 **TCLC 64; DAB**
    See also CA 108; 136; CANR 80; CLR 5; DA3; DLB 34, 141, 178; MAICYA; MTCW 2; SATA 100; YABC 1
Granovsky, Timofei Nikolaevich 1813-1855 **NCLC 75**
    See also DLB 198
Grant, Skeeter
    See Spiegelman, Art
Granville-Barker, Harley 1877-1946 **TCLC 2; DAM DRAM**
    See also Barker, Harley Granville
    See also CA 104
Grass, Guenter (Wilhelm) 1927- **CLC 1, 2, 4, 6, 11, 15, 22, 32, 49, 88; DA; DAB; DAC; DAM MST, NOV; WLC**
    See also CA 13-16R; CANR 20, 75; DA3; DLB 75, 124; MTCW 1, 2
Gratton, Thomas
    See Hulme, T(homas) E(rnest)
Grau, Shirley Ann 1929- **CLC 4, 9; SSC 15**
    See also CA 89-92; CANR 22, 69; DLB 2; INT CANR-22; MTCW 1
Gravel, Fern
    See Hall, James Norman
Graver, Elizabeth 1964- **CLC 70**
    See also CA 135; CANR 71
Graves, Richard Perceval 1945- **CLC 44**
    See also CA 65-68; CANR 9, 26, 51
Graves, Robert (von Ranke) 1895-1985 **CLC 1, 2, 6, 11, 39, 44, 45; DAB; DAC; DAM MST, POET; PC 6**
    See also CA 5-8R; 117; CANR 5, 36; CDBLB 1914-1945; DA3; DLB 20, 100, 191; DLBD 18; DLBY 85; MTCW 1, 2; SATA 45
Graves, Valerie
    See Bradley, Marion Zimmer
Gray, Alasdair (James) 1934- **CLC 41**
    See also CA 126; CANR 47, 69; DLB 194; INT 126; MTCW 1, 2
Gray, Amlin 1946- **CLC 29**
    See also CA 138
Gray, Francine du Plessix 1930- **CLC 22; DAM NOV**
    See also BEST 90:3; CA 61-64; CAAS 2; CANR 11, 33, 75, 81; INT CANR-11; MTCW 1, 2
Gray, John (Henry) 1866-1934 **TCLC 19**
    See also CA 119; 162
Gray, Simon (James Holliday) 1936- **CLC 9, 14, 36**
    See also AITN 1; CA 21-24R; CAAS 3; CANR 32, 69; DLB 13; MTCW 1
Gray, Spalding 1941- **CLC 49, 112; DAM POP; DC 7**
    See also CA 128; CANR 74; MTCW 2
Gray, Thomas 1716-1771 **LC 4, 40; DA; DAB; DAC; DAM MST; PC 2; WLC**

    See also CDBLB 1660-1789; DA3; DLB 109
Grayson, David
    See Baker, Ray Stannard
Grayson, Richard (A.) 1951- **CLC 38**
    See also CA 85-88; CANR 14, 31, 57
Greeley, Andrew M(oran) 1928- **CLC 28; DAM POP**
    See also CA 5-8R; CAAS 7; CANR 7, 43, 69; DA3; MTCW 1, 2
Green, Anna Katharine 1846-1935 **TCLC 63**
    See also CA 112; 159; DLB 202, 221
Green, Brian
    See Card, Orson Scott
Green, Hannah
    See Greenberg, Joanne (Goldenberg)
Green, Hannah 1927(?)-1996 **CLC 3**
    See also CA 73-76; CANR 59
Green, Henry 1905-1973 **CLC 2, 13, 97**
    See also Yorke, Henry Vincent
    See also CA 175; DLB 15
Green, Julian (Hartridge) 1900-1998
    See Green, Julien
    See also CA 21-24R; 169; CANR 33, 87; DLB 4, 72; MTCW 1
Green, Julien CLC 3, 11, 77
    See also Green, Julian (Hartridge)
    See also MTCW 2
Green, Paul (Eliot) 1894-1981 **CLC 25; DAM DRAM**
    See also AITN 1; CA 5-8R; 103; CANR 3; DLB 7, 9; DLBY 81
Greenberg, Ivan 1908-1973
    See Rahv, Philip
    See also CA 85-88
Greenberg, Joanne (Goldenberg) 1932- **CLC 7, 30**
    See also AAYA 12; CA 5-8R; CANR 14, 32, 69; SATA 25
Greenberg, Richard 1959(?)- **CLC 57**
    See also CA 138
Greene, Bette 1934- **CLC 30**
    See also AAYA 7; CA 53-56; CANR 4; CLR 2; JRDA; MAICYA; SAAS 16; SATA 8, 102
Greene, Gael CLC 8
    See also CA 13-16R; CANR 10
Greene, Graham (Henry) 1904-1991 **CLC 1, 3, 6, 9, 14, 18, 27, 37, 70, 72, 125; DA; DAB; DAC; DAM MST, NOV; SSC 29; WLC**
    See also AITN 2; CA 13-16R; 133; CANR 35, 61; CDBLB 1945-1960; DA3; DLB 13, 15, 77, 100, 162, 201, 204; DLBY 91; MTCW 1, 2; SATA 20
Greene, Robert 1558-1592 **LC 41**
    See also DLB 62, 167
Greer, Germaine 1939- **CLC 131**
    See also AITN 1; CA 81-84; CANR 33, 70; MTCW 1, 2
Greer, Richard
    See Silverberg, Robert
Gregor, Arthur 1923- **CLC 9**
    See also CA 25-28R; CAAS 10; CANR 11; SATA 36
Gregor, Lee
    See Pohl, Frederik
Gregory, Isabella Augusta (Persse) 1852-1932 **TCLC 1**
    See also CA 104; 184; DLB 10
Gregory, J. Dennis
    See Williams, John A(lfred)
Grendon, Stephen
    See Derleth, August (William)
Grenville, Kate 1950- **CLC 61**
    See also CA 118; CANR 53
Grenville, Pelham
    See Wodehouse, P(elham) G(renville)

Greve, Felix Paul (Berthold Friedrich)
1879-1948
See Grove, Frederick Philip
See also CA 104; 141, 175; CANR 79;
DAC; DAM MST

Grey, Zane 1872-1939 **TCLC 6; DAM POP**
See also CA 104; 132; DA3; DLB 212;
MTCW 1, 2

Grieg, (Johan) Nordahl (Brun) 1902-1943
TCLC 10
See also CA 107

Grieve, C(hristopher) M(urray) 1892-1978
CLC 11, 19; DAM POET
See also MacDiarmid, Hugh; Pteleon
See also CA 5-8R; 85-88; CANR 33;
MTCW 1

Griffin, Gerald 1803-1840 **NCLC 7**
See also DLB 159

Griffin, John Howard 1920-1980 **CLC 68**
See also AITN 1; CA 1-4R; 101; CANR 2

Griffin, Peter 1942- **CLC 39**
See also CA 136

Griffith, D(avid Lewelyn) W(ark)
1875(?)-1948 **TCLC 68**
See also CA 119; 150; CANR 80

Griffith, Lawrence
See Griffith, D(avid Lewelyn) W(ark)

Griffiths, Trevor 1935- **CLC 13, 52**
See also CA 97-100; CANR 45; DLB 13

Griggs, Sutton (Elbert) 1872-1930 **TCLC 77**
See also CA 123; 186; DLB 50

Grigson, Geoffrey (Edward Harvey)
1905-1985 **CLC 7, 39**
See also CA 25-28R; 118; CANR 20, 33;
DLB 27; MTCW 1, 2

Grillparzer, Franz 1791-1872 **NCLC 1; SSC 37**
See also DLB 133

Grimble, Reverend Charles James
See Eliot, T(homas) S(tearns)

Grimke, Charlotte L(ottie) Forten
1837(?)-1914
See Forten, Charlotte L.
See also BW 1; CA 117; 124; DAM MULT,
POET

Grimm, Jacob Ludwig Karl 1785-1863
NCLC 3, 77; SSC 36
See also DLB 90; MAICYA; SATA 22

Grimm, Wilhelm Karl 1786-1859 **NCLC 3,
77; SSC 36**
See also DLB 90; MAICYA; SATA 22

**Grimmelshausen, Johann Jakob Christoffel
von** 1621-1676 **LC 6**
See also DLB 168

Grindel, Eugene 1895-1952
See Eluard, Paul
See also CA 104

Grisham, John 1955- **CLC 84; DAM POP**
See also AAYA 14; CA 138; CANR 47, 69;
DA3; MTCW 2

Grossman, David 1954- **CLC 67**
See also CA 138

Grossman, Vasily (Semenovich) 1905-1964
CLC 41
See also CA 124; 130; MTCW 1

Grove, Frederick Philip TCLC 4
See also Greve, Felix Paul (Berthold
Friedrich)
See also DLB 92

Grubb
See Crumb, R(obert)

Grumbach, Doris (Isaac) 1918- **CLC 13, 22,
64**
See also CA 5-8R; CAAS 2; CANR 9, 42,
70; INT CANR-9; MTCW 2

Grundtvig, Nicolai Frederik Severin
1783-1872 **NCLC 1**

Grunge
See Crumb, R(obert)

Grunwald, Lisa 1959- **CLC 44**
See also CA 120

Guare, John 1938- **CLC 8, 14, 29, 67; DAM
DRAM**
See also CA 73-76; CANR 21, 69; DLB 7;
MTCW 1, 2

Gudjonsson, Halldor Kiljan 1902-1998
See Laxness, Halldor
See also CA 103; 164

Guenter, Erich
See Eich, Guenter

Guest, Barbara 1920- **CLC 34**
See also CA 25-28R; CANR 11, 44, 84;
DLB 5, 193

Guest, Edgar A(lbert) 1881-1959 **TCLC 95**
See also CA 112; 168

Guest, Judith (Ann) 1936- **CLC 8, 30; DAM
NOV, POP**
See also AAYA 7; CA 77-80; CANR 15,
75; DA3; INT CANR-15; MTCW 1, 2

Guevara, Che CLC 87; HLC 1
See also Guevara (Serna), Ernesto

Guevara (Serna), Ernesto 1928-1967 **CLC
87; DAM MULT; HLC 1**
See also Guevara, Che
See also CA 127; 111; CANR 56; HW 1

Guicciardini, Francesco 1483-1540 **LC 49**

Guild, Nicholas M. 1944- **CLC 33**
See also CA 93-96

Guillemin, Jacques
See Sartre, Jean-Paul

Guillen, Jorge 1893-1984 **CLC 11; DAM
MULT, POET; HLCS 1**
See also CA 89-92; 112; DLB 108; HW 1

Guillen, Nicolas (Cristobal) 1902-1989 **CLC
48, 79; BLC 2; DAM MST, MULT,
POET; HLC 1; PC 23**
See also BW 2; CA 116; 125; 129; CANR
84; HW 1

Guillevic, (Eugene) 1907- **CLC 33**
See also CA 93-96

Guillois
See Desnos, Robert

Guillois, Valentin
See Desnos, Robert

Guimaraes Rosa, Joao 1908-1967
See also CA 175; HLCS 2

Guiney, Louise Imogen 1861-1920 **TCLC 41**
See also CA 160; DLB 54

Guiraldes, Ricardo (Guillermo) 1886-1927
TCLC 39
See also CA 131; HW 1; MTCW 1

Gumilev, Nikolai (Stepanovich) 1886-1921
TCLC 60
See also CA 165

Gunesekera, Romesh 1954- **CLC 91**
See also CA 159

Gunn, Bill CLC 5
See also Gunn, William Harrison
See also DLB 38

Gunn, Thom(son William) 1929- **CLC 3, 6,
18, 32, 81; DAM POET; PC 26**
See also CA 17-20R; CANR 9, 33; CDBLB
1960 to Present; DLB 27; INT CANR-33;
MTCW 1

Gunn, William Harrison 1934(?)-1989
See Gunn, Bill
See also AITN 1; BW 1, 3; CA 13-16R;
128; CANR 12, 25, 76

Gunnars, Kristjana 1948- **CLC 69**
See also CA 113; DLB 60

Gurdjieff, G(eorgei) I(vanovich)
1877(?)-1949 **TCLC 71**
See also CA 157

Gurganus, Allan 1947- **CLC 70; DAM POP**
See also BEST 90:1; CA 135

Gurney, A(lbert) R(amsdell), Jr. 1930- **CLC
32, 50, 54; DAM DRAM**
See also CA 77-80; CANR 32, 64

Gurney, Ivor (Bertie) 1890-1937 **TCLC 33**
See also CA 167

Gurney, Peter
See Gurney, A(lbert) R(amsdell), Jr.

Guro, Elena 1877-1913 **TCLC 56**

Gustafson, James M(oody) 1925- **CLC 100**
See also CA 25-28R; CANR 37

Gustafson, Ralph (Barker) 1909- **CLC 36**
See also CA 21-24R; CANR 8, 45, 84; DLB
88

Gut, Gom
See Simenon, Georges (Jacques Christian)

Guterson, David 1956- **CLC 91**
See also CA 132; CANR 73; MTCW 2

Guthrie, A(lfred) B(ertram), Jr. 1901-1991
CLC 23
See also CA 57-60; 134; CANR 24; DLB
212; SATA 62; SATA-Obit 67

Guthrie, Isobel
See Grieve, C(hristopher) M(urray)

Guthrie, Woodrow Wilson 1912-1967
See Guthrie, Woody
See also CA 113; 93-96

Guthrie, Woody CLC 35
See also Guthrie, Woodrow Wilson

Gutierrez Najera, Manuel 1859-1895
See also HLCS 2

Guy, Rosa (Cuthbert) 1928- **CLC 26**
See also AAYA 4; BW 2; CA 17-20R;
CANR 14, 34, 83; CLR 13; DLB 33;
JRDA; MAICYA; SATA 14, 62

Gwendolyn
See Bennett, (Enoch) Arnold

H. D. CLC 3, 8, 14, 31, 34, 73; PC 5
See also Doolittle, Hilda

H. de V.
See Buchan, John

Haavikko, Paavo Juhani 1931- **CLC 18, 34**
See also CA 106

Habbema, Koos
See Heijermans, Herman

Habermas, Juergen 1929- **CLC 104**
See also CA 109; CANR 85

Habermas, Jurgen
See Habermas, Juergen

Hacker, Marilyn 1942- **CLC 5, 9, 23, 72, 91;
DAM POET**
See also CA 77-80; CANR 68; DLB 120

Haeckel, Ernst Heinrich (Philipp August)
1834-1919 **TCLC 83**
See also CA 157

Hafiz c. 1326-1389(?) **CMLC 34**

Hafiz c. 1326-1389 **CMLC 34**

Haggard, H(enry) Rider 1856-1925 **TCLC 11**
See also CA 108; 148; DLB 70, 156, 174,
178; MTCW 2; SATA 16

Hagiosy, L.
See Larbaud, Valery (Nicolas)

Hagiwara Sakutaro 1886-1942 **TCLC 60; PC
18**

Haig, Fenil
See Ford, Ford Madox

Haig-Brown, Roderick (Langmere)
1908-1976 **CLC 21**
See also CA 5-8R; 69-72; CANR 4, 38, 83;
CLR 31; DLB 88; MAICYA; SATA 12

Hailey, Arthur 1920- **CLC 5; DAM NOV,
POP**
See also AITN 2; BEST 90:3; CA 1-4R;
CANR 2, 36, 75; DLB 88; DLBY 82;
MTCW 1, 2

Hailey, Elizabeth Forsythe 1938- **CLC 40**
See also CA 93-96; CAAS 1; CANR 15,
48; INT CANR-15

Haines, John (Meade) 1924- **CLC 58**

See also CA 17-20R; CANR 13, 34; DLB 212

Hakluyt, Richard 1552-1616 **LC 31**

Haldeman, Joe (William) 1943- **CLC 61**
See also Graham, Robert
See also CA 53-56, 179; CAAE 179; CAAS 25; CANR 6, 70, 72; DLB 8; INT CANR-6

Hale, Sarah Josepha (Buell) 1788-1879 **NCLC 75**
See also DLB 1, 42, 73

Haley, Alex(ander Murray Palmer) 1921-1992 **CLC 8, 12, 76; BLC 2; DA; DAB; DAC; DAM MST, MULT, POP**
See also AAYA 26; BW 2, 3; CA 77-80; 136; CANR 61; CDALBS; DA3; DLB 38; MTCW 1, 2

Haliburton, Thomas Chandler 1796-1865 **NCLC 15**
See also DLB 11, 99

Hall, Donald (Andrew, Jr.) 1928- **CLC 1, 13, 37, 59; DAM POET**
See also CA 5-8R; CAAS 7; CANR 2, 44, 64; DLB 5; MTCW 1; SATA 23, 97

Hall, Frederic Sauser
See Sauser-Hall, Frederic

Hall, James
See Kuttner, Henry

Hall, James Norman 1887-1951 **TCLC 23**
See also CA 123; 173; SATA 21

Hall, Radclyffe
See Hall, (Marguerite) Radclyffe
See also MTCW 2

Hall, (Marguerite) Radclyffe 1886-1943 **TCLC 12**
See also CA 110; 150; CANR 83; DLB 191

Hall, Rodney 1935- **CLC 51**
See also CA 109; CANR 69

Halleck, Fitz-Greene 1790-1867 **NCLC 47**
See also DLB 3

Halliday, Michael
See Creasey, John

Halpern, Daniel 1945- **CLC 14**
See also CA 33-36R

Hamburger, Michael (Peter Leopold) 1924- **CLC 5, 14**
See also CA 5-8R; CAAS 4; CANR 2, 47; DLB 27

Hamill, Pete 1935- **CLC 10**
See also CA 25-28R; CANR 18, 71

Hamilton, Alexander 1755(?)-1804 **NCLC 49**
See also DLB 37

Hamilton, Clive
See Lewis, C(live) S(taples)

Hamilton, Edmond 1904-1977 **CLC 1**
See also CA 1-4R; CANR 3, 84; DLB 8

Hamilton, Eugene (Jacob) Lee
See Lee-Hamilton, Eugene (Jacob)

Hamilton, Franklin
See Silverberg, Robert

Hamilton, Gail
See Corcoran, Barbara

Hamilton, Mollie
See Kaye, M(ary) M(argaret)

Hamilton, (Anthony Walter) Patrick 1904-1962 **CLC 51**
See also CA 176; 113; DLB 191

Hamilton, Virginia 1936- **CLC 26; DAM MULT**
See also AAYA 2, 21; BW 2, 3; CA 25-28R; CANR 20, 37, 73; CLR 1, 11, 40; DLB 33, 52; INT CANR-20; JRDA; MAICYA; MTCW 1, 2; SATA 4, 56, 79

Hammett, (Samuel) Dashiell 1894-1961 **CLC 3, 5, 10, 19, 47; SSC 17**
See also AITN 1; CA 81-84; CANR 42; CDALB 1929-1941; DA3; DLBD 6; DLBY 96; MTCW 1, 2

Hammon, Jupiter 1711(?)-1800(?) **NCLC 5;**

BLC 2; DAM MULT, POET; PC 16
See also DLB 31, 50

Hammond, Keith
See Kuttner, Henry

Hamner, Earl (Henry), Jr. 1923- **CLC 12**
See also AITN 2; CA 73-76; DLB 6

Hampton, Christopher (James) 1946- **CLC 4**
See also CA 25-28R; DLB 13; MTCW 1

Hamsun, Knut **TCLC 2, 14, 49**
See also Pedersen, Knut

Handke, Peter 1942- **CLC 5, 8, 10, 15, 38; DAM DRAM, NOV**
See also CA 77-80; CANR 33, 75; DLB 85, 124; MTCW 1, 2

Handy, W(illiam) C(hristopher) 1873-1958 **TCLC 97**
See also BW 3; CA 121; 167

Hanley, James 1901-1985 **CLC 3, 5, 8, 13**
See also CA 73-76; 117; CANR 36; DLB 191; MTCW 1

Hannah, Barry 1942- **CLC 23, 38, 90**
See also CA 108; 110; CANR 43, 68; DLB 6; INT 110; MTCW 1

Hannon, Ezra
See Hunter, Evan

Hansberry, Lorraine (Vivian) 1930-1965 **CLC 17, 62; BLC 2; DA; DAB; DAC; DAM DRAM, MST, MULT; DC 2**
See also AAYA 25; BW 1, 3; CA 109; 25-28R; CABS 3; CANR 58; CDALB 1941-1968; DA3; DLB 7, 38; MTCW 1, 2

Hansen, Joseph 1923- **CLC 38**
See also CA 29-32R; CAAS 17; CANR 16, 44, 66; INT CANR-16

Hansen, Martin A(lfred) 1909-1955 **TCLC 32**
See also CA 167

Hanson, Kenneth O(stlin) 1922- **CLC 13**
See also CA 53-56; CANR 7

Hardwick, Elizabeth (Bruce) 1916- **CLC 13; DAM NOV**
See also CA 5-8R; CANR 3, 32, 70; DA3; DLB 6; MTCW 1, 2

Hardy, Thomas 1840-1928 **TCLC 4, 10, 18, 32, 48, 53, 72; DA; DAB; DAC; DAM MST, NOV, POET; PC 8; SSC 2; WLC**
See also CA 104; 123; CDBLB 1890-1914; DA3; DLB 18, 19, 135; MTCW 1, 2

Hare, David 1947- **CLC 29, 58**
See also CA 97-100; CANR 39, 91; DLB 13; MTCW 1

Harewood, John
See Van Druten, John (William)

Harford, Henry
See Hudson, W(illiam) H(enry)

Hargrave, Leonie
See Disch, Thomas M(ichael)

Harjo, Joy 1951- **CLC 83; DAM MULT; PC 27**
See also CA 114; CANR 35, 67, 91; DLB 120, 175; MTCW 2; NNAL

Harlan, Louis R(udolph) 1922- **CLC 34**
See also CA 21-24R; CANR 25, 55, 80

Harling, Robert 1951(?)- **CLC 53**
See also CA 147

Harmon, William (Ruth) 1938- **CLC 38**
See also CA 33-36R; CANR 14, 32, 35; SATA 65

Harper, F. E. W.
See Harper, Frances Ellen Watkins

Harper, Frances E. W.
See Harper, Frances Ellen Watkins

Harper, Frances E. Watkins
See Harper, Frances Ellen Watkins

Harper, Frances Ellen
See Harper, Frances Ellen Watkins

Harper, Frances Ellen Watkins 1825-1911 **TCLC 14; BLC 2; DAM MULT, POET; PC 21**

See also BW 1, 3; CA 111; 125; CANR 79; DLB 50, 221

Harper, Michael S(teven) 1938- **CLC 7, 22**
See also BW 1; CA 33-36R; CANR 24; DLB 41

Harper, Mrs. F. E. W.
See Harper, Frances Ellen Watkins

Harris, Christie (Lucy) Irwin 1907- **CLC 12**
See also CA 5-8R; CANR 6, 83; CLR 47; DLB 88; JRDA; MAICYA; SAAS 10; SATA 6, 74; SATA-Essay 116

Harris, Frank 1856-1931 **TCLC 24**
See also CA 109; 150; CANR 80; DLB 156, 197

Harris, George Washington 1814-1869 **NCLC 23**
See also DLB 3, 11

Harris, Joel Chandler 1848-1908 **TCLC 2; SSC 19**
See also CA 104; 137; CANR 80; CLR 49; DLB 11, 23, 42, 78, 91; MAICYA; SATA 100; YABC 1

Harris, John (Wyndham Parkes Lucas) Beynon 1903-1969
See Wyndham, John
See also CA 102; 89-92; CANR 84

Harris, MacDonald **CLC 9**
See also Heiney, Donald (William)

Harris, Mark 1922- **CLC 19**
See also CA 5-8R; CAAS 3; CANR 2, 55, 83; DLB 2; DLBY 80

Harris, (Theodore) Wilson 1921- **CLC 25**
See also BW 2, 3; CA 65-68; CAAS 16; CANR 11, 27, 69; DLB 117; MTCW 1

Harrison, Elizabeth Cavanna 1909-
See Cavanna, Betty
See also CA 9-12R; CANR 6, 27, 85

Harrison, Harry (Max) 1925- **CLC 42**
See also CA 1-4R; CANR 5, 21, 84; DLB 8; SATA 4

Harrison, James (Thomas) 1937- **CLC 6, 14, 33, 66; SSC 19**
See also CA 13-16R; CANR 8, 51, 79; DLBY 82; INT CANR-8

Harrison, Jim
See Harrison, James (Thomas)

Harrison, Kathryn 1961- **CLC 70**
See also CA 144; CANR 68

Harrison, Tony 1937- **CLC 43, 129**
See also CA 65-68; CANR 44; DLB 40; MTCW 1

Harriss, Will(ard Irvin) 1922- **CLC 34**
See also CA 111

Harson, Sley
See Ellison, Harlan (Jay)

Hart, Ellis
See Ellison, Harlan (Jay)

Hart, Josephine 1942(?)- **CLC 70; DAM POP**
See also CA 138; CANR 70

Hart, Moss 1904-1961 **CLC 66; DAM DRAM**
See also CA 109; 89-92; CANR 84; DLB 7

Harte, (Francis) Bret(t) 1836(?)-1902 **TCLC 1, 25; DA; DAC; DAM MST; SSC 8; WLC**
See also CA 104; 140; CANR 80; CDALB 1865-1917; DA3; DLB 12, 64, 74, 79, 186; SATA 26

Hartley, L(eslie) P(oles) 1895-1972 **CLC 2, 22**
See also CA 45-48; 37-40R; CANR 33; DLB 15, 139; MTCW 1, 2

Hartman, Geoffrey H. 1929- **CLC 27**
See also CA 117; 125; CANR 79; DLB 67

Hartmann, Sadakichi 1867-1944 **TCLC 73**
See also CA 157; DLB 54

Hartmann von Aue c. 1160-c. 1205 **CMLC 15**
See also DLB 138

Hartmann von Aue 1170-1210 **CMLC 15**

Haruf, Kent 1943- **CLC 34**
   See also CA 149; CANR 91
Harwood, Ronald 1934- **CLC 32; DAM DRAM, MST**
   See also CA 1-4R; CANR 4, 55; DLB 13
Hasegawa Tatsunosuke
   See Futabatei, Shimei
Hasek, Jaroslav (Matej Frantisek)
   1883-1923 **TCLC 4**
   See also CA 104; 129; MTCW 1, 2
Hass, Robert 1941- **CLC 18, 39, 99; PC 16**
   See also CA 111; CANR 30, 50, 71; DLB 105, 206; SATA 94
Hastings, Hudson
   See Kuttner, Henry
Hastings, Selina CLC 44
Hathorne, John 1641-1717 **LC 38**
Hatteras, Amelia
   See Mencken, H(enry) L(ouis)
Hatteras, Owen TCLC 18
   See also Mencken, H(enry) L(ouis); Nathan, George Jean
Hauptmann, Gerhart (Johann Robert) 1862-1946 **TCLC 4; DAM DRAM; SSC 37**
   See also CA 104; 153; DLB 66, 118
Havel, Vaclav 1936- **CLC 25, 58, 65; DAM DRAM; DC 6**
   See also CA 104; CANR 36, 63; DA3; MTCW 1, 2
Haviaras, Stratis CLC 33
   See also Chaviaras, Strates
Hawes, Stephen 1475(?)-1523(?) **LC 17**
   See also DLB 132
Hawkes, John (Clendennin Burne, Jr.) 1925-1998 **CLC 1, 2, 3, 4, 7, 9, 14, 15, 27, 49**
   See also CA 1-4R; 167; CANR 2, 47, 64; DLB 2, 7; DLBY 80, 98; MTCW 1, 2
Hawking, S. W.
   See Hawking, Stephen W(illiam)
Hawking, Stephen W(illiam) 1942- **CLC 63, 105**
   See also AAYA 13; BEST 89:1; CA 126; 129; CANR 48; DA3; MTCW 2
Hawkins, Anthony Hope
   See Hope, Anthony
Hawthorne, Julian 1846-1934 **TCLC 25**
   See also CA 165
Hawthorne, Nathaniel 1804-1864 **NCLC 39; DA; DAB; DAC; DAM MST, NOV; SSC 3, 29, 39; WLC**
   See also AAYA 18; CDALB 1640-1865; DA3; DLB 1, 74, 223; YABC 2
Haxton, Josephine Ayres 1921-
   See Douglas, Ellen
   See also CA 115; CANR 41, 83
Hayaseca y Eizaguirre, Jorge
   See Echegaray (y Eizaguirre), Jose (Maria Waldo)
Hayashi, Fumiko 1904-1951 **TCLC 27**
   See also CA 161; DLB 180
Haycraft, Anna (Margaret) 1932-
   See Ellis, Alice Thomas
   See also CA 122; CANR 85, 90; MTCW 2
Hayden, Robert E(arl) 1913-1980 **CLC 5, 9, 14, 37; BLC 2; DA; DAC; DAM MST, MULT, POET; PC 6**
   See also BW 1, 3; CA 69-72; 97-100; CABS 2; CANR 24, 75, 82; CDALB 1941-1968; DLB 5, 76; MTCW 1, 2; SATA 19; SATA-Obit 26
Hayford, J(oseph) E(phraim) Casely
   See Casely-Hayford, J(oseph) E(phraim)
Hayman, Ronald 1932- **CLC 44**
   See also CA 25-28R; CANR 18, 50, 88; DLB 155
Haywood, Eliza (Fowler) 1693(?)-1756 **LC 1, 44**

   See also DLB 39
Hazlitt, William 1778-1830 **NCLC 29, 82**
   See also DLB 110, 158
Hazzard, Shirley 1931- **CLC 18**
   See also CA 9-12R; CANR 4, 70; DLBY 82; MTCW 1
Head, Bessie 1937-1986 **CLC 25, 67; BLC 2; DAM MULT**
   See also BW 2, 3; CA 29-32R; 119; CANR 25, 82; DA3; DLB 117; MTCW 1, 2
Headon, (Nicky) Topper 1956(?)- **CLC 30**
Heaney, Seamus (Justin) 1939- **CLC 5, 7, 14, 25, 37, 74, 91; DAB; DAM POET; PC 18; WLCS**
   See also CA 85-88; CANR 25, 48, 75, 91; CDBLB 1960 to Present; DA3; DLB 40; DLBY 95; MTCW 1, 2
Hearn, (Patricio) Lafcadio (Tessima Carlos) 1850-1904 **TCLC 9**
   See also CA 105; 166; DLB 12, 78, 189
Hearne, Vicki 1946- **CLC 56**
   See also CA 139
Hearon, Shelby 1931- **CLC 63**
   See also AITN 2; CA 25-28R; CANR 18, 48
Heat-Moon, William Least CLC 29
   See Trogdon, William (Lewis)
   See also AAYA 9
Hebbel, Friedrich 1813-1863 **NCLC 43; DAM DRAM**
   See also DLB 129
Hebert, Anne 1916- **CLC 4, 13, 29; DAC; DAM MST, POET**
   See also CA 85-88; CANR 69; DA3; DLB 68; MTCW 1, 2
Hecht, Anthony (Evan) 1923- **CLC 8, 13, 19; DAM POET**
   See also CA 9-12R; CANR 6; DLB 5, 169
Hecht, Ben 1894-1964 **CLC 8**
   See also CA 85-88; DLB 7, 9, 25, 26, 28, 86
Hedayat, Sadeq 1903-1951 **TCLC 21**
   See also CA 120
Hegel, Georg Wilhelm Friedrich 1770-1831 **NCLC 46**
   See also DLB 90
Heidegger, Martin 1889-1976 **CLC 24**
   See also CA 81-84; 65-68; CANR 34; MTCW 1, 2
Heidenstam, (Carl Gustaf) Verner von 1859-1940 **TCLC 5**
   See also CA 104
Heifner, Jack 1946- **CLC 11**
   See also CA 105; CANR 47
Heijermans, Herman 1864-1924 **TCLC 24**
   See also CA 123
Heilbrun, Carolyn G(old) 1926- **CLC 25**
   See also CA 45-48; CANR 1, 28, 58
Heine, Heinrich 1797-1856 **NCLC 4, 54; PC 25**
   See also DLB 90
Heinemann, Larry (Curtiss) 1944- **CLC 50**
   See also CA 110; CAAS 21; CANR 31, 81; DLBD 9; INT CANR-31
Heiney, Donald (William) 1921-1993
   See Harris, MacDonald
   See also CA 1-4R; 142; CANR 3, 58
Heinlein, Robert A(nson) 1907-1988 **CLC 1, 3, 8, 14, 26, 55; DAM POP**
   See also AAYA 17; CA 1-4R; 125; CANR 1, 20, 53; DA3; DLB 8; JRDA; MAICYA; MTCW 1, 2; SATA 9, 69; SATA-Obit 56
Helforth, John
   See Doolittle, Hilda
Hellenhofferu, Vojtech Kapristian z
   See Hasek, Jaroslav (Matej Frantisek)
Heller, Joseph 1923- **CLC 1, 3, 5, 8, 11, 36, 63; DA; DAB; DAC; DAM MST, NOV, POP; WLC**

   See also AAYA 24; AITN 1; CA 5-8R; CABS 1; CANR 8, 42, 66; DA3; DLB 2, 28; DLBY 80; INT CANR-8; MTCW 1, 2
Hellman, Lillian (Florence) 1906-1984 **CLC 2, 4, 8, 14, 18, 34, 44, 52; DAM DRAM; DC 1**
   See also AITN 1, 2; CA 13-16R; 112; CANR 33; DA3; DLB 7; DLBY 84; MTCW 1, 2
Helprin, Mark 1947- **CLC 7, 10, 22, 32; DAM NOV, POP**
   See also CA 81-84; CANR 47, 64; CDALBS; DA3; DLBY 85; MTCW 1, 2
Helvetius, Claude-Adrien 1715-1771 **LC 26**
Helyar, Jane Penelope Josephine 1933-
   See Poole, Josephine
   See also CA 21-24R; CANR 10, 26; SATA 82
Hemans, Felicia 1793-1835 **NCLC 71**
   See also DLB 96
Hemingway, Ernest (Miller) 1899-1961 **CLC 1, 3, 6, 8, 10, 13, 19, 30, 34, 39, 41, 44, 50, 61, 80; DA; DAB; DAC; DAM MST, NOV; SSC 1, 25, 36, 40; WLC**
   See also AAYA 19; CA 77-80; CANR 34; CDALB 1917-1929; DA3; DLB 4, 9, 102, 210; DLBD 1, 15, 16; DLBY 81, 87, 96, 98; MTCW 1, 2
Hempel, Amy 1951- **CLC 39**
   See also CA 118; 137; CANR 70; DA3; MTCW 2
Henderson, F. C.
   See Mencken, H(enry) L(ouis)
Henderson, Sylvia
   See Ashton-Warner, Sylvia (Constance)
Henderson, Zenna (Chlarson) 1917-1983 **SSC 29**
   See also CA 1-4R; 133; CANR 1, 84; DLB 8; SATA 5
Henkin, Joshua CLC 119
   See also CA 161
Henley, Beth CLC 23; DC 6
   See also Henley, Elizabeth Becker
   See also CABS 3; DLBY 86
Henley, Elizabeth Becker 1952-
   See Henley, Beth
   See also CA 107; CANR 32, 73; DAM DRAM, MST; DA3; MTCW 1, 2
Henley, William Ernest 1849-1903 **TCLC 8**
   See also CA 105; DLB 19
Hennissart, Martha
   See Lathen, Emma
   See also CA 85-88; CANR 64
Henry, O. TCLC 1, 19; SSC 5; WLC
   See also Porter, William Sydney
Henry, Patrick 1736-1799 **LC 25**
Henryson, Robert 1430(?)-1506(?) **LC 20**
   See also DLB 146
Henry VIII 1491-1547 **LC 10**
   See also DLB 132
Henschke, Alfred
   See Klabund
Hentoff, Nat(han Irving) 1925- **CLC 26**
   See also AAYA 4; CA 1-4R; CAAS 6; CANR 5, 25, 77; CLR 1, 52; INT CANR-25; JRDA; MAICYA; SATA 42, 69; SATA-Brief 27
Heppenstall, (John) Rayner 1911-1981 **CLC 10**
   See also CA 1-4R; 103; CANR 29
Heraclitus c. 540B.C.-c. 450B.C. **CMLC 22**
   See also DLB 176
Herbert, Frank (Patrick) 1920-1986 **CLC 12, 23, 35, 44, 85; DAM POP**
   See also AAYA 21; CA 53-56; 118; CANR 5, 43; CDALBS; DLB 8; INT CANR-5; MTCW 1, 2; SATA 9, 37; SATA-Obit 47
Herbert, George 1593-1633 **LC 24; DAB; DAM POET; PC 4**

See also CDBLB Before 1660; DLB 126

Herbert, Zbigniew 1924-1998 **CLC 9, 43; DAM POET**
See also CA 89-92; 169; CANR 36, 74; MTCW 1

Herbst, Josephine (Frey) 1897-1969 **CLC 34**
See also CA 5-8R; 25-28R; DLB 9

Heredia, Jose Maria 1803-1839
See also HLCS 2

Hergesheimer, Joseph 1880-1954 **TCLC 11**
See also CA 109; DLB 102, 9

Herlihy, James Leo 1927-1993 **CLC 6**
See also CA 1-4R; 143; CANR 2

Hermogenes fl. c. 175- **CMLC 6**

Hernandez, Jose 1834-1886 **NCLC 17**

Herodotus c. 484B.C.-429B.C. **CMLC 17**
See also DLB 176

Herrick, Robert 1591-1674 **LC 13; DA; DAB; DAC; DAM MST, POP; PC 9**
See also DLB 126

Herring, Guilles
See Somerville, Edith

Herriot, James 1916-1995 **CLC 12; DAM POP**
See also Wight, James Alfred
See also AAYA 1; CA 148; CANR 40; MTCW 2; SATA 86

Herris, Violet
See Hunt, Violet

Herrmann, Dorothy 1941- **CLC 44**
See also CA 107

Herrmann, Taffy
See Herrmann, Dorothy

Hersey, John (Richard) 1914-1993 **CLC 1, 2, 7, 9, 40, 81, 97; DAM POP**
See also AAYA 29; CA 17-20R; 140; CANR 33; CDALBS; DLB 6, 185; MTCW 1, 2; SATA 25; SATA-Obit 76

Herzen, Aleksandr Ivanovich 1812-1870 **NCLC 10, 61**

Herzl, Theodor 1860-1904 **TCLC 36**
See also CA 168

Herzog, Werner 1942- **CLC 16**
See also CA 89-92

Hesiod c. 8th cent. B.C.- **CMLC 5**
See also DLB 176

Hesse, Hermann 1877-1962 **CLC 1, 2, 3, 6, 11, 17, 25, 69; DA; DAB; DAC; DAM MST, NOV; SSC 9; WLC**
See also CA 17-18; CAP 2; DA3; DLB 66; MTCW 1, 2; SATA 50

Hewes, Cady
See De Voto, Bernard (Augustine)

Heyen, William 1940- **CLC 13, 18**
See also CA 33-36R; CAAS 9; DLB 5

Heyerdahl, Thor 1914- **CLC 26**
See also CA 5-8R; CANR 5, 22, 66, 73; MTCW 1, 2; SATA 2, 52

Heym, Georg (Theodor Franz Arthur) 1887-1912 **TCLC 9**
See also CA 106; 181

Heym, Stefan 1913- **CLC 41**
See also CA 9-12R; CANR 4; DLB 69

Heyse, Paul (Johann Ludwig von) 1830-1914 **TCLC 8**
See also CA 104; DLB 129

Heyward, (Edwin) DuBose 1885-1940 **TCLC 59**
See also CA 108; 157; DLB 7, 9, 45; SATA 21

Hibbert, Eleanor Alice Burford 1906-1993 **CLC 7; DAM POP**
See also BEST 90:4; CA 17-20R; 140; CANR 9, 28, 59; MTCW 2; SATA 2; SATA-Obit 74

Hichens, Robert (Smythe) 1864-1950 **TCLC 64**
See also CA 162; DLB 153

Higgins, George V(incent) 1939-1999 **CLC 4, 7, 10, 18**
See also CA 77-80; 186; CAAS 5; CANR 17, 51, 89; DLB 2; DLBY 81, 98; INT CANR-17; MTCW 1

Higginson, Thomas Wentworth 1823-1911 **TCLC 36**
See also CA 162; DLB 1, 64

Highet, Helen
See MacInnes, Helen (Clark)

Highsmith, (Mary) Patricia 1921-1995 **CLC 2, 4, 14, 42, 102; DAM NOV, POP**
See also CA 1-4R; 147; CANR 1, 20, 48, 62; DA3; MTCW 1, 2

Highwater, Jamake (Mamake) 1942(?)- **CLC 12**
See also AAYA 7; CA 65-68; CAAS 7; CANR 10, 34, 84; CLR 17; DLB 52; DLBY 85; JRDA; MAICYA; SATA 32, 69; SATA-Brief 30

Highway, Tomson 1951- **CLC 92; DAC; DAM MULT**
See also CA 151; CANR 75; MTCW 2; NNAL

Higuchi, Ichiyo 1872-1896 **NCLC 49**

Hijuelos, Oscar 1951- **CLC 65; DAM MULT, POP; HLC 1**
See also AAYA 25; BEST 90:1; CA 123; CANR 50, 75; DA3; DLB 145; HW 1, 2; MTCW 2

Hikmet, Nazim 1902(?)-1963 **CLC 40**
See also CA 141; 93-96

Hildegard von Bingen 1098-1179 **CMLC 20**
See also DLB 148

Hildesheimer, Wolfgang 1916-1991 **CLC 49**
See also CA 101; 135; DLB 69, 124

Hill, Geoffrey (William) 1932- **CLC 5, 8, 18, 45; DAM POET**
See also CA 81-84; CANR 21, 89; CDBLB 1960 to Present; DLB 40; MTCW 1

Hill, George Roy 1921- **CLC 26**
See also CA 110; 122

Hill, John
See Koontz, Dean R(ay)

Hill, Susan (Elizabeth) 1942- **CLC 4, 113; DAB; DAM MST, NOV**
See also CA 33-36R; CANR 29, 69; DLB 14, 139; MTCW 1

Hillerman, Tony 1925- **CLC 62; DAM POP**
See also AAYA 6; BEST 89:1; CA 29-32R; CANR 21, 42, 65; DA3; DLB 206; SATA 6

Hillesum, Etty 1914-1943 **TCLC 49**
See also CA 137

Hilliard, Noel (Harvey) 1929- **CLC 15**
See also CA 9-12R; CANR 7, 69

Hillis, Rick 1956- **CLC 66**
See also CA 134

Hilton, James 1900-1954 **TCLC 21**
See also CA 108; 169; DLB 34, 77; SATA 34

Himes, Chester (Bomar) 1909-1984 **CLC 2, 4, 7, 18, 58, 108; BLC 2; DAM MULT**
See also BW 2; CA 25-28R; 114; CANR 22, 89; DLB 2, 76, 143; MTCW 1, 2

Hinde, Thomas CLC 6, 11
See also Chitty, Thomas Willes

Hine, (William) Daryl 1936- **CLC 15**
See also CA 1-4R; CAAS 15; CANR 1, 20; DLB 60

Hinkson, Katharine Tynan
See Tynan, Katharine

Hinojosa(-Smith), Rolando (R.) 1929-
See Hinojosa-Smith, Rolando
See also CA 131; CAAS 16; CANR 62; DAM MULT; DLB 82; HLC 1; HW 1, 2; MTCW 2

Hinojosa-Smith, Rolando 1929-
See Hinojosa(-Smith), Rolando (R.)
See also CAAS 16; HLC 1; MTCW 2

Hinton, S(usan) E(loise) 1950- **CLC 30, 111; DA; DAB; DAC; DAM MST, NOV**
See also AAYA 2, 33; CA 81-84; CANR 32, 62; CDALBS; CLR 3, 23; DA3; JRDA; MAICYA; MTCW 1, 2; SATA 19, 58, 115

Hippius, Zinaida TCLC 9
See also Gippius, Zinaida (Nikolayevna)

Hiraoka, Kimitake 1925-1970
See Mishima, Yukio
See also CA 97-100; 29-32R; DAM DRAM; DA3; MTCW 1, 2

Hirsch, E(ric) D(onald), Jr. 1928- **CLC 79**
See also CA 25-28R; CANR 27, 51; DLB 67; INT CANR-27; MTCW 1

Hirsch, Edward 1950- **CLC 31, 50**
See also CA 104; CANR 20, 42; DLB 120

Hitchcock, Alfred (Joseph) 1899-1980 **CLC 16**
See also AAYA 22; CA 159; 97-100; SATA 27; SATA-Obit 24

Hitler, Adolf 1889-1945 **TCLC 53**
See also CA 117; 147

Hoagland, Edward 1932- **CLC 28**
See also CA 1-4R; CANR 2, 31, 57; DLB 6; SATA 51

Hoban, Russell (Conwell) 1925- **CLC 7, 25; DAM NOV**
See also CA 5-8R; CANR 23, 37, 66; CLR 3; DLB 52; MAICYA; MTCW 1, 2; SATA 1, 40, 78

Hobbes, Thomas 1588-1679 **LC 36**
See also DLB 151

Hobbs, Perry
See Blackmur, R(ichard) P(almer)

Hobson, Laura Z(ametkin) 1900-1986 **CLC 7, 25**
See also CA 17-20R; 118; CANR 55; DLB 28; SATA 52

Hochhuth, Rolf 1931- **CLC 4, 11, 18; DAM DRAM**
See also CA 5-8R; CANR 33, 75; DLB 124; MTCW 1, 2

Hochman, Sandra 1936- **CLC 3, 8**
See also CA 5-8R; DLB 5

Hochwaelder, Fritz 1911-1986 **CLC 36; DAM DRAM**
See also CA 29-32R; 120; CANR 42; MTCW 1

Hochwalder, Fritz
See Hochwaelder, Fritz

Hocking, Mary (Eunice) 1921- **CLC 13**
See also CA 101; CANR 18, 40

Hodgins, Jack 1938- **CLC 23**
See also CA 93-96; DLB 60

Hodgson, William Hope 1877(?)-1918 **TCLC 13**
See also CA 111; 164; DLB 70, 153, 156, 178; MTCW 2

Hoeg, Peter 1957- **CLC 95**
See also CA 151; CANR 75; DA3; MTCW 2

Hoffman, Alice 1952- **CLC 51; DAM NOV**
See also CA 77-80; CANR 34, 66; MTCW 1, 2

Hoffman, Daniel (Gerard) 1923- **CLC 6, 13, 23**
See also CA 1-4R; CANR 4; DLB 5

Hoffman, Stanley 1944- **CLC 5**
See also CA 77-80

Hoffman, William M(oses) 1939- **CLC 40**
See also CA 57-60; CANR 11, 71

Hoffmann, E(rnst) T(heodor) A(madeus) 1776-1822 **NCLC 2; SSC 13**
See also DLB 90; SATA 27

Hofmann, Gert 1931- **CLC 54**

See also CA 128

Hofmannsthal, Hugo von 1874-1929 **TCLC 11; DAM DRAM; DC 4**
See also CA 106; 153; DLB 81, 118

Hogan, Linda 1947- **CLC 73; DAM MULT**
See also CA 120; CANR 45, 73; DLB 175; NNAL

Hogarth, Charles
See Creasey, John

Hogarth, Emmett
See Polonsky, Abraham (Lincoln)

Hogg, James 1770-1835 **NCLC 4**
See also DLB 93, 116, 159

Holbach, Paul Henri Thiry Baron 1723-1789 **LC 14**

Holberg, Ludvig 1684-1754 **LC 6**

Holcroft, Thomas 1745-1809 **NCLC 85**
See also DLB 39, 89, 158

Holden, Ursula 1921- **CLC 18**
See also CA 101; CAAS 8; CANR 22

Holderlin, (Johann Christian) Friedrich 1770-1843 **NCLC 16; PC 4**

Holdstock, Robert
See Holdstock, Robert P.

Holdstock, Robert P. 1948- **CLC 39**
See also CA 131; CANR 81

Holland, Isabelle 1920- **CLC 21**
See also AAYA 11; CA 21-24R, 181; CAAE 181; CANR 10, 25, 47; CLR 57; JRDA; MAICYA; SATA 8, 70; SATA-Essay 103

Holland, Marcus
See Caldwell, (Janet Miriam) Taylor (Holland)

Hollander, John 1929- **CLC 2, 5, 8, 14**
See also CA 1-4R; CANR 1, 52; DLB 5; SATA 13

Hollander, Paul
See Silverberg, Robert

Holleran, Andrew 1943(?)- **CLC 38**
See also Garber, Eric
See also CA 144

Hollinghurst, Alan 1954- **CLC 55, 91**
See also CA 114; DLB 207

Hollis, Jim
See Summers, Hollis (Spurgeon, Jr.)

Holly, Buddy 1936-1959 **TCLC 65**

Holmes, Gordon
See Shiel, M(atthew) P(hipps)

Holmes, John
See Souster, (Holmes) Raymond

Holmes, John Clellon 1926-1988 **CLC 56**
See also CA 9-12R; 125; CANR 4; DLB 16

Holmes, Oliver Wendell, Jr. 1841-1935 **TCLC 77**
See also CA 114; 186

Holmes, Oliver Wendell 1809-1894 **NCLC 14, 81**
See also CDALB 1640-1865; DLB 1, 189; SATA 34

Holmes, Raymond
See Souster, (Holmes) Raymond

Holt, Victoria
See Hibbert, Eleanor Alice Burford

Holub, Miroslav 1923-1998 **CLC 4**
See also CA 21-24R; 169; CANR 10

Homer c. 8th cent. B.C.- **CMLC 1, 16; DA; DAB; DAC; DAM MST, POET; PC 23; WLCS**
See also DA3; DLB 176

Hongo, Garrett Kaoru 1951- **PC 23**
See also CA 133; CAAS 22; DLB 120

Honig, Edwin 1919- **CLC 33**
See also CA 5-8R; CAAS 8; CANR 4, 45; DLB 5

Hood, Hugh (John Blagdon) 1928- **CLC 15, 28**
See also CA 49-52; CAAS 17; CANR 1, 33, 87; DLB 53

Hood, Thomas 1799-1845 **NCLC 16**
See also DLB 96

Hooker, (Peter) Jeremy 1941- **CLC 43**
See also CA 77-80; CANR 22; DLB 40

hooks, bell CLC 94; BLCS
See also Watkins, Gloria Jean
See also MTCW 2

Hope, A(lec) D(erwent) 1907- **CLC 3, 51**
See also CA 21-24R; CANR 33, 74; MTCW 1, 2

Hope, Anthony 1863-1933 **TCLC 83**
See also CA 157; DLB 153, 156

Hope, Brian
See Creasey, John

Hope, Christopher (David Tully) 1944- **CLC 52**
See also CA 106; CANR 47; SATA 62

Hopkins, Gerard Manley 1844-1889 **NCLC 17; DA; DAB; DAC; DAM MST, POET; PC 15; WLC**
See also CDBLB 1890-1914; DA3; DLB 35, 57

Hopkins, John (Richard) 1931-1998 **CLC 4**
See also CA 85-88; 169

Hopkins, Pauline Elizabeth 1859-1930 **TCLC 28; BLC 2; DAM MULT**
See also BW 2, 3; CA 141; CANR 82; DLB 50

Hopkinson, Francis 1737-1791 **LC 25**
See also DLB 31

Hopley-Woolrich, Cornell George 1903-1968
See Woolrich, Cornell
See also CA 13-14; CANR 58; CAP 1; MTCW 2

Horace 65B.C.-8B.C. **CMLC 39**
See also DLB 211

Horatio
See Proust, (Valentin-Louis-George-Eugene-) Marcel

Horgan, Paul (George Vincent O'Shaughnessy) 1903-1995 **CLC 9, 53; DAM NOV**
See also CA 13-16R; 147; CANR 9, 35; DLB 212; DLBY 85; INT CANR-9; MTCW 1, 2; SATA 13; SATA-Obit 84

Horn, Peter
See Kuttner, Henry

Hornem, Horace Esq.
See Byron, George Gordon (Noel)

Horney, Karen (Clementine Theodore Danielsen) 1885-1952 **TCLC 71**
See also CA 114; 165

Hornung, E(rnest) W(illiam) 1866-1921 **TCLC 59**
See also CA 108; 160; DLB 70

Horovitz, Israel (Arthur) 1939- **CLC 56; DAM DRAM**
See also CA 33-36R; CANR 46, 59; DLB 7

Horton, George Moses 1797(?)-1883(?) **NCLC 87**
See also DLB 50

Horvath, Odon von
See Horvath, Oedoen von
See also DLB 85, 124

Horvath, Oedoen von 1901-1938 **TCLC 45**
See also Horvath, Odon von; von Horvath, Oedoen
See also CA 118

Horwitz, Julius 1920-1986 **CLC 14**
See also CA 9-12R; 119; CANR 12

Hospital, Janette Turner 1942- **CLC 42**
See also CA 108; CANR 48

Hostos, E. M. de
See Hostos (y Bonilla), Eugenio Maria de

Hostos, Eugenio M. de
See Hostos (y Bonilla), Eugenio Maria de

Hostos, Eugenio Maria
See Hostos (y Bonilla), Eugenio Maria de

Hostos (y Bonilla), Eugenio Maria de 1839-1903 **TCLC 24**
See also CA 123; 131; HW 1

Houdini
See Lovecraft, H(oward) P(hillips)

Hougan, Carolyn 1943- **CLC 34**
See also CA 139

Household, Geoffrey (Edward West) 1900-1988 **CLC 11**
See also CA 77-80; 126; CANR 58; DLB 87; SATA 14; SATA-Obit 59

Housman, A(lfred) E(dward) 1859-1936 **TCLC 1, 10; DA; DAB; DAC; DAM MST, POET; PC 2; WLCS**
See also CA 104; 125; DA3; DLB 19; MTCW 1, 2

Housman, Laurence 1865-1959 **TCLC 7**
See also CA 106; 155; DLB 10; SATA 25

Howard, Elizabeth Jane 1923- **CLC 7, 29**
See also CA 5-8R; CANR 8, 62

Howard, Maureen 1930- **CLC 5, 14, 46**
See also CA 53-56; CANR 31, 75; DLBY 83; INT CANR-31; MTCW 1, 2

Howard, Richard 1929- **CLC 7, 10, 47**
See also AITN 1; CA 85-88; CANR 25, 80; DLB 5; INT CANR-25

Howard, Robert E(rvin) 1906-1936 **TCLC 8**
See also CA 105; 157

Howard, Warren F.
See Pohl, Frederik

Howe, Fanny (Quincy) 1940- **CLC 47**
See also CA 117; CAAS 27; CANR 70; SATA-Brief 52

Howe, Irving 1920-1993 **CLC 85**
See also CA 9-12R; 141; CANR 21, 50; DLB 67; MTCW 1, 2

Howe, Julia Ward 1819-1910 **TCLC 21**
See also CA 117; DLB 1, 189

Howe, Susan 1937- **CLC 72**
See also CA 160; DLB 120

Howe, Tina 1937- **CLC 48**
See also CA 109

Howell, James 1594(?)-1666 **LC 13**
See also DLB 151

Howells, W. D.
See Howells, William Dean

Howells, William D.
See Howells, William Dean

Howells, William Dean 1837-1920 **TCLC 7, 17, 41; SSC 36**
See also CA 104; 134; CDALB 1865-1917; DLB 12, 64, 74, 79, 189; MTCW 2

Howes, Barbara 1914-1996 **CLC 15**
See also CA 9-12R; 151; CAAS 3; CANR 53; SATA 5

Hrabal, Bohumil 1914-1997 **CLC 13, 67**
See also CA 106; 156; CAAS 12; CANR 57

Hroswitha of Gandersheim c. 935-c. 1002 **CMLC 29**
See also DLB 148

Hsun, Lu
See Lu Hsun

Hubbard, L(afayette) Ron(ald) 1911-1986 **CLC 43; DAM POP**
See also CA 77-80; 118; CANR 52; DA3; MTCW 2

Huch, Ricarda (Octavia) 1864-1947 **TCLC 13**
See also CA 111; DLB 66

Huddle, David 1942- **CLC 49**
See also CA 57-60; CAAS 20; CANR 89; DLB 130

Hudson, Jeffrey
See Crichton, (John) Michael

Hudson, W(illiam) H(enry) 1841-1922 **TCLC 29**
See also CA 115; DLB 98, 153, 174; SATA 35

Iskander, Fazil 1929- **CLC 47**
See also CA 102
Isler, Alan (David) 1934- **CLC 91**
See also CA 156
Ivan IV 1530-1584 **LC 17**
Ivanov, Vyacheslav Ivanovich 1866-1949
TCLC 33
See also CA 122
Ivask, Ivar Vidrik 1927-1992 **CLC 14**
See also CA 37-40R; 139; CANR 24
Ives, Morgan
See Bradley, Marion Zimmer
Izumi Shikibu c. 973-c. 1034 **CMLC 33**
J. R. S.
See Gogarty, Oliver St. John
Jabran, Kahlil
See Gibran, Kahlil
Jabran, Khalil
See Gibran, Kahlil
Jackson, Daniel
See Wingrove, David (John)
Jackson, Jesse 1908-1983 **CLC 12**
See also BW 1; CA 25-28R; 109; CANR
27; CLR 28; MAICYA; SATA 2, 29;
SATA-Obit 48
Jackson, Laura (Riding) 1901-1991
See Riding, Laura
See also CA 65-68; 135; CANR 28, 89;
DLB 48
Jackson, Sam
See Trumbo, Dalton
Jackson, Sara
See Wingrove, David (John)
Jackson, Shirley 1919-1965 **CLC 11, 60, 87;
DA; DAC; DAM MST; SSC 9, 39; WLC**
See also AAYA 9; CA 1-4R; 25-28R; CANR
4, 52; CDALB 1941-1968; DA3; DLB 6;
MTCW 2; SATA 2
Jacob, (Cyprien-)Max 1876-1944 **TCLC 6**
See also CA 104
Jacobs, Harriet A(nn) 1813(?)-1897 **NCLC
67**
Jacobs, Jim 1942- **CLC 12**
See also CA 97-100; INT 97-100
Jacobs, W(illiam) W(ymark) 1863-1943
TCLC 22
See also CA 121; 167; DLB 135
Jacobsen, Jens Peter 1847-1885 **NCLC 34**
Jacobsen, Josephine 1908- **CLC 48, 102**
See also CA 33-36R; CAAS 18; CANR 23,
48
Jacobson, Dan 1929- **CLC 4, 14**
See also CA 1-4R; CANR 2, 25, 66; DLB
14, 207; MTCW 1
Jacqueline
See Carpentier (y Valmont), Alejo
Jagger, Mick 1944- **CLC 17**
Jahiz, al- c. 780-c. 869 **CMLC 25**
Jakes, John (William) 1932- **CLC 29; DAM
NOV, POP**
See also AAYA 32; BEST 89:4; CA 57-60;
CANR 10, 43, 66; DA3; DLBY 83; INT
CANR-10; MTCW 1, 2; SATA 62
James, Andrew
See Kirkup, James
James, C(yril) L(ionel) R(obert) 1901-1989
CLC 33; BLCS
See also BW 2; CA 117; 125; 128; CANR
62; DLB 125; MTCW 1
James, Daniel (Lewis) 1911-1988
See Santiago, Danny
See also CA 174; 125
James, Dynely
See Mayne, William (James Carter)
James, Henry Sr. 1811-1882 **NCLC 53**
James, Henry 1843-1916 **TCLC 2, 11, 24, 40,
47, 64; DA; DAB; DAC; DAM MST,
NOV; SSC 8, 32; WLC**
See also CA 104; 132; CDALB 1865-1917;
DA3; DLB 12, 71, 74, 189; DLBD 13;
MTCW 1, 2
James, M. R.
See James, Montague (Rhodes)
See also DLB 156
James, Montague (Rhodes) 1862-1936 **TCLC
6; SSC 16**
See also CA 104; DLB 201
James, P. D. 1920- **CLC 18, 46, 122**
See also White, Phyllis Dorothy James
See also BEST 90:2; CDBLB 1960 to
Present; DLB 87; DLBD 17
James, Philip
See Moorcock, Michael (John)
James, William 1842-1910 **TCLC 15, 32**
See also CA 109
James I 1394-1437 **LC 20**
Jameson, Anna 1794-1860 **NCLC 43**
See also DLB 99, 166
Jami, Nur al-Din 'Abd al-Rahman
1414-1492 **LC 9**
Jammes, Francis 1868-1938 **TCLC 75**
Jandl, Ernst 1925- **CLC 34**
Janowitz, Tama 1957- **CLC 43; DAM POP**
See also CA 106; CANR 52, 89
Japrisot, Sebastien 1931- **CLC 90**
Jarrell, Randall 1914-1965 **CLC 1, 2, 6, 9,
13, 49; DAM POET**
See also CA 5-8R; 25-28R; CABS 2; CANR
6, 34; CDALB 1941-1968; CLR 6; DLB
48, 52; MAICYA; MTCW 1, 2; SATA 7
Jarry, Alfred 1873-1907 **TCLC 2, 14; DAM
DRAM; SSC 20**
See also CA 104; 153; DA3; DLB 192
Jawien, Andrzej
See John Paul II, Pope
Jaynes, Roderick
See Coen, Ethan
Jeake, Samuel, Jr.
See Aiken, Conrad (Potter)
Jean Paul 1763-1825 **NCLC 7**
Jefferies, (John) Richard 1848-1887 **NCLC
47**
See also DLB 98, 141; SATA 16
Jeffers, (John) Robinson 1887-1962 **CLC 2,
3, 11, 15, 54; DA; DAC; DAM MST,
POET; PC 17; WLC**
See also CA 85-88; CANR 35; CDALB
1917-1929; DLB 45, 212; MTCW 1, 2
Jefferson, Janet
See Mencken, H(enry) L(ouis)
Jefferson, Thomas 1743-1826 **NCLC 11**
See also CDALB 1640-1865; DA3; DLB
31
Jeffrey, Francis 1773-1850 **NCLC 33**
See also DLB 107
Jelakowitch, Ivan
See Heijermans, Herman
Jellicoe, (Patricia) Ann 1927- **CLC 27**
See also CA 85-88; DLB 13
Jemyma
See Holley, Marietta
Jen, Gish CLC 70
See also Jen, Lillian
Jen, Lillian 1956(?)-
See Jen, Gish
See also CA 135; CANR 89
Jenkins, (John) Robin 1912- **CLC 52**
See also CA 1-4R; CANR 1; DLB 14
Jennings, Elizabeth (Joan) 1926- **CLC 5, 14,
131**
See also CA 61-64; CAAS 5; CANR 8, 39,
66; DLB 27; MTCW 1; SATA 66
Jennings, Waylon 1937- **CLC 21**
Jensen, Johannes V. 1873-1950 **TCLC 41**
See also CA 170
Jensen, Laura (Linnea) 1948- **CLC 37**

See also CA 103
Jerome, Jerome K(lapka) 1859-1927 **TCLC
23**
See also CA 119; 177; DLB 10, 34, 135
Jerrold, Douglas William 1803-1857 **NCLC 2**
See also DLB 158, 159
Jewett, (Theodora) Sarah Orne 1849-1909
TCLC 1, 22; SSC 6
See also CA 108; 127; CANR 71; DLB 12,
74, 221; SATA 15
Jewsbury, Geraldine (Endsor) 1812-1880
NCLC 22
See also DLB 21
Jhabvala, Ruth Prawer 1927- **CLC 4, 8, 29,
94; DAB; DAM NOV**
See also CA 1-4R; CANR 2, 29, 51, 74, 91;
DLB 139, 194; INT CANR-29; MTCW 1,
2
Jibran, Kahlil
See Gibran, Kahlil
Jibran, Khalil
See Gibran, Kahlil
Jiles, Paulette 1943- **CLC 13, 58**
See also CA 101; CANR 70
Jimenez (Mantecon), Juan Ramon
1881-1958 **TCLC 4; DAM MULT,
POET; HLC 1; PC 7**
See also CA 104; 131; CANR 74; DLB 134;
HW 1; MTCW 1, 2
Jimenez, Ramon
See Jimenez (Mantecon), Juan Ramon
Jimenez Mantecon, Juan
See Jimenez (Mantecon), Juan Ramon
Jin, Ha
See Jin, Xuefei
Jin, Xuefei 1956- **CLC 109**
See also CA 152; CANR 91
Joel, Billy CLC 26
See also Joel, William Martin
Joel, William Martin 1949-
See Joel, Billy
See also CA 108
John, Saint 7th cent. - **CMLC 27**
John of the Cross, St. 1542-1591 **LC 18**
John Paul II, Pope 1920- **CLC 128**
See also CA 106; 133
Johnson, B(ryan) S(tanley William)
1933-1973 **CLC 6, 9**
See also CA 9-12R; 53-56; CANR 9; DLB
14, 40
Johnson, Benj. F. of Boo
See Riley, James Whitcomb
Johnson, Benjamin F. of Boo
See Riley, James Whitcomb
Johnson, Charles (Richard) 1948- **CLC 7,
51, 65; BLC 2; DAM MULT**
See also BW 2, 3; CA 116; CAAS 18;
CANR 42, 66, 82; DLB 33; MTCW 2
Johnson, Denis 1949- **CLC 52**
See also CA 117; 121; CANR 71; DLB 120
Johnson, Diane 1934- **CLC 5, 13, 48**
See also CA 41-44R; CANR 17, 40, 62;
DLBY 80; INT CANR-17; MTCW 1
Johnson, Eyvind (Olof Verner) 1900-1976
CLC 14
See also CA 73-76; 69-72; CANR 34
Johnson, J. R.
See James, C(yril) L(ionel) R(obert)
Johnson, James Weldon 1871-1938 **TCLC 3,
19; BLC 2; DAM MULT, POET; PC 24**
See also BW 1, 3; CA 104; 125; CANR 82;
CDALB 1917-1929; CLR 32; DA3; DLB
51; MTCW 1, 2; SATA 31
Johnson, Joyce 1935- **CLC 58**
See also CA 125; 129
Johnson, Judith (Emlyn) 1936- **CLC 7, 15**
See also Sherwin, Judith Johnson
See also CA 25-28R; 153; CANR 34

Johnson, Lionel (Pigot) 1867-1902 **TCLC 19**
See also CA 117; DLB 19

Johnson, Marguerite (Annie)
See Angelou, Maya

Johnson, Mel
See Malzberg, Barry N(athaniel)

Johnson, Pamela Hansford 1912-1981 **CLC 1, 7, 27**
See also CA 1-4R; 104; CANR 2, 28; DLB 15; MTCW 1, 2

Johnson, Robert 1911(?)-1938 **TCLC 69**
See also BW 3; CA 174

Johnson, Samuel 1709-1784 **LC 15, 52; DA; DAB; DAC; DAM MST; WLC**
See also CDBLB 1660-1789; DLB 39, 95, 104, 142

Johnson, Uwe 1934-1984 **CLC 5, 10, 15, 40**
See also CA 1-4R; 112; CANR 1, 39; DLB 75; MTCW 1

Johnston, George (Benson) 1913- **CLC 51**
See also CA 1-4R; CANR 5, 20; DLB 88

Johnston, Jennifer 1930- **CLC 7**
See also CA 85-88; DLB 14

Joinville, Jean de 1224(?)-1317 **CMLC 38**

Jolley, (Monica) Elizabeth 1923- **CLC 46; SSC 19**
See also CA 127; CAAS 13; CANR 59

Jones, Arthur Llewellyn 1863-1947
See Machen, Arthur
See also CA 104; 179

Jones, D(ouglas) G(ordon) 1929- **CLC 10**
See also CA 29-32R; CANR 13, 90; DLB 53

Jones, David (Michael) 1895-1974 **CLC 2, 4, 7, 13, 42**
See also CA 9-12R; 53-56; CANR 28; CD-BLB 1945-1960; DLB 20, 100; MTCW 1

Jones, David Robert 1947-
See Bowie, David
See also CA 103

Jones, Diana Wynne 1934- **CLC 26**
See also AAYA 12; CA 49-52; CANR 4, 26, 56; CLR 23; DLB 161; JRDA; MAI-CYA; SAAS 7; SATA 9, 70, 108

Jones, Edward P. 1950- **CLC 76**
See also BW 2, 3; CA 142; CANR 79

Jones, Gayl 1949- **CLC 6, 9, 131; BLC 2; DAM MULT**
See also BW 2, 3; CA 77-80; CANR 27, 66; DA3; DLB 33; MTCW 1, 2

Jones, James 1921-1977 **CLC 1, 3, 10, 39**
See also AITN 1, 2; CA 1-4R; 69-72; CANR 6; DLB 2, 143; DLBD 17; DLBY 98; MTCW 1

Jones, John J.
See Lovecraft, H(oward) P(hillips)

Jones, LeRoi **CLC 1, 2, 3, 5, 10, 14**
See also Baraka, Amiri
See also MTCW 2

Jones, Louis B. 1953- **CLC 65**
See also CA 141; CANR 73

Jones, Madison (Percy, Jr.) 1925- **CLC 4**
See also CA 13-16R; CAAS 11; CANR 7, 54, 83; DLB 152

Jones, Mervyn 1922- **CLC 10, 52**
See also CA 45-48; CAAS 5; CANR 1, 91; MTCW 1

Jones, Mick 1956(?)- **CLC 30**

Jones, Nettie (Pearl) 1941- **CLC 34**
See also BW 2; CA 137; CAAS 20; CANR 88

Jones, Preston 1936-1979 **CLC 10**
See also CA 73-76; 89-92; DLB 7

Jones, Robert F(rancis) 1934- **CLC 7**
See also CA 49-52; CANR 2, 61

Jones, Rod 1953- **CLC 50**
See also CA 128

Jones, Terence Graham Parry 1942- **CLC 21**

See also Jones, Terry; Monty Python
See also CA 112; 116; CANR 35; INT 116

Jones, Terry
See Jones, Terence Graham Parry
See also SATA 67; SATA-Brief 51

Jones, Thom (Douglas) 1945(?)- **CLC 81**
See also CA 157; CANR 88

Jong, Erica 1942- **CLC 4, 6, 8, 18, 83; DAM NOV, POP**
See also AITN 1; BEST 90:2; CA 73-76; CANR 26, 52, 75; DA3; DLB 2, 5, 28, 152; INT CANR-26; MTCW 1, 2

Jonson, Ben(jamin) 1572(?)-1637 **LC 6, 33; DA; DAB; DAC; DAM DRAM, MST, POET; DC 4; PC 17; WLC**
See also CDBLB Before 1660; DLB 62, 121

Jordan, June 1936- **CLC 5, 11, 23, 114; BLCS; DAM MULT, POET**
See also AAYA 2; BW 2, 3; CA 33-36R; CANR 25, 70; CLR 10; DLB 38; MAI-CYA; MTCW 1; SATA 4

Jordan, Neil (Patrick) 1950- **CLC 110**
See also CA 124; 130; CANR 54; INT 130

Jordan, Pat(rick M.) 1941- **CLC 37**
See also CA 33-36R

Jorgensen, Ivar
See Ellison, Harlan (Jay)

Jorgenson, Ivar
See Silverberg, Robert

Josephus, Flavius c. 37-100 **CMLC 13**

Josiah Allen's Wife
See Holley, Marietta

Josipovici, Gabriel (David) 1940- **CLC 6, 43**
See also CA 37-40R; CAAS 8; CANR 47, 84; DLB 14

Joubert, Joseph 1754-1824 **NCLC 9**

Jouve, Pierre Jean 1887-1976 **CLC 47**
See also CA 65-68

Jovine, Francesco 1902-1950 **TCLC 79**

Joyce, James (Augustine Aloysius) 1882-1941 **TCLC 3, 8, 16, 35, 52; DA; DAB; DAC; DAM MST, NOV, POET; PC 22; SSC 3, 26; WLC**
See also CA 104; 126; CDBLB 1914-1945; DA3; DLB 10, 19, 36, 162; MTCW 1, 2

Jozsef, Attila 1905-1937 **TCLC 22**
See also CA 116

Juana Ines de la Cruz 1651(?)-1695 **LC 5; HLCS 1; PC 24**

Judd, Cyril
See Kornbluth, C(yril) M.; Pohl, Frederik

Juenger, Ernst 1895-1998 **CLC 125**
See also CA 101; 167; CANR 21, 47; DLB 56

Julian of Norwich 1342(?)-1416(?) **LC 6, 52**
See also DLB 146

Junger, Ernst
See Juenger, Ernst

Junger, Sebastian 1962- **CLC 109**
See also AAYA 28; CA 165

Juniper, Alex
See Hospital, Janette Turner

Junius
See Luxemburg, Rosa

Just, Ward (Swift) 1935- **CLC 4, 27**
See also CA 25-28R; CANR 32, 87; INT CANR-32

Justice, Donald (Rodney) 1925- **CLC 6, 19, 102; DAM POET**
See also CA 5-8R; CANR 26, 54, 74; DLBY 83; INT CANR-26; MTCW 2

Juvenal c. 60-c. 13 **CMLC 8**
See also Juvenalis, Decimus Junius
See also DLB 211

Juvenalis, Decimus Junius 55(?)-c. 127(?)
See Juvenal

Juvenis
See Bourne, Randolph S(illiman)

Kacew, Romain 1914-1980
See Gary, Romain
See also CA 108; 102

Kadare, Ismail 1936- **CLC 52**
See also CA 161

Kadohata, Cynthia **CLC 59, 122**
See also CA 140

Kafka, Franz 1883-1924 **TCLC 2, 6, 13, 29, 47, 53; DA; DAB; DAC; DAM MST, NOV; SSC 5, 29, 35; WLC**
See also AAYA 31; CA 105; 126; DA3; DLB 81; MTCW 1, 2

Kahanovitsch, Pinkhes
See Der Nister

Kahn, Roger 1927- **CLC 30**
See also CA 25-28R; CANR 44, 69; DLB 171; SATA 37

Kain, Saul
See Sassoon, Siegfried (Lorraine)

Kaiser, Georg 1878-1945 **TCLC 9**
See also CA 106; DLB 124

Kaletski, Alexander 1946- **CLC 39**
See also CA 118; 143

Kalidasa fl. c. 400- **CMLC 9; PC 22**

Kallman, Chester (Simon) 1921-1975 **CLC 2**
See also CA 45-48; 53-56; CANR 3

Kaminsky, Melvin 1926-
See Brooks, Mel
See also CA 65-68; CANR 16

Kaminsky, Stuart M(elvin) 1934- **CLC 59**
See also CA 73-76; CANR 29, 53, 89

Kandinsky, Wassily 1866-1944 **TCLC 92**
See also CA 118; 155

Kane, Francis
See Robbins, Harold

Kane, Paul
See Simon, Paul (Frederick)

Kanin, Garson 1912-1999 **CLC 22**
See also AITN 1; CA 5-8R; 177; CANR 7, 78; DLB 7

Kaniuk, Yoram 1930- **CLC 19**
See also CA 134

Kant, Immanuel 1724-1804 **NCLC 27, 67**
See also DLB 94

Kantor, MacKinlay 1904-1977 **CLC 7**
See also CA 61-64; 73-76; CANR 60, 63; DLB 9, 102; MTCW 2

Kaplan, David Michael 1946- **CLC 50**

Kaplan, James 1951- **CLC 59**
See also CA 135

Karageorge, Michael
See Anderson, Poul (William)

Karamzin, Nikolai Mikhailovich 1766-1826 **NCLC 3**
See also DLB 150

Karapanou, Margarita 1946- **CLC 13**
See also CA 101

Karinthy, Frigyes 1887-1938 **TCLC 47**
See also CA 170

Karl, Frederick R(obert) 1927- **CLC 34**
See also CA 5-8R; CANR 3, 44

Kastel, Warren
See Silverberg, Robert

Kataev, Evgeny Petrovich 1903-1942
See Petrov, Evgeny
See also CA 120

Kataphusin
See Ruskin, John

Katz, Steve 1935- **CLC 47**
See also CA 25-28R; CAAS 14, 64; CANR 12; DLBY 83

Kauffman, Janet 1945- **CLC 42**
See also CA 117; CANR 43, 84; DLBY 86

Kaufman, Bob (Garnell) 1925-1986 **CLC 49**
See also BW 1; CA 41-44R; 118; CANR 22; DLB 16, 41

Kaufman, George S. 1889-1961 **CLC 38; DAM DRAM**

See also AAYA 1, 17; BEST 90:1; CA 61-64; CANR 1, 30, 52, 76; DA3; DLB 143; DLBY 80; JRDA; MTCW 1, 2; SATA 9, 55

King, Steve
See King, Stephen (Edwin)
King, Thomas 1943- **CLC 89; DAC; DAM MULT**
See also CA 144; DLB 175; NNAL; SATA 96
Kingman, Lee CLC 17
See also Natti, (Mary) Lee
See also SAAS 3; SATA 1, 67
Kingsley, Charles 1819-1875 **NCLC 35**
See also DLB 21, 32, 163, 190; YABC 2
Kingsley, Sidney 1906-1995 **CLC 44**
See also CA 85-88; 147; DLB 7
Kingsolver, Barbara 1955- **CLC 55, 81, 130; DAM POP**
See also AAYA 15; CA 129; 134; CANR 60; CDALBS; DA3; DLB 206; INT 134; MTCW 2
Kingston, Maxine (Ting Ting) Hong 1940- **CLC 12, 19, 58, 121; DAM MULT, NOV; WLCS**
See also AAYA 8; CA 69-72; CANR 13, 38, 74, 87; CDALBS; DA3; DLB 173, 212; DLBY 80; INT CANR-13; MTCW 1, 2; SATA 53
Kinnell, Galway 1927- **CLC 1, 2, 3, 5, 13, 29, 129; PC 26**
See also CA 9-12R; CANR 10, 34, 66; DLB 5; DLBY 87; INT CANR-34; MTCW 1, 2
Kinsella, Thomas 1928- **CLC 4, 19**
See also CA 17-20R; CANR 15; DLB 27; MTCW 1, 2
Kinsella, W(illiam) P(atrick) 1935- **CLC 27, 43; DAC; DAM NOV, POP**
See also AAYA 7; CA 97-100; CAAS 7; CANR 21, 35, 66, 75; INT CANR-21; MTCW 1, 2
Kinsey, Alfred C(harles) 1894-1956 **TCLC 91**
See also CA 115; 170; MTCW 2
Kipling, (Joseph) Rudyard 1865-1936 **TCLC 8, 17; DA; DAB; DAC; DAM MST, POET; PC 3; SSC 5; WLC**
See also AAYA 32; CA 105; 120; CANR 33; CDBLB 1890-1914; CLR 39, 65; DA3; DLB 19, 34, 141, 156; MAICYA; MTCW 1, 2; SATA 100; YABC 2
Kirkland, Caroline M. 1801-1864 **NCLC 85**
See also DLB 3, 73, 74; DLBD 13
Kirkup, James 1918- **CLC 1**
See also CA 1-4R; CAAS 4; CANR 2; DLB 27; SATA 12
Kirkwood, James 1930(?)-1989 **CLC 9**
See also AITN 2; CA 1-4R; 128; CANR 6, 40
Kirshner, Sidney
See Kingsley, Sidney
Kis, Danilo 1935-1989 **CLC 57**
See also CA 109; 118; 129; CANR 61; DLB 181; MTCW 1
Kivi, Aleksis 1834-1872 **NCLC 30**
Kizer, Carolyn (Ashley) 1925- **CLC 15, 39, 80; DAM POET**
See also CA 65-68; CAAS 5; CANR 24, 70; DLB 5, 169; MTCW 2
Klabund 1890-1928 **TCLC 44**
See also CA 162; DLB 66
Klappert, Peter 1942- **CLC 57**
See also CA 33-36R; DLB 5
Klein, A(braham) M(oses) 1909-1972 **CLC 19; DAB; DAC; DAM MST**
See also CA 101; 37-40R; DLB 68
Klein, Norma 1938-1989 **CLC 30**
See also AAYA 2; CA 41-44R; 128; CANR 15, 37; CLR 2, 19; INT CANR-15; JRDA; MAICYA; SAAS 1; SATA 7, 57

Klein, T(heodore) E(ibon) D(onald) 1947- **CLC 34**
See also CA 119; CANR 44, 75
Kleist, Heinrich von 1777-1811 **NCLC 2, 37; DAM DRAM; SSC 22**
See also DLB 90
Klima, Ivan 1931- **CLC 56; DAM NOV**
See also CA 25-28R; CANR 17, 50, 91
Klimentov, Andrei Platonovich 1899-1951
See Platonov, Andrei
See also CA 108
Klinger, Friedrich Maximilian von 1752-1831 **NCLC 1**
See also DLB 94
Klingsor the Magician
See Hartmann, Sadakichi
Klopstock, Friedrich Gottlieb 1724-1803 **NCLC 11**
See also DLB 97
Knapp, Caroline 1959- **CLC 99**
See also CA 154
Knebel, Fletcher 1911-1993 **CLC 14**
See also AITN 1; CA 1-4R; 140; CAAS 3; CANR 1, 36; SATA 36; SATA-Obit 75
Knickerbocker, Diedrich
See Irving, Washington
Knight, Etheridge 1931-1991 **CLC 40; BLC 2; DAM POET; PC 14**
See also BW 1, 3; CA 21-24R; 133; CANR 23, 82; DLB 41; MTCW 1
Knight, Sarah Kemble 1666-1727 **LC 7**
See also DLB 24, 200
Knister, Raymond 1899-1932 **TCLC 56**
See also CA 186; DLB 68
Knowles, John 1926- **CLC 1, 4, 10, 26; DA; DAC; DAM MST, NOV**
See also AAYA 10; CA 17-20R; CANR 40, 74, 76; CDALB 1968-1988; DLB 6; MTCW 1, 2; SATA 8, 89
Knox, Calvin M.
See Silverberg, Robert
Knox, John c. 1505-1572 **LC 37**
See also DLB 132
Knye, Cassandra
See Disch, Thomas M(ichael)
Koch, C(hristopher) J(ohn) 1932- **CLC 42**
See also CA 127; CANR 84
Koch, Christopher
See Koch, C(hristopher) J(ohn)
Koch, Kenneth 1925- **CLC 5, 8, 44; DAM POET**
See also CA 1-4R; CANR 6, 36, 57; DLB 5; INT CANR-36; MTCW 2; SATA 65
Kochanowski, Jan 1530-1584 **LC 10**
Kock, Charles Paul de 1794-1871 **NCLC 16**
Koda Rohan 1867-
See Koda Shigeyuki
Koda Shigeyuki 1867-1947 **TCLC 22**
See also CA 121; 183; DLB 180
Koestler, Arthur 1905-1983 **CLC 1, 3, 6, 8, 15, 33**
See also CA 1-4R; 109; CANR 1, 33; CD-BLB 1945-1960; DLBY 83; MTCW 1, 2
Kogawa, Joy Nozomi 1935- **CLC 78, 129; DAC; DAM MST, MULT**
See also CA 101; CANR 19, 62; MTCW 2; SATA 99
Kohout, Pavel 1928- **CLC 13**
See also CA 45-48; CANR 3
Koizumi, Yakumo
See Hearn, (Patricio) Lafcadio (Tessima Carlos)
Kolmar, Gertrud 1894-1943 **TCLC 40**
See also CA 167
Komunyakaa, Yusef 1947- **CLC 86, 94; BLCS**
See also CA 147; CANR 83; DLB 120

Konrad, George
See Konrad, Gyoergy
Konrad, Gyoergy 1933- **CLC 4, 10, 73**
See also CA 85-88
Konwicki, Tadeusz 1926- **CLC 8, 28, 54, 117**
See also CA 101; CAAS 9; CANR 39, 59; MTCW 1
Koontz, Dean R(ay) 1945- **CLC 78; DAM NOV, POP**
See also AAYA 9, 31; BEST 89:3, 90:2; CA 108; CANR 19, 36, 52; DA3; MTCW 1; SATA 92
Kopernik, Mikolaj
See Copernicus, Nicolaus
Kopit, Arthur (Lee) 1937- **CLC 1, 18, 33; DAM DRAM**
See also AITN 1; CA 81-84; CABS 3; DLB 7; MTCW 1
Kops, Bernard 1926- **CLC 4**
See also CA 5-8R; CANR 84; DLB 13
Kornbluth, C(yril) M. 1923-1958 **TCLC 8**
See also CA 105; 160; DLB 8
Korolenko, V. G.
See Korolenko, Vladimir Galaktionovich
Korolenko, Vladimir
See Korolenko, Vladimir Galaktionovich
Korolenko, Vladimir G.
See Korolenko, Vladimir Galaktionovich
Korolenko, Vladimir Galaktionovich 1853-1921 **TCLC 22**
See also CA 121
Korzybski, Alfred (Habdank Skarbek) 1879-1950 **TCLC 61**
See also CA 123; 160
Kosinski, Jerzy (Nikodem) 1933-1991 **CLC 1, 2, 3, 6, 10, 15, 53, 70; DAM NOV**
See also CA 17-20R; 134; CANR 9, 46; DA3; DLB 2; DLBY 82; MTCW 1, 2
Kostelanetz, Richard (Cory) 1940- **CLC 28**
See also CA 13-16R; CAAS 8; CANR 38, 77
Kostrowitzki, Wilhelm Apollinaris de 1880-1918
See Apollinaire, Guillaume
See also CA 104
Kotlowitz, Robert 1924- **CLC 4**
See also CA 33-36R; CANR 36
Kotzebue, August (Friedrich Ferdinand) von 1761-1819 **NCLC 25**
See also DLB 94
Kotzwinkle, William 1938- **CLC 5, 14, 35**
See also CA 45-48; CANR 3, 44, 84; CLR 6; DLB 173; MAICYA; SATA 24, 70
Kowna, Stancy
See Szymborska, Wislawa
Kozol, Jonathan 1936- **CLC 17**
See also CA 61-64; CANR 16, 45
Kozoll, Michael 1940(?)- **CLC 35**
Kramer, Kathryn 19(?)- **CLC 34**
Kramer, Larry 1935- **CLC 42; DAM POP; DC 8**
See also CA 124; 126; CANR 60
Krasicki, Ignacy 1735-1801 **NCLC 8**
Krasinski, Zygmunt 1812-1859 **NCLC 4**
Kraus, Karl 1874-1936 **TCLC 5**
See also CA 104; DLB 118
Kreve (Mickevicius), Vincas 1882-1954 **TCLC 27**
See also CA 170; DLB 220
Kristeva, Julia 1941- **CLC 77**
See also CA 154
Kristofferson, Kris 1936- **CLC 26**
See also CA 104
Krizanc, John 1956- **CLC 57**
Krleza, Miroslav 1893-1981 **CLC 8, 114**
See also CA 97-100; 105; CANR 50; DLB 147

See also BW 1; CA 125; CANR 83; DLB 51

Larson, Charles R(aymond) 1938- **CLC 31**
See also CA 53-56; CANR 4

Larson, Jonathan 1961-1996 **CLC 99**
See also AAYA 28; CA 156

Las Casas, Bartolome de 1474-1566 **LC 31**

Lasch, Christopher 1932-1994 **CLC 102**
See also CA 73-76; 144; CANR 25; MTCW 1, 2

Lasker-Schueler, Else 1869-1945 **TCLC 57**
See also CA 183; DLB 66, 124

Laski, Harold 1893-1950 **TCLC 79**

Latham, Jean Lee 1902-1995 **CLC 12**
See also AITN 1; CA 5-8R; CANR 7, 84; CLR 50; MAICYA; SATA 2, 68

Latham, Mavis
See Clark, Mavis Thorpe

Lathen, Emma CLC 2
See also Hennissart, Martha; Latsis, Mary J(ane)

Lathrop, Francis
See Leiber, Fritz (Reuter, Jr.)

Latsis, Mary J(ane) 1927(?)-1997
See Lathen, Emma
See also CA 85-88; 162

Lattimore, Richmond (Alexander) 1906-1984 **CLC 3**
See also CA 1-4R; 112; CANR 1

Laughlin, James 1914-1997 **CLC 49**
See also CA 21-24R; 162; CAAS 22; CANR 9, 47; DLB 48; DLBY 96, 97

Laurence, (Jean) Margaret (Wemyss) 1926-1987 **CLC 3, 6, 13, 50, 62; DAC; DAM MST; SSC 7**
See also CA 5-8R; 121; CANR 33; DLB 53; MTCW 1, 2; SATA-Obit 50

Laurent, Antoine 1952- **CLC 50**

Lauscher, Hermann
See Hesse, Hermann

Lautreamont, Comte de 1846-1870 **NCLC 12; SSC 14**

Laverty, Donald
See Blish, James (Benjamin)

Lavin, Mary 1912-1996 **CLC 4, 18, 99; SSC 4**
See also CA 9-12R; 151; CANR 33; DLB 15; MTCW 1

Lavond, Paul Dennis
See Kornbluth, C(yril) M.; Pohl, Frederik

Lawler, Raymond Evenor 1922- **CLC 58**
See also CA 103

Lawrence, D(avid) H(erbert Richards) 1885-1930 **TCLC 2, 9, 16, 33, 48, 61, 93; DA; DAB; DAC; DAM MST, NOV, POET; SSC 4, 19; WLC**
See also CA 104; 121; CDBLB 1914-1945; DA3; DLB 10, 19, 36, 98, 162, 195; MTCW 1, 2

Lawrence, T(homas) E(dward) 1888-1935 **TCLC 18**
See also Dale, Colin
See also CA 115; 167; DLB 195

Lawrence of Arabia
See Lawrence, T(homas) E(dward)

Lawson, Henry (Archibald Hertzberg) 1867-1922 **TCLC 27; SSC 18**
See also CA 120; 181

Lawton, Dennis
See Faust, Frederick (Schiller)

Laxness, Halldor CLC 25
See also Gudjonsson, Halldor Kiljan

Layamon fl. c. 1200- **CMLC 10**
See also DLB 146

Laye, Camara 1928-1980 **CLC 4, 38; BLC 2; DAM MULT**
See also BW 1; CA 85-88; 97-100; CANR 25; MTCW 1, 2

Layton, Irving (Peter) 1912- **CLC 2, 15; DAC; DAM MST, POET**
See also CA 1-4R; CANR 2, 33, 43, 66; DLB 88; MTCW 1, 2

Lazarus, Emma 1849-1887 **NCLC 8**

Lazarus, Felix
See Cable, George Washington

Lazarus, Henry
See Slavitt, David R(ytman)

Lea, Joan
See Neufeld, John (Arthur)

Leacock, Stephen (Butler) 1869-1944 **TCLC 2; DAC; DAM MST; SSC 39**
See also CA 104; 141; CANR 80; DLB 92; MTCW 2

Lear, Edward 1812-1888 **NCLC 3**
See also CLR 1; DLB 32, 163, 166; MAICYA; SATA 18, 100

Lear, Norman (Milton) 1922- **CLC 12**
See also CA 73-76

Leautaud, Paul 1872-1956 **TCLC 83**
See also DLB 65

Leavis, F(rank) R(aymond) 1895-1978 **CLC 24**
See also CA 21-24R; 77-80; CANR 44; MTCW 1, 2

Leavitt, David 1961- **CLC 34; DAM POP**
See also CA 116; 122; CANR 50, 62; DA3; DLB 130; INT 122; MTCW 2

Leblanc, Maurice (Marie Emile) 1864-1941 **TCLC 49**
See also CA 110

Lebowitz, Fran(ces Ann) 1951(?)- **CLC 11, 36**
See also CA 81-84; CANR 14, 60, 70; INT CANR-14; MTCW 1

Lebrecht, Peter
See Tieck, (Johann) Ludwig

le Carre, John CLC 3, 5, 9, 15, 28
See also Cornwell, David (John Moore)
See also BEST 89:4; CDBLB 1960 to Present; DLB 87; MTCW 2

Le Clezio, J(ean) M(arie) G(ustave) 1940- **CLC 31**
See also CA 116; 128; DLB 83

Leconte de Lisle, Charles-Marie-Rene 1818-1894 **NCLC 29**

Le Coq, Monsieur
See Simenon, Georges (Jacques Christian)

Leduc, Violette 1907-1972 **CLC 22**
See also CA 13-14; 33-36R; CANR 69; CAP 1

Ledwidge, Francis 1887(?)-1917 **TCLC 23**
See also CA 123; DLB 20

Lee, Andrea 1953- **CLC 36; BLC 2; DAM MULT**
See also BW 1, 3; CA 125; CANR 82

Lee, Andrew
See Auchincloss, Louis (Stanton)

Lee, Chang-rae 1965- **CLC 91**
See also CA 148; CANR 89

Lee, Don L. CLC 2
See also Madhubuti, Haki R.

Lee, George W(ashington) 1894-1976 **CLC 52; BLC 2; DAM MULT**
See also BW 1; CA 125; CANR 83; DLB 51

Lee, (Nelle) Harper 1926- **CLC 12, 60; DA; DAB; DAC; DAM MST, NOV; WLC**
See also AAYA 13; CA 13-16R; CANR 51; CDALB 1941-1968; DA3; DLB 6; MTCW 1, 2; SATA 11

Lee, Helen Elaine 1959(?)- **CLC 86**
See also CA 148

Lee, Julian
See Latham, Jean Lee

Lee, Larry
See Lee, Lawrence

Lee, Laurie 1914-1997 **CLC 90; DAB; DAM POP**
See also CA 77-80; 158; CANR 33, 73; DLB 27; MTCW 1

Lee, Lawrence 1941-1990 **CLC 34**
See also CA 131; CANR 43

Lee, Li-Young 1957- **PC 24**
See also CA 153; DLB 165

Lee, Manfred B(ennington) 1905-1971 **CLC 11**
See also Queen, Ellery
See also CA 1-4R; 29-32R; CANR 2; DLB 137

Lee, Shelton Jackson 1957(?)- **CLC 105; BLCS; DAM MULT**
See also Lee, Spike
See also BW 2, 3; CA 125; CANR 42

Lee, Spike
See Lee, Shelton Jackson
See also AAYA 4, 29

Lee, Stan 1922- **CLC 17**
See also AAYA 5; CA 108; 111; INT 111

Lee, Tanith 1947- **CLC 46**
See also AAYA 15; CA 37-40R; CANR 53; SATA 8, 88

Lee, Vernon TCLC 5; SSC 33
See also Paget, Violet
See also DLB 57, 153, 156, 174, 178

Lee, William
See Burroughs, William S(eward)

Lee, Willy
See Burroughs, William S(eward)

Lee-Hamilton, Eugene (Jacob) 1845-1907 **TCLC 22**
See also CA 117

Leet, Judith 1935- **CLC 11**

Le Fanu, Joseph Sheridan 1814-1873 **NCLC 9, 58; DAM POP; SSC 14**
See also DA3; DLB 21, 70, 159, 178

Leffland, Ella 1931- **CLC 19**
See also CA 29-32R; CANR 35, 78, 82; DLBY 84; INT CANR-35; SATA 65

Leger, Alexis
See Leger, (Marie-Rene Auguste) Alexis Saint-Leger

Leger, (Marie-Rene Auguste) Alexis Saint-Leger 1887-1975 **CLC 4, 11, 46; DAM POET; PC 23**
See also CA 13-16R; 61-64; CANR 43; MTCW 1

Leger, Saintleger
See Leger, (Marie-Rene Auguste) Alexis Saint-Leger

Le Guin, Ursula K(roeber) 1929- **CLC 8, 13, 22, 45, 71; DAB; DAC; DAM MST, POP; SSC 12**
See also AAYA 9, 27; AITN 1; CA 21-24R; CANR 9, 32, 52, 74; CDALB 1968-1988; CLR 3, 28; DA3; DLB 8, 52; INT CANR-32; JRDA; MAICYA; MTCW 1, 2; SATA 4, 52, 99

Lehmann, Rosamond (Nina) 1901-1990 **CLC 5**
See also CA 77-80; 131; CANR 8, 73; DLB 15; MTCW 2

Leiber, Fritz (Reuter, Jr.) 1910-1992 **CLC 25**
See also CA 45-48; 139; CANR 2, 40, 86; DLB 8; MTCW 1, 2; SATA 45; SATA-Obit 73

Leibniz, Gottfried Wilhelm von 1646-1716 **LC 35**
See also DLB 168

Leimbach, Martha 1963-
See Leimbach, Marti
See also CA 130

Leimbach, Marti CLC 65
See also Leimbach, Martha

Lispector, Clarice 1925(?)-1977 **CLC 43; HLCS 2; SSC 34**
See also CA 139; 116; CANR 71; DLB 113; HW 2

Littell, Robert 1935(?)- **CLC 42**
See also CA 109; 112; CANR 64

Little, Malcolm 1925-1965
See Malcolm X
See also BW 1, 3; CA 125; 111; CANR 82; DA; DAB; DAC; DAM MST, MULT; DA3; MTCW 1, 2

Littlewit, Humphrey Gent.
See Lovecraft, H(oward) P(hillips)

Litwos
See Sienkiewicz, Henryk (Adam Alexander Pius)

Liu, E 1857-1909 **TCLC 15**
See also CA 115

Lively, Penelope (Margaret) 1933- **CLC 32, 50; DAM NOV**
See also CA 41-44R; CANR 29, 67, 79; CLR 7; DLB 14, 161, 207; JRDA; MAICYA; MTCW 1, 2; SATA 7, 60, 101

Livesay, Dorothy (Kathleen) 1909- **CLC 4, 15, 79; DAC; DAM MST, POET**
See also AITN 2; CA 25-28R; CAAS 8; CANR 36, 67; DLB 68; MTCW 1

Livy c. 59B.C.-c. 17 **CMLC 11**
See also DLB 211

Lizardi, Jose Joaquin Fernandez de 1776-1827 **NCLC 30**

Llewellyn, Richard
See Llewellyn Lloyd, Richard Dafydd Vivian
See also DLB 15

Llewellyn Lloyd, Richard Dafydd Vivian 1906-1983 **CLC 7, 80**
See also Llewellyn, Richard
See also CA 53-56; 111; CANR 7, 71; SATA 11; SATA-Obit 37

Llosa, (Jorge) Mario (Pedro) Vargas
See Vargas Llosa, (Jorge) Mario (Pedro)

Lloyd, Manda
See Mander, (Mary) Jane

Lloyd Webber, Andrew 1948-
See Webber, Andrew Lloyd
See also AAYA 1; CA 116; 149; DAM DRAM; SATA 56

Llull, Ramon c. 1235-c. 1316 **CMLC 12**

Lobb, Ebenezer
See Upward, Allen

Locke, Alain (Le Roy) 1886-1954 **TCLC 43; BLCS**
See also BW 1, 3; CA 106; 124; CANR 79; DLB 51

Locke, John 1632-1704 **LC 7, 35**
See also DLB 101

Locke-Elliott, Sumner
See Elliott, Sumner Locke

Lockhart, John Gibson 1794-1854 **NCLC 6**
See also DLB 110, 116, 144

Lodge, David (John) 1935- **CLC 36; DAM POP**
See also BEST 90:1; CA 17-20R; CANR 19, 53; DLB 14, 194; INT CANR-19; MTCW 1, 2

Lodge, Thomas 1558-1625 **LC 41**

Lodge, Thomas 1558-1625 **LC 41**
See also DLB 172

Loennbohm, Armas Eino Leopold 1878-1926
See Leino, Eino
See also CA 123

Loewinsohn, Ron(ald William) 1937- **CLC 52**
See also CA 25-28R; CANR 71

Logan, Jake
See Smith, Martin Cruz

Logan, John (Burton) 1923-1987 **CLC 5**
See also CA 77-80; 124; CANR 45; DLB 5

Lo Kuan-chung 1330(?)-1400(?) **LC 12**

Lombard, Nap
See Johnson, Pamela Hansford

London, Jack TCLC 9, 15, 39; SSC 4; WLC
See also London, John Griffith
See also AAYA 13; AITN 2; CDALB 1865-1917; DLB 8, 12, 78, 212; SATA 18

London, John Griffith 1876-1916
See London, Jack
See also CA 110; 119; CANR 73; DA; DAB; DAC; DAM MST, NOV; DA3; JRDA; MAICYA; MTCW 1, 2

Long, Emmett
See Leonard, Elmore (John, Jr.)

Longbaugh, Harry
See Goldman, William (W.)

Longfellow, Henry Wadsworth 1807-1882 **NCLC 2, 45; DA; DAB; DAC; DAM MST, POET; PC 30; WLCS**
See also CDALB 1640-1865; DA3; DLB 1, 59; SATA 19

Longinus c. 1st cent. - **CMLC 27**
See also DLB 176

Longley, Michael 1939- **CLC 29**
See also CA 102; DLB 40

Longus fl. c. 2nd cent. - **CMLC 7**

Longway, A. Hugh
See Lang, Andrew

Lonnrot, Elias 1802-1884 **NCLC 53**

Lopate, Phillip 1943- **CLC 29**
See also CA 97-100; CANR 88; DLBY 80; INT 97-100

Lopez Portillo (y Pacheco), Jose 1920- **CLC 46**
See also CA 129; HW 1

Lopez y Fuentes, Gregorio 1897(?)-1966 **CLC 32**
See also CA 131; HW 1

Lorca, Federico Garcia
See Garcia Lorca, Federico

Lord, Bette Bao 1938- **CLC 23**
See also BEST 90:3; CA 107; CANR 41, 79; INT 107; SATA 58

Lord Auch
See Bataille, Georges

Lord Byron
See Byron, George Gordon (Noel)

Lorde, Audre (Geraldine) 1934-1992 **CLC 18, 71; BLC 2; DAM MULT, POET; PC 12**
See also BW 1, 3; CA 25-28R; 142; CANR 16, 26, 46, 82; DA3; DLB 41; MTCW 1, 2

Lord Houghton
See Milnes, Richard Monckton

Lord Jeffrey
See Jeffrey, Francis

Lorenzini, Carlo 1826-1890
See Collodi, Carlo
See also MAICYA; SATA 29, 100

Lorenzo, Heberto Padilla
See Padilla (Lorenzo), Heberto

Loris
See Hofmannsthal, Hugo von

Loti, Pierre TCLC 11
See also Viaud, (Louis Marie) Julien
See also DLB 123

Lou, Henri
See Andreas-Salome, Lou

Louie, David Wong 1954- **CLC 70**
See also CA 139

Louis, Father M.
See Merton, Thomas

Lovecraft, H(oward) P(hillips) 1890-1937 **TCLC 4, 22; DAM POP; SSC 3**
See also AAYA 14; CA 104; 133; DA3; MTCW 1, 2

Lovelace, Earl 1935- **CLC 51**

See also BW 2; CA 77-80; CANR 41, 72; DLB 125; MTCW 1

Lovelace, Richard 1618-1657 **LC 24**
See also DLB 131

Lowell, Amy 1874-1925 **TCLC 1, 8; DAM POET; PC 13**
See also CA 104; 151; DLB 54, 140; MTCW 2

Lowell, James Russell 1819-1891 **NCLC 2**
See also CDALB 1640-1865; DLB 1, 11, 64, 79, 189

Lowell, Robert (Traill Spence, Jr.) 1917-1977 **CLC 1, 2, 3, 4, 5, 8, 9, 11, 15, 37, 124; DA; DAB; DAC; DAM MST, NOV; PC 3; WLC**
See also CA 9-12R; 73-76; CABS 2; CANR 26, 60; CDALBS; DA3; DLB 5, 169; MTCW 1, 2

Lowenthal, Michael (Francis) 1969- **CLC 119**
See also CA 150

Lowndes, Marie Adelaide (Belloc) 1868-1947 **TCLC 12**
See also CA 107; DLB 70

Lowry, (Clarence) Malcolm 1909-1957 **TCLC 6, 40; SSC 31**
See also CA 105; 131; CANR 62; CDBLB 1945-1960; DLB 15; MTCW 1, 2

Lowry, Mina Gertrude 1882-1966
See Loy, Mina
See also CA 113

Loxsmith, John
See Brunner, John (Kilian Houston)

Loy, Mina CLC 28; DAM POET; PC 16
See also Lowry, Mina Gertrude
See also DLB 4, 54

Loyson-Bridet
See Schwob, Marcel (Mayer Andre)

Lucan 39-65 **CMLC 33**
See also DLB 211

Lucas, Craig 1951- **CLC 64**
See also CA 137; CANR 71

Lucas, E(dward) V(errall) 1868-1938 **TCLC 73**
See also CA 176; DLB 98, 149, 153; SATA 20

Lucas, George 1944- **CLC 16**
See also AAYA 1, 23; CA 77-80; CANR 30; SATA 56

Lucas, Hans
See Godard, Jean-Luc

Lucas, Victoria
See Plath, Sylvia

Lucian c. 120-c. 180 **CMLC 32**
See also DLB 176

Ludlam, Charles 1943-1987 **CLC 46, 50**
See also CA 85-88; 122; CANR 72, 86

Ludlum, Robert 1927- **CLC 22, 43; DAM NOV, POP**
See also AAYA 10; BEST 89:1, 90:3; CA 33-36R; CANR 25, 41, 68; DA3; DLBY 82; MTCW 1, 2

Ludwig, Ken CLC 60

Ludwig, Otto 1813-1865 **NCLC 4**
See also DLB 129

Lugones, Leopoldo 1874-1938 **TCLC 15; HLCS 2**
See also CA 116; 131; HW 1

Lu Hsun 1881-1936 **TCLC 3; SSC 20**
See also Shu-Jen, Chou

Lukacs, George CLC 24
See also Lukacs, Gyorgy (Szegeny von)

Lukacs, Gyorgy (Szegeny von) 1885-1971
See Lukacs, George
See also CA 101; 29-32R; CANR 62; MTCW 2

Luke, Peter (Ambrose Cyprian) 1919-1995 **CLC 38**
See also CA 81-84; 147; CANR 72; DLB 13

Lunar, Dennis
See Mungo, Raymond
Lurie, Alison 1926- **CLC 4, 5, 18, 39**
See also CA 1-4R; CANR 2, 17, 50, 88;
DLB 2; MTCW 1; SATA 46, 112
Lustig, Arnost 1926- **CLC 56**
See also AAYA 3; CA 69-72; CANR 47;
SATA 56
Luther, Martin 1483-1546 **LC 9, 37**
See also DLB 179
Luxemburg, Rosa 1870(?)-1919 **TCLC 63**
See also CA 118
Luzi, Mario 1914- **CLC 13**
See also CA 61-64; CANR 9, 70; DLB 128
Lyly, John 1554(?)-1606 **LC 41; DAM
DRAM; DC 7**
See also DLB 62, 167
L'Ymagier
See Gourmont, Remy (-Marie-Charles) de
Lynch, B. Suarez
See Bioy Casares, Adolfo; Borges, Jorge
Luis
Lynch, B. Suarez
See Bioy Casares, Adolfo
Lynch, David (K.) 1946- **CLC 66**
See also CA 124; 129
Lynch, James
See Andreyev, Leonid (Nikolaevich)
Lynch Davis, B.
See Bioy Casares, Adolfo; Borges, Jorge
Luis
Lyndsay, Sir David 1490-1555 **LC 20**
Lynn, Kenneth S(chuyler) 1923- **CLC 50**
See also CA 1-4R; CANR 3, 27, 65
Lynx
See West, Rebecca
Lyons, Marcus
See Blish, James (Benjamin)
Lyre, Pinchbeck
See Sassoon, Siegfried (Lorraine)
Lytle, Andrew (Nelson) 1902-1995 **CLC 22**
See also CA 9-12R; 150; CANR 70; DLB
6; DLBY 95
Lyttelton, George 1709-1773 **LC 10**
Maas, Peter 1929- **CLC 29**
See also CA 93-96; INT 93-96; MTCW 2
Macaulay, Rose 1881-1958 **TCLC 7, 44**
See also CA 104; DLB 36
Macaulay, Thomas Babington 1800-1859
NCLC 42
See also CDBLB 1832-1890; DLB 32, 55
MacBeth, George (Mann) 1932-1992 **CLC 2,
5, 9**
See also CA 25-28R; 136; CANR 61, 66;
DLB 40; MTCW 1; SATA 4; SATA-Obit
70
MacCaig, Norman (Alexander) 1910- **CLC
36; DAB; DAM POET**
See also CA 9-12R; CANR 3, 34; DLB 27
MacCarthy, Sir(Charles Otto) Desmond
1877-1952 **TCLC 36**
See also CA 167
**MacDiarmid, Hugh CLC 2, 4, 11, 19, 63; PC
9**
See also Grieve, C(hristopher) M(urray)
See also CDBLB 1945-1960; DLB 20
MacDonald, Anson
See Heinlein, Robert A(nson)
Macdonald, Cynthia 1928- **CLC 13, 19**
See also CA 49-52; CANR 4, 44; DLB 105
MacDonald, George 1824-1905 **TCLC 9**
See also CA 106; 137; CANR 80; DLB 18,
163, 178; MAICYA; SATA 33, 100
Macdonald, John
See Millar, Kenneth
MacDonald, John D(ann) 1916-1986 **CLC 3,
27, 44; DAM NOV, POP**

See also CA 1-4R; 121; CANR 1, 19, 60;
DLB 8; DLBY 86; MTCW 1, 2
Macdonald, John Ross
See Millar, Kenneth
Macdonald, Ross CLC 1, 2, 3, 14, 34, 41
See also Millar, Kenneth
See also DLBD 6
MacDougal, John
See Blish, James (Benjamin)
MacDougal, John
See Blish, James (Benjamin)
MacEwen, Gwendolyn (Margaret)
1941-1987 **CLC 13, 55**
See also CA 9-12R; 124; CANR 7, 22; DLB
53; SATA 50; SATA-Obit 55
Macha, Karel Hynek 1810-1846 **NCLC 46**
Machado (y Ruiz), Antonio 1875-1939 **TCLC
3**
See also CA 104; 174; DLB 108; HW 2
Machado de Assis, Joaquim Maria
1839-1908 **TCLC 10; BLC 2; HLCS 2;
SSC 24**
See also CA 107; 153; CANR 91
Machen, Arthur TCLC 4; SSC 20
See also Jones, Arthur Llewellyn
See also DLB 179; DLB 36, 156, 178
Machiavelli, Niccolo 1469-1527 **LC 8, 36;
DA; DAB; DAC; DAM MST; WLCS**
MacInnes, Colin 1914-1976 **CLC 4, 23**
See also CA 69-72; 65-68; CANR 21; DLB
14; MTCW 1, 2
MacInnes, Helen (Clark) 1907-1985 **CLC 27,
39; DAM POP**
See also CA 1-4R; 117; CANR 1, 28, 58;
DLB 87; MTCW 1, 2; SATA 22; SATA-
Obit 44
Mackenzie, Compton (Edward Montague)
1883-1972 **CLC 18**
See also CA 21-22; 37-40R; CAP 2; DLB
34, 100
Mackenzie, Henry 1745-1831 **NCLC 41**
See also DLB 39
Mackintosh, Elizabeth 1896(?)-1952
See Tey, Josephine
See also CA 110
MacLaren, James
See Grieve, C(hristopher) M(urray)
Mac Laverty, Bernard 1942- **CLC 31**
See also CA 116; 118; CANR 43, 88; INT
118
MacLean, Alistair (Stuart) 1922(?)-1987 **CLC
3, 13, 50, 63; DAM POP**
See also CA 57-60; 121; CANR 28, 61;
MTCW 1; SATA 23; SATA-Obit 50
Maclean, Norman (Fitzroy) 1902-1990 **CLC
78; DAM POP; SSC 13**
See also CA 102; 132; CANR 49; DLB 206
MacLeish, Archibald 1892-1982 **CLC 3, 8,
14, 68; DAM POET**
See also CA 9-12R; 106; CANR 33, 63;
CDALBS; DLB 4, 7, 45; DLBY 82;
MTCW 1, 2
MacLennan, (John) Hugh 1907-1990 **CLC 2,
14, 92; DAC; DAM MST**
See also CA 5-8R; 142; CANR 33; DLB
68; MTCW 1, 2
MacLeod, Alistair 1936- **CLC 56; DAC;
DAM MST**
See also CA 123; DLB 60; MTCW 2
Macleod, Fiona
See Sharp, William
MacNeice, (Frederick) Louis 1907-1963 **CLC
1, 4, 10, 53; DAB; DAM POET**
See also CA 85-88; CANR 61; DLB 10, 20;
MTCW 1, 2
MacNeill, Dand
See Fraser, George MacDonald
Macpherson, James 1736-1796 **LC 29**
See also Ossian

See also DLB 109
Macpherson, (Jean) Jay 1931- **CLC 14**
See also CA 5-8R; CANR 90; DLB 53
MacShane, Frank 1927-1999 **CLC 39**
See also CA 9-12R; 186; CANR 3, 33; DLB
111
Macumber, Mari
See Sandoz, Mari(e Susette)
Madach, Imre 1823-1864 **NCLC 19**
Madden, (Jerry) David 1933- **CLC 5, 15**
See also CA 1-4R; CAAS 3; CANR 4, 45;
DLB 6; MTCW 1
Maddern, Al(an)
See Ellison, Harlan (Jay)
Madhubuti, Haki R. 1942- **CLC 6, 73; BLC
2; DAM MULT, POET; PC 5**
See also Lee, Don L.
See also BW 2, 3; CA 73-76; CANR 24,
51, 73; DLB 5, 41; DLBD 8; MTCW 2
Maepenn, Hugh
See Kuttner, Henry
Maepenn, K. H.
See Kuttner, Henry
Maeterlinck, Maurice 1862-1949 **TCLC 3;
DAM DRAM**
See also CA 104; 136; CANR 80; DLB 192;
SATA 66
Maginn, William 1794-1842 **NCLC 8**
See also DLB 110, 159
Mahapatra, Jayanta 1928- **CLC 33; DAM
MULT**
See also CA 73-76; CAAS 9; CANR 15,
33, 66, 87
Mahfouz, Naguib (Abdel Aziz Al-Sabilgi)
1911(?)-
See Mahfuz, Najib
See also BEST 89:2; CA 128; CANR 55;
DAM NOV; DA3; MTCW 1, 2
Mahfuz, Najib CLC 52, 55
See also Mahfouz, Naguib (Abdel Aziz Al-
Sabilgi)
See also DLBY 88
Mahon, Derek 1941- **CLC 27**
See also CA 113; 128; CANR 88; DLB 40
Mailer, Norman 1923- **CLC 1, 2, 3, 4, 5, 8,
11, 14, 28, 39, 74, 111; DA; DAB; DAC;
DAM MST, NOV, POP**
See also AAYA 31; AITN 2; CA 9-12R;
CABS 1; CANR 28, 74, 77; CDALB
1968-1988; DA3; DLB 2, 16, 28, 185;
DLBD 3; DLBY 80, 83; MTCW 1, 2
Maillet, Antonine 1929- **CLC 54, 118; DAC**
See also CA 115; 120; CANR 46, 74, 77;
DLB 60; INT 120; MTCW 2
Mais, Roger 1905-1955 **TCLC 8**
See also BW 1, 3; CA 105; 124; CANR 82;
DLB 125; MTCW 1
Maistre, Joseph de 1753-1821 **NCLC 37**
Maitland, Frederic 1850-1906 **TCLC 65**
Maitland, Sara (Louise) 1950- **CLC 49**
See also CA 69-72; CANR 13, 59
Major, Clarence 1936- **CLC 3, 19, 48; BLC
2; DAM MULT**
See also BW 2, 3; CA 21-24R; CAAS 6;
CANR 13, 25, 53, 82; DLB 33
Major, Kevin (Gerald) 1949- **CLC 26; DAC**
See also AAYA 16; CA 97-100; CANR 21,
38; CLR 11; DLB 60; INT CANR-21;
JRDA; MAICYA; SATA 32, 82
Maki, James
See Ozu, Yasujiro
Malabaila, Damiano
See Levi, Primo
Malamud, Bernard 1914-1986 **CLC 1, 2, 3,
5, 8, 9, 11, 18, 27, 44, 78, 85; DA; DAB;
DAC; DAM MST, NOV, POP; SSC 15;
WLC**

See also AAYA 16; CA 5-8R; 118; CABS 1; CANR 28, 62; CDALB 1941-1968; DA3; DLB 2, 28, 152; DLBY 80, 86; MTCW 1, 2

Malan, Herman
See Bosman, Herman Charles; Bosman, Herman Charles

Malaparte, Curzio 1898-1957 **TCLC 52**

Malcolm, Dan
See Silverberg, Robert

Malcolm X CLC 82, 117; BLC 2; WLCS
See also Little, Malcolm

Malherbe, Francois de 1555-1628 **LC 5**

Mallarme, Stephane 1842-1898 **NCLC 4, 41; DAM POET; PC 4**

Mallet-Joris, Francoise 1930- **CLC 11**
See also CA 65-68; CANR 17; DLB 83

Malley, Ern
See McAuley, James Phillip

Mallowan, Agatha Christie
See Christie, Agatha (Mary Clarissa)

Maloff, Saul 1922- **CLC 5**
See also CA 33-36R

Malone, Louis
See MacNeice, (Frederick) Louis

Malone, Michael (Christopher) 1942- **CLC 43**
See also CA 77-80; CANR 14, 32, 57

Malory, (Sir) Thomas 1410(?)-1471(?) **LC 11; DA; DAB; DAC; DAM MST; WLCS**
See also CDBLB Before 1660; DLB 146; SATA 59; SATA-Brief 33

Malouf, (George Joseph) David 1934- **CLC 28, 86**
See also CA 124; CANR 50, 76; MTCW 2

Malraux, (Georges-)Andre 1901-1976 **CLC 1, 4, 9, 13, 15, 57; DAM NOV**
See also CA 21-22; 69-72; CANR 34, 58; CAP 2; DA3; DLB 72; MTCW 1, 2

Malzberg, Barry N(athaniel) 1939- **CLC 7**
See also CA 61-64; CAAS 4; CANR 16; DLB 8

Mamet, David (Alan) 1947- **CLC 9, 15, 34, 46, 91; DAM DRAM; DC 4**
See also AAYA 3; CA 81-84; CABS 3; CANR 15, 41, 67, 72; DA3; DLB 7; MTCW 1, 2

Mamoulian, Rouben (Zachary) 1897-1987 **CLC 16**
See also CA 25-28R; 124; CANR 85

Mandelstam, Osip (Emilievich) 1891(?)-1938(?) **TCLC 2, 6; PC 14**
See also CA 104; 150; MTCW 2

Mander, (Mary) Jane 1877-1949 **TCLC 31**
See also CA 162

Mandeville, John fl. 1350- **CMLC 19**
See also DLB 146

Mandiargues, Andre Pieyre de CLC 41
See also Pieyre de Mandiargues, Andre
See also DLB 83

Mandrake, Ethel Belle
See Thurman, Wallace (Henry)

Mangan, James Clarence 1803-1849 **NCLC 27**

Maniere, J.-E.
See Giraudoux, (Hippolyte) Jean

Mankiewicz, Herman (Jacob) 1897-1953 **TCLC 85**
See also CA 120; 169; DLB 26

Manley, (Mary) Delariviere 1672(?)-1724 **LC 1, 42**
See also DLB 39, 80

Mann, Abel
See Creasey, John

Mann, Emily 1952- **DC 7**
See also CA 130; CANR 55

Mann, (Luiz) Heinrich 1871-1950 **TCLC 9**
See also CA 106; 164, 181; DLB 66, 118

Mann, (Paul) Thomas 1875-1955 **TCLC 2, 8, 14, 21, 35, 44, 60; DA; DAB; DAC; DAM MST, NOV; SSC 5; WLC**
See also CA 104; 128; DA3; DLB 66; MTCW 1, 2

Mannheim, Karl 1893-1947 **TCLC 65**

Manning, David
See Faust, Frederick (Schiller)

Manning, Frederic 1887(?)-1935 **TCLC 25**
See also CA 124

Manning, Olivia 1915-1980 **CLC 5, 19**
See also CA 5-8R; 101; CANR 29; MTCW 1

Mano, D. Keith 1942- **CLC 2, 10**
See also CA 25-28R; CAAS 6; CANR 26, 57; DLB 6

Mansfield, Katherine TCLC 2, 8, 39; DAB; SSC 9, 23, 38; WLC
See also Beauchamp, Kathleen Mansfield
See also DLB 162

Manso, Peter 1940- **CLC 39**
See also CA 29-32R; CANR 44

Mantecon, Juan Jimenez
See Jimenez (Mantecon), Juan Ramon

Manton, Peter
See Creasey, John

Man Without a Spleen, A
See Chekhov, Anton (Pavlovich)

Manzoni, Alessandro 1785-1873 **NCLC 29**

Map, Walter 1140-1209 **CMLC 32**

Mapu, Abraham (ben Jekutiel) 1808-1867 **NCLC 18**

Mara, Sally
See Queneau, Raymond

Marat, Jean Paul 1743-1793 **LC 10**

Marcel, Gabriel Honore 1889-1973 **CLC 15**
See also CA 102; 45-48; MTCW 1, 2

March, William 1893-1954 **TCLC 96**

Marchbanks, Samuel
See Davies, (William) Robertson

Marchi, Giacomo
See Bassani, Giorgio

Margulies, Donald CLC 76

Marie de France c. 12th cent. - **CMLC 8; PC 22**
See also DLB 208

Marie de l'Incarnation 1599-1672 **LC 10**

Marier, Captain Victor
See Griffith, D(avid Lewelyn) W(ark)

Mariner, Scott
See Pohl, Frederik

Marinetti, Filippo Tommaso 1876-1944 **TCLC 10**
See also CA 107; DLB 114

Marivaux, Pierre Carlet de Chamblain de 1688-1763 **LC 4; DC 7**

Markandaya, Kamala CLC 8, 38
See also Taylor, Kamala (Purnaiya)

Markfield, Wallace 1926- **CLC 8**
See also CA 69-72; CAAS 3; DLB 2, 28

Markham, Edwin 1852-1940 **TCLC 47**
See also CA 160; DLB 54, 186

Markham, Robert
See Amis, Kingsley (William)

Marks, J
See Highwater, Jamake (Mamake)

Marks-Highwater, J
See Highwater, Jamake (Mamake)

Markson, David M(errill) 1927- **CLC 67**
See also CA 49-52; CANR 1, 91

Marley, Bob CLC 17
See also Marley, Robert Nesta

Marley, Robert Nesta 1945-1981
See Marley, Bob
See also CA 107; 103

Marlowe, Christopher 1564-1593 **LC 22, 47; DA; DAB; DAC; DAM DRAM, MST; DC 1; WLC**

See also CDBLB Before 1660; DA3; DLB 62

Marlowe, Stephen 1928-
See Queen, Ellery
See also CA 13-16R; CANR 6, 55

Marmontel, Jean-Francois 1723-1799 **LC 2**

Marquand, John P(hillips) 1893-1960 **CLC 2, 10**
See also CA 85-88; CANR 73; DLB 9, 102; MTCW 2

Marques, Rene 1919-1979 **CLC 96; DAM MULT; HLC 2**
See also CA 97-100; 85-88; CANR 78; DLB 113; HW 1, 2

Marquez, Gabriel (Jose) Garcia
See Garcia Marquez, Gabriel (Jose)

Marquis, Don(ald Robert Perry) 1878-1937 **TCLC 7**
See also CA 104; 166; DLB 11, 25

Marric, J. J.
See Creasey, John

Marryat, Frederick 1792-1848 **NCLC 3**
See also DLB 21, 163

Marsden, James
See Creasey, John

Marsh, (Edith) Ngaio 1899-1982 **CLC 7, 53; DAM POP**
See also CA 9-12R; CANR 6, 58; DLB 77; MTCW 1, 2

Marshall, Garry 1934- **CLC 17**
See also AAYA 3; CA 111; SATA 60

Marshall, Paule 1929- **CLC 27, 72; BLC 3; DAM MULT; SSC 3**
See also BW 2, 3; CA 77-80; CANR 25, 73; DA3; DLB 157; MTCW 1, 2

Marshallik
See Zangwill, Israel

Marsten, Richard
See Hunter, Evan

Marston, John 1576-1634 **LC 33; DAM DRAM**
See also DLB 58, 172

Martha, Henry
See Harris, Mark

Marti (y Perez), Jose (Julian) 1853-1895 **NCLC 63; DAM MULT; HLC 2**
See also HW 2

Martial c. 40-c. 104 **CMLC 35; PC 10**
See also DLB 211

Martin, Ken
See Hubbard, L(afayette) Ron(ald)

Martin, Richard
See Creasey, John

Martin, Steve 1945- **CLC 30**
See also CA 97-100; CANR 30; MTCW 1

Martin, Valerie 1948- **CLC 89**
See also BEST 90:2; CA 85-88; CANR 49, 89

Martin, Violet Florence 1862-1915 **TCLC 51**

Martin, Webber
See Silverberg, Robert

Martindale, Patrick Victor
See White, Patrick (Victor Martindale)

Martin du Gard, Roger 1881-1958 **TCLC 24**
See also CA 118; DLB 65

Martineau, Harriet 1802-1876 **NCLC 26**
See also DLB 21, 55, 159, 163, 166, 190; YABC 2

Martines, Julia
See O'Faolain, Julia

Martinez, Enrique Gonzalez
See Gonzalez Martinez, Enrique

Martinez, Jacinto Benavente y
See Benavente (y Martinez), Jacinto

Martinez Ruiz, Jose 1873-1967
See Azorin; Ruiz, Jose Martinez
See also CA 93-96; HW 1

Martinez Sierra, Gregorio 1881-1947 **TCLC 6**
  See also CA 115
Martinez Sierra, Maria (de la O'LeJarraga) 1874-1974 **TCLC 6**
  See also CA 115
Martinsen, Martin
  See Follett, Ken(neth Martin)
Martinson, Harry (Edmund) 1904-1978 **CLC 14**
  See also CA 77-80; CANR 34
Marut, Ret
  See Traven, B.
Marut, Robert
  See Traven, B.
Marvell, Andrew 1621-1678 **LC 4, 43; DA; DAB; DAC; DAM MST, POET; PC 10; WLC**
  See also CDBLB 1660-1789; DLB 131
Marx, Karl (Heinrich) 1818-1883 **NCLC 17**
  See also DLB 129
Masaoka Shiki TCLC 18
  See also Masaoka Tsunenori
Masaoka Tsunenori 1867-1902
  See Masaoka Shiki
  See also CA 117
Masefield, John (Edward) 1878-1967 **CLC 11, 47; DAM POET**
  See also CA 19-20; 25-28R; CANR 33; CAP 2; CDBLB 1890-1914; DLB 10, 19, 153, 160; MTCW 1, 2; SATA 19
Maso, Carole 19(?)- **CLC 44**
  See also CA 170
Mason, Bobbie Ann 1940- **CLC 28, 43, 82; SSC 4**
  See also AAYA 5; CA 53-56; CANR 11, 31, 58, 83; CDALBS; DA3; DLB 173; DLBY 87; INT CANR-31; MTCW 1, 2
Mason, Ernst
  See Pohl, Frederik
Mason, Lee W.
  See Malzberg, Barry N(athaniel)
Mason, Nick 1945- **CLC 35**
Mason, Tally
  See Derleth, August (William)
Mass, William
  See Gibson, William
Master Lao
  See Lao Tzu
Masters, Edgar Lee 1868-1950 **TCLC 2, 25; DA; DAC; DAM MST, POET; PC 1; WLCS**
  See also CA 104; 133; CDALB 1865-1917; DLB 54; MTCW 1, 2
Masters, Hilary 1928- **CLC 48**
  See also CA 25-28R; CANR 13, 47
Mastrosimone, William 19(?)- **CLC 36**
  See also CA 186
Mathe, Albert
  See Camus, Albert
Mather, Cotton 1663-1728 **LC 38**
  See also CDALB 1640-1865; DLB 24, 30, 140
Mather, Increase 1639-1723 **LC 38**
  See also DLB 24
Matheson, Richard Burton 1926- **CLC 37**
  See also AAYA 31; CA 97-100; CANR 88; DLB 8, 44; INT 97-100
Mathews, Harry 1930- **CLC 6, 52**
  See also CA 21-24R; CAAS 6; CANR 18, 40
Mathews, John Joseph 1894-1979 **CLC 84; DAM MULT**
  See also CA 19-20; 142; CANR 45; CAP 2; DLB 175; NNAL
Mathias, Roland (Glyn) 1915- **CLC 45**
  See also CA 97-100; CANR 19, 41; DLB 27

Matsuo Basho 1644-1694 **PC 3**
  See also DAM POET
Mattheson, Rodney
  See Creasey, John
Matthews, (James) Brander 1852-1929 **TCLC 95**
  See also DLB 71, 78; DLBD 13
Matthews, Greg 1949- **CLC 45**
  See also CA 135
Matthews, William (Procter, III) 1942-1997 **CLC 40**
  See also CA 29-32R; 162; CAAS 18; CANR 12, 57; DLB 5
Matthias, John (Edward) 1941- **CLC 9**
  See also CA 33-36R; CANR 56
Matthiessen, Peter 1927- **CLC 5, 7, 11, 32, 64; DAM NOV**
  See also AAYA 6; BEST 90:4; CA 9-12R; CANR 21, 50, 73; DA3; DLB 6, 173; MTCW 1, 2; SATA 27
Maturin, Charles Robert 1780(?)-1824 **NCLC 6**
  See also DLB 178
Matute (Ausejo), Ana Maria 1925- **CLC 11**
  See also CA 89-92; MTCW 1
Maugham, W. S.
  See Maugham, W(illiam) Somerset
Maugham, W(illiam) Somerset 1874-1965 **CLC 1, 11, 15, 67, 93; DA; DAB; DAC; DAM DRAM, MST, NOV; SSC 8; WLC**
  See also CA 5-8R; 25-28R; CDBLB 1914-1945; DA3; DLB 10, 36, 77, 100, 162, 195; MTCW 1, 2; SATA 54
Maugham, William Somerset
  See Maugham, W(illiam) Somerset
Maupassant, (Henri Rene Albert) Guy de 1850-1893 **NCLC 1, 42, 83; DA; DAB; DAC; DAM MST; SSC 1; WLC**
  See also DA3; DLB 123
Maupin, Armistead 1944- **CLC 95; DAM POP**
  See also CA 125; 130; CANR 58; DA3; INT 130; MTCW 2
Maurhut, Richard
  See Traven, B.
Mauriac, Claude 1914-1996 **CLC 9**
  See also CA 89-92; 152; DLB 83
Mauriac, Francois (Charles) 1885-1970 **CLC 4, 9, 56; SSC 24**
  See also CA 25-28; CAP 2; DLB 65; MTCW 1, 2
Mavor, Osborne Henry 1888-1951
  See Bridie, James
  See also CA 104
Maxwell, William (Keepers, Jr.) 1908- **CLC 19**
  See also CA 93-96; CANR 54; DLBY 80; INT 93-96
May, Elaine 1932- **CLC 16**
  See also CA 124; 142; DLB 44
Mayakovski, Vladimir (Vladimirovich) 1893-1930 **TCLC 4, 18**
  See also CA 104; 158; MTCW 2
Mayhew, Henry 1812-1887 **NCLC 31**
  See also DLB 18, 55, 190
Mayle, Peter 1939(?)- **CLC 89**
  See also CA 139; CANR 64
Maynard, Joyce 1953- **CLC 23**
  See also CA 111; 129; CANR 64
Mayne, William (James Carter) 1928- **CLC 12**
  See also AAYA 20; CA 9-12R; CANR 37, 80; CLR 25; JRDA; MAICYA; SAAS 11; SATA 6, 68
Mayo, Jim
  See L'Amour, Louis (Dearborn)
Maysles, Albert 1926- **CLC 16**
  See also CA 29-32R
Maysles, David 1932- **CLC 16**

Mazer, Norma Fox 1931- **CLC 26**
  See also AAYA 5; CA 69-72; CANR 12, 32, 66; CLR 23; JRDA; MAICYA; SAAS 1; SATA 24, 67, 105
Mazzini, Guiseppe 1805-1872 **NCLC 34**
McAlmon, Robert (Menzies) 1895-1956 **TCLC 97**
  See also CA 107; 168; DLB 4, 45; DLBD 15
McAuley, James Phillip 1917-1976 **CLC 45**
  See also CA 97-100
McBain, Ed
  See Hunter, Evan
McBrien, William (Augustine) 1930- **CLC 44**
  See also CA 107; CANR 90
McCaffrey, Anne (Inez) 1926- **CLC 17; DAM NOV, POP**
  See also AAYA 6, 34; AITN 2; BEST 89:2; CA 25-28R; CANR 15, 35, 55; CLR 49; DA3; DLB 8; JRDA; MAICYA; MTCW 1, 2; SAAS 11; SATA 8, 70, 116
McCall, Nathan 1955(?)- **CLC 86**
  See also BW 3; CA 146; CANR 88
McCann, Arthur
  See Campbell, John W(ood, Jr.)
McCann, Edson
  See Pohl, Frederik
McCarthy, Charles, Jr. 1933-
  See McCarthy, Cormac
  See also CANR 42, 69; DAM POP; DA3; MTCW 2
McCarthy, Cormac 1933- **CLC 4, 57, 59, 101**
  See also McCarthy, Charles, Jr.
  See also DLB 6, 143; MTCW 2
McCarthy, Mary (Therese) 1912-1989 **CLC 1, 3, 5, 14, 24, 39, 59; SSC 24**
  See also CA 5-8R; 129; CANR 16, 50, 64; DA3; DLB 2; DLBY 81; INT CANR-16; MTCW 1, 2
McCartney, (James) Paul 1942- **CLC 12, 35**
  See also CA 146
McCauley, Stephen (D.) 1955- **CLC 50**
  See also CA 141
McClure, Michael (Thomas) 1932- **CLC 6, 10**
  See also CA 21-24R; CANR 17, 46, 77; DLB 16
McCorkle, Jill (Collins) 1958- **CLC 51**
  See also CA 121; DLBY 87
McCourt, Frank 1930- **CLC 109**
  See also CA 157
McCourt, James 1941- **CLC 5**
  See also CA 57-60
McCourt, Malachy 1932- **CLC 119**
McCoy, Horace (Stanley) 1897-1955 **TCLC 28**
  See also CA 108; 155; DLB 9
McCrae, John 1872-1918 **TCLC 12**
  See also CA 109; DLB 92
McCreigh, James
  See Pohl, Frederik
McCullers, (Lula) Carson (Smith) 1917-1967 **CLC 1, 4, 10, 12, 48, 100; DA; DAB; DAC; DAM MST, NOV; SSC 9, 24; WLC**
  See also AAYA 21; CA 5-8R; 25-28R; CABS 1, 3; CANR 18; CDALB 1941-1968; DA3; DLB 2, 7, 173; MTCW 1, 2; SATA 27
McCulloch, John Tyler
  See Burroughs, Edgar Rice
McCullough, Colleen 1938(?)- **CLC 27, 107; DAM NOV, POP**
  See also CA 81-84; CANR 17, 46, 67; DA3; MTCW 1, 2
McDermott, Alice 1953- **CLC 90**
  See also CA 109; CANR 40, 90
McElroy, Joseph 1930- **CLC 5, 47**
  See also CA 17-20R

Michels, Robert 1876-1936 **TCLC 88**

Michener, James A(lbert) 1907(?)-1997 **CLC 1, 5, 11, 29, 60, 109; DAM NOV, POP**
See also AAYA 27; AITN 1; BEST 90:1; CA 5-8R; 161; CANR 21, 45, 68; DA3; DLB 6; MTCW 1, 2

Mickiewicz, Adam 1798-1855 **NCLC 3**

Middleton, Christopher 1926- **CLC 13**
See also CA 13-16R; CANR 29, 54; DLB 40

Middleton, Richard (Barham) 1882-1911 **TCLC 56**
See also DLB 156

Middleton, Stanley 1919- **CLC 7, 38**
See also CA 25-28R; CAAS 23; CANR 21, 46, 81; DLB 14

Middleton, Thomas 1580-1627 **LC 33; DAM DRAM, MST; DC 5**
See also DLB 58

Migueis, Jose Rodrigues 1901- **CLC 10**

Mikszath, Kalman 1847-1910 **TCLC 31**
See also CA 170

Miles, Jack CLC 100

Miles, Josephine (Louise) 1911-1985 **CLC 1, 2, 14, 34, 39; DAM POET**
See also CA 1-4R; 116; CANR 2, 55; DLB 48

Militant
See Sandburg, Carl (August)

Mill, John Stuart 1806-1873 **NCLC 11, 58**
See also CDBLB 1832-1890; DLB 55, 190

Millar, Kenneth 1915-1983 **CLC 14; DAM POP**
See also Macdonald, Ross
See also CA 9-12R; 110; CANR 16, 63; DA3; DLB 2; DLBD 6; DLBY 83; MTCW 1, 2

Millay, E. Vincent
See Millay, Edna St. Vincent

Millay, Edna St. Vincent 1892-1950 **TCLC 4, 49; DA; DAB; DAC; DAM MST, POET; PC 6; WLCS**
See also CA 104; 130; CDALB 1917-1929; DA3; DLB 45; MTCW 1, 2

Miller, Arthur 1915- **CLC 1, 2, 6, 10, 15, 26, 47, 78; DA; DAB; DAC; DAM DRAM, MST; DC 1; WLC**
See also AAYA 15; AITN 1; CA 1-4R; CABS 3; CANR 2, 30, 54, 76; CDALB 1941-1968; DA3; DLB 7; MTCW 1, 2

Miller, Henry (Valentine) 1891-1980 **CLC 1, 2, 4, 9, 14, 43, 84; DA; DAB; DAC; DAM MST, NOV; WLC**
See also CA 9-12R; 97-100; CANR 33, 64; CDALB 1929-1941; DA3; DLB 4, 9; DLBY 80; MTCW 1, 2

Miller, Jason 1939(?)- **CLC 2**
See also AITN 1; CA 73-76; DLB 7

Miller, Sue 1943- **CLC 44; DAM POP**
See also BEST 90:3; CA 139; CANR 59, 91; DA3; DLB 143

Miller, Walter M(ichael, Jr.) 1923- **CLC 4, 30**
See also CA 85-88; DLB 8

Millett, Kate 1934- **CLC 67**
See also AITN 1; CA 73-76; CANR 32, 53, 76; DA3; MTCW 1, 2

Millhauser, Steven (Lewis) 1943- **CLC 21, 54, 109**
See also CA 110; 111; CANR 63; DA3; DLB 2; INT 111; MTCW 2

Millin, Sarah Gertrude 1889-1968 **CLC 49**
See also CA 102; 93-96

Milne, A(lan) A(lexander) 1882-1956 **TCLC 6, 88; DAB; DAC; DAM MST**
See also CA 104; 133; CLR 1, 26; DA3; DLB 10, 77, 100, 160; MAICYA; MTCW 1, 2; SATA 100; YABC 1

Milner, Ron(ald) 1938- **CLC 56; BLC 3; DAM MULT**

See also AITN 1; BW 1; CA 73-76; CANR 24, 81; DLB 38; MTCW 1

Milnes, Richard Monckton 1809-1885 **NCLC 61**
See also DLB 32, 184

Milosz, Czeslaw 1911- **CLC 5, 11, 22, 31, 56, 82; DAM MST, POET; PC 8; WLCS**
See also CA 81-84; CANR 23, 51, 91; DA3; MTCW 1, 2

Milton, John 1608-1674 **LC 9, 43; DA; DAB; DAC; DAM MST, POET; PC 19, 29; WLC**
See also CDBLB 1660-1789; DA3; DLB 131, 151

Min, Anchee 1957- **CLC 86**
See also CA 146

Minehaha, Cornelius
See Wedekind, (Benjamin) Frank(lin)

Miner, Valerie 1947- **CLC 40**
See also CA 97-100; CANR 59

Minimo, Duca
See D'Annunzio, Gabriele

Minot, Susan 1956- **CLC 44**
See also CA 134

Minus, Ed 1938- **CLC 39**
See also CA 185

Miranda, Javier
See Bioy Casares, Adolfo

Miranda, Javier
See Bioy Casares, Adolfo

Mirbeau, Octave 1848-1917 **TCLC 55**
See also DLB 123, 192

Miro (Ferrer), Gabriel (Francisco Victor) 1879-1930 **TCLC 5**
See also CA 104; 185

Mishima, Yukio 1925-1970 **CLC 2, 4, 6, 9, 27; DC 1; SSC 4**
See also Hiraoka, Kimitake
See also DLB 182; MTCW 2

Mistral, Frederic 1830-1914 **TCLC 51**
See also CA 122

Mistral, Gabriela TCLC 2; HLC 2
See also Godoy Alcayaga, Lucila
See also MTCW 2

Mistry, Rohinton 1952- **CLC 71; DAC**
See also CA 141; CANR 86

Mitchell, Clyde
See Ellison, Harlan (Jay); Silverberg, Robert

Mitchell, James Leslie 1901-1935
See Gibbon, Lewis Grassic
See also CA 104; DLB 15

Mitchell, Joni 1943- **CLC 12**
See also CA 112

Mitchell, Joseph (Quincy) 1908-1996 **CLC 98**
See also CA 77-80; 152; CANR 69; DLB 185; DLBY 96

Mitchell, Margaret (Munnerlyn) 1900-1949 **TCLC 11; DAM NOV, POP**
See also AAYA 23; CA 109; 125; CANR 55; CDALBS; DA3; DLB 9; MTCW 1, 2

Mitchell, Peggy
See Mitchell, Margaret (Munnerlyn)

Mitchell, S(ilas) Weir 1829-1914 **TCLC 36**
See also CA 165; DLB 202

Mitchell, W(illiam) O(rmond) 1914-1998 **CLC 25; DAC; DAM MST**
See also CA 77-80; 165; CANR 15, 43; DLB 88

Mitchell, William 1879-1936 **TCLC 81**

Mitford, Mary Russell 1787-1855 **NCLC 4**
See also DLB 110, 116

Mitford, Nancy 1904-1973 **CLC 44**
See also CA 9-12R; DLB 191

Miyamoto, (Chujo) Yuriko 1899-1951 **TCLC 37**
See also CA 170, 174; DLB 180

Miyazawa, Kenji 1896-1933 **TCLC 76**
See also CA 157

Mizoguchi, Kenji 1898-1956 **TCLC 72**
See also CA 167

Mo, Timothy (Peter) 1950(?)- **CLC 46**
See also CA 117; DLB 194; MTCW 1

Modarressi, Taghi (M.) 1931- **CLC 44**
See also CA 121; 134; INT 134

Modiano, Patrick (Jean) 1945- **CLC 18**
See also CA 85-88; CANR 17, 40; DLB 83

Moerck, Paal
See Roelvaag, O(le) E(dvart)

Mofolo, Thomas (Mokopu) 1875(?)-1948 **TCLC 22; BLC 3; DAM MULT**
See also CA 121; 153; CANR 83; MTCW 2

Mohr, Nicholasa 1938- **CLC 12; DAM MULT; HLC 2**
See also AAYA 8; CA 49-52; CANR 1, 32, 64; CLR 22; DLB 145; HW 1, 2; JRDA; SAAS 8; SATA 8, 97; SATA-Essay 113

Mojtabai, A(nn) G(race) 1938- **CLC 5, 9, 15, 29**
See also CA 85-88; CANR 88

Moliere 1622-1673 **LC 10, 28; DA; DAB; DAC; DAM DRAM, MST; WLC**
See also DA3

Molin, Charles
See Mayne, William (James Carter)

Molnar, Ferenc 1878-1952 **TCLC 20; DAM DRAM**
See also CA 109; 153; CANR 83

Momaday, N(avarre) Scott 1934- **CLC 2, 19, 85, 95; DA; DAB; DAC; DAM MST, MULT, NOV, POP; PC 25; WLCS**
See also AAYA 11; CA 25-28R; CANR 14, 34, 68; CDALBS; DA3; DLB 143, 175; INT CANR-14; MTCW 1, 2; NNAL; SATA 48; SATA-Brief 30

Monette, Paul 1945-1995 **CLC 82**
See also CA 139; 147

Monroe, Harriet 1860-1936 **TCLC 12**
See also CA 109; DLB 54, 91

Monroe, Lyle
See Heinlein, Robert A(nson)

Montagu, Elizabeth 1720-1800 **NCLC 7**

Montagu, Elizabeth 1917- **NCLC 7**
See also CA 9-12R

Montagu, Mary (Pierrepont) Wortley 1689-1762 **LC 9, 57; PC 16**
See also DLB 95, 101

Montagu, W. H.
See Coleridge, Samuel Taylor

Montague, John (Patrick) 1929- **CLC 13, 46**
See also CA 9-12R; CANR 9, 69; DLB 40; MTCW 1

Montaigne, Michel (Eyquem) de 1533-1592 **LC 8; DA; DAB; DAC; DAM MST; WLC**

Montale, Eugenio 1896-1981 **CLC 7, 9, 18; PC 13**
See also CA 17-20R; 104; CANR 30; DLB 114; MTCW 1

Montesquieu, Charles-Louis de Secondat 1689-1755 **LC 7**

Montgomery, (Robert) Bruce 1921(?)-1978
See Crispin, Edmund
See also CA 179; 104

Montgomery, L(ucy) M(aud) 1874-1942 **TCLC 51; DAC; DAM MST**
See also AAYA 12; CA 108; 137; CLR 8; DA3; DLB 92; DLBD 14; JRDA; MAICYA; MTCW 2; SATA 100; YABC 1

Montgomery, Marion H., Jr. 1925- **CLC 7**
See also AITN 1; CA 1-4R; CANR 3, 48; DLB 6

Montgomery, Max
See Davenport, Guy (Mattison, Jr.)

Montherlant, Henry (Milon) de 1896-1972 **CLC 8, 19; DAM DRAM**
See also CA 85-88; 37-40R; DLB 72; MTCW 1

Monty Python
See Chapman, Graham; Cleese, John (Marwood); Gilliam, Terry (Vance); Idle, Eric; Jones, Terence Graham Parry; Palin, Michael (Edward)
See also AAYA 7

Moodie, Susanna (Strickland) 1803-1885 **NCLC 14**
See also DLB 99

Mooney, Edward 1951-
See Mooney, Ted
See also CA 130

Mooney, Ted CLC 25
See also Mooney, Edward

Moorcock, Michael (John) 1939- **CLC 5, 27, 58**
See also Bradbury, Edward P.
See also AAYA 26; CA 45-48; CAAS 5; CANR 2, 17, 38, 64; DLB 14; MTCW 1, 2; SATA 93

Moore, Brian 1921-1999 **CLC 1, 3, 5, 7, 8, 19, 32, 90; DAB; DAC; DAM MST**
See also CA 1-4R; 174; CANR 1, 25, 42, 63; MTCW 1, 2

Moore, Edward
See Muir, Edwin

Moore, G. E. 1873-1958 **TCLC 89**

Moore, George Augustus 1852-1933 **TCLC 7; SSC 19**
See also CA 104; 177; DLB 10, 18, 57, 135

Moore, Lorrie CLC 39, 45, 68
See also Moore, Marie Lorena

Moore, Marianne (Craig) 1887-1972 **CLC 1, 2, 4, 8, 10, 13, 19, 47; DA; DAB; DAC; DAM MST, POET; PC 4; WLCS**
See also CA 1-4R; 33-36R; CANR 3, 61; CDALB 1929-1941; DA3; DLB 45; DLBD 7; MTCW 1, 2; SATA 20

Moore, Marie Lorena 1957-
See Moore, Lorrie
See also CA 116; CANR 39, 83

Moore, Thomas 1779-1852 **NCLC 6**
See also DLB 96, 144

Moorhouse, Frank 1938- **SSC 40**
See also CA 118

Mora, Pat(ricia) 1942-
See also CA 129; CANR 57, 81; CLR 58; DAM MULT; DLB 209; HLC 2; HW 1, 2; SATA 92

Moraga, Cherríe 1952- **CLC 126; DAM MULT**
See also CA 131; CANR 66; DLB 82; HW 1, 2

Morand, Paul 1888-1976 **CLC 41; SSC 22**
See also CA 184; 69-72; DLB 65

Morante, Elsa 1918-1985 **CLC 8, 47**
See also CA 85-88; 117; CANR 35; DLB 177; MTCW 1, 2

Moravia, Alberto 1907-1990 **CLC 2, 7, 11, 27, 46; SSC 26**
See also Pincherle, Alberto
See also DLB 177; MTCW 2

More, Hannah 1745-1833 **NCLC 27**
See also DLB 107, 109, 116, 158

More, Henry 1614-1687 **LC 9**
See also DLB 126

More, Sir Thomas 1478-1535 **LC 10, 32**

Moreas, Jean TCLC 18
See also Papadiamantopoulos, Johannes

Morgan, Berry 1919- **CLC 6**
See also CA 49-52; DLB 6

Morgan, Claire
See Highsmith, (Mary) Patricia

Morgan, Edwin (George) 1920- **CLC 31**
See also CA 5-8R; CANR 3, 43, 90; DLB 27

Morgan, (George) Frederick 1922- **CLC 23**
See also CA 17-20R; CANR 21

Morgan, Harriet
See Mencken, H(enry) L(ouis)

Morgan, Jane
See Cooper, James Fenimore

Morgan, Janet 1945- **CLC 39**
See also CA 65-68

Morgan, Lady 1776(?)-1859 **NCLC 29**
See also DLB 116, 158

Morgan, Robin (Evonne) 1941- **CLC 2**
See also CA 69-72; CANR 29, 68; MTCW 1; SATA 80

Morgan, Scott
See Kuttner, Henry

Morgan, Seth 1949(?)-1990 **CLC 65**
See also CA 185; 132

Morgenstern, Christian 1871-1914 **TCLC 8**
See also CA 105

Morgenstern, S.
See Goldman, William (W.)

Moricz, Zsigmond 1879-1942 **TCLC 33**
See also CA 165

Morike, Eduard (Friedrich) 1804-1875 **NCLC 10**
See also DLB 133

Moritz, Karl Philipp 1756-1793 **LC 2**
See also DLB 94

Morland, Peter Henry
See Faust, Frederick (Schiller)

Morley, Christopher (Darlington) 1890-1957 **TCLC 87**
See also CA 112; DLB 9

Morren, Theophil
See Hofmannsthal, Hugo von

Morris, Bill 1952- **CLC 76**

Morris, Julian
See West, Morris L(anglo)

Morris, Steveland Judkins 1950(?)-
See Wonder, Stevie
See also CA 111

Morris, William 1834-1896 **NCLC 4**
See also CDBLB 1832-1890; DLB 18, 35, 57, 156, 178, 184

Morris, Wright 1910-1998 **CLC 1, 3, 7, 18, 37**
See also CA 9-12R; 167; CANR 21, 81; DLB 2, 206; DLBY 81; MTCW 1, 2

Morrison, Arthur 1863-1945 **TCLC 72; SSC 40**
See also CA 120; 157; DLB 70, 135, 197

Morrison, Chloe Anthony Wofford
See Morrison, Toni

Morrison, James Douglas 1943-1971
See Morrison, Jim
See also CA 73-76; CANR 40

Morrison, Jim CLC 17
See also Morrison, James Douglas

Morrison, Toni 1931- **CLC 4, 10, 22, 55, 81, 87; BLC 3; DA; DAB; DAC; DAM MST, MULT, NOV, POP**
See also AAYA 1, 22; BW 2, 3; CA 29-32R; CANR 27, 42, 67; CDALB 1968-1988; DA3; DLB 6, 33, 143; DLBY 81; MTCW 1, 2; SATA 57

Morrison, Van 1945- **CLC 21**
See also CA 116; 168

Morrissy, Mary 1958- **CLC 99**

Mortimer, John (Clifford) 1923- **CLC 28, 43; DAM DRAM, POP**
See also CA 13-16R; CANR 21, 69; CDBLB 1960 to Present; DA3; DLB 13; INT CANR-21; MTCW 1, 2

Mortimer, Penelope (Ruth) 1918- **CLC 5**
See also CA 57-60; CANR 45, 88

Morton, Anthony
See Creasey, John

Mosca, Gaetano 1858-1941 **TCLC 75**

Mosher, Howard Frank 1943- **CLC 62**
See also CA 139; CANR 65

Mosley, Nicholas 1923- **CLC 43, 70**
See also CA 69-72; CANR 41, 60; DLB 14, 207

Mosley, Walter 1952- **CLC 97; BLCS; DAM MULT, POP**
See also AAYA 17; BW 2; CA 142; CANR 57; DA3; MTCW 2

Moss, Howard 1922-1987 **CLC 7, 14, 45, 50; DAM POET**
See also CA 1-4R; 123; CANR 1, 44; DLB 5

Mossgiel, Rab
See Burns, Robert

Motion, Andrew (Peter) 1952- **CLC 47**
See also CA 146; CANR 90; DLB 40

Motley, Willard (Francis) 1909-1965 **CLC 18**
See also BW 1; CA 117; 106; CANR 88; DLB 76, 143

Motoori, Norinaga 1730-1801 **NCLC 45**

Mott, Michael (Charles Alston) 1930- **CLC 15, 34**
See also CA 5-8R; CAAS 7; CANR 7, 29

Mountain Wolf Woman 1884-1960 **CLC 92**
See also CA 144; CANR 90; NNAL

Moure, Erin 1955- **CLC 88**
See also CA 113; DLB 60

Mowat, Farley (McGill) 1921- **CLC 26; DAC; DAM MST**
See also AAYA 1; CA 1-4R; CANR 4, 24, 42, 68; CLR 20; DLB 68; INT CANR-24; JRDA; MAICYA; MTCW 1, 2; SATA 3, 55

Mowatt, Anna Cora 1819-1870 **NCLC 74**

Moyers, Bill 1934- **CLC 74**
See also AITN 2; CA 61-64; CANR 31, 52

Mphahlele, Es'kia
See Mphahlele, Ezekiel
See also DLB 125

Mphahlele, Ezekiel 1919- **CLC 25; BLC 3; DAM MULT**
See also Mphahlele, Es'kia
See also BW 2, 3; CA 81-84; CANR 26, 76; DA3; MTCW 2

Mqhayi, S(amuel) E(dward) K(rune Loliwe) 1875-1945 **TCLC 25; BLC 3; DAM MULT**
See also CA 153; CANR 87

Mrozek, Slawomir 1930- **CLC 3, 13**
See also CA 13-16R; CAAS 10; CANR 29; MTCW 1

Mrs. Belloc-Lowndes
See Lowndes, Marie Adelaide (Belloc)

Mtwa, Percy (?)- **CLC 47**

Mueller, Lisel 1924- **CLC 13, 51**
See also CA 93-96; DLB 105

Muir, Edwin 1887-1959 **TCLC 2, 87**
See also CA 104; DLB 20, 100, 191

Muir, John 1838-1914 **TCLC 28**
See also CA 165; DLB 186

Mujica Lainez, Manuel 1910-1984 **CLC 31**
See also Lainez, Manuel Mujica
See also CA 81-84; 112; CANR 32; HW 1

Mukherjee, Bharati 1940- **CLC 53, 115; DAM NOV; SSC 38**
See also BEST 89:2; CA 107; CANR 45, 72; DLB 60; MTCW 1, 2

Muldoon, Paul 1951- **CLC 32, 72; DAM POET**
See also CA 113; 129; CANR 52, 91; DLB 40; INT 129

Mulisch, Harry 1927- **CLC 42**
See also CA 9-12R; CANR 6, 26, 56

Mull, Martin 1943- **CLC 17**
See also CA 105

Muller, Wilhelm NCLC 73

Mulock, Dinah Maria
See Craik, Dinah Maria (Mulock)

Munford, Robert 1737(?)-1783 **LC 5**

See also DLB 31

Mungo, Raymond 1946- **CLC 72**
See also CA 49-52; CANR 2

Munro, Alice 1931- **CLC 6, 10, 19, 50, 95; DAC; DAM MST, NOV; SSC 3; WLCS**
See also AITN 2; CA 33-36R; CANR 33, 53, 75; DA3; DLB 53; MTCW 1, 2; SATA 29

Munro, H(ector) H(ugh) 1870-1916
See Saki
See also CA 104; 130; CDBLB 1890-1914; DA; DAB; DAC; DAM MST, NOV; DA3; DLB 34, 162; MTCW 1, 2; WLC

Murdoch, (Jean) Iris 1919-1999 **CLC 1, 2, 3, 4, 6, 8, 11, 15, 22, 31, 51; DAB; DAC; DAM MST, NOV**
See also CA 13-16R; 179; CANR 8, 43, 68; CDBLB 1960 to Present; DA3; DLB 14, 194; INT CANR-8; MTCW 1, 2

Murfree, Mary Noailles 1850-1922 **SSC 22**
See also CA 122; 176; DLB 12, 74

Murnau, Friedrich Wilhelm
See Plumpe, Friedrich Wilhelm

Murphy, Richard 1927- **CLC 41**
See also CA 29-32R; DLB 40

Murphy, Sylvia 1937- **CLC 34**
See also CA 121

Murphy, Thomas (Bernard) 1935- **CLC 51**
See also CA 101

Murray, Albert L. 1916- **CLC 73**
See also BW 2; CA 49-52; CANR 26, 52, 78; DLB 38

Murray, Judith Sargent 1751-1820 **NCLC 63**
See also DLB 37, 200

Murray, Les(lie) A(llan) 1938- **CLC 40; DAM POET**
See also CA 21-24R; CANR 11, 27, 56

Murry, J. Middleton
See Murry, John Middleton

Murry, John Middleton 1889-1957 **TCLC 16**
See also CA 118; DLB 149

Musgrave, Susan 1951- **CLC 13, 54**
See also CA 69-72; CANR 45, 84

Musil, Robert (Edler von) 1880-1942 **TCLC 12, 68; SSC 18**
See also CA 109; CANR 55, 84; DLB 81, 124; MTCW 2

Muske, Carol 1945- **CLC 90**
See also Muske-Dukes, Carol (Anne)

Muske-Dukes, Carol (Anne) 1945-
See Muske, Carol
See also CA 65-68; CANR 32, 70

Musset, (Louis Charles) Alfred de 1810-1857 **NCLC 7**
See also DLB 192

Mussolini, Benito (Amilcare Andrea) 1883-1945 **TCLC 96**
See also CA 116

My Brother's Brother
See Chekhov, Anton (Pavlovich)

Myers, L(eopold) H(amilton) 1881-1944 **TCLC 59**
See also CA 157; DLB 15

Myers, Walter Dean 1937- **CLC 35; BLC 3; DAM MULT, NOV**
See also AAYA 4, 23; BW 2; CA 33-36R; CANR 20, 42, 67; CLR 4, 16, 35; DLB 33; INT CANR-20; JRDA; MAICYA; MTCW 2; SAAS 2; SATA 41, 71, 109; SATA-Brief 27

Myers, Walter M.
See Myers, Walter Dean

Myles, Symon
See Follett, Ken(neth Martin)

Nabokov, Vladimir (Vladimirovich) 1899-1977 **CLC 1, 2, 3, 6, 8, 11, 15, 23, 44, 46, 64; DA; DAB; DAC; DAM MST, NOV; SSC 11; WLC**

See also CA 5-8R; 69-72; CANR 20; CDALB 1941-1968; DA3; DLB 2; DLBD 3; DLBY 80, 91; MTCW 1, 2

Naevius c. 265B.C.-201B.C. **CMLC 37**
See also DLB 211

Nagai Kafu 1879-1959 **TCLC 51**
See also Nagai Sokichi
See also DLB 180

Nagai Sokichi 1879-1959
See Nagai Kafu
See also CA 117

Nagy, Laszlo 1925-1978 **CLC 7**
See also CA 129; 112

Naidu, Sarojini 1879-1943 **TCLC 80**

Naipaul, Shiva(dhar Srinivasa) 1945-1985 **CLC 32, 39; DAM NOV**
See also CA 110; 112; 116; CANR 33; DA3; DLB 157; DLBY 85; MTCW 1, 2

Naipaul, V(idiadhar) S(urajprasad) 1932- **CLC 4, 7, 9, 13, 18, 37, 105; DAB; DAC; DAM MST, NOV; SSC 38**
See also CA 1-4R; CANR 1, 33, 51, 91; CDBLB 1960 to Present; DA3; DLB 125, 204, 206; DLBY 85; MTCW 1, 2

Nakos, Lilika 1899(?)- **CLC 29**

Narayan, R(asipuram) K(rishnaswami) 1906- **CLC 7, 28, 47, 121; DAM NOV; SSC 25**
See also CA 81-84; CANR 33, 61; DA3; MTCW 1, 2; SATA 62

Nash, (Frediric) Ogden 1902-1971 **CLC 23; DAM POET; PC 21**
See also CA 13-14; 29-32R; CANR 34, 61; CAP 1; DLB 11; MAICYA; MTCW 1, 2; SATA 2, 46

Nashe, Thomas 1567-1601(?) **LC 41**
See also DLB 167

Nashe, Thomas 1567-1601 **LC 41**

Nathan, Daniel
See Dannay, Frederic

Nathan, George Jean 1882-1958 **TCLC 18**
See also Hatteras, Owen
See also CA 114; 169; DLB 137

Natsume, Kinnosuke 1867-1916
See Natsume, Soseki
See also CA 104

Natsume, Soseki 1867-1916 **TCLC 2, 10**
See also Natsume, Kinnosuke
See also DLB 180

Natti, (Mary) Lee 1919-
See Kingman, Lee
See also CA 5-8R; CANR 2

Naylor, Gloria 1950- **CLC 28, 52; BLC 3; DA; DAC; DAM MST, MULT, NOV, POP; WLCS**
See also AAYA 6; BW 2, 3; CA 107; CANR 27, 51, 74; DA3; DLB 173; MTCW 1, 2

Neihardt, John Gneisenau 1881-1973 **CLC 32**
See also CA 13-14; CANR 65; CAP 1; DLB 9, 54

Nekrasov, Nikolai Alekseevich 1821-1878 **NCLC 11**

Nelligan, Emile 1879-1941 **TCLC 14**
See also CA 114; DLB 92

Nelson, Willie 1933- **CLC 17**
See also CA 107

Nemerov, Howard (Stanley) 1920-1991 **CLC 2, 6, 9, 36; DAM POET; PC 24**
See also CA 1-4R; 134; CABS 2; CANR 1, 27, 53; DLB 5, 6; DLBY 83; INT CANR-27; MTCW 1, 2

Neruda, Pablo 1904-1973 **CLC 1, 2, 5, 7, 9, 28, 62; DA; DAB; DAC; DAM MST, MULT, POET; HLC 2; PC 4; WLC**
See also CA 19-20; 45-48; CAP 2; DA3; HW 1; MTCW 1, 2

Nerval, Gerard de 1808-1855 **NCLC 1, 67; PC 13; SSC 18**

Nervo, (Jose) Amado (Ruiz de) 1870-1919 **TCLC 11; HLCS 2**
See also CA 109; 131; HW 1

Nessi, Pio Baroja y
See Baroja (y Nessi), Pio

Nestroy, Johann 1801-1862 **NCLC 42**
See also DLB 133

Netterville, Luke
See O'Grady, Standish (James)

Neufeld, John (Arthur) 1938- **CLC 17**
See also AAYA 11; CA 25-28R; CANR 11, 37, 56; CLR 52; MAICYA; SAAS 3; SATA 6, 81

Neville, Emily Cheney 1919- **CLC 12**
See also CA 5-8R; CANR 3, 37, 85; JRDA; MAICYA; SAAS 2; SATA 1

Newbound, Bernard Slade 1930-
See Slade, Bernard
See also CA 81-84; CANR 49; DAM DRAM

Newby, P(ercy) H(oward) 1918-1997 **CLC 2, 13; DAM NOV**
See also CA 5-8R; 161; CANR 32, 67; DLB 15; MTCW 1

Newlove, Donald 1928- **CLC 6**
See also CA 29-32R; CANR 25

Newlove, John (Herbert) 1938- **CLC 14**
See also CA 21-24R; CANR 9, 25

Newman, Charles 1938- **CLC 2, 8**
See also CA 21-24R; CANR 84

Newman, Edwin (Harold) 1919- **CLC 14**
See also AITN 1; CA 69-72; CANR 5

Newman, John Henry 1801-1890 **NCLC 38**
See also DLB 18, 32, 55

Newton, (Sir)Isaac 1642-1727 **LC 35, 52**

Newton, Suzanne 1936- **CLC 35**
See also CA 41-44R; CANR 14; JRDA; SATA 5, 77

Nexo, Martin Andersen 1869-1954 **TCLC 43**

Nezval, Vitezslav 1900-1958 **TCLC 44**
See also CA 123

Ng, Fae Myenne 1957(?)- **CLC 81**
See also CA 146

Ngema, Mbongeni 1955- **CLC 57**
See also BW 2; CA 143; CANR 84

Ngugi, James T(hiong'o) **CLC 3, 7, 13**
See also Ngugi wa Thiong'o

Ngugi wa Thiong'o 1938- **CLC 36; BLC 3; DAM MULT, NOV**
See also Ngugi, James T(hiong'o)
See also BW 2; CA 81-84; CANR 27, 58; DLB 125; MTCW 1, 2

Nichol, B(arrie) P(hillip) 1944-1988 **CLC 18**
See also CA 53-56; DLB 53; SATA 66

Nichols, John (Treadwell) 1940- **CLC 38**
See also CA 9-12R; CAAS 2; CANR 6, 70; DLBY 82

Nichols, Leigh
See Koontz, Dean R(ay)

Nichols, Peter (Richard) 1927- **CLC 5, 36, 65**
See also CA 104; CANR 33, 86; DLB 13; MTCW 1

Nicolas, F. R. E.
See Freeling, Nicolas

Niedecker, Lorine 1903-1970 **CLC 10, 42; DAM POET**
See also CA 25-28; CAP 2; DLB 48

Nietzsche, Friedrich (Wilhelm) 1844-1900 **TCLC 10, 18, 55**
See also CA 107; 121; DLB 129

Nievo, Ippolito 1831-1861 **NCLC 22**

Nightingale, Anne Redmon 1943-
See Redmon, Anne
See also CA 103

Nightingale, Florence 1820-1910 **TCLC 85**
See also DLB 166

Nik. T. O.
See Annensky, Innokenty (Fyodorovich)
Nin, Anais 1903-1977 **CLC 1, 4, 8, 11, 14, 60, 127; DAM NOV, POP; SSC 10**
See also AITN 2; CA 13-16R; 69-72; CANR 22, 53; DLB 2, 4, 152; MTCW 1, 2
Nishida, Kitaro 1870-1945 **TCLC 83**
Nishiwaki, Junzaburo 1894-1982 **PC 15**
See also CA 107
Nissenson, Hugh 1933- **CLC 4, 9**
See also CA 17-20R; CANR 27; DLB 28
Niven, Larry CLC 8
See also Niven, Laurence Van Cott
See also AAYA 27; DLB 8
Niven, Laurence Van Cott 1938-
See Niven, Larry
See also CA 21-24R; CAAS 12; CANR 14, 44, 66; DAM POP; MTCW 1, 2; SATA 95
Nixon, Agnes Eckhardt 1927- **CLC 21**
See also CA 110
Nizan, Paul 1905-1940 **TCLC 40**
See also CA 161; DLB 72
Nkosi, Lewis 1936- **CLC 45; BLC 3; DAM MULT**
See also BW 1, 3; CA 65-68; CANR 27, 81; DLB 157
Nodier, (Jean) Charles (Emmanuel) 1780-1844 **NCLC 19**
See also DLB 119
Noguchi, Yone 1875-1947 **TCLC 80**
Nolan, Christopher 1965- **CLC 58**
See also CA 111; CANR 88
Noon, Jeff 1957- **CLC 91**
See also CA 148; CANR 83
Norden, Charles
See Durrell, Lawrence (George)
Nordhoff, Charles (Bernard) 1887-1947 **TCLC 23**
See also CA 108; DLB 9; SATA 23
Norfolk, Lawrence 1963- **CLC 76**
See also CA 144; CANR 85
Norman, Marsha 1947- **CLC 28; DAM DRAM; DC 8**
See also CA 105; CABS 3; CANR 41; DLBY 84
Normyx
See Douglas, (George) Norman
Norris, Frank 1870-1902 **SSC 28**
See also Norris, (Benjamin) Frank(lin, Jr.)
See also CDALB 1865-1917; DLB 12, 71, 186
Norris, (Benjamin) Frank(lin, Jr.) 1870-1902 **TCLC 24**
See also Norris, Frank
See also CA 110; 160
Norris, Leslie 1921- **CLC 14**
See also CA 11-12; CANR 14; CAP 1; DLB 27
North, Andrew
See Norton, Andre
North, Anthony
See Koontz, Dean R(ay)
North, Captain George
See Stevenson, Robert Louis (Balfour)
North, Milou
See Erdrich, Louise
Northrup, B. A.
See Hubbard, L(afayette) Ron(ald)
North Staffs
See Hulme, T(homas) E(rnest)
Norton, Alice Mary
See Norton, Andre
See also MAICYA; SATA 1, 43
Norton, Andre 1912- **CLC 12**
See also Norton, Alice Mary

See also AAYA 14; CA 1-4R; CANR 68; CLR 50; DLB 8, 52; JRDA; MTCW 1; SATA 91
Norton, Caroline 1808-1877 **NCLC 47**
See also DLB 21, 159, 199
Norway, Nevil Shute 1899-1960
See Shute, Nevil
See also CA 102; 93-96; CANR 85; MTCW 2
Norwid, Cyprian Kamil 1821-1883 **NCLC 17**
Nosille, Nabrah
See Ellison, Harlan (Jay)
Nossack, Hans Erich 1901-1978 **CLC 6**
See also CA 93-96; 85-88; DLB 69
Nostradamus 1503-1566 **LC 27**
Nosu, Chuji
See Ozu, Yasujiro
Notenburg, Eleanora (Genrikhovna) von
See Guro, Elena
Nova, Craig 1945- **CLC 7, 31**
See also CA 45-48; CANR 2, 53
Novak, Joseph
See Kosinski, Jerzy (Nikodem)
Novalis 1772-1801 **NCLC 13**
See also DLB 90
Novis, Emile
See Weil, Simone (Adolphine)
Nowlan, Alden (Albert) 1933-1983 **CLC 15; DAC; DAM MST**
See also CA 9-12R; CANR 5; DLB 53
Noyes, Alfred 1880-1958 **TCLC 7; PC 27**
See also CA 104; DLB 20
Nunn, Kem CLC 34
See also CA 159
Nye, Robert 1939- **CLC 13, 42; DAM NOV**
See also CA 33-36R; CANR 29, 67; DLB 14; MTCW 1; SATA 6
Nyro, Laura 1947- **CLC 17**
Oates, Joyce Carol 1938- **CLC 1, 2, 3, 6, 9, 11, 15, 19, 33, 52, 108; DA; DAB; DAC; DAM MST, NOV, POP; SSC 6; WLC**
See also AAYA 15; AITN 1; BEST 89:2; CA 5-8R; CANR 25, 45, 74; CDALB 1968-1988; DA3; DLB 2, 5, 130; DLBY 81; INT CANR-25; MTCW 1, 2
O'Brien, Darcy 1939-1998 **CLC 11**
See also CA 21-24R; 167; CANR 8, 59
O'Brien, E. G.
See Clarke, Arthur C(harles)
O'Brien, Edna 1936- **CLC 3, 5, 8, 13, 36, 65, 116; DAM NOV; SSC 10**
See also CA 1-4R; CANR 6, 41, 65; CD-BLB 1960 to Present; DA3; DLB 14; MTCW 1, 2
O'Brien, Fitz-James 1828-1862 **NCLC 21**
See also DLB 74
O'Brien, Flann CLC 1, 4, 5, 7, 10, 47
See also O Nuallain, Brian
O'Brien, Richard 1942- **CLC 17**
See also CA 124
O'Brien, (William) Tim(othy) 1946- **CLC 7, 19, 40, 103; DAM POP**
See also AAYA 16; CA 85-88; CANR 40, 58; CDALBS; DA3; DLB 152; DLBD 9; DLBY 80; MTCW 2
Obstfelder, Sigbjoern 1866-1900 **TCLC 23**
See also CA 123
O'Casey, Sean 1880-1964 **CLC 1, 5, 9, 11, 15, 88; DAB; DAC; DAM DRAM, MST; DC 12; WLCS**
See also CA 89-92; CANR 62; CDBLB 1914-1945; DA3; DLB 10; MTCW 1, 2
O'Cathasaigh, Sean
See O'Casey, Sean
Ochs, Phil(ip David) 1940-1976 **CLC 17**
See also CA 185; 65-68
O'Connor, Edwin (Greene) 1918-1968 **CLC 14**

See also CA 93-96; 25-28R
O'Connor, (Mary) Flannery 1925-1964 **CLC 1, 2, 3, 6, 10, 13, 15, 21, 66, 104; DA; DAB; DAC; DAM MST, NOV; SSC 1, 23; WLC**
See also AAYA 7; CA 1-4R; CANR 3, 41; CDALB 1941-1968; DA3; DLB 2, 152; DLBD 12; DLBY 80; MTCW 1, 2
O'Connor, Frank CLC 23; SSC 5
See also O'Donovan, Michael John
See also DLB 162
O'Dell, Scott 1898-1989 **CLC 30**
See also AAYA 3; CA 61-64; 129; CANR 12, 30; CLR 1, 16; DLB 52; JRDA; MAI-CYA; SATA 12, 60
Odets, Clifford 1906-1963 **CLC 2, 28, 98; DAM DRAM; DC 6**
See also CA 85-88; CANR 62; DLB 7, 26; MTCW 1, 2
O'Doherty, Brian 1934- **CLC 76**
See also CA 105
O'Donnell, K. M.
See Malzberg, Barry N(athaniel)
O'Donnell, Lawrence
See Kuttner, Henry
O'Donovan, Michael John 1903-1966 **CLC 14**
See also O'Connor, Frank
See also CA 93-96; CANR 84
Oe, Kenzaburo 1935- **CLC 10, 36, 86; DAM NOV; SSC 20**
See also CA 97-100; CANR 36, 50, 74; DA3; DLB 182; DLBY 94; MTCW 1, 2
O'Faolain, Julia 1932- **CLC 6, 19, 47, 108**
See also CA 81-84; CAAS 2; CANR 12, 61; DLB 14; MTCW 1
O'Faolain, Sean 1900-1991 **CLC 1, 7, 14, 32, 70; SSC 13**
See also CA 61-64; 134; CANR 12, 66; DLB 15, 162; MTCW 1, 2
O'Flaherty, Liam 1896-1984 **CLC 5, 34; SSC 6**
See also CA 101; 113; CANR 35; DLB 36, 162; DLBY 84; MTCW 1, 2
Ogilvy, Gavin
See Barrie, J(ames) M(atthew)
O'Grady, Standish (James) 1846-1928 **TCLC 5**
See also CA 104; 157
O'Grady, Timothy 1951- **CLC 59**
See also CA 138
O'Hara, Frank 1926-1966 **CLC 2, 5, 13, 78; DAM POET**
See also CA 9-12R; 25-28R; CANR 33; DA3; DLB 5, 16, 193; MTCW 1, 2
O'Hara, John (Henry) 1905-1970 **CLC 1, 2, 3, 6, 11, 42; DAM NOV; SSC 15**
See also CA 5-8R; 25-28R; CANR 31, 60; CDALB 1929-1941; DLB 9, 86; DLBD 2; MTCW 1, 2
O Hehir, Diana 1922- **CLC 41**
See also CA 93-96
Ohiyesa
See Eastman, Charles A(lexander)
Okigbo, Christopher (Ifenayichukwu) 1932-1967 **CLC 25, 84; BLC 3; DAM MULT, POET; PC 7**
See also BW 1, 3; CA 77-80; CANR 74; DLB 125; MTCW 1, 2
Okri, Ben 1959- **CLC 87**
See also BW 2, 3; CA 130; 138; CANR 65; DLB 157; INT 138; MTCW 2
Olds, Sharon 1942- **CLC 32, 39, 85; DAM POET; PC 22**
See also CA 101; CANR 18, 41, 66; DLB 120; MTCW 2
Oldstyle, Jonathan
See Irving, Washington
Olesha, Yuri (Karlovich) 1899-1960 **CLC 8**

Park, Jordan
　See Kornbluth, C(yril) M.; Pohl, Frederik
Park, Robert E(zra) 1864-1944 **TCLC 73**
　See also CA 122; 165
Parker, Bert
　See Ellison, Harlan (Jay)
Parker, Dorothy (Rothschild) 1893-1967 **CLC 15, 68; DAM POET; PC 28; SSC 2**
　See also CA 19-20; 25-28R; CAP 2; DA3; DLB 11, 45, 86; MTCW 1, 2
Parker, Robert B(rown) 1932- **CLC 27; DAM NOV, POP**
　See also AAYA 28; BEST 89:4; CA 49-52; CANR 1, 26, 52, 89; INT CANR-26; MTCW 1
Parkin, Frank 1940- **CLC 43**
　See also CA 147
Parkman, Francis Jr., Jr. 1823-1893 **NCLC 12**
　See also DLB 1, 30, 186
Parks, Gordon (Alexander Buchanan) 1912- **CLC 1, 16; BLC 3; DAM MULT**
　See also AITN 2; BW 2, 3; CA 41-44R; CANR 26, 66; DA3; DLB 33; MTCW 2; SATA 8, 108
Parmenides c. 515B.C.-c. 450B.C. **CMLC 22**
　See also DLB 176
Parnell, Thomas 1679-1718 **LC 3**
　See also DLB 94
Parra, Nicanor 1914- **CLC 2, 102; DAM MULT; HLC 2**
　See also CA 85-88; CANR 32; HW 1; MTCW 1
Parra Sanojo, Ana Teresa de la 1890-1936
　See also HLCS 2
Parrish, Mary Frances
　See Fisher, M(ary) F(rances) K(ennedy)
Parson
　See Coleridge, Samuel Taylor
Parson Lot
　See Kingsley, Charles
Parton, Sara Payson Willis 1811-1872 **NCLC 86**
　See also DLB 43, 74
Partridge, Anthony
　See Oppenheim, E(dward) Phillips
Pascal, Blaise 1623-1662 **LC 35**
Pascoli, Giovanni 1855-1912 **TCLC 45**
　See also CA 170
Pasolini, Pier Paolo 1922-1975 **CLC 20, 37, 106; PC 17**
　See also CA 93-96; 61-64; CANR 63; DLB 128, 177; MTCW 1
Pasquini
　See Silone, Ignazio
Pastan, Linda (Olenik) 1932- **CLC 27; DAM POET**
　See also CA 61-64; CANR 18, 40, 61; DLB 5
Pasternak, Boris (Leonidovich) 1890-1960 **CLC 7, 10, 18, 63; DA; DAB; DAC; DAM MST, NOV, POET; PC 6; SSC 31; WLC**
　See also CA 127; 116; DA3; MTCW 1, 2
Patchen, Kenneth 1911-1972 **CLC 1, 2, 18; DAM POET**
　See also CA 1-4R; 33-36R; CANR 3, 35; DLB 16, 48; MTCW 1
Pater, Walter (Horatio) 1839-1894 **NCLC 7**
　See also CDBLB 1832-1890; DLB 57, 156
Paterson, A(ndrew) B(arton) 1864-1941 **TCLC 32**
　See also CA 155; SATA 97
Paterson, Katherine (Womeldorf) 1932- **CLC 12, 30**
　See also AAYA 1, 31; CA 21-24R; CANR 28, 59; CLR 7, 50; DLB 52; JRDA; MAICYA; MTCW 1; SATA 13, 53, 92

Patmore, Coventry Kersey Dighton 1823-1896 **NCLC 9**
　See also DLB 35, 98
Paton, Alan (Stewart) 1903-1988 **CLC 4, 10, 25, 55, 106; DA; DAB; DAC; DAM MST, NOV; WLC**
　See also AAYA 26; CA 13-16; 125; CANR 22; CAP 1; DA3; DLBD 17; MTCW 1, 2; SATA 11; SATA-Obit 56
Paton Walsh, Gillian 1937-
　See Walsh, Jill Paton
　See also AAYA 11; CANR 38, 83; DLB 161; JRDA; MAICYA; SAAS 3; SATA 4, 72, 109
Patton, George S. 1885-1945 **TCLC 79**
Paulding, James Kirke 1778-1860 **NCLC 2**
　See also DLB 3, 59, 74
Paulin, Thomas Neilson 1949-
　See Paulin, Tom
　See also CA 123; 128
Paulin, Tom **CLC 37**
　See also Paulin, Thomas Neilson
　See also DLB 40
Pausanias c. 1st cent. - **CMLC 36**
Paustovsky, Konstantin (Georgievich) 1892-1968 **CLC 40**
　See also CA 93-96; 25-28R
Pavese, Cesare 1908-1950 **TCLC 3; PC 13; SSC 19**
　See also CA 104; 169; DLB 128, 177
Pavic, Milorad 1929- **CLC 60**
　See also CA 136; DLB 181
Pavlov, Ivan Petrovich 1849-1936 **TCLC 91**
　See also CA 118; 180
Payne, Alan
　See Jakes, John (William)
Paz, Gil
　See Lugones, Leopoldo
Paz, Octavio 1914-1998 **CLC 3, 4, 6, 10, 19, 51, 65, 119; DA; DAB; DAC; DAM MST, MULT, POET; HLC 2; PC 1; WLC**
　See also CA 73-76; 165; CANR 32, 65; DA3; DLBY 90, 98; HW 1, 2; MTCW 1, 2
p'Bitek, Okot 1931-1982 **CLC 96; BLC 3; DAM MULT**
　See also BW 2, 3; CA 124; 107; CANR 82; DLB 125; MTCW 1, 2
Peacock, Molly 1947- **CLC 60**
　See also CA 103; CAAS 21; CANR 52, 84; DLB 120
Peacock, Thomas Love 1785-1866 **NCLC 22**
　See also DLB 96, 116
Peake, Mervyn 1911-1968 **CLC 7, 54**
　See also CA 5-8R; 25-28R; CANR 3; DLB 15, 160; MTCW 1; SATA 23
Pearce, Philippa **CLC 21**
　See also Christie, (Ann) Philippa
　See also CLR 9; DLB 161; MAICYA; SATA 1, 67
Pearl, Eric
　See Elman, Richard (Martin)
Pearson, T(homas) R(eid) 1956- **CLC 39**
　See also CA 120; 130; INT 130
Peck, Dale 1967- **CLC 81**
　See also CA 146; CANR 72
Peck, John 1941- **CLC 3**
　See also CA 49-52; CANR 3
Peck, Richard (Wayne) 1934- **CLC 21**
　See also AAYA 1, 24; CA 85-88; CANR 19, 38; CLR 15; INT CANR-19; JRDA; MAICYA; SAAS 2; SATA 18, 55, 97; SATA-Essay 110
Peck, Robert Newton 1928- **CLC 17; DA; DAC; DAM MST**

　See also AAYA 3; CA 81-84, 182; CAAE 182; CANR 31, 63; CLR 45; JRDA; MAICYA; SAAS 1; SATA 21, 62, 111; SATA-Essay 108
Peckinpah, (David) Sam(uel) 1925-1984 **CLC 20**
　See also CA 109; 114; CANR 82
Pedersen, Knut 1859-1952
　See Hamsun, Knut
　See also CA 104; 119; CANR 63; MTCW 1, 2
Peeslake, Gaffer
　See Durrell, Lawrence (George)
Peguy, Charles Pierre 1873-1914 **TCLC 10**
　See also CA 107
Peirce, Charles Sanders 1839-1914 **TCLC 81**
Pellicer, Carlos 1900(?)-1977
　See also CA 153; 69-72; HLCS 2; HW 1
Pena, Ramon del Valle y
　See Valle-Inclan, Ramon (Maria) del
Pendennis, Arthur Esquir
　See Thackeray, William Makepeace
Penn, William 1644-1718 **LC 25**
　See also DLB 24
PEPECE
　See Prado (Calvo), Pedro
Pepys, Samuel 1633-1703 **LC 11, 58; DA; DAB; DAC; DAM MST; WLC**
　See also CDBLB 1660-1789; DA3; DLB 101
Percy, Walker 1916-1990 **CLC 2, 3, 6, 8, 14, 18, 47, 65; DAM NOV, POP**
　See also CA 1-4R; 131; CANR 1, 23, 64; DA3; DLB 2; DLBY 80, 90; MTCW 1, 2
Percy, William Alexander 1885-1942 **TCLC 84**
　See also CA 163; MTCW 2
Perec, Georges 1936-1982 **CLC 56, 116**
　See also CA 141; DLB 83
Pereda (y Sanchez de Porrua), Jose Maria de 1833-1906 **TCLC 16**
　See also CA 117
Pereda y Porrua, Jose Maria de
　See Pereda (y Sanchez de Porrua), Jose Maria de
Peregoy, George Weems
　See Mencken, H(enry) L(ouis)
Perelman, S(idney) J(oseph) 1904-1979 **CLC 3, 5, 9, 15, 23, 44, 49; DAM DRAM; SSC 32**
　See also AITN 1, 2; CA 73-76; 89-92; CANR 18; DLB 11, 44; MTCW 1, 2
Peret, Benjamin 1899-1959 **TCLC 20**
　See also CA 117; 186
Peretz, Isaac Loeb 1851(?)-1915 **TCLC 16; SSC 26**
　See also CA 109
Peretz, Yitzkhok Leibush
　See Peretz, Isaac Loeb
Perez Galdos, Benito 1843-1920 **TCLC 27; HLCS 2**
　See also CA 125; 153; HW 1
Peri Rossi, Cristina 1941-
　See also CA 131; CANR 59, 81; DLB 145; HLCS 2; HW 1, 2
Perlata
　See Peret, Benjamin
Perrault, Charles 1628-1703 **LC 3, 52; DC 12**
　See also MAICYA; SATA 25
Perry, Anne 1938- **CLC 126**
　See also CA 101; CANR 22, 50, 84
Perry, Brighton
　See Sherwood, Robert E(mmet)
Perse, St.-John
　See Leger, (Marie-Rene Auguste) Alexis Saint-Leger
Perutz, Leo(pold) 1882-1957 **TCLC 60**

See also CA 147; DLB 81

Peseenz, Tulio F.
See Lopez y Fuentes, Gregorio

Pesetsky, Bette 1932- **CLC 28**
See also CA 133; DLB 130

Peshkov, Alexei Maximovich 1868-1936
See Gorky, Maxim
See also CA 105; 141; CANR 83; DA;
DAC; DAM DRAM, MST, NOV; MTCW
2

Pessoa, Fernando (Antonio Nogueira)
1888-1935 **TCLC 27; DAM MULT;**
HLC 2; PC 20
See also CA 125; 183

Peterkin, Julia Mood 1880-1961 **CLC 31**
See also CA 102; DLB 9

Peters, Joan K(aren) 1945- **CLC 39**
See also CA 158

Peters, Robert L(ouis) 1924- **CLC 7**
See also CA 13-16R; CAAS 8; DLB 105

Petofi, Sandor 1823-1849 **NCLC 21**

Petrakis, Harry Mark 1923- **CLC 3**
See also CA 9-12R; CANR 4, 30, 85

Petrarch 1304-1374 **CMLC 20; DAM POET;**
PC 8
See also DA3

Petronius c. 20-66 **CMLC 34**
See also DLB 211

Petrov, Evgeny TCLC 21
See also Kataev, Evgeny Petrovich

Petry, Ann (Lane) 1908-1997 **CLC 1, 7, 18**
See also BW 1, 3; CA 5-8R; 157; CAAS 6;
CANR 4, 46; CLR 12; DLB 76; JRDA;
MAICYA; MTCW 1; SATA 5; SATA-Obit
94

Petursson, Halligrimur 1614-1674 **LC 8**

Peychinovich
See Vazov, Ivan (Minchov)

Phaedrus c. 18B.C.-c. 50 **CMLC 25**
See also DLB 211

Philips, Katherine 1632-1664 **LC 30**
See also DLB 131

Philipson, Morris H. 1926- **CLC 53**
See also CA 1-4R; CANR 4

Phillips, Caryl 1958- **CLC 96; BLCS; DAM**
MULT
See also BW 2; CA 141; CANR 63; DA3;
DLB 157; MTCW 2

Phillips, David Graham 1867-1911 **TCLC 44**
See also CA 108; 176; DLB 9, 12

Phillips, Jack
See Sandburg, Carl (August)

Phillips, Jayne Anne 1952- **CLC 15, 33; SSC**
16
See also CA 101; CANR 24, 50; DLBY 80;
INT CANR-24; MTCW 1, 2

Phillips, Richard
See Dick, Philip K(indred)

Phillips, Robert (Schaeffer) 1938- **CLC 28**
See also CA 17-20R; CAAS 13; CANR 8;
DLB 105

Phillips, Ward
See Lovecraft, H(oward) P(hillips)

Piccolo, Lucio 1901-1969 **CLC 13**
See also CA 97-100; DLB 114

Pickthall, Marjorie L(owry) C(hristie)
1883-1922 **TCLC 21**
See also CA 107; DLB 92

Pico della Mirandola, Giovanni 1463-1494
LC 15

Piercy, Marge 1936- **CLC 3, 6, 14, 18, 27, 62,**
128; PC 29
See also CA 21-24R; CAAS 1; CANR 13,
43, 66; DLB 120; MTCW 1, 2

Piers, Robert
See Anthony, Piers

Pieyre de Mandiargues, Andre 1909-1991
See Mandiargues, Andre Pieyre de
See also CA 103; 136; CANR 22, 82

Pilnyak, Boris TCLC 23
See also Vogau, Boris Andreyevich

Pincherle, Alberto 1907-1990 **CLC 11, 18;**
DAM NOV
See also Moravia, Alberto
See also CA 25-28R; 132; CANR 33, 63;
MTCW 1

Pinckney, Darryl 1953- **CLC 76**
See also BW 2, 3; CA 143; CANR 79

Pindar 518B.C.-446B.C. **CMLC 12; PC 19**
See also DLB 176

Pineda, Cecile 1942- **CLC 39**
See also CA 118

Pinero, Arthur Wing 1855-1934 **TCLC 32;**
DAM DRAM
See also CA 110; 153; DLB 10

Pinero, Miguel (Antonio Gomez) 1946-1988
CLC 4, 55
See also CA 61-64; 125; CANR 29, 90; HW
1

Pinget, Robert 1919-1997 **CLC 7, 13, 37**
See also CA 85-88; 160; DLB 83

Pink Floyd
See Barrett, (Roger) Syd; Gilmour, David;
Mason, Nick; Waters, Roger; Wright, Rick

Pinkney, Edward 1802-1828 **NCLC 31**

Pinkwater, Daniel Manus 1941- **CLC 35**
See also Pinkwater, Manus
See also AAYA 1; CA 29-32R; CANR 12,
38, 89; CLR 4; JRDA; MAICYA; SAAS
3; SATA 46, 76, 114

Pinkwater, Manus
See Pinkwater, Daniel Manus
See also SATA 8

Pinsky, Robert 1940- **CLC 9, 19, 38, 94, 121;**
DAM POET; PC 27
See also CA 29-32R; CAAS 4; CANR 58;
DA3; DLBY 82, 98; MTCW 2

Pinta, Harold
See Pinter, Harold

Pinter, Harold 1930- **CLC 1, 3, 6, 9, 11, 15,**
27, 58, 73; DA; DAB; DAC; DAM
DRAM, MST; WLC
See also CA 5-8R; CANR 33, 65; CDBLB
1960 to Present; DA3; DLB 13; MTCW
1, 2

Piozzi, Hester Lynch (Thrale) 1741-1821
NCLC 57
See also DLB 104, 142

Pirandello, Luigi 1867-1936 **TCLC 4, 29;**
DA; DAB; DAC; DAM DRAM, MST;
DC 5; SSC 22; WLC
See also CA 104; 153; DA3; MTCW 2

Pirsig, Robert M(aynard) 1928- **CLC 4, 6,**
73; DAM POP
See also CA 53-56; CANR 42, 74; DA3;
MTCW 1, 2; SATA 39

Pisarev, Dmitry Ivanovich 1840-1868 **NCLC**
25

Pix, Mary (Griffith) 1666-1709 **LC 8**
See also DLB 80

Pixerecourt, (Rene Charles) Guilbert de
1773-1844 **NCLC 39**
See also DLB 192

Plaatje, Sol(omon) T(shekisho) 1876-1932
TCLC 73; BLCS
See also BW 2, 3; CA 141; CANR 79

Plaidy, Jean
See Hibbert, Eleanor Alice Burford

Planche, James Robinson 1796-1880 **NCLC**
42

Plant, Robert 1948- **CLC 12**

Plante, David (Robert) 1940- **CLC 7, 23, 38;**
DAM NOV
See also CA 37-40R; CANR 12, 36, 58, 82;
DLBY 83; INT CANR-12; MTCW 1

Plath, Sylvia 1932-1963 **CLC 1, 2, 3, 5, 9, 11,**
14, 17, 50, 51, 62, 111; DA; DAB; DAC;
DAM MST, POET; PC 1; WLC
See also AAYA 13; CA 19-20; CANR 34;
CAP 2; CDALB 1941-1968; DA3; DLB
5, 6, 152; MTCW 1, 2; SATA 96

Plato 428(?)B.C.-348(?)B.C. **CMLC 8; DA;**
DAB; DAC; DAM MST; WLCS
See also DA3; DLB 176

Platonov, Andrei TCLC 14; SSC 38
See also Klimentov, Andrei Platonovich

Platt, Kin 1911- **CLC 26**
See also AAYA 11; CA 17-20R; CANR 11;
JRDA; SAAS 17; SATA 21, 86

Plautus c. 251B.C.-184B.C. **CMLC 24; DC 6**
See also DLB 211

Plick et Plock
See Simenon, Georges (Jacques Christian)

Plimpton, George (Ames) 1927- **CLC 36**
See also AITN 1; CA 21-24R; CANR 32,
70; DLB 185; MTCW 1, 2; SATA 10

Pliny the Elder c. 23-79 **CMLC 23**
See also DLB 211

Plomer, William Charles Franklin 1903-1973
CLC 4, 8
See also CA 21-22; CANR 34; CAP 2; DLB
20, 162, 191; MTCW 1; SATA 24

Plowman, Piers
See Kavanagh, Patrick (Joseph)

Plum, J.
See Wodehouse, P(elham) G(renville)

Plumly, Stanley (Ross) 1939- **CLC 33**
See also CA 108; 110; DLB 5, 193; INT
110

Plumpe, Friedrich Wilhelm 1888-1931 **TCLC**
53
See also CA 112

Po Chu-i 772-846 **CMLC 24**

Poe, Edgar Allan 1809-1849 **NCLC 1, 16, 55,**
78; DA; DAB; DAC; DAM MST,
POET; PC 1; SSC 34; WLC
See also AAYA 14; CDALB 1640-1865;
DA3; DLB 3, 59, 73, 74; SATA 23

Poet of Titchfield Street, The
See Pound, Ezra (Weston Loomis)

Pohl, Frederik 1919- **CLC 18; SSC 25**
See also AAYA 24; CA 61-64; CAAS 1;
CANR 11, 37, 81; DLB 8; INT CANR-
11; MTCW 1, 2; SATA 24

Poirier, Louis 1910-
See Gracq, Julien
See also CA 122; 126

Poitier, Sidney 1927- **CLC 26**
See also BW 1; CA 117

Polanski, Roman 1933- **CLC 16**
See also CA 77-80

Poliakoff, Stephen 1952- **CLC 38**
See also CA 106; DLB 13

Police, The
See Copeland, Stewart (Armstrong); Sum-
mers, Andrew James; Sumner, Gordon
Matthew

Polidori, John William 1795-1821 **NCLC 51**
See also DLB 116

Pollitt, Katha 1949- **CLC 28, 122**
See also CA 120; 122; CANR 66; MTCW
1, 2

Pollock, (Mary) Sharon 1936- **CLC 50; DAC;**
DAM DRAM, MST
See also CA 141; DLB 60

Polo, Marco 1254-1324 **CMLC 15**

Polonsky, Abraham (Lincoln) 1910- **CLC 92**
See also CA 104; DLB 26; INT 104

Polybius c. 200B.C.-c. 118B.C. **CMLC 17**
See also DLB 176

Pomerance, Bernard 1940- **CLC 13; DAM**
DRAM
See also CA 101; CANR 49

See also CA 1-4R; CANR 6, 22, 38, 87; CLR 24; JRDA; MAICYA; SATA 22, 75, 111

Reilly, William K.
See Creasey, John

Reiner, Max
See Caldwell, (Janet Miriam) Taylor (Holland)

Reis, Ricardo
See Pessoa, Fernando (Antonio Nogueira)

Remarque, Erich Maria 1898-1970 **CLC 21; DA; DAB; DAC; DAM MST, NOV**
See also AAYA 27; CA 77-80; 29-32R; DA3; DLB 56; MTCW 1, 2

Remington, Frederic 1861-1909 **TCLC 89**
See also CA 108; 169; DLB 12, 186, 188; SATA 41

Remizov, A.
See Remizov, Aleksei (Mikhailovich)

Remizov, A. M.
See Remizov, Aleksei (Mikhailovich)

Remizov, Aleksei (Mikhailovich) 1877-1957 **TCLC 27**
See also CA 125; 133

Renan, Joseph Ernest 1823-1892 **NCLC 26**

Renard, Jules 1864-1910 **TCLC 17**
See also CA 117

Renault, Mary CLC 3, 11, 17
See also Challans, Mary
See also DLBY 83; MTCW 2

Rendell, Ruth (Barbara) 1930- **CLC 28, 48; DAM POP**
See also Vine, Barbara
See also CA 109; CANR 32, 52, 74; DLB 87; INT CANR-32; MTCW 1, 2

Renoir, Jean 1894-1979 **CLC 20**
See also CA 129; 85-88

Resnais, Alain 1922- **CLC 16**

Reverdy, Pierre 1889-1960 **CLC 53**
See also CA 97-100; 89-92

Rexroth, Kenneth 1905-1982 **CLC 1, 2, 6, 11, 22, 49, 112; DAM POET; PC 20**
See also CA 5-8R; 107; CANR 14, 34, 63; CDALB 1941-1968; DLB 16, 48, 165, 212; DLBY 82; INT CANR-14; MTCW 1, 2

Reyes, Alfonso 1889-1959 **TCLC 33; HLCS 2**
See also CA 131; HW 1

Reyes y Basoalto, Ricardo Eliecer Neftali
See Neruda, Pablo

Reymont, Wladyslaw (Stanislaw) 1868(?)-1925 **TCLC 5**
See also CA 104

Reynolds, Jonathan 1942- **CLC 6, 38**
See also CA 65-68; CANR 28

Reynolds, Joshua 1723-1792 **LC 15**
See also DLB 104

Reynolds, Michael S(hane) 1937- **CLC 44**
See also CA 65-68; CANR 9, 89

Reznikoff, Charles 1894-1976 **CLC 9**
See also CA 33-36; 61-64; CAP 2; DLB 28, 45

Rezzori (d'Arezzo), Gregor von 1914-1998 **CLC 25**
See also CA 122; 136; 167

Rhine, Richard
See Silverstein, Alvin

Rhodes, Eugene Manlove 1869-1934 **TCLC 53**

Rhodius, Apollonius c. 3rd cent. B.C.- **CMLC 28**
See also DLB 176

R'hoone
See Balzac, Honore de

Rhys, Jean 1890(?)-1979 **CLC 2, 4, 6, 14, 19, 51, 124; DAM NOV; SSC 21**

See also CA 25-28R; 85-88; CANR 35, 62; CDBLB 1945-1960; DA3; DLB 36, 117, 162; MTCW 1, 2

Ribeiro, Darcy 1922-1997 **CLC 34**
See also CA 33-36R; 156

Ribeiro, Joao Ubaldo (Osorio Pimentel) 1941- **CLC 10, 67**
See also CA 81-84

Ribman, Ronald (Burt) 1932- **CLC 7**
See also CA 21-24R; CANR 46, 80

Ricci, Nino 1959- **CLC 70**
See also CA 137

Rice, Anne 1941- **CLC 41, 128; DAM POP**
See also AAYA 9; BEST 89:2; CA 65-68; CANR 12, 36, 53, 74; DA3; MTCW 2

Rice, Elmer (Leopold) 1892-1967 **CLC 7, 49; DAM DRAM**
See also CA 21-22; 25-28R; CAP 2; DLB 4, 7; MTCW 1, 2

Rice, Tim(othy Miles Bindon) 1944- **CLC 21**
See also CA 103; CANR 46

Rich, Adrienne (Cecile) 1929- **CLC 3, 6, 7, 11, 18, 36, 73, 76, 125; DAM POET; PC 5**
See also CA 9-12R; CANR 20, 53, 74; CDALBS; DA3; DLB 5, 67; MTCW 1, 2

Rich, Barbara
See Graves, Robert (von Ranke)

Rich, Robert
See Trumbo, Dalton

Richard, Keith CLC 17
See also Richards, Keith

Richards, David Adams 1950- **CLC 59; DAC**
See also CA 93-96; CANR 60; DLB 53

Richards, I(vor) A(rmstrong) 1893-1979 **CLC 14, 24**
See also CA 41-44R; 89-92; CANR 34, 74; DLB 27; MTCW 2

Richards, Keith 1943-
See Richard, Keith
See also CA 107; CANR 77

Richardson, Anne
See Roiphe, Anne (Richardson)

Richardson, Dorothy Miller 1873-1957 **TCLC 3**
See also CA 104; DLB 36

Richardson, Ethel Florence (Lindesay) 1870-1946
See Richardson, Henry Handel
See also CA 105

Richardson, Henry Handel TCLC 4
See also Richardson, Ethel Florence (Lindesay)
See also DLB 197

Richardson, John 1796-1852 **NCLC 55; DAC**
See also DLB 99

Richardson, Samuel 1689-1761 **LC 1, 44; DA; DAB; DAC; DAM MST, NOV; WLC**
See also CDBLB 1660-1789; DLB 39

Richler, Mordecai 1931- **CLC 3, 5, 9, 13, 18, 46, 70; DAC; DAM MST, NOV**
See also AITN 1; CA 65-68; CANR 31, 62; CLR 17; DLB 53; MAICYA; MTCW 1, 2; SATA 44, 98; SATA-Brief 27

Richter, Conrad (Michael) 1890-1968 **CLC 30**
See also AAYA 21; CA 5-8R; 25-28R; CANR 23; DLB 9, 212; MTCW 1, 2; SATA 3

Ricostranza, Tom
See Ellis, Trey

Riddell, Charlotte 1832-1906 **TCLC 40**
See also CA 165; DLB 156

Ridge, John Rollin 1827-1867 **NCLC 82; DAM MULT**
See also CA 144; DLB 175; NNAL

Ridgway, Keith 1965- **CLC 119**
See also CA 172

Riding, Laura CLC 3, 7
See also Jackson, Laura (Riding)

Riefenstahl, Berta Helene Amalia 1902-
See Riefenstahl, Leni
See also CA 108

Riefenstahl, Leni CLC 16
See also Riefenstahl, Berta Helene Amalia

Riffe, Ernest
See Bergman, (Ernst) Ingmar

Riggs, (Rolla) Lynn 1899-1954 **TCLC 56; DAM MULT**
See also CA 144; DLB 175; NNAL

Riis, Jacob A(ugust) 1849-1914 **TCLC 80**
See also CA 113; 168; DLB 23

Riley, James Whitcomb 1849-1916 **TCLC 51; DAM POET**
See also CA 118; 137; MAICYA; SATA 17

Riley, Tex
See Creasey, John

Rilke, Rainer Maria 1875-1926 **TCLC 1, 6, 19; DAM POET; PC 2**
See also CA 104; 132; CANR 62; DA3; DLB 81; MTCW 1, 2

Rimbaud, (Jean Nicolas) Arthur 1854-1891 **NCLC 4, 35, 82; DA; DAB; DAC; DAM MST, POET; PC 3; WLC**
See also DA3

Rinehart, Mary Roberts 1876-1958 **TCLC 52**
See also CA 108; 166

Ringmaster, The
See Mencken, H(enry) L(ouis)

Ringwood, Gwen(dolyn Margaret) Pharis 1910-1984 **CLC 48**
See also CA 148; 112; DLB 88

Rio, Michel 19(?)- **CLC 43**

Ritsos, Giannes
See Ritsos, Yannis

Ritsos, Yannis 1909-1990 **CLC 6, 13, 31**
See also CA 77-80; 133; CANR 39, 61; MTCW 1

Ritter, Erika 1948(?)- **CLC 52**

Rivera, Jose Eustasio 1889-1928 **TCLC 35**
See also CA 162; HW 1, 2

Rivera, Tomas 1935-1984
See also CA 49-52; CANR 32; DLB 82; HLCS 2; HW 1

Rivers, Conrad Kent 1933-1968 **CLC 1**
See also BW 1; CA 85-88; DLB 41

Rivers, Elfrida
See Bradley, Marion Zimmer

Riverside, John
See Heinlein, Robert A(nson)

Rizal, Jose 1861-1896 **NCLC 27**

Roa Bastos, Augusto (Antonio) 1917- **CLC 45; DAM MULT; HLC 2**
See also CA 131; DLB 113; HW 1

Robbe-Grillet, Alain 1922- **CLC 1, 2, 4, 6, 8, 10, 14, 43, 128**
See also CA 9-12R; CANR 33, 65; DLB 83; MTCW 1, 2

Robbins, Harold 1916-1997 **CLC 5; DAM NOV**
See also CA 73-76; 162; CANR 26, 54; DA3; MTCW 1, 2

Robbins, Thomas Eugene 1936-
See Robbins, Tom
See also CA 81-84; CANR 29, 59; DAM NOV, POP; DA3; MTCW 1, 2

Robbins, Tom CLC 9, 32, 64
See also Robbins, Thomas Eugene
See also AAYA 32; BEST 90:3; DLBY 80; MTCW 2

Robbins, Trina 1938- **CLC 21**
See also CA 128

Roberts, Charles G(eorge) D(ouglas) 1860-1943 **TCLC 8**
See also CA 105; CLR 33; DLB 92; SATA 88; SATA-Brief 29

See also CA 163; CANR 90; DLBY 97

Roy, Gabrielle 1909-1983 **CLC 10, 14; DAB; DAC; DAM MST**
See also CA 53-56; 110; CANR 5, 61; DLB 68; MTCW 1; SATA 104

Royko, Mike 1932-1997 **CLC 109**
See also CA 89-92; 157; CANR 26

Rozewicz, Tadeusz 1921- **CLC 9, 23; DAM POET**
See also CA 108; CANR 36, 66; DA3; MTCW 1, 2

Ruark, Gibbons 1941- **CLC 3**
See also CA 33-36R; CAAS 23; CANR 14, 31, 57; DLB 120

Rubens, Bernice (Ruth) 1923- **CLC 19, 31**
See also CA 25-28R; CANR 33, 65; DLB 14, 207; MTCW 1

Rubin, Harold
See Robbins, Harold

Rudkin, (James) David 1936- **CLC 14**
See also CA 89-92; DLB 13

Rudnik, Raphael 1933- **CLC 7**
See also CA 29-32R

Ruffian, M.
See Hasek, Jaroslav (Matej Frantisek)

Ruiz, Jose Martinez CLC 11
See also Martinez Ruiz, Jose

Rukeyser, Muriel 1913-1980 **CLC 6, 10, 15, 27; DAM POET; PC 12**
See also CA 5-8R; 93-96; CANR 26, 60; DA3; DLB 48; MTCW 1, 2; SATA-Obit 22

Rule, Jane (Vance) 1931- **CLC 27**
See also CA 25-28R; CAAS 18; CANR 12, 87; DLB 60

Rulfo, Juan 1918-1986 **CLC 8, 80; DAM MULT; HLC 2; SSC 25**
See also CA 85-88; 118; CANR 26; DLB 113; HW 1, 2; MTCW 1, 2

Rumi, Jalal al-Din 1297-1373 **CMLC 20**

Runeberg, Johan 1804-1877 **NCLC 41**

Runyon, (Alfred) Damon 1884(?)-1946 **TCLC 10**
See also CA 107; 165; DLB 11, 86, 171; MTCW 2

Rush, Norman 1933- **CLC 44**
See also CA 121; 126; INT 126

Rushdie, (Ahmed) Salman 1947- **CLC 23, 31, 55, 100; DAB; DAC; DAM MST, NOV, POP; WLCS**
See also BEST 89:3; CA 108; 111; CANR 33, 56; DA3; DLB 194; INT 111; MTCW 1, 2

Rushforth, Peter (Scott) 1945- **CLC 19**
See also CA 101

Ruskin, John 1819-1900 **TCLC 63**
See also CA 114; 129; CDBLB 1832-1890; DLB 55, 163, 190; SATA 24

Russ, Joanna 1937- **CLC 15**
See also CA 5-28R; CANR 11, 31, 65; DLB 8; MTCW 1

Russell, George William 1867-1935
See Baker, Jean H.
See also CA 104; 153; CDBLB 1890-1914; DAM POET

Russell, (Henry) Ken(neth Alfred) 1927- **CLC 16**
See also CA 105

Russell, William Martin 1947- **CLC 60**
See also CA 164

Rutherford, Mark TCLC 25
See also White, William Hale
See also DLB 18

Ruyslinck, Ward 1929- **CLC 14**
See also Belser, Reimond Karel Maria de

Ryan, Cornelius (John) 1920-1974 **CLC 7**
See also CA 69-72; 53-56; CANR 38

Ryan, Michael 1946- **CLC 65**
See also CA 49-52; DLBY 82

Ryan, Tim
See Dent, Lester

Rybakov, Anatoli (Naumovich) 1911-1998 **CLC 23, 53**
See also CA 126; 135; 172; SATA 79; SATA-Obit 108

Ryder, Jonathan
See Ludlum, Robert

Ryga, George 1932-1987 **CLC 14; DAC; DAM MST**
See also CA 101; 124; CANR 43, 90; DLB 60

S. H.
See Hartmann, Sadakichi

S. S.
See Sassoon, Siegfried (Lorraine)

Saba, Umberto 1883-1957 **TCLC 33**
See also CA 144; CANR 79; DLB 114

Sabatini, Rafael 1875-1950 **TCLC 47**
See also CA 162

Sabato, Ernesto (R.) 1911- **CLC 10, 23; DAM MULT; HLC 2**
See also CA 97-100; CANR 32, 65; DLB 145; HW 1, 2; MTCW 1, 2

Sa-Carniero, Mario de 1890-1916 **TCLC 83**

Sacastru, Martin
See Bioy Casares, Adolfo

Sacastru, Martin
See Bioy Casares, Adolfo

Sacher-Masoch, Leopold von 1836(?)-1895 **NCLC 31**

Sachs, Marilyn (Stickle) 1927- **CLC 35**
See also AAYA 2; CA 17-20R; CANR 13, 47; CLR 2; JRDA; MAICYA; SAAS 2; SATA 3, 68; SATA-Essay 110

Sachs, Nelly 1891-1970 **CLC 14, 98**
See also CA 17-18; 25-28R; CANR 87; CAP 2; MTCW 2

Sackler, Howard (Oliver) 1929-1982 **CLC 14**
See also CA 61-64; 108; CANR 30; DLB 7

Sacks, Oliver (Wolf) 1933- **CLC 67**
See also CA 53-56; CANR 28, 50, 76; DA3; INT CANR-28; MTCW 1, 2

Sadakichi
See Hartmann, Sadakichi

Sade, Donatien Alphonse Francois, Comte de 1740-1814 **NCLC 47**

Sadoff, Ira 1945- **CLC 9**
See also CA 53-56; CANR 5, 21; DLB 120

Saetone
See Camus, Albert

Safire, William 1929- **CLC 10**
See also CA 17-20R; CANR 31, 54, 91

Sagan, Carl (Edward) 1934-1996 **CLC 30, 112**
See also AAYA 2; CA 25-28R; 155; CANR 11, 36, 74; DA3; MTCW 1, 2; SATA 58; SATA-Obit 94

Sagan, Francoise CLC 3, 6, 9, 17, 36
See also Quoirez, Francoise
See also DLB 83; MTCW 2

Sahgal, Nayantara (Pandit) 1927- **CLC 41**
See also CA 9-12R; CANR 11, 88

Saint, H(arry) F. 1941- **CLC 50**
See also CA 127

St. Aubin de Teran, Lisa 1953-
See Teran, Lisa St. Aubin de
See also CA 118; 126; INT 126

Saint Birgitta of Sweden c. 1303-1373 **CMLC 24**

Sainte-Beuve, Charles Augustin 1804-1869 **NCLC 5**

Saint-Exupery, Antoine (Jean Baptiste Marie Roger) de 1900-1944 **TCLC 2, 56; DAM NOV; WLC**
See also CA 108; 132; CLR 10; DA3; DLB 72; MAICYA; MTCW 1, 2; SATA 20

St. John, David
See Hunt, E(verette) Howard, (Jr.)

Saint-John Perse
See Leger, (Marie-Rene Auguste) Alexis Saint-Leger

Saintsbury, George (Edward Bateman) 1845-1933 **TCLC 31**
See also CA 160; DLB 57, 149

Sait Faik TCLC 23
See also Abasiyanik, Sait Faik

Saki TCLC 3; SSC 12
See also Munro, H(ector) H(ugh)
See also MTCW 2

Sala, George Augustus NCLC 46

Saladin 1138-1193 **CMLC 38**

Salama, Hannu 1936- **CLC 18**

Salamanca, J(ack) R(ichard) 1922- **CLC 4, 15**
See also CA 25-28R

Salas, Floyd Francis 1931-
See also CA 119; CAAS 27; CANR 44, 75; DAM MULT; DLB 82; HLC 2; HW 1, 2; MTCW 2

Sale, J. Kirkpatrick
See Sale, Kirkpatrick

Sale, Kirkpatrick 1937- **CLC 68**
See also CA 13-16R; CANR 10

Salinas, Luis Omar 1937- **CLC 90; DAM MULT; HLC 2**
See also CA 131; CANR 81; DLB 82; HW 1, 2

Salinas (y Serrano), Pedro 1891(?)-1951 **TCLC 17**
See also CA 117; DLB 134

Salinger, J(erome) D(avid) 1919- **CLC 1, 3, 8, 12, 55, 56; DA; DAB; DAC; DAM MST, NOV, POP; SSC 2, 28; WLC**
See also AAYA 2; CA 5-8R; CANR 39; CDALB 1941-1968; CLR 18; DA3; DLB 2, 102, 173; MAICYA; MTCW 1, 2; SATA 67

Salisbury, John
See Caute, (John) David

Salter, James 1925- **CLC 7, 52, 59**
See also CA 73-76; DLB 130

Saltus, Edgar (Everton) 1855-1921 **TCLC 8**
See also CA 105; DLB 202

Saltykov, Mikhail Evgrafovich 1826-1889 **NCLC 16**

Samarakis, Antonis 1919- **CLC 5**
See also CA 25-28R; CAAS 16; CANR 36

Sanchez, Florencio 1875-1910 **TCLC 37**
See also CA 153; HW 1

Sanchez, Luis Rafael 1936- **CLC 23**
See also CA 128; DLB 145; HW 1

Sanchez, Sonia 1934- **CLC 5, 116; BLC 3; DAM MULT; PC 9**
See also BW 2, 3; CA 33-36R; CANR 24, 49, 74; CLR 18; DA3; DLB 41; DLBD 8; MAICYA; MTCW 1, 2; SATA 22

Sand, George 1804-1876 **NCLC 2, 42, 57; DA; DAB; DAC; DAM MST, NOV; WLC**
See also DA3; DLB 119, 192

Sandburg, Carl (August) 1878-1967 **CLC 1, 4, 10, 15, 35; DA; DAB; DAC; DAM MST, POET; PC 2; WLC**
See also AAYA 24; CA 5-8R; 25-28R; CANR 35; CDALB 1865-1917; DA3; DLB 17, 54; MAICYA; MTCW 1, 2; SATA 8

Sandburg, Charles
See Sandburg, Carl (August)

Sandburg, Charles A.
See Sandburg, Carl (August)

Sanders, (James) Ed(ward) 1939- **CLC 53; DAM POET**
See also CA 13-16R; CAAS 21; CANR 13, 44, 78; DLB 16

Scotland, Jay
See Jakes, John (William)

Scott, Duncan Campbell 1862-1947 **TCLC 6; DAC**
See also CA 104; 153; DLB 92

Scott, Evelyn 1893-1963 **CLC 43**
See also CA 104; 112; CANR 64; DLB 9, 48

Scott, F(rancis) R(eginald) 1899-1985 **CLC 22**
See also CA 101; 114; CANR 87; DLB 88; INT 101

Scott, Frank
See Scott, F(rancis) R(eginald)

Scott, Joanna 1960- **CLC 50**
See also CA 126; CANR 53

Scott, Paul (Mark) 1920-1978 **CLC 9, 60**
See also CA 81-84; 77-80; CANR 33; DLB 14, 207; MTCW 1

Scott, Sarah 1723-1795 **LC 44**
See also DLB 39

Scott, Walter 1771-1832 **NCLC 15, 69; DA; DAB; DAC; DAM MST, NOV, POET; PC 13; SSC 32; WLC**
See also AAYA 22; CDBLB 1789-1832; DLB 93, 107, 116, 144, 159; YABC 2

Scribe, (Augustin) Eugene 1791-1861 **NCLC 16; DAM DRAM; DC 5**
See also DLB 192

Scrum, R.
See Crumb, R(obert)

Scudery, Madeleine de 1607-1701 **LC 2, 58**

Scum
See Crumb, R(obert)

Scumbag, Little Bobby
See Crumb, R(obert)

Seabrook, John
See Hubbard, L(afayette) Ron(ald)

Sealy, I(rwin) Allan 1951- **CLC 55**
See also CA 136

Search, Alexander
See Pessoa, Fernando (Antonio Nogueira)

Sebastian, Lee
See Silverberg, Robert

Sebastian Owl
See Thompson, Hunter S(tockton)

Sebestyen, Ouida 1924- **CLC 30**
See also AAYA 8; CA 107; CANR 40; CLR 17; JRDA; MAICYA; SAAS 10; SATA 39

Secundus, H. Scriblerus
See Fielding, Henry

Sedges, John
See Buck, Pearl S(ydenstricker)

Sedgwick, Catharine Maria 1789-1867 **NCLC 19**
See also DLB 1, 74

Seelye, John (Douglas) 1931- **CLC 7**
See also CA 97-100; CANR 70; INT 97-100

Seferiades, Giorgos Stylianou 1900-1971
See Seferis, George
See also CA 5-8R; 33-36R; CANR 5, 36; MTCW 1

Seferis, George CLC 5, 11
See also Seferiades, Giorgos Stylianou

Segal, Erich (Wolf) 1937- **CLC 3, 10; DAM POP**
See also BEST 89:1; CA 25-28R; CANR 20, 36, 65; DLBY 86; INT CANR-20; MTCW 1

Seger, Bob 1945- **CLC 35**

Seghers, Anna CLC 7
See also Radvanyi, Netty
See also DLB 69

Seidel, Frederick (Lewis) 1936- **CLC 18**
See also CA 13-16R; CANR 8; DLBY 84

Seifert, Jaroslav 1901-1986 **CLC 34, 44, 93**

See also CA 127; MTCW 1, 2

Sei Shonagon c. 966-1017(?) **CMLC 6**

Séjour, Victor 1817-1874 **DC 10**
See also DLB 50

Sejour Marcou et Ferrand, Juan Victor
See S

Selby, Hubert, Jr. 1928- **CLC 1, 2, 4, 8; SSC 20**
See also CA 13-16R; CANR 33, 85; DLB 2

Selzer, Richard 1928- **CLC 74**
See also CA 65-68; CANR 14

Sembene, Ousmane
See Ousmane, Sembene

Senancour, Etienne Pivert de 1770-1846 **NCLC 16**
See also DLB 119

Sender, Ramon (Jose) 1902-1982 **CLC 8; DAM MULT; HLC 2**
See also CA 5-8R; 105; CANR 8; HW 1; MTCW 1

Seneca, Lucius Annaeus c. 1-c. 65 **CMLC 6; DAM DRAM; DC 5**
See also DLB 211

Senghor, Leopold Sedar 1906- **CLC 54, 130; BLC 3; DAM MULT, POET; PC 25**
See also BW 2; CA 116; 125; CANR 47, 74; MTCW 1, 2

Senna, Danzy 1970- **CLC 119**
See also CA 169

Serling, (Edward) Rod(man) 1924-1975 **CLC 30**
See also AAYA 14; AITN 1; CA 162; 57-60; DLB 26

Serna, Ramon Gomez de la
See Gomez de la Serna, Ramon

Serpieres
See Guillevic, (Eugene)

Service, Robert
See Service, Robert W(illiam)
See also DAB; DLB 92

Service, Robert W(illiam) 1874(?)-1958 **TCLC 15; DA; DAC; DAM MST, POET; WLC**
See also Service, Robert
See also CA 115; 140; CANR 84; SATA 20

Seth, Vikram 1952- **CLC 43, 90; DAM MULT**
See also CA 121; 127; CANR 50, 74; DA3; DLB 120; INT 127; MTCW 2

Seton, Cynthia Propper 1926-1982 **CLC 27**
See also CA 5-8R; 108; CANR 7

Seton, Ernest (Evan) Thompson 1860-1946 **TCLC 31**
See also CA 109; CLR 59; DLB 92; DLBD 13; JRDA; SATA 18

Seton-Thompson, Ernest
See Seton, Ernest (Evan) Thompson

Settle, Mary Lee 1918- **CLC 19, 61**
See also CA 89-92; CAAS 1; CANR 44, 87; DLB 6; INT 89-92

Seuphor, Michel
See Arp, Jean

Sevigne, Marie (de Rabutin-Chantal) Marquise de 1626-1696 **LC 11**

Sewall, Samuel 1652-1730 **LC 38**
See also DLB 24

Sexton, Anne (Harvey) 1928-1974 **CLC 2, 4, 6, 8, 10, 15, 53; DA; DAB; DAC; DAM MST, POET; PC 2; WLC**
See also CA 1-4R; 53-56; CABS 2; CANR 3, 36; CDALB 1941-1968; DA3; DLB 5, 169; MTCW 1, 2; SATA 10

Shaara, Jeff 1952- **CLC 119**
See also CA 163

Shaara, Michael (Joseph, Jr.) 1929-1988 **CLC 15; DAM POP**
See also AITN 1; CA 102; 125; CANR 52, 85; DLBY 83

Shackleton, C. C.
See Aldiss, Brian W(ilson)

Shacochis, Bob CLC 39
See also Shacochis, Robert G.

Shacochis, Robert G. 1951-
See Shacochis, Bob
See also CA 119; 124; INT 124

Shaffer, Anthony (Joshua) 1926- **CLC 19; DAM DRAM**
See also CA 110; 116; DLB 13

Shaffer, Peter (Levin) 1926- **CLC 5, 14, 18, 37, 60; DAB; DAM DRAM, MST; DC 7**
See also CA 25-28R; CANR 25, 47, 74; CDBLB 1960 to Present; DA3; DLB 13; MTCW 1, 2

Shakey, Bernard
See Young, Neil

Shalamov, Varlam (Tikhonovich) 1907(?)-1982 **CLC 18**
See also CA 129; 105

Shamlu, Ahmad 1925- **CLC 10**

Shammas, Anton 1951- **CLC 55**

Shandling, Arline
See Berriault, Gina

Shange, Ntozake 1948- **CLC 8, 25, 38, 74, 126; BLC 3; DAM DRAM, MULT; DC 3**
See also AAYA 9; BW 2; CA 85-88; CABS 3; CANR 27, 48, 74; DA3; DLB 38; MTCW 1, 2

Shanley, John Patrick 1950- **CLC 75**
See also CA 128; 133; CANR 83

Shapcott, Thomas W(illiam) 1935- **CLC 38**
See also CA 69-72; CANR 49, 83

Shapiro, Jane CLC 76

Shapiro, Karl (Jay) 1913- **CLC 4, 8, 15, 53; PC 25**
See also CA 1-4R; CAAS 6; CANR 1, 36, 66; DLB 48; MTCW 1, 2

Sharp, William 1855-1905 **TCLC 39**
See also CA 160; DLB 156

Sharpe, Thomas Ridley 1928-
See Sharpe, Tom
See also CA 114; 122; CANR 85; INT 122

Sharpe, Tom CLC 36
See also Sharpe, Thomas Ridley
See also DLB 14

Shaw, Bernard TCLC 45
See also Shaw, George Bernard
See also BW 1; MTCW 2

Shaw, G. Bernard
See Shaw, George Bernard

Shaw, George Bernard 1856-1950 **TCLC 3, 9, 21; DA; DAB; DAC; DAM DRAM, MST; WLC**
See also Shaw, Bernard
See also CA 104; 128; CDBLB 1914-1945; DA3; DLB 10, 57, 190; MTCW 1, 2

Shaw, Henry Wheeler 1818-1885 **NCLC 15**
See also DLB 11

Shaw, Irwin 1913-1984 **CLC 7, 23, 34; DAM DRAM, POP**
See also AITN 1; CA 13-16R; 112; CANR 21; CDALB 1941-1968; DLB 6, 102; DLBY 84; MTCW 1, 2

Shaw, Robert 1927-1978 **CLC 5**
See also AITN 1; CA 1-4R; 81-84; CANR 4; DLB 13, 14

Shaw, T. E.
See Lawrence, T(homas) E(dward)

Shawn, Wallace 1943- **CLC 41**
See also CA 112

Shea, Lisa 1953- **CLC 86**
See also CA 147

Sheed, Wilfrid (John Joseph) 1930- **CLC 2, 4, 10, 53**
See also CA 65-68; CANR 30, 66; DLB 6; MTCW 1, 2

Sheldon, Alice Hastings Bradley
1915(?)-1987
See Tiptree, James, Jr.
See also CA 108; 122; CANR 34; INT 108;
MTCW 1
Sheldon, John
See Bloch, Robert (Albert)
Shelley, Mary Wollstonecraft (Godwin)
1797-1851 **NCLC 14, 59; DA; DAB;**
DAC; DAM MST, NOV; WLC
See also AAYA 20; CDBLB 1789-1832;
DA3; DLB 110, 116, 159, 178; SATA 29
Shelley, Percy Bysshe 1792-1822 **NCLC 18;**
DA; DAB; DAC; DAM MST, POET;
PC 14; WLC
See also CDBLB 1789-1832; DA3; DLB
96, 110, 158
Shepard, Jim 1956- **CLC 36**
See also CA 137; CANR 59; SATA 90
Shepard, Lucius 1947- **CLC 34**
See also CA 128; 141; CANR 81
Shepard, Sam 1943- **CLC 4, 6, 17, 34, 41, 44;**
DAM DRAM; DC 5
See also AAYA 1; CA 69-72; CABS 3;
CANR 22; DA3; DLB 7, 212; MTCW 1,
2
Shepherd, Michael
See Ludlum, Robert
Sherburne, Zoa (Lillian Morin) 1912-1995
CLC 30
See also AAYA 13; CA 1-4R; 176; CANR
3, 37; MAICYA; SAAS 18; SATA 3
Sheridan, Frances 1724-1766 **LC 7**
See also DLB 39, 84
Sheridan, Richard Brinsley 1751-1816 **NCLC**
5; DA; DAB; DAC; DAM DRAM, MST;
DC 1; WLC
See also CDBLB 1660-1789; DLB 89
Sherman, Jonathan Marc CLC 55
Sherman, Martin 1941(?)- **CLC 19**
See also CA 116; 123; CANR 86
Sherwin, Judith Johnson 1936-
See Johnson, Judith (Emlyn)
See also CANR 85
Sherwood, Frances 1940- **CLC 81**
See also CA 146
Sherwood, Robert E(mmet) 1896-1955 **TCLC**
3; DAM DRAM
See also CA 104; 153; CANR 86; DLB 7,
26
Shestov, Lev 1866-1938 **TCLC 56**
Shevchenko, Taras 1814-1861 **NCLC 54**
Shiel, M(atthew) P(hipps) 1865-1947 **TCLC**
8
See also Holmes, Gordon
See also CA 106; 160; DLB 153; MTCW 2
Shields, Carol 1935- **CLC 91, 113; DAC**
See also CA 81-84; CANR 51, 74; DA3;
MTCW 2
Shields, David 1956- **CLC 97**
See also CA 124; CANR 48
Shiga, Naoya 1883-1971 **CLC 33; SSC 23**
See also CA 101; 33-36R; DLB 180
Shikibu, Murasaki c. 978-c. 1014 **CMLC 1**
Shilts, Randy 1951-1994 **CLC 85**
See also AAYA 19; CA 115; 127; 144;
CANR 45; DA3; INT 127; MTCW 2
Shimazaki, Haruki 1872-1943
See Shimazaki Toson
See also CA 105; 134; CANR 84
Shimazaki Toson 1872-1943 **TCLC 5**
See also Shimazaki, Haruki
See also DLB 180
Sholokhov, Mikhail (Aleksandrovich)
1905-1984 **CLC 7, 15**
See also CA 101; 112; MTCW 1, 2; SATA-
Obit 36

Shone, Patric
See Hanley, James
Shreve, Susan Richards 1939- **CLC 23**
See also CA 49-52; CAAS 5; CANR 5, 38,
69; MAICYA; SATA 46, 95; SATA-Brief
41
Shue, Larry 1946-1985 **CLC 52; DAM**
DRAM
See also CA 145; 117
Shu-Jen, Chou 1881-1936
See Lu Hsun
See also CA 104
Shulman, Alix Kates 1932- **CLC 2, 10**
See also CA 29-32R; CANR 43; SATA 7
Shuster, Joe 1914- **CLC 21**
Shute, Nevil CLC 30
See also Norway, Nevil Shute
See also MTCW 2
Shuttle, Penelope (Diane) 1947- **CLC 7**
See also CA 93-96; CANR 39, 84; DLB 14,
40
Sidney, Mary 1561-1621 **LC 19, 39**
Sidney, Sir Philip 1554-1586 **LC 19, 39; DA;**
DAB; DAC; DAM MST, POET
See also CDBLB Before 1660; DA3; DLB
167
Siegel, Jerome 1914-1996 **CLC 21**
See also CA 116; 169; 151
Siegel, Jerry
See Siegel, Jerome
Sienkiewicz, Henryk (Adam Alexander Pius)
1846-1916 **TCLC 3**
See also CA 104; 134; CANR 84
Sierra, Gregorio Martinez
See Martinez Sierra, Gregorio
Sierra, Maria (de la O'LeJarraga) Martinez
See Martinez Sierra, Maria (de la
O'LeJarraga)
Sigal, Clancy 1926- **CLC 7**
See also CA 1-4R; CANR 85
Sigourney, Lydia Howard (Huntley)
1791-1865 **NCLC 21, 87**
See also DLB 1, 42, 73
Siguenza y Gongora, Carlos de 1645-1700
LC 8; HLCS 2
Sigurjonsson, Johann 1880-1919 **TCLC 27**
See also CA 170
Sikelianos, Angelos 1884-1951 **TCLC 39; PC**
29
Silkin, Jon 1930-1997 **CLC 2, 6, 43**
See also CA 5-8R; CAAS 5; CANR 89;
DLB 27
Silko, Leslie (Marmon) 1948- **CLC 23, 74,**
114; DA; DAC; DAM MST, MULT,
POP; SSC 37; WLCS
See also AAYA 14; CA 115; 122; CANR
45, 65; DA3; DLB 143, 175; MTCW 2;
NNAL
Sillanpaa, Frans Eemil 1888-1964 **CLC 19**
See also CA 129; 93-96; MTCW 1
Sillitoe, Alan 1928- **CLC 1, 3, 6, 10, 19, 57**
See also AITN 1; CA 9-12R; CAAS 2;
CANR 8, 26, 55; CDBLB 1960 to Present;
DLB 14, 139; MTCW 1, 2; SATA 61
Silone, Ignazio 1900-1978 **CLC 4**
See also CA 25-28; 81-84; CANR 34; CAP
2; MTCW 1
Silver, Joan Micklin 1935- **CLC 20**
See also CA 114; 121; INT 121
Silver, Nicholas
See Faust, Frederick (Schiller)
Silverberg, Robert 1935- **CLC 7; DAM POP**
See also AAYA 24; CA 1-4R, 186; CAAE
186; CAAS 3; CANR 1, 20, 36, 85; CLR
59; DLB 8; INT CANR-20; MAICYA;
MTCW 1, 2; SATA 13, 91; SATA-Essay
104
Silverstein, Alvin 1933- **CLC 17**

See also CA 49-52; CANR 2; CLR 25;
JRDA; MAICYA; SATA 8, 69
Silverstein, Virginia B(arbara Opshelor)
1937- **CLC 17**
See also CA 49-52; CANR 2; CLR 25;
JRDA; MAICYA; SATA 8, 69
Sim, Georges
See Simenon, Georges (Jacques Christian)
Simak, Clifford D(onald) 1904-1988 **CLC 1,**
55
See also CA 1-4R; 125; CANR 1, 35; DLB
8; MTCW 1; SATA-Obit 56
Simenon, Georges (Jacques Christian)
1903-1989 **CLC 1, 2, 3, 8, 18, 47; DAM**
POP
See also CA 85-88; 129; CANR 35; DA3;
DLB 72; DLBY 89; MTCW 1, 2
Simic, Charles 1938- **CLC 6, 9, 22, 49, 68,**
130; DAM POET
See also CA 29-32R; CAAS 4; CANR 12,
33, 52, 61; DA3; DLB 105; MTCW 2
Simmel, Georg 1858-1918 **TCLC 64**
See also CA 157
Simmons, Charles (Paul) 1924- **CLC 57**
See also CA 89-92; INT 89-92
Simmons, Dan 1948- **CLC 44; DAM POP**
See also AAYA 16; CA 138; CANR 53, 81
Simmons, James (Stewart Alexander) 1933-
CLC 43
See also CA 105; CAAS 21; DLB 40
Simms, William Gilmore 1806-1870 **NCLC 3**
See also DLB 3, 30, 59, 73
Simon, Carly 1945- **CLC 26**
See also CA 105
Simon, Claude 1913- **CLC 4, 9, 15, 39; DAM**
NOV
See also CA 89-92; CANR 33; DLB 83;
MTCW 1
Simon, (Marvin) Neil 1927- **CLC 6, 11, 31,**
39, 70; DAM DRAM
See also AAYA 32; AITN 1; CA 21-24R;
CANR 26, 54, 87; DA3; DLB 7; MTCW
1, 2
Simon, Paul (Frederick) 1941(?)- **CLC 17**
See also CA 116; 153
Simonon, Paul 1956(?)- **CLC 30**
Simpson, Harriette
See Arnow, Harriette (Louisa) Simpson
Simpson, Louis (Aston Marantz) 1923- **CLC**
4, 7, 9, 32; DAM POET
See also CA 1-4R; CAAS 4; CANR 1, 61;
DLB 5; MTCW 1, 2
Simpson, Mona (Elizabeth) 1957- **CLC 44**
See also CA 122; 135; CANR 68
Simpson, N(orman) F(rederick) 1919- **CLC**
29
See also CA 13-16R; DLB 13
Sinclair, Andrew (Annandale) 1935- **CLC 2,**
14
See also CA 9-12R; CAAS 5; CANR 14,
38, 91; DLB 14; MTCW 1
Sinclair, Emil
See Hesse, Hermann
Sinclair, Iain 1943- **CLC 76**
See also CA 132; CANR 81
Sinclair, Iain MacGregor
See Sinclair, Iain
Sinclair, Irene
See Griffith, D(avid Lewelyn) W(ark)
Sinclair, Mary Amelia St. Clair 1865(?)-1946
See Sinclair, May
See also CA 104
Sinclair, May 1863-1946 **TCLC 3, 11**
See also Sinclair, Mary Amelia St. Clair
See also CA 166; DLB 36, 135
Sinclair, Roy
See Griffith, D(avid Lewelyn) W(ark)
Sinclair, Upton (Beall) 1878-1968 **CLC 1, 11,**

15, 63; DA; DAB; DAC; DAM MST, NOV; WLC
See also CA 5-8R; 25-28R; CANR 7; CDALB 1929-1941; DA3; DLB 9; INT CANR-7; MTCW 1, 2; SATA 9

Singer, Isaac
See Singer, Isaac Bashevis

Singer, Isaac Bashevis 1904-1991 **CLC 1, 3, 6, 9, 11, 15, 23, 38, 69, 111; DA; DAB; DAC; DAM MST, NOV; SSC 3; WLC**
See also AAYA 32; AITN 1, 2; CA 1-4R; 134; CANR 1, 39; CDALB 1941-1968; CLR 1; DA3; DLB 6, 28, 52; DLBY 91; JRDA; MAICYA; MTCW 1, 2; SATA 3, 27; SATA-Obit 68

Singer, Israel Joshua 1893-1944 **TCLC 33**
See also CA 169

Singh, Khushwant 1915- **CLC 11**
See also CA 9-12R; CAAS 9; CANR 6, 84

Singleton, Ann
See Benedict, Ruth (Fulton)

Sinjohn, John
See Galsworthy, John

Sinyavsky, Andrei (Donatevich) 1925-1997 **CLC 8**
See also CA 85-88; 159

Sirin, V.
See Nabokov, Vladimir (Vladimirovich)

Sissman, L(ouis) E(dward) 1928-1976 **CLC 9, 18**
See also CA 21-24R; 65-68; CANR 13; DLB 5

Sisson, C(harles) H(ubert) 1914- **CLC 8**
See also CA 1-4R; CAAS 3; CANR 3, 48, 84; DLB 27

Sitwell, Dame Edith 1887-1964 **CLC 2, 9, 67; DAM POET; PC 3**
See also CA 9-12R; CANR 35; CDBLB 1945-1960; DLB 20; MTCW 1, 2

Siwaarmill, H. P.
See Sharp, William

Sjoewall, Maj 1935- **CLC 7**
See also CA 65-68; CANR 73

Sjowall, Maj
See Sjoewall, Maj

Skelton, John 1463-1529 **PC 25**

Skelton, Robin 1925-1997 **CLC 13**
See also AITN 2; CA 5-8R; 160; CAAS 5; CANR 28, 89; DLB 27, 53

Skolimowski, Jerzy 1938- **CLC 20**
See also CA 128

Skram, Amalie (Bertha) 1847-1905 **TCLC 25**
See also CA 165

Skvorecky, Josef (Vaclav) 1924- **CLC 15, 39, 69; DAC; DAM NOV**
See also CA 61-64; CAAS 1; CANR 10, 34, 63; DA3; MTCW 1, 2

Slade, Bernard CLC 11, 46
See also Newbound, Bernard Slade
See also CAAS 9; DLB 53

Slaughter, Carolyn 1946- **CLC 56**
See also CA 85-88; CANR 85

Slaughter, Frank G(ill) 1908- **CLC 29**
See also AITN 2; CA 5-8R; CANR 5, 85; INT CANR-5

Slavitt, David R(ytman) 1935- **CLC 5, 14**
See also CA 21-24R; CAAS 3; CANR 41, 83; DLB 5, 6

Slesinger, Tess 1905-1945 **TCLC 10**
See also CA 107; DLB 102

Slessor, Kenneth 1901-1971 **CLC 14**
See also CA 102; 89-92

Slowacki, Juliusz 1809-1849 **NCLC 15**

Smart, Christopher 1722-1771 **LC 3; DAM POET; PC 13**
See also DLB 109

Smart, Elizabeth 1913-1986 **CLC 54**
See also CA 81-84; 118; DLB 88

Smiley, Jane (Graves) 1949- **CLC 53, 76; DAM POP**
See also CA 104; CANR 30, 50, 74; DA3; INT CANR-30

Smith, A(rthur) J(ames) M(arshall) 1902-1980 **CLC 15; DAC**
See also CA 1-4R; 102; CANR 4; DLB 88

Smith, Adam 1723-1790 **LC 36**
See also DLB 104

Smith, Alexander 1829-1867 **NCLC 59**
See also DLB 32, 55

Smith, Anna Deavere 1950- **CLC 86**
See also CA 133

Smith, Betty (Wehner) 1896-1972 **CLC 19**
See also CA 5-8R; 33-36R; DLBY 82; SATA 6

Smith, Charlotte (Turner) 1749-1806 **NCLC 23**
See also DLB 39, 109

Smith, Clark Ashton 1893-1961 **CLC 43**
See also CA 143; CANR 81; MTCW 2

Smith, Dave CLC 22, 42
See also Smith, David (Jeddie)
See also CAAS 7; DLB 5

Smith, David (Jeddie) 1942-
See Smith, Dave
See also CA 49-52; CANR 1, 59; DAM POET

Smith, Florence Margaret 1902-1971
See Smith, Stevie
See also CA 17-18; 29-32R; CANR 35; CAP 2; DAM POET; MTCW 1, 2

Smith, Iain Crichton 1928-1998 **CLC 64**
See also CA 21-24R; 171; DLB 40, 139

Smith, John 1580(?)-1631 **LC 9**
See also DLB 24, 30

Smith, Johnston
See Crane, Stephen (Townley)

Smith, Joseph, Jr. 1805-1844 **NCLC 53**

Smith, Lee 1944- **CLC 25, 73**
See also CA 114; 119; CANR 46; DLB 143; DLBY 83; INT 119

Smith, Martin
See Smith, Martin Cruz

Smith, Martin Cruz 1942- **CLC 25; DAM MULT, POP**
See also BEST 89:4; CA 85-88; CANR 6, 23, 43, 65; INT CANR-23; MTCW 2; NNAL

Smith, Mary-Ann Tirone 1944- **CLC 39**
See also CA 118; 136

Smith, Patti 1946- **CLC 12**
See also CA 93-96; CANR 63

Smith, Pauline (Urmson) 1882-1959 **TCLC 25**

Smith, Rosamond
See Oates, Joyce Carol

Smith, Sheila Kaye
See Kaye-Smith, Sheila

Smith, Stevie CLC 3, 8, 25, 44; PC 12
See also Smith, Florence Margaret
See also DLB 20; MTCW 2

Smith, Wilbur (Addison) 1933- **CLC 33**
See also CA 13-16R; CANR 7, 46, 66; MTCW 1, 2

Smith, William Jay 1918- **CLC 6**
See also CA 5-8R; CANR 44; DLB 5; MAICYA; SAAS 22; SATA 2, 68

Smith, Woodrow Wilson
See Kuttner, Henry

Smolenskin, Peretz 1842-1885 **NCLC 30**

Smollett, Tobias (George) 1721-1771 **LC 2, 46**
See also CDBLB 1660-1789; DLB 39, 104

Snodgrass, W(illiam) D(e Witt) 1926- **CLC 2, 6, 10, 18, 68; DAM POET**
See also CA 1-4R; CANR 6, 36, 65, 85; DLB 5; MTCW 1, 2

Snow, C(harles) P(ercy) 1905-1980 **CLC 1, 4, 6, 9, 13, 19; DAM NOV**
See also CA 5-8R; 101; CANR 28; CDBLB 1945-1960; DLB 15, 77; DLBD 17; MTCW 1, 2

Snow, Frances Compton
See Adams, Henry (Brooks)

Snyder, Gary (Sherman) 1930- **CLC 1, 2, 5, 9, 32, 120; DAM POET**
See also CA 17-20R; CANR 30, 60; DA3; DLB 5, 16, 165, 212; MTCW 2

Snyder, Zilpha Keatley 1927- **CLC 17**
See also AAYA 15; CA 9-12R; CANR 38; CLR 31; JRDA; MAICYA; SAAS 2; SATA 1, 28, 75, 110; SATA-Essay 112

Soares, Bernardo
See Pessoa, Fernando (Antonio Nogueira)

Sobh, A.
See Shamlu, Ahmad

Sobol, Joshua CLC 60

Socrates 469B.C.-399B.C. **CMLC 27**

Soderberg, Hjalmar 1869-1941 **TCLC 39**

Sodergran, Edith (Irene)
See Soedergran, Edith (Irene)

Soedergran, Edith (Irene) 1892-1923 **TCLC 31**

Softly, Edgar
See Lovecraft, H(oward) P(hillips)

Softly, Edward
See Lovecraft, H(oward) P(hillips)

Sokolov, Raymond 1941- **CLC 7**
See also CA 85-88

Solo, Jay
See Ellison, Harlan (Jay)

Sologub, Fyodor TCLC 9
See also Teternikov, Fyodor Kuzmich

Solomons, Ikey Esquir
See Thackeray, William Makepeace

Solomos, Dionysios 1798-1857 **NCLC 15**

Solwoska, Mara
See French, Marilyn

Solzhenitsyn, Aleksandr I(sayevich) 1918- **CLC 1, 2, 4, 7, 9, 10, 18, 26, 34, 78; DA; DAB; DAC; DAM MST, NOV; SSC 32; WLC**
See also AITN 1; CA 69-72; CANR 40, 65; DA3; MTCW 1, 2

Somers, Jane
See Lessing, Doris (May)

Somerville, Edith 1858-1949 **TCLC 51**
See also DLB 135

Somerville & Ross
See Martin, Violet Florence; Somerville, Edith

Sommer, Scott 1951- **CLC 25**
See also CA 106

Sondheim, Stephen (Joshua) 1930- **CLC 30, 39; DAM DRAM**
See also AAYA 11; CA 103; CANR 47, 68

Song, Cathy 1955- **PC 21**
See also CA 154; DLB 169

Sontag, Susan 1933- **CLC 1, 2, 10, 13, 31, 105; DAM POP**
See also CA 17-20R; CANR 25, 51, 74; DA3; DLB 2, 67; MTCW 1, 2

Sophocles 496(?)B.C.-406(?)B.C. **CMLC 2; DA; DAB; DAC; DAM DRAM, MST; DC 1; WLCS**
See also DA3; DLB 176

Sordello 1189-1269 **CMLC 15**

Sorel, Georges 1847-1922 **TCLC 91**
See also CA 118

Sorel, Julia
See Drexler, Rosalyn

Sorrentino, Gilbert 1929- **CLC 3, 7, 14, 22, 40**
See also CA 77-80; CANR 14, 33; DLB 5, 173; DLBY 80; INT CANR-14

Soto, Gary 1952- **CLC 32, 80; DAM MULT; HLC 2; PC 28**
See also AAYA 10; CA 119; 125; CANR 50, 74; CLR 38; DLB 82; HW 1, 2; INT 125; JRDA; MTCW 2; SATA 80

Soupault, Philippe 1897-1990 **CLC 68**
See also CA 116; 147; 131

Souster, (Holmes) Raymond 1921- **CLC 5, 14; DAC; DAM POET**
See also CA 13-16R; CAAS 14; CANR 13, 29, 53; DA3; DLB 88; SATA 63

Southern, Terry 1924(?)-1995 **CLC 7**
See also CA 1-4R; 150; CANR 1, 55; DLB 2

Southey, Robert 1774-1843 **NCLC 8**
See also DLB 93, 107, 142; SATA 54

Southworth, Emma Dorothy Eliza Nevitte 1819-1899 **NCLC 26**

Souza, Ernest
See Scott, Evelyn

Soyinka, Wole 1934- **CLC 3, 5, 14, 36, 44; BLC 3; DA; DAB; DAC; DAM DRAM, MST, MULT; DC 2; WLC**
See also BW 2, 3; CA 13-16R; CANR 27, 39, 82; DA3; DLB 125; MTCW 1, 2

Spackman, W(illiam) M(ode) 1905-1990 **CLC 46**
See also CA 81-84; 132

Spacks, Barry (Bernard) 1931- **CLC 14**
See also CA 154; CANR 33; DLB 105

Spanidou, Irini 1946- **CLC 44**
See also CA 185

Spark, Muriel (Sarah) 1918- **CLC 2, 3, 5, 8, 13, 18, 40, 94; DAB; DAC; DAM MST, NOV; SSC 10**
See also CA 5-8R; CANR 12, 36, 76, 89; CDBLB 1945-1960; DA3; DLB 15, 139; INT CANR-12; MTCW 1, 2

Spaulding, Douglas
See Bradbury, Ray (Douglas)

Spaulding, Leonard
See Bradbury, Ray (Douglas)

Spence, J. A. D.
See Eliot, T(homas) S(tearns)

Spencer, Elizabeth 1921- **CLC 22**
See also CA 13-16R; CANR 32, 65, 87; DLB 6; MTCW 1; SATA 14

Spencer, Leonard G.
See Silverberg, Robert

Spencer, Scott 1945- **CLC 30**
See also CA 113; CANR 51; DLBY 86

Spender, Stephen (Harold) 1909-1995 **CLC 1, 2, 5, 10, 41, 91; DAM POET**
See also CA 9-12R; 149; CANR 31, 54; CDBLB 1945-1960; DA3; DLB 20; MTCW 1, 2

Spengler, Oswald (Arnold Gottfried) 1880-1936 **TCLC 25**
See also CA 118

Spenser, Edmund 1552(?)-1599 **LC 5, 39; DA; DAB; DAC; DAM MST, POET; PC 8; WLC**
See also CDBLB Before 1660; DA3; DLB 167

Spicer, Jack 1925-1965 **CLC 8, 18, 72; DAM POET**
See also CA 85-88; DLB 5, 16, 193

Spiegelman, Art 1948- **CLC 76**
See also AAYA 10; CA 125; CANR 41, 55, 74; MTCW 2; SATA 109

Spielberg, Peter 1929- **CLC 6**
See also CA 5-8R; CANR 4, 48; DLBY 81

Spielberg, Steven 1947- **CLC 20**
See also AAYA 8, 24; CA 77-80; CANR 32; SATA 32

Spillane, Frank Morrison 1918-
See Spillane, Mickey
See also CA 25-28R; CANR 28, 63; DA3; MTCW 1, 2; SATA 66

Spillane, Mickey CLC 3, 13
See also Spillane, Frank Morrison
See also MTCW 2

Spinoza, Benedictus de 1632-1677 **LC 9, 58**

Spinrad, Norman (Richard) 1940- **CLC 46**
See also CA 37-40R; CAAS 19; CANR 20, 91; DLB 8; INT CANR-20

Spitteler, Carl (Friedrich Georg) 1845-1924 **TCLC 12**
See also CA 109; DLB 129

Spivack, Kathleen (Romola Drucker) 1938- **CLC 6**
See also CA 49-52

Spoto, Donald 1941- **CLC 39**
See also CA 65-68; CANR 11, 57

Springsteen, Bruce (F.) 1949- **CLC 17**
See also CA 111

Spurling, Hilary 1940- **CLC 34**
See also CA 104; CANR 25, 52

Spyker, John Howland
See Elman, Richard (Martin)

Squires, (James) Radcliffe 1917-1993 **CLC 51**
See also CA 1-4R; 140; CANR 6, 21

Srivastava, Dhanpat Rai 1880(?)-1936
See Premchand
See also CA 118

Stacy, Donald
See Pohl, Frederik

Stael, Germaine de 1766-1817
See Stael-Holstein, Anne Louise Germaine Necker Baronn
See also DLB 119

Stael-Holstein, Anne Louise Germaine Necker Baronn 1766-1817 **NCLC 3**
See also Stael, Germaine de
See also DLB 192

Stafford, Jean 1915-1979 **CLC 4, 7, 19, 68; SSC 26**
See also CA 1-4R; 85-88; CANR 3, 65; DLB 2, 173; MTCW 1, 2; SATA-Obit 22

Stafford, William (Edgar) 1914-1993 **CLC 4, 7, 29; DAM POET**
See also CA 5-8R; 142; CAAS 3; CANR 5, 22; DLB 5, 206; INT CANR-22

Stagnelius, Eric Johan 1793-1823 **NCLC 61**

Staines, Trevor
See Brunner, John (Kilian Houston)

Stairs, Gordon
See Austin, Mary (Hunter)

Stairs, Gordon
See Austin, Mary (Hunter)

Stalin, Joseph 1879-1953 **TCLC 92**

Stannard, Martin 1947- **CLC 44**
See also CA 142; DLB 155

Stanton, Elizabeth Cady 1815-1902 **TCLC 73**
See also CA 171; DLB 79

Stanton, Maura 1946- **CLC 9**
See also CA 89-92; CANR 15; DLB 120

Stanton, Schuyler
See Baum, L(yman) Frank

Stapledon, (William) Olaf 1886-1950 **TCLC 22**
See also CA 111; 162; DLB 15

Starbuck, George (Edwin) 1931-1996 **CLC 53; DAM POET**
See also CA 21-24R; 153; CANR 23

Stark, Richard
See Westlake, Donald E(dwin)

Staunton, Schuyler
See Baum, L(yman) Frank

Stead, Christina (Ellen) 1902-1983 **CLC 2, 5, 8, 32, 80**
See also CA 13-16R; 109; CANR 33, 40; MTCW 1, 2

Stead, William Thomas 1849-1912 **TCLC 48**
See also CA 167

Steele, Richard 1672-1729 **LC 18**
See also CDBLB 1660-1789; DLB 84, 101

Steele, Timothy (Reid) 1948- **CLC 45**
See also CA 93-96; CANR 16, 50; DLB 120

Steffens, (Joseph) Lincoln 1866-1936 **TCLC 20**
See also CA 117

Stegner, Wallace (Earle) 1909-1993 **CLC 9, 49, 81; DAM NOV; SSC 27**
See also AITN 1; BEST 90:3; CA 1-4R; 141; CAAS 9; CANR 1, 21, 46; DLB 9, 206; DLBY 93; MTCW 1, 2

Stein, Gertrude 1874-1946 **TCLC 1, 6, 28, 48; DA; DAB; DAC; DAM MST, NOV, POET; PC 18; WLC**
See also CA 104; 132; CDALB 1917-1929; DA3; DLB 4, 54, 86; DLBD 15; MTCW 1, 2

Steinbeck, John (Ernst) 1902-1968 **CLC 1, 5, 9, 13, 21, 34, 45, 75, 124; DA; DAB; DAC; DAM DRAM, MST, NOV; SSC 11, 37; WLC**
See also AAYA 12; CA 1-4R; 25-28R; CANR 1, 35; CDALB 1929-1941; DA3; DLB 7, 9, 212; DLBD 2; MTCW 1, 2; SATA 9

Steinem, Gloria 1934- **CLC 63**
See also CA 53-56; CANR 28, 51; MTCW 1, 2

Steiner, George 1929- **CLC 24; DAM NOV**
See also CA 73-76; CANR 31, 67; DLB 67; MTCW 1, 2; SATA 62

Steiner, K. Leslie
See Delany, Samuel R(ay, Jr.)

Steiner, Rudolf 1861-1925 **TCLC 13**
See also CA 107

Stendhal 1783-1842 **NCLC 23, 46; DA; DAB; DAC; DAM MST, NOV; SSC 27; WLC**
See also DA3; DLB 119

Stephen, Adeline Virginia
See Woolf, (Adeline) Virginia

Stephen, SirLeslie 1832-1904 **TCLC 23**
See also CA 123; DLB 57, 144, 190

Stephen, Sir Leslie
See Stephen, SirLeslie

Stephen, Virginia
See Woolf, (Adeline) Virginia

Stephens, James 1882(?)-1950 **TCLC 4**
See also CA 104; DLB 19, 153, 162

Stephens, Reed
See Donaldson, Stephen R.

Steptoe, Lydia
See Barnes, Djuna

Sterchi, Beat 1949- **CLC 65**

Sterling, Brett
See Bradbury, Ray (Douglas); Hamilton, Edmond

Sterling, Bruce 1954- **CLC 72**
See also CA 119; CANR 44

Sterling, George 1869-1926 **TCLC 20**
See also CA 117; 165; DLB 54

Stern, Gerald 1925- **CLC 40, 100**
See also CA 81-84; CANR 28; DLB 105

Stern, Richard (Gustave) 1928- **CLC 4, 39**
See also CA 1-4R; CANR 1, 25, 52; DLBY 87; INT CANR-25

Sternberg, Josef von 1894-1969 **CLC 20**
See also CA 81-84

Sterne, Laurence 1713-1768 **LC 2, 48; DA; DAB; DAC; DAM MST, NOV; WLC**
See also CDBLB 1660-1789; DLB 39

Sternheim, (William Adolf) Carl 1878-1942 **TCLC 8**
See also CA 105; DLB 56, 118

Stevens, Mark 1951- **CLC 34**
See also CA 122

Stevens, Wallace 1879-1955 **TCLC 3, 12, 45;**

Swados, Elizabeth (A.) 1951- **CLC 12**
See also CA 97-100; CANR 49; INT 97-100

Swados, Harvey 1920-1972 **CLC 5**
See also CA 5-8R; 37-40R; CANR 6; DLB 2

Swan, Gladys 1934- **CLC 69**
See also CA 101; CANR 17, 39

Swanson, Logan
See Matheson, Richard Burton

Swarthout, Glendon (Fred) 1918-1992 **CLC 35**
See also CA 1-4R; 139; CANR 1, 47; SATA 26

Sweet, Sarah C.
See Jewett, (Theodora) Sarah Orne

Swenson, May 1919-1989 **CLC 4, 14, 61, 106; DA; DAB; DAC; DAM MST, POET; PC 14**
See also CA 5-8R; 130; CANR 36, 61; DLB 5; MTCW 1, 2; SATA 15

Swift, Augustus
See Lovecraft, H(oward) P(hillips)

Swift, Graham (Colin) 1949- **CLC 41, 88**
See also CA 117; 122; CANR 46, 71; DLB 194; MTCW 2

Swift, Jonathan 1667-1745 **LC 1, 42; DA; DAB; DAC; DAM MST, NOV, POET; PC 9; WLC**
See also CDBLB 1660-1789; CLR 53; DA3; DLB 39, 95, 101; SATA 19

Swinburne, Algernon Charles 1837-1909 **TCLC 8, 36; DA; DAB; DAC; DAM MST, POET; PC 24; WLC**
See also CA 105; 140; CDBLB 1832-1890; DA3; DLB 35, 57

Swinfen, Ann **CLC 34**

Swinnerton, Frank Arthur 1884-1982 **CLC 31**
See also CA 108; DLB 34

Swithen, John
See King, Stephen (Edwin)

Sylvia
See Ashton-Warner, Sylvia (Constance)

Symmes, Robert Edward
See Duncan, Robert (Edward)

Symonds, John Addington 1840-1893 **NCLC 34**
See also DLB 57, 144

Symons, Arthur 1865-1945 **TCLC 11**
See also CA 107; DLB 19, 57, 149

Symons, Julian (Gustave) 1912-1994 **CLC 2, 14, 32**
See also CA 49-52; 147; CAAS 3; CANR 3, 33, 59; DLB 87, 155; DLBY 92; MTCW 1

Synge, (Edmund) J(ohn) M(illington) 1871-1909 **TCLC 6, 37; DAM DRAM; DC 2**
See also CA 104; 141; CDBLB 1890-1914; DLB 10, 19

Syruc, J.
See Milosz, Czeslaw

Szirtes, George 1948- **CLC 46**
See also CA 109; CANR 27, 61

Szymborska, Wislawa 1923- **CLC 99**
See also CA 154; CANR 91; DA3; DLBY 96; MTCW 2

T. O., Nik
See Annensky, Innokenty (Fyodorovich)

Tabori, George 1914- **CLC 19**
See also CA 49-52; CANR 4, 69

Tagore, Rabindranath 1861-1941 **TCLC 3, 53; DAM DRAM, POET; PC 8**
See also CA 104; 120; DA3; MTCW 1, 2

Taine, Hippolyte Adolphe 1828-1893 **NCLC 15**

Talese, Gay 1932- **CLC 37**
See also AITN 1; CA 1-4R; CANR 9, 58; DLB 185; INT CANR-9; MTCW 1, 2

Tallent, Elizabeth (Ann) 1954- **CLC 45**
See also CA 117; CANR 72; DLB 130

Tally, Ted 1952- **CLC 42**
See also CA 120; 124; INT 124

Talvik, Heiti 1904-1947 **TCLC 87**

Tamayo y Baus, Manuel 1829-1898 **NCLC 1**

Tammsaare, A(nton) H(ansen) 1878-1940 **TCLC 27**
See also CA 164; DLB 220

Tam'si, Tchicaya U
See Tchicaya, Gerald Felix

Tan, Amy (Ruth) 1952- **CLC 59, 120; DAM MULT, NOV, POP**
See also AAYA 9; BEST 89:3; CA 136; CANR 54; CDALBS; DA3; DLB 173; MTCW 2; SATA 75

Tandem, Felix
See Spitteler, Carl (Friedrich Georg)

Tanizaki, Jun'ichiro 1886-1965 **CLC 8, 14, 28; SSC 21**
See also CA 93-96; 25-28R; DLB 180; MTCW 2

Tanner, William
See Amis, Kingsley (William)

Tao Lao
See Storni, Alfonsina

Tarantino, Quentin (Jerome) 1963- **CLC 125**
See also CA 171

Tarassoff, Lev
See Troyat, Henri

Tarbell, Ida M(inerva) 1857-1944 **TCLC 40**
See also CA 122; 181; DLB 47

Tarkington, (Newton) Booth 1869-1946 **TCLC 9**
See also CA 110; 143; DLB 9, 102; MTCW 2; SATA 17

Tarkovsky, Andrei (Arsenyevich) 1932-1986 **CLC 75**
See also CA 127

Tartt, Donna 1964(?)- **CLC 76**
See also CA 142

Tasso, Torquato 1544-1595 **LC 5**

Tate, (John Orley) Allen 1899-1979 **CLC 2, 4, 6, 9, 11, 14, 24**
See also CA 5-8R; 85-88; CANR 32; DLB 4, 45, 63; DLBD 17; MTCW 1, 2

Tate, Ellalice
See Hibbert, Eleanor Alice Burford

Tate, James (Vincent) 1943- **CLC 2, 6, 25**
See also CA 21-24R; CANR 29, 57; DLB 5, 169

Tauler, Johannes c. 1300-1361 **CMLC 37**
See also DLB 179

Tavel, Ronald 1940- **CLC 6**
See also CA 21-24R; CANR 33

Taylor, C(ecil) P(hilip) 1929-1981 **CLC 27**
See also CA 25-28R; 105; CANR 47

Taylor, Edward 1642(?)-1729 **LC 11; DA; DAB; DAC; DAM MST, POET**
See also DLB 24

Taylor, Eleanor Ross 1920- **CLC 5**
See also CA 81-84; CANR 70

Taylor, Elizabeth 1912-1975 **CLC 2, 4, 29**
See also CA 13-16R; CANR 9, 70; DLB 139; MTCW 1; SATA 13

Taylor, Frederick Winslow 1856-1915 **TCLC 76**

Taylor, Henry (Splawn) 1942- **CLC 44**
See also CA 33-36R; CAAS 7; CANR 31; DLB 5

Taylor, Kamala (Purnaiya) 1924-
See Markandaya, Kamala
See also CA 77-80

Taylor, Mildred D. **CLC 21**
See also AAYA 10; BW 1; CA 85-88; CANR 25; CLR 9, 59; DLB 52; JRDA; MAICYA; SAAS 5; SATA 15, 70

Taylor, Peter (Hillsman) 1917-1994 **CLC 1, 4, 18, 37, 44, 50, 71; SSC 10**
See also CA 13-16R; 147; CANR 9, 50; DLBY 81, 94; INT CANR-9; MTCW 1, 2

Taylor, Robert Lewis 1912-1998 **CLC 14**
See also CA 1-4R; 170; CANR 3, 64; SATA 10

Tchekhov, Anton
See Chekhov, Anton (Pavlovich)

Tchicaya, Gerald Felix 1931-1988 **CLC 101**
See also CA 129; 125; CANR 81

Tchicaya U Tam'si
See Tchicaya, Gerald Felix

Teasdale, Sara 1884-1933 **TCLC 4**
See also CA 104; 163; DLB 45; SATA 32

Tegner, Esaias 1782-1846 **NCLC 2**

Teilhard de Chardin, (Marie Joseph) Pierre 1881-1955 **TCLC 9**
See also CA 105

Temple, Ann
See Mortimer, Penelope (Ruth)

Tennant, Emma (Christina) 1937- **CLC 13, 52**
See also CA 65-68; CAAS 9; CANR 10, 38, 59, 88; DLB 14

Tenneshaw, S. M.
See Silverberg, Robert

Tennyson, Alfred 1809-1892 **NCLC 30, 65; DA; DAB; DAC; DAM MST, POET; PC 6; WLC**
See also CDBLB 1832-1890; DA3; DLB 32

Teran, Lisa St. Aubin de **CLC 36**
See also St. Aubin de Teran, Lisa

Terence c. 184B.C.-c. 159B.C. **CMLC 14; DC 7**
See also DLB 211

Teresa de Jesus, St. 1515-1582 **LC 18**

Terkel, Louis 1912-
See Terkel, Studs
See also CA 57-60; CANR 18, 45, 67; DA3; MTCW 1, 2

Terkel, Studs **CLC 38**
See also Terkel, Louis
See also AAYA 32; AITN 1; MTCW 2

Terry, C. V.
See Slaughter, Frank G(ill)

Terry, Megan 1932- **CLC 19**
See also CA 77-80; CABS 3; CANR 43; DLB 7

Tertullian c. 155-c. 245 **CMLC 29**

Tertz, Abram
See Sinyavsky, Andrei (Donatevich)

Tesich, Steve 1943(?)-1996 **CLC 40, 69**
See also CA 105; 152; DLBY 83

Tesla, Nikola 1856-1943 **TCLC 88**

Teternikov, Fyodor Kuzmich 1863-1927
See Sologub, Fyodor
See also CA 104

Tevis, Walter 1928-1984 **CLC 42**
See also CA 113

Tey, Josephine **TCLC 14**
See also Mackintosh, Elizabeth
See also DLB 77

Thackeray, William Makepeace 1811-1863 **NCLC 5, 14, 22, 43; DA; DAB; DAC; DAM MST, NOV; WLC**
See also CDBLB 1832-1890; DA3; DLB 21, 55, 159, 163; SATA 23

Thakura, Ravindranatha
See Tagore, Rabindranath

Tharoor, Shashi 1956- **CLC 70**
See also CA 141; CANR 91

Thelwell, Michael Miles 1939- **CLC 22**
See also BW 2; CA 101

Theobald, Lewis, Jr.
See Lovecraft, H(oward) P(hillips)

Theodorescu, Ion N. 1880-1967
See Arghezi, Tudor
See also CA 116; DLB 220

Theriault, Yves 1915-1983 **CLC 79; DAC;
DAM MST**
See also CA 102; DLB 88

Theroux, Alexander (Louis) 1939- **CLC 2, 25**
See also CA 85-88; CANR 20, 63

Theroux, Paul (Edward) 1941- **CLC 5, 8, 11,
15, 28, 46; DAM POP**
See also AAYA 28; BEST 89:4; CA 33-36R;
CANR 20, 45, 74; CDALBS; DA3; DLB
2; MTCW 1, 2; SATA 44, 109

Thesen, Sharon 1946- **CLC 56**
See also CA 163

Thevenin, Denis
See Duhamel, Georges

Thibault, Jacques Anatole Francois
1844-1924
See France, Anatole
See also CA 106; 127; DAM NOV; DA3;
MTCW 1, 2

Thiele, Colin (Milton) 1920- **CLC 17**
See also CA 29-32R; CANR 12, 28, 53;
CLR 27; MAICYA; SAAS 2; SATA 14,
72

Thomas, Audrey (Callahan) 1935- **CLC 7,
13, 37, 107; SSC 20**
See also AITN 2; CA 21-24R; CAAS 19;
CANR 36, 58; DLB 60; MTCW 1

Thomas, Augustus 1857-1934 **TCLC 97**

Thomas, D(onald) M(ichael) 1935- **CLC 13,
22, 31, 132**
See also CA 61-64; CAAS 11; CANR 17,
45, 75; CDBLB 1960 to Present; DA3;
DLB 40, 207; INT CANR-17; MTCW 1,
2

Thomas, Dylan (Marlais) 1914-1953 **TCLC
1, 8, 45; DA; DAB; DAC; DAM DRAM,
MST, POET; PC 2; SSC 3; WLC**
See also CA 104; 120; CANR 65; CDBLB
1945-1960; DA3; DLB 13, 20, 139;
MTCW 1, 2; SATA 60

Thomas, (Philip) Edward 1878-1917 **TCLC
10; DAM POET**
See also CA 106; 153; DLB 98

Thomas, Joyce Carol 1938- **CLC 35**
See also AAYA 12; BW 2, 3; CA 113; 116;
CANR 48; CLR 19; DLB 33; INT 116;
JRDA; MAICYA; MTCW 1, 2; SAAS 7;
SATA 40, 78

Thomas, Lewis 1913-1993 **CLC 35**
See also CA 85-88; 143; CANR 38, 60;
MTCW 1, 2

Thomas, M. Carey 1857-1935 **TCLC 89**

Thomas, Paul
See Mann, (Paul) Thomas

Thomas, Piri 1928- **CLC 17; HLCS 2**
See also CA 73-76; HW 1

Thomas, R(onald) S(tuart) 1913- **CLC 6, 13,
48; DAB; DAM POET**
See also CA 89-92; CAAS 4; CANR 30;
CDBLB 1960 to Present; DLB 27; MTCW
1

Thomas, Ross (Elmore) 1926-1995 **CLC 39**
See also CA 33-36R; 150; CANR 22, 63

Thompson, Francis Clegg
See Mencken, H(enry) L(ouis)

Thompson, Francis Joseph 1859-1907 **TCLC
4**
See also CA 104; CDBLB 1890-1914; DLB
19

Thompson, Hunter S(tockton) 1939- **CLC 9,
17, 40, 104; DAM POP**
See also BEST 89:1; CA 17-20R; CANR
23, 46, 74, 77; DA3; DLB 185; MTCW
1, 2

Thompson, James Myers
See Thompson, Jim (Myers)

Thompson, Jim (Myers) 1906-1977(?) **CLC
69**
See also CA 140

Thompson, Judith CLC 39

Thomson, James 1700-1748 **LC 16, 29, 40;
DAM POET**
See also DLB 95

Thomson, James 1834-1882 **NCLC 18; DAM
POET**
See also DLB 35

Thoreau, Henry David 1817-1862 **NCLC 7,
21, 61; DA; DAB; DAC; DAM MST;
PC 30; WLC**
See also CDALB 1640-1865; DA3; DLB 1,
223

Thornton, Hall
See Silverberg, Robert

Thucydides c. 455B.C.-399B.C. **CMLC 17**
See also DLB 176

Thumboo, Edwin 1933- **PC 30**

Thurber, James (Grover) 1894-1961 **CLC 5,
11, 25, 125; DA; DAB; DAC; DAM
DRAM, MST, NOV; SSC 1**
See also CA 73-76; CANR 17, 39; CDALB
1929-1941; DA3; DLB 4, 11, 22, 102;
MAICYA; MTCW 1, 2; SATA 13

Thurman, Wallace (Henry) 1902-1934 **TCLC
6; BLC 3; DAM MULT**
See also BW 1, 3; CA 104; 124; CANR 81;
DLB 51

Tibullus, Albius c. 54B.C.-c. 19B.C. **CMLC
36**
See also DLB 211

Ticheburn, Cheviot
See Ainsworth, William Harrison

Tieck, (Johann) Ludwig 1773-1853 **NCLC 5,
46; SSC 31**
See also DLB 90

Tiger, Derry
See Ellison, Harlan (Jay)

Tilghman, Christopher 1948(?)- **CLC 65**
See also CA 159

Tillich, Paul (Johannes) 1886-1965 **CLC 131**
See also CA 5-8R; 25-28R; CANR 33;
MTCW 1, 2

Tillinghast, Richard (Williford) 1940- **CLC
29**
See also CA 29-32R; CAAS 23; CANR 26,
51

Timrod, Henry 1828-1867 **NCLC 25**
See also DLB 3

Tindall, Gillian (Elizabeth) 1938- **CLC 7**
See also CA 21-24R; CANR 11, 65

Tiptree, James, Jr. CLC 48, 50
See also Sheldon, Alice Hastings Bradley
See also DLB 8

Titmarsh, Michael Angelo
See Thackeray, William Makepeace

**Tocqueville, Alexis (Charles Henri Maurice
Clerel, Comte) de** 1805-1859 **NCLC 7,
63**

Tolkien, J(ohn) R(onald) R(euel) 1892-1973
**CLC 1, 2, 3, 8, 12, 38; DA; DAC; DAB;
DAM MST, NOV, POP; WLC**
See also AAYA 10; AITN 1; CA 17-18; 45-
48; CANR 36; CAP 2; CDBLB 1914-
1945; CLR 56; DA3; DLB 15, 160;
JRDA; MAICYA; MTCW 1, 2; SATA 2,
32, 100; SATA-Obit 24

Toller, Ernst 1893-1939 **TCLC 10**
See also CA 107; 186; DLB 124

Tolson, M. B.
See Tolson, Melvin B(eaunorus)

Tolson, Melvin B(eaunorus) 1898(?)-1966
**CLC 36, 105; BLC 3; DAM MULT,
POET**
See also BW 1, 3; CA 124; 89-92; CANR
80; DLB 48, 76

Tolstoi, Aleksei Nikolaevich
See Tolstoy, Alexey Nikolaevich

Tolstoy, Alexey Nikolaevich 1882-1945 **TCLC
18**
See also CA 107; 158

Tolstoy, Count Leo
See Tolstoy, Leo (Nikolaevich)

Tolstoy, Leo (Nikolaevich) 1828-1910 **TCLC
4, 11, 17, 28, 44, 79; DA; DAB; DAC;
DAM MST, NOV; SSC 9, 30; WLC**
See also CA 104; 123; DA3; SATA 26

Tomasi di Lampedusa, Giuseppe 1896-1957
See Lampedusa, Giuseppe (Tomasi) di
See also CA 111

Tomlin, Lily CLC 17
See also Tomlin, Mary Jean

Tomlin, Mary Jean 1939(?)-
See Tomlin, Lily
See also CA 117

Tomlinson, (Alfred) Charles 1927- **CLC 2, 4,
6, 13, 45; DAM POET; PC 17**
See also CA 5-8R; CANR 33; DLB 40

Tomlinson, H(enry) M(ajor) 1873-1958
TCLC 71
See also CA 118; 161; DLB 36, 100, 195

Tonson, Jacob
See Bennett, (Enoch) Arnold

Toole, John Kennedy 1937-1969 **CLC 19, 64**
See also CA 104; DLBY 81; MTCW 2

Toomer, Jean 1894-1967 **CLC 1, 4, 13, 22;
BLC 3; DAM MULT; PC 7; SSC 1;
WLCS**
See also BW 1; CA 85-88; CDALB 1917-
1929; DA3; DLB 45, 51; MTCW 1, 2

Torley, Luke
See Blish, James (Benjamin)

Tornimparte, Alessandra
See Ginzburg, Natalia

Torre, Raoul della
See Mencken, H(enry) L(ouis)

Torrence, Ridgely 1874-1950 **TCLC 97**
See also DLB 54

Torrey, E(dwin) Fuller 1937- **CLC 34**
See also CA 119; CANR 71

Torsvan, Ben Traven
See Traven, B.

Torsvan, Benno Traven
See Traven, B.

Torsvan, Berick Traven
See Traven, B.

Torsvan, Berwick Traven
See Traven, B.

Torsvan, Bruno Traven
See Traven, B.

Torsvan, Traven
See Traven, B.

Tournier, Michel (Edouard) 1924- **CLC 6,
23, 36, 95**
See also CA 49-52; CANR 3, 36, 74; DLB
83; MTCW 1, 2; SATA 23

Tournimparte, Alessandra
See Ginzburg, Natalia

Towers, Ivar
See Kornbluth, C(yril) M.

Towne, Robert (Burton) 1936(?)- **CLC 87**
See also CA 108; DLB 44

Townsend, Sue CLC 61
See also Townsend, Susan Elaine
See also AAYA 28; SATA 55, 93; SATA-
Brief 48

Townsend, Susan Elaine 1946-
See Townsend, Sue
See also CA 119; 127; CANR 65; DAB;
DAC; DAM MST

Townshend, Peter (Dennis Blandford) 1945-
CLC 17, 42

Valdez, Luis (Miguel) 1940- **CLC 84; DAM MULT; DC 10; HLC 2**
See also CA 101; CANR 32, 81; DLB 122; HW 1

Valenzuela, Luisa 1938- **CLC 31, 104; DAM MULT; HLCS 2; SSC 14**
See also CA 101; CANR 32, 65; DLB 113; HW 1, 2

Valera y Alcala-Galiano, Juan 1824-1905 **TCLC 10**
See also CA 106

Valery, (Ambroise) Paul (Toussaint Jules) 1871-1945 **TCLC 4, 15; DAM POET; PC 9**
See also CA 104; 122; DA3; MTCW 1, 2

Valle-Inclan, Ramon (Maria) del 1866-1936 **TCLC 5; DAM MULT; HLC 2**
See also CA 106; 153; CANR 80; DLB 134; HW 2

Vallejo, Antonio Buero
See Buero Vallejo, Antonio

Vallejo, Cesar (Abraham) 1892-1938 **TCLC 3, 56; DAM MULT; HLC 2**
See also CA 105; 153; HW 1

Valles, Jules 1832-1885 **NCLC 71**
See also DLB 123

Vallette, Marguerite Eymery 1860-1953 **TCLC 67**
See also CA 182; DLB 123, 192

Valle Y Pena, Ramon del
See Valle-Inclan, Ramon (Maria) del

Van Ash, Cay 1918- **CLC 34**

Vanbrugh, Sir John 1664-1726 **LC 21; DAM DRAM**
See also DLB 80

Van Campen, Karl
See Campbell, John W(ood, Jr.)

Vance, Gerald
See Silverberg, Robert

Vance, Jack CLC 35
See also Vance, John Holbrook
See also DLB 8

Vance, John Holbrook 1916-
See Queen, Ellery; Vance, Jack
See also CA 29-32R; CANR 17, 65; MTCW 1

Van Den Bogarde, Derek Jules Gaspard Ulric Niven 1921-1999 **CLC 14**
See also CA 77-80; 179; DLB 19

Vandenburgh, Jane CLC 59
See also CA 168

Vanderhaeghe, Guy 1951- **CLC 41**
See also CA 113; CANR 72

van der Post, Laurens (Jan) 1906-1996 **CLC 5**
See also CA 5-8R; 155; CANR 35; DLB 204

van de Wetering, Janwillem 1931- **CLC 47**
See also CA 49-52; CANR 4, 62, 90

Van Dine, S. S. TCLC 23
See also Wright, Willard Huntington

Van Doren, Carl (Clinton) 1885-1950 **TCLC 18**
See also CA 111; 168

Van Doren, Mark 1894-1972 **CLC 6, 10**
See also CA 1-4R; 37-40R; CANR 3; DLB 45; MTCW 1, 2

Van Druten, John (William) 1901-1957 **TCLC 2**
See also CA 104; 161; DLB 10

Van Duyn, Mona (Jane) 1921- **CLC 3, 7, 63, 116; DAM POET**
See also CA 9-12R; CANR 7, 38, 60; DLB 5

Van Dyne, Edith
See Baum, L(yman) Frank

van Itallie, Jean-Claude 1936- **CLC 3**
See also CA 45-48; CAAS 2; CANR 1, 48; DLB 7

van Ostaijen, Paul 1896-1928 **TCLC 33**
See also CA 163

Van Peebles, Melvin 1932- **CLC 2, 20; DAM MULT**
See also BW 2, 3; CA 85-88; CANR 27, 67, 82

Vansittart, Peter 1920- **CLC 42**
See also CA 1-4R; CANR 3, 49, 90

Van Vechten, Carl 1880-1964 **CLC 33**
See also CA 183; 89-92; DLB 4, 9, 51

Van Vogt, A(lfred) E(lton) 1912- **CLC 1**
See also CA 21-24R; CANR 28; DLB 8; SATA 14

Varda, Agnes 1928- **CLC 16**
See also CA 116; 122

Vargas Llosa, (Jorge) Mario (Pedro) 1936- **CLC 3, 6, 9, 10, 15, 31, 42, 85; DA; DAB; DAC; DAM MST, MULT, NOV; HLC 2**
See also CA 73-76; CANR 18, 32, 42, 67; DA3; DLB 145; HW 1, 2; MTCW 1, 2

Vasiliu, Gheorghe 1881-1957
See Bacovia, George
See also CA 123; DLB 220

Vassa, Gustavus
See Equiano, Olaudah

Vassilikos, Vassilis 1933- **CLC 4, 8**
See also CA 81-84; CANR 75

Vaughan, Henry 1621-1695 **LC 27**
See also DLB 131

Vaughn, Stephanie CLC 62

Vazov, Ivan (Minchov) 1850-1921 **TCLC 25**
See also CA 121; 167; DLB 147

Veblen, Thorstein B(unde) 1857-1929 **TCLC 31**
See also CA 115; 165

Vega, Lope de 1562-1635 **LC 23; HLCS 2**

Venison, Alfred
See Pound, Ezra (Weston Loomis)

Verdi, Marie de
See Mencken, H(enry) L(ouis)

Verdu, Matilde
See Cela, Camilo Jose

Verga, Giovanni (Carmelo) 1840-1922 **TCLC 3; SSC 21**
See also CA 104; 123

Vergil 70B.C.-19B.C. **CMLC 9, 40; DA; DAB; DAC; DAM MST, POET; PC 12; WLCS**
See also DA3; DLB 211

Verhaeren, Emile (Adolphe Gustave) 1855-1916 **TCLC 12**
See also CA 109

Verlaine, Paul (Marie) 1844-1896 **NCLC 2, 51; DAM POET; PC 2**

Verne, Jules (Gabriel) 1828-1905 **TCLC 6, 52**
See also AAYA 16; CA 110; 131; DA3; DLB 123; JRDA; MAICYA; SATA 21

Very, Jones 1813-1880 **NCLC 9**
See also DLB 1

Vesaas, Tarjei 1897-1970 **CLC 48**
See also CA 29-32R

Vialis, Gaston
See Simenon, Georges (Jacques Christian)

Vian, Boris 1920-1959 **TCLC 9**
See also CA 106; 164; DLB 72; MTCW 2

Viaud, (Louis Marie) Julien 1850-1923
See Loti, Pierre
See also CA 107

Vicar, Henry
See Felsen, Henry Gregor

Vicker, Angus
See Felsen, Henry Gregor

Vidal, Gore 1925- **CLC 2, 4, 6, 8, 10, 22, 33, 72; DAM NOV, POP**

See also AITN 1; BEST 90:2; CA 5-8R; CANR 13, 45, 65; CDALBS; DA3; DLB 6, 152; INT CANR-13; MTCW 1, 2

Viereck, Peter (Robert Edwin) 1916- **CLC 4; PC 27**
See also CA 1-4R; CANR 1, 47; DLB 5

Vigny, Alfred (Victor) de 1797-1863 **NCLC 7; DAM POET; PC 26**
See also DLB 119, 192

Vilakazi, Benedict Wallet 1906-1947 **TCLC 37**
See also CA 168

Villa, Jose Garcia 1904-1997 **PC 22**
See also CA 25-28R; CANR 12

Villarreal, Jose Antonio 1924-
See also CA 133; DAM MULT; DLB 82; HLC 2; HW 1

Villaurrutia, Xavier 1903-1950 **TCLC 80**
See also HW 1

Villehardouin 1150(?)-1218(?) **CMLC 38**

Villiers de l'Isle Adam, Jean Marie Mathias Philippe Auguste, Comte de 1838-1889 **NCLC 3; SSC 14**
See also DLB 123

Villon, Francois 1431-1463(?) **PC 13**
See also DLB 208

Vine, Barbara CLC 50
See Rendell, Ruth (Barbara)
See also BEST 90:4

Vinge, Joan (Carol) D(ennison) 1948- **CLC 30; SSC 24**
See also AAYA 32; CA 93-96; CANR 72; SATA 36, 113

Violis, G.
See Simenon, Georges (Jacques Christian)

Viramontes, Helena Maria 1954-
See also CA 159; DLB 122; HLCS 2; HW 2

Virgil 70B.C.-19B.C.
See Vergil

Visconti, Luchino 1906-1976 **CLC 16**
See also CA 81-84; 65-68; CANR 39

Vittorini, Elio 1908-1966 **CLC 6, 9, 14**
See also CA 133; 25-28R

Vivekananda, Swami 1863-1902 **TCLC 88**

Vizenor, Gerald Robert 1934- **CLC 103; DAM MULT**
See also CA 13-16R; CAAS 22; CANR 5, 21, 44, 67; DLB 175; MTCW 2; NNAL

Vizinczey, Stephen 1933- **CLC 40**
See also CA 128; INT 128

Vliet, R(ussell) G(ordon) 1929-1984 **CLC 22**
See also CA 37-40R; 112; CANR 18

Vogau, Boris Andreyevich 1894-1937(?)
See Pilnyak, Boris
See also CA 123

Vogel, Paula A(nne) 1951- **CLC 76**
See also CA 108

Voigt, Cynthia 1942- **CLC 30**
See also AAYA 3, 30; CA 106; CANR 18, 37, 40; CLR 13, 48; INT CANR-18; JRDA; MAICYA; SATA 48, 79, 116; SATA-Brief 33

Voigt, Ellen Bryant 1943- **CLC 54**
See also CA 69-72; CANR 11, 29, 55; DLB 120

Voinovich, Vladimir (Nikolaevich) 1932- **CLC 10, 49**
See also CA 81-84; CAAS 12; CANR 33, 67; MTCW 1

Vollmann, William T. 1959- **CLC 89; DAM NOV, POP**
See also CA 134; CANR 67; DA3; MTCW 2

Voloshinov, V. N.
See Bakhtin, Mikhail Mikhailovich

Voltaire 1694-1778 **LC 14; DA; DAB; DAC; DAM DRAM, MST; SSC 12; WLC**
See also DA3

von Aschendrof, BaronIgnatz
  See Ford, Ford Madox
von Daeniken, Erich 1935- **CLC 30**
  See also AITN 1; CA 37-40R; CANR 17,
  44
von Daniken, Erich
  See von Daeniken, Erich
von Hartmann, Eduard 1842-1906 **TCLC 96**
von Heidenstam, (Carl Gustaf) Verner
  See Heidenstam, (Carl Gustaf) Verner von
von Heyse, Paul (Johann Ludwig)
  See Heyse, Paul (Johann Ludwig von)
von Hofmannsthal, Hugo
  See Hofmannsthal, Hugo von
von Horvath, Odon
  See Horvath, Oedoen von
von Horvath, Oedoen -1938
  See Horvath, Oedoen von
  See also CA 184
von Liliencron, (Friedrich Adolf Axel) Detlev
  See Liliencron, (Friedrich Adolf Axel) Detlev von
Vonnegut, Kurt, Jr. 1922- **CLC 1, 2, 3, 4, 5, 8, 12, 22, 40, 60, 111; DA; DAB; DAC; DAM MST, NOV, POP; SSC 8; WLC**
  See also AAYA 6; AITN 1; BEST 90:4; CA
  1-4R; CANR 1, 25, 49, 75; CDALB 1968-
  1988; DA3; DLB 2, 8, 152; DLBD 3;
  DLBY 80; MTCW 1, 2
Von Rachen, Kurt
  See Hubbard, L(afayette) Ron(ald)
von Rezzori (d'Arezzo), Gregor
  See Rezzori (d'Arezzo), Gregor von
von Sternberg, Josef
  See Sternberg, Josef von
Vorster, Gordon 1924- **CLC 34**
  See also CA 133
Vosce, Trudie
  See Ozick, Cynthia
Voznesensky, Andrei (Andreievich) 1933-
  CLC 1, 15, 57; DAM POET
  See also CA 89-92; CANR 37; MTCW 1
Waddington, Miriam 1917- **CLC 28**
  See also CA 21-24R; CANR 12, 30; DLB
  68
Wagman, Fredrica 1937- **CLC 7**
  See also CA 97-100; INT 97-100
Wagner, Linda W.
  See Wagner-Martin, Linda (C.)
Wagner, Linda Welshimer
  See Wagner-Martin, Linda (C.)
Wagner, Richard 1813-1883 **NCLC 9**
  See also DLB 129
Wagner-Martin, Linda (C.) 1936- **CLC 50**
  See also CA 159
Wagoner, David (Russell) 1926- **CLC 3, 5, 15**
  See also CA 1-4R; CAAS 3; CANR 2, 71;
  DLB 5; SATA 14
Wah, Fred(erick James) 1939- **CLC 44**
  See also CA 107; 141; DLB 60
Wahloo, Per 1926-1975 **CLC 7**
  See also CA 61-64; CANR 73
Wahloo, Peter
  See Wahloo, Per
Wain, John (Barrington) 1925-1994 **CLC 2, 11, 15, 46**
  See also CA 5-8R; 145; CAAS 4; CANR
  23, 54; CDBLB 1960 to Present; DLB 15,
  27, 139, 155; MTCW 1, 2
Wajda, Andrzej 1926- **CLC 16**
  See also CA 102
Wakefield, Dan 1932- **CLC 7**
  See also CA 21-24R; CAAS 7
Wakoski, Diane 1937- **CLC 2, 4, 7, 9, 11, 40; DAM POET; PC 15**
  See also CA 13-16R; CAAS 1; CANR 9,
  60; DLB 5; INT CANR-9; MTCW 2

Wakoski-Sherbell, Diane
  See Wakoski, Diane
Walcott, Derek (Alton) 1930- **CLC 2, 4, 9, 14, 25, 42, 67, 76; BLC 3; DAB; DAC; DAM MST, MULT, POET; DC 7**
  See also BW 2; CA 89-92; CANR 26, 47,
  75, 80; DA3; DLB 117; DLBY 81;
  MTCW 1, 2
Waldman, Anne (Lesley) 1945- **CLC 7**
  See also CA 37-40R; CAAS 17; CANR 34,
  69; DLB 16
Waldo, E. Hunter
  See Sturgeon, Theodore (Hamilton)
Waldo, Edward Hamilton
  See Sturgeon, Theodore (Hamilton)
Walker, Alice (Malsenior) 1944- **CLC 5, 6, 9, 19, 27, 46, 58, 103; BLC 3; DA; DAB; DAC; DAM MST, MULT, NOV, POET, POP; PC 30; SSC 5; WLCS**
  See also AAYA 3, 33; BEST 89:4; BW 2, 3;
  CA 37-40R; CANR 9, 27, 49, 66, 82;
  CDALB 1968-1988; DA3; DLB 6, 33,
  143; INT CANR-27; MTCW 1, 2; SATA
  31
Walker, David Harry 1911-1992 **CLC 14**
  See also CA 1-4R; 137; CANR 1; SATA 8;
  SATA-Obit 71
Walker, Edward Joseph 1934-
  See Walker, Ted
  See also CA 21-24R; CANR 12, 28, 53
Walker, George F. 1947- **CLC 44, 61; DAB; DAC; DAM MST**
  See also CA 103; CANR 21, 43, 59; DLB
  60
Walker, Joseph A. 1935- **CLC 19; DAM DRAM, MST**
  See also BW 1, 3; CA 89-92; CANR 26;
  DLB 38
Walker, Margaret (Abigail) 1915-1998 **CLC 1, 6; BLC; DAM MULT; PC 20**
  See also BW 2, 3; CA 73-76; 172; CANR
  26, 54, 76; DLB 76, 152; MTCW 1, 2
Walker, Ted CLC 13
  See also Walker, Edward Joseph
  See also DLB 40
Wallace, David Foster 1962- **CLC 50, 114**
  See also CA 132; CANR 59; DA3; MTCW
  2
Wallace, Dexter
  See Masters, Edgar Lee
Wallace, (Richard Horatio) Edgar 1875-1932
  TCLC 57
  See also CA 115; DLB 70
Wallace, Irving 1916-1990 **CLC 7, 13; DAM NOV, POP**
  See also AITN 1; CA 1-4R; 132; CAAS 1;
  CANR 1, 27; INT CANR-27; MTCW 1,
  2
Wallant, Edward Lewis 1926-1962 **CLC 5, 10**
  See also CA 1-4R; CANR 22; DLB 2, 28,
  143; MTCW 1, 2
Wallas, Graham 1858-1932 **TCLC 91**
Walley, Byron
  See Card, Orson Scott
Walpole, Horace 1717-1797 **LC 49**
  See also DLB 39, 104
Walpole, Hugh (Seymour) 1884-1941 **TCLC 5**
  See also CA 104; 165; DLB 34; MTCW 2
Walser, Martin 1927- **CLC 27**
  See also CA 57-60; CANR 8, 46; DLB 75,
  124
Walser, Robert 1878-1956 **TCLC 18; SSC 20**
  See also CA 118; 165; DLB 66
Walsh, Jill Paton CLC 35
  See also Paton Walsh, Gillian
  See also CLR 2, 65

Walter, Villiam Christian
  See Andersen, Hans Christian
Wambaugh, Joseph (Aloysius, Jr.) 1937- **CLC 3, 18; DAM NOV, POP**
  See also AITN 1; BEST 89:3; CA 33-36R;
  CANR 42, 65; DA3; DLB 6; DLBY 83;
  MTCW 1, 2
Wang Wei 699(?)-761(?) **PC 18**
Ward, Arthur Henry Sarsfield 1883-1959
  See Rohmer, Sax
  See also CA 108; 173
Ward, Douglas Turner 1930- **CLC 19**
  See also BW 1; CA 81-84; CANR 27; DLB
  7, 38
Ward, E. D.
  See Lucas, E(dward) V(errall)
Ward, Mary Augusta
  See Ward, Mrs. Humphry
Ward, Mrs. Humphry 1851-1920 **TCLC 55**
  See also DLB 18
Ward, Peter
  See Faust, Frederick (Schiller)
Warhol, Andy 1928(?)-1987 **CLC 20**
  See also AAYA 12; BEST 89:4; CA 89-92;
  121; CANR 34
Warner, Francis (Robert le Plastrier) 1937-
  CLC 14
  See also CA 53-56; CANR 11
Warner, Marina 1946- **CLC 59**
  See also CA 65-68; CANR 21, 55; DLB
  194
Warner, Rex (Ernest) 1905-1986 **CLC 45**
  See also CA 89-92; 119; DLB 15
Warner, Susan (Bogert) 1819-1885 **NCLC 31**
  See also DLB 3, 42
Warner, Sylvia (Constance) Ashton
  See Ashton-Warner, Sylvia (Constance)
Warner, Sylvia Townsend 1893-1978 **CLC 7, 19; SSC 23**
  See also CA 61-64; 77-80; CANR 16, 60;
  DLB 34, 139; MTCW 1, 2
Warren, Mercy Otis 1728-1814 **NCLC 13**
  See also DLB 31, 200
Warren, Robert Penn 1905-1989 **CLC 1, 4, 6, 8, 10, 13, 18, 39, 53, 59; DA; DAB; DAC; DAM MST, NOV, POET; SSC 4; WLC**
  See also AITN 1; CA 13-16R; 129; CANR
  10, 47; CDALB 1968-1988; DA3; DLB
  2, 48, 152; DLBY 80, 89; INT CANR-10;
  MTCW 1, 2; SATA 46; SATA-Obit 63
Warshofsky, Isaac
  See Singer, Isaac Bashevis
Warton, Thomas 1728-1790 **LC 15; DAM POET**
  See also DLB 104, 109
Waruk, Kona
  See Harris, (Theodore) Wilson
Warung, Price 1855-1911 **TCLC 45**
Warwick, Jarvis
  See Garner, Hugh
Washington, Alex
  See Harris, Mark
Washington, Booker T(aliaferro) 1856-1915
  TCLC 10; BLC 3; DAM MULT
  See also BW 1; CA 114; 125; DA3; SATA
  28
Washington, George 1732-1799 **LC 25**
  See also DLB 31
Wassermann, (Karl) Jakob 1873-1934 **TCLC 6**
  See also CA 104; 163; DLB 66
Wasserstein, Wendy 1950- **CLC 32, 59, 90; DAM DRAM; DC 4**
  See also CA 121; 129; CABS 3; CANR 53,
  75; DA3; INT 129; MTCW 2; SATA 94
Waterhouse, Keith (Spencer) 1929- **CLC 47**
  See also CA 5-8R; CANR 38, 67; DLB 13,
  15; MTCW 1, 2

Waters, Frank (Joseph) 1902-1995 **CLC 88**
See also CA 5-8R; 149; CAAS 13; CANR 3, 18, 63; DLB 212; DLBY 86

Waters, Roger 1944- **CLC 35**

Watkins, Frances Ellen
See Harper, Frances Ellen Watkins

Watkins, Gerrold
See Malzberg, Barry N(athaniel)

Watkins, Gloria Jean 1952(?)-
See hooks, bell
See also BW 2; CA 143; CANR 87; MTCW 2; SATA 115

Watkins, Paul 1964- **CLC 55**
See also CA 132; CANR 62

Watkins, Vernon Phillips 1906-1967 **CLC 43**
See also CA 9-10; 25-28R; CAP 1; DLB 20

Watson, Irving S.
See Mencken, H(enry) L(ouis)

Watson, John H.
See Farmer, Philip Jose

Watson, Richard F.
See Silverberg, Robert

Waugh, Auberon (Alexander) 1939- **CLC 7**
See also CA 45-48; CANR 6, 22; DLB 14, 194

Waugh, Evelyn (Arthur St. John) 1903-1966 **CLC 1, 3, 8, 13, 19, 27, 44, 107; DA; DAB; DAC; DAM MST, NOV, POP; WLC**
See also CA 85-88; 25-28R; CANR 22; CD-BLB 1914-1945; DA3; DLB 15, 162, 195; MTCW 1, 2

Waugh, Harriet 1944- **CLC 6**
See also CA 85-88; CANR 22

Ways, C. R.
See Blount, Roy (Alton), Jr.

Waystaff, Simon
See Swift, Jonathan

Webb, Beatrice (Martha Potter) 1858-1943 **TCLC 22**
See also CA 117; 162; DLB 190

Webb, Charles (Richard) 1939- **CLC 7**
See also CA 25-28R

Webb, James H(enry), Jr. 1946- **CLC 22**
See also CA 81-84

Webb, Mary Gladys (Meredith) 1881-1927 **TCLC 24**
See also CA 182; 123; DLB 34

Webb, Mrs. Sidney
See Webb, Beatrice (Martha Potter)

Webb, Phyllis 1927- **CLC 18**
See also CA 104; CANR 23; DLB 53

Webb, Sidney (James) 1859-1947 **TCLC 22**
See also CA 117; 163; DLB 190

Webber, Andrew Lloyd CLC 21
See also Lloyd Webber, Andrew

Weber, Lenora Mattingly 1895-1971 **CLC 12**
See also CA 19-20; 29-32R; CAP 1; SATA 2; SATA-Obit 26

Weber, Max 1864-1920 **TCLC 69**
See also CA 109

Webster, John 1579(?)-1634(?) **LC 33; DA; DAB; DAC; DAM DRAM, MST; DC 2; WLC**
See also CDBLB Before 1660; DLB 58

Webster, Noah 1758-1843 **NCLC 30**
See also DLB 1, 37, 42, 43, 73

Wedekind, (Benjamin) Frank(lin) 1864-1918 **TCLC 7; DAM DRAM**
See also CA 104; 153; DLB 118

Weidman, Jerome 1913-1998 **CLC 7**
See also AITN 2; CA 1-4R; 171; CANR 1; DLB 28

Weil, Simone (Adolphine) 1909-1943 **TCLC 23**
See also CA 117; 159; MTCW 2

Weininger, Otto 1880-1903 **TCLC 84**

Weinstein, Nathan
See West, Nathanael

Weinstein, Nathan von Wallenstein
See West, Nathanael

Weir, Peter (Lindsay) 1944- **CLC 20**
See also CA 113; 123

Weiss, Peter (Ulrich) 1916-1982 **CLC 3, 15, 51; DAM DRAM**
See also CA 45-48; 106; CANR 3; DLB 69, 124

Weiss, Theodore (Russell) 1916- **CLC 3, 8, 14**
See also CA 9-12R; CAAS 2; CANR 46; DLB 5

Welch, (Maurice) Denton 1915-1948 **TCLC 22**
See also CA 121; 148

Welch, James 1940- **CLC 6, 14, 52; DAM MULT, POP**
See also CA 85-88; CANR 42, 66; DLB 175; NNAL

Weldon, Fay 1931- **CLC 6, 9, 11, 19, 36, 59, 122; DAM POP**
See also CA 21-24R; CANR 16, 46, 63; CDBLB 1960 to Present; DLB 14, 194; INT CANR-16; MTCW 1, 2

Wellek, Rene 1903-1995 **CLC 28**
See also CA 5-8R; 150; CAAS 7; CANR 8; DLB 63; INT CANR-8

Weller, Michael 1942- **CLC 10, 53**
See also CA 85-88

Weller, Paul 1958- **CLC 26**

Wellershoff, Dieter 1925- **CLC 46**
See also CA 89-92; CANR 16, 37

Welles, (George) Orson 1915-1985 **CLC 20, 80**
See also CA 93-96; 117

Wellman, John McDowell 1945-
See Wellman, Mac
See also CA 166

Wellman, Mac 1945- **CLC 65**
See also Wellman, John McDowell; Wellman, John McDowell

Wellman, Manly Wade 1903-1986 **CLC 49**
See also CA 1-4R; 118; CANR 6, 16, 44; SATA 6; SATA-Obit 47

Wells, Carolyn 1869(?)-1942 **TCLC 35**
See also CA 113; 185; DLB 11

Wells, H(erbert) G(eorge) 1866-1946 **TCLC 6, 12, 19; DA; DAB; DAC; DAM MST, NOV; SSC 6; WLC**
See also AAYA 18; CA 110; 121; CDBLB 1914-1945; CLR 64; DA3; DLB 34, 70, 156, 178; MTCW 1, 2; SATA 20

Wells, Rosemary 1943- **CLC 12**
See also AAYA 13; CA 85-88; CANR 48; CLR 16; MAICYA; SAAS 1; SATA 18, 69, 114

Welty, Eudora 1909- **CLC 1, 2, 5, 14, 22, 33, 105; DA; DAB; DAC; DAM MST, NOV; SSC 1, 27; WLC**
See also CA 9-12R; CABS 1; CANR 32, 65; CDALB 1941-1968; DA3; DLB 2, 102, 143; DLBD 12; DLBY 87; MTCW 1, 2

Wen I-to 1899-1946 **TCLC 28**

Wentworth, Robert
See Hamilton, Edmond

Werfel, Franz (Viktor) 1890-1945 **TCLC 8**
See also CA 104; 161; DLB 81, 124

Wergeland, Henrik Arnold 1808-1845 **NCLC 5**

Wersba, Barbara 1932- **CLC 30**
See also AAYA 2, 30; CA 29-32R, 182; CAAE 182; CANR 16, 38; CLR 3; DLB 52; JRDA; MAICYA; SAAS 2; SATA 1, 58; SATA-Essay 103

Wertmueller, Lina 1928- **CLC 16**
See also CA 97-100; CANR 39, 78

Wescott, Glenway 1901-1987 **CLC 13; SSC 35**
See also CA 13-16R; 121; CANR 23, 70; DLB 4, 9, 102

Wesker, Arnold 1932- **CLC 3, 5, 42; DAB; DAM DRAM**
See also CA 1-4R; CAAS 7; CANR 1, 33; CDBLB 1960 to Present; DLB 13; MTCW 1

Wesley, Richard (Errol) 1945- **CLC 7**
See also BW 1; CA 57-60; CANR 27; DLB 38

Wessel, Johan Herman 1742-1785 **LC 7**

West, Anthony (Panther) 1914-1987 **CLC 50**
See also CA 45-48; 124; CANR 3, 19; DLB 15

West, C. P.
See Wodehouse, P(elham) G(renville)

West, (Mary) Jessamyn 1902-1984 **CLC 7, 17**
See also CA 9-12R; 112; CANR 27; DLB 6; DLBY 84; MTCW 1, 2; SATA-Obit 37

West, Morris L(anglo) 1916- **CLC 6, 33**
See also CA 5-8R; CANR 24, 49, 64; MTCW 1, 2

West, Nathanael 1903-1940 **TCLC 1, 14, 44; SSC 16**
See also CA 104; 125; CDALB 1929-1941; DA3; DLB 4, 9, 28; MTCW 1, 2

West, Owen
See Koontz, Dean R(ay)

West, Paul 1930- **CLC 7, 14, 96**
See also CA 13-16R; CAAS 7; CANR 22, 53, 76, 89; DLB 14; INT CANR-22; MTCW 2

West, Rebecca 1892-1983 **CLC 7, 9, 31, 50**
See also CA 5-8R; 109; CANR 19; DLB 36; DLBY 83; MTCW 1, 2

Westall, Robert (Atkinson) 1929-1993 **CLC 17**
See also AAYA 12; CA 69-72; 141; CANR 18, 68; CLR 13; JRDA; MAICYA; SAAS 2; SATA 23, 69; SATA-Obit 75

Westermarck, Edward 1862-1939 **TCLC 87**

Westlake, Donald E(dwin) 1933- **CLC 7, 33; DAM POP**
See also CA 17-20R; CAAS 13; CANR 16, 44, 65; INT CANR-16; MTCW 2

Westmacott, Mary
See Christie, Agatha (Mary Clarissa)

Weston, Allen
See Norton, Andre

Wetcheek, J. L.
See Feuchtwanger, Lion

Wetering, Janwillem van de
See van de Wetering, Janwillem

Wetherald, Agnes Ethelwyn 1857-1940 **TCLC 81**
See also DLB 99

Wetherell, Elizabeth
See Warner, Susan (Bogert)

Whale, James 1889-1957 **TCLC 63**

Whalen, Philip 1923- **CLC 6, 29**
See also CA 9-12R; CANR 5, 39; DLB 16

Wharton, Edith (Newbold Jones) 1862-1937 **TCLC 3, 9, 27, 53; DA; DAB; DAC; DAM MST, NOV; SSC 6; WLC**
See also AAYA 25; CA 104; 132; CDALB 1865-1917; DA3; DLB 4, 9, 12, 78, 189; DLBD 13; MTCW 1, 2

Wharton, James
See Mencken, H(enry) L(ouis)

Wharton, William (a pseudonym) CLC 18, 37
See also CA 93-96; DLBY 80; INT 93-96

Wheatley (Peters), Phillis 1754(?)-1784 **LC 3, 50; BLC 3; DA; DAC; DAM MST, MULT, POET; PC 3; WLC**

BLC 3; DA; DAB; DAC; DAM DRAM,
MST, MULT; DC 2; WLCS
See also AAYA 16; BW 2, 3; CA 115; 122;
CANR 42, 54, 76; DA3; MTCW 1, 2
Wilson, Brian 1942- CLC 12
Wilson, Colin 1931- CLC 3, 14
See also CA 1-4R; CAAS 5; CANR 1, 22,
33, 77; DLB 14, 194; MTCW 1
Wilson, Dirk
See Pohl, Frederik
Wilson, Edmund 1895-1972 CLC 1, 2, 3, 8,
24
See also CA 1-4R; 37-40R; CANR 1, 46;
DLB 63; MTCW 1, 2
Wilson, Ethel Davis (Bryant) 1888(?)-1980
CLC 13; DAC; DAM POET
See also CA 102; DLB 68; MTCW 1
Wilson, John 1785-1854 NCLC 5
Wilson, John (Anthony) Burgess 1917-1993
See Burgess, Anthony
See also CA 1-4R; 143; CANR 2, 46; DAC;
DAM NOV; DA3; MTCW 1, 2
Wilson, Lanford 1937- CLC 7, 14, 36; DAM
DRAM
See also CA 17-20R; CABS 3; CANR 45;
DLB 7
Wilson, Robert M. 1944- CLC 7, 9
See also CA 49-52; CANR 2, 41; MTCW 1
Wilson, Robert McLiam 1964- CLC 59
See also CA 132
Wilson, Sloan 1920- CLC 32
See also CA 1-4R; CANR 1, 44
Wilson, Snoo 1948- CLC 33
See also CA 69-72
Wilson, William S(mith) 1932- CLC 49
See also CA 81-84
Wilson, (Thomas) Woodrow 1856-1924
TCLC 79
See also CA 166; DLB 47
Winchilsea, Anne (Kingsmill) Finch Counte
1661-1720
See Finch, Anne
Windham, Basil
See Wodehouse, P(elham) G(renville)
Wingrove, David (John) 1954- CLC 68
See also CA 133
Winnemucca, Sarah 1844-1891 NCLC 79
Winstanley, Gerrard 1609-1676 LC 52
Wintergreen, Jane
See Duncan, Sara Jeannette
Winters, Janet Lewis CLC 41
See also Lewis, Janet
See also DLBY 87
Winters, (Arthur) Yvor 1900-1968 CLC 4, 8,
32
See also CA 11-12; 25-28R; CAP 1; DLB
48; MTCW 1
Winterson, Jeanette 1959- CLC 64; DAM
POP
See also CA 136; CANR 58; DA3; DLB
207; MTCW 2
Winthrop, John 1588-1649 LC 31
See also DLB 24, 30
Wirth, Louis 1897-1952 TCLC 92
Wiseman, Frederick 1930- CLC 20
See also CA 159
Wister, Owen 1860-1938 TCLC 21
See also CA 108; 162; DLB 9, 78, 186;
SATA 62
Witkacy
See Witkiewicz, Stanislaw Ignacy
Witkiewicz, Stanislaw Ignacy 1885-1939
TCLC 8
See also CA 105; 162
Wittgenstein, Ludwig (Josef Johann)
1889-1951 TCLC 59
See also CA 113; 164; MTCW 2
Wittig, Monique 1935(?)- CLC 22

See also CA 116; 135; DLB 83
Wittlin, Jozef 1896-1976 CLC 25
See also CA 49-52; 65-68; CANR 3
Wodehouse, P(elham) G(renville) 1881-1975
CLC 1, 2, 5, 10, 22; DAB; DAC; DAM
NOV; SSC 2
See also AITN 2; CA 45-48; 57-60; CANR
3, 33; CDBLB 1914-1945; DA3; DLB 34,
162; MTCW 1, 2; SATA 22
Woiwode, L.
See Woiwode, Larry (Alfred)
Woiwode, Larry (Alfred) 1941- CLC 6, 10
See also CA 73-76; CANR 16; DLB 6; INT
CANR-16
Wojciechowska, Maia (Teresa) 1927- CLC 26
See also AAYA 8; CA 9-12R, 183; CAAE
183; CANR 4, 41; CLR 1; JRDA; MAI-
CYA; SAAS 1; SATA 1, 28, 83; SATA-
Essay 104
Wojtyla, Karol
See John Paul II, Pope
Wolf, Christa 1929- CLC 14, 29, 58
See also CA 85-88; CANR 45; DLB 75;
MTCW 1
Wolfe, Gene (Rodman) 1931- CLC 25; DAM
POP
See also CA 57-60; CAAS 9; CANR 6, 32,
60; DLB 8; MTCW 2
Wolfe, George C. 1954- CLC 49; BLCS
See also CA 149
Wolfe, Thomas (Clayton) 1900-1938 TCLC
4, 13, 29, 61; DA; DAB; DAC; DAM
MST, NOV; SSC 33; WLC
See also CA 104; 132; CDALB 1929-1941;
DA3; DLB 9, 102; DLBD 2, 16; DLBY
85, 97; MTCW 1, 2
Wolfe, Thomas Kennerly, Jr. 1930-
See Wolfe, Tom
See also CA 13-16R; CANR 9, 33, 70;
DAM POP; DA3; DLB 185; INT
CANR-9; MTCW 1, 2
Wolfe, Tom CLC 1, 2, 9, 15, 35, 51
See also Wolfe, Thomas Kennerly, Jr.
See also AAYA 8; AITN 2; BEST 89:1;
DLB 152
Wolff, Geoffrey (Ansell) 1937- CLC 41
See also CA 29-32R; CANR 29, 43, 78
Wolff, Sonia
See Levitin, Sonia (Wolff)
Wolff, Tobias (Jonathan Ansell) 1945- CLC
39, 64
See also AAYA 16; BEST 90:2; CA 114;
117; CAAS 22; CANR 54, 76; DA3; DLB
130; INT 117; MTCW 2
Wolfram von Eschenbach c. 1170-c. 1220
CMLC 5
See also DLB 138
Wolitzer, Hilma 1930- CLC 17
See also CA 65-68; CANR 18, 40; INT
CANR-18; SATA 31
Wollstonecraft, Mary 1759-1797 LC 5, 50
See also CDBLB 1789-1832; DLB 39, 104,
158
Wonder, Stevie CLC 12
See also Morris, Steveland Judkins
Wong, Jade Snow 1922- CLC 17
See also CA 109; CANR 91; SATA 112
Woodberry, George Edward 1855-1930
TCLC 73
See also CA 165; DLB 71, 103
Woodcott, Keith
See Brunner, John (Kilian Houston)
Woodruff, Robert W.
See Mencken, H(enry) L(ouis)
Woolf, (Adeline) Virginia 1882-1941 TCLC
1, 5, 20, 43, 56; DA; DAB; DAC; DAM
MST, NOV; SSC 7; WLC
See also Woolf, Virginia Adeline

See also CA 104; 130; CANR 64; CDBLB
1914-1945; DA3; DLB 36, 100, 162;
DLBD 10; MTCW 1
Woolf, Virginia Adeline
See Woolf, (Adeline) Virginia
See also MTCW 2
Woollcott, Alexander (Humphreys)
1887-1943 TCLC 5
See also CA 105; 161; DLB 29
Woolrich, Cornell 1903-1968 CLC 77
See also Hopley-Woolrich, Cornell George
Woolson, Constance Fenimore 1840-1894
NCLC 82
See also DLB 12, 74, 189, 221
Wordsworth, Dorothy 1771-1855 NCLC 25
See also DLB 107
Wordsworth, William 1770-1850 NCLC 12,
38; DA; DAB; DAC; DAM MST,
POET; PC 4; WLC
See also CDBLB 1789-1832; DA3; DLB
93, 107
Wouk, Herman 1915- CLC 1, 9, 38; DAM
NOV, POP
See also CA 5-8R; CANR 6, 33, 67;
CDALBS; DA3; DLBY 82; INT CANR-6;
MTCW 1, 2
Wright, Charles (Penzel, Jr.) 1935- CLC 6,
13, 28, 119
See also CA 29-32R; CAAS 7; CANR 23,
36, 62, 88; DLB 165; DLBY 82; MTCW
1, 2
Wright, Charles Stevenson 1932- CLC 49;
BLC 3; DAM MULT, POET
See also BW 1; CA 9-12R; CANR 26; DLB
33
Wright, Frances 1795-1852 NCLC 74
See also DLB 73
Wright, Frank Lloyd 1867-1959 TCLC 95
See also AAYA 33; CA 174
Wright, Jack R.
See Harris, Mark
Wright, James (Arlington) 1927-1980 CLC
3, 5, 10, 28; DAM POET
See also AITN 2; CA 49-52; 97-100; CANR
4, 34, 64; CDALBS; DLB 5, 169; MTCW
1, 2
Wright, Judith (Arandell) 1915- CLC 11, 53;
PC 14
See also CA 13-16R; CANR 31, 76; MTCW
1, 2; SATA 14
Wright, L(aurali) R. 1939- CLC 44
See also CA 138
Wright, Richard (Nathaniel) 1908-1960 CLC
1, 3, 4, 9, 14, 21, 48, 74; BLC 3; DA;
DAB; DAC; DAM MST, MULT, NOV;
SSC 2; WLC
See also AAYA 5; BW 1; CA 108; CANR
64; CDALB 1929-1941; DA3; DLB 76,
102; DLBD 2; MTCW 1, 2
Wright, Richard B(ruce) 1937- CLC 6
See also CA 85-88; DLB 53
Wright, Rick 1945- CLC 35
Wright, Rowland
See Wells, Carolyn
Wright, Stephen 1946- CLC 33
Wright, Willard Huntington 1888-1939
See Van Dine, S. S.
See also CA 115; DLBD 16
Wright, William 1930- CLC 44
See also CA 53-56; CANR 7, 23
Wroth, LadyMary 1587-1653(?) LC 30
See also DLB 121
Wu Ch'eng-en 1500(?)-1582(?) LC 7
Wu Ching-tzu 1701-1754 LC 2
Wurlitzer, Rudolph 1938(?)- CLC 2, 4, 15
See also CA 85-88; DLB 173
Wyatt, Thomas c. 1503-1542 PC 27
See also DLB 132

Literary Criticism Series
Cumulative Topic Index

This index lists all topic entries in Gale's *Classical and Medieval Literature Criticism, Contemporary Literary Criticism, Literature Criticism from 1400 to 1800, Nineteenth-Century Literature Criticism,* and *Twentieth-Century Literary Criticism.*

overviews, 1-27
the nature of dramatic performances, 27-42
the medieval worldview and the mystery cycles, 43-67
the doctrine of repentance and the mystery cycles, 67-76
the fall from grace in the mystery cycles, 76-88

The English Realist Novel, 1740-1771 LC 51: 102-98
Overviews, 103-22
From Romanticism to Realism, 123-58
Women and the Novel, 159-175
The Novel and Other Literary Forms, 176-197

English Revolution, Literature of the LC 43: 1-58
overviews, 2-24
pamphlets of the English Revolution, 24-38
political Sermons of the English Revolution, 38-48
poetry of the English Revolution, 48-57

English Romantic Hellenism NCLC 68: 143-250
overviews, 144-69
historical development of English Romantic Hellenism, 169-91
influence of Greek mythology on the Romantics, 191-229
influence of Greek literature, art, and culture on the Romantics, 229-50

English Romantic Poetry NCLC 28: 201-327
overviews and reputation, 202-37
major subjects and themes, 237-67
forms of Romantic poetry, 267-78
politics, society, and Romantic poetry, 278-99
philosophy, religion, and Romantic poetry, 299-324

Espionage Literature TCLC 50: 95-159
overviews, 96-113
espionage fiction/formula fiction, 113-26
spies in fact and fiction, 126-38
the female spy, 138-44
social and psychological perspectives, 144-58

European Romanticism NCLC 36: 149-284
definitions, 149-77
origins of the movement, 177-82
Romantic theory, 182-200
themes and techniques, 200-23
Romanticism in Germany, 223-39
Romanticism in France, 240-61
Romanticism in Italy, 261-4
Romanticism in Spain, 264-8
impact and legacy, 268-82

Existentialism and Literature TCLC 42: 197-268
overviews and definitions, 198-209
history and influences, 209-19
Existentialism critiqued and defended, 220-35
philosophical and religious perspectives, 235-41
Existentialist fiction and drama, 241-67

Familiar Essay NCLC 48: 96-211
definitions and origins, 97-130
overview of the genre, 130-43
elements of form and style, 143-59
elements of content, 159-73
the Cockneys: Hazlitt, Lamb, and Hunt, 173-91
status of the genre, 191-210

The Faust Legend LC 47: 1-117

Fear in Literature TCLC 74: 81-258
overviews, 81
pre-twentieth-century literature, 123
twentieth-century literature, 182

Feminism in the 1990s: Commentary on Works by Naomi Wolf, Susan Faludi, and Camille Paglia CLC 76: 377-415

Feminist Criticism in 1990 CLC 65: 312-60

Fifteenth-Century English Literature LC 17: 248-334
background, 249-72
poetry, 272-315
drama, 315-23
prose, 323-33

Film and Literature TCLC 38: 97-226
overviews, 97-119
film and theater, 119-34
film and the novel, 134-45
the art of the screenplay, 145-66
genre literature/genre film, 167-79
the writer and the film industry, 179-90
authors on film adaptations of their works, 190-200
fiction into film: comparative essays, 200-23

Finance and Money as Represented in Nineteenth-Century Literature NCLC 76: 1-69
historical perspectives, 2-20
the image of money, 20-37
the dangers of money, 37-50
women and money, 50-69

Folklore and Literature TCLC 86: 116-293
overviews, 118-144
Native American literature, 144-67
African-American literature, 167-238
Folklore and the American West, 238-57
Modern and postmodern literature, 257-91

French Drama in the Age of Louis XIV LC 28: 94-185
overview, 95-127
tragedy, 127-46
comedy, 146-66
tragicomedy, 166-84

French Enlightenment LC 14: 81-145
the question of definition, 82-9
Le siècle des lumières, 89-94
women and the salons, 94-105
censorship, 105-15
the philosophy of reason, 115-31
influence and legacy, 131-44

French Realism NCLC 52: 136-216
origins and definitions, 137-70
issues and influence, 170-98
realism and representation, 198-215

French Revolution and English Literature NCLC 40: 96-195
history and theory, 96-123
romantic poetry, 123-50
the novel, 150-81
drama, 181-92
children's literature, 192-5

Futurism, Italian TCLC 42: 269-354
principles and formative influences, 271-9
manifestos, 279-88
literature, 288-303
theater, 303-19
art, 320-30
music, 330-6
architecture, 336-9
and politics, 339-46
reputation and significance, 346-51

Gaelic Revival See Irish Literary Renaissance

Gates, Henry Louis, Jr., and African-American Literary Criticism CLC 65: 361-405

Gay and Lesbian Literature CLC 76: 416-39

German Exile Literature TCLC 30: 1-58
the writer and the Nazi state, 1-10
definition of, 10-4
life in exile, 14-32
surveys, 32-50
Austrian literature in exile, 50-2
German publishing in the United States, 52-7

German Expressionism TCLC 34: 74-160
history and major figures, 76-85
aesthetic theories, 85-109
drama, 109-26
poetry, 126-38
film, 138-42
painting, 142-7
music, 147-53
and politics, 153-8

The Gilded Age NCLC 84: 169-271
popular themes, 170-90
Realism, 190-208
Aestheticism, 208-26
socio-political concerns, 226-70

***Glasnost* and Contemporary Soviet Literature** CLC 59: 355-97

Gothic Novel NCLC 28: 328-402
development and major works, 328-34
definitions, 334-50
themes and techniques, 350-78
in America, 378-85
in Scotland, 385-91
influence and legacy, 391-400

Graphic Narratives CLC 86: 405-32
history and overviews, 406-21
the "Classics Illustrated" series, 421-2
reviews of recent works, 422-32

Greek Historiography CMLC 17: 1-49

Greek Mythology CMLC 26: 193-320
overviews, 194-209
origins and development of Greek mythology, 209-29
cosmogonies and divinities in Greek mythology, 229-54
heroes and heroines in Greek mythology, 254-80
women in Greek mythology, 280-320

Harlem Renaissance TCLC 26: 49-125
principal issues and figures, 50-67
the literature and its audience, 67-74
theme and technique in poetry, fiction, and drama, 74-115
and American society, 115-21
achievement and influence, 121-2

Havel, Václav, Playwright and President CLC 65: 406-63

Historical Fiction, Nineteenth-Century NCLC 48: 212-307
definitions and characteristics, 213-36
Victorian historical fiction, 236-65
American historical fiction, 265-88
realism in historical fiction, 288-306

Holocaust and the Atomic Bomb: Fifty Years Later CLC 91: 331-82
the Holocaust remembered, 333-52
Anne Frank revisited, 352-62
the atomic bomb and American memory, 362-81

Holocaust Denial Literature TCLC 58: 1-110
overviews, 1-30
Robert Faurisson and Noam Chomsky, 30-52
Holocaust denial literature in America, 52-71
library access to Holocaust denial literature, 72-5
the authenticity of Anne Frank's diary, 76-90
David Irving and the "normalization" of Hitler, 90-109

Topic Index

CMLC Cumulative Nationality Index

"Ali the Son of Bakkar and Shems-en-Nahar"
2:14
Alimonia Romuli et Remi (Naevius) **37**:185, 223
Alimonium Remi et Romuli (Naevius)
   See *Alimonium Remi et Romuli*
Alku Kalevala
   See *Kalevala*
"Alladin and the Wonderful Lamp" **2**:1-2, 8,
   21, 23-24, 72
Allegoria mitologica (Boccaccio) **13**:63-4
"Alliterative Morte Arthure"
   See *Morte Arthure "Alliterative"*
Al-Nubl wa l-tannabbal wa-dhamm al-kibr
   25:332
Al-Qanūn al Masūdu (Biruni)
   See *Kitāb al-Qānūn al Mas'ūdī fi'l-Hay'a*
   w-an-nujim
Al-Risalah fi Nafy al-tashbih **25**:329
Al-Saidana (Biruni)
   See *Kītb al-Sydānāh*
al-Tacliqat (Avicenna) **16**:167
Al-Tahdīd (Biruni)
   See *Kitāb Tahdīd Nihāyāt al-Amākin*
Al-Tanbīh 'Alā Sinā'at al Tamwīh (Biruni)
   28:155
Ameto (Boccaccio) **13**:9, 18, 23, 27-8, 30, 32-3,
   44-5, 48, 61
De amicitia (Cicero) **3**:193, 195, 202
"Amor, tu vedi ben che quesra donna"
   (Petrarch) **20**:283
Amores (Ovid) **7**:292-93, 295-97, 299, 305, 323,
   326, 329, 336, 343, 346-49, 353, 355-56,
   376-79, 388, 390, 393, 396, 398, 413, 417,
   419-21, 423, 426-27, 436, 441, 444
Amorosa visione (Boccaccio) **13**:18, 27-8, 32-3,
   68, 72, 87
Amphitruo (Plautus) **24**:170-72, 175-78, 184,
   199
Amphitryon (Plautus)
   See *Amphitruo*
Anabasis (Xenophon) **17**:322, 324, 326, 327,
   328, 330, 339, 340, 341, 342, 348, 349, 354,
   357 358, 359, 360, 361, 362, 364, 365, 366,
   372, 374
Anacharsis (Lucian) **32**:17, 25, 39
Analects (Confucius)
   See *Lun Yu*
Analysis of the Analects (Su Shih) **15**:407
Analytics (Aristotle) **31**:64, 86
Ancient History of the Jews (Josephus)
   See *Antiquitates Judaicae*
Ancient Poems (Confucius)
   See *Shih Ching*
Andria (Terence) **14**:302-08, 311-13, 315-17,
   331, 333-35, 337-41, 344-45, 347-49, 352,
   355-356, 358, 363-65, 369-70, 383-85, 389-
   90, 392-93
"Androcles and the Lion" (Aesop) **24**:58
Andromache (Euripides) **23**:114, 121-22, 125,
   127-30, 174, 182-83, 185, 189, 207
Andromache (Naevius) **37**:185, 223
Andromeda (Euripides) **23**:120, 174, 182
Androtion (Demosthenes)
   See *Against Androtion*
Anger (Menander)
   See *Orgē*
Anglo-Saxon Chronicle **4**:1-33
De anima (Albert the Great) **16**:7, 61, 106, 109,
   113, 115
De Anima (Aristotle) **31**:65, 86-87, 274-75, 305,
   327, 337, 358-66, 370, 374, 379
De anima (Avicenna) **16**:176
De anima (Tertullian)
   See *On the Soul*
De animalibus (Albert the Great) **16**:18, 21,
   35-7, 61, 64, 82-3, 103, 107, 110
Animals (Albert the Great)
   See *De animalibus*
Annals of Lu (Confucius)
   See *Ch'un Ch'iu*
Annapurna-stotra (Sankara) **32**:390

"Answering a Layman's Question" (Li Po)
   2:140
"The Ant and the Fly" (Aesop) **24**:36
Antigonē (Sophocles) **2**:289, 296, 299-301, 303-
   04, 306-09, 311, 314-15, 318-20, 324-25,
   327, 331, 334-35, 338-40, 342-43, 345, 349-
   55, 360, 366, 368, 377-78, 380-83, 393-97,
   417-19, 423, 426-28
Antiope (Euripides)
Antiquitates Judaicae (Josephus) **13**:199-207,
   211-3, 215-8, 220, 224, 226-35, 239, 242,
   247-51, 256-65, 268-71, 286, 291-2, 294-7,
   299-300, 302, 305, 308-9, 311-3, 315-20
Antiquities of the Jews (Josephus)
   See *Antiquitates Judaicae*
Apella (Naevius) **37**:223
"Aphrodite Ode" (Sappho)
   See "Ode to Aphrodite"
Apion Answered (Josephus)
   See *Contra Apionem*
Apionem (Josephus)
   See *Contra Apionem*
Apocalypse (Hroswitha of Gandersheim) **29**:183
Apocalypse (Rolle) **21**:351
Apocolocyntosis Divi Claudii (Seneca) **6**:244,
   374, 382-84
Apologeticum (Tertullian)
   See *Apology*
Apologeticus (Tertullian)
   See *Apology*
Apologia (Plato) **8**:250, 260, 277, 306, 357
Apologia sive oratoria de magia (Apuleius)
   1:7-8, 10, 12-13, 20, 23, 26, 33-4
Apologia Socratis (Xenophon)
   See *Apology*
Apology (Apuleius)
   See *Apologia sive oratoria de magia*
Apology (Plato)
   See *Apologia*
Apology (Tertullian) **29**:310, 311, 312, 329, 330,
   334, 338, 346-349, 367, 384
Apology (Xenophon) **17**:342, 343, 369-71
Apology for 'On Salaried Posts' (Lucian) **32**:39
Apology of Origen (Origen) **19**:188-89, 199
Apomnemoneumata (Xenophon)
   See *Memorabilia*
Apophoreta (Martial) **35**:303-04, 331, 364, 375,
   377
Apophthegmata (Cato) **21**:22, 41, 54
Apotheosis of Arsinoe (Callimachus)
   See *Deification of Arsinoe*
"The Apples of Paradise" **2**:40
The Arabian Nights
   See *Alf Layla wa-Layla*
The Arabian Nights' Entertainments
   See *Alf Layla wa-Layla*
The Arbitrants (Menander)
   See *Epitrepontes*
The Arbitration (Menander)
   See *Epitrepontes*
Arbor scientiae (Llull) **12**:108-11, 115, 125
El arbre de filosofia d'amor (Llull)
   See *The Tree of the Philosophy of Love*
Arbre de Sciencia (Llull)
   See *Arbor scientiae*
Archias (Cicero) **3**:198-99, 210
Argo (Aeschylus) **11**:124
Argolica (Pausanias)
   See *Periegesis*
Argonautica (Rhodius) **28**:2-27, 29-110
Argonautika (Rhodius)
   See *Argonautica*
Arithmetic (Boethius)
   See *De Arithmetica*
De Arithmetica (Boethius) **15**:63, 69, 86
Der arme Heinrich (Hartmann von Aue)
   15:148-54, 164, 191, 194, 205-07, 209, 220,
   224, 241-44, 244-49
"Arrius and His Aitches" (Catullus)
   See "Poem 84"
"Arriving at Principles" (Po Chu-i) **24**:311

Ars Amandi (Ovid)
   See *Ars amatoria*
Ars amatoria (Ovid) **7**:281-83, 292-98, 304-06,
   309-10, 326, 329, 331, 342-47, 349, 353,
   377-79, 386-87, 396-98, 401-02, 404, 412-
   13, 416-19, 421-23, 426, 430, 435-43, 446
Ars brevis (Llull) **12**:106-07, 109, 133
Ars demonstrativa (Llull) **12**:105-06, 110, 117,
   134
Ars generalis (Llull) **12**:104, 107-08
Ars generalis ultima (Llull) **12**:114-16, 128
Ars inventiva (Llull) **12**:97, 109, 114-15, 120,
   128, 132
Ars magna (Llull) **12**:93-4, 104, 111, 132
Ars Poetica (Horace) **39**:116, 144, 171, 180,
   186, 247, 252, 273-75
Art of Contemplation (Llull) **12**:125, 129
Art of Finding Truth (Llull)
   See *Ars inventiva*
Art of Love (Ovid)
   See *Ars amatoria*
The Art of Poetry (Horace)
   See *Ars Poetica*
Art of Rhetoric (Hermogenes) **6**:186
De Arte metrica (Bede) **20**:42, 93, 120
De Arte Poetica liber (Horace)
   See *Ars Poetica*
Ascensio (Hroswitha of Gandersheim) **29**:123
The Ascension of our Lord (Hroswitha of
   Gandersheim) **29**:136
"Asceticon" (Basil of Caesaria) **35**:91, 92
"The Ash Tree" (Marie de France)
   See "Le Fraisne"
Asinaria (Plautus) **24**:170-73, 175, 218, 220-21,
   233, 235, 240, 244, 248-49, 263-64, 270-
   71, 273
Asinus aureus (Apuleius) **1**:6-9, 11-12, 14-18,
   20, 22-23, 26, 32, 37-38, 46-50
Aspis (Menander) **9**:253-58, 260-61, 263, 265,
   267-70, 276-77
"Ass in the Lion's skin" (Aesop) **24**:43
Assembly of Women (Aristophanes)
   See *Ekklesiazousai*
"At Kuo Hsiang-cheng's When I was Drunk I
   Painted" (Su Shih) **15**:402
"At the Serpentine Moved by Autumn" (Po
   Chu-i) **24**:338
Athamas (Aeschylus) **11**:122
Atomic Films (Epicurus) **21**:73
Atoms and Space (Epicurus) **21**:73
"Atretan deu ben chantar finamen" (Sordello)
   15:362-63, 368
Attica (Pausanias)
   See *Periegesis*
"Attis" (Catullus)
   See "Poem 63"
"Atys" (Catullus)
   See "Poem 63"
Auge (Euripides) **23**:203
"Augustinus" (Petrarch) **20**:286-87
Aulularia (Plautus) **24**:171-73, 175-76, 178-79,
   181, 184, 218, 258
Authorized Doctrines (Epicurus)
   See *Principal Doctrines*
Autolycus (Euripides) **23**:173
"Autumn Banks Song" (Li Po) **2**:161, 164
"Autumn Day" (Po Chu-i) **24**:335
"Autumn Evening" (Po Chu-i) **24**:336, 339
"Autumn Feelings" (Po Chu-i) **24**:336
"Autumn Hibiscus" (Po Chu-i) **24**:337
"Autumn Moon" (Po Chu-i) **24**:336
The Babylonians (Aristophanes) **4**:99, 126, 159,
   163, 165
Bacchae (Euripides) **23**:103-04, 108, 110, 114,
   120, 122, 124-26, 131, 136-38, 140, 142-
   44, 146-50, 153, 171, 173-76, 186, 189,
   204-07, 212, 219-22
Bacchanals (Euripides)
   See *Bacchae*
The Bacchants (Euripides)
   See *Bacchae*
Bacchides (Plautus) **24**:170-73, 175, 180, 184,

Title Index

Title Index

ISBN 0-7876-4382-3

90000

9 790787 643828